For Mrs. Hunnewell.

I hope _____ me
and the _____ of
silver from _____
America, with warmest regards,
Elliot   May 2008
    +
the Art of the Americas
department at the
Museum of Fine Arts,
Boston

Silver of the Americas, 1600–2000

Edited by Jeannine Falino and Gerald W. R. Ward

with texts by Jeannine Falino, Jane L. Port, Rebecca A. G. Reynolds, and Gerald W. R. Ward

Silver of the Americas, 1600–2000

AMERICAN SILVER IN THE MUSEUM OF FINE ARTS, BOSTON

mfa
BOSTON

MFA Publications
Museum of Fine Arts, Boston

MFA Publications
Museum of Fine Arts, Boston
465 Huntington Avenue
Boston, Massachusetts 02115
www.mfa-publications.org

© 2008 by Museum of Fine Arts, Boston

ISBN 978-0-87846-721-1
Library of Congress Control Number: 2007927114

The Museum of Fine Arts, Boston, is a nonprofit institution devoted to the promotion and appreciation of the creative arts. The Museum endeavors to respect the copyrights of all authors and creators in a manner consistent with its nonprofit educational mission. If you feel any material has been included in this publication improperly, please contact the Department of Rights and Licensing at 617 267 9300, or by mail at the above address.

While the objects in this publication necessarily represent only a small portion of the MFA's holdings, the Museum is proud to be a leader within the American museum community in sharing the objects in its collection via its Web site. Currently, information about more than 330,000 objects is available to the public worldwide. To learn more about the MFA's collections, including provenance, publication, and exhibition history, kindly visit www.mfa.org/collections.

For a complete listing of MFA Publications, please contact the publisher at the above address, or call 617 369 3438.

Front Cover: *Pitcher* (cat. 243), detail
Back Cover: *Missal stand* (cat. 379), detail
Title page: *Three-piece tea service* (cat. 225)
Dedication: *Bowl* (cat. 337)

Unless otherwise noted, all photography by Museum of Fine Arts, Boston.

Edited by Mary Ellen Wilson
Copyedited by Julia Gaviria
Designed and produced by Dean Bornstein
Printed and bound by Capital Offset

Trade distribution:
Distributed Art Publishers / D.A.P.
155 Sixth Avenue, 2nd floor
New York, New York 10013
Tel. 212 627 1999 Fax 212 627 9484

FIRST EDITION
Printed in the U.S.A.
This book was printed on acid-free paper.

This publication was made possible in large part through the generosity of

Chelsey and David Remington in memory of his aunt, Virginia Wireman Cute

Additional support was provided by

The National Endowment for the Arts
Nathaniel T. Dexter
The Seminarians
Museum Loan Network
Flagler College
Stephen and Leigh Braude

NATIONAL ENDOWMENT FOR THE ARTS

The publisher also wishes to acknowledge the generous support of the Andrew W. Mellon Publications Fund.

Contents

Director's Foreword

The Museum of Fine Arts, Boston, has been a leader in collecting, exhibiting, and publishing American silver for more than a century. The collection began in 1877 with the acquisition of a then-contemporary Tiffany & Co. mixed-metals pitcher exhibited at the Philadelphia Centennial Exhibition. A major milestone came with the groundbreaking exhibition of American church silver held at our original Copley Square location in 1906. Since those beginnings, the Museum has developed a collection of American silver that is unparalleled in works from early New England and is strong in objects from all time periods. Today, our American silver can be seen at the Museum in the context of outstanding collections of English, French, and German silver, as well as examples from the ancient world and from other cultures across the globe.

In 1972, our American holdings were catalogued by Kathryn C. Buhler, the leading silver scholar of her generation, in two massive volumes that remain a cornerstone of any library on American silver. By the 1990s, however, the growth in the collection made it evident that a new catalogue was necessary. Moreover, a catalogue was needed that not only would document the growth of the collection, but that would do justice to the Museum's holdings in silver from 1825 to the present, as well as in objects from the rich traditions of Mexico and South America.

The present catalogue addresses those needs. The challenge of preparing such a work was undertaken with enthusiasm by the authors of this volume—Jeannine Falino, Jane L. Port, Rebecca Reynolds, and Gerald W. R. Ward—and many other staff members who contributed to this book in myriad ways. We are indebted to them all for their hard work during the long course of research, writing, photography, design, and production. Even as this book goes on press, of course, the collection continues to grow. Silver enthusiasts of all types will be glad to know that all examples from our collection—indeed, the Museum's collection as a whole—are recorded on the museum's web site (www.mfa.org) that is updated regularly.

An initial grant from the National Endowment for the Arts started the process of preparing this substantial volume. Significant funding for research, photography, and other attendant costs was later supplied by generous gifts from The Seminarians, the estate of Nathaniel T. Dexter, and other private sources acknowledged with gratitude here.

Principal funding for the publication of this catalogue was provided by Chelsey and David Remington, in honor and memory of Virginia Wireman Cute, David's aunt and herself a distinguished modern silversmith represented in our collection. It is a great pleasure to recognize their essential and generous support of this endeavor.

MALCOLM ROGERS
Ann and Graham Gund Director

This publication has been made possible by a generous gift from

DAVID AND CHELSEY REMINGTON

in memory of his aunt

VIRGINIA WIREMAN CUTE

silversmith, professor of metalsmithing,
Distinguished Daughter of Pennsylvania,
and direct descendant of the noted
Richardson family of Philadelphia silversmiths

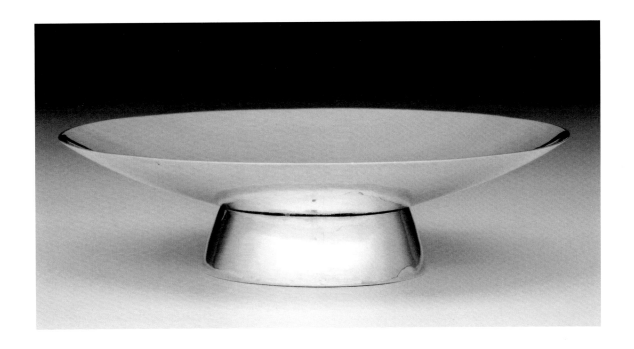

Preface

Silver—a "Mineral of that Excellent Nature," according to the seventeenth-century Englishman William Badcock—is literally a key element in the art and material culture of the Americas. Much of the silver used in the works of art included in this catalogue, for example, initially came out of the earth from the legendary mines of Potosí in South America, the product of inhumane slave labor, or was excavated from the mammoth deposits of the Comstock Lode and the surrounding territory, discovered and exploited in the late nineteenth century in the North American West at a time when people were, as Mark Twain put it, "smitten with the silver fever." This raw material from the Americas, often recycled over time through the proverbial melting pot, has been fashioned and refashioned into the stylish objects seen here.

The qualities of silver as a noble metal make it an ideal medium for artistic expression. Because of its nature as a crystal, it can be hammered repeatedly, and then, as the crystals harden, they can be reformed through annealing and hammered again. Malleable and ductile, it can easily be cast, drawn into thin wire, flattened into sheets, and otherwise manipulated by a wide range of techniques. Its reflectivity makes it an ideal canvas for the manipulation of light through plain or embellished surfaces. Silver's purity and thermal conductivity make it useful for a wide array of pouring, drinking, and serving vessels as well as for a rich variety of spoons and flatware. These properties challenge the artist in metal each time he or she begins to design an object, allowing for innovation and creativity.

Endowed with intrinsic value by millennia of tradition, silver has been principally a "luxury" material, and thus most objects made of silver have been commissioned or purchased by people of ample means. Many of the objects included here were indeed the possessions of the wealthy. However, a wider circle of people have owned silver in small quantities—perhaps just a spoon, for example, in seventeenth-century New England, where a family might have used it for medicinal purposes due to silver's purity—or encountered it in communal circumstances,

including religious services. Easily engraved, this durable and valuable metal has been in ideal material for objects that often have become icons of family continuity, passed down as heirlooms from generation to generation.

The seven hundred objects catalogued here represent many, but by no means all, of the forms produced in the Americas during roughly four centuries, in the small shops of eighteenth-century goldsmiths such as Paul Revere or the studios of contemporary metalsmiths, and in the large factories of such industrial leaders as Tiffany and Gorham. They range from monumental punch bowls to humble spoons, from stylish chocolate pots to utilitarian child's cups, from commodious tankards to mate cups and bombillas. As a whole, they provide for a fuller understanding of silver objects as art, as craft, and as commodity, in a way that only a collection that contains masterpieces in abundance as well as a broad assortment of forms and makers can achieve. Each object adds depth and richness to the Museum's great collection of silver from the Americas, which can be seen and studied in an historical and international context of other objects ranging from the ancient world to significant holdings of comparable silver from England and France.

As the reader here will discover, silver objects shed light on the human condition in a manifold variety of ways that touch on many aspects of life, from the domestic to the ecclesiastical, from the prosaic to the profound, from the technological to the gustatory. Each object is a polysemous three-dimensional embodiment of memory—of the stories of its maker, its original and subsequent owners, of the techniques of its manufacture, of the social customs it enlivened, and of many other facets of our history. Thus the objects cataloged here, meticulously preserved and cared for, like the other examples in the collection, provide abundant information for the historian, collector, student, and layman to analyze in the ongoing quest to more fully understand the beauty and fullness of life.

GERALD W. R. WARD

Acknowledgments

I would like to express my own appreciation to the curators and donors, and the Museum's administration for supporting this endeavor. Malcolm Rogers, Ann and Graham Gund Director, and Katherine Getchell, Deputy Director, Curatorial, provided support for this catalogue, and we are grateful to them.

This catalogue is chiefly indebted, however, to David and Chelsey Remington. As a descendant of the Richardsons, Philadelphia's great colonial silversmithing family, and the nephew of Virginia Wireman Cute, professor of metalsmithing at the Museum School of Art in Philadelphia (now University of the Arts), David Remington understands and appreciates the art of the silversmith. It was through a chance conversation with David's wife, Chelsey, that we first discussed Virginia Cute's contributions, and I learned of their interest in silver. Ever since that time I have been deeply grateful for their continued interest and support.

Additional funding came from several sources. The National Endowment for the Arts, a federal agency, provided seed money for the project. These funds were followed by a bequest from the estate of Nathaniel Dexter, a longtime friend of the department, and gifts from Stephen and Leigh Braude, The Seminarians, and The Museum Loan Network. Mr. William L. Proctor, chancellor of Flagler College and administrator of the Flagler Foundation, awarded funds for research on Latin American silver.

Jonathan L. Fairbanks, the Katharine Lane Weems Curator of American Decorative Arts and Sculpture, Emeritus, and head of the former Department of American Decorative Arts and Sculpture, was supportive of this venture from its beginnings, and his enthusiasm, guidance, and example are an inspiration. Most of the objects in this book were collected during his remarkable tenure at the Museum. Our fellow department staff members, who included Terry Cyr, Anne Dort Moffett (whose special role is discussed elsewhere), Linda Foss Nichols, Maria Pulsone Woods, Rachel Monfredo, and Rose Verheul-Goosen, were instrumental in taking on additional tasks, while Patrick McMahon clarified budgetary tangles. Grants administrators Marjorie Saul and Jennifer Cooper aided in securing funds for the project. But most important of all were the efforts of my co-contributors Jane Port, Rebecca Reynolds, and Gerald Ward, whose catalogue entries and essays comprise a large part of this volume.

We are grateful for the assistance of present and former members of the Department of the Art of the Americas, including Elliot Bostwick Davis, chair of Art of the Americas; Nonie Gadsden; Kelly H. L'Ecuyer; Danielle Kachapis; Toni Pullman; Angela Segalla Breeden; and Katie DeMarsh.

The staffs at numerous institutions have been helpful in researching the histories of the objects recorded in this volume: Stanley Ellis Cushing, Boston Athenaeum; Alana Bubnis, Cumberland County Historical Society; Jamelle Lyons, Archivist, Fall River Historical Society; Diane Shepherd, Lynn Historical Society; Peter Drummey, Anne Bentley, and Seth M. Vose III, under the direction of William Fowler at the Massachusetts Historical Society; Brenda Lynn, Museum of Polo and Hall of Fame, Lake Worth, Florida; John Wood, Public Record of the National Archives of Great Britain; William A. Peniston and Jeffrey V. Moy, The Newark Museum; David Eagleton, Sheffield Hallam University (formerly Sheffield College of Art); and Bert Denker and Margaret Welch, Decorative Arts Photograph Collection, Winterthur Museum. At the Museum of Fine Arts, Boston, we have been assisted by librarians Nancy Allen, Maureen Melton, and Debbie Barlow-Smedstead and their staff.

Scholars, silversmiths, dealers, genealogists, armorial specialists, and historians have offered the benefit of their expertise. These include Ellenor Alcorn, Henry Beckwith, Robert Butler, Elenita Chickering, Judith Graham, Merri Lou Schaumann, Iris and the late Seymour Schwartz, J. Peter Spang, Michael Weller of Argentum Antiques, Stephen Vaughan, and William Voss.

The following colleagues shared their knowledge regarding the works in their care: Kevin L. Stayton, Brooklyn Museum; Janine Skerry, Colonial Williamsburg; Amanda Lange, Historic Deerfield; Frances Safford and Beth Carver Wees, Metropolitan Museum of Art; Deborah Dependahl Waters, Museum of the City of New York; Michel Harvey, Museum of Modern Art; Pamela Stewart, St. Louis Art Museum; Thomas Michie and Jayne Stokes, Museum of Art, Rhode Island School of Design; David Brigham, formerly of the Worcester Art Museum; Patricia E. Kane and David Barquist, Yale University Art Gallery; Donald Fennimore, Winterthur Museum; and Barbara McLean

Ward, Moffatt-Ladd House. For translations, Pamela Russell, John Hermann, and Mary Comstock of the Museum's Art of the Ancient World department were especially helpful. Nancy Wilson and Wendy Swanton volunteered hours documenting history of ownership. Their searches at the New England Historic Genealogical Society Library were aided by reference staff directed by David C. Dearborn, library supervisor of the members' reference room, and the staff of the Massachusetts Archives. Many donors provided information on their ancestors, and we are very grateful to all of them for the time and effort they expended on locating family histories and sharing them with our staff. Within the Museum, recorders Bonnie Porter and Julia McCarthy opened their records to us in our search for the history of works that had been on loan for decades. Nevertheless, any and all errors are my responsibility.

Chapters on silver dating to the twentieth and twenty-first centuries were dependent upon many of the artists themselves, who responded to questions about their formative years, their education, and their careers. We wish to thank members of this group who shared their perspectives on the aesthetics and techniques of their day. They are Bernard Bernstein, Margret Craver, John Davis, John Paul Miller, Fred Miller, John Prip, Maria Regnier, Margarete Seeler, Henry Shawah, Carlyle Smith, and Lorna Belle Watkins. Family members Henrietta Wireman Shuttleworth and Judith Skoogfors provided critical information on Virginia Wireman Cute and Olaf Skoogfors, respectively.

For the chapter on Latin American silver, I offer thanks to Vanessa Davidson, who translated large tracts of Spanish text and served as translator for silver scholar Cristina Esteras Martin of Madrid. Professor Esteras Martin provided her time and energy, long after her visit to Boston, and identified objects made for the church of St. Augustine, Florida, during the seventeenth and eighteenth centuries. With the support of the Flagler Foundation we engaged Susan R. Parker, who conducted extensive research in St. Augustine that supported Professor Esteras Martin's theory. Professor Gauvin Bailey of Clark University reviewed the manuscript of this chapter and offered comments. For other aspects of research relating to Latin America and Florida, I am grateful to Pedro Querejazu; Charles Tingley, St. Augustine Historical Society Research Library; Carl Halbert, archeologist, City of St. Augustine; John Padberg, S.J., The Institute of Jesuit Sources; John T. Render, C.P., D.Min.; Debra Wynne, Florida Historical Society; Christopher Hartop; and John Vanderplank.

Project assistants Jennifer Jensen, Holly Collado, and Alex Huff handled the movement of the silver to the polishers and photographers, and recordkeeping of the same. Samantha Gore assisted with recordkeeping at a later stage in the project. Research was conducted by Emily Broekemeier, Sarah Clark, Abby Dorman, Myriam Gorske, Cameron Hall, Kathleen Henderson, Jeanne Hoefliger, Julia Jiannacopoulos, Susmita Lavery, Kathleen Lawrence, Marcia Lomedico, Blake Morandi, Dawn Piscitello, Tania Ralli, and Clare Talbot.

Metalsmithing students and others, including Kerry Ackerman, Susmita Lavery, Stephen O'Neil, Leah Piken, Dawn Piscitello, Audrey Oster, Veronica Tucker, and Sung-Hae Yun, volunteered to polish more than five hundred pieces of silver; Museum Associate Jane Hinkley was a devoted silver polisher who gave us several years of assistance. Funds secured by conservation director Arthur Beale enabled the Museum to hire Martha Shaw, who has worked on the collection since 2000. Collections care staff members Seth Waite and Brett Angell moved silver from vault to photographers to conservation labs.

Conservation scientists Richard Newman and Michele Derrick and conservators Susanne Gansicke, Abigail Hyman, Marie Svoboda, and Mei-An Tsu examined many of the objects illustrated in this volume. Dr. George Taylor of Children's Hospital provided CT scans of the resinous portion of the St. Augustine cross. Karen Gausch and Will Jeffers provided assistance on care of the collection.

Silver is a difficult subject to photograph, and we were rewarded by the services of staff photographers beginning with John Woolf, who worked with us in the first months of the project. He was succeeded by Gary Ruuska, whose work can be seen on nearly every page. Additional photographs were supplied by John Lutsch, David Mathews, Greg Heins, and Michael Gould. Jennifer Riley and Nicole Crawford, under the direction of Tom Lang, oversaw the paperwork connected with each photograph.

Former Information Technology head Sam Quigley ably guided the project through several stages of database development; his successor, Linda Pulliam, continued his work.

The staff of MFA Publications, including Mark Polizzotti, Matthew Battles, Emiko Usui, Terry McAweeney, and Jodi Simpson, brought our manuscript to life. Mary Ellen Wilson did an incredible job of copyediting a complicated manuscript, and Dean Bornstein designed the book with flair and grace.

JEANNINE FALINO

Notes to the Catalogue

In 1972 Kathryn C. Buhler published *American Silver, 1655–1825, in the Museum of Fine Arts, Boston*. This monumental two-volume work contains detailed entries on more than six hundred objects dating from the seventeenth through the early nineteenth centuries. However, that catalogue, a standard reference in the field of American decorative arts, no longer fully reflects the Museum's remarkable holdings in American silver.

This publication, a third volume to Buhler's work, principally presents objects acquired by the Museum from 1972 through 2004. Most entered the collection during the extraordinary tenure of Jonathan L. Fairbanks, the Katharine Lane Weems Curator of American Decorative Arts and Sculpture from 1971 to 1999 and now curator emeritus. The objects on the following pages reflect his appreciation of all types of American silver as well as his understanding of silver objects as both beautiful artworks and significant historical documents. They range in date from the extraordinary vessels produced by Hull and Sanderson in colonial Boston to masterpieces of contemporary design created by metalsmiths working today. Many are generous gifts made possible through the efforts of Anne Dort Moffett, who worked diligently for several years to convert long-term loans to gifts, thus enriching the Museum's collections enormously.

In addition, this volume catalogues several works made after 1825 that formed part of the Museum's collection prior to 1972 but were omitted by Buhler because of their late date of manufacture. Among these is the first piece of American silver acquired by the Museum—a Tiffany & Co. pitcher purchased at the Philadelphia Centennial in 1876 and given to the Museum in 1877 (cat. no. 248).

The creation of the Department of the Art of the Americas in 1999 brought the opportunity to include several silver objects in the Spanish-colonial mode that were made in Mexico and South America. Some are recent acquisitions, including many gifts from Lavinia and Landon Clay, but many have been in the collection for nearly a century.

The principal author of the catalogue is Jeannine Falino, who conceived of the project in the early 1990s and has been involved throughout its development. She prepared the essays and entries for colonial (chap. 1), twentieth-century (chap. 6), and Spanish colonial (chap. 7) objects; in addition, she contrib-uted to the introductory essays for chapters 4 and 5; some of the entries in chapters 2, 4, and 5; and the appendix on church silver. Jane L. Port prepared the essay and entries for mid nineteenth-century objects (chap. 3) and also contributed some major entries on federal-period objects in chapter 2. Rebecca Reynolds wrote the entries for the aesthetic (chap. 4) and arts and crafts (chap. 5) movements as well as contributing to the essays for those chapters. Gerald W. R. Ward contributed the essay and most of the entries for federal-period silver (chap. 2). He and Jeannine Falino shepherded the manuscript through compilation and editing. In the end, the catalogue is a group effort, reflecting not only the scholarship of these contributors but the efforts of many curators in the American decorative arts department between 1972 and the present.

Unlike the regional organization chosen by Buhler, this book is divided chronologically into chapters. This structure results in the appearance in more than one chapter of an individual or firm, principally Paul Revere, Gorham Manufacturing Company, and Tiffany & Co. Each chapter begins with a short introductory essay. Within each of the first six chapters, objects are arranged alphabetically by maker, with each maker's work then presented chronologically. (An exception is the silver of Arthur Stone, which is divided into several groupings.) The last chapter is devoted to Spanish-colonial works, which are arranged by form. We hope this categorization will serve a wide audience.

Each entry begins with a heading containing the maker's name and vital dates (or working dates), the name of the form, the place and date of its manufacture, and the Museum's credit line and accession number. Dimensions (in inches and centimeters) and troy weight (in ounces, pennyweight, and grains as well as in grams) are provided for each piece. The following abbreviations are used: H. (height), W. (width), D. (depth), L. (length), Diam. (diameter), Wt. (weight), in. (inches), cm (centimeters), oz (troy ounces), dwt (pennyweight), gr. (grains), gm (grams). Unless otherwise noted, dimensions are "outside," or maximum, measurements. Diameter is given (instead of depth) for rounded objects and is taken at both the widest point or base and the lip. For flatware, the length was measured from the tip of the handle to the tip of the bowl or tine, and the width refers to the width of the bowl at its widest point. Marks and inscriptions are given in full, and their locations are noted. Armorials, when present, are described under a separate heading.

Each object is discussed in a brief interpretive essay that places it in context and highlights relevant issues of manufacture, attribution, use, history, and aesthetic quality. Basic biographical information is given in the first entry for a person or company. We recognize that, on early silver, a maker's mark is a "shop mark" and that several people were involved in the fabrication of every object. When known, the names of craftsmen, designers, or other contributors are noted in the heading.

The objects included are of silver, unless gilding or other materials are noted under *Description*. Although the Museum's object files often contain information about an object's alloy content, as determined by X-ray fluorescence spectrometry, those details are included only if germane to the discussion. Provided is a description of the appearance and construction of each object, along with a note on condition. The reader should understand that each object has suffered wear and tear commensurate with its age; for the most part, only major replacements, restorations, and other alterations are noted.

We have paid great attention to tracing the provenance of each object, and a summary of that research appears in the *History* section. We have recorded as well each time an object has been shown publicly; these instances are listed chronologically in *Exhibitions and publications*. If an exhibition was accompanied by a catalogue, the book alone is cited; the note "none" appears if an object has not been previously exhibited or published.

Full citations for frequently cited sources and abbreviations are provided at the beginning of the catalogue. For nearly all objects, additional information appears in the Museum's object data files in the Department of the Art of the Americas, which are available to researchers by appointment. This volume does not include every object in the Museum's collection that falls within the above-mentioned parameters. For more information on the Museum's complete holdings, contact the Department of the Art of the Americas.

Frequently Cited Sources and Abbreviations

AIC 1902–

Art Institute of Chicago. *Exhibition of Original Designs for Decorations and Examples of Arts Crafts Having Distinct Artistic Merit.* Chicago: Art Institute of Chicago, 1902–10.

AFA 1994

American Federation of the Arts. *Arthur J. Stone: Master Silversmith.* New York: American Federation of the Arts, 1994.

Alcorn 2000

Alcorn, Ellenor. *English Silver in the Museum of Fine Arts, Boston.* Vol. 2. Boston: Museum of Fine Arts, Boston, 2000.

Anderson 1941

Anderson, Lawrence. *The Art of the Silversmith in Mexico, 1519–1936.* 2 vols. New York: Oxford University Press, 1941.

Avery 1920

Avery, Louise C. *American Silver of the Seventeenth and Eighteenth Centuries: A Study Based on the Clearwater Collection.* New York: Metropolitan Museum of Art, 1920.

Avery 1930

Avery, C. Louise. *Early American Silver.* New York: Century Company, 1930.

Avery 1931

Avery, C. Louise. "One Hundred Notable Examples of Early New York Silver." *Bulletin of the Metropolitan Museum of Art* 26, no. 12 (December 1931): 17–21.

Avery 1932

Avery, C. Louise. *Early New York Silver.* New York: Metropolitan Museum of Art, 1932.

Belden 1980

Belden, Louise Conway. *Marks of American Silversmiths in the Ineson-Bissell Collection.* Charlottesville: University Press of Virginia, 1980.

Belden 1983

Belden, Louise Conway. *The Festive Tradition: Table Decoration and Desserts in America, 1650–1900.* New York: W.W. Norton, 1983.

Bigelow 1917

Bigelow, Francis Hill. *Historic Silver of the Colonies and Its Makers.* Rev. ed. New York: Macmillan Company, 1917.

Bigelow 1941

Bigelow, Francis Hill. *Historic Silver of the Colonies and Its Makers.* New York: Macmillan Company, 1941.

BGMI

Herbert, Mirana C., and Barbara McNeil, comps. *Biography & Genealogy Master Index.* Detroit: Gale Research Co., 2000. (http://www.ancestry.com/search/rectype/biolist/bgmi/main.htm)

Bohan and Hammerslough 1970

Bohan, Peter, and Philip Hammerslough. *Early Connecticut Silver, 1700–1840.* Middletown, Conn.: Wesleyan University Press, 1970.

Bolton 1927

Bolton, Charles Knowles. *Bolton's American Armory.* Boston: F. W. Armory Faxon Company, 1927.

Boston Assessors Taking Books

Boston, City of. *Taking Books of Assessors of the Town of Boston*, on deposit in the Boston Public Library, Rare Books and Manuscripts Department.

Boston Tercentenary 1930

Boston Tercentenary Fine Arts and Crafts Exhibition. Exh. cat. Boston: Horticultural Hall, 1930.

Bostonian Society 1979

Cabot, Harriet Ropes. *Handbook of the Bostonian Society.* Boston: Bostonian Society, 1979.

Buck 1888

Buck, John H. *Old Plate.* New York: Gorham Manufacturing Company, 1888.

Buck 1903

Buck, John H. *Old Plate: Ecclesiastical, Decorative, and Domestic.* Rev. ed. New York: Gorham Manufacturing Company, 1903.

Buhler 1956

Buhler, Kathryn C. *Colonial Silversmiths: Masters and Apprentices.* Boston: Museum Fine Arts, Boston, 1956.

Buhler 1960

Buhler, Kathryn C. *Masterpieces of American Silver.* Exh. cat. Richmond: Virginia Museum of Fine Arts, 1960.

Buhler 1965

Buhler, Kathryn C. *Massachusetts Silver in the Frank L. and Louise C. Harrington Collection.* Worcester, Mass.: Privately printed, 1965.

Buhler 1972

Buhler, Kathryn C. *American Silver, 1655–1825, in the Museum of Fine Arts, Boston.* 2 vols. Boston: Museum of Fine Arts, Boston, 1972.

Buhler 1979

Buhler, Kathryn C. *American Silver from the Colonial Period through the Early Republic in the Worcester Art Museum.* Worcester, Mass.: Worcester Art Museum, 1979.

Buhler and Hood 1970

Buhler, Kathryn C., and Graham Hood. *American Silver: Garvan and Other Collections in the Yale University Art Gallery.* 2 vols. New Haven: Yale University Press, 1970.

Carcedo 1997

Carcedo, Paloma, et al. *Plata y plateros del Perú.* Lima: Patrono Plate del Perú, 1997.

Carpenter 1954

Carpenter, Ralph E., Jr. *The Arts and Crafts of Newport, Rhode Island, 1640–1820.* Newport: Preservation Society of Newport County, 1954.

Carpenter 1978

Carpenter, Charles H., Jr., with Mary Grace Carpenter. *Tiffany Silver.* New York: Dodd, Mead, 1978.

Carpenter 1982

Carpenter, Charles H., Jr. *Gorham Silver, 1881–1981.* New York: Dodd, Mead, 1982.

Carpenter and Carpenter 1987

Carpenter, Charles H., Jr., and Mary Grace Carpenter. *The Decorative Arts and Crafts of Nantucket*. New York: Dodd, Mead, 1987.

Chickering 1989

Chickering, Elenita C. "Arthur J. Stone, 1847–1938, An Anglo-American Silversmith." *Apollo* 130, no. 330 (new series) (August 1989): 95–101.

Chickering 1994

Chickering, Elenita C., with Sarah Morgan Ross. *Arthur J. Stone, 1847–1938: Designer and Silversmith*. Boston: Boston Athenaeum, 1994.

Clarke 1932

Clarke, Hermann F. *John Coney, Silversmith, 1655–1722*. Boston: Houghton Mifflin, 1932.

Clarke 1940

Clarke, Hermann F. *John Hull: A Builder of the Bay Colony*. Portland, Me.: Southworth-Anthoenson Press, 1940.

Clayton 1971

Clayton, Michael. *The Collector's Dictionary of the Silver and Gold of Great Britain and North America*. New York and Cleveland: World Publishing Company, 1971.

Cleveland 1908

Cleveland Decorative Arts Club. *Catalogue of the Arts & Crafts Exhibition, Cleveland School of Art*. Exh. booklet, 1908.

Cooper 1993

Cooper, Wendy A. *Classical Taste in America, 1800–1840*. New York: Baltimore Museum of Art and Abbeville Press, 1993.

Currier 1938

Currier, Ernest M. *Marks of Early American Silversmiths*. Portland, Me.: Southworth-Anthoensen Press, 1938.

Curtis 1913

Curtis, George Munson. *Early Connecticut Silver and Its Makers*. Meriden, Conn.: International Silver Company, 1913.

Cutten 1950

George B. Cutten, "Sucket Forks," *Antiques* 57, no. 6 (June 1950): 440-41.

DAB

Dictionary of American Biography, under the auspices of the American Council of Learned Societies; edited by Allen Johnson et al. 20 vols. plus 10 supplements and indexes. New York: Charles Scribner's Sons, 1928–1985.

DAPC

Decorative Arts Photographic Collection, Winterthur Museum, Winterthur, Del.

Darling 1964

Darling, Herbert F. *New York State Silversmiths*. Eggertsville, N.Y.: Darling Foundation of New York State Early American Silversmiths and Silver, 1964.

Darling 1977

Darling, Sharon S. *Chicago Metalsmiths: An Illustrated History*. Chicago: Chicago Historical Society, 1977.

Deutsch 1995

Deutsch, Alexandra. "George Christian Gebelein: The Craft and Business of a 'Modern Paul Revere.'" Master's thesis, University of Delaware, 1995.

Dexter and Lainhart 1989

Dexter, John Haven, and Ann Smith Lainhart, eds. *First Boston City Directory (1789) Including Extensive Annotations by John Haven Dexter (1791–1876)*. Boston: New England Historic Genealogical Society, 1989.

Doty 1987

Doty, Robert M., ed. *Henry Petzal, Silversmith*. Manchester, N.H.: Currier Gallery of Art, 1987.

Ellis Memorial 1984

[Catalogue of] *The Twenty-Fifth Ellis Memorial Antiques Show 1984*. Boston, 1984.

Emlen 1984

Emlen, Robert P. "Wedding Silver for the Browns: A Rhode Island Family Patronizes a Boston Goldsmith." *American Art Journal* 16 (spring 1984): 39–50.

English-Speaking Union 1960

[English-Speaking Union]. *An Exhibition of American Silver and Art Treasures*. London: English-Speaking Union, 1960.

Failey 1998

Dean F. Failey, with Robert J. Hefner and Susan E. Klaffky, *Long Island Is My Nation: The Decorative Arts and Craftsmen, 1640–1830*. Setauket, N.Y.: Society for the Preservation of Long Island Antiquities and Mount Ida Press, 1998.

Fairbanks 1975

Fairbanks, Jonathan L., et al. *Paul Revere's Boston, 1734–1818*. Boston: Museum of Fine Arts, Boston, 1975.

Fairbanks 1981

Fairbanks. Jonathan L. "A Decade of Collecting Decorative Arts and Sculpture at the Museum of Fine Arts, Boston." *Antiques* 120, no. 3 (September 1981): 590–636.

Fairbanks 1991

Fairbanks, Jonathan L., et al. *Collecting American Decorative Arts and Sculpture, 1971–1991*. Boston: Museum of Fine Arts, Boston, 1991.

Fairbanks and Trent 1982

Fairbanks, Jonathan, and Robert Trent. *New England Begins: The Seventeenth Century*. 3 vols. Boston: Museum of Fine Arts, Boston, 1982.

Fales 1970

Fales, Martha Gandy. *Early American Silver for the Cautious Collector*. New York: Funk & Wagnalls, 1970.

Fales 1995

Fales, Martha Gandy. *Jewelry in America, 1600–1900*. Woodbridge, Eng.: Antique Collectors' Club, 1995.

Falino and Ward 2001

Falino, Jeannine, and Gerald W. R. Ward, eds. *New England Silver and Silversmithing, 1620–1815*. Boston: Colonial Society of Massachusetts; distributed by University Press of Virginia, 2001.

Fane 1996

Fane, Dianna, ed. *Converging Cultures: Art and Identity in Spanish America*. New York: Brooklyn Museum in association with Harry N. Abrams, 1996.

Fennimore 1971

Fennimore, Donald L. "Elegant Patterns of Uncommon Good Taste: Domestic Silver by Thomas Fletcher and Sidney Gardiner." Masters thesis, University of Delaware, 1971.

Fennimore 1996

Fennimore, Donald L. *Metalwork in America: Copper and Its Alloys from the Winterthur Collection*. Winterthur, Del.: Henry Francis du Pont Winterthur Museum, 1996. Distributed by Antique Collectors' Club.

Flynt and Fales 1968

Flynt, Henry, and Martha Gandy Fales. *The Heritage Foundation Collection of Silver, with Biographical Sketches of New England Silversmiths.* Old Deerfield, Mass.: Heritage Foundation, 1968.

Freedley 1856

Freedley, Edwin T. *Leading Pursuits and Leading Men: A Treatise on the Principal Trades and Manufactures of the United States.* Phildaelphia: E. Young, 1856.

French 1939

French, Hollis. *Jacob Hurd and His Sons, Nathaniel and Benjamin, Silversmiths, 1702–1781.* Walpole Society, 1939.

Gibb 1969

Gibb, George Sweet. *The Whitesmiths of Taunton: A History of Reed and Barton, 1824–1943.* Cambridge: Harvard University Press, 1943. Reprint, New York: J & J Harper Editions, 1969.

Glendenning 1973

Glendenning, Herman W. "Arthur J. Stone, Master Craftsman, Dean of American Silversmiths, 1847–1938." *Silver* 6, no. 5 (September/October 1973): 27–28.

Goldsborough 1975

Goldsborough, Jennifer Faulds. *Eighteenth- and Nineteenth-Century Maryland Silver in the Collection of the Baltimore Museum of Art.* Edited by Ann Boyce Harper. Baltimore: Baltimore Museum of Art, 1975.

Goldsborough 1983

Goldsborough, Jennifer Faulds. *Silver in Maryland.* Baltimore: Museum and Library of Maryland History, Maryland Historical Society, in cooperation with Historic Annapolis, the Baltimore Museum of Art, and the Peale Museum, 1983.

Gourley 1965

Gourley, Hugh J. *The New England Silversmith: An Exhibition of New England Silver from the Mid-Seventeenth Century to the Present, Selected from New England Collections.* Providence: Rhode Island School of Design, 1965.

Halsey 1911

Halsey, R. T. Haines. *Catalogue of an Exhibition of Silver Used in New York, New Jersey, and the South.* Exh. cat. New York: Metropolitan Museum of Art, 1911.

Hammerslough and Feigenbaum 1958–73

Hammerslough, Philip H., and Rita F. Feigenbaum. *American Silver Collected by Philip H. Hammerslough.* 4 vols. Hartford: Privately printed, 1958–73.

Harvard Tercentenary Exhibition 1936

[Harvard University]. *Catalogue of Furniture, Silver, Pewter, Glass, Ceramics, Paintings, Prints, Together with Allied Arts and Crafts of the Period 1636–1836.* Cambridge: Harvard University Press, 1936.

Herndon 1892

Herndon, Richard, comp. *Boston of To-Day: A Glace at Its History and Characteristics, with Biographical Sketches and Portraits of Many of Its Professional and Business Men.* Edited by Edwin M. Bacon. Boston: Post Publishing Company, 1892.

Hollan 1994

Hollan, Catherine B. *In the Neatest, Most Fashionable Taste: Three Centuries of Alexandria Silver.* Alexandria, Va.: Lyceum, 1994.

Hood 1971

Hood, Graham. *American Silver: A History of Style, 1650–1900.* New York: Praeger Publishers, 1971.

Howard 1895

Howard, J. P. *Novelties for Christmas.* Trade cat. New York: J. P. Howard, 1895.

IGI

International Genealogical Index. http://www.familysearch.org

Jackson 1911

Jackson, Sir Charles James. *An Illustrated History of Silver Plate, Ecclesiastical and Secular.* 2 vols. London: B. T. Batsford, 1911.

Jackson 1949

Jackson, Sir Charles James. *English Goldsmiths and Their Marks.* London: B. T. Batsford, 1949.

Jamestown 1907

The Massachusetts Colonial Loan Exhibit at the Jamestown Ter-Centennial Exposition, 1607–1907. Boston: Wright and Potter Printing Company, 1907.

Johnston 1994

Johnston, Phillip M. *Catalogue of American Silver: The Cleveland Museum of Art.* Cleveland: Cleveland Museum of Art, 1994.

Jones 1913

Jones, E. Alfred. *The Old Silver of American Churches.* Letchworth, Eng.: National Society of Colonial Dames of America, 1913.

Kane 1987

Kane, Patricia E. "John Hull and Robert Sanderson: First Masters of New England Silver." Ph.D. diss., Yale University, 1987.

Kane 1998

Kane, Patricia E., Jeannine J. Falino, Deborah A. Federhen, Barbara McLean Ward, and Gerald W. R. Ward, with the assistance of Karen L. Wight and Edgard Moreno. *Colonial Massachusetts Silversmiths and Jewelers: A Biographical Dictionary Based on the Notes of Francis Hill Bigelow and John Marshall Phillips.* New Haven: Yale University Art Gallery, 1998. Distributed by University Press of New England.

Kaplan 1987

Kaplan, Wendy, et al. *"The Art That Is Life": The Arts and Crafts Movement in America, 1875–1920.* Boston: Museum of Fine Arts, Boston, 1987.

Kirkham 2000

Kirkham, Pat, ed. *Women Designers in the USA, 1900–2000: Diversity and Difference.* New Haven and London: Yale University Press for the Bard Graduate Center for Studies in the Decorative Arts, New York, 2000.

Leighton 1976

Leighton, Margaretha Gebelein, in collaboration with Esther Gebelein Swain and J. Herbert Gebelein. *George Christian Gebelein, Boston Silversmith, 1878–1945.* Boston: Privately printed, 1976.

Louisiana Purchase 1904

Official Catalogue of Exhibitors, Universal Exposition, St. Louis, U.S.A. St. Louis, Mo.: Official Catalogue Company, 1904.

Esteras Martín 1992a

Esteras Martín, Cristina. *La platería del Museo Franz Mayer: obras escogidas, siglos XVI–XIX.* Mexico: Museo Franz Mayer, 1992.

Esteras Martín 1992b

Esteras Martín, Cristina. *Marcas de Platería Hispanoamericana, Siglos XVI–XX* (Madrid: Ediciones Tuero, 1992).

Esteras Martín 1993

Esteras Martín, Cristina. *Arequipa y el arte de la platería: Siglos XVI–XX.* Madrid: Ediciones Tuero, 1993.

Esteras Martín 1997

Esteras Martín, Cristina. *Platería del Perú virreinal, 1535–1825.* Madrid: Gruppo BBV; Lima: Banco Continental, 1997.

Matthews 1907

Matthews, John, ed. *Matthews American Armory and Blue Book.* London: John Matthews, 1907.

McClinton 1968

McClinton, Katherine Morrison. *Collecting American 19th-Century Silver.* New York: Bonanza Books, 1968.

MCMA 1892

Annals of the Massachusetts Charitable Mechanic Association, 1795–1892. Boston, Press of Rockwell and Churchill, 1892.

Mexican Silver 1993

Mexican Silver. Brussels: Foundation Europalia International, 1993.

Meyer 1997

Meyer, Marilee Boyd, et al. *Inspiring Reform: Boston's Arts and Crafts Movement* Wellesley and New York: Davis Museum and Cultural Center, 1987. Distributed by Harry N. Abrams.

MFA

Museum of Fine Arts, Boston

MFA 1906

[Museum of Fine Arts, Boston]. *American Silver: The Work of Seventeenth- and Eighteenth-Century Silversmiths.* Boston: Museum of Fine Arts, Boston, 1906.

MFA 1911

[Museum of Fine Arts, Boston]. *American Church Silver of the Seventeenth- and Eighteenth-Centuries, with a Few Pieces of Domestic Plate.* Boston: Museum of Fine Arts, 1911.

MFA 1932

[Museum of Fine Arts, Boston]. *Exhibition of Silversmithing by John Coney, 1655–1722.* Exh. booklet. Boston: Museum of Fine Arts, Boston, 1932.

MHS 1991

[Massachusetts Historical Society]. *Witness to America's Past: Two Centuries of Collecting by the Massachusetts Historical Society.* Exh. cat. Boston: Massachusetts Historical Society, 1991.

Miller 1937

Miller, V. Isabelle. *Silver by New York Makers,*

Late 17th Century to 1900. Exh. cat. New York: Museum of the City of New York, 1937.

Miller 1962

Miller, V. Isabelle. *New York Silversmiths of the Seventeenth Century.* Exh. cat. New York: Museum of the City of New York, 1962.

MMA

Metropolitan Museum of Art, New York City.

Mo 1992

Mo, Charles L., *Splendors of the New World: Spanish Colonial Masterworks from the Viceroyalty of Peru.* Charlotte, N.C.: Mint Museum of Art, 1992.

Moore Collection 1980

[Providence College]. *American Silver, 1670–1830: The Cornelius C. Moore Collection at Providence College.* Providence: Rhode Island Bicentennial Foundation and Providence College, 1980.

NEHGR

New England Historic Genealogical Register

NEHGS

New England Historic Genealogical Society, Boston, Massachusetts.

Okie 1928

Okie, Howard Pitcher. *Old Silver and Old Sheffield Plate.* Garden City, N.Y.: Doubleday, Doran, 1928.

Oxford Compact Dictionary 1987

The Compact Edition of the Oxford English Dictionary. 2 vols. Oxford: Oxford University Press, 1987.

Paul Revere 1988

[Paul Revere Association]. *Paul Revere—Artisan, Businessman, and Patriot: The Man Behind the Myth.* Boston: Paul Revere Memorial Association, 1988.

Phillips 1939

Phillips, John Marshall. *Masterpieces of New England Silver, 1650–1800.* New Haven: Yale University Art Gallery, 1939.

Phillips, Parker, and Buhler 1955

The Waldron Phoenix Belknap, Jr., Collection of Portraits and Silver. Edited by John Marshall Phillips, Barbara N. Parker, and Kathryn C. Buhler. Biographical note by Edward Weeks. Cambridge, Harvard University Press, 1955.

Pristo 2002

Pristo, L. J. *Martelé 950-1000 Fine: Gorham's Art Nouveau Silver.* Privately printed, 2002.

Providence 1901

Arts and Crafts Exhibition. Providence, R.I.: Providence Art Club, 1901.

Puig 1989

Puig, Francis J., Judith Banister, Gerald W. R. Ward, and David McFadden, *English and American Silver in the Collection of the Minneapolis Institute of the Arts.* Minneapolis: Institute of the Arts, 1989.

Querejezu and Ferrer 1997

Querejazu, Pedro and Elizabeth Ferrer. *Potosí: Colonial Treasures and the Bolivian City of Silver.* New York: Americas Society Art Gallery, New York, in association with Fundación BHN, La Paz, Bolivia, 1997.

Quimby 1995

Quimby, Ian M. G. *American Silver at Winterthur.* Winterthur, Del.: Henry Francis du Pont Winterthur Museum, 1995.

Rainwater 1986

Rainwater, Dorothy T. *Encyclopedia of American Silver Manufacturers.* Atglen, Pa.: Schiffer Publishing, 1986.

Rainwater and Redfield 1998

Rainwater, Dorothy T., and Judy Redfield. *Encyclopedia of American Silver Manufacturers.* 4th rev. ed. Atglen, Pa.: Schiffer Publishing, 1998.

Revere daybooks

Daybooks of Paul Revere. 2 vols. Massachusetts Historical Society, Boston. Photocopies, Department of the Art of the Americas, Museum of Fine Arts, Boston.

Rollins 1991

Rollins, Alexandra, ed. *Treasures of State: Fine and Decorative Arts in the Diplomatic Reception Rooms of the U.S. Department of State.* New York: Harry N. Abrams, 1991.

Safford 1983

Safford, Frances Gruber. *Colonial Silver in the American Wing.* New York: Metropolitan Museum of Art, 1983.

SACB

Society of Arts and Crafts, Boston.

SACB 1899

Exhibition of the Society of Arts & Crafts, Together with a Loan Collection of Applied Art. Boston: George H. Ellis, 1899.

SACB 1907

Exhibition of the Society of Arts & Crafts, Copley Hall. Boston: Heinzemann Press, 1907.

SACB 1927

Tricennial Exhibition of the Society of Arts & Crafts. Boston: Museum of Fine Arts, Boston, 1927.

Sibley's Harvard Graduates

Sibley, John Langdon, and Clifford K. Shipton. *Biographical Sketches of Graduates of Harvard University* [and variant titles]. 17 vols. Vols. 1–3: Cambridge: Charles William Sever, 1873–85. Vol. 4: Cambridge: Harvard University Press, 1933. Vols. 5–17: Boston: Massachusetts Historical Society, 1937–75.

Silver Supplement 1973

United States Department of State. *Silver Supplement to the Guidebook to the Diplomatic Reception Rooms.* Washington, D.C.: Department of State, 1973.

Simple Elegance 1998

Simple Elegance: Generations of Newburyport Silversmiths. Newburyport, Mass.: Historical Society of Old Newbury, 1988.

Skerry 1981

Skerry, Janine Ellen. "Mechanization and Craft Structure in Nineteenth-Century Silversmithing: The Laformes of Boston." Masters thesis, University of Delaware, 1981.

Smith College 1958

[Smith College Museum of Art]. *Early New England Silver.* Exh. cat. Smith College Museum of Art, 1958.

Spofford 1929

Spofford, Ernest. *Armorial Families of America.* Philadelphia: Bailey, Banks and Biddle Co., 1929.

SSDI

Social Security Death Index

Staatliche Museum 1981

Silberschätze aus Südamerika, 1700–1900. Exh. cat. Munich: Hirmer Verlag, 1981.

Taullard 1947

Taullard, A. *Platería Sudamericana.* Peuser Ltda., Buenos Aires, Argentina, 1947.

Ulehla 1981

Ulehla, Karen Evans, ed. *The Society of Arts and Crafts, Boston, Exhibition Record, 1897–1927.* Boston: Boston Public Library, 1981.

Urgell 1988

Urgell, Guiomar de, et al. *El Mate de plata.* Buenos Aires: Associación Amigos del Museo Municipal de Arte Hispanoamericano "Isaac Fernández Blanco," 1988.

Venable 1994

Venable, Charles L. *Silver in America, 1840–1940.* Dallas: Dallas Museum of Art, 1994. Distributed by Harry N. Abrams.

Vermont 1886

Vermont, Edgar deV., ed. *America Heraldica: A Compilation of Coats of Arms, Crests, and Mottoes of Prominent American Families Settled in This Country before 1800.* New York: Brentano Brothers, 1886–89.

B. Ward 1983

Ward, Barbara McLean. "The Craftsman in a Changing Society: Boston Goldsmiths, 1690–1730." Ph.D. diss., Boston University, 1983.

B. Ward 1984

Ward, Barbara McLean. "Boston Goldsmiths, 1690–1730." In *The Craftsman in Early America.* Edited by Ian M. G. Quimby. New York and London: W.W. Norton, 1984.

Ward and Ward 1979

Ward, Barbara McLean, and Gerald W. R. Ward, eds. *Silver in American Life: Selections from the Mabel Brady Garvan and Other Collections at Yale University.* New York and New Haven: American Federation of Arts and Yale University, 1979.

Ward and Hosley 1985

Ward, Gerald W. R., and William N. Hosley Jr., eds. *The Great River.* Hartford: Wadsworth Atheneum, 1985.

Warren 1975

Warren, David B. *Bayou Bend: American Furniture, Paintings, and Silver from the Bayou Bend Collection.* Houston: Museum of Fine Arts, Houston, 1975.

Warren 1987

Warren, David B., et al. *Marks of Achievement: Four Centuries of American Presentation Silver.* Houston: Museum of Fine Arts, 1987.

Warren 1998

Warren, David B., et al. *American Decorative Arts and Paintings in the Bayou Bend Collection.* Houston: Museum of Fine Arts, Houston, in association with Princeton University Press, 1998.

Waters 2000

Waters, Deborah Dependahl, et al. *Elegant Plate.* 2 vols. New York: Museum of the City of New York, 2000.

Wees 1997

Wees, Beth Carver. *English, Irish, and Scottish Silver at the Sterling and Francine Clark Art Institute.* New York: Hudson Hills Press, 1997.

Whitehill 1970

Whitehill, Walter Muir. *Museum of Fine Arts, Boston: A Centennial History.* 2 vols. Cambridge: Belknap Press, 1970.

Winsor 1881

Winsor, Justin, ed. *The Memorial History of Boston, Including Suffolk County, 1630–1880.* 4 vols. Boston: J. B. Osgood, 1880–81.

WM

The Henry Francis du Pont Winterthur Museum, Winterthur, Delaware.

Wohlauer 1999

Wohlauer, Gilian Shallcross. *MFA: A Guide to the Collection of the Museum of Fine Arts, Boston.* Boston: Museum of Fine Arts, Boston, 1999.

Worthley 1970

Worthley, Harold Field. *Harvard Theological Studies XXV: An Inventory of the Records of the Particular (Congregational) Churches of Massachusetts Gathered 1620–1805.* Cambridge: Harvard University Press; London: Oxford University Press, 1970.

YUAG

Yale University Art Gallery, New Haven, Connecticut.

Silver of the Americas, 1600–2000

CHAPTER I

SILVER IN COLONIAL NORTH AMERICA

Jeannine Falino

Founded in 1630, Boston was one of the first continuously settled British colonies of the Americas. Far to the south lay the territories of Spain, including Florida. There, in the 1620s, the Catholic Church celebrated Mass with sophisticated Mannerist-style vessels fashioned in silver-rich Mexico.[1] North of Boston was New France, where congregations used primarily imported French domestic and liturgical silver until the end of the seventeenth century, when a larger population could support local silversmiths.[2]

When Boston was founded, colonists had little need for such specialized craftsmen since the tasks at hand concerned housing, farming, and establishing Gov. John Winthrop's ideal "city upon a hill."[3] What silver existed had arrived with the colonists, and some had brought considerable quantities.[4] Domestic silver probably served as the first communion vessels for Congregational church services and, in the case of the First Church in Boston (established 1630), included the use of an English steeple cup (fig. 1), an elite form with elaborate Mannerist decoration, that was brought by Winthrop on the *Arbella* and later made a gift to the church.[5] However, as new Separatist worshippers arrived and the population grew, churches began to order sets of communion silver that included multiple drinking vessels; these sets became a distinctive feature of the Congregational service.[6]

In time, silver became a concern for the leadership of the Massachusetts Bay Colony as well, for the lack of hard currency in New England was hampering free trade. Foreign currency fluctuated, and the practice of clipping coins undermined public confidence. The colony was determined to counter this trend by issuing its own coinage. John Hull and Robert Sanderson Sr. formed a partnership to meet these needs.

As the fledgling colony's first mintmasters, Hull and Sanderson developed the initial dies and struck the original coinage in 1652. That same year, they fashioned the first pieces of church silver in English-speaking North America. Norwich-born Sanderson had apprenticed in London, whereas English-born Hull learned the craft in Massachusetts under his half-brother Richard Storer (about 1615–1657+), who later returned to England. Together, Hull and Sanderson trained the first generation of American-born silversmiths, including Jeremiah Dummer, Timothy Dwight (1654–1691/92), Samuel Clarke (1659–1705), and Samuel Paddy (1645–1686).[7] From this small start, a community of silversmiths steadily grew. The fraternity passed along skills and styles to peers and apprentices, and it gained in strength and number along with the expansion of Boston.

Hull and Sanderson's role as mintmasters and silversmiths reflects the essential meaning of the craft as it was conceived in its day. They established the purity of the metal through assaying to assess its value by weight (fig. 2) and to serve as trusted

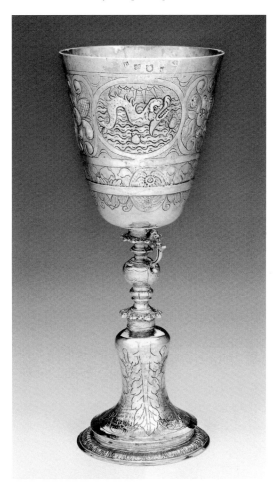

FIG. 1. Cup, London, 1610–11. Silver. Museum of Fine Arts, Boston; Lent by the First and Second Church in Boston.

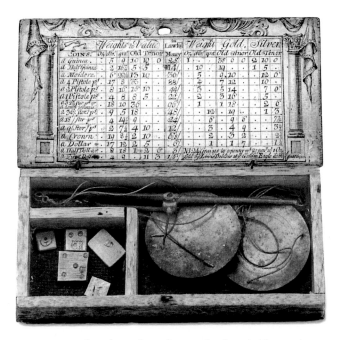

FIG. 2. Box with scales and weights, England, probably London, retailed in Boston by Lewis Deblois, printed ephemera by Nathaniel Hurd. Steel, brass, oak, lead, green baize lining, engraved paper label. Museum of Fine Arts, Boston; American Decorative Arts Curator's Fund (1999.187a–i).

bankers to their clients. As mintmasters, they were charged with transforming the metal into coinage of an established value. And as silversmiths, they sought to create beautiful objects in the service of God and man. When judge and diarist Samuel Sewall (1652–1730) wrote in 1714, "Let us Labour to be Vessels of Gold, or at least of Silver,"[8] he was echoing a biblical sentiment of pre-Christian origins. Yet the paradox of wrought silver lies in its dual role as an ancient symbol of ethereal purity and artfulness as well as a traded commodity in the material world. Thus, the handsome vessels shared at the communion service, or "eyed mightily" in a "handsome cupboard of plate," were admired for not only their beauty but also the prestige and power their monetary value conferred upon the owners.[9]

The lack of local raw materials represented the chief difficulty for New England silversmiths. As mintmasters, Hull and Sanderson had access to silver and thus enjoyed a steady income. Their successors, however, were not as fortunate. They depended on clients to bring outmoded or damaged English silver that could then be sent into the melting pot. English or foreign coinage, such as the Spanish dollar, obtained from patrons through trade and privateering offered another source for the crucible. The scarcity of silver made craftsmen vulnerable to suppliers, who could overcharge with impunity. In such cases,

silversmiths were forced to pass on the costs to their clients or suffer the financial consequences. John Edwards charged his patrons 7.5 percent above the cost of materials and labor if the customer did not supply the metal. In 1755, faced with a 30 percent metal surcharge, the great eighteenth-century silversmith Jacob Hurd was forced into bankruptcy.[10]

Without a doubt, the most productive, innovative, and talented Boston silversmith of the early eighteenth century was John Coney. An apprentice of Dummer, and thus one generation removed from Hull and Sanderson, Coney enjoyed a forty-five-year career that spanned the Mannerist and Baroque eras, all while keeping in touch with the latest trends in English silver. He received important commissions from private citizens such as Samuel Sewall and prominent members of the English government, including Capt. Walter Riddell of Scotland who, for a time, was assigned to the region. Coney filled orders for civic groups and churches and apparently worked until his death; a full complement of silversmithing tools were recorded at the inventory of his estate. In all, his shop executed more than 225 surviving pieces of silver, and it was responsible for fabricating an array of forms, ranging from cups and porringers to such rare and impressive items as grace cups, an inkstand, monteiths, punch bowls (cat. no. 32), and sugar boxes. Coney excelled at engraving as well. Early in his career he produced a salver that is ornamented with fluid and detailed floral decoration; he also fashioned a seal for Harvard College and engraved paper money. When tea and chocolate became fashionable in Boston, Coney was the first to create specialized forms for these imported beverages (cat. no. 35).[11]

How did these colonial silversmiths learn about these new styles and specialized vessels? Hull occasionally traveled to England, but most colonial silversmiths could not spare time away from their workshops. Their ability to offer stylish silver was partially dependent upon the imported plate that sometimes arrived in their shop for repairs. Paul Revere II, for instance, performed many repairs for his patrons and, in so doing, gained a close look at English silver.[12] Others, such as Dummer, may have had access to newly fashionable items through wares imported on merchant ships they owned. Among the best methods of keeping abreast of the latest developments, however, was to hire an immigrant craftsman with mature skills and experience in a London or Continental workshop. These men performed an invaluable service by stimulating the Boston silversmithing community through the introduction of novel concepts and approaches to the craft.

Among such immigrants were William Rouse of Holland; Henry Hurst of Sweden; and Richard Conyers, David Jesse, and Edward Webb of London. Rouse was an elegant engraver, and Hurst and Webb were accomplished chasers; Conyers and Jesse were adept at gadrooning and cut-card ornaments. Of these men, only Webb was truly successful in establishing himself as an independent craftsman in Boston. Most became journeymen in workshops where they were valued for their special skills. As a result, the majority labored in anonymity, placing their master's mark on finished work instead of their own. Edward Winslow employed Hurst when his varied and increasing civic duties kept him from the bench. Like Coney, Winslow produced many unusual and highly ornamented forms, such as chocolate pots and sugar boxes. The knowledge and skills of foreign-trained immigrants may have given the local silversmiths a competitive advantage in fashioning silver for a taste-conscious elite.

By the 1730s, Hurd had succeeded Coney as the most productive silversmith in Boston. More than five hundred objects of a high quality and sophistication were produced in his workshop, which must have been a lively establishment employing many apprentices and specialized journeymen chasers, burnishers, and turners. Hurd's son Nathaniel was an accomplished engraver. Along with producing an abundance of domestic silver, Hurd enjoyed special commissions. He created the admiralty oar, a symbol of power for the Admiralty Court, and cast an engraved silver key for the Charitable Irish Society. Hurd was also commissioned to fashion large two-handled covered cups for presentation purposes and church silver for twenty-five New England congregations.[13]

By the time Paul Revere II came of age in the mid-1750s, he had already learned much about the craft from his father, Apollos Rivoire (who later anglicized his name to Paul Revere). The elder Revere was a French Huguenot émigré who was apprenticed to Coney and was a contemporary of Hurd. The younger Revere had not yet completed his traditional seven-year apprenticeship when his father died, but even before that time, he had already mastered his craft. His earliest documented work is a beaker (cat. no. 111) made in 1753 for the Arlington Street Church; it is stamped with his "pellet Revere" mark a year before his father's death in 1754. The sociable Revere was an active Mason, and despite his artisanal origins, the young patriot was a political maverick well connected to Boston's most elite revolutionary groups. This web of cultural relationships brought him considerable business and may have made the difference between his phenomenal productivity and that of his contemporaries such as Samuel Minott, Zachariah Brigden, and Benjamin Burt.[14]

The young Revere quickly mastered his father's standard repertoire of cream jugs, beakers, and tankards and, later in his career, developed new forms that proved popular with Bostonians. He handled a large business in flatware and harness goods while continuing to fashion elegant hollowware for the city's elite. In his later career (see chapter 2), Revere embraced new technological developments and used them to great advantage.

Populated by such productive silversmiths as Coney, Hurd, and Revere, Boston became the silversmithing center in eighteenth-century New England. Nevertheless, the craft was practiced in many outlying areas, albeit to a lesser degree.

Between 1697 and 1714, Salem was the only other Massachusetts port authorized by the British crown to accept foreign goods. From an early date, therefore, port business attracted a wealthy merchant class, many of whom had both the desire and the means to purchase silver. Boston's talented pool of craftsmen actively served this population, thus preventing Salem from becoming a major silversmithing center until the late eighteenth century.

The same was true for silversmiths working in the Connecticut River valley of western Massachusetts and Connecticut who found it difficult to establish workshops on a scale comparable to those in Boston. Fewer patrons had the means to purchase silver, and the region's wealthy "mansion people" preferred to order from Boston craftsmen who were better equipped to deliver current, fashionable silver goods. The frustrations of the rural, or "micropolitan," silversmith stemmed from the hegemony of the metropolitan craftsmen, who, by virtue of location and training, often fashioned domestic and church goods for the rural smith's own neighbors.[15]

Without the same commissions or opportunities, most rural craftsmen produced modest wares. They fashioned spoons, performed repairs to existing plate, and, if fortunate, raised the occasional cann or porringer. Many led itinerant lives, often advertising their new locations in the newspaper. Their efforts garnered little business, if one judges by the few surviving pieces that carry their touchmarks. Some turned to clockmaking to make ends meet, whereas others, like Benjamin Tappan and John Potwine, became dry-goods merchants and jewelry merchants. Less successful men, such as Jeremiah Snow Jr. (about 1705–after 1778) and his son Jeremiah Snow III (1735–1803), gradually sold off real estate to make ends meet.[16]

One silversmith in western Massachusetts who escaped this fate was William Swan. Born in Charlestown, Swan apprenticed with an unknown master, presumably in Boston. Based on his surviving work, Swan developed creditable skills. While living in Boston in 1749, he produced his greatest achievement in hollowware, a covered two-handled cup fashioned for Col. Benjamin Pickman, who had led the Louisburg expedition. Swan had served in this conflict and may have received the commission for the cup through this association.[17] In 1754 he moved to Worcester, some fifty miles west of Boston, where he enjoyed a long and comfortable career. Perhaps word of the Pickman cup kept his name in high regard, for apparently he enjoyed local patronage that other silversmiths working outside Boston found difficult to attain.

In the early eighteenth century, Rhode Island silversmiths worked primarily for the landed gentry from the colony's southern tip, where a generous port and an accommodating coastline sheltered an elite population whose wealth was derived from the merchant trade, piracy, and privateering. Founded by Roger Williams on the principle of the separation of church and state, Rhode Island attracted people of many faiths. As a result, its communion silver differs markedly from that of Massachusetts, which was dominated by Congregational churches. Newport silversmiths provided most of the silver for Rhode Island's Anglican churches, in contrast to the English plate typically presented to Massachusetts churches of this faith.[18] Despite their proximity to Boston, southern Rhode Island silversmiths such as Samuel Vernon were only occasionally successful in obtaining commissions from a wide geographic area; others, such as the infamous counterfeiter Samuel Casey (1724–1780), introduced the Rococo style to the colony. However, British occupation of Newport during the War of Independence ruined prospects for local craftsmen, and by the end of the eighteenth century, silversmithing activities had permanently shifted to Providence.[19] In addition, some wealthy patrons consistently chose Boston craftsmen for their special commissions, a preference demonstrated by the wedding silver commissioned from Benjamin Burt by the Brown family of Providence (cat. nos. 12–13).

Southwest of New England were the Dutch colonists who settled in New Netherlands. Considered the greatest merchants of Europe, the Dutch valued silver and textiles for their color, sheen, texture, and reflective qualities. Long after England absorbed the colony in 1664, the Dutch clung to their cultural traditions, and for their family silver, they patronized New York silversmiths of similar origin.

Before 1750, fifty-nine silversmiths were working in the province of New York: more than 50 percent were of Dutch descent, 27 percent were Huguenot, 11 percent were English, and 6 percent were of unknown ethnic origin. Some were apprenticed in the Netherlands or England, and one (Kiliaen Van Rensselaer [1663–1719]) apprenticed with Dummer in Boston; most prac-ticed in Manhattan or Albany, farther north. Their forms were comparable to those popular with the English, but they were often heavier and decorated with Dutch ornament.[20]

Most of the communion silver made in New York was produced for the Dutch Reformed Church, which offered broad social programs in addition to spiritual leadership. The church's emphasis on the Dutch language, as late as the 1820s in some parishes, provided another source of comfort and cultural continuity.[21] Favored were tall trumpet-shaped church beakers, which had origins in a domestic Continental form that was adopted as a communion vessel after the Reformation. This vessel was produced most frequently in the New York region. Yet, notably, at least three such beakers were produced for Boston churches by Robert Sanderson, who was raised in the Puritan center of Norwich, England, and his partner John Hull; Sanderson also owned one such Dutch-made cup.[22]

Like other American colonists, the Dutch adapted domestic forms for specific rites of passage. As in New England, mourning rings were common, and in addition engraved spoons were given to pallbearers; birth spoons (*gebortelepel*) celebrated the birth of children. The earliest domestic spoons were cast in an auricular style (cat. no. 3) and were probably used with broad brandywine (*brandewijnskom*) bowls that held brandy and raisins and were passed at family gatherings.[23] A more formal vessel was the covered two-handled cup, a rare and magnificent late-seventeenth-century form. Unlike the taller grace cups of New England, these New York examples were elaborately chased with foliate decoration and engraved with heraldic emblems. Their lids are notable for having three cast feet, allowing them to serve as salvers when inverted.

The transformation of New Netherlands into an English colony was nearly complete by the mid eighteenth-century if one uses silver made in this period as an indicator. The international Rococo style had entered wealthy New York households, as demonstrated by a Paul de Lamerie kettle-on-stand owned by the David family.[24] Myer Myers, America's first Jewish silversmith, emerged as a major New York craftsman during the mid-eighteenth century; he provided his clientele with American adaptations of high-style English forms such as candlesticks and dish rings while producing traditional interpretations of ceremonial silver for the synagogue.[25] After the British occupation of New York between 1776 and 1783, many silversmiths were forced to relocate to Connecticut and elsewhere. By the time they returned, the Rococo had given way to a Neoclassical trend in the decorative arts.

South of New York was Philadelphia, formed in the 1680s when proprietor and governor William Penn offered freedom from religious persecution to settlers. Some 15,000 colonists arrived between 1681 and 1700. The Quaker preference for "plain things" and their avoidance of the "pomp of the world," as Penn wrote to his wife in 1682, led to a taste for unadorned English forms and styles that shared similarities with those of New England.[26] The early English Quaker settlers were moderately wealthy, and many came from the artisan class. They were joined by Irish, German, Swedish, and French immigrants heeding Penn's invitation to worship in freedom. In time, this international mix of colonists resulted in the Quakers' appreciation for the "vain arts and inventions of a luxurious world."[27]

Despite his protestations regarding such "vain arts and inventions," Penn enjoyed beautifully wrought silver and brought several English-made items to Philadelphia. By 1700 he added examples by several local silversmiths, including Johannis Nys (1671–1734), who may have learned his craft in New York. Cesar Ghiselin (about 1670–1734) of Rouen, France, arrived in Philadelphia in 1681 and maintained workshops there as well as in Annapolis, the home of his wife's family. Ghiselin produced a wide range of domestic forms and provided a church plate for Christ Church in Philadelphia.[28] He was probably master to Francis Richardson (1681–1729), who founded a family dynasty that included his son Joseph Sr. (1711–1784) and grandsons Joseph Jr. and Nathaniel (about 1785–1791).[29] Their legacy continued into the twentieth century with the work of their descendant Virginia Wireman Cute (cat. no. 337).

Other notable Philadelphia silversmiths included Irish émigré Philip Syng (1676–1739),[30] whose son and namesake, Philip Jr. (1703–1789), provided the handsomely articulated inkstand that was used at the signing of the Declaration of Independence. The younger Syng also fashioned silver for Lynford Lardner (1715–1774), a Philadelphia attorney and friend of the Penn family who owned fine English silver, such as a handsome silver cruet stand by Samuel Wood (1704–1794). Lardner purchased canns decorated with Rococo engraving by Syng Jr. and ordered stylish candlesticks by Philadelphia silversmith Edmund Milne (d. 1822), who cast them from an English example by John Preist (or Priest).[31]

The exuberant Rococo ornamentation found in Philadelphia silver and furniture far exceeded that produced by Boston, which had been in decline relative to both that city and New York by the second quarter of the eighteenth century.[32] The era is best summarized by an extraordinary teakettle-on-stand made about 1745–55 by Joseph Richardson (1711–1784). Its surface has been repousséd and chased with a profusion of foliage, shell forms, and an asymmetrical cartouche.[33] Joseph Richardson Jr., with Philip Syng Jr., also operated a successful business

in Indian trade silver, in addition to serving an elite clientele in Philadelphia.[34] By contrast, a more conservative and rural style prevailed in western Pennsylvania, as was true in western Massachusetts and elsewhere in New England. This prevalence can be seen in the work of Charles Hall (1742–1783), Peter Getz (1764–1809), and John Ewing (1755–1799).[35]

Farther south, in Maryland and Virginia, there was apparently less incentive for silversmiths to flourish since leading plantation families frequently obtained their silver from England, exchanging crops for manufactured goods. The English crown provided communion silver for local Anglican churches, thus removing another avenue of patronage that had otherwise supported New England and New York silversmiths.[36] Local silversmiths seemingly received few commissions from the planter aristocracy or the church. Nevertheless, within the region's metropolitan centers were several talented craftsmen working in the Rococo style; these included Gabriel Lewyn (w. 1770) of Baltimore, John Inch (1720–1763) of Annapolis, and Alexander Petrie (w. 1744–d. 1768) of Charleston.[37] The high quality of their design and repoussé work suggests that the southern Atlantic states indeed boasted talented silversmiths as well as willing buyers for their hollowware.

Colonial silver—particularly by Boston makers but also those from other regions—has long been an important area of collecting activity for the Museum of Fine Arts, beginning with the initial acquisitions in 1888. In the chapter that follows, the strength of the Museum's interest and commitment is amply demonstrated in some 134 entries embracing major masterpieces, such as First Church silver by Hull and Sanderson (cat. nos. 70–71), John Coney's punch bowl for the Riddell family (cat. no. 32), many works by Paul Revere, and a host of other objects that are important elements in understanding the nature of seventeenth- and eighteenth-century silversmithing in Boston, New York, Philadelphia, and elsewhere.

Notes

1. For Spanish colonial silver, see chapter 7.

2. Jean Trudel, *Silver in New France* (Ottawa: National Gallery of Canada, 1974), 33–37; Rene Villeneuve, *Quebec Silver from the Collection of the National Gallery of Canada* (Ottawa: National Gallery of Canada, 1997).

3. The phrase "For wee must consider that wee shall be as a citty upon a hill" was written by Gov. John Winthrop while sailing the *Arabella* to the New World; John Winthrop, *A Modell of Christian Charity (1630),* Collections of the Massachusetts Historical Society (Boston, 1838), 3d ser., 7:31–48.

4. For several early inventories rich in wrought silver, see Gerald W. R. Ward, "'An Handsome Cupboard of Plate': The Role of Silver in American Life," in Ward and Ward 1979, 33–45; Albert S. Roe and Robert F. Trent, "Robert Sanderson and the Founding of the Boston Silversmiths' Trade," in Fairbanks and Trent 1982, 3:480–89.

5. Roe and Trent 1982, 3:382–84, cat. no. 386. The cup now lacks its original lid.

6. Barbara McLean Ward, "'In a Feasting Posture': Communion Vessels and Community Values in Seventeenth- and Eighteenth-Century New England," *Winterthur Portfolio* 23, no. 1 (spring 1988): 1–24.

7. On Hull and Sanderson, see Kane 1987.

8. M. Halsey Thomas, ed., *The Diary of Samuel Sewall, 1674–1729*, 2 vols., (New York: Farrar, Strauss and Giroux, 1973), 2:757 (May 16, 1714).

9. For a broad discussion on the cultural meanings of silver, see Richard Lyman Bushman, "The Complexities of Silver," in Falino and Ward 2001, 1–15.

10. Barbara McLean Ward, "Forging the Artisan's Identity: Tools and the Goldsmithing Trade in Colonial Massachusetts," in Kane 1998, 28.

11. Kane 1998, 315–34.

12. Between 1781 and 1791, Paul Revere II performed the following tasks for Foster Bosinger, Esq.: mending teapot (1781), mending two silver branches (1792), mending and fixing five plated candlesticks (1792), putting a new joint to a teapot (1788). Paul Revere Daybooks, 1:66, 2:71, 117–18.

13. Kane 1998, 578–614. See department files, Art of the Americas.

14. Jeannine Falino, "'The Pride Which Pervades thro every Class': The Customers of Paul Revere II," Falino and Ward 2001, 152–82.

15. Barbara McLean Ward has noted that 27 of 33 vessels owned by Connecticut River valley churches before 1775 were made in Boston; Barbara McLean Ward, "Metalwares," in Ward and Hosley 1985, 273–75. Gerald W. R. Ward, "Micropolitan and Rural Silversmiths in Eighteenth-Century Massachusetts," in Kane 1998, 11–138; the word *micropolitan* was coined by Kenneth Clark, *Moments of Vision and Other Essays* (New York: Harper and Row, 1981), 57ff., as cited by Ward.

16. Kane 1998, 781, 902–5, 920–21.

17. Kane 1998, 913–16, 1189. Other grace cups were made by John Burt, John Coney, Peter Feurt, Jacob Hurd, Nathaniel Hurd, Paul Revere II, and Edward Winslow.

18. It is possible that English-made Anglican silver was removed, lost, or destroyed during the Revolutionary War.

19. Avery 1930, 90–111.

20. Waters 2000, 39.

21. Waters 2000, 55.

22. Albert S. Roe and Robert F. Trent, in Fairbanks and Trent 1982, 3:493–94, cat. nos. 461–62.

23. Rodric H. Blackburn and Ruth Piwonka, *Remembrance of Patria: Dutch Arts and Culture in Colonial America, 1609–1776* (New York: Publishing Center for Cultural Resources for the Albany Institute of History and Art, 1988), 278–79.

24. Morrison H. Heckscher and Leslie Greene Bowman, *American Rococo, 1750–1775: Elegance in Ornament* (New York and Los Angeles: Metropolitan Museum of Art and Los Angeles County Museum of Art, 1992), fig. 27; Waters 2000, 42.

25. David L. Barquist et al., *Myer Myers: Jewish Silversmith in Colonial New York* (New Haven: Yale University Art Gallery, 2001), 154.

26. William Penn to his wife, Gulielma, 1682, cited in Jack L. Lindsey, *Worldly Goods: The Arts of Early Pennsylvania, 1680–1758* (Philadelphia: Philadelphia Museum of Art, 1999), 21.

27. William Penn to his children Springett, Laetitia, and Billy, 1682, cited in Lindsey, *Worldly Goods*, 1999, 21.

28. Warren 1987, 37–8, cat. no. 22.

29. Buhler 1956, 37.

30. Syng's three sons and two grandsons were silversmiths, according to Avery 1930, 178. The inkstand is in the collection of Independence National Historic Park, National Park Service, U.S. Department of the Interior (INDE 11860).

31. Jack L. Lindsey, "Lynford Lardner's Silver: Early Rococo in Philadelphia," *Antiques* 143, no. 4 (April 1993), 608–15, fn. 24, pl. IX.

32. The population of Pennsylvania had passed those of New York by 1750 and Massachusetts by 1770, according to the federal census of 1770, as cited in Lindsey, *Worldly Goods*, 17.

33. Heckscher and Bowman, *American Rococo*, 71, no. 88.

34. On the many American and Canadian makers of Indian trade silver, see Martha Wilson Hamilton, *Silver in the Fur Trade, 1680–1820* (Chelmsford, Mass.: Martha Hamilton Publishing, 1995), 190–91, 198–99, 211.

35. Henry J. Kauffman, "Peter Getz of Lancaster," *Antiques* 58, no. 2 (August 1950), 112–13.

36. London silver was recorded in 29 of 30 churches founded in Virginia, while American, or possibly American, pieces were recorded in 3, according to Jones 1913, 1, 6, 141, 161, 168, 179, 204, 207, 214, 219, 231, 252, 258, 269, 341, 390, 404, 407, 411, 415, 418, 472, 473, 479, 488, 494, 496, 507, 510.

37. Heckscher and Bowman, *American Rococo*, cat. nos. 54, 64, fig. 29.

1

Josiah Austin (1719/20–about 1780)
Creampot

Charlestown, Massachusetts, 1740–60
Gift of Martha May Eliot and Abigail Adams Eliot
1975.280

H. 3⅞ in. (9.9 cm); W. 3⁵⁄₁₆ in. (8.4 cm); D. 2³⁄₁₆ in. (5.5 cm); Diam. 2⅜ in. (7 cm); Wt. 3 oz 2 dwt 21 gr (97.8 gm)

Marks: "J [pellet] AUSTIN" in roman letters within a rectangle struck on base.

Inscriptions: "L / I*M" in roman capitals engraved below mark. "ALDLD" in sprigged script added later on body, below spout.

JOSIAH AUSTIN was the oldest member of the silversmithing family that bears his name. He probably apprenticed to his cousin Jacob Hurd and, in turn, may have trained his nephews Nathaniel (1734–1818) and James (b. 1750) Austin in addition to Thomas Lynde (1745–1811) and Eleazer Wyer Sr. (1752–1800). Wyer married his daughter Lydia.[1]

Austin lived and worked in Charlestown. The Massachusetts tax list for 1771 notes that he owned a quarter of a house with an adjoining shop, presumably for silversmithing activities. More than forty-five works by Austin survive in both hollow-ware and flatware; they range in date from the 1740s through the 1770s. It is possible that he produced silver for or with other silversmiths in the area, as evidenced by two tankards that also bear the mark of Samuel Minott (see cat. no. 2).[2]

After Austin's death, his initial and surname mark, the same as on this creampot, was used by his nephew Nathaniel Austin.[3]

Reassessment of the marks of John Allen (1671/2–1760) and Josiah Austin has led to the reassignment, in some cases, of variants of the "I [pellet] A" mark from Allen to Austin. Since Allen may have ceased working after 1702, when his partnership with John Edwards ended, silver made during the 1740s and later can be considered the product of Austin's workshop. A creampot in the Museum's collection belonging to the latter group, attributed to Austin in 1911 and reassigned to Allen in 1972, can now be returned to Austin's oeuvre.[4]

This gourd-shape creampot is similar in form to the previously cited example once attributed to John Allen. Austin has updated the C-scroll handle and ring foot of the older vessel by replacing them with a broken-scroll handle and three pad feet.

1

Description: The raised pear-shape creampot has a cast scrolled handle and three pad feet. An applied drawn, molded rim leads into a spout that has a small baluster drop. The legs have been pushed into the body, and an old, repaired break is visible in the handle.

History: Possibly owned by the May family of Roxbury, Massachusetts; by descent to the donors.[5]

Exhibitions and publications: Kane 1998, 154–55.

NOTES TO THIS ENTRY ARE ON PAGE 151.

Josiah Austin (1719/20–ca. 1780)
Probably engraved and retailed by Samuel Minott (1732–1803)

Tankard

Charlestown and Boston, Massachusetts, 1768
Gift of the First Church in Newton
1973.18

H. 8¹¹/₁₆ in. (22.1 cm); W. 7⁵/₁₆ in. (18.5 cm); Diam. rim 3⅞ in. (10 cm); Diam. base 5³/₁₆ in. (13.1 cm); Wt. 27 oz 2 gr (839.9 gm)

Marks: "I [pellet] A" within a rectangle struck below center point. "Minott" in script within a rectangle struck on bottom, above center point.

Inscriptions: "The Gift of / Deacon John Stone to the / Church of Christ in Newton / 1768." in script engraved on body, opposite handle. The value "£ 90.6." lightly scratched above Minott's mark.

THE WORKING RELATIONSHIPS between silversmiths in Boston have always been difficult to discern, given the dearth of surviving account books and receipts to indicate a division of labor. It is rare to discover the identity of individual craftsmen who performed specific workshop tasks, such as raising or chasing, or to separate fabricator from retailer or partner. In a few exceptional cases, discoveries of collaborative efforts have been made.[1] Without documentation, it is difficult to clarify these relationships, that is, to identify the silversmith, engraver, and retailer.

So it is for Samuel Minott, a productive silversmith who made at least twenty-five tankards, six of which carry the mark of a second maker.[2] Minott's mark has appeared on objects also bearing the touchmark of William Simpkins, likely Minott's master, as well as those of silversmiths Samuel Bartlett, William Homes Sr., Thomas Townsend, and, as on this tankard, Josiah Austin.[3]

In view of his impressive volume of trade, Minott may possibly have called upon other craftsmen to assist with complex works and complete commissions, such as in this tankard probably made by Austin and engraved by Minott for the First Church in Newton.

Josiah Austin's career was more circumscribed than that of Minott, for although he produced some forty-five surviving objects, his mark has been found in conjunction with only that of Minott. Their marks appear together on two tankards, this example and another made for the Watertown Church.[4]

If Minott did occasionally retail the work of other silversmiths, he may have engraved the vessels himself. One such example may be the beaker Minott made for the Newton church (cat. no. 95), which bears elegant, flourished script similar to that on this tankard. The same engraver's hand may have produced the inscription on a beaker made for the First Church in Bedford that was marked by Minott and William Simpkins, indicating that perhaps Minott engraved silver for both his master and himself.[5]

Description: The raised tankard tapers inward from the base and has an applied midband above the lower handle attachment. A tall, cast flame finial tops the domed stepped lid. The cast scrolled thumbpiece and four-part hinge descend to a baluster-shape drop on the shoulder of a hollow seamed handle; a convex oval disk is visible at lower terminal, with a half-round air vent below. The finial has been reattached

History: Deacon John Stone (1692–1769), a weaver, was the son of Ebenezer Stone (1662–1754), the donor of the John Edwards tankard made for the First Church in Newton (cat. no. 95). The tankard was made a gift shortly before Stone's death in 1769.

Exhibitions and publications: Jones 1913, 323, pl. XCVIII; Kane 1998, 157. See also appendix 8.

NOTES TO THIS ENTRY ARE ON PAGE 151.

3

Henricus Boelen (1697–1755)
Spoon

New York, New York, 1720–40
Gift of a Friend of the Department of American Decorative Arts and Sculpture and the Frank Bemis Fund
1992.512

L. 6⅝ in. (16.7 cm); W. bowl 2 in. (5.1 cm); Wt. 1 oz 11 dwt 13 gr (49.1 gm)

Marks: "HB" conjoined in a faint crowned shield struck on back of bowl.

Inscriptions: "A R" in roman letters engraved on back of bowl, above mark.

A group of spoons produced in seventeenth-century New York by newly arrived immigrants from the Netherlands and their progeny are notable for richly modeled handles influenced by the Dutch auricular style, aspects of which evoke the bud, leaf, and stem.[1] The irregular casting quality, and the likely shared use of the same or similar molds by more than one generation of silversmiths, has hampered a full understanding of these designs. Spoons bearing hoof handles and caryatids in addition to the vegetal forms described above were also favored by New York silversmiths.[2]

Scholars once believed the production of such spoons had ceased by 1700. However, Ian Quimby's reassignment of the mark of the conjoined "HB" within a shaped shield from Hendrick Boelen (1666–1691), now thought to be a gunsmith, to the younger silversmith Henricus Boelen suggests that this form, like the ubiquitous New England porringer, may have remained popular with Dutch descendants long after it had passed out of use in the Netherlands.[3] A small group of these spoons has been found to play a commemorative role in marking birth or death, and these customs may have sustained the use of this form into the early decades of the eighteenth century.

Henricus may have had access to the spoon molds used by his father, Jacob, although few examples by the elder Boelen are known. Several auricular-style spoons bearing the latter's "IB" barred mark do not resemble the spoon in this entry; however, about five examples in the midrib or wavy style demonstrate the elder Boelen's facility with a later design. The close resemblance of Henricus's spoon to one by Cornelius van der Burch in the Yale collection suggests that such swages were probably available to the Boelens.[4]

Since this spoon and a two-handled bowl by Jacob Boelen (cat. no. 4) bear the same "AR" initials, they may have been fabricated contemporaneously. If so, the order was probably placed in the Boelen workshop between about 1718 and 1729, when father and son may have been working together.

Description: The spoon has a cast handle with upturned tip in a vegetal auricular style soldered to a large wide bowl with slender, pointed rattail drop.

History: The original owners have not been identified. Family history indicates that this spoon and its related bowl (cat. no. 4) descended along New York family lines to Mason Meyers Phelps of Newtonville, Massachusetts. Placed on loan to the Museum by Mr. Phelps in 1946 and sold by his heirs to the Museum in 1992.

Exhibitions and publications: MFA Annual Report 1992–93, 19.

NOTES TO THIS ENTRY ARE ON PAGE 151.

4

Jacob Boelen I (about 1657–1729/30)

Two-handled bowl

New York, New York, 1690–1710
Gift of a Friend of the Department of American Decorative
Arts and Sculpture and the Frank B. Bemis Fund
1992.511

H. 1⅘ in. (4.6 cm); W. 6⅝ in. (16.7 cm); Diam. rim 4¹³⁄₁₆ in.
(12.3 cm); Wt. 3 oz 16 dwt 17 gr (119.3 gm)

Marks: "IB" barred in a crowned shield struck on base.

Inscriptions: "A★R" in roman letters engraved on base.

A "CUP WITH TWO TWISTED EARS chas'd with Skutchens"
by Jacob Boelen that was stolen in 1733 was probably two handled, a form popular in New York at the turn of the eighteenth
century.[1] Originally a Renaissance form adopted in northern
Europe, these vessels are sometimes called "brandywine cups"
to recall those filled with brandy and raisins on feast days in
the Netherlands. Eighteen cups of this type by such New York
makers of Huguenot and Dutch descent as Bartholomew Le
Roux, Benjamin Wynkoop, and Jesse Kip were recorded by
John Pearce in 1961; Pearce ascribed three bowls to Boelen.[2]

Today scholars have identified at least seven surviving cups, in
varying forms, by this New York silversmith.

Boelen made shallow vessels with an undecorated body and
flat or twisted wire handles. The majority of his cups, however,
were ornamented with six chased and repousséd panels or sections, some defined with an undulating, chased line and others with simple vertical divisions. The latter group was usually
enlivened with a stylized leaf or flower design.

The Museum's bowl is one of at least three known examples
in the flowered style by Boelen.[3] The richly chased and repousséd flowers are reminiscent of those found in northern European engravings and silver, as is to be expected of New York
silversmiths with strong links to the Netherlands. Jacob and his
son, Henricus Boelen, also made slender beakers with interlaced patterns and foliate designs based upon Dutch examples
in their churches.

Just as Henricus Boelen, with his father, produced Dutch-
influenced spoons and church beakers, so too did he fashion a
two-handled bowl with flowers that is similar to the Museum's
example.[4] That bowl's slender, cast handles and applied foot differ from those on this, his father's, bowl; however, the five-petal

design with a central, trumpetlike center are closely related. Still more remarkable is the similarity in punchwork that enlivens the outline of each flower. The two men also shared similar design solutions, as seen in the faint volutes adorning the base of each lobe, a vestige of paneled and anthemion-decorated vessels. Together, these features demonstrate beautifully the transmission of skills and style from father to son.

Description: The raised two-handled vessel has a stepped base, with a flower in its center, and is divided into six lobes, each with horizontal volutes at base and decorated with flowers. Five of the flowers have similar elongated petals; the sixth has overlapping, rounded, rose-like petals. The drawn, twisted wire handles, shaped into S curves, are soldered to the body.

History: See cat. no. 3.

Exhibitions and publications: Buhler 1956, 74, cat. no. 172, fig. 73.

NOTES TO THIS ENTRY ARE ON PAGE 151.

5

5

Jacob Boelen I (about 1657–1729/30)

Pair of spoons

New York, New York, 1700–20
Gift of Mrs. Warren Christie Moffett in honor of her Grandfather, Francis Henry Bergen, and her Mother, Ruth Bergen Dort
1992.274–75

1992.274: L. 11⅞ in. (30.1 cm); W. bowl 2 in. (5 cm); Wt. 1 oz 16 dwt (56 gm)

1992.275: L. 11⅞ in. (30.1 cm); W. bowl 1⅞ in. (4.7 cm); Wt. 1 oz 16 dwt 16 gr (57.1 gm)

Marks: "IB" barred within a crowned shield struck on back of each handle, above bowl.

Inscriptions: "WH" conjoined, over "H*M," engraved on back of each handle tip.

THIS PAIR OF WAVY-HANDLE spoons is among a handful of utensils by Jacob Boelen that are known. Although most bear engraved initials, none has been ascribed to specific owners, and thus their fabrication dates remain inconclusive. Until further research reveals the life and marriage dates of their owners, a date range of 1700 to 1720 affixed to a spoon in the Yale collection may serve as a useful frame of reference.[1]

Description: Each swaged spoon has an upturned wavy-handle tip with a long tapered rattail on back of elliptical bowl.

History: The initials "WH" probably refer to a member of the Hubbard or Holmes family of New Jersey. Known ownership begins with Huldah Holmes (1779–1851) of Monmouth County, New Jersey, and Elias Hubbard (1776–1864) of Flatlands, New Jersey, m. 1801. To their daughter Mary Hubbard (1819–1858) and Garret G. Bergen (b. 1817) m. 1841, or to Bergen's second wife, Sarah Conover (b. 1835), m. 1861, the grandchild of Elias and Huldah (Holmes) Hubbard, through their daughter Sarah Hubbard (1805–1867), wife of Garret P. Conover of Middletown Point, New Jersey. To Francis Henry Bergen (1863–1932), son of Sarah Conover and Garret G. Bergen, who in 1882 m. Meta Johnson (1862–1939). By descent to their daughter Ruth Bergen (1893–1966) and Robert G. Dort (1891–1950), m. 1928; to their daughter, Anne Dort Moffett (Mrs. Warren C. Moffett) of Boston, Massachusetts, the donor.[2]

Exhibitions and publications: None.

NOTES TO THIS ENTRY ARE ON PAGE 152.

6

John Brevoort (1715–1775)
Tankard

New York, New York, about 1760
Gift of Mrs. Craig Wylie
1979.192

H. 8 in. (20.2 cm); W. 8⅝ in. (21.8 cm); Diam. rim 4⅝ in. (11.7 cm); Diam. foot 5¹¹⁄₁₆ in. (14.5 cm); Wt. 43 oz 8 dwt 3 gr (1350.1 gm)

Marks: "IBV" in an ellipse struck to left and right of handle, below rim.

Inscriptions: "P★M" in shaded roman letters engraved on handle. "Louisa Bronson Hunnewell / from her / Great Great Aunt / Louisa Troup / March 1882." in script added later.

Armorials: On body, to right of handle, the Greene/Charnock arms are displayed in a rococo cartouche with Greene impaling Charnock, vert three stags trippant; or on a bend gules three crosses-crosslets, crescent in chief; crest is a lion rampant on a torse. The whole is engraved within an elaborate scrolled, foliated cartouche. Latin motto *VINCET QUI PATITUR* ("He who is patient prevails") appears in swags below.[1]

JOHN BREVOORT established himself as a silversmith of rank in eighteenth-century New York. The son of Elias and Margaret (Sammans) Brevoort of New York, he was baptized on September 18, 1715, in the Reformed Dutch Church of New York City. His master is unknown, but by 1739, shortly after he would have completed his apprenticeship, he married Louisa-Abigail Kockerthal (1710–after 1775), daughter of the Rev. Joshua and Sybilla Charlotta Kockerthal.[2] Brevoort was admitted freeman on November 23, 1742.

His good standing within the community, which included English patrons, may be inferred from the 1757 marriage of his daughter Charlotte (1740–1790) to Whitehead Hicks (1728–80), who served as New York mayor from 1766 to 1773. Tankards and teapots by Brevoort survive, along with sugar bowls, spoons, and at least one covered porringer. Membership in the Collegiate Reformed Protestant Dutch Church provided him with the opportunity to produce three particularly ambitious tankards, each bearing the elaborate arms of the corporation but otherwise executed in a plain style similar to both the tankard seen here and another made for his father-in-law.[3] The presence of Brevoort's mark on an older porringer by Jacobus van der Spiegel (1668–1708) may indicate that Brevoort traded in or repaired older silver.[4] A collaboration with Thauvet Besley (d. 1757), his contemporary, may be inferred from a

porringer bearing their marks and formerly owned by Almy Townsend Hicks (1795–1862), Brevoort's granddaughter.[5]

The florid, rococo-style Greene-Charnock arms are not clearly understood in light of the tankard's history of ownership, which lacks an association with the Charnock family. They may indicate the somewhat idiosyncratic choice of heraldic imagery found on American silver.[6]

Description: The raised tankard has tapering sides and is covered with a flat lid having a serrated lip and an applied, drawn, molded base. A tall, scrolled thumbpiece is soldered to the lid and descends to a five-part hinge and flattened baluster drop on a seamed double-scroll handle terminating in a scroll. An added spout was removed at an unknown date.

History: The tankard's history is complicated. It appears that the Greene family of Rhode Island were early owners and accounted for half the vessel's heraldic arms. The first owner was likely Gen. Nathaniel Greene (1742–1786) of Newport and Katharine Littlefield (1755–1814) of New Shoreham, Block Island, Rhode Island, m. 1774. War-related debts forced Greene to sell most of his Newport property, and about 1785, a year before his death, the family relocated to Mulberry Grove, Cumberland Island, Georgia.[7] The later initials "P*M" coarsely engraved on the handle may be those of Phineas Miller (1764–1803) of Middletown, Connecticut. The son of Isaac and Hannah (Coe) Miller, he briefly attended Yale College and later became a tutor to the Greenes' children. Miller remained with the family as manager and married Greene's widow in 1796.[8]

The tankard passed to Martha Washington Greene (b. 1777), daughter of Nathaniel and Katherine Greene and wife of John Corlis Nightingale (b. 1771), m. 1795; to their son Phineas Miller Nightingale (b. 1803) and his wife, Mary King (about 1810–1894), m. 1836; to their daughter Mary Ray Nightingale and Robert Troupe (d. 1874), m. 1866.

Subsequent history in the Troupe family is unclear, but the tankard was apparently transferred cross-generationally to Louisa Troup (b. 1791), the unmarried daughter of Lt. Col. Robert Troupe (1757–1832) and Janet (Jennet) Goulet (b. 1758).[9] It is Louisa Troup's inscription, which includes the incorrect phrase "great-great aunt," that appears on the tankard to her grand-niece Louisa Bronson (1843–1890) of New York.

Louisa Bronson was the granddaughter of Louisa Troup's sister Charlotte Troup (b. 1792), who m. James Lefferts Brinkerhoff (b. 1791) in 1815. Louisa Bronson was the daughter of Charlotte Brinkerhoff (1818–1861) and Frederick Bronson (1802–1868), m. 1838. Louisa Bronson m. Hollis Horatio Hunnewell (1836–1884) of Wellesley, Massachusetts, in 1867; the tankard descended to their son Hollis Horatio Hunnewell Jr. (1868–1922) and his wife, Maude Somerville Jaffray (b. 1871); thence to their daughter Louisa Bronson Hunnewell, who m. diplomat Franklin-Mott Gunther (1885–1941) in 1918. To her cousin Charlotte Winthrop Cram (b. 1893), daughter of Charlotte Troup Bronson Winthrop (1865–1893) and Henry Spencer

Cram (1852/3–95). Charlotte Winthrop Cram m. Robert Ludlow Fowler Jr. in 1914. To their daughter Angela Fowler (1915–1989), the donor, and her husband, Craig Wylie (1908–1976), of Cambridge, Massachusetts.[10]

Exhibitions and publications: MFA Annual Report 1978–79, 16.

NOTES TO THIS ENTRY ARE ON PAGE 152.

7

Zachariah Brigden (1734–1787)
Pair of wine cups

Boston, Massachusetts, 1767
Gift of the First Church Parish, Unitarian, Medfield, in memory of Virginia Hagberg McQuillan
1980.490–91

1980.490: H. 6½ in. (16.5 cm); Diam. rim 3¹¹⁄₁₆ in. (9.5 cm); Diam. base 3½ in. (8.8 cm); Wt. 7 oz 5 dwt 11 gr (226.2 gm)

1980.491: H. 6½ in. (16.6 cm); Diam. rim 3¹¹⁄₁₆ in. (9.5 cm); Diam. base 3½ in. (9 cm); Wt. 7 oz 6 dwt 18 gr (228.2 gm)

Marks: "Z [four-pointed star] B" in roman letters, within a rectangle, struck between rim of each cup and its inscription.

Inscriptions: 1980.490: "The Gift of / Eleazer Bullard / To the Church:of:Christ / in / Medfeild" within an ellipse engraved on bowl. 1980.491: "The Gift of / Elizth (Adams) Richardson / To [pellet] the [pellet] Church [pellet] of Christ / in / Medfeild" in script, within an ellipse, engraved on bowl.

ACCORDING TO Zachariah Brigden's daybooks, these communion cups were ordered by Medfield Church Deacon Peter Cooledge (also spelled Coolidge) (1703–1792) on October 24, 1767. He arranged for "2 cups to be made weighing / 8oz 10dwt 0gr a peice . . . to be done / in five weeks." A receipt signed only four weeks later by Deacon James Boyden (d. 1779) acknowledged payment of £60 for their fabrication and his acceptance of the two church cups for conveyance to Deacon Cooledge.[1] The discrepancy in weight as measured today is difficult to explain. Some silver may have been lost due to years of polishing. It is also possible that Brigden felt rushed to meet the deadline and so made the cups of a lesser weight.

One cup (1980.490) was purchased with £5 bequeathed in 1753 by Eleazer Bullard; the matching vessel (1980.491) was purchased with an unknown sum provided by Elizabeth Adams Richardson (1694–1766), probably as a bequest. The church retained the funds for about a year after Richardson's death before commissioning the vessels.

7

Scholars have noted certain aesthetic and textual decisions that were undoubtedly made at the time of the commission. They have interpreted the crowding of letters on both as evidence that Brigden engraved the cups himself rather than engaging a proficient engraver such as Joseph Callender (1751–1821) as he was wont to do. Brigden's mark appears near the engravings, perhaps a subtle indication of authorship. Similar engravings are found on the Hadley church silver made by Brigden, but in these examples the marks do not appear in a prominent location.[2]

Bridgen was one of the more prolific silversmiths of mid-eighteenth-century Boston; more than 120 examples of his work are known. Through his marriage to Sarah Edwards, daughter of Thomas Edwards, his master, Brigden inherited Edwards's clientele and his shop on Cornhill. He produced a wide range of domestic silver, including a presentation teapot and tankard commissioned by the Proprietors of the Charles River Bridge.[3] Beakers, two-handle cups, standing cups, tankards, and mugs make up the liturgical silver he produced for Congregational churches in Massachusetts, Maine, and Connecticut.[4]

Description: Each inverted bell-shape vessel rests above a small baluster stem and has a splayed, slightly domed foot with foot ring. The border of each elliptical cartouche is decorated with a wavy line that contains an alternating dot-and-leaf pattern.

History: Funds for 1980.490 were provided to the church through the bequest of Eleazer Bullard (1676–1753) of Medfield, son of Benjamin Bullard of Sherman, Massachusetts.[5] Funds for 1980.491 were likely provided through a bequest of Elizabeth Adams (1694–1766), daughter of Henry Adams (1657–1733) and Prudence Frairy (1662–1750) of Medfield. She m. Solomon Clark (1678–1748) in 1740 and then Clark's first cousin, Joseph Richardson (1687–1768), in 1756.[6] The cups were made a gift to the Museum in 1980.

Exhibitions and publications: Kane 1998, 216–17. See also appendix 7.

NOTES TO THIS ENTRY ARE ON PAGE 152.

8

Zachariah Brigden (1734–1787)

Set of three teaspoons

Boston, Massachusetts, about 1760
Gift of Mr. and Mrs. Julius McNutt Ramsay, Jr.
1990.364–66

1990.364: L. 5¹¹⁄₁₆ in. (14.6 cm); W. bowl 1⅛ in. (2.9 cm); Wt. 15 dwt 21 gr (24.7 gm)

1990.365: L. 5⅞ in. (14.9 cm); W. bowl 1⅛ in. (2.9 cm); Wt. 15 dwt 18 gr (24.5 gm)

1990.366: L. 5¹¹⁄₁₆ in. (14.6 cm); W. bowl 1⅛ in. (2.9 cm); Wt. 16 dwt 22 gr (26.3 gm)

Marks: "Z [pellet] Brigden" in italics, within a shaped cartouche, struck on back of each stem.

Inscriptions: None.

THESE THREE SPOONS descended in the donor's family, along with a fourth of the same size and pattern made by Samuel Edwards (cat. no. 55). The set of four matched spoons provides a lesson in the transmission of style to apprentices and among family members.

Bridgen may have received or purchased the swages for these spoons through Thomas Edwards, who has traditionally been considered his master. The identical spoon marked by Samuel Edwards, Thomas's younger brother, highlights the fluid relationships among colonial silversmiths and their workshops,

assistants, and tools. The potential for sharing silversmithing resources generationally is well illustrated by Samuel's bequest of "a swage for tea and large spoons" of unknown design to his nephew, silversmith Joseph Edwards Jr. (1737–1783).[1]

Description: Each teaspoon has a round upturned handle with midrib on front and an elliptical bowl having a drop on the back and a finely modeled twelve-lobe shell pattern.

History: The original owners are unknown, but family history of descent is claimed through Sarah Winslow West Deming (1722–1788), daughter of mariner John Winslow (1693–1731) and Sarah Pierce (1697–1771) of Boston, m. 1721. Sarah Winslow m. John West (1722–1750) of Yarmouth, Massachusetts; in 1752 she m. Boston merchant John Deming (d. 1797).[2] The spoons were probably acquired sometime after her marriage to Deming. Subsequent descent is unknown until 1946, when the set, described by the donors as the "Winslow spoons," was received as a wedding gift from a family member.[3]

Exhibitions and publications: Kane 1998, 216.

NOTES TO THIS ENTRY ARE ON PAGE 152.

9

Zachariah Brigden (1734–1787)

Creampot

Boston, Massachusetts, about 1770
Gift of Mrs. Guy Warren Walker, Sr.
1980.629

H. 4¹³⁄₁₆ in. (12.2 cm); W. 4⅛ in. (10.3 cm); Diam. foot 2³⁄₁₆ in. (5.5 cm); Wt. 4 oz 3 dwt 11 gr (129.8 gm)

Marks: "Z [pellet] B" struck on bottom.

Inscriptions: "W / I E" in roman letters engraved under foot rim.

THE INVERTED PEAR FORM, scalloped rim, and finely cast double-scrolled handle of Brigden's creampot is reminiscent of the rococo style, whereas the vertical stance and finely reeded band encircling the central foot anticipates the neoclassical

taste. Brigden made numerous creampots in this style; all have a similar handle, form, and foot.[1] Perhaps in an effort to update his creamer, Brigden experimented subtly with the form's height and girth by altering the relationships between vessel and base. The Museum's creampot may be among his earlier works, for its scalloped rim would have been an outdated feature compared to other creampots having a beaded or pearled edge on the rim and, occasionally, the foot.

Description: This raised double-bellied vasiform vessel has a scalloped lip, a cast broken-scrolled handle, and a tall splayed foot with reeded border.

History: Early history unknown.

Exhibitions and publications: Kane 1998, 212.

NOTES TO THIS ENTRY ARE ON PAGE 152.

10

Benjamin Bunker (1751–1842)

Porringer

Nantucket, Massachusetts, 1775–1800
Gift of the Wunsch Americana Foundation
1977.745

H. 1¹³⁄₁₆ in. (4.5 cm); W. 8⅛ in. (20.5 cm); Diam. rim 5⁵⁄₁₆ in. (13.5 cm); Wt. 7 oz 6 dwt 4 gr (227.3 gm)

Marks: "BB" in roman letters, within a rectangle, struck twice on back of handle.

9

Inscriptions: Entwined monogram "PMC" in sprigged script engraved on top of handle, with letters facing toward bowl.

BENJAMIN BUNKER was the most prolific eighteenth-century silversmith in Nantucket, Massachusetts. Although his master is unknown, Bunker may have apprenticed with Samuel Barrett (about 1735–1815), who probably arrived on the island about 1763. Bunker was listed as an armorer during the Revolution. For many years he was a Mason at the Nantucket Union Lodge, to which he made several gifts, including a ladle in 1774 and "too Complet Ivory Tipt Rolls and one Ivory mallet" in 1775. Bunker produced about ten porringers, and at least thirty spoons bear his mark.[1]

The porringer remained popular with Americans long after it had passed out of fashion in England. This example bears a keyhole handle that was most commonly used by New England silversmiths during the last half of the century.

Description: The low circular vessel has convex sides, an everted rim, and a dome in the bottom. The cast keyhole handle is soldered at a right angle to the rim; a center point appears in bottom of vessel. Evidence exists of an old repair to the porringer wall, opposite handle.

History: Early history unknown.

Exhibition and publications: Kane 1998, 221.

NOTES TO THIS ENTRY ARE ON PAGE 152.

11

Benjamin Burt (1729–1805)
Pair of salts

Boston, Massachusetts, about 1760–70
Gift of Rosamond G. Heard
1991.671–72

1991.671: H. 1³⁄₁₆ in. (3 cm); Diam. rim 2³⁄₁₆ in. (5.7 cm); Wt. 1 oz 18 dwt 22 gr (60.5 gm)

1991.672: H. 1³⁄₁₆ in. (3 cm); Diam. rim 2³⁄₁₆ in. (5.7 cm); Wt. 1 oz 17 dwt 4 gr (57.8 gm)

Marks: "B [pellet] BURT" within a rectangle struck on each base, over center point.

Inscriptions: "R * W / to / S* S," with "to / E * S" in another hand, engraved on each. "Rd * Warren / to / Sh Sumner. / to / E * S / to / Elizabeth Sumner Lewis. / to George Lewis / 1771." added later to initials.

SMALL FOOTED SALTS such as these were commonly made during the mid-1700s; they succeeded the low circular trenchers of the early 1700s. The cast trifid-foot arrangement found on the salts is also typical of creampots and chafing dishes made during the same period. The cast cabriole legs with "molded pads" and "pad feet" described by Kathryn C. Buhler are similar to those produced by Jacob Hurd during the 1740s and 1750s and bear a close resemblance to those made by Paul Revere (cat. no. 113). The Burt salt bowls are more rounded than the broad flat-bottom salts by Hurd. Despite an active career in Boston, Benjamin Burt made few salts; only about five are known.[1]

11

Description: Each salt is a shallow, raised, circular vessel with convex sides and scored rim, supported on three cast, cabriole-style legs with hooflike feet. Accompanying boxes for each salt, made in the nineteenth century, display silk fittings with gilt block letters that read "JOSEPH WARREN TO SUSANNAH SUMNER 1771."

History: Despite the prominence of the Boston families whose names grace these salts and their stamped custom-made cases, discrepancies in their texts obscure the identities of the original donor and first owner. The gift of the salts from the Warren family to the Sumner family was no doubt due to their relationship through sisters Mary Stevens Warren (about 1710–1800/3), mother of the patriot Joseph Warren, and Susannah Stevens Sumner (1709–1733). The gift was probably made by a member of the Warren family whose initials were "RW" to Susannah Boylston (1741–1781), who in 1757 m. Samuel Sumner (1732–1813), the son of Susannah Stevens Sumner. The salts descended to her daughter Elizabeth Sumner (1770–post-1854) and Jesse Doggett (1761–1813), m. 1790.[2] By descent to their daughter Elizabeth Sumner Doggett (1791–1874) and Elijah Lewis (1773–1858), m. 1819;[3] to their son George Lewis (1820–1887) and Susan Minns Wheelwright (1827–1876), m. 1850; to their daughter Adeline Wheelwright Lewis (1858–1939) and John Heard (1859–1895), m. 1887;[4] to their son John Heard Jr. (1889–1949) and his wife, Rosamond Gregor Marshall, the donor, m. 1939.

Exhibitions and publications: MFA 1911, 14, cat. no. 120 (one only), pl. 5; Kane 1998, 237.

NOTES TO THIS ENTRY ARE ON PAGE 152.

12

Benjamin Burt (1729–1805)
Engraved by Nathaniel Hurd (1729/30–1777)
Teapot

Boston, Massachusetts, 1762
Gift of Jane Bortman Larus in Memory of Mark Bortman
1983.210

H. 5⅞ in (15 cm); W. 8⅞ in (22.5 cm); Diam. shoulder 4¹³⁄₁₆ in. (12.3 cm); Diam. foot 3¼ in. (8.4 cm); Wt. 17 oz 16 dwt 20 gr (555 gm)

Marks: "BENJAMIN / BURT" within a shaped cartouche struck on base, above center point.

Inscriptions: "O=B to S=B" in shaded roman letters engraved beneath crest on body, to right of handle.

Armorials: Displayed to left of handle are the Brown family arms, an eagle volant in a bordure, the whole within an asymmetrical cartouche and surrounded by foliate decoration. To right of handle is the crest of a double-headed eagle displayed above a torse.[1]

Commentary, see cat. no. 13.

Description: The teapot has a raised, inverted pear-shape body, with a center point on the bottom. The body is soldered to a stepped, splayed, cast foot with an applied foot rim. The round inset lid has a

12

History: Funds probably provided by Obadiah Brown (1712–1762) for his daughter Sarah (1742–1800) on her 1762 marriage to Jabez Bowen (1739–1815).[2] Subsequent history unknown until the twentieth century, when the teapot was acquired by Mark Bortman (1896–1967); by descent to his daughter Jane Bortman Larus, the donor

Exhibitions and publications: Smith College 1958, cat. no. 22; Gourley 1965, cat. no. 34, fig. 54; *MFA Annual Report* 1982–83, 19; Emlen 1984, 40–41, fig. 3; Kane 1998, 242.

NOTES TO THIS ENTRY ARE ON PAGE 152.

13

Benjamin Burt (1729–1805)
Engraved by Nathaniel Hurd (1729/30–1777)
Teapot

Boston, Massachusetts, 1763
Gift of Jane Bortman Larus in honor of Mrs. Llora Bortman
1985.16

H. 5¹¹⁄₁₆ (14.4 cm); W. 9⅛ in. (23 cm); Diam. shoulder 4³⁄₁₆ in. (12.2 cm); Diam. foot 3³⁄₁₆ in. (8.1 cm); Wt. 16 oz 13 dwt 18 gr (519.1 gm)

Marks: "BENJAMIN / BURT" within a cartouche struck on base, above center point.

Inscriptions: "O=B *to* A=B" engraved beneath crest on body, to right of handle.

Armorials: Displayed to left of handle are the Brown family arms, three gambs between a chevron in a bordure or below an eagle displayed in chief; to right of handle is the Brown family crest, an eagle or griffin head on a torse.[1]

TWO SURVIVING TEAPOTS (cat. nos. 12–13) offer a glimpse into a prominent Providence family's patronage of a Boston silversmith and a Boston engraver.[2] This entry's teapot, bearing the initials "O=B *to* A=B," formed part of a larger service made by Benjamin Burt in 1763 for the marriage of Anna, the daughter of Providence merchant Obadiah Brown. Anna married her first cousin Moses Brown, who as a youth had come to live in her home; his father, James, had died shortly after Moses's birth. The close relationship of uncle and nephew is evident in Obadiah's will of 1762, which divided his estate into five equal portions for his four daughters and Moses, his "well beloved kinsman." Obadiah had indirectly provided for the silver service through this will, as documented in the engraved initials described above.

pineapple finial and a three-part hinge set flush to the shoulder. The S-scroll spout has applied foliate decoration on its receding upper tip; reeded decoration on its lower section spreads downward and is affixed over strainer holes. The upper socket is angled, and its simple foliate decoration ends in nodelike tendrils. The lower socket is circular and extends from the body at a slight angle. Both sockets are chased with a single line at edge of socket; pins secure the replaced wooden handle with scrolled thumbgrip.

Deeply punched and chased decoration around shoulder and handle consists of rosettes set amid leafy, scrolled, and raffled surface decoration. Four leafy triangular forms extend from the shoulder onto the lid; a six-leaved engraved decoration radiates from the center of the domed lid.

13

Surviving drafts of Moses's correspondence with Burt, dated August 19, 1763, reveal the extent of his order for wedding silver. Burt was requested to produce "one Silver Tankard, 6 porringers Teapots, point cans, Cream pott, pepper Caster 1 doz Table & 1 doz tea spoons and 1 pr Tea Tongs, made in the Neatest manner and in ye same fashion of those you Lateley made for Mr. Jabez Bowen of this place."[3]

Brown's brother-in-law was Jabez Bowen, who in 1762 married Anna's older sister Sarah. Although it cannot be ascertained whether the Bowen family silver was ordered from Burt by Obadiah Brown or his son-in-law, Jabez Bowen, Moses followed the lead established by the Bowen service, as can be noted in his choice of the same style and silversmith as well as similar brief dedications from Obadiah to his daughters (see cat. no. 12). A magnificent tankard, two porringers, and two creampots bearing the arms, crest, and description also survive from Moses Brown's original order to Burt.[4]

The remarkable productivity of Burt's workshop can be assessed in light of his response to Brown. Three days after receiving the order, Burt replied, "I . . . can make the Plate therin mention'd in four Week's or less," indicating his ability to produce or procure work on short notice. In the same letter,

Burt requested the name of an appropriate engraver, indicating that this specialized task was one that his own shop would not directly handle. Early in September, Moses responded to Burt, adding a "mustard" to his order and describing the arms he desired: "a chevron between Three Lyons Paws Erected with in a bordure and an Eagle display'd and the same as that Mr. N.

Description: The raised teapot has an inverted pear-shaped body with center point on bottom; the body is soldered to a stepped splayed foot with an applied foot rim. The round inset lid is domed and has a pineapple finial and three-part hinge set flush to the shoulder. The S-scroll spout has applied foliate decoration on its receding upper tip; reeded decoration on the lower section spreads downward and is affixed over strainer holes. The upper socket is angled, and its simple foliate decoration terminates in a nodelike tendril. The circular lower socket extends at a slight angle, and both sockets are scored at the edge with a pair of pins securing the wooden replacement handle with scrolled grip. The teapot's deeply chased decoration consists of broken scrolls with lacy edges on the sides and above the spout and handle. Below the scrolls, along the sides of the vessel, appear three prominent rosettes amid floral and punched surface decoration. Chasing encircles the shoulder and surrounds the upper socket, and four triangular forms extend from scrolls onto the lid; a six-leaved design is set at the center of the dome. Armorial engraving appears to left of handle, with the crest on opposite side. Some modern hammer marks are visible inside the lid, caused by the finial reattachment; also visible are small dents at the shoulder, to left of handle, and stress cracks inside the body, near the foot and upper socket.

History: Funds provided by Providence merchant Obadiah Brown (1712–1762), as indicated by the inscription to his daughter Anna Brown (1744–1762), although correspondence indicates that her husband, Moses Brown (1738–1836), ordered the silver. By descent to his granddaughter Avis Harris (d. 1892). Subsequent history unknown until acquired in the twentieth century by Mark Bortman (1896–1967); by descent to his daughter Jane Bortman Larus, the donor.

Exhibitions and publications: Smith College 1958, cat. no. 21; Emlen 1984, 42, figs. 4–5; Warren 1987, 69, cat. no. 76; Fairbanks 1991, 71 (with image of 1983.210); Kane 1998, 243.

NOTES TO THIS ENTRY ARE ON PAGE 153.

Hurd Ingraved on a Seal for me Some time past." In the 1760s the Brown family had engaged Nathaniel Hurd to engrave a plate for paper labels used on spermaceti candles, and, as noted, he had made a seal at a previous date. Thus Brown's choice of Hurd, who was also one of the most respected engravers of his time, was based upon these previous experiences and Hurd's reputation.

The teapots are nearly identical in form, cast elements, and decoration. The horizontal band of broken C scrolls, with raffles and rosettes, follows a pattern seen in the work of several Boston silversmiths, including Thomas Edwards and William Simpkins.[5] In these two teapots, subtle disparities appear in the handling of the chased ornament. The earlier teapot dated 1762 has a linear design that gives prominence to elements such as the punched scalloped edge and repoussé rosettes. The teapot fashioned one year later displays an integrated flowing design that allows the eye to meander within a broader field of ornament. These differences reveal divergent approaches to the choice and handling of chasing tools; they may indicate a growing level of proficiency by the same unidentified artist rather than the work of two individuals.

Both teapots show that Burt produced silver that was at the height of fashion. The inverted pear form, with its dynamic rococo engraving and lavishly chased decoration, indicates that Burt closely followed London styles. The masterful integration of these elements demonstrates how the silversmith strove to fashion the best possible work in the most advanced taste for his wealthy patrons.

14

John Burt (1692/93–1745/46)

Porringer

Boston, Massachusetts, 1719–20
Gift in memory of Helen and David Craig
1992.270

H. 1⅞ in. (4.7 cm); W. 8³⁄₁₆ in. (20.8 cm); Diam. rim 5⁵⁄₁₆ in. (13.5 cm); Wt. 7 oz 1 dwt 10 gr (219.9 gm)

Marks: "IB" crowned in a shaped shield struck on back of handle, with a second fragmentary strike inside bowl, on center point.

Inscriptions: "M * A" in shaded roman letters engraved on handle, facing bowl. "H [cross] Gibbs / to / M [cross] A" in shaded roman capitals inscribed on base of porringer, within dome.

Armorials: The Appleton crest, a pineapple on a torse, appears below initials on handle.[1]

THE REMARKABLE SURVIVAL of this porringer in the Gibbs family adds to our knowledge of not only the possessions of an early and prominent American family but also the occasions they chose for making gifts of silver. The Gibbs family is well known to historians of colonial New England. Henry Gibbs, whose name appears on this porringer, was a minister of First Church, Watertown. He was the son of Boston merchant Robert Gibbs (about 1634–1674/75) and the namesake of his paternal grandfather, Sir Henry Gibbs, a knight from Homington, County Warwick, near Stratford on Avon.

Having limited financial prospects as the younger son in his family, Henry Gibbs's father, Robert, chose to establish himself in New England. He married Elizabeth Sheafe (1644–1718) of Cambridge, whose inheritance from her grandfather Henry Webb (d. 1660) was substantial. The couple built an impressive stone residence in Boston valued at £3,000 by John Josselyn, author of *New England's Rareties Discovered* (1672). It is likely that the mansion was graced with portraits by the Freake-Gibbs painter of Gibbs's children Margaret, Robert, and Henry.[2] The children's gentrified dress was no doubt intended to demonstrate their wealth and elevated social status, as was the silver that Robert received from his father in England. His wife, Elizabeth, who later married Jonathan Corwin (also spelled Curwen and Curwin) of Salem upon Robert's death, enumerated many of these objects in her will of 1717. To their son Henry she gave a "Grate Silver Tankard which his Grandfather Sir Henry Gibbs sent me as a present also my Grate Silver Salt seller," and to Henry's daughter Margaret (1699–1771) she gave a "silver mustard pott & a silver knob'd spoon."[3]

The porringer's engraving suggests that it was given by Henry Gibbs to his daughter Margaret either on her marriage to Rev. Nathaniel Appleton in 1719 or for the birth in 1720 of her daughter and namesake, Margaret. The Gibbs tradition of inscribing silver with the names or initials of donor and recipient is also recorded on an Edward Webb tankard that was given by Henry's mother, Elizabeth, to her granddaughter Mary Gibbs sometime after the latter's birth in 1699. The couple also owned a pepper box and chafing dish by John Coney, the former received by inheritance.[4]

The crest displayed on the porringer handle is probably a variant of one found on the tombstone carved for Samuel Appleton (1653–1725) of Ipswich.

14

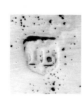

Description: The raised vessel has a center point on bottom, a domed base with convex sides, and a small everted rim. The cast keyhole-style handle is soldered at a right angle to the rim.

History: The porringer was purchased by Henry Gibbs (1668–1723), who in 1692 m. Mercy Greenough (1674/75–1716), daughter of William Greenough.[5] A largely matrilineal line of ownership to the donors can be established, beginning with its likely gift from the above-mentioned Henry Gibbs to his daughter Margaret (1699–1771), who m. Rev. Nathaniel Appleton (1693–1784) of Cambridge in 1719.[6] It may also have been given to commemorate the birth of his granddaughter Margaret Appleton (1720–1768), who m. the Rev. Joshua Prentiss (1719–1788) of Holliston, Massachusetts, in 1755.[7] The porringer descended to their daughter Margaret Prentiss (1759–1839), who m. the Rev. Timothy Dickinson (1761–1813) of Holliston in 1789; to their son Thomas Dickinson (1794–1844) and his wife, Rhoda Adams (1794–1833), m. 1817; to their daughter Annie (Nancy) Louisa Dickinson (1827–1912) of Holliston, m. Henry Woods (1820–1901) of Barre in 1851;[8] to their daughter Helen Margarett Woods (1864–1941), m. David Rankin Craig (1854–1918) in 1891; to their son James Wallace Craig (1893-1973), m. Margaret Crane (1897–1972) in 1927;[9] to their daughter Margaret Oliver Craig Locke (b. 1928), the donor.

Exhibitions and publications: Kane 1998, 253.

NOTES TO THIS ENTRY ARE ON PAGE 153.

15

John Burt (1692/93–1745/46)

Pair of flagons

Boston, Massachusetts, 1722
Gift of a Friend of the Department and Edward J. and
Mary S. Holmes Fund
1984.204–5

1984.204: H. 14⅛ in. (35.9 cm); W. 10 in. (25.5 cm); Diam. rim 4⅝ in.
(11.8 cm); Diam. base 7½ in. (19.1 cm); Wt. 56 oz 17 dwt 15 gr
(1769.2 gm)

1984.205: H. 14⅜ (36.5 cm); W. 9⅜ in. (24 cm); Diam rim 4⅝ in. (11.8
cm); Diam. base 7½ in. (19.1 cm); Wt. 54 oz 1 dwt 18 gr (1682.3 gm)

Marks: "IB" crowned above a pellet, all within a shield, struck to
left of each upper handle join and below each midband.

Inscriptions: "Belonging / to that Church / of Christ in Marblehead / of which the Rev^d M^r. / Edward Holyoke / is the pastor / 1722" in script engraved on each. The text appears within an elliptical cartouche surrounded by foliate decoration; a cherubim surmounts the whole.

AT LEAST FOUR FLAGONS are known to have originated in the shop of John Burt. The two for the Marblehead church, seen here, were made in 1722. About one year later, Burt fashioned a flagon, a legacy of John Frizzell, for the Second Church in Boston. More than twenty years after that, he made another example for the New North Church of Boston.[1]

Description: Each flagon is a tall raised vessel tapering toward its opening and supported by a broad, stepped, raised base and applied foot molding. A drawn molded midband appears below each handle join. The high, stepped, and domed lid with a button finial is seated upon the applied everted rim, with a flange within. The scrolled thumbpiece descends to a five-part hinge and a short, applied baluster decoration on seamed C-scroll handle, which is scribed vertically along its flat exterior. The handle is attached to the body at its upper joint with a short, rounded rattail drop and at lower section with a flat oval disk. A cast grotesque mask appears at terminus, with a crescent-shaped air vent below.

History: See appendix 6.

Exhibitions and publications: Kane 1998, 352; see appendix 6 for additional citations.

NOTES TO THIS ENTRY ARE ON PAGE 153.

16

John Burt (1692/93–1745/46)
Tankard

Boston, Massachusetts, 1724
Gift of Abby S. Niss, in memory of Ruth Morison Sharples
1981.504

H. 7¹³⁄₁₆ in. (19.9 cm); W. 7⁵⁄₁₆ in.(18.5 cm); Diam. rim 4⅛ in. (10.4 cm); Diam. foot 5⅛ in. (13 cm); Wt. 24 oz 9 dwt 6 gr (760.9 gm)

Marks: "JOHN / BURT" in roman letters, within an ellipse, struck to left of handle. "IB" in small roman letters, within a rectangle, struck on top of hinge plate.

16

Inscriptions: "G / P + M / 1724 / G / J + T / 1828 / A.T.G.E. / 1848 / C.G.E. / 1904 / J.W.N. / 1911 / to / R.M. / February 21 st 1911" in roman letters engraved on handle. Inscribed on bottom is scratch weight "24 oz – 16 Dw – o."

THE REASON IS UNCLEAR for Burt's placement of a small "IB" mark inside the hinge of this conventional Boston tankard. The English assay office required silversmiths to place their touchmarks on each element of a finished piece, such as the lid and handle, but colonial silversmiths were guided by no such rules. When two marks were used by such silversmiths as John Coney or Jacob Hurd—an infrequent occurrence—they were usually of the same scale. The tiny size of this "IB" mark was usually intended for jewelry, and this example is the only one that appears with the larger and more common "John Burt" mark. It helps substantiate marks found on a pair of sleeve buttons made about 1725–30.[1]

Description: The raised tankard has tapering sides, a drawn molded base and lip, and one midband slightly below center. The domed and stepped lid with button finial bears two pairs of scored lines at lip. A cast scrolled thumbpiece is atttached to a five-part hinge that descends to short split-baluster decoration on the seamed scroll-shaped handle. A long rounded drop connects the handle to the upper section of the body, while an oval disk connects the lower portion to the handle. A grotesque mask appears at the terminus, with an oval air vent below.

History: Descent of the tankard in the Gilman family has been ascertained through the inscriptions and significant marriage and death dates engraved on the handle. Based on the initials "G/P & M," the vessel was probably made for Peter Gilman (1703/4–1788) of Exeter, New Hampshire, and Mary (Thing) Gilman (b. 1702), widow of John and of the same town, m. 1724. It passed to Ann Taylor (1732–1783), one of many stepchildren of Gilman's second wife, Dorothy (Sherburne) Rymes Rogers Taylor (1712–1761), m. 1751. Ann Taylor (1732–1783) was the child of Elizabeth Rogers (m. 1730, d. 1735) and Rev. John Taylor (1704–1749/50) of Milton, Massachusetts. The tankard passed to Gov. John Taylor Gilman (1753–1828), the first-born son of Ann Taylor and her husband, Nicholas Gilman (1731–1783), of Exeter, New Hampshire, m. 1752. Governor Gilman m. Deborah Folsom (1753–1791) in 1775, and upon his death the tankard was inscribed with his initials and death date and inherited by his daughter Ann Taylor Gilman, m. the Hon. Nicholas Emery (1776–1861) of Portland, Maine, in 1807, as noted by the initials "ATGE / 1848." Upon her death in 1848, the tankard passed to their daughter Charlotte Gilman Emery (1817–1904), who died unm.[2] The tankard was inherited by her niece Julia Webster Abbot (1848–1920), wife of Edgar H. Nichols (1856–1910), m. 1884.[3] Having no issue, the tankard was given to their niece Ruth Morison (1877–1924) of Montclair, New Jersey, on her marriage in 1911 to Philip Price Sharples (1873–1965) and inherited in 1965 by their daughter, Abby Sharples Niss (Mrs. William U. Niss) (1917–1991) of Portland, Maine, who is the donor.[4]

Exhibitions and publications: Kane 1998, 257.

NOTES TO THIS ENTRY ARE ON PAGE 153.

John Burt (1692/93–1745/46)

Tankard

Boston, Massachusetts, about 1725–40
Bequest of Esther M. Boylston
1975.34

H. 7⅞ in. (20 cm); W. 9⁵⁄₁₆ in. (10.5 cm); Diam. rim 4⅛ in. (10.5 cm); Diam. foot 5⁵⁄₁₆ in. (13.4 cm); Wt. 24 oz 3 dwt 21 gr (752.5 gm)

Marks: "JOHN BURT" within an ellipse struck on bottom of vessel, above center point.

Inscriptions: "WN / and / AB" entwined monograms in later script engraved on handle. A scratch weight of "24" ounces inscribed on bottom, to left of center point. The same scratch weight appears faintly above the mark and near edge of base. Effaced coat of arms appears faintly around spout.

THIS CLASSIC BOSTON TANKARD, with its tapering walls, low midband, domed lid, and grotesque terminal, is nearly identical to the previous Burt example (cat. no. 16) but is notable for the spout that it received sometime in the nineteenth century.[1] The transformation of colonial-era tankards into pitchers has been commonly attributed to the influence of the temperance movement beginning in the mid-1820s.[2] The first documented "spouting" of a tankard occurred as early as 1816, however, suggesting that a trend to adapt tankards to new uses was already under way by this date.[3]

The tankard's traditional use as a drinking form was likely dealt a deathblow by the temperance movement, but its morphology may have more to do with changing attitudes toward health, etiquette, and taste. Due to their size, most tankards were considered communal vessels to be shared among friends, family, and church. The cup as a symbol of fellowship, for instance, was a medieval convention born of necessity in an era with few individual drinking cups. As cheap imports and new American products made glass and ceramic drinking cups affordable to many Americans, private use or ownership of such vessels became a reality for those who previously made do with inexpensive treen or horn. An increasing awareness of good hygiene also led to the demise of shared vessels. Beginning in the mid-sixteenth century, it was understood that contagious diseases could be passed from one person to another.[4] Personal etiquette gradually changed to reflect this concern, as books on manners of the period urged their readers to wipe their mouths before sharing in drink. Yet Americans in the late eighteenth century still retained the tradition of communal vessels. An American traveller in France decried the practices of his countrymen, which risked the contraction of disease, and noted that in France, "every man has his own glass, and risks no one's lips but his own."[5]

The Museum of Fine Arts has some spouted tankards in the permanent collection, along with others that were "despouted" in the twentieth century by owners who wished to return the vessels to their original form. The residual engraving on the body opposite the handle suggests that this tankard may have sacrificed a coat of arms to the new spout.

As with pewter, untold numbers of silver hollowware and flatware pieces were regularly melted down and remade into newly fashionable works during the eighteenth and nineteenth centuries. The spout was a frugal and efficient method of retaining an old-fashioned yet pleasant form while adapting it to new uses. For Americans who continued to purchase outmoded tankards and porringers until the end of the eighteenth century, improvisation on an old form was one manner of bridging cultural gaps, keeping the familiar at hand while bringing in the new.

Description: The tankard has straight tapering sides, with an applied molding at base band, on body, and at lip. Incised lines appear below the lip. The stepped domed cover has a narrow flange and a cast bell-shaped finial. A four-ridged scroll thumbpiece is above a five-part hinge plate; molded drop appears below. The seamed scroll handle has a rounded drop at upper joining; disk at lower end with grotesque mask terminus; and oval air vent below. At a later date, a large spout with a molded lip was applied on side opposite handle, obliterating all but a faint remnant of a coat of arms; large, evenly spaced holes were drilled into the body to accommodate the spout. The difference between the current and scratch weight is due to the addition of this spout.

History: It is possible that the original owner was the merchant Nicholas Boylston (1716–1771). Having no wife or children, he adopted his nephew Ward Nicholas Hallowell (1747/49–1828), son of his sister Mary, whose Loyalist husband, Capt. Benjamin Hallowell, fled to Halifax and then England in 1776.[6] The inscription "WN" on the handle suggests ownership by Ward Nicholas Boylston, who took his adopted uncle's surname. The second set of initials may refer to Ann Molineux (m. 1770, d. 1779), Boylston's first wife, or his second wife, Alicia Darrow (b. England), m. 1807.[7] The tankard descended to John Lane Boylston (1789–1847), the first son of Ward Nicholas and Alicia (Darrow) Boylston, m. Sarah/Sally Brooks (1793–1881); to their son Thomas Boylston (b. 1819) and his wife, Caroline A. Fowle; to their son Thomas Boylston Jr. (1845–1870), m. Florence Randall (b. about 1851); to their son Ward Nicholas Boylston (1871–1924) and his first wife, Nellie Frances Eayrs (b. 1874), m. 1895; to their son Ward Nicholas Boylston Jr. (1896–1966), thence to his wife Esther (Moore) Boylston (1903–1974), the donor.[8]

Exhibitions and publications: Kane 1998, 256.

NOTES TO THIS ENTRY ARE ON PAGE 153.

18

John Burt (1692/93–1745/46)

Mug

Boston, Massachusetts, about 1725
Gift of Anne, George, and Jessie Furness
1991.668

H. 4¹¹/₁₆ in. (11.9 cm); W. 5¹¹/₁₆ in. (14.6 cm); Diam rim. 3⅛ in. (8 cm); Diam. base 4⅛ in. (10.5 cm); Wt. 9 oz 9 dwt 4 gr (294.2 gm)

Marks: "JOHN / BURT" in roman letters, within an ellipse struck to right of handle.

18

Inscriptions: Faint initials "R / C * E" engraved on handle. Scratch weight of "9 " 15 -," the halo of former museum loan number "2.39," and faint crude initials that include the letter "I" engraved on base.

Armorials: Worn engraving of the Andrews or Storer arms displayed within an asymmetrical cartouche, emblazoned argent on a chevron gules between three mullets gules, three quatrefoils pierced. Crest, an unidentified animal. The whole surrounded by broken scrolls and raffles and flanked by floral standards.[1]

Barbara McLean Ward has suggested that John Edwards was the probable source for the grotesque mask found on this mug's terminal since, as early as 1695, Edwards had been actively creating unusual forms, such as the head of a lion and one of a lady.[2] Specialization in areas such as engraving and casting was practical since these tasks required significant working space and particular skills. However, Burt's partiality to the grotesque face, which he applied to the two tankards and a pair of flagons represented in this catalogue (cat. nos. 15–17), along with many others, suggests that he produced them in his own workshop.[3]

This mug appears to be a unique example by Burt, although he made numerous tankards, canns, and other drinking vessels. Most mugs are unembellished; however, Burt added the grotesque mask, a typical tankard ornamentation, on this vessel.

Description: The raised straight-sided cann, tapering slightly toward rim, has a drawn molded base and lip, with drawn midband near lower terminus. The S-scroll handle is heavily worn and dented, with breaks at several points in seam. A rounded drop appears at the upper terminus. The grotesque mask at the repaired lower terminus has a semicircular air vent below.

History: The arms on the mug are those of either the Andrews or Storer family, yet neither is easily connected by marriage to the Fur-ness family of Boston. It is unclear how or when the mug came into their possession, although it possibly came through a member of the Henchman or Hurd families, with whom they intermarried.[4]

Exhibitions and publications: Kane 1998, 252.

NOTES TO THIS ENTRY ARE ON PAGE 154.

19

John Burt (1692/93–1745/46)
Two-handled cup

Boston, Massachusetts, 1728
Gift of the family of Alice Storrow Rotch
1991.1041

H. 6⁵⁄₁₆ in. (16.1 cm); W. 8½ in. (21.5 cm); Diam. rim 3⅞ in. (9.9 cm); Diam. foot 4⁵⁄₁₆ in. (10.8 cm); Wt. 16 oz 18 gr (498.8 gm)

Marks: "I.BURT" in italics, within a shaped cartouche struck to right of each handle.

Inscriptions: "The Gift of Mr Samel Barrett to The New North / Church of Christ In Boston May 4th 1728" in script engraved between lower handle joins. Scratch weight "16-4" incised on bottom.

19

Two-handled communion cups were common in Congregational churches beginning in the early eighteenth century and persisted in use and production for about 140 years. A hybrid form derived from the slender beaker and the shorter caudle cup, these vessels enabled churches to use fewer pieces of communion plate to circulate wine among the congregation. The handles allowed congregants to pass the cup securely and comfortably, and the large size allowed many to drink from the same cup. As the eighteenth century progressed, taller foot rings and stems shifted the vessel's balance upward. Otherwise, they remained faithful to the form introduced earlier in the century.

Drawn and molded silver strips—similar to those used for cup handles, applied rims, and foot rings—were the preferred means of creating handles for most two-handled cups. Such elements were easily fashioned by pulling metal through a shaped device at the drawing bench; on occasion, they were simply cut from flat sections and chased. Either way, the handles were usually of a gauge similar to the vessel walls. Their slender silhouette gave a light and airy appearance to the communion cups.

The hollow handles found on this cup are an early departure from this convention. They are of a good size to grip, similar to those normally found on tankards, many canns, and mugs. Burt produced this cup in 1728, the same year he made a similar pair for the Essex, Massachusetts, congregation. A second pair that he produced four years later for the Essex church was also fashioned in the same manner. However, at least seven other examples Burt made between 1724 and 1730 follow the traditional pattern of strap handles.[1] Perhaps the cost of fabricating such handles prevented him from making others of this type. A survey of makers in his generation shows that strap handles were the typical choice for these cups. Force of habit and style, as well as cost, may have prevented hollow-handled cups from finding a greater appreciation among their makers and users.[2]

Ironically, beakers by John Coney and John Dixwell that were also owned by New North Church received hollow handles later in the eighteenth century.[3] For unknown reasons, the Coney cup received two handles, one of which was later removed, and the Dixwell cup was given one, perhaps to unify its appearance with the Burt cup.

Burt's 1714 marriage to Abigail, sister of merchant Joshua Cheever (1686/87–about 1750), an original church member, deacon, and ruling elder, may have brought this commission, his only marked piece among the church plate. In 1723 Samuel Barrett, patron of the Burt cup, had given a two-handled cup with strap handles, made by John Dixwell. After Dixwell's death in 1725, Barrett, or more likely a high-ranking member of the church such as Cheever, would have ordered the plate and thus may have turned to John Burt.[4]

In view of Burt's family relationship to the Cheevers, he may have also made an unmarked two-handled cup with strap handles, engraved in 1727 with the name of Joshua Cheever, that figures among the communion plate at New North Church.[5] If so, it stands as a traditional version made for his brother-in-law, created one year before he experimented briefly with the hollow handle form.

Description: The raised vessel is pear shaped and narrows upward to a generous drawn and molded rim; a drawn, molded, and splayed foot ring is soldered to the base. The hollow, seamed scroll handles have long flat tongues at the shoulder, which end in an ogee shape; they have a rounded drop at the upper joint with the body and are directly soldered without an intervening disk at each lower section. The terminus is spade shaped; a crescent-shaped air hole appears below.

History: Given to New North Church (also known as Fifth Church) Boston by Samuel Barrett, who was elected deacon in 1723 and elevated to the position of ruling elder in 1736. An 1863 merger of New North Church with the Bulfinch-Street Church and Society was followed about 1884 by the church's complete dissolution. Sometime before the church was disbanded, a quantity of the silver was sold to King's Chapel, which had lost much of its communion plate during the Revolution; a smaller quantity was sold through Bigelow, Kennard, and Co. to Mrs. Samuel Cabot.[6] By descent to Edward Cabot Storrow (1867–1933) of Milton, Massachusetts.[7] The cup was placed on loan to the Museum in 1911, with ownership transferred in 1929 to his wife, the former Caroline MacKay Richardson (1871–1965).[8] By descent to their daughter Alice Gedney Storrow (1900–1971) and Arthur Rotch (1899–1973), m. 1935, and thence to her children Anne Rotch Magendantz, Edward C. Rotch, and A. Lawrence Rotch, the donors.

Exhibitions and publications: MFA 1911, 18, cat. no. 160, pl. 6; Jones 1913, 66, pl. XXVI; Kane 1998, 259.

NOTES TO THIS ENTRY ARE ON PAGE 154.

20

John Burt (1692/93–1745/46)

Pair of caudle cups

Boston, Massachusetts, 1728
Gift of the First Church in Malden, Congregational
1991.497–98

21

John Burt (1692/93–1745/46)

Tablespoon

Boston, Massachusetts, about 1740
A gift from the collection of Dr. Arthur DuBois Brundidge,
Walden, N.Y., and Northport, N.Y.
1981.427

1991.497: H. 4 in. (10.1 cm); W. 6⅞ in. (17.5 cm); Diam. rim 4 in.
(10.1 cm); Diam. foot 3⁷⁄₁₆ in. (9 cm); Wt. 9 oz 11 dwt 9 gr (297.6 gm)

1991.498: H. 4⅛ in. (10.3 cm); W. 6¹¹⁄₁₆ in. (17.1 cm); Diam. rim 3⅞ in.
(9.9 cm); Diam. foot 3⁹⁄₁₆ in. (9.1 cm); Wt. 9 oz 10 dwt 11 gr (296.2 gm)

Marks: "I.BURT" within a shaped cartouche struck on each base,
above center point.

Inscriptions: 1991.497: "M+ Church Plate 1728" in shaded roman
letters engraved on base, with evidence of scribed guidelines.
1991.498: "M+ Church Plate 1728," with evident scoring of lines,
engraved in same manner.

See appendix 5.

Description: These two raised and undecorated gourd-shaped vessels
have a flaring rim. Two cast scrolled handles are affixed at rim and
sides.

History: See appendix 5.

Exhibitions and publications: Kane 1998, 251; see also appendix 5.

L. 7¹³⁄₁₆ in. (19.8 cm); W. bowl 1⅝ in. (4 cm); Wt. 1 oz 9 dwt 3 gr (45.3 gm)

Marks: "I.BURT" in roman letters, within a shaped cartouche, struck on back of handle.

Inscriptions: "A [cross] L" in roman letters engraved on back of handle tip.

A MATE TO THIS SPOON, engraved with identical initials and in the same style, was sold in 1992 by Gebelein Silversmiths, Inc.[1]

Description: The spoon has an upturned midrib handle terminating in an elliptical bowl, flattened and slightly worn at tip, with rattail on back.

History: Original owners unknown. Acquired by the donor, a silver collector, sometime during the twentieth century.

Exhibitions and publications: Kane 1998, 255.

NOTE TO THIS ENTRY IS ON PAGE 154.

22

Samuel Burt (1724–1754)

Teapot

Boston, Massachusetts, about 1745–54
Gift of Dr. and Mrs. Somers H. Sturgis
1982.651

H. 5 in. (12.7 cm); W. 9 in. (22.8 cm); Diam. shoulder 4½ in. (11.5 cm); Diam. foot 3⅜ in. (8.5 cm); Wt. 18 oz 6 dwt 16 gr (570.2 gm)

Marks: "SAMUEL BURT" in script, within a shaped cartouche, struck four times around center point.

Inscriptions: "85863," "84008," "84043," "85439" incised on base.

Armorials: The Barrett family arms on a shield are emblazoned ermine, on a fess, three lions rampant. Crest is a lion couchant ppr.[1] The whole surrounded by a broad scrolled, foliate, and diapered cartouche.

22

examples by Jacob Hurd and Josiah Austin, among others, may point to the existence of one shop that provided spouts and other cast elements for craftsmen in the close-knit Boston silversmithing community.[3] Since the forms of both teapots are nearly identical—they are distinguished solely by their engraving—they demonstrate the choices made by patrons willing to pay for this additional decoration.

Description: The raised apple-shaped teapot has a drawn, molded, splayed foot ring. The lower section of the cast twelve-sided scallop-edged spout is affixed over strainer holes; the upper section is in the form of a C scroll; the V-shaped spout has retracted upper lip. The five-part hinge, set flush with the body, operates a flat bezel-set circular lid with small circular air vent. The finial has a bell-shaped tip, turned wooden knob, and turned base and is attached inside the lid with notched silver nut and screw. The wooden handle, probably replaced, has been set into sockets with pins. The cast upper socket has an abstract leaf motif above and a drop below; the lower socket is unadorned. Both are circular and scored at end. Engraved ornamentation on shoulder consists of foliate and scrolled decoration within which are set diaper-patterned sections. Leafy repeating pattern scrolls appear at perimeter of lid.

History: No history of descent is known. The family suggests possible descent through the Codman and Paine families, but the arms appear to be those of the Barrett family. The Barrett arms as seen here were probably adapted from Blyth, as recorded in the *Promptuarium Armorum* of 1610. The arms are documented in this country on the tombstone of Col. James Barrett of Concord, who died in 1779.[4]

Exhibitions and publications: Kane 1998, 263.

NOTES TO THIS ENTRY ARE ON PAGE 154.

23

Samuel Burt (1724–1754)

Teapot

Boston, Massachusetts, about 1745–54
Gift of Mr. and Mrs. Franklin H. Williams in memory of Louise Bodine Wallace
1985.327

H. 4⅞ in. (12.4 cm); W. 9³⁄₁₆ in. (23.4 cm); Diam. shoulder 4½ in. (11.5 cm); Diam. foot 3⅜ in. (8.5 cm); Wt. 15 oz 10 dwt 23 gr (483.6 gm)

Marks: "SAMUEL / BURT" in a shaped cartouche struck four times on bottom, around center point.

Inscriptions: "E * F" in shaded roman capitals engraved on top of handle socket. "The Gift of Mrs. Sarah Ch [illegible] to Sarah [illeg-

As with the Hurd and Edwards families, John Burt and his three sons, Samuel, William, and Benjamin, formed a multigenerational silversmithing dynasty in colonial Boston. Samuel, the eldest, fashioned an impressive amount of silver during his brief career.

Burt would have just finished his apprenticeship at the time of his father's death in 1745. He probably ran the workshop after that date while completing the training of his younger brothers. A wide range of hollowware among Samuel's three dozen known works demonstrates his full mastery of his father's skills. Nearly one-third of Samuel's silver is in the Museum's collection, including this teapot and another (cat. no. 23), the only known examples of this form to survive with his mark.[2]

Both teapots are of the globular apple form popular during the early and mid-eighteenth century and resemble those produced by his father. Samuel may have used the molds in his father's shop, for the faceted scalloped spout appears to be the same as that used by John Burt. The spout's similarity to

ible]" in script engraved on base, around maker's marks. Scratch weight "15 5" incised in a modern hand at center of base.

THIS TEAPOT is the plainer of two examples by Samuel Burt in the Museum's collection (see also cat. no. 22). It bears the initials of a member of the Vergoose family and offers an opportunity to consider how many silversmiths could be patronized by related members of a Boston family. The accompanying photograph (fig. 1) also demonstrates how later generations used colonial silver along with silver of more recent vintage. A Hull and Sanderson porringer bears the initials of Isaac (1637–1710) and his first wife, Mary Vergoose (1648–1690); a spoon by Jeremiah Dummer (Yale University Art Gallery) carries the initals "M : V," thought to be for the same Mary Vergoose. A Jacob Hurd teapot (27.192) bearing the Fleet arms may have been owned by Isaac's daughter Elizabeth Vergoose (b. 1694), who m. Thomas Fleet (1685–1758) in 1715, or their son John Fleet (1734–1806), who m. Elizabeth Cazneau (1742–1827) in 1764. A porringer by David Jesse in this volume (cat. no. 90) may also have been owned by the elder Elizabeth Fleet.[1]

FIG. 1. Alice Wight Alden and Louise Duane, the donor's mother and her cousin, seated at 23 Wave Street, Cambridge, Massachusetts, at Christmas, between 1892 and 1902. Alden, at left, is holding the Burt teapot. Museum of Fine Arts, Boston; department files, Art of the Americas

Description: The raised globular vessel, with center point visible at base, has a splayed molded foot soldered to its body. A flat circular lid seats in a bezel soldered inside the rim. The three-part hinge, probably modern, rises above the lid, partially obscuring engraved decoration at the shoulder. The three-part finial has a bell-shaped tip, turned wooden center, and small base; an air vent is adjacent to the finial, facing the handle. The original or early wooden handle bears traces of paint and is set into circular handle sockets. The upper larger socket has foliate decoration at the thumbgrip and a delicate baluster drop below. The lower section of the cast twelve-sided scallop-edged spout is affixed over strainer holes; the upper section is in the form of a C scroll; the V-shaped spout has a retracted upper lip. Foliate and diaper-patterned engraving appears around the edge of the lid and on shoulder.

History: The initials "E * F" may stand for Elizabeth (Cazneau) Fleet (1742–1827), who m. John Fleet (1734–1806) in 1764. If so, the teapot would have been made very early in her youth and engraved with her married initials sometime after her marriage. A porringer by David Jesse (cat. no. 90) given by the donors and bearing the same initials, may have belonged to her mother-in-law, Elizabeth (Vergoose) Fleet (b. 1694).[2] According to family history, this Burt teapot, the Jesse porringer (cat. no. 90), a London-made creampot, a cup by Nathan Hobbs (cat. no. 156), and a small cann by Harris, Stanwood and Company (cat. no. 211), all of which were made a gift to the Museum, were acquired at different dates and passed along the matrilineal line.[3] The teapot descended in the following manner:

From John and Elizabeth (Cazneau) Fleet to their daughter Mary Fleet (1770–1815) and Ephraim Eliot, M.D. (1761–1827), m. 1793;[4] to their daughter Mary Fleet Eliot (1808–1897) and her husband, Ezekiel Lincoln (1796–1869), of Hingham, Massachusetts, m. 1835; to their daughter Emma Cushman Lincoln (1843–1930), wife of Rev. Charles Williams Duane (1837–1915), m. 1870;[5] to their daughter Louisa Duane (1879–1947), wife of Bodine Wallace (1866–1952), m. 1913; first to their daughter Louise Bodine Wallace (1914–1972) and thence to her sister Emily Duane Wallace (1918–1997), who, with her husband, Franklin H. Williams, donated the teapot. The creampot and teapot are visible in a photograph that dates from 1892–1902, demonstrating the familial pride in possessions owned by their ancestors.[3]

Exhibitions and publications: Kane 1998, 263.

NOTES TO THIS ENTRY ARE ON PAGE 154.

24

John Coburn (1724–1803)
Saucepan

Boston, Massachusetts, about 1749
Gift of Mary F. Sutherland
1991.779

H. 2³⁄₁₆ in. (5.5 cm); W. 9⅝ in. (24.5 cm); Diam. rim 3½ in. (9 cm); Diam. foot 3¹¹⁄₁₆ in. (9.5 cm); Wt. 5 oz 15 dwt 2 gr (179 gm)

Marks: "J. COBURN" in roman letters, within a rectangle, struck on bottom, below center point.

Inscription: "The Gift / of / Mary Storer / to / Isaac Smith Junr / May 7th 1749" in italics engraved on body opposite handle. "Hannah Smith / to / Charles Wendell Townsend / 1898" in script engraved in a later hand above and below center point. Scratch weight of "5oz" inscribed above the latter text.

SILVER SAUCEPANS HELD LIQUIDS that were prepared in the kitchen and transferred to the vessel for use at the dining table. Colonial examples have not survived in large numbers, perhaps due to the damage they suffered while resting in heated chafing dishes. Among Massachusetts makers, few are known.[1] Warmed brandy and butter were but two liquids served in saucepans, and these diminutive pans undoubtedly served many other purposes as well.

This example and a similar one by Samuel Edwards (cat. no. 56), Coburn's likely master, are of the reel-shaped variety that appeared briefly in the mid-eighteenth century. Therefore, Coburn likely learned to fashion this form while working as an

24

apprentice in Edwards's shop. Coburn's uncle Ebenezer Storer was married to Mary Edwards, sister to the Edwards silversmiths, and this family connection may have led to his apprenticeship and to commissions such as this sauceboat.

Description: The raised, cylindrical, staight-sided saucepan has an everted lip and applied stepped foot ring. A round disk, soldered to the body below the lip, serves as the footing for a slightly tapered, seamed handle socket that is circular in section. The socket is applied at a slight angle and holds an old, if not original, turned-baluster wooden handle secured with a brass pin.

History: Mary Edwards (1700–1772), wife of Ebenezer Storer (1699–1761), m. 1723, was the daughter of silversmith John Edwards and sister of silversmithing brothers Thomas and Samuel. The inscription implies that she gave the sauceboat as a baby gift to her grandson Isaac Smith Jr. (1749–1829). By descent to his great-niece Hannah Smith (1835–about 1880), who in turn gave it to her nephew Charles Wendell Townsend (1859–1934) and Gertrude Flint (1870–1917), m. 1891. By descent to their daughter Margaret Townsend (b. 1894) and C. Hale Sutherland (b. 1884), m. 1920; by descent to their daughter Mary Flint Sutherland (b. 1928), the donor.[2]

Exhibitions and publications: MFA 1906, 49, cat. no. 55, pl. 26; Buhler 1960, 48, cat. no. 19; Kane 1998, 302.

NOTES TO THIS ENTRY ARE ON PAGE 154.

25

John Coburn (1724–1803)
Strainer

Boston, Massachusetts, about 1750–75
Anonymous Gift
1991.690

L. 10⅞ in. (27.6 cm); W. 1⅛ in. (2.8 cm); Diam. rim 4⅛ in. (10.4 cm); Wt. 4 oz 8 dwt 21 gr (138.2 gm)

Marks: "J . COBURN" within a rectangle struck under each handle, below loop.

Inscriptions: "E [pellet] O [pellet] P" engraved off-center on bottom.

OF THE FOUR published punch strainers made by John Coburn, two have cast Rococo-style handles in the mid-eighteenth-century style like the one seen here; two later examples have a simple, elongated U-shaped frame with a circular ring at each end. This punch strainer, along with a cann made about 1765, may be one of two pieces of silver that Coburn made for the Orne family of Salem.[1]

Description: The shallow, raised, circular bowl has an applied molded rim. The bowl is pierced with a central star-shaped design, interspersed with densely arranged square, circular, and triangular elements. The cast handles of leafy, broken scroll design end in tipped loops.

History: Since Coburn made little silver by the 1780s, it is unlikely that the initials "EOP," probably for Esther Orne Paine (1774–1854), are those of the original owners. Coburn fashioned a cann about 1765 for the Orne family of Salem, and this strainer possibly passed to Esther from an Orne relative at the time of her 1795 marriage to Joseph Cabot (1770–1799) of Salem.[2] By descent to the anonymous donors.

Exhibitions and publications: Kane 1998, 303.

NOTES TO THIS ENTRY ARE ON PAGE 154.

26

Seth Storer Coburn (1744–after 1796)

Nutmeg grater

Probably Boston, Massachusetts, 1770
Gift of Miss Elizabeth Morford in memory of her late partner, Lucy Massenberg
1973.123

H. 2¹³⁄₁₆ in. (7 cm); Diam. ⅞ in. (2.2 cm); Wt. cylinder and lid 1 oz 7 dwt (42 gm)

Marks: "S [pellet] S [pellet] C," within a cartouche with a shaped top, struck inside lid and on bottom of case.

Inscriptions: "Mary / Storer / 1770" in italics engraved on circular lid; "M ★ S" in shaded roman capitals engraved on base of cylinder.

SETH STORER COBURN should have flourished as a silversmith in a family that boasted connections to some of the major Boston craftsmen of the eighteenth century: John Coburn was

his uncle; his great-aunt Mary Coney was the daughter of silversmith John Coney; and through his great-uncle Ebenezer Storer, he was related to the Edwards family of silversmiths.[1] These relationships undoubtedly contributed to the high concentration of silver that descended in these families.

Despite such genetic predispositions to silversmithing fame, Coburn was a n'er-do-well whose nutmeg grater, perhaps his greatest achievement, was fashioned in 1770, when he was about twenty-six years old. Engraved with the name of Mary Storer, the grater could have been made for one of two great-aunts who married brothers in the Storer family. Each was the daughter of a preeminent Boston silversmith. Mary Coney (1699–after 1774), daughter of John Coney, married the Rev. Seth Storer in 1720; and Mary Edwards (1700–1771), daughter of silversmith John Edwards, married merchant Ebenezer Storer (1699–1761) in 1723.[2]

Kathryn C. Buhler believed that Seth Storer Coburn apprenticed with his uncle John Coburn, a conclusion based partly on this nutmeg grater, which is modeled after one made by the latter in 1750 for his fiancée, Susanah Greenleaf. John Coburn would have been the silversmith most closely related to Seth Storer and thus was the natural choice for an apprenticeship. Although the two graters are separated by twenty years, both follow the cylindrical form favored in England.[3] Each was made when the men were about the same age. Yet even a cursory examination reveals John Coburn's superior engraving skills compared to those of his nephew.

Coburn probably worked for a time in Boston after his apprenticeship. He purchased two ounces of silver from Zachariah Brigden in 1767, enough to make a few spoons or graters, but little else. He moved to the Springfield area by 1775, the year of his marriage to Elizabeth Day of West Springfield, where he may have retailed and repaired watches and other small accessories. His apprentice, Nathan Storrs (1768–1839) of Northampton, witnessed a deed for Coburn in 1786, suggesting that the latter practiced his craft as late as that date. However, Coburn's income seems to have come largely from the sporadic sale of land inherited by his wife rather than from his own workshop. Aside from one spoon, this nutmeg grater stands as the only record of Coburn's unfulfilled promise as a member of Boston's silversmithing elite.

Description: This narrow, cylindrical, seamed form has an applied circular base that is slightly larger than the vessel. A molded strengthening band soldered slightly below a scalloped rim serves as a guard for a deep lid that is similarly seamed and capped. The cylindrical, seamed, metal grater is scalloped at each end, and the border is lightly engraved with abstracted foliate designs. Its surface is densely filled with a diagonal pattern of circular piercings that were punched while the metal was flat.

History: Early history unknown. On loan by the donor to the Museum since 1952 and given in 1973.

Exhibitions and publications: Kathryn C. Buhler, "Seth Storer Coburn: Boston Silversmith," *Silver Magazine* 20, no. 1 (January/February 1987), 8–9 and cover illustration; Kane 1998, 308.

NOTES TO THIS ENTRY ARE ON PAGE 154.

27

John Coney (1655/56–1722)

Set of four caudle cups

Boston, Massachusetts, about 1680
Gift of the First Church in Malden, Congregational
1991.493–96

1991.493: H. 4⅛ in. (10.5 cm); W. 7⁵⁄₁₆ in. (18.5 cm); Diam. rim 4⅛ in. (10.5 cm); Diam. foot 3¹¹⁄₁₆ in. (9.3 cm); Wt. 10 oz 1 dwt 22 gr (314 gm)

1991.494: H. 4⅛ in. (10.5 cm); W. 7⅛ in. (18 cm); Diam. rim 4 in. (10.2 cm); Diam. foot 3½ in. (8.9 cm); Wt. 10 oz 3 dwt 8 gr (316.2 gm)

1991.495: H. 4⅛ in. (10.5 cm); W. 7 in. (17.8 cm); Diam. rim 3¹⁵⁄₁₆ in. (10 cm); Diam. foot 3¹¹⁄₁₆ in. (9.3 cm); Wt. 9 oz 8 dwt 24 gr (293.9 gm)

1991.496: H. 4⅛ in. (10.5 cm); W. 7 in. (17.7 cm); Diam. rim 3⅞ in. (9.9 cm); Diam. foot 3⁷⁄₁₆ in. (9 cm); Wt. 9 oz 13 dwt 2 gr (300.3 gm)

Marks: "IC" with annulet between, over a fleur-de-lis, within a heart-shaped punch, struck twice on 1991.493 and 1991.495, once on base at center, once on body between handles, below rim. "IC" over a fleur-de-lis, within a heart-shaped punch, struck similarly on 1991.494 and 1991.496.

Inscriptions: 1991.493–94: "M : C : Plate." in shaded roman letters engraved on each base, above center point. 1991.495–96: "M : Church Plate." in shaded roman letters engraved on each, below center point.

JOHN CONEY produced at least seventeen caudle cups during his career. Of these, twelve were made for churches, including this set of four made for the church in Malden, Massachusetts, attesting to the adaptation of this domestic form for liturgical use.

Description: Each cup is a raised, plain, gourd-shaped vessel with flaring rim, flanked by two cast scrolled handles. One (1991.496) has repairs to one handle at three points, with solder visible, and tears in the metal are visible from inside the cup.

History: See appendix 5.

Exhibitions and publications: Coney 1932, cat. no. 14; Clarke 1932, nos. 26–27; Kane 1998, 324; see also appendix 5.

28

John Coney (1655/56–1722)

Spout cup

Boston, Massachusetts, 1688
Gift of Cortlandt and James Parker in memory of Major
General and Mrs. Cortlandt Parker
1991.687

H. 5⅜ in. (13.8 cm); W. 5³⁄₁₆ in. (13.3 cm); Diam rim. 3 in. (7.6 cm);
Diam. foot 2¹⁵⁄₁₆ in. (7.5 cm); Wt. 11 oz 16 dwt 7 gr (367.5 gm)

Marks: "IC" crowned over a coney, within a shield-shaped cartouche, struck to left of handle. "IC" within an ellipse struck on
bezel of lid.

Inscriptions: "B / W * M" in roman letters engraved on base.
"William & Mary Bowditch / Joseph & Sarah Hawthorne / Daniel
& Rachael Hawthorne / Simon & Rachael Forrester / Eleanor
Forrester. / dau. of Simon & Rachael Forrester" in script added
later.

THE AMERICAN SPOUT CUP is derived from delft posset pots
made in England from the early seventeenth century. These
were used to serve posset, a drink of "hot milk curdled with
ale, wine, or other liquors, often with sugar, spices, or other
ingredients; formerly much used as a delicacy, and as a remedy
for colds or other affections."[1] This form is essentially a caudle
cup with two handles and a spout. A two-handled version was
made by Jeremiah Dummer; also known are a rare New York
example by Jacob Boelen and an unusual, late Philadelphia
form by Joseph Richardson.[2]

In America, the form is considered particular to Massachusetts, where it was used primarily between 1690 and 1725 for
invalids, women in childbirth, and children. Colonial spout
cups may be related to a small number of English examples in
silver made in Norwich, Plymouth, and London.[3] In New England, the form was typically lidded to prevent spillage. A very
low spout was set at right angles to a single handle. The broad,
teardrop base of the spout, similar to those found on posset
pots, may have been used to cool liquids before being sipped.
Its slender, snaking form clung to the vessel's body and curved
above its rim, enabling the user to drink while reclining.

Many Boston silversmiths during this period were known to
have made at least one or two spout cups. The earliest examples by John Dixwell, John Coney, Andrew Tyler, and Jeremiah
Dummer were squat vessels having a spherical base, ribbed
neck, and friction-fitted lid and were reminiscent of Rhenish
forms in clay. But early in the eighteenth century, the fashion
shifted toward a Georgian ideal in which the S-curve predominated. Early examples by John Coney include a tall, domed
cover, similar to the teapot he made about 1710; his apprentice Nathaniel Morse made at least one similar in appearance.
Edward Winslow created a coverless beaker-style cup with a
strap handle and spout; his nephew and apprentice Moody Russell re-created this form at least four times. Seven spout cups
have been attributed to John Edwards, probably the largest
number yet ascribed to a single maker.[4]

William Bowditch was a wealthy mariner from Salem whose
large estate included 145½ troy ounces of household plate. In
addition to the spout cup, a one-handled cup and a gadrooned
salver, both by Jeremiah Dummer, were among his family possessions; George Hanners of Boston made eleven gold rings for
Bowditch's funeral in 1728.[5]

Description: The spherical body with a molded foot ring rises to a
cylindrical neck. An applied lip is scored and slightly everted. The
S-scroll spout is affixed over a teardrop-shaped opening in the
body. The cast handle has scroll returns at upper and lower points
of attachment and a beaded rattail on outer edge, terminating at

semicircular thumbpiece. The friction-fitted stepped lid has a button finial.

History: The spout cup is thought to have been made for William (1663–1728) and Mary Gardner Bowditch (1669–1724) of Salem, m. 1688. The cup passed down in their family as follows: To their daughter Sarah Bowditch (1695/96–1761), m. Joseph Hawthorne (1692–1762) in 1715.[6] To their son Daniel Hawthorne (1731–1796), a ship captain, m. Rachel Phelps (about 1734–1813) in 1756. To their daughter Rachel Hawthorne (1757–1823), m. Simon Forrester (1748–1817), a Salem ship captain, in 1776.[7] To their daughter Nancy Forrester (1790–1881), m. Gideon Barstow II (1783–1852) in 1812. To their daughter Eleanor Forrester Barstow (1826–1887), m. Caleb Harrison Condit (1826–1881) in 1854. To their daughter Charlotte Mathilda Condit (1856–1933), m. Maj. Gen. James Parker (b. 1854) in 1879.[8] To their son Maj. Gen. Cortlandt Parker (1884–1960), m. Elizabeth Gray (1886–1969) in 1918. To their sons Cortlandt Jr. (b.1921) and James Parker (1924–2001), the donors.[9]

Exhibitions and publications: Okie 1928, 238; Clarke 1932, no. 83, pl. 29; Kane 1998, 328.

NOTES TO THIS ENTRY ARE ON PAGES 154–55.

29

John Coney (1655/56–1722)
Set of three spoons

Boston, Massachusetts, about 1690
Gift in memory of Ruth P. and Pauline Dennis
1990.348
Gift in memory of Mrs. Oakes I. Ames
2001.742.1–2

1990.348: L. 7⅜ in. (18.7 cm); W. bowl 1¹¹⁄₁₆ in. (4.3 cm); Wt. 1 oz 16 dwt 23 gr (57.5 gm)

2001.742.1: L. 7½ in. (19.1 cm); W. bowl 1¾ in (4.4 cm); Wt. 1 oz 16 dwt 8 gr (56.5 gm)

2001.742.2: L. 7⅜ in. (18.8 cm); W. bowl 1¾ in. (4.5 cm); Wt. 1 oz 16 dwt 23 gr (57.5 gm)

Marks: "IC" with annulet between, over a fleur-de-lis, all within a heart-shaped device, struck on back of handle, near bowl; a second oval obliterated mark, possibly a flaw, struck on back of handle.

Inscriptions: "MS" in shaded roman letters engraved on back of handle; "H / I * E," in a similar lettering style, added later above the former, at tip of handle.

29

(1990.348)

THESE ARE AMONG at least five trifid-handled spoons made by Coney for the Shrimpton family; all bear foliated bowl and scrolled handle decoration. Kathryn C. Buhler believed that the presence of an obliterated heart-shaped mark on a Coney spoon in the Yale collection pointed to the use of an English model cast by Coney. Certainly many spoons in this style were brought to this country through trade or immigration, whereas others were made here using English or colonial-made swages. An example of imported swages may be inferred from the "plaine and flower'd Spoon Swages" noted in the 1718 shop inventory of Edward Webb; these were probably brought here by the silversmith in 1704 upon his emigration from London. Other Boston makers who produced trifid-handled spoons with similar bowls include Jeremiah Dummer, John Edwards, and Edward Winslow.[1]

Description: The slightly upturned trifid-end handle of each has a swaged shell over scrolled and beaded design on handle at tip. The back of each elliptical bowl has tapered scroll and foliate ornament flanking a slender ribbed rattail.

History: Initials engraved on the back of each spoon identify as the original owner Mary Shrimpton (1667–1746) of Salem. She m. Salem merchant Robert Gibbs (1665–1702) in 1692. By descent to her daughter and namesake, Mary Gibbs (1699–1761), who m. the Rev. John Cotton (1693–1757) in 1719. To their daughter Elizabeth Cotton (1722–1782), who in 1750 m. Jonathan Hastings (1708/9–1783) and for whom the second set of initials was engraved.[2]

Of the four children of Elizabeth (Cotton) and Jonathan Hastings, only the youngest child, Rebecca, was female, and one spoon (1990.348) descended to their son John (1754–1839) and Lydia Trowbridge Dana (1755–1808), m. 1783. The spoon descended to their daughter Elmira Hastings (1794–1857), wife of Reuben Parker, m. 1815; to their son Samuel Parker (1824–1894), m. Thirza Burrage Ballard (1828–1904) in 1846; to their daughter Mary Louise Parker Fairbanks Clark (b. 1862) and her second husband, Charles Clark (b. 1859), and thence to their daughter Thirza Fairbanks Clark (1884–1978), wife of William B. Esselen, m. 1911; and to their daughter Helen Esselen (1916–1992), wife of Charles Mandell (1916–1986) of Millis, Massachusetts; to her sister Lois Esselen (b. 1918), wife of Arthur R Currier (1918–1988) and the donor.[3]

The other two spoons (2001.742.1–2) began with the same ownership and descended to John Hastings (1754–1839) and Lydia Trowbridge Dana (1755–1808), m. 1783, passing to members of the Hatch and Ames family, as seen in the Edward Webb tankard (cat. no. 126).

Exhibitions and publications: Kane 1998, 329 (1990.348 only).

NOTES TO THIS ENTRY ARE ON PAGE 155.

30

John Coney (1655/56–1722)
Engraved by unknown artist, about 1725
Tankard

Boston, Massachusetts, about 1695–1710
Gift Mr. and Mrs. William W. Dunnell, Jr.
1978.198

H. 8⅝ in. (21.8 cm); W. 9¹⁄₁₆ in. (23.1 cm); Diam. rim 5⅜ in. (14 cm); Diam. base 5⅞ in. (15 cm); Wt. 41 oz 17 dwt 4 gr (1302 gm)

Marks: "IC" crowned over a coney, within a shield-shaped cartouche, struck on lid, handle, and base.

Inscriptions: "C / I * M" in shaded roman letters engraved on center of base, above mark.

Armorials: Shield-shaped armorial of the Cranston family is emblazoned gules three cranes argent within an embattled bordure; the crest a crane passant ppr. facing dexter, on a torse. The whole surrounded by stylized foliate, fishscale, and scrolled decoration. The motto *DUM VIGILO CURO* ("careful while watching" or "I care while I watch") engraved below on a banner.[1]

30

THIS MAJESTIC TANKARD is one of several made by Coney at midcareer. Almost too large to pass from one drinker to another, the vessel would have been admired by visitors, who would have easily grasped the wealth and importance of its owner.

The unusual eagle or griffin thumbpiece is a rare cast that has been found on several other tankards of about the same date. A tankard by Coney with a Hartford provenance (Wadsworth Atheneum) displays the same eagle thumbpiece and cherub terminus. A related example with a low stepped lid, made by Samuel Vernon (MMA), is perhaps slightly later. An Edward Winslow tankard (Albany Institute of History and Art) has been heavily altered but features the same eagle. It is possible that Vernon apprenticed with Winslow, since they were first cousins, related through their Hutchinson mothers; this relationship may account for the use of the same thumbpiece. Due to the similarities, it is likely that one individual cast the thumbpiece and sold it to the others, a division of labor that is still little understood due to lack of period documentation.[2]

Description: The large, raised, cylindrical tankard tapers slightly toward the rim. It features an applied baseband and applied and scored lip. The flat-topped lid has a scored and crenate rim. A large cast and chased eagle thumbpiece descends to a five-part hinge and molded hingeplate. The seamed scrolled handle is attached to the body with a slender rattail at upper joining and has a cast pierced cherub at terminus, with rounded vent hole below.

History: According to tradition, the tankard was made for Samuel Cranston (1659–1727), who served as Rhode Island governor between 1698 and 1710, under the Charter of 1663. The engraved initials are probably those of his son James (1701–1732), born to the aforementioned Samuel and his first wife, Mary Hart (1663–1710). In 1721 James m. Mary Ayrault (1704–1764).[3] The tankard was probably given as a gift to William Wanton (1670–1733), who became governor in 1732, the same year that James Cranston died. If so, the tankard may have been used by the elder Cranston while serving as governor and was made a gift to the new governor upon taking office. Wanton served as governor from 1732 to 1733.[4] By descent to the donors, William Wanton Dunnell Jr. (1894–1980) and his wife, Ellen Frothingham (d. 2001), of Wayland, Massachusetts.

Exhibitions and publications: Avery 1930, 301; MFA 1932, cat. no. 68; Clarke 1932, no. 94; Fairbanks 1981, 627, fig. 31; Kane 1998, 331.

NOTES TO THIS ENTRY ARE ON PAGE 155.

31

John Coney (1655/56–1722)

Mug with added lid

Boston, Massachusetts, about 1705–15
Gift of Barbara Greenough Bradley, H. Vose Greenough, Jr., and Peter B. Greenough
1974.497

H. 5⅜ in. (13.7 cm); W. 5⅜ in. (13.7 cm); Diam. rim 3⅛ in. (7.8 cm); Diam. base 3¾ in. (9.5 cm); Wt. 11 oz 11 dwt 4 gr (359.5 gm)

Marks: "IC" crowned over a coney, within a shield-shaped cartouche, struck on base at center; the same mark struck faintly to left of handle.

Inscriptions: "I / S + R" in roman capitals engraved on base, the "I" and "S" over effaced initials. "F.V . / 1856 / R.G.K. / 1880; C.F.B. / 1890 / H.V.G. / 1916." in script added later on base. "E. V." in a modern hand engraved on body of mug, opposite handle.

THIS MUG IS IDENTICAL in its original appearance and probable ownership to another by Coney in the Museum's collection.[1] The inscription "I / S + R" over effaced script on each may represent the initials of the first or second unidentified owner. Sometime in the nineteenth century, when the vessels were separated, each mug was altered to suit changes in taste.

The nineteenth-century bias against alcoholic drinking vessels may have prompted the fashioning of a spout on the mate to this mug, which was published in 1972 by Kathryn C. Buhler. This example was given a lid to emulate a larger tankard or perhaps to protect a sauce or drink from the air. Together, these vessels bear witness to changing American taste in the use of domestic silver.

31

scroll handle has a thumbgrip at shoulder. The handle is attached to the body with rounded drop at shoulder and with shaped tongue at terminus; a small circular vent hole is below. The domed bezel-set lid with button finial and beaded edge was added later.

History: Original owners unknown, although the mug was probably made as a pair with the Museum's other example by Coney (21.1256). The earliest likely ownership, as indicated by the later engraved text, can be dated to the early nineteenth century, beginning with Elijah Vose (1790–1856), m. Rebecca Gorham Bartlett in Charlestown, Massachusetts, in 1816. Upon his death, the mug may have passed first to his son Francis Vose (1821–1880), who died unm.; and upon his death to his sister Rebecca Gorham Vose (1819–1890), m. John Brooks Kettell in 1838. Their daughter Caroline Freeman Kettel (1846–1924) inherited the mug. Having no children through her 1878 marriage to William Brewster, she returned the silver to the patrilineal line through a gift to Henry Vose Greenough (1883–1973), the grandson of her uncle Henry Vose (1817–1869), who passed the vessel to his children, the donors.[2]

Exhibitions and publications: None.

NOTES TO THIS ENTRY ARE ON PAGE 155.

The passage of this mug through the Vose family during the nineteenth century illustrates one family's approach to the inheritance of silver. The mug was engraved with the initials of each new owner, followed by the death date of the preceding owner, and descended to male and female members alike. However, the importance of keeping family silver in the patrilineal line is borne out by the gift of Caroline Freeman Kettell Brewster, one of the later owners, who returned the silver to the Vose family.

Description: The mug has straight tapering sides; molded rim with applied molding below; and broad stepped baseband. The hollow

32

John Coney (1655/56–1722)
Punch bowl

Boston, Massachusetts, 1708–9
Theodora Wilbour Fund in memory of Charlotte Beebe Wilbour
1972.913

H. 4⅞ in. (12.5 cm); Diam. rim 9⅝ in. (24.5 cm); Diam. base 7 in. (17.8 cm); Wt. 32 oz 16 dwt 11 gr (1020.9 gm)

Marks: "I C" crowned over a coney, within a shield-shaped cartouche, struck on bottom.

Inscriptions: Except for motto, as noted in armorial.

Armorial: Riddell coat of arms within an elliptical shield is emblazoned argent a chevron argent between three ears of rye, all within a foliated and scrolled mantling. The motto *HOPE TO SHARE* inscribed on a scroll below arms.[1]

PERHAPS THE earliest-known example of monumental late baroque American silver, this punch bowl by John Coney marks the fruitful relationship between colonial and English cultures during the early eighteenth century. Along with the teapot and chocolate pot, the punch bowl is one of several stylish English forms that Coney was the first to make in the colonies.

32

The bowl was fashioned for Capt. Walter Riddell of Granton, a harbor near Edinburgh, Scotland. Riddell commanded the man-of-war *Falmouth*, arrived off the coast of Cape Ann on November 10, 1708, and returned to England in May 1709. Riddell kept a watchful eye on the valuable fisheries at Marblehead, Cape Ann, and the Piscataqua River near Portsmouth, which were vulnerable to attack from the French. He played an important role during this period of intense hostility between the English and French and participated in high-level negotiations with Philippe de Rigeau, the marquis de Vaudreuil, governor of North France (Canada) in 1710 for the release of Esther Williams, the celebrated "unredeemed captive" abducted during the Deerfield massacre of 1704.[2]

In short, Riddell was a royal appointee among many who arrived in Massachusetts following the 1692 charter that established English hegemony over the region's political affairs. Many of these newly settled officials desired furnishings for their homes and were potential sources of income for those

Boston craftsmen who could deliver work in an urban style to suit the patrons' taste. Silversmiths met the demand by keeping abreast of the latest fashions through the examination of newly imported examples that they repaired or sold. Recently arrived London craftsmen also brought a knowledge of new designs to Boston.

The hemispherical form of the punch bowl is derived from porcelain prototypes made in the Wan-li style of early-seventeenth-century China and exported to England, exerting a powerful influence on ceramics and metalwork.[3] The English affinity for the form held considerable sway over colonial styles as well, for John Coney's early Baroque style of silversmithing, as learned from his master, Jeremiah Dummer, was tempered by this aesthetic. For this punch bowl, which Coney produced as a mature craftsman, he fashioned a simple volumetric form with restrained ornament that had become stylish in England. As with all the arts produced at this time, the punch bowl demonstrates the close cultural ties between colony and mother country, despite the era's political tensions.

During Riddell's six-and-a-half-month stay in the colonies, it is unclear whether he set foot in Boston. Nevertheless, he did have contact with a "Mr. Faneuil," presumably Andrew Faneuil (d. 1738), as well as Gov. Joseph Dudley (1647–1720), among other dignitaries, who might have directed Riddell to Coney.[4]

The Riddell arms of Roxburghshire, Scotland, are displayed on the punch bowl, with the pronoun "I" removed from the original motto "I hope to share." The heraldic insignia definitively establishes the bowl's date of purchase before 1715, when the arms were modified as a consequence of Riddell's naval exploits in 1709 and 1715. Upon his return to England in May 1709, Riddell successfully defended the *Falmouth* and a convoy of vessels against the French, thereby saving £20,000 of "New England money" on board. In 1715, as commander of the frigate of war *Phoebe*, Riddell captured thirty-seven vessels in a second major battle with the French fleet. Following this encounter, Riddell was authorized to change the family escutcheon to reflect his accomplishments. One ear of rye was substituted with a boat with oars, and for the Granton branch of the family, the motto "Row and Retake" replaced "I hope to share." Riddell also acquired the barony of West Granton at this time, probably a result of his naval service.[5] The volumetric, architectural treatment of the mantling, with its interlocking scrolls, is nearly identical to those found on the great Colman monteith, made about the same time as the punch bowl, as well as a covered two-handled cup made by Coney in 1718 for Harvard tutor Henry Flynt.[6]

Description: The heavy-gauge raised vessel has a scribed, thin, applied, molded rim and nearly straight sides, curving to a flat bottom supported by a molded splayed foot ring.

History: Walter Riddell (about 1679–1738) of Granton, Scotland, son of the Rev. Archibald Riddell (d. 1708), m. Sarah Nisbet of nearby Dean, Scotland; they had no issue. Following Riddell's death, Sarah m. Sir John Rutherford from a nearby town by the same name.[7] Subsequent history unknown until February 1972, when the punch bowl was sold at Phillips Auctioneers, London. The consigner, Mrs. Yvonne Riddell Crow, discovered it while clearing out family belongings at East Nisbet Farm, Jedburg, which had been leased from Lord Lothian's estate in Roxburghshire. The bowl was misidentified in the Phillips catalogue as the work of English silversmith J. Cornasseau, now called Isaac Cornafleau (w. 1722–24). Purchased by London dealer Thomas Lumley for Boston dealers Firestone and Parson and acquired by the Museum in September 1972.[8]

Exhibitions and publications: Phillips Auctioneers, London, sale 18,923, February 11, 1972, lot 183; advertisement, Firestone and Parson, *Antiques* 101, no. 4 (April 1972): 618; Bettie Wysor, "Art and Antiques Newsletter," *Town and Country* 126, no. 4597 (August 1972): 84–89, fig. 2; Ruth Davidson, "Museum Accessions," *Antiques* 104, no. 6 (December 1972): 990; Fales 1973, 2; Fairbanks 1981, fig. 32; Fairbanks 1991, 69, cat. no. 50; Kane 1998, 322.

NOTES TO THIS ENTRY ARE ON PAGE 155.

33

John Coney (1655/56–1722)

Porringer

Boston, Massachusetts, 1710–15
Gift of Barbara Zinszer Hyre and Paul Harvey Zinszer
1997.305

H. 2 in. (5 cm); W. 7⅞ in. (20 cm); Diam. rim 5⅜ in. (13.7 cm); Wt. 6 oz 17 dwt 14 gr (214 gm)

Marks: "IC" over a coney, within a heart-shaped device, struck to left of handle at rim.

Inscriptions: "E N" in shaded roman letters engraved on handle, facing away from bowl.

THIS PREVIOUSLY UNPUBLISHED porringer is one of at least twenty-four known examples that Coney fashioned between 1695 and 1715. Its geometric-style handle, which the silversmith favored, is similar to another he fashioned in 1710, which is in the Museum's collection (31.219).[1]

The porringer is one of a group of early Massachusetts silver owned by the Norton and Mason families of Hingham.

33

John Coney (1655/56–1722)
Pair of trencher salts

Boston, Massachusetts, 1710–20
Gift of Mr. and Mrs. William L. Payson
1973.618–19

1973.618: H. 1⅛ in. (2.8 cm); W. 3⅛ in. (7.8 cm); D. 2⅜ in. (6.1 cm);
Wt. 2 oz 2 dwt 7 gr (65.8 gm)

1973.619: H. 1⅛ in. (2.9 cm); W. 3 in. (7.7 cm); D. 2⅜ in. (6 cm); Wt. 2
oz 1 dwt 4 gr (64 gm)

Marks: "I C" crowned over a coney, all within a shield, struck on
underside of each bowl.

Inscriptions: "A / T * H" in roman capitals engraved on base of
each. "W" in Gothic capitals inscribed later along exterior.

In addition, Coney made a sugar box and tankard, the latter
bearing the Norton arms, for Elizabeth Norton's parents, the
Rev. John and Mary (Mason) Norton. John Edwards produced a
tankard for the family, and William Cowell Sr. fashioned a pepper box. Elizabeth's maternal grandparents, Arthur and Joanna
(Parker) Mason, owned a porringer with a trefoil handle, made
by John Hull and Robert Sanderson. That porringer descended
in a family line closely related to the donors of this example.[2]

Description: The raised porringer has convex sides and a center point
in its large domed base. The cast geometric-style handle is soldered
at right angles to the everted rim. A repair is visible at the rim, to
right of handle.

History: Made for Elizabeth Norton (1695–1769) of Hingham, daughter of the Rev. John Norton (about 1651–1716) and Mary Mason
(1661–1740), m. 1678, possibly on the occasion of her marriage in
1715 to John Quincy (1689–1767) of Braintree. To their daughter
Lucy Quincy (1729–1785) and Cotton Tufts (1732–1815) of North
Weymouth, Massachusetts, m. 1755. To their son Cotton Tufts II
(1757–1833) and Mercy Brooks (1763–1849), m. 1788; at this point the
porringer probably crossed to the Brooks family. Possibly to Margaret Austin Brooks (1817–1886), niece of Mercy Brooks Tufts, and
her husband, William Brigham (1806–1869), m. 1840; to their daughter Mary Brooks Brigham (1851–1919) and McPherson LeMoyne
(1835–1900), m. 1875; to their son Charles LeMoyne (1876–1952) and
Clara Marcus; to his daughter Mary Brooks LeMoyne (1917–2000)
and William K. Zinszer (1914–2000); to their children, the donors.[3]

Exhibitions and publications: None.

NOTES TO THIS ENTRY ARE ON PAGE 155.

THE TRENCHER SALT, intended for placement at each diner's
trencher, or plate, was first used at English and American tables
during the early eighteenth century. Its modest scale followed
the majestic spool-shaped salts of the late seventeenth century
that were traditionally placed near the head of the household
and whose size alone commanded respect for the rare commodity they contained. As local saltworks became established
along the Massachusetts coast, and the spice was obtained
locally, the trencher salt came into use in several low forms that
were sometimes made in pairs.[1]

The octagonal trencher salt, actually a rectangular form with
canted corners and an oval interior, was popular in England
but rarely seen in the colonies. This pair is unique in Coney's
oeuvre. According to family tradition, the salts were a wedding
gift to Lydia Bowes from John Hancock; but due to their likely
date of fabrication, he probably inherited them from his uncle
Thomas Hancock (1703–1763), a merchant. Aside from another
pair by Coney that are oval, an example made about 1730 by
Jacob Hurd, and a pair dated 1745 and made by Joseph Richardson Sr., apparently few salts of this shape were made in the
colonies.[2]

According to family history, the salts were traditionally used
with a pair of later Jacob Hurd salt spoons (cat. no. 81). Hancock's wedding gift to Bowes also included a tankard by London silversmith Thomas Moore II and a creampot by Samuel
Gray.[3]

Description: Each low octagonal salt is of roughly rectangular shape
with two long and six shorter sides. The shallow oval bowl is set

34

within a faceted body having concave sides that splay inward from wide, scored base. Each foot is reinforced with applied wire.

History: The original owner, whose initials "A / T * H" are engraved on the salts, is unknown. According to the donor, the patriot John Hancock gave the salts to his first cousin Lydia Bowes (1749–1805), on her marriage in 1770 to Rev. Phinehas Whitney (1740–1819) of Shirley; the Gothic *W* was added later in the nineteenth century. By descent to their son Thomas Whitney (1771–1884) and Henrietta Parker (1775–1864) of the same town, m. 1799; to their son James Phineas Whitney (1802–1847) and Lydia Bowes Parker Treadwell (b. 1815), m. 1836; to their daughter Henrietta Parker Whitney (1837–1900) and Andrew McFarland Davis (b. 1833) of Worcester, m. 1862. To their daughter Frederica King Davis (1869–before 1964) and Thomas Russell Watson (1850–1920) of Plymouth and Middletown, m. 1901; to their three daughters, Eleanor Whitney Watson (Mrs. Thomas B. Coolidge) (b. 1902), Marjorie (Mrs. T. Dana Hill) (b. 1903), and Mrs. William Payson. Purchased from Mrs. Coolidge and Mrs. Hill by the donors and made a gift.[4]

Exhibitions and publications: Kane 1998, 328.

NOTES TO THIS ENTRY ARE ON PAGES 155–156.

35

John Coney (1655/56–1722)
Chocolate pot

Boston, Massachusetts, 1715–20
Gift of Dr. Lamar Soutter and Theodora Wilbour Fund in memory of Charlotte Beebe Wilbour
1976.771

H. 9½ in. (24.1 cm); W. 8¹¹⁄₁₆ in. (22.2 cm); Diam. rim 3⅛ in. (8 cm); Diam. base 4⅜ in. (11.1 cm); Wt. 28 oz 7 dwt 5 gr (882.1 gm)

Marks: "I C," with a crown above and a coney below, within a shaped cartouche, struck below rim near spout, on flange, and on bottom.

Inscriptions: "C / W D [tilde] E" engraved later on mantling, to left of handle. Scratch weight "27 oz 10 dwt 0 g" incised on base.

JOHN CONEY is considered the first New England silversmith to make both teapots and chocolate pots for the newly fashionable, imported beverages. His domed teapot, made about 1710–20 for the Mascarene family of Boston (MMA), is among the earliest of its kind. Along with Edward Webb, Peter Oliver, and Edward Winslow, Coney produced chocolate pots during the first fifteen years of the eighteenth century; Zachariah Brig-

35

History: Original owners are unknown. Initials engraved on the vessel are of later owners William Downes (1720–1788) and Elizabeth (Edwards) Cheever (1729–1802), m. 1749;[3] by descent in the matrilineal line to their daughter Eleanor Cheever (1749/50–1825) and the Hon. Caleb Davis (1738–1797), m. 1787; to their daughter Eliza Cheever Davis (1790–1828) and Dr. George Cheyne Shattuck (1783–1854), m. 1811; to their son, who was his father's namesake, Dr. George Cheyne Shattuck Jr. (1813–1893) and Anne Henrietta Brune (1809–1894),[4] m. 1840; to their daughter Eleanor A. B. Shattuck (also called Elizabeth) (1842–1918) and Alexander Whiteside (1825–1903), m. 1871;[5] to their daughter Helen Whiteside (1876–1940) and Dr. Robert Soutter (1870–1933), m. 1904; to their son Lamar Soutter (1909–1996), the donor.[6]

Exhibitions and publications: MFA 1911, 29, cat. no. 259, pl. 7; Jones 1913, 35, pl. XIII; Bigelow 1917, 269–70, fig. 263; Clarke 1932, no. 19, pl. 15; MFA 1932, cat. no. 80; "Museum of Fine Arts Acquires John Coney Chocolate Pot," *Antiques and the Arts Weekly* (January 21, 1977), 19; Fairbanks 1981, pl. XLII; Fairbanks 1991, 70, cat. no. 51; Kane 1998, 324; Falino and Ward 2001, 68–69, fig. 7.

NOTES TO THIS ENTRY ARE ON PAGE 156.

den created two during the 1750s, for a total of eight known chocolate pots. This gourd-shaped example and another in the shape of a ginger jar made by Coney that is in the Museum's collection are unique forms of this rare vessel.[1]

The 1749 union of Elizabeth Edwards and William Downes Cheever brought together a quantity of silver that predated their marriage by more than twenty years. In addition to the chocolate pot, the heirlooms included a porringer by Coney, a chafing dish by Winslow, a child's porringer by Thomas Savage, a cann by Nathaniel Morse, and a tankard possibly by Timothy Dwight.[2]

William Downes Cheever was a successful sugar refiner who had inherited a fortune and was well able to purchase silver of his choice. Yet it is more likely these older pieces were inherited from the Edwards side of the family. Elizabeth was the daughter of Thomas Edwards (1701–1755) and hence part of the Edwards silversmithing dynasty. She was also the great-niece of John Noyes and the sister-in-law of Zachariah Brigden. Thus, the chocolate pot, along with these additional pieces of silver, may have been received as wedding gifts from her family.

Description: The raised, tall, gourd-shaped vessel has a splayed molded foot with foot ring. Circular tapered sockets hold a replacement scrolled, carved wooden handle with thumbgrip. Opposite the handle is the cast and chased panelled spout, with the head of a collared serpent at its tip. A domed multistepped lid rises to a spherical finial and has a small hole, now filled with a cupped device with a protruding pin on reverse. The lid has a wide rim, scored several times; inside, a deep flange sets the friction-fitted lid. A section of chain, about 4 inches (10 cm) and probably replaced, has rings at each end that encircle the finial and upper socket. The decorative elements consist of cut-card ornamentation that rises from the spout and engraved triangular mantling with an oval reserve, which contains the later owner's initials.

36

John Coney (1655/56–1722)
Pair of tankards

Boston, Massachusetts, 1716
Gift of a Friend of the Department and the Edward J. and Mary S. Holmes Fund
1984.206–7

1984.206: H. 7½ in. (19 cm); W. 6½ in. (16.6 cm); Diam. rim 3¹⁵⁄₁₆ in. (10 cm); Diam. base 5¹⁄₁₆ in. (12.9 cm); Wt. 26 oz 6 dwt 3 gr (818.2 gm)

1984.207: H. 7⁹⁄₁₆ in. (19.2 cm); W. 6⅞ in. (17.6 cm); Diam. rim 3⅞ in. (9.9 cm); Diam. base 4¹³⁄₁₆ in. (12.2 cm); Wt. 25 oz 17 dwt 21 gr (805.4 gm)

Marks: "IC" crowned above a coney, within a shield-shaped cartouche, struck on bottom of each and to left of each handle, near rim; "IC" within an ellipse struck on each cover bezel.

Inscriptions: 1984.206: "A Gift to Mr Holyokes Church: / Marble head / 1716" in script engraved on body. 1984.207: "A Gift to Mr Holyoaks Church / Marblehead / 1716" in script engraved on body.

SEE APPENDIX 6 for silver commissioned by the Second Congregational Church (now the Unitarian Universalist Church of Marblehead), Marblehead, Massachusetts.

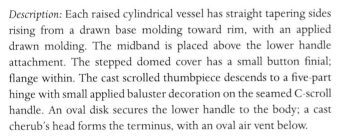

36

Description: Each raised cylindrical vessel has straight tapering sides rising from a drawn base molding toward rim, with an applied drawn molding. The midband is placed above the lower handle attachment. The stepped domed cover has a small button finial; flange within. The cast scrolled thumbpiece descends to a five-part hinge with small applied baluster decoration on the seamed C-scroll handle. An oval disk secures the lower handle to the body; a cast cherub's head forms the terminus, with an oval air vent below.

History: See appendix 6.

Exhibitions and publications: Clarke 1932, no. 106; MFA 1932, cat. no. 57; Kane 1998, 322; see also appendix 6.

37

John Coney (1655/56–1722)

Set of four beakers

Boston, Massachusetts, 1716
Gift of a Friend of the Department and Edward J. and Mary
S. Holmes Fund
1984.209–12

1984.209: H. 5¹¹⁄₁₆ in. (14.6 cm); Diam. rim 4⅛ in. (10.2 cm); Diam.
foot 2¹¹⁄₁₆ in. (6.9 cm); Wt. 8 oz 19 dwt 20 gr (279.7 gm)

1984.210: H. 5¹¹⁄₁₆ in. (14.6 cm); Diam. rim 4⅛ in. (10.3 cm); Diam.
foot 2⅝ in. (6.7 cm); Wt. 9 oz 4 dwt 8 gr (286.7 gm)

1984.211: H. 5⅞ in. (15.1 cm); Diam. rim 4⅛ in. (10.3 cm); Diam. foot
2¹¹⁄₁₆ (6.9 cm); Wt. 9 oz 4 dwt 2 gr (286.3 gm)

1984.212: H. 5¹³⁄₁₆ in. (14.7 cm); Diam. rim 4⅛ in. (10.3 cm); Diam.
foot 2¾ in. (7 cm); Wt. 9 oz 8 dwt 17 gr (293.5 gm)

Marks: "IC" crowned above a coney, all within a shield, struck twice
on each, above inscription and on bottom.

Inscriptions: 1984.209: "A Gift to Mr Holyoks Church /
Marble=head / 1716" engraved on body. 1984.210: "A Gift to Mr
Holyoke's Church / Marble=head / 1716" in script engraved on
body. 1984.211–12: "E:Brattle to Mr Holyokes Church." in script
engraved on wall of each.

ALL THESE BEAKERS have been dated to 1716: two are inscribed
with that date, and all are nearly identical in size, shape, and
moldings. See appendix 6 for silver commissioned by the Second Congregational Church (now the Unitarian Universalist
Church of Marblehead), Marblehead, Massachusetts.

Description: Each raised inverted bell-shaped beaker rises from a
small mold-drawn foot ring and flares outward at applied molded
rim. Imperfections from the latter are evident inside rim. A center
point is evident on the bottom.

History: Two of the cups (1984.211–12) were given to the church
by the Marblehead merchant Edward Brattle (1670–1719), son of
Thomas and Elizabeth (Tyng) Brattle of Boston and brother to Rev.
Thomas Brattle of Cambridge.[1]

Exhibitions and publications: Clarke 1932, no. 34; MFA 1932, cat. no. 58;
Kane 1998, 322. See also appendix 6.

NOTES TO THIS ENTRY IS ON PAGE 156.

38

John Coney (1655/56–1722)

Baptismal basin

Boston, Massachusetts, 1718
Gift of a Friend of the Department and the Edward J. and
Mary S. Holmes Fund
1984.208

H. 3⁵⁄₁₆ in. (8.5 cm); Diam. 16⅞ in. (43 cm); Wt. 50 oz 3 dwt 23 gr
(1561.3 gm)

Marks: "IC" above a coney, within a shield, struck between inscription and rim.

Inscriptions: "Doms. Johannes Legg Arm gr, Ecclesiam J. Christi apud Marbleh-d / eujus Revd D. Edwd Holyoke est Paftor, hoc pietatis testimonio religiofe donavit. / Anno 1718" in Latin engraved on rim.

As DONALD FENNIMORE has pointed out, the Congregational church strove to reduce the number of liturgical forms as a means of distancing themselves from the ritualistic accoutrements employed by the Roman and Anglican churches.[1]

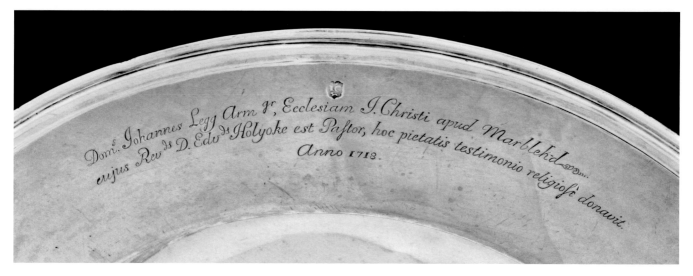

38

The large, wide bowl, or basin, was a secular vessel appropriated for christening. The plain form, graced only with a lively inscription, was at the opposite extreme from the lavish baptismal fonts often built into the fabric of the Roman churches. Effaced evidence of an unfinished S-scrolled decorative pattern at the rim and a compass design in the central dome of the vessel suggests that Coney had originally been commissioned to embellish the basin but stopped for unknown reasons early in his efforts.

For further information, see appendix 6.

Description: The large basin with a broad everted rim has a drawn, applied, molded edge. The sides of the basin descend vertically before curving inward toward a small central dome and center point. Faint remains of incomplete compass-patterned engraving are visible on the central dome; two S-scrolls for an intended repeating border appear on the rim to the right of the inscription. Two solder repairs appear under the rim.

History: In 1674, John Legg (d. 1718) was among 114 householders recorded in Marblehead. His will provided for "twenty five pounds to be layd out for a Silver Bason for ye perpetuall use & service of ye said Church." Edward Brattle, donor of the Coney beakers, m. his daughter Mary in 1692/93.[2]

Exhibitions and publications: Clarke 1932, no. 2; MFA 1932, cat. no. 56; Kane 1998, 321. See also appendix 6.

NOTES TO THIS ENTRY ARE ON PAGE 156.

39

Richard Conyers (about 1666–1708/9)

Tankard

Boston, Massachusetts, 1698–1708
Gift of Stuart Alan Goldman and Marion E. Davis Fund
1980.278

H. 5⅛ in. (13 cm); W. 5¹¹⁄₁₆ in. (8.2 cm); Diam. rim 3¼ in. (8.2 cm); Diam. base 3⅞ in. (9.9 cm); Wt. 15 oz 7 dwt 16 gr (478.5 gm)

Marks: "RC" below a crown, within a shield-shaped cartouche, struck to right of handle and on top of lid.

Inscriptions: "R / T * I" in shaded roman letters engraved on bottom, over center point.

THE SON OF A SADDLER, Richard Conyers was trained in London before arriving in Boston about 1698. Despite his London apprenticeship, and the chasing assistance of Swedish-born Henry Hurst (about 1666–1717/18), who for a brief time served as his indentured servant, Conyers encountered financial troubles and was unable to fully establish himself in his adopted city. Only seven known examples bear Conyers's mark.[1] Despite the lack of finished, marked work, Conyers's talent and knowlege of recent English fashions likely made him attractive to established Boston silversmiths as a journeyman or special-order silversmith. Future scholars may discern his

39

accomplishments in objects made in the shops of better-established Boston silversmiths.

This diminutive tankard's crisp detailing, as found in the gadrooned lid, crenate lip, and cast cherub's mask terminal, exemplifies the urbane high style that Conyers and other English immigrants imparted to the Boston trade at the turn of the century.[2] His mark, placed in the English manner on both the lid and body, is perhaps a vestige of his early training.

Description: The small raised tankard has straight tapering sides and crisply drawn, molded base and lip, all of finely scaled proportions. The gadrooned stepped lid has a scored crenate lip. The scrolled thumbpiece descends to a five-part hinge with wigglework decoration, and the seamed S-scroll handle has chased reeding that ends in a small scroll, with a cast cherub at terminus. It is attached to the vessel with an attenuated rattail drop at upper join and directly to handle at the base. An added spout was removed at an unknown date.

History: Early history of ownership is unknown; provenance attributed to Thomas and Jane Redmond of Boston, which was first sug-

gested in the Bigelow-Phillips files at the Yale University Art Gallery and published elsewhere, must be considered speculative. The late-twentieth-century history of ownership begins with Andrew Metropolis of Peabody, Massachusetts, to Stuart Alan Goldman of Randolph, Massachusetts. Acquired by the Museum in 1980.

Exhibitions and publications: B. Ward 1983, 160, fn. 9, 350; Fairbanks 1991, 69, cat. no. 49, checklist no. 22; Kane 1998, 338.

NOTES TO THIS ENTRY ARE ON PAGE 156.

40

William Cowell Sr. (1682/83–1736)
Tankard

Boston, Massachusetts, 1705
Museum purchase with funds provided by Mr. and Mrs. Joseph P. Pellegrino; the estate of Rosamond Sears, by exchange; the estate of Ada Belle Winthrop-King, by exchange, and the Marion E. Davis Fund
1998.48

H. 8⅛ in. (20.5 cm); W. 9⅝ in. (24.5 cm); Diam. rim 5¹/₁₆ in. (12.9 cm); Diam. base 6⅛ in. (15.5 cm); Wt. 34 oz 15 dwt 7 gr (1081.3 gm)

Marks: "W C" within an ellipse struck to left of handle and on lid, near thumbpiece.

Inscriptions: "This belongs to / the Church in / Brattle-street / 1705" in script, within a stylized foliate cartouche, engraved on body, opposite handle. "This Flagon / was given by the Proprietors of / The Brattle Street Church, / Boston / to / The Reverend Samuel Kirkland Lothrop, D.D. / and to / All Saints Church Dorchester, Boston. / by his daughter / Mary Lothrop Peabody, / All Saints' Day, / 1901." in script added later on base.

WILLIAM COWELL SR. may have apprenticed with John Allen (1671/72–1760), whose father held the mortgage to Cowell's family home, or with John Edwards (about 1671–1746), Allen's partner and brother-in-law. His apprenticeship complete by 1704, Cowell fashioned this tankard soon after for the Brattle Street Church, to which he and Allen belonged.[1]

Along with this tankard, Cowell produced, in the years following his apprenticeship, a nutmeg grater engraved with a carnation (MMA), a gadrooned cup with one handle (MFA), a plain dram cup (Historic Deerfield), and one beaker engraved with text for the Congregational Church of Windham, Connecticut.[2] Excepting the nutmeg grater, none demonstrates his ability to engrave the sophisticated design on this tankard.

40

The stylized mantling of angels and floral elements is similar to that found on seven pieces of communion plate made by four Boston silversmiths and members of the congregation. Although separated by as many as twenty-eight years, the engravings follow the one first used by John Noyes in 1704. In addition to the Cowell tankard made in 1705, two tankards by John Edwards dated 1728, a tankard by Andrew Tyler from 1732, and one communion cup by Edwards dated 1732 all bear similar designs.[3]

Close examination of the Noyes and Cowell tankards reveals a nearly identical engraving style that extends beyond lettering to the treatment of the curly-haired angel, its slender outstretched wings extending behind the mantling, and its pointed body. Later tankards and cups depict an angel having smooth hair parted in the center and combed into a "flip" (upturned ends), shorter articulated wings, and a rounded body. The Noyes and Cowell tankards also share similarities in the mantling, particularly in the engraving of berries and scrolls flanking the inscription. Fine cross-hatching at the base of the berries' spherical forms lends volume, and the closely spaced, vertical lines under the large scrolls give the illusion of depth. Later engravings treat these two features more broadly, with a resulting loss of subtlety.

The Noyes and Cowell tankards are of similar height and share physical characteristics that include a crenate lid, long rattail joining at the upper handle, mask and dolphin thumbpiece, and shield-shaped terminus, suggesting that they were intended to be a pair. Perhaps young Cowell was chosen to make the tankard at the urging of his former masters, Edwards and Allen, with the engraving completed by Noyes.

Description: The tapered cylindrical form has a drawn molded base and lip, scored twice below the lip. Its flat stepped lid has a broad rim, scored twice, and crenate decoration near handle and at the later, applied spout. A cast dolphin-and-grotesque thumbpiece descends to a five-part hinge with wigglework straps on the seamed handle. A prominent rattail drop appears below the upper join of handle, with a flat shield terminus and a crescent-shaped air vent below. The broadly engraved cartouche of stylized foliage appears on the body, opposite the handle.

History: The tankard was made by Cowell for the Brattle Street Church in 1705, although the source of funds for its purchase remains unknown. Along with approximately nineteen other pieces of church silver, the tankard was put up for auction by the Brattle Street Church in 1839. When no buyer materialized, the congregation voted to give the tankard to the church minister, the Rev. Samuel Kirkland Lothrop (d. 1886).[4] By descent to his daughter Mary Lothrop Peabody (1837–1910), who, on All Saints' Day 1901, made it a gift to the Parish of All Saints, Ashmont (Dorchester, Massachusetts). Acquired from the church in April 1998.

Exhibitions and publications: Jones 1913, 67–71, pl. XXVII; Kane 1998, 354. See also appendix 3.

NOTES TO THIS ENTRY ARE ON PAGE 156.

41

William Cowell Sr. (1682/83–1736)
Tankard

Boston, Massachusetts, 1727
Gift of the First Church in Newton
1973.17

H. 7¹³⁄₁₆ in. (19.7 cm); W. 7⅛ in. (18.1 cm); Diam. rim 4⅛ in. (10.5 cm); Diam. base 4¹⁵⁄₁₆ in. (12.6 cm); Wt. 24 oz 18 dwt 5 gr (774.8 gm)

Marks: "WC" in a shield, with a star above flanked by two pellets and one pellet below, struck to left of handle and on base at center. "W. Cowell" in script, within a shaped rectangle, struck on lid between finial and thumbpiece.

Inscriptions: "The Gift of / Mr. John Staples / TO THE / Church of Christ / in / Newtown May 28th / 1727" in script, within a circle of modest foliate decoration, engraved opposite handle. Scratch weight "24 13" incised on bottom.

WILLIAM COWELL SR. was a prolific silversmith who produced both domestic and ecclesiastical silver. He received commissions from many Congregational churches and at least one Episcopal church.[1] Cowell was patronized by local churches in Boston, Hull, and Newton, Massachusetts, and also received more distant requests from Stratford and Farmington, Connecticut. The tankard produced for the First Church in Newton was made during a period of great activity in his workshop, when Cowell was in his prime.

Description: The raised straight-sided tankard is slightly wider at base and has a drawn stepped base molding and a single midband in the lower third. A domed stepped lid has downturned lip with scored edge and a flange within. The small button finial is seated upon a swelled center with evidence of solder, suggesting a later repair. The scrolled thumbpiece is cast, and the five-part hinge descends to a short molded drop on seamed handle. The handle is joined to the body at lower terminus by a flat oval disk. Terminal has convex oval disk and semicircular air vent below.

History: Yeoman John Staples (d. 1740) was the sponsor for the Cowell tankard, which he gave in 1727. Staples's continued support of the church is recorded in his will, dated April 24, 1740, and proved January 5, 1740–41. He bequeathed "seventeen acres of land available towards the support of ye Ministerial use from year to year annually for so long as it shall be continued for a woodlot & I do desire & empower the Selectman of sd town to appoint what Trees shall be cut down annually so as that no strip or waste shall be made of wood or timber for any other use whatsoever save only for the ministers use."[2]

Exhibitions and publications: MFA 1911, 31, cat. no. 281, pl. 8; Jones 1913, 332; Kane 1998, 355; see also appendix 8.

NOTES TO THIS ENTRY ARE ON PAGE 156.

42

William Cowell Jr. (1713–1761)

Porringer

Boston, Massachusetts, about 1750
Bequest of Charles Hitchcock Tyler
32.381

H. 2³/₁₆ in. (5.5 cm); W. 8⁵/₁₆ in. (21 cm); Diam. rim 5½ in. (13.9 cm);
Wt. 6 oz 16 dwt 22 gr (212.9 gm)

Marks: "W:Cowell" in italics, within a rectangular punch with
shaped top, struck under handle.

Inscriptions: "Gelston" in script engraved later on base.

WHEN KATHRYN C. BUHLER published her two-volume work
on the Museum's silver collection, she omitted this porringer,
although it had been in the collection since 1932. Its added spout
may have led to her decision to exclude an altered object. However, this modification suggests how changing tastes or needs
have shaped the types of forms used over time.

The addition of a spout to a porringer allowed its owner
to extend its use as a type of low saucepan for serving liquids.
Porringers were popular in the colonies long after the taste for
this form had faded in England, but it is unclear how these vessels were used in the nineteenth century. The large number of
surviving porringers suggests that some must have remained in
use, whereas others were retained out of respect for the ances-

tors who first owned them. The survival of this curious spouted porringer allows us to consider how some were adapted for
continued use at the table.

Description: The raised low vessel with a center point has a defined
dome in the base and steps upward to low convex walls and everted
rim. A cast keyhole handle is soldered at a slight angle to the rim. At
an undetermined date, a spout having a shaped upper section was
added at left of handle. A failed repair to a tear at the rim is evident,
and numerous small dents appear along the sides.

History: None known prior to its acqusition by Boston collector
Charles Hitchcock Tyler (1863–1931).

Exhibitions and publications: Kane 1998, 346.

43

John Dixwell (1680/81–1725)

Porringer

Boston, Massachusetts, about 1715–25
Gift of Catherine Cooper-Morison
1991.586

H. 1⁷/₈ in. (4.8 cm); W. 8 in. (20.4 cm); Diam rim 5⁵/₈ in. (14.2 cm);
Diam. foot 2⅛ in. (5.3 cm); Wt. 8 oz 3 dwt 20 gr (254.8 gm)

Marks: "ID" in roman letters within an ellipse struck to left of
handle.

Inscriptions: "G / D * M" in roman letters engraved on handle, with
letters facing bowl. "ETA" in sprigged script added later on convex
side of porringer, opposite handle.

AS ONE OF THE LEADING Boston silversmiths of the early eighteenth century, John Dixwell operated a moderately sized shop
that received many important church and private commissions.
He also appears to have been among the first American-born
silversmiths to be influenced by the prevailing baroque style,
the result of a trip to England in 1710. The fashion for designs
introduced by French Huguenot silversmiths then working in
London, with their emphasis on simple forms, can be seen in
the two-handled bell-shaped beakers and dome-top tankards
that Dixwell introduced to his Boston patrons in the years after
his voyage.[1]

The exact origin of the ubiquitous so-called keyhole porringer handle, popular throughout the colonies in the eighteenth
century, is unclear. Nevertheless, Dixwell was possibly the first
silversmith to abandon the geometric handle style in favor of

this new decorative embellishment. He made several keyhole-handled porringers prior to his death in 1725.[2]

Description: The raised vessel has a central dome with convex sides and a vertical rim. Its center point is visible on the dome, both inside and underneath the bowl. A pierced keyhole-style handle is soldered at right angles to rim. The handle has been bent downward at the tip.

History: Family history places original ownership in the Greenleaf family, but that cannot be proven. The later script monogram is probably that of Elizabeth Turner Amory (1820–1898),[3] m. Ivers James Austin (1808–1889) in 1846.[4] To their daughter Catherine Austin (b. 1850), died unm.; to her niece Elizabeth Shaw Greene (1886–1945) and Harvard historian Samuel Eliot Morison (1887–1976), m. 1910; to the donor, their daughter Catherine Victoria Morison (b. 1925), wife of Julian Cooper.[5]

Exhibitions and publications: Kane 1998, 380.

NOTES TO THIS ENTRY ARE ON PAGE 156.

44

John Doane (1719–1767)

Cann

Boston, Massachusetts, about 1750
Gift of the Wunsch Foundation in Recognition of Kathryn C. Buhler
1982.799

H. $5\frac{5}{16}$ in. (13.5 cm); W. $5\frac{1}{2}$ in. (14 cm); Diam rim. $3\frac{3}{16}$ in. (8.1 cm); Diam. foot $3\frac{5}{16}$ in. (8.5 cm); Wt. 14 oz 5 gr (435.8 gm)

Marks: "I [pellet] DOANE" in roman letters within a rectangle struck to left of handle.

Inscriptions: Later engraving in two areas opposite handle: "MW / 1858" entwined monogram below lip; below, a larger circular device surrounded by crossed palms is similarly engraved "WW to TLJ" within reserve.

ALONG WITH A TANKARD and a porringer bearing the same maker's mark, this cann was once attributed to John Doane's older brother Joshua Doane (1717–1753), of Providence, Rhode Island.[1] Both men probably apprenticed with John Burt, and in the 1740s the younger Doane may have worked with William

44

DOANE

45

Simpkins. Despite John Doane's respectable career in public service as a constable and treasurer in Boston, his grandfather left him only twenty shillings in 1755 as punishment for his "ill, wild Carriage." Doane may have left Boston shortly thereafter for Barbados, where he died in 1767.

Doane's pride in workmanship is evident in this cann, which has cleanly cast elements and ample proportions The tiny air vents on the handle are carefully made and delicately placed, unlike the coarse gashes found on the work of most silver-smiths of the period, including that of his master. This cann is one of only three objects that have been identified by Doane's rectangular mark.

Description: The raised tulip-shaped vessel is soldered to a splayed, molded, cast foot with an applied foot ring. A stepped molded band is applied to the lip. The cast double-scrolled handle has a foliate thumbgrip, flattened buds, and a tendril at its terminus. A small circular air vent is found underneath the bud and the tendril. An extended socket is used for upper joining, and an elliptical disk is employed at lower join of handle to body.

History: Original owners unknown; purchased in the twentieth century by the donor and made a gift in 1992.

Exhibitions and publications: Kane 1998, 383.

NOTES TO THIS ENTRY ARE ON PAGE 156.

Jeremiah Dummer (1645–1718)

Spoon

Boston, Massachusetts, 1665–84
Gift of Mrs. Alexander Van R. Halsey, in memory of her
Father, Marshall P. Blankarn
1990.484

L. 7⅛ in. (18.1 cm); W. bowl 2 in. (5 cm); Wt. 1 oz 13 dwt 7 gr (51.8 gm)

Marks: "I [pellet] D/ [fleur de lis]," within a heart-shaped device, struck on bowl. Similar, less distinct mark appears on back of handle.

Inscriptions: Roman letter "W" engraved on back of handle, above bowl; "A/AA" engraved on back of bowl.

RELATED TO THE more common slip-top and apostle spoons, this so-called stump-end spoon was a rare form in England and the colonies. George Evelyn Paget How notes that early London examples date from 1635 and 1660 and have stems that are roughly octagonal.[1] With its somewhat bulbous tip and rounded stem, the spoon may have been among the earliest that Dummer attempted. He produced one Puritan and one slip-top spoon about 1675, but mostly trifid-end and wavy-end spoons from about 1680 to 1710.[2]

Description: The spoon has a worn, somewhat rounded, fig-shaped bowl with raised V-shaped drop and a rounded handle, culminating in a wide rounded tip.

History: Although no family history accompanies this spoon, earlier scholars have suggested descent in the Nicholas and Adams families of Boston, based upon the engraved initials.[3] However, further research demonstrates at least one other genealogical scenario for ownership in the Waight and Anderson families. These alternate interpretations point out the hazards of establishing a history of ownership without a secure provenance. The spoon was purchased in the twentieth century by collector Marshall Blankarn; by descent to his daughter, the donor.

Exhibitions and publications: Fairbanks and Trent, 1982 2:292, cat. no. 289; Kane 1998, 393.

NOTES TO THIS ENTRY ARE ON PAGE 156.

46

Jeremiah Dummer (1645–1718)

Porringer

Boston, Massachusetts, 1690–1700
Gift of a Friend of the Department of American Decorative Arts and Sculpture
1985.410

H. 1⁵⁄₁₆ in. (3.3 cm); W. 6⅛ in. (15.6 cm); Diam. rim 4³⁄₁₆ in. (10.6 cm); Wt. 3 oz 15 dwt 18 gr (117.8 gm)

Marks: "I [pellet] D" within a heart-shaped device, over a fleur-de-lis, struck under handle.

Inscriptions: Small, incuse fleur-de-lis engraved above inscription, on top of handle. "M * S" in shaded roman letters engraved on handle, facing bowl.

PORRINGERS WERE widely used in the colonial period, judging from the numbers that have survived. After spoons, they were probably the most commonly listed piece of silver in colonial inventories, attesting to their usefulness in the household. Hot liquids no doubt made the decorative piercings both handsome and functional, for they cooled the handle for users such as Judge Samuel Sewall (1652–1730), who wrote on September 11, 1704, that he was "threaten'd with my sore throat: but I went to Bed early . . . pin'd m y Stocking about my Neck, [and] drunk a porringer of Sage Tea upon which I sweat very kindly."[1]

Jeremiah Dummer produced a variety of porringer handles, ranging from simple trefoils to complicated geometric compositions. This early porringer is one of a small group notable for their geometric handles bearing nine pierced forms, a style seen in few others by Dummer from this early period. One

46

remarkable example bears the mark of René Grignon (about 1652–1714/15) along with an erased Dummer mark (now in the Yale collection). It prompts the theory advanced by Kathryn C. Buhler and Graham Hood that Grignon, a French Huguenot who worked briefly in Boston and later settled in Norwich, Connecticut, may have "repaired or resold an original Dummer porringer."[2] Since the Grignon porringer handle has a smooth and fully articulated surface, the cast may have been enhanced by him or taken from a Dummer example other than this one, which is flat and somewhat worn.

Dummer's mark on the Grignon porringer demonstrates the practicality of colonial silversmiths, who readily used the decorative silver elements that passed through their workshops. The presence of an incuse fleur-de-lis on the handle is unexplained.

Description: The small raised porringer, with a center point visible inside its domed bowl, has convex sides and an everted rim. The cast pear-shaped handle has nine pierced geometric shapes, at least two of which resemble tulips. It is soldered at right angles to the rim. A repair to a vertical break on the wall is visible to the right of the handle.

History: Early history unknown. Probably owned by Francis Hill Bigelow and sold at American Art Association/Anderson Galleries, Inc., in 1936; owned in 1939 by William T. H. Howe (Yale College, Class of 1893); later purchased by Mark Bortman; to Bortman-Larus Americana Foundation; purchased by the Museum.

Exhibitions and publications: "The Francis Hill Bigelow Collection of Early American Furniture, together with rare early American and English Silver, Property of Several owners including Mrs. Martha D. Johnston, Yorktown Heights, N.Y. and a Boston Private Collector sold by his order," American Art Association/Anderson Galleries, Inc., New York, sale 4232, February 8, 1936, lot no. 48; Phillips 1939, 40, cat. no. 75; Buhler 1956, 58, cat. no. 55; Kane 1998, 392.

NOTES TO THIS ENTRY ARE ON PAGE 156.

47

John Edwards (about 1671–1746)
Serving spoon

Boston, Massachusetts, about 1710–30
Gift of a Friend of the Department of American Decorative Arts and Sculpture
1985.411

L. 18⅛ in. (46 cm); W. bowl 3³⁄₁₆ in. (8.1 cm); Wt. 7 oz 17 dwt 16 gr (245.2 gm)

Marks: "I E" crowned over a fleur-de-lis, within a shield-shaped cartouche, struck on back of bowl, at center.

Inscriptions: "W / I A" in shaded roman letters engraved on back of bowl, above mark.

FEW EXAMPLES SURVIVE of early-eighteenth-century monumental serving spoons. Although it is difficult to identify the various forms and purposes of these utensils, such as this example by John Edwards, Kathryn C. Buhler suggests they may have been called goose spoons, for the purpose of serving stuffing; basting or ragout spoons; and hash spoons. Since all these tasks involved working with hot foods, the spoon's unusually long, hollow handle would have offered the server some protection from heat. Their usefulness at the dinner table can also be inferred by one known English example that conceals a marrow scoop within its removable handle.[1]

Serving spoons with hollow octagonal handles and crown-like faceted finials were also made by Jacob Hurd (MMA) and William Homes Sr. (1716/17–1785).[2] Both are closely related to the Edwards spoon, although each lacks the distinctive hook between the bowl and handle. Slightly smaller examples with hollow circular, or "cannon," handles were made by Peter Van Dyck (1684–1750/51) and Edward Winslow; a later example by Benjamin Burt in the Museum's collection is an updated version of these spoons and features a more attenuated handle and a shell motif on the back of the bowl.[3]

These large spoons, with their deep oblong bowls, also may have served as early punch ladles. Charles Jackson illustrated a closely related Irish example made in 1702 and speculated that,

in addition to serving hash or "Irish stew," the spoons were probably used to ladle large quantities of punch into a jug used at the table for filling drinking glasses.[4] The introduction in the 1740s of smaller ladles with deeper bowls set at right angles to the handle, more suitable for pouring, coincided with a trend to drink more potent punch in lesser quantities.[5]

Buhler also theorized that the prominent hook at the junction of the handle and bowl was used to rest the spoon on the edge of a punch bowl; however, the implement's length seems to prevent such a use. The hook allows for the spoon to be hung vertically, with its bowl pointing upward. Perhaps it provided a way to store this oversized and somewhat awkward implement in a cabinet or kitchen setting. A serving spoon by Benjamin Burt, made about 1750, included a ring at the end of the handle for this purpose.[6]

Description: This large serving spoon, with deep elliptical bowl, has a long handle made of two sections seamed lengthwise and bound laterally with three soldered midbands. The handle is octagonal, tapering toward a deep elliptical bowl. The handle tip is likewise faceted, having a tall pawn or crown-shaped finial soldered to the handle with midband decoration. Small circular air vents appear on the back, at the base of the handle tip and below the midband. A small midband and C-scroll hook connect the handle with the rat-tail bowl.

History: Early history is unknown. Purchased in the twentieth century by Massachusetts collector Mark Bortman (1896–1967) and placed on loan to the Museum in 1948. By descent to his daughter Jane Bortman Larus and sold to the Museum in 1985.

Exhibitions and publications: English-Speaking Union 1960, 19, cat. no. 27, pl. 12; *MFA Annual Report* 1985–86, 24; Kane 1998, 416.

NOTES TO THIS ENTRY ARE ON PAGES 156–57.

48

John Edwards (about 1671–1746)

Spout cup

Boston, Massachusetts, 1712
Gift of Mrs. Richard W. Hale, Jr., in memory of her husband
1980.628

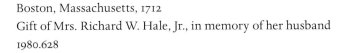

H. 5⁵⁄₁₆ in. (13.5 cm); W. 4½ in. (11.4 cm); Diam rim 4⅛ in. (10.5 cm);
Diam foot 2⅝ in. (6.5 cm); Wt. 8 oz 3 dwt 16 gr (254.5 gm)

Marks: "I E" with a crown above and a fleur-de-lis below, within a
shaped cartouche, struck to left of handle and on base, over center
point.

Inscriptions: "L / C S" in shaded roman letters engraved on base.

JOHN EDWARDS's early spout cups were spherical with cylindrical necks and relate stylistically to an example made during
his partnership with John Allen. One was in the shape of a gal-

lipot, a wide, urnlike form that was used for medicinal purposes and was based on ceramic vessels. Three of Edwards's
seven spout cups, dating from about 1712 to 1728, were made
in a bulbous, pear-shaped form.[1] The Museum's two examples
(see also cat. no. 50) are in this style, and each displays finely
cast handles comprised of S-scrolls, sprigs, and bud terminals
that delicately turn to and fro, with beaded rattail decoration
on the outer curves.

The Museum's two examples and a related third in the Winterthur collection reveal Edwards's ability to fabricate small
vessels incrementally different in size yet proportionately made
to scale.[2] Each would have required that Edwards use handles,
foot rings, and spouts that differed by about ¼ inch (1.5 cm),
which he accomplished without any loss of refinement. The
Museum's cups each bear the same tender heart-shaped space
cut into the vessel that leads to the spout, similar to at least one
example made in London about 1697.[3] Perhaps the little symbol, visible only to the server and user, offers mute testimony
of familial love.

Description: The raised pear-shaped vessel has an applied, molded,
and scored lip and a drawn, molded, splayed foot with an applied
foot ring. Its cast S-scroll handle is composed of several broken C
scrolls, ornamented with sprigs, bud terminals, and a beaded rattail thumbgrip. The seamed teardrop-shaped spout begins above the
foot, rising upward in a tubular shape and turning outward at the
rim. The raised lid is composed of several stepped forms rising from
a flat horizontal rim; the deep flange provides a friction fit between
lid and body. The lid is slightly dented below the flattened sphere
finial, which is secured from within by peening.

History: The engraved initials are for Charles Little (1685–1724) and
Sarah Warren (1692–1756), m. 1712 in Plymouth, Massachusetts. In
1728, Sarah Warren Little m. second, former Harvard tutor and Fellow of the House, Rev. Nicholas Sever (also Seaver) (1680–1764), the
owner of a large body of tutorial plate. The spout cup descended
through the Sever family as follows: to their son William (1729–1809)
and his wife Sarah Warren (1730–1797), m. 1755;[4] to William's son
John (1766–1803) and Nancy Russell (1767–1848), m. 1790; to their son
John (1792–1855) and Anna Dana (1800–1864), m. 1825; to their daughter Ellen (1835–1904) and George Silsbee Hale (1825–1897), m. 1868;
to their son Richard Walden Hale (1871–1943) and Mary Newbold
Patterson, m. 1903;[5] to their son Richard W. Hale Jr. (1909–1976),
who in 1940 m. Elisabeth Fairbanks, the donor.

Exhibitions and publications: Jamestown 1907, 20, cat. no. 298; Richard
Walden Hale, *Catalogue of Silver Owned by Nicholas Sever, A.B. 1701 in
1728, Now Owned by His Descendants and Exhibited at the Fogg Art Museum of Harvard University 1931* (Boston: Tudor Press, 1931), 16; Harvard
Tercentenary Exhibition 1936, 32, cat. no. 116; Kane 1998, 417.

NOTES TO THIS ENTRY ARE ON PAGE 157.

ety illustrated here, with a tapered cylindrical form that grows wider at its base and has a substantial hollow, seamed handle. The most elaborate of this latter group also has a prominent midrib decoration and a unique cherub's-head terminal.[3]

When the mate to this mug entered the Museum's collection in the 1960s, it was unknown that it was one of a pair.[4] Now united, the two were clearly fashioned at the same time. Their weights differ by scarcely a pennyweight, and the engraving of the initials is identical, even to the slight curve in the letter "S," for Sarah (Oliver) Wendell. From their worn and well-used appearance, and the clumsy repairs made to both, the mugs were probably kept in the family for some time before being separated.

Description: The raised straight-sided mug, with center point on bottom, is in the shape of a tapered cylinder with a shallow multiple-stepped base molding and an applied molded rim. The plain, seamed S-scrolled handle has a simple thumbgrip and upturned terminus, with an air vent below. An oval section is soldered between lower handle tip and body, for strength. Extensive poorly executed repairs have been made to the handle at its joints with the rim and body.

History: The cup was made for Jacob Wendell (1691–1761) and Sarah Oliver (1696–1762) of Boston, m. 1714.[5] Subsequent ownership unknown until acquired in the twentieth century by the donor.

Exhibitions and publications: Kane 1998, 415 (mate only).

NOTES TO THIS ENTRY ARE ON PAGE 157.

49

John Edwards (about 1671–1746)

Mug

Boston, Massachusetts, about 1714
Gift of the Wunsch Foundation, Inc.
1982.800

H. 4⅜ in. (11.1 cm); W. 5⅜ in. (13.6 cm); Diam. rim 3⅝ in. (9.1 cm); Diam. foot 3⅛ in. (7.8 cm); Wt. 7 oz 16 dwt 9 gr (243.2 gm)

Marks: "I E" over a device, within a crowned shaped shield, struck to left of handle.

Inscriptions: "W / I S" in roman letters engraved on base, above center point.

SUBTLE STYLISTIC CHANGES can be observed in the dozen or so mugs made by Edwards between 1695 and 1730. A spherical vessel with a tall neck by the silversmith and his partner John Allen is probably the earliest variant of this form, derived from Westphalian-style stoneware jugs.[1] The Museum possesses a related cup, dated 1708, that is in the shape of a short beaker; it has a reel-shaped body and molded strap handle.[2] However, the larger and later group consisted of the plain, sturdy vari-

50

John Edwards (about 1671–1746)

Spout cup (missing lid)

Boston, Massachusetts, about 1720
Gift of Mrs. Charles F. Hovey in memory of Mrs. Chandler Hovey
1983.682

H. 3³⁄₁₆ in. (8.2 cm); W. 3½ in. (9 cm); Diam. rim 1¹⁵⁄₁₆ in. (4.9 cm); Diam. foot 2 in. (5.1 cm); Wt. 4 oz 8 dwt 15 gr (137.8 gm)

Marks: "IE" within a shaped cartouche, with a crown above and a fleur-de-lis below, struck twice to left of handle and on base, over center point.

Inscriptions: "R / I x M" in shaded roman letters engraved on body, opposite handle. "I" in a similar hand engraved on base, to left of mark.

See cat. no. 48.

Description: The pear-shaped raised vessel has a drawn, splayed, and molded foot with an applied foot ring. Its seamed spout has a slender teardrop shape that begins above the foot and snakes upward, beyond the lip. A small heart-shaped opening leads from the vessel wall to the spout. The cast handle is scrolled, with sprigs, bud terminals, and beaded rattail decoration on its exterior. The tip of the spout is worn and slightly torn from use. A lid, now lost, once completed this vessel.

History: Josiah Richmond (1697–1763), a blacksmith from Middleboro, Massachusetts, and his first wife, Mehitable Deane (1697–1744/45), by descent through either the Richmond or Deane families, who intermarried about one hundred years after the fabrication of the vessel.[1] Subsequent history uncertain until the late nineteenth century, when the vessel was inherited by Dorothy Allen (1880–1956), the only child of Francis Richmond Allen (1843–1931) and Elizabeth Bradlee Wood (b. 1848), m. 1875. Dorothy Allen m. Chandler Hovey (1880–1971/72) in 1906.[2] By descent to their son Charles F. Hovey (1909–1992) and subsequently to his wife, Anita C. (Hinckley) Hovey, the donor.[3]

Exhibitions and publications: Jamestown 1907, cat. no. 121; Kane 1998, 417.

NOTES TO THIS ENTRY ARE ON PAGE 157.

51

John Edwards (about 1671–1746)

Flagon

Boston, Massachusetts, 1726
Anonymous Gift
1999.92

H. 13³⁄₁₆ in. (33.5 cm); W. 9³⁄₈ in. (24 in.); Diam rim 4½ in. (11.4 cm); Diam. foot 6⅞ in. (17.4 cm); Wt. 56 oz 3 dwt 16 gr (1747.5 gm)

Marks: "I E" crowned, over a fleur-de-lis, all within a shaped shield, struck on lid of and to left of handle. A third mark may be obscured by a circular disk applied later to base.

Inscriptions: "The Gift of the Honorable William Dummer Esqr. / to the first Church in Boston 1726." within a scrolled reserve, engraved below Dummer crest.

Armorials: The Dummer crest is of a demi-lion on a torse holding a fleur-de-lis in his dexter paw.[1]

MASSACHUSETTS LIEUTENANT GOVERNOR William Dummer, the donor of this magnificent flagon to the First Church of Boston, was the son of silversmith Jeremiah Dummer and his wife, Anne (Atwater), and the grandson of Richard Dummer (about 1598–1678/79), a wealthy Newbury landowner and cattleman. The First Church of Boston was probably William Dummer's family church; a communion cup made by his father was given to the church as a bequest from his maternal grandfather, Joshua Atwater.[2]

Dummer made an excellent political marriage in 1714 to Catherine Dudley (1690–d. before 1756), the daughter of Gov. Joseph Dudley. Dummer became lieutenant governor in 1716, and served as acting governor and commander-in-chief of the colony between 1722 and 1728. He settled one of the French and Indian wars in 1726 that was known as "Dummer's Indian War," or "Râle's War," the same year in which he gave this finely engraved flagon.[3]

Dummer gave generously to churches. The Hollis Street Church in Boston received a flagon in 1753 bearing the Dummer arms; he also gave two wine cups to his ancestral church, the Byfield Parish Church of Newbury, Massachusetts. A gold snuffbox, one of the handsomest of the colonial era, belonged to Dummer; it carries the fully engraved family arms.[4]

The crest on the Edwards flagon was one granted in 1711 by the College of Arms to Dummer's English cousins, based upon ancient seals held by the family. However, the crest was later found to be that of the Pyldren family, who had married into the Dummer family in the sixteenth century. The English

51

branch of the Dummer family discovered the error in 1720 and received a modified coat of arms in 1721. The lieutenant governor nevertheless employed the Pyldren crest for this flagon and the complete arms and crest on his gold snuffbox.[5]

The flagon is one of only two known examples made by Edwards. The other, fashioned more than a dozen years earlier for the Brattle Street Church and also in the Museum's collection, is about eight ounces lighter and slightly shorter, having a compressed stepped lid and contracted body.[6] This example shows a more fluid line from foot to finial, with only a slight alteration in proportions.

Description: The tall, raised, tapering cylindrical form has a drawn molded rim. Its seamed scroll handle has a pointed tonguelike terminal. The five-part hinge has a molded drop and a double-cusped thumbpiece. The stepped flat-topped lid has an inner flange and turned finial. Bands appear below lip and above a tall convex foot with applied foot rim. The donor's crest and inscription are placed directly opposite the handle.

History: Given by William Dummer (1677–1761) to the First Church in 1726. For more information, see appendix 4. The flagon was owned continuously by the First Church, Boston, later organized as the First and Second Churches of Boston, until acquired by the MFA in 1999 as an anonymous gift in honor of Jonathan L. Fairbanks.

Exhibitions and publications: MFA 1911, 47, cat. no. 42; Jones 1913, 31, pl. XIII; *Loan Exhibition of Early American Furniture and the Decorative Crafts for the Benefit of Free Hospital for Women, Brookline, Mass.* (Boston: n.p., 1925), 121, cat. no. 287; Kane 1998, 414.

NOTES TO THIS ENTRY ARE ON PAGE 157.

THE MODEST SCALE and low dome of this John Edwards tankard, as well as its lack of a midband, illustrate that it was made in the period between the broad-bodied flat-topped tankards of the 1710s and 1720s and the taller high-domed works that prevailed after the 1740s.

Description: The raised straight-sided tankard with center point is slightly wider at its base. The vessel displays drawn, high, stepped base molding and an everted lip molding. The domed stepped lid has a wide button finial pinned through and peened on the inside. The downturned edge of the flanged lid is scored on its perimeter. A scrolled thumbpiece above a five-part hinge descends to a cast, molded, baluster drop. The seamed handle is attached at its upper section with a shaped drop and at the lower end with an oval disk. The terminus has an oval convex disk with a roughly shaped air vent below.

History: Ebenezer Stone Sr. (1662/63–1754), the donor, was patriarch of the Stone and Trowbridge families who provided three pieces of ecclesiastical plate for the First Church in Newton between 1730 and 1768. In 1686 Stone m. Margaret Trowbridge (1666–1710). Their son John (1692–1769) gave a tankard marked by Minott and Austin to the First Church in Newton (cat. no. 2, 1973.18). Stone's brother-in-law Deacon William Trowbridge (1684–1744) gave a Jacob Hurd beaker (cat. no. 85, 1973.22).[1]

Exhibitions and publications: Kane 1998, 419; see also appendix 8.

NOTE TO THIS ENTRY IS ON PAGE 157.

52

John Edwards (about 1671–1746)
Tankard

Boston, Massachusetts, 1730
Gift of the First Church in Newton
1973.20

H. 7⅞ in. (20.1 cm); W. 6⅞ in. (17.6 cm); Diam. rim 4 in. (10.2 cm); Diam. foot 5 in. (12.6 cm); Wt. 19 oz 16 dwt 7 gr (616.3 gm)

Marks: "IE" within a shield and crowned over a device, probably a fleur-de-lis, struck twice, on lid between finial and thumbpiece and on body to left of handle, below lip

Inscriptions: "The Gift of Ebenezer Stone Senr. / to the Church of Christ in Newtown / 1730" in italics engraved on body, oppposite handle.

53

Joseph Edwards Jr. (1737–1783)
Cann

Boston, Massachusetts, about 1760–80
Gift of Mrs. Samuel Nickerson in memory of Samuel Mayo Nickerson
1977.769

H. 4¹³⁄₁₆ in. (12.3 cm); W. 5³⁄₁₆ in. (13.3 cm); Diam. rim 3⅛ in. (8 cm); Diam. foot 3⅞ in. (10 cm); Wt. 13 oz 5 dwt 15 gr (413.1 gm)

Marks: "IEdwards" within a rectangle struck on base, above center point.

Inscriptions: "M / T * A" engraved on bottom, below center point. Also on base is the modern inventory number "191," engraved twice, each time within an ellipse; the number "316" is underlined.

AN INCH SMALLER but slightly heavier than a cann Edwards made about 1765 for Joshua and Hannah (Storer) Green, this

53

example shares the same type of cast foot.[1] The edge of this foot is sharply delineated and may indicate an earlier manufacture date. Its crisply detailed handle is just slightly smaller in height and width, a subtle difference that suits the slender girth of this cann made for an unknown patron.

Description: The raised tulip-shaped vessel has a prominent applied, molded rim. A cast, splayed, molded foot with applied foot ring is soldered to the base. A double-scrolled cast handle has an acanthus thumbgrip and tendril at its terminus; a circular air vent appears below the thumbgrip. A separately cast elliptical disk and socket receive the upper handle; a repaired circular disk meets the lower join to the vessel. A triangular repair to the foot, below the handle, may have occurred during fabrication.

History: Early history unknown.

Exhibitions and publications: Kane 1998, 425.

NOTE TO THIS ENTRY IS ON PAGE 157.

54

Samuel Edwards (1705–1762)
Salver

Boston, Massachusetts, 1743
Anonymous Gift
1992.269

H. 1 in. (2.5 cm); Diam. 7⅞ in. (20 cm); Wt. 8 oz 15 dwt 2 gr (272.3 gm)

Marks: "S [pellet] E" over a device and within a shaped shield struck on top and near border.

Inscriptions: "W / W ⋆ R" in shaded roman letters engraved on bottom.

THE TERM *salver*, from the Spanish word *salva* (referring to the tasting of foods prior to serving) and the French and Latin words *salvar* and *salvare* (meaning "to save" or "to render safe by tasting"), had evolved by the eighteenth century in England to describe a serving plate, particularly a footed tray, used to offer food or drink.[1] Such trays were a staple at the table, where they were used to protect expensive, often imported, linens from dirty spoons, hot teapots, saucepans, and the like.

Early colonial salvers were round, with a plain applied rim or a gadrooned edge and a single trumpet foot. From the 1730s through the 1760s, some square salvers with four feet were made, but over time a tripod form prevailed; it featured cabriole legs and increasingly elaborate octagonal or circular forms with cast shell-and-scroll borders.

The flat expanse of the salver offered a challenge to the silversmith, who, before the age of rolled metal, was obliged to hammer the silver from an ingot into a uniformly even, reflecting surface. Larger examples such as this are rarer because of the increasing difficulty in raising a larger sheet. Few salvers have survived in pairs (cat. no. 88), but all were intended to be used in concert with other salvers of various sizes to support food and drink.

Of the three published salvers by Edwards, one was produced in the earlier trumpet-foot style, whereas a second, slightly smaller example bears six cast-shell forms rather than the seven seen here.[2]

The salver was one of many silver items that Boston merchant William White and his wife, Rebecca, owned and gave as gifts. They had a creampot by John Coburn[3] as well as two curious sauce dishes that were more likely reworked from tankard bases marked by Rufus Greene.[4] Kathryn C. Buhler has

NOTES TO THIS ENTRY ARE ON PAGE 157.

History: According to the donor, the initials are those of William White (1717–1773) and Rebecca Stoddard (about 1723–1773) of Boston, Massachusetts, m. 1743.[7] By descent to the anonymous donor.

Exhibitions and publications: Kane 1998, 451.

54

noted that the Whites owned a chafing dish by Paul Revere I, for the initials "W/WR" appear over a partially erased engraving "G/ TI M," initials of their contemporaries Thomas James Grouchy and Mary Dumaresque, who were married in 1741.[5] The Whites also gave silver to their first cousins. To Sarah Phillips (1735–1764), William gave a tankard by Daniel Henchman, probably for her wedding to Nathaniel Taylor (b. 1734) in 1759. The couple gave a salver by Paul Revere II to Sarah's brother William Phillips, probably at the time of his wedding in 1760 to Margaret Wendell (1739–1823). At White's death in 1774, he bequeathed six silver candlesticks and a few pairs of porringers, items he undoubtedly had enjoyed in his Charter Street "mansion house."[6] It may be that White's liking for silver was due to the influence of his maternal grandfather, Samuel Phillips (1657/58–1722), a Salem silversmith.

Description: The small, raised, circular tray displays a cast border of molded cyma curves interspersed with seven abstracted shell motifs. It is supported by three cast, broad, quadriped feet. Subtle wear marks appear directly over each of the feet, evidence of regular use.

55

Samuel Edwards (1705–1762)

Teaspoon

Boston, Massachusetts, about 1750–60
Gift of Mr. and Mrs. Julius McNutt Ramsay, Jr.
1990.367

L. 5¹¹⁄₁₆ in. (14.4 cm); W. bowl 1⅛ in. (2.7 cm); Wt. 15 dwt 13 gr (24.2 gm)
Marks: "SE" within a rounded rectangle struck on back.
Inscriptions: None.

FOR A DISCUSSION of this spoon, along with three others by Zachariah Brigden, see cat. no. 8.

Description: This small spoon with an elliptical bowl has a rounded upturned handle with a long midrib. The delicate twelve-lobed shell engraving on the back of the bowl descends from a long oval drop.

History: See cat. no. 8.

Exhibitions and publications: None.

 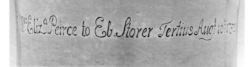

56

Samuel Edwards (1705–1762)

Saucepan

Boston, Massachusetts, about 1752
Gift of Grace and Malcolm Storer
1991.607

H. 2⅜ in. (6 cm); W. 8½ in. (21.5 cm); Diam. rim 3¹¹/₁₆ in. (9.5 cm); Diam. foot 3½ in. (9 cm); Wt. 6 oz 10 dwt 5 gr (202.5 gm)

Marks: "S [pellet] E," with a crown above and a device below, all within a notched shield, struck on bottom, over center point.

Inscriptions: "The Gift of Mrs Eliza Peirce to Eb. Storer Tertius Augt 10th 1752" in italics engraved in a single line around center of vessel.

THREE GENERATIONS of the Storer family of Boston were conspicuous consumers of New England silver. This was due in part to two daughters-in-law who hailed from silversmithing families. Mary Edwards (1700–1772), who married Ebenezer Storer (1699–1761), was the daughter of John Edwards. Mary Coney (1695/99–1781), the daughter of John Coney, married Seth Storer.

The union of Mary Edwards and Ebenezer Storer, a merchant, resulted in the acquisition of some of the most spectacular forms concentrated in one colonial Boston family. These ranged from a chocolate pot, salver, and saucepan to cups, mugs, and spoons, some of which carried the Storer family arms. Many were made by Mary's silversmithing brothers, Samuel and Thomas Edwards, although Zachariah Brigden and John Coburn, both of whom probably apprenticed with the Edwards brothers, also produced several objects.[1]

Their daughter Elizabeth (1726–1786) married merchant Isaac Smith (1719–1786/87) and followed the family tradition of acquiring silver made by members of their extended family.[2] Their son William Smith (1755–1816) and his wife, Hannah Carter (1764–1836), patronized Paul Revere II for tea equipage. John Coburn made a saucepan for Isaac and Elizabeth's son Isaac Smith Jr. (1749–1829) as a gift from his grandmother Mary Edwards Storer (cat. no. 24).[3]

The tradition of baby gifts was strong in the Storer family. Just as Isaac Smith Jr. received the above-mentioned saucepan, so too was his first cousin Ebenezer Storer (b. 1752) feted upon his birth with the saucepan in this entry.[4]

For a discussion of saucepans in the colonial period, see cat. no. 24.

Description: The raised cylindrical vessel has an everted lip and a stepped, slightly splayed foot ring soldered to its base. A round disk is soldered below the lip and opposite the engraving. It supports a seamed circular socket that is soldered at right angles to the vessel. The socket tapers slightly toward the saucepan and has an applied band of molding at its outer edge. A silver pin secures the modern baluster-style turned wooden handle.

History: The 1752 birth of Ebenezer Storer, Tertius, was commemorated with the gift of this saucepan from his maternal great-grandmother. Elizabeth (Gerrish) Wade Pierce (b. 1674) of Dover, New Hampshire, was the daughter of John and Elizabeth (Waldron) Gerrish and the second wife of Portsmouth merchant Joshua Pierce (1670/71–1742/43), m. 1718/19.[5] Ebenezer was the grandson of their daughter Anna Pierce (1702–1770) and Boston merchant Joseph Green (1703–1765), m. 1727, and the son of their daughter Elizabeth Green (1734–1774) and Ebenezer Storer (1729–1807), m. 1751.[6]

Ebenezer Storer died in infancy, and the saucepan descended to his namesake and brother, born in 1754, who m. Eunice Brewster in 1780. By descent to his sister Mary Storer (b. 1758) and Seth Johnson (b. 1767), m. 1796. To their son Charles John Johnson (1797/8–1843) and Mary Noel Neilson (1803–1863); to their niece Mary Storer Martha Annis Neilson (1833–1929) and David Murray (1830–1905) of New Brunswick, New Jersey, m. 1867. By descent to their kinsman, the antiquarian and genealogist Malcolm Storer (1862–1935) and his wife, Grace Ayrault (1868–ca. 1963).[7] By descent to their daughter Muriel Storer (b. 1904), the donor, and Egerton Burpee Sawtell, m. 1931, who made the gift in her parents' name.

Exhibitions and publications: Buhler 1956, 59, cat. no. 65, fig. 59; Kane 1998, 451.

NOTES TO THIS ENTRY ARE ON PAGES 157–58.

57

Samuel Edwards (1705–1762)

Patch box

Boston, Massachusetts, 1759
Gift of Grace and Malcolm Storer
1991.608a-b

H. ³⁄₁₆ in. (.4 cm); W. 1⁵⁄₁₆ in. (3.2 cm); D. ⅞ in. (2.4 cm);Wt. 4 dwt 4 gr (6.5 gm)

Marks: "S [pellet] E" within a rectangle struck inside base.

Inscriptions: "Mary ★ Storer / [tilde] 1759 [tilde]" in script engraved on base.

PATCH BOXES, like snuff boxes and chatelaines, are small personal items meant to be carried and held by their owners. These diminutive fashionable boxes held ornamental patches of various shapes for beautifying the face and were used by women and men despite sumptuary laws decrying such vanities. Early examples were circular until the first quarter of the century, when the elliptical form, as seen in this example, prevailed. Nearly all have delicate engraving atop their friction-fitted lids. Comparable elliptical examples were fashioned by Samuel Vernon, Benjamin Brenton, William Whitemore, and Jacob Hurd, among others.[1]

Small talismanic possessions such as patch boxes often carry much symbolic content. This tiny patch box was likely made by Samuel Edwards for his fifty-nine-year-old sister, Mary Edwards Storer, as a token of his affection rather than for its cosmet-

ic function. That such containers were used at various times and valued in both town and country can be inferred from a close study of this example and another made by John Dixwell for Sarah Pierpont (1709/10–1758) of New Haven, Connecticut. Sarah, daughter of the Rev. James Pierpont (1660–1714), received her patch box sometime before her sixteenth birthday. She became the wife of the Rev. Jonathan Edwards (1703–1758), who inspired the controversial revival called the "Great Awakening" in his Northampton, Massachusetts, congregation.[2] The Edwardses were sharply criticized by their detractors, especially Sarah for her "lavish" ways. Her patch box was found on the grounds of their farm in Stockbridge, Massachusetts, a rural outpost where Jonathan Edwards ministered after his dismissal in 1751 from the Northampton ministry. In both cases, the patch boxes were made for women of some social standing; Sarah was the daughter of a minister and Mary the wife of a Boston merchant. However, age, religion, and geography had little influence on their ownership of such elegant objects, which served primarily as symbols of gentility and taste.[3]

Description: The constructed patch box is composed of two elliptical disks and matching narrow sides that form the lid and base. The soldered sides of the lid and base overlap for friction fitting. The top of the lid is engraved with a figure-eight design having a lozenge at its center; a herringbone pattern adorns the border.

History: Although the significance of the engraved date "1759" is unknown, the box was most likely made by Edwards for his sister Mary (Edwards) Storer (1700–1771), rather than her daughter Mary (b. 1725), whose name would have changed after her marriage to Edward Green in 1757. Mary Edwards m. York, Maine, merchant Ebenezer Storer (1699–1761) in 1723. Descent in the Storer family, possibly through her granddaughter and namesake, Mary Storer (b. 1758), and Seth Johnson, m. 1796.

The box may have accompanied the Samuel Edwards saucepan (cat. no. 56) that was given by Mary Storer Johnson to her niece Martha Wilson and David Murray of New Brunswick, New Jersey; by descent to her kinsman Malcolm Storer (1862–1935) and his wife, Grace Ayrault (1868–about 1963), m. 1899. By descent to their daughter Muriel Storer (b. 1904), the donor, and Egerton Burpee Sawtell, m. 1931, who made the gift in her parents' name.[4]

Exhibitions and publications: Buhler 1956, cat. no. 66; Kane 1998, 449.

NOTES TO THIS ENTRY ARE ON PAGE 158.

The chafing dish joins its mate, which has been in the Museum's collection since 1956. Stylistically, it resembles examples made by John Burt, several by Jacob Hurd, and one by John Potwine.[2]

Description: The raised bowl-shaped dish with everted rim and recessed ember box is supported on three broken-scroll legs attached at rim and base. The vessel's wall is pierced in a stylized and symmetrical foliate pattern, which alternates at each leg with a pattern of five vertical panels. The circular grate with pierced whorl-like, design with star at center is secured by a nut-and-bolt arrangement. The legs have hoof feet and scrolled supports at rim. The original silver socket and wooden handle are missing. The Storer arms are engraved within an asymmetrical cartouche ornamented with raffles, diapers, scrolls, and flowers. One rim repair is located at the juncture with a scrolled support.

History: Ebenezer Storer (1699–1761) and Mary Edwards (1700–1772), m. 1723; to their daughter Elizabeth Storer (1726–1786) and Isaac Smith (1719–1787), m. 1749. By descent to their son William Smith (1755–1816) and Hannah Carter (1764–1836), m. 1787; to their son Capt. Thomas Carter Smith (1796–1880) and Frances Barnard (1804–1885), m. 1831; to their daughter Frances Barnard Smith (1832–1916) and Thomas Davis Townsend (1826–1880), m. 1854; to their son Dr. Charles Wendell Townsend (1859–1934) and Gertrude Flint (about 1870–1917), m. 1891; to their daughter Margaret Townsend (b. 1894) and C. Hale Sutherland (b. about 1884), m. 1920; to their daughter Mary Flint Sutherland, the donor.

Exhibitions and publications: The mate has been published in Buhler 1972, 2:175–76, cat. no. 141; Kane 1998, 462.

NOTES TO THIS ENTRY ARE ON PAGE 158.

58

Thomas Edwards (1701/2–1755)
Chafing dish

Boston, Massachusetts, about 1740
Gift of Mary F. Sutherland
1991.778

H. 3¹¹⁄₁₆ in. (9.4 cm); W. 6⅞ in. (17.6 cm); Diam rim. 6 in. (15.2 cm); Wt. 16 oz 17 dwt 14 gr (525 gm)

Marks: "T [pellet] Edwards" in italics within a rectangle struck on base, below bolt.

Inscriptions: "Storer 1723" in later script engraved on base, above "S / E M" in shaded roman letters.

Armorial: The Storer arms, adopted from those of the Andrews family, emblazoned argent on a chevron gules between three mullets of the last gules, three quatrefoils pierced. The crest, an unidentified animal couped.[1]

ORIGINALLY ONE OF A PAIR, this chafing dish and its mate may be those recorded as "2 Chaffing dishes 35 oz 15 dwt" in the 1787 estate of Isaac Smith, son-in-law of the original owners.

59

Benjamin Goodwin (about 1731–1792)
Cann

Boston, Massachusetts, about 1760
Gift of Mr. and Mrs. Charles D. Gowing, in memory of Anne Locke Gowing
1974.455

H. 4⅞ in. (12.4 cm); W. 5⁵⁄₁₆ in. (13.4 cm); Diam. rim 3³⁄₁₆ in. (8.1 cm); Diam. foot 3¹¹⁄₁₆ in. (9.4 cm); Wt. 11 oz 16 dwt 20 gr (368.3 gm)

Marks: "B:Goodwin," in upper and lower case letters, within a rectangle, struck on base, below center point.

Inscriptions: "G / N * L" in shaded roman letters engraved on thumbgrip.

59

MULTIPLE INTERMARRIAGES AMONG eighteenth-century families were common. However, when two Goodwin brothers and two LeBaron sisters married, a rising Boston family was joined with that of a revered French Huguenot family from Plymouth. Silversmith Benjamin Goodwin fashioned this cann for his older brother Nathaniel, who married Lydia LeBaron of Plymouth in 1745. Twelve years later, Benjamin married Lydia's younger sister Hannah (1734–1775).

This cann was made sometime after 1752, by which time Benjamin had completed his apprenticeship with Jacob Hurd. Its standard tulip shape is much like those made by Hurd, whose shop produced more than fifty examples between 1735 and 1750. It is one of three objects that the craftsman made for his brother and sister-in-law, which include a tankard bearing the Goodwin arms and a porringer dating from the same period. Despite his long career as a Boston silversmith who probably trained his own son Joseph (1761–1821+) in the craft, Goodwin flourished as a merchant and distiller. Five objects are attributed to him.[1]

Description: The raised tulip-shaped vessel is soldered to a cast splayed foot with an applied foot ring. The scrolled cast handle has a

thumbgrip and double drop at upper joining to body; the lower section has a simplified bud-and-tendril terminus, a distinctively broad gap for the air vent, and an elliptical disk where it joins the body. Pitting is visible along the seam of the handle.

History: Fashioned by the silversmith for his brother Nathaniel Goodwin (1724–1766) and Lydia LeBaron (also spelled LeBarron) (1724–1801), m. 1745/46. She was the daughter of physician Lazarus LeBaron (1698–1773) of Plymouth, Massachusetts, and his first wife, Lydia Bartlett LeBaron (1697/98–1742).[2] The cann descended to their son Nathaniel (1748–1819), a trader, and his wife, Mary Jackson (d. 1779), m. 1769; by descent to their daughter Lydia Goodwin (1779–1846) and Joseph Locke (1772–1853) of Billerica, Massachusetts, m. 1803; to their daughter Harriet Locke (b. 1807) and John Donaldson Locke (b. 1791) of Louisville, Kentucky, m. 1838. To their son Joseph Henry Locke (b. 1841) and Fannie Buckminster Churchill; by descent to their son Hersey Goodwin Locke (1863–1922)[3] and Julia Delaplaine Williams Emory (d. after 1922); to their daughter Anne Locke (1903–1971) of New York City and her husband, Charles Darrow Gowing (1905–1990), of Brookline, Massachusetts, m. 1932.[4]

Exhibitions and publications: MFA 1911, cat. no. 521; Kane 1998, 493.

NOTES TO THIS ENTRY ARE ON PAGE 158.

60

Thomas Grant (1731–1804)

Tankard

Marblehead, Massachusetts, 1773
Gift of a Friend of the Department and Edward J. and Mary S. Holmes Fund
1984.215

H. 8⅝ in. (21.9 cm); W. 7³⁄₁₆ in. (18.4 cm); Diam. rim 3⅞ in. (9.9 cm); Diam foot 5³⁄₁₆ in. (13.2 cm); Wt. 26 oz 17 dwt 10 gr (835.8 gm)

Marks: "T [pellet] GRANT" within a rectangle struck to left of handle and on bottom of tankard, above center punch.

Inscriptions: "Belonging to yt. Church of Christ in M'Head / wherof ye. Revd. Mr. Storey is Pastor / 1773" in italics engraved on side of tankard, opposite handle.[1]

THE DETAILS OF Thomas Grant's silversmithing career are somewhat hazy. Silversmith John Touzell (about 1727–1785), of Salem, Massachusetts, may have been his master or employer. From Touzell, Grant apparently purchased chisels and a "Tea Spoone punch of your Large Size." Although Grant's estate included a "Small Goldsmiths Shop," the silversmith owned a

60

thumbpiece descends to five-part hinge. A short baluster drop below hinge is applied to seamed C-scroll handle. A long rounded drop is below the upper join of handle; elliptical disk and terminal appear at lower join; crescent-shaped air vent below. The lid does not seat properly on the rim.

History: The church recorded "that there be a quart silver tankard purchased for the Communion table out of the Church Stock" on January 4, 1773.

For further information, see appendix 6 for silver commissioned by the Second Congregational Church (now the Unitarian Universalist Church of Marblehead), Marblehead, Massachusetts.

Exhibitions and publications: Jones 1913, 265–66; Kane 1998, 498.

NOTES TO THIS ENTRY ARE ON PAGE 158.

61

Halstead and Myers (active 1756–1766) Benjamin Halstead (1734–1817) and Myer Myers (1723–1795)

Creampot

New York, New York, 1756–66
Gift of Patricia Kramer Welte
1990.216

H. 4¹¹⁄₁₆ in. (12 cm); W. 4⁵⁄₁₆ in. (11 cm); D. 2⅝ in. (6.3 cm); Wt. 4 oz 5 dwt 8 gr (132.7 gm)

Marks: "H&M" within a rectangle and "N-York" in a shaped cartouche struck on bottom.

Inscriptions: "R / W S" and "M TE" (conjoined) in roman letters engraved on bottom.

SILVERSMITH MYER MYERS was well established in New York by the 1750s, but he lacked the kinship network that had enabled the Le Roux and Van Dyck silversmithing families to prosper. Without other family members or fellow Jewish silversmiths to call upon, Myers formed a partnership about 1756 with Benjamin Halstead. It was only the second time such an arrangement had occurred among silversmiths, the first being the joint venture of John Hull and Robert Sanderson Sr. in 1652. The partners commemorated their new relationship with two innovations. They devised a single touchmark bearing their surname initials "H&M," the first time such a mark had been employed anywhere in the British colonies, and they used a city mark as well. Both were frequently emulated by American silversmiths during the nineteenth century.[1]

schooner that saw action in the Revolutionary War and may have been a source of income in peacetime. Grant produced several spoons and a few examples of hollowware, including casters and a pair of beakers also made for the Marblehead church. This is his only known tankard.[2]

Description: The raised cylindrical vessel has a drawn molded foot, tapering sides, and a midband. A stepped domed lid with flame finial extends around edge of an applied rim; flange within; scrolled

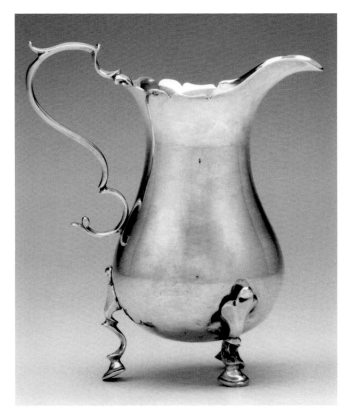

61

Despite their nearly eight-year partnership, surprisingly few objects bearing the joint "H&M" mark have survived. David L. Barquist has observed that the two men continued to fashion silver with their personal marks during the same period, with the majority by Myers. It may be that Halstead provided more capital than silversmithing skills, for he was styled "squire" in area records, usually an indicator of independent wealth. Barquist speculates that the objects bearing their joint mark could represent those in which both men had a financial interest. Halstead, who did not register as a Freeman in New York, may not have completed or even served an apprenticeship; he worked as a retail jeweler after the partnership ended.[2]

The Halstead and Myers creampot or milk pot is a modest form and stylistically indistinguishable from New England vessels of the same type. Such works could have been fashioned in quantity for sale in their shop. Similar creampots marked individually by Myers and Halstead were made during their partnership.[3]

Description: The raised vessel with pear-shaped body is ornamented with a cast broken-scroll handle and scalloped rim; the whole is supported by three cabriole legs with hoof-shaped feet.

History: Original owners unknown; Allen A. Rabineau (1808–1893) and Mary Frances Zabriskie (1810–1863), m. about 1829; to their great-granddaughter Elizabeth (Penny) Hart; to her niece Patricia (Kramer) Welte, the donor.[4]

Exhibitions and publications: David L. Barquist et al., *Myer Myers: Jewish Silversmith in Colonial New York* (New Haven: Yale University Art Gallery, 2001), cat. no. 12.

NOTES TO THIS ENTRY ARE ON PAGE 158.

62

George Hanners Sr. (about 1696–1740)
Tankard (missing lid)

Boston, Massachusetts, 1717–30
Gift of Mrs. Elliot P. Cogswell
1991.661

H. 5½ in. (14 cm); W. 7⅞ in. (20 cm); Diam. rim: 4⁵⁄₁₆ in. (11 cm); Diam. foot 5 in. (12.6 cm); Wt. 18 oz 6 dwt 19 gr (570.4 gm)

Marks: "GH" in roman capitals within a rectangle struck twice to left of the handle. "GH" in roman capitals, within a crowned shield and a device below, struck twice on bottom.

Inscriptions: "P / S ∗ H / 1709 / 1719" engraved on base below mark; "17 £ = 14 s / 26 oz - 8 wt." engraved on base, above marks.

GEORGE HANNERS SR. may have trained under Boston silversmith Andrew Tyler (1692/93–1741), for he witnessed the will of Tyler's mother in 1716/17. He had artisanal dealings with silversmiths Thomas Mullins (1680–1744) and Benjamin Hiller (1687/88–about 1745) and in 1739 successfully sued Thomas Townsend (1703/4–1757) for nonpayment for a ring, tankard, gold, several pounds of allum, and two nests of crucibles. The suit demonstrates Hanners's ability to produce hollowware and jewelry for others to retail and to provide supplies to fellow craftsmen.[1]

During his short career, spent "at his House at the Dock-Head, Boston," Hanners produced much hollowware but comparatively little flatware. He fashioned mourning rings, as noted in at least two estate records, for which he may have used the "Deaths head Stamp" listed in the detailed inventory of his tools. Hanners made ecclesiastical silver for Second

62

Church, Boston; First Church, Woburn; and other congregational churches farther afield in Greenland, New Hampshire, and Branford, Connecticut.

Stylistically, this tankard may be the earliest of its type by the smith.[2] The ribbed handle, with its delicate butterlike scroll, was already outdated when Hanners made it after completing his apprenticeship about 1716. Perhaps he had a model to draw upon, since Andrew Tyler, who has been theorized as Hanners's master, was not known to fashion such intricate handles.

This silver tankard and its related porringer (cat. no. 63) were made for the Rev. Samuel Phillips and his wife, Hannah (White), of Andover, a few years after their marriage in 1711. The two pieces were nearly contemporaneous, as is suggested by the distinctive notations found on each base, possibly in Hanners's own hand. The scratch weight engraved on the tankard's base, typically a guide to an object's original weight, is twelve ounces more than its current weight, proving that the lid was later removed. Despite this lack, the presence of two rare "GH" touches within rectangles, together with a pair of Hanners's better-known shield marks, make this work an extremely rare and significant document of the silversmith's skill.

Description: This short-bodied cylindrical tankard has straight sides that taper inward toward the rim. No center point is visible, but clearly the vessel was raised. Finely stepped applied molding on the base is repeated in a smaller, more delicate version at the lip. The lid and hinge plate were removed at an unknown date. The hollow seamed scroll handle has three ridges running vertically between a punched meander decoration near the hinge and a curled device below; a cast cherub perches on an upward-bent terminus. A cleanly cut crescent-shaped air vent is located beneath the terminal. The handle is soldered to the body at the top join with a long slender rat-tail. Below the terminus is a small rectangular repair, which partly remedied the metal fatigue on the inner walls.

History: According to the donor, the initials are those of the Rev. Samuel Phillips (1689–1771) of Andover, Massachusetts, m. Hannah White (1691–1775) of Haverhill in 1711/12.[3] By descent to their daughter Lydia Phillips (1717–1749) and Dr. Parker Clark (b. 1718),[4] m. 1742; Lydia was the sister of Samuel and John Phillips, founders of Phillips Academy, Andover. To their daughter Hannah Clark (1743–1832) and Dr. Edward Russell (1736–1785)[5] of Andover, m. 1767; to their son Gen. Edward Russell (1782–1835) and Lucy Stevens (1787–1870), m. 1812; to their daughter Margaret Elizabeth Russell (1815–1860) and the Hon. Charles Northend Cogswell (1797–1843), m. 1839. To their son Dr. Edward Russell Cogswell (1841–1914)[6] and Sarah Parks Proctor (d. 1907), m. 1864; to their son Dr. George Proctor Cogswell (1867–about 1953)[7] and Anna Willis Bumstead, of Cambridge, Massachusetts, m. 1895; to their son Elliot Proctor Cogswell (1905–1988) and the donor, Marion Park (1907–1995), of Weston, Massachusetts, m. 1930.[8] The dates 1709 and 1719 engraved on the handle remain unexplained.

Exhibitions and publications: Kane 1998, 531.

NOTES TO THIS ENTRY ARE ON PAGE 158.

63

George Hanners Sr. (about 1696–1740)
Porringer

Boston, Massachusetts, 1720–30
Gift of Mrs. Elliot P. Cogswell
1991.662

H. 1⅞ in. (4.8 cm); W. 8 in. (20.4 cm); Diam. rim 5⅜ in. (13.8 cm); Wt. 7 oz 6 gr (218.1 gm)

Marks: "GH" in roman capitals, in a crowned shield with a device below, struck near center point inside porringer.

Inscriptions: "P / S * H" in shaded roman capitals engraved on handle, initials facing away from bowl; "oun /7" and "pw / 7 –" with star between incised on base.

63

See cat. no. 62.

Description: The porringer has a small center dome and inclined base leading to convex sides and everted rim. The cast keyhole-style handle bears cast and chased decoration. Dents are visible in the sides directly opposite from and to proper right of handle, and a sharp dent appears on the base, below handle.

History: Phillips family of Andover; see cat. no. 62.

Exhibitions and publications: Kane 1998, 530.

64

Daniel Henchman (1730–1775)

Cann

Boston, Massachusetts, about 1755–69
Gift of William B. Osgood in memory of the cann's first owner, Edward Holyoke (1689–1769)
1983.550

H. 4¹¹⁄₁₆ in. (12 cm); W. 5⁵⁄₁₆ in. (13.5 cm); Diam. rim 3½ in. (8.9 cm); Diam. foot 3¹³⁄₁₆ in. (9.7 cm); Wt. 11 oz 17 dwt 7 gr (369 gm)

Marks: "Henchman" within a rectangle struck on bottom, below center point.

Inscriptions: None.

Armorials: The Holyoke arms, blazoned azure a chevon argent coticed or between three crescents. The crest a cubit arm erect habited gules, cuff argent, holding in the hand a branch fructed.[1]

The arms are engraved within an asymmetrical shield, surrounded by an elaborate mantling of broken scrolls and foliate decoration, and located on the vessel opposite the handle.

TRADITION HAS HELD that this cann was owned by the Rev. Edward Holyoke, minister of the Second Church in Marblehead. However, the vessel's late date has made this attribution problematic, given that Holyoke would have been at least sixty-five years old at the time he would have purchased it from Daniel Henchman. It is possible that the Holyoke's son Edward Augustus Holyoke bought the cann or that Holyoke purchased it for his son about the time of the latter's marriage, in 1759.

A graduate of Harvard College in 1705, Reverend Holyoke served as tutor from 1712 to 1716. Soon after, he was voted pas-

64

tor of the Second Church in Marblehead, where he served until his appointment in 1737 as president of Harvard.[2]

Despite the lack of surviving tutorial silver that should have marked his tenure at Harvard, it is known that Holyoke owned several pieces of domestic silver. A Jacob Hurd teapot was said to have been given upon Holyoke's second marriage in 1725 to Margaret Appleton. Shortly after and upon his departure for Harvard, the Marblehead church presented him with a tankard by John Coney, possibly one already owned by the church and engraved with his arms. All three bear the Holyoke arms, as seen on this cann. An early porringer by Coney simply bears the initials "E H" and was most likely purchased by Holyoke shortly before embarking on his pastorate in Marblehead. A third Coney piece, a large and early caudle cup of about 1690 bearing later arms, was probably owned by Holyoke's father, Eliazur, and descended to him.[3]

Nathaniel Hurd may be the engraver of the splendidly arrayed Holyoke arms on this cann, as Henchman had married Hurd's sister Elizabeth in 1753. Their collaboration is firmly documented in a commission for another college president—a silver monteith made in 1771 for the Rev. Eleazer Wheelock, the first president of Dartmouth College. The monteith bears Henchman's mark and Hurd's engraved signature.[4]

Description: The raised tulip-shaped vessel has an applied rim and a splayed molded foot with applied foot ring. The cast broken-scroll handle with foliate thumbgrip and sprigged terminus is soldered directly to the cann at the upper joining and below at an oval disk.

History: Probably purchased by Rev. Edward Holyoke (1689–1769) and Margaret Appleton (1701–1740), m. 1725, for their son Dr. Edward Augustus Holyoke (1728–1829), m. Mary Vial (1737–1802) in 1759;[5] to their daughter Susannah Holyoke (1779–1860) and Joshua Ward (1776–1840), m. 1799; to their daughter Susannah (Susan) Ward (1813–1844) and Salem portrait painter Charles Osgood (1809–1890), m. 1838;[6] to their son the Hon. Charles Stuart Osgood (1839–1897) and Elizabeth White Batchelder (b. 1846), m. 1867; to their son, a namesake of the original owner, Edward Holyoke Osgood (1882–1952), and Mary Nickerson (1888–1975), m. 1915; by descent to their son William Osgood, the donor.

Exhibitions and publications: Harvard Tercentenary Exhibition 1936, cat. no. 150; Kane 1998, 540.

NOTES TO THIS ENTRY ARE ON PAGE 158.

65

Daniel Henchman (1730–1775)

Porringer

Boston, Massachusetts, about 1755–75
Bequest of Sydney DeYoung
1988.281

H. 2 in. (5 cm); W. 8³⁄₁₆ in. (20.9 cm); Diam. rim 5⅛ in. (13.3 cm); Wt. 9 oz 7 dwt 7 gr (291.3 gm)

Marks: "Henchman" in upper and lower case letters, within a rectangle, struck under handle.

Inscription: "I * P / to / H * P" in shaded roman letters engraved on handle, facing bowl.

THIS CONVENTIONAL PORRINGER is one of only two published examples by Henchman.[1]

Description: The raised porringer has convex sides, an everted rim, and a stepped and high-domed base. One center point appears inside bowl; two appear outside. The cast keyhole-style handle is soldered at right angles to the rim. Five closely grouped dents and a second group of two dents appear on the side.

History: Traditional history of ownership in the family of John Quincy Adams, by descent to a member of the Beckwith family, who sold it to the donor.

Exhibitions and publications: Kane 1998, 541.

NOTES TO THIS ENTRY ARE ON PAGE 158.

66

Daniel Henchman (1730–1775)

Coffeepot

Boston, Massachusetts, about 1760–75
Marion E. Davis Fund and gift in memory of Emma Jane
Henchman Kimball and Harriet Kimball Williams by Phebe
W. Summers
1981.171

H. 11½ in. (29.2 cm); W. 9³⁄₁₆ in. (23.3 cm); Diam. rim 3½ in. (9 cm);
Diam. foot 4⅜ in. (11.2 cm); Wt. 33 oz 6 dwt 12 gr (1036.5 gm)

Marks: "Henchman" within a rectangle struck on base, above
center point.

Inscriptions: "CCW" in Federal-style, entwined sprigged script
engraved later on body, to left of handle; to right of handle in same
late script appears "CCW / to JWP."

THE TAPERING, CYLINDRICAL FORMS that characterized mid-eighteenth-century coffeepots can be seen in an example made by Daniel Henchman between 1755 and 1765 for a member of the Winthrop family.[1] Shortly after, however, a newer rococo form came into vogue in Boston; it featured a swelled body and tall stepped foot. Henchman's version of this coffeepot bears lively cast decoration on the spout and finely delineated details on the handle sockets, with matched stepped conical forms on the lid and foot. Henchman produced a slightly smaller example, with similar cast elements and a lower foot ring, for the Codman family.[2] The initials on the body of the coffeepot have not been identified.

Description: The raised gourd-shaped body is set on a molded and stepped foot. The cast S-scrolled spout has a baluster drop at base; a leaf-and-scroll ornament adorns the spout, and leafy decoration appears on its retracted upper lip. The stepped high dome is surmounted by a cast pinecone finial. A four-part hinge attaches the cover to scroll and leaf socket. The lower socket has scrolled elements and is adhered to body with a circular boss. The wooden double-scrolled handle is a replacement, and a repair has been made to the body, at the center point.

History: Purchased at a Sotheby Parke-Bernet sale in 1978 by S. J. Shrubsole Corporation of New York. Subsequently purchased in 1979 by Mrs. Richard E. Summers (Phebe Gould Williams) of Frederick, Maryland, and made a partial sale/partial gift to the Museum in 1981.[3]

Exhibitions and publications: Sotheby Parke-Bernet, New York, sale 4180, November 16–18, 1978, lot no. 410; advertisement, S. J. Shrubsole Corp., New York, N.Y., *Antiques* 115, no. 2 (February 1979), 220; *MFA Annual Report,* 1980–81, 15; Kane 1998, 541.

NOTES TO THIS ENTRY ARE ON PAGE 158.

67

Daniel Henchman (1730–1775)
Pair of sauceboats

Boston, Massachusetts, about 1770
Gift of Mrs. John Sylvester in memory of her grandfather, Desmond FitzGerald, and her mother Harriot F. Clark
1979.408–9

1979.408: H. 4⅛ in. (10.3 cm); W. 7⅜ in. (18.9 cm); D. 4⅜ in. (11.2 cm); Wt. 12 oz 15 dwt 22 gr (398 gm)

1979.409: H. 4⅛ in. (10.3 cm); W. 7⅜ in. (18.9 cm); D. 4⅜ in. (11.1 cm); Wt. 12 oz 19 dwt 11 gr (403.5 gm)

Marks: "Henchman" within a rectangle struck on each bottom, near center point.

Inscriptions: "W" in later script engraved above mark on base.

Armorials: Each engraved on side, to left of handle, with Barrett arms, blazoned ermine, on a fess three lions rampant; crest a lion couchant proper on a torse.[1]

THE DOUBLE-PAD FEET and knees on these sauceboats are identical to those on an unengraved version by the silversmith that was formerly in the Cornelius C. Moore Collection at Providence College. The rococo handles—each with acanthus-

67

leaf thumbgrip, broken scrolls, and sprigged terminus—are similar to one used by Henchman's master, Jacob Hurd, about 1750. Henchman has updated the body by emphasizing a scalloped rim and shortened spout. The unusually heavy weight of the sauceboats is comparable to a pair made by Hurd for the Pickering family of Salem.[2]

As with the Samuel Burt teapot (cat. no. 22), the Barrett arms were probably adapted from Blyth, as recorded in the *Promptuarium Armorum* of 1610.[3]

Description: Each raised elliptical vessel has double-pad feet and knees, a scalloped rim, and a broad curving spout. Each cast broken-scroll handle with foliate thumbgrip is soldered to rim at upper section and affixed to oval disk at lower terminal.

History: The donor's family history and the Barrett family arms indicate that Samuel Barrett (1738–1798) and his second wife, Elizabeth Salisbury (1744–1796) of Boston, m. 1771, were likely the first owners.[4] Probable descent suggests that the silver passed to Elizabeth's brother Samuel Salisbury (1739–1818) and his first wife, Elizabeth Sewall (1740–1789), m. 1768; by descent to their son Samuel Salisbury (1769–1849) and Nancy Gardner (1786–1865), m. 1806; to their son Dr. Stephen Salisbury (1812–1875) and Elizabeth Parker Clark (b. 1824), m. 1844;[5] to their daughter Elizabeth Parker Clark Salisbury (b. 1849) and Desmond FitzGerald (1846–1926), Museum trustee and civil engineer, m. 1870; to their daughter Harriot FitzGerald (b. 1872) and Robert Jones Clark, m. 1897.[6] The sauceboats were inherited by their daughter Geraldine Clark (b. 1902), the donor, and her second husband, Vice Admiral John Sylvester (1904–1990).[7] The initial "W" engraved at a later date remains unexplained.

Exhibitions and publications: Buhler 1956, 61, cat. no. 76; *MFA Annual Report* 1979–80, 15; Kane 1998, 542.

NOTES TO THIS ENTRY ARE ON PAGES 158–59.

68

Benjamin Hiller (1687/88–about 1745)

Caster

Boston, Massachusetts, 1720–30
Marion E. Davis Fund
1982.503

H. 6⁵⁄₁₆ in. (16 cm); Diam. foot 2 in. (5 cm); Wt. 6 oz 7 gr (187.1 gm)

Marks: "BH" over addorsed crescents, all within a shield, struck on base.

Inscriptions: "E : J" in roman letters, within scribed lines, engraved on base, below touchmark.

68

Armorials: The Dudley family crest, a lion's head erased on a torse, is engraved within an ellipse and surrounded by broad scrolled and foliate decoration.[1]

HOLLOWWARE WITH PANELLED or faceted sides found special favor in the early eighteenth century among silversmiths who made casters and pepper pots. Complex in shape and execution, octagonal and hexagonal forms were also well suited to the hand, which may account for the preponderance of smaller objects made in this style.[2]

John Coney produced a pair of hexagonal pear-shaped casters about 1710–20 for the Charnock family of Boston.[3] Kathryn C. Buhler believed that Hiller's version of this form was informed by his apprenticeship or journeyman experience with Coney, as documented in a 1709 deed that Hiller witnessed for Coney. By this date, Hiller would have completed his apprenticeship or recently begun work as a journeyman. Coney also fashioned an octagonal pepper box, or spice dredger, during the same period.

A slightly smaller version of this caster by Hiller, bearing the same arms and initials, is in the Yale collection. The discovery of the Museum's larger example indicates that the two were probably from an original set of three, few of which survive en suite.[4]

Description: The slender pear-shaped vessel is raised and has octagonal facets; the body is soldered to a simple concave foot with applied foot ring. An applied collar at rim receives a pair of cast, scrolled, bayonet-style mounts affixed below molding of a similarly faceted, tall, domed lid. A pierced and engraved four-petaled pattern decorates the lid, at the top of which is applied a circular disk and spherical finial.

History: The Dudley arms suggest that the caster was perhaps made for Col. William Dudley (1686–1743) and Elizabeth Davenport (1704–1750), m. 1721. By descent to their daughter Catherine (1729–1769), who m. the Loyalist Boston merchant Peter Johonnot (1729–1809) in 1751; they had no issue. The initials "E : J" may signify one of Peter's two unmarried sisters, Elizabeth (b. 1731) or Esther (b. about 1743–1748) Johonnot.[5] Subsequent history unknown until the twentieth century, when the caster was purchased in Canada by Ivor Cornman of Woods Hole, Massachusetts, and sold to the Museum.

Exhibitions and publications: Kathryn C. Buhler, "Two Angular New Englanders," *Antiques* 51, no. 3 (March 1947), 195; Kane 1998, 551.

NOTES TO THIS ENTRY ARE ON PAGE 159.

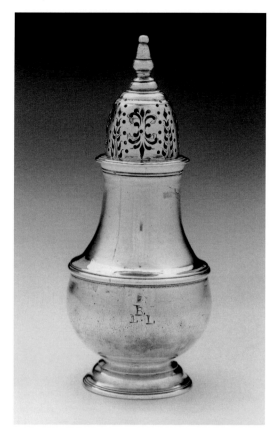

69

69

William Homes Sr. (1716/17–1785)

Caster

Boston, Massachusetts, 1743
Gift of Mrs. Robert E. Montgomery
1973.626

H. 5 in. (12.7 cm); W. 2³⁄₁₆ in. (5.6 cm); Diam. base 1⅜ in. (3.3 cm); Wt. 3 oz 15 dwt 13 gr (117.5 gm)

Marks: "HO . . ." within a rectangle struck indistinctly below rim and opposite seam.

Inscriptions: "LB [conjoined] / L [pellet] L" engraved below midband.

THIS CASTER is one of four currently known by Homes.[1] The pierced foliate decoration on the lid is unusual for a Boston-made caster, which ordinarily had more geometric piercings by this date.

Description: The raised pear-shaped caster with a center punch has a raised bowl-shaped lower section, to which a cast and molded circular foot has been soldered. An applied midband conceals the joint with the upper body, which has a seamed concave form that tapers inward to form a cylinder; applied molding is soldered at its rim. The tall domed lid with acorn finial has a flared rim and pierced and engraved foliate decoration. It has a friction-fitted lid with a worn flange.

History: According to the donor, the caster was originally owned by Gov. William Bradford (1589–1657), but the engraved initials suggest that a more likely owner was Bradford's great-granddaughter Lydia Bradford (1719–1756). In 1743 she became the second wife of Dr. Lazarus LeBaron (1698–1773) of Plymouth, Massachusetts, the son of Francis LeBaron, first doctor of the Plymouth Colony.[2] The caster passed to their daughter Elizabeth (1745–1829) and Ammi

Ruhami Robbins (1740–1813), m. 1762. Due to family history claiming descent through the eldest daughter, the caster probably passed to their daughter Elizabeth Robbins (1770–1815) and Grove Lawrence (b. 1766), m. 1789;[3] to their daughter Eliza Lawrence (1793–1850) and Timothy J. Gridley (b. 1788); to their daughter Sarah Battell Gridley (b. 1825) and Charles E. Delano (1820–1883), m. 1848.[4] The caster was transferred to her third cousin, the Rev. Howard Chandler Robbins, M.D. (1876–1952), and Mary Louise Bayles (1879–1965), m. 1907, and thence to their niece, the donor.[5]

Exhibitions and publications: Kane 1998, 563.

NOTES TO THIS ENTRY ARE ON PAGE 159.

70

John Hull (1624–1683) and Robert Sanderson Sr. (about 1608–1693)

Beaker

Boston, Massachusetts, 1659
Anonymous Gift
1999.90

H. 3⅞ in. (9.9 cm); Diam. rim 3¹¹⁄₁₆ in. (9.3 cm); Diam. base 3¼ in. (8.3 cm); Wt. 6 oz 4 dwt 2 gr (193 gm)

Marks: "IH" within a square, surmounted by a shaped reserve with four clustered shapes, struck on base. "RS" within a circle, surmounted by a radiant sun within a shaped device, struck to right of Hull touchmark.

Inscriptions: "T / B ⋆ C / 1659" within a shield faintly pricked on side of beaker, below lip.

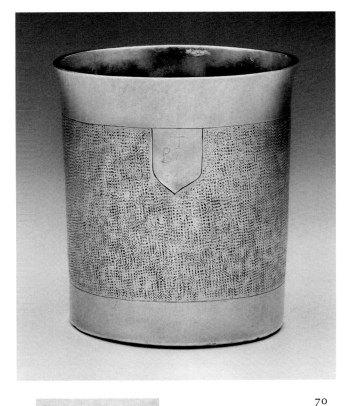

70

IN THE SEVENTEENTH CENTURY, beakers of this type were occasionally referred to as "tunns," a term possibly of Celtic origin. Defined as a large cask for holding wine or beer, the word also described a large barrel or unit of liquid capacity. It was used as early as 1555 to refer to a vessel that was no doubt derived from such utilitarian objects.[1] The tunn was an appropriately humble and secular choice for the Congregational communion table, far removed from the rich trappings of the Church of Rome.

As with the taller Dutch-style beakers made by Hull and Sanderson that Albert Roe termed "curious hybrids" inspired by Sanderson's native Norwich, so, too, these small beakers (or tunns) have a distinctive appearance that sets them apart from their English counterparts.[2] In its short and stocky appearance, the tunn is similar to, but slightly larger than, most related Eng-

lish beakers. Relatively straight sides and the lack of a foot also set this example apart from contemporaneous English examples, as does its chaste, finely punched surface, which serves as primary decoration while providing a secure grip. The source for the matte decoration may be the English wine cup among the First Church plate given by Jeremy Houchin, who arrived in the colony in 1635 and died in 1670.[3]

The tunn most closely related to the Museum's example in both date and form is also the earliest piece of colonial silver made for the church; it bears the single touchmark of John Hull. Hull and Sanderson also made two cups for the First Church of Dorchester and a fifth for Old South Church. These bear punched pattern in a broad field but lack the scored lines that mark the upper and lower border and the shield reserve, as seen on those of the First Church. Another beaker, now unlocated and known only through a period photograph, appears to be closely related to the First Church examples.[4]

Description: The raised, short, cylindrical form with a flat bottom flares slightly at lip; the center point is evident on the base. A broad lightly hatched field encircling the beaker is contained between two scribed lines placed ¾ inch (1.9 cm) from lip and base. A shield-shaped device descends from upper scored line.

History: Original patron unknown. The tunn, owned continuously by the First Church, Boston, later organized as the First and Second Churches of Boston, was acquired by the MFA in 1999 as an anonymous gift in honor of Jonathan L. Fairbanks.

Exhibitions and publications: See appendix 4; Buck 1888, 163; Buck 1903, 194; Jones 1913, 2; Bigelow 1917, 23, 66; Avery 1930, 22–23, pl. 2; Clarke 1940, 206, no. 2; Fales 1970, 5–6; Hood 1971, 20, fig. 1; Kane 1987, 1:appendix A, 422, cat. 23, 2:figs. 33a, b; Kane 1998, 569.

NOTES TO THIS ENTRY ARE ON PAGE 159.

71

John Hull (1624–1683) and
Robert Sanderson Sr. (about 1608–1693)
Wine cup

Boston, Massachusetts, 1660–80
Anonymous Gift
1999.91

H. 8 in. (20.3 cm); Diam. rim 4½ in (11.4 cm); Diam. base 4½ in. (11.5 cm); Wt. 12 oz 19 dwt 22 gr (404.2 gm)

Marks: "IH" with pellets above, all within a square shield surmounted by a circle, and "RS" flanked by pellets, with a partly effaced radiant sun above, struck below rim.

Inscriptions: "T / B C" pricked decoration, within a foliated trefoil design, appears below rim. "The Gift of A Freinde T ✴ C" to right of letters.

THIS VESSEL is the most impressive of the wine cups by Hull and Sanderson that embody Mannerist elements then on the wane in England.[1] The bowl has a wide rim that extends beyond the perimeter of the foot, and its stem, with inverted egg-shaped knop, adds to the unstable feeling. The cast beaded collar and petals below the knop have technical and aesthetic merit that is absent in the other cups.

The cast decoration emulates an English vessel marked "T. G.," also in the First Church communion service, that was giv-

en by Jeremy Houchin between 1635, the time of his arrival in the colony, and his death in 1670.[2] This is the second time that Houchin's cup may have served as a model for Hull and Sanderson, who probably knew of its matte punched surface when fashioning their tunns (cat. no. 70). The delicately pricked initials of the owner, The Boston Church, within a cloud of foliate ornamentation are a more elaborate version of those found on a cup that the partners made for Richard and Alice Brackett of the Braintree Church.

Description: The raised straight-sided bowl opens outward from its base toward a flaring lip. A strengthening disk has been applied to the base. Some repair continues below to the first of two reel-shaped elements that form the top of the stem. The central baluster is in the shape of an inverted egg; below is a cast floral design with petals and beads. At the base, the baluster is soldered to a splayed foot with an applied, stepped ring at its perimeter.

History: The will of wealthy merchant Thomas Clarke included a bequest of £50 to the First Church of Boston, some of which may have been put toward this wine cup bearing his initials. Clarke emigrated from England to Dorchester; by 1647 he had moved to Boston and joined the church, where in 1673 he was made ruling elder.[3] The cup was owned continuously by the First Church, Boston, later organized as the First and Second Churches of Boston, until acquired by the MFA in 1999 as an anonymous gift in honor of Jonathan L. Fairbanks.

Exhibitions and publications: Jones 1913, 23–24, pl. XI, no. 13; C. Louise Avery, "The Beginnings of American Silver," *Antiques* 18, no. 2 (August 1930), 122, fig. 1; Kane 1987, 1:cat. no. 22, 2:fig. 31; Kane 1998, 571. See also appendix 4.

NOTES TO THIS ENTRY ARE ON PAGE 159.

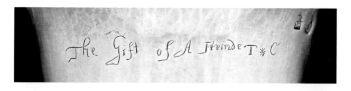

Description: The small spoon has a flat worn stem, rectangular in section, and a V-shaped drop on the back of a fig-shaped bowl; it terminates in a rounded tip. Numerous dents appear on the bowl; the handle is uneven. A horizontal break cuts across the bowl from proper right; a small secondary crack appears at center.

History: No original owner can be determined with certainty; indeed, it is unclear whether the engraved initials read "MY" or "MV."[3] It is possible that "MV" could be for Mary Balson (1648–1690), wife of Isaac Vergoose (1637–1710) of Boston. The Vergooses patronized Hull and Sanderson at least twice, for a porringer and a tankard, each of which bears their joint initials "V/IM."[4] Subsequent history unknown until the twentieth century, when owned by Maria Clark (b. about 1840) of South Boston and her husband, Henry Greene. By descent to to their son Frederick Greene; thence to his niece Florence A. Bessey (1906–1997) of Maine, until acquired by the Wunsch Foundation and made a gift.[5]

Exhibitions and publications: Clarke 1940, cat. nos. 22, 30; Kane 1987, cat. no. 51, figs. 75, 75a–d; Kane 1998, 570, 885.

NOTES TO THIS ENTRY ARE ON PAGE 159.

72

John Hull (1624–1683) and Robert Sanderson Sr. (about 1608–1693)

Spoon

Boston, Massachusetts, 1670–83
Gift of the Wunsch Foundation in Recognition of Kathryn C. Buhler
1983.134

L. 4½ in. (11.5 cm); Diam. bowl 1½ in. (3.9 cm); Wt. 7 dwt (10.9 gm)

Marks: "IH" over a fleur-de-lis, both within a heart-shaped device, struck inside bowl. "RS" (the worn surviving lower portion of Robert Sanderson Sr.'s mark), with a rosette above, both within a conforming punch, struck on back of stem.

Inscriptions: "MV" or "MY" engraved on handle tip.

A RARE SURVIVAL, this variant of the slip-end spoon is one of a group made during the early partnership of Hull and Sanderson. It is one of four spoons, each having a rectangular or otherwise faceted handle.[1] Two of the spoons have an oblique slant at the tip, described in seventeenth-century records as being "slipped in les stalkes," and one has a blunter, so-called Puritan-style end,[2] in contrast to the bulbous tip on the Museum's example. This spoon is about two inches shorter than the others, indicating that it may have been for a child.

73

Benjamin Hurd (1739–1781)

Creampot

Boston, Massachusetts, about 1750–60
Gift from the nieces and grandnephews of Mrs. Alice-Lee T. Stevenson, late of Boston: Alice Lee Thomas Bradlee, Rosamond Whitridge Thomas Oppersdorff, Elizabeth Chadwick Thomas Gwin, Hans Rolle Oppersdorff and Mathias Thomas Oppersdorff in memory of General Robert Hooper Stevenson
1974.434

H. 3⅞ in. (10 cm); W. 3¹¹⁄₁₆ in. (9.4 cm); D. 2⅝ in. (6.6 cm); Wt. 3 oz 9 dwt 5 gr (107.6 gm)

Marks: "B [device] H" within a rectangle struck twice on base.

Inscriptions: "CJY" entwined monogram engraved later on body, opposite handle.

THIS ROCOCO-STYLE CREAMER by Benjamin Hurd, with its scalloped rim and elegant extended spout, has been made in the economical manner often found in the work of Boston silversmiths. Like this example, many Boston creamers have curved spouts that are applied to their raised forms with an overlapping scarf joint. The approach follows the tradition of previous decades, when small, pinched, V-shaped spouts were

73

end of the handle, which terminates in a forked tip, has been reattached, as have the two front legs. An additional repair has been made to the body, around the left front leg.

History: Original owner unknown. The initials, engraved in the second or third decade of the nineteenth century, stand for Caroline James (b. 1807) of Boston, who m. the Rev. Alexander Young (1800–1854) in 1826. By descent to their daughter Caroline James Young (b. about 1838/39) and Gen. Robert Hooper Stevenson (b. 1838),[2] m. 1872, and thence to their son Robert Hooper Stevenson (1876–1965) and his wife, Alice-Lee Whitridge Thomas (d. 1972), m. 1916.[3] The creampot descended to their nieces and grandnephews, the donors.

Exhibitions and publications: French 1939, cat. no. 324; Kane 1998, 576.

NOTES TO THIS ENTRY ARE ON PAGE 159.

74

Benjamin Hurd (1739–1781)

Teaspoon

Boston, Massachusetts, about 1770–80
Gift of Mrs. Peter Christian Beer
1973.15

L. 4⅞ in. (12.4 cm); W. ⅞ in. (2.2 cm); Wt. 7 dwt 9 gr (11.5 gm)

Marks: "B [device] H" in roman letters, within a rectangle, struck on back of stem.

Inscriptions: "P G" in roman letters engraved on front of handle tip.

added to pear-shaped bodies. This method neatly solved the problem of raising a vessel in the new, asymmetrical style featuring an integral spout, which would otherwise have required a disproportionate amount of silver, much of which would have been sawn away, to form the pouring lip. With the loss of silver surface through polishing, the telltale U-shaped shadow of solder marks can sometimes be discerned.

This practice was handed down in at least two instances, by Paul Revere I to his son and, as demonstrated in this example, by Jacob Hurd to his son Benjamin.[1]

Description: The raised bulbous body ascends to a narrow neck and everted scalloped rim. A high curved pouring lip has been added by means of a scarf joint. Three cast cabriole legs have shells at the body and webbed trifid feet. The cast double-scroll handle, with its narrow thumbgrip, is attached at right angles to the rim. The lower

THIS DELICATE TEASPOON by Benjamin Hurd is one of a group that shares a distinctive lobed and webbed shell decoration on the back of the bowl.[1]

Description: Round-tipped handle with feather-edge decoration has short midrib on back; stem is rectangular in section. The elliptical bowl has a rounded drop with seven-lobed webbed shell decoration. Foliate bright-cut decoration appears under owner's initials. The bowl tip is somewhat worn.

History: Early history unknown.

Exhibitions and publications: Kane 1998, 577.

NOTES TO THIS ENTRY ARE ON PAGE 159.

75

Jacob Hurd (1702/3–1758)

Alms dish

Boston, Massachusetts, 1728
Gift of a Friend of the Department and Edward J. and Mary S. Holmes Fund
1984.214

H. 1⅞ in. (4.8 cm); Diam. 13⅜ in. (34 cm); Wt. 31 oz 14 dwt 8 gr (986.5 gm)

Marks: "IHURD" in a shaped cartouche struck directly over center point, within vessel.

Inscriptions: "Belonging to that Church of Christ in / Marblehead of whc the Revd Mr. Edwd. Holyoke / is the Pastor" in flowing script, within a scrolled entablature, engraved on rim.

THIS ALMS DISH was one of two commissioned by the Second Congregational Society of Marblehead, Massachusetts. For the purchase of the first dish, £30 were bequeathed to the church in the 1726/27 will of Deacon Richard Skinner, shoreman; the Skinner arms and a Latin inscription are emblazoned on the rim. The second dish, seen here, was purchased the following year. In contrast to the Skinner basin, this example bears only the name of the church and a simple dedication to Reverend Holyoke, following the pattern for most of the Marblehead silver.[1]

These alms dishes were the only two that Jacob Hurd made during his long career. Of large diameter and exceptionally heavy weight, they added considerable luster to a communion service that was already impressive by the late 1720s. Hurd was a

75

natural choice for the congregation, for in the previous decade, they had chosen his chief predecessors, John Coney and John Burt, whose careers were similarly long and prolific, to provide silver for the communion table.

Description: The large circular dish has a center point in its broad flat base and a wide brim with applied molding at the rim.

History: See appendix 6.

Exhibitions and publications: French 1939, no. 2; Kane 1998, 584; see also appendix 6.

NOTES TO THIS ENTRY ARE ON PAGE 159.

ringer; a second possibility is her daughter Elizabeth (1729–1777), for young unmarried women often possessed silver engraved with their maiden initials. The latter Elizabeth m. Capt. Solomon Davis (1715–1791) about 1750.[2] The porringer descended through their daughter Elizabeth Davis (1758–1833) and Dr. David Townsend (1753–1829), m. 1785.[3] By descent to their son David S. Townsend (1790–1852) and Elizabeth Gerry (1790–1882), m. 1816. To their daughter Catherine Augusta Townsend (1823–1902) and Edward Standish Sherman (1818–1882), m. 1852. To their daughter Katherine Wendell Sherman (1854–1927), who became second wife of her first cousin Edward Britton Townsend (1848–1910), m. 1892. By descent to their son Wendell Townsend (1893–1963), who made it a gift to his cousin, Anne Torbet, the donor and wife of Horace A. White (1914–1979), m. 1937.[4]

Exhibitions and publications: Kane 1998, 597.

NOTES TO THIS ENTRY ARE ON PAGE 159.

76

Jacob Hurd (1702/3–1758)

Porringer

Boston, Massachusetts, about 1730–40
Gift of Mrs. Horace A. White
1980.323

H. 1⅞ in. (4.9 cm); W. 7⅞ in. (20 cm); Diam. rim 5⅛ in. (13 cm); Wt. 7 oz 18 dwt 9 gr (246.3 gm)

Marks: "Hurd" in script, within an ellipse, struck to left of handle. "Jacob / Hurd" in upper- and lowercase letters, within a shield-shaped cartouche, struck on back of handle.

Inscriptions: "E * W" in shaded roman letters engraved on handle, facing bowl.

THIS PORRINGER is one of about forty-eight surviving examples made by the prolific Jacob Hurd, many of which were executed with the traditional keyhole-style handle.[1]

Description: The raised vessel has a domed center, convex sides, and a slightly everted rim. A center point is visible inside and underneath the bowl. Many dents mark the side, and two large unskilled repairs are visible on the bottom.

History: The initials "E * W" were engraved for one of two women in the Wendell family of Boston. Elizabeth Quincy (1706–1746), m. John Wendell (about 1703–1762) in 1724, may have owned the por-

77

Jacob Hurd (1702/3–1758)

Baptismal basin

Boston, Massachusetts, 1733
Anonymous Gift
1999.89

H. 2¹³⁄₁₆ in. (7 cm); Diam. rim 13⅜ in. (34.1 cm); Wt. 27 oz 1 dwt 13 gr (842.2 gm)

Marks: "IHURD" in a scalloped cartouche struck at center of basin, above center point.

Inscriptions: Scratch weight of "27-5" engraved on base; a nineteenth-century metal disk with the engraved numeral "7" soldered to base.

Armorials: The rim of the basin is ornamented with the Byfield family arms on a shield bearing gules, five bezants in saltire, a chief or; crest is a demi-lion rampant holding bezant.[1] Elaborate scrolled and swagged mantling surrounds the whole.

IT IS UNCLEAR with whom Jacob Hurd apprenticed or where he obtained the funds or connections to establish himself as one of the preeminent silversmiths of eighteenth-century Boston. Yet, influential patrons such as Samuel Sewall and Harvard tutor Henry Flynt knew enough of his work to make purchases from him beginning in the mid-1720s, soon after he first opened his shop. Important commissions, such as alms basins for the Second Congregational Society of Marblehead in 1727 and 1728

77

(cat. no. 75) and this baptismal basin (along with silver for the First Church of Lynn and Christ Church, Boston), were among his first pieces of ecclesiastical silver. The broad, flat alms dishes, which are technically difficult to produce, may have helped establish Hurd in the religious community as an extraordinarily talented silversmith.

This deep baptismal basin was the second of four by Hurd and one of three made during the 1730s, when his shop saw spectacular growth. In all, he fashioned communion silver for twenty-five regional churches.[2]

A legacy from Judge Nathaniel Byfield provided fifty ounces of plate each to Thomas Foxcroft and Charles Chauncy, the two ministers of the First Church. This basin, weighing more than twenty-seven troy ounces, was purchased with a portion of Byfield's bequest. Hurd's skill in raising large amounts of silver is evident in the smoothly raised form with undulating curves that lead from the domed center, up the broadly convex walls, and to the wide brim. The richly engraved arms are evidence of Hurd's skill with the burin.

Byfield, a wealthy merchant and public official, was closely linked to the church on both sides of his family. He was the son of the Rev. Richard Byfield, rector of Long Ditton in Surrey, England, and one of the Westminster assembly of divines; his maternal uncle William Juxon, bishop of London, became archbishop of Canterbury under Charles II. Shortly after his arrival in Boston in 1674, he married Deborah, daughter of Capt. Thomas and Mary Clarke, and moved to Bristol, Rhode Island, after King Philip's War. He was an active member of the town, serving as judge of the Bristol County court of common pleas for thirty-eight years and as judge of the vice admiralty for a time.[3]

In 1714/15 Byfield traveled to England, where he unsuccessfully petitioned to replace Gov. Joseph Dudley. His wife, Deborah, died in 1717; shortly after he married Sarah, daughter of Gov. John and Sarah Leverett, and relocated to Boston in 1724. A man of considerable means, his bequest was large for its day.

In addition to the First Church of Boston, recipient of this basin, Byfield made generous gifts of communion plate to two other churches. In 1693 he presented two beakers to the First Congregational Church of Bristol. About the time this basin was given, he gave to the Byfield parish near Newbury, Massachusetts, two beakers made by Hurd and similarly emblazoned with his family arms. Such a gift, made by kindness toward the congregation that bore his name, may have also been a symbol of his rivalry with the Dummer family, whose ancestors had established the church and whose descendants, brothers Jeremiah and Lieut. Gov. William Dummer, he opposed in the

political arena. The same sense of competitiveness may have guided Byfield's bequest to the First Church of Boston, where William Dummer had already made a prominent gift of a flagon in 1726 (cat. no. 51).[4]

Description: This large circular basin with center point has a raised dome at center, gently curving convex sides, and a wide brim with applied molding. The brim is engraved with the Byfield arms on a shield, which is surrounded by elaborate scrolled and swagged mantling.

History: Made from the bequest of Nathaniel Byfield (1653–1733), which arranged for "Fifty ounces of Good Silver" each to the Rev. Thomas Foxcroft and the Rev. Charles Chauncy, ministers of the First Church, Boston, which was later organized as the First and Second Churches of Boston. Owned continuously by the church until acquired by the MFA in 1999 as an anonymous gift in honor of Jonathan L. Fairbanks. See also appendix 4.

Exhibitions and publications: Jones 1913, 33–34, pl. XI; *Loan Exhibition of Early American Furniture and the Decorative Crafts for the Benefit of Free Hospital for Women, Brookline, Mass.* (Boston: n.p., 1925), 121, cat. no. 288; French 1939, no. 3; Kane 1998, 584–85.

NOTES TO THIS ENTRY ARE ON PAGE 160.

78

Jacob Hurd (1702/3–1758)
Small sword with scabbard and waistbelt

Boston, Massachusetts, 1735
Gift of Jane Bortman Larus in honor of Kathryn C. Buhler and in recognition of her warm friendship and association with Mark Bortman and Jane B. Larus
1984.109

L. 30½ in. (77.5 cm)

Marks: "Hurd" within an ellipse struck on shell of hilt.

Inscriptions: "R.H." engraved on one counter guard, "1735" on the other. "R. Hazen of / Haverhill A:D./1735" and "Cost £13= 15= 9" engraved on scabbard mount.

RARE IN ITS SURVIVAL from the colonial era, this sword by Jacob Hurd is even more remarkable for the detailed inscriptions on the blade that identify the owner, Col. Richard Hazen, and for the fine condition of its original red leather fittings. Hurd fashioned the silver hilt and mounts; he likely also provided the silver buckles and scabbard tip, called a chape; the

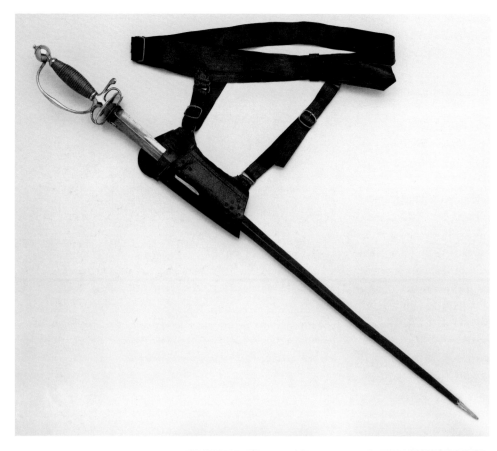

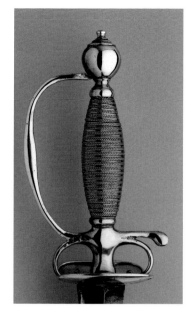

78

leather belt and scabbard were probably made by a local craftsman. The forged steel blade may have been made locally or procured from abroad.[1]

In his long career, Hurd produced domestic and ecclesiastical silver. Between 1730 and 1750, he made about ten swords, far more than his peers, most of whom made only one or two.[2] Two of his distinguished patrons include Col. William Prescott (1726–1795), commander of the American forces at the Battle of Bunker Hill, and Gen. John Winslow (1703–1774), grandson of Gov. Josiah Winslow.[3]

Richard Hazen (also Hazzen), eldest son of Richard (1669–1733) and Mary (Peabody) Hazen (1672–1731) of Haverhill, graduated from Harvard in 1717. By 1726 he had become one of the original proprietors of Pennycook (also Pennicook,

Penacook), now Concord, New Hampshire, where he took an active role in its settlement by undertaking land surveys. In 1741 he was appointed by Governor Belcher and the Council of New Hampshire to establish the boundary between Massachusetts and New Hampshire. The settlement of this border ended a long and bitter struggle between the two colonies that was caused by an error in the original royal charters. In his report to Belcher, Hazen described the wintry weather that he and his chainmen encountered while performing their job in March of that year:

The Journey was very fatiguing the Snow for 60 or 70 miles was near three feet deep & in many places four or five so that we were oblig'd to wear snow shoes till the very last day. We lodg'd about twenty nights on the snow without building any Camp to Cover us being favour'd with fair weather & we were oblig'd to wade some Rivers which we could not raft over & climb such Mountains as seem'd to over Top the Alps but through Divine goodness all are return'd in perfect health in thirty seven days.[4]

As is true for most American silver-mounted swords of the eighteenth century, Hurd's example is characterized by clean lines and simply formed elements, unlike its European counterparts, which were elaborately pierced and modeled. A member of the small sword family because of its light weight, it was the preferred shape for fencing in late-seventeenth-century England, which may account for its rather formal use in the colonies. Delicate in appearance but lethal in use, this example is of a type known as a "simple small sword," a term referring to the blade that tapers evenly from hilt to point.[5] Austerely handsome in line and form, silver-hilted swords were worn as an accessory in civilian life or as a dress sword when in uniform. The survival of a sword such as this can be attributed to its largely ceremonial function.

Description: The sword has a silver hilt with turned tip; flattened spherical pommel; and twisted wire-wound grip with plain ferrel. The knuckle guard and *pas d'anes* are simply curved and slightly molded. The quillion ends in a bulb form; the bivalve shell guard has molded edges. The plain, unmarked tapering steel blade is hollow ground and triangular in section. The tooled red leather scabbard, waist belt, and frog are original.

History: Col. Richard Hazen (1696–1754) and Sarah Clement of Newbury, m. 1719; to their daughter Elizabeth Hazen (1734/35–1808), m. Joseph Little (1730–1792) of Newbury, Massachussetts, in 1757;[6] to their daughter Lucretia Little (1759–1851) and her second cousin Silas Little (1754–1845), m. 1786. By descent to their son Joseph Little (b. 1799) and Elizabeth Moody (b. 1799) of Newbury, m. 1821;[7] to their son Joseph Little (b. 1833) and Sarah C. Hale (b. 1840), m. 1861. By descent to their son Joseph Danforth Little (b. 1868) of Nutley, New Jersey, who placed the sword on loan to the Metropolitan Museum of Art from 1926 to 1940.[8] Purchased sometime thereafter by Mark Bortman (1896–1967); by descent to his daughter Jane Bortman Larus, who made it a gift to the Museum in 1984.

Exhibitions and publications: *Masterpieces* 4, no. 1 (April 1927), 3; "The Editor's Attic," *Antiques* 17, no. 3 (March 1930), 209–10; French 1939, 41, no. 169; Smith College 1958, 18, cat. no. 14; *Silver Supplement* 1973, 34, cat. no. 56; Fairbanks 1991, 71, cat. no. 53, 91, cat. no. 30; John D. Hamilton, "Jacob Hurd and the Boston Smallsword," *American Society of Arms Collectors* (1993), 79–89; Kane 1998, 604–5.

NOTES TO THIS ENTRY ARE ON PAGE 160.

79

Jacob Hurd (1702/3–1758)
Cann

Boston, Massachusetts, 1740
Gift of Mrs. Charles C. Cabot
1996.401

H. 4¹³⁄₁₆ in. (12.2 cm); W. 5 in. (12.6 cm); Diam. rim 3 in. (7.6 cm); Diam. base 3⅛ in. (8 cm); Wt. 10 oz 10 dwt 13 gr (327.4 gm)

Marks: "Hurd" in script, within an ellipse, struck to left of handle.

Inscriptions: "Ex dono Pupillorum" [Given by the students] in script engraved above armorial. "Rev. Daniel Rogers / Exeter, / died, 1785" in script engraved later on base; "1740" engraved on front edge of foot, below arms.

Armorials: Elaborate engraving of Rogers family arms is found on the body opposite handle, the shield emblazoned argent a chevron sable between three bucks trippant azure, in a scroll and acanthus cartouche. The crest is of a buck sable trippant on a torse. Below the mantling, the motto *AD ASTRA PER ASPERA* (To the star through hardship) in shaded roman letters is engraved in a banner.[1]

THE PRESENTATION of specially engraved silver to tutors by their grateful students was practiced in England long before the custom was emulated in colonial America. Such gifts served as a show of appreciation even as they augmented a tutor's modest income. Tutors were aware of how much each student may have contributed toward these gifts, as proved by one teacher's surviving records. Therefore, tutorial silver may also have been used by students to secure favor. At Harvard College, tutorial silver was traditionally given until 1767, when reformation of the educational system improved faculty salaries and rendered such gifts unnecessary.[2]

The handsomely engraved cann bearing the Rogers family arms was given to Daniel Rogers by the Harvard class of 1740. It shares the same engraving and presentation inscription as an unmarked elliptical tobacco box, which may be the same one stolen from Rogers in a student prank of about 1735, along with wine and Bristol beer.

A grandson of the Rev. John Rogers (about 1630–1684), Harvard's fifth president, and a graduate of the class of 1725, Daniel Rogers served a rocky tenure as tutor from 1732 to 1741. Called "a cussed Fellow, Ignoramus, [and] Blockhead" by fellow tutor Nathan Prince, who also claimed that his colleague "was not fit to be admitted a freshman," Rogers displayed an arrogance toward his charges that made him rather unlikable.[3] Yet, in keeping with tradition, he received at least two such works. Still, the low esteem in which he was held might be inferred from a pilfered tutorial tobacco box, which was the smallest sort of gift students could have bestowed.[4] After a series of false starts, Rogers became minister of the Second Church of Exeter, New Hampshire, where he remained until his death in 1785.

Description: The raised baluster-form cann has a center point visible on the bottom. The cast stepped and splayed foot has been trimmed on the lathe on the underside and then thickly soldered to vessel. The applied molding has paired scored lines at the flaring lip. A cast two-section scroll handle with plain thumbgrip has a molded drop at its upper joining and a disk at the lower end. A flattened sphere forms the terminal, with an oval air vent below.

History: Commissioned by the Harvard class of 1740 for Daniel Rogers (1707–1785).[5] Descended to his son Daniel Dennison Rogers (1751–1825) and Elizabeth Bromfield (1763–1833), m. 1796, and

thence to their daughter Hannah Rogers (1806–1872) and William Powell Mason (1791–1867), m. 1831;[6] to their daughter Elizabeth Rogers Mason (1834–1920) and Walter Channing Cabot (1829–1904), m. 1860;[7] to their son Henry Bromfield Cabot (1861–1932) and Anne McMasters Codman (1864–1944), m. 1892; to their son Charles Codman Cabot (1900–1976) and the donor, his wife, Ellen P. White Cabot (1903–1997), m. 1929.[8]

Exhibitions and publications: Kane 1998, 591 (MFA ownership not indicated).

NOTES TO THIS ENTRY ARE ON PAGE 160.

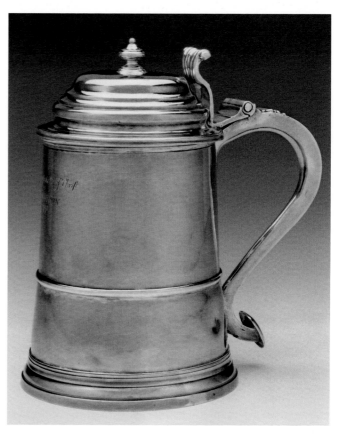

80

Jacob Hurd (1702/3–1758)

Tankard

Boston, Massachusetts, 1740
Gift of the First Church in Newton
1973.19

H. 7¹¹/₁₆ in. (19.6 cm); W. 7⅜ in. (18.7 cm); Diam. rim 4 in. (10.2 cm); Diam. base 5 in. (12.7 cm); Wt. 24 oz 18 dwt 13 gr (775.3 gm)

Marks: "Hurd" in script, within an ellipse, struck to left of handle; "Jacob / Hurd" within a shield struck on base, at center.

Inscriptions: "Belonging to the Chh of Christ / in NEWTOWN / 1740" in script engraved on body, opposite handle.

THIS CLASSIC BOSTON TANKARD, with its stepped lid, capstan finial, scrolled thumbpiece, and oval domed terminal, was a staple of Hurd's workshop in the 1730s and 1740s.[1] See also appendix 8.

Description: The raised straight-sided tankard is wider at the base; a center point is not visible. One midband appears above lower handle join, and an applied stepped molding appears at the base. The domed and stepped lid with inner flange has a downturned rim and scored edge. The tankard has capstan finial, scrolled cast thumbpiece, and five-part hinge. The raised seamed handle has short baluster drop at shoulder. A rounded drop appears under handle at top join to body; an oval disk is used at the lower point of attachment. The convex oval terminal has a lozenge-shaped air vent below.

History: The lack of a donor's name led Kathryn C. Buhler to surmise that this tankard was purchased by the church with general funds.[2]

Exhibitions and publications: French 1939, no. 244; Kane 1998, 606. See also appendix 8.

NOTES TO THIS ENTRY ARE ON PAGE 160.

81

Jacob Hurd (1702/3–1758)
Pair of salt spoons

Boston, Massachusetts, about 1740–50
Gift of Mr. and Mrs. William L. Payson
1973.735–36

1973.735: L. 3⅝ in. (9.2 cm); W. bowl 11/16 in. (1.8 cm); Wt. 2 dwt 20 gr (4.4 gm)

1973.736: L. 3⅝ in. (9.2 cm); W. bowl 11/16 in. (1.8 cm); Wt. 2 dwt 15 gr (4.1 gm)

Marks: "HURD" in roman capitals, within a rectangular cartouche, struck on back of handle.

Inscription: "A" in roman letter engraved on back of each handle, near tip. "C.T. to T. E. W." in script engraved later on stem, near tip.

SALT SPOONS appeared in England beginning in the seventeenth century and were made in some quantity during the eighteenth. In England, the first and preferred form for the

bowl was the shovel shape, which was gilded for protection against the corrosive effects of salt.[1]

Colonial American salt spoons, by contrast, appear infrequently with a shovel-shaped bowl. That is particularly true for those made in eighteenth-century New England; few examples can be identified, and the use of a spoon was more likely to be inferred by its scale rather than its specialized shape.

This pair constitutes the only known shovel-shaped salt spoons to have been made in Jacob Hurd's shop. An unmarked pair made for Benjamin and Mary (Toppan) Pickman has been attributed to John Coburn by Kathryn C. Buhler. In 1796 Paul Revere made four "salt shovels" for Jonathan Hunnewell, a bricklayer and president of the Massachusetts Charitable Mechanics Association.[2] As the number of silversmiths and the demand for silver grew in nineteenth-century America, the shovel-shaped bowl attained latter-day popularity.[3]

According to family history, these spoons were traditionally associated with a pair of trencher salts made by John Coney between 1710 and 1720 (cat. no. 34).[4]

Description: These delicate salt spoons have upturned midrib handles and slender stems terminating in flat shovel-shaped bowls curving gently outward at flattened end; a worn shell drop appears on the back of each bowl.

History: See cat. no. 34.

Exhibitions and publications: French 1939, 45, nos. 233–34; Kane 1998, 599.

NOTES TO THIS ENTRY ARE ON PAGE 160.

and Rococo shells at the handle tips. They are exceptionally decorative examples by Hurd, who produced numerous teaspoons with plain midrib handles and simple drops or shells on bowls.[2]

The Wendells owned several pieces of silver that carry their initials, names, arms, or crests. An example of the family arms and crest, accompanied by a magnificently engraved mantling, can be found on a tankard that Peter Van Dyck made about 1705–15 for Harmanus Wendell (1678–1731), Jacob's first cousin. A sugar bowl that Hurd made for Anne Wendell also bears the family arms. John Edwards produced a pair of mugs for Jacob and Sarah (Oliver) Wendell (cat. no. 49), and Edward Webb crafted a porringer that bears the initials "IW" (or "MI"), which have been interpreted by Kathryn C. Buhler as those of Jacob Wendell or Mary Jackson, his descendant.[3]

One of the handles bears an inscription that was probably engraved for Thomas Smith, who married Jacob Wendell's widow, Elizabeth Hunt Wendell, in 1766.

82

Jacob Hurd (1702/3–1758)
Pair of teaspoons

Boston, Massachusetts, 1740–50
Gift of Annie L. E. and Francis Dane
1992.230–31

1992.230: L. 5⅛ in. (12.9 cm); W. bowl ⅞ in. (2.4 cm); Wt. 10 dwt 1 gr (15.6 gm)

1992.231: L. 5⅛ in. (12.9 cm); W. bowl ⅞ in. (2.4 cm); Wt. 9 dwt 14 gr (14.9 gm)

Marks: 1992.230: "Hurd" in roman letters stuck within a shaped cartouche. 1992.231: Original mark obscured by old repair to stem.

Inscriptions: 1992.231: "T. S./ 1728" in shaded roman letters engraved below crest.

Armorials: Each spoon is engraved on back of handle tip with the Wendell family crest, a three-masted vessel to sinister having furled sails.[1]

THIS DIMINUTIVE PAIR of spoons was probably commissioned by Boston merchant Jacob Wendell. Their delicate form is enhanced with a family crest, swaged palmette bowls,

Description: The pair of slender teaspoons bears swaged Rococo shells within a cartouche on upturned handle tips; a single drop and palmette motif adorn the back of each bowl.

History: According to the donor, the teaspoons were first owned by Jacob Wendell (1715–1753) and Elizabeth Hunt (1717–1799), m. 1736.[4] Elizabeth Hunt Wendell m. second, Thomas Smith (1702–1795), in 1766. The spoons probably descended to Elizabeth Wendell (1742–1799), daughter of the above-mentioned Jacob and Elizabeth Hunt Wendell, m. Rev. Peter Thacher Smith (1731–1826) of Portland and Wyndham, Maine, in 1763 (or 1765). Smith was the son of the aforementioned Thomas Smith and his first wife, Sarah Tyng (d. 1742).[5] By descent to their daughter Lucy Smith (1769–1864) and Abraham Anderson (1758–1844), m. 1788; to their son John Anderson (1792–1853) and his second wife, Ann Williams Jameson (b. 1804), m. 1822. To their son John Farwell Anderson (1823–1887) and Marcia Bowman Winter (b. 1827), m. 1847/48;[6] to their daughter Anne Hichborn Anderson (1849–1919) and Charles William Lord (1845–1917), m. 1870;[7] to their niece Annie L. Edmands (1878–1977) and Francis Smith Dane (1874–1964), m. 1903; to their daughter Marcia Winter Anderson Dane (1905–1977), the donor.[8]

Exhibitions and publications: These teaspoons are probably the same as those in MFA 1906, 68, cat. nos. 155–56, described as "two teaspoons: about 1750; ship on back."[9] French 1939, 44, nos. 223–24; Buhler 1956, 62, cat. no. 88; Kane 1998, 613.

NOTES TO THIS ENTRY ARE ON PAGE 160.

83

Jacob Hurd (1702/3–1758)
Ladle

Boston, Massachusetts, about 1740–56
Gift of the Estate of George Stevens
1991.694

L. 12¹¹⁄₁₆ in. (32.2 cm); W. bowl 3⅝ in. (9.2 cm); D. bowl 2³⁄₁₆ in.
(5.5 cm) ; Wt. 2 oz 13 dwt 20 gr (83.7 gm)

Marks: "HURD" in roman capitals within a rectangle struck inside
bowl, above center point.

Inscription: "N / I*M" in shaded roman letters engraved on back of
bowl.

This Hurd ladle is similar to one by William Swan (cat. no.
119), although it is executed with less refinement, as seen in the
shaping of the bowl and the cast elements.

Description: The raised elliptical bowl with a center point has a scalloped rim and corresponding fluted sides, with broad pouring lips
at each end. The stem is forked and scrolled and soldered to bowl
with circular prunts. The stem is attached to a solid, tapering circular handle socket, which receives the friction-fitted replacement
wooden handle. An old repair to stem is visible at juncture between
fork and bowl.

History: According to family history, George Stevens (1867–1953), the
donor, inherited the ladle from Daniel L. Hazard (b. 1865), Nancook
Farm, Narragansett, Rhode Island. The initials "N / I*M" may stand
for a member of the Nichols family, possibly a relative of Susannah
Nichols (1662–1746), wife of Thomas Hazard (1660–1746), m. 1682.[1]

Exhibitions and publications: French 1939, no. 134; Kane 1998, 595.

NOTES TO THIS ENTRY ARE ON PAGE 160.

84

Jacob Hurd (1702/3–1758)

Bowl

Boston, Massachusetts, about 1740–58
Gift of Beatrice Hardcastle Magruder in memory of her
father Alfred Putnam Lowell
1991.789

H. 3³⁄₁₆ in. (8.1 cm); Diam. rim 7³⁄₈ in. (18.7 cm); Diam. base 3³⁄₈ in.
(8.6 cm); Wt. 13 oz 14 dwt 3 gr (426.3 gm)

Marks: "HURD" in small roman capitals within a rectangle struck
on base, below center point.

Inscriptions: "E / I = L" in roman capitals, over lightly scored
guidelines, engraved on base; scratch weight of "14 oz [illegible] 7"
faintly visible.

Armorials: Unidentified arms are engraved within a Rococo cartouche, surrounded with shell and scroll forms, flanked by slender
leaves and swagged below. The arms, emblazoned on a field argent,
a fess or between two barrulet azur cotised.

EMBELLISHED WITH A dynamic, asymmetrical Rococo engraving of unidentified arms, the bowl is one of the largest of five
surviving examples by Jacob Hurd that range in diameter from
4 to 7½ inches.[1] Its simple hemispherical shape recalls the Sons
of Liberty bowl by Revere and the grand punch bowl made
about 1708–9 by John Coney for Walter Riddell (cat. no. 32). All
these vessels emulate imported Chinese forms then popular in
England and the colonies.

Description: The raised hemispherical bowl with everted walls has an
applied rim and a small circular base with slight exterior molding.
Firescale is noticeable.

History: The vessel was possibly owned by Elizabeth Cutt (1709–1805) and the Rev. Joseph Whipple (1701–1757), m. 1727, or by Elizabeth Cutt Whipple through her second marriage of 1758 to the Rev. John Lowell (1704–1767).[2] At the time of this later marriage, the initials "E / I = L" were added, an unusual arrangement of letters that appears to be an anomaly. The bowl descended to Judge John Lowell (1743–1802), Reverend Lowell's son by his first wife, Sarah Champney (1704–1756). Judge Lowell m. his third wife, Rebecca (Russell) Tyng (1746–1816), in 1778, and the bowl descended to their son the Rev. Charles Lowell (1782–1861), pastor of West Congregational Church in Boston, m. Harriett Brackett Spence (1783–1850) in 1806.[3] By descent to their daughter Mary Traill Spence Lowell (1810–1898) and Samuel Raymond Putnam (1797–1861), m. 1832.[4] The vessel probably descended to their daughter Georgina Lowell Putnam (b. 1835), d. unm., and thence to her cousin Charles Lowell (1855–1905), who in 1885 m. Beatrice Kate Hardcastle (about 1852–1932).[5] By descent to their daughter Mary Beatrice Lowell (b. 1888) and Frederick Southgate Bigelow (1871–1954), m. 1915,[6] and thence to her brother Alfred Putman Lowell (1890–1954) and Catherine Hay Bowles (1890–1969), m. 1915,[7] by descent to the donor.

Exhibitions and publications: MFA 1911, 76, cat. no. 647; French 1939, 33, no. 37; *Ellis Memorial* 1984, no. 13; Kane 1998, 587.

NOTES TO THIS ENTRY ARE ON PAGES 160–61.

85

Jacob Hurd (1702/3–1758)

Beaker

Boston, Massachusetts, 1744
Gift of the First Church in Newton
1973.22

H. 5⅝ in. (14.1 cm); Diam. rim 3¹¹⁄₁₆ in. (9.4 cm); Diam. base 3⅛ in. (8 cm); Wt. 10 oz 2 dwt 1 gr (314.2 gm)

Marks: "Hurd" in a shaped cartouche struck between lip and inscription.

Inscriptions: "The Gift of / Deacon William Trowbridge / to / The Church of Christ / in / Newtown / 1744" engraved below mark on body.

THE INVERTED bell- or tulip-shaped beaker, with its low center of gravity and broad base, was the successor to the squatter flat-bottomed tunns or beakers of the seventeenth century (see cat. no. 70). Such vessels were made in large quantities for Congregational churches and often assembled over years through gifts and bequests. Many churches owned at least two beakers,

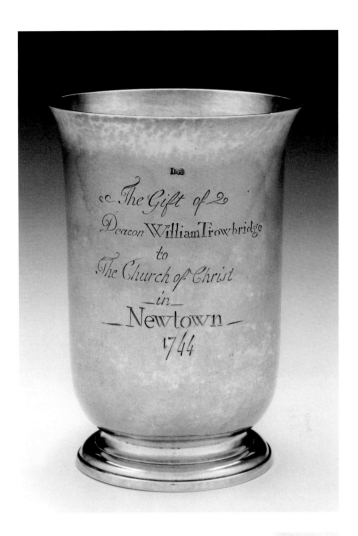

and often more, which were passed among the congregants to drink sacramental wine. Jacob Hurd made this beaker in 1744 through the legacy of deacon William Trowbridge. E. Alfred Jones speculated that it was remade from a silver tankard that Trowbridge had left to his wife, Sarah, but that cannot be proved.[1] It was not until 1768 that a second beaker, made by Samuel Minott, joined this example in the church's collection.

Description: The inverted bell-shaped beaker has a flaring applied lip and a drawn stepped base, with applied foot rim.

History: Deacon William Trowbridge (1684–1744) was the brother of Margaret Trowbridge (1666–1710), whose husband, Ebenezer Stone (1662/63–1754), gave the John Edwards tankard to the First Church in Newton (cat. no. 52). Trowbridge's will, dated July 2, 1744, and proved January 7, 1744/45, included a bequest of £5 to be provided for poor widows in the congregation but made no specific mention of a gift of communion silver.[2]

Exhibitions and publications: MFA 1911, 79; Jones 1913, 324; French 1939, 32. See also appendix 8.

NOTES TO THIS ENTRY ARE ON PAGE 161.

86

Jacob Hurd (1702/3–1758)
Beaker

Boston, Masschusetts, 1744
Gift of Lavinia and Landon T. Clay
2002.225

H. 5 1/16 in. (13 cm); Diam. rim 3¾ in. (9.5 cm); Diam. foot 3⅛ in. (8 cm); Wt. 9 oz 5 dwt 12 gr (288.5 gm)

Marks: "Hurd" within a shaped cartouche struck twice, below rim and on body, opposite engraving.

Inscriptions: "The Gift of / Mr. Brice and Mrs: Ann Blair / For the Use of the presbyteria /Church in Long-Lane. where of. / The Revd: M. Iohn Moorhead is. / Pastor / in Gratitude to God for / His. Goodnefs. / to them and thiers in a Strange / Land / BOSTON: may 1:1744. / Set Deo Maxima Laus." in varied styles, within a bellflower and shell cartouche, engraved on side.

THIS BEAKER by Jacob Hurd was the third piece of communion silver (the second by the silversmith) to be acquired by the fledgling Presbyterian church that had formed in 1729. The vessel is of a standard midcentury form and size, similar to the beaker that Hurd fashioned for the Newton church that same year (cat. no. 85). The tablet-shaped escutcheon, with its architectural, bellflower, and foliate decoration, was one favored by Hurd.[1] It served as a template for Paul Revere when, in 1753, he was given the charge of fashioning three more beakers for the church.

Description: The raised bell-shaped beaker with slightly everted lip and rounded base is soldered to a drawn and molded circular foot.

History: Brice Blair (d. 1758), tailor, and his wife, Ann Blair (d. 1756), to the Church of Presbyterian Strangers in Long-Lane, later known as Arlington Street Church. Beaker retained by the church until 2002, when it failed to sell at Christie's. It was offered a second time by Northeast Auctions in 2002, when it was purchased by the donors and made a gift.

Exhibitions and publications: MFA 1911, 79, cat. no. 676; Jones 1913, 78; French 1939, no. 25; Kane 1998, 587; Christie's, New York, sale 1003, January 18, 2002, lot no. 324; Northeast Auctions, Portsmouth, New Hampshire, August 3–4, 2002, lot no. 868. See also appendix 2.

NOTE TO THIS ENTRY IS ON PAGE 161.

sometime after 1760, the year she married her third husband, Ebenezer Brooks, of Medford, Massachusetts. Brooks was elected deacon of the nearby Medford church in 1759, and perhaps this cann served as a parting gift to her family church.[1]

Description: The cann has a raised bulbous body on a splayed, drawn, molded foot. The flaring lip has a molded edge, and the scrolled seamed handle has a thumbgrip of midrib design. The handle is attached at the shoulder with an elongated drop and near the base with an oval disk. It has an oval terminus and a crescent-shaped air vent.

History: The donor, Elizabeth Sweetser (1697/98–1782), was the daughter of Samuel and Elizabeth (Sprague) Sweetser of Mystic Side, Massachusetts, a region of Charlestown that was annexed to Malden in 1725.[2] She m. Samuel Tufts (1697–1735) of Medford in 1723; Daniel Mansfield (1689/90–1758) of Lynn in 1735/36; and Ebenezer Brooks, yeoman of Medford (1697–1781), in 1760.[3]

Exhibitions and publications: Jones 1913, 257–58; French 1939, 36, no. 87; Kane 1998, 590. See also appendix 5.

NOTES TO THIS ENTRY ARE ON PAGE 161.

87

Jacob Hurd (1702/3–1758)
Cann

Boston, Massachusetts, 1746
Gift of the First Church in Malden, Congregational
1991.499

H. 5⅝ in. (14.3 cm); W. 6⅜ in. (16.2 cm); Diam. rim 3¾ in. (9.3 cm); Diam. foot 4 in. (10.2 cm); Wt. 13 oz 19 dwt 14 gr (434.8 gm)

Marks: "HURD" in small roman capitals within a rectangle struck to left of handle.

Inscriptions: "M / D*E / 1746" in roman letters engraved on handle. "The Gift / of / Elizabeth Brooks / To the / First Church of Christ / in / Malden." in script, within a circular band, engraved later, opposite handle.

THIS HURD CANN is a fine example of domestic silver that came into a church through a congregant. According to the initials on the handle, Elizabeth Brooks, the donor, owned the cann at the time of her second marriage to Daniel Mansfield of Lynn, Massachusetts. She likely gave the vessel to the church

88

Jacob Hurd (1702/3–1758)
Salver

Boston, Massachusetts, about 1750
Marion E. Davis Fund
1982.183

H. 1³⁄₁₆ in. (3 cm); Diam. 7⅜ in. (18.8 cm); Wt. 7 oz 5 dwt 23 gr (227 gm)

Marks: "HURD" in small roman capitals within a rectangle struck near rim, below engraving.

Inscriptions: "The pair at 14 oz 16 dw 12 gr" in script engraved on underside.

Armorials: The Greene family arms engraved at the center of the salver depict azure three stags trippant. They are engraved within a rocaille shell and flanked by wheat sheaves. The crest is of a stag's head, or, on a torse.[1]

ACCORDING TO THE SCRATCH WEIGHT, the salver was originally one of a pair and was probably used as a serving piece in the household of the governor of Rhode Island. Although the mate is lost, it joins a small group of similar pairs recorded in mid-eighteenth-century Boston. Hurd produced an octagonal

pair in the 1750s that bear the Hastings arms, and Paul Revere II fashioned "2 small scoloppd Salvers" in 1762 for Nathaniel Hurd, who engraved them for the Franklin family. The lively Rococo border on this example suggests that it was made between 1745 and 1755, near the end of Hurd's productive career. A larger example made in 1761 by Paul Revere II for Lucretia Chandler possesses a similarly complex arrangement of cyma curves with alternating shells.[2]

A prolific silversmith, Hurd was particularly adept at producing salvers of varying sizes and shapes; he made about twenty-four between 1730 and 1745.[3] The technical challenge posed by the flat serving surface suggests that Hurd employed a journeyman who specialized in this form.

Among the many known examples of the Greene arms, especially fine ones include an embroidered hatchment made in 1745 by Katherine Greene (1731–1777), daughter of silversmith Rufus Greene; a tankard engraved in 1762 by Paul Revere II for Thomas Greene (1705–1763); and a richly engraved cann by Hurd.[4]

Description: The circular scalloped salver has a cast rim featuring conjoined curves and scrolls. Twelve points on the rim are marked by alternating small and large fluted-shell decoration. A conforming molded edge appears on the underside. The salver is supported by three cast cabriole legs with pad feet.

History: The original owner was probably William Greene (1695–1758), governor of the Colony of Rhode Island and Providence Plantations from 1743 to 1758, and his wife, Catharine Greene (1698–1777), a second cousin, m. 1719.[5] By descent to their son William Greene (1731–1809), governor of Rhode Island 1778–1785, and his wife, Catharine Ray (1731–1794), m. 1758.[6] By descent through their daughter Phebe Greene (1760–1828) and her husband and first cousin, Samuel Ward (1756–1832), Lieut. Col. in the Continental Army, m. 1778.[7] Ward was named for his father, Samuel Ward (1725–1776), who was governor of Rhode Island in 1762 and 1765–68; the elder Ward was also a delegate to the Continental Congress from 1774 to 1776.[8] Probable descent through their son William Greene Ward (1802–1848) and Abby Maria Hall (1802–1887) of New York City, m. 1830; to their son Charles Henry Ward (1833–1905) and Mary Montagu Parmely (1830–1913), m. 1857; to their son Henry Merion Ward (1870–1949) and Lucy Bond Morgan of Washington, D.C., to their son Samuel Bond Ward (1905–1982) of La Plata, Maryland, and acquired by the Museum.[9]

Exhibitions and publications: MFA Annual Report, 1981–82, 21 (in which the accession number is incorrectly published as 1991.183); Kane 1998, 601.

NOTES TO THIS ENTRY ARE ON PAGE 161.

88

HURD

89

Nathaniel Hurd (1729/30–1777)

Marrow scoop

Boston, Massachusetts, about 1751–77
Gift of Nathaniel T. Dexter
1983.223

L. 7¹³⁄₁₆ in. (19.7 cm); W. ⅝ in. (1.6 cm); Wt. 1 oz 0 dwt 14 gr (32 gm)

Marks: "N [pellet] Hurd" in italics, within a cartouche shaped on top, struck on flat side of stem.

Inscriptions: None.

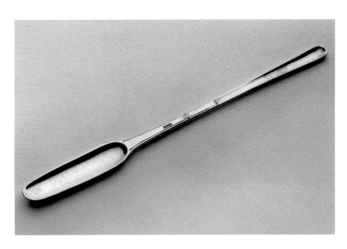

THIS SLENDER BUT STURDY implement was a popular form in England and America since colonial times. This practical tool was developed sometime after the evolution of the marrow spoon, which has an ordinary bowl with a stem in the form of a narrow scoop. The uneven widths of the scoop offered the user an advantage when extracting protein-rich marrow from bones of different diameters once these were cooked and broken open.[1]

Although marrow spoons and marrow scoops had been used in England as recently as this century, the utensil experienced a more narrow range of popularity beginning in the mid-eighteenth century. Aside from this example, several other mid- to late-eighteenth-century marrow utensils are known, including two from Massachusetts (one is by John Jackson [d. 1772] of Nantucket) and another with a stepped handle that was made by John Coburn. Examples by Hugh Wishart (about 1784–1819) and Charles Le Roux (1689–1748) have also survived, among New York makers. Two small revivals of the form took place. The first emerged in Connecticut at the beginning of the nineteenth century, with known examples by Charles Brewer (1778–1860) of Middletown and Joseph Church (1794–1876) of Hartford. The second occurred in Albany, New York, where Shepherd and Boyd produced marrow scoops notable for a lozenge design on the stem.[2]

English marrow scoops and spoons were undoubtedly used in the colonies, as proved by an example dated 1764/65 by London silversmith Thomas Tolman that was recorded in the estate of Sally Pickman Dwight.[3] Marrow scoops and spoons of unknown manufacture sometimes appeared in the public record. In a 1773 advertisement, silversmith William Whetcroft of Annapolis enumerated "soop-ladles and spoons, table, desert, marrow, and teaspoons" along with a mountain of domes-

tic goods and and personal accessories, most of which were probably imported from England. It is probable that the "Silver Table, Marrow and Tea-spoons . . . from London," offered in a 1784 South Carolina advertisement by Roger Fursdon, were also of foreign manufacture.[4] In view of such advertisements and the scarcity of documented American pieces, many of these utensils were likely imported.

Few early New England–made marrow spoons are known. Aside from the Coburn and Jackson examples, Joseph Edwards Jr. made one in 1765 for Joshua Green, and Paul Revere II sold two pairs in 1785 and 1786 to miniature painter James Dunkelly (also spelled Dunckley), according to receipts and account records.[5] Thus, the Hurd example is a rare surviving colonial New England version of this specialized utensil.

Description: The narrow utensil has a thin channel at one end that is about 3½ inches long, widening slightly to a flattened end. A deeper wider bowl on the opposite end is 2½ inches long. The stem between the two upward-facing bowls is flat, with scribed lines at each edge, and rounded below. An old repair to stem is located ⅜ of an inch to right of mark.

History: Early history unknown. Purchased earlier in this century by Hermann F. Clarke (1882–1947); purchased by Mark Bortman (1896–1967), of Massachusetts; by descent to his daughter Jane Bortman Larus. Purchased for the Museum in 1983.

Exhibitions and publications: French 1939, 52, cat. no. 306; Gourley 1965, cat. no. 117; *Silver Supplement* 1973, 35, cat. no. 60; Kane 1998, 619; *Masterpiece in Context*, Memorial Art Gallery, Rochester, New York, September 1999 to June 2001; *Porticus* 20 (2001), 62.

NOTES TO THIS ENTRY ARE ON PAGE 161.

90

David Jesse (about 1669–1705/6)

Porringer

Boston, Massachusetts, about 1700
Gift of Mr. and Mrs. Franklin H. Williams in memory of
Louise Bodine Wallace
1984.515

H. 1¹³⁄₁₆ in. (4.5 cm); W. 7³⁄₁₆ in. (18.3 cm); Diam. rim 5 ³⁄₁₆ in.
(13.1 cm); Wt. 8 oz 18 dwt 21 gr (278.2 gm)

Marks: "DI" in roman capitals within a circle, having an annulet
above and a pellet below, struck on everted rim, to right of handle.

Inscriptions: "E ✳ F" in shaded roman letters engraved on handle,
facing bowl and over effaced engraving. The scratch weight of "9-
0-0" incised later on bottom of bowl.

DAVID JESSE was apprenticed to London goldsmith Alexander
Roode in 1682 and probably immigrated to Boston shortly after
becoming freeman of the company in 1691. He married Mary
Wilson, originally of Hartford, Connecticut, about 1698. This
marriage once led scholars to believe that Jesse was born in
Hartford, but he may have met his future wife or father-in-law,
merchant Phineas Wilson, during one of the latter's business
trips to Boston.[1]

 Jesse's London training and his wife's considerable dowry
provided him with the necessary skills to establish himself in
the colonies. The quality of the surviving objects bearing his
mark—two of which were purchased by churches in Dorchester and farther afield, in Farmington, Connecticut—suggest

that his work was esteemed. The paucity of surviving examples
can be partly explained by Jesse's early death, in his mid-thirties.
In addition, he may have encountered difficulties in becoming
established in the Boston community, which was already close-
knit by his arrival in the 1690s.[2] He may have supplemented his
income by lending money, weighing hard currency, and cutting
down foreign coinage for local use. His widow and three small
children were in difficult straits by the time of his death. This
early porringer, despite the loss of the geometric handle tip, is
an important record of the silversmith's small oeuvre.

Description: The porringer, with center point, has a wide dome in
the base and a convex bulge in the side walls, rising to a slightly
everted rim. The cast handle, broken at its tip, has a pierced geometric pattern with seven voids and two open circles. A pitted area
under handle may be an unidentified mark. The bottom has been
reattached.

History: The original owners are unknown due to the effaced initials
over which appears the engraving "E ✳ F." The first known owner
was probably Elizabeth Vergoose (1694–1727), m. Thomas Fleet
(1685–1758) in 1715. For additional history, see cat. no. 23.

Exhibitions and publications: Kane 1998, 633.

NOTES TO THIS ENTRY ARE ON PAGE 161.

91

Jesse Kip (about 1660–1722)

Tankard

New York, New York, about 1700–1709
Gift of Mary Eliot Fay and Curator's Fund
1991.623

H. 2⅝ in. (6.7 cm); W. 7⅝ in. (19.3 cm); Diam. rim 4¹⁄₁₆ in. (10.3 cm);
Diam. base 4⅞ in. (12.4 cm); Wt. 24 oz 14 dwt 1 gr (768.3 gm)

Marks: "I K" within a rectangle struck below rim, to left of handle.

Inscriptions: None.

Armorials: Worn engraving of Granthan arms on a shield, emblazoned ermine a griffin segreant gules; crest a demi griffin. Swirled
foliate mantling symmetrically surrounds the whole.

OF FRENCH HUGUENOT and Dutch parentage, Jesse Kip was
born into a politically active New York family. He was the fourth
son of Jacob Hendrickzen Kip (1631–1690), who was a member
of the governor's council and provincial secretary. His mother,
Maria de la Fontaine, was the daughter of Huguenot physician

91

Johannes de la Montagne, who also served on the governor's council and was vice director of Fort Orange.[1]

During his thirty-year career, Kip was involved with a number of New York silversmiths through his extended family. John Marshall Phillips has suggested that Kip was responsible for the apprenticeships of his brother Benjamin (1678–1702) and his cousin Peter Van Imburgh (1689–1740). Cornelius Kierstede (1674–1757) and Benjamin Wynkoop (1675–1751) were his kinsman through marriage and young enough to have benefited by working in his shop.

Kip is noted in New York land and city records as a merchant and goldsmith. While engaged in public service, he was linked with two other silversmiths in the North Ward of New York. As an assessor in 1697, he served with alderman Jacob Boelen. The following year, he and Gerrit Onckelbag (1670–1732) were collectors, while Boelen remained an alderman. In 1699 Kip and Onkelbag continued as collectors, and Boelen became examin-

er.[2] Kip ceased his silversmithing activities sometime after 1709, when he left New York and joined his and his wife's family in Newtown, Long Island, where he operated a fulling mill for the thickening of fabric.[3]

This tankard may have been the smaller of two noted in the 1741 will of Edmund Kingsland, ancestor of the donor. Diminutive in scale, it is executed in the signature style of New York silversmiths, with its flat lid, crenate lip, cut-leaf ornamentation at the base, and traces of meander wirework. It is one of about fifteen examples made by Kip, who produced a variety of forms in silver, including several tankards, two-handled cups, a porringer, and several sucket forks.[4]

Description: The tankard is raised and has tapered sides and a drawn and molded base with leaf decoration. The flat lid with one shallow step and crenate lip has a scrolled thumbpiece that descends to a five-part hinge and seamed scroll handle with baluster decoration. A U-shaped air vent appears below the upper join. A cast cherub relief is applied to shield-shaped terminus, beneath which is an even-sided cross air vent. The elaborate but worn scrolled and foliated cartouche appears opposite the handle. The flange within the lid and portions of the baluster drop are clumsily repaired.

History: The engraved Grantham arms may signal a matrilineal origin, for they have not yet been linked with the known history of ownership. Family history and probate records indicate that the tankard was passed down in the matrilineal line, as first outlined in the will of Edmund Kingsland (1680–1742) of New Barbadoes, New Jersey, who beqeathed to his daughter Mary his "large Silver Tankard" and, for Anna, his "small Silver Tankard." In all likelihood, Anna's tankard was this one.[5]

The vessel probably descended from one of the two Kingsland women to their niece Elizabeth Kingsland (1734–1808), daughter of their brother Col. William Kingsland (1704–1770) and Margarreta Coerten (Courten) (1704–1756) of New Barbadoes Neck, New Jersey, m. 1732. Elizabeth Kingsland m. Josiah Hornblower (1729–1809) of Newark, New Jersey, in 1755, and the tankard passed to their daughter-in-law Mary Burnet (d. 1836) and Chief Justice Joseph Coerten Hornblower (1777–1864), m. 1803.[6] By descent to their daughter Mary Hornblower (1816–1896) and the Hon. Joseph P. Bradley (1813–1892), Justice of the United States Supreme Court, m. 1844; to their daughter Mary Burnet Bradley (b. 1845) and Henry Varnum Butler (b. 1821) of Patterson, New Jersey, m. 1870;[7] by descent to their daughter Mary Hornblower Butler and Bancroft Gherardi (1873–1941), m. 1898, who died without issue.[8] Mrs. Gherardi gave the tankard to her cousin Anne Brown Bradley (b. 1894) and Samuel Eliot of Manchester, Massachusetts, from whom it descended to their daughter Mary Eliot (Mrs. Grafton Fay), the donor.

Exhibitions and publications: Buhler 1956, 79, cat. no. 200, fig. 71.

NOTES TO THIS ENTRY ARE ON PAGE 161.

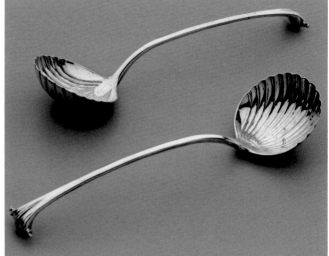

92

John Burt Lyng (d. 1785)
Pair of tablespoons

New York, New York, about 1760–80
Gift of James R. Larus, Diana L. Stone, and John M. Larus in
honor of Mrs. Llora Bortman
1985.938–39

1985.938: L. 8½ in. (21.5 cm); W. bowl 1⅞ in. (4.6 cm); Wt. 2 oz 5
dwt 2 gr (70.1 gm)

1985.939: L. 8⅝ in. (21.8 cm); W. bowl 1⅞ in. (4.6 cm); Wt. 2 oz 6
dwt 4 gr (71.8 gm)

Marks: "LYNG" within a serrated rectangle and "N-YORK" within
a rectangle struck on back of each handle.

Inscriptions: "C - R" in shaded roman letters engraved on front of
each handle tip.

See cat. no. 93.

Description: These tablespoons, with an elongated oval bowl, have
a long, rounded, upturned drop. Each downturned handle tip has a
short midrib on back.

History: Purchased by Mark Bortman (1896–1967); by descent to his
family, who made them a gift.

Exhibitions and publications: Silver Supplement 1973, 55, cat. no. 108a-b.

93

John Burt Lyng (d. 1785)
Pair of ladles

New York, New York, 1761–75
Gift of Jane Bortman Larus
1985.940–41

1985.940: L. 7³⁄₁₆ in. (18.3 cm); W. bowl 2 in. (5.2 cm); Wt. 1 oz 9 dwt
12 gr (45.9 gm)

1985.941: L. 7⅛ in. (18.1 cm); W. bowl 2 in. (5.2 cm); Wt. 1 oz 11 dwt
11 gr (48.9 gm)

Marks: "LYNG" within a serrated rectangle and "N-YORK" within
a rectangle struck on back of each handle.

Inscriptions: None.

NOTHING IS KNOWN of either John Burt Lyng's origins or his
master, but several records identify his activities in New York
City by the mid-eighteenth century. He married Magdalane
Jandine on September 11, 1759, and was identified as a silversmith on March 3, 1761, when he was made a freeman in New
York. In addition to his work as a silversmith, Lyng apparently
engaged in real estate speculation, for he owned several houses
and undeveloped lots. One house lot that he sold in 1773 was
adjacent to that of Myer Myers.[1]

Silver by John Burt Lyng is uncommon. In addition to a
range of such flatware as a marrow spoon, soup spoon, tablespoons, and ladles, existing hollowware includes a cann prob-

ably crafted shortly after he was made a freeman; a coffeepot and sugar bowl in the Rococo style; a tankard or ewer; and a small jug.[2]

The flatware in the Museum's collection offers a view to Lyng's clientele, some of whom required basic well-made utensils, as indicated by the undecorated tablespoons (cat. no. 92), with their somewhat old-fashioned roman lettering and plain, rounded handle tips. By comparison, his elegantly wrought ladles—with their delicately chased bowls, slender arching handles, and finely cast scrolled tips—are in the best Rococo style and would have appealed to moneyed families interested in fashionable tableware. The quality of their execution suggests that Lyng apprenticed with a skilled master, perhaps in England, or with a stylish New York workshop such as that of Swiss-trained Daniel Christian Fueter (w. 1720–1785), who arrived in New York in 1745.

An English origin for Lyng may be inferred from an advertisement he placed in 1781, in which he indicated that he was leaving New York for England. He offered land and his silversmithing tools for sale. It appears that he did not carry out his plans, however, but instead remained in New York, where he died in 1785.[3]

Description: The ladles have cast ribbed handles, scrolled downturned tips, and broad chased and scalloped bowls. The drop is short and square, with an upturned tip.

History: See cat. no. 92.

Exhibitions and publications: None.

NOTES TO THIS ENTRY ARE ON PAGE 161.

94

Samuel Minott (1732–1803)

Teapot

Boston, Massachusetts, about 1760
Gift of Mr. and Mrs. Walter Amory
1991.655

H. 7½ in. (19 cm); W. 8⅞ in. (22.6 cm); Diam. shoulder 4½ in. (11.4 cm); Diam. base 3⅛ in. (8 cm); Wt. 18 oz 13 dwt 20 gr (581.4 gm)

Marks: "Minott" within a rectangle struck on base, below center point.

Inscriptions: "Ex Dono Hon. di Dom. ni Thomae Hancock Armigeri" (The gift of the Honorable Sir/Mr. Thomas Hancock, armsbearer) engraved on a scrolled banner beneath armorial. Scratch price of "£ 74=16-0" incised on base.

Armorials: The Hancock arms engraved to the left of the handle display a dexter hand couped and erect gules on a chief gules three cocks; crest a phoenix or a demi-griffin erased on a torse. The whole surrounded by asymmetrical Rococo decoration of raffles, diaper patterning, scrolls, and pendant foliate decoration; swagged below.[1]

MERCHANT THOMAS HANCOCK and his wife, Lydia, daughter of bookseller Daniel Henchman, were wealthy Bostonians in the eighteenth century. Much of their silver was probably purchased abroad, but some pieces, such as three elaborate chafing dishes made by Jacob Hurd, were gifts from Lydia's father prior to her marriage in 1731.[2] At Hancock's death, he bequeathed

94

Hancock's name and the announcement of his gift are engraved on the teapot, yet the identity of its intended recipient remains uncertain. Family history maintains that the pot was a gift from Hancock to his nephew Ebenezer, who worked for his uncle upon graduation from Harvard College in 1760. That may have been one way in which the elder Hancock occasionally bestowed gifts upon Ebenezer, whose brother John had been adopted at the age of nine into the merchant's household. The teapot may be the same as one recorded with a value of $15 in the 1819 inventory of Ebenezer Hancock's estate.[4]

Similar in form, detail, and engraving to the Hancock teapot is a second example made by Minott in 1763 for tutor William Kneeland of Harvard College.[5] The symmetrical arrangement of arms and mantling amid the raffles and offset swags on the Hancock teapot are a somewhat more conservative expression of the Rococo style, which received livelier treatment in the Kneeland example.

Description: The globular apple-shaped teapot was raised upside down and tapers to a flat inset base with cast, molded, splayed foot. The low domed lid has a circular air vent; pinecone finial is riveted to lid within a small depression. A three-part hinge is set flush with the lid; an applied hingeplate is soldered underneath lid and body. The cast upper-handle socket is squared at shoulder and has leafy decoration, whereas the lower socket is round, tapering toward vessel. The wooden handle is a replacement. Chased and hatched leafy decoration appears on underside of cast S-scrolled spout having foliated, retracted upper lip; spout is affixed over strainer holes. Decorative engraving of scallop shells, fish scales, diaper patterns, and broken scrolls encircles the lid; a draped mask points toward the spout. Overlapping leaves are engraved at base of the finial; a border of stippled scrolls appears on edge of lid.

History: According to family history, the teapot was a gift from Boston merchant Thomas Hancock (1703–1764) to his nephew Ebenezer Hancock (1741–1819) and his wife, Elizabeth Lowell (b. 1744), m. 1767. The teapot descended to Ebenezer's son John Hancock (1774–1859) and Elizabeth Scott (d. London 1830/31), m. 1799.[6] It then descended matrilineally to their daughter Elizabeth Lowell Hancock (1814–1857) and Dr. Joseph Moriarty (1810–1847), m. 1839;[7] to their daughter Elizabeth Lowell Hancock Moriarty (1844–1929) and Charles Henry Wood (1843–1923), m. 1868;[8] to their daughter Mary Elizabeth Wood (b. about 1876) and George Albert Cole (b. 1877), m. 1901;[9] to their daughter Elizabeth Lowell Hancock Cole (1902–1983) and Walter Amory Jr. (1899–1937), m. 1923.[10] The teapot passed to their son Walter Amory (b. 1924) and his wife, Shirley Gay Waterman (b. 1923), m. 1947, the donors.[11]

Exhibitions and publications: Kane 1998, 697.

NOTES TO THIS ENTRY ARE ON PAGE 162.

two silver cups to the church in Lexington where his father John was minister, and two silver flagons to the Brattle Street Church.[3] The three communion plates that Hancock gave to the Brattle Church in 1764 were made and engraved with the family arms by Minott shortly after he made this teapot.

along with that of another silversmith is considered an indicator of a collaborative or retail arrangement, although the exact nature of such relationships is unclear. Minott produced some 170 pieces of silver before the Revolution, when his Loyalist sympathies ended his career.[1]

Description: The tall raised beaker has an inverted bell form, with a stepped and splayed foot and applied foot ring.

History: The donor, Abigail Parker (about 1690–1767), was the daughter of Isaac and Mary (Parker) Parker. Her will, dated April 7, 1767, and proved May 5, 1767, provided £5 6s. 3d. "for some utensil for the use of said Church," presumably this beaker.[2]

Exhibitions and publications: Kane 1998, 690; see also appendix 8.

NOTES TO THIS ENTRY ARE ON PAGE 162.

96

Attributed to Gideon Myrick (b. after 1735–d. about 1760)

Spoon

Possibly Eastham, Massachusetts, about 1755–60
Gift in memory of Ruth P. and Pauline Dennis
1990.349

L. 8 in. (20.3 cm); W. bowl 1⅝ in. (4.1 cm); Wt. 1 oz 12 dwt 10 gr (50.4 gm)

Marks: "G : M" within a rectangle struck on back of stem.

Inscriptions: "I * N / E * B" in roman letters engraved on back of handle, near tip.

95

Samuel Minott (1732–1803)

Beaker

Boston, Massachusetts, 1768
Gift of the First Church in Newton
1973.21

H. 5⁵⁄₁₆ in. (13.5 cm); Diam. rim 4³⁄₁₆ in. (10.7 cm); Diam. foot 3⅛ in. (7.9 cm); Wt. 11 oz 3 dwt 20 gr (348.1 gm)

Marks: "S [pellet] M" in roman letters within a rectangle struck below center point.

Inscriptions: "The Gift of Miss Abigal Parker / to the Church of Chrift in Newton / 1768" in script engraved below lip. Scribed guidelines are faintly visible.

MINOTT WAS ONE of the most successful silversmiths of his day. In addition to being a productive craftsman, he was adept at retailing the works of others. Silver that carries his mark

The sparse record of Gideon Myrick's short life notes that "he was a goldsmith by trade; went to sea, fell overboard in the night and was drowned." Although no birth record exists, he was probably born between 1734 and 1741 to Elizabeth Osborne (1715–1798) and Capt. William Myrick (d. 1742) of Eastham, on Cape Cod, who married in 1734/35.[1]

This spoon is one of only four known to carry the "G : M" mark, which has recently been ascribed to Myrick.[2]

Description: The midrib spoon with upturned tip has a handle that is rectangular in section; it terminates in a rounded and slashed drop on elliptical bowl.

History: Although the engraved initials are unidentified, this spoon descended to the donors along with an earlier spoon (1990.348) that John Coney made for the Gibbs/Shrimpton/Hastings families of Boston and Salem (see cat. no. 29).[3]

Exhibitions and publications: Brian Cullity, *'A Cubberd, Four Joyne Stools & Other Smalle Thinges': The Material Culture of Plymouth Colony and Silver and Silversmiths of Plymouth, Cape Cod & Nantucket* (Sandwich, Mass.: Heritage Plantation of Sandwich, 1994), 159–60, cat. no. 7; Kane 1998, 725–26.

NOTES TO THIS ENTRY ARE ON PAGE 162.

97

John Noyes (1674–1749)

Tankard

Boston, Massachusetts, about 1710–20
Bequest of Mrs. Carle R. Hayward
1983.382

H. 7³⁄₁₆ in. (18.3 cm); W. 7¹¹⁄₁₆ in. (19.6 cm); Diam. rim 4¼ in. (10.8 cm); Diam. base 5³⁄₁₆ in. (13.1 cm); Wt. 23 oz 19 dwt 12 gr (745.7 gm)

Marks: "IN" in roman capitals within an oval struck on top of lid at center, at center of base, and to left of handle.

Inscriptions: "David Parker. / BORN IN / West Barnstable Mass. / 1740. / DIED 1813. Hannah . Parker . Howland . / BORN 1778 / DIED 1862." in Gothic, script, italic, and block letters, and enlivened with flourishes, engraved later on body, opposite handle. "Hannah" engraved over an effaced area on body.

JOHN NOYES was the son of a minister and a member of the Third, or Old South, Church and later a founder of the Brattle Street Church. He was well known to diarist Samuel Sewall, who, along with the silversmith, his father, and his brother Oli-

ver Noyes, was a member of the Ancient and Honorable Artillery Company. Sewall awarded a silver cup to John Noyes for his superior marksmanship during a training day held by the company in May 1702.[1]

In 1691 Sewall had recorded in his diary that Noyes had accepted borax on behalf of Jeremiah Dummer. It is unclear why Sewall would have brought borax, a material used as flux in silversmithing, to Dummer. However, in recording its receipt, Sewall helped document Noyes's apprenticeship by placing him in Dummer's employ at about age seventeen.[2]

Less than thirty objects have survived bearing Noyes's mark. Yet, his level of accomplishment is clear from the variety of forms he fashioned—candlesticks, forks, beakers, and salvers—all of which demonstrate a high degree of skill in casting, decorative details, and finishing. This tankard was one of at least nine he made; many carry the dolphin-and-mask thumbpiece on a flat-topped lid. This thumbpiece is identical to one on a simpler example in the Museum's collection, which has a plain shield-shaped terminal.[3] When inventoried in the

1813 estate of David Parker, Esq., the first known owner, this tankard was valued at $30. It was the only piece of silver hollowware recorded in Parker's estate, along with seven silver spoons and twelve teaspoons.[4]

Description: The raised straight-sided tankard tapers inward from base to lip. The vessel displays a wide molded baseband, with no visible center point, and rises to applied, molded, slightly everted lip. The flat-topped stepped lid with inner flange bears two pairs of scored decoration at the wide crenate brim. A pair of dolphins flanking a fierce grotesque mask form the cast thumbpiece; wavy line decoration has been applied on the hinge plate before and after the five-part hinge. Prominent wear marks are visible on the seamed scroll handle as a result of contact with the thumbpiece. The handle is attached at its upper section with a long rattail drop and at its lower section with an oval disk. Below the cherub terminal is an oval air vent. The tankard has been repaired in two areas to the right of the handle, as evidenced by solder marks.

History: The original owner was probably David Parker (1699/ 1700/1–1788) of Barnstable, Massachusetts. It likely passed to his namesake, David Parker (1740–1813), of Barnstable, by his second wife, Mercy Crosby (1703–1785). According to the engraved inscription, and corroborated by Parker's surviving will, the tankard was passed to his daughter Hannah Parker (1778–1862), wife of Jabez Howland (1775–1848), m. 1797.[5] By descent to their daughter Hannah Howland (1806–1833), m. Ambrose Haywood in 1833; by descent to their son Albert Francis Hayward (1842–1873) and Louise Miranda Belden (1846–1911), m. 1873; to their son Carle Reed Hayward (1880–1965) and the donor, his widow, Mary Murray (1889–1983), m. 1915.[6]

Exhibitions and publications: Kane 1998, 738.

NOTES TO THIS ENTRY ARE ON PAGE 162.

98

Daniel Parker (1726–1785)

Cann

Boston, Massachusetts, about 1750–60
Gift of the Misses Aimée and Rosamund Lamb
67.1072

H. 5³⁄₁₆ in. (13.2 cm); W. 5⁵⁄₁₆ in. (13.5 cm); Diam. rim 3¼ in. (8.2 cm); Diam. base 3⁵⁄₁₆ in. (8.4 cm); Wt. 10 oz 7 dwt 1 gr (322 gm)

Marks: "D [pellet] PARKER" in roman letters overstruck three times on base, above center point.

Inscriptions: None.

THIS CANN is one of at least seven made by patriot and silversmith Daniel Parker, most of which have been dated to the 1760s and 1770s.[1] This example may be among the earliest, as it has a simple, hollow scroll handle and an unadorned thumbgrip, in contrast to most others, which have double-scrolled handles and acanthus-leaf thumbgrips.

Description: The raised tulip-shaped vessel is soldered to a cast splayed foot with applied foot ring. An applied molded rim projects a noticeable profile. The cast two-part scrolled handle has a triple drop at the upper joint and an elliptical disk below. A crescent-shaped air vent appears below the handle. This cann has seen considerable use, as indicated by the fine network of surface wear, small random indentations, and noticeable list away from the handle. Several stress cracks are visible on the interior.

History: Although the original owner is unknown, the cann descended in the donors' Boston family along with numerous examples of eighteenth-century paintings, glass, furniture, and silver.

Exhibitions and publications: Kane 1998, 755.

NOTE TO THIS ENTRY IS ON PAGE 162.

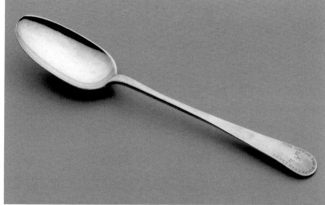

99

Daniel Parker (1726–1785)

Pair of tablespoons

Boston, Massachusetts, about 1750–70
Gift of Mrs. James R. Carter
1977.738–39

1977.738: L. 7⅞ in. (20 cm); W. bowl 1¾ in. (4.5 cm); Wt. 1 oz 12 dwt 24 gr (51.3 gm)

1977.739: L. 9⁷⁄₁₆ in. (24 cm); W. bowl 1¾ in. (4.5 cm); Wt. 1 oz 15 dwt 9 gr (55 gm)

Marks: "D [pellet] PARKER" in roman letters within a rectangle struck on back of each stem.

Inscriptions: "I ⋆ B / to / L ⋆ B" engraved on back of each handle tip.

TWO OF ABOUT THIRTY surviving spoons (see cat. no. 100) known by Parker (some of which also bear the mark of Stephen Emery), these examples were probably owned by a family whose last name started with the letter *B.* Parker also made a caster engraved "LB," but the family name is unknown.[1]

Description: The spoons have an upturned handle tip with short midrib and rectangular stem, ending in an elliptical bowl. The back of each bowl has a broad drop with worn webbed-shell decoration.

History: History unknown prior to their gift to the Museum.

Exhibitions and publications: Kane 1998, 757.

NOTE TO THIS ENTRY IS ON PAGE 162.

100

Daniel Parker (1726–1785)

Tablespoon

Boston, Massachusetts, 1774
Gift of Miss Martha May Eliot and Miss Abigail Adams Eliot
1971.319

L. 8½ in. (21.7 cm); W. bowl 1⅝ in. (4.1 cm); Wt. 1 oz 16 dwt 13 gr (56.8 gm)

Marks: "D [pellet] PARKER" in roman letters within rectangle struck on back of stem.

Inscriptions: "THE GIFT OF THE DORCHESTER LADYS" in roman letters engraved on perimeter of handle tip. "E / M = L" engraved at center of handle tip. "1774" inscribed on back of handle, below midrib.

THIS SPOON, the survivor of six given to the Rev. Moses Everett by the "Dorchester Ladies," presumably a church group affiliated with First Church, Dorchester, was probably intended as a wedding gift. He was married two months after his arrival at the Dorchester church.

Description: The spoon has a downturned rounded handle tip with short midrib on back and a rectangular stem. A rounded drop and worn eleven-ribbed shell decoration appear on back of the elliptical bowl.

History: Presented by the "Ladies of Dorchester," members of First Parish, Dorchester, to the Rev. Moses Everett (1750–1813) and his bride-to-be, Lucy Balch (1748–1776), m. November 24, 1774. By descent to Everett's son Francis Everett (1795–1835), the child of his third wife, Hannah Clap (also Clapp) (1759–1819), and thence to his daughter Mary C. Everett (1824–post 1901) and William Page Barnard (1812–1858), m. 1854.[1] Made a gift by Mary C. Everett to "Mr. Eliot," presumably the Rev. Christopher Rhodes Eliot, pastor of the First Church, Dorchester, about 1888; by descent to his daughters, the donors.[2]

Exhibitions and publications: Kane 1998, 757.

NOTES TO THIS ENTRY ARE ON PAGE 162.

101

Samuel Parmelee (1737–1807)

Cann

Guilford, Connecticut, 1756–70
Gift of Mrs. Samuel Nickerson in memory of Samuel Mayo Nickerson
1977.768

H. 5⅞ in. (15.1 cm); W. 5⅞ in. (14.9 cm); Diam. rim 3³⁄₁₆ in. (8.1 cm); Diam. foot 3¹¹⁄₁₆ in. (9.4 cm); Wt. 13 oz 9 dwt 16 gr (419.4 gm)

Marks: "S [pellet] P" in a shaped cartouche struck on base, below center point.

Inscriptions: "B / I * E" in shaded roman letters engraved over center point.

AFTER TRAINING WITH an unknown smith, perhaps in nearby New Haven, Connecticut, Parmelee spent his silversmithing career in the town of Guilford, his birthplace. From about 1756 until 1770, when he began his service as a lieutenant in the Seventh Regiment during the Revolutionary War, Parmelee produced a small but fine assortment of Georgian and Rococo forms, beginning with his earliest dated work, a heart-shaped engraved pendant dated 1756.[1] His other silver works include three-legged creamers and salts, shell-backed spoons, and a snuffbox of tortoiseshell and silver. Prestigious commissions from the First Church of Guilford include a baptismal basin and beaker. Following the war, he may have sold some jewelry but little or no hollowware. The few tools enumerated in an inventory of his estate in 1807 suggest that by that date, Parmelee had long since ceased silversmithing.[2]

This cann is one of at least two made by Parmelee. Nearly identical in weight and size, they also share a double-scroll handle with acanthus thumbgrip. The similarly awkward treatment of these pear-shaped vessels, each perched on a tall splayed foot with a thinly applied lip molding, indicate that they were probably made within a short time of each other.[3]

Description: The raised tulip-shaped vessel has a broad base that tapers inward near upper join of handle before expanding to a small mouth with thin molding. The cast splayed foot is thickly soldered to the body. A cast double-scroll handle with acanthus leaf at thumbgrip and tendril near teminus is soldered directly to the vessel; a circular air vent is beneath the terminus. At the foot of the vessel, opposite the handle, is a large poorly executed repair to a crack about 2 inches (5.1 cm) long.

History: Unknown prior to the donor's gift to the Museum.

Exhibitions and publications: None.

NOTES TO THIS ENTRY ARE ON PAGE 162.

102

Probably by John Patterson
(active about 1750)

Standing cup

Probably Annapolis, Maryland, about 1750
Marion E. Davis Fund
68.57

H. 6¹³⁄₁₆ in. (17.2 cm); Diam. rim 3⁷⁄₁₆ in. (8.8 cm); Diam. base 3⁵⁄₁₆ in. (8.4 cm); Wt. 7 oz 8 dwt 4 gr (230.4 gm)

Marks: "I [pellet] P" in roman letters, within a rectangle, struck under base and less distinctly on rim.

Inscriptions: None.

THIS UNUSUAL DRINKING CUP, with its coconut bowl and silver mounts, was probably made by John Patterson of Annapolis, Maryland. He may be the maker who advertised in the

Maryland Gazette on January 23, 1751, stating his intention of "departing this Province by the 19th of March." A standing cup of similar form and materials that carries the "I [pellet] P" mark is in a private collection. A circular spirit lamp bearing the engraved inscription "JP / IP / Annapolis / 1751" is the only other object attributed to Patterson.[1]

There is a European tradition of fashioning mounts for exotic objects found in nature or for prized examples of Chinese porcelain, the latter considered more valuable than gold. Although extremely rare in the colonies, one such known example is a sugar dish made from an ostrich egg, which was created for Andrew Oliver by Paul Revere in 1764.[2]

In preconquest South America, nuts and gourds occasionally served as vessels. The Spanish later adapted these simple cups by adding European-style silver mounts. The English made drinking cups with coconuts as early as 1670; indeed, one known unmarked "coco-nut goblet" with a rim is similar to the Patterson example. In North America, coconuts were easier to procure than ostrich eggs or porcelain, and a few documented New York examples are known from published sources. One cup attributed to John Cluet (w. 1725–1787?) of the Hudson River valley is similar to the Patterson cup in its use of a decorated border at the juncture with the stem. Such a device no doubt served as an anchor for the coconut bowl. This cup has a lid with a large ringlike finial reminiscent of patens and suggesting ecclesiastical use. Thomas Hammersley (1727–1781) produced an elegantly carved coconut sugar bowl mounted on three silver hoof feet with shell knees and a silver rim and lid. The scalloped edge beneath the Hammersley rim is nearly identical to that found on the Patterson cup. Last, a domed vessel with finely carved Masonic symbols, made by William Thompson (w. 1809–1845), also survives.[3]

Description: The silver-mounted coconut or other tropical nut has an applied concave silver rim with band. A scalloped decorative edge below the rim is secured to the nut in two places. A beaded and gadrooned foot with an applied foot rim rises to a seamed stem having a similar band of applied beading. A scalloped edging similar to that found at the lip is attached to the base.

History: Early history unknown. Purchased from Mr. Everett A. Young, Coes and Young, Boston, Massachusetts.

Exhibtions and publications: None.

NOTES TO THIS ENTRY ARE ON PAGE 162.

103

Elias Pelletreau (1726–1810)

Teapot

Southhampton, Long Island, New York, 1750–75
Gift of Nathaniel T. Dexter
1997.260

H. 6¹⁵⁄₁₆ in. (17.6 cm); Diam. shoulder 5 in. (12.7 cm); Diam. foot 3¹⁄₁₆ in. (7.7 cm); Wt. 19 oz 18 dwt 16 gr (620 gm)

Marks: "EP" in roman letters within a square struck on base, over center point.

Inscriptions: "H / I★C" engraved on base, above mark.

INFORMATION ABOUT Elias Pelletreau is particularly abundant due to the survival of his account books and shop in Southampton. Of French Huguenot descent, Pelletreau was apprenticed to Simeon Soumaine of New York. His indenture of apprenticeship survives, proving a seven-year term of service beginning in

January 1741. Following that, Pelletreau remained in New York City, where he became a freeman in 1750. Shortly thereafter, he returned to Southampton, where he lived and worked for the rest of his life, except briefly during the American Revolution, when he relocated to Connecticut.[1]

Pelletreau's account books record orders for at least seventeen teapots. Despite the large number, few survive. One recently discovered example, whose appearance is identical to this one, was made by the silversmith for his own use and later given to his daughter Jane, probably upon her marriage to Judge Pliny Hillyer of Simsbury, Connecticut.[2] Aside from these two teapots, only two others are known.[3]

The delicate engraving around the shoulder of this otherwise unadorned vessel is in keeping with the plainer style that

Pelletreau and his clients apparently preferred. However, the finely cast and finished spout and sockets, as well as the unusually large chased finial, evoke the prevalent Rococo style.

Description: The inverted pear-style teapot has a molded and splayed foot with applied foot rim. The tall domed lid with air hole near finial has an inset three-part hinge. The broadly scalloped cast spout has prominent leafage on its retracted lip. The leafy upper socket, with side scroll and slender lower socket, is pinned into circular wooden handles, and both are scored at edge. Scalloped and foliated engraved decoration, interspersed with four lozenge-shaped elements, appears around the shoulder. The cast and chased finial is slightly tipped. The handle is replaced; a repair was made to the hinge and possibly another on the side, to right of handle.

History: Original owner unknown. Inherited by the donor from his mother, Constance V. R. Dexter, on February 17, 1976, and later made a gift to the museum.

Exhibitions and publications: Dean F. Failey, with Robert J. Hefner and Susan E. Klaffky, "A Checklist of the Exhibition," *Long Island Is My Nation: The Decorative Arts & Craftsmen, 1640–1830* (Setauket, N.Y.: Society for the Preservation of Long Island Antiquities, 1976), cat. 81.

NOTES TO THIS ENTRY ARE ON PAGE 162.

104

Elias Pelletreau (1726–1810)

Tankard

Southhampton, Long Island, New York, about 1760–80
Gift of Ada Belle Winthrop-King
1993.128

H. 6¹¹⁄₁₆ in. (16.9 cm); W. 7⅞ in. (20 cm); Diam. rim 4³⁄₁₆ in. (10.6 cm); Diam. base 5⁵⁄₁₆ in. (13.5 cm); Wt. 31 oz 18 dwt 18 gr (993.4 gm)

Marks: "EP" in roman capitals within a rectangle struck to left and right of handle.

Inscriptions: "TSB" or "TLB" conjoined in sprigged script engraved on lid. "W" in shaded Gothic letter engraved on body, opposite handle. Scratch weight of "32 oz - 17 dwt 14 g [m?]" and "37 dol" incised lightly on base.

Armorials: An engraving of the Winthrop crest, centered on the vessel to the right and left of the handle, is displayed on a mound vert, a hare courant ppr.[1]

ACCORDING TO THE DONOR, this tankard descended in the Winthrop family of Massachusetts, in the line established by John Winthrop (1588–1649), first governor of the Massachu-

setts Bay Colony.[2] If so, the family crest was probably engraved about the time the tankard was made, when such devices were popular. The Gothic letter *W*, presumably for Winthrop, was probably added sometime in the mid- to late nineteenth century. The sprigged script initials "TSB" or "TLB" have yet to be explained; also unknown is how the work of a Long Island silversmith found its way into a Massachusetts family with no evident ties to that region. The Winthrop family ownership can be supported only by the fact that the population of eastern Long Island was of English stock, much of it by way of New England.[3]

Dating the tankard sylistically is hampered by Pelletreau's preference for making silver in a generally conservative style to suit his Long Island patrons. The majority of his known tankards had flat-topped lids; domed examples are noted only four times in his meticulously maintained account books. Therefore, this example was conceivably made between 1760 and 1798, the years during which he recorded orders for such forms.[4]

A possible aid in dating the tankard is found in the scratch price of $37. Written in an eighteenth-century hand contemporaneous with that of the scratch weight, the inscription could be interpreted as an indication that the tankard was fashioned sometime after 1792, the year in which the Coinage Act established the dollar as a standard monetary unit, although that date seems late.

Description: The raised body has a center point in the base and slightly tapering sides. A large stepped molding is soldered to base, and a smaller molding with score markings appears at lip. The lid, with center point appearing on both sides, has broad brim with scored edge and a crenate lip opposite and flanking handle. The flat-top lid has a wide and narrow step rising from the rim. A cast scrolled thumbpiece and five-part hinge lead to an extended baluster-shaped cast decoration on a seamed scrolled handle, which is attached to body with a rounded drop having a U-shaped air vent. The handle ends in a plain oval terminal, beneath which is an X-shaped air vent. The base is scored with concentric circles evenly spaced at quarter-inch intervals. A spout was added at an unknown date but later removed. The spout has been retained as an artifact of the passing fashion for making pitchers out of tankards; see cat. no. 17. New solder on the base was probably added when tankard was despouted.

History: According to donor, the tankard descended in the Winthrop family of Massachusetts.

Exhibition and publications: None known.

NOTES TO THIS ENTRY ARE ON PAGE 163.

105

Elias Pelletreau (1726–1810)

Tankard

Southampton, Long Island, New York, 1765
Bequest of Katharine Lane Weems
1989.515

H. 7⅝ in. (19.4 cm); W. 8⅜ in. (21.3 cm); Diam. rim 4¾ in. (12 cm); Diam. base 5¹¹⁄₁₆ in. (14.2 cm); Wt. 35 oz 12 dwt 10 gr (1107.9 gm)

Marks: "E P" in roman letters within a rectangle struck below lip, to right and left of handle.

Inscriptions: "C ⋆ F" engraved on handle, below baluster decoration. Scratch weight of "36 / oz" incised on base; "88691" engraved later above.

PELLETREAU WAS ESPECIALLY SUCCESSFUL in selling his work to a geographically dispersed population, ranging from Connecticut and New Jersey to the environs of New York, including his native Long Island. He was aided by his sons John and

Elias Jr. and by a grandson, William Smith Pelletreau. Dean Failey has noted that Pelletreau's account books recorded the sale of fifty-seven tankards, most of which had broad and plain bodies, a flat-topped lid, rigorous base molding, and cast scrolled thumbpieces, as found in both this example and the preceding Winthrop family vessel (cat. no. 104).[1]

This tankard, engraved "C ⋆ F," links three Long Island families distinguished by patriotic service during the American Revolution and for their patronage of this successful local silversmith. Pelletreau made silver for Charity Floyd, sister of William Floyd (1734–1821), a signer of the Declaration of Independence, and wife of Yale-educated Ezra L'Hommedieu, who was a participant in the New York Provincial Congress, delegate to the Continental Congress, and a framer of the Constitution of 1777. Pelletreau also made two canns for William Floyd's daughter Mary (1763–1805), the first wife of soldier and congressman Benjamin Tallmadge (1754–1835).[2]

Description: The broad tankard has slightly tapering sides, with a large stepped molding applied to the base and a proportionately smaller molding, with two narrow scored bands, at lip. The broad lid has a scored edge and a crenate edge opposite the handle and to each side of the hingeplate. The flat-top lid is lightly scored with several concentric circles and has a narrow and wider step that rises from the flange. The cast thumbpiece is scrolled on the side facing the lid. A five-part hinge leads to a baluster-shaped decoration on the raised, seamed, scroll handle, which ends in a plain oval terminus, with a round air vent below. The handle is attached to the body at the top with a short, wide rattail that has a circular air vent at tip. A small round disk attaches the lower handle section to body, above baseband.

History: The tankard was probably made for Charity Floyd (1739/40–1785) about the time of her 1765 marriage to the Hon. Ezra L'Hommedieu (1734–1811), whose portrait by Ralph Earl is in the Museum's collection.[3] The tankard passed to his daughter by his second marriage to Mary Catherine Havens, Mary Catherine L'Hommedieu (1806–1838), m. Samuel Smith Gardiner (1789–1859) of Shelter Island, New York, in 1823. By descent to their daughter Frances Eliza Gardiner (1832–1876) and George Martin Lane (1824–1897), professor of Latin at Harvard College, m. 1857.[4] The tankard passed to their son Gardiner Martin Lane (1859–1914), president of the Museum of Fine Arts, Boston, from 1907 until his death in 1914, and Emma Louise Gildersleeve (1872–1954), m. 1898; thence to their daughter, the *animalier* Katharine Lane Weems (Mrs. F. Carrington Weems) (1899–1989), whose many sculptures are in the Museum's collection.[5]

Exhibitions and publications: Marvin D. Schwarz and Arthur Pulos, *Elias Pelletreau, Long Island Silversmith and His Sources of Design* (Brooklyn, N.Y.: Brooklyn Museum, 1959), fig. 10; *MFA Annual Report* 1989–90, 21.

NOTES TO THIS ENTRY ARE ON PAGE 163.

106

John Potwine (about 1698–1792)

Tankard

Boston, Massachusetts, about 1730–34
Gift of Edwin and Helen Crawford
1993.643

H. 7¹³⁄₁₆ in. (19.7 cm); W. 7 in. (17.8 cm); Diam. rim 3⅞ in. (10 cm); Diam. base 4¹¹⁄₁₆ in. (12 cm); Wt. 25 oz 1 dwt 21 gr (780.5 gm)

Marks: "I:Potwine" in script, within a rectangular cartouche with a shaped top, struck to left of handle and on lid.

Inscriptions: "Presented / to / Joseph Tolman / by his Father / 1749" in script engraved later on body opposite handle. "To Joseph Tolman Hartt / in 1859 / To Joseph Tolman Hartt Jr. / Oct. 23d 1868" engraved below midband. Scratch weight of "26 2 0" incised twice on base.

JOHN POTWINE, son of a Huguenot physician, may have become apprenticed to William Cowell Sr. due to physical proximity as well as friendship. It is known that the two families lived adjacent to each other; Joseph Cowell, probably William Cowell Sr.'s uncle, witnessed the will of Potwine's father, and both families attended the Brattle Street Church. Potwine probably began working independently in Boston from about 1719 until his departure in 1734 for Hartford, Connecticut.[1]

In Boston, Potwine enjoyed patronage from South Church as well as area churches in Weston and Charlestown and prominent mercantile families, including those of Ebenezer and Mary (Edwards) Storer and Edward and Abigail (Coney) Bromfield. Potwine also sold general goods, some of which were purchased from merchant Peter Faneuil. Among his political customers were Roger Wolcott (1679–1767), governor of Connecticut from 1750 to 1754, and Maj. William Pynchon (1739–1808) of Springfield, Massachusetts, for whom he made a sword and cann, respectively.[2]

This tankard descended in the Tolman/Hartt family of Dorchester and Scituate, Massachusetts; it probably dates to the second quarter of the eighteenth century, for it exhibits a somewhat shorter profile and smaller dome than appear in classic Boston tankards made during the middle and latter part of the century. It is similar to several others by Potwine that have been dated to the 1730s.[3] Assuming that the inscription refers to the first owner, the tankard was probably made before Potwine left Boston in 1734.

Description: A straight-sided raised vessel with center point on base, the tankard tapers inward toward lip, with applied and stepped base molding, one midband soldered above lower handle juncture, and flared molding at lip. The domed and stepped lid has a reel-turned finial and is scored at lip and once at its downturned edge. It has a cast scrolled thumbpiece, five-part hinge, and molded drop hinge-plate. The seamed scroll handle is attached at upper juncture with a broad drop having three horizontal bands; a circular disk has been applied to lower juncture. Prominent dents on handle reveal consistent contact with the thumbpiece. Beneath the domed terminal is a crescent-shaped air vent.

History: The inscription was added years later, although it may identify the original owners. The text identifies the patrilineal owners, beginning with Benjamin Tolman (b. 1676) of Dorchester and later Scituate, Massachusetts, who gave the tankard to his son Joseph (b. 1715/16) in 1749.[4] Joseph Tolman m. Bertha May (Mary) Turner (b. 1717) of Scituate in 1738. The tankard descended to their son Joseph (1750–1831) of the same town, m. Bethiah Turner (1753–1846) in 1771; to their daughter Mary Turner Tolman (1792/93–1876) and Samuel Hartt (1786–1860), m. 1813. Samuel Hartt was the third son of Edmund Hartt (1744–1824), noted shipbuilder of the U.S.S. *Constitution* (1812). To their sixth son, Joseph Tolman Hartt (1830–1888), and Nellie L. Brownell (1847–1925), m. 1867; to their son Joseph Tolman Hartt Jr. (1868–1941)[5] of Scituate and Mary Agnes Moore (1880–1980) of Norwood, m. 1920. By descent to a daughter of Mary Agnes Moore, Alice Mary (Hamilton) Hartt (1906–1987), m. Edwin A. Crawford in 1932; to their son Edwin A. Crawford Jr. (b. 1934), the donor, and Helen Feaver of Westwood, m. 1956.[6]

Exhibitions and publications: Kane 1998, 783.

NOTES TO THIS ENTRY ARE ON PAGE 163.

107

Probably by Paul Revere I (1702–1754)

Creampot

Boston, Massachusetts, about 1727
Gift of Frances Lowell Hunsaker, Beatrice Hardcastle Magruder, and Christina Lowell Brazelton in memory of their father Alfred Putnam Lowell
1991.1022

H. 4⅝₆ in. (11 cm); W. 3¹¹⁄₁₆ in. (9.4 cm); D. 2⅝ in. (6.7 cm); Wt. 4 oz 9 dwt 15 gr (139.4 gm)

Marks: "P [pellet] REVERE" in roman letters struck on base, above center point.

Inscriptions: "M. S. L." in large shaded roman capital letters engraved later underneath creampot; scratch weight of "4 oz 12" incised above mark.

THE "P [PELLET] REVERE" mark in roman letters was used by Paul Revere I near the end of his life and during the early career of Paul Revere II. Stylistically, few differences can be discerned between the work of father and son during this period. This creamer illustrates the point, for both men produced forms with similar profiles, trifid feet, and double-scroll strap handles.[1] The younger Revere undoubtedly used casts from his father's workshop, hence the similar results, especially in the early years of his career.

The likely owner of the creamer was Elizabeth Cutt (1709–1805), who married first in 1727 and again in 1758. In view of a Paul Revere I teapot (cat. no. 108) that Cutt probably acquired during her first marriage, it is probable that Revere senior made this creamer as well.

Description: The raised, bulbous, gourd-shaped vessel tapers upward to scalloped rim and attached spout. The cast double-scroll handle with thumbgrip is attached at rim and below, directly to body. Three cast cabriole legs with trifid feet support the creampot.

History: Working backward in time from the initials "M. S. L.," said to be for Mary Traill Spence Lowell (1810–1898), it is likely that the first owner was Elizabeth Cutt (or Cutts) (1709–1805), probably after her first marriage in 1727 to the Rev. Joseph Whipple (1701–1757).[2] For the rest of the line of descent, see cat. no. 84.

Exhibitions and publications:; Fairbanks 1975, cat. no. 367; *Ellis Memorial* 1984, 31, no. 12; Kane 1998, 813.

NOTES TO THIS ENTRY ARE ON PAGE 163.

108

Paul Revere I (1702–1754)
Teapot

Boston, Massachusetts, about 1727
Gift of Frances Lowell Hunsaker, Beatrice Hardcastle Magruder, and Christina Lowell Brazelton in memory of their father Alfred Putnam Lowell
1991.790

108

H. 5¹¹⁄₁₆ in. (14.6 cm); W. 8¹¹⁄₁₆ in. (22.2 cm); Diam. shoulder 4¹⁵⁄₁₆ in. (12.5 cm); Diam. foot 3⅜ in. (8.5 cm); Wt. 19 oz 19 dwt 11 gr (621.2 gm)

Marks: "P [pellet] REVERE" in roman letters within a rectangle struck on bottom of teapot, above center point.

Inscriptions: Scratch weight of "oz /18 : ¾" and, in another hand, "oz w / 18 - 12" on bottom.

THIS TEAPOT'S DISTINCTLY GLOBULAR SHAPE and finely engraved scroll and bellflower decoration at the shoulder are stylistically within the oeuvre of Revere I and unlike any produced by the son.[1]

Description: The globular vessel was raised and then turned upside down so that the original base could be cut out and remade as a lid. A flat three-part hinge and applied ring seated within the rim ensure that the lid is flush with the vessel exterior; a cast and chased conical pineapple finial is pinned at the center of the lid, near a small air vent. The original open rim of the raised form has been closed with a base that has been let in and soldered in place.

The replaced silver and ivory handle is set into an existing upper socket having a scored edge and stylized foliate decoration. The reverse-curved spout is affixed over strainer holes; attenuated baluster decoration appears below spout; twelve panels with scalloped edges form the lower portion of the spout, and the curved upper portion terminates in foliate decoration on retracted upper lip. A broad, splayed cast foot with applied foot ring is soldered to the body.

A broad band of engraving at the shoulder consists of large shells at sides and mask facing spout, interspersed with diaper fields, broken scrolls, and foliate decoration. A narrow border around the edge of the lid has scallop decoration, with a sixteen-point flower at center.

History: It is likely that the first owner was Elizabeth Cutts (1709–1805), who acquired the teapot about the time of her first marriage in 1727 to the Rev. Joseph Whipple (1701–1757). The teapot could also have been brought into the marriage by Whipple, or by Cutts's second husband, the Rev. John Lowell (1704–1767).[2] For the history of descent to the donors, see cat. no. 84.

Exhibitions and publications: Ellis Memorial 1984, 34, no. 31; Kane 1998, 852.

NOTES TO THIS ENTRY ARE ON PAGE 163.

109

Paul Revere I (1702–1754)
Teapot

Boston, Massachusetts, about 1730
Gift of Mrs. George P. Montgomery
1972.122

H. 5¹³⁄₁₆ in. (14.8 cm); W. 9⅜ in. (24 cm); Diam. shoulder 4¾ in. (12 cm); Diam. foot 3¼ in. (8.3 cm); Diam. 4¹³⁄₁₆ in. (12.3 cm); Wt. 17 oz 10 dwt 6 gr (544.7 gm)

Marks: "P [pellet] Revere" in italics and within a rectangle struck on bottom, above center point.

Inscriptions: Scratch weight of "17: oz" in a contemporaneous hand and a later notation of "16 = 15" scratched on bottom.

THIS HANDSOME TEAPOT BY PAUL REVERE I carries the restrained engraving and globular, or apple-shaped, profile typical of Boston teapots from the 1730s through the 1750s. It is one of three in the Museum's collection, from a total of four that Revere I is believed to have made.[1] Its spout is original, unlike the one on the Foster/Hutchinson family teapot published by Kathryn C. Buhler, which was "changed within the memory of the donor."[2] The engraving on both is similar, but this teapot has a condensed design that is handled with a far more delicate touch than the broadly conceived scrolls and leafage on the Foster teapot. The 1730 marriage date of the original owners and the italic text of the "P [pellet] Revere" mark suggest that this teapot was one of the elder Revere's early attempts at this form.

Description: As with the teapot Revere made for the Foster family, this vessel was raised and then turned upside down so that the original base could be cut out and remade as a close-fitting lid. A flat three-part hinge and applied ring seated within the rim of the teapot ensure that the lid is flush with the vessel exterior. A wood and silver capstan-style finial is soldered to the lid, on which has been cut a small air vent. The original open rim of the raised form has been closed with a base that has been let in and soldered in place.

A broad, splayed, cast foot with an applied foot ring is soldered to the body. The seamed S-shaped spout has a baluster drop and a foliate bud above the extended lip. Two section sockets secure the old, possibly original, handle. The upper socket, mounted high on the shoulder, bears side volutes and a triangular engraved foliate section at center. The lower socket is unadorned, its portion of the handle secured with a large replaced pin driven inside the socket rather than from the sides, as in the typical working method. The

109

edge of lid and the shoulder are encircled with an engraved scrolled and foliate design filled with a fine pattern of diapers, fish scales, and parallel hatch marks.

The teapot's hinge and rim, which receives the lid, show signs of corrosion that suggest later repairs. The handle is worn and has been crudely repaired near the lower socket.

History: The teapot was made for shopkeeper and mariner John Pulling [Pullen] (about 1700–about 1770) of Boston and his first wife, Martha Mountjoy (d. before 1753), m. 1730.[3] The vessel passed to Edward Pulling (1755–1796) of Salem, son of John Pulling's second wife, Jerusha Bradbury (b. 1711), m. 1753. Edward Pulling m. Lois Robinson in 1796.[4] The teapot descended to their daughter Mary Robinson Pulling (1797–1882) of Salem and Daniel Oliver (1787–1842) of Marblehead, m. 1817; to their son Andrew Oliver (1824–1897) and Adelaide Imlay (1829–1898) of New York City;[5] to their daughter Mary Pulling Imlay Oliver (b. 1860), d. unm.; to her niece Katharine Alice Crane (1890–1980) of New York City, the donor and wife of George Peabody Montgomery (1885–1972), m. 1918.[6]

Exhibitions and publications: Fairbanks 1975, 232, cat. no. 358; Fairbanks 1981, 629, fig. 33; Kane 1998, 852.

NOTES TO THIS ENTRY ARE ON PAGE 163.

110

Paul Revere I (1702–1754)

Punch strainer

Boston, Massachusetts, about 1745–50
Gift in memory of Henry Wilder Foote, 1875–1964
1991.1011

L. 9½ in. (24.1 cm); W. 1⅜ in. (3.5 cm); Diam. circular strainer 4³⁄₁₆ in. (10.7 cm); Wt. 4 oz 12 dwt (143.1 gm)

Marks: "P. Revere" in script within a rectangle struck under outermost section of each handle.

Inscriptions: None.

ORANGE STRAINERS, or "cullenders," were used by the English as early as 1533. In that year, "a Strayner of golde for orrenges X oz" appeared in the inventory of the Royal Jewel House. The scarcity of oranges in England at this early date probably accounts for the special name given to the form, which evolved into "punch strainer" due to not only the rising popularity of that beverage but also the regular shipments of Spanish oranges to England by the mid-eighteenth century.

Some early English strainers resembled large spoons whose bowls were pierced with small holes. A hook opposite the handle was used to secure the utensil to one side of the punch bowl, thereby steadying the user's hand. In time, versions emerged with two handles, which were long enough to extend across the diameter of period punch bowls. Such forms allowed the juice of oranges and lemons to be introduced into the punch within a restricted area and enabled smooth ladling unencumbered

by citrus pulp and seeds. Most bowls were pierced with simple uniform rows, but over time some received elaborately pierced decorative patterns, which guests could admire while waiting to be served. Strainers fell out of fashion in the late eighteenth century, when wine funnels, introduced for the decanting of sediment, were used for citrus fruits as well.[1]

In the colonies, punch strainers typically had two handles, which progressed in style from flat shaped sheets or simple wire to elongated cast versions of porringer handles as well as more delicate forms in the Rococo style. Pierced decoration, achieved with a drill and jeweler's saw, rapidly progressed from the above-mentioned simple circular arrangements to lively patterns that included text. Jonathan Clarke, of Providence and Newport, made such a strainer for Jabez Bowen of Providence; it bears his name, that of his city, and the date of January 1765 in a circle below the rim and around a flower-shaped central design.[2]

Paul Revere I's dome-shaped strainer bowl shows the result of successful experimentation with a pierced cross-shaped design, and its plain wire handles are in keeping with its early date.

Description: The large shallow bowl with applied rim has delicate pierced decoration of numerous small crosses that form a circular field in the lower half of the bowl; an intermittent band of floral elements appears above. A stylized geometric and floral frieze is pierced below the rim. Two simple, flat scrolled handles diametrically opposite each other are soldered below the rim at an angle to the strainer. Substantial and unskilled repairs, probably made in the nineteenth century, are located on the bowl at the juncture with each handle.

History: Early history unknown, with possible descent in the family of Gershom (1705–1771) and Hannah (1711–1784) Flagg of Boston, ancestors of the donor. In this century, the punch strainer descended from the Rev. Henry Wilder Foote (1875–1964), a Massachusetts antiquarian, to his son Caleb Foote, the donor.

Exhibitions and publications: Fairbanks 1975, 226, cat. no. 205; Kane 1998, 851.

NOTES TO THIS ENTRY ARE ON PAGE 163.

111

Paul Revere II (1734–1818)

Beaker

Boston, Massachusetts, 1753
Gift of Lavinia and Landon T. Clay
2002.226

H. 5⅝ in.; (14.2 cm); Diam. rim 3¼ in. (9.5 cm); Diam. base 3⅛ in. (8 cm); Wt. 9 oz 16 dwt 23 gr (306.3 gm)

Marks: "[pellet] REVERE" within a rectangle struck under foot.

Inscriptions: "This Cup is / Generously Dedicated by the Con / tributors for the sole use and benefit / of the Presbyterian Church and Co / ngregation in Bury Street of which / the Revd. Mr. Moorhead is Minister / N=England. 8br ye 1753" in script, within a bellflower scrolled and foliated cartouche, engraved on side.

THIS BEAKER is one of three commissioned in 1753 by unnamed members, called the "contributors," of the Presbyterian Church originally in Long Lane, now known as Arlington Street Church. It is somewhat unusual for a church to acquire an odd number of cups, but the three beakers were undoubtedly intended to join one fashioned by Jacob Hurd in 1744 (cat. no. 86) to create a set of four.

Although these beakers were first published in 1913 and are well known to scholars, their recent sale has focused fresh attention on the marks used in the 1750s by the Reveres, father and son.[1] In particular, the combination of the "[pellet] Revere" mark and an engraved date of "1753" raises questions regarding the maker of this cup and its two mates.

The first concerns the "[pellet] REVERE" maker's mark, which has always been ascribed to Paul Revere II.[2] It has generally been understood that this mark was first used by the patriot after his father's death in July 1754. Despite being two years shy of completing his apprenticeship, the younger Revere was a competent craftsman by that date, for he carried on the trade under the supervision of his mother, who acted in her husband's stead.[3] These church beakers demonstrate that Revere was a skilled silversmith who used this mark before his father's death and probably with his father's consent.[4]

In all likelihood, the elder Revere allowed his son to produce works and stamp them with a mark modified from one he had used since about 1750. Such an unorthodox arrangement would have occurred only between silversmiths related by blood, when one silversmith was a headstrong son or the master was also a father who had complete confidence in his apprentice son. Indeed, by adapting the new mark from an old one, described by Kathryn C. Buhler as appearing "almost as if [Revere] had cut the initial from the earlier mark," the elder Revere put his "P [pellet] REVERE" mark out of commission, tacitly approving work made and stamped by his son.[5]

The assured construction of the beaker is completely in keeping with fabrication methods common in mid-eighteenth-century Boston, demonstrating the apprentice's skill. However, awkward line breaks in the text suggest that Revere Jr. had not yet learned to plan his engraved designs. The text on the related two beakers is arranged more smoothly, with no hyphenated words, and may demonstrate that the young silversmith learned an important lesson while working on this commission.

If one accepts the theory regarding the engravings, the Museum's beaker is an important document in Revere's career, for it could be the very first piece of church silver he fashioned and his first documented use of this mark. If so, it marked an auspicious start for an ambitious young silversmith.

Description: The raised vessel, of inverted bell form, has an everted rim and slightly rounded base; the vessel is soldered to a drawn and stepped circular foot rim. The presentation inscription is engraved on the side within a bellflower and scroll cartouche.

History: Commissioned by contributors to the Presbyterian Church in 1753, the beaker remained in the church until January 2002, when it was placed at auction at Christie's, New York. It was not purchased and thereafter sold through Northeast Auctions on August 3–4, 2002, when it was purchased by the donors and made a gift.

Exhibitions and publications: MFA 1911, 105, cat. no. 873, pl. 31; Jones 1913, 78, pl. XXX; Kane 1998, 806–7; Christies, New York, sale 1003, January 18–19, 2002, lot 324; Northeast Auctions, Portsmouth, New Hampshire, August 3–4, 2002, lot 869. See also appendix 2.

NOTES TO THIS ENTRY ARE ON PAGE 163.

112

Paul Revere II (1734–1818)
Porringer

Boston, Massachusetts, 1755–1800
Gift of Peter Waldo
1991.783

H. 2 in. (5 cm); W. 8⅜ in. (21.4 cm); Diam. rim 5½ in. (13.9 cm); Wt. 8 oz 15 dwt 13 gr (273 gm)

Marks: "P [pellet] REVERE" within a rectangle struck in center of bowl and faintly on back of handle.

Inscriptions: "M S" in entwined script engraved on handle, facing bowl. Scratch weight of "9-. oz- 9" engraved on base; in a large modern hand "8 = 14" appears to right of "K J [J?] / $15.00."

DESPITE THE NAME of the donor and the prominence of the Waldo family in colonial Boston, it is unknown whether this porringer descended in this line to Denman Waldo Ross, the first known owner. It is more likely that Ross acquired it along with the many works of art from around the world that he accumulated as a Harvard professor and trustee of the Museum. A scratch price of $15 on the base suggests that Ross purchased the porringer during his lifetime and later gave it to his cousin Gretchen Howes Waldo.

Description: The raised vessel has a stepped and domed base rising to convex sides and everted rim. A center point is evident in center and underside of bowl. The keyhole-style handle is soldered at right angles to the rim.

History: Early history unknown. The porringer was loaned to the Museum in 1916 by Denman Waldo Ross (1853–1935), former trustee of the MFA and son of Frances Walker Waldo (b. 1825) and John Ludlow Ross (1813–1884), m. 1848.[1] Ross transferred ownership in 1930 to Gretchen Howes Waldo (1884–1976) (later Mrs. Thomas Mott Shaw) of Concord, Massachusetts, whose husband, Charles Sidney Waldo Jr. (1883–1964), was Ross's first cousin once removed.[2] In 1952 she transferred ownership to her son, the donor, Peter Waldo (b. 1917) of Carmel, New York.

Exhibitions and publications: None.

NOTES TO THIS ENTRY ARE ON PAGE 163.

113

Paul Revere II (1734–1818)
Pair of salts

Boston, Massachusetts, about 1760
Gift of Jane M. Pray in memory of her Grandparents James E. and Anna Hayley Pray and her Parents Francis G. and Anna Aylward Pray
1992.276–77

1992.276: H. 1½ in. (3.8 cm); Diam. rim 2⅜ in. (6.1 cm); Wt. 2 oz 9 dwt 21 gr (77.6 gm)

1992.277: H. 1½ in. (3.8 cm); Diam. rim 2⅜ in. (6.1 cm); Wt. 2 oz 11 dwt 12 gr (80.1 gm)

Marks: "PR" in roman letters within a rectangle struck on each bottom, above and below center point (marks on 1992.277 are incomplete).

Inscriptions: Engraved letters on both salts have been effaced. 1992.277: remains of the letter "E" are visible.

113

Paul Revere produced some nine sets of salt spoons in sets of two and four as well as about five single salt spoons that probably had mates when first fashioned. Although Revere's spoon production was always high, it is surprising that so few salts with his mark have survived; aside from this pair, only four single salts are known.[1] This pair closely resembles a pair by Benjamin Burt (cat. no. 11).

Description: Each salt is a raised, flattened, shallow sphere with a circular opening that has an applied rim. The vessels are supported by three cast cabriole-style legs with triple pads at foot and knee.

History: Original owners unknown; inherited by the donor and made a gift.

Exhibitions and publications: Fairbanks 1975, 232, cat. nos. 343–44; Kane 1998, 823.

NOTE TO THIS ENTRY IS ON PAGE 163.

114

Paul Revere II (1734–1818)

Tankard

Boston, Massachusetts, 1768
Gift of Edward N. Lamson, Barbara T. Lamson, Edward F. Lamson, Howard J. Lamson and Susan L. Strickler
1986.678

H. 9⅛ in. (23 cm); W. 7⅜ in. (18.9 cm); Diam. rim 4¹/₁₆ in. (10.3 cm); Diam. base 4¹⁵/₁₆ in. (12.6 cm); Wt. 30 oz 2 dwt 23 gr (937.7 gm)

Marks: "REVERE" within a rectangle struck on base, above center point.

Inscriptions: "Stephano Scales / HARVARDINATES / A.D. MDCCLXVIII. / Conscripti, / Biennio sub ejus Tutelâ peracto / Hoc Poculum / Grati Animi Monimentum, / DONANT" (Presented to Stephen Scales by his students at Harvard in the year 1768. Having passed two years under his tutelage, they give this drinking vessel as a symbol of their gratitude) within scrolled and foliated Rococo-style decoration, in a large squared cartouche, engraved on body, on opposite side of handle. A pair of books lying on their sides, *Price's Mor* on top of *Locke's Essay,* is engraved in the position normally reserved for the crest.

GIFTS OF SILVER to educational institutions in colonial America were first made in the mid-seventeenth century, when student Richard Harris presented an English standing salt to Harvard College. More important corporate gifts included the magnificent two-handled cup by John Coney that was given to Harvard in 1701 by William Stoughton, lieutenant governor and chief justice of Massachusetts, who was a major benefactor and a member of the class of 1650. These infrequent gifts signified affiliations of a varied, but commemorative, nature.[1]

Harris's gift of the standing salt helped establish his rank among students, a practice based upon traditions at Oxford and Cambridge. As early as 1655, those who provided silver for Harvard valued at £3 or more were entitled to privileged treatment

114

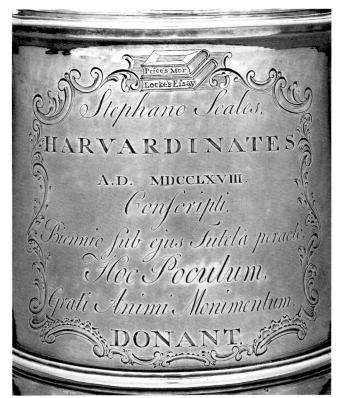

as Fellow Commoners. With this status came attendance at a special Fellow Commoners table, preferential listing in classes, and exemption from errands and physical tasks, all of which made them in many ways the near equal of faculty. The gifts, called commoner silver, were to be engraved with the donor's name, used while attending classes, and given to the college upon graduation.[2]

The gift of tutorial silver was also a Harvard tradition, in this case a class gift by undergraduate students in honor of the assigned tutor responsible for their studies. Unlike the English practice, in which the school retained all silver, tutorial silver at Harvard was considered a gift to the tutors, as a form of compensation. The custom ended sometime after 1767, when college laws assigned an additional student fee of "one shilling and nine pence lawful money quarterly" to compensate the tutors for the loss of these valuable gifts.[3]

This Revere tankard was given by the Harvard class of 1768 as an expression of their gratitude to Stephen Scales, a 1763 Harvard graduate and a law student while serving as tutor. He taught Harvard students from 1767 until 1770, when he left to practice law in Concord, New Hampshire.[4]

With its tall profile, high dome, and midband decoration, the tankard is a solid, if unexceptional, example of a standard form that was produced by many Massachusetts silversmiths of the period. The Scales tankard was accompanied by a pair of canns by Revere with a similar motif and the same inscription; they are the only known examples of tutorial silver made by Revere.[5] The elaborately worded Latin and English dedication and its personalized emblems symbolize the significant reform that took place at Harvard in 1767. Formerly responsible for teaching the complete curriculum to the students, after this date tutors were assigned to one of four specialties: Greek; Latin; natural philosophy, mathematics, and geography; or logic, metaphysics, and ethics. Scales taught the last group, as evidenced by the engraved books depicted in the cartouche: *Price's Mor* (Richard Price's *Review of the Principle Questions in Morals*, 1758) and *Locke's Essay* (Thomas Locke's *Essay Concerning Human Understanding*, 1690).[6]

Description: The raised vessel has tapering sides, a center point at base, and a wide drawn base molding with S-curve and two narrow steps at top and bottom; the midband appears above lower handle join. A twisted flame finial appears above domed and stepped lid; the peened pin for finial appears inside flanged lid. A cast thumbpiece descends to five-part hinge with cast drop. The cast, seamed, scrolled handle has rounded drop at upper join; round disk at lower attachment; concave spade-shaped terminal with crescent air vent below.

History: Presented to Stephen Scales (1741–1772), along with a pair of canns also made by Revere, from his students, the Harvard class of 1768. According to family history, the tankard descended to Mary G. Lamson (1883–1982), and thence to her children, the donors.[7]

Exhibitions and publications: MFA Annual Report 1986–87, 27; Fairbanks 1991, 72, cat. no. 55, checklist cat. no. 36; Kane 1998, 837; Falino and Ward 2001, 194, 196, figs. 10a–b.

NOTES TO THIS ENTRY ARE ON PAGES 163–64.

115

Joseph Richardson Sr. (1711–1784)
Pair of sauceboats

Philadelphia, Pennsylvania, 1755–65
Gift of a Friend of the Department of American Decorative Arts and Sculpture
1985.412–13

1985.412: H. 4⅛ in. (10.4 cm); W. 7⅝ in. (19.4 cm); D. 3⅝ in. (9.2 cm); Wt. 8 oz 14 dwt 23 gr (272.1 gm)

1985.413: H. 4 in. (10.2 cm); W. 7³⁄₁₆ in. (18.3 cm); D. 3½ in. (9 cm); Wt. 8 oz 15 dwt 19 gr (273.4 gm)

Marks: "IR" within a rectangle struck on each base; separate incuse leaf device appears above.

Inscriptions: "CW" or CWC" cypher monogram engraved on each body, to left of handle.

SAUCEBOATS, sometimes called "butter boats" or "butter cups" by Paul Revere, were of a low-slung elliptical shape. Their dynamic presence was derived from a lively scalloped rim and tall scrolled handle that punctuated the air with a flourish.[1] Often made in pairs to serve warm sauces quickly, the three-legged sauceboat came into use in England during the second and third decades of the eighteenth century and were soon found in Boston homes. For example, shortly after their marriage in 1728, merchant Joshua Winslow and his wife, Anna (Green) Winslow, of Hanover Street in Boston, acquired two London-made sauceboats that were probably used as a pair. Each features scalloped edges, an everted pouring spout, a broken scroll handle with foliate decoration, and cast feet with shell decoration, elements also favored by American silversmiths.[2]

American sauceboats first appeared in New England by the 1740s, with examples introduced by John Burt and Jacob Hurd. Their efforts were followed in later decades by those of John Coburn, Daniel Parker, Nathaniel Hurd, Daniel Henchman (see cat. no. 67), Benjamin Burt, Samuel Burt, and Paul Revere II, among many others, attesting to the serving vessels' popularity.[3]

The prolific craftsman Joseph Richardson was the second in the line of a distinguished Philadelphia silversmithing dynasty founded by his father, Francis. Joseph Richardson produced only two sauceboats prior to 1748, but by the 1750s and 1760s, the form gained in popularity and was often requested in pairs. The shape varied little among the pairs that Richardson made, but the level of decoration ranged from a highly chased pair in the Hammerslough collection, made for Joseph Emlen Miller, to these relatively simple examples, unadorned except for the elegant cypher monogram.[4] Richardson also emplyed a fleur-de-lis design on the knee of the sauceboats, a variant of which is in the Metropolitan Museum.[5]

Description: Each raised elliptical vessel has a scalloped rim and a broad, extended spout. A cast double-scrolled handle with leafy acanthus thumbgrip rises above each sauceboat. A rectangular notch cut into the handle secures the solder seam of the handle to the rim; the lower scroll is adhered directly to the body. Three cast cabriole legs have stylized shell patterns at each knee; triple pad feet support each vessel.

History: Early history unknown. Purchased in the twentieth century by silver collector Mark Bortman (1896–1967) and lent to the Museum in 1948; by descent to his daughter Jane Bortman Larus (b. 1927); sold to the Museum in 1985.

Exhibitions and publications: Buhler 1956, 95, cat. no. 316; Kathryn C. Buhler, "Colonial Silversmiths–Masters and Apprentices," *Antiques* 70, no. 6 (December 1956), 552–55; Martha Gandy Fales, *Joseph Rich-*

ardson and Family: Philadelphia Silversmiths (Middletown, Conn.: Wesleyan University Press for the Historical Society of Pennsylvania, 1974), fig. 109; Fairbanks 1991, checklist, 92, cat. no. 40.

NOTES TO THIS ENTRY ARE ON PAGE 164.

116

Daniel Rogers (1735–1816)

Porringer

Ipswich, Massachusetts, about 1760
Gift of Rosamond G. Heard
1991.670

H. 2 3/16 in. (5.5 cm); W. 8 7/16 in. (21.5 cm); Diam. rim 5 3/8 in. (13.6 cm); Wt. 9 oz 2 dwt 23 gr (284.5 gm)

Marks: "D [pellet] ROGERS" in a rectangle struck on top of handle.

Inscriptions: "I*H" in shaded roman letters engraved on handle (initials interpreted as facing bowl).

ESSEX COUNTY SILVERSMITH Daniel Rogers produced a number of canns, a few creamers, and many spoons. Rogers's specialty may have been gold beads, however, for surviving account books document his painstaking fabrication of these items for the regional silversmithing community. Among the purchasers

were William Homes (1742–1825), Robert Evans (1768–1812), David Tyler (about 1760–1804), Isaac Townsend (1760–1812), Joseph Loring (1743–1815), Samuel Minott (1732–1803) of Boston, and Samuel Davis (1765–1839) of Plymouth.[1] The Museum owns an engraved gold locket by Rogers, the only known marked example of his jewelry.[2]

This keyhole-handled porringer is similar to another by Rogers in the Cleveland Museum of Art. Both share generously proportioned bowls and display an unusual lengthwise placement of the touchmark on top of the keyhole handle.[3]

Description: The raised vessel, with center point, has a large domed base and tall convex sides rising to an everted rim. The keyhole handle is soldered to the rim at a slight angle, with tip extending upward. Several dents appear on the vessel wall.

History: Original owner unknown; the porringer descended in the family of the donor along with a pair of three-legged salts by Benjamin Burt (cat. no. 11), believed to have descended in the Warren/Sumner families of Boston, Massachusetts.

Exhibitions and publications: Kane 1998, 861.

NOTES TO THIS ENTRY ARE ON PAGE 164.

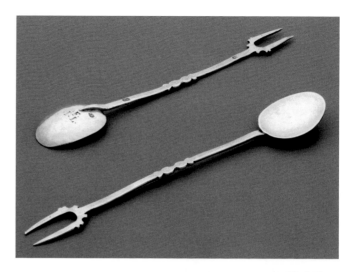

117

117

William Rouse (about 1640–1704/5)
Pair of sucket forks

Boston, Massachusetts, 1677
Gift of John and Mary Coolidge
1996.122.1–2

1996.122.1: L. 6 in. (15.3 cm); W. bowl 1 in. (2.5 cm); Wt. 9 dwt 6 gr (14.4 gm)

1996.122.2: L. 6⅛ in. (15.4 cm); W. bowl 1 in. (2.6 cm); Wt. 9 dwt 9 gr (14.6 gm)

Marks: "WR" in an oval struck twice on back of each handle and once on back of each bowl.

Inscriptions: "F / I L" in shaded roman capitals engraved on back of each bowl.

THE SUCKET FORK was an extremely rare form of late-seventeenth-century American silver. A practical utensil with English origins, it had a tined fork at one end and the bowl of a spoon on the other. Such forks were designed to eat sucket (or succade), fruits preserved in heavy syrup. The consump-

tion of these sweet luxuries was made famous by Elizabeth I (1533–1603), who held banquet pavilions filled with sucket, raisins, figs, currants, and comfits of sugared seeds, nuts, and fruits. An inventory of the jewelhouse of Henry VII (1457–1509) included "Item one spone wt suckett fork at thend of silver and gilt." By the late seventeenth century, when the second generation of settlers had become established in the New World, maturing orchards and vineyards offered an abundance of materials to satisfy the sweet tooth, and a variety of so-called sweetmeats were produced along with the proper tableware to display and consume them.[1]

The fashion for sweetmeats in this country continued through the early nineteenth century, but the use of the sucket fork seems to have ended in the early decades of the eighteenth, when smaller knives, forks, and spoons came into use. At least one set of six was observed with antiquarian interest by Salem diarist William Bentley (1759–1819), who, while visiting the "Widow Hawthorne" in 1790, saw "½ dozen Sweetmeet Silver Spoons, with Round Ladle Bowls, twisted Shafts, & two pronged forks on the Handle."[2]

That sucket forks may have persisted in some areas has been demonstrated by Louise Belden, who noted they were imported as late as 1743, when "silver spoon-handled forks imported from London" were advertised in the *South Carolina Gazette*.[3] Today less than twenty American-made examples of this unusual form are known.

Although the English sucket fork has traditionally been considered an influence on the colonial form, there may have been a Dutch precedent as well. With the exception of those by John Coney, the majority of surviving sucket forks were made by an early generation of silversmiths of Dutch or Continental heritage, including Jesse Kip (1660–1722), Bartholomew Le Roux (1663–1713), Johannis Nys (1671–1734), and Cornelius Kierstede (1674–1757). Some of these silversmiths were patronized by the van Rensselaer and Schuyler families, also of Dutch extraction.[4] Boston silversmith William Rouse, the maker of the Museum's pair, was the oldest. Born in 1639 in the Duchy of Cleves, which bordered the Netherlands, Rouse received his training abroad before arriving in Boston in the late 1660s.[5]

The Rouse sucket forks most closely resemble those made by Coney, an unidentified maker (private collection), and Johannis Nys. All are lightweight and have twisted handles and a small egg-shaped bowl.[6] The Rouse set differs in its flat handles with cyma-curve decoration cut in profile. John and Lydia (Turell) Foster, for whom Rouse made these sucket forks, also ordered a covered skillet, a handsomely engraved patch box, and a small cup with handle.[7] The descent of the forks in the matrilineal line is a remarkable demonstration of preservation and survival across eight generations.

Description: Each sucket fork has a flat stem, shaped in reverse curves, terminating at one end in a bowl and at the other in a flat two-tined fork with sprocketlike protrusions near handle. The bowls are rounded, with a V-drop on the back.

History: Col. John (1644–1710) and Lydia (Turell) Foster (1660–1689), m. 1677.[8] The sucket forks passed in the matrilineal line as follows: To their daughter Lydia Foster (1686–1748) and her husband, Edward Hutchinson (1678–1752), m. 1706; to Elizabeth Hutchinson (1731–1793) and Rev. Nathaniel Robbins (1726–1795), m. 1757; by descent to their son Edward Hutchinson Robbins (1758–1829) and Elizabeth Murray (1756–1837), m. 1785; to their daughter Mary Robbins (1794–1879) and Joseph Warren Revere (1777–1868), m. 1821;[9] to Jane Minot Revere (1834–1910) and Dr. John Phillips Reynolds (1825–1909), m. 1859; to Theresa Reynolds (1874–1972) and her husband, Julian Lowell Coolidge (1873–1954), m. 1901; to the donors, John Phillips Coolidge (1913–1995) and Mary Elizabeth Welch (b. 1912), m. 1935.[10]

Exhibitions and publications: George Barton Cutten, "Sucket Forks," *Antiques* 57, no. 6 (June 1950): 440–41, 444; Flynt and Fales 1968, 79; Kane 1998, 866; Sarah D. Coffin et al., *Feeding Desire: Design and the Tools of the Table, 1500–2005* (New York: Assouline Publishing in association with Cooper-Hewitt, National Design Museum, 2006), 118.

NOTES TO THIS ENTRY ARE ON PAGE 164.

118

Bartholomew Schaats
(about 1683–about 1758)

Porringer

New York, New York, ca. 1730
Gift of Mrs. Thomas P. Beal
1975.350

H. 2⅛ in. (5.3 cm); W. 7⅞ in. (20 cm); Diam. rim 5⁵⁄₁₆ in. (13.5 cm); Wt. 8 oz 12 dwt 11 gr (268.2 gm)

Marks: "B [pellet] S" over a stylized leaf, all within a heart-shaped device, struck on bottom of bowl, below center point.

Inscriptions: "N / M * P" in shaded roman letters engraved on handle, facing bowl.

MARRIED IN 1706 and made a freeman of the city of New York by 1708, Bartholomew Schaats enjoyed a long career as a silversmith. He produced numerous tankards, spoons, and porringers and fashioned more ambitious forms such as candlesticks, a salver, a two-handled bowl, a caster, and a teapot. Schaats supplemented his trade by subletting the docks and slips of New York between 1740 and 1746 as well as stalls in the city marketplaces in 1747. He served as collector of the East Ward between 1737 and 1745.[1]

Of his known porringers, one has an early tripartite handle, and another bears an intricate "flowered" form popular in eighteenth-century New York. This example, its handle pierced with circles, tablets, and hearts, echoes those made in New England in the early eighteenth century. It is identical to another porringer by Schaats that is engraved "T / E * E."[2] C. Louise

Avery has pointed out that both Schaats and Peter Van Dyck (1684–1751) made porringers with this type of handle.[3]

Description: The deep raised vessel, with central boss and stepped bottom, has convex sides and a tall everted rim. The geometric handle with circles, tablets, and a heart at its center is soldered at right angles to the rim.

History: Original owner unknown. According to family history, the porringer passed through the Peltz, Nexson, and Bogart families of New York, by descent to Frederick Grinnell Morgan (b. 1866); to his niece May Lefferts Morgan (Mrs. Thomas Prince Beal) (1899–1980).[4]

Exhibitions and publications: None.

NOTES TO THIS ENTRY ARE ON PAGE 164.

119

William Swan (1715–1774)
Ladle

Worcester, Massachusetts, 1740–65
Gift of Mrs. Graham P. Teller. In memory of Charles and Jean Gorely
1973.643

L. 15⅝ in. (39.7 cm); W. bowl 3⅞ in. (10 cm); Wt. (including wooden handle) 3 oz 15 dwt 7 gr (117.1 gm)

Marks: "Swan" in italics within a shaped cartouche struck inside bowl, at center.

Inscriptions: None.

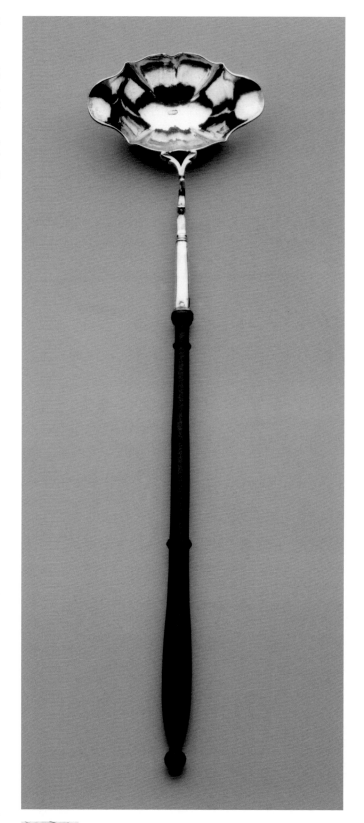

LADLES WITH RAISED, fluted bowls and exaggerated pouring lips were the most elegant forms of their type. With their extended wooden handles, most were probably used to dispense punch from large porcelain vessels imported from China or, less frequently, from silver bowls such as the one made by John Coney for Capt. Walter Riddell (cat. no. 32).

The refined forked and scrolled elements connecting the bowl with the handle add to the delicacy of the ladle. When guests gathered for refreshments, such ladles would reflect light from many angles as they dipped and swayed in the service of drink. However, the fragility of their construction may account for the few surviving examples. Similar ladles were made in New England by Jacob Hurd (cat. no. 83), Samuel Edwards, and Paul Revere II. Closely related to this group are New York examples having shell decoration made by Elias Pelletreau and Myer Myers and dating from the 1740s to 1760s.[1]

Ladles were not made en suite with punch bowls until the mid- to late nineteenth century. In the eighteenth century, they were purchased separately for use at family and larger social gatherings. The Masonic Order, a fraternal organization with many lodges, ordered ladles from Paul Revere, presumably to serve libations for their events.[2]

Description: The ladle has a raised, fluted, elliptical bowl with flared pouring lips at each end of the ellipse. Silver portions of the handle, possibly repaired, include a cast forked section having articulated elements that are composed of notched arms with curling tendrils at the juncture with the bowl. The cast C scroll with scrolled return is soldered to a ferule with seamed, tapering cylinder. The turned wooden handle of later date is secured to the cylinder with a silver pin.

History: Original owner unknown.

Exhibitions and publications: Kane 1998, 915.

NOTES TO THIS ENTRY ARE ON PAGE 164.

120

Benjamin Tappan (1742–1831)

Tablespoon

Northampton, Massachusetts, about 1770–80
Gift of H. Bowen White
1975.394

L. 8⅛ in. (20.5 cm); W. bowl 1⅝ in. (4.1 cm); Wt. 1 oz 7 dwt 17 gr (43.1 gm)

Marks: "B T" within a serrated rectangle struck on back of stem.

Inscriptions: None.

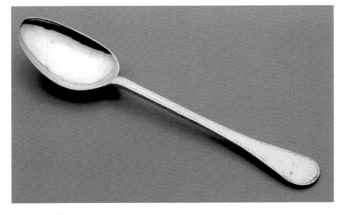

NORTHAMPTON HISTORIANS of the early twentieth century remembered Benjamin Tappan as a successful merchant whose portrait was painted by Gilbert Stuart, but they omitted any mention of his silversmithing activities.[1] In fact, Tappan probably began to sell dry goods soon after 1768, the year he arrived in Northampton, and gradually abandoned his silversmithing trade as his business expanded. This spoon's history of ownership among Tappan descendants demonstrates their knowledge and pride in his work as a craftsman whose accomplishments might otherwise have been forgotten.

Description: The spoon has a slightly downturned round-handled tip, with feather-edged decoration, a sharp midrib on the back, and a thick stem that is rectangular in section. The back of the elliptical bowl has a long rounded drop and fifteen-lobed shell decoration. The bowl of the shell is dented and worn at its tip; three small sharp dents appear in the handle tip.

History: This spoon was retained by Tappan and his wife, Sarah Homes (1748–1826), daughter of silversmith William Homes Sr. (1716/17–1785), and descended in the family for five generations.[2] It was inherited by Tappan's son Lewis (1788–1873), m. Susannah Aspinwall (1790–1853) in 1813.[3] The couple removed to Brooklyn, New York, where the spoon was inherited by their daughter Lucy Maria Tappan (1825–1863) and Henry Chandler Bowen (1813–1896), m. 1844; by descent to their son Henry Elliot Bowen (b. 1845) and Elizabeth White Plummer (b. 1848) of Roxbury, Massachusetts, m. 1869;[4] to their daughter Ethel Plummer Bowen (1879–1965) and Dr. Franklin Warren White (about 1869–1950) of Charlestown, Massachusetts, m. 1904;[5] to their son Henry Bowen White (b. 1911) of Boston, the donor.

Exhibitions and publications: Kane 1998, 921.

NOTES TO THIS ENTRY ARE ON PAGE 164.

121

Andrew Tyler (1692–1741)

Serving spoon

Boston, Massachusetts, 1730–40
Gift of Harriet Winslow Lowell
1991.601

L. 14⁵⁄₁₆ in. (36.4 cm); W. bowl 2⅝ in. (6.6 cm); Wt. 6 oz 18 dwt 23 gr (216.1 gm)

Marks: "A [pellet] TYLER" in broad roman letters, within a rounded rectangle, struck on back of handle.

121

Inscriptions: "W / S ✳ L" in exaggerated script engraved later on back of handle tip.

WITH THEIR MIDRIB DECORATION and rounded handles, large serving spoons of the 1730s and 1740s resembled the tea- and tablespoons of the same period. These oversized utensils are the likely successors to the rare hollow-handled serving spoons of the type made in the first decades of the century (see cat. no. 47). Other makers of midrib serving spoons include Thomas Edwards (YUAG), William Pollard (MFA), and Daniel Boyer (MFA) of Boston. Philip Syng Jr. of Philadelphia made a similar example with a pierced bowl (MFA), and a "stuffing spoon" by Tobias Stoughtenburgh of New York has a straight handle with a central rib (WM).[1]

Description: This large serving spoon has an upturned midrib handle tip and a shallow oval bowl with an attentuated rattail on back.

History: Although engraved at a later date, the initials are believed to be for Samuel Waldo (1695–1759) of Roxbury and Lucy Wainwright (1704–1741) of Ipswich, Massachusetts, m. 1722.[2] The spoon probably descended to their daughter Lucy Waldo (1724–1768) and Isaac Winslow (1709–1777), m. 1747,[3] and to their daughter Sarah Tyng Winslow (1765–1826), m. her first cousin, Samuel Waldo (1764–1798) in 1789. The spoon descended to their son William Tyng Waldo (1793–1844). The latter Waldo, being unm., probably gave the spoon to his second cousin Elizabeth Winslow (1787–1866) and William Pickering (b. England; d. 1813), m. 1807; to their nephew Francis Winslow (1818/19–1862) and his wife, Mary Sophia Nelson (1827–1903), m. 1846; to their son Arthur (1860–1938) and Mary L. Devereux (d. 1944);[4] to their daughter Charlotte Winslow (1890–1954) and her

husband, Robert Traill Spence Lowell (1887–1947), m. 1916;[5] to their son, poet Robert Traill Spence Lowell Jr. (1917–1977), and his second wife, writer Elizabeth Hardwick (b. 1916), m. 1949;[6] to their daughter Harriet Winslow Lowell (b. 1957), the donor.

Exhibitions and publications: Kane 1998, 942.

NOTES TO THIS ENTRY ARE ON PAGE 164.

122

Peter Vergereau (1700–1755)
Bowl

New York, New York, 1743–55
Gift of Geoffrey B. Torney and Ian Wynkoop Torney in memory of the Wynkoop Family of New York City and Kinderhook, New York
1992.286

H. 3⁵⁄₁₆ in. (8.5 cm); Diam. rim 7³⁄₈ in. (18.8 cm); Diam. foot 3⁹⁄₁₆ in. (9 cm); Wt. 19 oz 7 dwt 7 gr (602.3 gm)

Marks: "PV" within a rounded rectangle struck twice, once on each side of center point, underneath bowl.

Inscriptions: "G ✳ M P" in shaded roman letters engraved below center point and marks. The scratch weight of "19½ oz" in an early hand is engraved above center point.

PETER VERGEREAU is probably the individual born into New York City's French community and baptised at the Église Française à la Nouvelle York on August 21, 1700. He was granted freeman status in 1721, which would have been the logical time for him to begin practicing his craft after an average apprenticeship. Vergereau was married in 1737, rather late in life, to Susana(h) Boudinot, sister of silversmith Elias Boudinot (1706–1770).[1] Although his career lasted for some thirty years, few works bearing his mark are known. Nevertheless, this small body of silver proves that he was a talented silversmith and engraver who made forms ranging from tablespoons to tankards and including salvers, saucepans, and this commodious bowl.[2]

Bowls such as this were based upon Chinese porcelain forms. Despite the modest size, it was probably intended as a punch bowl. It is unadorned except for the owner's initials. Vessels of similar size were fashioned by New York silversmiths Myer Myers, Thauvet Besley, Bartholomew Le Roux II, and Cornelius Wynkoop, to mention only a few, as well as by Boston

craftsmen such as John Coney (cat. no. 32) and Jacob Hurd (cat. no. 86).[3] The best-known example in a larger size is the Sons of Liberty bowl made by Paul Revere in 1768, which stands about 5½ inches (14 cm) tall and measures 11 inches (28 cm) in diameter.

Description: The raised hemispherical bowl has convex sides and an applied rim; the drawn, splayed, and stepped foot has an applied foot ring.

History: Despite the unusual spacing in the initials, the likely original owners are Marytje Roel and George Petterson (d. 1764) of New York City, m. March 18, 1743. The bowl descended to her daughter by her first marriage, Maria Catharina Roel (Ruehl) (b. 1733/39), and

Capt. Cornelius C. Wynkoop (1732–1796) of Kingston, New York, m. 1760. To their son Augustus Wynkoop (1777–1836) and Anna Maria Sylvester (1780–1825) of Kinderhook, New York, m. 1808/9; to their son Augustus Wynkoop (1812–1862) and Anna Whiting (1815–1863), m. 1843; to their son Augustus Whiting Wynkoop (1844–1886) and Mary Lydia Talcott (b. 1846), m. 1873;[4] to their son Augustus Talcott Wynkoop (1878–1940); to his sister Anna Strong Wynkoop (1880–1958) and George Henry Torney (1872–1948);[5] to their son Geoffrey Barton Torney (b. 1914), the donor, and his nephew Ian Wynkoop Torney (b. 1963).[6]

Exhibitions and publications: None.

NOTES TO THIS ENTRY ARE ON PAGE 165.

123

Samuel Vernon (1683–1737)

One-handled cup

Newport, Rhode Island, 1704–28
Gift of Dr. Benjamin Wood in memory of Anna Wharton
Wood, and Marion Davis Fund
1976.65

H. 2¹³⁄₁₆ in. (7.1 cm); W. 3⅞ in. (9.9 cm); Diam. rim 2¾ in. (7 cm);
Diam. base 2⅜ in. (6 cm); Wt. 3 oz 7 dwt 8 gr (104.7 gm)

Marks: "SV" over a fleur-de-lis, all within a heart, struck to left of
handle.

Inscriptions: "1691 E ✱ W / 1729 M R 1793 / 1761 A H 1845 / 1795
D. F. W. 1888 / 1834 A. W. 1863 / [then upside down and proceeding away from preceding initials] 1864 A. W. S. / 1905 B. S.W" in
shaded roman letters engraved on base at successively later dates.
Later script initials and one date engraved on the vessel opposite its
handle reiterate those on base: "EW / MR / AH / DFW / AW /
AWS / 1864 / BSW."

THIS MODESTLY SCALED domestic vessel was probably similar
to the "Silver Cup with one ear, weighing about 3 ounces and
12 grains" given in 1728 by diarist Samuel Sewall to Elizabeth
Sewall, wife of his son Joseph Sewall, a minister.[1] This small
cup, essentially a short beaker with handle, is one of about
eight made by Vernon; each has a plain or drawn molded strap
handle and stepped baseband. All were probably fashioned
within the first several decades of the eighteenth century.[2]

The cup was passed down for six generations in the matrilineal line and is engraved with the women's birth dates; Elizabeth Wanton was the first owner. Despite the engraved date
of "1691," it probably came into her possession sometime after
1704, the earliest possible date that Vernon could have fashioned it. Wanton's birth date and initials were engraved later,
perhaps at or near her death, establishing precedent for later
inscriptions.

Description: The small, raised, cylindrical cup with a flaring rim has
a stepped, molded base and a molded, scrolled strap handle. Metal
fatigue from use is evident at contact points between vessel and handle, and a large repair has been made to the upper junction using a
shaped piece of silver. A second repair has been made to a tear in the
rim, opposite the handle.

History: The cup was made for Elizabeth Wanton (b. 1690/91–1762),
m. mariner Abraham Borden (1690–1732) of Newport, Rhode
Island, in 1713;[3] to their daughter Mary Borden (1728/29–1798) of
Newport and New Bedford, m. Capt. Thomas Rodman of Newport
(1724–1766)[4] in 1750; to their daughter Anna Rodman (1761–1845) and
Thomas Hazard (1758–1828), m. 1780;[5] to their niece Deborah Fisher
(1795–1888) and William Wharton (1790–1856) of Philadelphia, m.
1817;[6] to their daughter Anna Wharton (1834–1863), d. unm.; to her
niece Anna Wharton Smith (1864–1945) and Dr. Henry Austin Wood
of Waltham (1855–1942), m. 1898; to their son Dr. Benjamin Smith
Wood (b. 1905) of Waltham, Massachusetts, and later Roanoke, Virginia, from whom the cup was purchased.[7]

Exhibitions and publications: Gourley 1965, cat. no. 310.

NOTES TO THIS ENTRY ARE ON PAGE 165.

124

Samuel Vernon (1683–1737)

Tankard

Newport, Rhode Island, about 1720
Gift of Jean Ritchie Dingerson and Celia Ann Ritchie
1999.13

H. 7⅛ in. (18 cm); W. 7⅝ in. (19.2 cm); Diam. rim 4¼ in. (10.8 cm); Diam. base 5 in. (12.8 cm); Wt. 30 oz 13 dwt 23 gr (954.8 gm)

Marks: "SV" over a fleur-de-lis, both within a heart, struck on vessel to left of handle; a portion of same mark is visible on base; a third mark on lid has been overstruck with "IC" within an oval.

Inscriptions: "A / D ＊ B" in roman letters engraved on handle, below hinge; "1757" engraved in a later hand, below initials.

124

LITTLE IS KNOWN about Samuel Vernon's youth aside from the names of his parents, Daniel and Ann (Dyer) Hutchinson Vernon, of Narragansett, Rhode Island, and his familial link to silversmith Edward Winslow, who was his mother's nephew.[1] Vernon may have served as Winslow's apprentice, but some aspects of his silver are similar to the work of John Coney. In particular, an eagle thumbpiece, unique in colonial New England silver, has been found on tankards by both men. At the same time, Vernon's use of New York–style decorative leafy basebands, meander wirework, and flat-topped tankard lids point to influences west of Boston. His 1707 marriage to Elizabeth Fleet of Long Island would have taken place shortly after his apprenticeship or during his employment as a young journeyman. It is possible that a silversmith in the New York area provided Vernon with a new stylistic vocabulary, resulting in his unique fusion of New York and New England styles.[2]

After his apprenticeship, Vernon returned to Rhode Island, where he established a shop in Newport and produced silver for local and Providence patrons, including the Malbone family, Nathaniel Paine, Benjamin Ellery, Job Almy, and Peleg Brown. He received a prestigious commission from the General Assembly of the Colony of Rhode Island, which in 1733 purchased three tankards for New York commissioners Col. Isaac Hicks of Hempstead, James Jackson of Flushing, and Col. Lewis Morris Jr. of Westchester. The assembly's choice of Vernon may be indicative of the silversmith's connections to New York as well as his prominence in Rhode Island civic affairs. Patrons north of Providence included Josiah Salisbury of Worcester, Massachusetts, and Daniel Arnold of Woonsocket, Rhode Island, the first owner of this tankard.

The plain-bodied tankard, New England in style, shares two unusual details with another, more ambitious example made for Josiah Salisbury.[3] The classical portrait medallion on the terminus of each suggests that Vernon found or adapted this form from an unknown source. Although coins were occasionally used in colonial silver, Vernon incorporated them into at least three tankards, one of which was the General Assembly commission. In the case of the tankards for Arnold and Salisbury, he may have been emulating a Roman or later source with his image of a toga-clad youth reminiscent of the young Augustus. He imposed this classical form on a shield-shaped terminus, which he favored.[4]

Both tankards also possess mask-and-dolphin thumbpieces, a decorative device in the Mannerist style that was popular among early New England silversmiths but often cast with little concern for detail. The Vernon tankards, by contrast, have cleanly cast and chased thumbpieces. The silversmith customized his decoration with grimacing masks that display bone-shaped mouths and bulging eyes and balanced them between the tails of open-mouthed grinning dolphins with ribbed bodies.[5]

Still unexplained is a second touchmark on the lid that was struck squarely over one by Vernon. The "IC" mark within an ellipse is not that of John Coney, nor does it resemble the known marks of Vernon's contemporaries, his kinsman John Coddington (1690–1743) or Jonathan Clarke (1706–1766). The mark probably belongs to a silversmith who repaired the vessel, perhaps sometime after Vernon's death in 1737.

Description: The raised vessel has straight, tapering sides and a drawn and molded baseband; a center point is not evident. Below the applied and molded lip, the vessel is scored three times. The stepped lid with flat top and center point has a broad scored rim with a serrated edge near hinge and opposite handle. A five-part hinge with meander wire and short baluster drop is set below a repaired dolphin-and-mask thumbpiece. A hollow seamed S-scroll handle has a long rattail with rounded tip; the lower join is soldered to an elliptical disk. A shield-shaped terminus with acanthus border decoration displays a portrait bust at its center; a crude round air vent is beneath the terminus.

History: Daniel Arnold (1699–1773) and Bathsheba Ballou (1698–1790) m. 1720, of Smithfield, Rhode Island; by descent to their daughter Rachel Arnold (1730–1820)[6] of Smithfield, Rhode Island, and Stephen Arnold (1728–1796) m. 1746/49; to their son Cyrus Arnold (1774–1850) and Ruth Arnold (1778–1849) of Smithfield;[7] by descent to their son Cyrus Arnold (1815–1902) and Celia Ann Ballou (1825–1906), m. 1846;[8] to their daughter Lillian Alpha Arnold (1864–1906) and William E. Williams (1867–1954); to their daughter Ruth Virginia Williams (1903–1987) and Russell E. Ritchie (1903–1991), m. 1928; by descent to their daughters Celia Ann Ritchie and Jean Ritchie Dingerson, the donors.

Exhibitions and publications: Buhler 1956, 72, cat. no. 155.

NOTES TO THIS ENTRY ARE ON PAGE 165.

125

William Ward (1678–1768)

Spoon

Guilford or Wallingford, Connecticut, 1698–1715
Gift of Mrs. Warren Christie Moffett in honor of her Grandfather, Francis Henry Bergen, and her Mother, Ruth Bergen Dort
1992.273

L. 7³⁄₁₆ in. (18.4 cm); W. bowl 1¹¹⁄₁₆ in. (4.4 cm); Wt. 1 oz 11 gr (31.8 gm)

Marks: "WW," with two stars above and one below, all within a shield shape having a serrated top, struck three times on back of stem. A second unidentified mark may be a symbol or pseudohall-mark.

Inscriptions: "[pellet] T [pellet] B [pellet] / [pellet] M [pellet] R [possibly reconfigured as an "A" or vice versa] [pellet] / 1696" engraved on back of stem.

FEW WORKS ARE KNOWN by William Ward of Killingworth, Connecticut, whose progeny worked as silversmiths and possibly as clockmakers. These include his sons Macock Ward (1702–1783) and William Jr. (1705/6–1761). His grandson Bilious Ward (1729–1777), son of William Jr., was known to have made a paten for Dr. Samuel Johnson, first president of Kings College (now Columbia University).[1]

This early trifid-handled spoon may have been made in Guilford, Connecticut, where Ward worked at the start of his career. Two spoons bearing the "WW" and stars mark are in the collection of Historic Deerfield; one is trifid handled, and the other is a round-ended example having a front midrib and an upturned handle.[2]

Description: The spoon has an upturned trifid-end handle with flat stem terminating in an elliptical bowl with rounded drop and a ridged rattail.

History: Original owner unknown, although the initials could be those of Tunis Bergen (1679–1755) and his wife, Mary or Marritje, of Jamaica, New York.[3] The spoon descended in the Bergen family in a similar fashion as the Henricus Boelen spoons (cat. no. 3) owned by the same family.

Exhibition and publications: None.

NOTES TO THIS ENTRY ARE ON PAGE 165.

126

Edward Webb (about 1666–1718)
Tankard

Boston, Massachusetts, about 1700–10
Gift of Mr. and Mrs. Francis W. Hatch
1992.268

H. 5⁵⁄₁₆ in. (13.5 cm); W. 6³⁄₈ in. (16.3 cm); Diam. rim 3½ in. (8.9 cm); Diam. base 3¹⁵⁄₁₆ in. (10 cm); Wt. 13 oz 4 dwt 24 gr (412.1 gm)

Marks: "EW" in roman letters within a rectangle struck twice: on lid in front of thumbpiece and to left of handle.

Inscriptions: "The gift of her honoured / Grandmother Eliz : Corwin. / to Mary Gibbs" in script engraved on bottom of vessel. A crude "H" incised later on base, near molding.

ELIZABETH (SHEAFE GIBBS) CORWIN, the original owner of this magnificent tankard, was a woman of means. The eldest daughter of Jacob and Margaret (Webb) Sheafe of Cambridge, she inherited £500 from her maternal grandfather, Henry Webb (d. 1660), along with his mansion house, land at Fort Hill, and one-third of a sawmill at York, Maine.[1] She married wealthy merchant Robert Gibbs in 1660 and, after his death, wed Judge Jonathan Curwin of Salem. Financially independent, she commissioned this fine tankard for a granddaughter.

The year in which the tankard was made is difficult to ascertain since no date accompanies the inscription to Mary Gibbs from her "honoured Grandmother Eliz : Corwin." A conjectural date ranges from 1699, the birth date of Mary Gibbs, to 1718,

126

the death date of its maker, Edward Webb, and of Corwin. The earlier date, if deemed acceptable, would precede Webb's earliest documented presence in Boston in 1704, when he "served as security" for Peter Patey's admittance as an inhabitant of the city.[2]

Elizabeth Corwin's personal collection of English and American silver is well documented in her will of 1717, which includes items that had been given to her by her father-in-law, Sir Henry Gibbs, a knight from Homington, county Warwick. Mary Gibbs, the recipient of this tankard, was about eighteen years old at the time the will was written. She received a silver caudle silver cup and a sucking bottle, both symbolizing the duties of motherhood and care for family members that lay in her future.[3]

This tankard was not among the bequeathed items, and because of its small size and early style, it is possible that Corwin purchased it sometime after 1699 to celebrate her granddaughter's birth. There is also the possibility that it was intended as a dowry gift, perhaps in anticipation of Mary Gibbs's marriage to the Rev. John Cotton in 1719. That the tankard received no mention in Corwin's will demonstrates how easily such gifts could be passed along the matrilineal line during the life of the donor.

During his time in Boston, Webb employed several types of cast elements and forged forms for tankards, and he was among the first to experiment with domed lids.[4] His early flat-lidded tankards are ornamented with corkscrew, scrolled, and dolphin-and-mask thumbpieces. They all display long rattails below the hinge, a small curl on the outer edge of the handle, and a variety of termini. When Webb progressed to domed lids, he continued to decorate these new forms with the same old-fashioned casts. One example in the Museum's collection shows an attempt to update the form with a domed lid and midband, yet the vessel still retains a long rattail beneath the handle joining and a curl on the outer edge of the handle, two elements that point to Webb's lingering preference for a style that would soon be outmoded.[5] This tankard, with its gadrooned lid, finely cast elements, and delicate proportions, is one of the finest examples Webb produced in Boston.

Description: The raised tankard has a slightly tapered straight-sided body with center point evident in base. A center point is also visible on the inside of the raised, gadrooned, flat-topped lid. The wide crenate lip displays one pair and one single scored line at its edge; a flange is underneath the lid. The corkscrew thumbpiece descends to a five-part hinge with flanking meander lines on the hingeplate. The cast and seamed scroll handle with attenuated rattail drop at its upper joining has an additional tightly rolled scroll above the cherub terminal and an oval air vent below.

History: The tankard was acquired by Elizabeth (Sheafe Gibbs) (1644–1718), m. second, about 1675/76, Jonathan Corwin (Curwin, Curwen) of Salem, Justice of the Superior Court of Judicature, Province of Massachusetts Bay. It was made a gift to her granddaughter Mary Gibbs (1699–1761), m. the Rev. John Cotton (1693–1757) in 1719.[6] The tankard passed to their daughter Elizabeth Cotton (1722–1782) and Jonathan Hastings (1708/9–1783), m. 1750. The initial "H" was probably engraved for him or one of his descendants; to their son John Hastings (1754–1839) and Lydia Dana (1755–1808),[7] m. 1783; to their son Edmund Trowbridge Hastings (1789–1861) and Elizabeth Spring, m. 1815; to their daughter Harriet Elizabeth Hastings (1818–1887) and John Bryant Hatch (1817–1890), m. 1841; to their son George Stanley Hatch (1855–1931), Mary Kidder Whiting (b. 1861), m. 1891; to their son Francis Whiting Hatch (1897–1975), and Katherine Marjory Kennard, m. 1922; to their son Francis Whiting Hatch Jr. (b. 1925), the donor.[8]

Exhibition and publications: Buhler 1956, cat. no. 139; Kane 1998, 956.

NOTES TO THIS ENTRY ARE ON PAGE 165.

127

Edward Webb (about 1666–1718)

Chocolate pot

Boston, Massachusetts, about 1706–18
Gift of a Friend of the Department of American Decorative Arts and Sculpture, and Marion E. Davis Fund
1993.61

H. 9¹³⁄₁₆ in. (25 cm); W. 6⅞ in. (17.5 cm); Diam. rim 3⁷⁄₁₆ in. (8.7 cm); Diam. base 3¹¹⁄₁₆ in. (9.4 cm); Wt. 28 oz 2 dwt 12 gr (874.8 gm)

Marks: "EW" within a rectangle struck right of handle and within undecorated band on lid, opposite hinge.

Inscriptions: "P / T [pellet] A" in roman letters engraved on a later applied shield surrounded by shell and scroll mantling.

CHOCOLATE POTS, like sugar boxes, were among the rarest silver forms in the early eighteenth century. Fashioned for an elite clientele to serve imported luxury foodstuffs from the Caribbean and its southern neighbors, many of these vessels were lavishly decorated in the international Baroque style.[1]

The desire for such fine goods came from wealthy local merchants and a succession of royal appointees from abroad who had sufficient funds and an appetite for the latest styles. For instance, while stationed in New England between 1708 and 1709, Scottish captain Walter Riddell purchased a large unadorned punch bowl from John Coney in the newly fashionable Georgian style (cat. no. 32). Many recently arrived craftsmen served as transmitters of the latest trends while working as journeymen for established Boston artisans. They enabled the city's workshops to deliver goods in current London fashions for discriminating patrons and, ultimately, through diffusion to the general population.[2]

Such objects offer a useful corrective to the modern image of an unrelentingly dour Puritan existence. More than a few colonists showed an inclination for personal adornment despite religious teachings against vanity. They dressed in handsome clothes and decorated their homes according to their means. Only a few could afford the elaborately worked surfaces of sugar boxes and chocolate pots. The commanding sculptural presence of these forms and the rare commodities they held provide us with a perspective on the tastes and culture of an assuredly small but very cosmopolitan group.

London-trained silversmith Edward Webb was an active member of the craftsman community, arriving in Boston after 1704. More than forty examples bearing his mark have

127

Of the eight chocolate pots by five Boston silversmiths that have survived, six were made before 1720. Of these, four are distinguished by a tall domed lid and ribbed or fluted decoration derived from English precedent. The group of four includes this example by Webb; one made by Peter Oliver (about 1682–1712), possibly for Beulah (Jacquett) Coates; and two by Edward Winslow, who fashioned one vessel for the Auchmuty family and the other for merchant Thomas Hutchinson.[4] Stylistically, this group is as advanced as any created abroad.

Webb differed from Winslow and Oliver in his method of creating the broad bands of vertical decoration seen on this vessel. Following the practice of Denny's shop, Webb flat-chased the narrow concave or fluted channels, rather than taking the extra time to fashion reeds, which involved repoussé work as well as chasing. Webb's narrow irregular flutes, with their erratic punctuated borders, were characteristic of silver from Denny's shop, as can be seen in a monteith dated 1702 and a mug from 1703, both ostensibly made before Webb's departure for Boston. This distinctive treatment points to Webb as a likely journeyman for John Coney, whose monteith for Boston merchant John Coleman has fluted sides and a contrasting gadrooned foot similar to those seen here.[5]

Aside from the mildly stimulating medicinal properties attributed to chocolate, it was considered a relaxing social drink. Dissolved in a solution of claret, milk, egg, sugar, and spices, and stirred with a rod or paddle inserted through the lid, chocolate was prepared slowly, which no doubt contributed to the ceremony and enjoyment of the beverage. An export of provinces belonging to Catholic Spain, chocolate may have offered a brief mental escape from reformist strictures. Often set against a background of "studied leisure," the luxury of chocolate drinking may have fallen out of fashion among the wealthy, who found the connotations of idleness and even licentiousness to be not in keeping with their Protestant upbringing.[6]

The popularity of chocolate never matched that of tea or coffee, this last being politically preferable to tea during the Revolutionary War. However, its consumption perhaps should not be judged according to the survival of chocolate pots, for these specialized forms may have proved too expensive for many households. Julie Emerson notes that coffeepots and chocolate pots were "interchangeable" in Europe, and perhaps in the colonies the same proved true. The need for stirring rods (molinets) to dissolve the chocolate may have been rendered less necessary with the availability of improved grinding methods, as advertised in 1737 by an unnamed Salem gentleman. Still, only two Boston silver chocolate pots dated after 1750 are

survived—a large group considering that Webb's career in Massachusetts lasted only about fourteen years, until his death in 1718. Most of his silver is undecorated, perhaps to suit the majority of his colonial customers, but the impressive range of tools recorded in an inventory of his estate proves that he was well equipped to create forms such as those he crafted as an apprentice in the London shop of William Denny (active 1679–d. 1709).[3] This chocolate pot, a recent discovery, is stylistically closest (presumably) to the silver he fashioned in England, and it is unarguably his masterpiece.

known, both made by Zachariah Brigden. The presence of two chocolate grinders in the Boston directory of 1789 proves that the market for the beverage, if not the form itself, continued through the end of the eighteenth century.[7]

Description: The chocolate pot is a raised straight-sided vessel with a center point that tapers inward from a broad rounded base toward a tall domed cover. The vessel is soldered to a splayed gadrooned foot with an applied foot ring.

The lowest portion is composed of a fluted design with decorative punchwork surrounding its base. The spout, with acanthus-leaf decoration, and lower join of handle are attached to this section. A broad central area, flanked by drawn and molded midbands, is unornamented save for an applied shield with shell and leafy mantling that postdates the vessel's production. The rim has an applied and molded lip.

At the top of the tall domed lid is a removable screw-style finial in the shape of a tea caddy. Cut-card decoration radiates outward from the finial, below which is a band of fluted decoration like that found at the base. Drawn molded midbands flank the lower plain section, in which the maker's mark appears. An applied rim with alternating fluted and concave decoration is soldered at an angle to the rim of the lid, adding an additional flourish that serves to draw the eye upward. A shallow flange secures the lid in place.

The tall scrolled thumbpiece descends to a right-angled five-part hinge with molded decoration. The hinge extends downward to sockets that are circular in section, with applied molding at its outer edge; the socket tapers toward the body. Old, possibly original, C-shaped handle with broken thumbgrip is secured to sockets with pins.

History: Original owner unknown. The later initials "P / T [pellet] A" on the applied escutcheon may refer to one of several Boston couples who were married in the decades after the chocolate pot was made.[8] Subsequent history unknown until the twentieth century, when the vessel was apparently acquired by the Cryder family of South Center, Pennsylvania. Gaylord M. Cryder (b. 1896), owner of Cryder Candies, known locally for chocolates, may have acquired the work in connection with his business;[9] by descent to his brother Dr. Elton Cryder (1900–1991) of South Center, Pennsylvania. The vessel was purchased on June 13, 1992, by Susan Lee of Lightstreet, Pennsylvania, at the Cryder estate auction held by Nevius Auction Service of Mifflinville, Pennsylvania; purchased in 1993 at Christie's, New York.

Exhibitions and publications: Christie's, New York, sale 7604, January 22, 1993, lot 241; Lita and Sally Solis-Cohen, "Auction-goer Hits the Jackpot by Snagging Rare Piece for $75" *Sunday Star-Ledger* (New Jersey), January 10, 1993; Virginia Bohlin, "From Attic to Museum, in a $110,000 Bid," *Boston Sunday Globe,* January 31, 1993, 40; Lita Solis-Cohen, "Americana Discoveries," *Maine Antique Digest* (February 1993), 13A; Lita Solis-Cohen, "Silver and Old English Pottery Star," *Maine Antique Digest* (March 1993), 1C; Francis Russell, ed., *Christie's*

Review of the Season 1993 (New York: Christie's, 1993), 191; Falino and Ward 2001, 72.

NOTES TO THIS ENTRY ARE ON PAGES 165–66.

128

Edward Webb (about 1666–1718)
Porringer

Boston, Massachusetts, about 1710
Gift in loving memory of John Lowell Lyman
1992.271

H. 2⅛ in. (5.4 cm); W. 7⅞ in. (20 cm); Diam. rim 5⅜ in. (13.6 cm); Wt. 7 oz 13 dwt 15 gr (238.9 gm)

Marks: "EW" within a rectangle struck within bowl and above center point.

Inscriptions: "G / R ↑ K" over effaced initials engraved on handle, facing away from bowl. "Rufus Greene & Katherine Stanbridge / Married / December 11. 1728" in script engraved later on base of bowl.

THE HANDSOME GEOMETRIC HANDLE of this porringer is seemingly identical to at least three other known examples by Edward Webb, attesting to the popularity of this design in Boston at the beginning of the eighteenth century.[1] The vessel is also one of several works in the Museum's collection

that were owned by Loyalist and silversmith-turned-merchant Rufus Greene. In addition to a pepper box, or caster, made by Greene and owned by the craftsman and his wife, Katherine Stanbridge, the couple also owned a tankard by Boston silversmith David Jesse.[2]

Both Webb and Jesse were dead before Greene came of age, and their silver was probably made when he was a child. How the vessels came into his possession is unclear.

In the years between 1728, the year in which Greene began to practice independently as a silversmith, and 1749, when he is first listed in the public records as a merchant, the former craftsman gradually turned to more profitable mercantile pursuits that included land speculation and the sale of rum and sugar. Success in these enterprises brought the means to furnish Greene's comfortable household with such items as heraldic embroideries, leather chairs, and other upholstered goods; portraits of the couple were painted by John Singleton Copley about 1758–61.[3] It is possible that the Webb porringer, Jesse tankard, and Greene pepper box were the same as those listed in the former silversmith's probate inventory.[4]

Description: The raised porringer has a center punch evident inside its domed bowl; convex sides and everted rim; and a cast geometric handle soldered to rim.

History: Original owners unknown. Acquired by silversmith and merchant Rufus Greene (1707–1777) and his wife, Katherine Stanbridge (about 1709–1768), m. 1728.[5] By descent to their daughter Katherine Greene (1731–1778) and John Amory (1728–1803), m. 1757; to their daughter Rebecca Amory (1771–1842) and John Lowell (1769–1840), m. 1793; to their son the Hon. John Amory Lowell (1798–1881) and his second wife, Elizabeth Cabot Putnam (1807–1881), m. 1829[6]; to their daughter Ella Bancroft Lowell (1837–1894) and Arthur Theodore Lyman (1832–1915), m. 1858[7]; to their son Ronald Theodore Lyman (1879–1962) and Elizabeth van Cortlandt Parker (about 1883–1953), m. 1904.[8] By descent to their son John Lowell Lyman (1915–1986) and Cynthia Forbes (b. 1918), m. 1942, the donor.

Exhibitions and publications: English-Speaking Union 1960, no. 17, pl. 12; Kane 1998, 954.

NOTES TO THIS ENTRY ARE ON PAGE 166.

129

Edward Winslow (1669–1753)
Child's porringer

Boston, Massachusetts, about 1690–1720
Gift of the Wunsch Americana Foundation in recognition of Kathryn C. Buhler
1983.760

H. 1½ in. (3.9 cm); W. 6¹¹⁄₁₆ in. (17 cm); Diam. rim 4⁵⁄₁₆ in. (11 cm); Wt. 4 oz 5 dwt 14 gr (133.1 gm)

Marks: "EW" over a fleur-de-lis, in a shaped cartouche, struck on back of handle, over faint mark "WR" conjoined with a coronet above, all within a circle. Incomplete mark "EW" over a fleur-de-lis, within a shaped cartouche, struck to left of handle.

Inscriptions: "Mary Lowell / 1833 / Mary Lowell Coolidge / 1891" in script engraved later underneath bowl.

EDWARD WINSLOW is known for his skill in fashioning ambitious forms. His chocolate pots, candlesticks, and sugar boxes are considered among the most outstanding accomplishments of colonial American silversmiths.

Following his likely apprenticeship to Jeremiah Dummer, which would have ended about 1690, Winslow enjoyed his most productive period from about 1695 to about 1720, even as his growing civic and military duties required him to take on journeymen to handle daily shop activities. He was prominent in civil and military affairs in Boston beginning about 1700, when he became a member of the Ancient and Honorable Artillery Company. In addition to several other offices throughout his life, in 1743, at age seventy-four, Winslow was appointed judge of the Inferior Court of Common Pleas, a post he held until his death in 1753.

This child's porringer offers evidence of one means of the transmission of silver styles from England to America. Any enterprising silversmith who found himself with London-made goods, whether for repair or for sale, would have found it a simple task to appropriate useful decorative elements to cast for future use. It may have been especially attractive for Winslow to cast a small porringer handle. Since commissions for children's silver were infrequent, he would have been able to satisfy a patron without resorting to the labor-intensive fabrication of a new handle.

The unusual strike of the Winslow mark over another by maker "WR" indicates that the Boston silversmith had access to an English porringer, which he cast for his own use. The original porringer handle was made by an unnamed London goldsmith whose mark was recorded in 1674–75. A second porringer carrying a vestige of this English mark was made by Rhode Island silversmith Isaac Anthony (1690–1773), likely a Winslow apprentice. The "WR" mark occurrs in the same location as on the Winslow vessel. The handles of both porringers are identical, and they undoubtedly came from the same mold.[1]

Given the relationship between the two vessels, Anthony probably obtained a cast of the handle during his years with Winslow. Anthony was born in Portsmouth, Rhode Island, but appeared in Boston by 1712, when he was taken to court for debt. Two years later, he married Marcy Chamberlain of Boston in a Quaker service; he purchased goods from Boston stationer Daniel Henchman in 1715. Anthony probably became Winslow's apprentice through the influence of Rhode Island silversmiths Samuel Vernon (1683–1737) and John Coddington (1690–1743) and Boston silversmith Thomas Savage Sr. (1664–1749), to whom Winslow was related through his mother, Elizabeth Hutchinson (1639–1728).[2]

Description: The small raised porringer with geometric handle has convex sides and a slightly everted rim. The faint small dome in the bottom of the bowl has a center punch. The cast handle has pronounced filing marks on its underside, perpendicular to bowl.

History: Early history unknown. By the nineteenth century, the porringer was owned by Mary Lowell (1833–1915) of Waltham, Massachusetts, daughter of textile manufacturer Francis Cabot Lowell (1803–1894) and Mary Gardner (b. 1808), m. 1826; she m. Boston physician Algernon (Sidney) Coolidge (1830–1912) in 1856.[3] The por-

ringer was given to her granddaughter and namesake, Wellesley College professor Mary Lowell Coolidge (1891–1958), eldest daughter of their third son, Sidney (1864–1939), and his wife, Mary Laura Colt (b. 1866), m. 1890.[4] Subsequent ownership unknown until 1971, when the porringer was purchased by the donor from Gebelein Silversmiths, Boston.[5]

Exhibitions and publications: Advertisement, Gebelein Silversmiths, *Antiques* 100, no. 2 (August 1971), 162; Wendy A. Cooper, "New Findings on Colonial New England Goldsmiths and English Sources," *American Art Journal* 10, no. 2 (November 1978), 107–9, fig. 6; Kane 1998, 979

NOTES TO THIS ENTRY ARE ON PAGE 166.

130

Edward Winslow (1669–1753)
Tankard

Boston, Massachusetts, 1690–1704
Gift in memory of John Bryant Paine and Louise Frazer Paine from their children and grandchildren
1980.242

H. 6⅞ in. (17.5 cm); W. 5 in. (12.8 cm); Diam. rim 4⅛ in. (10.5 cm); Diam. base 5 in. (12.8 cm); Wt. 23 oz 10 dwt 23 gr (732.4 gm)

Marks: "EW" within a shaped mark, over a fleur-de-lis, struck on lid and to left of handle.

Inscriptions: "P / T M" in shaded roman capitals engraved on handle.

ABOUT TWENTY-FOUR TANKARDS bearing Winslow's mark are known, most dated between 1700 and 1730. The tankard for the Paine family of Eastham, Massachusetts—with its plain body and flat lid, handle accented with a cast dolphin-and-mask thumbpiece, and cherub terminal—is characteristic of many that Winslow made.[1]

Family history records that this tankard was originally owned by Thomas and Mary Paine, who were married in 1650. If they did purchase it, they acquired it some forty years after their marriage, an unusual acquisition made late in their lives.[2]

Description: The raised tankard with straight tapering sides has a center point on base. The drawn and stepped base molding rises to an applied everted rim; a pair of scored lines appears below the lip. The raised, two-stepped, flat-topped lid also has a center punch; two pairs of scored lines encircle the rim, and there is a crenate lip.

130

Eastham, Massachusetts, who in 1650 m. Mary Snow (1627–1704), daughter of Nicholas (1602–1676) and Constance (Hopkins) Snow (about 1605–1677) of Eastham.[3] However, it is more likely the tankard was first owned by their son James (1665–1728) and his wife, Bethiah Thacher (1671–1734). The tankard passed by descent to their son the Rev. Thomas Paine (1694–1757) and Eunice Treat (1704–1747), thence to Thomas's son Robert Treat Paine (1731–1814), a signer of the Declaration of Independence, and his wife, Sarah (Sally) Cobb (1740–1816). The tankard briefly entered the matrilineal line when it was given to Paine's eldest daughter, Mary (1780–1842), m. the Rev. Elisha Clap (also Clapp) (1783–1869).[4] As the couple had no issue, the tankard returned to the patrilineal line when it was inherited by their nephew Charles Cushing Paine (1808–1874) and his wife, Fanny Cabot Jackson (1812–1878). The tankard was given to their son Charles Jackson Paine (1833–1916) and his wife, Julia Lee Bryant (1847–1901), and thence to their son John Bryant Paine (1870–1951). The tankard was made a gift in honor of John Bryant Paine and his wife, Louise Rue Frazer (1879–1968), by their children and grandchildren: Helen Sumner Paine Dickson; Caroline Satterthwait Paine Ganson; Julia Lee Paine Wakefield; her children Elizabeth W. Doermann, Julia W. Proctor, Joan W. Millspaugh, and Sarah K. Wakefield; Louise Frazer Paine Erickson; Sarah Cushing Paine Forbes; Henrietta N. Paine.[5]

Exhibitions and publications: Kane 1998, 981.

NOTES TO THIS ENTRY ARE ON PAGE 166.

131

Edward Winslow (1669–1753)
Chafing dish

Boston, Massachusetts, about 1710–25
Gift of Mrs. James B. Peabody in memory of the late James Bishop Peabody
1980.627

H. 4⁵⁄₁₆ in. (10.8 cm); W. 10³⁄₁₆ in. (26 cm); Diam. 5⁷⁄₈ in. (15 cm); Wt. 13 oz 8 dwt 20 gr (418.1 gm)

Marks: "EW" over a fleur-de-lis, within a shaped cartouche, struck on bottom.

Inscription: "G / T ★ R / to / L H" in shaded roman letters engraved on bottom. Later script engraving notes history of ownership: "Thomas R. Goodwill / to / Lydia Holmes (Bishop) / to Rebecca Bishop / to / John Bishop / to / Lydia H. Bishop (Jones) / to Heber R. Bishop / 1861 / to Ogden M. Bishop / 1903; Known to have been in the family over 100 Years." At the request of the donor, after its acquisition by the Museum, the following text was added below the date "1903": "to / James Bishop Peabody / 1955."

The cast thumbpiece consists of a pair of dolphins flanking a circular mask of a mustachioed man; meander wire is below. The five-part hinge has a cast linen-fold hingeplate, again with meander wire below. The raised and seamed scroll handle is attached to the body with a long rattail drop at upper join. The terminus is a cast winged cherub's head; a coarse triangular air vent is below. The lid and stepped section near hinge have been reworked. The handle bears significant wear marks consistent with contact to thumbpiece.

History: According to family history and the engraved initials, the tankard was made for Thomas Paine (1612–1706) of Yarmouth and

131

CONSIDERED "among the chief aristocrats in the category of old plate," chafing dishes are among the rarest forms of colonial silver tableware. Primarily of Dutch and French origin, they are related to humbler examples, also called braziers, that served as simple space or food warmers and that were made of common materials such as clay, brass, or copper.[1] In the hands of talented silversmiths, the utilitarian brazier was transformed into an elegant accessory whose delicate cast elements and lively saw-pierced decoration added a refined note to the colonial table.

The term *chafing dish* is derived from the French word for the form, *réchauffé*, meaning "a dish that has been warmed or reheated."[2] Designed to keep food warm at the dining table, chafing dishes were a welcome addition to colonial homes lacking in modern insulation. Plates of food were positioned on three supports and heated from below by a dish filled with burning charcoal. Embers glowed through the pierced sides of the bowl, which provided necessary ventilation for combustion, and the ashes fell through a pierced grill into a small receptacle. The heat generated during use may have damaged many silver examples and account for the rare survival of the form. The popularity of chafing dishes extended from the 1690s until the 1740s, with only a few later examples dating from the 1750s.

Of the thirty-five or so extant examples of colonial chafing dishes, most were fashioned in Massachusetts by at least seventeen silversmiths. Jacob Hurd was the most prolific, and about a dozen examples bear his mark.[3]

Far fewer examples hail from New York and Philadelphia. In those cities, Peter Van Dyck (1684–1751), Adrian Bancker (1703–1772), Johannis Nys (1671–1734), and Philip Syng II (1703–1789) were among the few silversmiths known to fashion this useful table accessory.[4] Curiously, the two known chafing dishes by Winslow are closer in style to the Van Dyck and Bancker examples than to their Boston counterparts. They can be considered as part of a larger group, categorized by Barbara McLean Ward as "type B" for having the ember box and vessel raised as a single unit; they also form a subgroup with the New York/Philadelphia examples in that their convex sides are pierced with a stylized fleur-de-lis pattern, and each displays deep ash receptacles.[5] The three strap legs that form the feet and supports are likewise similar in that they conform to the bowl and have flattened shell supports.

The chief differences between the above-mentioned chafing dishes and those by Winslow can be discerned in the handling of the feet and the placement of the handle socket. The Museum's chafing dish has a modified pad-and-sphere foot that houses a wooden insulating ball. By contrast, the New York examples terminate in flat chased forms that echo the shell supports. The handle of each Winslow chafing dish is soldered to the vertical supports rather than to the body, as found in the New York examples.

Many similarities exist between the two Winslow chafing dishes, but subtle differences in proportions and details suggest that they might have been made as many as ten or fifteen years apart.[6] The bowl portion of the Museum's example has a more horizontal profile, in keeping with early-eighteenth-century silver, whereas the taller form of the second vessel offers a vertical orientation that found favor as the decades progressed. Similarly, a comparison of the lower section of the Museum's chafing dish has circular piercings in a shallow ash receptacle instead of the inverted teardrops over a deeper container that are found in the second version. In this analysis, the teardrops may be construed as looking toward the inverted pear form that became a fashionable rococo statement. Last, the Museum's dish sports silver hemispherical cups to which are affixed wooden feet, a feature that adds to its horizontal axis and one that is missing from the other example. Given these differences, Winslow's "EW" conjoined mark, found on the latter chafing dish and thought to indicate works made after 1720, may be offered as further proof that it was the second of the two works.

Description: The raised bowl-shaped chafing dish has a depressed center; the scored rim has drawn and applied molding. The side of the body is pierced in a repeating foliate pattern. A circular pierced grate seats over a recessed ember box and is secured beneath the vessel with a threaded silver nut and bolt having a domed head. Three vertical, flat supports conform to the convex sides. The supports terminate above the rim in chased shell-pattern dish rests and extend outward at base to form a rounded pad foot over a hemispherical section, housing spherical wooden feet. The exterior of each leg is reinforced with a narrow band of silver applied between the ember box and foot. The modern turned wooden handle is secured to a tapering socket, circular in section, and fitted over vertical side supports.

History: The chafing dish was probably made for Thomas Goodwill (1687–1749), Boston selectman and shipwright, and Rebecca Blakeman (bap. 1689) of Boston, sometime after their marriage in 1710. Although their daughter Rebecca Goodwill (1717–1800) was not mentioned in the engraving, the chafing dish probably descended to her and her husband, Nathaniel Holmes (1703–1774), m. 1747.[7] The chafing dish descended to their daughter Lydia Holmes (1758–1807), m. John Bishop (1755–1833) in 1782; by descent to their daughter Rebecca Bishop (1785–1807), d. unm.; to either her brother John Bishop (1787–1830), d. unm., or her father, both of whom were alive in 1807; to Lydia H. Bishop (1828–1860), niece or granddaughter to the John Bishops and wife of Samuel Howell Jones (1818–1883), m. 1862, who died without issue; to her brother Heber Reginald Bishop (1840–1902), m. Mary Cunningham; to his son Ogden Mills Bishop (1878–1955),[8] d. unm.; to his grandnephew James Bishop Peabody (1922–1978), a trustee of the Museum of Fine Arts, Boston, and secretary of the Museum from 1971 until his death in 1978; made a gift by his wife, the former Ann Reinecke.[9]

Exhibitions and publications: Kane 1998, 977.

NOTES TO THIS ENTRY ARE ON PAGES 166–67.

132

Edward Winslow (1669–1753)

Porringer

Boston, Massachusetts, 1715
Bequest of Barbara Boylston Bean
1976.640

H. 2 in. (5 cm); W. 8⅛ in. (20.5 cm); Diam. rim 5¼ in. (13.4 cm); Wt.
8 oz 5 dwt 1 gr (256.7 gm)

Marks: "EW" over a fleur-de-lis within a shield struck to left of
handle, on everted rim.

Inscriptions: "B / T S" in shaded roman capitals engraved on
handle, facing bowl.

THIS EARLY KEYHOLE-STYLE porringer, which descended in
the Boylston family, is said to be related to another made by
Edward Winslow for the same family and engraved "B / W
E."[1]

Description: The raised vessel with center point visible on both sides
of bowl has a wide low dome in its base, rising to a broad convex
side, and a nearly vertical rim. A cast keyhole-style handle is soldered to the body.

History: The porringer was probably made for Thomas Boylston (d.
1739) and Sarah Morecock (1696–1774), daughter of Nicholas Morecock, at about the time of their marriage on May 4, 1715. Descended
to their daughter Mary (b. 1722), wife of Capt. Benjamin Hallowell

(1724–1799), a Loyalist customs commissioner who fled to Canada
in 1776. By descent to their son Ward Hallowell (1747–1828), who
was adopted by his mother's unmarried brother, Nicholas Boylston
(1716–1771), who made him his namesake.[2] The porringer descended
to John Lane Boylston (1789–1847), son of Ward Nicholas (Hallowell) Boylston and his second wife, Alicia Darrow, of England. John
Lane Boylston m. Sarah Brooks (b. 1793) in 1813; by descent to their
son Thomas (b. 1819) and his wife, Caroline A. Fowle; to their son
Thomas Boylston Jr. (1848–1870) and his wife, Florence Randall (b.
about 1851); to their son Ward Nicholas Boylston (1871–1924) and
his second wife, Alice Meehan (d. 1938);[3] to their daughter Barbara Boylston Bean (1913–1975), the donor and wife of Paul W. Bean
(1914–1971).[4] The porringer was part of a large bequest from a
Boylston family descendant.

Exhibitions and publications: Kane 1998, 979.

NOTES TO THIS ENTRY ARE ON PAGE 167.

133

Edward Winslow (1669–1753)

Pair of candlesticks

Boston, Massachusetts, about 1715–20
Bequest of Mr. and Mrs. Horace Havemeyer
1983.162–163

1983.162: H. 7⅝ in. (19.4 cm); W. 4⅞ in. (12.4 cm); Wt. 14 oz 5 dw 15
gr (444.2 gm)

1983.163: H. 7⅝ in. (19.4 cm); W. 4⅞ in. (12.4 cm); Wt. 14 oz 0 dwt 8
gr (436.8 gm)

Marks: "EW" over a fleur-de-lis within a shield struck on exterior of
domed portion of each base.

Inscriptions: None.

FEW COLONIAL SILVER CANDLESTICKS by American makers
have survived. It is likely that the need for them was obviated by
the presence of imported silver and brass candlesticks, which
were as handsome as they were affordable.[1] The popularity of
candlesticks in the eighteenth century was probably enhanced
by their inclusion in period furniture designs. Candlestick slides
made for desks and bookcases and the reserves set into the corners of card tables are but two examples of how these lighting
devices were accommodated in the home.[2]

A few silver candlesticks were forged and fabricated in the
early colonial period. By the eighteenth century, however, most
were cast, as in the case of this pair by Edward Winslow. Other

133

known examples of cast silver candlesticks of the period were made by John Coney, John Burt, Myer Myers, and Nathaniel Morse.[3] The presence of two such molds in the inventory of John Coney's estate demonstrates that colonial silversmiths had the means to cast such forms.[4] Some American makers, including Thomas Dane (1726–1759) of Boston, Samuel Tingley (active about 1767–about 1796) of New York, and Edmund Milne (d. 1822) of Philadelphia, used imported candlesticks as models to cast new works.[5] In some cases, the colonial touch-mark appears over effaced English hallmarks. These examples prove the readiness of colonial silversmiths to sell and appropriate foreign imports when available.

The Winslow candlesticks may be the earliest of his three known pairs. Colonial Williamsburg and the Metropolitan Museum of Art each possess similar pairs by the maker; the latter's pair bears the arms of Edward Hutchinson.[6] These examples are notable for the inverted trumpet form found on each baluster, a detail that appears in English and French forms in the 1720s and 1730s. The densely packed octagonal knops of the Museum's candlesticks suggest a somewhat earlier style but one that postdates a pair by John Coney in the Museum's collection, which was dated about 1710 by Kathryn C. Buhler.[7]

Description: The octagonal socket and baluster candlesticks are cast in halves vertically. Each baluster consists of an urn-shaped socket, bulb, vase, and reel column, terminating in spreading octagonal section that merges with domed base. Each splayed, stepped, octagonal foot is formed in separate sections and soldered to a raised domed center; a narrow strengthening band is applied at lower edge. One candlestick (1983.163) shows a break in strengthening band at one joint.

History: Original owner unknown; owned by architect Adolph Mollenhauer Dick (1894–1956). The candlesticks were purchased from his estate by his sister Doris Dick (1890–1982) and sugar refiner Horace Havemeyer (1886–1956), m. 1911, who later bequeathed them to the Museum.[8]

Exhibitions and publications: Parke-Bernet, New York, sale 1669, April 14, 1956, lot 301; Fairbanks 1991, 91, cat. no. 23; Kane 1998, 976.

NOTES TO THIS ENTRY ARE ON PAGE 167.

134

Edward Winslow (1669–1753)

Tankard

Boston, Massachusetts, about 1720–30
Gift of Dorothy B. Hammond in memory of Roland B.
Hammond
1995.801

H. 7¹¹⁄₁₆ in. (19.6 cm); W. 7¹¹⁄₁₆ in. (19.5 cm); Diam. rim 4⅛ in. (10.5 cm); Diam. base 5⅛ in. (13 cm); Wt. 28 oz 3 dwt 2 gr (875.7 gm)

Marks: "EW" in double circle struck to left of handle.

Inscriptions: Crude "E * D" engraved later on handle; scratch weight of "28 oz 9 dwt 8 gr" on bottom.

SILVER WAS PRODUCED in Edward Winslow's shop long after he assumed civic responsibilities with the Ancient and Honorable Artillery Company and as sheriff of Suffolk County from 1716 to 1743. The style of this tankard, with its tapering body and domed lid, indicates that it was probably made during the 1720s or 1730s by either Thomas Mullins, John Banks, or Thomas McCullough, three journeymen known to have worked for Winslow between 1715 and 1742/43.[1]

It is doubtful that Winslow's shop would have produced such crudely engraved initials as those on this handle, which were probably added later by an untrained hand.

Description: The raised tankard with tapering cylindrical body has an applied midband, rim, and drawn and molded foot. The stepped domed cover with scored rim has a peened-in button finial and flange within. A tall scroll thumbpiece descends to the five-part hinge and seamed S-scroll handle with baluster decoration. Prominent wear marks appear on the handle as a result of contact with thumbpiece. The handle is attached to the body with rounded drop at upper join; an oval disk is below. Plain convex disk appears at terminus, with semicircular air vent below.

History: The initials "E * D," combined with oral history of ownership in the Jewett family, points to Edward Dearborn as the probable first owner. The tankard descended as follows: Edward Dearborn

(1702–1746) and Mary Foss (d. after 1746), both of Greenland, New Hampshire, m. 1724; to their daughter Mary Dearborn (bap. 1735) and Benjamin Jewett (d. after 1777), m. about 1761; to their son Dearborn Jewett (1765/66–1854) and Mary Furber (1760–1837), m. about 1786; to their son Capt. Theodore Furber Jewett (b. 1787) and Sarah Orne (d. 1819), m. 1812; to their son Dr. Theodore H. Jewett (1815–1878) and Caroline Frances Perry (b. 1820), m. 1842;[2] to their daughter Caroline Augusta Jewett (b. 1855) and Edwin C. Eastman (b. 1849), m. 1878; to their only son, Theodore Jewett Eastman (1879–1931), d. unm.;[3] made a gift to his cousin Charles French Perry (1833–1897) and Georgianna West Graves (1852–1934), m. 1872; to their daughter Elizabeth Lejee Perry (1879–1969) and Henry Hyslop Richardson (1872–1932), son of the Boston architect, m. 1906.[4] Mrs. Richardson placed the tankard on loan to the Museum in 1948 and transferred ownership in 1952 to her brother, architect William Graves Perry (1883–1975), and his first wife, Eleanor Bodine (b. 1886), m. 1908. To their son William Graves Perry Jr. (1913–1998) and his first wife, Helen Knowles.[5] The tankard was recalled from the Museum in 1991 and then purchased by North Andover, Massachusetts, antiques dealer Roland Bowman Hammond (1917–1993); by descent to his wife, Dorothy B. Hammond, the donor.

Exhibitions and publications: The Winslows: Pilgrims, Patrons, and Portraits (Boston: Museum of Fine Arts, Boston, 1974), 52, cat. no. 48; Northeast Auctions, Portsmouth, New Hampshire, November 4, 1995, lot 743; Kane 1998, 982.

NOTES TO THIS ENTRY ARE ON PAGE 167.

Notes

1

1. Kane 1998, 154–55.

2. Kane 1998, 157.

3. Jones 1913, 323–24, 482; Kane 1998, 159.

4. MFA 1911, 4, cat. no. 27, pl. 3; Buhler 1972 1:93, cat. no. 75; Kane 1998, 155–56.

5. *A Genealogy of the Descendants of John May Who Came from England to Roxbury in America, 1640* (Boston: Franklin Press, 1878), 4, 43–44, 53, 83; Kane 1998, 256.

2

1. For other collaborative work in this volume, see cat. nos. 12–13, 165–66, 172.

2. Kane 1998, 695–97.

3. For objects marked by Minott with a second mark of William Simpkins, Samuel Bartlett, William Homes Sr., Thomas Townsend, or Josiah Austin, see Kane 1998, 689–690, 694, 696.

4. Jones 1913, 482.

5. Departmental files, Art of the Americas; Kane 1998, 157, 696.

3

1. For a discussion of the auricular style, whose origins in Utrecht date to the the early seventeenth century, see R. W. Lightbown, "Christian van Vianen at the Court of Charles the First," *Proceedings of the Society of Silver Collectors* 2 (1966), 2–11; J. R. ter Molen, "The Van Vianen Family, Utrecht Silversmiths of International Renown," *International Silver & Jewellery Fair & Seminar* (London: The Dorchester, 1986), 22–31.

2. Other New York makers of these spoons include Jurian Blanck Jr. (about 1645–1714), Jesse Kip (1660–1722), Benjamin Wynkoop (1675–1751), Bartholomew Le Roux (1663–1713), Jacobus van der Spiegel (1668–1708), and Ahasuerus Hendricks (w. 1675–1727). See "An Early New York Spoon" in "The Editor's Attic," *Antiques* 40, no. 5 (November 1941), 300; Helen Burr Smith, "Four Hoof-Spoons," *Antiques* 45, no. 6 (June 1944), 292–94; Albert Scher, "Two Hoof Spoons," *Antiques* 114, no. 3 (September 1972), 567–69; Buhler and Hood 1970, 2:cat. nos. 550–52, 554; Warren 1987, cat. nos. 68–69; advertisement, William Core Duffy, *Maine Antique Digest* (November 1988); Quimby 1995, 196, 201, cat. no. 158.

3. Quimby 1995, 196, 201, cat. no. 158.

4. For the mark of Henricus Boelen, see Waddington's auction catalogue, Toronto, Canada, June 11–15, 1984, lot 667, ill. 68; advertisement, William Core Duffy, *Maine Antique Digest* (August 1984), 15-A; Deborah Dependahl Waters to Jeannine Falino, December 14, 1998.

4

1. Quotation from Rita Susswein Gottesman, comp., *The Arts and Crafts in New York, 1726–1776* (New York: New-York Historical Society, 1968), 31.

2. John N. Pearce, "New York's Two-handled Paneled Silver Bowls," *Antiques* 80, no. 4 (October 1961), 341–45.

3. The two other flowered vessels by Jacob Boelen are published in Buhler and Hood 1970, 2:12, cat. no. 556; and Miller 1937, 47, cat. no. 36.

4. In addition to the three floral vessels, the four additional forms in plain, anthemion, and paneled styles are illustrated in Avery 1932, fig. 17, and recorded in DAPC 69.1561, 71.2940, and 68.3352. For examples of Dutch- and New York–engraved beakers, see Halsey 1911, frontispiece, xvii, opp.

14, 40; Avery 1932, figs. 10–11, 15–16. The Henricus Boelen bowl (Albany Institute of History and Art) was included in Buhler 1956, 74, cat. no. 168.

5

1. For other flatware by Jacob Boelen, see DAPC 72.3001, 75.2772, 77.2231; Buhler and Hood 1970 2:cat. no. 558; Miller 1962, cat. no. 17; Johnston 1994, 8.

2. Teunis G. Bergen, *The Bergen Family; or, the Descendants of Hans Hansen Bergen, One of the Early Settlers of New York and Brooklyn, L.I.* (New York: Bergen & Tripp, 1866), 80–86, 99–104, 120, 122, 156.

6

1. Vermont 1886, 160; Bolton 1927, 71. The identification of Greene and Charnock arms is indisputable, yet no member of the Charnock family can be discerned in the Greene family history. The motto appears not to originate with either family, lending credence to the theory that in this instance arms were creatively or liberally used. Although many objects bear the Greene arms, only three bearing the Charnock arms are known: two casters (one in the Museum's collection) and a hatchment. See Buhler 1972, 1:73–74, cat. no. 62; auction catalogue, Christie, Manson & Woods, Intl., New York, sale 5264, January 22, 1983, lot 425; Bolton 1927, 32–33.

2. Deborah Dependahl Waters to Jeannine Falino, August 25, 1997; Waters 2000, 1:124–25.

3. For other works by Brevoort, see Avery 1920, 68–69, cat. no. 70; Avery 1932, cat. no. 24; Buhler 1956, 75, cat. nos. 176–78; Buhler and Hood 1970, 2:83–86, cat. nos. 639–42; Buhler 1979, 83, cat. no. 122; Warren 1987, 45, cat. no. 35. An unpublished sugar bowl and cover made by Brevoort for Anne Smith of Smithtown, Long Island, is in the New-York Historical Society (1965.15a–b).

4. Buhler 1972, 2:574–75, cat. no. 497.

5. Miller 1937, 7, cat. nos. 62–65.

6. Henry L. P. Beckwith to Jeannine Falino, May 19, 1998.

7. Louise Brownell Clarke, *The Greenes of Rhode Island with Historical Records of English Ancestry, 1534–1902* (New York: Knickerbocker Press, 1903), 126, 200; Mary Granger, ed., *Savannah River Plantations* (Savannah: Georgia Historical Society, 1947), 71–80; Virgil D. White, abstr., *Genealogical Abstracts of Revolutionary War Pension Files,* Vol. III N–2 (Waynesboro, Tenn.: National Historical Pub. Co., 1992), 3540.

8. Franklin Bowditch Dexter, *Biographical Sketches of the Graduates of Yale College* (New York: Henry Holt, 1907), 4:430–31; Edwin P. Hoyt, *The Whitneys* (New York: Weybright and Talley, 1976); Kenneth Scott, *Marriages and Deaths from the New Yorker, 1836–1841* (Washington, D.C.: National Genealogical Society, 1980), 143.

9. Clarke, *Greenes of Rhode Island,* 328.

10. Gertrude Montague Graves, *A New England Family and Their French Connections* (Boston: privately printed, 1930), 202, 204, 206, 210, 214; Lawrence Shaw Mayo, *The Winthrop Family in America* (Boston: Massachusetts Historical Society, 1948), 347, 408–9; Michael A. Cram, *The Cram Sourcebook* (Bowie, Md.: Heritage Books, 1995), 2:398; Obituaries, *Boston Globe* (December 5, 1976, June 21, 1989).

7

1. Zachariah Brigden Papers, Beinecke Library, Yale University, gen. mss. 86, box 1, folder 29, 38; William S. Tilden, ed., *The History of the Town of Medfield, Massachusetts, 1650–1886* (Boston: George H. Ellis, 1887), 36, 157, 331.

2. Hilary Anderson, "Earning a Living in Eighteenth-Century Boston: Silversmith Zachariah Brigden" (Master's thesis, University of Delaware, 1996), 36, 40–43, 62.

3. Buhler 1972, 2:348–49, 377–78, cat. nos. 307, 331.

4. Kane 1998, 208–18.

5. Tilden, *History of the Town of Medfield,* 331; Kane 1998, 216. See appendix 7 for more on Medfield church silver.

6. Harold Field Worthley, *An Inventory of the Records of the Particular Congregational Churches of Massachusetts, Gathered 1620–1805,* Harvard Theological Studies (Cambridge: Harvard University Press, 1970), 25:359–61; Tilden, *History of the Town of Medfield,* 281–82.

8

1. Buhler 1972, 1:239.

2. Albert H. Hoyt, "Daniel Peirce, of Newbury, Mass., 1638–1677, and His Descendants," *NEHGR* 29 (July 1875), 278; Judson Keith Deming, comp. and ed., *Genealogy of the Descendants of John Deming of Wethersfield, Connecticut, with Historical Notes* (Dubuque, Iowa: Press of Mathis-Mets Col, 1904), 61–62; Robert M. Sherman, *Mayflower Families through Five Generations,* vol. 2, *Chilton, More, Rogers* (Baltimore, Md.: Genealogical Society of Mayflower Descendants, 1978), 2:66.

3. The donors also gave the Museum a cut-paper landscape made by Sarah Winslow West Deming (1990.368). See Alice Morse Earle, ed., *Diary of Anna Green Winslow, A Boston School Girl of 1771* (Williamstown, Mass.: Corner House Publishers, 1974), cover ill. and 74.

9

1. Kane 1998, 212.

10

1. Carpenter and Carpenter 1987, 130; Everett Crosby, *Ninety-Nine Per Cent Perfect* (Nantucket, Mass.: Tetaukimmo Press, 1953), 189–90; Kane 1998, 173–75, 220–22.

11

1. Buhler and Hood 1970, 1:167, cat. no. 215; Buhler 1972, 1:343, cat. 303, 2:645, cat. no. 544; advertisement, Firestone and Parson, *Antiques* 152, no. 5 (November 2002), 98.

2. "Genealogy of the Sumner Family," *NEHGR* 8 (April 1854), 128j, 128m–o; Richard Frothingham, *Life and Times of Joseph Warren* (Boston: Little, Brown, 1865), 545–46; William Sumner Appleton, *Record of the Descendants of William Sumner, of Dorchester, Mass., 1636* (Boston: David Clapp & Son, 1879), 13, 31.

3. Samuel Bradlee Doggett, *A History of the Doggett-Daggett Family* (Boston: Rockwell and Churchill, 1894), 415, 440–45.

4. Doggett, *History of the Doggett-Daggett Family,* 487–88, 547–48; Edward W. Hanson, "The Heards of Ipswich, Massachusetts" (typescript, New England Historic Genealogical Society Library, Boston, 1986), 211, 244. For silhouettes, a sampler, a tea caddy, and additional articles owned by the Sumner family and lent by Mrs. John Heard, see Jamestown 1907, 35, 49, 58–59, 65.

12

1. Bolton 1927, 23–24.

2. Portraits of Jabez and Sarah (Brown) Bowen are discussed in Jules David Prown, *John Singleton Copley,* 2 vols. (Cambridge: Harvard University Press, 1966), 1:209–10.

13

1. These arms were published by John Guillim, *A Display of Heraldry*, 6th ed. (London, 1724), sec. 6, 432.

2. Emlen 1984, 39–50.

3. Brown and Burt correspondence is cited in Emlen 1984, 41–43.

4. Emlen 1984, 46–49.

5. Patricia E. Kane, "Artistry in Boston Silver of the Colonial Period," in Kane 1998, 96, figs. 102–3.

14

1. Bolton records the funeral monument of Col. Samuel Appleton (1653/54–1725) of Ipswich, Mass., with the crest of "an apple of the field." The *Heraldic Journal* notes that the elephant's head couped is also much used in this country, but that "three pine-apples vert, the tops purfled or, in a crown ppr." were also used; Bolton 1927, 5. The crest on the porringer appears to be a simplified version of the latter. See also "The Family of Appleton," *Heraldic Journal* 7 (July 1865), 97–107; William Sumner Appleton, *A Genealogy of the Appleton Family* (Boston: T. R. Marvin & Son, 1874), 7.

2. The portraits are in the following collections: Margaret (MFA, 1995.800), Robert (MFA, 1969.1227), and Henry (Sunrise Museum, Charleston, W. Va.). Fairbanks and Trent 1982, 3:458–59, cat. nos. 433–35; Walter Kendall Watkins, "The Robert Gibbs House, Boston," *Old-Time New England* 22, no. 4 (April 1932), 193–96.

3. Will of Elizabeth Corwin in Curwen Papers, Peabody Essex Museum, Salem, Mass., MSS45, box 1, folder 1.

4. Buhler 1956, 70, cat. no. 139; Buhler 1972, 1:72, cat. no. 61; Kane 1998, 253, 316, 324, 326.

5. Hamilton Perkins Greenough, *Some Descendants of Captain William Greenough of Boston, Massachusetts and Notes on Related Families* (Santa Barbara, Calif.: privately printed, 1969), xxvi; *Sibley's Harvard Graduates*, 3:327–32.

6. John Appleton, *Monumental Memorials of the Appleton Family* (Boston: privately printed, Edward S. Coombs, 1868), 18; *Sibley's Harvard Graduates*, 5:599–605.

7. *Vital Records of Holliston, Massachusetts (to the year 1850)* (Boston: New England Historic Genealogical Society, 1908), 52, 127, 199, 259, 309–10, 344; Dorothy Drinkwater Rees, *Holliston, Massachusetts, 1724–1974: The Story of a New England Town* (Holliston, Mass.: By the town, about 1976), 52, 199, 259, 309, 344; *Sibley's Harvard Graduates*, 10:312–14.

8. *Vital Records of Barre, Mass., to the end of 1849* (Worcester, Mass.: Franklin P. Rice, 1903), 199; Dr. Elinor V. Smith, comp., *Descendants of Nathaniel Dickenson* (n.p.: Dickenson Family Association, 1978), 205, 223, 241.

9. Massachusetts Bureau of Vital Statistics, microfilm (James Craig 1:51); death certificates for James Wallace Craig Sr. (65:121); Margaret Crane Craig (39:330); Helen Margarett Craig (10:10); David Rankin Craig (126:152); Annie L. Woods (10:697).

15

1. Kane 1998, 252.

16

1. Kane 1998, 254.

2. Arthur Gilman, comp., *A Genealogical & Biographical Record of that Branch of the Family of Gilman Descended form the Hon. Counsellor John Gilman of Exeter, N.H.* (Albany, N.Y.: J. Munsell, 1863), 17, 26, 104, 151; Arthur Gilman, *The Gilman Family Traced in the Line of Hon. John Gilman of Exeter, New Hampshire* (Albany, N.Y.: Joel Munsell, 1869), 67; "Notes and Queries," *NEHGR* 30 (April 1876), 221–23; *NEHGR* 32 (October 1878), 424; Major Lemuel Abijah Abbott, comp., *Descendants of George Abbott of Rowley, Massachusetts, of His Joint Descendants with George Abbott, Sr. of Andover, Massachusetts*, 2 vols. (by the author, 1906), 2:679, no. 797; *Milton Records, Births, Marriages, and Deaths, 1662–1843* (Boston: A. Mudge and Sons, 1900), 178; *Who Was Who in America, Historical Volume, 1607–1896* (Chicago: A. N. Marquis, 1963), 379; Maine Vital Records to 1892 (microfilm reel no. 40); Julia Abbot Nichols death recorded in Massachusetts Vital Records, Deaths 1916–20, 72:101. For Edgar Hamilton Nichols, see *Thirty-ninth Reunion of Harvard Class of 1878* (Cambridge: The University Press, 1917), 40–42.

3. Willard A. Nichols, *Ancestors of Willard Atherton Nichols* (n.c.: privately printed, 1911), 49–51.

4. Abbott, *Descendants of George Abbott*, 679–81. Based upon the initials of the tankard, a porringer by Burt may also have been purchased by the Gilmans. See Kane 1998, 254.

17

1. For similar examples by Burt, see Avery 1920, 35, cat. no. 20, fig. 76; Buhler 1972, 1:149, cat. no. 121; and Christie's, New York, sale 9054, January 15, 1999, lot 87.

2. Although the harmful effects of alcohol were discussed as early as the 1780s, the American Society for the Promotion of Temperance, established by Boston clergymen in 1826, was the first organization of its kind. See *Family Encyclopedia of American History* (Pleasantville, N.Y.: Reader's Digest Association, 1975), 1108–9.

3. On the evolution of tankards and a documented alteration of a tankard dated 1816, see Puig 1989, 124–39, fn. 70.

4. Italian scholar and physician Girolamo Fracastoro (1478–1553) first advanced the theory that contagious illnesses can be transferred by direct contact, using intermediaries such as clothing or utensils or through the air.

5. "Comparison between certain French and American customs," by "A Sentimental traveller," March 20, 1781, published in *The American Museum* (Philadelphia: Mathew Carey, 1788), 4:121, cited in Puig 1989, 129, fn. 57.

6. Thomas B. Wyman Jr., "Pedigree of the Family of Boylston," *NEHGR* 7 (April 1853), 145–50; James H. Stark, *The Loyalists of Massachusetts and the Other Side of the American Revolution* (Boston: W. B. Clarke, 1910), 281–83; Lawrence Park, comp., *Gilbert Stuart: An Illustrated, Descriptive List of His Works* (New York: William Edwin Rudge, 1926) 1:172–74, cat. nos. 106–8; Mary Caroline Crawford, *Famous Families of Massachusetts* (Boston: Little, Brown, 1930), 9–12.

7. *A Volume of Records Relating to the Early History of Boston Containing Boston Marriages from 1752–1809* (Boston: Municipal Printing Office, 1903), 414. Darrow's name is spelled Darrham in this entry. For Chester Harding's 1840 portrait of Mrs. Ward Nicholas Boylston (Alicia Darrow), see *American Paintings in the Museum of Fine Arts, Boston*, 2 vols. (Boston: Museum of Fine Arts, 1969), 1:129, cat. no. 475, fig. 206.

8. Massachusetts Vital Records, Births, 35:66, 459:551; Massachusetts Vital Records, Marriages, 227:341; Massachusetts Vital Records, Deaths 1847–48, 33:205; *Princeton, Massachusetts, Vital Records to the end of the year 1849* (Worcester, Mass.: F. P. Rice, 1902), 81, 151; *Roxbury, Massachusetts, Vital Records to the year 1849* (Salem, Mass.: Essex Institute, 1925–26), 1:36, 470–71; obituary, *Boston Herald*, August 17, 1966.

18

1. Bolton 1927, 4. Although the Storer family may have mistakenly adopted the Andrews arms as their own, it is unclear here for whose family these arms were intended. For the Andrews arms, see French 1939, 92–93.

2. B. Ward 1983, 262, figs. 119–20.

3. The grotesque mask can be found on Burt tankards published in MFA 1911, 17, cat. nos. 140–44; Avery 1920, cat. no. 20, fig. 76; Buhler 1972, 1:149, cat. no. 121; Johnston 1994, 17; Christie's, New York, sale 9054, January 15, 1999, lot 87.

4. Buhler 1972, 1:172, cat. no. 137. For other examples of Storer arms and/or crests on Boston silver, see Buhler 1972, 1:cat. nos. 135, 138, 141, 207, 258–59, 326.

19

1. Kane 1998, 258–59.

2. The additional weight required by the hollow handles may have made them too expensive to purchase. In a comparison between the weight of the Burt cup and two by John Dixwell (Barrett gift and Caleb Lyman gift), also made for New North Church, each of the Dixwell pieces weighed between 5 and 6 troy ounces less than the Burt cup. See Jones 1913, 59–66.

3. Jones 1913, 63.

4. Jones 1913, 66.

5. Jones 1913, 61.

6. Henry Wilder Foote, *Annals of King's Chapel from the Puritan Age of New England to the Present Day*, 2 vols. (Boston: Little, Brown, 1896), 2:616–18; Worthley 1970, 72–74.

7. Jones 1913, 59–67.

8. Walnut Hill Cemetery, Brookline, Mass. (Edward C. Storrow and Caroline MacKay Richardson Storrow); *Indices to Massachusetts Deaths*, Massachusetts Archives, 9:452, 12:163, 44:340, 71:118.

[no note on 20]

21

1. Kane 1998, 255; departmental files, Yale University Art Gallery.

22

1. Bolton 1927, 10.

2. Kane 1998, 260–63.

3. For a related teapot by John Burt, see Puig 1989, 236, cat. no. 194. For similar examples by Jacob Hurd, see Johnston 1994, 83; Buhler 1972, 1:205–7, cat. nos. 167–68; by Josiah Austin, see Buhler and Hood 1970, 1:152–53, cat. no. 188; and Safford 1983, 45, fig. 56.

4. "Monumental Inscriptions," *Heraldic Journal* 3, no. 20 (1867), 155–57; Bolton 1927, 10; Spofford 1929, 247–48. The engraving is lacking the helmet seen in the crest of the Barrett gravestone.

23

1. Buhler 1972, 1:233–34, cat. no. 194; Quimby 1995, 119, cat. no. 76.

2. *NEHGR* 25 (January 1871), 67–68. The additional engraving on the teapot base remains unexplained. It is doubtful that the teapot would have belonged to her mother since it was made in the 1740s, long after her marriage in 1715.

3. For the creamer, see Alcorn 2000, cat. no. 118.

4. Mrs. Bertram Stahl, "Eliot Bible Record," *NEHGR* 125 (October 1971),

283–85; Ann Smith Lainhart, "Descendants of Paix Cazneau," *NEHGR* 142 (April 1988), 127–33, 147–48.

5. Waldo Lincoln, *History of the Lincoln Family: An Account of the Descendants of Samuel Lincoln of Hingham, Ma., 1637–1920* (Worcester, Mass.: Commonwealth Press, 1923), 147–48, 264–65.

24

1. For related Massachusetts examples, see Clarke 1932, no. 72; Parke-Bernet, New York, sale 778, May 17–18, 1946, lot 294; Buhler 1956, 59, cat. no. 65, fig. 59; Buhler 1972, 1:190, cat. no. 153, 1:213, cat. no. 175.

2. "Necrology of Historic, Genealogical Society," *NEHGR* 35 (April 1881), 193–94; *Harvard Class of 1906, 25th Anniversary Report* (Cambridge: Privately printed for the class by the Cosmos Press, 1931), 523–24. FamilySearch™ International Genealogical Index v4.02, film no. 457920 (Hannah Smith).

25

1. Avery 1920, 77, cat. no. 93, fig. 94; Karen M. Jones, "Museum Accessions," *Antiques* 106, no. 3 (September 1974), 478; Robert H. Tannahill, "Silver," *Bulletin of the Detroit Institute of Arts of the City of Detroit* 24 (1944), 20.

2. L. Vernon Briggs, *History and Genealogy of the Cabot Family, 1475–1927* (Boston: Goodspeed, 1927), 268–69; Louisa Dresser, "The Orne Portraits by Joseph Badger," *Worcester Art Museum Bulletin* 1, no. 2 (February 1972), 1–16; Kane 1998, 300.

26

1. Flynt and Fales 1968, 186; Kathryn C. Buhler, "Seth Storer Coburn: Boston Silversmith," *Silver Magazine* 20, no. 1 (January/February 1987): 8–9 and cover; Kane 1998, 306–8. The genealogical references to Coburn's great-uncles are incorrect in Kane 1998, 306–7.

2. Buhler 1972, 1:306, cat. no. 260.

3. Elizabeth B. Miles, "The English Silver Pocket Nutmeg Grater," *Antiques* 90, no. 6 (December 1966), 828–31.

[no notes on 27]

28

1. The definition of a posset pot from *The Oxford English Dictionary*, cited in Frank Britton, *English Delftware in the Bristol Collection* (London: Sotheby Publications, 1984), 68–75; John Austin, *British Delft at Williamsburg* (Williamsburg, Va., and London: Colonial Williamsburg Foundation in association with Jonathan Horne Publications, 1994), 68–69, cat. nos. 11–16.

2. V. Isabelle Miller, "American Silver Spout Cups," *Antiques* 44, no. 2 (August 1943), 73–75; Miller 1962, cat. no. 16, pl. 20; Buhler 1972, 1:18–19, cat. no. 16.

3. Miller, "American Silver Spout Cups," 75.

4. Kane 1998, 144, 147, 254, 292, 303, 317, 328, 347, 353, 381, 393, 408, 417, 451, 506, 527, 531, 537, 551, 704, 875, 942, 980. See also DAPC 68.3345.

5. Essex County Probate Records, Salem, Mass., docket no. 2896; Buhler 1956, 57, cat. no. 50, fig. 10; Buhler 1972, 1:24, cat. no. 21; Kane 1998, 528.

6. Harold Bowditch, *The Bowditch Family of Salem, Massachusetts* (Boston: Press of Recording and Statistical Corp., 1936), 4; *Salem Vital Records* (Salem, Mass.: Essex Institute, 1916), 1:103–5; IGI Record, film no. 170558 (Joseph Hawthorne).

7. Henry Wycoff Belknap, *Simon Forrester of Salem and His Descendants* (Salem, Mass.: Essex Institute, 1935), 2, 30–31, 40.

8. Belknap, *Simon Forrester*, 40; IGI film nos. 1985650 (Eleanor F. Barstow), 1985599, 2034646 (Charlotte M. Condit).

9. "Memoirs," *NEHGR* 85 (July 1931): 329–30; *Harvard Class of 1943, Twenty-fifth Anniversary Report* (Cambridge, printed for the class, 1968), 975–76; James Parker, curator emeritus, European Sculpture and Decorative Arts, The Metropolitan Museum of Art, to Jeannine Falino, July 9, 1991; March 14, 1996.

29

1. For the Shrimpton-owned spoons and a tankard made by Coney, see Buhler and Hood 1970, 1:32–34, cat. nos. 25–26; Sotheby Parke-Bernet, New York, sale 3972, April 12–13, 1977, lot 168; *Antiques* 112, no. 1 (July 1977), 22; Clarke 1932, no. 75; Comm. George Evelyn Paget How, in collaboration with Jane Penrice How, *English and Scottish Silver Spoons, Mediaeval to Late Stuart and Pre-Elizabethan Hall-Marks on English Plate* (London: privately printed, 1952), 2:293–97. For spoons with similar bowls, see Buhler 1972, 1: cat. nos. 25, 66, 78; Kane 1988, 951–54; a related spoon by Jeremiah Dummer, engraved "MA," is in a private collection; department files, Art of the Americas.

2. Fairbanks and Trent 1982, 3:458, cat. no. 434, pl. 20; family correspondence, department files, Art of the Americas. Webb's inventory is reprinted in the biography by Barbara McLean Ward in Kane 1998, 953.

3. Index to Massachusetts Births, vol. 152 (1862), 266; Index to Massachusetts Marriages, vol. 336 (1882), 408; Index to Massachusetts Births, vol. 351 (1884), 440; Index to Massachusetts Deaths, vol. 447 (1894), 757; Index to Massachusetts Marriages, vol. 443 (1894), 334; Massachusetts Department of Vital Statistics, vol. 636 (1916), 54, 69. Franklin P. Rice, comp., *Worcester Births, Marriages, and Deaths* (Worcester, Mass.: Worcester Society of Antiquity, 1894), 401.

30

1. John Guillim, *A Display of Heraldry*, 6th ed. (London, 1724), 208; Vermont 1886, 101; Bolton 1927, 41. For the arms and inscriptions on the tombstone of Gov. John Cranston (d. 1680), see "Monumental Inscriptions," *Heraldic Journal* 3, no. 15 (April 1867), 58–60. According to Henry L. P. Beckwith, the Patent of Matriculation for a coat of arms was approved on June 29, 1724, and arrived in Newport in mid-September 1725, as recorded in a letter written by Samuel Cranston on September 16, 1725. Given this correspondence, it is likely the arms were engraved sometime after that date, which would have been after Coney's death in 1722. Henry L. P. Beckwith to Jonathan L. Fairbanks, November 10, 1996, department files, Art of the Americas.

2. Buhler 1956, 72, cat. no. 156; Buhler 1960, 49, cat. no. 24; department files, Art of the Americas. Vernon's master is unknown, although Winslow was likely to have trained him, as he did Vernon's cousin John Coddington (1690–1743) of Rhode Island; see Kane 1998, 989.

3. Charles Albert DuBosq and William Jones, "Descendants of Gov. John Cranston of Rhode Island," *NEHGR* 79 (July 1925): 247–53, 261.

4. *DAB* 4:512; 19:412; department files, Art of the Americas.

31

1. Buhler 1972, 1:69, cat. no. 59. The spout was removed in 1931 by George Christian Gebelein.

2. Ellen F. Vose, *Robert Vose and His Descendants* (Boston: privately printed, 1932), 146, 257, 415.

32

1. G. T. Ridlon, *History of the Ancient Ryedales, and Their Descendants in Normandy, Great Britain, Ireland, and America, from 1860 to 1884* (Manchester, N.H.: by the author, 1884), 87.

2. Master's Log and Captain's Log, *Falmouth*, Public Records of the National Archives of Great Britain, ADM 51/341, ADM 52/170, ADM 1/2377, ADM 33/265; John Charnock, *Biographica Navalis, the Lives and Characters of the Officers of the Navy of Great Britain from the Year 1660*, 6 vols. (London: R. Faulder, 1795), 3:281–83; *Calendar of State Papers, Colonial Series, America and West Indies, 1710–1711* (London: Her Majesty's Stationery Office, 1922), 230–31; John Campbell, Esq., *Lives of the Admirals and Other Eminent British Seamen*, 6 vols. (London: J. and H. Pemberton, and T. Waller, n.d.), 1:113; John Wood, Public Record Office, National Archives of Great Britain, July 25, 1998. Subsequent references to Riddell's life and career are drawn from these sources.

3. Jean McClure Mudge, *Chinese Export Porcelain for the American Trade* (Newark: University of Delaware Press, 1962), 67.

4. Master's Log and Captain's Log, *Falmouth*.

5. Ridlon, *History of the Ancient Ryedales*, 32, 70, 85–88.

6. For the two-handled cup, see *American Silver and Pressed Glass: A Collection in the R. W. Norton Art Gallery* (Shreveport, La.: R. W. Norton Art Foundation, 1967), 15, pl. 5; the Colman monteith is discussed in Buhler and Hood 1972, 1:40, cat. no. 31.

7. Ridlon, *History of the Ancient Ryedales*; *Macdonald's Tourists' Guide to Scotland* (Edinburgh: William Macdonald, n.d.), 68–69, 114–15; L. Russell Muirhead, ed., *The Blue Guides: Scotland* (Chicago: Rand McNally, 1949). Riddell's birth date has also been listed as about 1667 according to Family-Search™ Ancestral File v4.19 (AFN:THGC-VB).

8. Phillips Auctioneers, sale 18,923, February 11, 1972, lot. 183; Geraldine Norman, "US silver bowl sells for record £15,500," *Manchester [England] Guardian*, n.d., n.p.; Arthur G. Grimwade, *London Goldsmiths, 1697–1837* (London: Faber and Faber, 1976), 472–73.

33

1. For a related geometric handle, see Buhler 1972, 1:64, cat. no. 54; Kane 1988, 326–27.

2. Kane 1998, 69, fig. 50, 328, 330, 352, 420, 570, 885; Buhler 1972 1:5, cat. no. 2.

3. W. H. W., "The Norton Family," *NEHGR* 13 (July 1859), 229; *Sibley's Harvard Graduates* 2:394; *Vital Records of Medford, Massachusetts, to the Year 1850* (Boston: New England Historic Genealogical Society at the Charge of the Eddy Town Record Fund, 1907), 31, 180, 194, 348–49; W. I. Tyler Brigham, *The History of the Brigham Family, Descendants of Thomas, 1603–1653* (New York: Grafton Press, 1907), 332; Edith Austin Moore and William Allen Day, *The Descendants of Richard Austin of Charlestown, Massachusetts 1638* (St. Petersberg, Fla.: Privately printed, 1968), 38; Herbert Freeman Adams, *The Compendium of Tufts Kinsmen* (Boston: Tufts Kinsmen Project, 1975), 10–11, 22, 46; *Descendants of Edmund Quincy, 1602–1637* (Quincy, Mass.: Quincy Historical Society, 1977), no. 4.1.

34

1. Early saltworks were established in Plymouth, Salem, Salisbury, and Gloucester, but the British supplied the colonists additional quantities needed for the local cod and fur industries. The colonies remained largely dependent upon Great Britain for salt until the Revolution, when Cape

Cod became one of the premier saltworks locations. Mark Kurlansky, *Salt: A World History* (New York: Walker & Co., 2002), 216–23, 238–41.

2. *Metropolitan Museum Bulletin* 21, no. 1 (January 1926), 23; Fales 1970, 65, fig. 62. For trencher salts with the forged marks of Jacob Hurd, see Johnston 1994, 88. Jack L. Lindsey, *Worldly Goods: The Arts of Early Pennsylvania, 1680–1758* (Philadelphia: Philadelphia Museum of Art, 1999), 194, checklist no. 252.

3. Alcorn 2000, cat. no. 114 (19.261); Buhler 1972, 1:263, cat. no. 222. Each is engraved with a dedication from Hancock to Bowes.

4. [Drake, Samuel G.], "Brief Memoirs and Notices of Prince's Subscribers," *NEHGR* 6 (October 1852), 371; "The Hancock Family," *NEHGR* 9 (October 1855), 352; Arthur Bowes, "Stoddard, Bowes, and Hancock Pedigree," *NEHGR* 10 (January 1856), 81–82; W. H. W., "Memoirs of Prince's Subscribers," *NEHGR* 13 (April 1859), 137–38; *Vital Records of Shirley, Massachusetts, to the Year 1850* (Boston: New England Historic Genealogical Society at the charge of the Eddy Town-Record Fund, 1918), 93–94, 172; *Sibley's Harvard Graduates* 14:528–32; department files, Art of the Americas.

35

1. Buhler 1972, 1:59–60, cat. no. 50; Safford 1983, 33, fig. 39.

2. For a review of the Edwards-Cheever family silver, see Malcolm Stearns Jr., "Two in One Family: Two Pieces of Cheever Silver," in *Ellis Memorial* (1984), 69–72.

3. John T. Hassam, "Bartholomew and Richard Cheever and Some of Their Descendants," *NEHGR* 36 (July 1882), 305–13; IGI Records, batch nos. C502202 (Elizabeth Cheever), 8220204 (Caleb Davis), C500781, M502201 (Eleanor Cheever).

4. Rev. Caleb Davis Bradlee, "George Cheyne Shattuck, M.D.," *NEHGR* 48 (July 1894), 277–80; Henry Lee, *Pro Bono Publico: The Shattucks of Boston* (Boston: Massachusetts Historical Society, 1971), foreword; Beatrix Marie Larson, *Shattuck Memorials No. II* (Richland Center, Wis.: Richland County Publishers, 1977), 321–22, 324, 328.

5. Ida Whiteside, *A History of Phineas Whiteside and His Family* (n.p., 1961), 28–29, 92–94; Index to Massachusetts Marriages, 237 (1871), 112; Massachusetts Vital Records, 19 (1940): 377.

6. *Harvard Class of 1931, Twenty-Fifth Anniversary Report* (Cambridge: printed for the class, 1956), 951–53; obituary, *Concord Journal* (October 17, 1996), 32.

[no notes on 36]

37

1. Jones 1913, 266; Edward Doubleday Harris, comp., *An Account of Some of the Descendants of Captain Thomas Brattle* (Boston: D. Clapp and Son, 1867), 4–5; Joseph W. Chapman, comp., *Marblehead Vital Records*, 3 vols. (Salem, Mass.: Essex Institute, 1903–8), 2:49, 603.

38

1. Donald Fennimore, "Religion in America: Metal Objects in Service of the Ritual," *American Art Journal* 10, no. 2 (November 1978), 25–27.

2. Cited in Jones 1913, 267; Harris, *An Account of Some of the Descendants of Captain Thomas Brattle*, 28.

39

1. B. Ward 1983, 350; Quimby 1995, 81–82; Kane 1998, 334–39.

2. Fairbanks 1991, 69, cat. no. 49.

40

1. Kane 1998, 349–50.

2. Jones 1913, 501–2. For an image of the carnation, see Avery 1920, title page, 42, cat. no. 25. For the MFA cup, see Buhler 1972, 1:124, cat. no. 98.

3. Buhler 1972, 1:101, cat. no. 82; 1:105–6, cat. no. 87; 1:115, cat. no. 93; Buhler 1979, 19–20, cat. no. 11; Warren 1987, 33–35; Christie's, New York, sale 8578, January 18, 1997, lot no. 75; Kane 1998, 349–55, 500; Andrew Tyler tankard, Sterling and Francine Clark Institute, acc. no. TR524/80.

4. Jones 1913, 70–71.

41

1. Kane 1998, 349–50.

2. Cited in Jones 1913, 322–23.

[no notes on 42]

43

1. Buhler 1972, 2:119, cat. no. 96; Kane 1998, 376.

2. Kane 1998, 380.

3. Emma Worcester Sargent, *Epes Sargent of Gloucester and His Descendants* (Boston: Houghton, Mifflin, 1923), 146, 148. "Sargent Genealogy: William Sargent and His Descendants to the Children of the Sixth Generation" (typescript, NEHGS Library, about 1951), 56, 145.

4. Moore and Day, *Descendants of Richard Austin of Charlestown, Massachusetts, 1638*, 102, 186.

5. George Abbot Morison, *Nathaniel Morison and His Descendants* (Peterborough, N.H.: Peterborough Historical Society, 1951), 150; Gary Boyd Robert, "New England Ancestry of HRH Princess of Wales," *NEHGR* 136 (October 1982), 324.

44

1. The work of John Doane has also been confused with that of his uncle, a clockmaker by the same name, as well as with silver made by his elder brother Joshua. See Kane 1998, 382–85, 1010–11.

45

1. Comm. George Evelyn Paget How, in collaboration with Jane Penrice How, *English and Scottish Silver Spoons, Mediaeval to Late Stuart and Pre-Elizabethan Hall-Marks on English Plate*, 3 vols. (London: Privately printed, 1952), 2:293–97.

2. Buhler and Hood 1970, 1:12, cat. no. 7; Buhler 1972, 1:11, cat. no. 7; Fairbanks and Trent 1982, 2:292, cat. no. 289; Kane 1998, 393–94.

3. The names of Abraham and Abigail Adams were first put forward by Albert S. Roe in Fairbanks and Trent 1982, 2:292, cat. no. 289.

46

1. M. Halsey Thomas, ed., *The Diary of Samuel Sewall, 1674–1729*, 2 vols. (New York: Farrar, Straus and Giroux, 1973), 1:513.

2. Buhler and Hood 1970, 1:26, cat. no. 20; Buhler 1979, 9, cat. no. 1.

47

1. Kathryn C. Buhler, unpublished manuscript of the Mark Bortman collection; department files, Art of the Americas; Ian Pickford, *Silver Flatware, English, Irish, and Scottish* (Woodbridge, Eng.: Antique Collectors' Club, 1983), 179, figs. 312, 314.

2. Jacob Hurd serving spoon (MMA, 23.130.1). William Homes Sr. spoon discussed in Hammerslough and Feigenbaum 1958–73, 4:107.

3. Hugh Gourley III, "American Silver at the Currier Gallery of Art," *Currier Gallery of Art Bulletin* 1 (1971), fig. 5; Buhler and Hood 1970, 1:57, cat. no. 50, 2:46, cat. no. 592; Buhler 1972, 1:339, cat. no. 297.

4. Jackson 1911, 2:525–26, fig. 685; Clayton 1971, 272.

5. Bigelow 1917, 276, fig. 179.

6. Clayton 1971, 171–72.

48

1. For a pepper box made about the same time for the owners of the spout cup, and a discussion of the gallipot-shaped spout cup, see Buhler 1979, 18–19, cat. nos. 9–10; Kane 1998, 417.

2. Correspondence, Donald L. Fennimore, January 27, 1999. The shape of the opening on the Winterthur example is unclear since the spout had been torn away from the body and repaired. Fennimore conjectured, however, that Edwards originally created an elliptical access to the spout.

3. John A. Hyman, *Silver at Williamsburg: Drinking Vessels* (Williamsburg, Va.: Colonial Williamsburg Foundation, 1994), cat. no. 44.

4. *NEHGR* 26 (July 1872), 306–18; *NEHGR* 55 (April 1901), 162; Raeola Ford Cooke, "My Own Record of Descendants of Richard Warren" (typescript, Twin Falls, Idaho, n.d.), 6, 15; William T. Davis, *Genealogical Register of Plymouth Families* (Baltimore, Md.: Genealogical Publishing Co., 1985), 173; Ruth Wilder Sherman, ed., *Plymouth, Massachusetts, Vital Records to 1850* (Providence: Society of Mayflower Descendants in the State of Rhode Island and Providence Plantations, 1993), 194; Robert S. Wakefield, et al., *Richard Warren of the Mayflower, and His Descendants for Four Generations*, 6th ed. (Plymouth, Mass.: General Society of Mayflower Descendants, 1997), 37–38, 83–84, 156, 158–59.

5. Rev. George M. Adams, "Necrology of the New England Historic Genealogical Society," *NEHGR* 52 (July 1898), 386; *Record of the Class of 1892, Secretary's Report No. IV for the Fifteenth Anniversary* (Cambridge: University Press, 1907), 69; *NEHGR* 97 (October 1943), 386.

49

1. *Antiques* 41, no. 6 (June 1942), 378, cited in Kane 1998, 414.

2. Buhler 1972, 1:98, cat. no. 80.

3. Buhler 1972, 1:105, cat. no. 79.

4. On the Wendell, Jackson, and Holmes families in which its mate descended, see Buhler 1972, 1:cat. nos. 34 and 86.

50

1. William R. Deane, *Brief Memoirs of John & Walter Deane of Taunton, Massachusetts* (Chicago: Dean Brothers Blank Book and Printing Co., 1893), 13–14, 18–19; "The Deane Family," *NEHGR* 3 (October 1849), 384–85; *NEHGR* 10 (July 1856), 225; Joshua Bailey Richmond, *The Richmond Family, 1594–1896, and Pre-American Ancestors, 1040–1594* (Boston: By the compiler, 1897), 16, 26, 35, 79, 180–81, 356–58; *Mansfield, Massachusetts, Vital Records to 1850* (Salem, Mass.: Essex Institute, 1933), 10, 24–25, 176; Genealogical Committee of the Harlow Family Association, Alicia Crane Williams, *The Harlow Family, Descendants of Sgt. William Harlow (1624/5–1691) of Plymouth, Massachusetts* (Baltimore, Md.: Gateway Press, 1997), 14–15, 40, 48–50, 58, 179–80, 475–76. The letter "I" on the base is unexplained.

2. "A Branch of the Allen Family in New England," *NEHGR* 10 (July 1856), 225; 49 (April 1895), 225; 86 (April 1932), 225; Edward Franklin Everett, *Decendants of Richard Everett of Dedham* (Boston: privately printed, 1902),

40; *The Hovey Book Describing the English Ancestry & American Descendants of Daniel Hovey of Ipswich, Massachusetts* (Haverhill, Mass.: Press of Lewis R. Hovey, 1913), 266, 342; Massachusetts Vital Records, Deaths 1956–60, 75:21.

3. Dorothy Allen, listed in Pedigree of Members, NEHGS, Letters 1930, vol. 2, G-Mitchell; *Harvard College Class of 1932, Twenty-Fifth Anniversary Edition* (Cambridge: Harvard University Printing Office, 1932), 587–88; Masachusetts Vital Records, Deaths 1956–60, 77:104.

51

1. Matthews 1907, 28; Bolton 1927, 53.

2. Jones 1913, 31, pl. XIII.

3. "Governor Thomas Dudley and His Descendants," *NEHGR* 10 (October 1856), 341; "William Dummer," *American National Biography*, 34 vols. (New York: Oxford University Press, 1999), 7:53–54.

4. Jones 1913, 81–82; Buhler 1956, cat. no. 63; Buhler 1972 1:211, cat. no. 173; Kane 1998, 500.

5. Col. Joseph Lemuel Chester, "The Family of Dummer," *NEHGR* 35 (July 1881), 254–331.

6. Buhler 1972, 1:101–2, cat. no. 82.

52

1. Jones 1913, 323; *Vital Records of Newton* (Boston: New England Historic Genealogical Society, 1905), 193.

53

1. Buhler 1972, 2:473–74, cat. no. 424.

54

1. *Oxford Compact Dictionary* 1987, 2:2630, s.v. "salver."

2. Buhler 1956, 59, cat. no. 67; Moore Collection 1980, cat. no. 124.

3. Kane 1998, 301.

4. Rufus Greene sauce dishes, each roughly 5 in. (12.7 cm) in diameter and engraved "W/WR," have a history of descent in the White family; private collection.

5. Buhler 1972, 1:188, cat. no. 152.

6. "Boyle's Journal of Occurences in Boston," *NEHGR* 84 (April 1930), 167; William White, will, Suffolk County Probate Records, Boston, docket no. 15707; Kane 1998, 542, 824.

7. IGI, v.4.01 batch M502203, source 0928191 (marriage).

[no notes on 55]

56

1. Buhler 1972, 1:cat. nos. 137–39, 141–43, 202–4, 206–7, 209, 258–59.

2. Buhler 1972, 1:cat. nos. 257, 264.

3. Buhler 1972, 2:430–31, cat. no. 381.

4. In another example of silver bestowed upon family members, a cann by Samuel Edwards was given in 1758 by his sister Mary (Edwards) Storer to her namesake and grandchild, Mary Smith. Buhler 1972, 1:246, cat. no. 207.

5. Col. Joseph W. Peirce, "A Record of Births, Marriages and Deaths in Portsmouth, N.H., from 1706 to 1742," *NEHGR* 23 (October 1869), 395; Rev. Thomas F. Davies, "Memoir of Joshua Winslow Peirce," *NEHGR* 28 (October 1874), 368–69; Doris Powell Schultz, *Jonathan Wade of Ipswich, Mas-*

sachusetts (Immigrant 1632) and Descendants (Alexandria, Va.: D. P. Schultz, 1989), 18.

6. "Percival and Ellen Green," NEGHR 15 (April 1861, 107); G. Andres Moriarty Jr., "Hon. Samuel Abbott Green," NEHGR 74 (October 1920), 243; Sibley's Harvard Graduates 12:208–14.

7. Harvard Class of 1885, Fiftieth Anniversary Report (microfiche), 26; Malcolm Storer, Annals of the Storer Family (Boston: Wright and Potter, 1927), 48–50.

57

1. Buhler and Hood 1970, 1:11, cat. no. 6, 1:44, cat. no. 44, 1:120, cat. no. 137; Quimby 1995, 59, cat. no. 9, 172, cat. no. 130, 174, cat. no. 134.

2. Franklin Bowditch Dexter, Biographical Sketches of the Graduates of Yale College with Annals of the College History October, 1701–May 1745 (New York: Henry Holt, 1885), 218–21; Kane 1998, 380.

3. Ola Elizabeth Winslow, Jonathan Edwards 1703–1758, A Biography (New York: Macmillan, 1940), 216–17; Madeleine Siefke Estill, "Colonial New England Snuff, Tobacco, and Patch Boxes: Indices of Gentility and Gifts of Convention," in Falino and Ward 2001, 44–60.

4. See cat. no. 56 for early history of ownership.

58

1. Under the listings for "Andrews," Bolton 1927, 4. The manner in which the Andrews arms came to be used by the Storer family is explained in French 1939, 92–93.

2. Two chafing dishes would have weighed approximately 35 troy ounces. Buhler 1972, 1:175–76, cat. no. 141, 1:227–28, cat. no. 188; Bigelow 1917, 328.

59

1. Kane 1998, 490–94.

2. Mary LeBaron Stockwell, comp., Descendants of Francis LeBaron of Plymouth, Mass. (Boston: T. R. Marvin and Son, 1904), 49, 118, 254–255.

3. Hersey Goodwin Locke, Harvard Class of 1886, The Fiftieth Anniversary of the Class of 1886 and the Three Hundredth of the College, Class Secretary's Report (Boston: Anchor Linotype Printing Company, 1936), 279–80 (microfiche).

4. Massachusetts Vital Records, Deaths 1971, 24:376; SSDI for Charles Gowing (030-16-1216); Harvard Class of 1928, Fiftieth Anniversary Report (Cambridge: Printed for the university, 1978), 268.

60

1. Isaac Story was ordained a colleague of the church in 1771; he resigned in 1802 and died in 1816. Worthley 1970, 348.

2. Kane 1998, 496–99.

61

1. David L. Barquist et al., Myer Myers: Jewish Silversmith in Colonial New York (New Haven: Yale University Art Gallery, 2001), 33.

2. Barquist, Myer Myers, 33–34.

3. Barquist, Myer Myers, 92, cat. nos. 11–12.

4. Patricia Welte to Jeannine Falino, December 3, 1989, and January 23, 1990; department files, Art of the Americas. A pitcher by Baldwin Gardiner and presented to Allen Rabineau by members of the Lafayette Guards is now in the Museum of the City of New York, a gift of the same donor. Waters 2000, 2:345, cat. no. 181.

62

1. Kane 1998, 528.

2. Kane 1998, 531.

3. "Graduates of Harvard originating from Salem," NEHGR 5 (January 1851), 48; "Memoirs of Prince's Subscribers," NEHGR 6 (July 1852), 273; Daniel Appleton White, The Descendants of William White of Haverhill, Mass. (1863, 1889; reprint, Bowie, Md.: Heritage Books, 1993), 9, 11, 13–14.

4. G. K. Clarke, Nathaniel Clarke of Newbury, Massachusetts (facsimile copy, n.p., 1902), 238–43.

5. "Russell-Phillips, A Note upon Title 'Phillips' in Appendix to Bond's Genealogies of Watertown," NEHGR 27 (July 1873), 289–91.

6. "Memoirs," NEHGR 69 (supplement to April 1915), lxxv–lxxvi.

7. Harvard College, Class of 1888, Secretary's Report No. 7, Twenty-Fifth Anniversary (Boston: Rockwell and Churchill Press, 1913), 35.

8. SSDI for Marion Cogswell (184-24-8470) and Elliot Cogswell (028-01-3939); Massachusetts Index to Marriages 17 (1930): 301.

[no notes on 63]

64

1. Vermont 1886, 89, and Bolton 1927, 83, describe the arms emblazoned as those of Holyoke. Matthews 1907, addenda, 42, describes the crest used here as an "oak branch vert" while this version is of an unidentifiable plant.

2. Sibley's Harvard Graduates 5:265–78.

3. Jones 1913, 264; Avery 1920, 38, cat. no. 23; Harvard Tercentenary Exhibition 1936, cat. nos. 96, 107, 109, 140, 150; Buhler 1956, cat. no. 78; Kane 1998, 316, 323, 327, 332, 540, 611.

4. Kane 1998, 541.

5. George Francis Dow, The Holyoke Diaries 1709–1856 (Salem, Mass.: Essex Institute, 1911), xii–xvii; John Gibbs Holyoke, comp., Holyoke: A North American Family 1637–1992 (Baltimore, Md.: Gateway Press, 1993), 27–28, 31, 36–37, 42, 49–50.

6. Ira Osgood and Frank Story Osgood, A Genealogy of the Descendants of John, Christopher, and William Osgood, (Salem, Mass.: Salem Press, 1894), 243. Additional Osgood family history kindly supplied by the donor.

65

1. Kane 1998, 541.

66

1. Buhler and Hood 1970, 1:172–24, cat. no. 221.

2. Kane 1998, 541.

3. Department files, Art of the Americas.

67

1. Bolton 1927, 10.

2. Buhler and Hood 1970, 1:131, cat. no. 152; Moore Collection 1980, 95, cat. no. 111; Quimby 1995, 129, cat. no. 84; Kane 1998, 542.

3. "Monumental Inscriptions," Heraldic Journal 3, no. 20 (1867), 155–57; Bolton 1927, 10; Spofford 1929, 247–48. The engraving is lacking the helmet seen in the crest of the Barrett gravestone.

4. George Castor Martin, comp., Barrett Ancestry (New York: Martin & Allardyce, 1912), 4.

5. Edward Elbridge Salisbury, *Family-Memorials: A Series of Genealogical and Biographical Monographs on the Families of Salisbury, Aldworth-Elbridge, Sewall, Pyldren-Dummer, Walley, Quincy, Gookin, Wendell, Breese, Chevalier-Anderson, and Phillips* (New Haven: Tuttle, Morehouse & Tayler, 1885), 37, 57, 643.

6. Obituary, *Boston Transcript*, September 22, 1926; Alfred Johnson, "Desmond FitzGerald," *NEHGR* 81 (January 1927), 63–72; Walnut Hill Cemetery, Brookline, Mass. (Eliz. Parker Clark Fitzgerald; Desmond FitzGerald).

7. *Social Register* 92 (1978), 953; department files, Art of the Americas.

68

1. Bolton 1927, 51.

2. For a survey of hexagonal silver by Boston silversmiths, see Kathryn C. Buhler, "Two Angular New Englanders," *Antiques* 51, no. 3 (March 1947), 195. Of 60 casters, also called spice dredgers or pepper boxes, surveyed by Norman-Wilcox, nearly half were octagonal in section. Gregor Norman-Wilcox, "American Silver Spice Dredgers, Part I," *Antiques* 45, no. 1 (January 1944), 20–21; Gregor Norman-Wilcox, "American Silver Spice Dredgers, Part II," *Antiques* 45, no. 2 (February 1944), 80–84.

3. Buhler 1972, 1:72–73, cat. nos. 61–62; Christie's, New York, sale 5809, January 22, 1983, lot 425.

4. For a rare surviving set of three casters by New York silversmith Adrian Bancker (1703–1772), see Buhler 1956, cat. no. 163, fig. 90; and Safford 1983, fig. 43. For the smaller mate by Hiller, see Buhler and Hood 1970, 1:91–92, cat. no. 103.

5. This line of descent was advanced in Buhler and Hood 1970, 1:91–92, cat. no. 103. Andrew Johonnot, "The Johonnot Family," *NEHGR* 7 (April 1853), 141–42; D.D [poss. Dean Dudley], "Gov. Thomas Dudley and His Descendants," *NEHGR* 10 (October 1856), 338–39.

69

1. Kane 1998, 563

2. FamilySearch™ International Genealogical Index v4.19, AFN:2JV5-GX, AFN:BSQT-BF.

3. FamilySearch™ International Genealogical Index v4.19, AFN:S6CS-FW, AFN:S6CS-G3, AFN:S6CS-N4.

4. FamilySearch™ International Genealogical Index v4.19, AFN:W64T-TH, AFN:W64T-VN, AFN:W05F-7F, AFN:W0K7-LQ.

5. FamilySearch™ International Genealogical Index v4.19, AFN:1VSF-KQK, AFN:1VSF-KWL.

70

1. *Oxford Compact Dictionary* 1987, 3431.

2. Roe's observation is in Fairbanks and Trent 1982, 3:494, cat. no. 462. For two related English examples dated 1667 and 1674, see John A. Hyman, *Silver at Williamsburg: Drinking Vessels* (Williamsburg, Va.: Colonial Williamsburg Foundation, 1994), cat. nos. 64, 66.

3. Jones 1913, 20–21, pl. X. Jones describes the allover stamped pattern as granulated, although a more correct term might be *punched*, or *pounced*. See Kane 1987, 1:62–63; *Oxford Compact Dictionary* 1987, 2:2260.

4. Kane 1987, cat. nos. 52–54, 64, figs. 34, 76–78.

71

1. Kane 1987, 1:23, 59–62, cat. nos. 17–22, figs. 25–26, 28–31.

2. Jones 1913, 20–23, pls. X–XI.

3. Jones 1913, 23–34.

72

1. Buhler and Hood 1970, 1:6–7; Martha Gandy Fales, *Silver at the Essex Institute* (Salem, Mass.: Essex Institute, 1983), 8–9, fig. 1; Kane 1987, 53–54, app. A, 453–54, 457–58, 463–64, cat. nos. 52, 56, 60; Quimby 1995, 120, cat. no. 77; Kane 1998, 567–72, 882–86.

2. Quotation is from the will of Thomas Rotherham, archbishop of York, as cited by Kathryn C. Buhler, "Exhibit of the Week, August 15th to August 21st, 1936: No. 8: Silver—English and American Spoons, 1527–c. 1827," department files, Art of the Americas.

3. Kane 1998, 570, describes the initials as "MY."

4. Kane 1998, 570, 885.

5. Department files, Art of the Americas.

73

1. This feature is discussed in detail by Janine Skerry, "The Revolutionary Revere, A Critical Assessment of the Silver of Paul Revere," in *Paul Revere* 1988, 43–44; Buhler 1972, 2:388, cat. no. 338. Many examples exist of applied spouts on creamers by Jacob Hurd; for two, see Buhler and Hood 1970, cat. nos. 149–50. See also Kane 1998, 593–94.

2. Alfred S. Roe, *The Twenty-Fourth Regiment, Massachusetts Volunteers 1861–1866, "New England Guard Regiment"* (Worcester, Mass.: Twenty-Fourth Veteran Association, 1907), 452; Charles Henry Pope and Thomas Hooper, comps., *Hooper Genealogy* (Boston: Charles H. Pope, 1908), 126–27; *DAB* 20:618–19.

3. *Harvard Class of 1897, Twenty-fifth Anniversary Report* (Cambridge: Harvard University, 1922), 530; Massachusetts Vital Records, Index to Marriages 1871–75, box 3, vol. 246, 165.

74

1. Sotheby's, New York, January 27, 1989, sale 5809, lot 907. This lot is described as having "shell-back bowls," maybe not strong enough to fit the above description. However, French notes a spoon of the same size and general description with matching initials; French 1939, no. 336. For another Benjamin Hurd spoon with shells on the back, see DAPC 73.3034.

75

1. Jones 1913, 265–68.

76

1. Kane 1998, 597–99.

2. James Rindge Stanwood, "The Direct Ancestry of the Late Jacob Wendell of Portsmouth, N.H.," *NEHGR* 36 (July 1882), 248–49.

3. *Sibley's Harvard Graduates*, 17:442–45.

4. Social Security Admin., *Social Security Death Index, Master File* (Orem Utah: Ancestry Inc., 2000), SSN:085-28-9869; department files, Art of the Americas.

77

1. Vermont 1886, 159; Jones 1913, 33–34; Bolton 1927, 27; and Kane 1998, 584–85, all describe the Byfield arms with an azure or sable field, but the vertical lines in the basin's shield denote gules. For arms engraved on Byfield's tombstone, see "Monumental Inscriptions," *Heraldic Journal* 2,

no. 15 (July 1866), 126–27. Byfield's tomb is located in the Granary Burying Ground, Boston.

2. Kane 1998, 578–84.

3. Biographical details are found in William Heath Byford, "Nathaniel Byfield," *The Twentieth-Century Biographical Dictionary of Notable Americans*, 10 vols. (Boston: Biographical Society, 1904), 2:79.

4. John Louis Ewell, *The Story of Byfield, A New England Parish* (Boston: George E. Littlefield, 1904), 73–75. The Byfield church beakers were sold at Christie's, New York, sale 5153, June 12, 1982, lot no. 40. Kane 1998, 322, 585.

78

1. The source of blades for American silver-hilted swords is unclear. Some were undoubtedly made locally, but scholars generally believe that imported Spanish, French, and German blades were typically attached to American-made hilts. Philip Medicus, "American Silver-Hilted Swords, Part I," *Antiques* 46, no. 5 (November 1944), 264–66; Hermann Warner Williams, "American Silver-Hilted Swords," *Antiques* 67, no. 6 (June 1955), 510–13.

2. French 1939, nos. 168–72, 172a; Kane 1998, 604–5, 1233. Although no swords have been attributed to Paul Revere II, his daybooks record five instances in which he made repairs to existing ones. His tasks included "to new mounting [?] a sword and winding grip," "grinding sword blade," making a "new silver chape," "putting a new shaft to a sword," "mounting and cleaning," and a "new scabbard"; see Revere daybooks, 1:23, 67; 2:54, 135–35, 144, 146.

3. French 1939, 42, no. 171; MHS 1991, 87, cat. no. 53.

4. *Sibley's Harvard Graduates*, 6:186–91.

5. Harold L. Peterson, *American Silver Mounted Swords, 1700–1815* (Washington, D.C.: privately printed, 1955), 7–12.

6. Henry Allen Hazen, "The Hazen Family," *NEHGR* 33 (April 1879), 231, 234; George Thomas Little, *The Descendants of George Little Who Came to Newbury, Massachusetts in 1640* (Auburn, Me.: By the author, 1882), 43–44.

7. Little, *Descendants of George Little*, 217–18; *Vital Records of Newbury, Massachusetts, to the End of the Year 1849*, 2 vols. (Salem, Mass.: Essex Institute, 1911), 1:281, 330; 2:226, 292, 294.

8. Little, *Descendants of George Little*, 385; correspondence, Metropolitan Museum of Art, October 15, 1999, department files, Art of the Americas.

79

1. The casual handling of colors in the arms is evident in the chevron, which is sable on the left side and becomes azure to the right. Similarly, the bucks in the shield are largely azure, but occasional vertical hatchmarks suggest sable. The general shape of the arms follows, Vermont 1886, 114–15; Matthews 1907, 66; and Bolton 1927, 141; but the finer points of color and the pose of the bucks (courant versus trippant) suggest that the engraver took liberties with the design.

2. Janine E. Skerry, "'Ancient and Valuable Gifts': Silver at Colonial Harvard," in Falino and Ward 2001, 183–209.

3. *Sibley's Harvard Graduates*, 7:554–60.

4. Skinner's, Bolton, Mass., sale 1766, March 23, 1977, lot no. 112.

5. "Genealogical Memoir of the Family of Rev. Nathaniel Rogers," *NEHGR* 5 (April 1851), 322–330.

6. "Rev. Nathaniel Rogers of Ipswich," *NEHGR* 13 (January 1859), 68; P. A. M. Taylor, *More Than Common Powers of Perception: The Diary of Elizabeth Rogers Mason Cabot* (Boston: Beacon Press, 1991).

7. L. Vernon Briggs, *History and Genealogy of the Cabot Family, 1475–1927*, vol. 2 (Boston: Charles E. Goodspeed, 1927), 699–700; "The Fayerweather Family of Boston," *NEHGR* 145 (January 1991), 66–67.

8. SSDI, Ellen P. White, November 11, 1997, Dedham.

80

1. Kane 1998, 606–9.

2. Department files, Art of the Americas.

81

1. Wees 1997, 253–54, cat. no. 169.

2. Revere daybooks, 2:154; Buhler 1972, 1:315, cat. no. 270.

3. For an example of a nineteenth-century shovel-shaped salt spoon, see Belden 1980, 485, figs. 7–8.

4. Department files, Art of the Americas.

82

1. The crest is similar to that of the Wendell family but is not in full agreement with published sources. Bolton 1927, 177, notes several Wendell crests of ships traveling both sinister and dexter and in full sail.

2. Kane 1998, 612–13.

3. Buhler and Hood 1970, 2:39, cat. no. 587; Buhler 1972, 1:36, cat. no. 29, 1:105, cat. no. 86; Kane 1998, 604.

4. *Sibley's Harvard Graduates*, 9:365–67.

5. "Extracts from the Diary of Rev. Samuel Dexter, of Dedham," *NEHGR* 13 (October 1859), 20; Rev. George M. Bodge, "Anderson Pedigree," *NEGHR* 43 (April 1889), 198–99; *Vital Records of Tyngsboro, Massachusetts, to End of the Year 1849* (Salem, Mass.: Essex Institute, 1913), 19, 55; Samuel Thomas Dole, ed., *Frederick Howard Dole, Wyndham (Maine) in the Past* (Auburn, Me.: Merril & Webber, 1916), 529–30.

6. Rev. George Madison Bodge, "John Farwell Anderson," *NEHGR* 43 (April 1889), 124–28.

7. Charles Edward Lord, *The Ancestors and Descendants of Lieutenant Tobias Lord* (Boston: privately printed, 1913), 40, 57.

8. *General Catalogue of Bowdoin College and the Medical School of Maine, A Biographical Record of Alumni and Officers, 1794–1950* (Brunswick, Me.: Bowdoin College, 1950), 322.

9. Although no owner's name was published in the catalogue, it was probably Mrs. C. W. Lord, as recorded in French 1939.

83

1. See genealogical sources in department files, Art of the Americas.

84

1. Kane 1998, 587–88.

2. Cecil Hampden Cutts Howard, *Genealogy of the Cutts Family in America* (Albany, N.Y.: Joel Munsell's Sons, 1892), 12, 18.

3. "Marriages and Death," *NEHGR* 15 (April 1861), 187; Delmar R. Lowell, comp. and ed., *The Historic Genealogy of the Lowells of America, 1639–1899* (Rutland, Vt.: The author, 1899), 22, 34, 58, 119.

4. "Records of the West Church," *NEHGR* 92 (July 1938), 251; IGI Record, film no. 458347.

5. Lowell, *Historic Genealogy*, 119, 226, 285; "Records of the West Church," *NEHGR* 93 (April 1929), 122.

6. *Who's Who in the East* (Chicago: Marquis, 1948), 165.

7. *Boston Marriages* 2 (1915), 318; IGI Record, film no. 178023.

85

1. Jones 1913, 324.

2. Jones 1913, 324; Worthley 1970, 426–27.

86

1. For another example of the tablet-style reserve, see Buhler 1972 1:222, cat. no. 183.

87

1. Jones 1913, 257–58; Worthley 1970, 361–62.

2. Jones 1913, 257–58; Philip Starr Sweetser, *Seth Sweetser and His Descendants* (Philadelphia: Integrity Press, 1938), 155.

3. "Tufts Genealogy," *NEHGR* 51 (July 1897), 301; *Vital Records of Lynn, Massachusetts, to End of Year 1849*, 2 vols. (Salem, Mass.: Essex Institute, 1906), 1:253, 2:66, 242, 532; Herbert Freeman Adams, *The Compendium of Tufts Kinsmen* (Boston: Tufts Kinsmen Project, 1973), 7.

88

1. The Greene arms were first published in John Guillim, *A Display of Heraldry*, 6th ed. (London, 1724), sec. III, 157; Bolton 1927, 71.

2. Buhler 1972, 2:392–93, cat. no. 343; Buhler 1976, 7; Johnston 1994, 81; Kane 1998, 600; Revere daybooks 1:8.

3. Kane 1998, 599–601.

4. Louise Brownell Clarke, comp., *The Greenes of Rhode Island with Historical Records of English Ancestry, 1534–1902* (New York: Knickerbocker Press, 1903), ill. unpag.; Buhler and Hood 1970, 1:185–87, cat. 240; Betty Ring, *American Samplers and Pictorial Needlework, 1650–1850*, 2 vols. (New York: Alfred A. Knopf, 1993), 1:67, figs. 66–71; the Hurd cann is in a private collection.

5. Clarke 1903, 82–83, 100–2, 112–13, 174.

6. G. Andrews Moriarty, "Early Block Island Families: VII: The Ray Family," *NEHGR* 86 (July 1932), 329–30.

7. Clarke 1903, 293–94.

8. Clifford P. Monahon, *Correspondence of Governor Samuel Ward, May 1775–March 1776* (Providence: Rhode Island Historical Society, 1952), 3–5, 35; Herringshaw, *Herringshaw's Encyclopedia of American Biography*, 977.

9. The later generations of the Ward family are found in Monahon, *Correspondence*, 220, 225, 228.

89

1. Clayton 1971, 175; Harold Newman, *An Illustrated Dictionary of Silverware* (London: Thames and Hudson, 1987), 205.

2. See Alice Winchester, "Some Heirloom Silver from an Old New York Family," *Antiques* 47, no. 6 (June 1947), 390–91; Gourley 1965, cat. no. 117; Buhler and Hood 1970, 1:260, cat. no. 426, 2:116, cat. no. 684; Fales 1970, 62, fig. 57; Hammerslough and Feigenbaum 1958–73, 1:123, 4:117, 121; Johnston 1994, 28; Northeast Auctions, Portsmouth, N.H., March 2, 1996, lot 698, Kane 1998, 423–24.

3. Bigelow 1917, 279, fig. 182.

4. Alfred Coxe Prime, comp., *The Arts and Crafts in Philadelphia, Maryland, and South Carolina, Part 1: 1721–1785* (Topsfield, Mass.: Wayside Press for The Walpole Society, 1929), 62, 96–97.

5. Revere daybooks, 2:37, 44; MFA 1911, pl. 12.

90

1. Kane 1998, 633.

2. B. Ward 1983, 48.

91

1. Biographical information on Kip can be found in John Marshall Phillips, "Identifying the Mysterious IK," *Antiques* 43, no. 1 (July 1943), 19–21; Quimby 1995, 259–60; and Waters 2000, 1:149–50.

2. Collaboration between the two silversmiths has been inferred by Ian Quimby from a saucepan with lid that carries the touchmark of Kip on the lid and Gerrit Onckelbag's mark on the saucepan. Quimby 1995, cat. no. 223.

3. Waters 2000, 149–50.

4. For a sampling of Kip's silver, see Avery 1932, fig, 31; Phillips 1943, figs. 2–7; Warren 1987, 52, cat. no. 49; Waters 2000, 1:150, cat. no. 36.

5. Bergen County Probate Records, Book D, p. 48; Francis Bazley Lee, ed., *Genealogical and Memorial History of the State of New Jersey* (New York: Lewis Historical Publishing Co., 1910), 2:739–40. Related family names include Pinhorne, Graevenraet, de Riemer, and Van Meeunwis, but none of the family coats of arms matches that on the tankard. Additional silver bequeathed by Kingsland included six silver spoons each for his daughters Hester and Catherine.

6. *Memorial Biographies of the New-England Historic Genealogical Society, 1862–1864,* vol. 5 (Boston: NEHGS, 1894), 445–47, 465–66. FamilySearch™ International Genealogical Index v4.01, film no. 184229, p. 1153, ref. no. 25664.

7. Joseph P. Bradley, *Family Notes Respecting the Bradley Family of Fairfield and Our Descent Therefrom* (Newark, N.J.: Amzi Pierson, 1894), sec. 6, n.p.,58. William Nelson, ed., *Nelson's Biographical Cyclopedia of New Jersey* (New York: Easter Historical Publishing Society, 1913), 1:244–47. FamilySearth™ International Genealogical Index v4.01, film no. 1985527.

8. *The National Cyclopaedia of American Biography, Being the History of the United States* (New York: James T. White, 1948), 34:121.

[no notes to 92]

93

1. For the most recent assessment of Lyng's career, see Waters 2000, 159–60.

2. Parke-Bernet Galleries, Inc., New York, sale 805, November 2, 1946, lot no. 22; sale 2400, January 21, 1966, lot no. 135; Hammerslough and Feigenbaum 1958–73, 1:18; Buhler and Hood 1970, 2:141, cat. nos. 727–28; advertisement, Jonathan Trace, *Antiques* 105, no. 4 (April 1974): 775; Ward and Ward 1979, 161, cat. no. 169; Belden 1980, 281; Johnston 1994, 102; Waters 2000, 160, cat. nos. 44–45.

3. Waters 2000, 159–60; see also department files, Art of the Americas.

94

1. Bolton 1927, 75. The arms of Hancock were not used in this country before the time of Boston merchant Thomas Hancock (1703–1764). Church silver engraved with the family arms includes six communion dishes made for the Church in Brattle Street, two beakers for the Church of Christ in Lexington, and two cups for the First Church of Boston. Jones 1913, 26, 69, 246; Buhler 1972, 1:316, cat. 272, 1:364–65, cat. no. 321.

2. Kane 1998, 592.

3. Suffolk County Probate Records (SCPR), Boston, 63.278 Thomas Hancock; Buhler 1972, 1:316, cat. no. 272, 1:364–65, cat. no. 321.

4. Ebenezer Hancock inventory, SCPR, docket no. 24050. *Sibley's Harvard Graduates*, 13:416; *Sibley's Harvard Graduates*, 14:619–23.

5. Harvard Tercentenary Exhibition 1936, 40, cat. no. 152, pl. 24; Kane 1998, 697.

6. Edward Wheelwright, "The Lowell Pedigree," *NEHGR* 54 (July 1900), 315–19; *Sibley's Harvard Graduates*, 14:619–23.

7. G. Andrews, "Moriarty Family of Salem, Massachusetts," *NEHGR* 101 (July 1947), 227–28.

8. *Vital Records of Gardner, Massachusetts, to the End of the Year 1849* (Worcester, Mass.: Franklin P. Rice, 1907), 66–67.

9. Massachusetts Census of 1880, ED509, vol. 22, sheet 52, line 1; Ernest Byron Cole, *The Descendants of James Cole of Plymouth, 1633* (New York: Genealogical Publishers, 1908), 270.

10. Social Register, Boston (New York: Social Register Association, 1939), 38; Social Register, Boston (New York: Social Register Association, 1950), 152; SSDI, Ancestry.com for Elizabeth [Lowell Hancock Cole Amory Cabot] McRoberts (1902–1983), 029-30-0209.

11. Edgar Francis Waterman, notes, Donald Lines Jacobus, comp., *The Descendants of Robert Waterman of Marshfield, Massachusetts* (New Haven: Edgar Francis Waterman, 1942), 322; department files, Art of the Americas.

95

1. Figures relating to Minott's production and retail work were extracted from Kane 1998, 689–98.

2. Jones 1913, 324, pl. XCVIII.

96

1. Alfred Alder Doane, *The Doane Family: I. Deacon John Doane, of Plymouth: II. Doctor John Doane, of Maryland; and Their Descendants* (Boston: A. A. Doane, 1902), 75, 508–9; Flynt and Fales 1968, 286. Gideon Myrick may have been born in 1736, for a child by that name was recorded in his father's birthplace, in nearby Harwich, Mass. FamilySearch™ International Genealogical Index v4.01, film no. 2034562.

2. Kane 1998, 726.

3. A spoon by Myrick bearing the initials "H / C R" is associated with the Hastings family. Kane 1998, 726.

97

1. Kane 1998, 736–39.

2. Samuel Sewall account book, as cited in Kane 1998, 736.

3. Buhler 1972, 1:112, cat. no. 91; Kane 1998, 738.

4. Barnstable Probate Records 37:32–34, 39:5, Barnstable, Mass.

5. Maclean W. McLean, "Robert Parker of Barnstable, Mass." *NEHGR* 13 (January 1959), 17–18; *NEHGR* 13 (April 1959), 116–18.

6. SSDI (024–24–4408) for Carle Hayward. Membership records, NEHGS, submitted by Mrs. Carle Reed Hayward (Mary Murray).

98

1. *Antiques* 109, no. 3 (March 1976), 470; Kane 1998, 750–55. For another example in the Museum's collection, see Buhler 1972, 1:293.

99

1. Kane 1998, 756.

100

1. Edward Franklin Everett, *Descendants of Richard Everett of Dedham, Mass.* (Boston: T.R. Marvin & Sons, 1902), 64–65.

2. Everett, *Descendants of Richard Everett*, 118; correspondence, Mary C. Everett Barnard to Mr. [Christopher Rhodes] Eliot or Abigail Adams Eliot, June 28, 1888, department files, Art of the Americas.

101

1. Buhler and Hood 1970, 1:248–49, cat. no. 371.

2. P. H. Hammerslough, "A Master Craftsman of Early Guilford," *Connecticut Historical Society Bulletin* 19 (October 1954), 123–28; Hammerslough and Feigenbaum 1958–73, 1:62, 79, 2:30; Flynt and Fales 1968, 294–95; Buhler and Hood 1970, 1:48–49, cat. nos. 371–75.

3. Rollins 1991, 326–27, cat. no. 201.

102

1. A John Patterson was said to be in Pittsburgh, Pa., from 1797 to 1815 and in 1816/17. He was in Alexandria, Va., in 1815 and in Nottingham, Pa., in 1819. If so, then he may be the same silversmith recorded in an advertisement in the July 14, 1815, *Alexandria Herald* by goldsmith John Potter of Alexandria, which stated that "a certain John Patterson who lately came from Pittsburg to this place and was taken into partnership by me" had stolen goods from his shop. J. Hall Pleasants and Howard Sill, *Maryland Silversmiths, 1715–1830* (Baltimore, Md.: Lord Baltimore Press, 1930), 61–62, 302, plate IV; "Silversmiths of Alexandria," *Antiques* 47, no. 2 (February 1945), 93–95; George Barton Cutten, *The Silversmiths of Virginia (Together with Watchmakers and Jewelers), from 1694 to 1850* (Richmond, Va.: Dietz Press, 1952), 19; Hollan 1994, 188.

2. Revere daybooks, 1:23–34.

3. John D. Kernan Jr., "Further Notes on Albany Silversmiths," *Antiques* 80, no. 1 (July 1961), 60–61, figs. 1, 6; Buhler and Hood 1970, 2:112–14, cat. no. 679; Hammerslough and Feigenbaum 1958–73, 4:50–51. For a silver-mounted coconut ladle with wooden handle from Lynchburg, Va., see Lucille McWane Watson, "Silversmiths of Lynchburg, Virginia," *Antiques* 59, no. 1 (January 1951), 40–43.

103

1. Marvin D. Schwarz and Arthur Pulos, *Elias Pelletreau, Long Island Silversmith and His Sources of Design* (Brooklyn, N.Y.: Brooklyn Museum, 1959), cat. no. 78, fig. 10; Quimby 1995, 274–76; Failey 1998, 300–01.

2. Failey 1998, 9–46, cat. no. 63A.

3. Christie's, New York, sale 7624, January 22, 1993, lot 119; Puig 1989, 255, cat. no. 209.

104

1. The crest is found on the seal of Gov. John Winthrop. W. H. Whitmore, "Official Seals," *Heraldic Journal* 1, no. 1 (January 1865), 18; Bolton 1927, 184.

2. Department files, Art of the Americas.

3. Failey 1998, 11. For one other example of New York silver bearing the Winthrop arms and crest, see a cann by Lewis Feuter in Buhler and Hood 1970, 2:146–47, cat. 748.

4. Dean Frederick Failey, "Elias Pelletreau Long Island Silversmith" (masters thesis, University of Delaware, 1971), 70–71, table 1.

105

1. Failey, "Elias Pelletreau Long Island Silversmith", 70–71, table 1; Failey 1998, 68–73, 156–60, figs. 82, 243.

2. *DAB*, 18:284–85.

3. Edward Doubleday Harris, Esq., "Ancient Burial Grounds of Long Island, New York," *NEHGR* 53 (April 1899), 169–70; Barrington S. Havens, *American Paintings in the Museum of Fine Arts, Boston,* 2 vols. (Boston: Museum of Fine Arts, 1969), 1:103–4, 2:fig. 101; acc. no. 1989.634.

4. Curtiss C. Gardiner, *Lion Gardiner and His Descendants* (St. Louis, Mo.: A. Whipple, 1900), 150–51.

5. James Hill Fitts, comp., *Lane Genealogies* (Exeter, N.H.: Newsletter Press, 1897), 2:33–35, 47–49, 64–65; Willard Harvey Gildersleeve, *Gildersleeve Pioneers* (Rutland, Vt.: Tuttle Publishing, 1941), 246–48; obituary, *Boston Globe,* February 15, 1989.

106

1. Kane 1998, 780–81.

2. Kane 1998, 781–84.

3. Jones 1913, 38; Ward/Hosley 1985, 285–86, cat. nos. 169–70; Buhler and Hood 1972, 1:112–13, cat. no. 127.

4. Gerald Lee Tolman, *The Descendants of Thomas Tolman (1608)* (Bountiful, Utah: Thomas Tolman Family Genealogy Center, 1996), 1, 5–6, 14, 29–30, 61–62, 127–28.

5. James A. Hart, comp., *Genealogical History of Descendants of Samuell Hartt of Lynn, Mass., 1640–1903* (Pasadena, Calif.: by the author, 1903), 3, 18, 71–72, 77, 79.

6. Massachusetts Vital Records and Statistics for Edwin Alexander Crawford Jr. (marriage), Joseph Hartt and Mary Agnes Hamilton (death), Joseph Hartt, Mary A. Hartt; Nellie B. Hartt; Alice M. Crawford; department files, Art of the Americas.

107

1. Buhler 1972, 2:388, cat. no. 338; Buhler 1979, 24, cat. no. 18, 42, cat. no. 48.

2. Howard, *Genealogy of the Cutts Family in America,* 12, 18; "Joseph Whipple" in *Sibley's Harvard Graduates,* 6:415–17.

108

1. Kane 1998, 852.

2. Howard, *Genealogy of the Cutts Family in America,* 12, 18; "Joseph Whipple" in *Sibley's Harvard Graduates,* 6:415–17.

109

1. Kane 1998, 852.

2. Buhler 1972, 1:185, cat. no. 149.

3. Mary Keny (Davey) Babcock, "Christ Church, Boston, Records," *NEHGR* 100 (July 1946), 239; Thwing Index, Massachusetts Historical Society, Boston.

4. Boston Registry Department, *Boston Births from A.D. 1700 to A.D. 1800* (Boston: Rockwell & Churchill, 1894); FamilySearch™ International Genealogical Index v4.01, ref. no. 37644, film no. 446255, film no. 457757 (Edward Pulling, Lois Robinson).

5. FamilySearch™ International Genealogical Index v4.01, ref. no. 35556, film no. 446253, batch no. A457758 (Mary Robinson Pulling, Daniel Oliver). William H. P. Oliver, comp., *Descendants of the Honorable Andrew Oliver of Boston (1706–1774) and His First Wife Mary (Fitch) Oliver* (1937), 6–8, 10, 12.

6. *Social Register* (New York: Social Register Association, 1952) LXVI (November 1951), 1:160, 512, 544, 563.

110

1. G. Bernard Hughes, "Evolution of the Orange Strainer," *Country Life* (May 9, 1968), 1240, 1242; Clayton 1972, 191–92, figs. 389a–c, 390–92.

2. Buhler and Hood 1972, 1:282–83, cat. no. 471.

111

1. Jones 1913, 79, pl. XXX.

2. Buhler 1972, 1:385.

3. Buhler 1972, 2:384; Janine Skerry, "The Revolutionary Revere: A Critical Assessment of the Silver of Paul Revere," in *Paul Revere* 1988, 46, fig. 14, 59, fn. 13.

4. On rare occasions, dates engraved on church silver are much earlier than the date of fabrication. In the case of bequests, funds provided in a donor's will may not be spent until enough monies are gathered or church leadership determines that communion silver is needed. As no surviving papers record when the beakers were purchased, or when they were first used at the church, the inscribed dates are accepted as correct.

5. Buhler 1972, 2:385. Kane 1998, 849–52, notes that at least 14 objects can be attributed to either Paul Revere I or II, illustrating the difficulty of distinguishing between the late work of the father and the early work of the son.

112

1. "Notes," *NEHGS* 113 (January 1959), 66; BMGI, no. 983583; IGI v4.02, film nos. 457981, 184220.

2. SSDI for Gretchen Shaw (017–36–1710).

113

1. Kane 1998, 822–23.

114

1. Warren 1987, fig. 11, 26–27, 30, 47–50.

2. The chief source on Harvard tutorial silver is Skerry, "'Ancient and Valuable Gifts': Silver at Colonial Harvard," in Falino and Ward 2001, 183–209.

3. Falino and Ward 2001, 192.

4. *Sibley's Harvard Graduates,* 15:492–93.

5. Harvard Tercentenary Exhibition 1936, 41, 110; *Exhibition of American Silver and Pressed Glass* (Shreveport, La.: R. W. Norton Art Gallery, 1967), 21.

6. *Paul Revere* 1988, 49–50, fn. 23; Fairbanks 1991, 72, 92, cat. no. 55.

7. SSDI for Mary Lamson (011–36–1681); Kane 1998, 810.

115

1. Revere daybooks, 1:60, 65, 164, 2:113.

2. One sauceboat was marked by Phillips Garden (first mark entered 1738) and the other by Richard Pargeter (first mark entered 1730). These were presented as a pair and engraved in 1802 as a gift to Anne (Green) Winslow's nephew, Judge Joshua Green (Harvard College, Class of 1784). Bigelow 1941, 415–18, fig. 306; Alcorn 2000, 140, cat. no. 80.

3. Kane 1998, 228, 254, 262, 302, 451, 463, 541–42, 601, 620, 824–25.

4. Hammerslough and Feigenbaum 1958–73, 4:6.

5. Martha Gandy Fales, *Joseph Richardson and Family: Philadelphia Silversmiths* (Middletown, Conn.: Wesleyan University Press for the Historical Society of Pennsylvania, 1974), 126–27, figs. 109–10a.

116

1. Martha Gandy Fales, "Daniel Rogers, Ipswich Goldsmith (The Case of the Double Identity)," *Essex Institute Historical Collections* 101, no. 1 (January 1965), 40–49; Kane 1998, 858–63.

2. Buhler 1972, 1:382, cat. no. 334.

3. Johnston 1994, 132.

117

1. Miller 1963, cat. nos. 32, 47, 48; Graham Hood, "A New Form in American Seventeenth-Century Silver," *Antiques* 94, no. 6 (December 1968), 879–81.

2. William Bentley, *The Diary of William Bentley*, 4 vols. (Salem: Essex Institute, 1905–14), 1:147.

3. Belden 1983, 95–115.

4. Avery 1931, fig. 104; Miller 1937, 17, cat. no. 164; Miller 1963, nos. 32, 47, 48; Flynt and Fales 1968, 78–79; Ward and Ward 1979, 131, cat. no. 137; Quimby 1995, 259, cat. no. 222; Waters 2000, 149–50, cat. no. 36.

5. Kane 1998, 864–67.

6. George B. Cutten, "Sucket Forks," *Antiques* 57, no. 6, (June 1950), 441; Northeast Auctions, Portsmouth, N.H., March 2, 1996, lot 696; department files, Art of the Americas.

7. Buhler and Hood 1970, 1:11, cat. no. 6; Kane 1998, 866.

8. "Memoirs of Governor Hutchinson," *NEHGR* 1 (October 1847), 301–2.

9. Donald Nielsen, "The Revere Family," *NEHGR* 145 (October 1991), 301, 309, 313.

10. Index to Marriages in Massachusetts, 107 (1931–1935), 25:21; George Walter Chamberlain, "The New England Coolidges and Some of Their Descendants," *NEHGR* 77 (October 1923), 300.

118

1. Waters 2000, 183–84.

2. Buhler and Hood 1970, 2:27, 29, cat. no. 575; Waters 2000, 99, 118; DAPC 77.2459, 68.5093.

3. Avery 1920, cxxvi, fig. 41.

4. For Frederick Grinnell Morgan: FamilySearch™ International Genealogical Index v4.02, batch no. F877708, source call no. 1396449; May Lefferts Morgan SSDI records (029-36-5914). The donor also gave an altered cup marked by Koenraet Ten Eyck (1975.349) that has the same history of descent.

119

1. Jeannette W. Rosenbaum, *Myer Myers, Goldsmith, 1723–1795* (Philadelphia: Jewish Publication Society of America, 1954), pl. 15, illus. b; Flynt and Fales 1968, 117, pl. 101; Buhler and Hood 1970, 2:112, cat. no. 676. For a Samuel Edwards ladle having a circular bowl with a similar forked and scrolled joint, dated 1750, see Buhler 1972, 1:244, cat. no. 204. For a period image containing a punch bowl and ladle, see Belden 1983, 237, plate 6:17; *Paul Revere* 1988, 184, cat. no. 218; Quimby 1995, 100; Kane 1998, 915.

2. Kane 1998, 220, 817.

120

1. Kane 1998, 921–22.

2. Daniel Langdon Tappan, *Tappan-Toppan Genealogy, Ancestors & Descendants of Abraham Toppan of Newbury, Massachusetts, 1606–1672* (Arlington, Mass.: privately printed, 1915), 24–25, 40–42.

3. Algernon Akin Aspinwall, comp., *The Aspinwall Genealogy: Peter Aspinwall & Descendants* (Rutland, Vt.: Tuttle, 1901), 53, 76, 82–83, 124.

4. Edward Augustus Bowen, *Lineage of the Bowens of Woodstock, Ct.* (Cambridge: Riverside Press, 1897), 154, 157; Sidney Perley, *The Plumer Genealogy—Francis Plumer, Who Settled at Newbury, Massachusetts, and Some of His Descendants* (Salem, Mass.: Essex Institute, 1917), 199–200; Richard N. Gookins, comp., *A History and Genealogy of the Gookin Family of England, Ireland and America* (typescript, Salem, Ore., 1983; NEHGS library), 372.

5. Hon. Daniel Appleton White, *The Descendants of William White of Haverhill, Massachusetts, Genealogical Notices* (Boston: J. Wilson and Son, 1863), 34, 44–46.

121

1. Buhler and Hood 1970, 1:114, cat. no. 130; Buhler 1972, 1:331, cat. no. 290, 1:137, cat. no. 110; Quimby 1995, 286, cat. no. 255; 291, cat. no. 260.

2. Waldo Lincoln, "Waldo Family in America," *NEHGR* 52 (April 1898), 221, 228; Waldo Lincoln, comp., *The Genealogy of the Waldo Family, A Record of the Descendants of Cornelius Waldo of Ipswich, Massachusetts from 1647–1900*, 2 vols. (Worcester, Mass.: Press of Charles Hamilton, 1902), 96, 183–87, 311–12; undated correspondence from Arthur Winslow to Kathryn C. Buhler suggests Samuel and Lucy Waldo as owners of the serving spoon; department files, Art of the Americas.

3. Arthur Winslow, *Francis Winslow, His Forebears & Life* (Norwood, Mass.: privately printed at Plimpton Press, 1935), 1, 24, 32, 37, 48–49; Massachusetts Vital Records, Deaths, 1938, 10:485.

4. Clifford Lewis III and John Devereux Kernan, *Devereux of the Leap, County Wexford, Ireland, and Utica, New York; Nicholas Devereux, 1791–1855* (n.p.: Lewis, 1974), 88.

5. Lowell, *Historic Genealogy of the Lowells*, 120, 226, 285; Sarah Payne Stuart, *My First Cousin, Once Removed: Money, Madness, and the Family of Robert Lowell* (New York: HarperCollins, 1998), 2–11, 13–14, 17, 33–38, 49, 52, 95–96, and *passim*; *Harvard Class of 1939* (Cambridge: Harvard University Printing Office, 1964), 660; Harvard Class of 1939, *50th Anniversary Report* (Cambridge: Class of 1939, 1989), 324; Department of Vital Statistics, Massachusetts, Marriages 1 (1916), 158.

6. *Who's Who in America*, 44th ed., 1986–87 (Wilmette, Ill.: Marquis Who's Who, Macmillan Directory Division, 1987), 1:1187.

122

1. For further biographical information on Vergereau, see Waters 2000, 218–19.

2. DAPC 71.2220, 71.2222, 71.2439, 74.2150, 92.3000; Waters 2000, 220–21, cat. nos. 86–87; Sotheby's, New York, sale 7521, October 13, 2000, lot 136.

3. Phillips, Parker, and Buhler 1955, 77, 82; Buhler and Hood 1970, 2:74–77, cat. no. 627; Christie's, New York, sale 9054, January 15, 1999, lot 89.

4. Richard Wynkoop, *Wynkoop Genealogy in the United States of America* (New York: Knickerbocker Press, 1904), 39–41, 79, 115, 165. The bowl came into the Wynkoop family through the maternal side; however, silversmiths Benjamin and Cornelius Wynkoop were great-uncle and uncle to Capt. Cornelius C. Wynkoop. Wynkoop, *Wynkoop Genealogy*, 15, 23.

5. *Social Register, New York, 1941* (New York: Social Register Association, LV, no. 1, November 1940), 42; Newton Cemetery, Newton, Mass.

6. Harvard Class of 1937, *Twenty-fifth Anniversary Report* (Cambridge: Printed for the class, 1962), 1076–77; Harvard Class of 1941, *Fiftieth Anniversary Report* (Cambridge: Printed for the class, 1991), 569.

123

1. M. Halsey Thomas, ed., *The Diary of Samuel Sewall, 1674–1729*, 2 vols. (New York: Farrar, Straus, and Giroux, 1973), 2:1063.

2. Carpenter 1954, 168, 170, cat. nos. 110, 112; Gourley 1965, cat. nos. 308–10; Buhler and Hood 1970, 1:271, 173, cat. no. 456; Sotheby's, New York, sale 5357, June 17–28, 1985, lot 57; Moore Collection 1980, 46–47, cat. no. 3; DAPC 74.3354.

3. John Russell Bartlett, "History of the Wanton Family of Newport, Rhode Island," *Rhode Island Historical Tracts No. 3* (Providence, R.I.: Sidney S. Rider, 1878), 12.

4. Charles Henry Jones, *Genealogy of the Rodman Family, 1620–1886* (Philadelphia, Pa.: n.p., 1886), 27–28, 42–44, 74, 97, 131.

5. Caroline E. Robinson, *The Hazard Family of Rhode Island, 1635–1894* (Boston: printed for the author, 1895), 75–77.

6. Anne H. Wharton, *Genealogy of the Wharton Family of Philadelphia* (Philadelphia, Pa.: Collins Printers, 1880), 16–22, 28–31, 104.

7. Obituary, *Waltham News Tribune*, February 24, 1942,; June 14, 1945; Harvard Class of 1925, *Fiftieth Anniversary Report* (Cambridge: Printed for the university, 1975), 704–5.

124

1. For the Vernon family, see Harrison Ellery, "The Vernon Family and Arms," *NEHGR* 33 (July 1879), 312, 315–16; John O. Austin, *The Genealogical Dictionary of Rhode Island*, rev. ed. (Baltimore: Genealogical Publishing Co., 1995), 402.

2. Carpenter 1954, 155–56, cat. no. 119; Buhler 1956, 72, cat. no. 153; Buhler 1972, 554.

3. Buhler 1979, 79–80.

4. The Rhode Island General Assembly gift was made in thanks for the New York commissioners' assistance in a boundary dispute with the Massachusetts Bay Colony. One of the three tankards is in the Yale University Art Gallery. Buhler and Hood 1972, 1:273–75. For a shield-shaped terminus, see Johnston 1994, 170.

5. Three colonial silversmiths were interrelated as first cousins through the marriage of three daughters of Edward Hutchinson. Elizabeth Hutchinson (1639–1728) married Edward Winslow (about 1634–1682), and their son Edward was a goldsmith. Ann Hutchinson (1643–1716/17) married second, Daniel Vernon, and their son Samuel was a goldsmith. Last, Susanna Hutchinson (1649–1716) married Nathaniel Coddington, son of Rhode Island Governor William Coddington. They were the parents of Newport silversmith John Coddington (1690–1743). See "Brief Genealogy of the Hutchinson Family," *NEHGR* 19 (January 1865), 15; Wayne Howard Miller Wilcox, "The Ancestry of Katherine Hamby, Wife of Captain Edward Hutchinson of Boston, Massachusetts," *NEHGR* 146 (April 1991), 99, 258–63.

6. Adin Ballou, comp. and ed., *An Elaborate History and Genealogy of the Ballous in America* (Providence, R.I.: Press of E. L. Freeman & Son, 1888), 51, 108, 1048.

7. Robert F. Kirkpatrick, "A Record of Deaths in Rhode Island and Massachusetts, 1813–1852," *NEHGR* 138 (April 1984), 125–26.

8. Ballou, *History and Genealogy of the Ballous*, 501, 1048.

125

1. Curtis 1913, pl. xxii; Flynt and Fales 1968, 349–51; Bohan and Hammerslough 1970, 256–57, 277–78; *Antiques* 103, no. 4 (April 1973), 631.

2. The spoons in the collection of Historic Deerfield are engraved "SM / 1702" (75.498) and "SC / RS / 1714" (75.515). The spoon engraved 1702 has a trifid handle and pseudohallmark, as found in the MFA's example.

3. Teunis G. Bergen, *The Bergen Family; or, the Descendants of Hans Hansen Bergen, One of the Early Settlers of New York and Brooklyn, L.I.* (New York: Bergen & Tripp, 1866), 60–61.

126

1. Henry Webb (d. 1660) and silversmith Edward Webb were unrelated. Walter Kendall Watkins, "The Robert Gibbs House, Boston," *Old-Time New England* 22, no. 4 (April 1932), 193–96. Portraits of Henry, Robert, and Margaret Gibbs, three of her children, by the Freake-Gibbs painter are illustrated in Fairbanks and Trent 1982, 3:458–59, cat. nos. 433–35.

2. Kane 1998, 951–52.

3. Will of Elizabeth Corwin in Curwen Papers, Peabody Essex Museum, Salem, Mass., MSS45, box 1, folder 1.

4. Kane 1998, 954.

5. Buhler 1972, 1:37–38, cat. no. 31.

6. *Vital Records of Newton, Massachusetts, to the Year 1850* (Boston: New England Historic Genealogical Society, 1905), 263, 303; *Vital Records of Salem, Massachusetts, to the End of the Year 1849*, 6 vols. (Salem, Mass.: Essex Institute, 1916–25), 3:412, 5:177, 190, 412.

7. Thomas W. Baldwin, *Vital Records of Cambridge, Massachusetts, to the Year 1850*, 2 vols. (Boston: Wright & Potter Print Co., 1914–15), 2:187; *Sibley's Harvard Graduates*, 7:720–23.

8. Ruth A. Hatch-Hale, *Genealogy & History of the Hatch Family, Descendants of Thomas & Grace Hatch of Dorchester, Yarmouth & Barnstable, Mass., Part V* (Salt Lake City, Utah: Hatch Genealogical Society, 1928), 413–14, 655; George Walter Chamberlain, "Old Boston Families, Number 6, The Bryant Family," *NEHGR* 97 (January 1943), 45; Elizabeth Ellery Dana, *The Dana Family in America* (Boston: Wright & Potter, 1956), 473–74.

127

1. For the most comprehensive volume on the role of chocolate in the Americas and Europe, see Sophie D. Coe and Michael D. Coe, *The True History of Chocolate* (London: Thames and Hudson, 1996).

2. For a comparable piece of furniture that was probably made by an English-trained cabinetmaker in Boston and purchased by the Warland family of Cambridge, see Fairbanks 1991, 32, cat. no. 5.

3. Kane 1998, 954–57.

4. Buhler 1956, 65–66, cat. no. 111, fig. 45; Buhler and Hood 1970, 1:54–56, cat. no. 49. For other chocolate pots in the Museum's collection, see Buhler 1972, 1:59–60, cat. no. 50, 1:373, cat. no. 326; for an early example by John Coney, see cat. no. 35; Kane 1998, 212, 324, 741–42, 977. A third chocolate pot by Winslow is cited in Kane 1998, 777.

5. For an analysis of Webb's technique, see Gerald W. R. Ward, "The Silver Chocolate Pots of Colonial Boston," in Falino and Ward 2001, 61–88, fig. 11. Jackson 1911, 2:272; Buhler and Hood 1970, 1:38–41, cat. no. 31; Georgina

E. Lee, *Monteith Bowls, Including American and European Examples* (Byfleet, Eng.: Manor House Press, 1978), fig. 2; Safford 1983, 22–23. Two London precedents for this form, by William Charnelhouse (free 1696; d. 1711/12) from 1703/4 and Joseph Ward (free 1689) from 1702 are published in Wees 1997, 267–68, 274–76, cat. no. 182, 309–10, cat. no. 209.

6. Ward, "The Silver Chocolate Pots of Colonial Boston," 83; Julie Emerson notes that chocolate was used as a beverage, and occasionally as a spice, until the early nineteenth century, when it was first developed by the Dutch as a confection. Julie Emerson, *Coffee, Tea, and Chocolate Wares in the Collection of the Seattle Art Museum* (Seattle, Wash.: Seattle Art Museum, 1991), 3.

7. George Francis Dow, *Domestic Life in New England in the Seventeenth Century* (Topsfield, Mass.: Perkins Press, 1925), 22–23; George Francis Dow, comp., *The Arts and Crafts in New England, 1704–1775* (Topsfield, Mass.: Wayside Press, 1927), 258, 260; Dexter and Lainhart 1989, 86; Emerson, *Coffee, Tea, and Chocolate Wares*, 3; department files, Art of the Americas.

8. *Boston Marriages, 1752–1809* (Boston: Municipal Printing Office, 1898), 115, 233, 331.

9. Department files, Art of the Americas.

128

1. Buhler 1972, 1:34–35, cat. no. 28; Quimby 1995, 173, cat. no. 32; porringer engraved "B / I [barred] M" facing bowl, private collection; department files, Art of the Americas.

2. Buhler 1972, 1:90–91, cat. no. 74, 1:256, cat. no. 216.

3. Jules David Prown, *John Singleton Copley in America, 1738–1774* (Cambridge and Washington, D.C.: Harvard University Press and National Gallery of Art, 1966), 217, pls. 61–62; Quimby 1995, 111.

4. Greene's probate record is cited in Kane 1998, 512.

5. Kane 1998, 509–10.

6. Elizabeth Cabot Putnam and Harriet Silvester Tapley, comps., *Samuel and Sarah Putnam; with a Genealogical Record of Their Descendants* (Danvers, Mass.: reprinted from the Danvers Historical Collections, 1922), 35–36.

7. Lowell, *Historic Genealogy of the Lowells*, 221.

8. *Fiftieth Anniversary Report, Harvard Class of 1902* (Cambridge: printed for the class, 1952), 415–16; *Fiftieth Anniversary Report, Harvard Class of 1937* (Cambridge: Printed for the class, 1986), 451–52; Massachusetts Vital Records, Index to Marriages, 547–654.

129

1. Jackson 1949, 134; Wendy A. Cooper, "New Findings on Colonial New England Goldsmiths and English Sources," *American Art Journal* 10, no. 2 (November 1978), 107–9. It was on the basis of these porringers that Cooper advanced the theory that Anthony apprenticed with Winslow.

2. Kane 1998, 150, 979; department files, Art of the Americas.

3. Lowell, *Historic Genealogy of the Lowells*, 119; Emma Downing Coolidge, *Descendants of John and Mary Coolidge of Watertown, Massachusetts, 1630* (Boston: Wright & Potter Printing Co., 1930), 348–50.

4. Faculty records, Wellesley College, Wellesley, Mass.

5. Advertisement, Gebelein Silversmiths, *Antiques* 100, no. 2 (August 1971), 162.

130

1. Winslow tankards accented with dolphin-and-mask thumbpieces and cherub termini have been published in Buhler 1956, cat. nos. 142, 145; War-

ren 1975, cat. no. 285; and Quimby 1995, cat. no. 136; and are in private collections. See also David A. Hanks, "Recent Acquisitions of American Silver," *Bulletin of the Detroit Institute of Arts* 55 (1977), 109–14, fig. 1; department files, Art of the Americas.

2. Thomas Paine became a landowner in the North End in 1696, and perhaps travel to Boston brought him into contact with Winslow. The initials on the tankards do not appear to match any of the Paines' immediate descendants. Kane 1998, 967–84, incorrectly notes that the Paine arms appear on the MFA vessel. A tankard by Winslow that bears the Payne arms has a similar thumbpiece and cherub's head, but it does not appear to have any family relationship to this example; Warren 1975, cat. no. 285.

3. Sarah Cushing Paine, comp., Charles Henry Pope, ed., *Paine Ancestry: The Family of Robert Treat Paine, Signer of the Declaration of Independence* (Boston: printed for the family, 1912), 9–12; Thomas M. Paine, *Growing Paines* (Wellesley, Mass.: privately printed, 1991), chart 1.

4. D. W. Allen, *Genealogy and Biographical Sketches of the Descendants of Thomas and Anthony Thacher, from Their Settlement in New England, June 4, 1635* (Vineland, N.J.: Independent Printing House, 1872), 32–33; Ebenezer Clapp, comp., *The Clapp Memorial: Record of the Clapp Family in America* (Boston: David Clapp & Son, 1876), 257–58; "Memoirs of Mrs. Gino Lorenzo (Caroline Thacher)," *NEHGR* 103 (January 1949), 69.

5. Department files, Art of the Americas.

131

1. Quotation from H. E. K., "Braziers as Collectibles, A Gallery Note," *Antiques* 25, no. 3 (September 1933), 106–7. For a fine Continental brazier made of brass, see Fennimore 1996, cat. no. 31.

2. The definition of the French term *eschauffement*, meaning "chafing, warming, heating," cited by Claude Hollyband, *The Treasurie of the French Tong* (London: Bynneman, 1580). However, it had already entered general usage in the English language by the late fifteenth century; *The Compact Edition of the Oxford English Dictionary* (Oxford: Oxford University Press), 1:372, s.v. "chafing."

3. Kane 1998, 592–93.

4. Samuel W. Woodhouse Jr., "John De Nys, Philadelphia Silversmith," *Antiques* 21, no. 5 (May 1932), 217–18; Russel Hastings, "Two Chafing Dishes by Peter Van Dyck," *Antiques* 30, no. 4 (October 1936), 152–54; Helen Comstock, "Chafing Dishes by New York Silversmiths, *Connoisseur* 110, no. 484 (October 1942), 66; Kurt M. Semon, "Small but Useful American Silver," in *A Treasury of Old Silver* (New York: Robert M. McBride, 1947), 76; Buhler 1956, 71, cat. no. 148, fig. 28; *English-Speaking Union* 1960, 8, cat. no. 23, pl. 12; Buhler 1972, 1:68, cat. no. 58, 1:70, cat. no. 60, 1:175, cat. no. 141, 1:188–89, cat. no. 152, 1:227–29, cat. no. 188–89, 1:284, cat. no. 237; Kane 1998, 592–93, 1184.

5. B. Ward 1983, 125–27, fig. 19, fnn. 25–31.

6. *Ellis Memorial* 1984, 69–72; Kane 1998, 977.

7. Thomas and Rebecca Goodwill also gave to their daughter Lydia a tankard engraved "T.R.G." and "Sept. 7, 1747," probably the date of her marriage intentions with Nathaniel Holmes. The tankard was fashioned by Paul Revere II. G. Arthur Gray, Esq., "George Holmes of Roxbury, Mass. and Some of His Descendants," *NEHGR* 58 (January 1904): 28, 143–44; Thomas J. Goodwill, *300 Years in America: A History of the Goodwill Family* (Jamestown, N.Y.: T. J. Goodwill, 1985), 11–12.

8. Herbert Freeman Adams, *The Compendium of Tufts Kinsmen* (Boston: Tufts Kinsman Project, 1975), 11; Diana L. Smith, comp., *The Heber Reginald Bishop Genealogy* (Jamestown, R.I.: privately printed, 1987), charts 1, 5–6;

Vital Records of Medford, Massachusetts, to the Year 1850 (Boston: NEGHS, 1907), 20, 185, 339.

9. "Reviews of Books," *NEHGR* 136 (July 1982), 261.

132

1. Advertisement, Gebelein Silversmiths, *Antiques* 108, no. 4 (October 1975), 594; Kane 1998, 979.

2. Thomas B. Wyman Jr., "Pedigree of the Family of Boylston," *NEHGR* 7 (April 1853), 145–50; Thomas Bellows Wyman, *The Genealogies and Estates of Charlestown* (Boston: David Clapp and Son, 1879), vol. A–J, 105–8; David E. Maas, *Divided Hearts—Massachusetts Loyalists, 1765–1790* (Boston: Society of Colonial Wars in the Commonwealth of Massachusetts and the New England Genealogical Society, 1980), 74; Eugene Chalmers Fowle, comp., *Descendants of George Fowle (1610/11?–1682) of Charlestowne, Massachusetts* (Boston: New England Historical Genealogical Society, 1990), 139. Ogden Codman, comp., *Index of Obituaries in Boston Newspapers, 1704–1800*, 3 vols. (Boston: G. K. Hall, 1968), 1:35. A portrait of Mrs. Thomas Boylston (Sarah Morecock), the porringer's original owner, is in the Harvard University Portrait Collection, Bequest of Ward Nicholas Boylston.

3. Massachusetts Vital Records, Index to Marriages, 227 (1869–1870), 341; Massachusetts Archives, Marriages 452 (1895): 459; Massachusetts Vital Records, Births 233, (1870–1871): 423; *Princeton, Massachusetts, Vital Records to the End of the Year 1849* (Worcester, Mass.: Franklin P. Rice, 1902), 13, 81, 151; *Roxbury Vital Records to the End of the Year 1849*, 2 vols. (Salem, Mass.: Essex Institute, 1925–26), 1:36, 2:470–71.

4. Obituary, *Portland, Maine Press Herald* (June 30, 1975), 2; telephone inquiry, February 5, 1998, Lone Oak Cemetery, Leesburg, Fla.

133

1. For related English examples, see John Davis, *English Silver at Williamsburg* (Williamsburg, Va.: Colonial Williamsburg Foundation, 1976), 23–24, cat. no. 8; Peter, Nancy, and Herbert Schiffer, *The Brass Book, American, English and European, Fifteenth Century through 1850* (Atglen, Pa.: Schiffer Publishing, 1978), 145–93; and Fennimore 1996, 192–201, cat. nos. 105–17. In some cases, Fennimore attributes candlesticks to England or America, but for the most part, brass candlesticks were imported.

2. Jonathan L. Fairbanks and Elizabeth Bidwell Bates, *American Furniture, 1620 to the Present* (New York: Richard Marek Publishers, 1981), 119, 123.

3. Bigelow 1917, 289–90, fig. 191; Edward Wenham, "Candlesticks and Snuffers by American Silversmiths," *Antiques* 18, no. 6 (December 1930), 491–93; Joseph T. Butler, *Candleholders in America, 1650–1900* (New York: Bonanza Publishers, 1967), 33–34, figs. 15–17; Fales 1970, 108–9, fig. 109a, 110, 155; Ward and Ward 1979, 155–56, cat. no. 163; Quimby 1995, 65–67, cat. no. 20.

4. Kane 1998, 321.

5. On the Milne candlesticks, see Jack L. Lindsey, "Lynford Lardner's Silver: Early Rococo in Philadelphia," *Antiques* 143, no. 4 (April 1993), 608–15.

6. Silver candlesticks by Winslow at the Colonial Williamsburg Foundation, acc. no. 1962.263.1–2, DAPC 73.3130; at the Metropolitan Museum of Art, acc. no. 1973.152.1–2, Safford 1983, 34, fig. 41.

7. Buhler 1972, 1:67, cat. no. 57.

8. Wedding announcement, *New York Times*, January 4, 1911, March 1, 1911; obituaries, *New York Times*, October 26, 1956, September 22, 1982; *Social Register, New York, 1911* (New York: Social Register Association, 1911), vol. 25, no. 1, 270; Parke-Bernet, New York, sale 1669, April 14, 1956, lot 301;

NEHGR 111 (April 1957), 147; Adolph Dick death date courtesy of Yale Alumni Records.

134

1. Kane 1998, 970–84.

2. Arthur Gilman, *The Gilman Family Traced in the Line of Hon. John Gilman of Exeter, New Hampshire* (Albany, N.Y.: Joel Munsell, 1869), 152; Frederick Clarke Jewett, *History and Genealogy of the Jewetts of America*, 2 vols. (Baltimore, Md.: Genealogical Publishers, 1908); David Curtis Dearborn, *The Dearborn Family* (Boston: NEHGS, forthcoming).

3. *Harvard University, Class of 1901, Thirtieth Anniversary Report* (Cambridge: for the university, 1931), 123.

4. Obituary, *NEHGR* 89 (January 1935), 70; obituary, *Boston Globe*, December 17, 1969; Massachusetts Vital Records (microfilm), 306:140, 342:94. Ownership in the Richardson and Perry family is documented in Registrar's Department, MFA. The history of ownership through Dr. Theodore Jewett Eastman was related by former museum curator Timothy Kendall, whose cousin Juliet (Richardson) French was the daughter of Mr. and Mrs. Henry Hyslop Richardson Jr.; see department files, Art of the Americas.

5. William A. Warden, *Warden Family Genealogy: The Ancestors, Kin, and Descendants of John Warden and Narcissa (Davis) Warden* (Worcester, Mass.: Wm. A. Warden, 1901), 137; *Harvard Class of 1905, Third Report* (Cambridge: for the university, 1915), 431–42; obituary, *NEHGR* 87 (January 1933), 59.

CHAPTER 2

NEOCLASSICISM IN AMERICAN SILVER

Gerald W. R. Ward

The decades after the American Revolution were a liminal period in the development of American silversmithing, as craft stood on the threshold of industry. Traditional elements of the creation, design, and marketing of silver wares continued, but the era saw dramatic changes as well—changes that would come to fruition later in the nineteenth century. The population of the United States doubled, from about 860,000 in 1790 to 1,750,000 in 1820, and the Louisiana Purchase dramatically expanded the geographic extent of the new nation, which grew from about 4 million square miles at the beginning of the period to some 10 million by the end. The population growth and enlarged territory opened up new markets for producers of material goods, including silversmiths. Throughout this roughly fifty-year period, the nation's economy fluctuated greatly due to wars and political turmoil, among other factors. Yet the period was booming, a fact reflected in the material culture and in the silver discussed in this chapter.[1]

The political independence achieved as a result of the Revolutionary War did not bring with it a drive for artistic independence. American decorative arts objects, including silver, made during the federal period are even more closely related to English prototypes than those made before the war. Neoclassicism—the revival of the arts and architecture of the ancient worlds of Greece, Rome, and to some extent Egypt—became the dominant international stylistic language. Although the American idiom varied, for the most part American silversmiths moved in step with their English counterparts.

Precursors of Neoclassicism can be found in a few objects made before the Revolution, such as the famous silver urn fashioned in 1774 by Richard Humphreys of Philadelphia for Charles Thomson. But these are exceptions. Although Neoclassicism took a firm hold in the 1780s, the popularity of the Rococo style endured into the 1790s. Some traditional forms—such as the so-called keyhole-handled porringer introduced in the early 1700s—persisted into the 1800s, as seen in an example (cat. no. 142) made about 1820 by the Boston firm of Davis, Watson & Co.

During the federal period, the style of silver changed significantly, shifting away from robust and fanciful forms of the Rococo and toward those of elegant simplicity and grace. The era also saw a technological transition, as silver making grew from craft into industry. Silversmiths continued the centuries-old manner of raising the metal from ingots through repeated hammer blows, but they often augmented the process with rolled-sheet silver. These thin sheets, prepared in flatting mills through compression and heat, could then be bent into the desired form and joined with solder, saving both time and energy. Although some of this labor-saving machinery existed prior to the 1790s, it became more commonplace after the Revolution, as seen in such objects as Paul Revere's famous fluted teapots (cat. no. 171). The widespread use of specialists such as engravers also continued, reflecting the interconnectedness of the silversmiths' craft evident since the 1600s. Toward the 1820s, silversmiths in urban shops increasingly incorporated into their work die-stamped decoration in the form of beading, pieced work, and relief ornament. With little effort, designs could be repeated endlessly and without variation, thus adding another layer of the "workmanship of certainty" to the creation of silver objects. The use of sheet silver also allowed silversmiths to create larger, more bulbous forms characteristic of so-called empire silver of the period from about 1810 to 1840. Such forms appear massive but are in fact relatively light compared to hand-raised objects.[3]

In the colonial period, the luxury craft of silversmithing had been largely confined to urban centers, principally Boston, New York, Philadelphia, and, to some extent, Albany and Newport, Rhode Island. Makers in these cities dominated the market for not only major church commissions and presentation pieces but also most domestic hollowware. Their rural and smaller-city counterparts practiced almost a different trade, making primarily flatware, executing repairs, and retailing goods imported from the urban centers and abroad. By the federal period, however, the growth of smaller cities—including Portsmouth, New Hampshire; Salem, Massachusetts; Providence, Rhode Island; and Wilmington, Delaware—enabled those populations to support more silversmiths. The tea wares (cat. nos. 137–38) by Charles A. Burnett of Alexandria, Virginia, are testimony to the diffusion of the craft into emerging urban areas.[4]

Yet the old centers of Boston, New York, and Philadelphia remained prominent. Shops there grew in size; in 1815 the prominent Philadelphia firm of Fletcher and Gardiner, maker of the most ambitious American silver in this era, employed as many as twenty-two workmen, including apprentices, journeymen, and "burnishers."[5] Repair work remained an important part of the craft, and most large shops also carried on retail trade in imported wares, such as large quantities of fused-plate candlesticks, baskets, and varied forms produced in Sheffield and other areas of England.

The work of Boston silversmiths, including Paul Revere, is especially well represented in the Museum's collections. After the stress, turmoil, and population loss of the war years, by about 1790 Boston's residents once again numbered approximately 18,000. The loss of the wealthy Loyalist population was offset by the arrival of merchants from Essex County.[6] In this port, traditional livelihoods connected to the sea—trade, privateering, fishing, and shipbuilding—reasserted themselves, strengthening the town's economic life. New ventures were undertaken, including in 1787 the advent of trade with the Northwest Coast and the opening of the China Trade in 1790.

The social life of Boston and America was in flux as well. Increased wealth resulted in the construction of luxurious houses whose interiors needed fashionable goods in the latest style. As the lingering vestiges of Puritanism began to fade, more relaxed views about recreational activities took hold, and new entertainments and pursuits appeared. In Boston in 1784–85, Sarah Morton and Hepzibah Swan founded the Sans Souci Club as a tea assembly that encouraged dancing, drinking, and gambling. In 1792 a law prohibiting the performance of stage plays in Boston was repealed, and plans were quickly drawn for the city's first theater. Supported by Harrison Gray Otis and Perez Morton, the Federal Street Theater was designed in 1793–94 by Charles Bulfinch and built at the corner of Federal and Franklin streets. In addition to diversions such as gambling and the theater, the period also saw the publication of the first American novels, a dramatic rise in the consumption of alcoholic beverages, and the adoption of clinging, transparent, and otherwise revealing dress among ladies of fashion.[7]

Against this backdrop of revised social conventions and novel architecture, federal-period silversmiths plied their craft. The international fashion of Neoclassicism, expressed in early and late phases, dominated the era. The early neoclassical style was linear and delicate in proportion, with an emphasis on two-dimensional surface ornament and pattern. In furniture, this emphasis was expressed through the use of veneers, especially mahogany accented and trimmed with light and dark woods

FIG. 1. Gilbert Stuart (1755–1828), *Paul Revere*, 1813. Oil on panel 28¼ x 22½ in. (71.75 x 57.15 cm.). Museum of Fine Arts, Boston; Gift of Joseph W. Revere, William B. Revere and Edward H. R. Revere (30.782).

in both pictorial and patterned modes, or through colorful painted decoration. In silver it was achieved through engraving or bright-cutting, a technique in which the object's surface is gouged to form facets that catch light and sparkle, taking advantage of the metal's remarkable reflectivity. Geometric forms, such as the ellipse, and classical silhouettes, especially the urn, were used for the bodies of silver objects or for discrete parts such as finials.[8]

Paul Revere retained his status as the leading figure in Boston during this early phase of Neoclassicism. After the Revolution, he resumed silversmithing as early as 1779, but not until 1781 does he seem to have returned to his prewar activity level. By 1813, the date of his portrait (fig. 1) by Gilbert Stuart, he had largely moved on to coppersmithing while well on his way to becoming a legend. His postwar silver is notable for its innovative translation of ceramic forms into metal, as seen in the so-called Liverpool creamware pitchers (fig. 2). Revere is also

FIG. 2. An English creamware pitcher flanked by two silver examples by Paul Revere. Museum of Fine Arts, Boston. Left: Gift of Joseph W.R. Rogers and Mary C. Rogers (42.462). Center: Bequest of William Lambert Barnard (55.678). Right: Gift of William Westfall (1991.1083).

recognized for his adoption of designs prominent in English fused-plate and sterling wares.[9]

The later phase of the Neoclassical style appears in objects dating from the mid-1810s to the 1830s. Often called Empire, the style displays a more massive, monumental, and literal reiteration of ancient motifs. With its well-articulated feet, dolphin finial, and three-dimensional leaf decoration, a water pitcher (cat. no. 150) by the prominent Philadelphia firm of Fletcher and Gardiner reflects this later mode. Also representative are the swelled, lobate bodies of a three-piece tea set by Higbie and Crosby (cat. no. 155) or that made by Chitry and Gale (cat. no. 139). These are further embellished with rolls of die-stamped floral ornament, the successor to the bright-cut decoration on earlier pieces.

The social functions of silver in this period remained largely those it had served for hundreds of years, but with significant alterations. In the domestic arena, the vocabulary of specialized forms expanded, and, even though silver remained a luxury, ownership of the precious metal extended to a greater population. The norm became large tea and coffee services (in some cases containing as many as nineteen pieces) in which each object was fashioned en suite, in contrast to colonial times when tea sets tended to be assembled piece by piece. In the home, silver was often displayed on the sideboard, itself a new furniture form in fashionable interiors. Presentation silver continued to play an important role in society, particularly in the form of grand pieces presented to heroes of the War of 1812.

Two such examples are the pitcher and monteith made by the Boston firm of Churchill and Treadwell as part of a large silver service presented by the grateful citizens of Boston to Oliver Hazard Perry (cat. no. 141).[10]

The early and late phases of Neoclassicism were the first of many successive yet overlapping revival styles, including the Gothic revival and the Rococo revival, that would come to characterize the nineteenth century, as explored in chapter 3.

Notes

1. Overviews of political and social life in this formative period are in Stanley M. Elkins, with Eric McKitrick, *The Age of Federalism* (New York: Oxford University Press, 1993); and Jack Larkin, *The Reshaping of Everyday Life, 1790–1840* (New York: Harper and Row, 1988).

2. A useful introduction to the stylistic developments of this period is Hood 1971, 160–212.

3. For technological changes in this period, see Stephen K. Victor, "'From the Shop to the Manufactory': Silver and Industry, 1800–1970," in Ward and Ward 1979, 23–32.

4. For a profile of one maker in an emerging small city, see Gerald W. R. Ward, "Jabez Baldwin, Silversmith-Entrepreneur of Salem, 1802–1819," *Winterthur Portfolio* 23, no. 1 (spring 1988), 51–62.

5. Cited in Victor, "'From the Shop to the Manufactory,'" 29.

6. On Boston during this period, see Fairbanks 1975, 143–96.

7. For changing mores during this period, see Gerald W. R. Ward, "'Avarice and Conviviality': Card Playing in Federal America," in Benjamin A. Hewitt, Patricia E. Kane, and Gerald W. R. Ward, *The Work of Many Hands: Card Tables in Federal America, 1790–1820* (New Haven: Yale University Art Gallery, 1982), 15–38.

8. Hood 1971.

9. For Revere's later career, see *Paul Revere* 1988, 75–90; and Fairbanks 1975, 197–211.

10. Presentation pieces of this period are discussed in Warren 1987, 75–131.

135

Joseph Anthony Jr. (1762–1814)

Camp cup

Philadelphia, Pennsylvania, 1783
Gift of Mr. and Mrs. Sargent Bradlee
1978.679

H. 1⅝ in. (4 cm); Diam. rim 1⅜ in. (3.5 cm); Diam. base 1¹³⁄₁₆ in. (4.5 cm); Wt. 1 oz 3 gr (31.3 gm)

Marks: "J [pellet] A" within a rectangle struck twice on base.

Inscriptions: "WS" entwined monogram in sprigged script engraved on side. "from / Camp Chest of / Major Winthrop Sargent / U.S.A. / 1776–1785" in script engraved later on base.

SIMPLE, STACKABLE, and portable silver camp cups were commonly included among a well-equipped officer's possessions. They offered, in miniature, an elegant respite from the rigors of war. Typically monogrammed or engraved with heraldic crests and made in sets of two to twelve, these cups were used to serve strong spirits and wine. Their capacity, as noted by Jennifer Goldsborough, was similar to that of glassware of the period, which was designed to hold about two ounces and often replenished in social settings. It is perhaps due to their

small size and hard use that many camp cups have disappeared, lost on the battlefield or in the melting pot.[1]

Newport-trained silversmith Joseph Anthony Jr. enjoyed access to patronage of the political and mercantile elite, thanks in part to the success of his merchant father and through his own marriage to Henrietta Hillegas, daughter of the first treasurer of the United States. As an enterprising and prolific silversmith with a showroom and workshop in his Philadelphia home, Anthony counted George Washington, the Penn family, and the Cadwaladers among his patrons.[2]

The son of a Gloucester, Massachusetts, merchant by the same name, Winthrop Sargent Jr. purchased domestic silver from Revere, as his father did before him. In 1782, while serving as aide-de-camp to Maj. Gen. Robert Howe, Sargent bought spoons and cups with engraved crests from Revere and engaged him to repair a holster. In view of these purchases, family history may be correct in noting that Sargent's "army kit was furnished with plate made for him by Paul Revere." In 1783 Sargent's military service took him to Philadelphia, where he ordered from Anthony twelve camp cups, including the Museum's example, and a ladle, all bearing the "WS" monogram. Five of the cups are now in the collection of the U.S. Department of State, a gift of the donor of the Museum's camp cup; the other six were sold at auction in 1971.[3]

Among surviving camp cups is a group by Philadelphia silversmith Richard Humphreys, who fashioned a half dozen large examples and two smaller ones for George Washington; one for Jeremiah Wadsworth of Connecticut; and a pair for Nathaniel Greene, who was second-in-command to Washington. Boston silversmith Joseph Edwards Jr. also produced six seamed camp cups for Greene. Philadelphia silversmith Allen Armstrong produced a pair of camp cups for Col. Jonas Simmons of Massachusetts.[4]

Description: The small, raised, straight-sided cup with center point flares outward from a flat base and is scored twice below rim.

History: Maj. Winthrop Sargent (1753–1820), Gloucester, Massachusetts. Probable descent through the children of Sargent's first cousin John Turner Sargent (1769–1813): Howard Sargent (1810–1872), and his wife, Charlotte Cunningham (1818–1888); to their daughter Mary Sarah Sargent (1844–1908) and her husband, Arthur Malcolm Thomas (1844–1879); to their daughter Elizabeth Whitwell Thomas (b. 1868) and her husband, Frederick Josiah Bradlee; to their son, a namesake of the original owner and donor, Sargent Bradlee (1898–1987).[5]

Exhibitions and publications: None.

NOTES TO THIS ENTRY ARE ON PAGE 221.

136

Samuel Buel (1742–1819)

Bowl

Hartford or Westfield, Connecticut, 1790–1810
Gift of the Nathaniel T. Dexter Fine Arts Trust
2000.690

H. 3⅝ in. (9.2 cm); Diam. rim 7⅛ in. (18.1 cm); Diam. base 3¹⁵⁄₁₆ in. (10.1 cm); Wt. 10 oz 10 dwt 10 gr (328.1 gm)

Marks: "S[pellet]B" within a rectangle struck twice on base.

Inscriptions: Crest of a goat on a torse over the letter "H" within an ellipse engraved on side, pendant from a bowknot.

BORN IN BRANFORD, Connecticut, Samuel Buel was a third cousin of silversmith Nathaniel Crittenden (1752–1828) and a second cousin, once removed, to the engraver and counterfeiter Abel Buel (1738–1822). It is likely that Samuel Buel's master was Ebenezer Chittenden (1726–1821) of Madison and later New Haven, Connecticut. Chittenden produced communion silver for nearby Connecticut churches, and his mechanical ingenuity brought him into association with Eli Whitney, inventor of the cotton gin. As Chittenden was Abel Buel's brother-in-law and master, Samuel Buel may have learned the craft from him as well.[1]

By 1777 Buel had established his own shop and advertised the sale of "hangars," or broad swords for officers, "made in the neatest manner." In 1780 he announced the move of his shop to Hartford, where he sought the assistance of a journeyman.[2] In later years, he moved to Westfield, where he died in 1819. Silver by Buel ranges in form from spoons to a cream jug, bowl, beaker, and coffeepot, although scarcely ten objects are known.[3]

Buel's skill as an engraver is evident in the light and assured touch seen in the bowknot, swags, and crest of this bowl. The elliptical reserve, surmounted by this delicate ornamentation, was at the time the classic method for rendering an owner's initials; the engraving of a crest in this location was somewhat unusual in American silver. The unidentified owner, whose surname begins with the letter "H," was probably from Connecticut, where Buel spent his career.

Description: The raised hemispherical bowl with applied rim has a splayed foot with an applied foot rim. Bands of bright-cut swags encircle the rim beneath its molding edge.

History: Early history unknown; collected by Nathaniel T. Dexter of Boston, Massachusetts, and bequeathed to the Museum.

Exhibitions and publications: None.

NOTES TO THIS ENTRY ARE ON PAGE 221.

137

Charles Alexander Burnett (1769–1848)

Teapot and creampot

Alexandria, Virginia, or Georgetown, District of
Columbia, 1790–1825
Marion D. Davis Fund
1971.334–35

Teapot (1971.334): H. 9 in. (22.9 cm); W. 12 in. (30.6 cm); D. 4⅜ in.
(11.2 cm); Wt. 23 oz 17 dwt 20 gr (743.1 gm)

Creampot (1971.335): H. 7⅜ in. (18.8 cm); W. 5⅞ in. (15 cm); D. 3⅞
in. (10 cm); Diam. base 3⅜ in. (8.5 cm); Wt. 11 oz 4 dwt 2 gr
(348.5 gm)

Marks: "C.A. BURNETT" in roman letters within a rectangle,
flanked by eagle's head device, struck on foot of teapot. "C.A.
BURNETT" in roman letters within a rectangle struck on bottom
of creampot, below center point.

Inscriptions: "BW" in entwined, superimposed, sprigged script
engraved on body of teapot, to right of handle. "BW" monogram
in entwined sprigged script engraved on creampot, to right of
handle; "3033" scratched lightly inside foot rim.

In the early decades of the new republic, as Americans
from every state in the union were called to serve their country, many began to settle in the shadow of the nation's capital.
These elected officials and their families sought to purchase
well-appointed homes and furnishings for their new surround-
ings. These new arrivals were served by a growing body of
Washington-area mercantile establishments and craftspeople
who prospered in their wake.

Charles Alexander Burnett was among the most prominent
silversmiths to serve this burgeoning population during the
early federal years. Due to the similarities of Burnett's work
to silver produced in Philadelphia and particularly Baltimore,
Jennifer Goldsborough has conjectured that Burnett received
his training in the Mid-Atlantic region and later used his early
craft relationships to purchase milled bands and other decorative elements from these more active silversmithing centers.[1]

Burnett worked in Alexandria, Virginia, by the 1790s and
shortly thereafter moved to Washington, D.C., where his work
was in demand in government circles. He made a skippet that
housed the seal for the Treaty of Ghent, many domestic services, presentation silver, and Indian trade silver. His patrons
included George Washington, Thomas Jefferson, and Henry
Clay.

The Neoclassical style of this service, with its elliptical form and narrow bands of stamped gadrooning, was popular throughout the eastern seaboard from about 1790 to 1825. The engraved initials "BW" on the teapot body have been ascribed to Bushrod Washington, who trained as a lawyer and worked in Alexandria, Virginia. He married Julia Ann Blackburn in 1785 and moved to Richmond in 1790. Washington was appointed associate justice to the Supreme Court by President John Adams in 1798. Given the dates of Washington's career, his marriage date, and his Alexandria origins, the tea service could have been made by Burnett shortly after he began working on his own, or later, when both men were working in the capital. Twelve goblets engraved with the family arms were also made for Bushrod Washington by Burnett and date to the same period.

These two pieces are linked by the monogram of its original owner, but their dissimilar styles indicate that they may have been made at different dates or assembled from two services. The distinctive looped handle of the creamer is stylistically similar to one on a coffeepot by Burnett that is dated 1795. The engraved cartouche of the teapot is closely related to one found on another service dated 1815–25 and bearing the initials "L. B. B."[2] As the taste of the period favored increasingly larger services for display on sideboards and entertaining, the teapot and creamer may have originally been accompanied by a sugar bowl and waste bowl, as in the service made by Burnett for Richard Cutts (cat. no. 138).

Description: The tall, raised, elliptical teapot has a raised stepped foot. The convex sides of the vessel rise to an urn-shaped finial through a series of undulating curves, punctuated by two narrow rows of applied and soldered bands of gadrooning. An engraved shield shape with palm leaf above surrounds the monogram and is encircled with foliate decoration. The elliptical, domed lid with flat five-part hinge is set upon the uppermost band of gadrooning; it has an urn-shaped finial and an air vent. A plain S-scroll spout is affixed over strainer holes and displays an applied boss on retracted upper lip. The original wooden handle has carved leafy decoration on its thumbgrip.

The capacious, raised, helmet-shaped pitcher has an elliptical, stepped foot and a bulbous lower portion. Sections of applied gadrooning are soldered at shoulder, below vessel, and on foot. The broad spout is accented with narrow gadrooned decoration. The tall two-part cast handle is soldered vertically to the top of the vessel, with curled thumbgrip at apex. The handle curves steeply downward to a C-scroll element that is soldered to lower section of the creamer; air vent appears on scrolled section inside handle.

History: Probably purchased from Burnett by Bushrod Washington (1762–1829) of Alexandria, Virginia, a nephew of George Wash-

ington. In 1785 the younger Washington m. Julia Ann Blackburn (1768–1829) of Rippon Lodge, Virginia, daughter of Col. Thomas Blackburn, an aide-de-camp to General Washington. The couple had no issue. Subsequent ownership is unknown until 1938, when it was placed on loan to the MFA by Mrs. Fiske Warren (Gretchen Osgood) (1871–1961) of Boston, and transferred in 1962 to her children, Mrs. R. C. Barton (Rachel Warren) (b. 1892) and Hamilton Warren, of Harvard, Massachusetts, and County Wicklow, Ireland, who sold it to the Museum in 1971.[3]

Exhibitions and publications: None.

NOTES TO THIS ENTRY ARE ON PAGE 221.

138

Charles Alexander Burnett (1769–1848)
Four-piece tea service

Georgetown, District of Columbia, about 1825
Gift of Robert Whipple Cutts and Henry Madison Cutts
1993.218.1–4

Teapot (1993.218.1): H. 8⅛ in. (20.5 cm); W. 11¹¹⁄₁₆ in. (29.6 cm); Diam. base 4½ in. (11.4 cm); Wt. 27 oz 8 dwt 7 gr (852.7 gm)

Waste bowl (1993.218.2): H. 5¹³⁄₁₆ in. (14.7 cm); W. 5⅞ in. (15 cm); Diam. base 4⁵⁄₁₆ in. (11 cm); Wt. 14 oz 1 dwt 17 gr (438.1 gm)

Sugar bowl with lid (1993.218.3a, b): H. 7⁵⁄₁₆ in. (18.5 cm); W. 7⅞ in. (20.1 cm); Diam. base 4⅜ in. (11.3 cm); Wt. 20 oz 3 dwt 12 gr (627.5 gm)

Creampot (1993.218.4): H. 6¹¹⁄₁₆ in. (16.9 cm); W. 5⁵⁄₁₆ in. (13.5 cm); D. 3⅞ in. (9.8 cm); Diam. base 2⅞ in. (7.3 cm); Wt. 8 oz 13 dwt 19 gr (270.3 gm)

Marks: "C. A. BURNETT" in a rectangle, below an eagle's-head device in a circle, struck on bottom of teapot and sugar bowl, near center point. The waste bowl is unmarked. An incuse fleur-de-lis is struck on bottom of creampot, at center point.

Inscriptions: Scratch weight of "26 5" appears on bottom of teapot, above center point; otherwise the set is uninscribed.

AS WITH THE SERVICE that Justice Bushrod Washington commissioned from Charles Alexander Burnett (cat. no. 137), this tea set was ordered by a member of the federal government who had moved to the District of Columbia. The owner, Richard Cutts of Cutts Island, Maine, was a direct descendant of John Cutts, the seventeenth-century governor of New Hampshire. Cutts followed his distinguished ancestor in public service when, in 1801, he became the first member of Congress to

138

hail from Maine. He later served as Comptroller of the Treasury under President James Madison, among other posts.

Cutts's relationship to the Madison presidency was more than official, for in 1804 he had married Anna Payne, sister of Dolley Madison (Dorothy Payne Todd, 1768–1849). That same year, the two couples patronized painter Gilbert Stuart, who produced likenesses of both. Although it is unknown whether the Madisons owned a Burnett tea service, the president owned a snuffbox that the craftsman made between 1815 and 1825.[1] The Cuttses probably acquired this set from Burnett in the mid- to late 1820s, judging from its ample proportions, prominent lobes, and broad bands of milled decoration that characterize early Empire-era silver. The vessel form closely resembles a teapot in the Hammerslough collection, although the simple treatment of the spout and wooden handle is modest compared to the vigorously chased animal figures on the latter.[2]

Description: The teapot has been raised with repoussé lobes that extend vertically from the foot. It stands on an applied, low, round foot having a die-stamped band of oak-and-grape-leaf clusters applied to the vertical edge of the foot. The side of the body flares to a convex die-stamped band of same ornament below a milled band of gadrooning at shoulder. The teapot narrows to a round neck edged with a gadrooned bezel. The high curved spout is rectangular in section, with a star-patterned boss soldered to a retracted upper lip. The round cover has smaller lobes on a raised dome and a flat five-part hinge. The finial is a replacement. The handle sockets are rectangular in section and hold an angled wooden handle that retains traces of original black paint.

The wastebowl is a raised round vessel with lobes emanating from bottom; it is soldered to a low round foot having a vertical edge of die-stamped ornament with oak-and-grape-leaf clusters. The bowl flares outward to a convex die-stamped band with the same ornament below an applied gadrooned lip.

The sugarbowl is similar. The two angular strap handles with scroll termini are soldered to the body. The round stepped cover has lobed sections at its domed center; the finial is a replacement. The creampot has a flared spout rim edged with gadrooning. The angular strap handle is scrolled at its base.

History: Originally owned by Anna Payne Cutts (1779–1832), daughter of John and Mary (Coles) Payne and sister of First Lady Dolley Madison, and Richard Cutts, son of Col. Thomas and Elizabeth (Scammon), m. 1804. The set descended to their son Richard Dominicus Cutts (1817–1883), m. Martha Jefferson Hackley in 1845. In turn, the set was made a gift to their son Harry Madison Cutts, M.D. (1858–1918), of Brookline, Massachusetts, m. Marion Belcher in 1891. Their son George Cutts (1895–1976) inherited the service. His wife, Priscilla (Whipple) Cutts (1903–1994), of Wellesley, Massachusetts, gave the service to her sons, the donors.[3]

Exhibitions and publications: None.

NOTES TO THIS ENTRY ARE ON PAGE 221.

139

Peter Chitry (active 1812–1836) and William Gale (1799–1867)

Three-piece tea service

New York, New York, 1824
Gift of Mr. and Mrs. Hugh B. Darden
1977.742–44

Cream pitcher (1977.742): H. 7⅝ in. (19.5 cm); W. 7³⁄₁₆ in. (18.7 cm); D. 4⅛ in. (10.5 cm); Wt. 11 oz 10 dwt 4 gr (358.0 gm)

Sugar bowl (1977.743): H. 9⅛ in. (23.2 cm); W. 9½ in. (24 cm); D. 5½ in. (13.9 cm); Wt. 19 oz 17 dwt 10 gr (618.1 gm)

Teapot (1977.744): H. 10⁵⁄₁₆ in. (26.2 cm); W. 13⅜ in. (34 cm); D. 6⅛ in. (15.5 cm); Wt. 30 oz 15 dwt 15 gr (957.4 gm)

Marks: "P. Chitry" in italic letters, in a rectangle with rounded corners, struck on bottom of teapot. "W. GALE" in roman letters, in a rectangle with a four-part stamped manufacturing logo, struck on bottom of cream pitcher and sugar bowl. The logo consists of a male profile within an oval, a star, a crowned head within a shield, and a lion walking within a cartouche; distributed one to each side around the maker's mark.

Inscriptions: "Presented by Morton Encampment No 4 to Wm F. Piatt M.E.P.G. / Commander as a testimony of respect & esteem New York Nov 26th 1824" in script engraved on right side of each piece; "WFP" in sprigged script engraved below, on center lobe of each piece.

THIS ROBUST, richly decorated tea service was presented on November 24, 1824, to Dr. William Fleet Piatt (1788–1849), a leading figure in New York's Free Masonry movement, by his Masonic lodge known as Morton Encampment No. 4.[1]

The fashionably large elliptical bodies, broad melon gadrooning, and multiple decorative bands are characteristic of the period's exuberant loosening of the restraints of the earlier Neoclassical forms and motifs. Although presented as a matching set, the service was produced by two New York City silversmiths working in separate shops. Perhaps time constraints or cost concerns determined the use of two shops. The applied bands, cast finials, and handles may have been produced by either silversmith (or another supplier) and wholesaled to the other. The inscriptions are identical on all three pieces and appear to be the hand of a single engraver.

139

The teapot bears the mark of Peter Chitry, who appeared in the city directories from 1812 through 1836. The details of Chitry's early life are unknown, but scholars have surmised that he was born in France and as a child immigrated with his family to the island of Santo Domingo and then to New York City, where he may have received his training from the Forbes family of silversmiths.[2]

The matching creampot and sugar bowl carry the mark of William Gale.[3] A native of New York State, Gale was said to have apprenticed with and subsequently purchased the silversmithing business of John and Peter Targee. Gale worked with John Stickler (Gale & Stickler) from 1821 to 1822, the first two years of his long career in New York City. He worked alone in 1823/24, the period during which this creampot and sugar bowl were made. Although he later formed various partnerships, from the start Gale's inventive and entrepreneurial talents drove his silverware business.[4] In 1826, early in his career, he obtained a patent for improved roller dies for the manufacture of patterned flatware, which gave him a leading role in the industry for the fourteen years he controlled the patent (see cat. nos. 190–93).[5]

Description: The teapot, creampot, and sugar bowl have raised bodies, elliptical in form, with large lobes and applied bands of floral decoration. The teapot has a raised domed and stepped five-part hinged cover; the sugar bowl has a separate matching cover. Both have compote-shaped cast finials with floral decoration. The teapot's S-shaped spout terminates in a greyhound head. The scrolled, cast, hollow handles have wooden separators. All three pieces sit on raised and stepped elliptical bases.

Each piece has a stamped floral molding below a stepped foot that forms the shaft supporting the oval body. The lowest part of the body is melon ribbed, the central rib bearing the engraved initials. Above the melon ribbing is the engraved inscription, with another stamped band of flowers above. Encircling the lip of the creamer is a stamped leaf pattern with floral blossoms. The covers of the teapot and creamer fit into a stamped floral band, identical to the one around the base and above the engraved inscription. The stepped lids terminate in a floral compote. Each piece has scrolled handles.

History: Dr. William Fleet Piatt to his daughter Eliza Piatt Burgess; to her son William Piatt Burgess; to his sister Clara Nye Burgess Marston; to her son James H. C. Marston; to his daughter Genevieve Burgess Marston Darden, the donor.

Exhibitions and publications: None.

NOTES TO THIS ENTRY ARE ON PAGE 221.

140

Jesse Churchill (1773–1819)

Pitcher

Boston, Massachusetts, about 1810
Gift of Sargent Bradlee
1973.411

H. 7¾ in. (19.5 cm); W. 9½ (24 cm); Diam. rim 4½ in. (11.4 cm); Diam. foot 4 in. (10.2 cm); Wt. 28 oz 19 dwt 9 gr (901.3 gm)

Marks: "CHURCHILL" within a rectangle struck twice on bottom.

Inscriptions: "A Token of Affection, / bequeathed to / Gorham Thomas / by his Grandfather. / Thomas K. Thomas. / February A.D. 1849" in script engraved under spout.

JESSE CHURCHILL belonged to the first generation of New England silversmiths to mature during the era of the new republic and the last generation to practice before the factory system and steam power began its slow but inevitable domination. The earliest documented objects bearing his mark are a flagon made about 1802 for the South Congregational Church in Andover, Massachusetts, and flagons and plates made in 1805 for the first Religious Society in nearby Newburyport.[1] Churchill may have trained with Newburyport's Moulton family of silversmiths and continued to work in the area as a journeyman. Boston's *Columbian Centinel* (February 15, 1804) announced his January 13, 1804, marriage to Hannah Brown in Concord, Massachusetts.

Churchill's first recorded appearance as a goldsmith in Boston was in the Tax Assessor's Taking Books of 1808. The following year he was listed in the *Boston Directory* (published every two to three years at that time). Before launching his own Boston shop, Churchill may have had ties to Ebenezer Moulton (1768–1824), who relocated from Newburyport to Boston in the mid-1790s, the only one of his family to do so.[2] This sturdy barrel-shaped water or beer pitcher is similar to two of Moulton's barrel-shaped pitchers in the collection of the MFA.[3] Churchill's marks (like those of Moulton, Paul Revere, and Samuel Bartlett of Concord) appear occasionally with that of Boston silversmith Joseph Loring, who was known to retail the work of a few colleagues. About 1810, when this pitcher was made, Churchill also made a pair of matching barrel-shaped pitchers (plain, without reeded bands) that bear both his and Loring's marks.[4]

In 1808 Churchill's shop was located at 88 Newbury Street in Ward 11, part of today's Washington Street and east of the south end of Boston Common, between Essex and Summer streets. He lived on Pleasant Street, a few blocks west of the shop. The 1810 tax records note the presence of an assistant in Churchill's shop, perhaps Elizur/Eleazur Holyoke, and a second shop in Ward 12 (its location is not given) with an assistant or apprentice.[5] Also about this time, Daniel Treadwell arrived in Boston to finish his apprenticeship with Churchill after the failure of his brother's shop in Ipswich, Massachusetts, in 1809. A pair of flagons and a basin dated 1811, made for the West Boston Society or "West Church" built in 1809, bear Churchill's mark.[6] His shop remained at the Newbury Street address in 1813, and his home was at Newbury Place. Treadwell and Holyoke were listed as journeymen silversmiths living at Newbury Place, presumably with Churchill.[7]

During the autumn of 1813 and spring of 1814, the Churchill shop produced the silver presentation service of more than three dozen hollowware pieces that was commissioned by citizens of Boston for Comm. Horatio Oliver Perry, hero of the battle of Lake Erie (see cat. no. 141). Each piece bears the mark "Churchill & Treadwell."[8] In 1816 the partners produced an elaborate presentation urn for Boston Masonic chaplain Thaddeus M. Harris, probably the most ambitious object of their careers.[9] Despite the firm's success, sometime before 1817 Treadwell left the silversmithing profession to forge a career as an inventor and, eventually, to become a professor at Harvard College.

A respected member of the community, Churchill was one of the appraisers of Joseph Loring's estate in 1815. Loring's executors also made two payments to Churchill for earlier work, indicating that Churchill continued to wholesale goods through Loring after 1810.[10] The tax records indicate that Churchill was working with three unnamed apprentices in 1817, with his shop now on Marlboro Street in Ward 8. He made two flagons in 1817 and 1818 for the Church of Christ in Bedford. In 1818 Churchill's shop moved again, to 8 Hawley Place. Little else is known of his life before his death in 1819. The modest value of his estate inventory suggests that much was sold or lost to creditors before his death.[11]

Description: Two reeded bands divide the barrel-shaped body of the pitcher into three sections. Graduated two-part rounded molding is applied at the upper rim of the body and inset V-shaped spout. The angular three-part hollow handle is attached at the rim and lower midsection. The handle is square in section with beveled corners. The pitcher rests on an applied and molded base.

History: Thomas Kemble Thomas (b. 1771); to grandson Gorham Thomas (b. 1831); through the Thomas family to Elizabeth Whitwell Thomas (b. 1868) and her husband, Frederick Josiah Bradlee; to their son Sargent Bradlee (1898–1987), the donor.

Exhibitions and publications: None.

NOTES TO THIS ENTRY ARE ON PAGE 222.

141

Churchill & Treadwell (active 1814–1816)
Jesse Churchill (1773–1819)
Daniel Treadwell (1791–1872)

Engraved by Joseph Callender (1751–1821)

Monteith and pitcher

Boston, Massachusetts, 1814
Gift of the Storrow Family
1999.133–34

Monteith (1999.133): H. 7⁹⁄₁₆ in. (19.2 cm); W. 15⅞ in. (40.5 cm); D. 8 in. (20.2 cm); Wt. 45 oz 15 dwt 5 gr (1423.3 gm)

Pitcher (1999.134): H. 9⅛ in. (23.1 cm); W. 9 in. (23 cm); Diam. rim 4⅛ in. (10.4 cm); Diam. foot 4⅛ (10.5 cm); Wt. 33 oz. 14 dwt 22 gr (1049.6 gm)

Marks: "Churchill & / Treadwell" within a rectangle struck twice on bottom of monteith; "5 (or 8?) 73–842 / S19596" scratched lightly on surface. "Churchill & / Treadwell" within a rectangle struck on bottom of pitcher; "OZ>DWT41.4" scratched in place.

Inscriptions: "Com. O.H. Perry / Conquered the Enemy / on Lake Erie / Sept. 10, 1813" engraved on center front; "Presented / by the Citizens / of Boston" engraved on center back of monteith. "Com. O.H. Perry / Conquered the Enemy / on Lake Erie / Sept. 10, 1813" engraved to left of handle; "Presented / by the Citizens / of Boston" engraved to right of handle on pitcher.

THE TOWN OF BOSTON responded exuberantly to the nation's first great naval victory of the War of 1812, when Comm. Oliver Hazard Perry (1785–1819) defeated the entire British fleet on Lake Erie, regaining control of the lake and, thereby, the Northwest Territory. In the tradition of the tea service made by Paul Revere and presented to Edmund Hartt, builder of the frigate *Constitution*, funds were raised through public subscription to commission a much larger silver service containing more than three dozen pieces. A part of that tribute for the hero of Lake Erie, this monteith and pitcher, each originally one of a pair, represent nationally significant nineteenth-century presentation silver that is important in Boston as well.

FIG. 3. Jesse Churchill and Daniel Treadwell, wine cooler awarded to Commodore Perry, about 1813. Silver. Mead Art Museum, Amherst College, Bequest of Herbert L. Pratt (Class of 1895) (AC 1945.161).

The *Columbian Centinel* described the service as "of the most elegant order, and executed with a skill and workmanship, which does honor to the Mecanics of Boston . . . massy and rich . . . equally calculated for ornament and usefullness. . . . The inscriptions were engraved by Mr. Joseph Callender in his well-known excellent style." The report listed the major pieces in the service as "A Saber . . . Two ice pails or decanter Coolers, barrel shape [see fig. 3] . . . Two pitchers, of a large size, Chinese shape . . . Two dozen tumblers, plain barrel shape, Wine Glass Coolers, each to hold a dozen glasses . . . A Coffee Pot, Tea Pot, Sugar Bowl, Cream Ewer, Tea Cady, and Slop Bowl." The oblong shapes, ball feet, "bright" gadrooned decoration, and (on the tea service) bands of "impressed roses" were all noted proudly.[1]

The monteith's high-style English origins lend dignity and importance to Churchill and Treadwell's example, doubly so when originally presented as a pair. Although oblong-shaped bodies were common in teapots, coffeepots, creamers, and sugar bowls, this rectangular monteith and its mate may be unique.[2] The term "Wine Glass Coolers" describes the purpose of the bowls to hold stemmed glasses, safely separated by the rim's crevices, inverted in cold water.

Much of Churchill's known work is severely plain. However, the clean, graceful lines and highly polished, smooth surfaces of both wine glass cooler and pitcher contrast with a variety of rich but subtle embellishments. The pitcher's ginger-jar-shaped body and handle, whose form resembles the brushstrokes of a Chinese character, reflect the prized porcelain vessels of Boston's famous China Trade. The rich texture and quick rhythm of bright gadrooned edges balance the slower curves and plain surfaces of the vessels. The inscriptions set under a hero's laurel wreath were engraved by Joseph Callender, whose hand is found on the work of Zachariah Brigden, among other prominent Boston smiths of the previous generation.[3]

By 1812, in a series of silver eagle standards made for local military groups, Churchill began to incorporate into his work the most popular of the new national American symbols.[4] The ring handles of the Perry decanter coolers are suspended from the beaks of eagles' heads.[5] In 1816 the partners produced a presentation piece in the form of a large covered vase that incorporated all the embellishments used in the Perry service, with the addition of paw feet, a lobed body, a fluted cover, and a lush fruit finial, in an expression of the fully developed American Empire style.[6]

Although the establishment of their partnership demonstrates Daniel Treadwell's competence as a silversmith and his importance to Churchill, he did not linger in the trade. By 1817 Treadwell is absent from the Boston tax records, and Churchill is listed alone. Treadwell's passion lay in mechanical experiments. He invented screw-making and nail-making machines, devised improvements for printing presses, and patented "Treadwells Power Press" on March 2, 1826. More inventions and patents in other industrial processes followed, with Treadwell eventually being recruited by Harvard College in 1834 as Rumford Professor and Lecturer on the Application of Science to the Useful Arts.[7]

Description: A narrow stamped band with a delicate acorn-and-oak-leaf motif enlivens and strengthens the crenelated rim of the oblong bowl of the monteith, which curves down and in toward the conforming short-waisted base trimmed with an applied band of gadrooning and set on ball feet. Looped cast handles are attached to each narrow side of the bowl at the rim.

The wide rounded shoulders of the pitch curve inward toward the base. A short cylindrical neck with inset spout is joined to the body. A gadrooned band rings the pitcher at the top and bottom. The flat beveled sides of the three-part hollow handle contrast with the curved lines of the handle's profile.

History: From Oliver Hazard Perry (1785–1819), m. Elizabeth Champlin Mason (1791–1858) in 1811; to their son Oliver Hazard Perry

(1815–1878), m. Elizabeth Ann Randolph (1816–1847) in 1837; to their daughter Annie Maria Perry (1838–1865), m. James Jackson Storrow (1837–1897) in 1861; to their son James Jackson Storrow (1864–1926), m. Helen Osborne (b.1864) in 1891; to their son James Jackson Storrow (1892–1977), m. Margaret Randolph Rotch (1896–1945) in 1916; to their son James Jackson Storrow (1917–1984); to his son James Storrow, the donor.[8]

Exhibitions and publications: None.

NOTES TO THIS ENTRY ARE ON PAGE 222.

142

Davis, Watson & Co. (active about 1820)
Samuel Davis (active 1807–1842)
Edward Watson (d. 1839)
Bartlett M. Bramhill

Porringer

Boston, Massachusetts, ca. 1820
Bequest of Mrs. Arthur Croft
01.6449

H. 2 in. (5 cm); W. 8⅛ in. (20.5 cm); Diam. rim 5⅛ in. (13.1 cm); Wt. 10 oz 4 dwt 8 gr (317.8 gm)

Marks: "DAVIS [pellet] WATSON & CO." in rectangle struck on underside of handle.

Inscriptions: "W" engraved on top of handle.

ACQUIRED IN 1901, this modest keyhole-handled porringer was omitted by Kathryn C. Buhler from her two-volume catalogue of the Museum's silver published in 1972, probably on the grounds that it fell outside the temporal boundaries of her book. It is included here as a representative example of a form that enjoyed a long popularity in this country.

The little-known firm of Davis, Watson & Co. was working in Boston in 1820 and consisted of the partnership of Samuel Davis, Edward Watson, and Bartlett M. Bramhill. Davis, active in Boston as a jeweler as early as 1807, and Watson may have been in partnership as early as 1815. By 1825 the Boston Directory indicates that they were "importers."[1]

The Museum's collection also includes a pair of sugar tongs (1971.317) and a tablespoon (1971.318) by the same firm.

Description: The raised porringer is of standard form, with convex sides, domed bottom with center punch, everted rim, and applied cast handle in the so-called keyhole pattern.

History: Early history unknown. The engraved initial on the handle may stand for a member of the Weld family. Probably collected by Gardner Brewer, Boston. Part of the large and diverse bequest from the Gardner Brewer Collection by his daughter, Mrs. Arthur Croft, in July 1901.

Exhibition and publications: None.

NOTE TO THIS ENTRY IS ON PAGE 222.

143

Thomas Aspinwall Davis (1798–1845)
Pair of beakers

Boston, Massachusetts, 1822–35
Gift of the First Church in Newton
1973.23, 1973.28

1973.23: H. 6 in. (15.2 cm); Diam. rim 4⅛ in. (10.7 cm); Diam. base 3⅛ in. (8.2); Wt. 9 oz 18 dwt 7 gr (308.4 gm)

1973.28: H. 5⅞ in. (15.1 cm); Diam. rim 4³⁄₁₆ in. (10.8 cm); Diam. base 3⅛ in. (8.2 cm); Wt. 9 oz 10 dwt 2 gr (295.6 gm)

Marks: "T. A. Davis" in roman letters within a rectangle struck twice on bottom of each vessel, above and below center point.

Inscriptions: "The Gift of / Mrs. Anna Longly / to the Church of Christ / in Newton Mar. 23. / 1733." in flowing script engraved on body of one beaker (1973.23). The other (1973.28) is similarly engraved "This belongs to the / Church of Christ / in Newton / 1729."

143

ALTHOUGH THEIR INSCRIPTIONS COMMEMORATE the years 1729 and 1733, these two beakers were produced in the nineteenth century to maintain the memories of gifts to the church during its early history. Boston jeweler and retailer Thomas A. Davis used this mark until 1835, when he formed a partnership with Julius A. Palmer. Boston silversmiths were known to wholesale marked and unmarked wares to the trade. Davis may have purchased the beakers umarked and stamped them with his retail mark.

Born into one of Brookline's founding families, Thomas Aspinwall Davis (fig. 4) was the fifth of seven children born to Ebenezer and Lucy Aspinwall Davis. He attended public schools and was probably apprenticed to a Boston jeweler. Davis was first listed in the Boston Directory of 1820 as a jeweler at 83 Market Street, in partnership with Thomas N. Marong. Both

men disappeared from the following year's directory, and only Davis resurfaced in 1822, listed on his own as a jeweler at 2 Market Row. He married Sarah Jackson of Newton on November 11, 1824.[1] In 1825 Davis moved his shop to 1 Washington Street, where he remained for a decade as a retailer of imported watches. In 1835 he formed T. A. Davis & Co., another short-lived partnership with A. Langford, and in 1836 Davis moved the shop a few blocks south, to 87 Washington Street.

During these years, T. A. Davis's mark appeared on these two beakers, several other pieces of ecclesiastical hollowware, and some spoons.[2] Although some jewelers were trained as silversmiths, it is unclear whether Davis was the maker or the retailer of the silver wares that carry his mark. In 1837 Julius A. Palmer, formerly a partner in a retail hardware business in Boston, and Josiah G. Bachelder joined Davis to form Davis,

FIG. 4. Lithograph portrait of Thomas A. Davis (1798–1845) by E. W. Bouve, from a daguerreotype by Litch and Whipple. Photograph courtesy of Boston Public Library.

Palmer & Co., retailers of imported watches, jewelry, coin flatware, and hollowware (see cat. nos. 187–88). They were located at 87 Washington Street, Davis's longtime address.

Like the majority of other Boston shop owners in the early nineteenth century, Davis lived in the city where he worked.[3] Involved in politics and especially interested in the drive to purify the local water supply, Davis ran as the candidate of the new Native American party and was elected mayor of Boston. He was sworn in on February 27, 1845, but served only a short time before his death in November of that year.[4] Reorganized as Palmer & Bachelder, Davis's former partners remained in business at various addresses on Washington Street for at least the next twenty-five years.

Description: Each raised beaker has a bell-shaped form with a thick, applied rim and a splayed, stepped foot.

History: The "1729" beaker (1973.28) may have been made for the church, not an individual. The beaker inscribed with the name of Anna Longley (1973.23) was fabricated in the early nineteenth century, about one hundred years after its donor made her gift. Anna Shepherd (about 1677–1758), daughter of Francis and Sara (Osburne) Shepherd of Charlestown, Massachusetts, m. Nathaniel Longley

(1676–1732), son of John and Hannah Longley, in 1699. In 1734 Anna Longley m. Thomas Hammond (1686–1753), who predeceased her. A beaker, perhaps lost or damaged, or funds for that purpose were probably given to the First Church in Newton by Longley shortly after the death of her first husband, as indicated by the engraved date and her surname. For further information on silver previously owned by the First Church in Newton, see appendix 8.

Exhibitions and publications: See appendix 8.

NOTES TO THIS ENTRY ARE ON PAGE 222.

144

Samuel Drowne (1749–1815)

Sugar tongs

Portsmouth, New Hampshire, about 1800
Gift of Kathryn C. Buhler
1984.183

L. 5¹¹⁄₁₆ in. (14.4 cm); W. 2⅛ in. (5.4 cm); Wt. 1 oz 13 dwt 4 gr (51.6 gm)

Marks: "S x Drowne" in a rectangle with shaped ends struck on inside of bow, at joint with arm.

Inscriptions: "M.W." in script engraved on inside of bow; "E C" on outside of bow.

IN THE FEDERAL PERIOD, the luxury craft of silversmithing spread from the established colonial urban centers of Boston, New York, and Philadelphia to growing cities such as Portsmouth, New Hampshire, where these high-quality sugar tongs were made. Samuel Drowne, a minister's son, was a member of that seaport community's small but active group of silver-

smiths, which included his brother Benjamin (1759–1793) and his two sons, Daniel Pickering Drowne (1784–1863) and Thomas Pickering Drowne (1782–1849).[1] Samuel, although known as a craftsman and the owner of a house on State Street, near the Piscataqua River, was perhaps better known for his activities as a patriot during the Revolution and for his service to the town in the years after independence.[2]

Elegantly pierced, with multiple voids resembling those of a high-style Federal chair back, these tongs are perhaps the most beautiful example of the form fashioned by Drowne. His shop produced primarily flatware, but some hollowware by him is known.[3]

Description: The tongs are of bow form, with cast reticulated arms embellished with a double row of serpentine piercing, shell-shaped hollow grips, and a chased border on the shoulders and bow.

History: Made for Eleanor Clark (1765–1830), m. Edmund Wingate in 1788. Descended in the family to one of their daughters, probably (based on the initials) Mary Ann (b. 1789) or Maria (b. 1795).[4] Acquired at an unknown date by Mrs. Kathryn C. Buhler, Boston, and given to the Museum in 1984.

Exhibitions and publications: The Decorative Arts of New Hampshire, 1725–1825 (Manchester, N.H.: Currier Gallery of Art, 1964), cat. no. 94; Charles S. Parsons, *New Hampshire Silver* (n.p.: Adams Brown, 1983), 31.

NOTES TO THIS ENTRY ARE ON PAGE 222.

145

Abraham Dubois (about 1751–1807)

Soup ladle and ten teaspoons

Philadelphia, Pennsylvania, about 1790
Gift of the Grandchildren of Jane Coy Derr
1989.166–76

Soup ladle (1989.166): L. 14 in. (35.5 cm); W. 3⅞ in. (9.8 cm); D. 2⁵⁄₁₆ in. (5.9 cm); Wt. 5 oz 4 dwt 18 dwt (162.9 gm)

1989.167: L. 9⅝ in. (24.3 cm); W. 1¹¹⁄₁₆ in. (4.4 cm); Wt. 2 oz 4 dwt 21 gr (69.8 gm)

1989.168: L. 9⅜ in. (24 cm); W. 1¹³⁄₁₆ in. (4.5 cm); Wt. 2 oz 4 dwt 10 gr (69.1 gm)

1989.169: L. 9½ in. (24.1 cm); W. 1¹¹⁄₁₆ in. (4.3 cm); Wt. 2 oz 4 dwt 21 gr (69.8 gm)

1989.170: L. 9⅝ in. (24.3 cm); W. 1¹¹⁄₁₆ in. (4.3 cm); Wt. 2 oz 3 dwt 7 gr (67.3 gm)

145

1989.171: L. 9½ in. (24.2 cm); W. 1¹¹⁄₁₆ in. (4.4 cm); Wt. 2 oz 3 dwt (66.9 gm)

1989.172: L. 9⅝ in. (24.3 cm); W. 1¹¹⁄₁₆ in. (4.4 cm); Wt. 2 oz 2 dwt 17 gr (66.4 gm)

1989.173: L. 9⅝ in. (24.3 cm); W. 1¹¹⁄₁₆ in. (4.4 cm); Wt. 2 oz 3 dwt 16 gr (67.9 gm)

1989.174: L. 9⅝ in. (24.3 cm); W. 1¹¹⁄₁₆ in. (4.4 cm); Wt. 2 oz 5 dwt 22 gr (71.4 gm)

1989.175: L. 9⅝ in. (24.3 cm); W. 1¹¹⁄₁₆ in. (4.3 cm); Wt. 2 oz 5 dwt 6 gr (70.4 gm)

1989.176: L. 9⅝ in. (24.3 cm); W. 1¹¹⁄₁₆ in. (4.3 cm); Wt. 2 oz 5 dwt 6 gr (70.4 gm)

Marks: "A. DUBOIS" in roman capitals within a rectangle struck on back of each handle.

Inscriptions: "JSM" in script engraved on top of handle.

Although relatively little of his work is known, Abraham Dubois was an accomplished silversmith in Philadelphia during the federal period.[1] The teaspoons, with their bright-cut borders and medallions with bellflowers on the end, demonstrate the high quality of engraved work produced by his shop. The ladle varies in detail but is engraved with the same original initials.

The bird figure on the back of the teaspoon bowls is the result of the skills of a diesinker, a specialist craftsman who created the image on an iron die that the silversmith later used to transfer to the spoon. Several diesinkers were active in Philadelphia at the time these spoons were made.[2]

Description: The large soup ladle has a scalloped bowl and an engraved ropelike edge to the handle. Each teaspoon has a slightly pointed spatulate handle with bright-cut edges and a medallion enclosing script initials, bellflowers, short midrib on back, and pointed oval bowl decorated on back with crested bird on a perch, holding a branch in its beak, and rounded drop.

History: Early history unknown. Presumably owned by Jane Coy Derr (d. 1955) and inherited by her daughter-in-law Mrs. Thomas (Mary S.) Derr (d. 1988) of Brookline, Massachusetts, who placed them on loan to the Museum in 1952. They descended in the family and were given by the grandchildren of Jane Coy Derr in 1996.

Exhibitions and publications: None.

NOTES TO THIS ENTRY ARE ON PAGE 222.

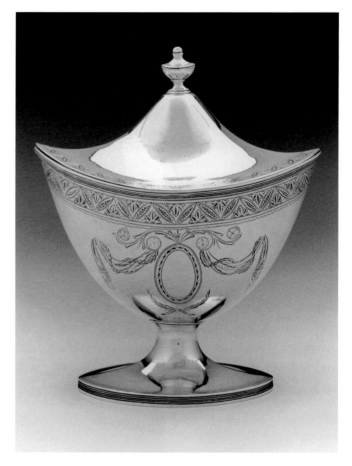

146

146

Joseph DuBois (1767–1798)

Sugar bowl

New York, New York, about 1795
Gift of the Nathaniel T. Dexter Fine Arts Trust
2000.689a–b

H. 7⅜ in. (18.7 cm); W. 6⅛ in. (15.6 cm); D. 6⅛ in. (10.5 cm); Wt. 12 oz 10 dwt 6 gr (389.2 gm)

Marks: "J [pellet] D" within an ellipse; a sheaf of wheat within a rectangle; and a bird's head within a rectangle all struck on bottom.

Inscriptions: "GJF" intertwined monogram within an ellipse engraved on front of bowl.

THIS ELEGANTLY SHAPED sugar bowl, with its delicate bright-cut engraving, is the product of the shop of Joseph DuBois, active in New York City from 1790 to about 1798. He worked in partnership with his younger brother Teunis DuBois in 1796.[1] A more typical urn-shaped sugar bowl by the maker is in the collection of the Museum of the City of New York.[2]

Description: The raised boat-shaped bowl rests on an oval foot with a reeded edge. The conforming, separate, raised cover terminates in a finial echoing the shape of the bowl and the lid. The top edge of the bowl is engraved with bright-cut leafage, and the center of the front is engraved with an oval medallion surrounded by swags. The edge of the lid has bright-cut decoration as well.

History: Early history unknown. Acquired by the Boston collector Nathaniel T. Dexter and bequeathed to the Museum in 2000.

Exhibitions and publications: None.

NOTES TO THIS ENTRY ARE ON PAGE 222.

147

Thomas Knox Emery (1781–1815)

Porringer

Boston, Massachusetts, about 1805–15
Bequest of Charles Hitchcock Tyler
32.385

H. 2 in. (5.2 cm); W. 8⁵⁄₁₆ in. (21 cm); Diam. rim 5⅝ in. (14.1 cm); Wt. 8 oz 11 dwt 6 gr (266.3 gm)

Marks: "T. Emery" in a cartouche struck on back of handle.

Inscriptions: "EW" in sprigged entwined script engraved on side of vessel, opposite handle.

ALONG WITH Thomas Bentley (1764–1804) and Robert Dawes (b. 1767), who preceded him, Thomas Knox Emery was probably the last silversmith to apprentice in the large shop run by his father, Stephen (1749–1801). Thomas began working independently about the time of his father's death, with the likely inheritance of the "sundry Shop tools & Utensils" valued at $30 that was listed in his father's inventory. The mark he employed—that of his first initial and full surname within a shaped cartouche—resembles the one used by his father.[1]

Description: A raised keyhole-handled porringer of standard form, with convex sides, domed bottom with center punch, everted rim, and applied cast handle.

History: Early history unknown. Part of the large bequest in 1932 from the noted Boston collector Charles Hitchcock Tyler.

Exhibitions and publications: None.

NOTE TO THIS ENTRY IS ON PAGE 222.

148

Thomas Knox Emery (1781–1815)

Pair of wine cups

Boston, Massachusetts, 1801–15
Gift of the First Church Parish, Unitarian, Medfield, in memory of Virginia Hagberg McQuillan
1980.492–93

1980.492: H. 5⅞ in. (15 cm); Diam. rim 4⅛ in. (10.4 cm); Diam. base 3⅛ in. (7.8 cm); Wt. 7 oz 13 dwt 19 gr (239.2 gm)

1980.493: H. 5¹³⁄₁₆ in. (14.8 cm); Diam. rim 4⅛ in. (10.4 cm); Diam. base 3⅛ (7.9 cm); Wt. 8 oz 13 dwt 22 gr (270.5 gm)

Marks: 1980.492: "T. Emery" within a shaped cartouche struck inside foot ring. 1980.493: Unmarked.

Inscriptions: None.

THE UNMARKED communion cup is similar in size, form, and fabrication to its marked mate, which suggests that Thomas Knox Emery was the maker of both. During his fifteen-year career, Emery produced hollowware and flatware in a plain, early Federal style, as seen in these examples. The relatively modest stature of the wine cups is in keeping with those made by Emery's contemporaries. They are small compared to robust cups produced in the seventeenth century by Hull and Sanderson (cat. no. 71).[1]

Description: Each vessel has a raised V-shaped bowl, a wide flaring lip, a small stem, and a round stepped base.

History: Acquired by the First Congregational Church in Medfield, about 1801–15; made a gift to the Museum in 1980.

Exhibitions and publications: See appendix 7 for further information on silver of First Congregational Parish, Medfield.

NOTE TO THIS ENTRY IS ON PAGE 222.

149

Farnam and Ward (active about 1816)
Rufus Farnam (b. 1771)
Richard Ward (active about 1809–1820)

Spout cup

Boston, Massachusetts, about 1816
Gift of Miss Emma L. Coleman in the name of Mrs. Polly Hollingsworth
17.1079

H. 3⁵⁄₁₆ in. (8.5 cm); W. 4 in. (10.2 cm); D. 3⅞ in. (10 cm); Diam. base 2 in. (5.2 cm); Wt. 4 oz 12 dwt 10 gr (143.7 gm)

Marks: "Farnam & Ward" in rectangle struck on bottom.

Inscriptions: "P Hooper" in script engraved on body of vessel, opposite handle.

THIS BULBOUS LITTLE spout cup provides an interesting nineteenth-century counterpart to the seventeenth- and eighteenth-century examples in the Museum's collection. It was made during the apparently short-lived partnership of Farnam and Ward, who are listed in the Boston Directory for 1816 only, providing a narrow date range for this object. Each man was involved in other partnerships during the early nineteenth century.[1]

Description: This small raised cup has a center point on the bottom and is globular in form. It has a hinged cover with a knob finial; a flat curved spout; and a strap handle set at a right angle to the spout. It is supported by an applied foot ring.

History: Early history unknown.

Exhibitions and publications: None.

NOTE TO THIS ENTRY IS ON PAGE 223.

150

Fletcher and Gardiner (active 1808–1830)
Thomas Fletcher (1787–1866)
Sidney Gardiner (1785–1827)

Covered water pitcher

Philadelphia, Pennsylvania, about 1811–27
Gift of Family and Friends in memory of George Seybolt
1995.45

H. 13½ in. (34.3 cm); W. 10 in. (25.4 cm); D. 5½ in. (14 cm); Wt. 55 oz 9 dwt (1725 gm)

Marks: "PHILADA / F & G" both within a rectangle struck on base of vessel.

Inscriptions: None.

PHILADELPHIA SILVERSMITHS Thomas Fletcher and Sidney Gardiner established a reputation for creating some of the finest Neoclassical silver made in America. They succeeded in attracting and executing some thirty major commissions between 1812 and 1842 and set a high standard with their elaborate compositions, large and vertically scaled work, and highly skilled execution. The two men established a partnership in Boston in 1808, but its origins are obscure. Gardiner was born in Southold, Long Island; Fletcher was born in Alstead, New Hampshire, and as a youth lived in the Lancaster, Massachusetts, area.[1]

Fletcher was living in Boston as early as 1806 and by 1807, at age twenty, was engaged as an apprentice shopkeeper in the workshop and warehouse of jeweler Joseph C. Dyer. When Dyer was bought out by John McFarlane in April 1808, Fletcher worked for his new employer. McFarlane apparently intended to dissolve the business at auction in October 1808, but before the sale, Fletcher and Gardiner aranged to purchase most, if not all, of McFarlane's stock. Donald L. Fennimore has speculated that Gardiner had worked as a silversmith for Dyer and later McFarlane, thus coming into contact with Fletcher. In an announcement celebrating the new enterprise of Fletcher and Gardiner, customers were assured that "the whole attention of one of the partners will be devoted to this [manufacturing] part of the business." As Fletcher was listed as the manager in the publication, Gardiner was likely the silversmith.[2]

During their brief partnership in Boston, which lasted from November 1808 to September 1811, they sold a variety of imported plated goods, jewelry, and personal accessories along with silver and jewelry that they made in Boston. Among surviving items bearing their marks are plain two-handled beakers made for the Second Baptist Church in Boston and Church of Christ in Hadley; some fiddle-handled spoons made for the Salisbury family of Worcester; and a hair bracelet.[3]

These ambitious young men enjoyed a profitable business during their short tenure in Boston, and they arranged for their brothers Charles Fletcher (b. 1794), George Fletcher (b. 1796), and Baldwin Gardiner (1791–1869) to join them as either apprentices or employees. When James Fosdick Fletcher (1785–1820), an older brother of Thomas Fletcher, retailed their work in New Orleans in 1808, the partners could appreciate the opportunities that lay in such new and lucrative markets. Their decision to relocate to Philadelphia in 1811 was no doubt informed by such observations. Despite their financial success in Boston, New York and Philadelphia were rapidly emerging as important commercial centers. Their timing proved to be fortuitous, for in Philadelphia their reputation grew quickly as designers and makers of fashionable silver.[4]

It is unclear whether their marriages to members of the Veron family influenced the move to Philadelphia, their success in their adopted city, or their embrace of the French Neoclassical style. A Mrs. Veron took jewelry orders at the shop's 59 Cornhill location in Boston; Sidney Gardiner married Mary Holland Veron in Boston 1811; his younger brother Baldwin apprenticed with the partners in Boston and followed them to Philadelphia. In 1815 he married Louise-Leroy Veron, who was recorded as the daughter of Etienne and Melanie (Melina) Veron of St. Malo, France. Two years later, Baldwin Gardiner, together with

Lewis Veron (1793–1853), established the fancy hardware company of Gardiner, Veron, and Company. Last, partner Thomas Fletcher married Meline Degrasse Veron in 1818.[5]

The War of 1812 provided the silversmiths with some of the most prestigious commissions of the period, ordered by grateful citizens for victorious American commanders. The radical change in style from their earlier Boston-made silver may have been due to the influx of French imports to Philadelphia and a nexus of French-born silversmiths such as John Tanguy (1780–1858) and Simon Chaudron (1798–1814) who had settled in the area; it is probable that the partners employed émigré silversmiths from France or England to execute their designs. The firm's reputation continued to grow even after Gardiner's death in 1827. A tea service, made in 1838 for Nicholas Biddle at a cost of $15,000, was considered "superb" by New York City mayor Philip Hone (1780–1851), who remarked, "Nobody in this world of ours hereabouts can compete with them in their kind of work."[6]

The French Neoclassical style that characterized their presentation silver is also evident in the sculptural form and delicately cast and chased details of such domestic forms as this covered pitcher, which is a superb example of the silver they fashioned in Philadelphia. Several variations of the form survive. An identical example with an inscribed dedication is in the Bayou Bend collection; the Philadelphia Museum of Art, the Museum of the City of New York, and Winterthur Museum own related pitchers.[7]

Description: The water pitcher or urn with hinged cover is seated upon a square plinth supported by hairy paw feet. The cast hollow handle is in the form of an eagle's head that grasps the lid in its beak; the handle terminates in a scroll. Chased acorn leaves radiate from the center of the lid and base of the urn; the cast finial is in the form of a dolphin with tail upraised. A narrow milled band of repeating stars adorns the lip of ewer, and a broad milled band of stylized leaves is located at the shoulder. Repairs include the straightening of the dolphin's tail on the finial, the removal of a dent in the lid, and the removal of ten lead solder marks on the body, near the central milled band. Crossed palms are engraved on the side of the rectangular base.

History: Early history unknown. Purchased by Baldwin's Bookstore at the Hall Family Auction Gallery, Schnecksville, Pennsylvania, on February 6, 1995, and sold shortly thereafter to the Museum.

Exhibitions and publications: Advertisement, Hall Family Auction Gallery, Schnecksville, Pennsylvania, *Antiques and the Arts Weekly* (February 3, 1995), 151; Waters 2000, 70, fig. 4.

NOTES TO THIS ENTRY ARE ON PAGE 223.

151

William Garrett Forbes (1751–1840)

Sugar bowl

New York, New York, about 1800–09
Gift of Mrs. James Stuart Smith
63.635a–b

H. 7³⁄₁₆ in. (18.2 cm); W. 6½ in. (16.5 cm); D. 3¾ in. (10.5 cm); Wt. 12 oz 9 dwt 10 gr (387.9 gm)

Marks: "W.G. Forbes" in script, in a rectangle and with an eagle's head, struck on bottom.

Inscriptions: "W" engraved inside bowl; "13" scratched on base.

Armorials: Engraved on side within an ellipse with a crest of a griffin on a torse, above the motto "EN DIEU EST TOUT"; the ellipse on the other side is unengraved.

WITH ITS RING HANDLES and refined form, this sugar bowl was made by William Garrett Forbes, patriarch of a distinguished New York City silversmithing family. It represents one of the successful variations on the form produced during the federal period.[1] As Deborah Dependahl Waters has pointed out, the lower profile and gentle curves of this style of bowl, also seen on a closely related three-piece tea set in the collection of the Museum of the City of New York, represent a slightly later evolution of the more vertical, geometric forms of a few years earlier.[2]

Description: The sugar bowl has a seamed oval body, curved cushion shoulder, and a slightly convex side; it rests on an oval foot ring. The conforming separate lid has a boat-shaped urn finial and is fitted with pendant ring handles descending from shell-like cast scrolls. A band of bright-cut engraving is at the shoulder of the bowl, and a bright-cut engraved medallion on the front.

History: History unknown prior to its gift by Mrs. James Stuart Smith of North Chatham, Massachusetts.[3]

Exhibitions and publications: None.

NOTES TO THIS ENTRY ARE ON PAGE 223.

Philip Garrett (about 1780–1851)
Robert Wilson (active about 1802–1846)
William Wilson (active about 1825–1846)
and possibly others

Six-piece assembled tea service

Philadelphia, Pennsylvania, about 1813 and 1835
Anonymous Gift in honor of Eugenia Cassatt Madeira
1982.359–64

Teapot (1982.359): H. 8⁵⁄₁₆ in. (21 cm); W. 9 in. (22.8 cm); D. 4¹¹⁄₁₆ in. (12 cm); Wt. 26 oz 11 gr (809.4 gm)

Teapot (1982.360): H. 7⅞ in. (20 cm); W. 8¹³⁄₁₆ in. (22.3 cm); Diam. 4¹¹⁄₁₆ in. (12 cm); Wt. 23 oz 10 dwt 16 gr (732 gm)

Teapot (1982.361): H. 7½ in. (19 cm); W. 8½ in. (21.6 cm); D. 4⅛ in. (10.5 cm); Wt. 20 oz 16 dwt 16 gr (648 gm)

Creampot (1982.362): H. 5¹¹⁄₁₆ in. (14.5 cm); W. 5 in. (12.6 cm); D. 3³⁄₁₆ in. (8.1 cm); Wt. 6 oz 15 dwt 19 gr (211.2 gm)

Waste bowl (1982.363): H. 5⅝ in. (14.1 cm); W. 5⅞ in. (15 cm); D. 5 in. (12.7 cm); Wt. 16 oz 10 dwt 9 gr (513.8 gm)

Covered sugar bowl (1982.364): H. 7¹¹⁄₁₆ in. (19.5 cm); W. 6¹³⁄₁₆ in. (17.2 cm); D. 4½ in. (11.5 cm); Wt. 20 oz 5 dwt 18 gr (631 gm)

Marks: "P.GARRETT" in roman letters, within a rectangle, struck twice on bottom of teapot (1982.360), creamer, and sugar bowl. "R & WW" in roman letters struck twice within a rectangle on bottom of waste bowl. Two teapots (1982.359 and 1982.361) are unmarked.

Inscriptions: "MS / 1813 / KKJ" engraved on side of two teapots (1982.359 and 1982.360) and creampot, waste bowl, and sugar bowl. "RSC" engraved on side of teapot (1982.361).

THIS ASSEMBLED TEA SET (see *History*) is a fine representation of early-nineteenth-century Philadelphia silver by Philip Garrett, the partnership of Robert and William Wilson, and possibly an unidentified maker.[1] It has gained added atten-

tion due to its association with the family of Mary Stevenson Cassatt, the famous American artist. Initially made for the artist's grandmother, and presumably added to by her mother, the tea set became a treasured family heirloom. Two of the objects—the sugar bowl and a teapot—appear in *The Tea*, painted about 1879–80 and now in the Museum's collection (fig. 5), as well as in works on paper by the artist.[2]

Description: One unmarked teapot (1982.359) is a raised vessel, rectangular in section. It has a rounded rectangular base with a stamped base molding in a repeating flower pattern, with one step rising to stamped gadrooned neck and bulbous rectangular bowl. A rose pattern molding surrounds the vessel, to which the upper handle section is attached. The body rises upward to a rectangular lid with a squared top, cut-card applied decoration, and finial. The lid has a five-part hinge; the seamed handle is rectangular in section and fitted with pinned ivory insulators. The spout terminates in a chased eagle's head; strainer holes are within.

The Garrett teapot (1982.360) is similar in most details but varies in some of the stamped patterns. A third teapot (1982.361) is similar in form to the other teapots but also varies in decorative detail.

The creampot is seamed at the handle; it has panels on each side;

balls for feet; and a cast S-scroll handle with thumbgrip. It is stamped with stars and snowflakes and is engraved to the left of the handle. A tear appears at the handle, near its terminus.

The waste bowl, a vessel form with bulbous proportions, is decorated with bands of stamped decoration in a manner related to two of the teapots. The large sugar bowl has four ball feet; stamped decoration is related to that of the set but varies in detail and application. It has cast S-scroll handles and a friction-fitted lid with acorn finial. The feet are worn and dented on one side.

History: This assembled tea set includes a teapot, creamer, and sugar bowl marked by Philip Garrett of Philadelphia and engraved "M.S. 1813" for Mary Stevenson at the time of her marriage that year to Alexander Johnston. The "KKJ" added later stands for Katharine Kelso Johnston, m. Robert Simpson Cassatt in 1835. The waste bowl marked by the Wilsons (engraved "RSC," possibly for Robert Simpson Cassatt) and presumably the two unmarked teapots were added to the set about 1835, when Katharine Kelso Johnston Cassatt inherited her maternal grandmother's tea set and added these three pieces to it. All three of these later pieces may be by the partnership of Robert and William Wilson.

The assembled set descended in the family until it was given by the descendants of the original owners and of the artist Mary Stevenson Cassatt (1844–1926), a granddaughter of Mary Stevenson Johnston, in honor of Eugenia Cassatt Madeira.[3]

Exhibitions and publications: Barbara Stern Shapiro, *Mary Cassatt at Home* (Boston: Museum of Fine Arts, Boston, 1978); Barbara Stern Shapiro, *Mary Cassatt: Impressionist at Home* (New York: Universe, 1998), 36–37.

NOTES TO THIS ENTRY ARE ON PAGE 223.

spoons carry the serrated "G. GREENLEAF" mark seen on this cup. Many of these items were owned by relatives of the craftsman or by Newburyport residents.[2]

This beaker is similar to a pair that were engraved "A W," thought by Hammerslough to represent Greenleaf's father-in-law, Capt. Abraham Wheelwright.[3] Its form is an updated version of the seventeenth-century tunn, a short barrel-shaped vessel that is easy to grasp.

Description: The raised beaker has a center point on bottom and slightly convex sides that curve inward to a slightly flared rim.

History: Early history unknown. Sarah Gilbert Hammond (1815–1902) of Newburyport and William P. Tenney (1814–1881) of Westford, Massachusetts, m. 1838; to the donor, their daughter Grace Gorden Tenney (1855–1947), and Frederic O. North (1852–1910), m. 1876.[4]

Exhibitions and publications: None.

NOTES TO THIS ENTRY ARE ON PAGE 223.

153

George Greenleaf (1790–1872)
Beaker

Newburyport, Massachusetts, 1811–25
Gift of Mrs. Frederick O. North
29.915

H. 3⁵⁄₁₆ in. (8.5 cm); Diam. rim 2¾ (7 cm); Diam. base 2⅛ in. (5.4 cm); Wt. 3 oz 23 gr (94.8 gm)

Marks: "G.GREENLEAF" within a serrated rectangle struck on base.

Inscriptions: "AEH" entwined monogram in sprigged script engraved on midsection of vessel.

NOTED COLLECTOR Philip Hammerslough was probably the first to recognize the "G. Greenleaf" mark as being that of George Greenleaf of Newburyport, Massachusetts.[1] Greenleaf may not have worked long at his craft, for he was listed as an "auctioneer" as early as 1813, the same year in which he advertised himself as a silversmith. By 1847 his occupation was recorded as "commission merchant." A small number of objects survive with various marks that have been ascribed to Greenleaf. Of these, several beakers, a porringer, and some

154

George Hendel (1766–1842)
Tablespoon and two teaspoons

Carlisle, Pennsylvania, about 1803
Gift of Anne, George and Jessie Furness
1991.665–67

Tablespoon (1991.665): L. 9⁵⁄₁₆ in. (23.7 cm); W. bowl 1¾ in. (4.5 cm); Wt. 2 oz 1 dwt (64.2 gm)

Teaspoon (1991.666): L. 6⅛ (15.4 cm); W. bowl 1¹⁄₁₆ in. (2.7 cm); Wt. 10 dwt 12 gr (16.3 gm)

Teaspoon (1991.667): L. 6⁵⁄₁₆ in. (16 cm); W. bowl 1¹⁄₁₆ in. (2.7 cm); Wt. 9 dwt 23 gr (15.5 gm)

Marks: "GH" in roman letters within an oval struck on back of each handle; the tablespoon struck twice.

Inscriptions: "TRF" in entwined script engraved on end of each handle.

GEORGE HENDEL was the son of the Rev. Johan William Hendel (1740–1798) and Elizabeth Leroy of Lancaster County, Pennsylvania, who were married about 1766. He was born in 1776, probably in nearby Tulpehocken, where his German Reformed clergyman father was minister. In 1789 George Hendel enrolled in Franklin College (now Franklin and Marshall College) in Lancaster, where the elder Hendel was a founder and vice pres-

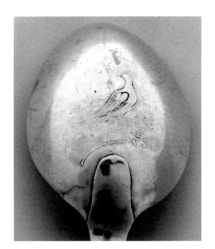

ident. How young Hendel obtained his silversmithing skills is unclear, since he should have begun his apprenticeship about this time. It is possible that he learned from his elder brother Jacob, a clockmaker and merchant who had established himself in Carlisle in 1796. By 1799 George Hendel had also moved to Carlisle, where the brothers probably worked together until 1806, when George Hendel acquired a residence and shop. A third brother, Bernard (b. 1777), joined Jacob as a clockmaker in 1811. George Hendel's marriage to Rosanna Jumper in 1807 was followed by his participation in the War of 1812.[1]

Following his military service, George Hendel built a large three-story brick building in the center of town, where presumably he practiced his trade. At this time, Carlisle was home to several other silversmiths, including John D. Haverstick and Robert Guthrie, and it is unclear whether the town could support three craftsmen. Hendel suffered financial pressures and briefly gave up silversmithing between 1817 and 1818 to run a tavern called the "Sign of General Washington," presumably at the same location. In 1826 he mortgaged his real estate, including his household goods and tools, although he was allowed to continue using them. He died in 1842.[2]

Surviving silver by Hendel and the assortment of tools that he mortgaged in 1826 indicate that he was well equipped to fashion a variety of goods. In addition to spoons, surviving works bearing his mark include a sugar bowl, teapots, a cream pitcher, and an ear trumpet. Clockmaking equipment listed below was perhaps a vestige of Hendel's early work with his brother Jacob. The "eight punches to make spoons" were probably among those used to make these teaspoons and table-

spoon. At the time of his mortgage, Hendel owned the following shop tools:

Two Ingots
one Rolling Mill
8 Hammers, 2 Vises
2 Anvils, 2 Stakes
8 punches to make spoons & Ladles
13 hollow punches
27 do. to make breast pins & lockets
Apparatus for melting silver
1 pair Bellows
2 Small desks
1 wire Bench and apparatus
1 Bick [?] iron
1 set of thimble tools
1 large Reamer
Apparatus for clock making
Apparatus for brass founding[3]

The spoons, engraved "TRF," were made for Thomas Foster and Rebecca Crawford of Carlisle, who were married in 1778. Foster owned the "Sign of the Sorrel Horse," the most fashionable tavern in the area. Next door was the home and possibly the shop of Jacob Hendel; thus he was near the clockmaking and silversmithing family at the time of his purchase.[4]

The spoons were probably part of a larger service that Foster purchased about 1803, when he and his wife would have celebrated their twenty-fifth wedding anniversary. Surviving pieces in the service include a coffeepot, two teapots, a sugar bowl and creamer, and spoons.[5] The ornamental bird and branch design on the bowl of the spoon was popular in the Mid-Atlantic states. For a similar example, see spoons by Baltimore silversmith Abraham Dubois (cat. no. 145).[6]

Description: The spoons have a pointed-end downturned handle and a slight midrib on back. Undecorated except for the owner's initials, each has an oval bowl with long rounded drop and, on the back, a swaged form of a bird holding a branch in its beak; the bird faces left on the tablespoon and right on the teaspoons.

History: The spoons were made for Thomas Foster (1753–1829) and Rebecca Crawford (1756–1812) of Carlisle, Pennsylvania, m. 1778. By descent to their children, Henrietta Foster, m. Jesse Castor of Philadelphia, in 1820; and Crawford Foster (1787–1853) m. Elizabeth Pattison (d. 1821), in 1816; to the children of these siblings, Josephine C. Castor (b. 1828?) and Alfred Holmes Foster (1819–1884), first cousins who married each other.[7] By descent to their daughter Jessie Crawford Foster (d. 1907) and her husband, William Theodore Furness (d. 1929), who placed them on loan to the MFA in 1919. They then descended to her brother Thomas C. Foster. By descent to the children of William and Jessie Furness: Thomas F. Furness (1892–1976); Emily D. Furness (1896–1970); George Abbot Furness (1896–1985). By descent to the donors, the children of George Abbot Furness and his first wife, Eleanor Winslow Williams, and second wife, Yasuko Kimio Suzuki: Anne Winslow Furness (b. 1926); George Abbot Furness Jr. (b. 1930); Jessie Caroline Furness (b. 1957).

Exhibitions and publications: None.

NOTES TO THIS ENTRY ARE ON PAGE 223.

155

Higbie and Crosby (active about 1825–1832)
Aaron H. Higbie
Ransom Crosby

Three-piece tea service

New York, New York, about 1825–30
Gift of Dr. and Mrs. Roger G. Gerry
1975.649–51

Teapot (1975.649): H. 10⅜ in.(26.5 cm); W. 12³⁄₁₆ in. (30.9 cm); D. 6⅜ in. (16.3 cm); Wt. 35 oz 3 gr (1088.8 gm)

Creamer (1975.650): H. 8 in. (20.2 cm); W. 7 in. (17.7 cm); D. 4⁵⁄₁₆ in. (11 cm); Wt. 14 oz 4 dwt 22 gr (443.1 gm)

Covered sugar bowl (1975.651a–b): H. 9⅝ in. (24.5 cm); W. 9⁵⁄₁₆ in. (23.5 cm); D. 5¹¹⁄₁₆ in. (14.5 cm); Wt. 25 oz 13 dwt 1 gr (797.9 gm)

Marks: "HIGBIE & CROSBY / [face in profile] / [crowned head] / C / [star]" struck on bottom of teapot. "[face in profile] / [crowned head] / C / [star] / HIGBIE & CROSBY" struck on bottom of covered sugar bowl. "[face in profile] / [crowned head] / C / [star]" struck on bottom of creamer.

Inscriptions: "A M S" in entwined script engraved on side of each piece; "XX" scratched on each bottom.

THE REFINED FORMS and simple geometry that were characteristic of Neoclassical silver in the late eighteenth and early nineteenth centuries gave way to a bolder and more robust expression in the 1820s. Holloware dating from this period, such as these examples, consisted of thin, rolled sheet silver hammered into complex, rotund shapes that were often accentuated with pronounced lobes and usually dominated by a reliance on milled and cast decoration.

Ransom Crosby and Aaron H. Higbie were working in New York when it became America's largest city and port. They were listed as jewelers in *Longworth's New York Directory* from 1825 to 1832, after which time Higbie apparently left the partnership.[1] The broad-hipped lobed body and the densely packed floral decoration of this tea service represent the aesthetic of the day, which combined the repoussé (made easy with sheet silver) with innovatively designed, milled bands of floral decoration.[2]

Description: The three pieces conform in shape and decoration. Made of thinly rolled sheet silver, each body rises from a round stepped foot to a bulbous body with pronounced lobed decoration. Each piece has bands of milled floral ornament at the foot and shoulder and on the covers of the teapot and sugar bowl. The scrolled handles of each piece and the spout of the teapot are cast. The handle of the teapot is protected with ivory insulators, and the spout has a touch of floral decoration on its tip. The teapot and sugar bowl are crowned with large floral finials.

History: Early history unknown.

Exhibitions and publications: Fairbanks 1991, 73, cat. no. 57.

NOTES TO THIS ENTRY ARE ON PAGE 223.

155

156

Nathan Hobbs (about 1792–1868)

Three cups

Boston, Massachusetts, about 1817
Gift of Mr. and Mrs. Franklin H. Williams in memory of
Louise Bodine Wallace
1984.513
Donated by Mrs. Kathryn Homes Yezek and Mrs. Nancy
Holmes Maxfield in memory of Mary Reno Eliot and Alice
Rebecca Eliot
1986.739–40

1984.513: H. 3⁵/₁₆ in. (8.5 cm); W. 2⁵/₁₆ in. (5.8 cm); Diam. 2⁷/₈ in.
(7.4 cm); Wt. 3 oz 19 dwt 16 gr (123.9 gm)

1986.739: H. 3⁵/₁₆ (8.3 cm); W. 2³/₁₆ in. (5.8 cm); D. 2⁵/₁₆ in. (7.3 cm);
Wt. 3 oz 19 dwt 1 gr (122.9 gm)

1986.740: H. 3⁵/₁₆ in. (8.5 cm); W. 2⁵/₁₆ in. (5.8 cm); Diam. 2⁷/₈ in.
(7.4 cm); Wt. 3 oz 16 dwt 23 gr (119.7 gm)

Marks: "HOBBS" within a rectangle, with an eagle facing right
within a serrated circle, struck on each bottom.

Inscriptions: "The New North Religious Society / - to - / Ephraim
Eliot / - Their Treasurer from 1794–1817 -" in script engraved on
body of each vessel. "J.F.E. / 1827 / J.E. 1882 A.R.E. 1909" engraved
on bottom of two cups (1986.739–40).

NATHAN HOBBS produced a body of silver that attests to his
presence in the local community. His master remains unknown;
he was listed as a jeweler, engraver, and silversmith in the Boston directories from 1816 to 1846. In addition to these three
cups, during his career Hobbs produced ecclesiastical silver for
the Church of Christ, Medford; First Congregational Society,
Cohasset; and First Parish, Scituate.

Ephraim Eliot, the recipient of these cups, was the son of
Andrew Eliot, who had graduated from Harvard College in
1737 and was ordained in 1742 at the New North Church in Boston. The elder Eliot was appointed president of Harvard College in 1773. It seems that Ephraim Eliot continued to serve the
church in which his father was ordained. The cup was given in
appreciation for his services as treasurer of the society.

Description: Each raised barrel-shaped beaker has a narrow gadrooned band at the foot and a lightly everted lip.

History: For the history of one cup (1984.513), see cat. no. 23, beginning with its ownership in the nineteenth century. The history of
the other two cups is unknown.

Exhibitions and publications: None.

157

Possibly Joseph Loring (1743–1815)

Teapot

Boston, Massachusetts, 1810–15
Gift of Elizabeth Quincy Fisher in memory of John Gardner
Fisher
1985.691

H. 6⅞ in. (17.6 cm); W. 11½ in. (29.2 cm); D. 4½ in. (11.5 cm); Wt. 18
oz 24 gr (561.4 gm)

Marks: "J [pellet] Loring" in a scalloped ellipse struck on base,
above center point.

Inscriptions: "MH" entwined monogram engraved on body of
vessel, to right of handle; "HTQ" engraved in similar, but later,
manner on the pourer's side, both within a foliated ellipse. Scratch
weight of "17 4" on base.

JOSEPH LORING produced a variety of forms, including baptismal basins, beakers, canns, wine cups, creampots, and porringers, but few teapots. On some occasions, he sold silver that also bore the mark of Jesse Churchill of Boston; Samuel Bartlett of Concord; or Ebenezer Moulton of Newburyport, Massachusetts. In such cases, it is likely that these men supplied one another with silver to meet market demands. What is not clear is which silversmiths made their work for others to retail.[1]

Because of the difficulty in unraveling the mystery of which silversmiths sold the work of their colleages, an unmarked fluted teapot and a marked stand in the Museum's collection that had formerly been attributed to Loring have been reassigned to Paul Revere II. The attribution was made on the basis of their similarity to other fluted teapots from Revere's workshop. Two fluted teapots marked by Loring in a private collection are also close matches to the fluted form that Revere made famous.[2] If Revere did indeed make all the above-mentioned fluted forms that were marked and retailed by Loring, it becomes even more

difficult to determine whether this late example is indeed by the silversmith.

This teapot's long, low profile recalls the late-eighteenth-century fluted style, but its slightly convex, elliptical shape and smooth, expansive surface reveal its production in the federal period. A tea service by William Moulton in the Museum's collection, which Kathryn C. Buhler dated to 1800–10, has a similar contour.[3] It calls to mind an unmarked teapot in the Bayou Bend collection that descended from the silversmith's family. That teapot has a Neoclassical form, with a slightly rounded contour, ball feet, and applied reeding, and could also have been made by Jesse Churchill.[4]

The shop tools and goods cited in the inventory of Loring's estate indicate that he was working as a silversmith until his death in 1815. It is unclear, however, whether Loring produced much hollowware in this new style. Since the teapot was probably made within several years before his death, one can only speculate whether Loring chose to subcontract with a maker proficient in the Neoclassical style.

Description: The raised teapot has an elliptical base with an applied foot, swelled sides, and concave rim. The domed lid has a three-part hinge; the baluster finial has an elliptical ebonized wooden separator. The scrolled spout, with an extended lower lip, is affixed over strainer holes. Angled cylindrical sockets with molded edges are set with a replaced, black-painted, wooden scroll handle. The difference in weight of one additional troy ounce than that recorded in the scratch weight may be due to this later handle.

History: The initials "MH" together with Loring's death in 1815 suggest that the teapot was made for Mary Hatch (1800–1835) sometime before her marriage in 1818 to Samuel Quincy (1791–1850) of Boston.[5] The teapot descended in a matrilineal line, for at her death it was given to her sister-in-law Harriet Tufts (1827–1867) of Plymouth, New Hampshire, second wife of the Hon. Josiah Quincy (1793–1875), m. 1845, whose initials "HTQ" are also engraved on the teapot;[6] to their daughter Mary Ann Quincy (b. 1854) and Willard F. Kinsman (b. 1849), m. 1876; to their daughter Elizabeth Grace Kinsman (b. 1879) and Charles Edward McGlashan (b. about 1879), m. 1909; to their daughter Elizabeth Quincy McGlashan (1910–1992), the donor, wife of John Gardner Fisher (about 1908–1973), m. 1938.[7]

Exhibitions and publications: Kane 1998, 672.

NOTES TO THIS ENTRY ARE ON PAGES 223–24.

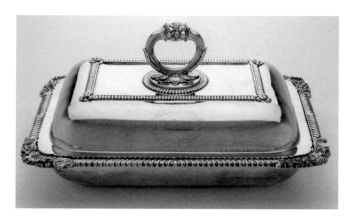

158

Edward Lownes (1792–1834)
Entree dish

Philadelphia, Pennsylvania, about 1820–30
Anonymous Gift
1994.33

H. 7½ in. (19.1 cm); W. 14³⁄₁₆ in. (36 cm); D. 10³⁄₁₆ in. (26 cm); Wt. 85 oz 17 dwt 4 gr (2670.5 gm)

Marks: "E. LOWNES" in a rectangle struck four times on underside of bottom.

Inscriptions: "A / TESTIMONY of AFFECTION / from / Charles Francis / to his Sister / Sophia Harrison" within wreath engraved on side. "GSH" engraved on side of lid.

ALTHOUGH NOT UNCOMMON in English silver and fused plate, large serving dishes such as this by Edward Lownes of Philadelphia are rare in American silver. It is an excellent example of the form, massive and weighty, with milled gadrooned borders and rocaille ornament at the corners. As is customary, the loop handle is removable, and the cover can be inverted to form a matching, smaller dish.[1]

Description: This large rectangular dish has a milled gadrooned border, with floral and C-scroll decoration at each corner. The removable lid has a loop handle of two conjoined cornucopiae sheathed in leaves. It swivels to unlock and detach, converting the lid into a smaller, matching dish, decorated en suite.

History: Given by Charles Francis to his sister Sophia Francis Harrison, probably on the occasion of her marriage to George Harrison. It descended to Sophia's sister Mary Francis Fisher and her husband, Joshua Fisher; to their son Joshua Francis Fisher and his wife, Eliza Middleton Fisher; then through the family to the parents of the donor and to the anonymous donor in 1963.

Exhibitions and publications: None.

NOTE TO THIS ENTRY IS ON PAGE 224.

159

Ebenezer Moulton (1768–1824)

Pitcher

Boston, Massachusetts, 1790–1810
Gift of Mrs. John W. Laverack, Mr. John L. Sabine, Mrs. Andrew C. Marsters in memory of our parents, Mr. and Mrs. Stephen Webb Sabine
1977.157

H. 10³⁄₁₆ in. (26 cm); W. 8 in. (20.3 cm); D. 5³⁄₁₆ in. (13.3 cm); Diam. base 4⅛ in. (10.4 gm); Wt. 21 oz 19 dwt 4 gr (683 gm)

Marks: "MOULTON" struck twice on underside of bottom.

Inscription: "SSW" within a circular garland engraved on side, under spout.

EBENEZER MOULTON was a member of the large Moulton family of silversmiths from Newbury and Newburyport. He worked in both the latter city and in Boston. As observed by Martha Gandy Fales, a noted silver scholar, "Of all the Moultons, it was Ebenezer who produced the most interesting silver, much of it while he had his shop in Boston."[1] This large pitcher, made for a Salem mariner, is a simple yet classically elegant example of his work. Moulton's best-known work is a large presentation pitcher in the Museum's collection, which was engraved by Thomas Wightman and presented to Isaac Harris in 1810 for his efforts in extinguishing a fire in the Old South Church.[2]

Description: The raised pitcher is of barrel form; it has an applied hollow handle set opposite the drawn flaring spout. The angular handle rises from the top edge and joins the body just below the center. There is an applied gadrooned molding at the top edge of the body and an applied molding at the circular base.

History: The family history indicates original ownership by Stephen

159

Webb (b. 1756), a mariner from Salem, Massachusetts. Presumably descended in the family to Mr. and Mrs. Stephen Webb Sabine; given in their memory by their children in 1977.

Exhibitions and publications: None.

NOTES TO THIS ENTRY ARE ON PAGE 224.

and before her death in 1814. It was a small part of a diverse range of American-made and imported English silver and Sheffield plate owned by the wealthy Derby-West family of Salem and Danvers.[1]

Description: Made in three parts in faux barrel form, when assembled the grater has four sets of applied bands over the simulated staves. A small ring handle is applied on one side at the center of the middle section. With a twist release, the small bottom section separates to allow access to the large center section, which is designed to hold the nutmeg and is fitted at its top with a perforated grater. The top, also fitted with a twist release, comes off.[2]

History: Probably owned originally by Elizabeth Derby (1762–1814), m. Nathaniel West in 1783. Descended in the family and included as part of a large body of Derby-West family material, much of it owned originally in the mansion known as Oak Hill and given by the donor in 1972.[3]

Exhibitions and publications: "300 Years of Newburyport Silver," Custom House Maritime Museum, Newburyport, Massachusetts, Oct. 16–18, 1981; Wendy A. Cooper, "The Furniture and Furnishings of the Farm at Danvers," *Museum of Fine Arts, Boston, Bulletin* 81 (1983), 44.

NOTES TO THIS ENTRY ARE ON PAGE 224.

160

Ebenezer Moulton (1768–1824)

Nutmeg grater

Boston, Massachusetts, about 1806–14
Gift of Richard Edwards
1972.517

H. 3 in. (7.6 cm); W. 2½ in. (6.4 cm); Diam. rim 1⅞ in. (4.8 cm); Diam. base 1⅞ in. (4.8 cm); Wt. 4 oz 14 dwt 0 gr (146.2 gm)

Marks: "MOULTON" struck on lid.

Inscriptions: "ED" in script engraved on bottom.

THIS SMALL BUT ELEGANT nutmeg grater was owned originally by Elizabeth Derby and was probably commissioned by her after her notorious divorce from Nathaniel West in 1806

161

Paul Revere II (1734–1818)

Set of three tablespoons

Boston, Massachusetts, about 1780–90
Gift of Mr. and Mrs. Charles F. Hovey
1973.620–22

1973.620: L. 8½ in. (21.6 cm); W. bowl 1¹¹⁄₁₆ in. (4.3 cm); Wt. 1 oz 18 dwt 4 gr (59.4 gm)

1973.621: L. 8½ in. (21.6 cm); W. bowl 1¹¹⁄₁₆ in. (4.3 cm); Wt. 2 oz 1 dwt 6 gr (64.2 gm)

1973.622: L. 8½ in. (21.6 cm); W. bowl 1¹¹⁄₁₆ in. (4.3 cm); Wt. 1 oz 16 dwt 20 gr (57.3 gm)

Marks: "REVERE" in rectangle struck on back of each handle.

Inscriptions: "JVR" or "IVR" in script within an oval engraved on top of each handle.

161

162

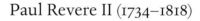

THE WAR YEARS caused a hiatus in Paul Revere's silversmithing career, from April 1775 until early 1779; his daybooks indicate that he was not back into full production until 1781.[1] He then embarked on a roughly twenty-five-year period as New England's leading producer of silver in the new Neoclassical, or Federal, style. His silversmithing career seems to have come to an end about 1806.

These three spoons, in excellent condition, demonstrate the finest quality of Revere's Federal-period flatware. They are but three of many known examples. Their original owner is, unfortunately, unknown.[2]

Description: Each spoon has an ovoid bowl and a slightly pointed, downturned handle. Each handle is engraved with initials in an oval, topped by a bowknot; bright-cut flowers decorate the stem. The handle joins the bowl at an elongated slashed drop.

History: Early history unknown.

Exhibitions and publications: Kane 1998, 832.

NOTES TO THIS ENTRY ARE ON PAGE 224.

Paul Revere II (1734–1818)

Creampot

Boston, Massachusetts, about 1780–85
Anonymous Gift
1976.43

H. 5⁵⁄₁₆ in. (13.5 cm); W. 4½ in. (11.5 cm); D. 2¹¹⁄₁₆ in. (6.8 cm); Wt. 4 oz 18 dwt 18 gr (153.6 gm)

Marks: "REVERE" in roman letters within a rectangle struck indistinctly to left of handle, near rim.

Inscription: A worn, entwined, script monogram that probably reads "EOT" engraved on vessel, opposite handle.

THE DESIGN OF THIS TALL double-bellied creamer, with its distinctive gadrooned edge, looks back to midcentury use of this decorative motif. Its vasiform profile, by contrast, anticipates the Neoclassical style. Gadrooned or more stylish beaded decoration can be found on a few cylindrical teapots that were made by Revere in the early 1780s, including one in the Museum's collection. That example displays gadrooned decoration that was fashioned in 1782 for his cousin Thomas Hitchborn.[1] The compatability of these two designs may explain how, in 1783, Revere made a creamer with a gadrooned rim and splayed beaded foot, along with a beaded cylindrical teapot for fellow Mason Michael Hays and his wife, Rachel (Myers) Hays, of Boston.[2] This creamer, similar to one in the Yale collection that is dated 1778, displays a gadrooned rim and splayed gadrooned foot.[3] Whether these examples were intended to accompany specific teapots is unknown. The style, however, was short-lived, for Revere soon adopted the helmet-shaped Neoclassical form that came into vogue at century's end.

Description: The raised double-bellied pitcher has a raised, stepped, trumpet foot and encircling, applied, gadrooned edge with matching rim. The upper portion of the cast double-scrolled handle with thumbgrip is soldered to the rim; the lower end of the handle is soldered directly to the body.

History: Early history unknown.

Exhibitions and publications: Kane 1998, 814.

NOTES TO THIS ENTRY ARE ON PAGE 224.

163

Paul Revere II (1734–1818)
Ladle

Boston, Massachusetts, 1781
Gift of Mary Sargent Thompson and Helena Apthorp Long
1991.1084

L. 14⅜ in. (36.5 cm); W. bowl 3¹¹/₁₆ in. (9.5 cm); Wt. 6 oz 6 dwt 2 gr (196.1 gm)

Marks: "[pellet] REVERE" in a rectangle struck on back of handle.

Inscriptions: "M / P * S" in shaded roman letters engraved on back of handle tip.

Armorials: The Apthorp family crest, a mullet on a torse, is engraved within a cartouche on the front tip of handle.

FOLLOWING HIS MARRIAGE to Sarah Apthorp in 1781, Boston patriot Perez Morton purchased a large amount of tea- and punch-related silver items from Paul Revere. Within the first year of his marriage, Morton bought a dozen large teaspoons, five salt spoons, two pair of sugar tongs, two small ladles, a "sil-

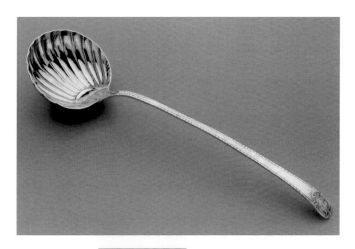

163

ver frame for Casters," and probably this large "tureen ladle," one of a pair to be engraved with crests, as was recorded in Revere's daybooks. Revere also mended candlesticks, fans, a "pudding Bason," and a "glass piramed" for Morton, some of which were surely imported.[1]

Because this ladle carries the Apthorp crest, it may have originated in the home of this prominent merchant family or been given to Sarah Apthorp before or after her marriage. Alternatively, the family may have ordered the ladle from Revere as a wedding gift or provided funds to Morton for its purchase. Although not widely recognized, there is precedent for wedding silver engraved with matrilineal family arms. One well-known example is a sugar bowl engraved with the Chandler arms and crest that was made by Revere for Lucretia Chandler upon her marriage in 1761 to John Murray of Rutland, Massachusetts.[2]

Since Revere's daybook does not record any purchases made by the Apthorp family, it is possible that Morton purchased the silver and arranged for his wife's family to be honored in the engraved crest. Fittingly, the ladle descended in the matrilineal line through five generations until it was made a gift by the donors.

Description: The large scallop-shaped bowl of this ladle is notable for the leafy pattern swaged on the back of its deep and broad drop. The handle extends from a rounded drop toward a rounded downturned handle. The feather-edged decoration ends in swaged asymmetrical cartouche at handle tip.

History: Possibly ordered from Revere by Perez Morton (1750–1837), Speaker of the Massachusetts House of Representatatives from 1806 to 1811 and Massachusetts Attorney General from 1811 to 1832. Morton m. Sarah Wentworth Apthorp (1759–1846) in 1781.[3] Sarah's parents were James and Sarah (Wentworth) Apthorp of Braintree (now Quincy).[4] By descent to their daughter Sarah Apthorp Morton (1782–1844) and Richard (or John) Cunningham, m. 1809; to their daughter Charlotte Cunningham (b. 1817/18) and Dr. Howard Sargent (1810–1872);[5] to their daughter Mary Sarah Sargent (1844–1908) and her second husband, John Vaughn Apthorp (b. 1844), m. 1882; to their daughter Helen Sargent Apthorp (1883–1982) and Henry Smith Thompson (1871–1944); to their daughters Mary Sargent Thompson (1909–1995) and Helena Apthorp Thompson Long (1903–1992), the donors.

Exhibitions and publications: Fairbanks 1975, cat. no. 206; Kane 1998, 818.

NOTES TO THIS ENTRY ARE ON PAGE 224.

164

Paul Revere II (1734–1818)
Four salt spoons

Boston, Massachusetts, about 1783
Gift of Mary Sargent Thompson and Helena Apthorp Long
1991.1085–88

1991.1085: L. 4 in. (10.2 cm); W. bowl 11/16 in. (1.9 cm); Wt. 4 dwt 10 gr (6.9 gm)

1991.1086: L. 4 in. (10.2 cm); W. bowl 11/16 in. (1.8 cm); Wt. 4 dwt 2 gr (6.4 gm)

1991.1087: L. 4 in. (10.1 cm); W. bowl 11/16 in. (1.8 cm); Wt. 4 dwt 12 gr (7 gm)

1991.1088: L. 4 in. (10.1 cm); W. bowl 11/16 in. (1.9 cm); Wt. 4 dwt 4 gr (6.5 gm)

Marks: "PR" in script within a rectangle struck on back of each handle.

Inscriptions: None.

Armorials: The unidentified crest, possibly adopted by the Swan family, is that of a long-necked bird standing in tall grass on a torse. The engraving is located on the top of each handle tip.[1]

SCOTTISH-BORN MERCHANT James Swan served in the Revolutionary War and fought at the Battle of Bunker Hill in 1775.[2] With the onset of peacetime, in 1783 Swan ordered from Revere

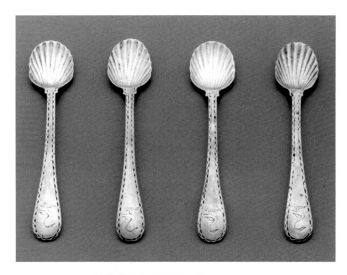

164

"6 large Silver Spoons," "10 large tea spoons," and "6 Silver Table Spoons," all engraved with crests. In 1785 and again in 1787, the patriot "clean[ed] and 'burnish[ed]" six salts, possibly English imports, no doubt pitted from frequent use.[3] Although Revere did not record the sale of these spoons to Swan, it is possible they were made within a short time of Swan's 1783 purchases.

Description: Each small salt spoon has a scallop shell bowl with squared shoulders that extends to a rounded, downturned handle with feather-edge decoration.

History: Family history records that James Swan (1755–1828) and his wife, Hepzibah Clarke (d. 1826), m. 1776, were the first owners, but the unidentifiable crest suggests that the silver probably entered the family through the marriage one of their three daughters, perhaps Chritiana Keadie Swan (1779–1867) and John Turner Sargent (1769–1813), m. 1806.[4] By descent to their son Howard Sargent (1810–1872) and Charlotte Cunningham (1818–1888), m. 1836; to their daughter Charlotte Howard Sargent (1840–1869) and John D. Parker (1841–1878), m. 1864; to Charlotte's sister Alice Wentworth Sargent (1851–about 1929), m. her sister's widower in 1871; to their niece Mary Frances Thomas (1873–1941), d. unm.; to her descendants Mary Sargent Thompson (1909–1995) and Helena Apthorp Thompson Long (1911–1994), the donors.[5]

Exhibitions and publications: Fairbanks 1975, cat. nos. 345–48; Kane 1998, 823.

NOTES TO THIS ENTRY ARE ON PAGE 224.

165

Attributed to Paul Revere II (1734–1818)

Creampot

Boston, Massachusetts, 1787
Marion Davis Fund
1973.214

H. 5¹³⁄₁₆ in. (14.8 cm); W. 5⁵⁄₁₆ in. (13.5 cm); D. 3 in. (7.7 cm); Wt. 4 oz
12 dwt 24 gr (144.6 gm)

Marks: Unmarked.

Inscriptions: "HC" entwined initials in sprigged script engraved
within an elliptical device; "1787." engraved below crossed palms.

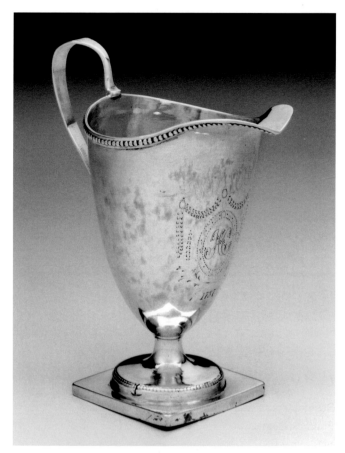

BEARING THE MONOGRAM "HC" within an oval garland, the
engraving on this unmarked creampot is closely related to a
teapot and stand by Paul Revere in the Museum's collection
that was fashioned in 1787 for the wedding of Hannah Carter
and William Smith.[1] Because the service postdates Josiah Austin's death by seven years, the presence of the "J [pellet] Austin"
mark on that teapot has caused much discussion. Fortunately,
surviving bills from Nathaniel Austin to William Smith, and
corresponding records in Paul Revere II's waste book, suggest
that Austin made use of his late uncle's mark in retailing the
work of Revere. William Smith did make a large purchase from
Austin on June 28, 1787, which did not include the creampot.
However, on the following day, Revere charged Austin £2.1.14
for "one Silver cream pot wt. 5 oz 2-." The Museum's creampot
is now lighter by 9 dwt, a small difference probably due to years
of polishing.

Despite Revere's daybook record, Kathryn C. Buhler conjectured that construction features in the creampot were unlike
those characteristic of Revere's work. She believed that Nathaniel Austin made the vessel.[2] Indeed, the rather small and light
base of the creamer, with its broken seam, is less well executed
than Revere's typical work. Furthermore, the beading on the
vessel is not found on the teapot and stand. These conflicting
results demonstrate how difficult it can be to make attributions
for colonial silver that was made by one party and retailed by
another. However, the delicate, swagged engraving was almost
certainly done by Revere or someone in his workshop, for it
closely matches that found on the Smith family silver made by
Revere.

Description: The raised helmet-shaped vessel has a square plinth supporting a circular splayed foot with a narrow vertical step. A slen-

der C-shaped strap handle is attached to rim opposite the V-shaped
mouth; an attenuated section of handle is soldered to body of vessel
at lower join. Beaded decoration appears at rim of pitcher and on
top edge of the foot. There is a break at the seam of the circular
foot. A decorative device below the spout is composed of swags and
ribbons over crossed stalks of flowers that surrounds an elliptical
shield bearing owner's initials.

History: Probably made for Hannah Carter and William Smith, m.
1787; subsequent history unknown until sold in 1973 to the Museum
by Firestone and Parsons, Boston.

NOTES TO THIS ENTRY ARE ON PAGE 224.

pierced shaker is surmounted by a twisted flame finial pinned in place.

History: Originally owned by William and Hannah (Carter) Smith; see also cat. no. 172. Descended to their son Thomas Carter Smith in 1831; to his son William Vincent Smith in 1877; he m. Alice Parkman in 1878 (and changed his name to William Smith Carter in 1880); to his son Theodore P. Carter. Purchased from the latter by noted collector Mark Bortman and placed on loan to the Museum from 1948 to 1966. By descent to his daughter Jane Bortman Larus. Purchased from William Core Duffy, New Haven, Connecticut, in 1983.

Exhibitions and publications: Motif and Meaning: Classicism in America (Brockton, Mass.: Brockton Art Center/Fuller Memorial, 1987), 26; Kane 1998, 812.

NOTES TO THIS ENTRY ARE ON PAGE 224.

166

Attributed to Paul Revere II (1734–1818)

Caster

Boston, Massachusetts, 1787
Frank B. Bemis Fund
1983.129

H. 6⅛ in. (15.4 cm); W. 1⅞ in. (4.9 cm); D. 1⅞ in. (4.9 cm); Wt. 3 oz 18 dwt 9 gr (121.9 gm)

Marks: Unmarked.

Inscriptions: "WHS / 1787." entwined script initials engraved within within an oval on one side, with ribbon-hung garland above and crossed sprays below. "TCS / to / WVS / 1877" in script engraved on opposite side.

THIS UNMARKED CASTER is thought to have been owned originally by William and Hannah Carter Smith of Boston and made at the time of their marriage in 1787. A teapot and stand in the Museum's collection, marked by Revere, has the same history (see cat. nos. 165 and 172 for related pieces owned in the same family).[1]

Only three other Revere casters are known in this same form.[2] The piece is also related to the small, unmarked gold urn made by Revere for the Grand Lodge of Massachusetts in 1799 to hold a lock of George Washington's hair.[3]

Description: The raised oviform vessel is soldered to a splayed foot, which in turn is supported by a squared plinth. Beaded decoration separates the shoulder of the vessel from its incurved neck; a domed

167

Paul Revere II (1734–1818)

Ladle

Boston, Massachusetts, about 1790
Gift of the grandchildren of James Dellinger Barney
1991.1089

L. 12¹³⁄₁₆ in. (32.5 cm); W. bowl 3⅛ in. (8 cm); Wt. 4 oz 11 dwt 3 gr (141.7 gm)

Marks: "[pellet] REVERE" within a rectangle struck on back of handle.

Inscription: "SH" entwined script initials within lozenge engraved at handle tip.

THIS LARGE AND SIMPLE ladle by Revere, with its round bowl and delicate engraving, was undoubtedly among the more popular utensils produced by his shop. In his daybooks, at least fifty are mentioned, most of them in the postwar era. These include salt and pepper ladles, cream ladles, tureen ladles, soup ladles, and punch ladles. Presumably, all but the cream and pepper ladles were of the sizable long-handled variety seen here. Revere produced a tureen ladle for taverner Andrew Cunningham; a punch ladle for Loyalist blacksmith Edward Foster; a tureen ladle for lumber merchant Samuel Dilloway; two tureen ladles for merchant Samuel Wells; and a tureen ladle for Col. Paul Dudley Sargent. Punch ladles were standard orders that Revere filled for his Masonic brothers at St. Andrew's Lodge, St. Paul Lodge, and Tyrian Lodge, among others.[1]

168

Description: The ladle has a rounded drop on its hemispherical bowl. Its handle arches to a downturned pointed tip on which is engraved a lozenge-shaped device with pendant flower motif. There is a poor repair to a tear on the edge of the bowl, opposite the handle.

History: As seen in cat. no. 168, in 1792 Capt. Samuel Howard purchased spoons and probably one other ladle from Revere. Howard may have also purchased this ladle from Revere; if so, the initials on this example could be his. Beyond this conjectural origin, little is known of the ladle until it was made a gift to the Museum in 1991.

Exhibitions and publications: Kane 1998, 817.

NOTE TO THIS ENTRY IS ON PAGE 224.

168

Paul Revere II (1734–1818)
Ladle

Boston, Massachusetts, ca. 1790
Gift of Elizabeth D. Geier and Thomas N. Dabney
1991.1002

L. 14⁵⁄₁₆ in. (36.4 cm); W. bowl 3¹³⁄₁₆ in. (9.6 cm); Wt. 5 oz 14 dwt 9 gr (177.9 gm)

Marks: "[pellet] REVERE" struck on back of handle.

Inscription: "SN Howard" in sprigged script engraved along length of handle, near tip.

IN 1792 CAPT. SAMUEL HOWARD purchased twelve large silver teaspoons from Revere, all with engraved cyphers.[1] Neither this ladle nor another engraved "SH" by Revere (cat. 167) appears in the silversmith's surviving daybooks. It is neverthe-

less possible that both were fashioned about the same time as the spoons.

Description: The ladle has a large scallop-shaped bowl with multiple squared drops on the back and extends to a long downturned handle with rounded tip. Feather-edge decoration is engraved along the perimeter of the handle. Poor repairs have been made around the squared drop.

History: Aside from a conjectural attribution to Capt. Samuel Howard, caulker of Boston, nothing is known of the ladle before it was made a gift to the Museum in 1991.

Exhibitions and publications: Kane 1998, 817.

NOTE TO THIS ENTRY IS ON PAGE 225.

169

Paul Revere II (1734–1818)
Coffeepot

Boston, Massachusetts, about 1795–1800
Bequest of Arthur D. Fay
1972.56

H. 13⁷⁄₈ in. (35.2 cm); W. 10 in. (25.5 cm); Diam. base 4½ in. (11.5 cm); Wt. 34 oz 7 dwt 15 gr (1069.4 gm)

Marks: "REVERE" in shaped rectangle struck on side of foot.

Inscriptions: "HCS" entwined monogram within bright-cut wreath engraved on each side.

TALL AND SLENDER, the basic form of this pear-shaped coffee-pot looks back to mid-eighteenth-century examples. However, its elongated proportions, high foot, and engraved decoration mark it as a product of the last few years of the century.[1] Perhaps ordered by a customer with more traditional tastes, the coffeepot was made at virtually the same time that Revere was also making his more typical fluted teapots (see cat. no. 171).[2]

Description: The tall, slender, raised oviform body is soldered to a round, stepped, raised foot with bands of border decoration. It has a long, undecorated, curved spout over rough strainer holes and a band of guilloche engraving at the neck, between bands of dotted border decoration. The hinged three-part lid is fitted with a bezel, and the domed cover has a pinecone finial pinned in place. The handle, old but not original, has been repaired.

History: Family history suggests that this coffeepot was made originally for Hepzibah Clarke Swan (1777–1833) of Boston, m. Dr. John Clarke Howard in 1800; to her great-granddaughter Katharine (Gray) Fay; to her son Arthur D. Fay of Nahant, Massachusetts, who lent it to the Museum in 1953 and subsequently bequeathed it to the Museum.[3]

Exhibitions and publications: Buhler 1956, cat. no. 123; Fairbanks 1981, 630, fig. 35; Kane 1998, 812.

NOTES TO THIS ENTRY ARE ON PAGE 225.

170

Paul Revere II (1734–1818)

Creampot

Boston, Massachusetts, about 1795–1800
Gift of John Robert Dyar and Diane Moore Dyar
2001.743

H. 6¹¹⁄₁₆ in. (17 cm); W. 5½ in. (14 cm); D. 2¹¹⁄₁₆ (6.8 cm); Wt. 6 oz 1 dwt 2 gr (188.3 gm)

Marks: "REVERE" within a rectangle doublestruck on sides of base.

Inscriptions: "ISD" entwined monogram in sprigged script, within an ellipse, engraved beneath spout.

REVERE MADE NEOCLASSICAL-STYLE creamers in a variety of forms, including the inverted helmet-shape seen here, although not all are as elaborately engraved.[1] A pair of Revere sugar tongs owned by the Museum bears the same engraved initials, thought to be those of James Dunbar and his wife, Sarah Templeton, who were married in 1792.[2]

Description: The raised helmet-shaped body is soldered to a tall, flaring, circular foot atop a square base plinth, which is engraved with leafage at the corners. The narrow scrolled strap handle has a high loop and bright-cut engraving on its upper edge; it is attached opposite the flaring lip to the rim at the top and to the lower body at the bottom. There is a molded edge at the top. The body is engraved with a pattern of bright-cut bowknots, ribbon swags, and floral sprigs, with an ellipse on the front containing the engraved initials.

History: The cream pitcher was collected by Hugh Huntington Dyar (1888–1969), who considered it a family piece. It descended to his son and daughter-in-law, the donors.

Exhibitions and publications: None.

NOTES TO THIS ENTRY ARE ON PAGE 225.

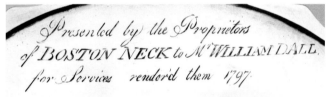

171

Paul Revere II (1734–1818)

Teapot

Boston, Massachusetts, 1797
Gift of Mr. Charles Whitney Dall Jr.
1981.39

H. 6⅛ in. (15.5 cm); W. 10¹³⁄₁₆ in. (27.4 cm); D. 3¹¹⁄₁₆ in. (9.3 cm); Wt.
19 oz 14 dwt 6 gr (613.1 gm)

Marks: "REVERE" within a rectangle struck at center of base.

Inscriptions: "Presented by the Proprietors / of BOSTON NECK
to Mr. WILLIAM DALL / for Services render'd them 1797" in
script and roman capitals engraved on base.

WILLIAM DALL, the recipient of this elegant teapot, was a
merchant who lived near Boston Neck, the narrow spit of land
that connected Boston with the mainland, an area now filled
in and known as the Back Bay.[1] Dall may have negotiated the
filling or development of the marshy region along the neck, or
performed some related service, for the dedication on the teapot acknowledges his assistance to the "proprietors" of Boston
Neck.

The teapot was probably purchased for Dall by one of these

proprietors. Fortunately, the Revere daybooks record that one of their number, merchant Amasa Davis, purchased a twenty-ounce silver teapot in 1797, the same year as that inscribed on the teapot. Davis was a good customer of Revere, having purchased canns, many teaspoons, ladles, porringers, and a tankard beginning in 1783, and he would have been a likely person to find a suitable gift of thanks for Dall. The current weight of this teapot is six pennyweight less than that recorded by Revere, a minor difference explained by years of polishing and the drying out of the handle.[2]

The fluted teapot is executed in Revere's signature style of the mid-1790s. Its elliptical design, made possible with the use of sheet silver, allowed him to produce this new and elegant shape with relative ease and consistency. The vessel found favor in the greater Boston area, for Revere produced at least seventeen examples for patrons as far west as Worcester.[3]

Description: The fluted elliptical teapot is made of sheet silver and seamed along the handle; the joints are pinned. The vessel has a slender, seamed, cone-shaped spout attached close to the base and an elliptical lid that is slightly domed above the flat shoulder. A tall pinecone/pineapple finial completes the lid. Angled sockets, circular in section and scored at their edges, hold a replaced wooden handle that has been pinned in place. A thick strengthening band of silver on the base follows the fluted perimeter of the vessel and protects the engraved text from wear. Banded and swagged decoration is strung along the base and below the shoulder.

History: Made a gift to William Dall (1753–1829), whose first wife was Mary Parker (1763–1783), m. 1781. The teapot descended in a patrilineal line through five generations, beginning with their son James Dall (1781–1863) of Baltimore, Maryland, and Henrietta Austin (1781–1866), m. 1812; to their son Rev. Charles Henry Appleton Dall (1816–1886) and Caroline Wells Healey (1822–1912), m. 1844; to their son William Cranch Healey Dall (1845–1927) and Annette Whitney (1859–1943), m. 1880; to their son Charles Whitney Dall (1881–1972) and Emily Marshall Maurice (1887–1975), m. 1911;[4] to their son Charles Whitney Dall Jr. (1913–1982), who bequeathed it to the Museum.

Exhibitions and publications: Paul Revere 1988, 160, cat. no. 69; Kane 1998, 838–39.

NOTES TO THIS ENTRY ARE ON PAGE 225.

172

Attributed to Paul Revere II (1734–1818)
Coffeepot

Boston, Massachusetts, 1798
Marion E. Davis Fund
2000.826

H. 12 in. (30.5 cm); W. 11½ in. (29.2 cm); D. 6½ in. (16.5 cm); Wt. 35 oz 16 dwt 11 gr (1114.2 gm)

Marks: None.

Inscriptions: "WHS" in entwined script within a buckled medallion engraved on side.

CLOSE STUDY of the engraving on this elegant, but unmarked, coffeepot, combined with its history of ownership, strongly suggests that the vessel was almost certainly produced by the shop of Paul Revere.

The distinctive acorn-and-leaf decoration also appears on at least six other examples of early American silver. A sugar urn, two bowls, and two teapots bearing this design are marked by Revere. A large urn-shaped coffeepot, marked by Nathaniel Austin, is the sixth example. Made for President John Adams, Austin's first cousin by marriage, and his wife, the former Abigail Smith, the Austin coffeepot was also probably made by Revere.[1]

The Revere bowls share two common elements with the coffeepot. In addition to a bowknot, the bowls display the unusual device of a buckled medallion encircling the owner's initials, a feature reminiscent of the Most Noble Order of the Garter, an English heraldic emblem that is found on no other colonial New England silver. Along with the coffeepot, the bowls, sugar urn, and teapots have nearly identical engraving styles; the Adams coffeepot exhibits less assured engraving of the acorn border.

The initials on this coffeepot probably stand for William and Hannah (Carter) Smith, who purchased quantities of silver through Nathaniel Austin, their cousin by marriage. Curiously, however, Austin produced little hollowware. Surviving bills of sale from Austin to William Smith document that a variety of tea equipage was "bot of Nathl Austin." The Revere daybooks prove that it was Revere who supplied the finished work, although in some cases it was marked by Austin using his own touchmark or that of his uncle, Josiah Austin.[2] By extension, the Adams coffeepot can be attributed to Revere.

The MFA coffeepot may be the same one listed in a receipt signed by Nathaniel Austin on October 22, 1798, accepting payment of $81 from William Smith for a "Coffee Pot."[3] Although there is no corresponding record in Revere's daybooks (the silversmith did not always enter work into his log), it is likely that, based on the engraving and known working relationship between Revere and Austin, the pot was also made by Revere.

Indeed, Revere was the leading maker of coffeepots in eighteenth-century Boston. The form gained popularity during the Revolution, when resistance to the tax on tea prompted colonists to change beverages. From the time of the Townsend Acts in 1767 until the end of the war in 1783, Revere made at least seven coffeepots. Following the war, the taste for coffee continued, as evidenced by this example, the closely related Adams pot, and at least five others. These late examples included retardataire double-bellied forms with Neoclassical engraving, one elegant and elongated variant thereof (cat. no. 169),

and one urn-shaped Neoclassical form with a pineapple finial, which was made for David Greene of Boston.[4]

Description: The raised coffeepot is urn shaped and has a reeded rim, concave neck, and reeded shoulder. The detached circular lid with a flange has a shallow dome and a spherical finial peened in place. The slender S-curved spout extends from the base of the urn and has a long lower lip. The upper handle socket has a stylized petal design; the lower socket is circular in section. The tiger-maple handle is a replacement. The splayed circular foot has a stepped edge with reeded banding. Bright-cut wavy lines frame a repeating band of acorns and leaves, which encircles the top of the urn. Wavy ribbons crown a buckled medallion on each side of the vessel.

History: The coffeepot was made for William Smith (1753/55–1816) of Boston and his wife, Hannah Carter (1764–1838), m. 1787.[5] It descended to their daughter Elizabeth Storer Smith (1789–1859) and her husband, Boston merchant Edward Cruft (1776–1866), m. 1810. It then likely descended to their daughter Harriet Otis Cruft (d. 1913), d. unm., who was a benefactor of the Museum and owner of other pieces of the Smith-Carter family wedding silver.[6] It then passed to one of her nieces, either Eunice McClellan Cruft (1872–1939) or Francis Cordis Cruft (1874–1941), both d. unm.[7] The next owner was their niece Anita Chandler Hinkley (b. 1911) and her husband, Charles F. Hovey, who consigned it to Shreve, Crump, and Low in Boston about 1970.[8] It was purchased by Gebelein Silversmiths of Boston before 1984 and acquired from them by the Museum in 2000.

Exhibitions and publications: Antiques 152, no. 6 (December 1997), 808.

NOTES TO THIS ENTRY ARE ON PAGE 225.

173

Paul Revere II (1734–1818)

Creampot

Boston, Massachusetts, about 1800
Gift of Robert A. Lawrence
1991.1037

H. 6 in. (15.3 cm); W. 5⁵⁄₁₆ in. (13.5 cm); D. 3 in. (7.5 cm); Wt. 7 oz 13 dwt 21 gr (239.3 gm)

Marks: "REVERE" in rectangle struck on base.

Inscriptions: "BEW" sprigged entwined monogram engraved below spout.

THIS EXAMPLE represents yet another variant on the cream pitcher produced in Revere's shop. It echoes the shape of the

173

174

Paul Revere II (1734–1818)

Pitcher

Boston, Massachusetts, about 1805
Gift of William Westfall
1991.1093

H. 5⅝ in. (14.3 cm); W. 6⅞ in. (17.4 cm); D. 4⅜ in. (11.2 cm);
Wt. 12 oz 8 dwt 6 gr (386.1 gm)

Marks: "REVERE" in rectangle struck on bottom.

Inscriptions: "L" in script engraved on front.

larger Revere pitchers that have become an icon of that colonial establishment.

Description: An elliptical seamed form, this pitcher has a swelling midsection that rises to an upturned spout with an applied and molded rim. A squared, ribbed strap handle rises vertically from the rim; its attenuated lower section is soldered to the body. An applied foot ring provides added reinforcement. An old repair to handle is evident at its juncture with the rim.

History: According to family history, the engraved initials refer to the original owner, Benjamin E. West (1792–1822) of Boston, m. Elisa Ann Jarvis (1797–1856) in 1817. It descended to their daughter Harriett Jarvis West (1820–1909), m. John Kuhn Fuller (1816–1905) in 1840. One of their children, Annie, m. Edward Lawrence Jr.; by descent to their son Edward Lawrence (d. 1957); by descent to his son Robert A. Lawrence. Placed on loan to the Museum in 1973 from Mr. and Mrs. Robert A. Lawrence and made a gift in 1991.

Exhibitions and publications: Kane 1998, 814.

PITCHERS OF THIS FORM, modeled after creamware examples imported from England, have become closely associated with the workshop of Paul Revere. At least fourteen known examples survive, of which this is an intermediate-sized version, larger than the smaller but related cream pitchers (see cat. no. 173) and the larger examples of the water pitcher.

Description: This small pitcher with curved sides is in the standard "barrel" form. Made of rolled and seamed sheet silver, it has an applied triangular spout opposite its applied, hollow, C-shaped handle.

History: Early history unknown. Placed on loan to the Museum by Miss Helen L. Adams in 1911; transferred to Mrs. William West in 1919; acquired by inheritance in 1962 by the donor, William Westfall of Montclair, New Jersey, and later Hudson, Ohio, and made a gift to the Museum in 1991.

Exhibitions and publications: Fairbanks 1991, 107, cat. no. 887; Kane 1998, 819; Falino and Ward 2001, 159.

175

Joel Sayre (1778–1818) or
John Sayre (1771–1852)
Cruet stand with glass bottles

New York, New York, about 1802–18
Gift of Mrs. Llora Bortman in memory of her late husband, Mark Bortman
1974.456

H. 9⅜ in. (24 cm); W. 8⅞ in. (22.5 cm); D. 6¹¹⁄₁₆ in. (17 cm); Wt. 29 oz 10 dwt 22 gr (919.0 gm)

Marks: "J.Sayre" in shaped rectangle struck twice on base, on each side of center column wing nut. "F." in square on one side. "F." in square on either side, with three pseudohallmarks consisting of a head, lion passant, and "D," each in shaped rectangle.

Inscriptions: None.

Armorials: Crest of a knight's arm raised holding a sword on a torse engraved on plaque attached to one side of the base.

SEPARATING THE WORK of brothers Joel and John Sayre is complicated. The division adopted here is based on the categorization of marks by Louise Conway Belden, who also noted that the two men may have used the marks interchangeably.[1] Thus, this cruet stand and two objects that follow (cat. nos. 176–77) should probably be considered as the work of either brother.[2]

Cruet stands are relatively rare in American silver. In the colonial period, most examples were imported, probably due to their complicated construction.[3] Early cruets were usually fitted with only two glass bottles for oil and vinegar. By the early nineteenth century, examples like this one commonly contained multiple spaces for glass containers. This stand originally held eight containers in three different sizes. The bottles probably held such condiments as soy, mustard, lemon, ketchup, pepper, cayenne, and other ingredients in addition to the traditional oil and vinegar.

Description: The stand, assembled from sheet soldered together, consists of a base, rectangular with rounded corners, supported by four cast and applied paw feet. A small oval plaque with engraved crest is applied to one side of the base.

Applied to the base are the carrying handle and the support system for six glass bottles. This system has a center column rising to the oval pierced handle, which is decorated with cast and chased leafage; the threaded column pierces the base and is secured with a wing nut underneath. At the top of the column, just below the handle, curved strips flare out and then down and are also secured to and through the sides of the base and underneath with wing nuts. At each side of these strips, three open rings are applied in line and conjoined; those on one side are larger than the three on the other. On the side with the larger rings, two small additional rings are soldered on either side of the center ring. Two of the faceted glass bottles are fitted with perforated silver lids, the others with glass stoppers (one stopper is missing, and one appears to have been cut to accommodate a spoon). The bottles designed to fit the small rings are missing.

History: Early history unknown; given by Llora Bortman in memory of her late husband, noted American silver collector Mark Bortman.

Exhibitions and publications: None.

NOTES TO THIS ENTRY ARE ON PAGE 225.

176

Joel Sayre (1778–1818) or
John Sayre (1771–1852)

Five-piece coffee and tea service

New York, New York, about 1821
Gift of Anne Sims Morison in memory of My Mother,
Mrs. William S. Sims
1994.293.1–5

Coffeepot (1994.293.1): H. 9¾ in. (24.8 cm); W. 12½ in. (31.8 cm); D. 4¼ in. (10.8 cm); Wt. 36 oz 10 dwt 2 gr (1135.4 gm)

Teapot (1994.293.2): H. 8¼ in. (21 cm); W. 11 in. (27.9 cm); D. 3¾ in. (9.5 cm); Wt. 24 oz 12 dwt 11 gr (765.9 gm)

Teapot (1994.293.3): H. 7½ in. (19.1 cm); W. 10 in. (25.4 cm); D. 3⅜ in. (8.6 cm); Wt. 21 oz 17 dwt 1 gr (679.7 gm)

Sugar bowl (1994.293.4): H. 7½ in. (19.1 cm); W. 8 in. (20.3 cm); D. 3¼ in. (8.3 cm); Wt. 18 oz 13 dwt 15 gr (581.1 gm)

Creamer (1994.293.5): H. 6⅜ in. (16.2 cm); W. 6 in. (15.2 cm); D. 2⅝ in. (6.7 cm); Wt. 10 oz 9 dwt 1 gr (325.1 gm)

Marks: "J. Sayre" in script in shaped cartouche struck on underside of each.

Inscriptions: "A E H" in shaded Old English capitals engraved, possibly later, on side of each vessel. Scratch weight of "24 [?]" on bottom of one teapot (1994.293.2); "22oz9" on bottom of other teapot (1994.293.3); "37oz6" on bottom of coffeepot.

THIS FIVE-PIECE TEA SET descended through four generations of the same family, from its original owners to its donor, and was a treasured, frequently used heirloom. Family members had distinguished careers in the law and in the Navy. [1] According to family history, the set was made for a wedding in 1821, suggesting that it may be the work of John Sayre, as opposed to his brother Joel, who died in 1818. However, the mark on the set is usually attributed to Joel. [2]

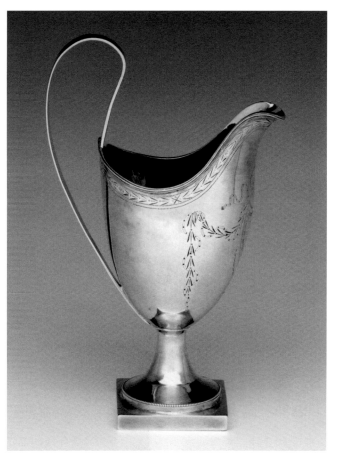

The set is distinguished by its imposing fluted form and its milled bands of gadrooning and oak leaves and grapes. Slightly lighter in feeling than later Empire forms, the set retains some of the flavor of earlier Federal forms. Its most distinctive feature, however, and the one that elevates it above the ordinary, is the superbly rendered cast terminals on the boldly curved handles. These eagle's-head ornaments reflect the Neoclassical emphasis on animal imagery and are seen on other examples of Sayre's work, including a closely related tea set made for John L. Woodworth of Albany, New York.[3]

Description: The coffeepot has a fluted paneled body with a milled band of oak leaves and grapes at the shoulder and a milled gadrooned border at the rim; the hinged lid has an oblong finial with a gadrooned rim; a plain, wrought, curved spout; a pedestal base with a conforming border; and a curved handle with wooden insulators terminating in an eagle's head. The two teapots are largely en suite. The sugar bowl has a separate unmarked cover and paired handles. The creamer has a flared lip and one handle; there has been a repair to the handle at the junction with the body.

History: Owned originally by Anne Erwin Hitchcock (1803–1854) and her husband, Henry Hitchcock (1792–1830), of Nashville, Tennessee, and Mobile, Alabama, probably at the time of their marriage in October 1821; descended to their son Ethan Allen Hitchcock and his wife, Margaret Collier, of St. Louis, Missouri; to their daughter Anne Erwin Hitchcock (1875–1960) and Adm. William S. Sims; to their daughter, the donor, Anne Sims Morison (b. 1914), in 1960.

Exhibitions and publications: None.

NOTES TO THIS ENTRY ARE ON PAGE 225.

177

John Sayre (1771–1852) or Joel Sayre (1778–1818)

Creampot

New York, New York, about 1800
Gift of Virginia N. Holly and Ruth N. McKittrick
1975.652

H. 8⅛ in. (20.7 cm); W. 5⁵⁄₁₆ in. (13.5 cm); D. 3 in. (7.5 cm); Wt. 7 oz 11 dwt 18 gr (236 gm)

Marks: "I [pellet] SAYRE" within a rectangle struck on side of squared foot, below spout.

Inscriptions: "JGAR" entwined sprigged initials, within a shield-shaped device, engraved below spout.

THIS SOMEWHAT LARGE CREAMER in the Neoclassical mode represents an addition to the forms in the collection by this New York maker(s).

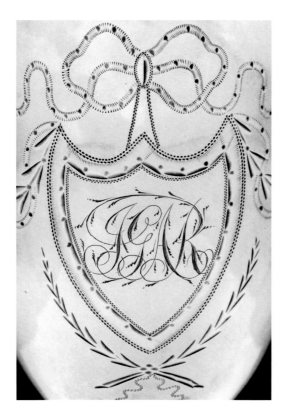

177

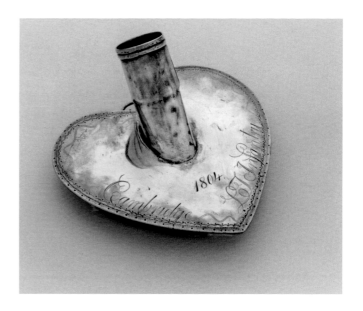

178

Unknown maker

Banner holder

Probably Boston, Massachusetts, about 1804
Gift of Lemuel Pope
1972.616

H. 4⁵⁄₁₆ in. (11 cm); W. 4⁵⁄₈ in. (11.7 cm); D. 2¹³⁄₁₆ in. (7.1 cm); Wt. 5 oz 18 dwt 4 gr (183.8 gm)

Marks: None.

Inscriptions: "Cambridge / 1804 / Lt. Infantry" engraved on top, at edge.

Description: The raised urn-shaped vessel has an elongated strap handle that rises above the spout and a round, splayed foot that, in turn, is soldered to a square plinth. Fine beading has been soldered to an applied rim and at base of a splayed foot ring. Bright-cut engraving of stylized foliage runs below the lip. A shield surrounding the monogram is surmounted by bowknot and swags; crossed palms with ribbon are below. Several dents appear on the body, to the left of the handle. The handle attachment at rim appears clumsy but is probably original.

History: If one accepts the letters "GA" in the initials "JGAR" as those of one individual rather than two, then the family history of descent in the Read (or Reed) family may be correct. The first owners were probably John and Glorianna Reed (or Read), m. about 1790; by descent to the donors.

Exhibitions and publications: None.

A RARITY IN AMERICAN SILVER, this banner holder was presumably made for a member of the Cambridge Light Infantry, a local militia unit that traces its origins to the seventeenth century.[1] Although unmarked, it was probably made in the Boston area. It is one of only two such examples in the Museum's collection.

The other (06.2402) is crescent shaped and has a brass back plate; it is engraved "The Property of the Housewrights of the Town of Boston" and bears the date 1816. The Society of Housewrights of the Town of Boston, founded in 1804, was a fraternal mutual-aid organization comprised of members of the building trades, including carpenters and architects. Members included Asher Benjamin, Solomon Willard, Ithiel Town, and Alexander Parris, among many others. It dissolved in 1837.[2]

Description: This heart-shaped banner holder retains its original padded leather backing, with a ring at the top for a leather shoulder strap. A single socket protrudes to hold the shaft of a banner pole or flagpole. There is a chased and punched geometric border.

History: According to family history and tradition, the original owner was Lemuel Pope (1777–1851) of Cambridge, Massachusetts. It descended in the family to the eponymous donor of Washington, D.C.

Exhibitions and publications: None.

NOTES TO THIS ENTRY ARE ON PAGE 225.

179

Thomas H .Warner (1780–1828) and Andrew Ellicott Warner (1786–1870)

Presentation sword and scabbard

Baltimore, Maryland, about 1805–12
William N. Banks Foundation
1973.481

L. 39 in. (99.1 cm); Wt. 58 oz 16 dwt 17 gr (1830 gm)

Marks: "T [pellet] & A [pellet] E [pellet] WARNER" within rectangle struck on underside of cross guard, and with an eagle's-head mark in a rectangle.

Inscriptions: "Liberty and Independence" engraved on one side of blade; "E PLURIBUS UNUM / 1783" on the other.

ALTHOUGH MANY American silversmiths are known to have made swords, relatively few have survived. This presentation or commemorative dress sword (or saber), complete with a rare silver scabbard, can be dated within the working years of the well-known and prolific Baltimore partnership of brothers Thomas and Andrew Warner.[1]

According to family history, the sword was owned by a member of the Van Deventer family, either Peter, who served with the New Jersey militia during the Revolution and was active during the War of 1812, or his son Christopher, a West Point graduate who fought with distinction in the War of 1812.[2] The engraved date of 1783 probably refers to the signing of the Treaty of Paris, and the nationalistic and classical emblems mark it as a product of its time.

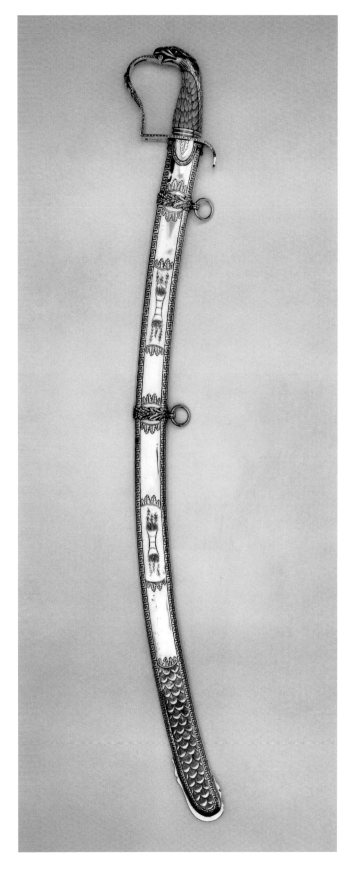

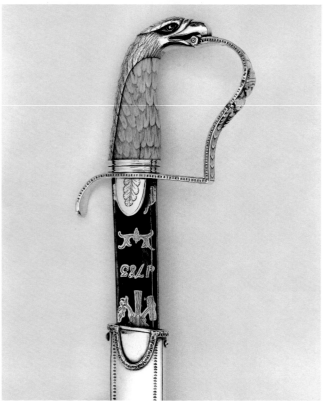

In a detailed, unpublished analysis of a related sword in the colletion of the Museum of Early Southern Decorative Arts, Gary Albert presents a subtle case study of the use and origin of such weapons, including the possibility that they were imported (in whole or in part) from Britain or France by the Warners. Albert suggests that the blades of the MESDA and MFA examples, in any event, were probably produced in Solingen, Germany.[3]

Description: This large sword has an eagle-head handle. The silver scabbard is engraved with a Greek fret border, overlapping eagle feathers at the end, and two passages of bundled lightning bolts between oak leaves. Two applied bands of holly leaves hold silver rings from which to hang the sword. The eagle's neck feathers on the handle are carved ivory, and the head is cast. A scroll handle, with a female head on the outside, emanates from the bird's beak. Each side of the steel blade is blued and etched in gilt. One side is inscribed with the motto "Liberty and Independence" and an arm wielding a sword. The other side is inscribed with "1783" and the motto "E PLURIBUS UNUM" and is decorated with an American eagle.

History: Probably made for Peter Van Deventer (1755–1837) or his son Christopher (1788–1838); by descent in the family; purchased from Firestone and Parson, Boston, in 1973.

Exhibitions and publications: Fairbanks 1981, 629, pl. 44; Fairbanks 1991, 92, cat. no. 50.

NOTES TO THIS ENTRY ARE ON PAGE 225.

180

Samuel Waters (active about 1803–1823)
Spoon

Boston, Massachusetts, about 1823
Gift of the First Church in Malden, Congregational
1991.500

L. 7 in. (17.7 cm); W. bowl 1½ in. (3.8 cm); Wt. 14 dwt 23 gr (23.3 gm)

Marks: "S W" within a serrated rectangle partially struck on back of stem.

Inscriptions: "First Church / Malden 1823" in flowing sprigged script engraved on top of handle.

SAMUEL WATERS is an obscure Boston silversmith who was active in the early nineteenth century.[1] He was apprenticed to Benjamin Burt and inherited Burt's tools in 1805.[2] Among other

180

objects known by him are a tankard (on loan to the MFA) and a creampot in the Chrysler Museum.[3] In some Congregational churches, silver spoons were used to add a few drops of water to the communion wine, following an Anglican practice.[4]

Description: The fiddlehead-style spoon has a pointed egg-shaped bowl with squared shoulders and a downturned tip.

History: In the collection of the First Church, Congregational, in Malden, Massachusetts, until given to the Museum in 1991.

Exhibitions and publications: See appendix 5.

NOTES TO THIS ENTRY ARE ON PAGE 225.

Notes

135

1. On camp cups, see Stephen Decatur, "Washington's Camp Silver, Pewter and Tin," in *American Collector*, republished in *Treasury of Old Silver* (Toronto, Can.: George J. McLeod, 1947), 90–91; Rollins 1991, 207, cat. no. 207.

2. Quimby 1995, 328.

3. For Sargent's military history and patronage of Revere, see Frances B. Heitman, *Historical Register of Officers of the Continental Army during the War of the Revolution, April, 1775 to December, 1783* (1914; reprint, Baltimore, Md.: Genealogical Publishing Co., 1982), 13, 481, 819–20. For correspondence between Winthrop and Gen. Lincoln, Philadelphia, June 17, 1783, and E. Boudinot, Philadelphia, August 10, 1783, see Records of the Continental and Confederation Congresses and the Constitutional Convention (record group 360), M247: Papers of the Continental Congress, 1774–1789, 3p, M247, r102, i78, v21, p311, and 4p, and M247, r102, i78, v21, p315. See also

Revere daybooks, 1:31–32, 45, 48, 53–54, 60, 62, 68, 69, 75; and Bradford Adams Whittemore, *Memorials of the Massachusetts Society of the Cincinnati* (Boston: Massachusetts Society of the Cincinatti, [1964]), 521–22.

4. A cup made for Washington by Edward Milne of Philadelphia is illustrated in *The Walpole Galleries*, sale no. 146, April 7, 1920, lot 50; Hammerslough and Feigenbaum 1958–73, 3:35–36, 4:58–59; Buhler and Hood 1970, 2:209, cat. no. 876; Parke-Bernet Galleries, sale 3265, November 12–13, 1971, lot nos. 338–89; "Mr. Custis' Collection," *The Mount Vernon Ladies' Association of the Union Annual Report 1980* (Mount Vernon, Va.: Mount Vernon Ladies' Association of the Union, 1981), 15–22.

5. Emma Worcester Sargent and Charles Sprague Sargent, *Epes Sargent of Gloucester and His Descendants* (Boston: Houghton, Mifflin, 1923), 48, 187.

136

1. Thanks to William Voss for amplifying life dates and relationships among these silversmiths, which were first published in Flynt and Fales 1968, 169–70, 181, 192.

2. Flynt and Fales 1968, 169–70.

3. Hammerslough and Feigenbaum 1958–73, 3:80; Bohan and Hammerslough 1970, 104–6, pl. 80, 274, 266. Other examples are in the collection of the Yale University Art Gallery.

137

1. For Burnett, see "Silversmiths of Alexandria," *Antiques* 47, no. 2 (February 1945), 93–95, figs. 1–2; Hollan 1994, 34; Rollins 1991, cat. nos. 228, 230; Goldsborough 1983, 100–01, cat. nos. 65–66; Buhler and Hood 1970, 2:252, cat. no. 970.

2. See *Southern Silver, An Exhibition of Silver Made in the South Prior to 1860* (Houston: Museum of Fine Arts, Houston, 1968), fig. C–1–F.

3. *American Paintings in the Museum of Fine Arts, Boston*, 2 vols. (Boston: Museum of Fine Arts, 1969), 1:228, cat. no. 868, 2:291, fig. 459; *DAB* 19:508–9; Vinetta Wells Ranke, comp., *The Blackburn Genealogy with Notes on the Washington Family through Intermarriage* (Washington, D.C.: V. W. Ranke, 1939), 14, 24–27, 37. *A Century of Silver, 1750–1850* (Washington, D.C.: Associates of The Corcoran Gallery of Art, 1966), 15, cat. nos. 58–59; "Silversmiths of Alexandria," 93–95, fig. 2.

138

1. *A Century of Silver, 1750–1850* (Washington, D.C.: Corcoran Gallery of Art, 1966), 23.

2. Hammerslough and Feigenbaum, 1957–73, 3:64.

3. Cecil Hampden Cutts Howard, *Genealogy of the Cutts Family in America* (Albany, N.Y.: Joel Munsell's Sons, 1892), 86, 168; Lawrence Park, comp., *Gilbert Stuart, An Illustrated, Descriptive List of His Works* (New York: William Edwin Rudge, 1926), 1:248–50, 499, 3:121–22, pls. 202–3, 515.

139

1. *Masonic Standard* (New York) 17, no. 17 (April 27, 1912), 1.

2. Waters 2000, 297–98. A nearly identical teapot marked by Chitry is in a private collection; see department files, Art of the Americas. A less elaborate three-piece tea set, each piece with Chitry's mark, is in the Worcester Art Museum; see Buhler 1979, cat. nos. 128–29.

3. For another illustration of Gale's early four-part manufacturing logo, see Darling 1964, 82.

4. Waters 2000, 331–33.

5. Venable 1994, 20.

140

1. Buhler 1972, 2:529.

2. *Simple Elegance* 1998, 21.

3. Buhler 1972, cat. nos. 461–62.

4. Kane 1998, 670. For the two Loring/Churchill marked pitchers, see Hammerslough and Feigenbaum 1958–73, 4:30–31; and *Antiques* 101, no. 5 (May 1972), 756.

5. Boston Assessors Taking Books for 1808 Ward 11, p. 15; 1810 Ward 11, p. 29, Ward 12, p. 41; 1812 Ward 11, p. 24, Ward 12, p. 38.

6. Buhler 1972, cat. nos. 471, 473.

7. Boston Assessors Taking Books 1813, Ward 11, p. 24. Daniel Treadwell is never listed in the Boston Directory, nor is the partnership Churchill and Treadwell. Elizur/Eleazur Holyoke was listed in the Boston Directory beginning only in 1820, after Churchill died.

8. A number of other pieces bear the "Churchill & Treadwell" mark. See, for example, a bread dish with cover, made in 1815 for Christ Church, Boston, on loan to the MFA (340.26); a teapot identical to those in the Perry service but bearing no inscription, in the collection of SPNEA, illustrated in Berry B. Tracy, "Late Classical Styles in American Silver," *Antiques* 86, no. 6 (December 1964), 702; a porringer illustrated in *Antiques* 92, no. 6 (December 1967), 773; and an elaborate presentation covered vase dated 1816, illustrated in Cooper 1993, 175.

9. Cooper 1993, 175, fig. 131.

10. Kane 1998, 666–70.

11. Boston Vital Records, fiche 398–99, states that he died January 1, 1820; the cause of death was not noted. The *Columbian Centinel* noted "Major Jesse Churchill died in Boston, aged 46" (January 1, 1820). The inventory of Colonel Jesse Churchill's will, dated March 8, 1820, shows a value of $229.72; Suffolk County Probate Records, Boston, docket 26056. The flagons (188–189.52) and two beakers (186–187.52) are on loan to the MFA.

141

1. Other surviving pieces of the Perry service are a matching monteith (Perry National Monument, Put-in-Bay, Ohio); a wine decanter cooler (Mead Art Museum, Amherst College, Amherst, Mass.); a seven-piece tea service (Smithsonian Institution, National Museum of American History, 1985.0121.1–.7); seven tumblers (one pair, Museum of Fine Arts, Houston [B.91.36.1-2; see Warren 1998, 285–86]; one pair Peabody Essex Museum, Salem, Mass. [M23,294-5]; one each at the Perry National Monument, Put-in-Bay, Ohio, and the Bostonian Society, Boston, Mass. [84.125], and one auctioned at Christie's, New York, sale 7624, January 22, 1993, lot 78). Objects now missing from those listed in the *Columbian Centinel* (Boston), May 28, 1814, include a sword, a second cooler, a second pitcher, seventeen tumblers, and various "small pieces" not described.

2. For the origins and history of monteiths, see Jessie McNab, "Monteiths: English, American, Continental," *Antiques* 129, no. 2 (August 1962), 156–60.

3. Neither Daniel Treadwell nor the partnership "Churchill and Treadwell" was ever listed in the *Boston Directory*.

4. Standard of the New England Guards, Bostonian Society, 84.125, illustrated in Bostonian Society 1979, 72.

5. Warren 1987, 107.

6. Cooper 1993, 175.

7. Kane 1998, 274–76.

142

1. Flynt and Fales 1968, 164, 199, 352. See also Belden 1980, 132, 433.

143

1. Samuel Forbes Rockwell, *Davis Families of Early Roxbury and Boston* (North Andover, Mass.: 1932), 126, 128.

2. DAPC files record a pair of salt shovels, a single teaspoon, and a set of five teaspoons with Davis's mark. See also a communion plate on loan to the MFA (188.67).

3. In the 1820s Davis lived on Hancock Street, in Beacon Hill; at 11 Chestnut Street in the 1830s; and finally at 6 Otis Place.

4. Winsor 1881, 3:250–51.

144

1. See Flynt and Fales 1968, 206–7; Charles S. Parsons, *New Hampshire Silver* (n.p.: Adams Brown, 1983), 94–96.

2. Stephen Decatur, "The Drowne Silversmiths of Portsmouth," in Kurt M. Semon, ed., *A Treasury of Old Silver* (New York: Robert M. McBride, 1947), 53–54.

3. For a plain version and one featuring bright-cut engraving, see Parsons, *New Hampshire Silver*, 31.

4. Genealogical information on the early owners of the tongs is recorded in the Wingate family Bible in the Museum's collection.

145

1. For an elegant tea set by Dubois originally owned by Aaron Burr, see Ward and Ward 1979, 168.

2. See Donald L. Fennimore, *Flights of Fancy: American Silver Bird-Decorated Spoons* (Winterthur, Del.: Henry Francis du Pont Winterthur Museum, 2000) for an analysis of the making and decorating of these spoons; Philadelphia diesinkers are on 16–17.

146

1. Waters 2000, 309–11. Among related examples are a bowl by James Douglas of New York at Amherst College and an example made by Hugh Wishart of New York (private collection); see Deborah Dependahl Waters, "American Neoclassical Silver," in *Decorative Arts at Amherst College, Mead Museum Monographs* 3 (winter 1981–82), fig. 1, and department files, Art of the Americas.

2. Waters 2000, 309. See also Christie's, New York, sale 1129, October 9, 2002, lot 21.

147

1. Buhler 1972, 2:500; Buhler 1979, 54, cat. no. 70; Kane 1998, 470, notes that four apprentices, journeymen, or servants were recorded in the 1790 census of Stephen Emery's household.

148

1. For related wine cups, see MFA 1906, 61, cat. no. 120; MFA 1911, 55, cat. no. 489; Avery 1920, 128, cat. no. 229; Buhler 1979, 71, cat. no. 103; Johnson 1994, 52.

8. *DAB* 18:631–33, and Wyman Morill, "Daniel Treadwell, Inventor," *Atlantic Monthly* 32, no.192 (October 1873), 470–82; H. G. Pearson, *Son of New England* (Boston, 1932).

149

1. Flynt and Fales 1968, 217, 351.

150

1. For earlier and more detailed studies of the partnership, see Elizabeth Ingerman Wood, "Thomas Fletcher: A Philadelphia Entrepreneur of Presentation Silver," *Winterthur Portfolio* 3 (1967), 136–71; Fennimore 1971; Donald L. Fennimore, "Thomas L. Fletcher and Sidney Gardiner: The Stylistic Development of Their Domestic Silver," *Antiques* 102, no. 4 (October 1972), 642–49; Quimby 1995, 357–59, cat. nos. 347–51; Waters 2000, 2:341–43.

2. *Columbia Centinel* (Boston), November 9, 1808, cited in Fennimore 1971, 3. Sidney Gardiner's mother, Abigail Worth, was born in Nantucket and may have been the reason for his move to Boston.

3. Jones 1913, 88; Buhler 1979, 72, cat. no. 105; Falino and Ward 2001, 92, fig. 1; Fletcher and Gardiner bracelet, Massachusetts Historical Society, artifact no. 0730. The silver made for the Hadley church was probably made before their move to Philadelphia.

4. Fennimore 1971, 5.

5. Fennimore 1971, 5; *Columbia Centinel*, May 25, 1811; November 4, 1815. U.S. Federal Census, Pennsylvania 1840, 95.

6. Bayard Tucker, ed., *The Diary of Philip Hone, 1828–1851*, 2 vols. (New York: Dodd, Mead, 1889), 2:288–89, cited in Wood, "Thomas Fletcher," 166; Fennimore "Thomas L. Fletcher and Sidney Gardiner," 642. The firm was listed as Fletcher & Gardiner until 1836. Quimby 1995, 357.

7. For the Bayou Bend example and references to additional pitchers, see Warren 1998, 305.

151

1. Two of William Garrett Forbes's sons also became silversmiths, and Forbes was related to others as well. See Waters 2000, 324–26; and Patricia E. Kane, "A Silver Presentation Pitcher by John Wolfe Forbes," *Yale University Art Gallery Bulletin* (2001), 23–32.

2. Waters 2000, 325, cat. no. 165.

3. The same donor also gave the Museum a pair of sugar tongs (63.636) by the same maker and bearing the same mark and engraving. The collection also includes a ladle (42.122) by Forbes, engraved "GP" on the handle, that Kathryn C. Buhler also omitted from her catalogue of the collection published in 1972.

152

1. For Garrett, see Belden 1980, 184, and Buhler and Hood 1972, cat. nos. 893–95. For the prolific firm of Robert and William Wilson, see Belden 1980, 450.

2. Barbara Stern Shapiro, *Mary Cassatt: Impressionist at Home* (New York: Universe, 1998), discusses the tea set and other three-dimensional objects as they were used by the artist in her work; see esp. 36–37.

3. Frederick A. Sweet, *Miss Mary Cassatt: Impressionist from Philadelphia* (Norman: University of Oklahoma Press, 1966), 52.

153

1. Philip Hammerslough, "G. Greenleaf, Silversmith," *Antiques* 72, no. 6 (December 1957), 559.

2. Hammerslough and Feigenbaum 1958–73, 1:98, 2:6, 4:61; Flynt and Fales 1968, 234; *Simple Elegance* 1998, 41–42, figs. 31–33.

3. Hammerslough, "G. Greenleaf," 559. A third beaker that shares the same form is in YUAG (1993.96.55).

4. IGI batch no. 7220314, source call no. 0820495 (Sarah Gilbert Hammond); IGI film no. 456277 (William Palmer Tenney); Frederick Stam Hammond, *Histories and Genealogies of the Hammond Families in America* (Oneida, N.Y.: Ryan & Burkhardt, 1902), 281, 322, 356–57.

154

1. *Franklin and Marshall College Catalogue of Officers and Students, 1787–1903* (Lancaster, Pa.: Alumni Association, 1903), 33; Milton E. Flower, "The Hendel Brothers," *Made in Cumberland County: The First Hundred Years, 1750–1850* (Carlisle, Pa.: Cumberland County Historical Society, 1991), 12–15; Direct Date Capture, comp., War of 1812 muster rolls, roll box 97, roll exct. 602, roll record 74, drawn from the "Index to the Compiled Military Service Records for the Volunteer Soldiers Who Served During the War of 1812," M602, 234 rolls, Washington, D.C.: National Archives and Records Administration as accessed on Ancestry.com; Archives, Franklin and Marshall College, Lancaster, Pa. Hendel's birth date was kindly provided by Merri Lou Schaumann; see correspondence, December 20, 1998, department files, Art of the Americas.

2. Advertisement, *American Volunteer*, July 3, 1817.

3. Recorder of Deeds, Cumberland County [Pennsylvania], record book 1, vol. 1, p. 41 (September 16, 1826); the repair bill is cited in Flower, "Hendel Brothers," 13; Cumberland County Historical Society, acc. nos. 1982.004, 1986.024, 1988.051.001-02, 1996.022.

4. Flower, "Hendel Brothers."

5. Sotheby's, New York, sale 6589, June 23–24, 1994, lot nos. 172–73. The coffeepot is pictured on the cover of the auction catalogue. Seven teaspoons bearing the same initials as these are in a private collection. On Hendel, see Merri Lou Schaumann, *Silversmiths of Cumberland County, Pennsylvania, and Its Surrounds* (forthcoming).

6. See Fennimore, *Flights of Fancy*.

7. For genealogical sources, see department files, Art of the Americas.

155

1. Higbie and Crosby were originally attributed to the Boston area by Stephen G. C. Ensko, *American Silversmiths and Their Marks II* (New York: Robert Ensko, 1927), 40. Wendy A. Cooper reattributed the silversmiths to New York; see Dorothy E. Ellison, ed., "Collector's Notes," *Antiques* 110, no. 6 (November 1976), 936.

2. The technological advances that made milled banding possible also enabled some silversmiths to specialize in selling these elements to other makers. A die-rolled grapevine ornament made by Moritz Furst (b. 1792) of Philadelphia was used by Nicholas Bogert of Newburgh, New York, in an 1835 tea service (Christie's, New York, sale 6536, January 23, 1988, lot 71).

[**no notes on 156**]

157

1. Kane 1998, 665–75.

2. Buhler 1972, 2:486–87, cat. no. 435; Janine E. Skerry, "The Revolutionary Revere: A Critical Assessment of the Silver of Paul Revere," in *Paul Revere* 1988, 53–55. Benjamin Burt also produced fluted teapots.

3. Buhler 1972, 2:526–28, cat. nos. 468–70.

4. Warren 1998, 299–300, cat. no. M61.

5. "Jabez Hatch, Ancestry and Descendants," *NEHGR* 51 (January 1897), 36–37; H. Hobart Holly, comp., *Descendants of Edmund Quincy, 1602–1637* (Quincy, Mass.: Quincy Historical Society, 1977), 21–22.

6. IGI film no. 447825, ref. no. 51348; film no. 455760, film no. 447870, ref. no. 36708.

7. *Vital Records of Ipswich, Massachusetts, to the End of the Year 1849* (Salem, Mass.: Essex Institute, 1910), 224; Herbert Freeman Adams, *The Compendium of Tufts Kinsmen* (Boston: Tufts Kinsmen Project, 1975), 216; Massachusetts Vital Records: Index to Births in Massachusetts 1876–1880, 304:209; Deaths 1973, 23:541; 1992, cert. no. 033254; Marriages 1909, 586:462; 1938, 60:253.

158

1. For a related pair by Hugh Wishart of New York, see Rollins 1991, cat. no. 232. For a discussion of the form and references to an example by Thomas Fletcher of Philadelphia, see Warren 1998, 314–15.

159

1. Martha Gandy Fales, "Silver in Old Newbury," *The Newburyport Maritime Society Antiques Show,* exh. cat. (Newburyport, Mass., 1981), 27. See also Buhler 1979, 59–61; *Simple Elegance* 1998, 21–22.

2. Buhler 1972, cat. no. 462. Another presentation pitcher made by Moulton in 1808 in varying form is discussed in Hammerslough and Feigenbaum 1958–73, 4:10–11.

160

1. Wendy A. Cooper, "The Furniture and Furnishings of the Farm at Danvers," *Museum of Fine Arts, Boston, Bulletin* 81 (1983), 24–45; the nutmeg grater is discussed on 43–44.

2. For a discussion of the form, see John D. Davis, *The Robert and Meredith Green Collection of Silver Nutmeg Graters* (Williamsburg, Va.: Colonial Williamsburg Foundation in association with the University Press of New England, 2002); barrel-shaped graters are discussed and illustrated on 26–27. Elizabeth B. Miles, *The English Silver Pocket Nutmeg Grater: A Collection of Fifty Examples from 1693 to 1816* (privately printed, 1966), esp. 36–37.

3. A special issue of the *Museum of Fine Arts, Bulletin* 81 (1983) is devoted to a discussion of the Derby-West family and the contents of their mansion called Oak Hill, three rooms of which are in the Museum's collection.

161

1. Fairbanks 1975, 197.

2. The same donors gave two other Revere tablespoons, and they may have descended in the same unknown family. One (1973.623) is engraved "V / IR" in block letters and is marked with the "[pellet] REVERE" mark; the other (1973.624) is engraved with the initials "PV" in script on handle and the "REVERE" mark.

162

1. Buhler and Hood 1970, 1:189–90, cat. no. 244; Buhler 1972, 2:420, cat. no. 368; Kane 1998, 838.

2. Fairbanks 1975, 187–88, cat. nos. 288–89.

3. Buhler and Hood 1970, 1:187–90, cat. no. 243.

163

1. Revere daybooks 1:59–63; 66, Jeannine Falino, "'The Pride Which Pervades thro every Class': The Customers of Paul Revere," in Falino and Ward 2001, 172.

2. Buhler 1972, 2:394–95, cat. no. 344.

3. Lawrence Park, comp., *Gilbert Stuart, An Illustrated, Descriptive List of His Works* (New York: William Edwin Rudge, 1926), 2:534–38, cat. nos. 561–63; Gilbert Stuart, *Mrs. Perez Morton (Sarah Wentworth Apthorp)*, 1802, Museum of Fine Arts, Boston (acc. no. 39.681), in Carol Troyen et al., *American Paintings in the Museum of Fine Arts, Boston, Summary Catalogue* (Boston: Museum of Fine Arts, 1997), 265.

4. John Wentworth, *Descendants of Samuel Wentworth*, 3 vols. (Boston: Little, Brown, 1978), 1:519–24.

5. Emma Worcester Sargent and Charles Sprague Sargent, *Epes Sargent of Gloucester and His Descendants* (Boston: Houghton Mifflin, 1923), 184–88.

164

1. According to Bolton, the crest of the family is of "an armed sinister arm embow holding a knight's helmet, front open," as found on a creampot by Paul Revere II. A mustard pot and pair of salt cellars by French silversmith Marc-Etienne Janety, owned by Swan, are each engraved with this crest, with a crown beneath; on the reverse is the Swan crest displayed vert on a shield, three swans two and one; an unidentified French ladle has the same arms (MFA, acc. no. 21.1278–81). Although it is possible that James Swan used the crest on the Revere salt spoons as his own, it seems more likely that the crest belonged to another family that intermarried with his descendants. Bolton 1927, 160–61; Kane 1998, 814.

2. For Swan's portrait by Gilbert Stuart, see Troyen et al., *American Paintings in the Museum of Fine Arts, Boston.* On Swan's patronage of Revere, see Jeannine Falino, "'The Pride Which Pervades thro every Class': The Customers of Paul Revere," in Falino and Ward 2001, 173.

3. Revere daybooks, 2:8, 10, 40, 55.

4. Lawrence Park, comp., *Gilbert Stuart, An Illustrated, Descriptive List of His Works* (New York: William Edwin Rudge, 1926), 2:729–31.

5. General information on Swan's activities and his descendants are found in Jeffrey Munger, "Royal French Furniture in 18th-Century Boston," in Howard Creel Collinson, comp. and ed., *Versailles: French Court Style and Its Influence* (Toronto: University of Toronto School of Continuing Studies, 1992), 124–25.

165

1. Buhler 1972, 2:430–31, cat. no. 381; Mary Lou Thomas, "Name Research on Silver," *Silver Magazine* 21, no. 2 (March/April 1988), 16–17.

2. Buhler and Hood 1970, 1:191, cat. no. 248; Janine Skerry, "The Revolutionary Revere, A Critical Assessment of the Silver of Paul Revere," in *Paul Revere* 1988, 47. Bills of sale from Austin to Smith are cited in Kane 1998, 159–60; Revere daybook, 2:58, 59 (1787), 86, 87 (1790); department files, Art of the Americas. See also cat. no. 172 for an unmarked coffeepot made for this family that has been attributed to Revere.

166

1. Buhler 1972, cat. no. 381.

2. A pair is in the collection of the Fogg Art Museum, Cambridge, Mass., and one is in a private collection; see Kane 1988, 811; *Paul Revere* 1988, 161; *American Art at Harvard* (Cambridge: Fogg Art Museum, Harvard University, 1972), cat. no. 175.

3. Fairbanks 1975, cat. no. 338.

167

1. Revere daybooks, 1:61 (1781), 2:145, 149, 162 (1795); Kane 1998, 817.

168

1. Revere daybooks 2:123 (1792).

169

1. For a fuller-bodied pear-shaped coffeepot made by Revere in 1792, now in the Worcester Art Museum, see Buhler 1979, cat. no. 59.

2. Fairbanks 1981, 630.

3. The Museum owns a portrait by Gilbert Stuart of Hepzibah Clarke Swan (27.540).

170

1. For a closely related example, see Moore Collection 1980, cat. no. 143. For plainer examples, see Buhler 1972, cat. nos. 391, 403.

2. See Buhler 1972, cat. no. 412.

171

1. Dexter and Lainhart 1989, 34.

2. Revere daybooks, 1:74, 2:108, 116, 123, 130, 133, 136, 139, 161. For the teapot purchase, see 2:165.

3. Kane 1998, 837–40. See Janine E. Skerry, "The Revolutionary Revere, A Critical Assessment of the Silver of Paul Revere," in *Paul Revere* 1988, 53.

4. John William Linzee Jr., *The History of Peter Parker and Sarah Ruggles of Roxbury, Mass. and Their Ancestors and Decendants* (Boston: privately printed, 1913), 129–34.

172

1. Andrew N. Adams, *A Genealogical History of Henry Adams of Braintree, Mass., and His Descendants* (Rutland, Vt.: Tuttle, 1898), 398; Kathryn C. Buhler, ms. cat. of the Mark Bortman collection, department files, Art of the Americas; Buhler and Hood 1970, 1:196–97, cat. no. 256; Elisabeth Donaghy Garrett, *The Arts of Independence: The DAR Museum Collection* (Washington, D.C.: National Society, Daughters of the American Revolution, 1985), 24, 183, cat. no. 10; Rollins 1991, 348–51, cat. no. 220; Christie's, New York, sale 7492, June 17, 1992, lot 65; Christie's, New York, sale 9592, January 18–19, 2001, lot 341.

2. Buhler and Hood 1970, 1:191, cat. no. 248; Buhler 1972, 2:430–31, cat. no. 381; Mary Lou Thomas, "Name Research on Silver," *Silver Magazine* 21, no. 2 (March/April 1988), 16–17. For a creamer and a caster also by Revere, the creamer bearing the retail mark of Austin, see cat. nos. 165 and 166; Kane 1998, 158–62.

3. Receipt, Smith-Carter Papers, reel 4, Massachusetts Historical Society.

4. Kane 1998, 812–13. Benjamin Burt, the only other silversmith of Revere's generation to make coffeepots in any quantity, produced at least five between 1765 and 1780; see Kane 1998, 234.

5. "Necrology of Historic, Genealogical Society," *NEHGR* 35 (April 1881), 194; IGI Record v. 4.01, ref. no. 14704; FamilySearch™ Ancestral File v. 4.19, http://www.familysearch.org/AFN:K175-LR, AFN:K175-0G3; IGI Record v. 4.01, ref. no. 29682, batch no. M502201.

6. "Deaths," *NEHGR* 21 (January 1867), 79; Suffolk County probate records, docket no. 162516, vol. 1043:115; Malcolm Storer, *Annals of the Storer Family* (Boston: Wright and Potter, 1927), 48; Buhler 1972, 2:430, cat. no. 381 (this teapot carries the dual marks of Josiah Austin and Revere II). IGI Record v. 4.01, film no. 458358.

7. *Massachusetts Vital Statistics* 24 (1939): 434 (Eunice McClellan Cruft), 19 (1941): 224 (Francis Cordis Cruft).

8. Brown University, Alumni Necrology Record for Frank L. Hinckley, class of 1891; correspondence, department files, Art of the Americas.

[no notes on 173–74]

175

1. Belden 1980, 373–74.

2. Waters 2000, 385–90, provides the most comprehensive biographical information on the brothers.

3. Warren 1998, 311–12, discusses early examples of the form. A set comparable in date to the MFA stand and made by Garret Eoff of New York is discussed in Waters 2000, cat. no. 155.

176

1. The donor provided a four-page memorandum detailing the provenance and use of the tea set within her family, as their lives took them to locations throughout the country and the world; see department files, Art of the Americas.

2. See Waters 2000, 385–90.

3. See Louisa Bartlett, "American Silver," *Saint Louis Art Museum Bulletin* (winter 1984), 30–31.

[no notes on 177]

178

1. We are grateful to Brian Youmans of the Cambridge Historical Society for his assistance with this entry.

2. See Gerald W. R. Ward, "The Society of Associated Housewrights of the Town of Boston, 1804–1837" (seminar paper, Boston University, 1973); copy in department files, Art of the Americas.

179

1. For the partnership, see J. Howard Pleasants and Howard Sill, *Maryland Silversmiths, 1715–1830* (1930; reprint, Harrison, N.Y.: Robert Alan Green, 1972), 193–200; Wilbur Harvey Hunter, *The Warner Family: Silversmiths to Baltimore* (Baltimore: Peale Museum, 1971); and Goldsborough 1975, 198.

2. Christobelle Van Deventer, *The Van Deventer Family* (Columbia, Mo.: E. W. Stephens, 1943), 38–42.

3. Correspondence, Gary Albert to Gerald W. R. Ward, February 2006, departmental files, Art of the Americas.

180

1. Flynt and Fales 1968, 352, suggests that his name may have been Nathaniel Samuel Waters, and elsewhere (Kane 1998, 225) he is referred to as Samuel B. Waters.

2. Kane 1998, 225.

3. See Kane 1998, 245, n.19.

4. See Barbara McLean Ward, "'In a Feasting Posture': Communion Vessels and Community Values in Seventeenth- and Eighteenth-Century New England," *Winterthur Portfolio* 23, no. 1 (spring 1988), 11, n19.

CHAPTER 3

TRADITION AND INNOVATION IN THE MID-NINETEENTH CENTURY: GOTHIC, ROCOCO, AND OTHER REVIVAL STYLES

Jane L. Port

The silver industry in America transformed itself during the middle decades of the nineteenth century. Small workshops of the 1820s, run by one master, still echoed colonial-era practices. By the 1860s, however, those shops had been replaced with a giant industry dominated by a few large companies employing hundreds. Such dramatic changes to the structure of the industry were largely the result of specialization, such as Newell Harding's focus on the manufacture of flatware; technical advancements including William Gale's roller dies; and John Gorham's innovative division of factory labor and his adaptation of English steam-powered machinery for flatware production. The rise of large silver-plating companies from midcentury onward (a development not represented by the objects in this volume) and the discovery of vast amounts of native silver in the Comstock Lode and other mines in the American West also transformed the relationship between silver objects and consumer, as more people were able to own wares with at least a veneer of precious metal.

Changes on the shop floor were accompanied by shifts in business models, as production separated from marketing. Fashionable salesrooms were luxuriously outfitted with mahogany or walnut cases filled with shining silver and silver plate, gleaming gold watches, sparkling gemstones, rich jewelry, music boxes, and other specialty items. Patrons could count on a dizzying variety of local and imported goods (fig. 1). Shopping had become an experience to delight the senses as well as a mission to procure the furnishings necessary to create a comfortable, tasteful home. If a firm produced silverware or jewelry, its "manufactory" was located in either a nonpublic part of the building or a separate facility, where dirt and noise would not disturb patrons.

Through this period of transition in the flourishing retail market, silver remained the material most esteemed for use as presentation pieces both public and private, grand and intimate. This was a century in which celebrations of military conquests and personal triumphs were commemorated in silver.

The victories of the War of 1812 provided opportunities for the best silversmiths to create splendid objects for the glorification of heroes and the young country they represented. The firm of Fletcher and Gardiner, in Philadelphia (relocated from Boston), produced an elegant covered urn in the Neoclassical style for presentation to Capt. Isaac Hull. The urn towered more than 28 inches and boasted 502 ounces of silver.[1] In 1814 the citizens of Boston presented to naval hero Oliver Hazard Perry a service of more than fifty pieces made by Churchill and Treadwell (cat. no. 141).

The Museum's collection is particularly rich in Boston silver of the nineteenth century, an era that, until recently, has received little attention. As in New York, Philadelphia, and other urban centers, the city of Boston commissioned grand silver trophies from prominent local retailers of luxury goods. Jones, Lows & Ball contracted with Obadiah Rich, then Boston's most accomplished silversmith, to produce trophies for presentation to local hero Daniel Webster and Canadian businessman Samuel Cunard, who brought the first transatlantic mail steamship service to the city. These magnificent works served as advertisements that prompted countless orders for domestically scaled pitchers, salvers, and tea services often inscribed with business- or family-related testimonials. Successful businessmen and public figures of all types, and sometimes their wives, were rewarded with silver objects inscribed by grateful employees or associates (cat. nos. 205, 207). Along with bankers and ministers, the founders of a New Hampshire shoe manufactory, a Roxbury soap and tar factory, and a South Boston engine works are all memorialized on pitchers or tea services now in the museum's collection.

In the domestic sphere, silver often played a large and usually ceremonial role. Brides and grooms presented inscribed silver wine goblets to each other, and a complete tea and coffee service displayed on the family sideboard remained a badge of gentility and solidity. Family members purchased monogrammed silver rattles, cups, napkin rings, and flatware as pres-

JONES, BALL & COMPANY,
No. 226 Washington, and 1 Summer Street,
IMPORT

Clocks, Watches,

JEWELRY,

Watch Makers' Tools & Materials,

SILVER PLATED & BRITANNIA WARE,

BRONZE,

MANTEL & TABLE CANDELABRAS,

CUTLERY, MILITARY

—AND—

RICH FANCY GOODS.

Manufacture in a superior style of workmanship,

SILVER WARE,

AND FINE GOLD JEWELRY,

IN THE GREATEST VARIETY.

BOSTON.

GEO. B. JONES,
TRUE M. BALL,

BENJ. SHREVE,
SETH E. BROWN.

FIG. 1. Advertisement for Jones, Ball & Co. From Boston Directory (1852), p. 3. (See cat. no. 215.)

ent for children. The growing custom of entertaining at home resulted in the invention of dozens of innovative hollowware and flatware forms for familiar and new foods. Boston jeweler Albert L. Lincoln patented an improved macaroni server.[2] Specialized forms appeared on the market for the service and consumption of such novel items as oysters, asparagus, celery, sardines, and ice cream.[3]

By the late eighteenth century, silver production in New York and other cities along the eastern seaboard surpassed that of Boston. Nevertheless, Boston's silversmithing tradition continued as the city itself grew. Between 1790 and 1825, the city's population more than tripled from 18,038 to 58,277. Those swelling the populace included young men from New England's countryside and smaller towns who came to work, develop their skills, or apprentice with local craftsmen. Boston's established base of wealthy residents, bolstered by a growing middle class, offered a steady market for household and personal luxuries such as solid silverware, jewelry, and watches. The 1825 city directory listed twenty-five jewelers, fourteen individual silversmiths, and sixteen watchmakers. Of these, silversmiths Jesse Churchill (1773–1819), John B. Jones (1782–1854), and Jabez Baldwin (1777–1819) were important early-nineteenth-century successors to the colonial craftsmen. Although a few older gold- or silversmiths were still located on Ann and Fish streets in the North End, the center of Boston's life in the 1700s, by the 1820s silversmiths, jewelers, and watchmakers had moved their shops to the fashionable retail area of Washington and Court streets, where Churchill, Jones, and Baldwin all worked.

Boston's young smiths of the 1830s and 1840s were largely native-born New Englanders of British descent; a few were of European stock, and only one had trained abroad. This next generation learned their trade in shops such as those of Churchill, Jones, and Baldwin, where handwork done for a local clientele was still the rule. Local tradition assigns the apprenticeship of Quincy-born Lewis Cary (1798–1834) to Churchill's shop. Like Baldwin, silversmiths John J. Low (1800–1876) and George B. Foster (1810–1881) also came to Boston from Salem. Brothers Hazen (1790–1874) and Moses (b. 1793) Morse and Newell Harding (1796–1862) arrived from Haverhill, Massachusetts. Obadiah Rich (1809–1888), born just across the river in Charlestown and perhaps the most talented silversmith of his generation, is said to have apprenticed with Moses Morse, who may have apprenticed with Churchill. Henry Haddock (1811–1892) was born in Haverhill, moved with his family to Lynn, and was sent to apprentice with a Boston silversmith, perhaps one with ties to Haverhill. In 1844 Seth E. Brown (1821–1884) arrived in Boston from Concord, in southern New Hampshire, to finish his apprenticeship. Samuel T. Crosby, one of the city's prominent midcentury retailers, came from Milton, Massachusetts, in 1835 to apprentice with Jones, Lows & Ball, his future rival. In the 1850s, John R. Wendt (1826–1907), born and trained in Germany, became well known in Boston, though ambition eventually took him to the larger commercial world in New York City.

With the early deaths of Churchill and Baldwin in 1819 and Cary fifteen years later, the field was clear for such ambitious and talented smiths as Rich, Harding, and Haddock to participate in both the wholesale and retail trades. In the 1830s, established retailers like John B. Jones, as well as newer firms such as that of brothers John and Joseph Bigelow, were competing for the city's luxury trade in silverware, watches, jewelry, and other goods. Such competition was sharpened during the first exhibition of the Massachusetts Charitable Mechanics Association in 1837, when Jones, Lows & Ball exhibited the so-called Webster vase, "manufactured under their direction by Obadiah Rich . . . in size, design and execution . . . superior to any specimen of silverware before made in this city."[4]

The decorative arts of the mid-nineteenth century drew forms and imagery from an accumulated storehouse of the world's past civilizations. The revival and reinterpretation of classical, Gothic, and Rococo styles from the West were augmented by not only a wide variety of Eastern motifs but also the affection of Americans for those forms and decorations that had furnished the colonial past of their youthful nation.

FIG. 2. Detail, S. T. Crosby and Lincoln & Foss storefronts. From "Grand Panoramic View of the West Side of Washington Street," *Gleason's Pictorial* 4, no. 20 (May 14, 1853), p. 313.

Through the mid-1800s, silversmiths in Boston, like their colleagues in other cities, produced silverware in numerous styles ranging from chaste Neoclassical forms to those boasting the most elaborate and up-to-date Rococo curves and flourishes. Obadiah Rich was among the first of his generation to mine colonial forms and adapt them in his own work.

Until the 1859 discovery of the rich veins of the Comstock Lode in Nevada, raw material for silver flatware and hollowware production was supplied by European and American coins and old silver items, just as in the colonial era. American silver was generally marked with the maker's name but never with the guild mark that, in the British system, assured quality. Beginning around the early 1830s, however, the maker's name was often joined by terms such as "Standard" and "Pure as Dollars," referring to the quality of the metal based on the U.S. dollar (892.4/1000 before 1837 and 900/1000 thereafter). To denote quality, New England silversmiths most often adopted the phrases "Pure Silver Coin," "Pure Coin," or simply "Coin." The first known use of "Pure Silver Coin" appears on a gob-

let inscribed "North Church / Newburyport [Massachusetts] 1833" and marked "John B. Jones & Co." British sterling quality (925/1000) or better was advertised by some American silversmiths for their finest wares.[5] Rich marked some of his wares as "Fine," perhaps to indicate a higher silver content (cat. no. 226).

The 1820s and 1830s saw the growth of American retail shops selling imported and American-made luxury goods. In New York, Marquand & Co. opened its doors in 1823, and Tiffany followed in 1837. Both Bailey, Banks & Biddle and J. E. Caldwell & Co. were established in Philadelphia in the early 1830s. In Boston, John and Joseph Bigelow specialized in watches imported from Liverpool, England, and Geneva, Switzerland. The firm's business records from the 1830s illustrate their day-to-day wholesale dealings with other Boston retailers and manufacturers such as J. B. Jones, whom they supplied with watches, and Ebed Whiton, who provided them with coin-silver flatware. The Bigelows also supplied watches, jewelry, and music boxes to shops in small towns like Edgartown and Amherst, Massachusetts, and Bangor, Maine. The country's sluggish economy of the 1810s and 1820s had improved by the early 1830s, and the Bigelows' business appeared steady, if not as vibrant as they wished. The economy fell again, however, and the Panic of 1837 created a harsh economic climate that lasted into the early 1840s.[6] In 1840 the Bigelow brothers wrote to decline a further shipment of watches from a Liverpool supplier, citing slow business. By 1843 they reported that business had improved but was "nothing to boast of," but, later in the decade, they began to flourish. Between 1848 and 1852, local silversmith Henry Haddock supplied the firm with close to 650 pieces of unmarked hollowware. Ebed Whiton remained the major supplier of flatware, although firm records indicate that it purchased flatware and other silver for retail sale from New York makers Michael Gibney, Albert Coles, Ball, Black & Co., and Wood and Hughes.[7]

By midcentury Samuel T. Crosby left the Jones firm to form his own establishment, which advertised silverware from the shop of the celebrated Obadiah Rich. Crosby also retailed silver made by Vincent Laforme & Brother (cat. no. 222) and others, including John R. Wendt (cat. no. 237) (fig. 2). By 1850 Boston's population had more than doubled, to 136,881. The 1854 city directory still included fourteen listings for silversmiths, but at least seven were now partnerships of two or more men, most of whom retailed other luxury goods in their shops. In contrast, the listings for jewelers who manufactured or retailed (or both) jewelry, watches, and silverware had doubled, numbering about fifty. The listings for watchmakers doubled as well.

FIG. 3. Detail of silver salver made for the First Baptist Church, Boston, inscribed with the year "1857" and marked "Bigelow Bros. & Kennard" (retailer) and with Gothic "L" and eagle used by Laforme & Brother. Private collection; photograph courtesy Museum of Fine Arts, Boston.

Occasionally, a name could be found under more than one occupation, but most appeared only once.[8]

Partnerships, as well as internal trade among retail and wholesale suppliers of parts and finished and unfinished products, made it increasingly difficult to identify the manufacturer of articles often marked only by the retailer. For example, the same stamped, decorative bands that appear on several pieces of New York hollowware also appear on a pair of pitchers produced in Boston about 1828 (cat. no. 184). Similarly, after describing as "magnificent" the presentation vase that Jones, Ball & Poor made for Col. William P. Winchester, the judges at the 1850 Massachusetts Charitable Mechanics Exhibition complained that the firm's other wares "closely resemble Lincoln and Foss and [are] believed to be [the] products of [that] workshop."[9]

In other instances, some skilled individuals may have offered their talents to multiple workshops. For example, a number of Boston manufacturers and retailers used the services of an as-yet-unidentified engraver whose recognizable, lively Rococo-revival designs appear on numerous wares. One such case is a salver (fig. 3), marked by Laforme and retailed by Bigelow Brothers about 1857, that carries a dense design of finely controlled but rapidly curving and turning scrolls and curling foliage and flowers. A lighter, more playful design cascades down the side of a small tumbler marked by Newell Harding & Co. (cat. no. 205), and merry, glittering, bright-cut scrolls encircle the pear-shaped body of a water pitcher marked by Harding as well (cat. no. 207)

By the 1860s, the silverware manufacturing industry had consolidated into a few large firms in New England, New York, Maryland, and Ohio.[10] In southern New England, Gorham & Company and Reed & Barton had grown into large wholesale manufacturers. Tiffany & Co. and Ball, Black & Co. in New York; Samuel Kirk & Son in Baltimore; and the Duhme Company in Cincinnati all operated large manufactories. Through the third quarter of the nineteenth century, American retail firms increasingly purchased stock items from these large manufacturers either to augment their inventory or for presentation engraving or further embellishment in their own or local shops. A few small, independent manufacturing shops remained. Vincent Laforme's Gothic "L" and stamped eagle marks can be found on wares marked by Boston retailers Samuel T. Crosby and Bigelow Brothers & Kennard as well as Hyde & Goodrich in New Orleans. Toward the end of his career, however, repair and gilding became Laforme's specialties.[11]

The collection of mid-nineteenth-century silver in the Museum of Fine Arts, Boston, began with the gift in 1877 of a ewer marked by Tiffany & Co. (cat. no. 248). By that time, Tiffany was a major force among national silversmithing firms, and the ewer was the first piece of contemporary decorative arts to enter the collection. The donor was Gideon F. T. Reed, who had left an early partnership with Boston jeweler Albert L. Lincoln (Lincoln & Reed; active 1841–1846/47), to establish Charles L. Tiffany's Paris branch. In 1913 Caroline Borden of Fall River, Massachusetts, presented another piece of New York silver, a coffee urn by made by Cann & Dunn that was part of a service presented to her father about 1855 (cat. no. 182). The Museum acquired few revival-era silver objects during the first half of the twentieth century, when the zeal for colonial- and federal-era silver, and a general distaste for revival ornament and form, reigned. Although they became properly accessioned in 1964, the sugar bowl and creampot by Davis, Palmer & Co. and the tea service by Harris & Stanwood (cat. nos. 187 and 210) were first used by the Museum in the 1950s for receptions and tea parties. In the last twenty-five years, the trend has been reversed, and most well-known Boston makers are now represented in the Museum's collection. With these acquisitions, the networks and relationships between silver makers and retailers in Boston and the eastern United States raise as many questions as answers.

Notes

1. Cooper 1993, 240–41.

2. U.S. patent no. 15,266, July 1, 1856; see also D. Albert Soeffing, "More on Macaroni Servers," *Silver Magazine* 25, no. 2 (March/April 1992), 28–29.

3. Venable 1994, 128.

4. *Program for the First Triennial Exhibition of the Massachusetts Charitable Mechanics Association* (Boston: Massachusetts Charitable Mechanics Association, 1837), n.p.

5. Deborah Dependahl Waters, "From Pure Coin: The Manufacture of American Silver Flatware, 1800–1860," in Ian M. G. Quimby, ed., *Winterthur Portfolio 12* (Charlottesville: University Press of Virginia for the Henry Francis du Pont Winterthur Museum, 1977), 20–24.

6. Venable 1994, 19.

7. Bigelow, Kennard and Company, Records, 1830–1925, R.G. Dun and Co. Collection, Baker Library, Harvard University Graduate School of Business Administration. For day-by-day business with others in the trade, see Journal 1, January 1830–33, and Journal 6, June 1845–May 1846. For Henry Haddock, production, see vol. 65, 1848–52.

8. For discussions of Philadelphia and New York directory listings in the precious metals trade, see Martha Gandy Fales, *Jewelry in America, 1600–1900* (Woodbridge, Eng.: Antique Collectors' Club, 1995), 275, 287.

9. *Program for the Triennial Exhibition of the Massachusetts Charitable Mechanics Association* (Boston: by the association, 1850), "Metals" section.

10. Venable 1994, 22.

11. Skerry 1981, 14.

181

Gerardus Boyce (1795/96–1880)

Pitcher

New York, New York, about 1832
Edwin E. Jack Fund
1971.269

H. 12½ in. (31.7 cm); W. 9¹³⁄₁₆ in. (25 cm); D. 6½ in. (16.5 cm);
Diam. foot 5⅛ in. (13 cm); Wt. 42 oz 2 dwt 21 gr
(1310.8 gm)

Marks: "G. BOYCE" and "N [pellet] YORK," both within rectangles, struck on bottom of body, above and below center point.

Inscriptions: "Offered to Captain / Beekman / by / General Santander / from Colombia" in serif script engraved and centered under spout.

GEN. FRANCISCO DE PAULA SANTANDER of Colombia offered this classically proportioned pitcher to Capt. Henry Beekman of the American packet brig *Montilla* in thanks for a safe voyage from New York to Colombia. General Santander had been living in exile in New York from 1828 to 1832, when he was recalled to Colombia to become president after Simon Bolivar's death. Santander was a law student in his native land when he joined Bolivar's 1813 campaign to liberate New Granada (modern-day Colombia), Venezuela, and Ecuador. His success in preparing an advance base for Bolivar in New Granada earned him a place as vice president in Bolivar's new regime, with the understanding that he would rule the newly formed Gran Granada while Bolivar fought to hold together the union. However, differing political ideologies divided the two leaders, and Santander subsequently led the people's opposition to Bolivar's continuing foreign campaigns to enlarge his domain. In 1828 Bolivar declared himself dictator of New Granada; following an assassination attempt, he jailed Santander for complicity but later allowed him to go into exile.[1]

Presumably made about the time of Santander's departure from New York, this pitcher was intended for domestic use. Its inscription is discreetly placed within a broad wreath of leaves and fruit, below the spout. The vessel's surface is a study in light and dark. The dense floral pattern of the decorative bands and textured handle create a dramatic contrast to the pitcher's polished, curvilinear form.

Gerardus Boyce worked from about 1820 to 1857 at 101 Spring Street in New York City. Elisha Jones joined Boyce from 1825 to 1830, and the firm was then known as Boyce & Jones.

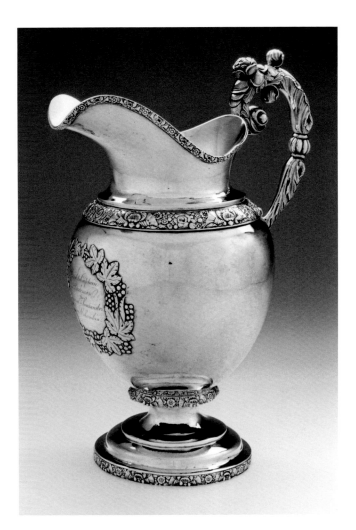

In 1835 Boyce moved to 110 Greene Street, where he remained for more than twenty years as the head of a small shop of five employees in 1850.[2]

Description: Stamped floral bands decorate the upper and lower rims and dress the joints between the raised bulb-shaped body, the domed and stepped foot, and the low-cut neck. The long and generous sweep of the spout balances the densely textured scrolled handle with a cabbage rose thumbpiece. The engraved inscription is wreathed by a repoussé and chased grapevine with neatly articulated fruit and leaves.

History: The history of the pitcher's ownership after Captain Beekman is unknown.

Exhibitions and publications: None.

NOTES TO THIS ENTRY ARE ON PAGE 309.

182

Cann & Dunn (active 1855–1857)
John Cann (active 1848–1867)
David Dunn (active 1848–1860)

Coffee urn

Brooklyn, New York, about 1855
Gift of Miss Caroline Borden
14.516a–b

H. 18½ in. (47 cm); W. 11³⁄₁₆ (28.5 cm); D. 11³⁄₁₆ in. (28.5 cm); Diam. rim 5⅛ in. (13 cm); Wt. 83 oz 1 dwt 13 gr (2584 gm)

Marks: Lion's head within an ellipse; "C & D" within a shaped lozenge; an arm and hammer within an ellipse, all struck on bottom of body, below center point.

Inscriptions: "To / Col. Richard Borden / As a Testimony of Esteem / From His Friends / George W. Quintard, Samuel Sneden / Bootman & Smith Joseph K. Comstock / E. V. Haughwout / Jackson & McDermott / August 1855" in a frontal reserve engraved on body, above spigot.

THIS SUMPTUOUS COFFEE URN was part of a six-piece tea and coffee service presented in 1855 to Col. Richard Borden (1795–1874), a Fall River businessman who earned his military rank during the War of 1812. He then began his career as a shipbuilder and founder of the Fall River Iron Works Company, organized in 1821. The company prospered and became the source of capital for the Fall River Steamboat Line, which became possible in 1845 with the establishment of the Old Colony railroad line from Boston to Fall River. Presented in 1855, this coffee urn and its accompanying pieces may have commemorated the date of Borden's decision to establish the steamship

line founded in 1847, which operated, in conjunction with the rail line, between Fall River and New York City until 1937. An elaborate scene of the Taunton River, bustling with steamboats and other water traffic set against the Fall River skyline, is engraved on the back of the urn, opposite the inscription.[1]

John Cann and David Dunn worked with Thomas Charters Jr. as Charters, Cann & Dunn from 1848 to 1854 on Frankfort Street in New York. When Charters departed, Cann and Dunn moved their shop to Jay Street in Brooklyn (see cat. no. 185), where they continued as Cann and Dunn from 1855 to 1857.[2] The earlier firm's three-part manufacturing logo featured a lion in the left position and the initials "C C & D" and an arm and hammer in the center and right positions. Cann & Dunn may have used the same three-part logo without the first "C" in the center position. The firm operated as a wholesaler specializing in hollowware for the trade. They were a popular source of presentation silver and esteemed for the quality of their work.[3]

Description: The bulb-shaped urn has a separate lid and scrolled foliate handles attached with split stem to the widest part of the body and curving up toward the extended neck. The urn's slender cylindrical stem broadens into a round base that sits on four cast shell and foliate feet. A hinged panel on the base provides access to the wick of the alcohol lamp, which twists in from below. The urn and base are elaborately decorated with a repoussé and chased design of panels, strapwork, and tassels above four large scroll-edged reserves for engraving and placement of the handles. Highly polished areas of the surface contrast with dark, heavily stippled surfaces and lighter areas, with a single curving line of stippling. The separate bezel-set domed lid is topped with a floral finial. The lid is fitted above a pierced silver ring to which is sewn a cloth filter to contain the ground coffee. To pour the beverage, the server lowers a scroll-shaped lever that loops above a spigot decorated with floral chasing.

History: The urn descended from Richard Borden (1795–1874) to his oldest child and only daughter, Caroline Borden (1829–1922), the donor.

Exhibitions and publications: None.

NOTES TO THIS ENTRY ARE ON PAGE 309.

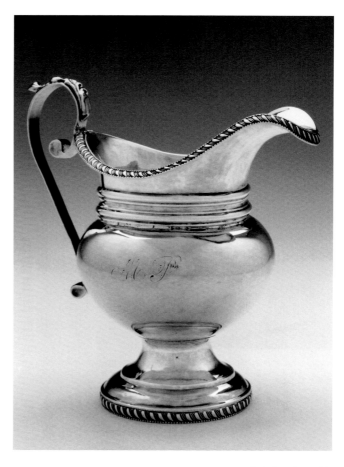

183

Lewis Cary (1798–1834)

Creampot

Boston, Massachusetts, about 1820–25
Gift of Mary B. Comstock
1981.354

H. 6¹³⁄₁₆ in. (17.3 cm); W. 6⁵⁄₁₆ in. (16 cm); D. 4⁵⁄₁₆ in. (11 cm); Diam. foot 3⅛ in. (8 cm); Wt. 9 oz 7 dwt 4 gr (291.1 gm)

Marks: "L. Cary" in roman letters struck within a serrated banner on bottom.

Inscriptions: "MP" in script engraved on side of vessel, to right of handle.

INSCRIBED "MP" for its original owner, Mary Porter, daughter of Dudley Porter of Salem, Massachusetts, this creampot may have been a bridal gift upon her marriage to Thomas Tileston in 1820. Tileston was born in Boston, where he first entered the printing trade. After a few years as editor of the *Merrimack Intelligencer* in Haverhill, Massachusetts, in 1818 he left with his family for New York City, where he became prominent in shipping and banking circles.[1]

During the early nineteenth century, the size of tea- and coffeepots, creampots, and sugar and slop bowls increased. Dainty creampots, previously large enough to hold only a few ounces, grew to almost pint-sized vessels such as this, capable of serving a large family or group. Manufactured using a combination of handwork and machine work, it exemplifies techniques common during this period. Cary laboriously hand raised the creampot's bowl and foot, with the sweep of the rim and wide curve of the urn-shaped body gathered in by the elegant detail of the ribbed neck.

Ornamental bands, such as the richly textured gadrooned ones encircling the rim and base, were made by various types of hand-operated pressing or stamping machines widely available to silversmiths. Produced in strips of varying widths, the bands could be cut to any length and soldered onto ornament to strengthen a rim or foot or to conceal a joint. Whether purchased from another shop or made in-house, these machined elements lowered the smith's production costs while raising profits.

The apprenticeship of Quincy-born silversmith Lewis Cary has long been assigned to the firm of Churchill & Treadwell (see cat. no. 141).[2] Boston tax records show that the firm had two apprentices in 1815, about the time Cary would have apprenticed.[3] Later, Cary was engaged to provide additional silver for Boston's West Church, whose early silver was made by Churchill. In 1814 Cary's sister Lucy (1790–1860) married Boston silversmith Hazen Morse (1790–1874), and, according to an 1856 account, Lewis Cary bought his brother-in-law's business in 1820, when Morse retired. However, Morse was only thirty years old in 1820 and apparently sold the silversmithing side of his business to his brother-in-law not to retire but to focus on a career as an engraver.[4]

Both Jesse Churchill and Jabez Baldwin died in 1819, and the unexpected loss of two of the city's leaders in the silver industry undoubtedly created opportunities for the youthful Cary. In 1821, owner of his own business, he married Adeline Billings in Dorchester, Massachusetts.[5] Cary is best known for the ecclesiastical silver he made for not only Boston churches but congregations as far away as Deerfield, Massachusetts, about ninety miles west.[6] Among a few surviving domestic forms from his shop are this cream pitcher, a large pair of presentation pitchers (cat. no. 184), and a three-piece tea set (1976.55–57) in the Museum's collection. A presentation pitcher dated 1827 is in the

collection of the Museum of Fine Arts, Houston. He also made an oval egg warmer with stand for a member of the Adams family.[7] Cary was admitted as a silversmith into the Massachusetts Charitable Mechanics Society in 1828.[8] Perhaps his most ambitious surviving work, the Lyman presentation pitchers of that year (cat. no. 184) may represent the summit of his career, for scarcely two years later he appeared in the Boston directory without occupation, and he died four years after that, at age thirty-six.

Description: The raised body is elliptical in form, with cylindrical neck and high-drawn spout. A strap handle curves above the rim. Stamped bands of gadrooned decoration encircle the rim and the stepped base.

History: Mary Porter (1797–1879) and Thomas Tileston (1793–1864), m. 1820; by descent to their daughter Clara Tileston (1827–1915) and her husband, William Bryce, m. 1849; by descent to their daughter Mary Tileston Bryce (1859–1953), d. unm.; bequeathed to her grandniece Mary B. Comstock.

Exhibitions and publications: None.

NOTES TO THIS ENTRY ARE ON PAGE 309.

184

Lewis Cary (1798–1834)
Pair of covered pitchers

Boston, Massachusetts, about 1828
Gift of Charles P. and Henry Lyman, and Richard Warren in Memory of Cora Lyman Warren
1991.249–50

1991.249: H. 12½ in. (31.8 cm); W. 11⅞ in. (30.2 cm); D. 7⁹⁄₁₆ (19.2 cm); Diam. base 5⅝ in. (14.3 cm); Wt. 56 oz 3 dwt 7 gr (1746.9 cm)

1991.250: H. 12½ in. (31.8 cm); W. 11¹¹⁄₁₆ in. (29.7 cm); D. 7¹³⁄₁₆ in. (19.8 cm); Diam. base 5⅝ in. (14.3 cm); Wt. 56 oz 16 dwt 11 gr (1767.4 cm)

Marks: "L. CARY" in roman letters within a rectangle struck on each neck, to left of handle.

Inscriptions: "Presented to / Brigadier General Lyman / by the Officers of the / Boston Brigade / May 1828" in script engraved below each spout. "Chosen / Brigadier General / February 17, 1823. / Resigned November 9th / 1827" engraved on each bottom.

THESE IMPRESSIVE PITCHERS were presented as a gift to Brig. Gen. Theodore Lyman Jr. upon his resignation from the Third Brigade of the First Division of the Ancient and Honorable

Artillery Company. The expansive size, in addition to the presentation of not one but a pair of grandly decorated vessels, underlines the importance of both the recipient and the occasion.

Like Cary's creampot (cat. no. 183), the Lyman pitchers were produced using handwork and machine work. The hand-raised, repoussé, and chased bodies, as well as the individually cast and cold-chased finials and handles, represent hours of labor. The wide and narrow die-rolled bands covering the junctures and rims of the pitchers are machined ornament that was readily available to the silversmith by the first decades of the nineteenth century.[1]

In contrast to the reserved gadrooned bands that quietly define the creampot's form, the bold floral bands of the pitchers compete for attention with their profiles. The remaining polished areas serve mainly as foils for the visually commanding ornament.

Description: The raised bulb-shaped bodies of these identical covered pitchers appear to nest within the four large repoussé and chased leaves that rise from the stem. A disk of silver carrying an additional inscription is inserted under each short-stemmed molded foot. Four die-rolled bands encrusted with floral ornament gird the base, rim, and joints of the pitchers. Each broad curved spout is set over plain piercings; the repoussé and chased domed cover is hinged at the back and finished with a basket-of-flowers finial. Each handle is ornamented with acanthus leaves curving out from the base of the bowl and scrolling in toward the rim of the neck.

History: Brig. Gen Theodore Lyman Jr. (1792–1849) and Mary Elizabeth Henderson (d. 1836), m. 1821; to their son Col. Theodore Lyman (1833–1897) and Elizabeth Russell; to their son Dr. Henry Lyman (b. 1878) and Elizabeth Cabot (b. 1880), m. 1907; to their children Cora (1910–1982), m. Richard Warren in 1933; Charles Peirson Lyman (b. 1912) and Henry Lyman (b. 1915); made a gift by Dr. Charles Pierson Lyman, Henry Lyman, and Dr. Richard Warren.[2]

Exhibitions and publications: None.

NOTES TO THIS ENTRY ARE ON PAGE 309.

185

Charters, Cann & Dunn (active 1848–1854)
Thomas Charters Jr. (active 1848–1859)
John Cann (active 1848–1860)
David Dunn (active 1848–1856)

Retailed by Ball, Tompkins & Black (active 1839–1851)

Five-piece tea service

New York, New York, about 1850
Bequest of Maxim Karolik
64.933–37

Kettle on stand (64.933): H. 8 in. (20.3 cm); W. 9⅝ in. (24.4 cm); D. 7¹³⁄₁₆ in. (19.7 cm); Wt. 31 oz 17 dwt 4 gr (990.9 gm)

Teapot (64.934): H. 7¹⁵⁄₁₆ in. (20.2 cm); W. 9¹³⁄₁₆ in. (25 cm); Diam. rim 3⅝ in. (9.4 cm); D. 6⅜ in. (16.2 cm); Wt. 27 oz 4 dwt 3 gr (846.2 gm)

Sugar bowl (64.935): H. 6½ in. (16.5 cm); W. 8⅝ in. (21.8 cm); Diam. rim 3⅜ in. (8.6 cm); D. 5⅞ in. (15 cm); Wt. 17 oz 13 dwt 24 gr (550.5 gm)

Creampot (64.936): H. 6¹¹⁄₁₆ in. (17 cm); W. 5¹¹⁄₁₆ in. (14.5 cm); Diam. rim 2¾ in. (7 cm); D. 4½ in. (11.5 cm); Wt. 12 oz 7 dwt 1 gr (384.2 gm)

Waste bowl (64.937): H. 4⅛ in. (10. 5 cm); Diam. 6⁵⁄₁₆ in. (16 cm); Wt. 11 oz 12 dwt 19 gr (362 gm)

Marks: "BALL TOMPKINS & BLACK" in an arched reserve curve; "N [pellet] Y" in a rectangle; lion's head within an ellipse; "C C & D" in a shaped lozenge; an arm and hammer in an ellipse,

all struck on base of each vessel. "NY" over "C C & D" struck on kettle, teapot, creampot, and sugar bowl. The kettle stand lacks the place mark. The burner carries the same retailer's and maker's marks, with accompanying pseudohallmarks. The waste bowl struck with maker's initials and place mark.

Inscriptions: "M P R" in entwined sprigged script, in a reserve framed by C scrolls and foliage, engraved to left of handle on kettle, teapot, and creampot and on side of sugar bowl and waste bowl.

Armorial: The crest of a running stag between two trees is engraved within an identical reserve on the opposite side of the initials on each piece. The family affiliation for the crest is unknown.

RIPENED PRODUCE fresh from the kitchen garden might have inspired the organic forms of this lavish tea service. Like bedding plants laid out in an orderly pattern, scrolls, foliage, and flowers embellish the lobes of the gourd-shaped vessels. Handles formed of twining grapevines and leafy bracket feet continue the playful conceit, which is completed by a plump melon finial atop the domed cover. Form and ornament combine to create a rich display of glittering silver likely intended for a dark walnut or mahogany sideboard. A number of firms may have produced this version of the Rococo-revival-style tea set. Several are known that either appear to be identical to this set or vary only in their finials, feet, or other details. Only one other bears the mark of Charters, Cann & Dunn.[1]

In 1839 New York City's Marquand & Co. was reorganized by its former partners, Henry Ball, Erastus O. Tompkins, William Black, and J. D. Williams, and renamed Ball, Tomkins & Black. The firm was the nation's most prestigious retailer of silverware and jewelry at the time this tea service was produced. The firm of Charters, Cann & Dunn served as wholesalers to the trade in New York from 1848 to 1854 and were one of Ball, Tompkins & Black's many suppliers. Known for the quality of their work, the firm specialized in hollowware and presentation silver.[2]

The Charters, Cann & Dunn manufactory was located at "rear 53 Mercer" through 1853 and, later, at 89 Mercer Street before relocating in 1854 to Frankfort Street. Charters left the firm in 1854, and the 1855–56 New York City directory listed Cann and Dunn at 144 & 146 Jay Street, Brooklyn (see cat. no. 182).[3]

Description: Each of the conforming five pieces has a raised, one-piece, gourd-shaped body, which is grooved into eight curved panels decorated with chased and repoussé daisies and scrolls. There are small variations in design; for example, the teapot spout is of a

simpler design than that of the kettle, and the creampot has a long V-shaped spout opposite the handle.

The kettle, teapot, and creampot have domed and hinged lids finished with bolted cast finials of a melon on leaves; the sugar bowl's lid is loose. The kettle has a bail handle, hinged on long leaf appliqués with reverse scrolls of grapevine pattern at the ends, ivory insulation, and a plain top. Below the kettle's ornamented spout is a tilting hinged slot for the linchpin connecting the kettle and stand. Another pin and slot secure the two pieces on the opposite side. The stand is pierced on the skirt near the edge; it has scrolled edges and four cast and leaf-ornamented scrolled legs on shell feet, with flanking leafy foliage. Simple straps hold the plain lamp in the center of the stand. The waste bowl has curved sides, a molded and scalloped

185

rim, and a flat bottom. Its foot rim and feet are simpler than those on the other pieces.

History: Early history unknown. From the collection of Maxim Karolik (1893–1963), noted collector of American art and benefactor of the MFA.

Exhibitions and publications: None.

NOTES TO THIS ENTRY ARE ON PAGE 309–10.

186

Cooper & Fisher (active 1854–1862)
Francis W. Cooper (1815–1898)
Richard Fisher (active 1858–1862)

Henry P. Horlor (1823–after 1881), enameler
[?] Segel, engraver
Chalice and paten

New York, New York, 1855
Gift of The Seminarians, Curator's Fund, and Ron Bourgeault
1996.27.1–2

Chalice (1996.27.1): H. 9⅞ in. (25.1 cm); Diam. rim 5½ in. (14 cm); Wt. 29 oz 9 dwt 2 gr (916.1 gm)

Paten (1996.27.2): H. ½ in. (.5 cm); Diam. 9½ in. (24.2 cm); Wt. 14 oz 6 dwt 16 gr (445.8 gm)

Marks: "COOPER & FISHER; 131 AMITY ST NY" in roman letters struck on each; the chalice is missing a portion of the street name. The chalice is marked on applied foot rim; the paten is marked on back.

Inscriptions: At the base of the chalice, a ribbon appears below the panel depicting the baptism of Christ. In Gothic-style script, it reads, "This is my / beloved Son / in whom I am well pleased." The crucifixion scene includes the Greek symbols "A" and "Ω" (alpha and omega) and "INRI," the initial letters of the Latin text *Iesus Nazarenvs Rex Ivdaeorum* (Jesus Christ, King of the Jews). Underneath the chalice, each section of the base has been scribed with numbers intended to match those on the pierced quatrefoil edge; numbering begins with 7, ends at 12, and contains other numbers, some duplicates. "holy ⋆ holy ⋆ holy ⋆ Lord ⋆ God ⋆" in shaded Gothic script, on a matte band of strapwork, engraved on rim of paten.

THIS EXCEPTIONAL EXAMPLE of Gothic-revival communion silver represents some of the most ambitious work produced for the Episcopal church in the nineteenth century; it is also

among the earliest enameled silver hollowware made in this country. Francis W. Cooper, the silversmith who fashioned the chalice and paten, is little known despite his fifty-year career in New York. Aside from church plate bearing his stamp, most of Cooper's secular production was retailed by larger firms such as Tiffany & Co. without his own touchmark. Cooper was active in New York from 1842 until 1890, but his greatest activity probably occurred between 1854 and 1862, when jeweler Richard Fisher became his financial partner. During that time, Cooper & Fisher became the eighth-largest silver manufacturer in New York City.[1]

Cooper's success, and that of the Cooper & Fisher partnership, rose along with reforming efforts within the American Episcopal church. Prompted in part by the secularization of industrial society, Anglicans and Episcopalians (their American counterparts) wished to revitalize their congregations by recapturing the innocence and spirituality of the early Christian church. The English Ecclesiological Society of London was prominent among the reformers. Their circle was composed of prominent High Church Anglicans who drew upon elements of historic church architecture and embellishments for a fresh interpretation. Its membership hoped to reestablish a medieval framework for worship through the careful selection of liturgical programs and close supervision of designers.

Designs for communion plate received similar scrutiny. An 1843 article by English architect William Butterfield (1814–1900)

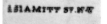

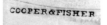

186

titled "The Proper Shape of Chalices" appeared in the society's publication, *The Ecclesiologist*. Butterfield invited the society to take a leadership role in establishing guidelines for the design and production of church plate. Within four years, *Instrumenta Ecclesiastica* was published under their guidance; it included 140 designs by Butterfield based upon medieval Gothic prototypes. The publication enabled the society to promote a sanctioned body of designs for churches wishing to order new communion silver. Church plate executed by London silversmith John James Keith (w. 1824–1870), under Butterfield's supervision, received a medal at the Crystal Palace exhibition of 1851.[2]

The New York Ecclesiological Society, formed in 1848, was the American counterpart to the English society. It appointed the Rev. John Henry Hopkins Jr. (1820–1891) to oversee the fabrication of silver using Butterfield's designs. Acting on behalf of Episcopal churches wishing to purchase communion silver, Hopkins engaged Francis W. Cooper in 1851 as the New York society's exclusive silversmith. Hopkins also made arrangements with Henry P. Horlor, an English enameler, who came with excellent credentials. Prior to his arrival in New York, Horlor had worked in London for the English Ecclesiastical Society, and the enamels he produced in New York are perhaps the first made for American hollowware. Engraving was performed by a craftsman named Segel, "an accomplished German artist in metal."[3] Chalices, patens, a footed paten, alms basins, and flagons were the chief forms of communion silver made under Hopkins's direction.

It is puzzling how Cooper achieved his exclusive distinction. His religious affiliation is unknown, and it is unclear whether he fashioned any domestic silver for society members. Certainly the choice was made by Hopkins, who exerted broad powers to select a craftsman for this purpose. The result was that Cooper became the only American metalsmith to fashion a quantity of silver hollowware in the Gothic mode.[4] James Cox (w. 1831–33) and Zalmon Bostwick (w. 1846–1852) of New York were notable craftsmen working in this style, as was Roswell Gleason (1799–1887) of Dorchester, Massachusetts, but their production was modest by comparison.

The chalice and paten originally formed part of a larger communion service that was made for Trinity Chapel in New York. As a satellite of Trinity Church, which today stands in Manhattan's financial district, Trinity Chapel was established at West Twenty-fifth Street, near Broadway, and was intended to serve the church's membership in what was then considered the town's northern reaches. Designed by Richard Upjohn (1802–1878), the architect of Trinity Church, the chapel was dedicated in 1855.[5] Upjohn's High Church design was in harmony with Cooper's paten, which displays broad Gothic lettering and a severe, frontal, Byzantine-style image of Christ. The pre-Reformation-style chalice resembles similar designs published by Augustus Welby North Pugin and updated by Butterfield.

The New York Ecclesiological Society was dissolved in 1855, but American Episcopal churches continued to request silver that followed Butterfield's designs. Francis W. Cooper filled these orders long after his association with Richard Fisher ended in 1862, fashioning variants of the same designs until about 1875. When the larger firms such as Tiffany & Co. and Gorham opened their own ecclesiastical departments in the late nineteenth century, they continued to draw upon Butterfield's designs as wrought by Cooper.

Description: The chalice stands on a splayed foot with applied twisted-chain edging and pierced quatrefoils on the applied vertical section of the foot. Lobed hexagonal sections rising from the foot contain three engraved panels with champlevé enamel in opaque blue, white, and translucent red that depict the Crucifixion, Pentecost, and Baptism of Christ. Interspersed within these are three panels engraved with the images of St. George slaying the dragon; St. John the Evangelist; and the martyrdom of a kneeling bearded man at the hands of a soldier. The figure may be St. Alban, Protomartyr of England.

The openwork stem consists of six twisted wire columns around a central pierced shaft; central baluster is chased with a cluster of prunts in the form of arches and quatrefoils.

The silver-gilt bowl (which has been regilded), with stylized floral engraving below the lip, is set in a silver calyx having egg-shaped reserves that reveal the bowl; the calyx framework is chased with the images of six angels whose outspread wings form spandrels between the reserves and below the gadrooned rim. Each angel displays an emblem of the Passion of Christ. Foliage is affixed between bowl and stem.[6]

The round shallow paten with worn gilding has a raised circular boss at center, on which has been applied a champlevé portrait bust of the Pantocrator, that of Christ wearing the royal crown and halo and holding the orb, with right hand raised, right forefinger extended. Surrounding the enamel is a simple engraved border leading to a broad rim ornamented with Gothic text against matte strapwork; a gadrooned edge surrounds the whole.

History: Originally made for Trinity Chapel, New York City. Probably dispersed by Trinity Church when the chapel was sold in 1942. Subsequent history unknown until consigned by the Rev. Gregory T. Bittner to Sotheby's in 1996, when it was purchased by the Museum.

Exhibitions and publications: Sotheby's, New York, sale 6800, January 19, 1996, lot 556; Jennifer M. Swope, "Francis W. Cooper, Silversmith," *Antiques* 55, no. 2 (February 1999), fig. 2; Wohlauer 1999, 328.

NOTES TO THIS ENTRY ARE ON PAGE 310.

187

Davis, Palmer & Co. (active 1837–1845)
Thomas Aspinwall Davis (1798–1845)
Julius A. Palmer (1803–1872)
Josiah G. Bachelder (active 1837–1870)

Sugar bowl and creampot

Boston, Massachusetts, 1837–45
Source unidentified
Res.64.10.1–2

Sugar bowl (Res.64.10.1a–b): H. 6⁵⁄₁₆ in. (16 cm); W. 9⅛ (23 cm); D. 6¹¹⁄₁₆ in. (16.9 cm); Diam. rim 4¾ in. (11.9 cm); Wt. 24 oz 1 dwt 10 gr (748.7 gm)

Creampot (Res.64.10.2): H. 4¾ in. (12.1 cm); W. 6¾ in. (17.1 cm); D. 4¾ in. (12.1 cm); Wt. 11 oz 20 dwt 8 gr (358.9 gm)

Marks: "Davis, Palmer & Co." and "Pure / coin" in italic letters within rectangles struck on bottom of each.

Inscriptions: "T & / MAS" in script engraved on sugar bowl, in center of body and between handles, and under spout of creampot.

DAVIS, PALMER & CO. offered a varied line of luxury goods to Boston's carriage trade (see cat. no. 143). This large sugar bowl and creampot, decorated with melon reeding and heavy bud-and-leaf finial, retain some of the plain surface of the late Neoclassical style while boasting elements of the new rococo revival, as seen in the winsome asymmetrical bud finial and the dense foliage of the bracket feet.

Description: The shallowly lobed and rounded body of the sugar bowl sits on cast, conjoined bracket feet composed of foliate decoration. Ear-shaped handles with acanthus grips and flat tips attach at the shoulders and body. The domed cover has conforming lobes and a flared rim. A bud-and-leaf finial is attached with a screw and bolt. The waist of the creamer ascends to a generous spout with an everted rim.

History: Accessioned September 23, 1964, from an unknown source.

Exhibitions and publications: None.

188

Davis, Palmer & Co. (active 1837–1845)
Thomas Aspinwall Davis (1798–1845)
Julius A. Palmer (1803–1872)
Josiah G. Bachelder (active 1837–1870)

Child's cup

Boston, Massachusetts, about 1842
Bequest of Annie Bolton Matthews Bryant
Res.34.5

H. 3⅛ in. (8 cm); W. 4⅛ in. (10.5 cm); Diam. rim 2¹³⁄₁₆ in. (7.2 cm); Diam. foot 2⅝ in. (6.7 cm); Wt. 3 oz 15 dwt 21 gm (118 gm)

Marks: "Davis Palmer and Co." in italic letters and "Pure Coin" in roman letters, within rectangles, struck on base.

Inscriptions: "Eliza Fay French" in script, within a reserve framed with chased C scrolls and foliage, engraved and centered on body, opposite handle.

Windsor Fay, a prominent Boston shipowner and India Wharf merchant, and his wife, Dorcas, purchased this elaborately chased cup for their granddaughter Eliza Fay French, who was born August 14, 1842. The couple bought the cup from Davis, Palmer & Co., retailers of imported jewelry, coin flatware, and hollowware (see cat. no. 143). Dorcas Fay also presented a silver cup (Res.34.2) to William Henry Fay (b. 1835), the child of her son William C. Fay. The presentation of a lavishly decorated silver cup signifies not only affection and high expectations for a child but also the donor's financial ability to afford such a substantial gift.

Description: The cup has a seamed straight-sided body that is divided into twelve panels engraved with upright acanthus leaves centered on each bend. A cartouche on the front of the cup interrupts the row of leaves. A band of gadrooned decoration encircles the rim, and the cup sits on an applied anthemion-stamped base band. The angular handle is hollow and impressed on three sides with a delicate scroll.

History: Given to Eliza Fay French (b. 1842) by her grandparents Dorcas Clark Fay (1785–1861) and Windsor Fay (1780–1844) of Boston, m. 1829. Eliza's cup descended through the Fay/French family to Annie Bolton (Fay) Bryant, m. William Matthews, to their daughter, the donor, Annie Bolton Matthews (1871–1933), m. Wallace Bryant.[1]

Exhibitions and publications: None.

NOTE TO THIS ENTRY IS ON PAGE 310.

189

Eoff and Shepard (active about 1852–1861)
Edgar Mortimer Eoff (active 1852–1860)
George L. Shepard (active 1852–1862)

Retailed by Ball, Black & Co. (1852–1874)

Ewer

New York, New York, about 1860
Helen and Alice Colburn Fund
1977.620

H. 19½ in. (49.5 cm); W. 9⅜ in. (24 cm); D. 7½ in. (19 cm); Diam. foot 6½ in. (16.5 cm); Wt. 67 oz 3 dwt 20 gr (2089.9 gm)

Marks: "E & S" and "N. YORK," each within rectangles; "BALL, BLACK & CO." within a semicircular band; "162" and "950" incuse, all struck on bottom.

New York April 18 1854
Purchased by John W. Barry at the grand
Metropolitan Fair

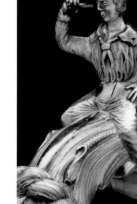

189

extraordinary ewer was exhibited by Ball, Black & Co. at New York's 1864 Metropolitan Fair, where it was purchased by Bostonian John Williams Quincy. The fair was one of a series held in the northern states to benefit the U.S. Sanitary Commission and its efforts to support hospitals and medical relief during the Civil War. The ewer may have been exhibited at the "Museum of Arms and Trophies for Exhibition and Sale" held at the fair.[2] The engravings were probably added by Quincy to honor the wishes of his late mother.

Bedecked with sea nymphs, dolphins, conch shells, and swirling waves, this tall, classically shaped domestic vessel has been cast in the role of an ocean-going ship. On the prow, under Neptune's vigilant eye, an angel figurehead thrusts forward above the breakwater. Three-dimensional anchors with draped chains complete the fantasy prow. Symbols of Christian faith, the angel and the anchors combine with nautical elements to create an impressive memorial to Captain Atkins.

Description: The raised urn-shaped body curves inward to a long, tapered neck and spout. It has a large cast double-curved handle and raised splayed foot. Applied ropelike beading extends around the spout's outer edge. A ringlet of "waves" at the top of the base cradles the body of the "vessel," as a ripple of frothy tide on the shoulder articulates the passage from body to neck. Applied three-dimensional anchors ride at either side of the shoulder, with their chain held up by a cast and applied female figure at the front. An engraved panel in front is surrounded by a repoussé and chased cartouche of watery scrolls couched in a patch of cattails. It is flanked by vignettes of sea nymphs and dolphins on the sides of the vessel, with oak branches toward the back, near the joining of the handle. The lower portion of the body and stem of the foot are ribbed in imitation of waves, with alternating applied oval and leafy rosettes. The rim of the flared foot is alive with repoussé and chased aquatic and vegetal motifs and alternating cast and applied dolphin heads and seashells. The double C-scroll handle is joined to the body just under the lip with applied coral-like fronds. Its larger top section simulates cresting waves and is surmounted by a cast and applied sailor figure. In the lower section, a small scroll terminates in a dolphin's head, which is attached to the body at the shoulder.

History: To honor his mother's request for a memorial to her father, Capt. Silas Atkins (1747–1835), the ewer was purchased by Bostonian John W. Quincy (1813–1883) at the 1864 Metropolitan Fair in New York City.[3] Its subsequent history is unknown until purchased by the museum in 1977 from Thurston H. Smith Jr. of Locust Valley, New York.

Exhibitions and publications: Fairbanks 1981, fig. 37.

NOTES TO THIS ENTRY ARE ON PAGE 310.

Inscriptions: "New York April 18th 1864 / Purchased by John W. Quincy at the great / Metropolitan Fair" in script engraved below rim, to right of handle. Engraved on front: "In Memorium. / This token of respect and affection to the memory of Captain Silas Atkins of Boston, Mass. / (Who died Dec. 7th. 1835. Aged 88 years) / is inscribed at the request of his daughter, / Abigail Atkins Quincy. / (Who died at Dorchester, Mass. Aug. 24th 1861. Aged 89 years.) / to perpetuate his name and memory as a faithful husband, / and an affectionate father. / He pursued Navigation and Commerce, / and early retired to enjoy the reward / of his industry."

EDGAR MORTIMER EOFF and George L. Shepard operated a modern steam-powered silverware manufactory that employed twenty-five workers. For nearly a decade, the firm supplied distinctive silverware to prestigious luxury-goods retailers such as Ball, Black & Co.[1] According to its marks and inscriptions, this

190

William Gale & Son (active 1850–1858 and 1863–1866)

William Gale Sr. (1799–1864)
William Gale Jr. (1825 or 1831–1885)

Retailed by Henry B. Stanwood (1818–1869), Boston, Massachusetts

Sugar sifter and sauce ladle

New York, New York, 1850
Gift of Robert F. Trent in memory of Emma Sophie Trent
(1881–1966)
1982.176–77

Sugar sifter (1982.176): L. 8½ in. (20.2 cm); W. bowl 2½ in. (6.4 cm); Wt. 2 oz 1 dwt 16 gr (64.8 gm)

Sauce ladle (1982.177): L. 7¹³⁄₁₆ in. (19.8 cm); W. bowl 2⅝ in. (7.2 cm); Diam. 2⅝ in. (6.7 cm); Wt. 2 oz 10 dwt 16 gr (78.7 gm)

Marks: "HENRY B STANWOOD" within a rectangle; "1850" within a diamond; "G & S" within an oval; and "PATENTED 1847" within a rectangle, all struck on back of each stem.

Inscriptions: 1982.176: "LA to EMB" in script engraved on back of handle tip. 1982.177: "AA / to / EMB" in script engraved on back of handle tip.

KNOWN BY THE 1750S, sugar sifters were produced in many flatware patterns by the 1850s. As in this example, they were about the size of sauce ladles, although the latter often had rounded bottoms, whereas sifters were flat bottomed.[1] This sugar sifter and sauce ladle are in the Gothic pattern that was first patented in 1848 by William Gale and partner Nathaniel Hayden. The mark of Gale & Son on the ladle indicates that Gale retained the patent in his next partnership with his son.[2] Although made in New York, these objects were retailed by Henry B. Stanwood in Boston (see also cat. nos. 210, 231).

Taking its vocabulary from architectural details, the Gothic-revival style was used to design nonecclesiastical wares for secular, domestic use during its surge of popularity in the 1840s and 1850s. Thereafter, it was largely limited to ecclesiastical objects.[3]

Description: The handles of this sugar sifter and sauce ladle are decorated with a stamped Gothic-style pattern with pointed arches, qua-trefoil, and crockets on the front and back of the upturned ends. The front and back of the sides of the handles are threaded. The sifter's flat, round bowl is perforated with circles and stars; the bowl of the sauce ladle is solid.

History: The history of the ladles prior to their gift to the Museum is unknown.

Exhibitions and publications: None.

NOTES TO THIS ENTRY ARE ON PAGE 310.

191

William Gale & Son (active 1850–1858 and 1863–1866)
William Gale Sr. (1799–1864)
William Gale Jr. (1825 or 1831–1885)

Four-piece tea service

New York, New York, 1852
Gift of Mrs. James O. Murray
65.1195–98

Teapot (65.1195): H. 11¹¹⁄₁₆ in. (29.7 cm); W. 10⅜ in. (26.5 cm); D. 6⁵⁄₁₆ in. (16 cm); Diam. foot 4⅞ in. (12.4 cm); Wt. 34 oz 7 dwt 9 gr (1069 gm)

Sugar bowl (65.1196): H. 9⅝ in. (24.4 cm); W. 7⅞ in. (20 cm); D. 5⅝ in. (11.5 cm); Diam. foot 4½ in. (11.4 cm); Wt. 24 oz 18 dwt 8 gr (775 gm)

Covered creampot (65.1197): H. 8¹¹⁄₁₆ in. (22.2 cm); W. 5⁵⁄₁₆ in. (13.5 cm); D. 4½ in. (11.4 cm); Diam. foot 3½ in. (8.9 cm); Wt. 17 oz 6 dwt 6 gr (538.5 gm)

Waste bowl (65.1198): H. 4¹¹⁄₁₆ in. (12 cm); Diam. rim 6⁵⁄₁₆ in. (16 cm); Diam. foot 4⅜ in. (11.1 cm); Wt. 14 oz 18 dwt 21 gr (464.8 gm)

Marks: "W͟m GALE & SON / NEW-YORK"; "G & S" within an oval; and "1852" within a diamond, all struck incuse on each. The date mark is obscured on the teapot.

Inscriptions: "M L T" in entwined script engraved on body of each.

THIS TEA SERVICE was produced two years after William Gale Sr. made his son a partner in the firm, which became a popular source for hollowware such as this matching tea service. By midcentury the firm's employees numbered seventy-five.[1] Presented as a wedding gift, the service was decorated in the fashionable Rococo-revival style. William Gale & Son apparently copied its scheme of rusticated grapevines that serve to cover joints and form handles from the design of a teakettle on stand made in 1850 by Edward Moore.[2] A stylish and costly service, elaborately repousséd and chased and marked by one of New York City's best-known silversmiths, it served to indicate the high social expectations of the newlyweds.

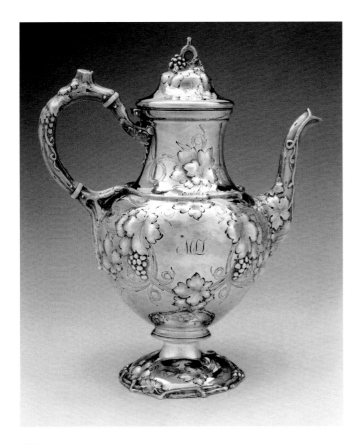

191

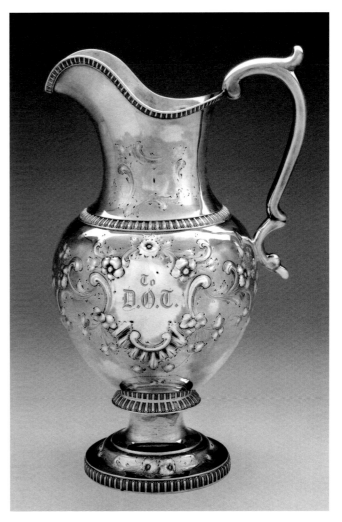

192

William Gale & Son (active 1850–1858 and 1863–1866)
William Gale Sr. (1799–1864)
William Gale Jr. (1825 or 1831–1885)

Pitcher

New York, New York, about 1855
Gift of Mrs. James O. Murray
65.1199

H. 13⅛ in. (33.3 cm); W. 8½ in. (21.5 cm); D. 6¹¹⁄₁₆ in. (17 cm); Diam. foot 4⅞ in. (12.2 cm); Wt. 32 oz 7 dwt 11 gr (1006.9 gm)

Marks: "WM GALE & SON" incuse; "W G & S" within an oval incuse; "1855" within a diamond; and "NEW-YORK" incuse, all struck above and below center point.

Description: The four pieces display an overall pattern of repoussé and chased leaves, tendrils, and grapes. The joints of the raised, inverted pear-shaped bodies and seamed, curved necks are concealed by a ropelike rusticated vine. On the teapot, the vines twist to form a cast C-scroll handle with ivory insulators. Flat-chasing simulates the bark of a woody stem, and a picturesque shorn outgrowth of the limb, textured with growth circles, forms the thumbpiece. The rustic decoration continues onto the curved cast spout. The hinged domed teapot cover is finished with a grapevine and twig finial, as is the sloping hinged creampot cover and the domed, but separate, sugar bowl lid. The short-stemmed round feet are edged with applied entwined vines, leaves, and grapes.

History: According to family history, the set was presented as a wedding gift in 1853 in Troy, New York, to Maria Louisa Tweedy (1832–before 1865) upon her marriage to Dexter Oliver Tiffany (b. 1825). However, the initials could indicate the bride's maiden or married name. The silver descended to their son Dexter O. Tiffany Jr. (b. 1854); to his half-sister Maria Louisa Tiffany (b. 1864) and William Haughton Murray (b. 1860), m. 1887; to their son James O. Murray (b. 1892); and made a gift by his widow.

Exhibitions and publications: None.

NOTES TO THIS ENTRY ARE ON PAGE 310.

192

Inscriptions: "LCL" entwined monogram in script engraved on body, to right of handle; "To / D.O.T." to left. Both inscriptions appear in reserves framed by C scrolls, flowers, and foliage.

THIS PITCHER is similar in style to the four-piece Gale tea set (cat. no. 191), which also belonged to the Tweedy/Tiffany family, although it displays delicate floral repoussé and chased decoration in lieu of the former's rusticated grapevine motif. Further, the less exuberant decoration is confined to specific areas of the vessel and not laced overall, as in the four-piece set. The variation in motif and the date mark of 1855 suggest that this pitcher was a later addition to the set.

Description: The pitcher's raised and inverted bulb-shaped body sits on a short-stemmed molded foot. Both the body and foot are encircled with deeply embossed flowers and scrolls. On the body, the decoration is arranged to terminate near the hollow double-scrolled handle. Its slender curving neck is flat-chased on both sides with squarish, foliate, cartouchelike decorations. Stamped bands of egg-and-dart molding decorate the rims and junctures of the body, neck, and foot.

History: This pitcher was presented to "D.O.T." (Dexter O. Tiffany) by "LCL," whose identity is unknown. It subsequently descended in the same manner as the Tweedy/Tiffany family tea set (see cat. no. 191).

Exhibitions and publications: None.

193

William Gale & Son (active 1850–1859 and 1863–1867)
William Gale Sr. (1799–1864)
William Gale Jr. (1825 or 1831–1885)
Child's cup

New York, New York, 1856
Gift of W. Ogilvie Comstock
1972.893

H. 4⅝ in. (11.6 cm); W. 4⁵⁄₁₆ in. (11 cm); Diam. rim 2¾ in. (7 cm); Diam. foot 2⅝ in. (6.7 cm); Wt. 4 oz 14 dwt 2 gr (146.3 gm)

Marks: "W. G & S" incuse within an ellipse; "1856" incuse in a diamond pattern; and "Wm GALE & SON / NEW-YORK" incuse, all struck above and below center point.

Inscriptions: "Frederick William" in script within a reserve engraved opposite handle.

It was a fortunate child who received this rich keepsake to celebrate his birth. The traditional cann-shaped form is updated by fashionable Rococo-style floral and scrolled repousséd and chased decoration that frames the inscription and trails around the cup toward the handle.

Description: A circular molded, domed foot, with delicately repousséd and chased foliate decoration and applied beaded trim, supports the raised bulb-shaped body. A matching beaded trim circles the flared lip. Profuse repousséd and chased floral ornament circles back from each side of the frontal cartouche toward the handle, in an asymmetrical manner. A boldly articulated double-scrolled cast handle rises above the rim and curves in to join the body at the waist.

History: Frederick William Dibblee, son of Frederick E. Dibblee (d. 1875), d. unm. about 1884; to his cousin William O. Comstock's (1815–1883) son, William O. Comstock (d. 1931); to his son W. Ogilvie Comstock (d. 1972?), the donor.[1]

Exhibitions and publications: None.

NOTE TO THIS ENTRY IS ON PAGE 310.

194

Baldwin Gardiner (1791–1869)
Ewer

New York, New York, 1833
Gift in honor of Jonathan Fairbanks on the occasion of the silver anniversary of the Department of American Decorative Arts and Sculpture by his many friends and supporters
1996.240

H. 17 11/16 in. (45 cm); W. 13 in. (33 cm); Diam. foot 5 7/8 in. (14.9 cm); Wt. 63 oz 4 dwt 1 gr (1965.8 gm)

Marks: "B [pellet] GARDINER" within a serrated rectangle, with pseudohallmarks of a head in profile, "G," and lion rampant, each within a rectangle with chamfered corners, struck on base.

Inscriptions: "As a Testimonial / of their estimation of his personal Character / and Seaman-like abilities, / the passengers of the Ship Natchez / on her Voyage from New Orleans to New York, in June 1833, / present this Pitcher / TO / Captain Hartwell Reed, / New York, July 4th 1833" in script engraved beneath spout.

This richly ornamented presentation ewer is a grand statement of the Neoclassical mode in early-nineteenth-century America. The frosty and richly repousséd handle, lip,

and body, with its anthemia, scrolled rinceaux decoration, and vigorous gadrooning, are elements derived from the French style. Similar to ambitious examples made in the Philadelphia shop of Fletcher and Gardiner (cat. no. 150), this ewer, marked by Baldwin Gardiner, may have been made by an immigrant craftsman who worked in one of these two shops and had the skills and talent to execute silver in the latest mode.

Baldwin Gardiner was the younger brother of Boston and Philadelphia silversmith Sidney Gardiner. Both men were born in Southold, Long Island, to John Gardiner (1752–1823) of that town and Abigail Worth (1760–1781) of Nantucket, Massachusetts. Baldwin Gardiner traveled to Boston to apprentice in the shop that his brother operated with Thomas Fletcher; he continued working for them when the firm moved south to Philadelphia in 1811. By 1815 he established a fancy hardware store called Gardiner, Veron & Co. on 98 Chestnut Street. His partner was Lewis Veron (1793–1853), a member of the Veron family into which Baldwin Gardiner, his brother Sidney, and Thomas Fletcher married.[1]

Shortly after the death of Sidney Gardiner in 1827, Baldwin Gardiner moved to New York, where he established a furnishings warehouse called B. Gardiner and Co. He sold imported French plateaus, candelabras, and lamps. By 1832 he was operating a steam-driven silver manufactory. However, not all silver marked by Baldwin Gardiner was completed on site. In 1828 he arranged for Fletcher and Gardiner to complete a commission that was to carry his marks, writing, "I should expect to have my name stamped upon the bottoms."[2] Such information makes it difficult to ascertain the maker of this presentation ewer dated 1833, which is among the most magnificent examples to display the Baldwin Gardiner mark.

The extent to which Gardiner shared craftsmen or patrons with Fletcher and Gardiner is unknown, but the quality of some surviving work, and this ewer in particular, suggests that highly skilled craftsmen may have come to New York through his older brother's shop or that this commission was carried out by his brother's company after his death in 1827. The touchmark "G" that appears along with two pseudohallmarks is not fully understood.[3]

Gardiner's manufactory produced an assortment of flatware including ladles, cheese knives, spoons of varying sizes, and tongs. His mark also appears on a set of knives in the Thread pattern that were also produced by Fletcher and Gardiner. Some larger examples of hollowware also survive, including ewers of similar scale and an elaborate wirework cake or fruit basket. By 1836 Gardiner moved to 39 Nassau, where he sold a variety of domestic ornamental wares, mostly imported from France

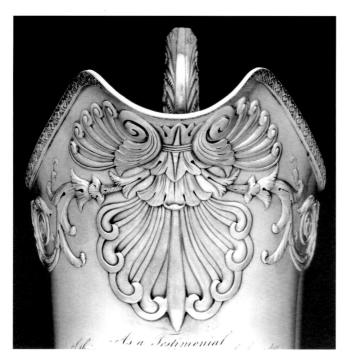

194

section; the short stem with a foliate baluster descends to a circular foot embellished with a radiating leaf pattern. A later inscription to the left of the spout has been removed, and the firescale restored.

History: Presented on July 4, 1833, to Capt. Hartwell Reed by the passengers of the packet ship *Natchez*. The ewer was subsequently owned in the 1940s by a private collector of West Hartford, Connecticut; by descent to her daughter; acquired in 1994 by Hirschl & Adler, New York; purchased by the Museum in 1996.

Exhibitions and publications: Waters 2000, 1:70, fig. 4.

NOTES TO THIS ENTRY ARE ON PAGE 310.

195

Gorham & Co. (active 1852–1865)
John Gorham (1820–1898)
Teapot and sugar bowl

Providence, Rhode Island, about 1852–68
Bequest of Barbara Boylston Bean
1976.641–42

Teapot (1976.641): H. 9⅝ in. (24.5 cm); W. 9¹³⁄₁₆ in. (25 cm); D. 6⁵⁄₁₆ in. (16 cm); Wt. 29 oz 10 dwt 22 gr (919 gm)

Sugar bowl (1976.642): H. 8⅝ in. (21.8 cm); W. 6¹³⁄₁₆ in. (17.3 cm); D. 5¹¹⁄₁₆ in. (14.5 cm); Wt. 22 oz 19 dwt 3 gr (714 gm)

Marks: "GORHAM & COMPANY / PROVIDENCE, RI / STERLING" and "GORHAM & CO. / PURE COIN" struck incuse on bottom of teapot. "GORHAM & CO. / PURE COIN" in incuse roman letters struck on bottom of sugar bowl.

Inscriptions: "M H B" in Gothic lettering, within a Rococo-style cartouche, engraved to left of teapot handle and on one side of sugar bowl.

Armorials: The Boylston family arms depicting gules, six cross-crosslets fitchee argent, on a chief gold three pellets, charger, and the crest is a lion pass guarde holding a cross-crosslet of the field, all within a Rococo-style cartouche, engraved to right of teapot handle and on one side of sugar bowl.[1]

and England. After a brief period in California in 1848, Gardiner moved to Newark, New Jersey, where he died in 1869.

The presentation of the ewer to Capt. Hartwell Reed, whose "personal Character and Seaman-like abilities" are extolled in the inscription, celebrated the packet ship's maiden voyage from New Orleans to New York. The *Natchez* was one of five new vessels built to increase travel between the two cities. The ship arrived in New York on July 5, but the ewer is engraved July 4, perhaps because that was the date it had been expected in port. Such honors paid to ship captains were not uncommon in the early to mid-nineteenth century. Gardiner produced a ewer in 1834 for Capt. George Maxwell, whose ship *Europe* traveled from Liverpool to New York.[4]

Description: The large, raised, helmet-shaped presentation ewer has a cast and chased scrolled handle with foliate decoration; an air vent is below. Under the flaring spout is chased a large anthemion, on each side of which extends scrolled rinceaux decoration that surrounds the vessel. The rim is edged with die-rolled floral ornamentation. Convex die-rolled midband decoration appears above a gadrooned

THE SEAMLESS hand-raised bodies of these objects offer a clean canvas for the lavish Rococo-revival motifs of branches, leaves, and flowers that erupt into three dimensions and ramble over the curvy forms in an informal, natural manner. Gorham adopted the English sterling standard of 92.5 percent silver alloy in 1868. These two pieces, from what was probably a larger matching service, are made of different alloys. That

195

the teapot bears the quality mark "Sterling" and the sugar bowl "Pure Coin" suggests that the sugar bowl may have been made somewhat earlier. Quality marks such as "Coin," "Pure Silver Coin," or "Pure Coin" had been used on American silver since the 1830s.[2]

Description: The raised and repoussé bodies of the teapot and sugar bowl have an overall chased floral and foliate decoration. Reserves framed by asymmetrical scrolls on the sides of the teapot and front and back of the sugar bowl hold a monogram and family crest. Leafy vines entwine the rusticated spout and handles of both. Bracket-shaped feet on both are composed of twigs, flowers, and leaves. Domed bezel-set lids, strewn with gadrooned leaves and repoussé and chased flowers and foliage, are surmounted by a pineapple finial secured with a nut and bolt. The teapot lid is attached with a five-part hinge; the lid for the sugar bowl is separate. The teapot's pineapple finial is slightly bent toward the handle.

History: This teapot and sugar bowl may have belonged to Mary Hallowell Boylston (b. 1824), subsequently passing through the Boylston family to Ward Nicholas (d. 1924) and Alice Meehan Boylston (d. 1938); to their daughter Barbara Hallowell Boylston (1913–1975) and Paul Webster Bean (b. 1914), m. 1937.[3]

Exhibitions and publications: None.

NOTES TO THIS ENTRY ARE ON PAGE 310.

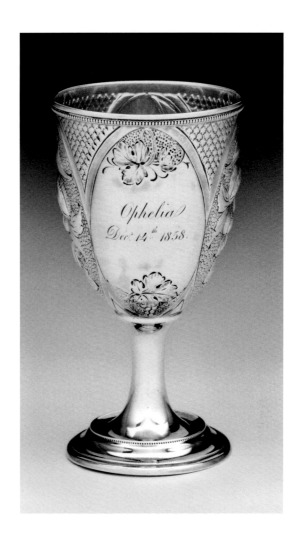

Gorham & Company (active 1852–1865)
John Gorham (1820–1898)

Goblet

Providence, Rhode Island, about 1858
Gift of Florence S. Baker
1983.268

H. 4⅞ in. (12.5 cm); Diam. rim 2¹¹⁄₁₆ in. (6.8 cm); Diam. foot 2⅜ in. (6 cm); Wt. 2 oz 17 dwt 4 gr (88.9 gm)

Marks: "[lion rampant] [anchor] [Gothic G] / 17 / COIN" struck incuse on bottom of bowl.

Inscriptions: "Ophelia / Decr 14th 1858" in script within an elliptical reserve engraved on bowl.

BY 1850 the ambitious and innovative John Gorham wished to expand the family operation from spoons and other small goods to include hollowware of the best quality and in the newest styles. To provide extra capital for machinery and skilled labor, he invited his cousins Gorham Thurber and Lewis Dexter Jr. to become partners in Gorham & Company. In this pivotal decade, the firm's sales increased fourteen-fold, from $29,000 in 1850 to $397,000 in 1859. The number of employees ballooned from fourteen to two hundred. By the end of the 1860s, with employees doubled and revenues almost tripled, Gorham was the largest fine silverware producer in the world.[1]

This richly textured goblet may have been presented to Ophelia Annie Smith of Cambridge on her wedding engagement to Atty. Samuel Snow, son of Caleb Hopkins Snow, M.D. (1796–1835), author of *A History of Boston, the Metropolis of Massachusetts* (Boston: Abel Bowen, 1828).

Description: Four oval panels divide the tulip-shaped bowl into quarters; two panels are embellished with repoussé and chased swags of pomegranates and leaves; one contains reserves carrying the inscription. Applied half-round and beaded bands encircle the rim. The waisted stem flares out to a stepped base.

History: Ophelia Annie Smith (1832–1876), m. Samuel Snow (1832–1900) in 1861; to their daughter Mabel Snow (b. 1862) and William Vaughn Moses, m. 1896; by descent to their nephew William Bradford Saunders and his wife, Florence S. Baker, the donor.[2]

Exhibitions and publications: Fitchburg Art Museum, Fitchburg, Massachusetts, "Made by Design: American Silver from the 17th to 20th Century," September 18, 1983–October 30, 1983.

NOTES TO THIS ENTRY ARE ON PAGE 310.

197

Gorham & Company (active 1852–1865)
  John Gorham (1820–1898)

Retailed by Newell Harding & Co.
(active 1851–1889), Boston, Massachusetts

Pitcher and salver

Providence, Rhode Island, and Boston, Massachusetts, about
1863–68
Gift of Mr. and Mrs. Henry L. Mason
1986.85–86

Pitcher (1986.85): H. 10⅜ in. (26.5 cm); W. 8¹¹⁄₁₆ in. (22 cm); D. 6³⁄₁₆
in. (15.8 cm); Diam. foot 4¼ in. (10.8 cm); Wt. 32 oz 9 dwt 18 gr
(1010.5 gm)

Salver (1986.86): H. 1 in. (2.6 cm); Diam. 10⅝ in. (26.8 cm); Wt. 18
oz 1 dwt 12 gr (562.2 gm)

Marks: "430"; lion passant within an octagon; anchor within a
shaped reserve; Gothic "G" within an octagon; "N. HARDING
& CO.," all struck incuse on base of pitcher. "N. HARDING &
CO. / PURE COIN" struck incuse on bottom of salver.

Inscriptions: None.

THIS GORHAM-MANUFACTURED pitcher was retailed as part
of a set by Newell Harding & Co. of Boston, a well-known
manufacturer of flatware; only the salver is marked by Harding. The firm's hollowware production, especially works dated
after the 1862 death of Newell Harding Sr., remains unclear.
The relationship with Gorham may have developed from Harding's early association with H. L. Webster of Providence. Webster worked with Jabez Gorham in that city in 1831 and invested
in Harding's firm in 1841.[1]

By the 1860s, Gorham offered hollowware in a wide variety of styles. The Harding firm may have purchased the water

197

pitcher and then further embellished it, along with a salver of their own or another's manufacture, to create a marketable set. Both pieces have central engravings of a complex strapwork design entwined with a sprigged vine within a reserve, which resemble the elaborate entwined monograms popular in the later nineteenth century. The newly fashionable Renaissance-revival-style strapwork and portrait medallions may have been engraved in Providence or Boston. Harding & Co.'s letterhead was embellished with a similar strapwork-style ornament.[2]

The delicately modeled and cast catfish mask at the base of the pitcher's spout is set against a grouping of cattails, providing a dramatic contrast to the smooth, highly polished surface of the body. The mark includes the pattern number "430," although Carpenter has noted that these numbers seem to have been assigned arbitrarily and not sequentially; nor do they always indicate the same form. The exact date of the first use of the "lion-anchor-G" logo is unknown, but it was in use by the mid-1850s. Silverware such as this pitcher, bearing only the logo and a pattern number, was known to have been made by Gorham from 1863 through 1865.[3] Gorham sold mainly to the trade during this period, and solid silver hollowware from the region's largest wholesaler stocked many shops, such as Newell Harding & Co. on Court Street in Boston.

Description: The vase-shaped spun body of the pitcher sits on a splayed ring base. A band of large beads ornaments the seam between the body and neck, under the beaded rim. The set-in spout with scrolled edge is adorned at its base with a stylized catfish head set against a group of repoussé-chased cattails with stippled background. The hollow ear-shaped handle features a long applied acanthus leaf that curls at the top to form a thumbpiece and continues down the length of the handle. A band of flat-chased leaves stretches around the middle of the body and frames a circular reserve below the spout, within which is a stylized strapwork design embellished with vines.

The salver is a stamped shallow form with three cast feet and an applied stamped band on the rim. The interior is densely engraved with concentric rings of flat geometric shapes, punctuated with medallions depicting a lady, a knight, and two interlaced strapwork motifs. The strapwork motif engraved under the pitcher's spout is repeated at the center of the salver.

History: Early history unknown. Purchased in 1986 from the Boston shop of J. Herbert Gebelein and presented as a gift to the Museum by Mr. and Mrs. Henry L. Mason.

Exhibitions and publications: None.

NOTES TO THIS ENTRY ARE ON PAGE 311.

198

Gorham & Company (active 1852–1865)
John Gorham (1820–1898)
George Wilkinson (1819–1894), designer

Ladle

Providence, Rhode Island, 1864
American Decorative Arts Curator's Fund
1987.515

L. 12½ in. (31.7 cm); W. bowl 4⅛ in. (10.5 cm); Wt. 5 oz 3 dwt 17 gr (161.3 gm)

Marks: Lion passant; anchor; Gothic letter "G"; "PAT.1864 / STERLING" struck incuse on back of stem.

Inscriptions: "C R" entwined in Gothic letters engraved on back of stem, near handle tip.

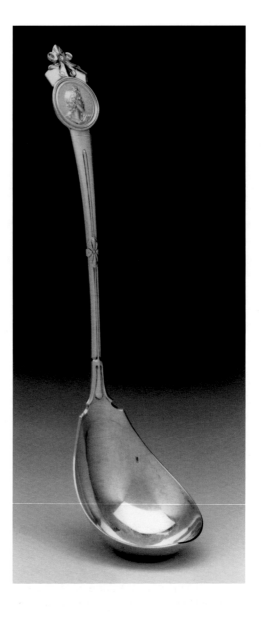

THIS PUNCH LADLE in the die-stamped Medallion pattern, with portrait profile, is characteristic of the period in which John Gorham's innovations in manufacturing gave him the lead in America as a maker of solid silver flatware. In 1852, twelve years before this ladle was made, Gorham engaged James Nasmyth (1808–1890), the English inventor of the steam hammer, to create a steam-powered drop press. Installed in Gorham's Providence factory in 1853 or 1854, the superior machine enabled the firm to dominate the American market.[1]

Gorham's Medallion pattern was designed in 1864 by English-trained silversmith George Wilkinson (1819–1894), a pivotal member of the firm for nearly four decades. Medallion flatware became widely popular in America and was emulated by many leading manufacturers.[2]

Description: This large punch ladle has a gold-washed, elongated, egg-shaped bowl. The stem terminates in a circular portrait profile of a youth crowned with laurel leaves.

History: Early history unknown. Museum purchase from E. J. Canton, Lutherville, Maryland.

Exhibitions and publications: None.

NOTES TO THIS ENTRY ARE ON PAGE 311.

199

Gorham Manufacturing Company
(active 1865–1961)
Thomas J. Pairpoint (1847–1902), designer
Ladle

Providence, Rhode Island, 1871
Gift of V. Stephen Vaughan in memory
of Robert E. Cleaves
1997.163

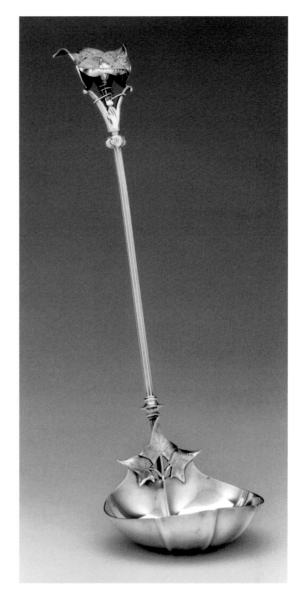

L. 13⅛ in. (33.3 cm); W. bowl 3¹¹⁄₁₆ (9.5 cm); D. 3 in. (7.5 cm); Wt. 5 oz
15 dwt 16 gr (179.9 gm)

Marks: Lion passant; anchor; Gothic "G"; "STERLING," all struck
incuse on exterior of bowl, below lip.

Inscriptions: None.

THE MORNING GLORY pattern was patented in 1871, during
the 1868–1877 tenure of Paris-trained Thomas Pairpoint as
Gorham's head designer. Although an example of Gorham's
production work and a traditional form in silver flatware, this
ladle illustrates the nineteenth-century drive to domesticate
nature. The vining morning glory grew wild but was commonly trained to climb a fence or trellis in a household garden. On
this utensil, silver replicas of the flower are brought indoors to
embellish the table of a dining room, where an oak or mahogany sideboard may have also been decorated with realistically
carved game, fish, or other fauna or flora.

Description: This large soup or punch ladle in the Morning Glory
pattern has a slender reeded handle terminating in a morning glory
flower set against three pointed veined leaves, with vinelike tendrils
wrapped around the foliate support. At the handle base, reeds are
clustered above the stamped bowl. A cluster of ivylike leaves are soldered above a lobed bowl, with three scalloped channels for pouring.

History: Early history unknown. Acquired by Stephen Vaughan of
Boston about 1980 and made a gift to the Museum in 1997.

Exhibitions and publications: None.

Gorham Manufacturing Company (active 1865–1961)

Child's cup and napkin ring

Providence, Rhode Island, about 1873
Gift of Frederick Winslow in Memory of his father Dr. Frederick Winslow
1991.784–85

Napkin ring (1991.784): H. 1⅝ in. (4 cm); Diam. 1¹³⁄₁₆ in. (4.5 cm); Wt. 2 oz 10 dwt 7 gr (78.2 gm)

Child's cup (1991.785): H. 3⅝ in. (9.2 cm); W. 5 in. (12.7 cm); Diam. rim 2⅞ on. (7.3 cm); Diam. foot 3 in. (7.6 cm); Wt. 6 oz 19 dwt 5 gr (216.5 gm)

Marks: Lion passant within an octagon; anchor within a shaped reserve; Gothic "G" within an octagon; "STERLING / 936 / F," the latter all incuse, struck on base of cup. "XVI" scratched above mark. Napkin ring unmarked.

Inscriptions: "Fred" in Gothic letters, within a lozenge-shaped reserve, engraved on exterior of napkin ring; "From Uncle Fred" in script engraved on interior edge. "July 27 1873 / FREDERIC B. WINSLOW. / from / Uncle Fred. / Dec. 25. 1873." in varied lettering engraved on body of cup, opposite handle.

SILVER SPOONS, cups, and bells had long been traditional presentation gifts for children. By the last quarter of the 1800s, children's ware had become a special category for silver manufacturers and was often featured in special sections of company catalogues, which offered a variety of individual pieces as well as matching boxed sets.[1] This Gothic-revival silver cup by Gorham and its related but unmatched and unmarked napkin ring (possibly by Gorham) have been personalized with inscriptions that allude to the tender affection and regard for their young recipient.

Description: The napkin ring is a seamed silver cylinder with mechanically produced bright-cut-style ornament. The cup is composed of a seamed cylindrical body with a wide base band of bright-cut style die-rolled decoration with a repeated design. Beaded bands are applied at upper and lower rims. A simulated branch with leaves and berries has been "trained" to the cast circular handle with neatly wound "twine"; its upper termial forms a thumbpiece.

History: Given to Dr. Frederick Bradley Winslow (1873–1937), son of Walter and Sarah Louisa (Sears) Winslow, by his paternal uncle Frederick Winslow. The set descended to the recipient's son Frederick Winslow of Wollaston, Massachusetts, the donor.

Exhibitions and publications: None.

NOTE TO THIS ENTRY IS ON PAGE 311.

Gorham Manufacturing Company
(active 1865–1961)

Pair of bud vases

New York, New York, 1876
American Decorative Arts Curator's Fund
1991.255–56

1991.255: H. 7³⁄₁₆ in. (18.3 cm); Diam. foot 2½ in. (6.3 cm); Wt. 3 oz 18 dwt 23 gr (122.8 gm)

1991.256: H. 7³⁄₁₆ in. (18.4 cm); Diam. foot 2⅜ in. (6.2 cm); Wt. 3 oz 18 dwt 20 gr (122.6 gm)

Marks: Lion rampant within an octagon; anchor within a shaped reserve; Gothic "G" within an octagon, all struck on each. Also marked "UNION SQUARE N.Y. / GORHAM & CO / 1465 / STERLING / I" in sans-serif letter.

Inscriptions: "M E L A" in Gothic letters engraved on each.

EVEN DURING THE MOST eclectic periods of nineteenth-century design, simple pieces of silver with plain surfaces and quiet ornament were available to the consumer. The restrained classical-style decoration and form, combined with their petite size, suggest that this pair of bud vases was intended to ornament a private space. During the second half of the nineteenth century, vases became increasingly popular as grand public presentation pieces and personal gifts for domestic use.

Even though the company was chartered in 1863 and incorporated in 1865, Gorham continued to stamp "Gorham & Co." on its Union Square silverware through the 1880s. Carpenter has noted that silver marked "Union Square" was probably made at the small shop Gorham operated in New York about 1875–1885.[1]

Description: Each slender amphora-shaped vase displays angular handles that extend from the lip to the shoulder. A band of swagged floral decoration has been placed above the engraving. A short stem with a reel-shaped baluster descends to a splayed circular foot.

History: Purchased by the Museum in 1979 from Eugene J. Carter, Baltimore, Maryland; formally accessioned in 1991.

Exhibitions and publications: None.

NOTE TO THIS ENTRY IS ON PAGE 311.

Henry Haddock (1811–1892)

Child's cup

Boston, Massachusetts, about 1850
Gift of Mabel Gurney Clark and F. Lyman Clark in memory
of their mother, Susan Ward Clark
54.514

H. 2⅝ in. (6.5 cm); W. 4⅞ in. (12.4 cm); D. 3¹¹⁄₁₆ in. (9.5 cm); Diam.
foot 2⅜ in. (6 cm); Wt. 4 oz 4 dwt 12 gr (131.4 gm)

Marks: "HADDOCK" within a rectangle, doublestruck; "BOS-
TON." incuse; and "Coin" in Gothic incuse lettering, all struck on
bottom of cup.

Inscriptions: "Susan Ward" in script engraved under rim of bowl,
opposite handle.

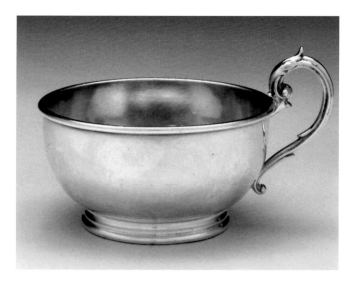

THIS DEMURE child's cup is undecorated except for its highly
polished finish, graceful form, and scrolled handle. The round,
wide bowl resembles that of a porringer and may have served
as both cup and bowl for its young owner.

Henry Haddock was born in Haverhill, Massachusetts, and
as a boy moved with his family to Boston, where he may have
apprenticed with silversmith Moses Morse.[1] Haddock first
appeared in the Boston directory of 1838, listed in partnership
with silversmith Henry Andrews (w. 1830–1847) on Hawley,
near Milk Street. By 1840 Haddock & Andrews, silversmiths,
were listed at 7 Williams Court, set amid Boston's best retail
establishments.[2] After six years, the firm relocated to nearby
Court Street. In 1848 Andrews disappeared from the listings,
but Haddock prospered on his own as a major supplier of silver
hollowware to Bigelow Brothers & Kennard, one of Boston's
large prominent purveyors of "Watches, Jewelry and Plate."
According to the retailer's account books, from 1848 to 1852
Haddock supplied close to seven hundred teapots, creamers,
sugar bowls, coffeepots, cups, goblets, salvers, toast racks,
mustard pots, vases, and other forms. A "plain cup" of similar weight to this child's cup (4 oz. 3 dwt) was entered in the
accounts on March 30, 1849. Haddock's wholesale charge for
the cup was $6.96, $4.46 for materials and $2.50 for labor.

In addition to plain wares, Haddock accommodated the burgeoning market for Rococo-revival-style silverware, which may
have been termed "Antique" in his production book. Haddock
produced wares in the following patterns: Octagonal, Chinese,
Chased, Fluted, Claw, Parian, and Egg and Grape, among others.[3]

No pieces have surfaced bearing marks by both Haddock
and Bigelow Brothers & Kennard, suggesting that Haddock
refrained from marking the wares he wholesaled, which presumably received the retailer's mark. As in the case of this
child's cup, he did sometimes mark his hollowware, perhaps to
retail in his own shop.

From 1859 until 1868, when he retired from silversmithing,
Haddock was the senior member of Haddock, Lincoln (Albert
L.) and Foss (Charles M.), jewelers, of 65 Washington Street.
The new partnership may have been formed to strengthen
the firm's financial base as well as to offer a broader selection
of wares. During this period, numerous New England retailers augmented their stock with solid silver goods purchased
wholesale from Gorham & Company in Providence, Rhode
Island.[4] By 1863, apparently thriving and with a spotless credit
record, Haddock, Lincoln & Foss had expanded to include a
factory at 13 Court Square, though the nature of its production
is unknown. The R. G. Dun and Company credit ledgers pronounced the firm "good for all engagements."[5]

Description: The low raised vessel sits on a molded ring foot and
features an applied rounded rim. A cast acanthus-leaf and scrolled
handle is applied to the rim and side.

History: Susan Nahum Ward (b. 1845) and Lyman Jabez Clark (b.
1835), m. 1866; to their children Mabel Gurney Clark (b. 1870) and
Francis Lyman Clark (b. 1877), the donors.[6] For two additional pieces of Ward family silver, see cat. nos. 205 and 207.

NOTES TO THIS ENTRY ARE ON PAGE 311.

203

Newell Harding (1796–1862)
Pitcher

Boston, Massachusetts, about 1824–50
Charles T. and Susan P. Baker by bequest of the latter
21.1258

H. 7⁵⁄₁₆ in. (18.5 cm); W. 7⁵⁄₈ in. (19.2 cm); D. 5½ in. (14 cm); Wt. 17 oz 19 dwt 5 gr (558.6 gm)

Marks: "N. Harding" in script within a banner; "BOSTON." incuse; and "Pure Silver Coin" in a rectangle, all struck on bottom.

Inscriptions: "Susan P. Baker" in script engraved on top of thumb-piece.

IN THIS SMALL but gracefully proportioned paneled pitcher, the plain, highly polished surfaces combine with the octagonal form to reflect light and create dramatic shadows. Newell Harding's reputation was based on the manufacture of flatware, and it is unclear whether the firm manufactured or only purchased solid silver hollowware for retail. Although marked with Harding's pre-1851 mark, this pitcher may have been produced by another silversmith and purchased for retail sale by Harding.

Harding was the son of Jesse and Hannah (Webster) Harding of Haverhill, Massachusetts. It has long been maintained that he apprenticed in Boston with Hazen Morse (1790–1874), the Haverhill-born silversmith and engraver.[1] Thirty years after his death, Harding was hailed in the *Annals of the Massachusetts Charitable Mechanics Association* as "probably the best known silversmith in New England in his day." He joined the association early in his career, in 1828, and in 1837 received a silver medal in its first exhibition, honored for "A case of Silver Table Ware, comprising spoons, forks, ladles, sugar tongs, fish and butter knives . . . 94 pieces all made in a finished, superior, massy manner."[2] He actively maintained his membership throughout his life and acted as a silverware judge at the 1848 and later exhibitions.

Harding commenced business shortly before Boston incorporated in 1822; the city's population had more than doubled since 1800, to approximately 57,000. Ambitious and graced with an entrepreneurial outlook, Harding flourished, and his firm continued in the Court Square area of upper Washington Street until 1889. Much of the information published to date about the firm has been drawn from the 1856 publication *Leading Men and Leading Pursuits*, produced to showcase the principal trades

and industries of the United States. The publication reported that early in his career, Harding confined his business to spoon-making, a practice seen as innovative since most silversmiths in the 1820s produced a variety of flatware and hollowware. His spoon business was described as so successful that "Newell Harding became a household word in New England." The publication further credited him with being the first in Boston to introduce power for the purpose of rolling silver; to segment the operation to increase production and allow for "more highly finished work"; and to introduce the "ornamental style of work now so much in vogue." The report claimed Newell Harding & Co., which had thirty-five workers, employed the "only silversmiths in Boston who make and sell their own work to consumers."[3] A large ad within lists more than fifty available flatware forms but mentions no hollowware. The firm did, however, advertise both flatware and hollowware in an ad in the Boston directory of 1857.[4]

In 1851 Harding, in business since 1821, entered into a partnership with his eldest son, Francis Low Harding (1806–1906), as well as Alexander H. Lewis (1815–1859) and Lewis A. Kimball (w. about 1851–85), to form Newell Harding & Co. According to contemporary R. G. Dun credit reports, Harding leased the land at 12 Court Street but owned the shop and store at that address. Known in 1852 as good mechanics with a solid retail business, they were considered safe credit risks. Two years later, Dun reported that the firm was known to "manufacture considerably for the dealers . . . though possibly not so much as before . . . and was known to seek family patronage."[5]

By 1860 large manufacturers such as Gorham had begun to dominate the industry, whereas small and medium-sized firms struggled to remain competitive. Internal problems beset Harding's firm as well. R. G. Dun reported that the "young Hardings habits [were] considered rather free" after the death of the remaining "substantial" member, partner Alexander H. Lewis, in 1859. Subsequently, caution was advised in dealing with the firm. It was noted that Francis Low Harding withdrew from the partnership and that the senior Harding was "drinking badly" when the firm's 12 Court Street land lease was not renewed in 1861. After Newell Harding Sr. died in 1862, the firm continued under his name, operated by Lewis Kimball and Harding's remaining sons.[6]

During the 1860s, in an effort to take advantage of the market for less expensive plated wares, Harding & Co., like many other retailers, operated their own plating department and purchased goods "in the metal" (unplated) from Reed & Barton in Taunton, Massachusetts.[7] Newell Harding Jr., who had separated from the family business for a few years after his father's death (apparently with feelings of ill will), maintained a separate listing in the Boston directory for several years; however, by 1868 he had rejoined the firm. In 1875 Julius L. D. Sullivan (born in 1833 in Cambridge, Massachusetts) is listed together with the reunited brothers, Francis Low Harding (1826–1906), Webb Harding (about 1832–after 1875), and Newell Harding Jr. (1834–1885), as Newell Harding & Co. Although it is unclear how the business was divided between retailing and manufacturing, the firm continued for another twenty years at Court Street, School Street, or Washington Street addresses, disappearing from the Boston directory in 1890.

Description: The vessel is octagonal in cross-section, its raised tulip-shaped body is faceted with eight panels. The scalloped rim, with an applied rounded edge, gives way to a large set-in spout that rises above the rim in a great curve complementing that of the lower body. The contrasting angular handle attaches to the rim; rises sharply; and curves down to the hip of the body, where its W-shaped bottom edge attaches near a small vent hole. The applied base is octagonal, and the center of the bottom is closed with a thinner circle of silver. An applied edge on the base conforms to that surrounding the upper rim.

History: This pitcher was probably first owned by Henry Porter (b. 1793) of Medford and his wife, Susan Simpson Tidd (1803–1853), of Boston, sometime after their marriage in 1824. Charles Tidd Porter (1825–1826), their firstborn son, died as an infant, and it is possible that one of two additional children, named Susan Emily Porter (bap. 1828) and Francis Henry Porter (bap. 1833), also died young. The donors Susan Porter Baker (1837–1921) and Charles Tidd Baker (1830–1905) were the namesakes and first cousins of the children and likely recipients of the family silver.[8]

NOTES TO THIS ENTRY ARE ON PAGE 311.

204

Newell Harding (1796–1862)
Tazza

Boston, Massachusetts, about 1830–40
Gift of Malcolm Parkes Hunt
1999.64.22

H. 5 5/16 in. (13.5 cm); Diam. rim 7 in. (17.7 cm); Diam. foot 4 5/8 in. (11.7 cm); Wt. 12 oz 7 dwt 6 gr (384.5 gm)

Marks: "NEWELL HARDING / PURE COIN" in roman letters struck incuse on foot, below beaded edge.

Inscriptions: None.

ALTHOUGH THIS SOPHISTICATED tazza bears the mark Harding used until 1851, it seems unlikely he was the maker, given his specialization in flatware. The graceful design and fine craftsmanship of the fluted bowl; dainty ribbon encircling the stem; lively flat-chased acanthus leaves of the base; finely cast claw feet; and deftly rendered grapevine indicate a hollowware maker of high ability. During this period, Obadiah Rich, the celebrated Boston silversmith, worked a few doors away from Harding's shop on Court Avenue. Like others, Rich may have wholesaled unmarked work, possibly this compote, for Harding to retail.

Description: The fluted bowl of the compote is encircled with a wide rim decorated with a repoussé and chased grapevine and edged with an applied beaded band. A two-part stem joined by a rounded baluster curves into the domed base, which is ornamented with swirling repoussé and chased acanthus leaves. An applied beaded band circles the lower rim of the base, which sits on four cast paw feet.

History: Purchased between the 1970s and 1990s by the donor.

Exhibitions and publications: None.

205

Newell Harding & Co. (active 1851–1889)
  Newell Harding (1796–1862)
  Francis Low Harding (1826–1906)
  Alexander H. Lewis (1815–1859)
  Lewis Kimball (active about 1851–1885)

Cup

Boston, Massachusetts, 1854
Gift of Mabel Gurney Clark and F. Lyman Clark in memory of their mother, Susan Ward Clark

54.513

H. 3¹³⁄₁₆ in. (9.7 cm); Diam. rim 3⅜ in. (8.6 cm); Diam. foot 2½ in. (6.4 cm); Wt. 5 oz 12 dwt 22 gr (175.6 gm)

Marks: "N. HARDING & CO." in roman letters struck incuse on bottom.

Inscriptions: "Mrs N. Ward. / Roxbury. / 1854." in script within a reserve engraved on side.

205

LIVELY FLAT-CHASED scrolls and flowers surround the somewhat formal inscription on this cup. It seems unlikely to have been a personal gift but rather one presented to Mrs. Ward by employees or other associates of her husband, Nahum.[1] Nahum Ward moved from his birthplace of Athol, Massachusetts, to Boston in 1825. He worked for two years in a soap and candle establishment and then entered the oil and tallow business, in neighboring Roxbury. After amassing a considerable fortune, Ward helped found the Rockland Bank of Roxbury and served on its board for twenty-seven years.[2] Ruth Ward would have celebrated her fortieth birthday in 1854. Five years later, she received a large pitcher also marked by Newell Harding & Co. and inscribed in the same manner to "Mrs. Ward" (cat. no. 207).

The deftly drawn scrolls and flowers in the exuberant, light-hearted engraving add interest and fashion to a plain, sturdy form. The work of the engraver can be seen on other silverware marked by Harding (cat. nos. 206–7) and on that marked by other Boston retailers.[3] Working in the mid-nineteenth century, this as-yet-unidentified craftsman seems to be looking back to the previous century, to the Rococo-style engraving on surviving works by Boston's colonial silversmiths such as Jacob Hurd or Paul Revere. However, the scrolls decorating this 1854 cup surround a reserve bearing an inscription to the wife of a self-made American businessman rather than the English-style family coat of arms characteristic of eighteenth-century silver.

Description: The body is raised, with straight sides curving inward at the base to a seamed and stepped ring foot. Heavy applied molding strengthens the upper rim. Chased and engraved foliate ornament surrounds the inscription.

History: Mrs. N. Ward was born Ruth Stetson Gurney (1814–1863) in Saco, Maine; m. Nahum Ward (1801–1858) in 1845 after his first wife, her sister, had died two years earlier. The cup descended from Ruth Ward to her daughter Susan Nahum Ward (b. 1845) and Lyman Jabez Clark (1835–1918), m. 1866; to their children Mabel Gurney Clark (b. 1870) and Francis Lyman Clark (b. 1877), the donors.

Exhibitions and publications: None.

NOTES TO THIS ENTRY ARE ON PAGE 311.

206

Newell Harding & Co. (active 1851–1889)
Newell Harding (1796/99–1862)
Francis Low Harding (1826–1906)
Alexander H. Lewis (1815–1859)
Lewis Kimball (active about 1851–1885)

Pitcher with two goblets

Boston, Massachusetts, 1855
Gift of Miss Florence Viaux and Frederic Ballou Viaux
62.202–4

Pitcher (62.202): H. 13⅜ in. (34 cm); W. 7⅝ in. (19.2 cm); D. 6³⁄₁₆ in. (15.7 cm); Diam. foot 4½ in. (11.4 cm); Wt. 26 oz 16 dwt 13 gr (834.4 gm)

Goblet (62.203): H. 6 in. (15.3 cm); Diam. rim 3⅜ in. (8.6 cm); Diam. foot 2⅞ in. (7.3 cm); Wt. 6 oz 5 dwt 5 gr (194.7 gm)

Goblet (62.204): H. 6 in. (15.3 cm); Diam. rim 3⅜ in. (8.6 cm); Diam. foot 2⅞ in. (7.3 cm); Wt. 6 oz 2 dwt 4 gr (190 gm)

Marks: "N. HARDING & CO." in roman letters struck incuse on bottom of each.

Inscriptions: "A Token / from the friends of the / Massachusetts / Volunteer Militia System / To / Colonel Isaac H. Wright / Rememorative of / his eloquent argument for the / perpetuation of the Institution / April 1855." engraved on front of pitcher. The Great Seal of the Commonwealth of Massachusetts engraved on body of each goblet.

THIS THREE-PIECE libation set saluted Col. Isaac Hull Wright (1814–1886) in appreciation of his "eloquent argument" for the preservation of the voluntary militia. Wright was a popular and respected Bostonian whose wit and eloquence meant that he was in great demand as a public speaker. An honored veteran of the Mexican War, he had enlisted as a private in Company B, Massachusetts Volunteers. He was elected lieutenant colonel and later made colonel of the regiment. Gen. Zachary Taylor appointed Colonel Wright to be military governor of Monterrey and Perote after their capture by U.S. forces. After the war, President Taylor made Wright a naval officer of Boston. He subsequently commanded the Boston Light Dragoons and commanded, for one year, the Ancient and Honorable Artillery Company.[1]

As illustrated by this handsome service, Newell Harding & Co. provided custom-engraved presentation pieces (see also cat. nos. 205, 207). The style is generally conservative, related

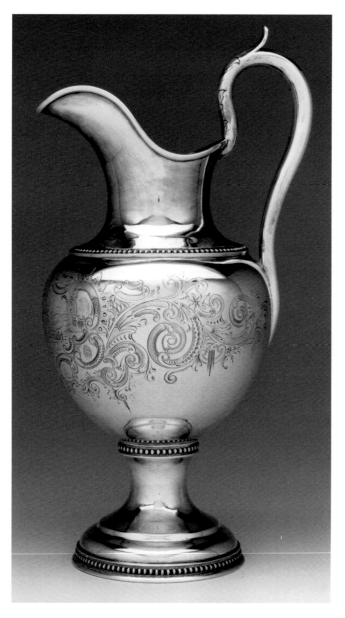

206

N. HARDING & CO

Massachusetts seal, and inscription. Crossed banners, cannons, and balls embellish the neck. The bowl of each goblet is raised and sits on a stemmed, domed foot. Beaded trim is applied to the rims of the cup and the foot, and a ribbed band embellishes the stem.

History: Col. Isaac Hull Wright (1814–1886) and Clementine G. Ballou (b. 1812) of New Hampshire, m. 1837;[2] to their niece Florence Ballou Farrar (b. 1843), who was the daughter of Clementine's sister Feducia Ballou and Abijah Farrer. Florence Ballou Farrar m. Frederick Henry Viaux (b. 1839) in 1873, and the pitcher descended to their daughter Florence Viaux (1878–1981) and her nephew Frederic Ballou Viaux, the donors.

Exhibitions and publications: None.

NOTES TO THIS ENTRY ARE ON PAGE 311.

to the elegant Neoclassical shapes and smooth, polished surface popular earlier in the century. By contrast, the exuberant engraving encircling the body of the pitcher reflects the newer Rococo-revival style fashionable at midcentury.

Description: The raised bulbous body of the pitcher sits on a high molded foot with stamped beaded bands at the rim and foot and at the juncture of the curved cylindrical neck and the body. The high spout is finished with an applied flat band. The hollow scrolled handle rises slighty above the height of the spout. Elaborate, chased, foliate scrolls wrap almost back to the handle from a central cartouche under the spout, which is emblazened with emblems of the

Newell Harding & Co. (active 1851–1889)
Newell Harding (1796–1862)
Francis Low Harding (1826–1906)
Alexander H. Lewis (1815–1859)
Lewis Kimball (active about 1851–1885)

Pitcher

Boston, Massachusetts, 1859
Gift of Mabel Gurney Clark and F. Lyman Clark in memory
of their mother, Susan Ward Clark
54.512

H. 12³⁄₁₆ in. (31 cm); W. 8⁵⁄₁₆ in. (21 cm); D. 6³⁄₈ in. (16.2 cm); Diam.
foot 3⁷⁄₈ in. (9.9 cm); Wt. 31 oz 2 dwt 1 gr (967.4 gm)

Marks: "N. HARDING & CO. / BOSTON" in roman letters,
and "Coin" in Gothic letters, struck incuse on bottom of vessel. A
second stamp of "Coin" has been effaced.

Inscriptions: "Mrs. N. Ward, / Roxbury. / 1859." in script within a
reserve engraved beneath spout.

THIS PITCHER was presented to Ruth Ward in 1859, the year
after the death of her husband Nahum. In 1854 she had received
from Harding's shop a silver cup bearing a similar inscription
(cat. no. 205).

The energetic, bold, and glittering bright-cut engraving on
this large, classically shaped pitcher covers nearly the entire
body. Although the engraving appears to be by the same hand, it
contrasts sharply with the loose, exuberant style of the engraving on the cup given to Mrs. Ward five years earlier; it also differs greatly from the subtle effect of the fine, delicate chasing
of Harding & Co.'s presentation ewer for Colonel Wright (cat.
no. 206), dated about the same time. The sweeping scrolls of
floral and foliate motifs gradually narrow as they approach the
handle, and mannered vertical tendrils extend below the lower
foliage.

Because of the widespread popularity of domestic silver presentation gifts, larger retailers probably maintained an inventory of wares, either of their own or others' manufacture, ready
to be engraved or further embellished at the customer's behest.
Without additional elaborate and expensive handmade decoration, this seamed pitcher may have been a less costly stock
item.

207

Description: The seamed bulbous body is joined to a tall concave neck
by a band of shaped beading and sits on a cast ring foot. The hollow
scrolled handle rises above the upper rim and attaches to the widest
part of the body. A beaded edge continues around the slightly angular applied lip. Engraved foliate ornament extends broadly over the
surface of the body, with a reserve below the spout.

History: See cat. no. 205.

Exhibitions and publications: None.

208

Newell Harding & Co. (active 1851–1889)
  Newell Harding (1796–1862)
  Francis Low Harding (1826–1906)
  Alexander H. Lewis (1815–1859)
  Lewis Kimball (active about 1851–1885)
  M & P (active about 1861)

Standing cup

Boston, Massachusetts, about 1870
Gift of the First Church in Newton
1973.29

H. 6¹¹⁄₁₆ in. (17 cm); Diam. rim 3⅜ in. (8.6 cm); Diam foot 3⅜ in.
(8.6 cm); Wt. 7 oz 18 dwt 10 gr (246.4 gm)

Marks: "N. HARDING & CO. / BOSTON / COIN / M & P /
N. HARDING & CO." in roman letters struck incuse under bowl.

Inscriptions: "First Church / Newton / 1861" in script engraved on
bowl.

THIS STANDING CUP was modeled after a seventeenth-century
English example in Newton's First Church that was given by
Abraham White (fig. 4). It is unclear that Newell Harding &
Co. manufactured silver hollowware. During the 1850s and
1860s, the firm did accept orders for presentation silver (see, for
example, cat. no. 206) and retail other makers' hollowware as
well. "M & P," whose mark is not yet identified, may have been
the maker.

In addition to this wine cup, Newell Harding & Co. created at least one other facsimile of early silver. The firm's mark
appears on a silver cruet stand bearing the Faneuil family arms.
It was commissioned as a copy of the English cruet stand made
in 1745/46 for Benjamin Faneuil by Samuel Wood (1704–about
1794).[1] When the original cruet stand descended to another
branch of the family, Dr. George Avery Bethune (1812–1886),
a direct descendant of Benjamin Faneuil and thus entitled to
use the Faneuil arms, commissioned Newell Harding & Co. to
reproduce it.[2] These two orders reflect the trust and confidence
that local patrons placed in the Harding firm, which had been
in business forty years at the time this cup was engraved.

Description: The bell-shaped bowl of this standing cup is raised and
has an applied flaring lip. A prominent center point suggests that the
vessel may have been lathe turned after it was raised. The spun stem
with applied midband descends to a stepped splayed base finished
with an applied foot ring.

History: See appendix no. 8.

Exhibitions and publications: None.

NOTES TO THIS ENTRY ARE ON PAGE 311.

FIG. 4. Unidentified
artist, standing cup,
London, 1618–19, with
later engraving. Silver.
Museum of Fine Arts,
16¹¹⁄₁₆ in (17 cm). Boston;
Gift of the First Church
in Newton (1973.24).

Newell Harding & Co. (active 1851–1889)
Newell Harding (1796–1862)
Francis Low Harding (1826–1906)
Alexander H. Lewis (1815–1859)
Lewis Kimball (active about 1851–1885)

Ladle

Boston, Massachusetts, about 1870
Gift of Malcolm Parkes Hunt
1999.64.19

L. 5¼ in. (13.3 cm); W. 1¼ in. (3.2 cm); Wt. 1 oz 8 dwt 16 gr (44.6 gm)

Marks: "COIN / N. HARDING & CO." struck incuse on back of stem.

Inscriptions: Gothic letter "L" engraved on back of stem tip.

PERHAPS INTENDED FOR serving cream or another rich liquid, this small, whimsical, barrel-shaped ladle fits snugly into its own satin-lined case for safe keeping. The handle pattern with Neo-Grec-style spirals is similar to others produced about 1870.[1]

Early in his career, Newell Harding manufactured the well-known fiddle- and olive-patterned spoons made by many other manufacturers. In 1841 Henry L. Webster, a Providence, Rhode Island, spoonmaker, joined Harding's firm.[2] After an apprenticeship in Boston, Webster had returned to his native Providence to become Jabez Gorham's first partner in a spoon manufacturing business. In 1841 Webster sold his share to Gorham and returned to Boston, where he was associated with Harding until 1851, the year Harding took his sons into his business and renamed the firm Newell Harding & Co. Webster returned to Providence after this date and formed a new silver flatware manufacturing company.

In the 1850s Lewis Kimball, another spoonmaker, joined Harding's firm. He remained until 1863, leaving soon after Newell Harding Sr.'s death in 1862. He remained in business for himself in Boston, producing "for the trade and to special order, both plain or the most elaborately ornamental silver spoons, knives, forks, ladles, etc., of his own or special designs furnished by his customers."[3]

The firm may have always retailed some wares by other makers. Yet, it becomes increasingly difficult to distinguish between the firm's manufacturing and retailing roles after Harding's death in 1862 and the departure of Kimball in 1863. The majority of flatware marked by Newell Harding and New-

ell Harding & Co. in the Museum's collection bears no other marks. However, a large ladle in the Prince Albert pattern in a private collection bears the marks of Newell Harding & Co. and Michael Gibney of New York, who patented the Prince Albert pattern in the 1850s. A jelly spoon (1999.64.6) in the Museum's collection bears only Harding & Co.'s mark but is identical to Knowles & Ladd's Emperor pattern, which was introduced in the early 1870s.

R. G. Dun & Co.'s last report on the firm in 1866 remained gloomy: "not much to them, drink too much" (see cat. no. 203).[4] Nevertheless, Newell Harding & Co. remained in business until 1889, perhaps due to the solid reputation built by its founder during his long career.

Description: The cast barrel-shaped bowl of this ladle is ornamented with three narrow bands of bright-cut engraving. A floral swag design rings the area between the middle and upper bands of engraving. The stem is attached to the bowl with a three-pronged end. The downturned stem tip is triangular, with spirals at each side. The ladle retains its original custom-fitted box with blue satin interior and exterior covered with simulated leather and gold trim.

History: Purchased about 1980 by the donor and made a gift to the Museum.

Exhibitions and publications: None.

NOTES TO THIS ENTRY ARE ON PAGE 311–12.

210

Harris & Stanwood (active 1839–1848)
William C. Harris (active about 1839–1848)
Henry B. Stanwood (1818–1868)

Five-piece tea service

Boston, Massachusetts, 1839–48
Gift of Beatrice P. Strauss, William Phillips Jr., Drayton
Phillips, Christopher H. Phillips and Anne P. Bryant
Res.69.2.1–5

Teapot (Res. 69.2.1): H. 9¹³⁄₁₆ in. (25 cm); W. 12 in. (30.6 cm); D. 6⁵⁄₁₆
in. (16 cm); Diam. foot 4⅝ in. (11.7 cm); Wt. 37 oz 11 dwt 4 gr
(1168.2 gm)

Teapot (Res. 69.2.2): H. 9⅝ in. (24.5 cm); W. 12³⁄₁₆ in. (31 cm); D.
6⁵⁄₁₆ in. (16 cm); Diam. foot 4½ in. (11.5 cm); Wt. 38 oz 4 dwt 16 gr
(1189.2 gm)

Sugar bowl (Res. 69.2.3a–b): H. 9⅝ in. (24.5 cm); W. 9⅛ in. (23.2);
D. 5¹¹⁄₁₆ in. (14.5 cm); Diam. foot 4⁵⁄₁₆ in. (10.9 cm); Wt. 29 oz. 12 dwt
17 gr (921.8 gm)

Creampot (Res.69.2.4): H. 7⅞ in. (20 cm); W. 6⅞ in. (17.5 cm); D.
4⅝ in. (11.7 cm); Diam. foot 3⅜ in. (8.6 cm); Wt. 19 oz 7 dwt 1 gr
(601.9 gm)

Waste bowl (Res.69.2.5): H. 6¹¹⁄₁₆ in. (17 cm); Diam. 5⅞ in. (15 cm);
diam. foot 4¼ in. (10.8 cm); Wt. 19 oz 8 dwt 15 gr (604.4 gm)

Marks: "Harris & Stanwood" in roman letters, "Pure Silver Coin"
twice in italics, and "BOSTON." in roman letters struck on base
of each teapot. The sugar bowl lacks the second "Pure Coin Silver"
mark. The creampot and waste bowl are unmarked.

Inscriptions: "A R" in script engraved on side of teapots, beneath
spout of creampot, and on bodies of sugar bowl and waste bowl.

MARKED BY ONE OF Boston's best jewelry houses, this large
and boldly shaped service is characterized by a playful sense of
fashion in its form and a more sober restraint in its plain and
highly polished surface. The sinuous lines of the bodies reflect
the popular interest in the rendering of natural forms. The
bulb shapes seem to grow from the foliage below and reach
"full bloom" in their ruffled rims.

Mechanics Association for their "tea sets, pitchers, [and] salt cellars . . . [that] as to style and work of plain silver ware is equal to the best foreign [wares]" (see cat. no. 211).[2]

An advertisement in the 1847–48 Boston directory describes the company as "Importers and Dealers in Silver and Plated Wares, Watches, Clocks, Lamps, Gas Fixtures, Candleabras, Tea Trays, Fine Table Cutlery, Rich Fancy Goods, &c., Watches and Clocks cleaned and repaired by an experienced workman." Harris seems to have retired soon after; his name appeared only in the directory's residential section. Stanwood worked alone until he was joined by James D. Stanwood and George D. Low, from 1853 to 1861, forming Henry B. Stanwood & Co. (see cat. no. 232). The following year, Henry B. Stanwood (and perhaps James D. Stanwood and George D. Low) joined his former rival at 123 Washington Street (at that time known as Shreve, Brown & Co.) to form Shreve, Stanwood & Co. (see cat. no. 231). Stanwood remained in business with Shreve until the former's death in 1868, when the company reorganized to become the familiar Shreve, Crump & Low.

Description: The identical teapots are raised in a lobed bulb form that nestles within a cast leafy support that springs from a narrow baluster. A conforming splayed foot, with undulating surface, is attached to the stem by a nut and bolt. The cast curved spout and scrolled handle with ivory insets are decorated with curving cast acanthus leaves. The domed cover rests inside a waved flaring collar and is finished with a bud finial. The matching sugar bowl has double handles and a separate cover. The conforming creamer carries a broad lip on a wavy collar. The generously sized waste bowl conforms to the set, with the exception of the foot, which is soldered in place and not bolted together.

History: Original owners unknown and "A R" monogram unidentified. The service was loaned to the Museum in 1948 by Mr. and Mrs. William Phillips for use at public functions and was acquired as a gift from their heirs in 1969.

Exhibitions and publications: None.

NOTES TO THIS ENTRY ARE ON PAGE 312.

The firm of Harris & Stanwood first appeared in the 1839 Boston directory. William C. Harris and Henry B. Stanwood manufactured and retailed "silver ware" at 29 Tremont Row until 1842, when the firm moved to 253 Washington Street, just a short distance from their main competitor, Lows, Ball & Co., located at 123 Washington. Both firms showed pieces at the second Massachusetts Charitable Mechanics Association exhibition in 1839. The judges noted that it was difficult to judge which was better, "each house excellent of their kind but so different in character . . . while Harris & Stanwood very rich and beautiful in pattern and finished in a superior manner the design and excellence of the Antique Chased Pitcher presented for competition by Jones Lows & Ball is preferred." Both firms were awarded a silver medal. The "Antique Chased Pitcher" probably referred to the new Rococo-revival style with chased and repousséd decoration, and its novelty may have appealed more than the plain surfaces characteristic of Harris & Stanwood.[1]

In 1844 the firm, renamed named Harris, Stanwood & Co., received another silver medal from Massachusetts Charitable

Inscriptions: "LL / to / ECL / 1843. / to / LBW / 1914." in entwined and sprigged script engraved on body, opposite handle.

HARRIS, STANWOOD & CO. were celebrated for the beauty and quality of their "plain" wares, such as this small cup. Its graceful, curved form and polished surface are reminiscent of larger canns of the previous century. First presented in 1843, probably as a baby gift to a child in the Lincoln family, and subsequently inscribed to Louise Bodine Wallace in 1914, the cup remained a part of the family's history for 140 years.

Description: This small bulb-shaped cup is raised and sits on a drawn foot ring. A rounded band is applied to the upper rim. The hollow ear-shaped handle is soldered directly to the body. One stress crack appears at juncture between body and lower handle joint.

History: The cup was probably acquired by the Lincoln family of Hingham and passed by descent to the Wallace and Williams families. See cat. no. 23 for other silver from these families.

Exhibitions and publications: None.

211

Harris, Stanwood & Co. (active 1842–1848)
William C. Harris (active about 1839–1848)
Henry B. Stanwood (1818–1868)

Cup

Boston, Massachusetts, about 1843
Gift of Mr. and Mrs. Franklin H. Williams in memory of Louise Bodine Wallace
1984.514

H. 3¹¹⁄₁₆ in. (9.5 cm); W. 4⅛ in. (10.5 cm); D. 3 in. (7.5 cm); Diam. foot 2¼ in. (5.7 cm); Wt. 3 oz 16 dwt 12 gr (119 gm)

Marks: "HARRIS STANWOOD & CO" in roman letters and "Pure Silver Coin" in italic letters, each within a rectangle, struck on base.

212

John B. Jones & Co. (active 1833–1834)
John B. Jones (1782–1854)
Samuel S. Ball (b. 1807)

Creampot

Boston, Massachusetts, 1833–34
Bequest of Annie Bolton Matthews Bryant
Res.34.3

H. 6⅝ in. (16.7 cm); W. 6⁵⁄₁₆ in. (16 cm); D. 4⅛ in. (10.5 cm); Diam. foot 3 in. (7.6 cm); Wt. 6 oz 17 dwt 5 gr (213.4 gm)

Marks: "J. B. Jones & Co." within a rectangle struck on base.

Inscriptions: "Mary B. Fay. / Jan. 1st 1857." in script engraved beneath spout.

JOHN B. JONES had been in the jewelry business twenty years when this large and inverted pear-shaped creampot was made. Jones began working in 1813, and in 1816 he became the junior partner of Jabez Baldwin, managing the Salem silversmith's new Boston store. Jones established himself independently

212

include a Boston shop, Jones became his partner. He dropped the "junior" from his name by 1818 and, in 1821, added the middle initial "B," for his mother's maiden name, Belknap.[3]

By the time Jones added a partner (to create John Jones & Co.), the city directory had a small, separate advertising section, and the enterprising Jones placed a large half-page ad in the 1833 edition, the only local jeweler to do so. Along with imported watches, plated and Brittannia ware, Japannery and other fancy goods, Jones proclaimed that he "Manufactures in a superior style all description of Silver Plate and variety of Rich Jewels, Diamonds and Precious Stones." An 1834 tutorial cup, struck with Jones's mark from this period, is in the collection of the Massachusetts Historical Society. Later work by the firm is included in this catalogue (cat. nos. 213–16, 231).

Description: Decorated with elaborate flat-chased leaves and circles on both sides, the creampot's pear-shaped body curves in to the neck, which is bound with three ribs, and out to a flaring lip and broad spout. The body sits on a domed foot edged with two stamped bands of stars set against a dark stippled background. The scrolled strap handle attaches to the upper rim and the lower body.

History: Mary B. (Carter) Fay (1808–1889) was the wife of Boston merchant/distiller William C. Fay (1811–1889), son of Winslow Fay, prominent shipowner and merchant on India Wharf. The creampot may have been inscribed as a New Year's gift to Mary in 1857, though the mark indicates the piece was made earlier.[4] The family also owned a silver cup (Res. 34.2) from the Boston firm of Jones, Lows & Ball (active 1835–1840). See cat. no. 188 for the donor's connection to the Fay family.

Exhibitions and publications: None.

NOTES TO THIS ENTRY ARE ON PAGE 312.

after Baldwin died in 1819; sometime between 1826 and 1829, he moved to 123 Washington Street, which would become the firm's longtime home. In 1833 he took into the firm Samuel S. Ball, twenty-five years his junior. Three years later, George B. Jones replaced John as head of the firm, though John maintained a business address "above" 123 Washington Street until at least 1840. The firm prospered, undergoing several changes in partnerships but continuing to build a reputation as one of Boston's two or three most prestigious jewelers. It survives today as the well-known Shreve, Crump & Low.[1]

Jones was born in Framingham, Massachusetts, in 1782 to John and Mary (Belknap) Jones and was trained by an unknown master. His early career is complicated by the existence of a second jeweler with the same name working in Boston from about 1810 to 1822.[2] Jones first appeared in the Boston directory of 1813, listed as "John Jones, junior, jeweller." When silversmith Jabez Baldwin of Salem expanded his business in 1816 to

213

Jones, Lows & Ball (active 1835–1841)
  John B. Jones (1792–1854)
  Samuel S. Ball (b. 1807)
  True M. Ball (1815–1890)
  George B. Jones (1815–1875)
  John J. Low (1800–1876)
  Francis Low (1806–1855)

Four-piece tea service

Boston, Massachusetts, 1837
Gift of Mark Healey Dall
2001.820.1–4

Teapot or water pot (2001.820.1): H. 8 in. (20.3 cm); W. 10¹³⁄₁₆ in. (27.5 cm); Diam. body 6¹¹⁄₁₆ in. (17 cm); Diam. foot 4⅞ in. (12.5 cm); Wt. 28 oz 19 dwt 19 gr (901.7 gm)

Cream pitcher (2001.820.2): H. 6⅞ in. (17.5 cm); W. 6¹¹⁄₁₆ in. (17 cm);

Diam. body 4⅞ in. (12.4 cm); Diam. foot 3⁵⁄₁₆ in. (8.4 cm); Wt. 11 oz 8 dwt 18 gr (355.8 gm)

Teapot (2001.820.3): H. 7½ in. (19 cm); W. 10⅝ in. (27 cm); Diam. body 6⁵⁄₁₆ in. (16 cm); Diam. foot 5 in. (12.7 cm); Wt. 26 oz 15 dwt 4 gr (823.3 gm)

Sugar bowl (2001.820.4): H. 7¹³⁄₁₆ in. (19.8 cm); W. 7⅞ in. (20 cm); Diam. body 8⅝ in. (21.9 cm); Diam. foot 6 in. (15.2 cm); Wt. 21 oz 7 dwt 22 gr (665.5 gm)

Marks: "JONES, LOWS & BALL / Boston / Pure Silver Coin / Boston," each in a rectangle and arranged to form a rough square, struck on bottom of all. The retailer's and place names are in roman letters, the quality mark in italics.

Inscriptions: "Presented by the Merchants Bank, Boston to Mark Healey, January 1837 / on his resignation of the Presidency of the Bank." in script, within a floral reserve, engraved on all, except sugar bowl. Healey is spelled "Healy" on cream pitcher. "MH" entwined script monogram engraved within floral reserve on one side of sugar bowl. A similar reserve on the reverse has been left blank.

213

set is accompanied by a water pitcher (cat. no. 214) apparently presented to Healey at the same time.[3]

Description: Each object has a raised body, applied floral concave decoration above the shoulder, exuberant floral decoration around the perimeter, and a large cast leafy floral element on the lid. The two teapots have hinged lids; the sugar bowl is separate. Ivory insulators are inserted in the hollow seamed handles of the two teapots. Each short splayed trumpet foot on the tea service is reeded along its side; the foot of the pitcher is plain. The matching cream pitcher has a generously sized self spout with an applied rounded band at the rim. The matching sugar bowl has double handles and a separate cover that matches those on the teapots.

History: Fashioned for Mark Healey (1791–1876), m. Caroline Foster (1800–1871) in 1821; by descent to their daughter Caroline Wells Healey (1822–1912) and Charles Henry Appleton Dall (1816–1886), m. 1844; to their son William Healey Dall (1845–1927) and Annette Whitney (1859–1943), m. 1880; to their daughter Marion Dall (1882–1962); to her son Mark Healey Dall (1915–2000), who retained the Dall family name, and Pauline Kingsland Dall (b. 1920), m. 1947, who made the gift in her husband's name.[4]

Exhibitions and publications: None.

NOTES TO THIS ENTRY ARE ON PAGE 312.

In 1835 partners John B. Jones and Samuel S. Ball (see cat. no. 215) enlarged their partnership. By 1836 George B. Jones replaced John B. Jones as head of the firm, but, according to the listings in the Boston directory, John maintained an office upstairs at 123 Washington Street, the firm's longtime address. By 1839 Samuel S. Ball disappeared from the list of partners, replaced by True M. Ball.

Born in Gloucester, Massachusetts, John J. Low apprenticed in the silver and jewelry trade in nearby Salem. He appeared in the 1822 Boston directory first as a partner in the firm of Putnam and Low. By 1825 he appeared on his own, and in 1828 was joined by Daniel W. Low (for that year only) and his brother Francis as partners in the Jones firm, where they remained until the late 1840s.[1]

Commissioned to deliver grand presentation pieces, such as the vase presented to Daniel Webster in 1835 and the Brittania Cup to Samuel Cunard (1787–1865) in 1840, the partners were fortunate in their alliance with Boston silversmiths, especially the talented Obadiah Rich (see cat. nos. 226–28).[2]

This rich, elaborately decorated service was presented in January 1837 by Merchant's Bank, Boston, to Mark Healey at the end of his tenure as bank president. The financial panic of that year led to the loss of Healey's fortune, and he declared bankruptcy in 1842. He later regained his fortune and built an estate in Lynn, Massachusetts, that he named Ashton. In 1855 he added a townhouse at 2 Pemberton Square, Boston. The tea

214

Jones, Lows & Ball (active 1835–1841)
John B. Jones (1792–1854)
Samuel S. Ball (b. 1807)
True M. Ball (1815–1890)
George B. Jones (1815–1875)
John J. Low (1800–1876)
Francis Low (1806–1855)

Pitcher

Boston, Massachusetts, 1837
Gift of Mark Healey Dall
2001.821

H. 11 in. (28 cm); W. 9⅜ in. (24 cm); Diam. body 6½ in. (16.5 cm); Diam. foot 5 in. (12.6 cm); Wt. 27 oz 16 dwt 2 gr (864.8 gm)

Marks: "JONES, LOWS & BALL / Boston / Pure Silver Coin / Boston," each in a rectangle and arranged to form a rough square, struck on bottom. The retailer's and place names are in roman letters; the quality mark in italics.

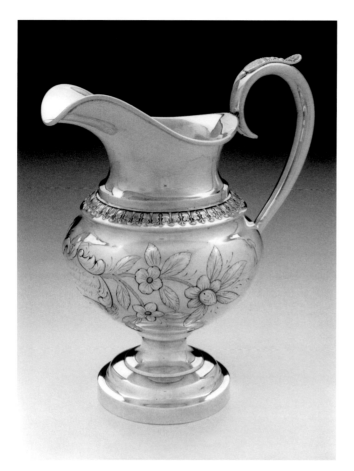

214

Inscription: "Presented by the Merchants Bank, Boston to Mark Healey, January 1837 / on his resignation of the Presidency of the Bank" engraved on front.

See cat. no. 213.

Description: En suite with the four-piece tea service (cat. no. 213).

History: See cat. no. 213.

Exhibitions and publications: None.

215

Jones, Ball & Co. (active 1852–1854)
  George B. Jones (1815–1875)
  Nathaniel C. Poor (1808–1895)
  True M. Ball (1815–1890)
  Benjamin Shreve (1813–1895)
  Seth E. Brown (1821–1884)
  John Damon (active about 1852–1854)

Cream pitcher

Boston, Massachusetts, about 1852
From the Estate of Alice Brooks Spark Wendling
1973.645

H. 6⅛ in. (15.5 cm); W. 5 in. (12.6 cm); D. 3¹³⁄₁₆ in. (9.6 cm); Diam. foot 2⅞ in. (7.3 cm); Wt. 7 oz 5 dwt 23 gr (227 gm)

Marks: "JONES, BALL & CO. / BOSTON / PURE COIN" in roman letters within rectangles struck on base.

Inscriptions: "Carrie / from a / Friend." in script within a cartouche engraved under spout.

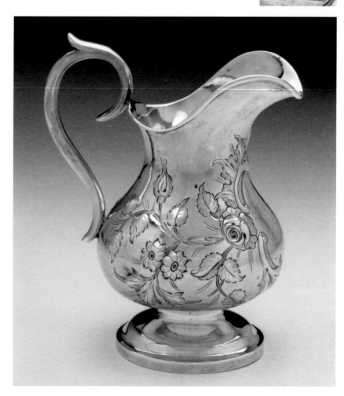

THIS PITCHER and two other pieces from the same donor (cat. no. 232) belonged to Mary Caroline ("Carrie") Brooks Champney and her husband, Benjamin Champney, an artist known in Boston for his landscapes and portrait work.[1] The artist said of his wife that she was born in "Indiana but of good New England stock." He also noted in his biography that "Mrs. Champney is very fond of flowers," a sentiment confirmed by the exuberant floral decoration of the silverware in her possession.[2]

Available from the firm from at least 1848 to 1858, this graceful pear-shaped cream pitcher could be purchased in several versions: with floral motif but supported by three paw feet or with an acorn-and-oakleaf pattern, either on paw feet or with a round and domed foot.[3] Until more is known about the relationships between members of the luxury metals trade, it is difficult to distinguish between maker and retailer. From the beginning, Jones and partners advertised themselves as retailers of both local and imported wares, though they may have manufactured some items as well.

By the 1850s, the company was nationally known, and partners Jones, Ball & Poor built a new "state-of-the-art" store at 226 Washington Street.[4] When True M. Ball (who replaced Samuel S. Ball by 1839) left the firm in the early 1850s, the company reformed, and "Shreve and Brown" was listed after George B. Jones in the company name. George B. retired in 1859, and Brown remained with Shreve until 1862, when the firm reformed once again, and Henry B. Stanwood became Shreve's partner (see cat. no. 231). Benjamin Shreve and Seth E. Brown were associated with the firm (Jones, Ball & Co.) by 1852, and by the mid-1850s, the two men were included in the company name of Jones, Shreve, Brown & Co. (see cat.no. 229).

When George B. Jones retired in 1858, Shreve and Brown continued at the head of the firm. When Brown left in 1862, Henry B. Stanwood joined the firm; he remained until his death in 1869. In 1870 Charles H. Crump and George P. Low joined Benjamin Shreve, and the company became known as Shreve, Crump & Low (1870–present).

Description: The cream pitcher has a pear-shaped body that sits on a circular domed foot. The narrow neck curves up into a generous spout. A scrolled handle with curved thumbgrip is attached at the rim and hip. Repoussé and chased flowers and foliage are rendered in a naturalistic manner and extend around the entire body.

History: Mary Caroline Brooks (1829–1876) and Benjamin Crackbone Champney (1817–1907), m. 1853 in Woburn, Massachusetts; to their granddaughter Alice Brooks Sparks Wendling (d. 1973), the donor.[5]

Exhibitions and publications: None.

NOTES TO THIS ENTRY ARE ON PAGE 312.

216

Jones, Shreve, Brown & Co.
(active 1855–1858)
 George B. Jones (1815–1875)
 Benjamin Shreve (1813–1896)
 Seth E. Brown (1821–1884)

Pitcher

Boston, Massachusetts, 1856
Gift of Mrs. MacKinley Helm, in memory of her father, Gardiner Greene Hammond, Jr.
56.611

H. 13³⁄₁₆ in. (33.5 cm); W. 10¹³⁄₁₆ in. (27.5 cm); D. 7½ in. (19 cm); Diam. foot 5½ in. (14 cm); Wt. 39 oz 18 dwt 15 gr (1242 gm)

Marks: "JONES. SHREVE. BROWN & CO. [incuse] / PURE COIN / BOSTON," the latter two within rectangles, all in roman letters, struck on bottom.

Inscriptions: "Dr. Charles Mifflin from / GGH / 1856" in Gothic letters engraved on central panel, to right of handle.

THE FLAT, linear character of the decoration on this bulb-shaped water pitcher illustrates a reserved aesthetic that contrasts with not only the exuberant naturalism of the Rococo style popular at midcentury but also the self-important large, lobed, gadrooned, and banded bodies of the 1820s and 1830s. Stylized foliage, symmetrical scrolls, and shells organize the six long, curved panels, and the crisp outline of the rim amplifies the linear effect. The swelling lobes that often formed the bodies of hollowware earlier in the century are relegated to the foot of this pitcher, where they conform to the lines of the flat panels of the upper body.[1]

Description: The raised vessel has a broad bulb-shaped lower section that curves inward and upward to a flared scalloped rim edged with applied cast scrolls and shells. A hollow, cast, broken-scroll handle, with floral chasing and an acanthus grip, rises high above the rim, opposite the inset triangular spout. Six floral-chased lobes on the body, corresponding to the upper panels, ring the round splayed foot.

History: Presented to Dr. Charles Mifflin (1805–1875) by Gardiner Greene Hammond (b. 1832), m. Elizabeth Crowninshield in 1856 in Watertown, Massachusetts. The pitcher descended to Gardiner Greene Hammond Jr. (b. 1859), who gave it to his daughter Frances Hammond, the donor, and her husband, MacKinley Helm.

Exhibitions and publications: None.

NOTE TO THIS ENTRY IS ON PAGE 312.

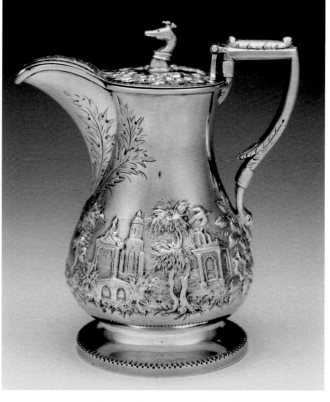

217

Samuel Kirk (1793–1872)
Pitcher

Baltimore, Maryland, 1830–46
Gift of Misses Aimée and Rosamond Lamb
58.1348

H. 8⅛ in. (20.7 cm); W. 7⁵⁄₁₆ in. (18.5 cm); D. 5⁵⁄₁₆ in. (13.5 cm); Diam. foot 4½ in. (10.8 cm); Wt. 22 oz 2 dwt 19 gr (688.6 gm)

Marks: "SAML KIRK / S : K / 11.OZ" in roman letters in rectangles struck on bottom.

Inscriptions: "AKL" in old English letters in a reserve engraved below spout. "Abbott and Katharine Lawrence 1844 22 oz 4 dwts" in script engraved inside applied foot ring.

217

SAMUEL KIRK was perhaps the earliest American exponent of Europe's new rage for the revival of the eighteenth-century Rococo style. From the beginning of his career, Kirk employed the technique of repoussé and chased foliate decoration characteristic of Rococo metalwork. Although some highly polished, plain surfaces remain on this pitcher, which was made early in Kirk's career, ornament frequently covered the entire surface of his wares, which was known as "Baltimore-style" repoussé work (see cat. no. 218).

Kirk's depictions of quaint country buildings and bridges, ruins of Gothic architecture, and children wandering through landscapes under trees and alongside brooks, as seen here, are derived from the romanticism of the mid-eighteenth century that found favor in Europe and America a century later. Sometimes referred to today as the "landscape" pattern, Kirk called it "Etruscan."[1] The wide traylike foot offers stability and adds to the decorative effect. Its flat polished surface and distinctive rippled edge reflect the shining brook pictured just above.

Description: This pitcher has a seamed bulbous body with inset base. A deep V-spout with foliate decoration is set into the neck. Repoussé and chased landscapes and flowers surround the lower body. The flat conforming cover follows the upward curve of the spout and features repoussé and chased floral ornament. The cover is hinged to the top of the seamed, angular handle, which is decorated with applied stylized leaf grips and banded near the upper and lower joinings.

A jaunty-eared greyhound-head finial perches above a scene of a boy wandering under weeping willows near cottages, a brook, and a stone bridge. The opposite side of the body features buildings with Gothic arches and towers, some in ruins, that line the water's edge. Curving acanthus leaves soften the seam joining the deep inset spout to the upper portion of the vessel. The finial is attached with a bolt and screw. The raised foot splays outward, and a repeating stamped decoration appears at the join with the foot ring.

History: Abbott and Katharine Lawrence, probably m. 1844; by descent through the Lamb family to sisters Aimée Lamb (1893–1989) and Rosamond Lamb (1898–1989), the donors.

Exhibitions and publications: Kirk Silver in United States Museums (Baltimore: Samuel Kirk and Sons, 1967), 12.

NOTE TO THIS ENTRY IS ON PAGE 312.

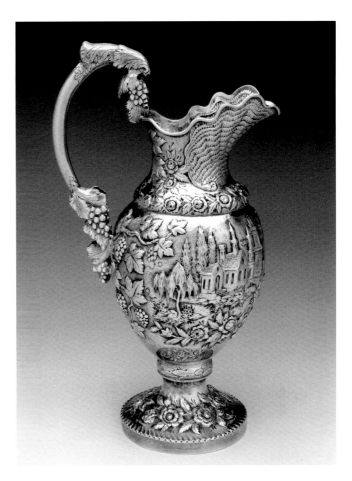

218

Samuel Kirk & Son (active 1846–1861)
Samuel Kirk (1793–1872)
Henry Child Kirk Sr. (1827–1914)

Pitcher

Baltimore, Maryland, 1846–61
Gift of Mrs. Haig P. Papazian in memory of Miss Xoa M. Shafer
1977.193

H. 14⅜ in. (36.5 cm); W. 8½ in. (21.5 cm); D. 6⅛ in. (15.5 cm); Diam. foot 4¹³⁄₁₆ in. (12.2 cm); Wt. 38 oz 11 dwt 18 gr (1200.2 gm)

Marks: "S. KIRK & SON [doublestruck] / 11.oz," all in roman letters and each within a rectangle, struck on base.

Inscriptions: "Susan Cotton / to / E. A. Cotton / 1850." in script within a reserve engraved below spout.

THE MAKER'S MARKS stamped on the base of this pitcher were used during the years 1846–1861, when Samuel Kirk's son Henry Child Kirk first worked with him.[1] By this time, the elder Kirk's distinctive "Baltimore" Rococo-revival style was fully developed, and the entire surface of this large pitcher is covered with hand-chased repoussé ornament. A late-summer landscape of trees surrounding a steepled church, adorned with two stately Italianate towers and set beside a stream with a bridge, surrounds the inscribed reserve under the spout. Roses in full bloom and grapevines laden with fruit form a meandering framework around the landscape. More orderly circles of roses ring the shoulder and base.

Description: The pitcher's ovoid body is raised and has a seamed and pinched neck; large drawn spout; large C-curved handle; and raised, splayed base. Repoussé work with stippled background covers most of the surface. The spout has an applied beaded edge with wavy contours; its underside has a rippled shell-like relief design. A raised floral band surrounds the shoulder; side vignettes of landscape and architectural scenes are surrounded by floral and grapevines in repoussé work. A band of leaves encircles the base, which is covered with a raised floral design and tightly rippled at the outer edge. The base rests on an applied and seamed vertical edge. The cast handle, decorated with grapes and leaves at each end, rises from the top rim opposite the spout and joins near the center of the body.

History: Early history unknown prior to its acquisition by Edna K. Papazian (Mrs. Haig P. Papazian), the donor.

Exhibitions and publications: Scarsdale (New York) Historical Society, "The Portrayal of Flowers in the Decorative Arts," December 4, 1988–March 19, 1989.

NOTE TO THIS ENTRY IS ON PAGE 312.

219

Samuel Kirk & Son (active 1846–1861)
Samuel Kirk (1793–1872)
Henry Child Kirk Sr. (1827–1914)

Salver

Baltimore, Maryland, 1846–61
Gift of Mr. and Mrs. Gordon Abbott
63.1041

H. ¹¹⁄₁₆ in. (1.9 cm); Diam. 6⅛ in. (15.5 cm); Wt. 4 oz 16 dwt 5 gr (149.6 gm)

219

Marks: "S. KIRK & SON" in italic letters and "11 oz" both struck incuse on bottom.

Inscriptions: None.

SMALL BUT RICHLY DECORATED salvers such as this were produced in Baltimore as early as the 1820s.[1] This example displays a variety of decorative techniques in its flat-chased wreath of foliage, ringed with a diapered surface and repousséd and chased floral band and tooled rim. The diminutive ball-and-claw feet add to the eclectic mixture of styles. The salver may have served in a front hall as a receiver for calling cards.

Description: This circular salver sits on three cast ball-and-claw feet. A chased rim surrounds a border of repousséd and chased flowers and foliage. A reserve wreathed in foliage marks the center of a diaper-patterned ground.

History: Early history unknown.

Exhibitions and publications: None.

NOTE TO THIS ENTRY IS ON PAGE 312.

220

Samuel Kirk & Son (active 1868–1896)
Samuel Kirk (1793–1872)
Henry Child Kirk Sr. (1827–1914)
Henry Child Kirk Jr. (joined firm in 1890)

Footed bowl

Baltimore, Maryland, about 1875
Gift of Anne Seddon Rutherfoord Lemaire
1996.263

H. 7¹¹⁄₁₆ in. (19.5 cm); W. 14¼ in. (36.2 cm); D. 7½ in. (19 cm); Wt. 24 oz 1 dwt 18 gr (749.2 gm)

Marks: "S. Kirk & Son" in italic letters and "11.oz" both struck incuse on base.

Inscriptions: "June 25, 1875" and "June 20th 1964" in script engraved beneath each end of elliptical bowl.

Armorial: Crest is the head of a panther on a coronet, engraved within a reserve on side of bowl.

THIS FOOTED BOWL still displays the deep relief characteristic of the Rococo-revival style, as seen in the encircling naturalistic band of flowers. However, the graphic outlines and flat interior markings of the butterfly's wings seem to relate it to the newer, flatter forms and more stylized design popular dur-

ing the last quarter of the nineteenth century. The sinuous line of the rim and elongated body suggest a natural pool of water that has attracted the two insects and may reflect an affinity for the Japanese aesthetic in vogue at the time.

Description: The shallow, oval, raised bowl of the compote has an undulating rim with a rounded applied band and sits on a spool-type pedestal with a wide oval foot. Large butterflies of indeterminate species (possibly a swallowtail butterfly, family Papilionidae), with stamped details, perch upon the ends of the bowl. A dense band of repoussé and chased floral decoration circles the bowl, under the rim. Clusters of naturalistic flowers embellish the front and back of the engraved and punched ground of the elliptical foot with applied foot ring.

History: Descended through the Lemaire family to Anne Johnson Matthews, who bequeathed it in June 1953 to the donor.

Exhibitions and publications: None.

221

Samuel Kirk & Son (active 1868–1896)
  Samuel Kirk (1793–1872)
  Henry Child Kirk Sr. (1827–1914)
  Henry Child Kirk Jr. (joined firm in 1890)

Monteith

Baltimore, Maryland, 1868–96
Gift of Joseph Randolph Coolidge IV
1989.810

H. 8⅛ in. (20.5 cm); Diam. rim 10⁵⁄₁₆ in. (26.2 cm); Diam. foot 6⅛ in. (15.6 cm); Wt. 42 oz 16 dwt 13 gm (1332.1 gm)

Marks: "S. KIRK & SON" in roman letters incuse, flanked at each end by "11.oz" within a rectangle, struck on base.

Inscriptions: "ALC" in entwined script, within a reserve of broken scrolls, engraved below rim.

Armorial: The Coolidge family crest, a griffin (a winged animal with a beak and birdlike forelegs, front proper right foot raised) on a torse, engraved within a second reserve of broken scrolls opposite monogram.

ENGLISH IN ORIGIN and a rare form in American silver (see cat. no. 141), the monteith was reserved for grand occasions, when it assumed pride of place on the tables of the wealthy. Produced during the last quarter of the nineteenth century, an era sometimes referred to as the "gilded age," this lavishly hand-decorated punch bowl with its crownlike rim belonged to one of Boston's most distinguished families.[1]

Description: The crenelated detachable rim, rounded bowl, and domed foot of this raised monteith are decorated with an elaborate overall pattern of repoussé and chased flowers and foliage.

History: According to Art of the Americas department files, the monteith was a gift from Isabella Stewart Gardner to Anna Lyman Cabot and Joseph Randolph Coolidge III at the time of their marriage in 1913. By descent to Joseph Randolph Coolidge IV, the donor.

Exhibitions and publications: None.

NOTE TO THIS ENTRY IS ON PAGE 312.

222

Probably Vincent Laforme & Brother (active 1850–1854)
Vincent Laforme (1823–1893)
Francis J. Laforme (1827–1895)

Retailed by J. C. Farnsworth (active about 1852)

Pitcher

Boston, Massachusetts, 1852
Gift of Mr. and Mrs. Walworth B. Williams
1985.1024

H. 13³⁄₁₆ in. (33.5 cm); W. 9⅜ in. (24 cm); D. 6½ in. (16.5 cm); Diam. foot 4⅜ in. (11.1 cm); Wt. 62 oz 10 dwt 5 gr (1944.3 gm)

Marks: "J. C. FARNSWORTH. / BOSTON." incuse and "Pure Silver Coin" in italics within a rectangle struck on bottom. An eleven-digit number in a modern hand is also scratched into base.

Inscriptions: "TO / James J. Walworth / A Tribute of Respect / from 126 Persons / formerly employed by / Walworth & Nason. / -in- / Boston and Malden. / April. / 1852." in a combination of script and Gothic letters, within a cartouche, engraved below spout.

SUBSTANTIAL IN WEIGHT and rich in decoration, this classically shaped pitcher was deemed a worthy gift to be presented to James J. Walworth (1808–1896) by 126 of his employees about ten years after the founding of the Walworth firm, a pioneer in the central heating business.[1] Heavy-gauge silver allowed for

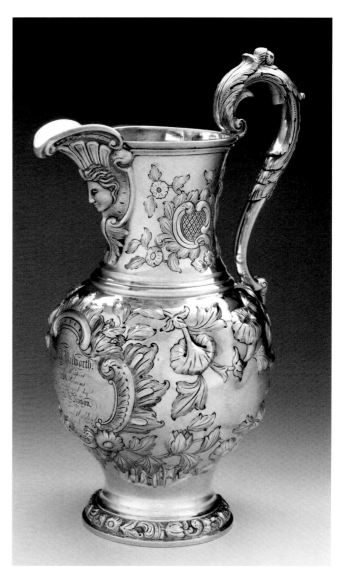

222

the deep rich-looking repoussé and chased Rococo-style decoration, and the many hours of hand labor to raise and decorate the vessel would have accounted for the major part of its undoubtedly high cost.

In 1841, about the same time the Walworth firm was founded, apprentice Vincent Laforme entered a belt buckle and a gilded watch case in the triannual Massachusetts Charitable Mechanics Association Exhibition. The buckle was judged "neatly made," though the watch case was deemed only "fair."[2] Laforme prob-

powered machinery in his firm, he gave up his silversmithing business that same year. For a short time, Vincent tried his hand in farming out West, but within a year he returned to Boston, where he remained in the silversmithing business at various addresses on Water Street until his death in 1893.[6] Vincent Laforme adopted an elegant English Gothic "L," along with a stamped spread-winged eagle gripping shield and arrows, as his manufacturing marks (see cat. no. 223).

During the third quarter of the nineteenth century, the Laformes chose to operate small, independent shops similar to those of the eighteenth century, even as large steam-powered manufactures began to dominate the field. Conservative in his private as well as his professional life, Vincent joined the Massachusetts Volunteer Militia in 1848 and the Ancient and Honorable Artillery Company in 1858, remaining a member until his death. After their marriage in 1845, Vincent and Sarah Laforme settled in South Boston and became prominent and well-known residents. The Laformes wholesaled their wares to Boston's most prestigious jewelry houses, including Lincoln & Foss; Jones, Ball & Co.; Samuel T. Crosby; and Bigelow Brothers & Kennard.[7] Gilding and repairs were always part of the shop's work, but gilding became Vincent's specialty during the last years of his career. During these years, R. J. Dunn & |Co. reported financial difficulties for the shop. When Sarah Laforme died a few months before her husband, her will disclosed that all the family's property was in her name and heavily mortgaged. None of the Laforme children entered the silversmithing profession of their grandfather, father, and uncle, though one son managed the business (keeping his regular job) until it was purchased in 1909 by Hallet & Smith, gilders and platers.[8]

ably apprenticed with his father, German-trained silversmith Anthony Laforme (d. 1846), who had arrived in Boston in the mid-1830s. In 1841 Anthony was listed in the Boston directory as a silversmith at 5 Water Street, next to the city's best retail shops on Washington Street. In 1844, at age twenty-one, Anthony's son Vincent was listed in his own shop, upstairs from his father at 5 Water Street.

Known as "Vincent Laforme & Brother" from 1850 to 1854, when his brother Francis became partner, the small firm employed five workers and used only manually operated equipment.[3] The repoussé and chased flowers on another pitcher marked "Vincent Laforme & Brother" and dated 1851 strongly resemble those on this 1852 example. The quality and place manufacturing marks are identical on both as well.[4] The attribution is further supported simply by the physical proximity of the silversmith and the pitcher's recipient. The Walworth firm began in the early 1840s on Water Street, one block from the Laforme shop, and remained on nearby Devonshire Street until 1869.[5] The retailer of the pitcher, J. C. Farnsworth, was located at 67 Washington Street, near both the Laforme and Walworth firms.

After only a few years, the Laforme brothers' business arrangement changed, and in the Boston directory they were listed separately at 1½ Water Street as "F. J. Laforme & Co." and "V. Laforme." Although it was claimed in an 1856 publication that Francis employed twenty workers and used steam-

Description: The raised body and seamed neck of this baluster-shaped pitcher are decorated with trailing repoussé and chased flowers and leaves. A cast female head wearing a gladiator's helmet decorates the inset spout, under which C scrolls frame a reserve for the inscription. The pitcher sits on a domed foot circled with chased flowers and leaves worked in repoussé. A scrolled handle with acanthus thumbpiece rises from the rim and joins the body at the shoulder. The neck rim is bent inward on the side, to the right of the handle, and the body is dimpled on each side.

History: Made for James J. Walworth, the pitcher descended in the Walworth/Williams family to James R. Walworth and in 1952 to his nephew Walworth B. Williams of Winchester, Massachusetts.

Exhibitions and publications: None.

NOTES TO THIS ENTRY ARE ON PAGES 312–13.

CUPS SIMILAR TO THIS were used to store the numerous silver spoons likely to be owned by well-to-do households at midcentury. Placed on a sideboard or table, spoonholders held a small cache of flatware for ready use.

The motif of acorns and oak leaves that decorates this goblet appeared on numerous wares marked by Vincent Laforme. Similar decoration rings a large salver engraved with an inscription of 1857 as well as two teapots and the creamer and sugar bowl of a five-piece tea set made after 1854.[1] The spoonholder was sold by Lincoln & Foss, a Boston retailer (see cat. no. 224).

Description: This raised tulip-shaped body sits on a short-stemmed domed foot encircled with a garland of repoussé and chased floral decoration. On the body, crisp oak leaves and acorns set in relief against a punched background frame an engraved inscription. The edges of the base and rim are beaded.

History: Presented to Anne Elizabeth Homer (b. 1830) of Boston by A. Adams; the goblet descended in the Homer/Adams/Eliot families to sisters Dr. Martha May Eliot (1891–1978) and Dr. Abigail Adams Eliot (1892–1992), the donors.

Exhibitions and publications: None.

NOTE TO THIS ENTRY IS ON PAGE 313.

223

Vincent Laforme (1823–1893)
Retailed by Lincoln & Foss
(active 1847–1858)

Spoonholder

Boston, Massachusetts, 1852
Gift of Miss Martha May Eliot and Miss Abigail Adams Eliot
1971.313

H. 5½ in. (14 cm); Diam. rim 3¹¹⁄₁₆ in. (9.5 cm); Diam. foot 3 in. (7.6 cm); Wt. 7 oz 10 dwt 7 gr (233.7 gm)

Marks: "LINCOLN & FOSS" within a rectangle struck above center point. Below are the incuse pseudohallmarks, quality, and place marks of an eagle in shaped cartouche, an eagle in shaped cartouche, and "L PURE COIN / BOSTON."

Inscriptions: "A.E. Homer / from / A. Adams / -1854.-" in script within a reserve engraved on front.

224

Retailed by Lincoln & Foss (active 1847–1858)
Albert L. Lincoln (d. 1903)
Charles M. Foss (d. 1892)

Pitcher with hinged lid

Boston, Massachusetts about 1847–58
Bequest of Maxim Karolik
65.438

H. 10 in. (25.4 cm); W. 6⅝ in. (16.8 cm); D. 4¾ in. (12.1 cm); Diam. foot 3⅝ in. (9.2 cm); Wt. 16 oz. 12 dwt. 18 gr (517.5 gm)

Marks: "LINCOLN & FOSS," "BOSTON" and "FINE" within rectangles struck on foot, near edge. Several sets of five-digit numbers scratched in a modern hand, near marks.

Inscriptions: "The Gift of / L. Rawlins Pickman / to / Martha Pickman Rogers" in script engraved below spout, on upper body.

THE PLEASING CURVES and highly polished surface of this graceful ewer are accented by the sturdy ribs marking the double convex flutes that ring the body. Although the identity of

224

239) and by Lincoln & Foss. Since Boston retailers drew their silver flatware and hollowware stock from many sources in and outside Boston, including New York manufacturers, it is difficult to identify the maker of this ewer.

Lincoln & Foss was reorganized as Haddock, Lincoln & Foss in 1859, when longtime independent Boston silversmith Henry Haddock (cat. no. 202) joined the firm as senior partner. Haddock remained until 1868, when he retired from the silverware and jewelry business. That Haddock, whose credit was considered "good for all engagements," chose to enter a partnership illustrates how large manufacturers had come to dominate the wholesale trade. Upon his retirement at age fifty-seven, Haddock engaged in the real estate business. At the time of his departure, the company was disbanded, and former partner Charles M. Foss joined the partnership of Samuel T. Crosby and Henry D. Morse, which was listed in the 1870 Boston directory as "Jewellers, Silversmiths, and Diamond Cutters. Also dealers of Rich Watches, Silver and Plated Wares." By 1890 Crosby had retired, and Morse and Foss had become specialists in "Diamonds and other gems."

By 1870 Albert L. Lincoln had become "reduced in means." Credit reports noted that he was known as a "high-minded man . . . at one time with Haddock, Lincoln & Foss . . . [but] now occupying part of a store and stocked by a friend on commission . . . and doing his own work at small expense and not asking much credit." The report also noted that Lincoln's wife was known to have money but was also prudent and thus "not likely to furnish him with funds."[2] By 1875 Lincoln had gone into bankruptcy.

the maker is unknown, the subtle lines and quality of construction indicate one of high ability.

Charles M. Foss and Albert L. Lincoln advertised their firm as "Importers and dealers in Rich Watches, Jewelry & Silver Ware."[1] Located at the corner of Court and Washington streets, the firm of Lincoln & Foss was within steps of Boston's best jewelry houses, including Brackett & Crosby with Obadiah Rich (69 Washington); Palmer & Bachelders (91 Washington); Jones, Ball & Poor (123 Washington); Bigelow Brothers & Kennard (124 Washington); and Harris & Stanwood (253 Washington).

As with the retail mark of Lincoln & Reed, that of Lincoln & Foss appears on many pieces of hollowware along with place and quality stamps but no maker's mark. As with the spoon-holder bearing Vincent Laforme's mark as well as the retail mark of Lincoln & Foss (cat. no. 223), other wares are marked both by Boston silversmiths Woodward & Grosjean (cat. no.

Description: The globular body of this small, spun, covered pitcher is decorated with ribbed pairs of wide convex flutes scalloped at the upper edge with ogee curves. Beading conceals the joint of the slender curved neck to the body. A flat cover with a five-part hinge follows the line of the applied molding at the rim and high curved spout with a cut tip for pouring. The hollow, cast, scrolled handle with inset wooden insulators curves above the rim and is affixed at the shoulder. The body sits on a molded spool-form stem and splayed and domed foot edged with applied beading.

History: The pitcher was a gift from Love Rawlins Pickman (1786–1863) to her great-neice Martha Pickman Rogers (1829–1905). It may have been a wedding gift, for it was made about the time that Rogers m. John Amory Codman (1824–1886) in 1850. By descent to their daughter Martha Catherine Codman (1858–1948) and Maxim Karolik (1893–1963), m. 1928; made a bequest by Mr. Karolik.[3]

NOTES TO THIS ENTRY ARE ON PAGE 313.

225

Pear & Bacall (active 1848–1876)
  Edward Pear (1805–1876)
  Thomas Bacall (1814–1879)

Three-piece tea service

Boston, Massachusetts, about 1870
Gift of Winthrop Hall in memory of Thalia James Hall
1999.63.1–3

Teapot (1999.63.1): H. 6 in. (15.2 cm); W. 9½ in. (24.1 cm); Diam. rim 2⅝ in. (6.6 cm); Diam. base 3¼ in. (8.3 cm); D. 5⅞ (15 cm); Wt. 33 oz 7 dwt 3 gr (1037.5 gm)

Cream pitcher (1999.63.2): H. 3⅜ in. (8.7 cm); W. 6¹³⁄₁₆ in. (17.2 cm); Diam. rim 3 in. (7.6 cm); Diam. base 2⅜ in. (6 cm); D. 3⅜ in. (8.6 cm); Wt. 14 oz 10 dwt 8 gr (451.5 gm)

Sugar bowl (1999.63.3): H. 4 in. (10.2 cm); W. 7⅞ in. (20 cm); Diam. rim 3¼ in. (9 cm); Diam. base 2⅞ in. (7.4 cm); D. 3⅞ in. (10 cm); Wt. 22 oz 7 dwt 7 gr (695.6 gm)

Marks: "Pear & Bacall" within a rectangle, "Boston" incuse, and "Coin" in Gothic letters struck incuse on bottom of each.

Inscriptions: None.

THE STRONG, inventive design of this tea service may refer to an ancient Roman motif used in ceramics, or it may be derived from an exotic, abstract Moorish textile design. The rich vocabulary employed by American artists in the third quarter of the nineteenth century illustrated the era's fascination with historic and exotic design sources from around the world.

Only a few other objects bearing the Pear & Bacall mark are known. Mostly flatware, these pieces are in the conventional "olive" or "tipped" patterns long produced by many makers and of conventional construction. The construction of this tea service, however, is highly unconventional. The decorative pattern on the body of the wares does not relate to the placement of the spout or handle: unlike the body design, they are neither unusual in form or manufacture but are simply placed where utility demands.

Born in Roxbury, Massachusetts, to English immigrant parents, Edward Pear probably apprenticed in Boston with Lewis Cary, Moses Morse, or John B. Jones, launching his own shop in 1829. He took his brother-in-law Thomas Bacall into the business in 1848 and probably taught his sons, who later began their own firm. Described as "thriving" in their fourth decade by the R. G. Dun financial report, this small family firm managed to compete with the large silverware manufacturers then coming of age in New England.

Description: Each vessel has a spherical body with an overall applied abstract decoration of double rows of button-centered bosses with raised outer rings and centers, separated by stylized vertical waves. All the pieces feature cast looped handles terminating in applied foliate ornament and ring feet with applied beaded decoration, repeated at the rim. The teapot has a cast finial and an attached domed lid with finial.

History: Early history unknown. The set passed from Thalia James Hall to her son Winthrop Hall, the donor.

Exhibitions and publications: None.

226

Obadiah Rich (1809–1888)
Pair of sauceboats

Boston, Massachusetts, 1830–50
Charles T. and Susan P. Baker by bequest of the latter
21.1261–62

21.1261: H. 5⅛ in. (13 cm); W. 8⅛ in. (20.5 cm); D. 3¹¹⁄₁₆ in. (9.5 cm); Wt. 11 oz 17 dwt 24 gr (370.1 gm)

21.1262: H. 5⅛ in. (13 cm); W. 8⅛ in. (20.5 cm); D. 3¹¹⁄₁₆ in. (9.5 cm); Wt. 11 oz 19 dwt 13 gr (372.5 gm)

Marks: "O. RICH." in Gothic letters and "fine / * BOSTON *" struck incuse on underside of each.

Inscriptions: "Porter" in Gothic script engraved on side of each vessel, to right of handle.

See cat. no. 227.

Description: Each raised sauceboat has an elliptical body and a large spout, with a center point evident on bottom. Each has a cast and chased double-scroll handle, with foliate decoration at thumbgrip, and three cast legs with scallop-shell feet and scrolled knees, above which scallop-shell decoration is soldered to body.

History: Probably made for Henry Porter (b. 1793) of Medford, and his wife, Susan Simpson Tidd (1803–1853) of Boston, sometime after their marriage in 1824. Charles Tidd Porter (1825–1826), their first-

226

born son, died as an infant, and it is possible that one or two additional children, named Susan Emily Porter (bap. 1828) and Francis Henry Porter (bap. 1833), also died young. The donors were siblings on the Tidd side of the family whose birthdates postdate those of their Porter cousins. Susan Porter Baker (1837–1921) and Charles Tidd Baker (1830–1905) were the namesakes and first cousins of the first two Porter children and likely recipients of the family silver.[1] Two additional objects in the MFA collection given by the same donors, a Zachariah Brigden porringer and a David Mosely cann, each bear the initials "T / I R," indicating likely ownership in the Tidd family.[2]

Exhibitions and publications: None.

NOTES TO THIS ENTRY ARE ON PAGE 313.

227

Obadiah Rich (1809–1888)

Teapot

Boston, Massachusetts, about 1840
Gift in honor of Jonathan Fairbanks on the occasion of the silver anniversary of the Department of American Decorative Arts and Sculpture by his current staff
1996.243

H. 7¹¹⁄₁₆ in. (19.5 cm); W. 10¹¹⁄₁₆ in. (27.1 cm); D. 6⅛ in. (15.6 cm); Diam. foot 3⅞ in. (10 cm); Wt. 26 oz 18 dwt 10 gr (837.3 gm)

Marks: "O. RICH" incuse and "BOSTON" in raised letters within a rectangle struck on base, above and below center point.

Inscriptions: "E.W.A." in Gothic script within oval reserve engraved on body, to right of handle.

THE GIFTED BOSTON ARTIST Obadiah Rich was one of the most accomplished silversmiths of his day before blindness abruptly ended his career while he was in his prime. Evidence of the esteem in which he was held was noted in the *Boston Evening Transcript* of July 3, 1840, which observed that Rich was "well known to our citizens as the best silver plate worker—taking the elegant and ornamental, with the useful and substantial—that we have in Boston. It would be hard for New York or Philadelphia to indicate his superior." The judges who praised Rich's work shown in an 1844 exhibition at the Massachusetts Charitable Mechanics Association noted that his "elegant specimens of Ornamental Silver Ware [were] in style and finish equal in all respects to the same class of English man-

ufacture; and in every way highly creditable to this celebrated manufacturer."[1]

Born in Charlestown, Massachusetts, of New Brunswick parentage, Rich was apprenticed to silversmith Moses Morse (w. 1815–1830) of Boston. Rich would have completed his apprenticeship about 1830, and that same year he opened his shop at 69 Washington Street.[2]

Apparently it was not long before the silversmith was recognized for his skills. He may have been engaged to produce silver for retail in the firm of Jones, Lows & Ball of Boston, for in 1835 he and his partner, Samuel L. Ward, exhibited a monumental two-handled vase honoring Daniel Webster. The commission demonstrated that Rich was conversant with the international taste for such antiquities as the monumental Warwick vase, which had created a sensation when it was excavated at Hadrian's Villa in 1771. It further proved his talent for executing challenging forms and repoussé decoration on a large scale. During the next decade Rich appears to have worked alone, producing other important works that placed him at the forefront of Boston's silversmithing craft. These included a half-size version of the Warwick vase, with more delicate chasing at the rim and flowers scattered on the body of the vessel, and the Britannia Cup, given by the citizens of Boston to shipowner Samuel Cunard (1787–1865) for establishing the first transatlantic mail steamship to sail from Liverpool to Boston.[3]

Rich also produced a varied body of domestic silver that possesses an originality and fine craftsmanship equal to his major commissions. In addition to sugar bowls, pitchers, and teapots, he fashioned inkwells with cast greyhounds, covered vessels based upon porcelain prototypes, and shaving mugs with French precedents.[4]

Rich may have been among the first silversmiths of his generation to revisit the colonial style. Martha Gandy Fales has demonstrated that while proportions and stylistic changes mark his silver as the product of the nineteenth century, Rich clearly based much of his work, either intentionally or unconsciously, upon New England forms of the pre-Revolutionary era.

Rich's reliance on colonial prototypes is evident in the ample sauceboats (cat. no. 226) that emulate mid-eighteenth-century examples. This oversized teapot, with its abundance of flat-chased engraving, is but a robust cousin of the Rococo examples made eighty years earlier by Paul Revere and his contemporaries. The plain foot of Rich's teapot that, at first glance, suggests modern taste may indeed have been drawn from a colonial example. By contrast, Rich's cast finial of a seated Chinese figure is indicative of the nineteenth century's fascination with such ancient cultures as Egypt and Greece. The finial was used on at least one other teapot. Another in the Art Institute of Chicago bears a cartouche chased with the scene of a palm tree and a bamboo structure; a water carrier labors in the foreground.[5] All three were probably intended as a symbol for the East, the source of tea.

Description: The raised and inverted pear-style teapot has a center point on bottom. A plain oval foot with vertical step is soldered in place, and a second step rises to the vessel. The S-scroll spout is affixed over strainer holes. The tall, hollow, C-shaped handle with curved thumbgrip and two wooden insulators terminates at its shoulder in leafy decoration; the lower section conforms to the shape of the teapot, ending in a rounded tip. The slightly convex lid, with bezel and applied rim, has a small five-part hinge and ridged hingeplate that sets into the applied, molded edge of teapot. The cast and chased finial in the form of a Chinese figure is bolted to the lid.

Lively bright-cut engraving of floral decoration appears on handle and spout. Two large oval reserves on body, to each side of handle, provide a focus of interest. One is engraved with initials; the opposite side displays a central floral design. Rococo scrolls filled with diaper patterns or fish-scale decoration surround the ovals; a large scallop shell appears below, extending to foot. Broken scroll band of floral decoration appears along shoulder, between oval reserves.

History: Original owner unknown. It has been suggested that the engraved initials, which also appear on a box or tea caddy by Rich in the collection of the Clark Art Institute in Williamstown, Massachusetts, are those of Emily Warren Appleton.[6] Purchased in 1996 from Argentum, The Leopard's Head, San Francisco, California.

Exhibition and publications: None.

NOTES TO THIS ENTRY ARE ON PAGE 313.

228

Possibly by Obadiah Rich (1809–1888)

Retailed by Lincoln & Reed (active 1841–1848)
Albert L. Lincoln (d. 1903)
Gideon F. T. Reed (d. 1892)
Covered shaving cup on stand

Boston, Massachusetts, 1841–48
Anonymous gift in honor of Jeannine Falino
2002.192a–c

Covered cup (2002.192a): H. 7⅛ in. (18 cm); W. 4⁵⁄₁₆ (11 cm); Diam. rim 2½ in. (6.3 cm); Wt. 8 oz 12 dwt 21 gr (268.9 gm)

Stand (2002.192b): H. 1⅜ in. (3.5 cm); Diam. 4⅝ in. (11.7 cm); Wt. 4 oz 0 dwt 21 gr (125.8 gm)

Burner (2002.192c): H. 1⅜ in. (3.5 cm); Diam. 1⅞ in. (4.8 cm); Wt. 1 oz 8 dwt 13 gr (44.4 gm)

Marks: "LINCOLN & REED / BOSTON / PURE COIN" each within a rectangle struck on base of cup and base of burner. Stand is unmarked.

Inscriptions: "J L L" entwined script monogram engraved on body, opposite handle.

HOLLOWWARE bearing the mark of Boston retailers Lincoln & Reed testifies to the firm's sale of tableware that supplemented their core business as jewelers. Silver bearing their retail mark, along with that of Albert Coles & Co. or of Garrett Eoff and William Phyffe, suggests that their offerings were in the mainstream. Several exceptional works indicate that the firm may have, on occasion, employed highly skilled craftsmen.

This shaving cup on stand is executed in the Queen Anne

This silver vessel is marked only by Lincoln & Reed, but it displays elements of Rich's style. The use of a stand and burner was rare in the second quarter of the nineteenth century, yet Rich has been attributed as the maker of a chafing dish marked by Boston silversmiths Jones, Ball & Poor.[2] Similarly, his use of shell supports for legs is also featured in the Museum's sauceboats. The only other known example of this rare form is marked by Rich.[3]

Description: The raised, elongated, gourd-shaped vessel is supported by three cast double-pad feet that scroll upward to seven-ribbed shells. The rim is accented with an applied, graduated, ribbed edge. A raised stepped dome with flange, air hole, and turned ivory finial forms the lid. The tall seamed handle rises above the lid; an abstracted leafy scroll forms the thumbgrip. Two ivory insulators are pinned into the handle, which is soldered to the body below the rim and at a lower swelling in the vessel. The circular stand has an applied ribbed rim similar to that on the vessel. Three double-pad feet with cabriole legs support the stand. The circular burner has a friction-fit lid with tubular extension to accommodate a wick. Below the lid, the burner curves downward and extends horizontally at shoulder to seat neatly within stand.

History: Original owner is unclear, but according to an old tag accompanying the object, it was J. L. Lloyd, which corresponds to the engraved initials. No further information until it was offered for sale at Northeast Auctions, about 1998–99, and purchased by silver dealers Spencer Marks of Massachusetts. Purchased by the donor about 1999 and made a gift in 2002.

Exhibitions and publications: None.

NOTES TO THIS ENTRY ARE ON PAGE 313.

228

style of the early eighteenth century, displaying the simple pad feet and shell ornaments of the era. It may have been made by Boston silversmith Obadiah Rich, who on at least one occasion sold work that was retailed by Lincoln & Reed.[1] Until blindness overtook him about 1850, Rich was considered the most talented Boston silversmith of his generation. He produced several monumental forms in the ancient style and fashioned tableware in a wide range of updated colonial forms (cat. nos. 226–27).

229

Rogers & Wendt (active 1853–1857)
   Augustus Rogers (active 1830–1871)
   Johan Rudolph Wendt (1826–1907)

Retailed by Jones, Shreve, Brown & Co.
(active 1855–1858)

Six-piece tea and coffee service

Boston, Massachusetts, about 1857
Gift of The Seminarians, other friends, and the Curator's
Fund in memory of Harry H. Schnabel, Jr.
1998.188.1–6

Gorham Manufacturing Company (active
1865–1961)

Kettle on stand

Providence, Rhode Island, ca. 1915
Gift of The Seminarians, other friends, and the Curator's
Fund in memory of Harry H. Schnabel, Jr.
1998.189.1–3

Sugar bowl and cover (1998.188.1a–b): H. 7⁵⁄₁₆ in. (18.5 cm); W. 8⁵⁄₁₆
in. (21 cm); D. 6½ in. (16.5 cm); Diam. foot 4⅛ in. (10.5 cm); Wt. 24
oz 13 dwt 2 gr (766.8 gm)

Waste bowl (1998.188.2): H. 4⅛ in. (10.5 cm); D. 6½ in. (16.5 cm);
Diam. foot 4⅛ in. (10.5 cm); Wt. 12 oz 2 dwt 4 gr (376.6 gm)

Teapot (1998.188.3): H. 7⅞ in. (20 cm); W. 12 in. (30.5 cm); D. 6½ in.
(16.5 cm); Diam. foot 4⅛ in. (10.5 cm); Wt. 30 oz 1 dwt 11 gr (935.4 gm)

Creampot (1998.188.4): H. 6⅞ in. (17.5 cm); W. 4⅞ in. (12.5 cm); D.
4⅛ in. (10.3 cm); Diam. foot 2⅝ in. (6.7 cm); Wt. 9 oz 10 dwt 23 gr
(297 gm)

Teapot (1998.188.5): H. 7¹¹⁄₁₆ in. (19.5 cm); W. 12 in. (30.5 cm); D.
6½ in. (16.5 cm); Diam. foot 4⅛ in. (10.5 cm); Wt. 29 oz 5 dwt 11 gr
(910.5 gm)

Coffeepot (1998.188.6): H. 12 in. (30.5 cm); W. 10¹³⁄₁₆ in. (27.5 cm); D.
6½ in. (16.5 cm); Diam. foot 4¼ in. (10.8 cm); Wt. 33 oz 13 dwt 10 gr
(1047.3 gm)

Kettle on stand (1998.189.1): Kettle: H. 11 in. (28 cm); W. 11⅜ in. (29
cm); D. 8⅞ in. (22.5 cm); Diam. foot 4¾ in. (12.1 cm); Wt. 48 oz 11
dwt 13 gr (1510.9 gm)

Base: H. 7⅛ in. (18 cm); W. 8½ in. (21.5 cm); D. 6⅞ in. (17.5 cm); Wt.
21 oz 13 dwt 17 gr (674.5 gm)

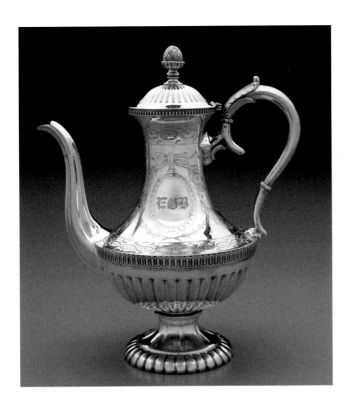

Burner: H. 2⅞ in. (7.3 cm); W. 3¹³⁄₁₆ in. (9.6 cm); D. 2 in. (5.2 cm); Wt. 5 oz 5 dwt 19 gr (164.5 gm)

Marks: "JONES, SHREVE, BROWN & CO. / STERLING" incuse; twice with an incuse eagle flanking "BOSTON" in a rectangle; above "R. & W." incuse, all struck on bottom of each Rogers & Wendt piece. Lion passant within an octagon, anchor within a shaped reserve, Gothic "G" within an octagon, and "STERLING / M T G." struck incuse on base of Gorham kettle on stand; the stand is marked underneath in the same manner with manufacturer's and quality marks and "H T G." The burner is similarly marked on base and carries additional "[P-shape] / PAT. APPLIED FOR / [dagger] 1915 date symbol]," all incuse.

Inscriptions: Entwined letters, within a medallion, engraved on concave shoulder of each Rogers & Wendt piece: "EAG" to right and "EGB" to left of handle of coffeepot, two teapots, and creampot and at front and back of sugar and waste bowls. "EGB" entwined letters within a medallion engraved on concave shoulder of side of kettle on stand, to right of handle. "from / W. B. and K. D'C. B. / June 28, 1915" in alternating script and Gothic letters engraved underneath base.

THIS LARGE COFFEE AND TEA SERVICE is composed of six pieces made by Rogers & Wendt in the mid-nineteenth century and a matching kettle on stand made by Gorham in the early twentieth. The addition succeeds beautifully and provides evidence of the high quality of workmanship available after the turn of the century.

Formed and decorated in the late classical style, the original six pieces are the work of Rogers & Wendt, a little-known Boston firm. Johan Rudolph Wendt apprenticed with master goldsmith Dietrich Heinrich Stadt II in his native Germany and immigrated to the United States during the 1848 revolution.[1] Listed as a chaser in the Boston directory of 1850, he prospered quickly. By 1853 he appeared in partnership with Augustus Rogers, who had begun his career in New York but established himself in Boston in the 1840s. Reported to have a large shop of forty workers, the firm prospered.[2] Rogers & Wendt retailed this service and other wares through Jones, Shreve, Brown & Co., one of Boston's largest and most prestigious retailers of luxury goods.[3]

This fully marked service is a major example of comparatively rare Boston silver by this firm. In 1860 Rogers & Wendt formed a partnership with George Wilkinson, Gorham's head designer, to supply the well-known New York firm of Ball, Black & Co. For unknown reasons, the partnership lasted only a few months, but Wendt retained his New York connection and, for more than a decade, occupied two floors of the firm's new building as an independent supplier. Although Wendt is recognized as a major New York City silversmith, his Boston work remains relatively unknown.

Description: The reeded kylix-shaped lower bodies of each piece are spun and joined to the concave shoulders and slender necks by an egg-and-dart decorated stamped band. A flat-chased Greek-key design with additional floral motifs above rings the shoulder of the upper part of each piece and the long neck of the coffeepot. The coffee- and teapot have domed and reeded hinged lids with cold-chased acorn finials; the conforming sugar bowl lid is separate. The cast spouts of the coffee- and teapot are reeded. Hollow cast C-scrolled handles curve above the upper rims and down to the bowls of the coffee- and teapot; the creampot's handle stops at the shoulder. The handles of the sugar bowl mimic split rusticated tendrils scrolled upward from an acanthus leaf to the shoulder. The short-stemmed feet are deeply gadrooned at the bottom edge. The matching kettle rests in a stand with curving brackets; its round flared base is encircled with the smaller scaled banding of the hollowware's upper bodies and sits on bun feet.

History: Elizabeth Ann Goddard (1829–1910) m. Thomas Perkins Shepard (1817–1877) of Salem, Massachusetts, in 1856 in Providence, Rhode Island; to their son William Binney Jr. (1858–1921) and his wife, Harriet D'Costa Rhodes; to their daughter Elizabeth Goddard Binney (b. 1893), whose monogram was inscribed on each piece probably about 1915, when she m. Barnes Newberry of Rhode Island and the Gorham kettle was added to the service.[4] The service descended to their son William Binney Newberry (b. 1928), who placed the service at auction. In 1998 it was purchased by dealer Spencer Marks and therafter purchased by the Museum.

Exhibitions and publications: None.

NOTES TO THIS ENTRY ARE ON PAGE 313.

230

Probably George B. Sharp (1819–1904)

Retailed by Bailey & Co. (active 1848–1878)

Child's cup

Philadelphia, Pennsylvania, about 1855–67
Gift of Mrs. H. S. Geery
1971.95

H. 3³⁄₁₆ in. (8.2 cm); W. 4⅛ in. (10.5 cm): D. 2¹³⁄₁₆ in. (7 cm); Diam. rim 2½ in. (6.4 cm); Wt. 2 oz 9 dwt 22 gr (77.6 gm)

Marks: "BAILEY & Cᵒ / CHESTNUT ST PHILA" retailer's mark, in the shape of enclosing ellipses, struck incuse on base of cup; "136" struck in center. Below is a lion passant, struck twice, each within a shaped reserve. Beneath these touchmarks appear the lion passant within a shaped reserve; "S" within an oval; and a shield.

Inscriptions: "From / M. S. Pyles, / to / M. G. Strean." in script within a reserve engraved on front.

THE PICTURESQUE LANDSCAPE of thatched-roof cottages and picket fence set among towering trees that embellishes the body of this presentation cup would have charmed a small child. The time-consuming handwork of the repousséd and

chased decoration made it a most luxurious gift from Philadelphia's prominent jeweler, Bailey & Co., which is today the well-known Bailey, Banks & Biddle.

Even though it bears only the retailer's marks, the cup may have been made by George B. Sharp, who managed Bailey & Co.'s silverware manufacturing production from 1852 to the mid-1860s. Bailey & Co.'s quality mark was introduced in 1855 and indicates an early adoption in this country of the English sterling standard. When the firm reverted to its earlier emphasis on manufacturing jewelry and retailing silverware, Sharp went into business for himself.[1]

Description: The seamed cylindrical body with heavily repousséd and chased landscape decoration, above a plain ogee-curved bottom, sits on a narrow ring base. A hollow S-shaped handle is attached at the upper rim and lower body of the cup.

History: Descended through the Strean/Greenleaf family of Cambridge, Massachusetts, to the donor.

Exhibitions and publications: None.

NOTE TO THIS ENTRY IS ON PAGE 313.

231

Shreve, Stanwood & Co. (active 1862–1869)
  Benjamin Shreve (1813–1896)
  Henry B. Stanwood (1818–1868)
  James Henry Kimball (b. 1827)

Seven-piece tea and coffee service

Boston, Massachusetts, about 1867
Gift of Priscilla L. Waite
1984.569–75

Coffeepot (1984.569): H. 10⁵⁄₁₆ in. (26.1 cm); W. 10⅝ in. (27 cm); D. 5⅛ in. (13 cm); Wt. 31 oz 2 dwt 17 gr (968.4 gm)

Sugar bowl with cover (1984.570): H. 7¹¹⁄₁₆ in. (19.5 cm); W. 8½ in. (21.5 cm); D. 4½ in. (11.5 cm); Wt. 18 oz 15 dwt 2 gr (583.3 gm)

Creampot (1984.571): H. 5¹¹⁄₁₆ in. (14.5 cm); W. 6¹³⁄₁₆ in. (17.7 cm); D. 3¹¹⁄₁₆ in. (9 cm); Wt. 8 oz 14 dwt 8 gr (271.1 gm)

Creampot (1984.572): H. 6⅝ in. (16.7 cm); W. 6¹³⁄₁₆ in. (17.2 cm); D. 3¹¹⁄₁₆ in. (9.5 cm); Wt. 18 oz 18 dwt 24 gr (589.4 gm)

Waste bowl (1984.573): H. 4½ in. (11.5 cm); D. 6¹³⁄₁₆ in. (17.2 cm); D. 4¹³⁄₁₆ in. (12.2 cm); Wt. 10 oz 15 dwt 10 gr (335.0 gm)

Teapot (1984.574): H. 8⅞ in. (22.5 cm); W. 10³⁄₁₆ in. (26 cm); D. 4⅞ in. (12.5 cm); Wt. 28 oz 17 dwt 13 gr (898.2 gm)

Teapot (1984.575): H. 8⅞ in. (22.5 cm); W. 10³⁄₁₆ in. (26 cm); D. 4⅞ in. (12.5 cm); Wt. 29 oz 11 dwt 23 gr (920.6 gm)

Marks: "SHREVE, STANWOOD & CO" incuse, "BOSTON" within a rectangle, and "STERLING" incuse, all struck on base of coffeepot, teapots, sugar bowl, small creampot, and waste bowl; "75279" scratched on bottom of these six pieces. The small creampot (1984.571) has an additional series, "L6772," scratched on bottom.

Inscriptions: Gothic "L" engraved on one side of each. "MGL / 1867 / TPL—TWL / 1928" in script engraved later on base of teapot (1984.574), sugar bowl, and large creampot (1984.572).

THIS LARGE SERVICE is executed in a restrained Neoclassical style and was purchased from one of Boston's most prestigious retail stores. It was presented to Margaret Gardner of Nantucket and Harrison Loring of Duxbury on their marriage in 1867, as a gift by the employees of Loring's steamship works in South Boston. The gleaming unornamented surface of the urn-shaped forms acts as a foil for the finely detailed cast fini-

231

als in the form of ram's heads. Along with the nautical-wheel finial, these wild animals may refer to the untamed Western market still served by water (and Loring's steamships) but not yet by rail. One of the teapots, the sugar bowl, and one of the creampots, perhaps composing a smaller set for daily use, were inscribed in memory of Margaret in 1928, when they were given to the donor's parents on their marriage.

Born in Duxbury, Massachusetts, Harrison Loring served his apprenticeship as a machinist in Jabez Coney's Foundry in South Boston. In 1847 he established his own business on First Street in South Boston and built stationary and marine engines and boilers, sugar mills, paper mill machinery, pumps, presses, shafting, and iron lighthouses; he employed more than five hundred skilled workers. Foreseeing the demand for iron steamships, Loring established the first iron shipbuilding facility in New England. In 1860–1861 four iron-screw merchant steamers were built for service to Charleston and New Orleans. Two of the vessels, the *Massachusetts* and the *South Carolina*, were later sold to the U.S. government for blockading the southern coast during the Civil War. Another, the *Merrimack*, fell into rebel hands. Renamed the *Virginia* and outfitted as an armored gunboat, she fought the Battle of Hampton Roads on March 9, 1862, with the U.S.S. *Monitor*.[1]

Benjamin Shreve began his career in Boston in 1852 with Jones, Ball & Co. (see cat. no. 215), already one of the city's most prestigious purveyors of luxury goods; Shreve was added to the firm's name in 1855 (see cat. no 216). After George B.

Jones retired and Seth E. Brown left the firm, Shreve joined with longtime Boston silversmith Henry B. Stanwood and J. H. Kimball to form Shreve, Stanwood & Co. The partnership remained in place until Stanwood's death in 1868. Although the partners may have trained as silversmiths, and some jewelry was manufactured by the firm, their stock of silverware was purchased wholesale from makers in Boston, Providence, New York, and other cities as well as sources outside the United States.[2]

Description: The seven urn-shaped pieces are seamed, elliptical in section, and footed. Angular hollow handles on each (with the exception of the sugar bowl) have square shoulders, with ivory insulating rings and cast ram's-head thumbpieces. Ram's heads with partial horns fit snugly under the rim on each side of the sugar bowl and were meant to be used as handles. The spouts are tall, slender, and vertical. On the coffeepot, teapots, and sugar bowl, the necks taper in, producing a cove molding, with an applied ribbed band at the upper edge and a beaded band at the shoulder and body joint. The bezel-set and domed lids are topped with a beaded ring finial reminiscent of a nautical wheel. The covers of the coffee- and teapot have five-part hinged covers; the sugar bowl cover is separate. The larger creampot has an integral spout, with applied beaded decoration along the rim, and a weighted foot. The small creampot has a set-in spout and narrow gadrooned decoration on the rim (except on the spout) and foot.

History: Harrison Loring (1822–1907) and Margaret Gardner (1838–1920), m. 1867; to their son Harrison Loring Jr. (b. 1868) and Clara Melville, m. 1892; to Theodore Plimpton Loring and Thelma Woodson, m. 1928; to their daughter Priscilla L. Waite, the donor.

Exhibitions and publications: Motif and Meaning: Classicism in America (Brockton, Mass.: Brockton Art Center/Fuller Memorial, 1987), 26.

NOTES TO THIS ENTRY ARE ON PAGE 313.

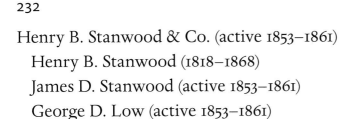

232

Henry B. Stanwood & Co. (active 1853–1861)
  Henry B. Stanwood (1818–1868)
  James D. Stanwood (active 1853–1861)
  George D. Low (active 1853–1861)

Sugar bowl with lid

Boston, Massachusetts, about 1853–61
From Estate of Alice Brooks Sparks Wendling
1973.644

H. 7¹¹⁄₁₆ in. (19.5 cm); W. 6½ in. (16.6 cm); D. 5⅜ in. (13.6 cm);
Diam. foot 3¹³⁄₁₆ in. (9.6 cm); Wt. 14 oz 5 dwt 9 gr (443.8 gm)

Marks: "H. B. STANWOOD & CO." twice, "BOSTON" twice,
and "Coin" struck incuse on bottom.

Inscriptions: "CBC" in entwined script within an asymmetrical
reserve engraved on side.

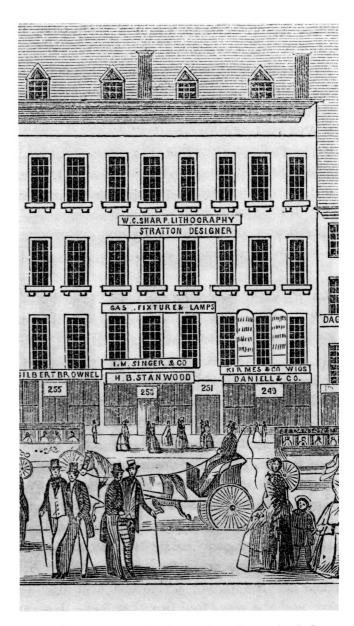

FIG. 5. The H. B. Stanwood & Co. storefront. From a detail of
"Grand Panoramic View of the West Side of Washington Street,"
Gleason's Pictorial 4, no. 20 (May 14, 1853), p. 312.

DURING THE 1850s, in the years between his partnerships with
William C. Harris and Benjamin Shreve, Henry B. Stanwood
worked alone before forming a partnership in 1853 with James
D. Stanwood and George D. Low, which continued until 1861
(see fig. 5).

In contrast to the more reserved style of wares that carried
the mark of his earlier partnership with William C. Harris (see
cat. nos. 210–11), during these years Stanwood's mark can be
found on wares in the Rococo style most admired at midcentury.[1]

Description: The raised one-piece body of the bowl is bulb shaped and has an everted and scalloped rim and circular splayed and stepped molded foot. Repoussé and chased grapes and leaves are arranged in an asymmetrical manner around the bowl. Reserves encircled with C scrolls and flowers are centered on the front and back of the bowl; one is empty, the other inscribed. The repoussé chasing extends to the separate bezel-set domed lid. Two bunches of grapes and leaves form the cast finial. Cast sprig-and-leaf handles are applied at the widest part of each side of the bowl.

History: Probably owned by Mary Caroline ("Carrie") Brooks Champney (see cat. no. 215). It descended through the Brooks family to the donor.

Exhibitions and publications: None.

NOTE TO THIS ENTRY IS ON PAGE 314.

233

Tiffany & Co. (active 1837–present)

Edward C. Moore (1827–1891), designer

Ten-piece punch service

New York, 1864
Gift of Elizabeth Roome Luquer in memory of her grandfather, General Charles Roome
1984.460–69

Punch bowl (1984.460): H. 10³⁄₁₆ in. (25.9 cm); Diam rim 11⁵⁄₁₆ in. (28.6 cm); Diam foot 6 in. (15.3 cm); Wt. 57 oz 20 gr (1774.2 gm)

Strainer (1984.461): H. 3½ in. (9 cm); Diam. 10⅜ in. (26.3 cm); Wt. 17 oz 7 dwt 19 gr (540.9 gm)

Ladle (1984.462): L. 13 in. (33 cm); Diam. 2¹³⁄₁₆ in. (7.2 cm); Wt. 5 oz 6 dwt 24 gr (166.4 gm)

Tray (1984.463): H. 1¹¹⁄₁₆ in. (4.2 cm); Diam. 16⅛ in. (41 cm); Wt. 52 oz 9 dwt 3 gr (1631.6 gm)

Goblet (1984.464): H. 4⅝ in. (11.8 cm); D. 2¹³⁄₁₆ in. (7 cm); Diam. rim 2¼ in. (5.7 cm); Diam. foot 2⅜ in. (6.2 cm); Wt. 3 oz 3 dwt 19 gr (99.2 gm)

Goblet (1984.465): H. 4⅝ in. (11.8 cm); D. 2¹³⁄₁₆ in. (7 cm); Diam. rim 2¼ in. (5.7 cm); Diam. foot 2⅜ in. (6.2 cm); Wt. 3 oz 8 dwt 10 gr (106.4 gm)

Goblet (1984.466): H. 4⅝ in. (11.8 cm); D. 2¹³⁄₁₆ in. (7 cm); Diam. rim 2¼ in. (5.7 cm); Diam. foot 2⅜ in. (6.2 cm); Wt. 3 oz 8 dwt 1 gr (105.8 gm)

Goblet (1984.467): H. 4⅝ in. (11.8 cm); D. 2¹³⁄₁₆ in. (7 cm); Diam. rim 2¼ in. (5.7 cm); Diam. foot 2⅜ in. (6.2 cm); Wt. 3 oz 8 dwt 22 gr (107.2 gm)

Goblet (1984.468): H. 4⅝ in. (11.8 cm); D. 2¹³⁄₁₆ in. (7 cm); Diam. rim 2¼ in. (5.7 cm); Diam. foot 2⅜ in. (6.2 cm); Wt. 3 oz 6 dwt 2 gr (102.8 gm)

Goblet (1984.469): H. 4⅝ in. (11.8 cm); D. 2¹³⁄₁₆ in. (7 cm); Diam. rim 2¼ in. (5.7 cm); Diam. foot 2⅜ in. (6.2 cm); Wt. 3 oz 7 dwt 17 gr (105.3 gm)

Marks: "TIFFANY & CO." within an arched reserve; "561" incuse; "ENGLISH STERLING / 925-1000" within a conforming reserve; "1049" incuse; "550 Broadway" within an arched reserve; and Gothic-style "M" within an ellipse struck twice, flanking the whole, all struck on punch bowl, inside trumpet foot. The strainer is unmarked and may be replated. "1550 / 563" incuse; Gothic "M" within an ellipse; "Tiffany & Co." incuse, all struck on back of ladle handle, near juncture with bowl. "TIFFANY & CO." within an arched reserve; "1181" incuse; "ENGLISH STERLING / 925-1000" within a conforming reserve; "9931"incuse; "550 Broadway" within an arched reserve; and Gothic "M" in an ellipse struck twice, flanking the whole, all struck on underside of tray. "TIFFANY & CO. / STERLING" both incuse; Gothic "M" in an ellipse; "1549" incuse; and "562" incuse, all struck inside foot of each goblet.

Inscriptions: "Presented / to / Colonel Charles Roome / by / the 37th Regiment, National Guard, / State of New York. / December 1864." in various lettering styles and accompanied by numerous flourishes, engraved on punch bowl, centered between handles. "IBIMUS QUOCUMQUE OFFICIUM VOCAT," in an ellipse on the Order of the Garter engraved on opposite side of bowl. The strainer lacks inscriptions. "CR" entwined monogram engraved on ladle handle tip and on bowl of each goblet. The coat of arms (see *Armorials*) is centered, with the same presentation inscription surrounding it.

Armorial: The coat of arms and crest of the 37th New York Regiment, with "37" at the center, surrounded by the Order of the Garter, engraved in Latin, and a crest of a raised knight's arm holding a hatchet, on a torse engraved on side of punch bowl, between the handles.

THIS LAVISH PRESENTATION punch service is distinguished by Neoclassical ornament and elaborate inscriptions. It consists of a footed bowl, tray, six goblets, a strainer, and a ladle. Its small, practical size suggests that it was intended for personal use, serving an intimate party of celebrants in a private setting rather than a crowd for a public occasion. The service was offered in 1864 to Col. Charles Roome by the 37th New York Militia, the regiment he commanded at the defense of Baltimore in 1862. Colonel (later General) Roome was a prominent Mason and served as president of both the Consolidated Gas Company and the St. Nicholas Society of New York City.

The service is an example of the high level of craftsmanship that continued in the silver trade past midcentury, evident

fits closely inside the punch bowl and is pierced in a dense geometric design at the bottom. Two small round ring handles are attached to the inner walls.

The ladle is kettle shaped; the bowed fiddle-end stem has a cast mask of Bacchus that serves as drop at the union of the bowl and stem. It has a gold-washed interior. The circular tray is wreathed with an engraved grapevine; edged with an applied egg-and-dart band along the molded rim; and set on four cast scrolled feet. The rounded stemmed goblets are trimmed with applied beaded bands and have gold-washed interiors.

History: Col. Charles Roome (1812–1890) to his son; to his daughter Elizabeth Roome Luquer, the donor.

Exhibitions and publications: None.

234

Tiffany & Co. (active 1837–present)

Edward C. Moore (1827–1891), designer

Coffeepot

New York, New York, about 1858–73
Marion E. Davis Fund
1981.403

H. 10¹¹⁄₁₆ in. (27.2 cm); W. 8⅛ in. (20.5 cm); D. 5⅝ in. (14.2 cm); Diam. foot 3⅛ in. (7.8 cm); Wt. 30 oz 15 dwt 3 gr (956.6 gm)

Marks: "TIFFANY & CO." within an arched reserve, "774" incuse; "ENGLISH STERLING / 925-1000" within a conforming reserve; "5245" incuse; "550 Broadway" within an arched reserve; and Gothic "M" within an ellipse struck twice, flanking the whole, all struck on bottom.

Inscriptions: "MCV" in script entwined inside a medallion engraved on shoulder, to right of handle.

THE BOLD, classically derived "Neo-Grec" style was born in France in the third quarter of the nineteenth century and adopted by English and American designers. It offered an alternative to the naturalistic foliage and flowers of Rococo-revival design. Although the motifs decorating this coffeepot are mainly Greek, characteristic of the era's free use of design vocabulary, Tiffany named the pattern Etruscan and produced it from 1858 until 1873. The coffeepot is modeled in the shape of a Greek oenochoe and banded with a flat-chased and engraved frieze that incorporates horse-drawn chariots and warriors accompanied by statesmen.[1]

in the judicious combination of modern manufacturing techniques and skilled handwork. The highly polished, plain surface of the hemispherical, spun bowl contrasts with the hand-chased complexity of the grotesque heads holding the unusual oval loop handles. Each element of the seven-part inscription is engraved in a different style, with the name of the recipient dominating in decorated Gothic-style letters. Silver remained a favorite medium for public testimonials during the nineteenth century. Tiffany & Co. produced many presentation and commemorative pieces and borrowed one hundred such examples to exhibit at the Philadephia Centennial Exhibition in 1876. This set was executed by the shop of Edward C. Moore, who for forty years guided the Tiffany silver business as designer and manager.

Description: The spun punch bowl is hemispherical in form; an applied egg-and-dart band joins the lower body of the bowl to a concave collar encircled with an engraved guilloche decoration on its upper rim. Two pendant oval handles are attached to the cast grotesque mounts. The bowl's trumpet-shaped base is decorated with beading at the upper and lower edges. The sieve, or strainer,

The theatrical helmet finial crowns the steeply domed lid and continues the frieze's warrior theme. Bands of anthemion and acanthus leaves, Greek-key fretwork, and classical beading continue the antique design references. Elements that distinguish the Neo-Grec from the Neoclassical style of the eighteenth and early nineteenth centuries are the stylized, flat chasing and the dramatic contrast of light and dark, seen especially in the smooth polish of the frieze's figures set against the matte, stippled background.[2]

Description: This vase-shaped coffeepot is composed of a spun three-part lower body, shoulder, and neck. The lower body joints are covered by two squared, applied beads enclosing a frieze of flat, chased figures. Stylized anthemion ring the slender neck under the rim, and more naturalistic trailing leaves are chased on the vessel's shoulder. The curved spout and handle are cast, the latter fitted with ivory separators. The domed, hinged lid is finished with a helmet finial, and the vessel sits on a beaded foot ring.

History: Early history unknown. Museum purchase in 1981.

Exhibitions and publications: "Made by Design: American Silver from the 17th to 20th Century," Fitchburg Art Museum, September 18–October 30, 1983; "The Silver of Tiffany & Co.," Place des Antiquaires, New York, November 1987–February 1988; Charles H. Carpenter Jr. and Janet Zapata, *The Silver of Tiffany & Co., 1850–1987* (Boston: Museum of Fine Arts, Boston, 1987), 27.

NOTES TO THIS ENTRY ARE ON PAGE 314.

235

Tiffany & Co. (active 1837–present)

Edward C. Moore (1827–1891), designer

Pair of pepper casters

New York, New York, about 1874
Gift of Ada Belle Winthrop-King
1993.120.1–2

1993.120.1: H. 4⅛ in. (10.5 cm); Diam. 2³⁄₁₆ in. (5.5 cm); Diam. foot 1³⁄₁₆ in. (3 cm); Wt. 2 oz 1 dwt 13 gr (64.6 gm)

1993.120.2: H. 3⅞ in. (10 cm); Diam. 2 in. (5 cm); Diam. foot 3³⁄₁₆ in. (3 cm); Wt. 2 oz 1 dwt 11 gr (64.5 gm)

Marks: "TIFFANY & Cº / 3147 M 3965 / STERLING SILVER," the latter two words in sans serif, struck incuse on each bottom.

Inscriptions: None.

FILLED WITH GROUND or cracked pepper, these dainty unlined casters may have been used on the dining table in combination with open salts and salt spoons. The flat-chased decoration in the Islamic style that rings the bowls provides the exotic flavor of the Eastern-influenced design that became increasingly popular after the Civil War. Carpenter notes that objects decorated in the Islamic taste were in steady production at Tiffany & Co. throughout the later part of the nineteenth century, although the style was "never all pervasive at any one time," as was Japanese design during the 1860s and 1870s.[1]

According to a recent study, the development of the use of Islamic sources by Edward C. Moore (1827–1891), Tiffany's head silversmith from 1851 to 1891, falls into three phases, beginning in the late 1860s. The order number on these casters (3147) indicates a production date that falls in the early 1870s, during the first phase of designs in which Moore relied upon Islamic objects and ornament found in his own and the firm's collection of artifacts and books. The second and third phases are characterized by Moore's interpretations of the Eastern sources.[2]

Description: The flattened spherical body of each caster sits on a ring foot and is surmounted by a vertical form or neck whose flared base is fitted with threaded rings that screw into the bowl. A reel-shaped finial is soldered to the rounded and perforated tip of the elongated form. A crimped and flared collar extends outward from the neck, below which flat geometric and floral patterns surrounding Islamic-style arches ornament the flared trumpet base and spherical bowl.

History: Early history unknown. To the donor at an unknown date and made a gift to the museum.

Exhibitions and publications: None.

NOTES TO THIS ENTRY ARE ON PAGE 314.

236

Tiffany & Co. (active 1837–present)
Edward C. Moore (1827–1891), designer
Pocket flask

New York, New York, about 1886–87
Gift of Mrs. Henry Buhler
1979.410

H. 5³/₁₆ in. (13.1 cm); W. 3³/₁₆ in. (8.2 cm); D. 1³/₁₆ in. (3 cm); Wt. 5 oz 1 dwt 16 gr (158.1 gm)

Marks: "TIFFANY & Cº / 8929 M 1635 / STERLING / 1½ GILLS" in roman letters struck incuse on bottom.

Inscriptions: "C C C" in script, in a central rounded reserve, engraved on side.

SLIPPED INTO A gentleman's pocket, this richly decorated silver flask signified the taste and wealth of its owner and served the practical purpose of a portable source of about six ounces of liquid refreshment. The sumptuous Rococo-revival decoration served especially well for a flask. Made to be held in the hand, its gently rounded form and highly textured surface offered a pleasant tactile experience and gave no evidence of fingerprints to mar its appearance. In the late nineteenth century, Tiffany and other luxury jewelers advertised an overwhelming variety of personal items made in sterling silver and decorated in many styles for men, women, and children. Along with pocket flasks, "Presents for Men" in Tiffany's 1880 catalogue included almost fifty categories, including silver-mounted canes, compass cases, ash receivers, telescoping drinking cups, silver bells for library or dinner table, claret pitchers with silver mountings, horse bits, match boxes, whistles, and wine labels.[1]

Description: The front and back halves of the flask's oval body are seamed at the perimeter. Both body and cap are deeply repoussé and chased with roses, peonies, violets, daisies, and ferns. The flask's capacity is 1½ gills (1 gill equals ¼ liquid pint). Though the cap screws down and is fitted with a cork to prevent leakage, it is secured to the neck of the flask by a ring, which is part of the five-part hinge that allows the cap to be swung aside for drinking.

History: Early history unknown. Acquired by former MFA curator Kathryn C. Buhler and made a gift.

Exhibitions and publications: None.

NOTE TO THIS ENTRY IS ON PAGE 314.

237

Possibly by John R. Wendt & Co., New York (active 1860–1871)

John R. Wendt (1826–1907)

Retailed by Crosby & Morse, Boston (active 1864–1869)

Samuel Trevett Crosby (1813–1908)

Henry D. Morse (b. 1826, active about 1847–1890)

Five-piece coffee and tea service for one

New York, New York, about 1865
Gift of Mr. and Mrs. Frederick C. Dumaine
1990.137–41

Teapot (1990.137): H. 5³⁄₁₆ in. (13.2 cm); W. 6⅝ in. (16.8 cm); D. 4 in. (10.2 cm); Wt. 10 oz 4 dwt 5 gr (317.6 gm)

Coffeepot (1990.138): H. 6½ in. (16.4 cm); W. 5⅝ in. (14.3 cm); D. 3¹¹⁄₁₆ in. (9.3 cm); Wt. 10 oz 18 dwt 9 gr (339.6 gm)

Sugar bowl with lid (1990.139): H. 4⅜ in. (11.2 cm); W. 5 in. (12.7 cm); D. 3⅝ in. (9.1 cm); Wt. 6 oz 9 dwt 17 gr (201.7 gm)

Creampot (1990.140): H. 4½ in. (11.5 cm); W. 3½ in. (8.8 cm); D. 2¹¹⁄₁₆ in. (6.8 cm); Wt. 4 oz 3 dwt 5 gr (129.4 gm)

Waste bowl (1990.141): H. 3⁵⁄₁₆ in. (8.3 cm); Diam. 3½ in. (8.9 cm); Wt. 4 oz 8 dwt 8 gr (137.4 gm)

Marks: "CROSBY & MORSE / 925/1000 [within a shield] / BOSTON" in roman letters struck incuse on each base. Waste bowl lacks maker and location marks.

Inscriptions: "C T D" ("D" smaller than "C" and "T") in applied, interlaced, and gilded Gothic letters, engraved to right of coffee-, tea-, and creampot handles and to one side of sugar and waste bowls.

INTENDED AS A service for one, both the coffeepot and teapot in this diminutive service hold one-half pint of liquid. In the latter half of the nineteenth century in Europe and America, the term *cabaret service* was applied to small services that included either a tea- or coffeepot, a creamer and sugar bowl, and often a tray. Those intended for two held one pint in the tea- and coffeepots and were called *tete à tetes*. Those intended for one were termed *solitaire* services.

Although lacking a tray, this elaborate set has both a coffee- and teapot as well as a creamer, sugar bowl, and waste bowl. It is characterized by the clean lines, symmetry, and polished surfaces of the Neo-Grec style introduced in this country by George Wilkinson, a professional English designer engaged by the Gorham Company in 1857. The jewelry-like gilded ajouré-work monogram emphasizes the intention of the service as a type of personal ornament. The new style offered a high contrast to the effusive naturalistic ornament and highly textured surfaces characteristic of the prevailing Rococo-revival style, and by 1870 it had spread to manufacturers throughout the United States.[1]

The set may have been made by John R. Wendt, a talented silversmith born and trained in Germany. Wendt's New York City shop provided silver for Ball, Black & Co. and others, such as Crosby & Morse of Boston, retailers of this service. Before moving to New York, he worked in Boston, earning recognition as a chaser. The refined flat-chased ornament that graces this service also appears on the Rogers & Wendt service (see cat. no. 229) and on hollowware marked by Ball, Black & Co.[2] It has been suggested that the quality mark "925/1000" within a shield, inscribed on each piece, may also support an attribution to Wendt.[3]

Samuel Trevett Crosby, the first-named partner of Crosby & Morse, was born in Charlestown, New Hampshire. In 1837 he began an apprenticeship with Jones, Lows & Ball (a forerunner of Shreve, Crump & Low), the Boston luxury goods retail house. It is unknown whether Crosby apprenticed as a smith, watchmaker, or shopkeeper.[4] A decade later he became associated with Jeffrey R. Brackett (about 1815–1876) and celebrated Boston silversmith Obadiah Rich. The three advertised in the 1847–48 Boston directory as "Importers, Wholesale and Retail Dealers in Rich Watches, Jewelry and Plated Wares . . . Silverware by O. Rich." By 1850 blindness caused Rich to retain only a financial interest in the trade, and Brackett left entirely to become a commercial broker. After a short period as sole name, as indicated on the company letterhead, Crosby took Seth E. Brown as a partner and, later, engraver and jeweler Henry D. Morse, with whom he retailed this service. In 1869 Charles M. Foss joined the firm.[5]

By the late 1860s both Crosby and his partner Morse had worked in Boston's jewelry trade for a generation, Crosby principally as a retailer. Morse began his career as an engraver in the 1840s; he became interested in the new popular diamond business, and, during his partnership with Crosby, diamond jewelry seems to have been the company's focus. In the 1865 triennial exhibition of the Massachusetts Charitable Mechanics Association, Crosby & Morse earned a gold medal for Morse's diamond-cutting expertise, which "introduced a new art to the mechanics of our country."[6] The firm competed directly with Boston's preeminent jewelry houses such as Shreve, Stanwood & Co. and Bigelow, Kennard & Co., all located within a few blocks of one another in Boston's fashionable shopping district on upper Washington Street.

These firms drew their inventories of silverware from large manufacturers, including Gorham in nearby Providence, Rhode Island, and from wholesalers such as the Laformes of Boston and John R. Wendt, who had moved from Boston to New York City in 1860.

According to the R. G. Dun reports of the early 1870s, the firm of Crosby & Morse suffered financial reverses due to "heavy expenses." Morse claimed that he had left the firm before it failed. Foss joined Crosby in 1876, and the Dun report noted that Crosby and Foss "finally settled their debts and are going on but there is great lack of confidence . . . [they are] not recommended for credit."[7] By 1890 Crosby left the jewelry trade for the insurance business, and Morse rejoined Foss at 120 Tremont Street, where they worked as diamond specialists.

Description: The spun spherical bodies are chased and engraved with Neo-Grec ornament in the form of palmettes and strapwork. The upper half of each vessel is ornamented with an applied gold monogram. Cast rectangular handles with rams' heads are interlaced with a cord. The vessels sit on cast hoof feet. The coffee- and teapot have domed five-part hinged lids, chased with a floral outline and topped with a button-shaped finial that becomes the center of the flower when viewed from above. The coffeepot is distinguished by its elongated neck.

History: Purchased at Sotheby's, New York, in 1990 and donated to the Museum by Mr. and Mrs. Frederick C. Dumaine.

Exhibitions and publications: Sotheby's, New York, January 24, 1990, lot 135.

NOTES TO THIS ENTRY ARE ON PAGES 314.

238

Whiting Manufacturing Company (active 1866–1924)

William D. Whiting (active about 1840–1875)

William M. Cowan (active about 1866–1875)

Charles E. Buckley (active about 1866–1875)

George E. Strong (active about 1870)

Pitcher and two cups

Providence, Rhode Island, about 1875–76
Marion E. Davis Fund
1975.669–671

Pitcher (1975.699): H. 11¹³⁄₁₆ in. (29.9 cm); W. 9⅜ in. (24 cm); Diam. rim 5½ in. (13.9 cm); Diam. base 6¾ in. (17.5 cm); D. 6¹³⁄₁₆ in. (17.2 cm); Wt. 41 oz 15 dwt 1 gr (1299.1 gm)

Cup (1975.670): H. 4⁵⁄₁₆ in. (11 cm); W. 4⅞ in. (12.5 cm); Diam. rim 2¹⁵⁄₁₆ in. (7.6 cm); Diam. foot 2¾ in. (7 cm); D. 3⁵⁄₁₆ in. (8.5 cm); Wt. 6 oz 4 dwt 15 gr (193.8 gm)

Cup (1975.671): H. 4⁵⁄₁₆ in. (11 cm); W. 4⅞ in. (12.5 cm); Diam. rim 3 in. (7.7 cm); Diam. base 2¾ in. (7 cm); D. 3⁵⁄₁₆ in. (8.5 cm); Wt. 6 oz 15 dwt 2 gr (210.1 gm)

Marks: Incuse marks of a lion holding an elliptical cartouche emblazoned with "W / STERLING / 406 / A" struck on pitcher; "x334" lightly scratched on bottom. Incuse marks of a lion holding an elliptical cartouche emblazoned with "W / STERLING / 121 / A" struck on both cups.

Inscriptions: "To / John Gilbert / on his Birthday / from his old friend and companion in Art / Lester Wallack / Feb. 27th 1876" in script engraved on front of pitcher, opposite handle; "Be So Good As To Pledge Me / She Stoops To Conquer " in script encircling cover. "JG from LW / Feb. 27th 1876" in script engraved on side of each cup.

THE ENTHUSIASTIC REVIVAL of interest in Egyptian styles in the decorative arts in the 1860s and 1870s has been credited to the construction of the Suez Canal (completed in 1870) and the Cairo opening of Verdi's *Aida* in 1871.[1]

This impressive beverage service, dramatically plain in form and embellished with bold Egyptian motifs, served as a rich and fashionable gift in 1876, when it was presented to John Gilbert, the prominent stage actor, on his sixty-sixth birthday. It was given by Lester Wallack, a fellow actor, manager of New York's Wallack's Theatre, and Gilbert's friend. Gilbert was known for his comedic roles, and the inscription encircling the cover is a toast from the second act of Oliver Goldsmith's comedy *She Stoops to Conquer* (1773). Gilbert remained with Wallack's company until it disbanded in 1888. Although Gilbert's work kept him in New York, he maintained a home in Boston, where he had been born and raised and where he made his acting debut in 1828.[2]

The Whiting Manufacturing Company was originally located in North Attleboro, Massachusetts. After a fire in 1875, F. Jones of Newark, New Jersey, salvaged the company's property and reestablished factory and commercial operations in a large corner building at Broadway and Fourth Street in New York City. Since wares made after the fire have "New York" as part of their manufacturing marks, this beverage service, which carries the earlier Whiting mark, was probably produced in Attleboro. Having survived the fire, it may have been sold in New York in January or February of 1876. In 1924 the Whiting firm was purchased by Gorham and merged with its Providence, Rhode Island, operations.[3]

Description: The straight sides of the seamed pitcher rise to a slight lip and rest on a large stepped, molded base. The domed cover is stepped and has a cast lotus finial. The cover features a five-part hinge and is shaped to overlap the spout. The cast applied handles on the pitcher and the cups are composed of sections of banded stalks of lotus blossoms. A cast seated Greek sphinx serves as the thumbpiece above the pitcher's handle, and the V-shaped spout is applied opposite the handle, over large strainer holes. The interior and exterior of the entire service were given a matte acid-etched surface before it was engraved; only the central dedicatory inscription appears on a polished ground. Engraved decoration consists of an Egyptian-style entranceway with cavetto molding, at the center of which is the inscription. At the base of the doorway are two floriform capitals and flanking it are a stringed instrument, two fans, and a vessel. Below is a sun disk flanked by uraei, with a lotus below and two lotus flowers (one in bud form) outstretched on long stalks. Engraved bands of stylized papyrus leaves, lotus flowers, and geometrical ornament encircle the domed cover, the upper and lower edges of the body, and the spout.[4]

The sides of each cup swell slightly out from the lip and then taper down to a molded edge; each body rests on a low, circular pedestal base. Their ornamental engraving is a simplified version of that found on the pitcher.

History: Given in 1876 to John Gilbert (1810–1889) by Lester Wallack (1819–1888); later history unknown until purchased in 1975 from Richard B. Pierce of Wellesley Hills, Massachusetts.

Exhibitions and publications: None.

NOTES TO THIS ENTRY ARE ON PAGE 314.

239

Woodward & Grosjean (active 1847–1850)
John H. [or Elijah?] Woodward (active about 1841–1866)
Charles [?] Grosjean (d. 1865)

Retailed by Jones, Ball & Poor (1848–1851)
George B. Jones (1815–1875)
True M. Ball (1815–1890)
Nathaniel C. Poor (1808–1876)

Coffeepot

Boston, Massachusetts, about 1847–50
Gift of Jane Sears Kostoff
1990.363

H. 11⅝ in. (29.5 cm); W. 10³⁄₁₆ in. (26 cm); Diam. 6½ in. (16.3 cm); D. 6⅞ in. (17.5 cm); Wt. 36 oz 15 dwt 22 gr (1144.5 gm)

Marks: "JONES, BALL & POOR / PURE COIN / W & G / BOSTON" within rectangles struck on bottom.

Inscriptions: None.

WITH ITS SCROLLS and repoussé and chased floral motifs confined to the lower section, this raised coffeepot is a somewhat conservative version of the often exuberant Rococo-revival style, the most current and popular of the midcentury. Several examples of silver hollowware retailed by Jones, Ball &

Poor, one of Boston's most prominent retail jewelers, bear the "W & G" mark identified as that of Woodward & Grosjean.[1] However, a number of questions remain about the identities and histories of the men.

The names Elijah Woodward and John H. Woodward appear separately in the Boston directory as silversmiths in 1841 (though no place of business is listed for either); John's home is listed as 12 Madison Place, and Elijah boarded at 34 Pitts.[2] No Grosjean appears in the Boston directories until 1847–1851, when one is listed as the second-named partner in the firm of Woodward & Grosjean at 13 Court Square.[3] In 1852 Woodward and Grosjean have disappeared from the directory. It is unclear whether Woodward is Elijah or John or what Grosjean's given name was.

Woodward and Grosjean apparently moved to New York

City to work by 1853, and the name of the firm was changed to Grosjean & Woodward. The pair worked there for some years as major suppliers for Tiffany & Co.[4] The obituary for Tiffany designer Charles T. Grosjean in the *Jewelers' Circular* of April 1888 notes that he "learnd the silversmith's trade from his father, of the late firm of Grosjean & Woodward." When the elder Grosjean died, his son joined the Tiffany firm.[5]

Description: Repoussé and chased floral and rocaille decoration and gadrooned C scrolls frame an asymmetrical cartouche on the front and back of the raised gourd-shaped vessel. The cast spout, handle, and scrolled feet are embellished with acanthus leaves. A dramatic flame finial sits atop the hinged, domed cover.

History: Early history unknown; to the donor at an unknown date and made a gift in 1990.

Exhibitions and publications: None.

NOTES TO THIS ENTRY ARE ON PAGE 314.

Notes

181

1. Malcolm Deas, "Venezuela, Colombia and Ecuador: The First Half-Century of Independence," in *The Cambridge History of Latin America*, 3 vols. (Cambridge: Cambridge University Press, 1985), 3:140.

2. Waters 2000, 285–88.

182

1. At the time she donated the urn, Caroline Borden presented a separate small identification plaque inscribed "Coffee-urn / belonging to a service of six pieces / made from exclusive designs / and presented to / Richard Borden Fall River / Presented by his daughter / Caroline Borden"; the location of the other five pieces is unknown. According to Jamelle Lyons, Fall River Historical Society archivist, files indicate that the men noted in the inscription were New Yorkers associated with Borden's steamship line. On Borden and the Fall River Line, see J. H. Beers & Co., *Representative Men and Old Families of Southeastern Massachusetts* (Chicago: J. H. Beers, 1912); A. Forbes and J. W. Greene, *The Rich Men of Massachusetts* (Boston: V. W. Spencer, 1861), 185; Roger Williams McAdam, *The Old Fall River Line* (New York: Stephen Daye Press, 1955); A. J. Slom, *The History of the Old Fall River Line* (Newport, R.I.: Newphoto Publishing Co., 1947). Michael Martins, curator, Fall River Historical Society, kindly provided life dates for Caroline Borden.

2. Waters 2000, 457.

3. The left edge of the diamond-shaped center part of the manufacturing mark on this piece seems to have been truncated to read "C & /D" instead of "C.C & D." No flatware is known to be marked by the firm. See Venable 1994, 317.

183

1. *DAB* 18:541; Mary W. Tileston, *Thomas Tileston 1793–1864* (Privately printed, about 1925), 32–35.

2. Buck 1903, preface, 49. In the preface for his pioneering American silver exhibition of 1903, scholar John H. Buck acknowledged the help of Samuel T. Crosby (1813–1908), a longtime Boston jeweler and businessman who began his career with Jones, Lows and Ball in 1837. Probably based mainly on Crosby's memory of the men who participated in Boston's nineteenth-century luxury trades, Buck compiled the first attempt to name and match the period's masters and apprentices; in many cases, his remains the last word on the subject. Buck assigned Cary's apprenticeship to the firm of Churchill and Treadwell and named a number of prominent smiths of the next generation as Cary's apprentices. They included Ebed Whiton (1813–1879), John Farrington (w. 1835–1885), Edward Pear (1805–1876), Henry Andrews (w. 1830–1847), and Newell Harding (1796–1862). Though the first four men were young enough to have apprenticed with Cary, Harding was two years older than Cary and not likely his apprentice.

3. Boston Assessors Taking Books, 1815, W11, p.4.

4. For births of Lewis and Lucy Cary in Quincy, Mass., see Samuel Fenton Cary, *Cary Memorials* (Cincinnati: J. J. Farrell, 1874), 91. For the marriage of Hazen Morse of Boston and Lucy Cary of Milton on November 6, 1814, see *Milton Vital Records to 1850, Births, Marriages & Deaths 1662–1843* (Boston: Alfred Mudge & Son, 1900), 101. For the account of Cary taking over Morse's business, see Freedley 1856, 393. According to listings in the Boston directories, by 1837 Morse had taken Joseph W. Tuttle (w. about 1837–1872) into his engraving business, now located at 70 Washington Street, and in 1842 his son George Hazen Morse (1820–1884) joined the firm, now called Morse, Tuttle & Co. In the mid-1840s, the elder Morse apparently moved his business to his hometown of Haverhill, Mass. He was listed as an engraver in Haverhill's first city directory, published in 1859. Tuttle and Morse remained in business in Boston until the early 1870s, while George Hazen Morse, engraver, was listed alone at 12 West Street by 1875.

5. *Columbian Centinel* (Boston), September 8, 1821; *NEHGR* 93 (July 1939), 275.

6. For a West Church communion cup, see Buhler 1972, 536–37.

7. The pitcher is in the Bayou Bend Collection, Museum of Fine Arts, Houston, Tex. (B.2000.21). The egg warmer with stand is illustrated in Parke-Bernet Galleries, New York, sale 724, January 12, 1946, lot 47.

8. J. T. Buckingham, comp., *Annals of the Massachusetts Charitable Mechanics Society* (Boston: Crocker and Brewster, 1853), 146.

184

1. The leafy rose pattern at the neck and rim is also found on New York silver made about the same time; see cat. no. 155. For a tea set marked by Baldwin Gardiner, a pitcher marked by William Gale, and a pitcher marked Gale & Moseley, each having die-rolled bands similar or identical to these pitchers, see Waters 2000, 332, 336.

2. Cora Lyman Warren, *Boston Globe*, September 29, 1983, 33–34; Charles Pierson Lyman, *Harvard College, Class of 1936, Twenty-fifth Anniversary Report* (Cambridge: printed for the class, 1961), 871–73; Henry Lyman, *Harvard College, Class of 1937, Twenty-fifth Anniversary Report* (Cambridge: printed for the class, 1962), 706–8.

185

1. A four-piece service that appears to be identical and bears the same maker's and retailer's marks as this set is illustrated in a dealer's advertise-

ment in *Antiques* 108, no. 4 (October 1975), 687. For a similar three-piece set with plain handles and a different pattern of foliate chasing, marked by Eoff & Shepard (active New York City about 1852–1861, about the same time as Charters, Cann & Dunn), see Waters 2000, 477–78. A six-piece service with swan finials, claw feet, and another variation of Rococo chasing is illustrated in Martha Gandy Fales, *Silver in the Essex Institute* (Salem, Mass.: Essex Institute, 1983), fig. 33. Marked by George B. Foster of Salem and Boston, the service may have been purchased wholesale for retail by Foster.

2. Venable 1994, 315.

3. See Waters 2000, 461–64.

186

1. Information on the silversmiths, the New York Ecclesiological Society, and the circumstances surrounding the commission of their church silver is drawn from research conducted by Jennifer Merritt [Swope], "Communion Plate of the Most Approved and Varied Patterns in True Ecclesiastical Style: The Gothic Revival Communion Plate made by Francis W. Cooper for the American Protestant Episcopal Church between 1851 and 1879" (master's thesis, Winterthur Program in Early American Culture, University of Delaware, 1997), and Jennifer M. Swope, "Francis W. Cooper, Silversmith," *Antiques* 55, no. 2 (February 1999), 291–97. The firm's productivity is drawn from Dun and Bradstreet report, vol. 322 (1858), 373, as cited in Swope, "Francis W. Cooper," fn. 27.

2. Simon Jervis, *The Penguin Dictionary of Design and Designers* (London: A. Lane, 1984), 94. The designs of Augustus W. N. Pugin (1812–1852) no doubt influenced Butterfield.

3. Hopkins was actively involved in the design of churches, stained-glass windows, furnishings, and vestments, and it was he who adapted Butterfield's designs to be fabricated by Cooper. See Merritt, "Communion Plate," 24.

4. Cooper produced 35 objects in 1851 for the New York Ecclesiological Society. Two years later, the society estimated that he fashioned more than $10,000 worth of church silver. At the society's final meeting in 1855, it was stated that more than $20,000 worth of silver had been commissioned of Cooper for Episcopal churches. Merritt, "Communion Plate," 5.

5. The original service cost $1,605.51. Morgan Dix, *An Inventory of Church Plate and Altar Ornaments* (New York: Corporation of Trinity Church, Knickerbocker Press, 1900), 41. The set consisted of two patens, two chalices, a large footed paten, and an alms basin.

6. For a full description of the iconographic program, see *Transactions of the New-York Ecclesiological Society, 1855* (New York: Daniel Dana Jr. 1857), 86.

[no notes on 187]

188

1. Orlin P. Fay, *Fay Genealogy* (Cleveland: J. B. Savage, 1898), 241. Known as "Nanna" Bryant, the donor was a sculptor; her *Head of a Woman* is in the Museum's collection (21.227).

189

1. For new information on Eoff & Shepard and their partnership, and for another example of this form produced by the firm, see Waters 2000, 477–79.

2. *Harper's Weekly* 8, no. 380 (Saturday, April 9, 1864), 225 [cover].

3. *NEHGR* 11 (April 1857), 157–58; *NEHGR* 35 (July 1881), 287.

190

1. Ian Pickford, *Silver Flatware: English, Irish, and Scottish, 1660–1980* (Woodbridge, Eng.: Antique Collectors' Club, 1985), 198.

2. For the most current information on William Gale and his numerous partnerships, see Waters 2000, 331–40, 483–87. For Gale's earlier career, see cat. no. 139.

3. For four pieces of Gale and Hayden's Gothic pattern, knife, fork, spoon, and perforated ladle (though bowl of ladle is fluted while 1982.176 is not), see Venable 1994, fig. 3.12. William Gale Sr. worked with Nathaniel Hayden from 1845 to 1849. For a fork in this Gothic pattern, see Ward and Ward 1979, cat. no. 180.

191

1. Waters 2000, 483.

2. Warren 1987, 93–94.

[no notes on 192]

193

1. Unpublished family geneology provided by Mary B. Comstock, November 1999, department files, Art of the Americas.

194

1. Waters 2000, 341–43; Baldwin Gardiner (AFN:1X5Z–596), Sidney Gardiner (AFN:1X5Z–57R), Intellectual Reserve, Inc., 1999–2002.

2. Waters 2000, 341–50.

3. Another Baldwin mark containing a "W," recorded by Belden, suggests that these initials do not necessarily refer to a surname. Thus the "G" on the MFA pitcher may not refer to Gardiner, as one might suspect, but may represent a different maker's surname, a date letter, or some other indicator; see Belden 1980, 182.

3. Department files, Art of the Americas.

4. Cooper 1993, 139, fig. 99.

195

1. "Bookplates," *Heraldic Journal Recording the Armorial Bearings and Genealogies of the American Families* 3, no. 17 (January 1867): 23; see also Bolton 1927, 20. For a related nineteenth-century fob seal in the MFA collection bearing similar arms and belonging to the Boylston family, see 1976.644.

2. Deborah Dependahl Waters, "From Pure Coin: The Manufacture of American Silver Flatware, 1800–1860," in Ian M. G. Quimby, ed., *Winterthur Portfolio 12* (Charlottesville: University Press of Virginia for the Henry Francis du Pont Winterthur Museum, 1977), 19–33.

3. Bernie Bean, *The Life and Family of John Bean of Exeter and His Cousins* (Seattle: Seattle Genealogical Society, 1970).

196

1. Carpenter 1982, 41.

2. Index to Massachusetts Births, Cambridge 1892, vol. 151, p. 109; Index to Massachusetts Marriages, 1861–1865, Cambridge 1861, vol. 145, p. 48, and Cambridge 1896, vol. 461, p. 111. Rev. George M. Adams, "Memoirs of the New-England Historic Genealogical Society," *NEHGR* 55 (April 1901), lxix–lxx; Thomas Baldwin, comp., *Vital Records of Cambridge, Massachusetts to the Year 1850*, 2 vols. (Boston: Wright & Potter Printing Co., 1914), 1:654–55.

197

1. Freedley 1856, 397.

2. Rainwater 1998, 141.

3. Carpenter 1982, 281–84.

198

1. Carpenter 1982, 48.

2. D. Albert Soeffing, *Silver Medallion Flatware* (New York: New Books, 1988), 50.

[no notes on 199]

200

1. Serena Totman Bechtel, "Changing Perceptions of Children, c. 1850–c. 1925, as Reflected in American Silver," *Studies in the Decorative Arts* 6, no. 2 (spring/summer 1999), 64–94.

201

1. Carpenter 1982, 286.

202

1. "Deacon Henry Haddock" obituary, *Lynn (Mass.) Transcript*, February 26, 1892; Buck 1903, 49. We are indebted to Diane Shepherd, reference librarian of the Lynn Historical Society, for Haddock's obituary. Moses Morse (b. 1793) grew up in Haddock's hometown of Haverhill, Mass., before he moved to Boston. Moses was listed in the city directory as a silversmith for a few years during the 1820s, though by 1830 he had disappeared from the publication.

2. Henry Andrews appeared in the Boston directory a few years before Haddock. By 1835 Andrews was listed as a silversmith at Hawley, near Milk Street. Haddock married Mary Farrington in 1838, and though his shop remained in Boston throughout his career, by 1841 he resided with his family in Lynn, Mass.

3. Bigelow, Kennard and Company, Records, 1830–1925, production 65, July 20, 1848–December 1, 1852, Baker Library, Harvard University Graduate School of Business Administration.

4. A trumpet-shaped vase (documented in DAPC) that is marked by both Gorham and Haddock, Lincoln & Foss demonstrates this practice.

5. Massachusetts, vol. 4, 350, R. G. Dun and Co. Collection, Baker Library, Harvard University Graduate School of Business Administration.

6. Charles Martyn, *The William Ward Genealogy: History of the Descendants of William Ward of Sudbury, Massachusetts, 1638–1925* (New York: Artemis Ward, 1925), 201.

203

1. For the first published material noting the relationship between the Harding and Morse families, see Buck 1903, 49; *Massachusetts Vital Statistics*, Deaths, vol. 265, p. 193 (Hazen Morse); *Vital Records of Haverhill, Massachusetts, to the End of the Year 1849*, 2 vols. (Topsfield, Mass.: Topsfield Historical Society, 1911), 150, 154–55, 413 (Harding family). Buck incorrectly identified Harding as Morse's brother-in-law. Town records show that some members of the Haverhill Morses and Hardings were connected by marriage in this generation; however, marriage records link Newell Harding's five sisters (a sixth sister died young) with other men, at least in their first unions. During the period that he worked in Boston, Hazen Morse married Lucy Carey (Cary), sister of Boston silversmith Lewis Cary, in Milton (*Columbian Centinel,* November 9, 1814). Harding married

Eliza Brewer in Boston on Sunday, May 29, 1822, the year after he opened his own shop in Cornhill Court. Newell Harding and Eliza Brewer Harding and twelve other members of their family are buried in Mt. Auburn Cemetery, Cambridge, Mass.

2. *First Exhibition Report of the Massachusetts Charitable Mechanics Association, 1837* (Boston: Massachusetts Charitable Mechanics Association, 1837), 17.

3. Freedley 1856, 393–94. The report also noted that the founders of the large Boston wholesale flatware firm of Farrington and Hunnewell (active 1835–1885) were former employees of Harding. In 1853–54 John Gorham installed the Nesmyth-designed steam drop press, which would allow him to dominate the manufacture of flatware within the next decade. The effect on Harding and Farrington and Hunnewell and other flatware specialists has not yet been studied.

4. Newell Harding advertisement, *Boston Directory for the Year 1856* (Boston: George Adams, 1856), 19; *Boston Directory for the Year 1857* (Boston: George Adams, 1857), 22.

5. Massachusetts, vol. 1, 118, R. G. Dun and Co. Collection, Baker Library, Harvard University Graduate School of Business Administration.

6. Massachusetts, vol. 1, 118, R. G. Dun and Co. Collection, Baker Library, Harvard University Graduate School of Business Administration.

7. Gibb 1969, 182–83. Palmer & Bachelder of Boston, Ball, Black & Co. of New York, and numerous other customers for Reed & Barton's unplated wares are listed.

8. See also cat. no. 226; and Buhler 1972, 1:375, 2:504.

[no notes on 204]

205

1. On the use of presentation gifts in the mid-nineteenth century and the relationship between employer and employees, see Warren 1987, 21.

2. Charles Martyn, *The William Ward Genealogy: History of the Descendants of William Ward of Sudbury, Massachusetts, 1638–1925* (New York: Artemis Ward, 1925), 201.

3. For an engraved serving tray marked by Bigelow Bros. & Kennard, see back cover of *Silver Magazine* 31, no. 4 (July/August 1999).

206

1. Wright's obituary appeared in the *Boston Transcript*, December 22, 1886.

2. Adin Ballou, comp., *An Elaborate History and Genealogy of the Ballous in America* (Providence: Ariel & Latimer, 1888).

[no notes on 207]

208

1. Alcorn 2000, 157–58, fig. 94.

2. Rita Feigenbaum, "A Faneuil Family Silver Cruet Stand Rediscovered," *Antiques* 112, no. 1 (July 1977), 120.

209

1. H. L. Webster & Co. and Knowles & Ladd introduced a pattern named Crete about 1870; see D. Albert Soeffing, "The Firms of Henry L. Webster, Knowles & Ladd, and J. B. & S. M. Knowles: History and Patterns," *Silver Magazine* 28, no. 5 (September/October 1996), 30–32.

2. Freedley 1856, 397.

3. *Leading Manufacturers and Merchants of the City of Boston* (Boston, New York, and Chicago: International Publishing Co., 1885), 297.

4. Massachusetts, vol.1, 118, R. G. Dun and Co. Collection, Baker Library, Harvard University Graduate School of Business Administration.

210

1. George B. Foster arrived in Boston from Salem in 1841 and was listed as a watchmaker at 29 Tremont Row, the address of Harris & Stanwood. However, when Harris & Stanwood moved to Washington Street the following year, Foster remained at the old address. *MCMA* 1892, 321; *Boston Directory for 1839* (Boston: Charles Stimpson Jr., 1839), 211; *Boston Directory for 1841* (Boston: Charles Stimpson, 1841), 196 (for Foster), 231 (Harris & Stanwood); *Boston Directory for 1842* (Boston: Charles Stimpson Jr., 1842), 245.

2. Since George B. Foster remained listed alone at 29 Tremont Row through the 1840s, the identity of the individual(s) who represented the "& Co." of Harris, Stanwood & Co. is unclear.

[no notes on 211]

212

1. According to *Our First Men: A Calendar of Wealth, Fashion, and Gentility* (Boston: The Booksellers, 1846), George B. Jones was "a well-known man; long a favorable jeweler, [worth] $100,000." It is unknown how (or whether) John B. and George B. were related. John Jones was born August 5, 1782, in Framingham, Mass., to John Jones and Mary Belknap, m. April 15, 1779 (see Thomas W. Baldwin, comp., *Vital Records of Framingham, Massachusetts, to the Year 1850* [Boston: Wright & Potter, 1911], 123, 321) and died May 7, 1854 (*Massachusetts Vital Statistics,* Death Records, 1854, 85:177).

2. Although the two John Jones appear to have worked in separate locations in Boston (see n. 3), a footed bowl of about 1820 marked "John and John B. Jones" is illustrated in Christie's, New York, sale 6666, October 1, 1988, lot 58.

3. A close reading of shop and home addresses of the two Boston jewelers named John Jones listed in the Boston directories from 1813 to 1822 produces a profile of the two men. The John Jones whose name in the directories always remained simply "John Jones" is first listed in the 1810 directory as a partner in the firm of "Jones (John) & Pierce (John)," jewelers, on Marlboro St. By 1813 Jones separated from Pierce and was in business with Richard Ward at 13 Cornhill Street; his home was listed at 10 Newbury Street. By 1818 Richard Ward formed a partnership with Henry Farnum. Jones is listed alone at several different addresses until 1822, after which he disappears from the directory. The shop and home addresses of the John Jones who begins as "John Jones, junior, jeweler, hs back 43 Cornhill" in 1813 and becomes "John B. Jones" in 1822 can be traced through the directories from 1813 to 1822 as the partner of Jabez Baldwin and principal of John B. Jones & Co.

4. Orlin P. Fay, *Fay Genealogy* (Cleveland: J. B. Savage, 1898), 241.

213

1. *MCMA* 1892, 222.

2. Fales 1968, 1982, and 1986.

3. Helen Deese, "'My life . . . reads to me like a Romance': The Journals of Caroline Healey Dall," *Massachusetts Historical Review* 3 (2001), 116–37. Meeting notes, Merchants National Bank of Boston, department files, Art of the Americas. Portraits of Mark Healey and his wife, Caroline (Foster)

Healey, and Healey family papers are located in the Massachusetts Historical Society, Boston.

4. Family history courtesy of the donors; department files, Art of the Americas.

[no notes on 214]

215

1. See cat. no. 232. An unmarked goblet (1973.646) bearing the inscription "B.C. / DEC. 25th 1853 / Carrie." was apparently a Christmas gift from Mrs. Champney to her husband in their first year of marriage.

2. Benjamin Champney, *Sixty Years' Memories of Art and Artists* (Boston: n.p., 1900); Charles O. Vogel, "'Wanderings after the Wild and Beautiful': The Life and Career of Benjamin Champney," in *Beauty Caught and Kept: Benjamin Champney in the White Mountains,* in *Historical New Hampshire* 51, nos. 3–4 (fall/winter 1996), 71–89.

3. For floral motif and paw feet, see DAPC (84.3349); for acorn-and-oak-leaf patterns on paw feet and a round foot, see the Paine collection, Worcester Art Museum (1907.239, 1937.67). The pieces are marked either by Jones, Ball & Poor (1848–1851), Jones, Ball & Co. (1852–1854), or Jones, Ball & Co. overstruck with Jones, Shreve, Brown & Co. (1855–1858).

4. Fales 1995, 278–79.

5. Copy of the will of Alice B. Wendling, dated August 4, 1969; department files, Art of the Americas.

216

1. A pitcher marked by New York manufacturers Wood and Hughes and bearing an inscription dated 1868 is identical except for addtitional floral decoration on the widest section of the body; illustrated in Christie's, New York, sale 8507, April 17, 2001, lot 16.

217

1. See Gregory R. Weidman et al., *Classical Maryland, 1815–1845: Fine and Decorative Arts from the Golden Age* (Baltimore: Maryland Historical Society, the Museum and Library of Maryland History, 1993), 156; and Goldsborough 1983.

218

1. Henry Child Kirk Sr.'s death date is given as 1894 in Goldsborough 1983, 264, and as 1914 in Rainwater 1998, 183.

219

1. Goldsborough 1975, 135.

[no notes on 220]

221

1. For a similar monteith produced by Kirk, see Louise Durbin, "Samuel Kirk, Nineteenth-Century Silversmith," *Antiques* 94, no. 6 (December 1968), 868, 873, fig. 16.

222

1. Walworth Reginald Wellington, *Walworth Genealogy, 1689–1962: Descendants Male and Female of William Walworth and Mary Abigail Seaton* (Centreville, Md.: n.p., 1962), 111.

2. *Massachusetts Charitable Mechanics Association Exhibition, 1841* (Boston: Massachusetts Charitable Mechanics Association, 1841), "Metals" section.

3. As quoted in Skerry 1981, 7, from the Schedule of Industry for Suffolk County Massachusetts, Ward 7, 1850 Census of Manufacturers, Records of the U.S. Bureau of the Census. Archives of the Commonwealth of Massachusetts, Dorchester, Mass.

4. For the mark that occurs on a pitcher in the Worcester Art Museum (1943.38), see Skerry 1981, fig. B. The pitcher is illustrated in Gourley 1965, fig. 76, cat. no. 128.

5. C. Bancroft Gillespie, comp., *Illustrated History of South Boston* (South Boston, Mass.: Inquirer Publishing Co., 1901), 147–48, 173–75. By 1901 the Walworth firm employed more than one thousand people in their South Boston plant. Included are a photograph and short biography of the "late" Vincent Laforme, who lived in South Boston from the time he married Sarah Jane Field (1845) until his death in 1893. The Laformes built homes on K Street for three of their nine children.

6. For Francis J. Laforme after 1854, see Freedley 1856, 396, as quoted in Skerry 1981, 8–10. Skerry speculates that Francis Laforme entered the business of marketing elixir for "pulmonary consumption" after becoming ill from his exposure to mercury in the gilding process used in silversmithing.

7. Herndon 1892, 284–85. For a goblet marked by both Laforme and Lincoln & Foss, see cat. no. 223; for a salt labeled by Laforme and Jones, Ball & Co., see DAPC 90.3070; for a coffee service labeled by Laforme and Brother and Samuel T. Crosby, see Philadelphia Museum of Art (1980-70-1-5), ill. in Venable 1994, fig 3.16 (identified only as by Samuel T. Crosby). Department files, Art of the Americas. For a salver marked by Laforme and Bigelow Brothers & Kennard, see department files, Art of the Americas.

8. Skerry 1981, 14.

223

1. The salver, owned by the First Baptist Church of Boston, is on loan to the MFA; the teapots, creamer, and sugar bowl are in a private collection, documented in DAPC (80.3932). Laforme closely followed John C. Moore's 1850 design for a hot-water kettle on stand (ill. in Warren 1984, 94, fig. 104) but substituted the acorn theme for the grapevine motif originally used by Moore.

224

1. On July 1, 1856, Lincoln patented a design for a macaroni server (U.S. patent no. 15,266); see D. Albert Soeffing, "More on Macaroni Servers," *Silver Magazine* 25, no. 11 (March/April 1992), 28–29.

2. R. G. Dun & Co. Collection, Baker Library, Harvard University Graduate School of Business Administration, Cambridge, Mass., vol. 11, 195.

3. For Rawlins/Pickman/Rogers/Codman genealogy, see department files, Art of the Americas.

[no notes on 225]

226

1. Henry S. Nourse, ed., *The Birth, Marriage, and Death Register, Church Records and Epitaphs of Lancaster, Massachusetts, 1643–1850* (Lancaster, Mass.: J. M. Coulter, Printer, 1890), 176, 237, 362; obituaries, *Boston Globe* 20 (1905): 210; I (1921): 336; *Vital Records of Medford to the Year 1850* (Boston: New England Historical Genealogical Society, 1907), 113, 277, 305, 417; Thomas W. Baldwin, comp., *Vital Records of Cambridge, Massachusetts to the Year 1850* (Boston: Wright & Potter Print Co., 1914); 1:33, 2:458; *Massachusetts Vital Records*, vol. 20, 210, 1921, vol. 1, 336; 1905.

2. Buhler 1972, 1:375, cat. no. 329, 2:594, cat. no. 451.

227

1. *Stimson's Boston Directory* for 1834 lists Obadiah Rich, of Ward (S. L.) & Rich, living at 320 Washington St. His first listing as a silversmith appears in 1837. *Stimson's Boston Directory* (Boston: Stimson's Directory, 1834), 296; *Stimson's Boston Directory* (Boston: Stimson's Directory, 1837), 323.

2. Biographical material drawn from Martha Gandy Fales, "Obadiah Rich, Boston Silversmith," *Antiques* 114, no. 4 (October 1968), 565–69; Martha Gandy Fales, "The Britannia Cup," *Antiques* 121, no. 1 (July 1982), 156–68; and Martha Gandy Fales, "Rich Silver," *Silver Magazine* 19, no. 4 (July/August 1986), 8–13.

3. Fales, "Rich Silver," figs. 1–2; Sotheby's, New York, sale 6660, January 26, 1995, lot 1427.

4. In addition to those examples cited by Fales (see n. 3), see also Cooper 1993, 64, fig. 41; *Antiques and the Arts Weekly* (January 3, 1997), 96; advertisement, Britannia House, *Maine Antique Digest* (August 2001), 18B; department files, Art of the Americas.

5. Donald C. Peirce, *Art & Enterprise, American Decorative Art, 1825–1917: The Virginia Carroll Crawford Collection* (Atlanta: High Museum of Art in association with Antique Collectors' Club, 1983), 79–80, cat. no. 39; a similar finial of a seated robed Chinese man can be found on a coffee pot in a private collection and on a pitcher by Jones, Shreve, Brown & Co.; department files, Art of the Americas.

6. We are grateful to Kate Lanford Joy for the suggestion of the possible Appleton ownership; see department files, Art of the Americas.

228

1. For an Obadiah Rich salver retailed by Lincoln & Reed, see Rich Neal Auction Co., New Orleans, La., Feb. 7, 1999, lot 221.

2. Cooper 1993, cat. no. 41.

3. Martha Gandy Fales calls this example, which lacks a stand with burner, a shaving mug in "Rich Silver," *Silver Magazine* 19, no. 4 (July/August 1986), 8–13, fig. 8.

229

1. Rainwater/Redfield 1998, 365.

2. Freedly 1856, 395.

3. A five-piece tea service (minus the coffeepot) almost identical to the Rogers & Wendt service but marked only by Jones, Shreve, Brown & Co., Boston, is illustrated in McClinton 1968, 73. Unlike the sugar bowl in the MFA service, that example displays the more conventional handles of the other pieces and is marked by retailer Bigelow, Kennard & Co.

4. Though the monogram was engraved in the same style as the older one, close observation shows different hands.

230

1. D. Albert Soeffing, "Some Bailey & Co. Marks and Their Significance," *Silver Magazine* 27, no. 6 (November/December 1995), 12–15.

231

1. Charles Henry Pope, *Loring Genealogy* (Cambridge: Murry & Emery, 1917).

2. Charles W. Kennard & Co. of Boston marked a four-piece sterling tea service of the same form but with different surface decoration and without the rams' heads. Department files, Art of the Americas.

232

1. For an illustration of a four-piece tea service in the same pattern and marked by Henry B. Stanwood & Co., see McClinton 1968, 50.

[no notes on 233]

234

1. Ward and Ward 1979, 174.

2. Kenneth L. Ames, "What Is Neo-Grec?" in *Nineteenth Century* 2 (summer 1976), 12–21.

235

1. Carpenter 1978, 201.

2. Elizabeth L. Kerr Fish, "Edward C. Moore and Tiffany Islamic-Style Silver, c. 1867–1889," *Studies in the Decorative Arts* 6, no. 2 (spring/summer 1999), 42–63.

236

1. Carpenter 1978, 135. See also Janet Zapata, "Flasks for All Seasons, Part II: Nature Motifs," *Silver Magazine* 27, no. 5 (September/October 1995), 18–22.

237

1. Venable 1994, 49–51.

2. For a full-size tea service with Neoclassical form and decoration attributed to John R. Wendt, see Venable 1994, fig. 3.3. For a three-piece tea service marked by Ball, Black & Co. and dated during the period of Wendt's association with the firm, see Skinner catalogue, sale 1912, April 17, 1999, lot 115.

3. Diana Cramer, "John R. Wendt of Boston and New York," *Silver Magazine* 25, no. 3 (May/June 1992), 12–13; D. Albert Soeffing, "Ball, Black & Co. Silverware Merchants," *Silver Magazine* 30, no. 6 (November/December 1998), 44–49. A water pitcher in the same pattern, retailed by J. E. Caldwell & Co. of Philadelphia and attributed to Rogers and Wendt, has recently appeared on the antiques market, expanding our understanding of the wider impact on the wholesale trade in silver during this period; see department files, Art of the Americas.

4. Obituary, Samuel T. Crosby, *Hingham Journal*, January 10, 1908, 5.

5. Apparently a less successful partnership, Crosby & Brown offered silverware at the 1850 Massachusetts Charitable Mechanics Association Exhibition that was dismissed as having an "indifferent finish . . . [and] . . . not good enough to show"; *Massachusetts Charitable Mechanics Association Triennial Exhibition Report* (Boston: MCMA, 1850), 137.

6. *Massachusetts Charitable Mechanics Association Triennial Exhibition Report* (Boston: MCMA, 1865), 106.

7. R. G. Dun and Co. Collection, Baker Library, Harvard University School of Graduate Business Administration, Mass., vol. 15, 31.

238

1. Gerald Boardman, *The Oxford Companion to American Theatre*, 2d ed. (New York: Oxford University Press, 1992), 291, 699.

2. Venable 1994, 64.

3. Venable 1994, 324.

4. Yvonne Markowitz, research fellow, Art of the Ancient World, MFA, kindly interpreted the engraved decoration.

239

1. See, for example, Sotheby, Parke-Bernet, November 17–19, 1977, lot 376.

2. Neither man is listed in the 1835 Boston directory, but Woodward's name appears in 1841.

3. According to Rainwater 1998, 134, a Charles Grosjean emigrated from Germany in 1836 through New York City and was listed with Woodward in the Boston directory of 1840.

4. Venable 1994, 316.

5. As quoted in Carpenter 1978, 98.

CHAPTER 4

DESIGN REFORM IN METALWORK: THE AESTHETIC STYLE

Jeannine Falino and Rebecca A. G. Reynolds

The Aesthetic movement in America was catalyzed by the Philadelphia Centennial Exposition of 1876, where legions of nations from the four corners of the globe converged to display their most refined works of art. By the 1880s a new "aesthetic" visual language emerged, sparked by the exposition. It was stoked by artists who continued their education abroad and tended by armchair travelers studying the myriad publications that were increasingly available, particularly Owen Jones's *The Grammar of Ornament* (1856), an exhaustive survey of historic and foreign designs, and Christopher Dresser's *Principles of Decorative Design* (1873), which offered new ways of interpreting these forms.

Working in all media, designers and artists of the aesthetic era endeavored to create only useful and beautiful works as set forth by English design reformers Augustus Welby Northmore Pugin, John Ruskin, and William Morris.[1] Dense ornamentation, repetition of pattern, fidelity to nature, and a fascination with historic and foreign designs characterize metalwork of the period. Some of the most successful examples subtly evoke color and the sense of touch through deft use of base metals, enamel, and surface ornamentation. The Museum's collection of Aesthetic-movement silver, although relatively small and principally domestic, began at an early date and contains several impressive examples.

The monumental punch bowl and ladle (cat. no. 244) by Gorham Manufacturing Company represent the refined elegance for which the era is known. A masterpiece of aesthetic-period metalwork, the bowl is ornamented overall with elegantly repoussé, cast, and chased sea life. With a leaping carp and coiled dragon featured on each side, the vessel incorporates two well-known symbols of the Far East. Such imagery was first known in this country through the China Trade but more recently had been evoked during the Centennial Exposition, where the Japanese pavilion inspired American artists working in all media. The vessel and ladle are encrusted with tiny marine animals in a faithful, Ruskinian rendering of nature that has parallels in Pre-Raphaelite painting. The resulting work reveals extraordinary creatures in a watery landscape and

is rendered in a sensuous hand that was a hallmark of aesthetic decorative arts.

The crowded field of American silversmithing firms put a premium on locating innovative artists who could provide a competitive edge in designing original wares. Talented designers were sought for their ability to render their ideas into drawings that diemakers would then translate onto steel plates, or dies, for practical application in the factory.[2] The constant demand for fresh designs prompted some companies to provide internal schooling opportunities, libraries, and study collections of objects that could offer inspiration for their artists. The repository of books and related works assembled by Tiffany design director Edward C. Moore (1827–1891) proved to be an enormously important resource and is among the best known of these collections.[3] An eclectic mix of designs grew from these varied visual resources that ranged from modern Gothic to Renaissance, Egyptian revival, and Oriental, with Japanese wares and ornamentation serving as prominent influences. Some artists closely followed original sources, whereas others freely adapted them to such an extent that several styles were often combined in a single piece, the imaginative result often having little in common with its prototype.

Tiffany & Co.'s slender and elegant pitcher (cat. no. 248), the first piece of "contemporary American silver" to enter the Museum's collection, exemplifies the innovative use of historic prototypes that distinguished the aesthetic mode as well as the repetitive pattern that often characterizes its decorative style. Acquired from the 1876 Centennial Exposition in Philadelphia, this pitcher represented Tiffany's experimentation with color in metal, in this case silver inlaid with copper. Trefoil in section and fashioned in the modern Gothic style, the work borrowed heavily from ecclesiastical metalwork and architecture of the Middle Ages and historicized English versions advanced by Ruskin and others.[4]

Gorham's tea caddy (cat. no. 241) further demonstrates the success with which designers compiled aesthetic decoration from multiple sources. The designer of this hollowware container adapted the Chinese ginger jar shape while drawing from Japanese Meiji-era metalwork to create the applied silver ornaments. Such mixed-metal pieces were advertised by Gorham through its distinctive Art Silver line of the early 1880s, which remained popular into the early 1900s.[5]

In 1897 Gorham introduced the Martelé line, named after the French word for "hand hammered." Although Art Nouveau (a subgenre of the broader Aesthetic movement) had limited appeal in America, Gorham's popular Martelé silver relates to this organically derived style. The Museum's delicately repoussèd and chased Turkish-style coffeepot (cat. no. 245) has a softly modulated, unplanished surface that was a feature of the new line. Also in the collection is a Gorham inkstand (cat. no. 246) distinguished more by its hand-chased floral elements than its cast body, the latter a production feature that enabled the firm to create a similar effect with less expense.[6]

Fortunately, the surviving Tiffany and Gorham archives provide valuable details about labor distribution, materials, designs, and expenses as well as the names of some craftsmen who sketched, raised, and embellished these remarkable works. The company records demonstrate that consumers enjoyed unprecedented choices in selecting silver, for vessels were available in a variety of ornamental styles. In the 1870s, for example, Gorham produced a teakettle and stand (cat. no. 240) in a simple, austere style that was available in ten variations.

These documents also help explain how American firms expanded to keep up with demand while maintaining high-quality products. By century's end, new and larger factories had been built, and production staff were efficiently organized into ever smaller divisions that worked the silver at different stages. With few technological advances aside from the drop press and sectional wedge, such economies of scale made it possible for silver to be efficiently moved through a many-faceted production process that included stamping, casting, raising, spinning, chasing, and polishing. Workers handled an ever-changing body of silver. Excluding flatware, most items were made in small quantities based on seasonal needs, the fashion for personalized engraving, and the wide selection of designs available to consumers. Some believed that the constantly changing forms, finishes, and ornament prevented "the artist [from becoming] an affected idler and the artizan an unartistic 'hand,'" as had been predicted by social reformers. Despite such claims, it was an undeniable fact that the factory system broke down the craft process into a series of repetitive tasks that prevented any individual from making an object from start to finish. The result was a rupture in the generational transmission of knowledge, from which the field has never completely recovered.[7]

By the last quarter of the nineteenth century, the number of workshops that fabricated silver on a small scale, and in which craftsmen exerted more control and artistry over the finished product, appears to have declined. Numerous independent workshops eventually reemerged during the Arts and Crafts period, as will be seen in the next chapter. Yet, complete artistic control was more of a romantic, utopian concept imposed on an ancient craft. Specialized silversmithing skills such as engraving had been valued in this country since the early eighteenth century and elsewhere since antiquity, and even the smallest of shops imposed a division of labor on staff. Indeed, the delicacy of execution found in the finest aesthetic silver might not have been achieved without the factory circumstances in which such a high degree of specialization could prosper.

Notes

1. For an introduction to the Aesthetic movement, see the preface to Doreen Bolger Burke et al., *In Pursuit of Beauty, Americans and the Aesthetic Movement* (New York: Rizzoli, 1986), 10–21.

2. Venable 1994, 49. Dies were among the most valuable company assets and were closely guarded from theft.

3. Burke, *In Pursuit of Beauty,* 472. Moore bequeathed his collection of art and his library to the Metropolitan Museum of Art; "The Moore Collection: A Valuable Gift to the Metropolitan Museum of Art," *The (New York) Sun,* March 6, 1892.

4. British metalwork by Bruce J. Talbert and designs by Gothic-revival advocate A. W. N. Pugin were suggested as English sources in David A. Hanks with Jennifer Toher, "Metalwork: An Eclectic Aesthetic," in Burke et al., *In Pursuit of Beauty,* 253–55.

5. For a discussion of this line introduced by Gorham in 1881, see Carpenter 1982, 112–16.

6. John Webster Keefe and Samuel J. Hough, *Magnificent, Marvelous Martelé: American Art Nouveau Silver* (New Orleans: New Orleans Museum of Art, 2001).

7. Ruskin's writings regarding the separation of art and labor and Morris's critique of factory work were carried forward in America by social reformers Oscar Lovell Triggs, Edward Pearson Pressey, and Leonard Abbott, among many others. Quotation from Leonard Abbott, "Art and Social Reform," in W. D. B. Bliss, ed., *Encyclopedia of Social Reform* (New York: Funk and Wagnall's, 1908), 67, cited in Kaplan 1987, 212 note 22; Eileen Cynthia Boris, "Art and Labor: John Ruskin, William Morris, and the Craftsman Ideal in America, 1876–1915" (Ph.D., Brown University, 1981), 297–98. For a broad assessment of labor and the silver industry, see Venable 1994, 74–76, 205–23.

240

Gorham Manufacturing Company
(active 1865–1961)

Teakettle on stand

Providence, Rhode Island, 1874–78
Marion E. Davis Fund
1990.466a–c

H. 13⅝ in. (34.6 cm); W. 6³/₁₆ in. (15.7 cm); D. 9⅛ in. (23 cm); Wt.
56 oz 2 dwt 1 gr (1745 gm)

Teakettle (1990.466a): H. 9 in. (22.9 cm); W. 8½ in. (21.6 cm); D.
4¾ in. (22.1 cm); Wt. 32 oz 19 dwt 21gr (1026.2 gm)

Stand (1990.466b): H. 7⅞ in. (20 cm); W. 6¾ in. (17.1 cm); D. 5¾ in.
(14.6 cm); Wt. 20 oz 3 dwt 9 gr (627.3 gm)

Spirit lamp (1990.466c): H. 2¼ in (5.7 cm); Diam. 2 in. (5.2 cm); Wt.
2 oz 18 dwt 20 gr (91.5 gm)

Marks: "1040" above a pellet and a lion passant hallmark, an anchor
hallmark, and a "G" in Gothic script, with "STERLING / K"

below, all struck on bottom of teakettle; "S" struck on handle,
close to spout, directly above insulators. "G " above a lion passant
hallmark, an anchor hallmark, and a "G" in Gothic script, with
"STERLING / 1040" below, all struck on bottom of stand. A lion
passant hallmark, an anchor hallmark, and a "G" in Gothic script,
above "STERLING," all struck on bottom of burner. An upside-
down "1" and "STERLING" struck on lamp, inside rim of top.

Inscriptions: None.

SOON AFTER THE OPENING of Japan to foreign trade in 1853,
Japanese woodblock prints, watercolors, architectural details,
and pattern books entered the libraries of American silver
manufacturers, inspiring designers to create a sumptuous
body of silver in the Japanesque style, popular from the 1860s
to the 1880s. Intended as part of a matching set, this teakettle
on stand, with its Japanese-inspired bamboo ties, is one of at
least ten variations produced by Gorham in the mid-1870s.[1] The
austere simplicity contrasts with the more lavish silver made
in America in the Japanese taste. It is nearly unique in an era
that favored ornamental eclecticism and has been described as
anticipating the streamline moderne look of the 1930s by more
than fifty years.[2]

Cost records for this model survive, providing information
on the time and division of labor required for its fabrication.
Silversmithing required sixty-seven hours, plus two and one-
half hours for spinning. Cast elements took one and two-thirds
hours. Finishing of the kettle and stand included five hours of
stoning, four hours of bobbing, and six hours of burnishing,
resulting in the superb surface it has retained. The projected
cost was $180.40: $82.35 for the silver and just under $100 for
labor. The record further documents that the ivory insulators
cost $1.[3]

Description: This elliptical straight-sided teakettle on stand was
formed from sheets of soldered silver. There are molded reedlike
horizontal bands at the kettle's base, lid, spout, and handle, which
are echoed in narrower bands on the spherical cast finial and feet.
The spout has an applied rim that flares at the bottom and forms an
inverted lip at the top. The stand has applied cross-banding on the
vertical kettle supports, which are screwed to the base. The spirit
lamp, which fits into an opening in the base, has a spun hinged cover
and seamed friction-fitting wick holder. The main body of the lamp
was cast and has an applied band. The insulators on the handle are
made of ivory.

History: Early history unknown; purchased from Historical Design,
New York City.

Exhibitions and publications: None.

NOTES TO THIS ENTRY ARE ON PAGE 329.

H. 4⅛ in. (10.5 cm); W. 4⅛ in. (10.3 cm); D. 3¹¹⁄₁₆ in. (9.5 cm); Diam. base 2⅞ in. (7.3 cm)

Marks: "Gorham CO / 160 / N" below an anchor hallmark struck on bottom; "H" and "13" scratched above marks.

Inscription: "C. J. [or S] B / from F. W. J [or S]" in script engraved on bottom. "21" stamped on both rim and inside lid.

ONE OF THE EARLIEST KNOWN copper pieces from Gorham's distinctive Art Silver line, this tea caddy represents a relatively small, but exclusive, body of work that was decorated with silver appliqués and fittings and produced between 1881 and 1885.[1] The design and decoration were clearly influenced by the extraordinary achievements of Japanese Meiji metalwork, despite the fact that Asian tea caddies were typically ceramic. Still, this vessel's shape does depend on Chinese Ming wares as adapted from the ginger jar, a form collected in America since colonial times.

In addition to its affordability, copper allowed for a wide range of color options, from warm reds to deep chocolate browns. Works such as this, with its pristine glazelike finish, are highly prized. Original matte surfaces rarely survive, and the process used to create them is no longer understood.

Description: This raised copper tea caddy has a ceramic glazelike finish and is ornamented in a highly naturalistic manner, with applied silver leaves, flowers, peppers, and a grasshopper. On the body, applied granules of copper and silver simulate the earth; a mouse appears on the separate lid.

History: Original owner unknown. Subsequent history unknown until purchased from W. M. Schwind Jr., Antiques of Yarmouth, Maine.

Exhibitions and publications: Gerald W. R. Ward, "West Meets East: American Furniture in the Anglo-American Taste at the Museum of Fine Arts, Boston," *Apollo* 157, no. 495 (May 2003), 25.

NOTE TO THIS ENTRY IS ON PAGE 329.

241

Gorham Manufacturing Company
(active 1865–1961)

Tea caddy

Providence, Rhode Island, 1881
Gift of Mr. and Mrs. Fred G. Peil, Irma M. Lampert, Henry B. and Klaudia S. Shepard Jr., Gage Bailey Jr., Dr. and Mrs. Francis de Marneffe, Charles S. Nichols, Frank and M. L. Coolidge, Jane E. Coolidge, Angela B. Fischer, Elisha W. Hall II, Ruth F. Hamlen, Faith Moore, Olivia and John Parker, Mr. and Mrs. Walter W. Patten, Jr., J. E. Robinson III, John and Patricia Rodgers, Irvin and Rebekah Taube, Anne D. Moffett, and Louise and Jonathan L. Fairbanks
1991.636

Gorham Manufacturing Company
(active 1865–1961)

Ewer

Providence, Rhode Island, 1880–90
Gift of The Seminarians
1983.21

H. 13 in. (33 cm); W. 5¹¹⁄₁₆ in. (14.4 cm); Diam. rim 1¼ in. (3.2 cm); Diam. base 3½ in. (8.9 cm); Wt. 28 oz 16 dwt 3 gr (896 gm)

Marks: "GORHAM CO / E40" below an anchor hallmark struck on bottom.

Inscriptions: None.

GORHAM, along with Tiffany and Whiting, produced the most innovative designs in the Japanesque style, often executed in mixed metals. This ewer is another outstanding example of the late-nineteenth-century penchant for combining exotic forms to fine effect. In this case, Japanesque decorative elements ornament a vessel of Near Eastern shape popularly known as "Moresque." Other examples of this design have silver spouts or finials.[1]

Description: This oviform copper ewer with tall neck was probably spun in two pieces and then soldered together; the seam is likely hidden under the silver floral die-rolled collar. The top of the narrow neck terminates with a silver reeded band at the rim, surmounted by a hinged ball cover with ball finial. The long spout and handle are seamed; the latter has ivory insulators pinned with silver rods. Applied silver pine boughs with four flying birds grace one side; a dragonfly flies above cattails on the other. The ewer retains much of its original red patina; however, it has lost its red luster on the top of the spout, the neck at the handle joint, lid, and handle.

History: Original owner unknown. Subsequent history unknown until purchased at auction at Christie's in 1982.

Exhibition and publications: Christie's, New York City, sale 5242, December 11, 1982, lot 203; "Gorham Silver, 1831–1981," Rhode Island School of Design, Providence, October 1983–February 1984, checklist no. 95;[2] Venable 1995, fig. 6.64.

NOTES TO THIS ENTRY ARE ON PAGE 329.

243

   1295

243

Gorham Manufacturing Company
(active 1865–1961)

Pitcher

Providence, Rhode Island, 1885
Edwin E. Jack Fund
1983.331

H. 10 in. (25.4 cm); W. 7⅝ in. (19.4 cm); D. 5³⁄₁₆ in. (13.2 cm); Diam. base 3¾ in. (8.3 cm); Wt. 32 oz 9 dwt 17 gr (1010.4 gm)

Marks: A lion passant hallmark, an anchor hallmark, the letter "G" within an escutcheon, "STERLING," "1295," and a boar's head hallmark, all struck in separate locations near bottom edge. "1 S E" scratched to right, below marks.

Inscriptions: None.

ALTHOUGH THE DESIGNER and silversmith are unknown, this snake pitcher is unquestionably an American masterpiece produced during a period of great experimentation and imaginative adaptations of traditional forms. During the 1870s and 1880s, Gorham produced trompe l'oeil "napkins" on plates, "silk" shawls wrapped around pitchers, and applied three-dimensional floral and vegetal elements made to scale, such as the pepper plant on a Gorham tea caddy (cat. no. 241). These objects of fantasy and whimsy relate closely to this pitcher, which represents two coiled life-size snakes. Few other examples of this vessel are known,[1] yet it epitomizes a pervasive fascination in the United States for the exotic and fantastic. It is reminiscent of contemporary snake jewelry, and this particular reptilian motif may have been derived from Egyptian imagery. It may reflect the renewed interest of Victorian audiences in the circumstances of Cleopatra's death, the result of a lethal self-induced asp bite.

No less masterful than the overall form of the pitcher is the silversmith's skillful handling of each surface detail. The body of the pitcher was raised and subsequently repousséd to create the desired contour and to form the bodies of the two snakes. The vessel was filled with molten pitch, which quickly hardened, allowing the silversmith to chase the delicate scales and other exterior surface details. When the work was complete, the pitch was melted and poured out.

The scratch marks indicate that the factory net price for this item was $160.[2]

Description: This raised body and functional elements, such as the handle and spout, are formed by the coiled bodies of two intertwin-

ing snakes, created through repoussé work. The handle is soldered in place.

History: Original owner unknown. Subsequent history unknown until purchased from Firestone and Parson, Inc., Boston, Massachusetts.

Exhibitions and publications: "Gorham Silver, 1831–1981," Rhode Island School of Design, October 1983–February 1984, checklist no. 43; Fairbanks 1991, cat. no. 59, ill. 74; Venable 1994, fig. 6.64, 195, 346; Marilyn Nissenson and Susan Jonas, *Snake Charm* (New York: Harry N. Abrams, 1995), figs. 144–45; Wohlauer 1999, 342.

NOTE TO THIS ENTRY IS ON PAGE 329.

244

Gorham Manufacturing Company
(active 1865–1961)

Punch bowl and ladle

Providence, Rhode Island, 1885
Edwin E. Jack Fund
1980.383–84

Punch bowl (1980.383): H. 10⅛ in. (25.7 cm); W. 15¼ in. (38.7 cm); Diam. rim 9¼ in. (23.5 cm); Diam. foot 7 in. (17.8 cm); Wt. 112 oz 10 dwt 13 gr (3500 gm)

Ladle (1980.384): L. 14 in. (35.6 cm); W. bowl 3¾ in. (9.5 cm); Wt. 7 oz 15 dwt 4 gr (241.3 gm)

Marks: A lion passant, an anchor, "G," "STERLING," "1980," and a boar's head within a shaped reserve, all struck in separate locations on bottom of punch bowl, near edge. "XE —" scratched on bottom. "STERLING" struck on back of ladle.

Inscriptions: None.

THIS MONUMENTAL PUNCH BOWL, with matching ladle, is a testament to the extraordinary technical and artistic prowess of Gorham's craftsmen in the late nineteenth century, an era otherwise noted for significant advances in machine production. Reflecting an interest in Japanese art and culture that predominated in the 1880s, this magnificent set demonstrates not only the influence of British reform, or craftsman, movement at century's end but also America's engagement with the Aesthetic style.

This raised bowl represents a tremendous technical achievement, evidenced by its broadly repousséd ornament of swirling waves, flying fish, and fantastic sea serpent.[1] Surviving compa-

244

ny records reveal that the retail cost was about $840, a considerable sum in 1885, and that the value of the gold on the piece far exceeded that used on other punch bowls created at the same time.[2] The interior, as well as the serpent's tongue and eyes and other details, were originally gilded.

Description: This raised bowl exhibits a chased swirling image of sea life, with waves, fish, seaweed, and other aquatic elements. The rim is encircled with a cast silver border imitating coral and applied shells, crabs, and seaweed. Similar ornamentation appears on the raised and soldered foot. Two large cast scallop shells, encrusted with cast seaweed, serve as handles. Traces of gilt can be found throughout the bowl's surface. The ladle has gilt accents and is made up of cast elements: a scallop shell bowl, oyster shell terminus, and applied sea-life ornamentation on the handle.

History: Original owner unknown. Subsequent history unknown until purchased from Firestone and Parson, Inc., Boston, Massachusetts.

Exhibitions and publications: MFA Annual Report 1980–81, 15; Carpenter 1982, 100–101; "Gorham Silver, 1831–1981," Rhode Island School of Design, October 1983–February 1984, checklist no. 42; Doreen Bolger Burke et al., *In Pursuit of Beauty: Americans and the Aesthetic Movement* (New York: Metropolitan Museum of Art, 1986), fig. 8.19, 271–72; Fairbanks 1991, cat. no. 58; Gerald W. R. Ward, "West Meets East: American Furniture in the Anglo-American Taste at the Museum of Fine Arts, Boston," *Apollo* 157, no. 495 (May 2003), 25.

NOTES TO THIS ENTRY ARE ON PAGE 329.

245

Gorham Manufacturing Company
(active 1865–1961)

Coffeepot (or ewer)

Providence, Rhode Island, 1898
Mary L. Smith Fund
1978.472

H. 11½ in. (29.2 cm); W. 6½ in. (16.5 cm); Diam. 4³⁄₁₆ in. (10.7 cm);
Diam. base 3⁷⁄₁₆ in. (8.8 cm); Wt. 23 oz 18 dwt 8 gr (743.9 gm)

Marks: A lion passant, an anchor surmounted by eagle, and a
Gothic script "G" with "950-1000 FINE. / 1413 [within an oval] /
1½ PINT," all struck on bottom, above engraved initials. A three-
spiked arrow year mark for 1898 struck to right of initials.

Inscriptions: "FS" in script engraved on bottom.

THE DECORATION OF this coffeepot displays sensuous floral
motifs, anticipating the spread of the Art Nouveau style in
America, whereas the form illustrates the fashion for Islamic-
inspired wares in the last quarter of the nineteenth century.[1]
By this period, Gorham had fully mechanized its methods and
developed one of the most efficient and modern factories of
its type. Yet, the firm repeatedly introduced handcrafted elements into its products and, in 1897, launched a line of silver
made entirely by hand. These wares, characterized by their Art
Nouveau style, were called Martelé, the French word for hand
hammered.[2]

Gorham's goal in producing the Martelé line was to reunite
the designer and the craftsman, an idea in harmony with the
philosophical outlook of the Arts and Crafts movement. Gorham's chief designer was English-trained silversmith William
Christmas Codman (1839–1921), who directed this initiative.[3] In
preparation for the introduction of the Martelé line, Gorham
provided instruction to its craftsmen in hand-raising hollowware from flat sheets of silver. Between 1897 and 1912, the company produced approximately 4,800 pieces of Martelé. The date
mark for 1898 on this object suggests that it was among the
earliest produced; the company typically did not mark these
hand-wrought pieces with the word *Martelé* until 1901.[4]

Description: Embellished with delicate repoussé and chased ornament of flowering vines, veined leaves, and budding flowers, this
vessel has a footed, bulbous, raised body tapering to a narrow neck
that flares slightly outward and then inward at the upper juncture
of the handle. The spout and pinned handle are seamed; the latter

has ivory insulators. The bottom is inset, and the hinged lid bears a
knob finial.

History: Original owner unknown. Subsequent history unknown
until purchased from Fred Silverman, New York City.

Exhibitions and publications: Fairbanks 1981, 627, pl. 42.

NOTES TO THIS ENTRY ARE ON PAGE 329–30.

246

Gorham Manufacturing Company
(active 1865–1961)

Inkstand

Providence, Rhode Island, 1903
Museum purchase with funds donated by Dr. and Mrs. James Rabb
2001.804

H. 2¹³⁄₁₆ in. (7.1 cm); W. 11¹³⁄₁₆ in. (30.0 cm); D. 6½ in. (16.5 cm); Wt. 22 oz 16 dwt 22 gr (710 gm)

Marks: A lion passant within a shaped cartouche; anchor within a shaped cartouche; Gothic-style "G" within a hexagon, and "STER-LING / B2342," all struck underneath. Scratch marks include "2242-2" among other less decipherable markings.

Inscriptions: None.

THE CONTINENTAL LOVE of Art Nouveau was only rarely reflected in objects produced for a more conservative American clientele. This inkstand is a rare exception, with its whiplash curves, floral ornament with swirling and entwined stems,

flower buds, and boldly undulating edge. Notable for its refined form and elegant embellishments, the inkstand was a product of Gorham's finest years. It was probably made under the direction of the firm's legendary designer, William Christmas Codman.

The inkstand, Gorham's production model number B 2342, sold for $37.50 when it was first produced in 1903; Gorham's profit was $6.79. In 1906 the price was raised to $41.35, but within four years, perhaps due to the decline of the Art Nouveau style, it was heavily discounted.[1]

Although not part of Gorham's glamorous Martelé line of hand-hammered silver, the inkstand achieved similar effects with less effort and expense. Gorham employed the more economical method of casting to establish the form and then used silversmiths to complete the finishing by hand. Thus, the time-intensive cost of raising the form was minimized while hand-work gave the object its glimmering surface and enhanced the delicate floral decoration.

Description: The inkstand has a shallow undecorated trough, intended to hold a pen, and rises to a flat lidded inkwell. The form is ornamented with an arrangement of California poppies, whose tendrils wind around the perimeter to create a bilaterally symmetrical design. A five-part hinge connects the square lid to the body. The lid has a thumbgrip and bears a stamped and chased image of a poppy with two pendant leaves. The interior of the lid is gilded. The form was first cast and then lightly chased to provide additional detail and a hand-worked finish. The glass inkwell is missing.

History: Acquired from a private New Hampshire collection by the firm of Spencer Marks, East Walpole, Massachusetts, from which it was purchased.

Exhibitions and publications: None.

NOTE TO THIS ENTRY IS ON PAGE 330.

247

Gorham Manufacturing Company
(active 1865–1961)

Seven-piece coffee and tea service

Providence, Rhode Island, 1906
In Loving Memory of Betty and Saul Palais
69.1291–97

Coffeepot (69.1291): H. 10¹³⁄₁₆ in. (27.5 cm); W. 10 in. (25.5 cm); D. 5 in. (12.6 cm); Wt. 36 oz 12 dwt (1138.4 gm)

Teapot (69.1292): H. 8³⁄₁₆ in. (20.8 cm); W. 10½ in. (26.6 cm); D. 6⅛ in. (15.5 cm); Wt. 35 oz 16 dwt 12 gr (1114.3 gm)

Sugar bowl (69.1293): H. 6½ in. (16.6 cm); W. 8⁵⁄₁₆ in. (21.2 cm); Diam. 5 in. (12.7 cm); Wt. 21 oz 19 dwt 9 gr (683.3 gm)

Creamer (69.1294): H. 6⅞ in. (17.5 cm); W. 6⅜ in. (16.3 cm); Diam. 3⅞ in. (9.8 cm); Wt. 15 oz 8 dwt 9 gr (479.6 gm)

Waste bowl (69.1295): H. 3⅞ in. (9.8 cm); W. 7³⁄₁₆ in. (18.4 cm); Diam. 5 in. (12.7 cm); Wt. 15 oz 17 dwt 2 gr (493.1 gm)

Teakettle on stand (69.1296a–c): H. 11¹¹⁄₁₆ in. (29.7 cm); W. 9⅜ in. (24 cm); D. 7⅜ in. (18.8 cm.); Wt. 71 oz 8 dwt 11 gr (2221.5 gm)

Waiter (69.1297): H. 2¾ in. (7 cm); W. 31½ in. (80 cm); D. 21⅛ in. (53.7 cm); Wt. 186 oz 9 dwt 12 gr (5800 gm)

Marks: "Martelé / [lion passant] [anchor surmounted by spread eagle] G / 9584 / H/ WZ" struck on base and under foot of each (except the waiter), with minor variations in locations and arrangements. A skeleton-key date mark struck in various locations on each base. "ISN" scratched onto bottom of teapot, to right of monogram. "-30." scratched next to silver composition mark, and "H/WZ." struck on foot of waste bowl. "H/WZ." also struck on foot of teakettle. "Martelé" / [lion passant] [anchor, surmounted by spread eagle] G / 9584 / LCH / 28 in." struck on bottom of waiter. "9584" struck on inside of burner top.

Inscriptions: None.

Description: Composed of ten parts, this tea service is embellished with flowering vines, veined leaves, and budding flowers. The teakettle includes a burner and chain. The elliptical vessels were raised and shaped with ribbed vertical sections that frame the broader right and left face of each form. The handles and spouts are seamed, and several of the lids are hinged. The lidded vessels have ornate seedpod finials. All insulators are ivory (part of insulator on teapot is missing). The handle on the burner also has a turned ivory knob. The burner has a cogwheel mechanism attached to the handle to lift the wick.

History: According to family tradition, this set was purchased from Gorham by a New York district attorney as a gift to celebrated New York singer Lillian "Diamond Lil" Russell (1861–1922). It was subsequently acquired by Eskind, an antiques dealer in Newton, Massachusetts, who sold it to Betty and Saul Palais about 1940.[5]

Exhibitions and publications: Pristo 2002, 91.

NOTES TO THIS ENTRY ARE ON PAGE 330.

247

ONE OF THE SIGNATURE ASPECTS of Martelé silver is a softly modulated finish that bears traces of the craftsman's hammer. As the background for the undulating organic shapes of Art Nouveau ornament, the shimmering hammer marks add a misty appearance to these works, contributing to their ethereal quality. The delicacy of Martelé wares has been attributed to William Christmas Codman, Gorham's chief designer from 1891 until the 1930s.[1] A pronounced respect for individual design and handcraftsmanship was part of the growing concern for integrity of materials and workmanship that characterize the Arts and Crafts movement. In practice, however, several hands were involved with the creation of this set, each contributing their specialty to realize a magnificent whole. The hollowware pieces were raised by William Hughes Jr. in February 1906 and then chased by five other craftsmen.[2] The waiter was made in August 1906 by F. O. Erichsen and chased by Otto Colmetz, who was responsible for decorating two of the vessels.

For economic as well as aesthetic reasons, several different alloys were used in the fashioning of Gorham's Martelé silver. Gorham gradually moved from the standard .925 sterling alloy used in 1897 to a higher silver content of .9684 in 1905 to allow a more fluid shaping of the metal. In economic terms, the increase in malleability also meant a 10–12 percent savings in time spent on an individual object. Regrettably, the softer silver is more delicate and readily damaged; thus, works that survive with their fragile surfaces intact are all the more coveted.[3] The complete service also included salt and pepper shakers.[4]

248

Tiffany & Co. (active 1837–present)

Pitcher

New York, New York, 1875
Gift of Gideon F. T. Reed
77.61

H. 8¼ in (20.5 cm); W. 4³⁄₁₆ in. (10.6 cm); D. 3¾ in. (9.5 cm); Wt. 8 oz 17 dwt 18 gr (276.4 gm)

Marks: "TIFFANY & Cº / 4065 MAKERS 5392" struck on bottom, above center point; "STERLING–SILVER / 925 - 1000" and roman letter "M" struck below center point. "209" scratched on bottom, to right of marks.

Inscriptions: none.

ACQUIRED AT THE 1876 Centennial Exposition, this pitcher represents Tiffany's new line of chromatically decorated silver utilizing mixed-metal techniques. It became the first piece of American silver to enter the Museum's collection and distinguished the institution for its early interest in contemporary, as well as historic, art. Former Boston jeweler Gideon F. T. Reed, who was then a major shareholder in Tiffany & Co. and head of its Paris office, engaged Frank Hill Smith to select and acquire metalwork for the Museum from the Philadelphia fair.[1] Despite an acknowledged conflict of interest, this pitcher became the first piece of Tiffany silver to enter a museum col-

TIFFANY&Cº
4065 MAKERS 5392
STERLING·SILVER
925-1000.
M

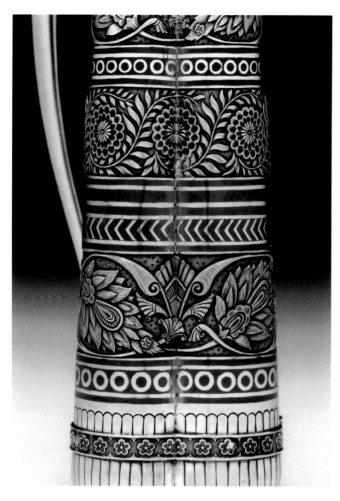

248

Quest for Unity: American Art Between World's Fairs, 1876–1893 (Detroit: Founders Society Detroit Institute of Arts, 1983), 199–200; Doreen Bolger Burke et al., *In Pursuit of Beauty: Americans and the Aesthetic Movement* (New York: Metropolitan Museum of Art, 1986), fig. 8.3, 253–55; "The Silver of Tiffany and Co.," Place des Antiquaires, New York City, November 1987–February 1988; Charles H. Carpenter Jr. and Janet Zapata, *The Silver of Tiffany and Company, 1850–1987* (Boston: Museum of Fine Arts, Boston, 1987), cat. no. 52, cover ill.; Venable 1994, 170–71; John Loring, *Magnificent Tiffany Silver* (New York: Harry N. Abrams, 2001), 62.

NOTES TO THIS ENTRY ARE ON PAGE 330.

249

Tiffany and Company (active 1837–present)
Pitcher

New York, New York, 1888
Gift of Mr. and Mrs. Joel Glassman in Memory of Parents,
Mr. and Mrs. Samuel D. Saxe
1990.625

H. 12⅛ in. (30.8 cm); W. 8½ in. (21.5 cm); Diam. base 5¹¹⁄₁₆ in. (14.5 cm); Wt. 41 oz 19 dwt 22 gr (1306.2 gm)

Marks: "TIFFANY & Cº" "6015 MAKERS 2128," "STERLING-SILVER," "925-1000," and roman letter "M" struck on bottom of base. "492" and "42/14" also scratched on bottom.

Inscriptions: none.

IN THE LATE NINETEENTH CENTURY, Tiffany gained international fame for its elaborately designed and chased wares. This handsome water pitcher adds credence to the firm's reputation. It is lavishly chased and covered with densely packed floral and broad-leaf patterns. Described as "High Old English" in the Tiffany records, this pitcher's elongated shape differs from the firm's usual globular pitchers, on which this type of floral decoration usually appears. The original pattern books, now at Tiffany archives, identify this pitcher as the first example of this particular model.[1] The cost before retail markup and ornamentation is listed as $50, a considerable sum for the time; chasing and decorative mounts would have added another $25 to $50.

Description: This slightly tapered cylindrical form, made from soldered sheets and perhaps a spun bottom, is richly ornamented with a bouquet of various flowers in repoussé. Divided into three sections. The upper section, which encompasses the spout, is topped by an unornamented band at the rim, with a wide band of floral

lection.[2] And although the designer of this pitcher is unknown, a Tiffany drawing of this vessel, dated April 29, 1875, indicates that it was "pitcher no. 4065, [made from] four pieces, [with a] handle made of plate."[3]

Description: This silver vessel with copper inlay has a tapering quatrefoil cross section. An acute triangular spout interrupts the uppermost band, which is unadorned. The bottom has incised vertical ribs, intersected by a die-rolled band of stylized flowers. Alternating bands of silver with chased floral decorations and bands of copper inlaid with silver chevrons or circles terminate with a thin band of chased waves and stylized egg-and-dart molding just below the uppermost plain silver band. It has an applied foot and S-scroll hollow cast handle; the interior shows traces of gilding.

History: Purchased from the Tiffany display at Philadelphia Centennial Exhibition for Museum of Fine Arts, Boston, by Frank Hill Smith with funds provided by Gideon F. T. Reed.[4]

Exhibitions and publications: Carpenter 1978, pl. 1; "Tiffany Silver," New-York Historical Society, 1979; Detroit Institute of Arts, *The*

249

decoration and a gadrooned band below. A wider band of floral decoration defines the center section. The lower section has vertical leaf decorations and a slightly flaring applied foot with foliate sprays. The double-scroll handle with foliate accents was cast.

History: Original owner unknown. Acquired by Mr. and Mrs. Samuel D. Saxe about 1910; inherited in 1970 by Eleanor Saxe Glassman, who, with her husband, Joel Glassman, gave the piece to the Museum in her parents' memory.

Exhibitions and publications: None.

NOTE TO THIS ENTRY IS ON PAGE 330.

Notes

240

1. Samuel Hough has provided documentation on this kettle from the Gorham Archive at Brown University in Providence, R.I., and conjectures that the date marks on the bottom, which represent the years 1874 (Gothic letter "G") and 1878 ("K"), could indicate that an 1874 teakettle was perfected in 1878 so that it swung more smoothly; see Hough correspondence dated May/June 1990, department files, Art of the Americas.

2. Carpenter 1982, 119–20.

3. Research at the Gorham Archive, Brown University, on labor and expenses provided by Samuel Hough, who has identified potential designers of this piece as George Wilkinson, Thomas Pairpoint, Antoine Heller, and Otto (last name unknown); see Hough correspondence, department files, Art of the Americas.

241

1. The letter "N" stamped on the bottom of the vessel corresponds to the Gorham date symbol for 1881, the year when such copper wares were introduced to the broader Art Silver line. Carpenter 1982, 112–16.

242

1. See Venable 1994, 164. For similar examples of this form, see Christie's, New York, sale 9592, January 19, 2001, lot 242; Sotheby's Auctions Online, offered January 21, 2000, lot D6L; Christie's, New York, sale 8894, June 18, 1998, lot 72; and Sotheby's, London, sale LN6195, March 29, 1996, lot 169. Unornamented versions of the ewer were also sold by Gorham.

2. Susan Bartlett, assistant registrar at the Rhode Island School of Design, provided this reference from the exhibition files.

243

1. Another example of this pitcher is in the Philadelphia Museum of Art, 1963-1-32.

2. On reading scratch marks, see Pristo 2002, 160–61.

244

1. About 1800, William Wilson and Son of Philadelphia fashioned a similar tureen displaying swirling wavelike surface repoussé with fish and crustaceans. See *Silver Magazine* 32, no. 3 (May/June 2000), 9.

2. Archival records indicate that this bowl cost $155.25 for the silver, $50 for chasing, $20.50 for applied work, and $20 for gilding. Its weight is listed as 115 troy ounces. Charles Carpenter has suggested that the name "White Jr.," which is associated with this piece as well as with other punch bowls, may identify the original client when the bowl was cost out in April 1885. Gorham made a similar bowl in 1886. See departmental files for Carpenter correspondence. Pristo 2002, 160–61, has identified the corresponding numerical values for the scratch marks that typically appear on Martelé pieces. The symbolic price codes scratched on the punch bowl indicate the factory net price was $440.

245

1. For examples of Martelé black coffee sets, which include comparable forms, see McClinton 1968, 114.

2. Carpenter 1982, 221–52.

3. Carpenter 1982, 203, 223.

4. The earliest use by Gorham of the word *Martelé* occurred in 1899; see Pristo 2002, 14; see also Carpenter 1982, 223, 285, 290; and John Webster

Keefe and Samuel J. Hough, *Magnificent, Marvelous Martelé: American Art Nouveau Silver, The Robert and Jolie Shelton Collection* (New Orleans: New Orleans Museum of Art, 2001), 56–57. Gorham's records, collected in Pristo 2002, 184, describe model "1413" as requiring 35 hours to make and 60 hours of chasing time. The net cost was $120. In the Gorham Archive at Brown University, no name is associated with the creation of this piece. A second example is in the Philadelphia Museum of Art (1963-1-32).

246

1. An identical inkwell is discussed in Keefe and Hough, *Magnificent, Marvelous Martelé*, 498–99, cat. no. 134.

247

1. Carpenter 1982, 231–32.

2. With 182 raised pieces documented to his name, Hughes was among the most prolific of Gorham's makers of Martelé; Pristo 2002, 32. For information regarding weight, making and chasing time, as well as net price, see Pristo 2002, 344, 376. The following craftsmen were responsible for chasing work: Henry Brooks, coffeepot; Walter C. Sanders, creamer; Emil Stursberg, kettle; F. Vierling, waste bowl; Otto Colmctz, sugar bowl and teapot.

3. Carpenter 1982, 225–27.

4. For correspondence related to these additional pieces, see department files, Art of the Americas.

5. Oral history account provided by Nancy Palais Levin, daughter of Saul and Elizabeth "Betty" Robinson Palais. See also McClinton 1968, 113, for comparable examples of Martelé tea sets with kettles.

248

1. Before joining Tiffany & Co., Gideon Reed was a partner in Lincoln, Reed, and Company, one of Boston's leading jewelry firms. Information about this gift is in an extract of a letter from Miss Alice A. Gray, May 1905, in department files, Art of the Americas. See also Joseph Purtell, *The Tiffany Touch* (New York: Random House, 1971), 24, 44; and John Loring, *Magnificent Tiffany Silver* (New York: Harry N. Abrams, 2001), 62. Reed donated more than 50 objects to the Museum from the Centennial Exhibition, mainly ancient Islamic arms and armor (and a few modern reproductions), and three pieces of Japanese ceramics.

2. Loring, *Magnificent Tiffany Silver*, 62.

3. A copy of the Tiffany drawing, in the Tiffany Archives, is in the department files, Art of the Americas.

4. For copies of correspondence and records relating to this gift, see department files, Art of the Americas.

249

1. Tiffany Archives, Hollowware Manufacturer Ledgers, vol. 204, book 3, pattern 6015, order 2128. This particular vessel is listed at $100. Another version of the same form, which wholesaled for $75, was chased and decorated with "heads" and parcel gilt.

CHAPTER 5

ARTS AND CRAFTS SILVER

Rebecca A. G. Reynolds and Jeannine Falino

The Arts and Crafts movement emerged in the late nineteenth century and predominated in England and the United States, where it was especially popular during the first two decades of the twentieth century. Artists drew upon many of the same stylistic sources as did proponents of the Aesthetic movement (see chapter 4), with which it initially overlapped. Yet they were soberly moralistic in their approach to design reform, espousing the basic tenets of handcraftsmanship, restrained design, and truth to materials.[1] Reinterpreted in the 1940s and 1950s by early modernist silversmiths, these principles resonate to this day in the field of American contemporary craft.

Arts and Crafts style, like the Aesthetic style, is an eclectic synthesis drawn from sources as varied as the Gothic and the Japanesque. These diverse influences are unified by a reductive and schematic approach that eschews excessive surface decoration. Following the call of English architect Augustus Pugin for form that follows function, Arts and Crafts ornament supports or enhances the purpose of the object. However, the sculptural potential of silver, like that of ceramics, inspired artists to break away from the style's characteristic restraint to create floral schemes, as seen in the work of Potter Studios, Arthur Stone (1847–1938), and Clemens Friedell (cat. nos. 274–75, 303, 424).

Copper also proved to be an attractive material, providing Arts and Crafts metalsmiths with similar visual and tactile pleasures. Among its many advantages to both craftsman and consumer were its malleability and its cost, often a fraction of that of silver. Copper's changeable quality was valued as well. It was easily treated to produce various patinas, and it combined beautifully with enamel.[2] Stone was particularly fond of the metal and produced a rich and varied group of objects for his personal pleasure. His copper jardiniere (cat. no. 290) earned a prize at the Louisiana Purchase Exposition of 1904 and is considered one of his greatest works.[3]

Certainly the leading style of this period and, indeed, the perennial favorite among New England artists was Colonial Revival. George Gebelein (1878–1945) pointed to his employment by Boston makers Goodnow and Jenks as evidence of his artistic link to that most celebrated of all colonial silversmiths, Paul Revere.[4] Gebelein, Stone, and Ernest Currier (1867–1936)

were all respected for their connection to traditional forms and styles because of the colonial silver they emulated or sold. By no means confined to Boston, the style was also used to good effect by Chicago artist Robert Jarvie (1865–1941) (cat. no. 264). The Museum of Fine Arts, Boston, contributed to the Colonial-Revival movement by mounting landmark exhibitions of colonial silver in 1906 and 1911, a time of growing interest in early American art.[5]

The practice of metalsmithing benefited from the craft revival of the era. By the late nineteenth century, skilled artists were scarce in a field in which manufacturers had risen as the dominant force (see chapter 3). The situation was acute by 1896, when Gorham Manufacturing Company established a school on factory grounds to train staff in fashioning the firm's select Martelé line (see cat. nos. 245 and 247). Tiffany & Co. also operated its own school and retained a pool of talented artists to produce their Special Hand Work line. Both companies exhibited magnificent tour-de-force examples of silversmithing, enameling, and the jeweler's art at international world fairs, but these remarkable objects were the exceptions in an industrial world that operated according to the standards of mass production. With increased mechanization and division of labor at the largest firms, the craft had become compartmentalized so that few individuals were responsible for creating a complete vessel or piece of flatware. Fortunately, a groundswell of interest in preindustrial crafts inspired some artists to reestablish earlier traditions. Aided by immigrant craftsmen who arrived with fully developed silversmithing skills and a new emphasis on craft education, these artists prospered until the era had run its course, about the time of World War I.

Talented immigrants, many of whom are included in this chapter, infused the American field with fresh ideas. Stone was most prominent. A founding member of Sheffield's Society of Arts and Crafts in his native England, he quietly operated a cooperative profit-sharing workshop in which staff cosigned works they helped create.[6] He encouraged the professional growth of his apprentices; arranged study trips for his employees; and sponsored their membership in the Society of Arts and Crafts, Boston, an organization in which Stone was a leader and active member. He was considered the "dean of American silversmiths," and his achievements are represented by more than fifty objects in the Museum's collection.[7]

The influence that Scandinavian immigrants exerted on American silver is most evident in the Midwest, where this population was especially concentrated. Kalo Shop (1900–1970) in Chicago is regarded as one of the era's most influential and successful enterprises. Initially, shop members engaged in a variety of media, from textiles to leather crafts, but soon specialized in metalwork after the 1905 marriage of founder Clara P. Barck to George P. Welles, an amateur metalworker.[8] Clara Welles founded an "art-craft community" that employed many newly arrived Scandinavian silversmiths, some of whom later established their own successful businesses. Kalo silver vessels and jewelry are characterized by the use of graceful lobes and occasional strapwork. The style varied little and received steady customer support throughout the exceptionally long period of the shop's operation.

Boston claimed at least two outstanding Scandinavian silversmiths from this period, Frans Gyllenberg (1883–1974) from Sweden and Karl F. Leinonen (1866–1957) from Finland (cat. nos. 262 and 271). Both craftsmen were affiliated with Handicraft Shop, a subsidiary of the Society of Arts and Crafts, Boston. German-born George Germer (1868–1936) produced handsomely wrought hollowware and jewelry, often featuring impressive, repoussé passages, which he executed primarily for ecclesiastical patrons (fig. 1).

Established in 1897 as the first organization of its type in the United States, the Society of Arts and Crafts, Boston, furthered the aesthetic ideals of the movement, both locally and nationally. It helped support the work of its membership and establish the city's preeminence as a leading Arts and Crafts community through the sale of members' work in its salesroom. It further promoted their work at its own annual exhibitions in Boston as well as those sponsored by corresponding organizations across the country, notably in Chicago and Detroit. Its mission statement reflected the ideals of the movement as a whole:

> The motives of the True Craftsman are the love of good and beautiful work as applied to useful service, and the need of making an adequate livelihood. . . . Artistic Cooperation: When the designer and the workman are not united in the same person, they should work together, each teaching the other his own special knowledge, so that the faculties of the designer and the workman may tend to become united in each.[9]

FIG. 1. George E. Germer, pectoral cross, about 1915. Silver, amethyst; H. 4¼ in. (10.8 cm); W. 2⅝ in. (6.7 cm). Museum of Fine Arts, Boston; Decorative Art Curators' Fund, 1985 (1985.816).

One of the major aims of Arts and Crafts ideology was to provide art education as a means of encouraging self-expression, offering not only direction in design reform but also marketable skills to young people and newly arrived immigrants. These goals followed an effort begun in 1870 with the Massachusetts Art Reform Act, the first such measure in the country to establish art education as a fundamental element of the public school system; its purpose was to train new generations of designers for industry. That same year, the state opened the Massachusetts Normal Art School so that properly trained art teachers could convey the principles of design and composition to students. In 1873 the Museum of Fine Arts, Boston, established the Museum School, where students first learned by drawing from classical casts and other facsimiles, in emulation of the British model advanced by the South Kensington Museum (now the Victoria and Albert Museum). In time, classes in the decorative arts, including metalsmithing, became part of the curriculum. By 1901 the first metalsmithing classes at the Massachusetts Normal Art School were being taught by Laurin Hovey Martin (1875–1939); Englishman George J. Hunt (1866–1947) began teaching the craft at the Museum School in 1905. Similar developments were taking place in cities nationwide, notably New York, Cleveland, and Minneapolis.[10]

Graduates of these schools became art educators who introduced students to drawing, design, and craft disciplines. The academic approach supplanted the traditional apprenticeship system that had been swept away by the Industrial Revolution. In so doing, it forever changed the relationship of craft with industry. Craft disciplines became one of many art forms that students could study, leading away from utilitarian forms and toward the deeply personal interpretations that emerged in the second half of the twentieth century.

The emphasis on handcraftsmanship was fully evident in studio silver of the period. Hammer marks were considered an imperfection to be cherished as a sign of humanity (much as John Ruskin had praised the chisel marks of medieval stone carvers), and irregular surfaces were preferred to the mirror finish of manufactured silver. In the United States, porringers, teapots, and similar historic forms, along with ornamental engravings of the Rococo and early Neoclassical eras, were faithfully, if sometimes romantically, interpreted by Arts and Crafts metalsmiths. Some chose the difficult task of sawcutting porringer handles despite the speed and ease of the casting method in use since antiquity. Others intentionally roughened edges to make vessels appear less refined, although such techniques would have been unacceptable in the eighteenth century.[11] So desirable was the hand-worked surface that, in later years, the shop of George Gebelein jobbed out vessels for spinning and regularly "finished" such forms with hammer marks to give the illusion of having been handmade. Makers engaged in these mechanical processes in order to increase efficiency and control costs, thereby passing on savings and expanding their customer base beyond traditional, wealthy patrons.

Women, as keepers of the domestic sphere, performed a vital function in furthering Arts and Crafts design through their efforts in the home. Furthermore, they also figured among some of its chief practitioners. In Massachusetts, women formed the largest group of metalsmithing members of the Society of Arts and Crafts, Boston, a fact that attests to their interest in the field as both diversion and livelihood. As designers, metalworkers, enamelists, and jewelers, many distinguished themselves through both their collaborations and individual production. Teacher and silversmith Katharine Pratt (1891–1978) gained her experience in a manner similar to that of male craftsmen. She pieced together the equivalent of a traditional apprenticeship by studying with, and later working alongside, established masters. She learned from George J. Hunt at the Museum School and later gained a prestigious internship in Gebelein's shop. She then worked briefly for Handicraft Shop before setting out on her own. Mary Catherine Knight (1876–active 1927) studied in Philadelphia and worked briefly for Gorham before settling into her work with Handicraft Shop.

Wealthy patrons, churches, and social organizations fueled the careers of many silversmiths. Some achieved renown by fashioning extraordinary ecclesiastical silver in collaboration with architects. As sacred objects of religious rituals, these precious, sumptuous works were rarely available for public viewing except by the congregation on special occasions. Detroit publisher and philanthropist George G. Booth commissioned Boston-area silversmiths to create some of their most ambitious religious pieces for Christ Church, Cranbrook, on the grounds of the artistic and educational community that he established in Bloomfield Hills, Michigan.[12] The Cliff Dwellers, a Chicago literary club, hired Robert Jarvie to fashion some of the era's most distinctive Arts and Crafts silver. In New England and elsewhere, Stone was chosen when presentation cups or ecclesiastical silver was required.[13] Sports clubs were fond of commissioning trophies for their membership. Among these, a massive punch bowl (cat. no. 424) ordered by the Pasadena Polo Club and made by California artist Clemens Friedell displays the ease with which artists met the needs of their clients for such large and handsomely chased vessels.

Aside from special commissions, silver made by studio craftsmen tended to be more modest in scale and number than that produced by manufacturers. Tea and beverage services of five and six pieces—such as those in the Museum's collection by Jarvie, Gebelein, and Stone—are among the largest known. Serving pieces with enameled ornament, including those by Frances (Barnum) Smith (active 1901–1904) and Jane (Carson) Barron (b. 1879, w. 1926) (cat. no. 250), were more typical than formal fifteen-piece table settings, such as the Puritan-style flatware by Gebelein (cat. no. 260). Small Chinese- or Revere-style bowls with everted rims; porringers; and the occasional *écuelle* followed the taste for preindustrial styles of colonial America. Diminutive personal items prevailed in the form of boxes, which were sometimes enameled and accented with cabochons, thus bearing medieval overtones; children's or youth sets; and toiletry and desk accessories. As twentieth-century tastes in tableware changed, so, too, did silversmiths, who turned to making candy dishes, ashtrays, and sandwich plates for their younger patrons.

The Arts and Crafts period is often considered to be most strongly represented by furniture, ceramics, and architecture. Yet one-third of the membership in the Society of Arts and Crafts, Boston was held by metalsmiths. The many forms, styles, and artists represented in this chapter attest to the wealth of skill and the vibrancy of work produced in silver during this era.

Notes

1. For a general style discussion, see Richard Guy Wilson, "American Arts and Crafts Architecture: Radical though Dedicated to the Cause Conservative," in Kaplan 1987, 101–31.

2. Jeannine Falino, "Circles of Influence: Metalsmithing in New England," in Meyer 1997, 71.

3. Artists in the Museum's collection who are solely represented by jewelry, works in copper, or works in other base metals are not included in this chapter.

4. Alexandra Deutsch, "George Christian Gebelein: The Craft and Business of a 'Modern Paul Revere'" (master's thesis, University of Delaware, 1995).

5. See MFA 1906 and MFA 1911.

6. Chickering 1994, 14.

7. Rosalie Berberian, "The Society of Arts and Crafts of Boston and Its Master Silversmiths," *Arts and Crafts Quarterly* 4, no. 1 (winter 1991), 16–23; Falino, "Circles of Influence," 70–85.

8. W. Scott Braznell, cited in Kaplan 1987, 279–80.

9. Ulehla 1981, 276.

10. For a summary of the organizations and schools that developed in the U.S. during the Arts and Crafts period, see Scott Braznell, "Metalsmithing and Jewelrymaking, 1900–1929," in Janet Kardon, ed., *The Ideal Home, 1900–1920: The History of Twentieth-Century American Craft* (New York: American Craft Museum, 1993), 55–63.

11. See, for example, a two-handled porringer by George C. Gebelein dated about 1930, having an intentionally roughened edge, in the collection of the Museum of Art, Rhode Island School of Design (85.02).

12. Falino, "Circles of Influence," 81.

13. A wide variety of Stone's patrons can be found in Chickering 1994.

250

Frances (Barnum) Smith (active 1901–1904) and Jane (Carson) Barron (b. 1879)

Salad servers

Cleveland, Ohio, about 1902–5
Gift of The Seminarians
1994.224a–b

Fork (1994.224a): L. 9 1/16 in. (23 cm); W. bowl 2 1/2 in. (6.3 cm); Wt. 3 oz 21 dwt 21 gr (94.7 gm)

Spoon (1994.224b): L. 9 1/16 in. (23 cm); W. bowl 2 1/2 in. (6.3 cm); Wt. 3oz 6 dwt 7 gr (103.1 gm)

Marks: "B" within a "C" monogram in sans-serif letters, all within a circle, and "STERLING" in sans-serif letters incuse, struck on back of each handle.

Inscriptions: None.

WOMEN FORMED THE MAJORITY of metalsmiths and enamelers during the Arts and Crafts period in America.[1] Their activities paralleled that of many women who moved from the household sphere into the working world. The applied arts, in particular, were considered a socially acceptable focus for their energies, and for some it proved an avenue to financial independence.

Cleveland artists Frances Barnum and Jane Carson were exceptionally active in the field during the first decade of the twentieth century.[2] Both attended school briefly in Boston. Bar-

num began her studies at the Cleveland School of Art (now the Cleveland Institute of Art), well known for its courses in the decorative arts, before continuing her education at the School of the Museum of Fine Arts, Boston. Carson attended the Massachusetts Normal Art School in the 1890s and the Museum School in 1900, participating in its exhibition in 1901.[3]

In that year, the women jointly opened a workshop in Cleveland that became known for its jewelry and decorative desk, table, and toiletry accessories; in 1902 both joined the Society of Arts and Crafts, Boston, at the craftsman level. The brief but prolific activity that followed garnered them national recognition. At the 1904 Louisiana Purchase International Exhibition, their efforts were recognized with a silver medal.[4]

Shortly after Barnum married Arthur Lawrence Smith in 1904, her exhibition career seems to have ended. Carson, however, continued to work until her own marriage to Amos N. Barron, about 1910. Between 1904 and 1910, she sometimes collaborated with fellow Cleveland artist Mildred Watkins (1883–1968), who had previously worked with Carson and Barnum and, like them, had briefly studied in Boston.[5] About 1904, she attended metalsmithing classes at the nearby Massachusetts Normal Art School (now the Massachusetts College of Art) taught by Laurin Hovey Martin before establishing a teaching career at the Cleveland School of Art.

Carson and Watkins participated together in the 1906 and 1907 Arts and Crafts exhibitions held by the Chicago Art Institute and in the 1907 Society of Arts and Crafts exhibition in Boston. That show included two pendants executed by them and designed by Amy Sacker (1876–1965), a Boston book artist with whom one or both women had studied. Their collaboration documents the continuing relationship between the Cleveland women and their Boston colleagues.

These serving pieces, small in scale and enlivened with colorful enameled panels, are typical of the workshop products of Barnum and Smith. They are just a few of the many surviving objects fashioned by these makers and may have been among those included in the 1904 or 1905 Cleveland Art Institute exhibition. A pair of silver and enamel salad servers priced at $40 was exhibited by Carson and Barnum in 1904; at the 1905 show they sold two pairs of servers for $45 each.[6] Although Barnum exhibited under her married name in 1905, the women may have retained the "B" within a "C" maker's mark for the works they sold that year.

Description: Each serving utensil is composed of two overlapping sections soldered together. Each large shallow bowl, in the shape of a leaf, bears hammer marks and extends to a broad handle with

V-shaped enameled panels displaying peacock feather designs. The bowl and handle section is soldered to a wider handle with cut-card design. Two pierced attenuated ovals flank a central enameled panel at the tip and lead downward to a narrow groove along each side of the handle. The enameled panel extends slightly beyond the handle tip; a supporting rectangular section has been soldered behind the enamel; the tines of the fork echo the shape of the bowl.

History: Early history unknown; purchased in October 1994 from ARK Antiques, New Haven, Connecticut.

Exhibitions and publications: None.

NOTES TO THIS ENTRY ARE ON PAGE 401.

251

Elizabeth Ethel Copeland (1866–1957)

Box

Boston, Massachusetts, 1912
Gift of Mrs. Horatio A. Lamb in memory of Mr. and Mrs. Winthrop Sargent
19.5

H. 3⅛ in. (7.9 cm); W. 5¹⁄₁₆ in. (12.8 cm); D. 4½ in. (11.4 cm)

Marks: "EC. / 1912" in crude sans-serif letters incised on bottom.

Inscriptions: None.

See cat. no. 252.

Description: The rectangular box has soldered sides, four small spherical feet, and a three-part hinged lid with a three-part hinged clasp. It is embellished on the exterior with prominent raised oval sections of floral cloisonné enamel in a cream, green, and purple palette. One large oval is soldered to the lid; two side-by-side ovals are set along the front and back, with a narrow oval along each side. Foliate wire decoration is soldered to the interstices around the enamels on each surface. Four amethyst cabochons are set in each corner of the lid; one appears on the latch. There has been some loss to the enamel on the top, near the hinges.

History: Acquired by the donor, presumably from the artist, and made a gift to the Museum.

Exhibitions and publications: None.

Elizabeth Ethel Copeland (1866–1957)

Candlestick

Boston, Massachusetts, 1917
Gift of The Seminarians in honor of J. E. Robinson III
1997.56

H. 7⅜ in. (18.7 cm); W. 4⅛ in. (10.5 cm); D. 4⅛ in. (10.5 cm)

Marks: "EC / 1917" crudely incised on base.

Inscriptions: None.

ELIZABETH COPELAND was one of New England's most prominent enamelists of the Arts and Crafts period. She was born in Revere, Massachusetts, and from 1900 to 1904 attended the Cowles Art School in Boston, where she studied design with Amy Sacker (1876–1965). Her influential metalsmithing teacher at Cowles was Laurin Hovey Martin, who became the first professor in this medium at the Massachusetts College of Art. Martin had recently returned from England, where he had studied at the Birmingham School of Art and with master enamelist Alexander Fisher (1864–1936) in London. In 1905 Copeland attended a summer course titled "Principles of Design," offered at Harvard College by Denman Ross, a Museum of Fine Arts trustee; there she met artists and teachers from around the country.[1]

Copeland was thirty-four years old when she began her studies at Cowles and wasted little time in establishing her career. Evidence of her talent was noted as early as 1903, when her enamelwork appeared in *The Craftsman*. Soon after, she was featured in an essay by Syracuse University professor Irene Sargent. The article recounted Copeland's student years spent commuting three times per week between Revere and Boston. The artist recalled performing her domestic duties at home while studying assigned design problems, which she pinned above her ironing board, noting dryly: "No doubt the garments suffered."[2]

At Cowles, Copeland was befriended by Sarah Choate Sears (1858–1935), a Boston collector, Museum of Fine Arts philanthropist, photographer, and fellow craftswoman. Sears supported the young artist by funding a tour to Europe in 1908 and, for a time, provided her with bench space in her own studio. By that date Copeland had achieved recognition for her silver boxes, which were often repoussé and always enameled in an evocation of medieval reliquaries. After a brief period with the Handicraft Shop, Copeland established a home and studio

at 296 Boylston Street that she maintained from 1905 to 1912; in 1913 she moved to 294 Boylston Street, staying there until at least 1927.[3]

Copeland supported herself through her craft, which she was able to promote by submitting work to exhibitions in the national Arts and Crafts community. Although her mainstay appears to have been small jewel boxes, she also produced hollowware and jewelry. She was recognized for her achievements in Boston, Detroit, and Chicago, three metropolitan cities that boasted strong Arts and Crafts communities. She also received a bronze medal at the 1915 Panama-Pacific Exposition and, in 1916, was appointed a medalist by the Society of Arts and Crafts, Boston, its highest honor reserved for lifetime achievement. By that date, her work was sought by museums and collectors, including Detroit philanthropist George C. Booth, the Detroit Art Institute, and the Cincinnati Art Museum.[4]

Copeland's contemporaries considered her work to be medieval in style, and indeed her use of heavy cloison wires to define enameling areas, as well as her liberal use of rich

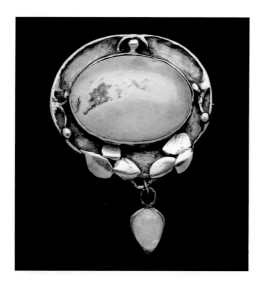

FIG. 2. Brooch, by Elizabeth Ethel Copeland, Boston, Massachu-setts, about 1907. Gold, turquoise, and opal cabochons; H. 1¾ in. (4.4 cm); W. 1⅛ in. (2.9 cm); D. ⅜ in. (1 cm). Museum of Fine Arts, Boston; Gift of Jane Kaufmann in memory of Charles L. Kaufmann (1997.160).

color, is reminiscent of that era. Her subject matter included stylized interpretations of flora and fauna and the occasional figure. Her loose and often asymmetrical style, sometimes accented with the irregular forms of unfaceted semiprecious gems and baroque or blister pearls, appears in both her jewelry and wrought forms (fig. 2). It bears some relation to the work of Janet Payne Bowles (1876–1948), her contemporary, and anticipates metalwork of the 1970s and 1980s, which may partly account for the recent revival of her reputation.

It is difficult to ascertain the length of Copeland's career. She resigned her membership in the Society of Arts and Crafts, Boston, in 1937, at age seventy-one, and died twenty years later, apparently indigent and unmarried.[5]

Description: The silver candlestick has a square base, with each side inclining slightly toward a single square column. Each side is deco-rated with cloisonné enamel decoration of pansy-like flowers and leaves. Concentric circles of blue and yellow enamel form bosses that are placed midway along the length of the column. Geometric wire decoration is applied throughout, surrounding the enameled base and extending along the column shaft; each wire terminates in a spherical ball.

History: Early history unknown; acquired from Christie's East, 1997.

Exhibitions and publications: Christie's East, New York, sale 7989, April 17, 1997, lot 101.

NOTES TO THIS ENTRY ARE ON PAGE 401.

253

Ernest M. Currier (1867–1936)
Coffeepot

New York, New York, 1920
Gift of Kathryn C. Buhler
1982.443

H. 8⅞ in. (22.5 cm); W. 8½ in. (21.5 cm); D. 1⅝ in. (4 cm); Wt. 18 oz 6 dwt 8 gr (569.7 gm)

Marks: "B 38494" scratched on bottom; "E. M. CURRIER / STERLING / 1097 [last two digits are a restamping correction] / 1½ PINTS." struck incuse on bottom.

Inscriptions: None.

ERNEST CURRIER is best known as the maker of such famil-iar trophies as the U.S. Golf Amateur Championship's Bobby

Jones Gold Cup. He retailed his silverwares through Tiffany, Gorham, and Gebelein as well as several retail stores that he operated, with Harry R. Roby (1862–about 1924), across the country. Currier and Roby may have met at A. F. Towle and Son in Newburyport, Massachusetts, where Roby served as foreman and later head of the samplemaking department, and Currier was a young apprentice.[1] They formed a partnership about 1901, opening a shop in New York City that specialized in reproducing colonial and early American and English silver.[2] An advocate for custom-made replicas rather than mass-produced works, Currier distinguished himself as a craftsman-scholar, publishing several articles on antique silver and hand-production techniques.[3] He is also credited with designing much of the silver produced by his firm.

According to Bennett Trupin, the firm's photographer and Currier's general assistant, this coffeepot is a prototype for one of Currier's favorite designs. Unlike later versions that were stamped from cast dies, this pot was shaped by hand.[4] It formed part of a larger set that included a creamer and sugar bowl; the model number for the set is "1097." It was illustrated in a more ornamental, engraved version as plate 209 in the company records.[5] Typically, Currier's name in script appeared on the bottom of his hollowware pieces, although that is not the case with this example, which, according to Trupin, Currier brought home for his personal use.

Description: The raised rectangular vessel has straight tapered sides and a high-curved spout affixed at the middle of body with a low-curved lip. The domed lid has a cast urn finial. Applied cast anthemia grace the top and bottom of the seamed handle and the base of spout. The insulators on the pinned handle are ivory. The seamed body is set on a cast and molded base with a vertical rim.

History: Given by the silversmith's widow, Lavinia Duchemin Currier, to Kathryn C. Buhler in gratitude for Buhler's role in editing her husband's manuscript on the marks of early American silversmiths in 1938. Made a gift to the Museum by Mrs. Buhler in 1982.

Exhibitions and publications: None.

NOTES TO THIS ENTRY ARE ON PAGE 401.

254

Seth Ek (active 1906–1912) for Handicraft Shop (1903–1907)

Bowl

Wellesley Hills, Massachusetts, 1906
Gift of Gertrude S. Atwood
1987.71

H. 1¾ in. (4.4 cm); Diam. rim 4 in. (10.2 cm); Diam. foot 2⅜ in. (6 cm); Wt. 4 oz 14 dwt 19 gr (147.4 gm)

Marks: "STERLING / H[anvil]S[in rectangle] / 1906 / E" struck incuse on bottom. "R U % = / 74204 A –" scratched on bottom.

Inscriptions: None.

THE YOUNGEST SON in a family of twenty-two children, Seth Ek immigrated to this country from Finland and established himself in 1901 as a silversmith working at the Handicraft Shop of Boston, located on Somerset Street in Beacon Hill. In 1906 Ek became a craftsman member of the Society of Arts and Crafts, Boston, describing himself as a silversmith and metalworker. He participated in the society's 1907 exhibition, to which he submitted work he had designed and crafted as well as work he had executed after the design of Mary Knight, (see cat nos. 267–269). During this time he maintained a studio in Wellesley Hills, at 392 Washington Street, where Handicraft Shop was then housed, as well as at the firm's Boston location, at 42 Stanhope Street, in 1908. In 1909 Ek relocated to Astoria, Oregon, to take up a career in the fishing industry, though he remained a member of the society and maintained a silver workshop there until 1912.[1]

This bowl reflects the colonial taste that was promoted by the society. It reveals an understanding of eighteenth-century forms and the influence of Chinese export porcelain during that period.

Description: Raised by hand, the small bowl rises to an everted lip and has an applied foot. Faint hammer marks are evident.

History: Descended in the family of silversmith George C. Gebelein (1878–1945), who worked with Ek at Handicraft Shop. Purchased from the estate of J. Herbert Gebelein (1906–1986), George's son, with funds provided by the donor.

Exhibitions and publications: None.

NOTE TO THIS ENTRY IS ON PAGE 401.

255

Seth Ek (active 1906–12) for Handicraft Shop (1903–1907)

Pitcher

Wellesley Hills, Massachusetts, 1907
Gift of Gertrude S. Atwood
1987.72

H. 3³⁄₁₆ in. (8.1 cm); W. 4⅜ in. (11.2 cm); Diam. lip 3⅛ in. (8 cm); Diam. base 1¹¹⁄₁₆ in. (4.3 cm); Wt. 5 oz 11 dwt 4 gr (172.9 gm)

Marks: "STERLING," "S. EK" within a conforming ellipse, and "1907" struck incuse on bottom.

Inscriptions: None.

The robust presence of this small pitcher suggests Seth Ek's Scandinavian heritage. The year in which Ek executed this piece, he entered a three-piece tea service, along with two ladles and a syrup jug and tray, in the Society of Arts and Crafts, Boston, exhibition. Also included were two silver finger bowls designed by Mary Knight, which Ek executed, reaffirming the close association and cooperation among society members.[1]

Description: This raised pitcher has a wide mouth, applied lip and foot, and cast handle. Hammer marks are evident.

History: See cat. no. 254.

Exhibitions and publications: None.

NOTE TO THIS ENTRY IS ON PAGE 401.

256

George C. Gebelein (1878–1945) for Gebelein Silversmiths (1908–about 1960)

Grape shears

Boston, Massachusetts, about 1910
Gift of Gertrude S. Atwood
1987.74

L. 6⁵⁄₁₆ in. (16 cm); W. 2⅜ in. (6.2 cm); Wt. 4 oz 5 dwt 5 gr (132.5 gm)

Marks: "G [in Gothic letter] / GEBELEIN / STERLING" struck incuse on underside of blade.

Inscriptions: None.

GEORGE CHRISTIAN GEBELEIN played a key role in the development of the handicraft movement in Boston during the early twentieth century. Born in Bavaria, he was brought to this country as an infant and, at age fourteen, was apprenticed to Goodnow and Jenks (1893–1905), a Boston silversmithing firm. Upon completing his apprenticeship, he moved to New York, where he worked at Tiffany & Co., and then Concord, New Hampshire, to continue his career with William B. Durgin and Company.[1] By 1903 he had returned to Boston and joined Hand-

256

icraft Shop, and in 1905 he became a craftsman member of the Society of Arts and Crafts, Boston (he was elected a medalist in 1919). In 1908 Gebelein achieved master status at the society and, the following year, opened his own shop at 79 Chestnut Street, with the help of David Mason Little (1860–1923), his patron and student (see cat. no. 425). Gebelein Silversmiths maintained this location and continued to be productive until Gebelein's death in 1945.

These grape shears reflect Gebelein's early training in a nineteenth-century shop, demonstrating his fluency in styles other than the colonial revival, for which he is best known.[2]

Description: The cast handles of the fancy grape shears are decorated with three-dimensional grapes and vine leaves, which have been chased to refine the ornament. The pivot hinge and surface show wear consistent with regular use.

History: See cat. no. 254.

Exhibition and publications: Society of Arts and Crafts, Boston, "Medals Centennial Exhibition," May 1–June 30, 1997.

NOTES TO THIS ENTRY ARE ON PAGE 401.

257

George C. Gebelein (1878–1945)

Gold two-handled cup

Boston, Massachusetts, about 1914
Gift of the Family of George Christian Gebelein
1986.796

H. 2⅞ in. (7.3 cm); W. 5⅛ in. (13.1 cm); D. 2¾ in. (7 cm); Wt. 2 oz 14 dwt 19 gr (85.2 gm)

Marks: "18 K G [in Gothic letter] GEBELEIN" struck on body near rim, to right of one handle.

Inscriptions: None.

AFTER ESTABLISHING HIS SHOP at 79 Chestnut Street in 1909, Gebelein concentrated on designing and overseeing the output of his skilled employees, who focused on production. In 1914, despite increasing demands as proprietor and manager of this busy enterprise, Gebelein personally executed a number of items, among them this gold cup, for exhibition at the Art Institute of Chicago. Traditionally, silversmiths worked in both silver and gold and, occasionally, base metals; in the United States, however, they rarely fashioned gold objects, and then only on special order. Undertaken as an exhibition piece, not a commission, this cup was designed and executed by Gebelein as a demonstration of his mastery of the metalworker's art, that is, his great technical skill and refined aesthetic. It is said that Gebelein raised the cup from a sheet he had hammered from melted gold filings, a remarkable effort supposedly undertaken

to obtain a metal content purer than that commercially available. In addition, although cast handles were available through the trade, Gebelein is purported to have modeled these by making the molds and casting them himself.[1]

Precious in material, skillful in execution, and adapted from venerated eighteenth-century English and American silverwares, this work was heralded at the time as the consummate example of the goldsmith's craft.[2] Gebelein's peers signaled their high esteem by awarding a bronze medal to this and his other entries at the 1915 Panama-Pacific Exposition in San Francisco.[3] In retrospect, however, this particular vessel does not hold up to the high standards of other work produced by Gebelein Silversmiths. Gebelein assigned to it a value of $150, a significant sum in 1914, when he sent it to Chicago. He never sold it, retaining it as a demonstration piece in his shop and sales office before removing it to his home as a personal memento.[4]

Description: The bowl of the diminutive hand-wrought gold vessel is elliptical, with a fluted dot-punched rim. The scrolled handles are documented as having been cast in a cuttlefish mold, and the bowl is set on a foot with faint beading and a scalloped edge. This dish is in remarkably fine condition despite the material's malleability.

History: Descended in the family of silversmith George C. Gebelein to his son Arthur D. Gebelein and his grandchildren—Mrs. Eleanor Gebelein Greene, Mrs. Margaretha Gebelein Leighton, Mr. Ernest G. Gebelein—who donated it to the Museum.

Exhibitions and publications: Art Institute of Chicago, 1914; Panama-Pacific Exposition, San Francisco, 1915; Irene Sargent, "Examples of 17th- and 18th-Century Domestic Silver with Interpretations of Same by George Christian Gebelein," *The Keystone* (September 1922), 131 (later reprinted as a Gebelein brochure).

NOTES TO THIS ENTRY ARE ON PAGES 402.

258

George C. Gebelein (1878–1945), designer, for Gebelein Silversmiths (1908–about 1960)

Bowl

Boston, Massachusetts, 1918
Bequest of Helen S. Coolidge, John Gardner Coolidge
Collection
Res.63.27

H. 2¹¹⁄₁₆ in. (6.8 cm); Diam. 5³⁄₁₆ in. (13.1 cm); Wt. 7 oz 17 dwt 2 gr (244.3 gm)

Marks: "GEBELEIN [in rectangle] / STERLING / Boston" struck incuse on bottom.

Inscriptions: "J * H / C / APRIL 3, 1918" in open roman letters engraved on side.

THIS SIMPLE, ELEGANT BOWL, engraved with a date of April 3, 1918, was a birthday gift to Helen Stevens Coolidge from her husband, John, who probably purchased it from the Gebelein Shop near their Boston residence.[1] Gebelein inverted the Coolidge's monogram from the customary colonial format, in which the surname initial appears above those of the husband and wife. The vessel's scalloped edge further defines the updated approach to this traditional form, which would have been well suited to the couple's Colonial Revival-style home in North Andover, Massachusetts.

Description: The spun bowl flares out from the base to a scalloped edge. The foot is applied.

History: Purchased as a birthday gift for the donor, Helen S. Coolidge (1876–1962), by her husband, John Gardner Coolidge (1863–1936), m. 1909. Made a bequest to the Museum upon the death of Helen Coolidge.

Exhibitions and publications: None.

NOTE TO THIS ENTRY IS ON PAGE 402.

259

George C. Gebelein (1878–1945), designer, for Gebelein Silversmiths (1908–about 1960)

Five-piece coffee and tea service

Boston, Massachusetts, 1929
Anonymous Gift
1986.778–82

Teakettle on stand (1986.778a–c): H. 12⁷⁄₁₆ in. (31.5 cm); W. 8⅞ in. (22.5 cm); D. 6¹¹⁄₁₆ in. (17 cm); Wt. 52 oz 6 dwt 17 gr (1627.8 gm)

Teakettle (1986.778a): H. 9½ in. (24 cm); W. 8⅞ in. (22.5 cm); D. 6½ in. (16.5 cm); Base 3⅛ in. (8.5 cm) x 3⅛ in. (8.5 cm); Wt. 24 oz 11 dwt 8 gr (764.1 gm)

Stand (1986.778b): H. 6½ in. (16.6 cm); W. 5⅝ in. (14.2 cm); D. 5½ in. (13.9 cm); Base 5⁵⁄₁₆ in. (14.2 cm) x 5⅝ in. (14.3 cm); Wt. 19 oz 15 dwt 8 gr (614.8 gm)

Spirit lamp (1986.778c): H. 1⅝ in. (4 cm); W. 5⅛ in. (13 cm); Diam. 2⅝ in. (6.5 cm); Wt. 3 oz 16 dwt 5 gr (118.5 gm)

Coffeepot (1986.779): H. 9½ in. (25 cm); W. 10⁷⁄₁₆ in. (26.4 cm); Diam. 4½ in. (11.5 cm); Base 3½ in. (8.7 cm) x 3⁷⁄₁₆ in. (8.6 cm); Wt. 22 oz 6 dwt 15 gr (694.6 gm)

Covered sugar bowl (1986.780): H. 8⁵⁄₁₆ in. (21 cm); Diam. rim 4³⁄₁₆ in. (10.5 cm); Diam. lid 4¼ in. (10.7 cm); Base 2½ in. (6.4 cm) x 2½ in. (6.4 cm); Wt. 12 oz 14 dwt 4 gr (395.3 gm)

Creamer (1986.781): H. 6⁵⁄₁₆ in. (16 cm); W. 4½ in. (11.5 cm); D. 2½ in. (6.3 cm); Base 2¹⁄₁₆ in. (5.4 cm) x 2¹⁄₁₆ in. (5.4 cm); Wt. 7 oz 4 dwt 9 gr (224.5 gm)

Teapot (1986.782): H. 8¹³⁄₁₆ in. (22.3 cm); W. 9⅝ in. (24.5 cm); Diam. 4⅜ in. (11.2 cm); Base 3⅛ in. (8 cm) x 3³⁄₁₆ in. (8.1 cm); Wt. 20 oz 8 dwt 17 gr (635.6 gm)

Marks: "GEBELEIN" in shaped rectangle, "STERLING" in sans-serif letters, "Boston" in italics, all struck incuse on base of teakettle and stand. "STERLING" in incuse sans-serif letters struck on spirit lamp. "Gebelein" in raised letters, within a shaped cartouche, and "STERLING" in sans-serif letters struck incuse on bottom of coffeepot, in one corner; "Boston" in incuse italics struck in second corner. "Gebelein" in shaped cartouche, "STERLING" in incuse

259

finial on the teapot and a flame finial on the lidded sugar bowl. Gebelein's teapot displays the same round foot on a square plinth as the other forms in the set; by contrast, Revere's teapots typically rested on a stand.[2]

Commissioned by a Boston patron as a wedding present in 1929, this service includes an unusual colonial form, the teakettle on stand, which late-nineteenth-century silversmiths reintroduced.[3] Gebelein jobbed out parts of this order, most likely to ensure his profit margin.[4] The bodies of the separate pieces are believed to have been created in the Gebelein shop; P. Charles Machon at Goodnow and Jenks supplied the cast handles, and Harold Small executed the engraving.[5] Despite Gebelein's cultivated reputation as a colonial-style silversmith who fashioned every piece from start to finish, the shop took advantage of methods that increased efficiency without sacrificing quality. These included spinning forms that were later hammered to suggest a completely handwrought vessel. It is known that Revere also jobbed out parts of his commissions and made use of new technological advances, such as prefabricated sheet silver, to enhance production and curtail costs.[6]

Description: The conforming pieces in the set are characterized by a fluted urn-shaped elliptical body with applied roulette-decorated rim; raised splayed foot soldered to a square plinth; bright-cut swags with ribboned tassels and border engraving; and cast flame finials. The C-scroll handles, with tendril thumbgrips on all but the creamer, are made of ebonized wood; the spirit lamp also has a wooden handle attached to a hinged, spun lid. The lids are typically spun, although the feet and teakettle were raised. The original owner's monogram appears in a cartouche on one side of each vessel except the teakettle and stand.

History: Given anonymously by the original owner.

Exhibitions and publications: Fairbanks 1991, cat. no. 61, 75–76; Janet Kardon, ed., *Revivals! Diverse Traditions, 1920–1945: The History of Twentieth-Century American Craft* (New York: Harry N. Abrams, 1994), 194, 284; Deutsch 1995, fig. 11, 48; William H. Truettner and Roger B. Stein, eds., *Picturing Old New England: Image and Memory* (New Haven: Yale University Press, 1999), 90.

NOTES TO THIS ENTRY ARE ON PAGE 402.

sans-serif letters, and "Boston" in italics struck in a third corner on bottom of sugar bowl, creamer, and teapot.

Inscriptions: "N.T." in roman letters, within an ellipse, engraved on body of each. "November 22, 1929" in script engraved on bottom of each base (inside foot of sugar bowl); burner is undated.

THIS TEA AND COFFEE service demonstrates Gebelein's indebtedness to colonial silversmith Paul Revere, from whom he traced his apprenticeship lineage through the firm Goodnow and Jenks (1893–1905). It is thought that Gebelein borrowed closely from a covered sugar bowl by Revere, now in the Museum's collection, that has the same shape, ornamentation, and pinecone finial and was displayed in the 1906 exhibition of American silver at the Museum of Fine Arts, Boston.[1] Gebelein made all the pieces in his set to match; Revere, however, would have combined more than one style body. For example, a typical Revere tea service might have a pinecone

George C. Gebelein (1878–1945), designer, for Gebelein Silversmiths (1908–about 1960)

Fifteen-piece place setting

Boston, Massachusetts, 1929
Gift of Mr. and Mrs. Laurence Batchelder
1981.379 a–o

Oyster fork (1981.379a): L. 5¹¹⁄₁₆ in. (14.6 cm); W. ¹¹⁄₁₆ in. (1.8 cm); Wt. 13 dwt 23 gr (21.7 gm)

Salad/dessert fork (1981.379b): L. 6³⁄₁₆ in. (15.8 cm); W. 1 in. (2.6 cm); Wt. 1 oz 1 dwt 21 gr (34 gm)

Luncheon fork (1981.379c): L. 7⁵⁄₁₆ in. (18.5 cm); W. ⅞ in. (2.3 cm); Wt. 1 oz 13 dwt 3 gr (51.5 gm)

Dinner fork (1981.379d): L. 7¹³⁄₁₆ in. (19.7 cm); W. ⅞ in. (2.3 cm); Wt. 1 oz 14 dwt 3 gr (53.1 gm)

Dinner knife (1981.379e): L. 9¹¹⁄₁₆ in. (24.6 cm); W. ¹³⁄₁₆ in. (2.1 cm); Wt. 2 oz 3 dwt 16 gr (67.9 gm)

Luncheon knife (1981.379f): L. 8⅜ in. (21.4 cm); W. ¹¹⁄₁₆ in. (1.9 cm); Wt. 1 oz 4 dwt 13 gr (50.6 gm)

Fruit knife (1981.379g): L. 3⅛ in. (7.8 cm); W. ¹¹⁄₁₆ in. (1.8 cm); Wt. 1 oz 6 dwt 1 gr (40.5 gm)

Bread and butter knife (1981.379h): L. 6⁵⁄₁₆ in. (15.9 cm), W. ¹¹⁄₁₆ in. (1.8 cm); Wt. 1 oz 4 dwt 23 gr (38.8 gm)

Serving spoon (1981.379i): L. 8⁵⁄₁₆ in. (21.1 cm); W. bowl 1⅜ in. (4.5 cm); Wt. 2 oz 12 gr (63 gm)

Dessert spoon (1981.379j): L. 7 in. (17.8 cm); W. bowl 1⁷⁄₁₆ in. (3.7 cm); Wt. 1 oz 6 dwt 12 gr (41.2 gm)

Clear soup spoon (1981.379k): L. 7 in. (17.8 cm); W. bowl 1⅞ in. (4.9 cm); Wt. 1 oz 10 dwt 21 gr (48 gm)

Cream soup spoon (1981.379l): L. 5⅝ in. (14.3 cm); W. bowl. 1⁹⁄₁₆ in. (3.9 cm); Wt. 18 dwt 3 gr (28.2 gm)

Melon spoon (1981.379m): L. 5¹¹⁄₁₆ in. (14.6 cm); W. bowl 1⅛ in. (2.7 cm); Wt. 16 dwt 22 gr (26.3 gm)

Teaspoon (1981.379n): L. 5¹³⁄₁₆ in. (14.7 cm); W. bowl 1¹⁄₁₆ in. (2.7 cm); Wt. 14 dwt 19 gr (23 gm)

Demitasse spoon (1981.379o): L. 4⁵⁄₁₆ in. (10.9 cm); W. bowl ⅞ in. (2.3 cm); Wt. 7 dwt 19 gr (12.1 gm)

Marks: "STERLING," "GEBELEIN" in a rectangle, and "Boston" in incuse italics struck on reverse of handle of most pieces, with slight variations. Oyster fork is doublestruck. "STAINLESS" or "GEBELEIN / STAINLESS" struck on knife blades, which often have "STERLING" stamped on side of handle as well. "GEBELEIN" in incuse letters and "STERL" struck on dinner

Illustrated are, from left to right, 1981.379 o, n, d, f, h.

GEBELEIN
STAINLESS

knife, on side of handle. "GEBELEIN" in raised letters, within a rectangle, and "STERLING" struck on demitasse spoon, on reverse of handle.

Inscriptions: "B / L N" engraved on each handle.

IN ADDITION TO MAKING contemporary pieces, Gebelein restored, replicated, bought, and sold antique silver.[1] This intimate contact with some of the finest eighteenth- and nineteenth-century Boston silver enabled him to develop a remarkable sensitivity to historic forms. When Gebelein later reinterpreted these pieces, often enhancing them with modern flourishes, he succeeded in preserving the aesthetic integrity of the older models.

This place setting, which looks back to eighteenth-century examples, was designed by Gebelein with the assistance of Nancy Thayer (d. 1995) as part of a service for twelve made at the time of her marriage to Laurence Batchelder.[2] The service represents every form appropriate to an elegant and fully equipped table in the early twentieth century, from individual fruit knives to oyster forks. It further reflects the refined and austere tastes of prominent Bostonians in the late 1920s. Flatware has been recognized as an important part of Gebelein's overall production. He also retailed the flatware of other firms, such as Gorham, Reed & Barton, and Currier and Roby reproductions.[3]

Description: Each utensil has a plain ovoid end; the spoons and forks have downturned handles.

History: Commissioned in 1929 from Gebelein by the donors, who gave it to the Museum in 1981.

Exhibitions and publications: None.

NOTES TO THIS ENTRY ARE ON PAGE 402.

261

261

George C. Gebelein (1878–1945), designer,
for Gebelein Silversmiths (1908–about 1960)
Copper bowl with silver lining

Boston, Massachusetts, 1930–40
Gift of Mr. and Mrs. Herbert F. Sacks
1992.386

H. 3⅞ in. (9.8 cm); Diam. rim 8¼ in. (21 cm); Diam. base 3¾ in. (9.5 cm)

Marks: "GEBELEIN" in a rectangle and "Boston" struck incuse on bottom. "F 1439" scratched on bottom, above marks.

Inscriptions: None.

IN THE 1920S to the mid-1940s, Gebelein enjoyed a good trade in copper bowls, partly due to the scarcity and subsequent prohibitive cost of silver. In addition to being more affordable than silver during the Depression, copper vessels may have been more popular in Boston because the corporate headquarters of Anaconda, a large copper mine, was located on Beacon Hill, and many Bostonians held shares in the company. During World War II, however, Gebelein's production of copper wares all but ceased when wartime restrictions prevented artists from using the material.[1]

According to Gebelein's daughter Eleanor, who worked in the family's retail store, copper pieces were common wedding presents for Beacon Hill brides. The shop promoted the firm's copper line through brochures distributed locally and nationally. Appealing to a broad economic base, Gebelein offered a wide assortment of shapes and sizes while emphasizing copper's innate qualities that "lend to home decoration that needed touch of color, and a certain feeling of hospitality which Copper of all metals alone imparts." This bowl was item number F210 and is listed as a flower or fruit bowl that "has proved a favorite." It was available with a regular or scalloped edge for $15; a hammered finish and silver lining were optional. Gebelein advertised his signature bowls as distinctive from other copperwares since the silver lining rendered them more inert and thus more practical for everyday use. The shop marketed this ware as having a classic, yet modern, modified Revere style.[2]

Although Gebelein marketed his work as "hand-wrought," much of it was made mechanically. The shop regularly contracted spinning work to a Boston South End spinner named Harry Allen and to Eastern Spinning, a Malden firm. Thus, most copper bowls were fully formed when they arrived at the Gebelein shop, where assistants lightly hammered them to eliminate the spinning marks, to harden the copper, and, above all, to impart a handmade look.[3] Ornamental details and the Gebelein touchmark were added then as well. Silver-lined bowls were individually plated in the Gebelein shop through an electroplating process that required two to three hours on average. The bowl received the last "coloring" polish, without diminishing the hammer marks, and the piece was prepared for shipment or sale in the shop.[4]

Description: The scallop-edged copper bowl has a spun and hammered body and spun applied foot. The silver lining was applied by an electroplating technique that enhanced the hammered appearance.

History: Original owner unknown; purchased privately by the donors, Mr. and Mrs. Herbert F. Sacks, at auction in the 1980s.

Exhibitions and publications: None.

NOTES TO THIS ENTRY ARE ON PAGE 402.

262

Frans J. R. Gyllenberg (1883–1974) and Alfred Henry Swanson (1899–1978)

Sandwich tray

Boston, Massachusetts, about 1929
Gift of Mrs. Irvin Taube in memory of Anne Murphy
1985.56

H. 1⅜ in. (3.6 cm); W. 14⁵⁄₁₆ in. (36.3 cm); Diam. base 8⅜ in. (21.3 cm); Wt. 14 oz 9 dwt 15 gr (450.4 gm)

Marks: "G / F J R / A.H.S. / STERLING / 5 9 2" struck incuse on bottom.

Inscription: "1929" engraved on one handle; "B / PC," with two notches on top of each other below "B" and between "P C," engraved on other handle.

FRANS GYLLENBERG probably served an apprenticeship in his native Sweden before moving to Boston and joining Handicraft Shop in 1906.[1] The following year Gyllenberg became a craftsman member of the Society of Arts and Crafts, Boston, and was promoted to master status in 1910.[2] Gyllenberg is listed in society records as having a bench in the Boston Handicraft shops at 42 Stanhope Street (1908–1913) and at 516 Atlantic Avenue (1914–1927).[3] In 1929 Gyllenberg was elected a medalist craftsman, the society's highest honor.

Letters in the society's archives reveal that Gyllenberg was often recommended to clients who wanted to commission matching silver pieces for an existing set. Correspondence further relates that, although Gyllenberg's prices tended to be higher than those of other silversmiths, he was the best craftsman for this work and always prompt in filling orders. Gyllenberg participated in the annual exhibitions organized by the society in Boston and Chicago, entering brass candlesticks and small silver wares such as bells, salt spoons, and salt cellars of his own designs as well as metalwork he executed that was designed by fellow Handicraft member Mary Knight (see cat. nos. 267–269)[4]

The society occasionally featured Gyllenberg's work in advertisements in magazines such as *Arts and Decoration* and *International Studio*. In fact, this sandwich tray is identical to one illustrated in an article on contemporary American silversmiths from the society. Although the maker is unidentified, the work is probably by Gyllenberg and perhaps also his assistant Alfred Swanson, with whom he formed a partnership at the shop about 1926.[5]

Gyllenberg established his reputation with reproductions of colonial silver, most notably replicas of works by Paul Revere now in the collection of the Museum of Fine Arts.[6] Some of his patrons, however, preferred work that adapted colonial forms to modern uses, such as this sandwich tray. Slightly shallower than the traditional mid-eighteenth-century porringer, the piece also has an extra handle and a foot that are lacking in colonial models.[7] Gyllenberg and Swanson's popular colonial-revival-style wares sold well until the Depression, when the partners moved their bench to a garage on Van Brunt Avenue in Dedham, Massachusetts, a Boston suburb. Eventually they turned to automobile repair to earn a living.

Description: Probably form-pressed on wood, this raised shallow dish with two soldered, keyhole, pierce-cut handles has a soldered foot and rim.

History: Original owner unknown. Subsequent owner unknown until purchased from Brodney Gallery of Fine Arts, Boston, Massachusetts, with funds provided by the donors.

Exhibitions and publications: Kaplan 1987, cat. no. 67, 180–81; "Medals Centennial Exhibition," Society of Arts and Crafts, Boston, May 1–June 30, 1997.

NOTES TO THIS ENTRY ARE ON PAGE 402.

263

George J. Hunt (1866–1947)

Teapot

Liverpool, England, 1904
Gift of Joseph B. and Edith Alpers
1991.929

H. 6⅛ in. (15.5 cm); W. 8⅜ in. (21.3 cm); Diam. 5⅜ in. (13.7 cm); Diam. base 3⅛ in. (8 cm); Wt. 20 oz 5 dwt 4 gr (630.1 gm)

Marks: "G. J. / H." in a triangle; lion passant within a shaped cartouche; Chester hallmark of three sheaves of wheat within a shield; and scrolled "C" within a shaped square (the date mark for 1904), all struck on body, to right of handle. The lion passant and scrolled "C" hallmarks also struck inside lid, wing nut, and underside of handle.

Inscriptions: None.

GEORGE HUNT served his apprenticeship in his native England before immigrating to the United States at age twenty. He became a member of the Society of Arts and Crafts, Boston, in 1903. By 1905 he opened his own shop and, one year later, established the "metalry" department at the School of the Museum of Fine Arts.[1]

This teapot was produced during a brief sojourn Hunt made to England, probably to his native Liverpool. In English fashion, the vessel carries numerous hallmarks on each of the separate-

ly fashioned parts. It bears the hallmark of the town of Chester (the assay office nearest Liverpool), Hunt's own mark, and the mark for 1904—a scrolled "C" within a shaped square—that documents the year he returned to England. The chaste profile is reminiscent of the designs of Christopher Dresser; its purity of form looks forward to the work of Rhode Island silversmith John Prip and the teapot he produced for Reed & Barton in the late 1950s (cat. no. 354).[2]

Hunt may have spent more time teaching than working in his own shop. He taught in Minneapolis; in Chautauqua, New York; at the Swain School in New Bedford, Massachusetts; and at the Museum School.[3] The few surviving pieces of his hollowware reveal a propensity for the Colonial Revival style. This teapot, with its design-reform aesthetic, shows Hunt's English leanings before his return to Boston and an American, ultraconservative clientele. His submissions to the society's 1907 exhibition included carved brass vases and candlesticks, made after the designs of Frank E. Cleveland; candlesticks he designed after an old English model; and a punch bowl and four-piece silver service, after Paul Revere. The latter were executed by Hunt and W. E. Manchester.[4]

Description: The teapot was hand-raised. It has a wide base that tapers to a small mouth. The handle and spout are seamed, and the insulators are ivory, as is the turned finial on the lid, which is held in place by a small silver knob.

History: Original owner unknown; subsequent history unknown until acquired by the donors, Dr. and Mrs. Joseph B. Alpers, about 1971.

Exhibitions and publications: Meyer 1997, 174–75, cat. no. 40.

NOTES TO THIS ENTRY ARE ON PAGE 402.

264

Robert Riddle Jarvie (1865–1941)

Hot-beverage service

Chicago, Illinois, about 1915
Gift of a Friend of the Department of American Decorative Arts and Sculpture, John H. and Ernestine A. Payne Fund, and Curator's Fund
1987.556–61

Tray (1987.556): H. 1⅛ in. (2.8 cm); W. 21 in. (53.5 cm); D. 15¹⁵⁄₁₆ in. (40.4 cm); Wt. 71 oz 18 dwt 4 gr (2236.6 gm)

264

Coffeepot (1987.557): H. 8⅝ in. (21.8 cm); W. 9¹¹⁄₁₆ in. (24.6 cm); D. 3⅞ in. (10 cm); Wt. 19 oz 2 dwt 2 gr (594.2 gm)

Hot-water pot (1987.558): H. 7¹¹⁄₁₆ in. (19.5 cm); W. 8⁵⁄₁₆ in. (21 cm); D. 3½ in. (9 cm); Wt. 15 oz 14 dwt 9 gr (488.9 gm)

Teapot (1987.559): H. 5¹¹⁄₁₆ in. (14.5 cm); W. 10 5⁄₁₆ in. (26.2 cm); D. 4⅝ in. (11.6 cm); Wt. 17 oz 6 dwt 11 gr (538.8 gm)

Sugar bowl (1987.560): H. with handle raised 6¹³⁄₁₆ in. (17.2 cm); W. 6⁷⁄₁₆ in. (16.2 cm); D. 4¹⁄₁₆ in. (11.2 cm); Wt. 6 oz 14 dwt 12 gr (209.2 gm)

Creamer (1987.561): H. 4¹³⁄₁₆ in. (12.2 cm); W. 6³⁄₁₆ in. (15.8 cm); D. 3 in. (7.6 cm); Wt. 6 oz 12 dwt 17 gr (206.4 gm)

Marks: "STERLING" in sans-serif letters, "Jarvie" in script, and "1" struck incuse on each. Incuse-style numbers struck to right of maker's mark: tray "2015"; coffeepot "2010"; hot-water pot "2011"; teapot "2012"; sugar bowl "2014"; creamer "2013."

Inscriptions: "F" engraved on side of each and in center of tray.

ROBERT RIDDLE JARVIE, the self-taught Chicago metalsmith, began to publicize his wares in *House Beautiful* in 1901.[1] Although he initially billed himself as "The Candlestick Maker," by 1904 Jarvie had expanded his wares and received special mention in *The Craftsman* for his graceful work in brass, copper, and silver. Between 1905 and 1910, he fashioned objects almost exclusively in silver and gold, many of which were commissioned as presentation gifts.[2]

About 1912 Jarvie attracted the attention of Arthur G. Leonard (1862–1949), president of the Union Stock Yard Company. Leonard became an important patron, providing Jarvie with a studio on the company compound and commissioning numerous trophies as prizes for cattlemen at local livestock fairs. According to oral history, this beverage service is associated with Leonard's firm. Presumably, it was purchased by a company vice president as a wedding gift for his daughter.[3]

The service owes a great debt to the work of colonial silver-

264

smith Paul Revere. A set that matches this one was illustrated as "Revere-Jarvie Silver" in the June 1914 issue of *Art Progress*. The accompanying article cited Jarvie's preference for Revere's domestic designs and explained that Jarvie adapted the forms from an original Revere teapot, altering the spouts and handle. Jarvie also designed and executed a complete set of flatware to accompany the service.[4]

The decoration and design relate directly to a Revere tea service that has been in the Museum of Fine Arts collection since 1896 (fig. 3). It has been suggested that Jarvie consulted published material, such as the 1906 or 1911 MFA exhibition catalogues that featured this Revere set.[5] Despite the professed homage to Revere, the work of William Moulton may have served as a design source as well. A Moulton teapot, which was also illustrated in the 1906 catalogue, has a similar pinecone finial with cut-silver leaves and curved spout.[6] Jarvie's handsomely designed and finely crafted hot-beverage service demonstrates the parallel evolution of the Colonial Revival style in Chicago, beyond its epicenter in Boston.

Description: All the vessels are elliptical in section, with seamed and very slightly curving sides. The bottoms are flat, and the concave shoulders have affixed bands of reeding. The covered vessels have a domed hinged lid with a pinecone finial made of wood and cut-

silver leaves. The handles, except the silver swing handle on the waste bowl, are made of wood. The curved and tapering spouts are seamed. Below the molded bands are bright-cut dotted lines and an engraved and chased floral band with a dotted line ground. Additional bands of engraved leaves ornament the shoulders of the lidded vessels.

History: Oral tradition relates that this coffee set was acquired from the silversmith by a vice president of Union Stock Yard Company for his daughter; it was sold at a Chicago auction house about 1984. Victorian Chicago, an antiques dealer, acquired the set and sold it to ARK Antiques. It was purchased from ARK Antiques, New Haven, Connecticut, in 1987.

Exhibitions and publications: "Revere-Jarvie Silver," *Art and Progress* 5, no. 10 (June 1914): 369; *MFA Annual Report 1987–88,* 21; Fairbanks 1991, cat. nos. 83, 94; Janet Kardon, ed., *The Ideal Home, 1900–1920: the History of Twentieth Century American Craft* (New York: Harry N. Abrams, 1993), 204.

NOTES TO THIS ENTRY ARE ON PAGE 402.

265

Kalo Shop (1900–1970)

Bowl

Chicago, Illinois, about 1921–41
Seth K. Sweetser Fund
1979.157

H. 2⁵⁄₁₆ in. (5.8 cm); Diam. 8⅛ in. (20.5 cm); Diam. base 5⅛ in.
(13 cm); Wt. 13 oz 1 gr (404.4 gm)

Marks: "STERLING / HAND WROUGHT [in a demilune] / AT
/ THE KALO SHOP / 5811 M" struck on bottom.

Inscriptions: None.

CHICAGO'S KALO SHOP, named after the Greek word meaning "good and beautiful," was one of the most successful and
long-lived Arts and Crafts silverware shops in the country. Initially, it offered leather and woven goods, expanding to include
metalwork and jewelry after the marriage in 1905 of its founder, Clara P. Barck (1867–1965), to metalsmith George S. Welles
(b. about 1857). The Kalo Art-Craft Community, which the
Welleses created in a home studio, served as both workshop and
school to scores of artisans, many of whom later established
their own thriving shops. Clara Welles employed many women
and Scandinavians; she was a strong supporter of women's participation in the arts, acting as their mentor and teacher.[1]

Kalo Shop sustained consumer interest even after the Arts
and Crafts style waned. Its finely crafted wares were not only
highly adaptable but also beautifully crafted. This bowl, for
example, could have served equally well as a centerpiece for
flowers or a serving dish.[2]

Almost from the beginning, Kalo silverwares were stamped
with their order number. About 1921, model numbers were
stamped onto the bottom of each piece, along with "S," "M,"
or "L," identifying the object's size. This bowl, design number
5811, proved to be popular and was a standard item in the Kalo
production line for at least two decades.[3]

Description: The raised, elliptical, scalloped bowl with applied rim
and raised foot retains its hammered surface.

History: Original owner unknown; subsequent history unknown
until given to the Art Institute of Chicago by the John L. and Helen
Kellogg Foundation in 1978; the bowl (one of a pair) was exchanged
with the Art Institute for duplicate examples of Stone silver in the
MFA's collection.

Exhibitions and publications: Darling 1977, fig. 57 (matches this example, unclear if the same).

NOTES TO THIS ENTRY ARE ON PAGE 402.

266

Kalo Shop (1900–1970)

Condiment dish

Chicago, Illinois, about 1921–41
Seth K. Sweetser Fund
1979.156

H. ⅞ in. (2.3 cm); W. 15 in. (38 cm); D. 5¹¹⁄₁₆ in. (14.4 cm); Wt. 19 oz
11 dwt 22 gr (609.5 gm)

Marks: "STERLING / HAND WROUGHT [in demilune shape]
/ AT / THE KALO SHOP / O C" struck on bottom.

Inscriptions: None.

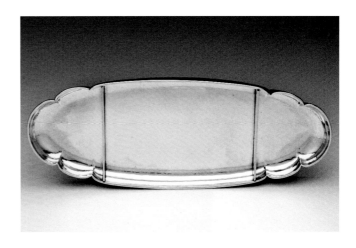

THE "O C" stamped on the bottom of this dish may refer to its maker and could possibly stand for Yngve Olsson (1896–1970) and John H. Cook, both of whom worked for Kalo during this period. A Danish emigré, Olsson assumed a leading role in the shop after founder Clara Welles retired to California in 1940.[1] The shop closed in 1970.[2] The dish was made as one of a pair.

Description: The serving dish has three lobes at each end and is divided into three sections. It has an applied silver course at the rim.

History: See cat. no. 265.

Exhibitions and publications: None.

NOTES TO THIS ENTRY ARE ON PAGE 403.

267

Mary Catherine Knight (b. 1876, active 1927) for Handicraft Shop (1901–1940)

Bowl

Boston or Wellesley Hills, Massachusetts, 1902–11
Gift of Gertrude S. Atwood
1987.68

H. 1¹¹⁄₁₆ in. (4.4 cm); Diam. rim 4⅜ in. (11.1 cm); Wt. 4 oz 7 dwt 11 gr (136 gm)

Marks: None.

Inscriptions: None.

267

See cat. no. 269.

Description: The raised bowl has a small rounded base and rises outward to a slightly everted rim; the foot ring is applied. A punched pattern of flowers and petals has been filled in with blue and white enamel.

History: Descended in the family of silversmith George C. Gebelein (1878–1945), who worked with Knight at Handicraft Shop. Purchased from the estate of the silversmith's son J. Herbert Gebelein (1906–1986) with funds provided by Gertrude Atwood.

Exhibitions and publications: None.

Gebelein (1906–1986). A Gebelein shop inventory tag accompanied each, although it is now difficult to discern which spoon was intended for which tag. One tag reads: "#25," "Jelly spoon by Mary C. Knight," "A8528 / 107548," and on the reverse "worked jointly with GCG in Handicraft Shop / Est. of Wm. R. Knox." The second tag reads: "#26," "TRE," "AM2152 / Handwrought spoon grape enamel," and "The Handicraft Shop / Miss Mary Knight / or Hersey." This last refers to Mary L. Hersey (a craftsman member of the Society of Arts and Crafts, Boston); however, given the Knight mark on one spoon, it seems unlikely that Hersey was involved in the creation of the other.[1] Purchased by the Museum from the estate of J. Herbert Gebelein with funds provided by Gertrude S. Atwood.

Exhibitions and publications: None.

NOTE TO THIS ENTRY IS ON PAGE 402.

268

Mary Catherine Knight (b. 1876, active 1927) for Handicraft Shop (1901–1940)

Pair of jelly spoons

Boston or Wellesley Hills, Massachusetts, 1906
Gift of Gertrude S. Atwood
1987.69–70

1987.69: L. 5½ in. (14 cm); W. bowl 1½ in. (3.8 cm); Wt. 1 oz 3 dwt 10 gr (36.4 gm)

1987.70: L. 6⅜ in. (16.3 cm); W. bowl 1¾ in. (4.3 cm); Wt. 1 oz 7 dwt 3 gr (42.2 gm)

Marks: 1987.69: "STERLING" incuse, in sans-serif letters; "H [anvil] S" within a rectangle; and "1906" incuse, all struck on back. 1987.70: Knight on horseback, "K" above, all within a shield; and "STERLING" incuse, struck on back.

Inscriptions: None.

See cat. no. 269.

Description: Each forged spoon has an oval bowl, upturned handle tip, and a punch-decorated grape design ornamented with blue enamel.

History: Although the early history of the spoons is unclear, they entered the Gebelein shop and were later acquired by J. Herbert

269

Mary Catherine Knight (b. 1876, active 1927) for Handicraft Shop (1901–1940)

Charger

Boston or Wellesley Hills, Massachusetts, 1902–11
Joyce Arnold Rusoff Fund
1993.532

Diam. 12¾ in. (32.4 cm); Wt. 31 oz 12 dwt (982.9 gm)

Marks: Knight on horseback, surmounted by "K" in the upper-left corner, all within a shield; "STERLING" incuse in sans-serif letters; "H [anvil] S" within a rectangle, all struck on base.

Inscriptions: "KCW" entwined script monogram engraved at center.

MARY CATHERINE KNIGHT was born in Flushing, New York, and passed her "childhood in the mountains of California." She studied design and decoration at the Drexel Institute in Philadelphia, where she became a student of Mary C. Ware (later Dennett), a teacher of artistic leatherworking. After graduating in 1897, Knight was briefly employed in Providence as a designer for Gorham. In the meantime, Dennett moved to Boston, where she practiced her craft and became an influential member of the Society of Arts and Crafts, Boston. Shortly after her marriage in 1900, Dennett gave up her workshop and was instrumental in bringing Knight to run the society's pioneering workshop beginning in 1902.[1]

Handicraft Shop was conceived as the educational arm of the Society of Arts and Crafts, Boston. Established in 1901, it

269

ited with being the "designer," "maker," and "exhibitor." Other times, she is listed as the designer, and chief Handicraft Shop silversmith Karl Leinonen or their colleague Frans Gyllenberg was credited as the maker. Yet it seems likely that all Handicraft Shop silver bearing stamped patterns was decorated by Knight.[4]

The interrelationship between Knight and other workshop members is evident when examining vessels made by her colleagues that are identical to ones she decorated. In the case of her enameled bowl (cat. no. 267), the form is the same as one crafted by Seth Ek (cat. no. 254). The punched charger in this entry is similar in execution and design to vessels marked solely by Leinonen.[5]

Knight's silver is sometimes unmarked, as in the enameled bowl, or struck with her "knight on horseback" mark as well as the Handicraft Shop mark. Knight appears in the exhibition record from 1904 until about 1911; she showed her work in Boston, St. Louis, Detroit, Chicago, and Cleveland. She remained a member of the Society of Arts and Crafts, Boston, until at least 1927, the last year in which membership records were kept.

Description: The raised circular charger with a flat tray rises to a concave rim with an applied edge. The rim has a repeating, punched, decorative pattern of stylized flowers.

History: Early history unknown; acquired by ARK Antiques of New Haven, Connecticut, and purchased by the Museum.

Exhibitions and publications: None.

NOTES TO THIS ENTRY ARE ON PAGE 403.

was largely supported by the society's first president, Arthur Astor Carey. The original intention was to offer classes and workspace for leather, wood, and metal crafts through Handicraft Shop, but the educational dimension was short lived, and metalworking rapidly became the sole focus. Knight served as chief designer, decorator, and silversmith.

Using leatherworking tools left to her by Dennett, Knight began to produce unique ornamental designs in silver. She produced delicate, repeating patterns—ranging in style from floral to strapwork, folk, and lace—expressed in a foliate vocabulary. Her silver was described in contemporary exhibition catalogues as "tooled," evoking the origins of her decorative method. On occasion, Knight pierced her forms, adding to the lacy designs that were noted in the press.[2] Enameling was also Knight's specialty; blue and turquoise were her preferred colors. Small bowls, plates, and spoons were her typical forms, although she exhibited an enameled parasol in 1905.[3]

Knight's role at the shop was to design, raise, and decorate silver, while her coworkers focused on raising vessels. The cooperative nature of shop work was clarified in contemporary exhibition catalogues that explicitly noted the division of labor in the fabrication of an object. Knight is sometimes cred-

270

Karl F. Leinonen (1866–1957) for Handicraft Shop (1901–1940)

Porringer

Boston or Wellesley Hills, Massachusetts, 1901–15
American Decorative Arts Curator's Fund
1991.465

H. 1⅝ in. (4 cm); W. 6 in. (15.2 cm); Diam. bowl 4 in. (10.1 cm); Wt. 5 oz 14 dwt 15 gr (178.3 gm)

Marks: "H [anvil] S" struck under porringer, near center. "L" in roman letter and "STERLING" in sans-serif letters, both incuse, struck on underside of handle, near join at body.

Inscriptions: "G · W · F" in shaded roman letters engraved on side of vessel, opposite handle.

BOSTON ESTABLISHED a reputation during the first decades of the twentieth century for small-scale workshops producing high-quality silver hollowware. Handicraft Shop was one such cooperative, established under the aegis of the Society of Arts and Crafts, Boston. The brief relocation of the studio to the pastoral remove of Wellesley Hills in 1903 was likely inspired by British craftsman C. R. Ashbee's Guild of Handicraft, which had relocated the previous year from London to rural Chipping Campden. Early shop members included George Christian

Gebelein, whose work favored the colonial-revival style, Seth Ek, F. J. R. Gyllenberg, Mary C. Knight, and C. G. Forssen.[1]

Shop member Karl Leinonen was born in Åbo, Finland, where he apprenticed for five years and worked five more as a silversmith before immigrating to Boston in 1893. He joined Handicraft Shop when it was founded in 1901 and became a long-standing member, serving as supervisor. He created work independently as well as with other members, including Ek, Knight, and his son K. Edwin Leinonen. Noting in his 1906 membership form that he worked "whit out machinery," Karl Leinonen was elected a craftsman of the society in 1901 and in 1918 was elected a medalist, its highest honor.[2]

Leinonen was an active participant in the era's exhibitions, beginning with the 1904 St. Louis Exposition, in which he collaborated with Knight on a range of flatware, salt cellars, and a child's silver mug. He showed his work independently at several exhibitions held by the Art Institute of Chicago; as late as 1930, he and his son K. Edwin, exhibiting together as Karl F. Leinonen and Son, were listed in the exhibition held at Boston's Horticultural Hall.[3] Although Leinonen did not teach formally, artist L. Cora Brown (1859–1937) of Concord attended private silversmithing lessons in his studio.[4]

The porringer demonstrates Leinonen's blending of the Colonial Revival style with the aesthetic of his Scandinavian homeland. Porringers were a popular form in colonial America and were briefly revived during the Arts and Crafts period. Unlike colonial porringers, whose convex sides are evenly rounded and feature keyhole-style handles, the walls of Leinonen's porringer swell below the rim and angle inward toward the base in a manner reminiscent of Chicago's Kalo Shop. The combination of old and new can also be discerned in the stylized handle, which owes a debt to the modern Neoclassical style pioneered by Danish craftsman Georg Jensen (1866–1935), even as the engraved initials, in shaded roman capitals, harken back to the colonial taste.

Description: The small raised vessel has sides extending outward and rising to an everted lip, with a small dome at center. The cast handle is soldered at right angles to the rim.

History: Original owner unknown. Estate of Mrs. Mason H. Stone, formerly of Boston, sold by Sanders & Mock Associates, of Moultonboro, New Hampshire, about 1988 to Mrs. Gardiner Greene (Eleanor Gebelein) of Laconia, New Hampshire, and acquired by the Museum in 1991.[5]

Exhibitions and publications: None.

NOTES TO THIS ENTRY ARE ON PAGE 403.

Description:
The body of this pot was fabricated from a single sheet of hammered silver that was seamed under the spout. The slightly bulbous lower body gently tapers to a molded rim and is hinged to a lid with cut-out end. The handle and knob are wood; the handle is attached with a silver bolt that extends through knob to nut inside, and the handle sockets have double-reeded molding.

History: From the artist to his daughter Ellen Leinonen, who honored her father's wishes by donating the coffeepot to the Museum.

Exhibitions and publications: "Medals Centennial Exhibition," Society of Arts and Crafts, Boston, May 1–June 30, 1997.

NOTE TO THIS ENTRY IS ON PAGE 403.

272

Edward Everett Oakes (1891–1960)
Jeweled casket

Boston, Massachusetts, 1929
Museum purchase with funds donated anonymously
2000.628.1–4

Box with tray (2000.628.1–2): H. 5⁵⁄₁₆ in. (13.5 cm); W. 7⅞ in. (20.1 cm); D. 6⁵⁄₁₆ in. (16.1 cm)

Base with lid (2000.628.3–4): H. 2⁵⁄₁₆ in. (5.8 cm); W. 9⅞ in. (25.15 cm); D. 8⅛ in. (20.7 cm)

Marked: "OAKES," within a small incuse mark in the shape of an oak leaf, struck underneath box and on base of rectangular silver plaque.

Inscriptions: None.

271

Karl F. Leinonen (1866–1957)
Coffeepot

Boston, Massachusetts, about 1945
Gift of Ellen Leinonen in memory of Karl F. Leinonen
1982.172

H. 7¹³⁄₁₆ in. (19.7 cm); W. 6⁵⁄₁₆ in. (15.9 cm); Diam. 3⅝ in. (9.2 cm); Diam. base 2¹³⁄₁₆ in. (7.2 cm); Wt. 15 oz 9 dwt 12 gr (481.3 gm)

Marks: "K. L F. / & SON" cipher and "STERLING" struck incuse on bottom.

Inscriptions: None.

THIS POT, made about 1945, when Leinonen was nearly eighty years old, is perhaps his last effort in silver. It closely resembles a chocolate pot he made for a four-piece set in 1905–6.[1]

JEWELER EDWARD EVERETT OAKES was a prominent member of the Society of Arts and Crafts, Boston. He began his training in 1909 with Boston jeweler Frank Gardner Hale (1876–1945), who had studied silversmithing and enameling with C. R. Ashbee, an English designer and utopian visionary. Oakes spent another three years working with Josephine Hartwell Shaw (1865–1941), a Pratt Institute–educated jeweler, before embarking on his own long career in 1917. Hale provided Oakes with a Renaissance design vocabulary, whereas Shaw offered a more sensitive appreciation of color, texture, and suitability to the client.[1]

While training with Shaw, Oakes was elected to craftsman membership by the society, and in 1917 he was advanced to master craftsman. A prolific artist, Oakes became a member of the society's Jewelers' Guild, showing his work regularly at the

272

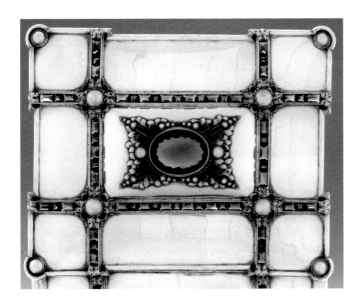

272

FIG. 4. Edward Everett Oakes (1891–1960), brooch, Boston, Massachusetts, about 1920. Silver, gold, moonstones, sapphires; Diam. 1½ in. (3.8 cm) Museum of Fine Arts, Boston; Benjamin Pierce Cheney Fund (1986.265).

Detroit Society of Arts and Crafts and similar locations nationwide. In 1923 the society awarded him the Medal of Excellence, their highest honor, and that same year the Metropolitan Museum of Art purchased a tasseled pendant from him.

Employing a naturalistic, asymmetrical style, Oakes selected moonstones, popular among Arts and Crafts artists, along with diamonds, sapphires, emeralds, and other richly colored stones, which he set amid tiny leaves he fabricated by hand (fig. 4). His delicate foliate decoration was a compositional device that led the eye lyrically from stone to stone; a simple, notched framing device usually enveloped the whole.

Having achieved significant success, Oakes nevertheless dreamt of creating a masterpiece, and he embarked on the fabrication of the jeweled casket seen here. He spent considerable time searching for the perfectly matched amethysts and pearls. Then, having assembled his materials with great care and expense from sources in Siberia, South America, and Asia, he

faced his greatest technical challenge: incorporating the jewels without endangering the leafy settings or warping the silver walls. The box took more than nine months to complete and was exhibited to great acclaim in October 1929 at the Society of Arts and Crafts in Boston.[2]

Called "architectural in miniature" by the press, the casket was lauded as the artist's crowning achievement. It was described as having a "cover designed in the spirit of a lightly vaulted roof with a large amethyst for the central dome." The stepped placement of gemstones at each corner and below the handles suggests an Art Deco aesthetic underlying an Arts and Crafts philosophy of construction. Although Oakes made little hollowware during his career, the bejeweled box functions as a brooch "writ large" and is the magnum opus of a world-class jeweler. Exhibited just days before the stock market crash of October 1929, the box was never sold, although it was widely exhibited until its acquisition by the Museum.[3]

Oakes trained his son Gilbert (1919–1987) in the craft and worked steadily until his death in 1960; nearly all seventy items shown at the artist's final exhibition in 1959 at the society were purchased, offering proof of his abilities and a devoted clientele during some forty years.[4]

Description: The rectangular paneled box is made of silver, green gold, 143 amethysts, 18 Japanese pearls, 68 oriental pearls, and 88 onyx, set on a laurel base. It has a hinged, slightly domed lid and round and faceted amethyst ball feet and sits on a narrow, two-tiered, shaped wooden plinth. Round columns form each of the four corners. Two pairs of channel-set amethysts intersect across the lid to create nine panels, at the center of which is a large faceted, elliptical amethyst, from which radiates rays of onyx and pearls. The amethyst bands continue down the sides of the box, where they flank triangular clusters of amethysts, onyx, and pearls; large rectangular amethysts form two shallow handles on the sides as part of these designs. At the base of each corner is a vertical cluster of graduated, rectangular onyx settings with pearls and auricular metalwork. Clusters of delicate gold foliate decoration are found throughout, and large pearls are featured prominently on the lid, at intersections of the amethyst bands and on each corner.

The box is completely finished on the interior, allowing the user to see the amethysts that adorn the exterior inside the box and lid. Additional pearls mounted with supporting gold settings adorn the lid interior. Concave onyx settings in each corner of the lid are complemented by faceted amethyst stones lodged at the top of the four corner columns. A rectangular wooden tray with silver, gold, pearl, and onyx fittings rests inside. The interior of the base, including the tray, is lined with black velvet.

A wooden stepped base made of laurel, having rounded corners, provides a setting on which the casket rests. At each corner, a circular depression set with onyx within a petaled silver frame is designed to receive each of the faceted amethyst feet of the box. A plain rectangular silver plaque, with small finger grips at each narrow end, serves as a handle for a chamfered lid that is seated above a small recess in the base.

History: By descent from the artist to his children, Norma Oakes Errico and Gilbert Oakes, and the family of Gilbert Oakes until acquired by the Museum.

Exhibitions and publications: G. H. C., "Silver and Precious Stones Make an Exquisite Jewel Casket," *Boston Evening Transcript*, October 16, 1929, part 3, p. 7; D. E., "Should Be Kept in Boston," *Boston Transcript*, November 16, 1929; Exhibition, Society of Arts and Crafts, Boston, October 17–23, 1929; Exhibition, The Little Gallery, New York, 1929; booklet, *A Jewel Casket That Is Itself a Jewel* (1929; reprint 1971); *Decorative Metalwork and Cotton Textiles* (New York: American Federation of Arts, 1930–31), cat. no. 402; *Tercentenary Celebration, 1630–1930: The Massachusetts Bay Colony and Boston; a Selected List of Works in the Public Library of the City of Boston* (Boston: Trustees of the Boston Public Library, 1930), cat. no. 11; *Arts and Crafts in Detroit, 1906–1976. The Movement, the Society, the School* (Detroit: Detroit Institute of Arts, 1976), cat. no. 58; Edith Alpers, "Edward Everett Oakes (1891–1960), A Craftsman from Boston, Massachusetts," *Jewellery Studies* 3 (1989), 73–79, fig. 8; Meyer 1997, cat. no. 67.

NOTES TO THIS ENTRY ARE ON PAGE 403.

273

Franklin Porter (1869–1935)
Four-piece coffee service

Danvers, Massachusetts, 1925–35
Harriet Otis Cruft Fund
1982.193–96

Coffeepot (1982.193): H. 7⅛ in. (18 cm); W. 5⅛ in. (13 cm); Diam. base 3¹¹⁄₁₆ in. (9.5 cm); Wt. 18 oz 9 dwt 16 gr (574.9 gm)

Sugar bowl (1982.194): H. 2⅝ in. (6.5 cm); W. 4⅜ in. (11.1 cm); Diam. rim 2¹¹⁄₁₆ in. (6.9 cm); Diam. base 3⅛ in. (8 cm); Wt. 7 oz 7 dwt 11 gr (229.3 gm)

Creampot (1982.195): H. 3½ in. (8.9 cm); W. 3¹³⁄₁₆ in. (9.7 cm); Diam. base 3 in. (7.5 cm); Wt. 8 oz 2 dwt 21 gr (253.3 gm)

Tray (1982.196): H. ⅜ in. (1 cm); W. 16⅛ in. (40.9 cm); D. 10 in. (25.3 cm); Wt. 33 oz 12 dwt 7 gr (1045.5 gm)

Marks: "F [reversed, with a conjoined] P / STERLING / F. Porter" struck incuse on all.

Inscriptions: None.

FRANKLIN PORTER was a self-professed morally earnest silversmith. With each piece sold, he included a card describing his noble intent to impart with his handiwork an ethic and aesthetic of "Simplicity and Service."[1] Unlike many other aspiring silversmiths from his generation, Porter worked alone. He never joined with a partner, nor did he participate in one of the shop collectives prevalent at the time. Remarkably, this independence did not limit his production, for he later applied efficient procedures learned as a machinist to his approach to silversmithing; he also benefited from the assistance of his daughter Helen L. Philbrick. Porter's work consists mostly of flatware and small accessories, such as mustard pots, bowls, and plates. His hollowware is rarely encountered today, though he did receive commissions for communion sets as well as tea and children's services.

Porter learned his trade through courses at the Rhode Island School of Design and technical training at Browne and Sharpe in Providence. From 1910 to 1914, he worked out of his home in Bristol Ferry, Rhode Island, selling to a local clientele and regular customers in Newport. He and his family eventually moved to Middleton, Massachusetts, where his wife, Ethel, operated a tearoom in the front of the house that also served as a salesroom. In the early years of automobile travel, such tearooms developed as popular roadside stops. World War I interrupted

273

Porter's silversmithing as he contributed to the war effort as a machinist and master mechanic at two local factories.

During this period, Porter and his family became caretakers of the historic Judge Samuel Holten House in Danvers. In 1924 Porter returned full-time to his craft, operating a workshop from Holten House. He capitalized on the appeal of traditional time-honored forms and offered many wares in the colonial style. This set, with its strap handles and pronounced hammered surface, displays an Arts and Crafts design. His fastidious attention to detail can be noted in the precision with which he tapered each vessel, leaving hammer marks as a testament to his skill and the fine-wrought construction. The ample tray was made to accommodate the service as well as ceramic cups and saucers.[2]

The set is characteristic of Porter's wares and is distinguished by its visual and physical weight. Given his proficiency as a machinist, he was preoccupied with the crafting of his wares, taking extra care with their mechanical functioning. For example, the hinging apparatus on the lid and the bolts

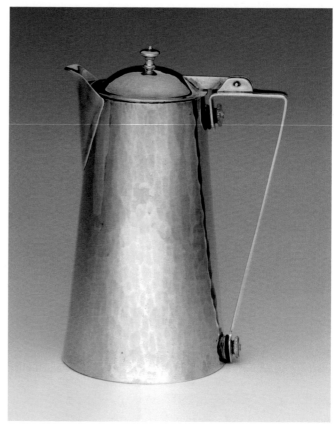

that attach the handle on the coffeepot are prominent features. Porter typically relied on his knowledge of practical mechanics to solve design issues, sometimes favoring technical solutions over generally accepted silversmithing methods.

Description: Made of seamed heavy-gauge sheet silver, the set has upset (or hammered and thickened) edges and a scintillating hammered surface. It was shaped by hammering. Each vessel has straight tapering sides that are seamed under strap handles, which are tapered and incised along the edges. The teapot has threaded rods that secure the handle over wooden insulators and knurled round nuts; the domed lid with narrow flange and bezel is seamed at the side. The turned spool finial has a threaded rod held by a square nut under the lid. The applied shallow spout has a high curved lip over a triangular hole. The drawn spout of the creampot has a body drop and low curved lip. The tray is rectangular with rounded corners and a narrow raised rim, which has been crimped, as have the rims of the vessels except at spouts.

History: Original owner unknown; subsequent ownership unknown until the Museum purchased the service from T. & R. Yonge, Cambridge, Massachusetts, in 1982.

Exhibitions and publications: Boston University Art Gallery, *Pilgrims and Progressives: The Colonial Revival in Massachusetts, 1863–1963,* March 2–April 7, 1996, 16.

NOTES TO THIS ENTRY ARE ON PAGE 403.

274

274

Horace E. Potter (1873–1947)

Porringer

Cleveland, Ohio, 1908–1920
Gift in memory of Rosamund Foote Brown
1999.20

H. 1¹¹⁄₁₆ in. (4.4 cm); W. 7³⁄₁₆ in. (18.2 cm); Diam. rim 5⁵⁄₁₆ in. (13.5 cm); Wt. 7 oz 14 dwt 15 gr (240.5 gm)

Marks: "POTTER / STUDIO" in stylized Arts and Crafts lettering struck incuse on base.

Inscriptions: None.

See cat. no. 275.

Description: The raised vessel with a pattern of visible hammer marks has a flat, small base with walls that extend sharply outward before turning inward to an applied vertical rim. An Art Nouveau-style handle frames a delicately cast and chased design of three

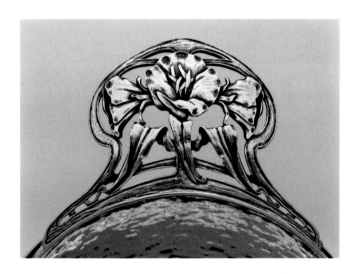

naturalistically rendered lilies. The downturned handle is soldered at right angles to the rim.

History: Original owner unknown; purchased at Skinner's in 1998 by Alexander Yale Goriansky; acquired from him in March 1999.

Exhibitions and publications: Skinner's, Bolton, Massachusetts, sale 1871, October 3, 1998, lot 40.

275

Horace E. Potter (1873–1947)

Porringer spoon

Cleveland, Ohio, 1908–20
Gift in memory of Rosamund Foote Brown
1999.21

L. 5⁵⁄₁₆ in. (13.5 cm); W. bowl 1⁷⁄₁₆ in. (3.8 cm); Wt. 16 dwt 14 gr (25.8 gm)

Marks: "POTTER / STUDIO" in stylized arts-and-crafts lettering struck incuse on back of handle.

Inscriptions: None.

HORACE E. POTTER, a native of Cleveland, was one of the city's most accomplished and long-lived artists of the Arts and Crafts era. Potter studied under Louis Rorimer (1872–1939) at the Cleveland School of Art, graduating about 1898, and shortly thereafter traveled to Boston, where he studied at the Cowles School of Art and perhaps also the Amy Sacker School. While a student, Potter exhibited a "silk repeat" and a "wall-paper repeat" at the 1899 exhibition held by the Society of Arts and Crafts, Boston. It was in Boston that Potter came under the tutelage of Sacker (1876–1965), who taught decorative design at both schools, and perhaps crossed paths with fellow artists Laurin Martin (1875–1939), who had returned to Boston in 1898 from the Birmingham School of Art in England, Elizabeth Copeland (1866–1957), and Sarah Choate Sears (1858–1935), all of whom produced enameled metalwork and jewelry.[1]

Potter traveled abroad shortly afterward, visiting the Guild of Handicraft in Chipping Camden, where he may have studied under Charles Robert Ashbee (1863–1942). While in England and through various publications, Potter undoubtedly became aware of the whiplash curves of Art Nouveau and Celtic interlace patterns that were popularized by Archibald Knox (1864–1933), designer for Liberty & Co. of London. Like his contemporaries Elizabeth Copeland and Augustus Rose (1873–1946), an educator in Providence, Rhode Island, Potter may have also met Alexander Fisher (1864–1936), who taught at the Central School of Art from 1896 to 1899 and privately thereafter. These English influences exerted a lasting influence on him.[2]

Upon returning to Cleveland, Potter taught historic ornament at the Cleveland School of Art under Rorimer and established the first of several studios where he taught and created works of art; Jane Carson (Barron) was one of his more celebrated students.[3] With his colleague Wilhelmina P. Stephan, also of Cleveland, Potter exhibited at the 1905 and 1906 Arts and Crafts exhibitions at the Art Institute of Chicago. Their goods included hollowware in silver and occasionally copper, some of which were enameled or set with semiprecious stones. They made syrup pitchers and trays, salt cups, bonbon spoons, and small desk accessories and jewelry. Prices for works shown in 1905 ranged from $8 for a spoon to $75 for a tea set made of silver and ebony or a bowl displaying a pierced and enameled border, with matching tongs. The enlargement of Potter's workshop had taken place by 1908, when The Potter Shop was established in a remodeled grain house on the family farm in Cleveland. H. E. Robus, H. R. Linn, and W. Burgdorff were three area artists whose names appeared under this rubric in a Cleveland exhibition catalogue of the same year. The shop became a center of activity for artists working in a variety of media. Ohio potter R. Guy Cowan (1884–1957) worked there for a time, as did metalsmith and enamelist Jane (Carson) Brown. Meanwhile, Potter's affiliation continued with the Society of Arts and Crafts, Boston. He was elected a craftsman in 1907 and elevated to master status in 1908.[4]

By that date, Potter occasionally took part in exhibitions, such as the Panama Pacific Exposition of 1914, but he apparently enjoyed sufficient support from local clientele to render participation in such venues unnecessary.[5] His business grew until 1921, when Louis Mellen joined the firm, giving rise to the Potter-Mellen name, which was a favorite Cleveland destination for fine jewelry and luxury goods.

Like artists Josephine Hartwell Shaw (1865–1941), William Brigham (1885–1962), and Marie Zimmermann (1878–1972),

Potter occasionally integrated the work of his colleagues and various exotic finds into his work. He set tiles by Ernest Batchelder into copper bookends and made a lid with accompanying spoon for a Marblehead bowl. It is unclear whether he obtained these materials directly from the artists, who were far from Cleveland, or through purchases. Potter also created new settings for non-Western discoveries, once creating a covered jar from a carved elephant tusk.[6]

The MFA porringer (cat. no. 274) may have been part of a larger set that included a matching spoon and plate. The handle and matching spoon of one known set are decorated with a richly chased bunny and interlace pattern; deep yellow enamel was fired on the bowl's interior. A "porringer, spoon and plate—Silver and enamel, Celtic Motif," published in the catalogue for the 1908 exhibition at the Cleveland School of Art, seems to be the complete version of what was probably a child's service.[7] The spoon accompanying the porringer in the collection has a different design; however, because of their consignment to auction by the same source, it is possible they were once used as a set.

Description: The small porringer spoon has a fig-shaped bowl. The lozenge-shaped handle tip is pierced with a naturalistic Art Nouveau-style rendering of grasses.

History: See cat. no. 274.

Exhibitions and publications: See cat. no. 274.

NOTES TO THIS ENTRY ARE ON PAGES 403.

276

Katharine Pratt (1891–1978)
Two-handled porringer

Dedham, Massachusetts, 1933–34
Gift of Mr. and Mrs. Herbert F. Sacks
1992.387

H. 2 in. (5.1 cm); W. 10¼ in. (25.7 cm); Diam. rim 4¹³⁄₁₆ in. (11.6 cm); Wt. 10 oz 17 dwt 19 gr (338.7 gm)

Marks: "STERLING / PRATT" in sans-serif letters struck under handle.

Inscriptions: "J · F · M · II" on one handle facing bowl; "JAMES FRANKLIN McELWAIN II FROM HIS GREAT UNCLE JAMES FRANKLIN McELWAIN" in a circular design on base; "DECEMBER 31, 1933" across center of bowl, on base, all in engraved shaded roman capitals.

THE WEB OF RELATIONSHIPS in the giving of silver is exemplified in this two-handled porringer by Katharine Pratt. The donor, shoe manufacturer James Franklin McElwain, was related to Pratt through his wife, Mary Barton Pratt (1875–1953), who was a first cousin to the silversmith and a supporter of the art department where she taught.[1] The porringer was intended as a baby gift for his namesake, James Franklin McElwain II.

Pratt studied metalsmithing under George Hunt at the Museum School of the Museum of Fine Arts, Boston, graduating in 1914. The following year, she held an exhibit of her work at the Women's Educational and Industrial Union (WEIU). A scholarship granted by the WEIU enabled her to continue her studies under George Christian Gebelein, a proponent of the colonial-revival style in New England. Pratt worked actively

and showed her silver, participating in the 1927 exhibition of the Society of Arts and Crafts, Boston; she became a medalist of the society in 1931. She exhibited at the 1937 Paris Exposition des Arts et Techniques and received the *diplôme de médaille d'or.*[2]

Pratt also served on the faculty of the Beaver Country Day School in Chestnut Hill, where she taught jewelrymaking and silversmithing from 1930 to 1949. The two McElwain children attended the progressive school, and their mother was especially supportive of the art department, which bears an engraved mantelpiece dedicated in her honor.[3]

Most New England silversmiths working during the Arts and Crafts period had access to or images of eighteenth-century silver upon which to base their work, yet they romanticized its manufacture out of admiration for the preindustrial craftsman. As a result, their work is stylistically in the colonial style but Arts and Crafts in its approach to fabrication. The Pratt porringer is a case in point. Despite its conformity in scale and form to colonial Massachusetts single-handled porringers, it is easily identifiable as a twentieth-century product. It is made of unusually heavy-gauge silver and displays softly modulated hammer marks, unlike most colonial examples, which are of moderate weight and have well-planished surfaces. Pratt laboriously saw-cut the handles, whereas, in the colonial era, casting was a more rapid and preferred technique. A two-handled sandwich plate by Frans J. R. Gyllenberg and Alfred Henry Swanson is an updated version of the same form, also with saw-cut handles (cat. no. 262), and Gebelein produced a very rough, almost medieval, interpretation of the vessel, with geometric handles.[4] Interestingly, all three Boston silversmiths chose to make variations on the two-handled porringer, a form that appeared infrequently in the colonies, in emulation of the French *écuelle* (which includes a cover). Collectively considered, these works illustrate three interpretations of the Colonial Revival in the close-knit Boston metalsmithing community and the choice of an archaic form over the ubiquitous American porringer.

Description: The heavy raised porringer with well-defined dome at center has convex sides and a thick everted rim. The saw-cut keyhole-style handles are soldered to the rim along one axis.

History: The porringer was a gift from James Franklin McElwain (1874–1958) to his great-nephew and namesake (b. 1933), who was the son of Alexander McElwain (b. 1897) and Beatrice Christina Stevens, m. 1928.[5] Subsequently sold at auction about 1992 in Foxboro, Massachusetts, where it was purchased by the donors and later made a gift.

Exhibitions and publications: None.

NOTES TO THIS ENTRY ARE ON PAGE 403–04.

277

The Randahl Company (1950–1963)

Tray

Skokie, Illinois, about 1950–54
Gift of Mrs. Mason Scudder
1982.452

H. 13/16 in. (2 cm); Diam. 12 in. (30.5 cm); Wt. 23 oz 1 dwt 10 gr (717.6 gm)

Marks: "RANDAHL / STERLING / 318 / 12 IN" struck incuse on bottom. "H – 11 – 166 M E W O – A W V E X." scratched on bottom, near edge.

Inscriptions: "C V" with a circular border engraved in center.

IN 1911 Swedish immigrant Julius Randahl (1880–1972) founded The Randahl Company, one of the largest and best-known metalwork firms in Chicago.[1] A skilled silversmith, Randahl was also a successful entrepreneur, developing a national distribution network that sold to distant retailers, such as Shreve,

Crump & Low of Boston, as well as locally through Marshall Field's. He received wide recognition in 1937 for the silverwares he included in the "Exhibition of Contemporary and Hand-wrought Silver" at the Brooklyn Museum. Later that year he won a silver medal in Paris at the Exposition International des Arts et Techniques for a silver centerpiece and pair of candlesticks.

A stock item, this model was identified as "318/12 Hand Wrought Waiter" in company records; it was available in at least four sizes. In 1965 the retail cost for a twelve-inch waiter of this design was listed as $125.[2] Randahl took advantage of all means to increase production and satisfy demand while realizing a considerable profit. He employed modern machinery and an army of specialized workmen, including skilled silversmiths, spinners, and polishers. Randahl's sons, Julius Jr. and F. Scott Randahl, sold their silver business to Reed & Barton, which established the Randahl Division in 1965.

Description: The circular tray is raised from sheet and bears five small lobes interspersed with five scalloped lobes. There is an applied rim.

History: Purchased at Shreve, Crump, & Low, one of the silversmith's retailers, and presented to Celia Vanderworde in 1954, when she left Museum of Fine Arts, Boston to marry Mason Scudder (1894–1971) of St. Louis. Mrs. Scudder donated the piece to the Museum in 1982.

Exhibitions and publications: None.

NOTES TO THIS ENTRY ARE ON PAGE 404.

278

Arthur Stone (1847–1938)
Masterwork

Gardner, Massachusetts, 1868
Gift of Miss Alma Bent in memory of Annie E. Priest
1978.306

H. 5½ in. (13.9 cm); W. 7¹¹⁄₁₆ in. (19.6 cm); D. ⅜ in. (1 cm)

Marks: "A J STONE" scratched on front; "AJS/1868" scratched on reverse.

Inscriptions: None.

WHEN ARTHUR STONE finished his indenture and apprenticeship in 1868, the ancient custom of presenting a demonstra-

tion piece to the goldsmith's guild for admission as a master craftsman was no longer practiced. Nonetheless, Stone created this "masterwork" to illustrate that he had successfully mastered the required skills and fully earned the honor. This copper relief reveals his competence as a chaser and designer of chased ornament, skills that would later distinguish him from his contemporaries.

Today, Stone is widely recognized as America's foremost Arts and Crafts silversmith. He was born in England and, from the age of fourteen, trained as an apprentice under Edwin Eagle; during his indenture, he also attended evening classes at the National School of Design, Sheffield. Stone was strongly influenced by William Morris's Arts and Crafts movement. Having engaged in much independent study at John Ruskin's Museum, he was involved in the formation of the Sheffield Society of Arts and Crafts.[1]

Discouraged by the reliance of local silver manufacturers on machines and the strict division of labor among craftsmen, Stone took hope in the promises offered by American advertisements trying to lure talented young silversmiths from England. He moved to the United States in 1884. His familiarity with the Arts and Crafts style proved instrumental in encouraging New England's interest in and perpetuation of historical crafts. He worked first for William B. Durgin Co. in Concord, New Hampshire, before moving in 1887 to Gardner, Massachusetts, to become designer, salesman, and manager of the hollow-ware department at the newly formed Frank W. Smith Company. In 1895 he moved to New York City to become a partner with J. P. Howard, a silversmith and retailer. By 1897 Stone had returned to Gardner, presumably to establish his own business and a home with his new wife, widow Elizabeth Bent Eaton, of Gardner.[2] She became a valuable partner and business manager; with her independent means and "rare business ability," she was instrumental in keeping the shop open and active during the Depression.[3]

Stone was engaged to create some of Boston's most important commissions, collaborating with imminent architects and designers on ecclesiastical and presentation pieces. Domestic wares, which formed the bulk of his production, were made with the assistance of apprentices. Between 1901 and 1936, Stone employed as many as twelve silversmiths. The atmosphere in the studio was most congenial; his employees recalled their loyalty to their paternalistic employer, who shared profits semiannually and allowed individual craftsmen to add their own mark beside that of their master.[4] Stone encouraged his staff's personal and professional development by arranging study trips and sponsoring their memberships in the Society

278

FIG. 5. Arthur Stone workshop, Gardner, Massachusetts, about 1908. Left to right: William Blair, Clinton Ogilvie, George Blanchard (at rear), and Arthur Stone. Museum of Fine Arts, Boston; Arthur Stone Papers, gift of Alma Bent.

FIG. 6. Arthur Stone wearing his Silversmith Guild artist's smock. Photograph, Museum of Fine Arts, Boston; Arthur Stone Papers, gift of Alma Bent.

FIG. 7. Detail of a hammer embroidered on the Silversmith Guild artist's smock seen in fig. 6, which belonged to Arthur Stone. The early twentieth-century smock, now in the Museum's collection, is of cotton plain weave with mother-of-pearl buttons; H. 47¼ in. (120 cm). Gift of Miss Alma Bent in memory of Annie E. Priest (1978.439). See also figs. 6 and 8.

FIG. 8. Detail of a dragon embroidered on Arthur Stone's Silversmith Guild smock, seen in fig. 6.

of Arts and Crafts, Boston. Several achieved master status, and three became medalists, the society's highest award. The quality of their skill and craftsmanship is evident in many works from Stone's shop that are now in the Museum's collection. Stone also contributed to the development of the careers of at least two recognized women artists, designer Charlotte Bone and silversmith Margret Craver.[5] After suffering a disabling stroke in 1926, Stone relied increasingly on assistants to execute his designs and on draftsmen, such as Bone, to provide working drawings for his craftsmen.

Stone's involvement with the Society of Arts and Crafts, Boston, was considerable. In 1913 he was one of three craftsmen to receive the society's inaugural Medal of Honor. He was the first metalsmith to earn this honor acknowledging his mastery of the medium, his profound commitment to the ideals of the Arts and Crafts movement, and his role in furthering the influence of the society both locally and nationally. Both husband and wife were active members in the society. Stone participated in its annual exhibitions and served as vice president; his wife gave lectures and wrote articles. He sold his wares primarily through the society's Boston and New York stores; he rarely sold wares from his Gardner shop, and then only to neighbors and close friends. Later he retailed stock items and flatware through the Little Gallery in New York City, John Kay in Detroit, and the Arts and Crafts Guild of Philadelphia, of which he was also a member.[6]

Stone was closely associated with the Museum of Fine Arts as well and was given permission to study, measure, and reproduce several pieces of American silver in the collection. About 1928, through Harvard's University Film Foundation, he helped the Museum produce a documentary of the silversmith's craft. Today, the Museum is the institution of record for this craftsman, with a representative collection of his production as well as a complementary study collection.[7] Stone retired in 1937, at the age of ninety. He died five months later.

Henry Heywood took over the shop in October 1937, calling it "The Stone Silver Shop," and subsequently "Stone Associates." Heywood continued to produce a number of Stone designs, with the assistance of some former employees, until he closed the establishment in 1957, and Ernest Lehtonen took over the flatware business and the Stone mark.[8]

Description: The three-part demonstration piece has a flat-chased strapwork design, a shield with a grotesque mask in bas-relief, and a chased and repoussé bouquet with a tulip, a lily, and a chrysanthemum. The corners of the plaque have been clipped, and pitch is retained in the recesses on the reverse.

History: Arthur and Elizabeth Bent Stone estate to their companion Annie E. Priest (1872–1972); by descent to Alma Bent (about 1921–1992), Stone's cousin, who donated it to the Museum.[9]

Exhibitions and publications: "76 Years a Silversmith," *Monday Evening Gardner News* (February 7, 1938), obituary with reference to masterwork; Elenita Chickering, "Arthur J. Stone, 1847–1938: An Anglo-American Silversmith," *Apollo* 130, no. 330 (August 1989), 101; Chickering 1994, fig. 2, cat. no. 1, 2–3, 95; AFA 1994, cat. no. 10.

NOTES TO THIS ENTRY ARE ON PAGE 404.

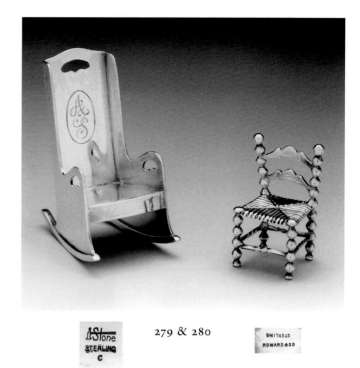

279 & 280

279

Arthur Stone (1847–1938), designer

David Carlson (active 1909–1919), maker

Miniature winged rocking chair with high back

Gardner, Massachusetts, 1909–19
Gift of Miss Alma Bent
1979.184

H. 2 3/16 in. (5.5 cm); W. 1 1/8 in. (2.9 cm); D. 1 11/16 in. (4.3 cm); Wt. 19 dwt 24 gr (31.1 gm)

Marks: "Stone," with profile of chasing hammer stamped across *St*, and "STERLING / C" struck on underside of seat.

Inscription: "A J S," overlapping one another as they descend within an oval, engraved on back of rocker.

ARTHUR STONE created miniature toys and silverware throughout his career. A comparison of the early less-restrained pieces made during his short-lived partnership with J. P. Howard & Company of New York, as well as the later miniatures designed for his own shop, reveals a notable contrast in aesthetic sensibilities. Stone's taste was for simple lines and chaste decoration.[1] Howard offered more than 180 patterns in his line of "solid silver toys," seventy-five of which he marketed in an 1895 brochure entitled "Novelties for Christmas."[2] The catalogue encouraged would-be buyers to start or expand their own collections, noting the centuries-old tradition in Holland of passing down large miniature collections. In offering an eighteenth-century-style two-handled cup, Howard may have been capitalizing on the appeal of heirlooms, just as Stone did with his mid-eighteenth-century-style tankard. Despite the diminutive size, great pride was taken in the skill and quality of production. Howard claimed that his miniatures were indestructible and far superior to the stamped antique versions; some pieces, such as Stone's candlesnuffer and tea caddy, even had moving workable parts.[3]

Description: Constructed from soldered silver, the rocking armchair has cut-out horizontal notched crescent shapes in the back and on each arm.

History: See cat. no. 278.

Exhibitions and publications: AFA 1994, cat. no. 12.

NOTES TO THIS ENTRY ARE ON PAGE 404.

280

Arthur Stone (1847–1938), maker

Retailed by Howard & Company (1866–about 1922)

Miniature ladder-back chair

New York, New York, 1895–97
Gift of Miss Alma Bent
1979.188

H. 1⅜ in. (3.6 cm); W. 11/16 in. (1.9 cm); D. 11/16 in. (1.7 cm); Wt. 6 dwt 12 gr (10.1 gm)

Marks: "STERLING [upside down] / HOWARD & CO." struck on underside of seat.

Inscriptions: None.

Description: Fashioned after a turned ladder-back rush-seat chair, the diminutive model was hand formed from twisted and articulated rods and chased and cut sheets of silver that were then soldered together.

History: See cat. no. 278.

Exhibitions and publications: Howard 1895, no. 4 (listed at $3).

281

Arthur Stone (1847–1938), maker

Retailed by Howard & Company (1866–about 1922)

Miniature two-handled covered cup

New York, New York, 1895–97
Gift of Miss Alma Bent
1979.190

H. 2³/16 in. (5.5 cm); W. 1¹³/16 in. (4.6 cm); Diam. lip 1¹/16 in. (2.6 cm); Diam. base ¾ in. (2 cm); Wt. 15 dwt 13 gr (24.2 gm)

Marks: "HOWARD / HOWARD [double struck] / STERLING" struck on inside of trumpet foot.

Inscriptions: None.

Description: The covered cup has applied C-scroll handles, a bulbous body with gadrooning on the bottom half, and a two-tiered spool-form foot. The domed lid has ornamental chasing and an urn finial.

History: See cat. no. 278.

Exhibitions and publications: Howard 1895, no. 94 (listed at $8); AFA 1994, cat. no. 12.

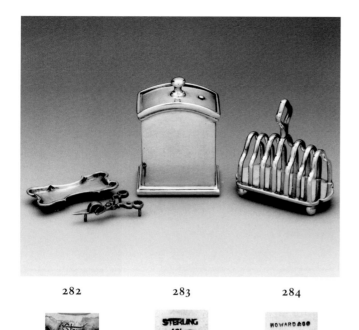

282   283   284

283

Arthur Stone (1847–1938), designer

Arthur Hartwell (active 1909–1937), maker

Miniature tea caddy

Gardner, Massachusetts, about 1925
Gift of Miss Alma Bent
1979.185

H. 1½ in. (3.9 cm); W. 1⅛ in. (2.8 cm); D. ¹¹⁄₁₆ in. (1.9 cm); Wt.
15 dwt 7 gr (23.8 gm)

Marks: "STERLING / Stone," with profile of an incuse chasing
hammer stamped across *St*, and "H" struck on bottom.

Inscriptions: None.

Description: The workable tea caddy has a curved top. Its sliding lid
is fitted with a knob finial and small applied button with rod extending into caddy, which acts as a stopping mechanism when opened.
The straight-sided rectangular body with applied molded rim and
baseband is rather restrained, although the interior is washed with
gold.

History: See cat. no. 278.

Exhibitions and publications: None.

282

Arthur Stone (1847–1938)

Miniature candle snuffer and stand

Gardner, Massachusetts, 1901–36
Gift of Miss Alma Bent
1979.187

H. snuffer ¼ in. (.6 cm); L. ⅞ in. (2.3 cm); W. ⅜ in. (.9 cm); H. stand
⅛ in. (.3 cm); W. 1³⁄₁₆ in. (3 cm); D. ½ in. (1.3 cm); Wt. snuffer 14 gr
(.9 gm); Wt. stand 1 dwt 5 gr (1.9 gm)

Marks: "Stone," with profile of chasing hammer stamped across *St*,
struck on bottom of stand. Snuffer is unmarked.

Inscriptions: None.

Description: Both the stand and candlesnuffer scissors are footed.
The scissors have circular finger holes, with scrolls leading to pivot
hinge; the stand has an articulated raised rim.

History: See cat. no. 278.

Exhibitions and publications: None.

284

Arthur Stone (1847–1938)

Retailed by Howard & Company
(1866–about 1922)

Miniature toast caddy

New York, New York, 1895–97
Gift of Miss Alma Bent
1979.186

H. 1⅜ in. (3.5 cm); W. 1⅜ in. (3.6 cm); D. ¹¹⁄₁₆ in. (1.8 cm); Wt. 10 dwt
10 gr (16.2 gm)

Marks: "HOWARD & CO / STERLING" struck; "2507"
scratched, both on bottom.

Inscriptions: None.

Description: This ball-footed caddy has seven ribbed supports; the central one is topped by an open diamond-shaped handle.

History: See cat. no. 278.

Exhibitions and publications: None.

285

Arthur Stone (1847–1938), designer

Arthur Hartwell (active 1909–1937), maker

Miniature tankard

Gardner, Massachusetts, about 1925
Gift of Miss Alma Bent
1979.183

H. 2³⁄₁₆ in. (5.5 cm); W. 1⅞ in. (4.7 cm); Diam. base 1½ in. (3.7 cm); Diam. rim 1⅛ in. (2.9 cm); Wt. 1 oz 8 dwt 21 gr (44.9 gm)

Marks: "STERLING / Stone," with profile of an incuse chasing hammer stamped across *St*, and "H" struck on bottom, near molded edge. "12" struck on both handle and lid where hinge causes them to meet.

Inscriptions: None.

Description: The tankard has straight tapering sides; applied bead midband; molded and splayed baseband; and reeded rim. The molded lid has a flange with incised lines; a five-part hinge; a molded scroll thumbpiece; and molded shape drop on shoulder of scroll handle. The interior is washed with gold.

History: See cat. no. 278.

Exhibitions and publications: AFA 1994, cat. no. 12.

286

Arthur Stone (1847–1938), maker

Retailed by Howard & Company (1866–about 1922)

Miniature pitcher

New York, New York, 1895–97
Gift of Miss Alma Bent
1979.189

H. 1⅛ in. (2.7 cm); D. 1³⁄₁₆ in. (3.1 cm); W. ⅞ in. (2.2 cm); Wt. 8 dwt 7 gr (12.9 gm)

Marks: "HOWARD & CO / STERLING" struck; "2310" faintly scratched, both on bottom. Interior may have been gold washed.

Inscriptions: None.

Description: The robust miniature has a full bulbous body with a simple applied C-scroll handle and three ball feet. The rim is scalloped with a wide pouring spout.

History: See cat. no. 278.

Exhibitions and publications: Howard 1895, no. 74 (listed at $4).

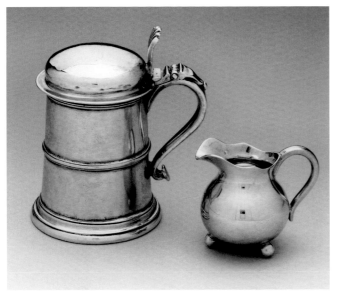

285   286

STERLING
Stone
H

HOWARD&CO
STERLING

287 288

287

Arthur Stone (1847–1938), designer

Benjamin "Henry" Harrison (active 1901–1937), maker

Miniature porringer

Gardner, Massachusetts, about 1905–12
Gift of Miss Alma Bent
1979.181

H. ¹³⁄₁₆ in. (2 cm); W. 2⅜ in. (6.2 cm); Diam. 1¹¹⁄₁₆ in. (4.2 cm); Wt. 16 dwt 17 gr (26 gm)

Marks: "Stone," with profile of incuse chasing hammer stamped across *St,* and "STERLING / H [pellet]" struck on bottom, near edge.

Inscriptions: None.

Description: The deep-bowl porringer has a slightly everted rim; curved sides with incised double lines that divide the double-lined arches springing from the stepped, flat base to the midpoint. The keyhole handle has chased lines to accent the floral design. The interior is gold washed.

History: See cat. no. 278.

Exhibitions and publications: AFA 1994, cat. no. 12.

288

Arthur Stone (1847–1938), designer

Arthur Hartwell (active 1909–1937), maker

Miniature porringer

Gardner, Massachusetts, about 1925
Gift of Miss Alma Bent
1979.182

H. ⅝ in. (1.4 cm); W. 1⅞ in. (4.8 cm); Diam. 1⁵⁄₁₆ in. (3.2 cm); Wt. 8 dwt 19 gr (13.7 gm)

Marks: "STERLING / Stone," with profile of incuse chasing hammer across *St,* and "H [pellet]" struck on bottom, near edge.

Inscriptions: None.

Description: This porringer has a straight rim; the sides curve to a stepped flat base. The keyhole handle has chased lines to accent the floral design.

History: See cat. no. 278.

Exhibitions and publications: None.

289

Arthur Stone (1847–1938)

Compote

Gardner, Massachusetts, about 1901
Gift of Mary Adams Scott Evans
1987.204

H. 4⅛ in. (10.3 cm); W. 7⁵⁄₁₆ in. (18.6 cm); Diam. base 3¹³⁄₁₆ in. (9.7 cm); Wt. 17 oz 11 dwt 2 gr (546 gm)

Marks: "STERLING" struck on underside of bowl, above center point. "Stone" incised below center point, with profile of incuse chasing hammer stamped across *St.*

Inscriptions: None.

JUDGING FROM ITS MARK, this compote dates to 1901, when Stone launched his own business and joined the Society of Arts and Crafts, Boston. He received a certificate of commendation from the society for this piece and three other works he submitted for exhibition in November 1903.[1] This achievement validated Stone's dream to "to work without stress in a little shop

289

STERLING

of his own."[2] The care taken in the execution of the bowl's shimmering, planished surface attests to his respect for materials and his sensitivity in representing the natural world. He often incorporated floral designs in his work, and the crocus is said to have been one of his favorite floral decorations.[3]

From the start, Stone employed his trademark "signature," which he used with minor variations until his retirement. His first initial "A" was suggested by the head of a chasing hammer, with the handle positioned horizontally to cross the "St" of his last name. He was proud of his chasing abilities, a skill few silversmiths master. Even when he had a full shop of able assistants, Stone continued to perform most of the chasing work himself until a disabling stroke in 1926 limited his technical abilities.[4]

Description: The raised bowl tapers outward and gently inward to a rounded everted rim. Alternating open and closed crocuses are chased and repoussé onto the bowl. It has a splayed trumpet foot that was raised and applied to the bottom of the bowl.

History: Early history unknown. According to family lore, it was received as a wedding present in 1905 by Mary Kennard Scott (1877–1960), who left it to her daughter Mary Adams Scott Evans (b. 1908) in 1959.

Exhibitions and publications: Elizabeth Emery, "Arts and Crafts: Some Recent Work," *The House Beautiful* 15 (1903–4), 132–33; AIC 1903, cat. no. 303; "Masters: Past and Present," The Society of Arts and Crafts, Boston, May 4–30, 1987; Chickering 1994, cat. no. 9, illus. 96; AFA 1994, cat. no. 17.

NOTES TO THIS ENTRY ARE ON PAGE 404.

FIG. 9. Arthur Stone in his workshop, Gardner, Massachusetts, about 1908. Museum of Fine Arts, Boston; Arthur Stone Papers, gift of Alma Bent.

290

Arthur Stone (1847–1938)

Jardinière

Gardner, Massachusetts, 1903
Gift of Miss Alma Bent
1987.464

H. 4¹³⁄₁₆ in. (12.2 cm); Diam. 9⅛ in. (23 cm); Diam. base 3⅞ in. (10 cm); Diam. lip 7½ in. (19 cm)

Marks: "Stone" incised, with profile of chasing hammer struck incuse across *St,* on bottom.

Inscriptions: None.

DESPITE ITS HUMBLE MATERIAL, this copper jardinière is considered to be one of Stone's finest works. The metal vessel reveals not only his technical virtuosity but also a sublime sensitivity to natural ornament and design. Stone entered this piece and three other works in the Louisiana Purchase Exposition in St. Louis in 1904 and received a silver medal.[1] Although Gorham, Roycroft, and other manufacturers had included copper and mixed-metal wares in their lines since the 1880s, Stone's copper work is rare. Most of his copper pieces were made for his own use. This bowl was displayed in the Stones' front living room, placed atop an upright piano.[2]

Description: The squat bulbous copper body was raised. It has naturalistic repoussé oak leaves and jewel-like inlaid silver acorns around its center, with a stepped flat foot and applied silver rim. The exterior has been lacquered.

History: See cat. no. 278.

Exhibitions and publications: AIC 1903, cat. no. 302; SACB 1903; Louisiana Purchase 1904, cat. no. 752; Chickering 1981, cat. no. 29; Elenita Chickering, "Arthur J. Stone, Silversmith," *Antiques* 129, no. 1 (January 1986), 276, 278, fig. 4; Kaplan 1987, 29, color pl. 144; Elenita Chickering, "Arthur J. Stone, 1847–1938: An Anglo-American Silversmith," *Apollo* 130, no. 330 (August 1989): 96, fig. 3; Fairbanks 1991, cat. no. 60; AFA 1994, cat. no. 18; Chickering 1994, cat. no. 13, illus. 10, 17, 98; "Metals Centennial Exhibition," Society of Arts and Crafts, Boston, May 1–June 30, 1997; "Drawn to Design," Museum of Fine Arts, Boston, June 5–November 7, 1999.

NOTES TO THIS ENTRY ARE ON PAGE 404.

Description: The raised and fluted copper vase has a deep red patina and five applied sprigs of mistletoe encircling its bulbous textured body, whose swirling surface is hammered. It has an applied silver band at the foot. The mouth rim has been scored with a line of slanted parallel marks directly below a wavy chased line.

History: See cat. no. 278.

Exhibitions and publications: AFA 1994, cat. no. 19; Chickering 1994, cat. no. 14.

NOTES TO THIS ENTRY ARE ON PAGE 404.

292

Arthur Stone (1847–1938)

Sauceboat

Gardner, Massachusetts, 1903
Seth K. Sweetser Fund
1978.232a

H. 3⅞ in. (9.9 cm); W. 7¹³⁄₁₆ in. (19.9 cm); D. 4⅛ in. (10.3 cm); Wt. 9 oz 7 dwt 7 gr (291.3 gm)

Marks: "STERLING" struck on bottom, away from rim; "Stone" incised, with profile of chasing hammer struck incuse across *St,* on bottom.

Inscriptions: None.

ASCRIBED ENTIRELY TO STONE, this sauceboat represents his work before he hired assistants to carry out his designs. It displays a tentative, yet sensitive, touch that translates into a wonderfully delicate line. Several years later, Herman Glendenning made an accompanying tray.[1]

Description: The vessel has a shallow elliptical bowl with delicate

291

Arthur Stone (1847–1938)

Vase

Gardner, Massarchusetts, 1903
Gift of Miss Alma Bent in memory of Annie E. Priest
1978.307

H. 4⅜ in. (11 cm); Diam. 3¼ in. (9.2 cm); Diam. base 1¹⁵⁄₁₆ in. (4.9 cm); Diam. lip 2⁵⁄₁₆ in. (5.9 cm)

Marks: "Stone" incised, with profile of chasing hammer struck incuse across *St,* on bottom.

Inscriptions: None.

THIS DELICATE COPPER VASE represents the type of ware Arthur Stone made for his own pleasure. The deep red patina was created by immersing the vase in a chemical solution.[1] Stone retailed works in mixed metals and retained pieces for his own use at home.[2]

chased lines that conform to the shape of the body. It rests on a wrought splayed and molded foot. The high, curved cast handles with applied central band rise from an everted rim and are placed at the narrow ends of the form.

History: Arthur and Elizabeth Bent Stone estate to their companion Annie E. Priest; by descent to Alma Bent, Stone's cousin, from whom the Museum purchased the piece.

Exhibitions and publications: AFA 1994, cat. no. 20; Chickering 1994, cat. no. 15.

NOTE TO THIS ENTRY IS ON PAGE 404.

293

Arthur Stone (1847–1938)

Plate

Gardener, Massachusetts, about 1905–6
Seth K. Sweetser Fund
1978.253

H. ⅝ in. (1.4 cm); Diam. 4¹¹⁄₁₆ in. (12 cm); Diam. base 3⁵⁄₁₆ (8.4 cm); Wt. 3 oz 2 dwt 7 gr (96.9 gm)

Marks: "STERLING" struck on bottom; "Stone" incised, with profile of chasing hammer struck incuse across *St,* on bottom.

Inscriptions: None.

THE EARLY MARK and incongruous combination of delicately engraved floral designs, with deeply chased ornaments obscuring the touchmark, suggest that this piece may have been an unfinished lid or dish that either Stone or one of his assistants used to try out his hand.

Description: This shallow bowl has an applied band at the edge of the raised rim. The bottom has an eight-petaled flower design in negative, created by chased floral decorations; the edge of the rim is encircled by an engraved leafy vine.

History: See cat. no. 292.

Exhibitions and publications: None.

294

Arthur Stone (1847–1938), designer and chaser

Arthur Hartwell (active 1909–1937), maker

Box

Gardner, Massachusetts, 1909–37
Helen and Alice Colburn Fund
1979.169

H. ⅝ in. (1.6 cm); W. 2³⁄₁₆ in. (5.5 cm); D. 1¹¹⁄₁₆ in. (4.2 cm); Wt. 1 oz 8 dwt 4 gr (43.8 gm)

Marks: "Stone," with profile of incuse chasing hammer across *St,* and "STERLING / H" struck on bottom, near edge. "15" struck inside lid and box.

Inscriptions: None.

SOMETIMES CALLED patch or pill boxes, these small containers were most likely used for personal effects such as pills or stamps.[1] Incorporating floral patterns and swirled lines, the boxes are representative of Stone's fine work and skill at chasing ornament. He often washed the interiors in gold, as he sometimes did with his miniatures, thus intentionally emphasizing their preciousness.

Description: The oval box is fitted with a molded flat foot and friction-fitted lid that is slightly domed and ornamented with chased panels and flowers. The interior is gold washed.

History: See cat. no. 292.

Exhibitions and publications: None.

NOTES TO THIS ENTRY ARE ON PAGE 404.

294

295

296

294 (upper right), 295 (upper left), 296 (bottom)

295

Arthur Stone (1847–1938), designer and chaser

Herman W. Glendenning (active 1920–1936), maker

Box

Gardner, Massachusetts, 1920–36
Helen and Alice Colburn Fund
1979.171

H. ⅝ in. (1.6 cm); W. 2³⁄₁₆ in. (5.5 cm); D. 1⅝ in. (4.1 cm); Wt. 1 oz 12 dwt 10 gr (50.4 gm)

Marks: "Stone," with profile of incuse chasing hammer across *St,* and "STERLING / G" struck on bottom. "10" struck inside rim of lid and outside rim of inner lip.

Inscriptions: None.

Description: The oval box has a molded flat foot and friction-fitted lid that is slightly domed and ornamented with a band of chased swirling lines. The interior is gold washed.

History: See cat. no. 292.

Exhibitions and publications: AFA 1994, cat. no. 23.

296

Arthur Stone (1847–1938), designer and chaser

Arthur Hartwell (active 1909–1937), maker

Box

Gardner, Massachusetts, 1909–15
Helen and Alice Colburn Fund
1979.176

H. ⅝ in. (1.5 cm); W. 2⅞ in. (7.4 cm); D. 1⁵⁄₁₆ in. (3.3 cm); Wt. 1 oz 4 dwt 12 gr (38.1 gm)

Marks: "Stone," with profile of incuse chasing hammer across *St,* and "STERLING / H" struck on bottom. "4" struck inside box, along bottom edge, and inside lid.

Inscriptions: None.

Description: The oblong box is fitted with a nine-part hinge that attaches the lid, which has a design of chased grapevines, leaves, and grape clusters. The interior is gold washed.

History: See cat. no. 292.

Exhibitions and publications: AFA 1994, cat. no. 23.

297

Arthur Stone (1847–1938), designer
and chaser

Arthur Hartwell (active 1909–1937), maker

Box

Gardner, Massachusetts, 1909–37
Helen and Alice Colburn Fund
1979.173

H. ¹³⁄₁₆ in. (2 cm); W. 2³⁄₁₆ in. (5.5 cm); D. 1⁵⁄₈ in. (4 cm); Wt. 1 oz 7 dwt 16 gr (43 gm)

Marks: "Stone," with profile of incuse chasing hammer across *St,* and "STERLING / H" struck on bottom, near edge. "14" struck inside box, along bottom edge, and inside lid.

Inscriptions: "A [pellet] E [pellet] P"¹ chased inside circular floral design.

Description: The oval box has a flat foot and a friction-fitted lid that is slightly domed and ornamented with a garland of chased flowers and leaves.

History: See cat. no. 292.

Exhibitions and publications: AFA 1994, cat. no. 23.

NOTE TO THIS ENTRY IS ON PAGE 404.

298

Arthur Stone (1847–1938), designer
and chaser

Arthur Hartwell (active 1909–1937), maker

Box

Gardner, Massachusetts, 1909–37
Helen and Alice Colburn Fund
1979.172

H. 1⅛ in. (2.8 cm); W. 3 in. (7.5 cm); D. 1⅞ in. (4.7 cm); Wt. 2 oz 8 dwt 16 gr (75.7 gm)

Marks: "Stone," with profile of incuse chasing hammer across *St,* and "STERLING / H" struck on bottom, near edge. "4" struck inside box, along bottom edge, and inside lid.

Inscriptions: "A P"¹ in script, within central cartouche, chased on lid.

Description: The rectangular box has rounded edges and a friction-fitted lid that is slightly domed and decorated with a Rococo cartouche, foliate C scrolls, and flower sprays on either side.

History: See cat. no. 292.

Exhibitions and publications: None.

NOTE TO THIS ENTRY IS ON PAGE 404.

299, 301, 300

299

Arthur Stone (1847–1938), designer
and chaser

Herbert A. Taylor (active 1908–1937), maker

Box

Gardner, Massachusetts, 1908–37
Helen and Alice Colburn Fund
1979.174

H. ⅞ in. (2.3 cm); W. 1½ in. (3.9 cm); Diam. 1½ in. (3.7 cm); Wt.
18 dwt 11 gr (28.7 gm)

Marks: "Stone," with profile of incuse chasing hammer across *St,*
and "STERLING / T" struck on base.

Inscriptions: None.

Description: The circular box, with a band at the rim and a flat foot,
has a scroll hinge and chased floral design on the lid. The interior is
gold washed.

History: See cat. no. 292.

Exhibitions and publications: AFA 1994, cat. no. 23.

300

Arthur Stone (1847–1938), designer
and chaser

Benjamin "Henry" Harrison
(active 1901–1937), maker

Box

Gardner, Massachusetts, 1905–12
Helen and Alice Colburn Fund
1979.170

H. ¹³⁄₁₆ in. (2.1 cm); W. 1¹¹⁄₁₆ in. (4.3 cm); Diam. 1¹¹⁄₁₆ in. (4.2 cm);
Wt. 19 dwt 10 gr (30.2 gm)

Marks: "Stone," with profile of incuse chasing hammer across *St,*
and "STERLING / H [pellet]" struck on base, near edge.

Inscriptions: None.

Description: The circular box has tapering sides, with knots encircling its center, and a scroll hinge with crossed lines. The lid is boldly
chased with a tripartite Celtic rope design covering the surface. The
interior is gold washed.

History: See cat. no. 292.

Exhibitions and publications: AFA 1994, cat. no. 23.

301

Arthur Stone (1847–1938)

Box

Gardner, Massachusetts, about 1906
Helen and Alice Colburn Fund
1979.175

H. 13⁄16 in. (2 cm); Diam. 1¹¹⁄16 in. (4.4 cm); Wt. 1 oz 6 gr (31.5 gm)

Marks: "STERLING" struck and "Stone" incised, and struck across *St* incuse chasing hammer, on center of base.

Inscriptions: None.

Description: The circular box has a friction-fitted lid ornamented with a large chased Tudor rose. The interior is gold washed.

History: See cat. no. 292.

Exhibitions and publications: AFA 1994, cat. no. 23; Chickering 1994, cat. no. 26.

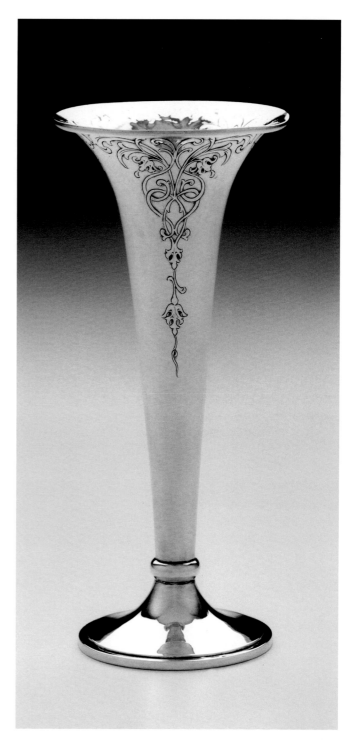

302

Arthur Stone (1847–1938)

Bud vase

Gardner, Massachusetts, 1906
Seth K. Sweetser Fund
1978.233

H. 5⁵⁄16 in. (13.4 cm); Diam. lip 2⁵⁄16 in. (6 cm); Diam. base 2 in. (5.1 cm); Wt. 3 oz 5 dwt 17 gr (102.2 gm)

Marks: "Stone," with profile of incuse chasing hammer across *St*, and "STERLING," both double struck on bottom.

Inscriptions: None.

According to Herman Glendenning, this piece was made entirely by Stone in 1906.[1]

Description: The vase has a small circular base that rises to a knob from which the vessel flares upward and outward, like a trumpet. Three divisions of leafy chased decoration embellish the sides.

History: See cat. no. 292.

Exhibitions and publications: Chickering 1994, cat no 26.

NOTE TO THIS ENTRY IS ON PAGE 404.

302

303

Arthur Stone (1847–1938), designer and maker, with various assistants

Five-piece tea set

Gardner, Massachusetts, about 1906–7
Gift of a Friend of the Department of American Decorative
Arts and Sculpture, John H. and Ernestine A. Payne Fund,
and Curator's Fund
1987.551–55

Kettle, stand, and burner (1987.551a–c): H. 12¼ in. (31.1 cm);
W. 9⁷⁄₁₆ in. (23.9 cm); D. 7⅜ in. (18.7 cm); Wt. 59 oz 17 dwt 4 gr
(1861.8 gm)

Kettle (1987.551a): H. 9½ in. (24 cm); W. 9⁷⁄₁₆ in. (23.9 cm); D. 7⅜ in.
(18.7 cm); Wt. 30 oz 15 dwt 23 gr (957.9 gm)

Stand (1987.551b): H. 7 in. (17.8 cm); W. 7¼ in. (18.4 cm); Diam. base
7¹⁄₁₆ in. (17.9 cm); Diam. base 4¹⁄₁₆ in. (24 cm); Wt. 23 oz 17 dwt 18 gr
(743 gm)

Burner (1987.551c): H. 2³⁄₁₆ in. (5.4 cm); W. 5¼ in. (13.3 cm); Diam.
3 in. (7.5 cm); Wt. 5 oz 3 dwt 17 gr (161.3 gm)

303

Sugar bowl (1987.552): H. 4½ in. (11.5 cm); W. 7¹³⁄₁₆ in. (19.8 cm); Diam. 5⁵⁄₁₆ in. (13.5 cm); Wt. 15 oz 4 dwt 14 gr (473.7 gm)

Teapot (1987.553): H. 5⁵⁄₁₆ in. (13.5 cm); W. 10¹¹⁄₁₆ in. (27.3 cm); Diam. 6 in. (15.3 cm); Diam. base 3⁷⁄₁₆ in. (8.8 cm); Wt. 23 oz 3 dwt 2 gr (720.2 gm)

Waste bowl (1987.554): H. 3 in. (7.6 cm); W. 7¹³⁄₁₆ in. (19.7 cm); Diam. 5¹³⁄₁₆ in. (14.8 cm); Diam. rim 4¹¹⁄₁₆ in. (12 cm); Diam. foot 3³⁄₁₆ in. (8 cm); Wt. 12 oz 15 dwt 5 gr (396.9 gm)

Creamer (1987.555): H. 4 in. (10.2 cm); W. 6 in. (15.3 cm); Diam. 4⅛ in. (10.3 cm); Diam. base 2³⁄₁₆ in. (6.9 cm); Wt. 8 oz 9 dwt 7 gr (263.3 gm)

Marks: "STERLING / Stone [with profile of incuse chasing hammer stamped across St] / T" struck on bottom of kettle, near edge of rim, and on bottom of stand, in center. Whiting trademark, a lion beside a script "W" within an ellipse; and company date mark for 1907, "3176" and inverted triangle with semicircle along each side, both struck on burner. "STERLING / [incised] Stone [with profile of incuse chasing hammer stamped across St] / 1906," with the *1, 9,* and *6* engraved and the *0* stamped, all on bottom of teapot, near edge. "STERLING / [incised] Stone [with profile of incuse chasing hammer stamped across St] / 1906" stamped on bottom of creamer, sugar bowl, and waste bowl.

Inscriptions: "LAB / 1906" in script engraved on bottom of teapot, creamer, sugar bowl, and waste bowl.

THE DECORATION OF this tea set is admired best when the pieces are in use and viewed at the proper height. The pleasing forms, refined lines, and delicate chasing demonstrate the aesthetic and technical ambition of Stone's shop.

Commissioned as a wedding present for Lawrence and Alice Bullard in 1906, the original four-piece set documents early workshop practices when Stone executed much of the raising

and chasing. After his stroke in 1926, much of that work was handled by his assistants. Stone was sufficiently proud of the group, and no doubt eager for similar commissions, to borrow the set from the Bullards in order to include it in the Society of Arts and Crafts exhibition the next year.[1] Some six years later, the set was augmented by the kettle and stand, which were perhaps given as an anniversary present to Mrs. Bullard.[2] By that time Stone's business had grown, and he employed several full-time assistants. Herbert Taylor (w. 1908–1937) was involved with the creation of the kettle and stand to such a degree that he was allowed to strike his initial on them. The burner, however, was purchased from Whiting, one of the period's foremost silver manufacturers.

Description: The pear-shaped forms, save the spun kettle, were raised. The parts soldered together to make the stand were probably hammered over a form. The feet were applied; that of the kettle has a perforated design. Chased crocuses framed by symmetrical scrolling vines divide the body of each vessel into twelve sections; however, the crocus bud was omitted behind handles and at the spout, except on the teapot. The creamer, sugar, and waste bowl have delicately scrolled thumb rests at the handle joins; the first two show evidence of gold wash, and the waste bowl and creamer have an applied band at the rim. The sugar, teapot, and kettle have button finials with chased leaf pattern. The teapot and kettle have five-part hinges and chased leaves extending the length of the top of the spouts. The kettle has four applied knobs for positioning the piece on the stand. The burner has its original fuel basket with batting insert, and the cogwheel mechanism for opening this device still works. The handles on the kettle, teapot, and burner have ivory or bone insulators.

History: The set, except the kettle, was purchased from Stone by Florence E. Bullard for her son Lawrence and his wife, Alice Lowell Kennedy Bullard. The kettle may have been commissioned by Lawrence Bullard in 1912 as an anniversary present. The set descended to the Bullards' daughter Margrette Bullard (1907–1983) and then to Alice Bullard's grandchildren Alice N. Mays and Barbara N. Ziems; they sold it to the Museum through ARK Antiques, New Haven, Connecticut.

Exhibitions and publications: Exhibition of the Society of Arts and Crafts, Copley Hall, Boston, February 5–26, 1907, 795 B (teapot, creamer, sugar, and waste bowl); Janet Kardon, ed., *The Ideal Home, 1900–1920: the History of Twentieth-Century American Craft* (New York: Harry N. Abrams, 1993), illus. 200, 294; AFA 1994 (first four venues only), cat. no. 28; Chickering 1994, cat. no. 36, color plate IV, 66; Jim Clancy, "Humanism and the Arts and Crafts Movement," *Silver Magazine* 35, no. 1 (January/February 2003), 39.

NOTES TO THIS ENTRY ARE ON PAGE 404–05.

lor was head craftsman in Stone's shop and achieved medalist status in the Society of Arts and Crafts. He helped fashion this delicate vase about the time that Stone created one of his most celebrated pieces of ecclesiastical silver, a gold monstrance for the Church of the Advent in Boston.

Description: The raised globular copper body tapers at the top and has decorative chased arches embellished with chased leaves and silver rosettes. The rim is finished with an applied silver band, and the rich red surface appears to have been selectively polished and then lacquered. The inside of the vase has become encrusted with verdigris, indicating regular use.

History: See cat. no. 292.

Exhibitions and publications: AFA 1994, cat. no. 32; Chickering 1994, cat no. 46, illus., 109.

304

Arthur Stone (1847–1938), designer and chaser

Herbert A. Taylor (active 1908–1937), maker

Vase

Gardner, Massachusetts, about 1908
Seth K. Sweetser Fund
1978.246

H. 4⅛ in. (10.4 cm); Diam. 4⅞ in. (12.4 cm); Diam. rim 3¹¹⁄₁₆ in. (9.3 cm); Diam. base 2⅞ in. (7.3 cm)

Marks: "Stone [with profile of incuse chasing hammer stamped across St] / T" struck on base, at center.

Inscriptions: None.

STONE'S CHIEF ASSISTANTS ably assimilated his hand and style, a fact well demonstrated by Herbert Taylor's skillful combination of the elements of this vessel. Note the way that the applied silver-and-chased ornament complement and harmonize with the modulated shape and hammered surface. Tay-

305

Arthur Stone (1847–1938)

Dish

Gardner, Massachusetts, 1908–11
Seth K. Sweetser Fund
1978.252

H. 1¹¹⁄₁₆ in. (4.2 cm); Diam. 10 in. (25.5 cm); Wt. 17 oz 17 dwt 20 gr (556.5 gm)

Marks: "Stone [with profile of an incuse chasing hammer stamped across *St*] / STERLING" struck on base, near edge.

Inscriptions: None.

ADVERTISED AS A VEGETABLE DISH, and offered in various sizes as wedding silver through the showrooms of the Society of Arts and Crafts, this form was a stock item. Nonetheless, this dish is believed to be solely by the master's hand, for only his mark appears on the base. Although Stone employed several assistants during this period, his reliance on them to fabricate and spin work to meet increasing demands changed gradually.[1]

Description: The sides of the raised fluted dish are divided into five sections. The scalloped rim has an applied molding.

History: See cat. no. 292.

Exhibitions and publications: None.

NOTE TO THIS ENTRY IS ON PAGE 405.

306

306

Arthur Stone (1847–1938), designer and chaser

Herbert A. Taylor (active 1908–1937), maker

Bowl

Gardner, Massachusetts, 1908–37
Benjamin Cheney Fund
1977.19

H. 4⅛ in. (10.5 cm); W. 9⅜ in. (23.9 cm); Diam. base 4 in. (10.1 cm); Diam. rim 9½ in. (24.1 cm); Wt. 26 oz 12 dwt 3 gr (827.6 gm)

Marks: "STERLING / Stone [with profile of incuse chasing hammer stamped across *St*] / T" struck on base, near edge.

Inscriptions: None.

THIS BOWL IS REMINISCENT of eighteenth-century Chinese export porcelain lotus bowls and thus relates to Boston's predominant taste for colonial design and ornament. The fluid, attenuated floral decoration, however, aligns it with the Art Nouveau style, which had become popular by the turn of the twentieth century. This piece was the first by Stone to enter the Museum's collection.

Description: The bowl has a slightly flaring lip with a molded edge. The sides are curved, and the foot band is splayed and molded. The sides contain nine incised lotus-petal panels, with a lily blossom and leaves between each, just below the bowl's lip.

History: Original owner unknown; purchased by the Museum in 1977 from Firestone and Parsons, Inc., Boston.

Exhibitions and publications: None.

307

Arthur Stone (1847–1938)

Kensington dish

Gardner, Massachusetts, 1908–36
Seth K. Sweetser Fund
1978.243

H. ¹¹⁄₁₆ in. (1.8 cm); Diam. 5⅞ in. (15 cm); Diam. base 4⁵⁄₁₆ in. (10.8 cm); Wt. 5 oz 11 dwt 23 gr (174.1 gm)

Marks: "Stone [with profile of incuse chasing hammer stamped across *St*] / Sterling / T" struck near edge.

Inscriptions: None.

307

The inspiration for this design came from Stone's study of work at London's South Kensington Museum (now the Victoria and Albert Museum). A popular pattern, the Kensington dish was offered in various sizes to suit different needs and budgets.[1]

Description: Probably form-pressed on wood, this shallow flat-bottomed bowl has nine chased panels and is divided by flutes, creating a subtle scalloped effect.

History: See cat. no. 292.

Exhibitions and publications: Chickering 1994, cat. no. 51, ill.

NOTE TO THIS ENTRY IS ON PAGE 405.

308

Arthur Stone (1847–1938)

Watering can

Gardner, Massachusetts, about 1910
Gift of Louisa and Jonathan Fairbanks
1991.744

H. 11⅞ in. (30.3 cm); W. 6⅜ in. (16.2 cm); D. 12⅝ in. (32 cm)

Marks: "Stone [with profile of incuse chasing hammer stamped across *St*]" struck on base.

Inscriptions: None.

THE RICH SURFACE and beautifully balanced design elevate this copper watering can above its utilitarian function. Tapering from the top, the sides seem to bulge closer to the bottom, as if the pressure from the contents had reshaped the form. The strong handles with ornamental rivets and the carefully angled spout further attest to Stone's masterful sense of line and proportion. Similar rivets were used in traditional colonial construction. Here they are purely decorative and do not penetrate the vessel's body. This design is closely related to a miniature silver watering can advertised by J. P. Howard & Company, which Stone likely designed and produced during his partnership with the firm.[1]

Description: The rectangular vessel is made of hammered sheet copper. It has a flat base and top, soldered handles with faux rivets, and a seamed spout with tip attached at an angle.

History: Arthur and Elizabeth Bent Stone estate to their companion Annie E. Priest; by descent to Stone's cousin Alma Bent. Purchased from Bent for the Museum by Jonathan and Louisa Fairbanks.

Exhibitions and publications: None.

NOTE TO THIS ENTRY IS ON PAGE 405.

309

Arthur Stone (1847–1938), designer and chaser

David Carlson (active 1909–1919), maker

Child's breakfast set

Gardner, Massachusetts, about 1913
Gift of Joseph Randolph Coolidge IV
1989.811–13

Cup (1989.811): H. 3⅜ in. (8.6 cm); W. 4¼ in. (11.3 cm); Diam. 3⅜ in. (8.4 cm); Diam. rim 3 in. (7.7 cm); Diam. base 2⅜ in. (6.1 cm); Wt. 8 oz 15 dwt 2 gr (272.3 gm)

Plate (1989.812): H. 1 in. (2.5 cm); Diam. 7½ in. (19 cm); Diam. foot 3¾ in. (9.5 cm); Wt. 10 oz 3 dwt 5 gr (316 gm)

Bowl (1989.813): H. 2⅝ in. (6.5 cm); Diam. 5¹¹⁄₁₆ in. (14.4 cm); Diam. foot 3⅜ in. (8.6 cm); Wt. 10 oz 8 dwt 20 gr (324.8 gm)

Marks: "Stone [with profile of incuse chasing hammer stamped across *St*] / STERLING / C" struck on bottom of each.

Inscriptions: None.

THIS CHILD'S SERVICE records a personal gift exchanged to and from prominent Bostonians at the turn of the twentieth century. It also documents a preference for marking important occasions with silverware. The set was presented in 1913 to Peggy Stuart Coolidge to celebrate her baptism. It is made of heavy-gauge metal and, despite use, has survived in good condition.

Description: The bulbous raised cup with C-scroll handle and the raised bowl with volutes each have center points on their bottoms. Each is similarly ornamented with ribbing or panels that divide the sides or plate rim and that have palmette decorations, which form the seam of these sections. The plate has a shallow basin and applied molded foot; the cup and bowl have a molded foot and rim.

History: Baptismal gift received by composer Peggy Stuart (1913–1981) in 1913; by descent to her husband, Joseph Randolph Coolidge IV, the donor.

Exhibitions and publications: None.

310

Arthur Stone (1847–1938), designer and chaser

Herbert A. Taylor (active 1908–1937), maker

Vase

Gardner, Massachusetts, 1914
Seth K. Sweetser Fund
1978.234

H. 7¹³⁄₁₆ in. (19.7 cm); Diam. 4⅜ in. (11.2 cm); Diam. rim 3⅛ in. (8 cm); Diam. base 2¹³⁄₁₆ in. (7.2 cm); Wt. 16 oz 15 dwt 14 gr (521.9 gm)

Marks: "Stone [with profile of incuse chasing hammer stamped across *St*] / STERLING / T" struck on base, near edge.

Inscriptions: None.

THIS VASE demonstrates Stone's consummate ability to combine elements associated with different historical periods, resulting in a beautifully unified modern expression. The overall design and delicacy of the piece recalls the Art Nou-

veau style, whereas the flat fluting was a common feature on Baroque art.

Description: The raised vase tapers gently outward and then quickly inward at the rim. An ornamental band of latticework is punctuated with floral cartouches alternating with single rose stems that extend above and below the band. A scalloped line creates the divisions for the flat fluting, which is terminated by two sets of scored lines above the splayed foot.

History: See cat. no. 292.

Exhibitions and publications: AFA 1994, cat. no. 36; Chickering 1994, cat. no. 65, 116; Jim Clancy, "Humanism and the Arts and Crafts Movement," *Silver Magazine* 35, no. 1 (January / February 2003), 35.

311

Arthur Stone (1847–1938)

Napkin ring

Gardner, Massachusetts, ca. 1920
Seth K. Sweetser Fund
1978.254

H. 1³⁄₁₆ in. (3.1 cm); Diam. 1¹³⁄₁₆ in. (4.5 cm); Wt. 1 oz 11 dwt 12 gr (49 gm)

Marks: "Stone [with profile of incuse chasing hammer stamped across *St*] / STERLING" struck on exterior edge of lower band.

Inscriptions: None.

STONE'S USE OF GOLD on this napkin ring, probably made for use in his own family, elevates it above the typical expression of the form.

Description: The ring is divided by scored lines into five bands; the center band has applied silver flowers and chased leaves that are separated by inlaid gold dots.

History: See cat. 292.

Exhibitions and publications: AFA 1994, cat. no. 49.

312

Arthur Stone (1847–1938), designer and chaser

Herbert A. Taylor (active 1908–1937), maker

Plate

Gardner, Massachusetts, about 1921
Seth K. Sweetser Fund
1978.247

H. ¹³⁄₁₆ in. (2 cm); Diam. 8⁵⁄₁₆ in. (21 cm); Wt. 11 oz 8 dwt 5 gr (354.9 gm)

Marks: "Stone [with profile of incuse chasing hammer stamped across *St*] / STERLING / T" struck on bottom.

Inscriptions: "TO / AJS AND EBS / 1896–1921 / THE GIFT OF / HERBERT A TAYLOR" engraved on bottom.

Description: The deep-bottomed plate has an upward curved border and a chased wavelike pattern on the rim.

History: Given to Arthur and Elizabeth Stone by Herbert A. Taylor, foreman of the Stone silver shop in 1921, on their twenty-fifth anniversary. From the Arthur and Elizabeth Bent Stone estate to their companion Annie E. Priest; by descent to Stone's cousin Alma Bent, from whom the Museum purchased the piece.

313

Arthur Stone (1847–1938), designer

Arthur Hartwell (active 1909–1937), maker

Four-piece tea service

Gardner, Massachusetts, about 1922
Seth K. Sweetser Fund
1978.228–31

Teapot (1978.228): H. 6⅛ in. (15.6 cm); W. 10¹¹⁄₁₆ in. (27.2 cm);
D. 4⅛ in. (10.4 cm); Wt. 16 oz 15 dwt 17 gr (522.1 gm)

Sugar bowl (1978.229): H. 4¹¹⁄₁₆ in. (12 cm); W. 6⁵⁄₁₆ in. (16 cm);
D. 3⁵⁄₁₆ in. (8.4 cm); Wt. 13 oz 4 dwt 13 gr (411.4 gm)

Cream pitcher (1978.230): H. 4⁵⁄₁₆ in. (11 cm); W. 5 in. (12.7 cm);
D. 2⁵⁄₁₆ in. (5.9 cm); Wt. 7 oz 7 dwt 9 gr (229.2 gm)

Teapot stand (1978.231): H. ¹¹⁄₁₆ in. (1.7 cm); W. 7⅛ in. (18 cm);
D. 5³⁄₁₆ in. (13.3 cm); Wt. 5 oz 7 dwt 9 gr (167 gm)

Marks: "Stone [with profile of incuse chasing hammer stamped
across *St*] / STERLING / H" struck on bottom of teapot, sugar

bowl, and cream pitcher, near edge. Teapot stand bears same mark but lacks the *H*.

Inscriptions: None.

REFLECTING THE STRONG Colonial Revival taste then prevalent in Boston, this set was made by Arthur Hartwell about 1922. The wooden handle of the teapot was fabricated from cokus wood, which is sometimes called grenadilla.[1]

Description: The teapot has an elliptical body with a hinged domed lid and turned oval finial. The spout is curved, and the handle and knob are made of cokus wood. The stand is a scalloped tray supported by four cabriole legs with pad feet. The sugar bowl and cream pitcher were formed into an elliptical form with shaped sides; they have solid curved handles. The bowl's domed top has a turned oval finial.

History: See cat. no. 292

Exhibitions and publications: Pilgrims and Progressives: The Colonial Revival in Massachusetts (Boston: Boston University Art Gallery, 1996), 16 (teapot, sugar bowl, creamer).

NOTE TO THIS ENTRY IS ON PAGE 405.

314

Arthur Stone (1847–1938), designer

Edgar L. Caron (active 1924–1937), maker

Bowl

Gardner, Massachusetts, 1923
Seth K. Sweetser Fund
1978.250

H. 2⅝ in. (6.6 cm); Diam. rim 3¹⁵/₁₆ in. (10 cm); Diam. foot 1⅞ in. (4.7 cm); Wt. 4 oz 12 gr (125.2 gm)

Marks: "Stone [with profile of incuse chasing hammer stamped across *St*] / STERLING / C" struck on bottom.

Inscriptions: None.

314

EDGAR CARON made this adaptation of a Paul Revere bowl in 1923, soon after leaving F. W. Smith Company, a commercial silverware firm. Caron became a master craftsman in the Society of Arts and Crafts, Boston, and specialized in hollowware fabrication in Stone's shop from 1924 to 1936.

Such diminutive bowls were first used as drip bowls, with a tea strainer. Later clients used them as small sugar bowls to accompany a creamer on breakfast trays.[1]

Description: The raised bowl with everted lip and curving sides has an applied and splayed molded footband.

History: See cat. no. 292.

Exhibitions and publications: None.

NOTE TO THIS ENTRY IS ON PAGE 405.

315

Arthur Stone (1847–1938), designer

Herman W. Glendenning (active 1920–1936), maker

Bowl

Gardner, Massachusetts, 1926
Seth K. Sweetser Fund
1978.251

H. 1¾ in. (4.4 cm); Diam. rim 4¾ in. (12.1 cm); Diam. foot 2¼ in. (5.7 cm); Wt. 4 oz 17 dwt 24 gr (152.4 gm)

Marks: "Stone [with profile of incuse chasing hammer stamped across *St*] / STERLING / G" struck on bottom.

Inscriptions: None.

HERMAN GLENDENNING made this bowl, after Stone's design, in 1926. Glendenning recalled that the form was first made for a client who had ordered a set of sixteen finger bowls. She had her name engraved on the bottom of each, and all were numbered with engraved numerals from 1 to 16 as well.[1]

Description: The sides of the raised bowl taper outward from the bottom to the flaring rim.

History: See cat. no. 292.

Exhibitions and publications: None.

NOTE TO THIS ENTRY IS ON PAGE 405.

316

Arthur Stone (1847–1938), designer and chaser

Herbert A. Taylor (active 1908–1937), maker

Avon bowl

Gardner, Massachusetts, about 1926
Seth K. Sweetser Fund
1978.248

H. 2⅞ in. (7.3 cm); Diam. rim 6⅞ in. (17.6 cm); Diam. foot 2¹¹⁄₁₆ in. (6.9 cm); Wt. 10 oz 8 dwt (323.5 gm)

Marks: "Stone [with profile of incuse chasing hammer stamped across *St*] / STERLING / T" struck on base, near edge.

Inscriptions: None.

ADAPTED FROM A GLASS BOWL that Stone had studied at Shakespeare's house in Stratford-upon-Avon, this so-called Avon design was based on the form of an ancient drinking vessel and was offered in various sizes and modified forms (fig. 10). Stone used the snarling technique to alter the encircling band into an alternating raised and hollow reverse fluting.[1] The first Avon bowl was made of 95 percent silver, at the client's request. All others were of the stronger .925 sterling composition. According to Herman Glendenning, this bowl was raised by Herbert Taylor and chased by Stone about 1926. It is thus one of the last works he chased before suffering a debilitating stroke in the fall of that year.[2]

FIG. 10. Arthur Stone seated at bench with the Avon bowl, Gardner, Massachusetts. Museum of Fine Arts, Boston; Arthur Stone Papers, gift of Alma Bent.

Description: This raised tapering bowl has a chased midband of flutes, with a band embellished with alternating punched crosses and circles above and a scored line below the bowl; it flares outward at the lip.

History: See cat. no. 292.

Exhibitions and publications: AFA 1994, cat. no. 35.

NOTES TO THIS ENTRY ARE ON PAGE 405.

317

Arthur Stone (1847–1938), designer and chaser

Herman W. Glendenning (active 1920–1936), maker

Bowl

Gardner, Massachusetts, about 1926
Seth K. Sweetser Fund
1978.249

H. 3⁵⁄₁₆ in. (8.3 cm); Diam. rim 5⅝ in. (14.3 cm); Diam. foot 2¹³⁄₁₆ in. (7.2 cm); Wt. 10 oz 15 dwt 10 gr (335 gm)

Marks: "Stone [with profile of incuse chasing hammer stamped across St] / STERLING / G" struck on bottom, near edge.

Inscriptions: None.

HERMAN GLENDENNING raised this bowl especially for the Stones' home about 1926. Arthur Stone was responsible for the chased elements. Glendenning worked with Stone from about the age of eight, gradually becoming an apprentice.[1] He learned to craft flatware but excelled at hollowware, becoming a master craftsman of the Society of Arts and Crafts, Boston. He worked in the workshop until Stone's death, upon which Glendenning established a hollowware department in the workshop of George C. Erickson, another former Stone employee who had specialized in flatware. In 1971 he retired to his own studio, where he continued to work under the name "Glendenning Sterling Handwrought." He taught classes in silversmithing and jewelrymaking as well.

Description: This raised bowl has a scalloped and stepped rim with chased shell ornament atop the deeply chased lines that divide the bowl into eight panels. The splayed molded foot is soldered.

History: See cat. no. 292.

Exhibitions and publications: None.

NOTE TO THIS ENTRY IS ON PAGE 405.

318

Arthur Stone (1847–1938), designer

Arthur Hartwell (active 1909–1937) and Herman W. Glendenning (active 1920–1936), makers

Set of five nut dishes

Gardner, Massachusetts, about 1932
Seth K. Sweetser Fund
1978.235–39

1978.235: H. 1³/₁₆ in. (2 cm); W. 4 in. (10 cm); D. 2⁵/₈ in. (6.7 cm); Wt. 2 oz 5 dwt 19 gr (71.2 gm)

1978.236: H. 1³/₁₆ in. (2 cm); W. 4 in. (10.1 cm); D. 2⁵/₈ in. (6.7 cm); Wt. 2 oz 7 dwt (73.1 gm)

1978.237: H. 1³/₁₆ in. (2 cm); W. 3⁷/₈ in. (9.9 cm); 2⁵/₈ in. (6.7 cm); Wt. 2 oz 1 dwt 2 gr (63.9 gm)

1978.238: H. 1³/₁₆ in. (2 cm); W. 3⁷/₈ in. (9.9 cm); D. 2⁵/₈ in. (6.7 cm); Wt. 2 oz 6 dwt 13 gr (72.4 gm)

1978.239: H. 1¹/₁₆ in. (1.9 cm); W. 4 in. (10.1 cm); D. 2¹¹/₁₆ in. (6.8 cm); Wt. 2 oz 6 dwt 10 gr (72.2 gm)

Marks: 1978.235: "Stone [with profile of an incuse chasing hammer stamped across *St*] / STERLING / G" struck on bottom. "Stone [with profile of incuse chasing hammer stamped across *St*] / STERLING / H" struck on bottom of the four others.

Inscriptions: None.

318

THIS SET, consisting of square nut dishes, was the only one made at the Stone workshop.[1] Originally a set of six, one of the dishes, along with a Stone condiment dish, was exchanged with the Art Institute of Chicago for works by Kalo Shop (see cat. no. 266).

Description: The square shallow dishes have rounded edges and saw-pierced handles in a foliate design.

History: See cat. no. 292.

Exhibitions and publications: None.

NOTE TO THIS ENTRY IS ON PAGE 405.

319

Arthur Stone (1847–1938)

Ashtray

Gardner, Massachusetts, 1934
Bequest of Helen S. Coolidge
Res.63.28

H. $^{11}/_{16}$ in. (1.9 cm); Diam. $3^{5}/_{8}$ in. (9.2 cm); Wt. 3 oz 2 dwt 23 gr (97.9 gm)

Marks: "Stone [with profile of incuse chasing hammer stamped across *St*] / STERLING" struck on bottom.

Inscriptions: "29 – APRIL – 1934" engraved on bottom.

IDENTIFIED AS ASHTRAYS, such small shallow dishes were often engraved with a wide assortment of floral decoration. Those made after 1926 usually do not have a craftsman's initial, perhaps because the form was spun and Stone executed the simple ornament.[1]

Description: The shallow spun dish with applied foot has chased trumpet flowers encircling its center.

History: Made for Mr. and Mrs. John Gardner Coolidge; bequeathed to the Museum by Mrs. Coolidge.

Exhibitions and publications: None.

NOTE TO THIS ENTRY IS ON PAGE 405.

320

Arthur Stone (1847–1938)

Coffee spoon

Gardner, Massachusetts, 1901
Seth K. Sweetser Fund
1978.256

L. $4^{11}/_{16}$ in. (12 cm); W. bowl $^{13}/_{16}$ in. (2.1 cm); Wt. 8 dwt 10 gr (13.1 gm)

Marks: "STERLING / [chasing hammer]" struck on reverse of handle.

Inscriptions: None.

THIS SPOON documents one of Stone's first marks. The delicate decoration is characteristic of his early work.

Description: The spoon has a straight spatulate handle engraved with alternating spirals, each successively smaller toward the bowl.

History: See cat. no. 292.

Exhibitions and publications: AFA 1994, cat. no. 57.

321

Arthur Stone (1847–1938)

Five o'clock teaspoon

Gardner, Massachusetts, 1901–12
Seth K. Sweetser Fund
1978.258

L. 4¹¹⁄₁₆ in. (11.9 cm); W. bowl ⅞ in. (2.3 cm); Wt. 8 dwt 10 gr (13.1 gm)

Marks: "STERLING" stamped and "S," incised with profile of incuse chasing hammer stamped across "S," struck on back of handle.

Inscriptions: Musical notes "A B," within a rectangular cartouche, engraved on back of handle.[1]

THIS SPOON WAS A GIFT from Stone to Adelaide Bent, his sister-in-law. Bent was a violinist, hence the musical notes from the Gregorian chant engraved on the handle. She also was a member of the Stone household until her death, at which time Annie Priest was asked to share their home.[2]

Much of the Museum's collection of silver by Stone was purchased from Priest. The Museum's collection of Stone drawings and working sketches include four images of spoons bearing a similar decoration. Two additional drawings at the Smithsonian Institution illustrate spoon handles with a twisted-leaf mistletoe; this example displays straight leaves.[3]

Description: The downturned oval handle is engraved with a mistletoe sprig having five gold berries.

History: Made for Adelaide Bent (1868–1916); by descent to Alma Bent, from whom the Museum purchased the piece.

Exhibitions and publications: AFA 1994, cat. no. 59.

NOTES TO THIS ENTRY ARE ON PAGE 405.

322

Arthur Stone (1847–1938)

Iced tea spoon

Gardner, Massachusetts, about 1901
Seth K. Sweetser Fund
1978.257

L. 6¹¹⁄₁₆ in. (17 cm); W. bowl ¹⁵⁄₁₆ in. (2.3 cm); Wt. 1 oz 5 gr (31.4 gm)

Marks: "STERLING" stamped and "Stone," incised with profile of incuse chasing hammer across *St,* struck on back of handle.

Inscriptions: None.

AS EARLY AS 1915, Stone began exhibiting his silverware at the Little Gallery in New York City. Sometime afterward, the gallery advertised four of Stone's flatware patterns for sale, including this Georgian design. It was twice as expensive as the others, indicative of the intensive labor required to hand file the scroll handles.[1]

Description: This spoon has a downturned scroll-end handle, rolled in upon itself, and a ridged rattail.

History: See cat. no. 292.

Exhibitions and publications: AFA 1994, cat. no. 58.

NOTE TO THIS ENTRY IS ON PAGE 405.

323

Arthur Stone (1847–1938), designer

Sylvanus E. Lamprey (active 1909–1912), maker

Dessert spoon

Gardner, Massachusetts, 1908–11
Seth K. Sweetser Fund
1978.261

L. 7½ in. (19 cm); W. bowl 1⅜ in. (3.5 cm); Wt. 1 oz 1 dwt 1 gr (32.7 gm)

Marks: "STERLING / Stone [with profile of incuse chasing hammer across *St*] / L" struck on back of handle.

Inscriptions: "E [pellet] B [pellet] S" in block letters engraved on handle.

THE ARTHUR STONE COLLECTION at the Museum, in addition to being representative of this master's oeuvre, also contains several personal items that were used daily by this silversmith and his family. These include this spoon, which is engraved with his wife's initials.

Description: The straight-handle spoon has a downturned coffin-shaped end.

History: Made for Elizabeth Bent Stone; Arthur and Elizabeth Bent Stone estate to their companion Annie E. Priest; by descent to Stone's cousin Alma Bent, from whom the Museum purchased the piece.

Exhibitions and publications: None.

324

Arthur Stone (1847–1938), designer and chaser

Sylvanus E. Lamprey (active 1909–1912), maker

Nut spoon

Gardner, Massachusetts, probably 1909
Seth K. Sweetser Fund
1978.260

L. 4⁵⁄₁₆ in. (10.8 cm); W. bowl 1¹³⁄₁₆ in. (4. cm); Wt. 14 dwt 14 gr (22.7 gm)

Marks: "STERLING / Stone [with profile of incuse chasing hammer across *St*] / L" struck on back of handle.

Inscriptions: None.

Description: The wide-bowl nut spoon has a flower-stalk decoration on the handle, which is engraved and pierced.

History: See cat. no. 292.

Exhibitions and publications: None.

325

Arthur Stone (1847–1938), designer

Sylvanus E. Lamprey (active 1909–1912), maker

Dessert spoon

Gardner, Massachusetts, 1909–12
Seth K. Sweetser Fund
1978.262

L. 7 in. (17.7 cm); W. bowl 1⁷⁄₁₆ in. (3.6 cm); Wt. 1 oz 6 dwt 10 gr (41.1 gm)

Marks: "STERLING / Stone [with profile of incuse chasing hammer stamped across *St*] / L" struck on back of handle.

Inscriptions: None.

Description: The straight-handle spoon has a downturned spatulate tip.

History: See cat. no. 292.

Exhibitions and publications: None.

326

Arthur Stone (1847–1938), designer and chaser

Charles Brown (active 1912–1937), maker

Demitasse spoon

Gardner, Massachusetts, 1912–15
Seth K. Sweetser Fund
1978.259

L. 5 in. (12.7 cm); W. bowl 1³⁄₁₆ in. (2.1 cm); Wt. 7 dwt 17 gr (12 gm)

Marks: "Stone [with profile of incuse chasing hammer stamped across *St*] / STERLING / B [sideways]" struck on back of handle.

Inscriptions: None.

CHARLES BROWN was the head of spoonmaking in Arthur Stone's shop from 1912 to 1937. The snowdrop pattern can also be found among Stone's working drawings, such as AS-1-2.[1]

Description: The straight downturned handle with pointed tip is engraved with a snowdrop flower.

History: See cat. no. 292.

Exhibitions and publications: None.

NOTE TO THIS ENTRY IS ON PAGE 405.

327

Arthur Stone (1847–1938), designer

Charles Brown (active 1912–1937), maker

Dessert spoon

Gardner, Massachusetts, 1912–37
Seth K. Sweetser Fund
1978.264

L. 7¹³⁄₁₆ in. (19.8 cm); W. bowl 1¹³⁄₁₆ in. (4.5 cm); Wt. 2 oz 4 dwt 10 gr (69.1 gm)

Marks: "Stone [with profile of incuse chasing hammer stamped across *St*] / STERLING / B [sideways]" struck on back of handle.

Inscriptions: None.

THE COMBINATION OF a trifid-end handle and a tapering rattail of raised metal down the center of the bowl indicates that the spoon was based on a London-made seventeenth-century prototype.[1]

Description: The trifid upturned-handle spoon was made in two pieces; the bowl is attached with a ridged rattail drop.

History: See cat. no. 292.

Exhibitions and publications: None.

NOTE TO THIS ENTRY IS ON PAGE 405.

328

Arthur Stone (1847–1938), designer

Charles Brown (active 1912–1937), maker

Jelly spoon

Gardner, Massachusetts, 1912–37
Seth K. Sweetser Fund
1978.263

L. 6¹¹⁄₁₆ in. (17.1 cm); W. bowl 1⅜ in. (3.5 cm); Wt. 1 oz 23 gr (32.6 gm)

Marks: "Stone [with profile of incuse chasing hammer across *St*] / STERLING / B [sideways]" struck on back of handle.

Inscriptions: None.

Description: The straight-handle spoon has engraved lines that follow and outline the contours of its handles. The arrow-shaped end is pierced to enclose an engraved bunch of grapes.

History: See cat. no. 292.

Exhibitions and publications: None.

330

Arthur Stone (1847–1938), designer

George P. Blanchard (active 1906–1909), maker

Tea strainer

Gardner, Massachusetts, 1906–9
Seth K. Sweetser Fund
1978.245

H. 1⁹⁄₁₆ in. (3.9 cm); L. 6⅞ in. (17.6 cm); Diam. strainer 2³⁄₁₆ in. (5.5 cm); Wt. 1 oz 11 dwt 4 gr (48.5 gm)

Marks: "STERLING / Stone [with profile of incuse chasing hammer stamped across *St*] / B" struck on bottom.

Inscriptions: None.

GEORGE PORTER BLANCHARD specialized in spoonmaking in Stone's shop between 1906 and 1909.[1] When he left Stone's employ, he opened his own shop with his two sons, Richard and Porter George Blanchard.[2]

Description: The raised tea strainer has a shallow circular bowl that is pierced with dots and lines within an engraved ten-pointed star. The longer handle is straight, with a spatulate end; the other has a narrow neck that opens onto a round end.

History: See cat. no. 292.

Exhibitions and publications: None.

NOTES TO THIS ENTRY ARE ON PAGE 405.

329

Arthur Stone (1847–1938), designer

Charles Brown (active 1912–1937), maker

Tea strainer

Gardner, Massachusetts, 1914–15
Seth K. Sweetser Fund
1978.244

H. 1½ in. (3.8 cm); L. 8⅛ in. (20.5 cm); Diam. strainer 2¹¹⁄₁₆ in. (6.9 cm); Wt. 1 oz 15 dwt 9 gr (55 gm)

Marks: "Stone [with profile of incuse chasing hammer stamped across *St*] / STERLING / B [sideways]" struck on bottom.

Inscriptions: None.

HERMAN GLENDENNING recalled that this strainer was made about 1914 or 1915.

Description: The raised tea strainer has a circular bowl pierced with dots arranged in an eight-pointed star; an engraved line forms a border on one of the handles, which is foliate shaped; the other is pointed and similarly engraved.

History: See cat. no. 292.

Exhibitions and publications: None.

331

Arthur Stone (1847–1938), designer
George C. Erickson (1896–1991), maker

Sugar spoon

Gardner, Massachusetts, 1918–32
Seth K. Sweetser Fund
1978.265

L. 6⅛ in. (15.5 cm); W. bowl 1⅜ in. (3.5 cm); Wt. 19 dwt 1 gr
(29.6 gm)

Marks: "Stone [with profile of incuse chasing hammer across *St*] /
STERLING / E" struck on back of handle.

Inscriptions: None.

GEORGE C. ERICKSON was one of Stone's few assistants capable of fine chasing work, yet he excelled in flatware above all else.[1] Erickson concentrated on producing flatware after Stone's designs from 1918 to 1932, at which time he went into business for himself in Gardner, Massachusetts, presumably as a result of the economic strain of the Depression on Stone's business.[2] Erickson's grandson Peter (b. 1951) continues to produce flatware and jewelry in Gardner, using his grandfather's tools.[3]

Description: The sugar spoon has an oval handle decorated with an engraved floral design, which was accented with saw-piercing.

History: See cat. no. 292.

Exhibitions and publications: None.

NOTES TO THIS ENTRY ARE ON PAGE 405.

332

Mary P. Winlock (active 1888–1927)

Small ladle

Cambridge, Massachusetts, 1914–27
Gift of Gertrude S. Atwood
1987.73

L. 5⁵⁄₁₆ in. (13.5 cm); W. bowl 1¹³⁄₁₆ in. (4.5 cm); Wt. 1 oz 4 dwt 3 gr
(37.5 gm)

Marks: "M. P. W. STERLING" struck incuse on back of handle.

Inscriptions: None.

THIS ENAMEL-DECORATED SPOON is a rare survival by Mary P. Winlock. A student of Denman Ross's design courses in the summer of 1899, Winlock also trained in the shop of George Gebelein, becoming one of several talented women who chose metalworking as a career.[1] In 1901 Winlock became a craftsman member of the Society of Arts and Crafts, Boston, achieving master status in 1920. She participated in the Handicraft Shop cooperative from 1903, exhibiting work at the society in 1907 as a jewelry and metalwork designer. From 1901 to 1927, Winlock also maintained a studio at 59 Langdon Street in Cambridge, Massachusetts.[2] Like many of the female decorative artists of her era, she produced designs for book covers, illustrations, bookplates, and posters.[3]

Description: The small ladle has a shallow, hammered, hemispherical bowl, with a notch at the point of attachment to the handle. The cut-out handle has a rounded tip whose interior is pierced and decorated with a red enameled strawberry design.

History: Descended in the family of silversmith George C. Gebelein, who worked with Winlock at Handicraft Shop. Purchased from the estate of J. Herbert Gebelein, George Gebelein's son, with funds provided by Gertrude Atwood.

Exhibitions and publications: None.

NOTES TO THIS ENTRY ARE ON PAGE 405.

Notes

250

1. Jeannine Falino, in Kirkham 2000, 223, fn. 2.

2. Janet Kardon, ed., *The Ideal Home, 1900–1920: The History of Twentieth-Century American Craft* (New York: Harry N. Abrams in association with the American Craft Museum, 1993), 237, 249; Kaplan 1987, 270, cat. no. 131.

3. *Museum of Fine Arts Twenty-Sixth Annual Report of the School* (1902), 16; *School of the Museum of Fine Arts: Thirtieth Annual Report* (1906), 10.

4. Providence 1901, 37, cat. no. 175; AIC 1902, 22, cat. nos. 163–72; AIC 1903, 16, cat. nos. 58–100; Isabel McDougall, "Some Recent Arts and Crafts Work," *The House Beautiful* 14 (June/November 1903), 69–75; AIC 1904, 17, cat. nos. 78–126; Louisiana Purchase 1904, 70, cat. nos. 58–64; Detroit 1905; AIC 1905, 16, cat. nos. 76–127; AIC 1906, 18, cat. nos. 103–11; AIC 1907, 21, cat. nos. 139–54; SACB 1907, 22, cat. nos. 346–54, 36, cat. nos. 591–93; Cleveland 1908, cat. nos. 56–90; AIC 1910, cat. nos. 270–76.

5. Frances Lawrence Barnum (b. 1874) m. Arthur Lawrence Smith, June 8, 1904. Carson exhibited under her married name for the first time in 1910 and was married to Amos N. Barron by this date, as proved by the Ohio Census of 1910 (Ohio 1910 Census Miracode Index, Ancestry.com). Ulehla 1981, 25.

6. AIC 1904, cat. no. 111; AIC 1905, cat. nos. 76–77. Prices for the servers were not published in the catalogue but rather added in an unknown hand.

[no notes on 251]

252

1. Archives of the Society of Arts and Crafts, Boston, Archives of American Art, Boston Public Library.

2. Henry W. Belknap, "Jewelry and Enamels," *Craftsman* 4 (June 1903), 178–81; Irene Sargent, "The Worker in Enamel, with Special Reference to Miss Elizabeth Copeland," *The Keystone* 27 (February 1906), 193–96; Lillian Leslie Tower, "Rich Designs for Metal Jewelry Boxes," *Craftsman* 21 (December 1911), 321–32.

3. Ulehla 1981, 59. Copeland also lived in Bedford, Mass., before establishing herself in Boston.

4. Robert Judson Clark, *The Arts and Crafts Movement in America* (Princeton, N.J.: Princeton University Press, 1972), 26; Kaplan 1987, 268, no. 129; Janet Kardon, ed., *The Ideal Home, 1900–1920* (New York: Harry N. Abrams in association with the American Craft Museum, 1993), 57, 62, 187, 239; Meyer 1997, 210, cat. nos. 35, 57.

5. Death Certificate, Massachusetts Dept. of Vital Statistics.

253

1. Robert Alan Green, "The Miniatures of Currier and Roby," *Silver Magazine* 11, no. 4 (July/August 1978), 6–11.

2. Some four years after Currier's death, the Currier firm absorbed George A. Henckel and Company and later became a division of Elgin Silversmith Company, Inc., which closed in 1976. See Rainwater 1998, 83–84.

3. See, for example, his pamphlets *Folding Spoons* and *Marks of Early American Silversmiths, with Notes on Silver, Spoon Types, and List of New York City Silversmiths, 1815–1841* (Portland, Me.: Southworth-Anthoensen Press, 1938); and "A Word on Reproductions of Old Silver," from *Timely Trade Topics* in *The Jewelers' Circular* (December 15, 1927), reprinted in *Silver* 16, no. 1 (January/February 1983), 10–16.

4. Bennett W. Trupin to Mrs. Yves Henry (Kathryn C.) Buhler, January 26, 1983, department files, Art of the Americas. See also Bennett Trupin, "Additional Information on Currier & Roby, Inc. Silversmiths," *Silver Magazine* 16, no. 3 (May/June 1983), 8–14; "Currier & Roby, Inc.: Silversmiths," *Silver Magazine* 16, no. 1 (January/February 1983): 8–10. Trupin also donated books from Currier's library and some of his drawings to the Museum of the City of New York.

5. See photocopies of plate ills. from Bennett Trupin's files, as well as a copy of the working drawing for this model, department files, Art of the Americas.

254

1. Ulehla 1984, 76. Information about Ek and other craftsmen associated with the society can be gleaned from the society's archives. In 1907 Ek exhibited a hammered silver bowl at the Art Institute of Chicago's contemporary craft exhibition. On Ek's workshop affiliations in the Boston area, see also Jeannine Falino, "Circles of Influence: Metalsmithing in New England," in Meyer 1997, 75, 85. Ek's Astoria, Ore., silver workshop was located at 130 Lincoln Street.

255

1. SACB 1907, 37, cat. nos. 614–20.

256

1. Leighton 1976. J. Herbert Gebelein, "George C. Gebelein and the Arts and Crafts Movement," *Silver Magazine* 18, no. 4 (July/August 1985), 22–28.

2. This piece entered the Museum's collection with its original Gebelein shop inventory tag, which included the following: "A5108/ made by GCG" and, on the reverse, "JHG pers" (indicating that it belonged to J. Herbert Gebelein personally), above "TEK," later covered by "DKK."

257

1. Department files, Art of the Americas.

2. This form has been compared with the kantharos, a classic Greek wine cup; see Irene Sargent, "Examples of 17th- and 18th-Century Domestic Silver with Interpretations of Same by George Christian Gebelein," *The Keystone* (September 1922), 131 (later reprinted as a Gebelein brochure).

3. Leighton 1976, 92.

4. See documentation in department files, Art of the Americas, as well as a copy of a period photograph from the Gebelein archives listing the price for this "solid gold bowl" as $150 and its weight as "55 dwts." Although the piece is marked "18 K," family records repeatedly indicate that it is made of "20–22 kt" gold.

258

1. The significance of the date and other biographical facts were confirmed by Susan Hill Dolan, Northeast Regional Historic Resources Manager, The Trustees of Reservations, which manages the Stevens-Coolidge Place in North Andover, Mass. The home, which the couple acquired from Helen's older sister Gertrude, was remodeled by the Coolidges in the Colonial Revival style between 1914 and 1918. The Coolidges were living on Commonwealth Ave., not far from the Gebelein shop, in April of 1918, as they had recently returned from Europe and their North Andover residence was not finished until that June.

259

1. See Buhler 1972, cat. no. 384; and MFA 1906, cat. no. 285, ill. opp. 84. This service relates to an original Gebelein drawing in the Winterthur Museum collection (94x1.92) of an urn-shaped fluted service featuring a teapot, coffeepot, and covered sugar bowl with flame finials. The pots have wooden handles with tendril thumbgrips. This later set appears to be the same as the Museum's except the Winterthur illustration lacks the square plinth under the round foot; the bright cutting differs slightly as well. Winterthur preserves many of Gebelein's extant drawings. Another tea set, presumably made to order in 1920 and 1927, after a Revere teapot in the Museum's collection, is in Kaplan 1987, cat. no. 65, and was sold at Christie's, New York, sale 1003, January 19, 2002, lot 217.

2. See, for example, Buhler 1972, cat. nos. 414–46.

3. Jacob Hurd's teakettle on stand is the only published example of this form made in New England in the colonial period; see Buhler 1972, cat. no. 543.

4. Alexandra Deutsch discusses how Gebelein was able to sustain his business by combining handwrought wares with machine production; see Deutsch 1995.

5. Kaplan 1987, 179.

6. Deborah Federhen, "From Artisan to Entrepreneur: Paul Revere's Silver Shop Operation," in *Paul Revere* 1988, 77.

260

1. Leighton 1976, 65–77.

2. See department files, Art of the Americas, for family history of set.

3. Leighton 1976, 52, 105.

261

1. Gebelein's son Arthur D. Gebelein provided an extensive written account about the fabrication of silver-lined copper bowls and their significance in Boston culture at this time; see department files, Art of the Americas.

2. See photocopies of company brochures provided by Dave Thomas of Gebelein Silversmiths in East Arlington, Vt. Despite Gebelein's claims about the uniqueness of his wares, Kalo Shop of Chicago also produced silver-lined copper bowls that were equally popular; Darling 1977, 45.

3. The details of fabrication were supplied by Arthur D. Gebelein; see department files, Art of the Americas; and also Deutsch 1995, 47–48.

4. Some of the records, tools, and artifacts from the Gebelein shop are at the Henry Ford Museum in Dearborn, Mich.

262

1. Gyllenberg had a bench at Handicraft Shop in Wellesley at 392 Washington St. in 1906–7.

2. Ulehla 1984, 97.

3. Meyer 1997, 75–76.

4. SACB 1907, cat. no. 649B, 38. See also catalogues to the annual exhibitions in Boston and Chicago between 1907 and 1914.

5. Handon Thomas, "Art in Every-day Life," *International Studio* 79, no. 323 (April 1924), 77–78; A. W. K., "The Society of Arts and Crafts, Boston," *American Magazine of Art* 17 (October 1926), 543–44. Gyllenberg and Swanson's collaborative efforts are noted in "The Society of Arts and Crafts, Boston," *American Magazine of Art* 17 (October 1926), 543–44. Swanson is listed as working in Handicraft Shop until 1927; Meyer 1997, 76.

6. *Bulletin of the Society of Arts and Crafts, Boston* 10, no. 6 (October 1926), n.p.

7. See Rosalie Berberian, "The Society of Arts and Crafts of Boston and Its Master Silversmiths," *Arts and Crafts Quarterly* 4, no. 1 (winter 1991), 23.

263

1. Students in this department studied jewelrymaking and silversmithing; Meyer 1997, 82.

2. Meyer 1997, 73.

3. Meyer 1997, 83.

4. SACB 1907, cat. nos. 265–68, 662–64.

264

1. Darling 1977, 55. See also Thomas Maher, *The Jarvie Shop: The Candlesticks and Metalwork of Robert R. Jarvie* (Philmont, N.Y.: Turn of the Century Editions, 1997).

2. One notable commission was a grand punch bowl ordered by Chicago Art Institute president Charles Hutchinson for the Cliff Dwellers Club of Chicago in 1910. See Darling 1977, 61.

3. Provenance provided by ARK Antiques.

4. *Art and Progress* 5 (June 1914), 369.

5. Compare with MFA 1906, cat. nos. 252–55, pl. XVIII; MFA 1911, cat. nos. 901–3.

6. Compare with MFA 1906, cat. no. 194, pl. XVIII. See department files, Art of the Americas.

265

1. Darling 1977, 45–55; Elyse Zorn Karlin, *Jewelry and Metalwork in the Arts and Crafts Tradition* (Atglen, Pa.: Schiffer Publishing, 1993), 240; and Kirkham 2000, 229. Swedish immigrant Julius Randahl (cat. no. 277) also trained under Welles.

2. For a 1939 *Chicago Tribune* description lauding the versatility of the wares, see Darling 1977, 53.

3. Darling 1977, 48, 50.

266

1. Clara Welles turned the workshop over to employees Robert R. Bower, Arne Myhre, Yngve Olsson, and Daniel P. Pederson, who continued to create the now-classic pieces, after their mentor's designs; Darling 1977, 48–49, 84. See also Robert Judson Clark, *The Arts and Crafts Movement in America* (Princeton: Princeton University Press, 1972), 76.

2. Kirkham 2000, 229.

[no notes on 267]

268

1. Ulehla 1981, 107.

269

1. A "May C. Knight" was recorded as a graduate of the Drexel Day School, earning a diploma in Design and Decoration in 1897. Drexel Institute of Technology, Day College Recipients of Certificates, Diplomas, and Degrees, 1893–1948 (typescript, Publications Department, Drexel Institute of Technology, November 1, 1948), 12. Mary Knight, artist questionnaire, Society of Arts and Crafts, Boston, Archives of American Art, Smithsonian Institution. Drexel professor Mary C. Ware (later Dennett) was a former Museum School student who, during a trip abroad, rediscovered the art of making Spanish and Italian leather wall hangings. Upon her return to Boston, she practiced leatherworking and briefly held a leadership role in the SACB. Handicraft Shop may have originated with her Somerset Street workshop. *American Biographical Library* (Salt Lake City, Utah: Ancestry Inc., 1996), records 6614–23. On Dennett and Knight, see "Idealism at 'The Handicraft Shop,'" *Providence Sunday Journal*, June 25, 1905.

2. An example of pierced and punched border decoration by "Miss Mary B. Knight of Boston" is illustrated in "Arts and Crafts," *The House Beautiful* 38, no. 11 (November 1915), 184. That Knight did all the decorative work is borne out in the 1905 article "Idealism at 'The Handicraft Shop,'" which stated "while she does the designing and decorating and has an oversight of the shop, she is also able to execute her designs and works in the shop with the rest."

3. *Catalogue, Second Annual Exhibition of Applied Arts* (Detroit: Detroit Museum of Art, 1905), 11.

4. In the 1905 Arts and Crafts exhibition in Chicago, cat. nos. 230–32 were made by Frans Gyllenberg, and Mary Knight was credited as designer; cat. no. 233 was made by Leinonen and designed by Knight; cat. nos. 251–54—a coffeepot, sugar bowl, creamer, and tray made of "tooled silver"—were credited entirely to Knight; AIC 1905, 25, 27.

5. For a vessel marked by Leinonen and ornamented with a punched design in Knight's style, see Rosalie Berberian, "The Society of Arts and Crafts of Boston and Its Master Silversmiths," *Arts & Crafts Quarterly Magazine* 4, no. 1 (1991), 17, fig. 2.

270

1. F. Scott Braznell, in Kaplan 1987, 273, cat. nos. 134–36; Jeannine Falino, in Meyer 1997, 75, fn. 13.

2. Karl F. Leinonen, membership form, Archives, Society of Arts and Crafts, Archives of American Art, Smithsonian Institution. Obituary, *Boston Daily Globe*, December 7, 1957, 16.

3. AIC 1903, cat. no. 237; Louisiana Purchase 1904, 81, cat. nos. 302–11; AIC 1905, cat. nos. 233–35; AIC 1906, cat. no. 306; AIC 1908, cat. nos. 394–98; Cleveland 1908, cat. nos. 201–2; AIC 1909, cat. nos. 315–16; AIC 1910, cat. nos. 715–24; Boston Tercentenary 1930, cat. nos. 109.56, 109.251, 109.2, 109.70, 109.244, 109.245.

4. Meyer 1997, 75.

5. Undated ad for auction by Sanders & Mock Associates, held June 17, 1988; the Leinonen porringer was misattributed to Gebelein; department files, Art of the Americas.

271

1. See Ward and Ward 1979, cat. nos. 54, 85; and Kaplan 1987, cat. nos. 135, 273.

272

1. Thanks are offered to Susan Oakes Peabody, Jon Peabody, and Edith Alpers for sharing their observations on Oakes's career. Most of the bio-graphical information is from Anne Webb Karnaghan, "Edward E. Oakes: Master Craftsman, Maker of Hand-wrought Jewelry," *American Magazine of Art* 17, no. 12 (December 1926), 625–29; Edith Alpers, "Edward Everett Oakes (1891–1960), a Craftsman from Boston, Massachusetts," *Jewellery Studies* 3 (1989), 73–79; and Meyer 1997, 226. For two brooches by Oakes in the Museum's collection, see 1986.764 and 1986.265.

2. G. H. C., "Silver and Precious Stones Make an Exquisite Jewel Casket," *Boston Evening Transcript*, October 16, 1929, pt. 3, 7. A matching pair of candlesticks was fashioned about 1952 by Oakes, with assistance from his son Gilbert.

3. Quotation from G. H. C., "Silver and Precious Stones." The artist completed his final payment for the gemstones in 1945.

4. Oakes's legacy was carried on by his son Gilbert and by Gilbert's daughter Susan Oakes Peabody (b. 1950) and her husband, Jon R. Peabody (b. 1944). Each has employed a variant of the Oakes mark so as to distinguish their work from that of Edward Everett Oakes.

273

1. Helen Porter Philbrick, "Franklin Porter, Silversmith (1869–1935)," *Essex Institute Historical Collections* 105, no. 3 (July 1969), 145–215. Porter's personal papers and financial records are at the Peabody Essex Museum, Salem, Mass.

2. A similar service sold at Northeast Auctions, Manchester, N.H., May 18–19, 2002, lot 3.

[no notes on 274]

275

1. SACB 1899, 25, cat. letters "o" through "p." Sacker's school was also called "School of Miss Amy Sacker"; Nancy Findlay, *Artists of the Book in Boston, 1890–1910* (Cambridge: Houghton Library, 1985), 103; William Robinson et al., *Transformations in Cleveland Art, 1796–1946: Community and Diversity in Modern America* (Cleveland: Cleveland Museum of Art, 1996), 166–71, 234–35.

2. Untitled article, probably *Cleveland Plain Dealer*, about August 1928, library files, Cleveland Museum of Art.

3. Grace V. Kelly, "Launch Scholarship Project as Tribute to Horace Potter," *Cleveland Plain Dealer*, Sunday, December 12, 1948.

4. AIC 1905, 36–37, cat. nos. 373–406; AIC 1906, 36–77, cat. nos. 399–417; J. A. Wadovick, "H. E. Potter's Craftsmanship Carves Place in Art History," *Cleveland Plain Dealer*, February 24, 1947; Ulehla 1981, 176.

5. Cleveland 1908, cat. nos. 254–87; untitled article, probably *Cleveland Plain Dealer*.

6. *ARK Antiques: Catalogue 94-1* (New Haven: ARK Antiques, 1994), cat. no. 7; *Affirmation and Rediscovery, a Centennial Exhibition and Sale, Objects from the Society of Arts & Crafts, Boston* (Boston: JMW Gallery, 1997), cat. nos. 145–46.

7. *Affirmation and Rediscovery*, cat. no. 143; Cleveland 1908, cat. nos. 254–87.

276

1. Telephone conversation with William Howe McElwain, December 10, 1996; with David McElwain, December 1996.

2. Scrapbook, School of the Museum of Fine Arts, Boston, vol. 8, 25; SACB 1925, 9, cat. nos. 115–19; Kaplan 1987, 180–81, cat. no. 66; Meyer 1997, 76, 82, 228.

3. Telephone conversation with Paul Banevicius, Art Department, Beaver Country Day School, January 6, 1997.

4. Gebelein two-handled porringer, Museum, Rhode Island School of Design, acc. no. 1985.202. For a pair of porringers by Pratt, see *ARK Antiques: Catalogue 93-1* (New Haven: ARK Antiques, 1993), cat. no. 49.

5. *Harvard Twenty-fifth Anniversary Report of Class of 1921* (Cambridge: Harvard University Printing Office, 1946), 466.

277

1. For an account of Randahl's companies and associations, see Darling 1977, 84–88. Randahl's two sons operated the business through the Cellini Shop, a retail store in Evanston, and Randahl Jewelers in Park Ridge, Ill. See Rainwater 1998, 69, 256.

2. See photocopies of Randahl Company literature in the department files, which were provided by W. Scott Braznell.

278

1. Elenita Chickering, Stone's great niece, has published extensively on her uncle's production and legacy; see esp. Chickering 1994. See the Stone archives at the MFA for correspondence documenting his work as a chaser at James Dixon and Sons in Sheffield from 1875 to 1884.

2. The Stones were married on June 2, 1896.

3. Newspaper clipping in Stone scrapbook by Henry P. Macomber, "Tomorrow an Antique, but Today It Is Art," *Boston Transcript* (November 19 [no year]), 6. Department files, Art of the Americas.

4. *Bulletin of the Society of Arts and Crafts* 10, no. 2 (March 1926), n.p.

5. Kirkham 2000, 230–31, 234–35.

6. See Stone archive, department files, Art of the Americas.

7. The study collection includes Stone's silversmithing tools, consisting of four hammers that he forged to meet specialized needs; his 120-volume reference library; account books; manuscript materials; design drawings; his Master Craftsman's gown; and four medals awarded. The hammers are illustrated in Chickering 1994, figs. 19, 24. The medals include Stone's Society of Arts and Crafts, Boston, medal; a silver medal from the Louisiana Purchase Exposition; a Boston Tercentenary Medal; and an Allied Relief Fund Medal from World War I.

8. On the continuation of the business and marks, see Glendenning 1973, 28, and Chickering 1994, 182. Windsor C. Robinson has also engaged in original archival research on individuals in the silversmith trade in Gardner, Mass. His generosity in sharing this information is gratefully acknowledged.

9. Annie Priest was engaged to a Bent cousin who died during the influenza epidemic of 1918. Although not a blood relative, the Stones considered her family.

279

1. Beverly Kay Brandt, "'Sturdy usefulness, exquisite perfection and restful beauty . . .': A Study of the Life, Philosophy, and Work of Arthur J. Stone, Silversmith (1847–1938)" (unpublished manuscript, 1980), 9. Howard & Company was located at 264 Fifth Ave. in New York City and also had offices in Newport, R.I., and London.

2. See Stone archive, department archives, Art of the Americas.

3. It is likely that some, if not all, of these miniatures were exhibited at the memorial exhibition "Silver by Arthur John Stone," Worcester Art Museum (May 28–June 18, 1941). No. 37 on the checklist describes "toys and other small objects" lent anonymously. See the Stone archive for Stone's scrapbook as well as a line drawing of the winged rocking chair.

[no notes on 280–88]

289

1. See Stone archive, folder 2, department files, Art of the Americas.

2. The 1901 date for this piece was assigned by Chickering 1994, 96. Herman Glendenning, "Arthur Stone, Master Craftsman, Dean of American Silversmiths, 1847–1938," *Silver Magazine* 6, no. 5 (September/October 1973), 28.

3. Chickering 1994, 96.

4. After his stroke, Stone hired Andrew Walker and Edward Billings to chase his work; see Chickering 1994, 31. The Museum also has another, more modest compote (1978.242) that was raised by Herman Glendenning in 1925.

290

1. An entry in Stone's guestbook firmly dates this piece to 1903; Stone archive, department files, Art of the Americas. On his awards, see May R. Spain, *The Society of Arts and Crafts* (Boston: Society of Arts and Crafts, 1924), 18. Stone's silver medal is in the Museum's collection; correspondence with members of the exposition committee is in the Stone archive at the MFA. Stone received a certificate of commendation for his four submissions to this exhibition, which also included a Georgian salt spoon, quaigh with base, and the crocus compote (cat. no. 289).

2. Chickering 1994, 10.

291

1. Chickering 1994, 98.

2. A bowl in the Museum's collection (1978.255; not included in this catalogue), raised by Herman Glendenning, was intended as part of a set of six ordered by a client. According to Glendenning, Andrew Walker made an error when dividing the vessel's flutes. (Walker was responsible for chasing wares after Stone's stroke in 1926.) Another was made to replace it, and Stone brought home the unmatched bowl for his family's use. See Glendenning's notes, department files, Art of the Americas.

292

1. See Glendenning's notes, department files, Art of the Americas. The tray (1978.232b) is not included in this catalogue.

[no notes on 293]

294

1. Chickering 1994, 38.

[no notes on 295–96]

297

1. The initials are those of Annie E. Priest, the Stones' companion.

298

1. The initials are those of Annie E. Priest, the Stones' companion.

[no notes on 299–301]

302

1. See department files, Art of the Americas.

303

1. The 1907 Society of Arts and Crafts catalogue describes a four-piece set,

cat. no. 195 B, as being on loan from Mrs. Bullard. It is listed as having been "designed by Mr. Stone and executed by Mr. Stone and assistants."

2. Florence E. Bullard to Stone, October 12, 1906; in Stone archive, folder 8, department files, Art of the Americas. Stone's guestbook includes some entries, probably written by his wife, that list his work by date. In 1906 a three-piece tea set valued at $290 is identified with Mrs. A. M. Bullard. It is unclear whether this entry is an error that should read "four-piece set." It is also possible that the service was added to over time or that Mrs. Bullard commissioned another tea set during this same period.

[no notes on 304]

305

1. See undated (probably about 1930) promotional brochure "Wedding Silver" in Stone scrapbook, Stone archive, department files, Art of the Americas.

[no notes on 306]

307

1. Chickering 1994, III.

308

1. Howard 1895, no. 124.

[no notes on 309–12]

313

1. See department files, Art of the Americas.

314

1. See Glendenning notes, department files, Art of the Americas.

315

1. See Glendenning notes, department files, Art of the Americas.

316

1. Chickering 1989, 100; Chickering 1994, 46–47.

2. Chickering 1989, 11.

317

1. See Alma Bent correspondence, department files, Art of the Americas; Glendenning 1973, 27. A 17-inch bowl of the same design is documented as a punch bowl in the Stone archive, department files, Art of the Americas.

318

1. See Glendenning notes, department files, Art of the Americas.

319

1. Chickering 1994, 155.

[no notes on 320]

321

1. See Bent's description of this spoon, department files, Art of the Americas.

2. Chickering 1994, 9.

3. See drawings numbered AS-6-10 through AS-6-13. For comparison, see another spoon with the mistletoe pattern in Chickering 1989, 100, fig. 7.

322

1. See copy of advertisement in Stone scrapbook, Stone archive, Art of the Americas; also noted within is a comparison between this spoon and a pair of ladles (cat. no. 93) made about 1760 by John Burt Lyng that was given to the Museum by Jane Bortman Larus.

[no notes on 323–25]

326

1. See Stone archive, department files, Art of the Americas.

327

1. For a history of the trifid spoon, see Simon Moore, "The Trefid Spoon: Its Importance in the Evolution of British Table Cutlery," *Silver Magazine* 28, no. 6 (November/December 1996), 42–45.

[no notes on 328–29]

330

1. The Art Institute of Chicago's 1910 *Arts and Crafts Exhibition* featured 16 entries (291–306) for various flatware and serving pieces and one napkin ring. These works were designed and made exclusively by Blanchard, who by this time was operating a shop at 192 Pearl St. in Gardner, Mass.

2. For an account of the handwrought silver and pewter made by Porter G. Blanchard and sold by the S. & G. Gump Company of San Francisco, see Louis Stanley Grohs, *The Renaissance of an Ancient Art* (San Francisco: S. & G. Gump, 1930). His son Porter (1886–1973) later distinguished himself as an Arts and Crafts silversmith in California; see Leslie Green Bowman, "Arts and Crafts Silversmiths: Friedell and Blanchard in Southern California," in *Silver in the Golden State: Images and Essays Celebrating the History and Art of Silver in California* (Oakland: Oakland Museum History Department, 1986), 46–48.

331

1. This appraisal was offered by designer Charlotte Bone and recorded by Chickering 1994, 31.

2. Chickering 1994, 46.

3. The close-knit community of silversmiths that grew from Stone's shop is illustrated by the lineage of tools and templates shared among his former staff. When Porter Blanchard moved to California, David Carlson acquired his templates. Following Carlson's death, George Erickson bought all his tools, which his grandson Peter now uses.

332

1. Meyer 1997, 75. For an extensive discussion on this topic, see Kirkham 2000.

2. Uhela 1984, 234.

3. This piece entered the Museum's collection with its original Gebelein shop inventory tag, which included the following: "181" in a circle beside the letters "RKK," which are above "HANDICRAFT." On one side of the tag is written "#24" and, on the opposite side, "WT. 1½ oz." The article is described as "STERLING + ENAMEL HANDMADE BY M. P. W." above the identifying number "B36047L [last letter in circle]." The reverse provides workshop information about Winlock and mentions that she "occupied [the] frontroom," presumably of the Gebelein shop. The society's exhibition catalogues list the various mediums and materials that engaged her creative spirit.

CHAPTER 6

MODERN METALSMITHING IN THE FACTORY AND STUDIO

Jeannine Falino

Surprising changes have swept through the silversmithing industry during the last century. Many of the most successful American silver companies of 1900 are today either defunct or scarcely recognizable as divisions of large conglomerates. At the same time, independent artists have survived and prospered. Moreover, women have strengthened their position in this traditionally male craft and now dominate the field. Within this same period, the silversmith has evolved from colonial craftsman to modern artist, as is true in all craft media in the twentieth and twenty-first centuries.

By the 1920s, makers and consumers of silver objects favored historical styles, a phenomenon true for most decorative arts during the conservative postwar period. Arts and crafts practitioners relied on the Colonial Revival style, which was best known through the work of George Christian Gebelein (cat. no. 259). Among silver manufacturers, a reductive, columnar Neoclassicism came into vogue, as seen in a candy dish designed in the mid-1920s by Erik Magnussen (cat. no. 340). Larger firms such as Gorham Manufacturing Company and Tiffany & Co. offered a smorgasbord of designs drawn from Rococo, Colonial, or Federal sources; few such pastiches are memorable today.

The lack of modernity in American design is said to have prevented the participation of the United States in France's Exposition internationale des arts décoratifs et industriels modernes of 1925. Herbert Hoover, then secretary of commerce, declined the planners' invitation on the grounds that American designers did not demonstrate the "new inspiration and real originality" expected of participants.[1] Yet by that date, the seeds of modernism had been sown in this country. Indeed, the dissemination of the style was encouraged through exhibitions organized by the Metropolitan Museum of Art between 1917 and 1929.[2] Such shows celebrated American industrial arts as expressed in architecture, interior design, and decorative arts and elevated the role of the industrial designer while relegating the craftsman to relative anonymity.

A selection from the French exposition arrived on American shores soon after the show closed in Paris, giving the American public their first taste of European modern design.[3] Some of the fair exhibitors, such as Edgar Brandt, established retail shops in Manhattan, furthering their penetration into American society.

Nevertheless, American consumers remained conservative. In 1925 Gorham gambled on modern design and public taste, hiring Danish artist Erik Magnussen to serve as creative director. Magnussen's Cubic pattern made a powerful statement about the modernity of the firm's wares, but it confused the public and was soon retracted as an example of "Fine Art" that was "intended merely for exhibition."[4] The Modern American design (cat. no. 341) that followed was a retreat into soothing neoclassicism that enjoyed a more favorable response.

Modern design reform, as featured in the Metropolitan Museum of Art exhibitions and the "Good Design" and "Useful Objects" series at the Museum of Modern Art during the 1930s and 1940s, was considered by the press to exert a positive influence on manufacturers and consumers. The success of these programs inspired the Institute of Contemporary Art in Boston to create a Design in Industry department in 1948. As part of this initiative, the institute launched a program to bring together manufacturers and young craftspeople through an innovative collaboration that organizers hoped would yield innovative, marketable ideas. In 1949 silver manufacturer Reed & Barton, of Taunton, Massachusetts, invited five craftsmen to consult on and create new designs. The results were marketed in 1950 as "the contemporary group," aimed at young households during the economic boom that followed World War II.[5]

Such collaborative projects form part of a brief period, from the late 1940s through the 1950s, when artists became allied with industry as designer-craftsmen, a term used to describe individuals who, because of their creative silversmithing skills, were called upon to develop designs for application in industry. One such designer-craftsman was Earl Pardon, who was hired by Towle Manufacturing Company at the behest of metalsmith Margret Craver, wife of company president Charles Withers. Pardon spent most of his career teaching at Skidmore College; his own work focused on enamel jewelry, which he used to good effect at Towle. His Contempra House flatware (cat. no. 369) sports turquoise enamel at the heel of each handle, which was protected from damage by a thick ferrule. Pardon later made expansive use of enamel in his designs for candy dishes and punch bowls, a popular concept that was produced by competitors Reed & Barton as well as Wallace Silversmiths.

Among the best-known designer-craftsmen was Danish artist John Prip, who first taught at the School for American Craftsmen. Employed by Reed & Barton beginning in 1957, Prip developed several designs, including the Dimension pattern (cat. no. 354) and the richly textured Tapestry flatware. A veteran silversmith, Prip had grown up on the shop floor working with his silver manufacturing family in Denmark, and he proved to be a natural for this type of arrangement.

Despite these innovative collaborations, the American silversmithing industry was shrinking by the 1950s and 1960s. Midcentury housewives, most of whom lacked servants, considered polishing and maintaining silver to be onerous work. Moreover, as the price of the raw material rose, silver became the target of theft. The cost of manufacturing increased as well, and stainless steel appeared as an affordable substitute for silver and silver plate, cutting into market share. Consequently, consumption of manufactured silver dropped precipitously throughout the 1960s and 1970s. Many reputable manufacturers either closed their doors or were absorbed into larger corporations with offshore production facilities.[6]

Nevertheless, the few remaining independent firms, such as Reed & Barton and Lunt Silversmiths, continue a robust operation. Tiffany & Co. in the 1990s introduced a line of electroformed pitchers that emulates inexpensive pottery of the 1930s and 1940s, an unusual step for a company associated with high-style forms but one that has proved appealing to customers. Strengthened by the allure of "old Europe," continental firms such as Buccellati and Orfèvrerie Christofle maintain a niche market among affluent buyers in the United States, and the occasional new American firm has attempted to do the same. In the 1980s and 1990s, Swid Powell briefly produced trophies and bold domestic silver, collaborating with such well-known architects as Michael Graves, Robert Venturi, and Richard Meier in the design of limited-edition works.

Although American silver manufacturing is in decline, the imminent demise of the studio craftsman has been greatly exaggerated. Long feared to be near extinction, independent silversmiths have proved to be a hardy lot. Indeed, they have managed to thrive while toiling in the shadow of industry giants.

Education, rather than traditional apprenticeship, has enabled the modern craftsman to continue practicing at the bench. The time-honored method of transferring skills from one generation to the next through apprenticeship became outmoded in the late nineteenth century, when the factory system separated the silversmithing process into many different departments. Fortunately, art schools have since taken the place of apprenticeships, and aspiring craftspeople are able to acquire both a broad artistic education and the necessary skills to compete successfully in the marketplace.

The first such schools were founded at museums, which established them as adjuncts to their institutional missions. The School of the Museum of Fine Arts, Boston, was founded on the model of the South Kensington Museum (now the Victoria and Albert Museum) to teach the principles of skillful design. These schools focused on drawing, painting, and design until the 1890s, when craft-related courses, including metalsmithing, were introduced. However, with the exception of the Cranbrook Academy of Art, founded in 1925 by Detroit philanthropist George Booth, course offerings at most institutions atrophied or remained static while industrial design programs gained ground during the postwar decades.

By 1930 American silversmithing companies and independent silversmiths appeared to be on an equal footing when the American Federation of Arts held an international exhibition of modern textiles and metalwork. Metalwork exhibitors were divided between manufacturers, including Gorham, Reed & Barton, International Silver Company, and Towle Manufacturing Company, and a range of studio artists. Studio silversmiths were represented by such old-guard members as Arthur J. Stone and Laurin H. Martin, whose outdated forms were balanced by the work of newly arrived Danish artist Adda Husted-Andersen, a former colleague of Jean Dunand in Paris, and Peter Müller-Munk, a German-born silversmith and designer. Bostonian Edward Everett Oakes, best known for delicate brooches in an Arts and Crafts style, submitted his greatest achievement, a gem-studded jewelry casket with terraced elements redolent with the aura of Art Deco (cat. no. 272).[7]

Regrettably, the exhibition took place nearly a year into the Great Depression, and purchases of costly silver were few. As the economy began to revive in 1937, an exhibition entitled "Contemporary Industrial and Handwrought Silver" at the Brooklyn Museum brought fresh attention to domestic silver. It marked the first time colonial American silver was shown alongside modern works.[8] As in the 1930 show, it featured a mixture of commercial manufacturers and private silversmiths. Of special note was Native American silver, produced under the direction of the Indian Arts and Crafts Board with the support of its director, René d'Harnoncourt, as well as Mexican silver produced after the designs of American William Spratling. The Native American and pre-Columbian designs found a ready audience among American consumers. Six women were also included (compared to three times as many men), a sizeable group that reflected a trend that began in the Arts and Crafts era, when, for the first time, significant numbers of female artists chose careers in metalsmithing.[9]

Not included in the 1937 exhibition was Margret Craver, a Kansas-born artist who has exerted a lasting influence on the field. Craver came of age at a time when industrial-design programs had begun to replace courses in traditional craft techniques. After graduating from the University of Kansas, she resolved to make her own way in the field. She arranged to work with established artists, including the workshop of Leonard Heinrich, arms and armor conservator at the Metropolitan Museum of Art; Tiffany jeweler Wilson Weir; former Cranbrook professor Arthur Neville Kirk in Detroit; and Stone Associates.[10]

Craver translated these experiences into wartime service with the metal-refining company Handy and Harman. There, as head of their Hospital Services Program, she taught therapeutic metalsmithing to veterans.[11] After the war, she led the company's Craft Service Department, which disseminated useful information to craftsmen. Between 1947 and 1951, she directed summer workshops, known as the Handy and Harman conferences, for aspiring silversmiths who were also educators. Each summer a new group of artists from around the country converged at the conference to hone their skills.[12] These men and women learned to raise silver; built valuable contacts with other artists; and then returned to school, where many directed their own departments. The timing was fortunate, for the GI Bill of 1944 had enabled many universities to expand programs to serve returning veterans.[13] Graduates included Thetis Lemmon, who led the State Industrial College for Women in Dallas, Texas; Virginia Cute and Richard Reinhardt of the University of the Arts in Philadelphia; Fred Miller and John Paul Miller of the Cleveland Art Institute; Alma Eikerman of Indiana University; and Ruth Pennington of the University of Washington, Seattle. Their influence spread as former students began working and teaching across the country, fueling a revival of silversmithing.

An example of the spread of such influence is Carlyle Smith, who had studied metalsmithing with Arts and Crafts professor Augustus Rose at the Rhode Island School of Design. He learned the principles of Arts and Crafts design and craftsmanship and, after graduation, taught manual arts at the grade-school level. In 1947 Smith was appointed professor of metal-

smithing at the University of Kansas. Before moving west, he attended that year's Handy and Harman workshop at the suggestion of Marjorie Whitney, Craver's former professor.

Smith's arrival in Kansas coincided with a period of impressive artistic development in that state. The "Wichita Nationals," an annual exhibition of crafts from around the nation, allowed the new professor and his students to study the latest developments firsthand. Smith maintained high standards of craftsmanship for his students, whose rigorous training prepared them well for graduate studies and employment with silver manufacturers. Although his aesthetic was informed by modern Scandinavian style, Smith encouraged students to follow their own creative path and thus guided some of the best-known metalsmiths of the late twentieth century, including Richard Mawdsley and Brent Kington, professor and professor emeritus at the University of Illinois at Carbondale, and Robert Ebendorf, who taught at the State University of New York at New Paltz.

As at the University of Kansas, many art departments were either created or enlarged to accommodate silversmithing programs. The School for American Craftsmen was founded in 1943 with the support of philanthropist Aileen Osborn Webb.[14] Danish silversmiths John Prip and Hans Christensen, early professors in the program, imparted to their students a Scandinavian aesthetic that held sway for more than a decade. In 1948 at the Cranbrook Academy of Art, Richard Thomas established a rich and rigorous program that has left a continuing legacy. The Rhode Island School of Design was one of the first museum schools; it founded its metalsmithing department in 1901. The school flourished near Gorham before losing momentum, like many programs and companies during the war, due to lack of raw materials. The department was revived in 1963, however, when Prip was hired to lead the program. Prip's exploration of pop and sculptural forms in the 1960s and 1970s opened the door for the metalsmithing of nonfunctional objects, a trend that flourishes today.

Along with an increase in silversmiths came a growth in artworks, and venues for the exhibition and sale of such works soon developed. Aileen Osborn Webb was ahead of her time when, in 1940, she opened America House as a retail arm of the American Craft Council. Another important venue was the "May Show," an exhibition of Ohio art held annually at the Cleveland Museum of Art from 1919 to 1973. The first national craft exhibition took place in 1946 in Wichita, Kansas. Soon artist-craftsmen organizations formed in many states and mounted their own exhibitions. When the Contemporary Craft Museum (now the Museum of Arts & Design) opened in

New York City in 1956, modern craftsmen were at last able to see their work displayed in a dignified setting and accorded the same respect as works in other media.

As these artists, professors, and students settled into teaching positions and independent studios around the country, a clear need arose for a national clearinghouse for ideas, a place where they could exchange techniques and keep abreast of changes in the field. In response, a group of eighteen artists founded the Society for North American Goldsmiths in 1969.[15] The organization has grown rapidly to include more than six thousand individual members and schools.

Recent economic conditions have caused several metalsmithing programs to be discontinued. Yet the public's interest in metalwork and the outlook for the field remain healthy. The chief concern among professors is students' preference for producing jewelry rather than hollowware, which often suffers a lower value in the marketplace compared to other craft media. Raising a vessel can be an expensive endeavor; it requires substantial raw material, deliberate and measured movements, and a sequence that can take days or weeks to complete. The investment rarely yields a substantial return.

During the last fifty years, more than a dozen metalsmithing programs have been founded. Geographically dispersed yet connected through workshops, conferences, and visiting faculty, many have become dynamic centers of activity. Aspiring metalsmiths learn design fundamentals and gain expertise in the technical aspects of metalsmithing. Most important, they contribute to the ongoing dialogue about art in our time. Today that discussion centers on the craft process, gender issues, conspicuous consumption, and the body, often to the detriment of function or form. Silver is not always the primary material of choice, as evidenced by the proliferation of the word "metalsmith." Artists today choose from a wide range of metals and a broad palette of colors and surface treatments to achieve their unique and creative ends.

Notes

1. Karen Davies, *At Home in Manhattan, Modern Decorative Arts, 1925 to the Depression* (New Haven: Yale University Art Gallery, 1983), 11. Hoover's citation is from Janet Kardon, "Craft in the Machine Age," in Janet Kardon, ed., *Craft in the Machine Age, 1920–1945: The History of Twentieth-Century American Craft* (New York: Harry N. Abrams in association with the American Craft Museum, 1995), 25.

2. Christine Wallace Laidlaw, "The Metropolitan Museum of Art and Modern Design: 1917–1929," *Journal of Decorative and Propaganda Arts, 1875–1945* 8 (spring 1988), 88–103; Craig Miller, "Modern Design at the Metropolitan Museum of Art," *Modern Design in the Metropolitan Museum of Art, 1890–1990* (New York: Metropolitan Museum of Art, 1990), 1–45.

3. *A Selected Collection of Objects from the International Exposition of Modern Decorative Arts at Paris 1925* (Washington, D.C.: American Association of Museums, 1925). In 1922 the Newark Museum hosted "Applied Arts of Modern Germany," which was organized by the German Werkbund.

4. Quotations from Gorham Manufacturing Company's *The Modern American* (New York, 1928), cited in Jewel Stern, *Modernism in American Silver: Twentieth Century Design* (New York and London: Dallas Museum of Art in association with Yale University Press, 2005), 30, note 33.

5. W. Scott Braznell, "'New Way of Life': A Candelabrum from Reed & Barton's 'Contemporary Group,'" *Yale University Art Gallery Bulletin, 1997–98*, 77–84. Reed & Barton undertook a similar venture in 1975, when they engaged five contemporary artists to design limited-edition jewelry named "Signature Five"; see Ward and Ward 1979, 89.

6. In late 2002, the Gorham Company, a former subsidiary of the conglomerates Textron and Dansk, was acquired by Brown-Forman of Louisville, Ky., joining Kirk Stieff and Lenox. Economies of scale undoubtedly were achieved by Syratech Corporation of Boston, which absorbed Towle, Wallace silversmiths, International Silver Company, Tuttle, and English manufacturer C. J. Vander before declaring bankruptcy in 2005; Lifetime Brands now owns the American silver firms once held by Syratech and Brown-Forman.

7. *Decorative Metalwork and Cotton Textiles, Third International Exhibition of Contemporary Industrial Art* (New York: American Federation of Arts, 1930–31). Designers included Donald Deskey, Eliel Saarinen, Walter von Nessen, and Russel Wright. The female designer, Belle Kogan, was represented with a covered vegetable dish manufactured by Reed & Barton, although she did not receive credit in the catalogue.

8. *Contemporary Industrial and Handwrought Silver* (Brooklyn, N.Y.: Brooklyn Museum, 1937). "Silver, An Exhibition of Contemporary American Design by Manufacturers, Designers, and Craftsmen," held at the Metropolitan Museum of Art, April 11–May 23, 1927, had a similar roster of participants, albeit with slightly more contemporary artists and no historical silver.

9. The women were Clara B. Welles of Kalo Shop of Chicago; Charlotte Bone, designer for Arthur Stone; Boston artist Rebecca Cauman, who later moved to New York; ecclesiastical silversmith Ilse von Drage; Thetis Lemmon of the State Industrial College for Women in Dallas, Texas; and California jeweler Esther Lewittes. For an assessment of women's role in Arts and Crafts metalsmithing, see Jeannine Falino, "Circles of Influence," in Meyer 1997, and "Women Metalsmiths," in Kirkham 2000, 223–46.

10. Jeannine Falino and Yvonne Markowitz, "Margret Craver, A Foremost 20th-Century Jeweler and Educator," *Jewelry: Journal of the American Soci-*

ety of Jewelry Historians 1 (1996–97), 9–23. By 1936 Kirk had already left Cranbrook, one of the few art programs in the country to offer a metalsmithing program, which closed after his departure.

11. The therapeutic value of metalsmithing is one that several artists have pursued. See W. Scott Braznell, "Silversmithing as a Treatment for Tuberculosis: William Waldo Dodge Jr. and the Beginnings of Gaylord Silvercraft," *Connecticut Historical Society Bulletin* 57, nos. 3/4 (summer/fall 1992), 174–86. Virginia Wireman Cute returned to the field of art therapy when she stepped down from leadership of the Philadelphia Museum School.

12. Falino and Markowitz, "Margret Craver," 15. Craver mounted an exhibition at the Metropolitan Museum of Art in 1949–50 entitled "Form in Handwrought Silver," featuring the work of Handy and Harman graduates.

13. These programs were called National Silversmithing Workshop Conferences. For a discussion of the graduates, see Jeannine Falino, "Metalsmithing at Midcentury," *Sculptural Concerns, Contemporary American Metalworking* (Cincinnati, Ohio: Fort Wayne Museum of Art and the Contemporary Arts Center, 1993), 10–27.

14. "The School for American Craftsmen, New England Division, Hanover, N.H." *Craft Horizons* 4, no. 10 (August 1945), 4–9, 35. The school was first established at Dartmouth College; it was later moved to Alfred, N.Y., and is now located at the Rochester Institute of Technology.

15. For a list of founders, see *The Founding Masters* (Saratoga Springs, N.Y.: Schick Art Gallery and Skidmore College, 1988).

333

Bernard Bernstein (b. 1928)

Elliptical bowl

Rochester, New York, 1960
Gift of the artist
2000.941

H. 5⁵⁄₁₆ in. (13.5 cm); W. 8⁵⁄₁₆ in. (21 cm); D. 6⅛ in. (15.5 cm); Wt. 23 oz 16 dwt 4 gr (740.5 gm)

Marks: "B. BERNSTEIN / 1960" engraved; "STERLING" in sans-serif letters and "BB," in angular figure-eight shape, struck on base, near center point.

Inscriptions: None.

New York artist Bernard Bernstein is a 1963 graduate of the School for American Craftsmen at the Rochester Institute of Technology. He has been a working silversmith, teacher, and writer for more than forty years. As a young craftsman, Bernstein's work was accepted in two national exhibitions, beginning with the groundbreaking "Young Americans," held at the Museum of Contemporary Arts (now the Museum of Arts & Design) in 1958, and the 1959 "Fiber-Clay-Metal" exhibition in St. Paul, Minnesota.[1] His early work consisted of jewelry and some domestic hollowware, as seen in this elliptical bowl; over time he specialized in religious and academic silver. He fashioned a mace for the City College of New York and many examples of Judaica for synagogues nationwide. A torah crown and a pair of torah finials are in the permanent collection of the Renwick Gallery, Smithsonian American Art Museum.

From 1962 to 1988, Bernstein taught in the Department of Industrial Education at the City College of New York. Since then, he has held Judaica silversmithing workshops at the Ninety-second Street YMCA.[2]

This work was produced at a key moment when Bernstein was studying for his master's degree at the School for American Craftsmen, under the guidance of Hans Christensen (1924–1983), professor of metalsmithing. With its swooping lip and softly curving sides, the bowl owes a debt to the aesthetics of midcentury Scandinavian silver as taught by his Danish-born professor.

An elliptical vessel, with its sharply delineated shoulder, is more challenging to produce than spherical forms. Even more difficult was the ogee-shaped foot ring on this example, which Bernstein chose to fabricate rather than follow Christensen's suggestion to use a scroll saw to cut the shape from sheet metal.[3] These aesthetic and technical choices were based in Bernstein's desire to set a high standard for his work, regardless of the time and effort required. His viewpoint echoes the sentiments of Arts and Crafts silversmiths, who often chose more difficult construction techniques, believing these were more in keeping with preindustrial standards.

Description: The raised elliptical bowl has a gently curved rim with a thick applied molding at edge. A concave neck descends from the rim, turning outward to an angled shoulder that curves down to an elliptical fabricated foot ring composed of ogee sections.

History: The artist retained this vessel until making it a gift in 2000.

Exhibitions and publications: None.

NOTES TO THIS ENTRY ARE ON PAGE 457.

334

Robert A. Butler (b. 1955)

Animal bowl

Northeast, New York, 1990
Anonymous gift
1990.604a–b

H. 8½ in. (21.6 cm); W. 12½ in. (31.8 cm); D. 8 in. (20. 3 cm); Wt. 31 oz 12 dwt (2630.4 gm)

Marks: "[thistle] / STERLING [in incuse sans-serif letters] / R A BUTLER [within shaped cartouche] / NY / 1990" struck on underside. "RAB [within shaped cartouche] / STERLING [in incuse sans-serif letters] / [thistle]" struck inside lid.

Inscriptions: None.

As a silversmith who came of age in the last quarter of the twentieth century, Robert Butler focuses on formal hollowware, an unusual choice in a generation that has generally favored jewelry as the primary form of expression. From 1972 to 1976, Butler studied with silversmith Michael Murray in London and registered his "RAB" mark at Goldsmiths' Hall. Upon his return to the United States about 1976, Butler worked briefly at Gebelein Silversmiths in Boston and soon established his own workshop.[1]

This elegant vessel, the sole commission of contemporary American silver ordered by the Museum, had its origins in a baby cup with an elephant-head handle fashioned by Butler. For this bowl, he used the elephant as a motif in a richly ornamented scene of African wildlife in which the creased and weathered heads serve as the support. Repoussé crocodiles emerge from a smoothly planished, "watery" base, while marsh grass, cut with a scroll saw, is reflected below. The handles are formed by delicate reeds, and intertwined gilded giraffes, made from lost-wax casts, surmount the whole.

Because of his contact with colonial silver at the Museum of Fine Arts, Boston, Butler enlarged his "RAB" mark, which he had used in London, to "RaBUTLER." He learned that the simple initials first used by colonial American silversmiths followed the pattern that was established by London's Goldsmiths' Hall and brought to this country by immigrant craftsmen. However, since American silversmiths were not administered by the English guild system, they were free to alter their marks, and, by the late eighteenth century, they commonly used full surnames. Like his colonial counterparts, Butler surmised that such a mark could bring his name to a wider clientele.[2]

The graceful profile and volume of the tureen, with its elliptical form, recall the achievements of nineteenth-century presentation silver. Yet despite the formality of the arrangement, the ornamentation is quite contemporary. The bowl showcases Butler's remarkable silversmithing skills in raising, lost-wax casting, and chasing.

Description: The elliptical bowl has a bezel setting to receive a conforming curved lid, which is ornamented with tall intertwined giraffe handles. Bowl handles are made of chased and saw-cut forms resembling marsh grasses; the base features repoussé crocodiles, elephant heads, and marsh grasses. Gilding was executed by P. J. Gill of Woburn, Massachusetts.

History: The bowl was commissioned by the Museum in 1988 with funds provided by an anonymous donor.

Exhibitions and publications: Fairbanks 1991, cat. no. 123, 97; Society of Arts and Crafts, Boston, "Celebration of Excellence," March 9–May 2, 1993; Malcolm Rogers and Gilian Wohlauer, *Treasures of the Museum of Fine Arts, Boston: A Tiny Folio* (New York: Abbeville Press, 1996), 299; Wohlauer 1999, 383.

NOTES TO THIS ENTRY ARE ON PAGE 457.

335

Margret Craver (b. 1907)

Teapot

Detroit, Michigan, and Wichita, Kansas, about 1936
Gift in Memory of Joyce Goldberg with funds provided by Mr. John P. Axelrod, Mr. and Mrs. Sidney Stoneman, Mr. Charles Devens, Mr. and Mrs. Peter S. Lynch, The Seminarians, Mr. James G. Hinkle, Jr., The MFA Council, and Friends
1988.533

H. 5½ in. (14 cm); W. 9⁵⁄₁₆ in. (23.5 cm); Diam. shoulder 5½ in. (13.9 cm); Diam. base 2 in. (5.1 cm); Wt. 27 oz 13 dwt 23 gr (861.5 gm)
Marks: "C" within a stylized six-petaled flower struck on underside.
Inscriptions: None.

AS A TEACHER, innovator, jeweler, and silversmith, Kansas-born Margret Craver is a twentieth-century artist of the first rank. Her work represents a link between Arts and Crafts silversmiths and artists of the postmodern era. In addition, Craver is one of the few women of her generation to have received international recognition for her achievements in metalsmithing.

Craver first encountered the craft as a young student at the University of Kansas. After graduation, she taught a variety of media, including silversmithing and jewelrymaking, at the Wichita Art Association. During the 1930s, the association was one of the few institutions committed to raising contemporary decorative arts to a national level. During the summers, she worked in the studios of established artists. She studied with Wilson Weir of Tiffany's; Stone Associates of Gardner, Massachusetts; and Arthur Nevill Kirk (1881–1958), a leading metalworker and first professor in the craft at Cranbrook Academy. From Leonard Heinrich, chief armor conservator at the Metropolitan Museum, Craver learned the silversmith's essential skill—the art of toolmaking. She maintained contact with the university, traveling to Europe with design department director Marjorie Whitney in 1938, the same year in which she studied with Baron Erik Fleming (1894–1954), silversmith to the king of Sweden.[1]

During the war, Craver worked with Handy and Harman, a leading refiner of precious metals, to develop therapeutic projects for returning veterans. She then directed Handy and Harman's newly formed Craft Service Department, which trained design teachers in the making of hollowware. As part of this effort, Handy and Harman sponsored five National Silversmithing Workshop Conferences between 1947 and 1959. Craver

335

enlisted Fleming and Sheffield College of Arts and Crafts professor William Ernest Bennett (1906–w. 1967) as instructors.[2] The conferences greatly influenced the direction of American silversmithing, as many of the graduates were responsible for the first wave of postwar metalsmithing departments organized throughout the country.

This teapot was the first major work in hollowware undertaken by the artist. It is entirely her own design and was made under Kirk's direction. Her personal aesthetic is evident in the lively profile, whose light, almost birdlike stance belies the capacious volume within. Fully conceived and executed, the teapot displays none of the hesitancy usually associated with an artist's early work.

Craver's lifelong dedication to metalwork and her revival and modern reinterpretation of the lost *en résille* enameling technique place her among the first rank of American silversmiths and jewelers. Her work has been seen in the groundbreaking "Objects: USA" exhibition of 1970 and, more recently, "The Eloquent Object" (1987) and "Women Designers in the USA, 1900–2000" (2000). Her honors include membership in the Master Gold and Silversmiths Guild of Sweden; fellowship in the American Crafts Council; and the council's Medal of Excellence. Her small but exceptional oeuvre can be seen at the Renwick Museum, the Metropolitan Museum of Art, and the Art Institute of Chicago.

Description: The raised vessel has an applied narrow ring foot that is roughly circular in section, with strainer holes cut in the body and a V-shaped spout affixed to the body. The shoulder soldered to the body is flat, lozenge-shaped, and upturned at each end, creating a transition to the spout and handle; a three-part hinge secures the lid, which has a finial made of Gabon ebony and a hollow silver sphere. The handle is formed with two sheets of silver that spring from above the foot and the shoulder. A shaped, Gabon ebony grip connects these elements and completes the whole.

History: The teapot remained in the artist's possession until acquired by the Museum in 1988.

Exhibitions and publications: Fairbanks 1991, 76, cat. no. 63; Kirkham 2000, 234–35, figs. 9–12; Jane Port, *Margret Craver and Her Contemporaries* (Boston: Museum of Fine Arts, 2002), cat. no. 1, cover ill.

NOTES TO THIS ENTRY ARE ON PAGE 457.

CHARLES CROWLEY is committed to producing innovative hollowware forms. To do so, he uses milling machines and lathes instead of stake and hammer. He was among the first contemporary studio artists to set aside the ancient traditions of the craft—which have placed a high premium on method and its aesthetic effects—in favor of industrial methods and appearances. What matters to Crowley is the idea; the execution is simply a means to that end. First, he shapes the vessel by machine. Then he uses traditional skills, mastered while a student of the Program in Artisanry at Boston University (B.F.A., 1984), to achieve his vision.

For this tea service on stand, Crowley spun the forms and milled the accompanying frame before proceeding with detailed work. The resulting appearance is one of hovering shapes at rest on slender towers, a delicate equipoise made dynamic by the arching teapot handle and the sleek profiles hinting at speed and modernity. With its highly reflective surface and machined forms, the service is characteristic of the artist's oeuvre. It addresses a modern sensibility, just as the painted surfaces and playful, sometimes illogical, details (as in the sugar handle masquerading as a spout) aim to amuse and engage.

Recently, metal-based furniture and lighting have taken up more of Crowley's time, partly because he has not found a ready market for his hollowware. In a lecture presented to the Society of North American Goldsmiths in 2000, Crowley acknowledged the difficulty of contemporary silversmiths to earn a living making hollowware. He challenged artists to find new ways of expressing themselves in hollowware, thereby controlling their future in the field.[1]

Recognition of Crowley's distinctive interpretation of contemporary silver came early, with a third-place award in Towle's Sterling Silver Design Competition (1983). Among later honors, Crowley received a fellowship from the Massachusetts Council for the Arts (1986); a first-prize award in the Fortunoff Sterling Silver Design Competition (1990); and a fellowship from the National Endowment for the Arts (1993). A one-man exhibition, organized by the Wetsman Collection of Birmingham, Michigan, traveled from 1991 to 1992.[2]

336

Charles Crowley (b. 1958)
Three-piece tea service on stand

Waltham, Massachusetts, 1987
Gift of Anne and Ronald Abramson
1987.232.1-4

Teapot (1987.232.1a–b): H. 12 in. (30.5 cm); Diam. base 9 in. (22.9 cm); Wt. 39 oz 12 dwt 17 gr (1232.8 gm)

Sugar bowl with spoon (1987.232.2a–c): H. 2⅝ in. (6.7 cm); Diam. base 4⅞ in. (12.5 cm); Wt. 11 oz 16 dwt 10 gr (367.7 gm)

Creamer (1987.232.3a–b): H. 2¹³⁄₁₆ in. (7 cm); Diam. base, 4⅞ in. (12.5 cm); Wt. 10 oz 18 dwt 12 gr (339.8 gm)

Stand (1987.232.4): H. 12 in. (30.5 cm); W. 8⅞ in. (22.5 cm); D. 11¼ in. (28.5 cm)

Marks: "Charlie Crowley / 1987." in the artist's script incised on bottom of all three vessels. Stand is unmarked.

Inscriptions: None.

Description: The wide, spun conical forms are smallest at openings and expand to a broad base. Disks soldered to the body have been machined to blend with the acute angle of the form. Narrow cylinders are used alternatively as tea and creamer spout or sugar spoon, with hollow triangular forms bridging the gap between cylinder and vessel. All three vessels have a small circular lid with one flat side. The lids have flanges and rectangular finials soldered along their length, with a notch cut that faces the flat side of the lid.

The handles on the sugar bowl and creamer are flat, solid, hemi-spherical disks, with a notch removed near the base, and they are seated within a seamed triangular wedge soldered to the body. The teapot handle is rectangular in section and curves in a large tall arc, tapering toward its end. All painted surfaces are made of enameled cast aluminum. A three-legged painted aluminum base, with three circular pedestals, supports the whole.

History: Created by the artist in 1987 and made a gift to the Museum by the donors.

Exhibitions and publications: Fairbanks 1991, 80, cat. no. 67; Society of Arts and Crafts, Boston, "Celebration of Excellence," March 9–May 2, 1993.

NOTES TO THIS ENTRY ARE ON PAGE 457.

337

Virginia Wireman Cute (1908–1985)
Bowl

Philadelphia, Pennsylvania, 1947
Gift of David and Chelsey Remington
1999.736

H. 1¾ in. (4.4 cm); Diam. rim 7 in. (17.8 cm); Diam. foot 3⅛ in. (7.9 cm); Wt. 9 oz 18 dwt 4 gr (308.2 gm)

Marks: None.

Inscriptions: "VWC" entwined monogram, in shaded script letters, engraved at center of bowl.

VIRGINIA WIREMAN CUTE (fig. 1) represents the old and the new in the world of American silversmithing. She is the daughter of illustrator Katharine Richardson Wireman (1878–1966) and a descendant of Francis Richardson (1681–1729), a colonial Philadelphia silversmith. Cute reinvigorated the city's reputation for fine craftsmanship when she was appointed director of silversmithing and jewelry at the Museum School of Art, now the University of the Arts.[1] As evidence of her energy and enthusiasm, enrollment in her department rose from 20 pupils in 1942, the year of her appointment, to 175 in 1950.[2]

Cute pursued two parallel and sometimes interconnected careers. Her first degree in 1929 was earned from the Philadelphia School of Occupational Therapy (University of Pennsylvania School of Auxiliary Medical Services). From 1931 to 1935, she continued her studies at the Philadelphia School of Art and graduated with a bachelor's degree in fine arts from the Moore Institute of Art. About the time of her appointment to the

FIG. 1. Virginia Wireman Cute. Photo, courtesy Mrs. David Remington.

Museum School, she studied briefly in New York with Swedish-born silversmith Adda Husted Anderson (w. in the United States about 1930, d. 1990) and with Walter Rhodes (1896–1968), probably at the Crafts Students League.

Cute's skills were honed at the 1947 Handy and Harman silversmithing conference run by Margret Craver, which reintroduced traditional hollowware-making skills to a new generation of American art students (figs. 2–3). William E. Bennett, professor of the Sheffield College of Arts and Crafts in England, taught the 1947 session. Upon her return to Philadelphia, she urged Richard Reinhardt (1921–1998), a Museum graduate and professor, to attend; he succeeded her as head of the department.

In 1949 Bennett invited Cute to study with him in England. While there, she became the first American woman whose touchmark was accepted into London's Goldsmiths' Hall. She traveled in 1953 to meet Baron Erik Fleming, silversmith to the Swedish court, and Count Sigvard Bernadotte (1907–2002), brother of the queen of Denmark and designer for Georg Jensen, the Sheffield College of Art, and the Worshipful Company of Goldsmiths. One of her travel companions was Phoebe Phillips Prime (Mrs. Alfred Coxe Prime), an antiquarian and silver specialist.[3] Throughout this period, Cute lectured, exhibited, and published in the field of American silver.[4]

337

FIG. 2. Silver exhibited by members of the 1947 Handy and Harman conference. Low bowl at far right by Virginia Wireman Cute; footed bowl with banded decoration below rim by Dooley Dewey Shorty; wine cup at far left by Gunda Lee Cornell; ladle by Ruth Pennington. Photo, courtesy Mary Lee Hu from the papers of Ruth Penington.

FIG. 3. Virginia Wireman Cute (at right) with Richard Reinhardt and an unidentified student. Undated photo, courtesy Mrs. David Remington.

In 1953 Cute returned to her earlier field to become assistant director of the Philadelphia School of Occupational Therapy. She remained with the department until the early 1980s.

This sleek bowl, with its low, almost space-age profile, was made in a manner taught at the Handy and Harman conferences. The technique of using a graver to insert small "stitches" underneath the bowl to center the foot ring is carefully explained in a 1948 Handy and Harman instructional film and booklet entitled "Handwrought Silver."[4] Stylistically, the bowl adheres to the Scandinavian modern style that is found in the work of all conference participants. The entwined script monogram of the artist's name, however, is a reminder of Cute's colonial ancestry.

Description: The shallow raised vessel with faint center point sits on a conical raised foot, with a reinforcing ring at juncture with vessel. Tiny burrs visible at the juncture between the foot and bowl were intended to stabilize the foot before soldering.

History: From the artist to her sister Mary Wireman Remington (b. 1906); to her son David Remington and his wife, Chelsey, the donors.

Exhibitions and publications: Kirkham 2000, 238–39, figs. 9–17.

NOTES TO THIS ENTRY ARE ON PAGE 457.

338

John F. Davis Jr. (b. 1924)

Three-piece tea service

Boston, Massachusetts, about 1948
Gift in memory of John F. Davis
1995.782.1–3

Teapot (1995.782.1): H. 6 in. (15.2 cm); W. 6½ in. (16.5 cm); Diam. shoulder 9⅝ in. (24.5 cm); Diam. foot 7¹¹⁄₁₆ in. (19.5 cm); Wt. 32 oz 4 dwt 5 gr (1001.9 gm)

Creamer (1995.782.2): H. 2⅞ in. (7.3 cm); W. 6⅛ in. (15.4 cm); Diam. rim 4 in. (10.2 cm); Diam. foot 2³⁄₁₆ in. (5.5 cm); Wt. 6 oz 12 dwt 17 gr (206.4 gm)

Sugar bowl (1995.782.3): H. 3¹¹⁄₁₆ in. (9.5 cm); W. 6⅞ in. (17.5 cm); Diam. base 4½ in. (11.5 cm); Wt. 13 oz 4 dwt 4 gr (410.8 gm)

Marks: "STERLING" in sans-serif letters, "ENTIRELY HAND / WROUGHT" in sans-serif letters, and "J.F. Davis, Jr." in script struck incuse on base of each.

Inscriptions: None.

THE UNADORNED MODERNE style of this service is in keeping with a contemporary Scandinavian aesthetic that was expressed in various media in the American decorative arts of the early to mid-twentieth century. As with many examples of the period, its gentle curves present a buoyant stance countered by strong geometry of the circular shoulder and prominent C-scroll handles.

John F. Davis Jr. was born in Cambridge and attended the Cambridge School, in nearby Weston. As a teenager, he studied painting on Saturdays at the Vesper George School in Boston and learned metalworking in summer workshops at Camp Idlewilde, Lake Winnipesaukee, where he was taught by Museum School professor Joseph L. Sharrock (d. 1962).

Davis's long-term affiliation with the Museum of Fine Arts, Boston, began with childhood visits and a membership that he has retained since 1942. He entered the Jewelry and Silversmithing Department at the School of the Museum of Fine Arts in 1946 (fig. 4). Davis received the Boit Prize in 1949 and, the following academic year, the Special Gem Prize, in which a precious stone is awarded to the winner. He also received a traveling fellowship in 1949, which he used to go to Denmark, Germany, and England.

Davis received prestigious commissions even before graduation in 1950. Among these were a baptismal bowl, a ciborium, a pair of altar cruets, and a chalice given to Trinity Church, Boston, in memory of its rector, Dr. Theodore P. Ferris.[1]

After graduation, Davis was appointed assistant professor to Sharrock in the Jewelry and Metalsmithing Department, a position he retained for several years before relocating to Philadelphia, where he worked as a jeweler for J. E. Caldwell. Several other secular and ecclesiastical commissions followed in the 1970s and 1980s, including a pair of candlesticks and a baptismal bowl for the First Presbyterian Church in Philadelphia. Davis worked independently as a studio silversmith and jeweler until his retirement in the mid-1980s.

This tea service was fashioned while Davis was enrolled in the Museum School. Beautifully raised, shaped, and planished, it admirably demonstrates the high level of skill expected of students during the late 1940s and 1950s, an era when silversmithing experienced a revival. A demitasse set with scroll-cut decoration, a bracelet, and two rings by Davis are also in the Museum's collection.[2]

Description: The three vessels share a similar form. Each is raised and has gently curving U-shaped sides and a drawn, seamed, stepped base and applied foot rim. An angular shoulder is soldered to each and slopes gently upward toward center.

338

FIG. 4. Silversmithing class at the School of the Museum of Fine Arts, about 1951–53. Joseph L. Sharrock, wearing a tie, is standing to the left; Davis is seated at the far right in the fourth row from the foreground. Museum of Fine Arts, Boston; department files, Art of the Americas.

The teapot has a depression around the rim to receive a slight domed lid with a stylized foliate, or wavelike, finial; it has a small five-part hinge hidden beneath the flat rectangular hinge plate. The seamed C-scroll handle is square in section, tapering at each end; two rosewood insulators are pinned into the handle. A V-shaped spout is affixed over a pierced strainer that conforms to the teapot's body. The sugar bowl has two scrolled handles; its lid is removable. The creamer has an open V-shaped spout that is soldered to the walls.

History: Retained by artist until made a gift in 1995.

Exhibitions and publications: None.

NOTES TO THIS ENTRY ARE ON PAGE 457.

339

Robert Ebendorf (b. 1938)
Traveling communion service

Fredrikstadö, Norway, 1967
Anonymous gift
1992.265.1–2

Communion vessel (1992.265.1a–d): H. 4⅝ in. (11.8 cm); Diam. 1⅝ in. (4 cm); Wt. 6 oz 13 dwt 16 gr (207.9 gm)

Walnut case (1992.265.2a–b): H. 5 in. (12.7 cm); W. 6 in. (15.2 cm); D. 3 in. (7.6 cm)

Marks: Fish and "925S E" struck; and "R EBENDORF / 1967" engraved on base. Inked letters on white tape affixed to base of wooden case "M-28a" and faintly below "E141b."

Inscriptions: None.

ROBERT EBENDORF has had a long and successful career as a silversmith and jeweler. Following his studies at the University of Kansas under Carlyle Smith (see cat. no. 364), in 1963 Ebendorf traveled on a Fulbright grant to Norway, studying at the State School for Applied Arts and Crafts. He returned there on a Louis Comfort Tiffany grant in 1966–67, working at the Norway Silver Design workshop, in Fredrikstadö, under the supervision of Erling Christofferson. By day, Ebendorf worked on production jewelry, and by night he was allowed use of the shop to create his own silver. This communion set, made during his second trip, demonstrates the formative influence of Scandinavian, and particularly Norwegian, design. The use of a simple cylindrical form, the shaped rosewood case, and the even-sided cross that ornaments the cup and pins of the

wooden case all recall the ancient and contemporary aesthetic of Nordic peoples.

Other works fashioned by Ebendorf while at Fredrikstadö show his fascination with texture and pattern, as contrasted with smooth surfaces. A tea infuser from 1967 is ornamented with links and small ball ornaments that are closely related to the stopper of this service. His hand gavel and striker block (1965) and umbrella handle (1967) are covered with intricate patterns of positive-negative space that enchant the eye and delight the touch.[1] Both are related to the cup in this traveling service.

Ebendorf left hollowware and the Scandinavian design aesthetic long ago to work almost exclusively in jewelry, which he crafts from nonprecious and discarded materials. An appropriationist at heart, he has made these unorthodox creations a hallmark of his career. He often juxtaposes society's detritus, such as bottle caps, sea glass, and chicken wire, with twigs, shells, and other natural scraps. Beautiful, strange, and never ordinary, these unique works may well be his major contributions to the field.

In 1971 Ebendorf became professor at the State University of New York at New Paltz, where he taught for twenty years, working with Kurt Matzdorf and Jamie Bennett. He was a founding member of the Society of North American Goldsmiths, serving as president from 1972 to 1977. He was made a Fellow of the American Craft Council in 1994. Ebendorf is presently Distinguished Professor of Art at East Carolina University in Greenville.[2]

Description: The seamed cylindrical vessel has a friction-fitted cover that is used as a cup. A flat circular disk secured to a cork stopper with a link and ball sets into the vessel. The cup decoration consists of equal-sided crosses soldered in a frieze on the exterior; the interior is gilded. A single equal-sided cross is soldered to the underside of the cup (which becomes the lid when assembled); the background has been oxidized to create contrast. A hidden container at the base of the cylinder is used to store holy wafers. Shaped rosewood case contains two silver pins that enable the lid to seat correctly; each pin has been ornamented with a similar equal-sided cross.

History: Given anonymously to the Museum in 1992.

Exhibitions and publications: None.

NOTES TO THIS ENTRY ARE ON PAGE 457.

339

Gorham Manufacturing Company
(active 1865–1961)

Erik Magnussen (1884–1961), designer
Candy dish

Providence, Rhode Island, 1926
Gift of John P. Axelrod
1999.254a–b

H. 8¾ in. (22.5 cm); Diam. rim 6½ in. (16.5); Wt. 23 oz 8 dwt 22 gr (729.3 gm)

Marks: Sequential incuse touchmarks "GORHAM" in roman letters; lion passant, anchor, and Gothic letter "G," each in a shaped device; "STERLING" in sans-serif lettering; incuse roman letters "F / Y N"; and sailboat date icon for 1926; all struck under foot ring. "1 6 7 8" incised alongside "sterling," with one number above the next.

Inscriptions: "★ EVERETT AND EVA BACON ★ 1936 ★" in roman letters engraved under foot ring.

BORN IN COPENHAGEN, Erik Magnussen was a product of the cultural Danish scene and a contemporary of Georg Jensen (1866–1935). From 1898 to 1901, Magnussen worked at Winkel and Magnussen, an art gallery run by his uncle, while studying sculpture with Stephan Sinding (1846–1922) and chasing with silversmith Viggo Hansen. By 1907 Magnussen had relocated to Berlin, where for two years he worked as a chaser in the workshop of Otto Rohloff at the Kunstgewerbeschule. In 1909 the artist returned to Copenhagen, where he opened his own studio. Soon thereafter, he began to exhibit his work both locally and more widely with shows in Berlin (1910, 1911), Paris (1922), and Rio de Janeiro (1922).[1]

In 1924 Georg Jensen established the company's first American showroom in New York City. Its success apparently prompted American firms to follow popular interest in Scandinavian-style silver designs.[2] The next year, Gorham Manufacturing Company of Providence, Rhode Island, hired Magnussen as art director, thus heralding a major change in their product line. This candy dish, designed shortly after his arrival in 1926, owes a stylistic debt to Jensen, as is evident in the double foot rim, stylized plant motifs, and glimmering planished surface. The reeded ivory column provides a Neoclassical reference that Magnussen reprised in later works, such as the Modern American series (cat. no. 341). The inscription is dated 1936, ten years

after the design was introduced, suggesting that the candy dish continued in popularity or that it was leftover stock.[3]

Description: The tall vessel has a raised bowl with a wide flaring rim and an applied bezel setting to receive the lid. The body is supported by a columnar ivory stem having spherical and stylized foliate decoration in silver at each end. A spreading, raised, circular foot flares slightly upward at edge. The cup is raised upward by a double foot ring having similar sphere and foliate brackets. A bell-shaped lid that echoes the shape of the bowl is ornamented with a spherical silver finial and scalloped, floral, ivory insert.

History: Purchased by the donor from Historical Design, Inc., New York City, July 1985, and made a gift to the Museum in 1999.

Exhibitions and publications: Karen Davies, *At Home in Manhattan: Modern Decorative Arts, 1925 to the Depression* (New Haven: Yale University Art Gallery, 1983), cat. no. 15.

NOTES TO THIS ENTRY ARE ON PAGE 457.

341

Gorham Manufacturing Company
(active 1865–1961)

Erik Magnussen (1884–1961), designer
The Modern American coffee service

Providence, Rhode Island, 1927–29
Estate of Rosamund Sears, by exchange
1996.242.1–4

Tray (1996.242.1): H. ¹³⁄₁₆ in. (2.1 cm); W. 14¹³⁄₁₆ in. (37.5 cm); Diam. 12 in. (30.6 cm); Wt. 27 oz 11 gr (840.5 gm)

Coffeepot (1996.242.2): H. 8⅜ in. (21.4 cm); W. 8³⁄₁₆ in. (20.8 cm); Diam. 3³⁄₁₆ in. (9.6 cm); Wt. 22 oz 4 dwt 11 gr (691.2 gm)

Sugar bowl (1996.242.3a–b): H. 4⅝ in. (11.8 cm); W. 6¹¹⁄₁₆ in. (16.9 cm); Diam. 3¹¹⁄₁₆ in. (9.5 cm); Wt. 13 oz 2 dwt 15 gr (408.4 gm)

Creamer (1996.242.4): H. 2⅞ in. (7.3 cm); W. 6³⁄₁₆ in. (15.7 cm); Diam. 3³⁄₁₆ in. (9.7 cm); Wt. 9 oz 14 dwt 14 gr (302.6 gm)

Marks: "EM." conjoined monogram above "14054 / STERLING / [lion] [anchor] G / GORHAM," each in a shaped device, all struck on tray. "EM." conjoined monogram above "14051 / STERLING / [lion] [anchor] [G] / GORHAM," each in a shaped device, all struck on coffeepot. "EM." conjoined monogram, above "A14052/ STERLING / GORHAM / [lion] [anchor] [G]," each in a shaped device, struck on sugar bowl. "EM." conjoined monogram, above "14053 / STERLING / [lion] [anchor] [G] / GORHAM," each in a shaped device, struck on creamer.

Inscriptions: "M.A.W." in broad, shaded, roman letters engraved on side of each vessel and on tray, on expanse between handles.

341

MAGNUSSEN ARRIVED AT GORHAM in 1927 with a mandate to create modern designs to invigorate the company's line of historically derived offerings. He designed the controversial Cubic service and serving pieces, later dubbed "The Lights and Shadows of Manhattan," which immediately drew a critical response, both positive and negative. Yet few, if any, examples were manufactured beyond the demonstration model, attesting to the difficulty in finding a market for avant-garde forms.[1] Thereafter, Magnussen shifted to designing silver in a conservative, classically inspired modernism. The Modern American line is the best-known example of this style.

According to promotional literature, Magnussen designed the service after he had traveled throughout the country in search of a style that epitomized contemporary American life. The clean lines, simple forms, and updated Neoclassical decoration were intended to provide a smart, if rather conservative, note to the upscale modern household. The lower register of each vessel and the tray features a repeating pattern of three closely spaced vertical lines, in emulation of triglyphs of classical Greek architecture. This reductive Neoclassicism, seen in the ivory stem of his covered candy dish (cat. no. 340), was a feature of Scandinavian workshops, most notably that of Georg Jensen.[2]

Magnussen had been hired to inspire Gorham's designers

and appeal to consumer interest in modernism. The Modern American line represented the company's best hope for a foothold in this new style. Despite such efforts, poor sales demonstrated the public's aversion to risking funds on avant-garde styles in silver. Cost was likely a major factor as well, for quantities of surviving chrome and aluminum table accessories fabricated after the Depression attest to the broad appeal of modern design to price- and style-conscious American consumers.

Magnussen left Gorham in October 1929 to work briefly for August Dingledein & Son of Hanau and Idar, Germany. He later worked in Chicago and Los Angeles before returning to Denmark in 1939.

The Modern American line blended historic forms in a contemporary mode. By using a simple design element drawn from ancient Greek sources to decorate columnar forms, Magnussen evoked the classical world. His rectilinear handles, derived from nineteenth-century American examples, softened the otherwise harsh machine-made cylinders that formed the modern core of the service.

Description: The set consists of three straight-sided machine-made cylindrical vessels and a machine-made tray. Along the base of each vessel is a conforming decorative band of triglyphs that is balanced below the rim with a stamped horizontal line. Squared ebony handles, rectangular in section, are set into conforming sockets. Four flattened bun feet carry the triglyph design and support each vessel.

The coffeepot has a straight tapered spout, round in section, affixed over strainer holes near its base. The spun lid with five-part hinge tapers slightly upward at center toward a plastic and silver finial, probably an early replacement for the original ivory finial, as on the sugar bowl; there is a bezel underneath the lid. The sugar bowl has a removable lid with flange. The flat circular tray, with shallow sides and no evident center point, is machine made; it has a narrow band of decoration on its exterior edge that continues the triglyph pattern. A pair of black plastic bars is set into rim on each side of the tray, each affixed at right angles to a pair of conforming sockets.

History: First owned by Ephraim Daniel Whitty (1910–1991) and Muriel Adelson Whitty (1911–1993), m. about 1929; they lived at 1120 Park Avenue, New York City. By descent in 1993 to their son Richard, who consigned the set to Moderne Gallery, Inc., of Philadelphia.[3] Purchased by the Museum in 1996.

Exhibitions and publications: None.

NOTES TO THIS ENTRY ARE ON PAGE 457.

342

Gorham Manufacturing Company
(active 1865–1961)

Erik Magnussen (1884–1961), designer

The Modern American cocktail service

Providence, Rhode Island, 1930
Gift of John P. Axelrod
1999.250.1–9

Cocktail shaker (1999.250.1): H. 12⅜ in. (31.4 cm); W. 6⁵⁄₁₆ in. (16.1 cm); Diam. foot 3¾ in. (9.5 cm); Wt. 34 oz 10 dwt 5 gr (1073.4 gm)

Martini stemware (1999.250.2–9): Each cup is about H. 5⅛ in. (13

cm); Diam. rim 3⅜ in. (8.6 cm); Diam. base 2⅜ in. (6 cm); Wt. 3 oz 12 dwt 22 gr (113.4 gm)

Marks: "GORHAM" in roman letters; lion passant, anchor, and Gothic letter "G," each within a device; "STERLING" in sans-serif letters; "A14082"; elephant date symbol for 1930; "3 PINT"; and "EM." conjoined monogram, all struck incuse on cocktail shaker. "GORHAM" in roman letters; lion passant, anchor, and Gothic letter "G", each within a device; "STERLING" in sans-serif letters; "A14083 / EM." conjoined monogram, all struck on martini stemware. Two cups display the elephant date symbol for 1930.

Inscriptions: None.

often substandard bathtub gin. Due in part to the furtiveness of this social activity, cocktail services of the era were chiefly made of inexpensive glass, steel, or chrome-plated brass; only a small number were produced in silver, a particularly elite material for such a newly fashionable purpose.

The martini, a gin-based mixed drink popular at the time, lent its name to the broad cone-shaped drinking glass in which it was served. Glass was the most common material for drinking vessels; yet as with most manufacturers of metal drinking services of the period, Gorham chose to market martini glasses in silver, then an uncharacteristic material.

Due to the interchangeability of items in the Modern American line, this cocktail service was intended to be used with the tray shown in the coffee service (cat. no. 341).

Description: The spun cocktail shaker is in the form of a truncated cone, widening at shoulders; the narrowing shoulder angles inward, where it is soldered to a circular neck. A flat strap handle is attached at the neck and shoulder. A shallow, conical, friction-fitted lid with deep bezel has square strainer holes arranged in a triangular pattern matching those in the shaker spout. The spun cups are broadly flaring, with slender, cast, rodlike stems and stepped circular feet. The shaker and cups share similar narrow borders with vertical markings in the Neoclassical manner.

History: Purchased by the donor from Lillian Nassau Antiques, New York City, in January 1986 and made a gift to the Museum in 1999.

Exhibitions and publications: None.

NOTE TO THIS ENTRY IS ON PAGE 457.

Health to the Bride and Groom. Modern—sophisticated—luxurious—toast happiness to the bride and groom, and present them with a beverage set to return the compliment when other members of the young aristocracy marry and also are made the proud recipients of such sterling splendor.[1]

AT THE HEIGHT OF Prohibition (1919–33) in the 1920s, the term "beverage set" became a euphemism for a cocktail set. Thus the above-mentioned toasts, published in Gorham's promotional text, were meant to accompany alcohol consumption, despite the federal ban. Cocktails became popular during Prohibition, for the ancillary juices or seltzers masked what was

343

Gorham Manufacturing Company (active 1865–1961)

Erik Magnussen (1884–1961), designer

The Modern American salt and pepper shakers

Providence, Rhode Island, 1927–29
Gift of John P. Axelrod
1999.252.1–2

1999.252.1: H. 5¾ in. (14.4 cm); Diam. foot 1⅞ in. (4.8 cm); Wt. 2 oz 17 dwt 14 gr (89.6 gm)

1999.252.2: H. 5¾ in. (14.4 cm); Diam. foot 1⅞ in. (4.8 cm); Wt. 2 oz 15 dwt 14 gr (86.5 gm)

Marks: "EM." conjoined monogram; "14076"; "STERLING" in sans-serif letters; "GORHAM" in roman letters; lion passant and anchor symbols; and Gothic letter "G," all struck incuse on each base.

Inscriptions: None.

See cat. no. 342.

Description: The tall cylindrical forms have a stepped base with a narrow border, whose vertical markings are in the Neoclassical manner. The removable lids have a radiating pierced pattern that rises to an antennalike finial at center.

History: See cat. no. 342.

Exhibitions and publications: None.

344

Gorham Manufacturing Company (active 1865–1961)

Erik Magnussen (1884–1961), designer

Bonbon dish

Providence, Rhode Island, about 1928
Gift of John P. Axelrod
1999.253

H. 3¹¹⁄₁₆ in. (9.3 cm); Diam. rim 4⅜ in. (11.2 cm); Diam. foot 3⅛ in. (8 cm); Wt. 7 oz 15 dwt 1 gr (241.1 gm)

Marks: "GORHAM" in roman letters; "EM." conjoined monogram; lion passant and anchor symbols; Gothic letter "G"; "62"; and "STERLING" in sans-serif letters, all struck incuse on base.

Inscriptions: "M [pellet] W" in shaded sans-serif letters engraved on circular foot.

The giraffes that serve as tripod supports for this petite candy dish were among a menagerie of designs that Erik Magnussen created for Gorham. Storks, deer, and pelicans are but three of the many animals the artist included in similar designs that Gorham put into production sometime in 1928. All featured a circular ring-shaped base. The pelican version, which included an agate ball beneath each of the three feet, cost $43.34 to produce and retailed at $75.[1]

Description: The wide spun bowl has a gilded interior and is stamped with a scored rim. The bowl is supported on the backs of three stamped two-dimensional giraffes. The giraffes are balanced on small spheres with collars, which in turn stand on a flat ring.

History: Purchased by the donor from Historical Design, Inc., New York City, October 1986, and made a gift to the Museum in 1999.

Exhibitions and publications: None.

NOTE TO THIS ENTRY IS ON PAGE 458.

345

Richard Mawdsley (b. 1945)
Standing cup with cover

Carterville, Illinois, 1986
Anonymous Gift
1988.535a–b

H. 17 3/16 in. (43.8 cm); Diam. rim 3 5/8 in. (9.2 cm); Diam. foot 3 5/8 in. (9.2 cm); Wt. 26 oz 5 dwt 10 gr (817.1 gm)

Marks: "RM STERLING" and "SN /AG" struck on base.

Inscriptions: None.

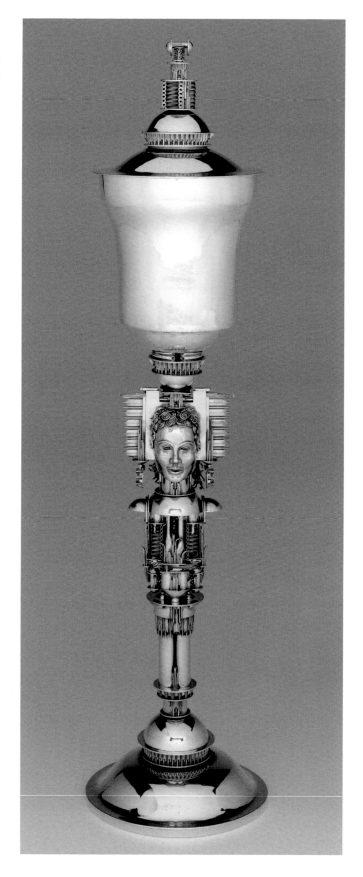

The mechanical, the miniature, and man have been the chief features of silver made by Richard Mawdsley. Since his graduation in 1969 from the University of Kansas, Lawrence, the artist has been preoccupied with using these subjects to create a microcosm of the world. *Feast Bracelet* (1974) was his first such work to attract national attention. More of a corsage than a bracelet, its principal feature is a "table" bearing a tiny teakettle on stand, a coffeepot, pouring and drinking vessels, a half-eaten berry pie, fruit, utensils, and linen, all fabricated by the artist. The lovingly detailed version of a Dutch still life won admiration. Critics hailed his precision in creating historical objects to scale as well as his uncanny ability to provide a

345

a male figure whose chest is a virtual engine of machine tubing. The figure's frontal pose and curly hair recall Leonardo da Vinci's *Vitruvian Man*. The vessel can be interpreted as a modern corollary to the progressive humanism of the fourteenth century.

The female form had been a subject for Mawdsley from the early years of his career, and in fact the Museum's example began as such.[2] The artist created female figures in repoussé (*Goneril, Regan, Cordelia*, 1976) and as a pendant with torso (*Wonderwoman in Her Bicentennial Finery*, 1976; *Medusa*, 1979–80; and *Headdress*, 1982).

The cup's male figure offers an optimistic view of the mechanical world by virtue of its dignified presence. Although Mawdsley has moved away from depicting the figure in his water tower series, humanity's place within these elaborate constructs can be gleaned from the tiny tools that are found scattered about the sculpture. The tools hint at the presence of workmen who have momentariy stepped away from the site. Like the cup's central figure, they are reminders of the human dimension in a perfectly conceived "Mawdsleyan" world.

Description: The tall raised bowl has a gradually everted rim and is surmounted by a tall steeple-shaped lid composed of a low dome and three stages of increasingly smaller tubular assemblages. The bowl is supported from below by a smaller corresponding dome and tubular mass. The tall stem is composed of a male head with curly locks made of hollow wire; a head formed in repoussé; and a stylized torso and legs. The body and headdress are composed of narrow tubes that have been shaped and cut to emulate a machine-like appearance. The domed and splayed foot is capped by a second, smaller dome and tubular pattern that echoes the lid.

History: Purchased by an anonymous donor in 1988 from Mobilia Gallery, Cambridge, Massachusetts, and made a gift to the Museum.

Exhibitions and publications: Linda Lindeen Raiteri, "Richard Mawdsley: Master Metalsmith" (exhibition review), *Metalsmith* 8, no. 2 (spring 1988), 52; "American Metalcraft Artists 24: Richard Mawdsley," *Monthly Crafts, A Companion to Monthly Design* (June 1988), 54–55; "National Ornamental Metal Museum, Collections and Exhibitions," *Fabricator* (January/February 1989), 14; *Explorations, The Aesthetic of Excess* (New York: American Craft Museum, 1990), 36–39; Fairbanks 1991, 79, cat. no. 66, checklist no. 121, ill.; "Precious Metals," *Perspectives, Research, and Creative Activities* (spring 1994), 10–12.

NOTES TO THIS ENTRY ARE ON PAGE 458.

dignified setting for the meal and its invisible guests, set within a futuristic environment.

The modernistic tubular elements that support and frame this standing cup with cover have come to dominate the artist's work. He uses them to evoke the mechanical elements of farm machinery that first entranced him as a midwestern boy. In the 1990s, he fabricated giant water towers, for which tubular and related mechanical forms constitute the structural basis. The variation in shape and scale conveys the feel of a miniature, yet the overall result is one of enormity, as the viewer is drawn ever deeper into the object and the immense world conjured by the artist. Moreover, the machine-made appearance of his creations belies the months of painstaking benchwork required to complete them.[1]

This standing cup with cover was inspired by ecclesiastical and Renaissance examples. Its stem is expressed in the form of

346

Frederick A. Miller (1913–2000)

Salt and pepper shakers

Cleveland, Ohio, 1949
Gift of Margret Craver Withers
1987.572a–b

1987.572a: H. 1½ in. (3.7 cm); Diam. body 1¹³⁄₁₆ in. (4.6 cm); Diam. foot 1⅝ in. (4 cm); Wt. 2 oz 6 dwt 17 gr (72.7 gm)

1987.572b: H. 1½ in. (3.7 cm); Diam. body 1¹³⁄₁₆ in. (4.6 cm); Diam. foot 1⅝ in. (4 cm); Wt. 2 oz 7 dwt 1 gr (73.2 gm)

Marks: "FM" in conjoined italics, "STERLING / STERLING [faint impression]" in sans-serif letters struck on base of each.

Inscriptions: None.

FRED MILLER was one of the most active and accomplished American silversmiths of his time, working steadily from the postwar era until the 1990s. Since his introduction to the craft in 1936, as a student at the Cleveland Art Institute, Miller was a committed artist and teacher. He specialized in raising and stretching hollowware into functional biomorphic forms. He was particularly influenced by Scandinavian modernism as well as the advances of modernism and abstraction during the 1940s and 1950s. Yet Miller was continually searching for a fresh approach. Inspired by organic natural forms, his silver is often energized by an asymmetrical dynamism. His most impressive aesthetic and technical accomplishment was a series of so-called bottle vases that were raised into partially closed forms.[1]

Following discharge from the army in 1946, Miller visited silversmith studios along the eastern seaboard before joining the fine jewelry and hollowware firm of Potter and Mellen in Cleveland, Ohio. (Miller purchased the firm in 1967, serving as president and chief designer until 1977.) In 1948 he participated in the silversmithing conference sponsored by Handy and Harman, studying with Baron Erik Fleming.

In addition to his work with Potter and Mellen, Miller also maintained a long-standing relationship with the Cleveland Art Institute, where he served as an instructor in silversmithing and jewelry from 1948 until 1975. Between 1948 and 1971, the artist was also a frequent exhibitor in the silver division of the annual *May Show*, organized by the Cleveland Museum of Art, garnering most of the top prizes in hollowware throughout that period.[2]

As a measure of Miller's skill with a hammer, photographs of him using the stretching method were illustrated in an article that featured silver made at the Handy and Harman conference. He later produced, with John Paul Miller, the film and booklet *Contemporary Silversmithing—The Stretching Method*, which was issued about 1952 by the Handy and Harman Craft Service Department.[3]

As a result of his involvement with the Handy and Harman silversmithing workshop, Miller participated in the Metropolitan Museum of Art's "Handwrought Silver" exhibition of 1949. He later exhibited his work in the exhibitions "Fiber-Clay-and-Metal" of 1953 and 1955 and "Objects: USA" of 1970. His silver is in the collections of the Renwick Gallery of the Smithsonian Institution of American Art, the Art Institute of Chicago, and the Cleveland Museum of Art.

These salt and pepper shakers were early examples of Miller's work, for which he won awards at the 1950 "May Show." Designed for ease of handling, the deceptively simple forms required considerable handworkmanship to create the smooth concave and convex surfaces as well as the tight relationship of parts in the snap bases.

Description: Each shaker was fabricated from a truncated cone of sheet silver that was soldered with a vertical seam. The wall of each vessel was hammered to create a convex bulge. Circles of sheet silver were planished slightly to create a shallow cup, which was then soldered to the top of the cone to form the top of each shaker. Each base was formed of two narrow ring sections planished together over graduated steel rods, such that one ring was able to fit into the other. When trimmed, the larger of the two tubes was soldered to the base of the shaker; the smaller tube was soldered to a disk of silver to create a removable snap base.[4]

History: The shakers were among a group of six objects that Miller entered into the 1950 "May Show" at the Cleveland Museum of Art. The group won the Special Award and the Horace E. Potter Memorial Award for excellence in craftsmanship. Purchased by Margret Craver Withers; made a gift to the Museum in 1987.

Exhibitions and publications: Bulletin of the Cleveland Museum of Art 37, no. 5 (May 1950), 101.

NOTES TO THIS ENTRY ARE ON PAGE 458.

347

John Paul Miller (b. 1918)

Covered urn

Rochester, New York, 1951
Gift of John Paul Miller
2001.158

H. 7¼ in. (18.41 cm); Diam. rim 2¹¹⁄₁₆ in. (6.83 cm); Diam. base 2⁷⁄₁₆ in. (6.19 cm); Wt. 12 oz 7 dwt 21 gr (385.5 gm)

Marks: "JPM" incuse and "STERLING" in sans-serif letters struck on base.

Inscriptions: None.

BEAUTIFULLY RAISED and perfectly planished, with a simple granulated design of a sunburst set into the short stem and finial, this covered vase exemplifies the high standards of mid-century silversmithing advanced by the Handy and Harman conferences. All the elements have been fully considered and developed, resulting in a well-balanced and elegant composition.

Internationally renowned for his enameled and granulated jewelry (see fig. 5), John Paul Miller produced this urn while enrolled as a participant in the 1951 Handy and Harman silversmithing conference. The conference was held that year at the School for American Craftsmen in Rochester, New York.

Miller had just begun to experiment with granulation, evident in the little sunbursts on the vase's baluster and lid. Miller recalled that "in 1940 I happened to come across photos of granulation by Elizabeth Treskow in a German art magazine called *Die Kunst*. I couldn't understand the German and I knew nothing about granulation—including its name—but the work fascinated me." He became one of the acknowledged masters of the technique.

Justly celebrated for his jewelry, Miller participated in numerous exhibitions, most frequently the "May Shows" organized by the Cleveland Museum of Art. A graduate of the Cleveland Art School (now the Cleveland Institute of Art), he went on to

teach at his alma mater. Among his best-known students are Frank Marshall, professor emeritus of the University of Washington, Seattle; enamelist William Harper; and Lisa Norton, professor of metalsmithing at the Art Institute of Chicago. The American Crafts Council awarded its gold medal for excellence to Miller in 1994.

Description: The tall raised vessel is of elongated convex form and rises to a slightly everted rim. Its short stem contains four rectangular reserves. Of these, two display a sun motif of saw-cut flames and a central gold disk, on which a face has been delineated in granulated gold. The design has been soldered to an oxidized silver ground for contrast. The two sun images alternate with undecorated reserves. A flat base with an applied edge supports the vessel. The circular lid has a narrow flange and a stepped edge. The finial, soldered to the lid, is in three sections. Of these, a small flat disk supports a wide

FIG. 5. John Paul Miller (b. 1918), "Fragments" brooch, Brecksville, Ohio, about 1963. Gold; h. 1½ in. (3.8 cm), w. 2¹³⁄₁₆ in. (7.1 cm), diam. ½ in. (1.27 cm). Museum of Fine Arts, Boston; Gift of John Paul Miller in memory of Mary W. Miller (2001.157).

cone that is 1¹⁄₁₆ in. (2.7 cm) in diameter. At the center of this form is a second cone that has been capped with a third sun disk.

History: The urn was made during the Handy and Harman silver-smithing conference of 1951; retained by the artist until made a gift to the Museum.

Exhibitions and publications: None.

348

Lorna Belle Pearson (b. 1925)

Decanter

Probably Alfred, New York, 1953
The Living New England Artists Purchase Fund, Created by Stephen and Sybil Stone Foundation
2001.258a–b

H. 17⅛ in. (43.51 cm); Diam. base 2½ in. (6.35 cm); Wt. excluding stopper 15 oz 9 dwt 3 gr (480.8 gm)

Marks: "PEARSON / STERLING" struck incuse on base. "188" in red paint and "C/G 43–4A" in blue ink on cloth tape, also on base.

Inscriptions: None.

348

TALENTED AND ADVENTUROUS, Lorna Belle Pearson was the daughter of New York City art educator Ralph M. Pearson and elder sister of silversmith Ronald Hayes Pearson (1924–1996). She was often involved with her father's work; as a teenager, she contributed images to his book *The New Art Education* (1951). Despite an illustrious start to her career, she ceased practicing her craft due to the demands of marriage and children.

Pearson was a student at Black Mountain College from 1944 to 1946, when she transferred to the School for American Craftsmen, then located in Alfred, New York. It was a seminal, formative time in the history of both institutions. At the School for American Craftsmen, she decided to pursue a career as a silversmith, graduating in 1948 with a certificate of Master Craftsmanship in Metal.

While at the school, Pearson studied under jeweler Philip Morton and silversmiths Alden Wood, Lauritz Eichner, Charles Reese, and John Prip (cat. no. 354). After graduation, she exhibited at several early craft venues, including the "Wichita National" exhibitions. In 1951 she was appointed Crafts Director for the U.S. Army Special Services in Japan. Upon her return to the United States, Pearson taught studio crafts at the University of New Hampshire from 1952 to 1954.

This decanter was one of two works honored at the 1953 Designer Craftsman Exhibition held at the Contemporary Craft Museum. She won first prize for a pitcher and honorable mention for the decanter.[1] These awards marked her as an artist of promise and were all the more meaningful since the field included silver by senior craftspeople, including her former professor Prip.

With its slender neck and broad base, the decanter was a complex work to achieve. Presenting a gleaming and seamless surface, the highly planished surface belies its complex construction. The carved ebony finial has abstract, African overtones and provides a contrast in color and texture, a combination occasionally found in midcentury silver.

Long in the shadow of her brother, Lorna Pearson is receiving late recognition for her achievements. Like many women who chose the path of wife and mother to that of artist, she fell into obscurity. Almost fifty years later, we can look back and appreciate the elegant and flawless lines of her silver, noting with admiration all she accomplished during her brief but brilliant career.

Description: The raised vessel is composed of a slightly convex base that is surmounted by a slender trumpet-shaped neck. The lower portion has been raised, and the long neck was made in two sections: the narrow neck and the trumpet-shaped base. Both have been secured with lap joints, and the whole is soldered to the lower section, at the shoulder. The vessel is capped by a tall ebony and cork stopper carved in an abstract design. The finial is set into a silver ferrule that is secured to a wooden disk with a cork stopper. The whole is secured by a silver bolt threaded through the cork.

History: In the artist's personal collection until acquired by the Museum.

Exhibitions and publications: The decanter is probably the "wine bottle" listed in *Decorative Arts & Ceramics Exhibition, April 16–May 15* (Wichita, Kan.: Wichita Art Association, 1949), cat. no. 332; *Designer–Craftsman U.S.A.: A National Competition Sponsored by the American*

Craftsman's Council on the Theme "Designed and Handicrafted for Use" (New York: American Federation of Arts, 1953), 71, cat. no. 188.

NOTE TO THIS ENTRY IS ON PAGE 458.

349

Henry Petzal (1906–2002)
Pair of salad servers

Shrewsbury, New Jersey, 1965
Gift of Henry Petzal
1979.411–12

Spoon (1979.411): L. 12 in. (30.5 cm); W. 2⅜ in. (6 cm); Wt. 4 oz 9 dwt 1 gr (138.5 gm);

Fork (1979.412): L. 12³⁄₁₆ in. (30.8 cm); W. 2⅕ in. (5.6 cm); Wt. 4 oz 3 dwt (129.1 gm)

Marks: "HP" monogram and "HANDWROUGHT / STERLING" struck incuse on back of each handle.

Inscriptions: None.

SILVERSMITH HENRY PETZAL came to his craft late in life. Born in Berlin, Petzal immigrated to the United States in 1935 and established himself in Shrewsbury, New Jersey, where he enjoyed a successful career as an executive in the textile indus-

try. Several years before his retirement in 1963, he discovered a natural facility with metal and began attending classes at the New York City YMCA on Fiftieth Street, where Rudolph Schumacher and William Seitz taught him raising. At the Craft Students League, he learned chasing from Adda Husted Andersen.[1]

Petzal developed contemporary interpretations of historic silver forms, as found in the scalloped trays and plates; other works are reminiscent of Chinese pottery (cat. no. 352). He relieved silver's monochromatic surface tone with finials made of semiprecious stones. He strove to attain a three-dimensional quality, as attested to in the leafy candlesticks (cat no. 351); his bold chased decoration could be read at ten paces, lending a scale to silver not yet seen in the twentieth century. He devised some ninety forms, which he numbered and reproduced on commission, but never exceeded each design by more than eight examples.[2]

Thanks to his natural facility with the hammer and good business sense, Petzal soon found favor with such elite American shops as Tiffany & Co. and Cartier in New York; Caldwell and Co. of Philadelphia; and Shreve, Crump & Low in Boston.[3] After he moved north to Lenox, Massachusetts, his work was exhibited regionally at the Museum of Fine Arts, Boston (1970); the Berkshire Museum (1974); the Lawrence Art Museum (now the Williams College Museum of Art) (1975); and the Currier Gallery of Art, which in 1984 organized a one-man exhibition, with accompanying catalogue, of Petzal's work.[4]

Description: The spoon and fork are elongated, slender, forged objects of biomorphic shape; they have squared coffin-style handle tips. Stylized leaf decoration is chased within the bowl of the spoon; the fork tines are shaped and chased in the manner of a crocus bud.

History: Retained by the artist until made a gift to the Museum

Exhibitions and publications: Doty 1987, 23, cat. no. 11.

NOTES TO THIS ENTRY ARE ON PAGE 458.

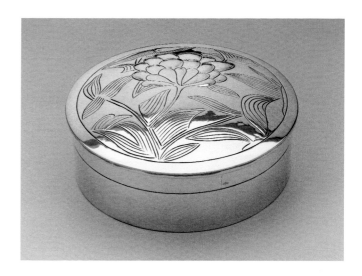

350

Henry Petzal (1906–2002)
Candy dish with lid

Shrewsbury, New Jersey, 1967
Gift of Henry Petzal
1979.413a–b

H. 2⅝ in. (6.5 cm); Diam. 6⅜ in. (16.2 cm); Wt. 28 oz 6 gr (871.3 gm)

Marks: "HANDWROUGHT," "HENRY PETZAL," and "STERLING," in sans-serif letters, struck incuse in different locations on base. A label affixed to the base reads "Display only 50/6593."

Inscriptions: None.

See cat. no. 349.[1]

Description: The friction-fitted domed lid of this vessel has been chased with the image of a peony flower and leaves; the design has an incised, circular border. The base has seamed sides and a soldered bottom.

History: Retained by the artist until made a gift in 1979.

Exhibitions and publications: None.

NOTE TO THIS ENTRY IS ON PAGE 458.

351

Henry Petzal (1906–2002)

Candleholder

Shrewsbury, New Jersey, 1968
Gift of Henry Petzal
1979.420

H. 3½ in. (9 cm); Diam. 10³⁄₁₆ in. (25.8 cm); Wt. 42 oz 15 dwt 8 gr
(1330.2 gm)

Marks: "HP" monogram and "HANDWROUGHT" and "STER-
LING," in sans-serif letters, struck incuse in various locations on
base.

Inscriptions: None.

See cat. no. 349.

Description: The candleholder is in the shape of a flower or leafy
cluster. It is formed of three layers of leaves, with chased veining,
that are bolted together. A shaped cylinder at the center serves as
the candlestick.

History: Retained by the artist until made a gift in 1979.

Exhibitions and publications: Doty 1987, 37, no. 46.

352

Henry Petzal (1906–2002)

Covered jar

Shrewsbury, New Jersey, 1968
Gift of Henry Petzal
1979.418a–b

H. 8½ in. (21.5 cm); Diam. 5¹¹⁄₁₆ in. (14.5 cm): Wt. 31 oz 13 dwt 7 gr
(984.9 gm)

Marks: "HP" monogram and "HANDWROUGHT" and "STER-
LING," in sans-serif letters, struck incuse in various locations on
base.

Inscriptions: None.

See cat. no. 349.

Description: The raised spherical jar with an applied rim bears an abstracted repoussé and chased design of leaves and flowers. The base is supported by an applied splayed foot with an applied vertical foot rim. The gently sloped, bell-shaped lid rises to a malachite finial.

History: Retained by the artist until made a gift in 1979.

Exhibitions and publications: Doty 1987, 36, no. 45.

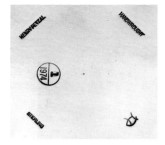 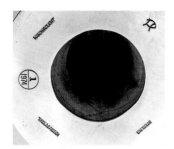

See cat. no. 349.[1]

Description: The raised bowl has a gilded interior, a flat base, and a slightly everted rim. The bowl is soldered to a raised trumpet stem that is attached to a flat ring-shaped foot. The drip plate with center point is surrounded by a cast seven-pointed openwork frame.

History: Retained by the artist until made a gift in 1979.

Exhibitions and publications: None.

NOTE TO THIS ENTRY IS ON PAGE 458.

353

Henry Petzal (1906–2002)
Cup with drip plate

Lenox, Massachusetts, 1975
Gift of Henry Petzal
1979.426a–b

Cup (1979.426a): H. 6⅞ in. (17.5 cm); Diam. 3¹¹⁄₁₆ in. (9.4 cm); Wt. 12 oz 8 dwt 20 gr (387 gm)

Drip plate (1979.426b): Diam. 5½ in. (14 cm); Wt. 5 oz 17 dwt (182 gm)

Marks: "HP" incuse monogram; "HENRY PETZAL," "HAND-WROUGHT," "STERLING," in incuse sans-serif letters; and "1/1974" within a circle, all struck on both.

Inscriptions: None.

354

John Axel Prip (b. 1922)
Onion teapot

Rochester, New York, 1954
Gift of Stephen and Betty Jane Andrus
1995.137

H. 6³⁄₁₆ in. (15.8 cm); W. 10¹³⁄₁₆ in. (27.5 cm); Diam. 7½ in. (19.1 cm); Diam. base 3 in. (7.62 cm); Wt. 23 oz 18 dwt (743.4 gm)

Marks: Three heart-shaped symbols in a row above "STERLING" in sans-serif letters, struck incuse on base.

Inscriptions: None.

JOHN PRIP is a pivotal figure in the history of American studio silver. Born in New York to a Danish metalsmithing family, Prip was a fourth-generation metalsmith familiar from childhood with workshop activities. His family returned to Denmark while Prip was a young child; he later attended Copenhagen Technical College, where for five years he was apprenticed to Evald Nielsen, graduating in 1942. He continued to build on his considerable technical skills between 1945 and 1948 while working for the family business and other Danish concerns. In 1948, at age twenty-six, he was recruited to head the metals

354

department at the newly founded School for American Craftsmen (SAC) in Alfred, New York.[1]

The school was an outgrowth of several crafts organizations spearheaded by Aileen Osborn Webb (1892–1979), founder of the Handicraft League of America, the American Craftsman's Council, and the Contemporary Craft Museum (now the Museum of Arts & Design). Webb's concern with the loss of traditional craft techniques, coupled with the return of many veterans in need of job training or rehabilitation, led to the school's creation in 1948. In their choice of Prip, the school was fortunate to engage an artist who had been thoroughly trained in all aspects of metalsmithing yet was willing to explore new forms and challenge functional aspects of the craft.

Prip left SAC in 1954 to pursue consulting and design work. He worked for a few years at Shop One, an early craft gallery that he established with professor and furnituremaker Tage Frid, potter Frans Wildenhain, and former student silversmith Ron Pearson.[2] He taught during the early 1960s at the School of the Museum of Fine Arts, Boston, during the tenure of Joseph Sharrock, while continuing to search for a different manner in which to express himself.

It was in the short-lived role of designer-craftsman that Prip saw the next chapter of his career unfold. Upon the recommendation of James S. Plout, first director of the Institute of Contemporary Art in Boston, to Roger Hallowell, then company president, he joined Reed & Barton, the silver manufacturer based in Taunton, Massachusetts.[3] Following developments at the Museum of Modern Art and the Metropolitan Museum of Art beginning in the late 1920s, Plout had created a Design in Industry department in 1948 to foster partnerships between rising designers and manufacturers.[4] Reed & Barton was the first company to participate, and Ronald Hayes Pearson (1924–1996), Prip's colleague from SAC, was among the first "Institute Associates" of 1955. It was through these associations that Prip's name came forward as company designer.

During his tenure as designer/craftsman-in-residence, Prip produced several designs for domestic wares that marked the brief union of craftsmen with industry during the 1950s and 1960s.[5] This teapot, called the "onion teapot" by the artist, was made in Rochester in 1954. It was shown in 1957 to Reed & Barton as an example of Prip's abilities. Shortly after he joined the company, the teapot became a signature piece for the production of Dimension hollowware and flatware. The technical skills needed to create the teapot exemplify Prip's exacting Danish training. However, his form and design solutions, such as the extended hinge and the tension achieved in the attenuated accents of the handle and finial, mark him as an innovative silversmith of first rank.

In 1963 Prip joined the faculty of the Rhode Island School of Design, where he taught until his retirement in 1980. He retained his affiliation with Reed & Barton, however, producing the Tapestry flatware pattern in 1964. He retired from the company in 1970.

Description: The onion-shaped teapot is in the form of a compressed sphere, from which the central cover and finial rise. The woven rattan handle forms a whiplash curve that widens before turning inward to the body. The cone-shaped lid seats seamlessly in the vessel's bezel-set opening. An ebony finial is shaped to meet the lid, extending vertically in a trumpet form.

History: Retained in artist's personal collection until purchased by the donors as a gift to the Museum.

Exhibitions and publications: C. B., "Shop One," *Craft Horizons* 16, no. 2 (March/April 1956), 18–23; "Dialogue in a Museum: Hui Ka Kwong and James Crumrine Discuss 'Acquisitions,' the Museum of Contemporary Crafts' 10th Anniversary Exhibition of Objects from Its Permanent Collection and Works to be Acquired," *Craft Horizons* 27, no. 4 (July/August 1967), 21; *John Prip: Master Metalsmith* (Providence, R.I.: Museum of Art, Rhode Island School of Design, 1987), 22; Arthur J. Pulos, "John Prip's Odyssey in Metal," *Metalsmith* 48, no. 4 (August/September 1988), 51; "Society of Arts and Crafts, Boston, Medal for Excellence in Craft Award and Exhibition," May 6–June 25, 1995; Jane Port, "John Prip: Medal for Excellence in Craft Award and Exhibition," *Metalsmith* 15, no. 4 (fall 1995), 44–45.

NOTES TO THIS ENTRY ARE ON PAGE 458.

355

Reed & Barton (active 1840–present)

Five-piece hot beverage service

Taunton, Massachusetts, 1928
Gift of The Seminarians
1990.323.1–5

Coffeepot (1990.323.1): H. 5⅛ in. (13 cm); W. 9⅛ in. (23.2 cm); Diam. 6⅛ in. (15.5 cm); Diam. foot 3¾ in. (9.5 cm); Wt. 15 oz 2 dwt 24 gr (471.2 gm)

Teapot (1990.323.2): H. 5 in. (12.6 cm); W. 8½ in. (21.5 cm); Diam. 5⅝ in. (14.2 cm); Diam. foot 3⅞ in. (8.7 cm); Wt. 13 oz 14 dwt 17 gr (427.2 gm)

Creamer (1990.323.3): H. 2¹¹⁄₁₆ in. (6.9 cm); W. 5⁵⁄₁₆ in. (13.5 cm); Diam. 4½ in. (11.5 cm); Diam. foot 2⅞ in. (6.9 cm); Wt. 6 oz 12 dwt 3 gr (205.5 gm)

Waste bowl (1990.323.4): H. 2 in. (5 cm); Diam. 4½ in. (11.5 cm); Diam. foot 2⅞ in. (6.9 cm); Wt. 5 oz 15 gr (156.5 gm)

Sugar bowl (1990.323.5): H. 4⅛ in. (10.3 cm); W. 6⁵⁄₁₆ in. (16 cm); Diam. 4½ in. (11.5 cm); Diam. foot 2⅞ in. (6.9 cm); Wt. 8 oz 4 dwt 18 gr (256.2 gm)

Marks: "[Reed & Barton trademark] / STERLING / 985 / 20 / 1 3 /4 PTS / [eagle]" struck incuse on base of coffeepot. "[trademark] / STERLING / 985 / 1½ PTS / [eagle]" struck incuse on base of teapot. "REED & BARTON / [trademark] / STERLING / 985 / [eagle]" struck incuse on base of creamer. "[Reed & Barton trademark] / STERLING / 985 / [eagle]" struck incuse on base of waste bowl. "[Reed & Barton trademark] / STERLING / 985 / [eagle]" struck incuse on base of sugar bowl.

Inscriptions: None.

IN THE EARLY 1900S, the low price of sterling silver, combined with a large number of immigrant metalsmiths and an increasing number of avocational artists, led to a rise in the popularity and production of silver hollowware. By the late 1920s, how-

355

all vessels except the waste bowl; hollow acorn-shaped finials bear a similar narrow reeded pattern.

History: Original owner unknown; sold to the Museum by Kurland-Zabar of New York City in 1990.

Exhibitions and publications: None.

NOTE TO THIS ENTRY IS ON PAGE 458.

356

Maria Regnier (1901–1994)
Three-piece tea service

St. Louis, Missouri, 1939
Gift of John E. Goodman
1989.60–62

Teapot (1989.60a–b): H. 6³⁄₁₆ in. (15.8 cm); W. 11¹³⁄₁₆ in. (30 cm); D. 6⅛ in. (15.5 cm); Wt. 42 oz 14 dwt 21 gr (1329.5 gm)

Creamer (1989.61): H. 2³⁄₁₆ in. (5.6 cm); W. 6¹¹⁄₁₆ in. (16.9 cm); D. 3½ in. (9 cm); Wt. 8 oz 16 dwt 4 gr (274 gm)

Sugar bowl (1989.62a–b): H. 3 in. (7.5 cm); W. 4⁵⁄₁₆ in. (11 cm); D. 3⅝ in. (9.1 cm); Wt. 12 oz 3 dwt 5 gr (378.2 gm)

Marks: "MR [conjoined within a square] / STERLING / HAND WROUGHT" struck incuse on each base.

Inscriptions: None.

ever, production had dropped considerably. A range of revival styles, but few new designs, was entering the market, possibly due to competition with electroplated silver and chrome-plate manufacturers. In 1925 Gorham Manufacturing Company of Providence, Rhode Island, hired Erik Magnussen to inject a modern look into their lines (cat. no. 340). Reed & Barton, in nearby Taunton, Massachusetts, issued a few contemporary designs, including this tea service that bears an eagle mark, the date symbol for 1928.

Unlike the tall and stately Neoclassical forms designed by Magnussen, the Reed & Barton service has more in common with machine imagery, with its narrow panels along the sides of the vessels and their spinning appearance, emphasized by a radiating design below the finials. From a manufacturing stand-point, the wide cone-shaped and paneled forms were simple to spin and stamp into the desired shape, with little or no chasing required. The vessels' two cone shapes were soldered together at their widest point, and a stamped foot was applied.

The largest pouring vessel was called a coffeepot by Reed & Barton, although it could also function as a hot-water pot. The service was originally sold with an elliptical waiter that bore a similarly patterned rim. The service with the tray sold for $450; the five-piece service alone for $200.[1]

Description: The vessels are composed of two wide truncated cones of differing sizes that have been stamped in a narrow pattern of panels and soldered together at their widest points. A conforming foot is soldered below. A related lid has a narrow band of panels below the hollow stamped finial; it is attached to the coffeepot and teapot by means of a projecting hinge. The sugar bowl lid is detachable. Hollow seamed handles with ivory insulators are attached to

As A YOUNG WOMAN, Hungarian-born and convent-educated Maria Regnier immigrated to the United States with her family, settling in Saint Louis, Missouri. While studying for her bachelor's degree at Washington University, Regnier took her first classes in metalwork and jewelry, studying with Ruth Barry and Noemi Madeline Walsh. In the summer of 1935, she studied with Sidney Rollins at the Rhode Island School of Design, and, in the summer of 1939, she completed her silversmithing courses at the Dixon School in New York, where she worked under Swedish designer Alex Hammer.[1]

By 1945 Regnier had found a market for her work in fine midwestern shops, such as the Warfield Shops and Lockhart's in St. Louis, Marshall Field's in Chicago, and Swanson's in Kansas City. Her talents were frequently noted in local and national newspapers.[2] By 1948 her clients included additional retailers from both coasts, including Georg Jensen, Inc., Gump's, and Nieman-Marcus.[3] Several solo exhibitions on the East Coast followed, including those at the Montclair Art Museum in 1949 and at Leah K. Curtiss Gallery in New York City in 1950. She

356

also participated in shows appealing to a broader audience, such as the "Wichita Nationals" in 1946 and an exhibition on American church silver at the Museum of the Cranbrook Academy in 1952.[4]

The streamlined appearance of her designs belies their time-consuming fabrication by hand. Regnier's silver often featured minimal decoration; many pieces are ornamented solely by planishing marks and the occasional bold applied monogram, circle pattern, or floral design, as seen on two compacts from about 1940–50 (cat. nos. 357–58). She explained: "I think that the beauty and glowing warmth of silver, whether in flat ware or hollow ware, is most evident when it is hand-crafted. I like simplicity but not the fancy nor gingerbread style of the Victorian era."[5]

Regnier produced dinner services, including place settings and plates for special clients; she also fashioned desk and home accessories that recall an age of cigarettes, mixed drinks, and rotary telephones. An energetic woman who took her craft seriously, she was dismissive of newspaper articles that focused solely on her sex and diminutive size.

Despite the acclaim she received in the 1940s and 1950s, Regnier's work did not enter museum collections until later in her life.[6] The Museum of Fine Arts owns a group of Regnier's jewelry in addition to the tea service and two compacts included in this catalogue.[7]

Description: The service, made of heavy-gauge silver, is composed of raised elliptical forms of two different sizes. Softly modulated plan-

ishing marks are visible. The teapot has a soldered rim; the strainer holes are cut through the body. The creamer displays a deep V-shaped spout with an applied lip; the rim of the creamer continues uninterrupted across the spout. Hollow, seamed, C-shaped handles are on the pitcher and creamer; the teapot handle includes ivory insulators. The elliptical finial on the teapot lid is made of ivory and secured with a silver screw and nut arrangement. The finial of the sugar bowl is made of silver.

History: Silver retained by artist until made a gift to the Museum.

Exhibitions and publications: Jessie Ash Arndt, "Mrs. Kaufman, Modern Jill of Many Trades Proves Herself Mistress of Them All," *The Christian Science Monitor*, Tuesday, November 1945, 80 (shown with tray, location unknown); Virgina Marmaduke, "Silver, Not Diamonds, This Girl's Best Friend," *Chicago Sun-Times*, November 5, 1950, 64; Fairbanks 1991, 77, cat. no. 64, checklist no. 92; Kirkham 2000, 235–37; figs. 9–13, checklist no. 67.

NOTES TO THIS ENTRY ARE ON PAGE 458.

357

Maria Regnier (1901–1994)
Circular compact

St. Louis, Missouri, about 1940–50
Gift of Maria Regnier
1988.145

H. ³⁄₁₆ in. (.5 cm); W. 1⅛ in. (2.8 cm); Wt. 4 oz 18 dwt 1 gr (152.5 gm)

Marks: "MR" conjoined within a square, and "STERLING" in incuse sans-serif letters struck on underside.

Inscriptions: None.

See cat. no. 356.

Description: The circular compact is cut from sheet silver; the sides are soldered. The applied floral design is ornamented with green and red enamel.

History: Retained by artist until made a gift to the Museum.

Exhibitions and publications: None.

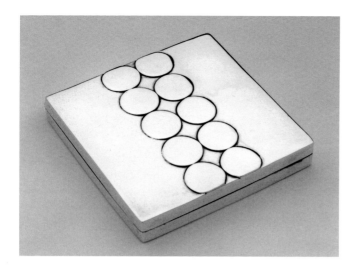

Margarete Seeler (1909–1996)

The Cup of '88

Kennebunkport, Maine, 1988
Gift in honor of Margarete Seeler
1999.135

H. 6 in. (15.2 cm); Diam. rim 4¼ in. (10.8 cm); Diam. foot 2¹¹⁄₁₆ in. (6.9 cm); Wt. 17 oz 1 dwt 20 gr (531.6 gm)

Marks: "S" within a circle, colored to appear as the symbol of yin and yang, formed with cloison wire.

Inscriptions: "+ ET NOS INDUCAS IN TENTATIONEM SE LIBERA NOS A MALO" (And lead us not into temptation, but deliver us from evil), in cloison wire, below rim of cup. "1988," to right of angel Gabriel; and "GENESIS / 1.26.27.28," to right of Adam and Eve, all in cloison wire, on bowl of cup. "GENESIS / 1.27" in cloison wire, on stem of cup, to left of skeleton.

FEW TWENTIETH-CENTURY decorative artists have chosen moral themes, but Margarete Seeler dedicated much of her career to such subjects. Her ineffably beautiful and often haunting enamels are suffused with the urgent message that humanity must find a way to care for itself or risk tragic consequences. She was born in Germany to printer and stationer Otto and Rose (Kempe) Seeler and barely survived World War II while living in Berlin with her two young sons. Some of her greatest enameled works bear witness to the cruelties wrought by war even as they resolutely retain hope for the future. Despite all she had seen, Seeler remained steadfast in her love of humanity and its potential.[1]

A student at the Berlin Academy of Art (Vereinigte Staatschulen für frei und angewandte Kunst), Seeler studied drawing, painting, goldsmithing, and enameling; she graduated about 1935. Among her professors were painter Bruno Paul (1874–1968) and anatomy professor Wilhelm Tank (b. 1888). She spent the next two years traveling around the world, drawing and painting along the way. From Italy, she traveled to Bali and India. In 1937 she returned to Berlin and married silversmith Herbert Zeitner (1900–1986), her former professor. The two later separated, leaving Seeler to raise their two children.

Seeler immigrated to the United States about 1957. She taught at the Putney School in Vermont until 1959 and then at the Wichita Art Association from 1959 to about 1961. Shortly afterward, she embarked on private studio work in Weston, Connecticut, where she occasionally collaborated with pewter

Maria Regnier (1901–1994)

Square compact

Probably St. Louis, Missouri, about 1940–50
Gift of Maria Regnier
1988.146

H. ⅜ in. (1 cm); W. 2½ in. (6.4 cm); D. 2½ in. (6.4 cm); Wt. 3 oz 2 dwt 9 gr (97 gm)

Marks: "MR" conjoined within a square, and "HAND [largely effaced] WROUGHT / STERLING" in incuse sans-serif letters struck on underside.

Inscriptions: None.

See cat. no. 356.

Description: The square compact is cut from sheet silver and soldered to form a shallow box. Two rows of circles are chased along the center of the lid and proceed from the hinge to the front opening.

History: Retained by artist until made a gift to the Museum.

Exhibitions and publications: None.

artist Frances Felton.[2] In 1980 she moved to Kennebunkport, Maine, and worked continuously until her death in 1996.

Much like an illuminated manuscript or a richly worked medieval chalice, this cup relies on brilliant colors and memorable biblical passages to convey a message. Using two paired images, representing the Old Testament and the modern apocalypse of nuclear war, Seeler distilled her hopes and fears for the future. By featuring images of a family and the archangel Michael, she implies that hope prevails over the devastation unleashed by nuclear war.

A close look at Seeler's enamels and her technical books reveal the painstaking efforts she took in creating a fully realized work of art. Her deft use of fine cloison wires yield lines as supple as those drawn on paper, and her chiaroscuro effects in enamel are worthy of any painter. A consummate artist, she was driven by the content of her work, writing, "We must never forget that design, skill, and precious metals are only the vehicles that give lasting form to a thought."[3]

Seeler's enamels are located in American churches, synagogues, and universities; many others were produced as private commissions. Her influence is wide, for many of her important projects were disseminated through her two technical books on enameling.[4]

Description: The standing cup bears polychromed enamel decoration depicting the birth and potential death of the world, expressed through religious and secular iconography. One side of the cup depicts a couple raising a child above their shoulders. To the left of the couple are a seated cow and a tree of knowledge, decorated with flowers, a bird, and a snake. To the right is a stand of flowers and birds, with "GENESIS / 1/26.27.28," formed by cloison wire, referring to God's creation of the world. Small fish create a border between the cup and stem. Below the family is a seated draped skeleton holding the atomic symbol in his right hand. In his left is a rope that secures a kneeling man to a ball and chain. To the right of the skeleton is the symbol "$" and two missiles.

Opposite the scene, the Angel Gabriel, with wings outstretched, plunges an arrow into a flaming crescent-shaped dragon at his feet. Below them is a nuclear explosion in which a mushroom cloud rises above flames and water. Burning ruins are to the left; a woman shielding a child is at the right, along with "GENESIS 1.27."

History: The artist gave the cup in 1991 to her son Hans Zeitner and his wife, Therese, who made it a gift to the Museum in 1999.

Exhibitions and publications: Glass on Metal 9, no. 3 (June 1990), 52–55 and cover; Margarete Seeler, *Enamel: Medium for Fine Art* (Pittsburgh, Pa.: Dorrance Publishing, 1997), 79–80; Kirkham 2000, 240–41, fig. 9-18.

NOTES TO THIS ENTRY ARE ON PAGE 458.

360

Henry Shawah (b. 1920)
Bird of the Nile salt cellar with spoon

Cambridge, Massachusetts, 1967
Gift of Mary and Martha Lorantos
1991.1039a–b

Salt cellar (1991.1039a): H. 4⁵⁄₁₆ in. (10.8 cm); W. 1¹³⁄₁₆ in. (4.5 cm); D. 3 in. (7.6 cm); 18K gold set with 5 sapphires (Wt. approx. 1.65 cts); two chrysoberyls (Wt. approx. 1.4 cts)

Spoon (1991.1039b): L. 1¹⁵⁄₁₆ in. (5 cm); Wt. 1 dwt 8 gr (2.1 gm)

Marks: "5/67/Shawah" engraved on foot of salt cellar. "H S" engraved on back of spoon handle.

Inscriptions: "18K" engraved on foot of salt cellar.

THE SON OF TURKISH immigrant silk weavers, Henry Shawah was born in Danbury, Connecticut, and spent his early years working in the fields of design, architecture, and art education before turning to goldsmithing. Following service in World War II, he made use of the GI Bill to study design and interior architecture at Pratt Institute, graduating in 1948. Shortly

thereafter, Shawah moved to Boston, where he worked for furnituremakers Irving & Casson as a designer of ship interiors. In the early 1950s, he worked for Boston architect Thomas Abyrd Epps and Newbury Street decorator Laura Appleton while teaching part-time at the Vesper George School of Art and the Fashion and Design Institute. Shawah held these various part-time jobs while earning a bachelor of science degree in Art Education from Boston University in 1953. For a few years, he taught full-time in the school's design department, where he discovered *Jewelrymaking as an Art Expression,* by D. Kenneth Winebrenner. The book helped him realize that "jewelry was based on the same premise as sculpture or other fine art forms," and he became "carried away with the idea of intimate sculpture."[1]

Shawah had experimented with metal from childhood, and Winebrenner's book stimulated the idea of establishing a jewelry studio on Nantucket. He spent a few years teaching design at Boston University and making jewelry in the summer and then enrolled in an intensive master's degree program in Fine Arts from Columbia University, graduating in 1958. After that date, he focused most of his energies on goldsmithing. He sold some work to the New York showroom of Georg Jensen and received encouragement from early exhibitions at Raybun Studios, America House, and Columbia University. Despite such exposure and a favorable review in *Craft Horizons* (1959), Shawah was unable to sell his jewelry to New York retailers, who felt that their clientele would not understand his aesthetic.[2]

By the 1970s, however, Shawah's jewelry had begun to receive recognition. In 1971 he became the first American to hold a one-man show at Goldsmiths' Hall in London. Perhaps the highest honor he has received came from the Goldsmith's Company, which invited him in 1981 to become one of their few international members.

Shawah made the *Bird of the Nile* salt cellar in honor of Julia Child, gourmet chef and television host from Cambridge, Massachusetts. He donated it to an annual fund-raising auction for the WGBH nonprofit television station. The salt cellar is one of Shawah's few vessels, but, as in his jewelry, its form is inspired by the animal world. The object's function relates to cuisine, the heart of Child's interests, while the lively stance of the bird and its sparkling tail convey, for Shawah, her "zany" personality.

The artist has developed a devoted circle of collectors. Among his many commissioned works are a hair ornament made for Hope Cook, the Queen of Sikkim, and a tie clip that included metal from the first Russian *Sputnik* spacecraft. Handsome presentation stands often complement his jewelry and enable the owner to enjoy the object as sculpture as well. Known for his easy laughter and ready smile, Shawah often shows his sense of humor in his work. His practical jokes in precious materials include dieter's spoons that are hinged above the bowl.

Shawah rarely draws a design beforehand. Instead, before turning to his workbench he seeks inspiration "sometimes by listening to music or by conversation, or the sky or an ice cream cone, by a dance or by recalling a previous sensation."[3] The result is a lively synthesis of his own personality and these far-flung ideas. He prefers to use high-carat gold and colored stones; a scintillating surface, created by cold-finishing tools, is a hallmark of his work.

These characteristics apply to the perky stance of the *Bird of the Nile* and its infinitesimally small spoon. They speak to the imaginative powers of the artist and his wish to communicate his love of form and metal, laughter, and life in an age in which information, rather than communication, rules the day.

Description: The body of the salt cellar is raised into the form of a bird; cold-worked decoration creates the look of feathers. The appendages are soldered to the body, and the five sapphires and two chrysoberyl stones are set with prongs. The little gold spoon is forged.

History: Purchased at the WGBH Boston television auction in 1967 by Mary C. Lorantos of South Natick, Massachusetts, and made a gift to the Museum in 1992.

Exhibitions and publications: None.

NOTES TO THIS ENTRY ARE ON PAGE 458–59.

361

Olaf Skoogfors (1930–1975)
Coffeepot

Rochester, New York, 1957
Gift of Judith Skoogfors
1999.132

H. 11⁵⁄₁₆ in. (28.6 cm); W. 6⅜ in. (16.2 cm); Diam. base 4⅛ in. (10.4 cm); Wt. 20 oz 18 dwt 10 gr (650.7 gm)

Marks: "HANDWROUGHT / STERLING / OS," the last within an oval device, in sans-serif letters, struck incuse on base.

Inscriptions: None.

OLAF SKOOGFORS was one of this country's most promising metalsmiths. His rigorous training and personal vision made him legendary among his peers long before his untimely death at age forty-five. Born Gustav Olaf Jansson in Bredsjo, Sweden, the artist and his family immigrated in 1934 to Wilmington, Delaware, where many immigrant Swedes had made their home. Upon becoming a U.S. citizen in 1945, his father, Gustav, changed the family name to Skoogfors, meaning "forest stream." The artist retained his birth name until attaining citizenship in 1955, when he legally became Olaf Gustav Skoogfors.

Following a brief stint in Sweden as a draftsman, Skoogfors returned to the United States, and, in 1949 he entered the Philadelphia Museum School of Art (formerly the Philadelphia School of Industrial Art), graduating in 1953. He studied metalsmithing and jewelry with Virginia Wireman Cute (later Curtin) (1908–1985) (cat. no. 337) and Richard Reinhardt (1921–1998). From 1951 to 1953, he exhibited in the sixth, seventh, and eighth "National Decorative Arts/Ceramics" exhibitions held in

Wichita, Kansas. "The Wichita Nationals," as they came to be known, provided a rare opportunity for craftsmen to compete and exhibit nationally; Skoogfors received honorable mention in 1951 and 1953. He exhibited as well in the 1953 *Young Americans* exhibition at America House in New York City.[1]

Skoogfors married the artist Judith Gesensway, daughter of musician Louis Gesensway, in 1954. Their marriage took place at the Radnor, Pennsylvania, home of magazine publisher Curtis Bok, which was designed by Wharton Esherick (1887–1970). The next year, the couple moved to Rochester, New York, where Skoogfors continued his education at the School for American Craftsmen in the Rochester Institute of Technology. There, he studied under Hans Christensen (1924–1983) and established lifelong friendships with such metalsmiths and jewelers as Svetozar (b. 1918) and Ruth Clark Radakovich (b. 1920); Ronald Hayes Pearson (1924–1996); and John Prip (b. 1922) (cat. no. 354).

Following Skoogfors's graduation in 1957, the couple returned to Philadelphia, where he established a private studio and began teaching. Beginning in 1959, he served first as a part-time instructor at his alma mater, renamed the Philadelphia Museum College of Art (now Universtiy of the Arts). He was appointed full professor in 1971. Skoogfors actively showed his work along with that of fellow professors, book artist Claire van Vliet; ceramicist William Paley; and furnituremaker Dan Jackson. Notable exhibitions include "Schmuck 70: Tendenzen at the Schmuckmuseum" in Pforzheim, Germany, "Jewelry by Olaf Skoogfors" at the Museum of Contemporary Crafts, New York (1968); and "Objects: U.S.A.," the landmark 1969 exhibition of the Johnson Wax Collection of Contemporary American Crafts. In addition, Skoogfors was a member of the First World Congress of Craftsmen, held by the World Craft Council (1964), and was a founding member of the Society of North American Goldsmiths (1970).[2]

Best known for his jewelry, Skoogfors was hailed for his abstract and sometimes enigmatic art. He created many pieces using the lost-wax casting process. Tyler School of Art professor Stanley Lechtzin has noted Skoogfors's close relationship to painters among the wider art community. This rapport may have influenced the reticulated surface and frontal emphasis of his work. Lechtzin observed that Abstract Expressionism especially informed Skoogfors's jewelry.

Description: The tall, cylindrical, seamed coffeepot of elongated pear form is seamed behind the handle. The cast silver handle brackets have a shaped rosewood insert. A forged spout with applied lip is seamed on the upper section. The form spreads, leaflike, against

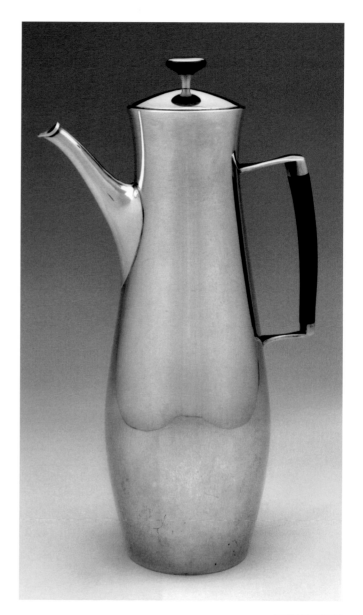

361

the body of the vessel, and its shape echoes the mouth of the spout. The friction-fitted lid has an inner flange and a slightly domed lid. A circular finial of silver and turned rosewood extends upward and outward to a flat silver top.

History: By inheritance to the artist's widow and made a gift.

Exhibitions and publications: Olaf Skoogfors, 20th-Century Goldsmith, 1930–1975 (Philadelphia and Washington, D.C.: Philadelphia College of Art and Renwick Gallery of the National Collection of Fine Arts, Smithsonian Institution, 1979), 53, cat. no. 10, fig. 10.

NOTES TO THIS ENTRY ARE ON PAGE 459.

With its trademark thin gauge and seamed form, this set follows Scandinavian metalsmithing practices that Olaf Skoogfors learned in Rochester from Hans Christensen and Jack Prip. The softly modulated surface, however, is at odds with the flawless mirror finish typically found among silver by graduates of the School for American Craftsmen. The surface treatment, achieved by thorough planishing and polishing, was specifically requested by Claire van Vliet, Skoogfor's colleague.

Description: The gourd-shaped seamed vessel has a soldered flat base. The raised bell-shaped lid rises to a tall, twisted ivory finial. A bezel soldered inside the rim of the lid seats on a flange inside the rim of the vessel. The slender spoon with forged, elongated lozenge-shaped handle is soldered to a shallow hemispherical bowl. Hammer marks are evident on the interior and exterior of the body and lid as well as the bowl of the spoon, as requested by the donor, who disliked finely planished silver. The spoon was designed to fit within the honey pot.

History: The donor, graphic designer Claire van Vliet, was a recipient of the John D. and Catherine T. MacArthur Foundation grant and faculty member with Skoogfors in Philadelphia during the 1960s. Van Vliet received the honey pot from the artist about 1966 in exchange for an example of her own work. Made a gift to the Museum in 1992.

Exhibitions and publications: None.

363

Olaf Skoogfors (1930–1975)
Chalice and paten

Philadelphia, Pennsylvania, 1968
Gift of Judith Skoogfors
1999.131.1–2

Chalice (1999.131.1): H. 7 in. (17.8 cm); Diam. rim 4¹¹⁄₁₆ in. (11.9 cm); Diam. base 2¹⁵⁄₁₆ in. (7.4 cm)

Paten (1999.132.2): H. ¹³⁄₁₆ in. (2 cm); Diam. 6 in. (15.3 cm)

Marks: "OLAF SKOOGFORS" in incuse sans-serif letters struck on exterior rim of chalice. Paten is unmarked.

Inscriptions: None.

This heavy, cast bronze chalice, with its scumbled exterior and projecting crystal, contrasts starkly with the smooth, lightweight paten. The artist's design choices reflect the taste of the era, in which stylish interiors featured combinations of

OLAF SKOOGFORS
STERLING

362

Olaf Skoogfors (1930–1975)
Honey pot with cover and spoon

Philadelphia, Pennsylvania, about 1966
Gift of Claire van Vliet
1992.287a–c

Honey pot with cover (1992.287a–b): H. 7⅞ in. (20 cm); Diam. foot 2¾ in. (7 cm); Wt. 11 oz 6 dwt 17 gr (352 gm)

Spoon (1992.287c): L. 6¼ in. (15.6 cm); Wt. 12 dwt 5 gr (19 gm)

Marks: "OLAF SKOOGFORS / STERLING" in block letters struck incuse on base, in center. Lid and spoon are unmarked.

Inscriptions: None.

363

364

Carlyle H. Smith (1912–2004)
Nut bowl and nut scoop

Princeton, New Jersey, 1945–46
Gift of Carlyle and Isabelle Smith
1993.593a–b

Bowl (1993.593a): H. 2⅝ in. (6.5 cm); W. 5⅜ in. (13.7 cm); D. 4³⁄₁₆ in. (12.2 cm); Wt. 7 oz 6 dwt 22 gr (228.5 gm)

Scoop (1993.593b): L. 4 in. (10.3 cm); W. ⅜ in. (.95 cm); Wt. 17 dwt 17 gr (27.6 gm)

Marks: "Smith 925" incised twice on base of bowl and once on back of spoon.

Inscriptions: None.

MANY OF THE ARTISTS in this chapter have spent their careers as teachers, and each can boast a devoted following of former students. Yet for personal modesty, high standards, and a broad-minded approach, Carlyle Smith holds a special place. He also forms an important link between the generation of silversmiths working during the Arts and Crafts period and those who came of age during the 1960s and 1970s. He studied with Augustus Rose (1873–1946), a pioneering professor in the field,

bold colors and varied textures, and middle-class homes sported long-fibered "shag" carpeting and sleek Scandinavian-style furniture. The chalice's nubby and distressed surface relates to fiber arts, then an ascendant craft medium, and gives a nod to similar accomplishments by such abstract sculptors of the period as Theodore Roszak, Seymour Lipton, and Herbert Ferber.

Olaf Skoogfors often incorporated precious stones into his abstract jewelry compositions. This ecclesiastical service marks an occasion in which the artist applied his jeweler's aesthetic to hollowware.[1]

Description: The chalice, of cast bronze, is composed of a small circular foot that rises, turning inward slightly toward the bowl, and then opens outward to the rim. A raised silver-gilt cup set inside the bronze form extends above the lip, forming a smooth rim. A rock crystal set into a copper bezel is attached near the foot of the chalice. The paten is a shallow, circular silver-gilt plate with three applied feet.

History: Originally made as a commission but never sold, the chalice and paten descended to the artist's wife, Judith Skoogfors, who made it a gift.

Exhibitions and publications: Olaf Skoogfors, 20th-Century Goldsmith, 1930–1975 (Philadelphia and Washington, D.C.: Philadelphia College of Art and Renwick Gallery of the National Collection of Fine Arts, Smithsonian Institution, 1979), 58, cat. no. 65.

NOTE TO THIS ENTRY IS ON PAGE 459.

and in the postwar era enthusiastically guided a diverse generation of young students.

Born in Connecticut, Smith studied metalsmithing with Rose at the Rhode Island School of Design in Providence, graduating in 1931. The Smith-Hughes Act, which funded part of his education, also required that he spend five years as a wage earner in a silversmithing shop before gaining a teaching certificate. This law was a distant echo of traditional apprenticeships, which typically involved seven years at the bench but no formal schooling. Although it was difficult to find suitable arrangements during the Depression, Smith was hired by Rose as an assistant in the Rose Metal Craft Shop, which he operated as an adjunct to teaching.[1]

Smith later taught silversmithing to students in the Providence public school system, a position that may have been arranged by Rose, who, by this time, had initiated a manual arts training program in his post as school superintendent. Smith then taught in the public school system in Princeton, New Jersey, until 1947. That year, he was invited by Marjorie Whitney, then chair of the Design Department, to become the first professor of metalsmithing at the University of Kansas, Lawrence.

Before leaving Princeton for Kansas in 1947, Smith followed Whitney's suggestion to attend the first Handy and Harman conference, organized by her former student, Margret Craver (cat. no. 335). To demonstrate his abilities as a metalsmith, Smith brought this silver nut bowl and spoon to his New York interview with Craver. The form's lightly planished surface and stretched oval shape were avant-garde for the time, and he was accepted. His attendance at the conference was well timed, for it enabled him to take full advantage of the program taught that summer by William Bennett, professor at the College of Art in Sheffield, England, before setting off to teach on his own.

During his second year at the University of Kansas, Smith established a degree program in metalsmithing, the first such four-year program offered by a state university. During his thirty-year career there, he left only briefly in 1965 to teach the first complete courses in silversmithing and jewelry at Costa Rica University. Upon his retirement in 1977, the department's metalsmithing studio was named in his honor.

Richard Mawdsley (cat. no. 345), Brent Kington, and Robert Ebendorf (cat. no. 339) are among the many nationally acclaimed artists who learned their craft from Smith. Their widely divergent styles blossomed, in part, because he encouraged their creative growth and supported their efforts. Each artist contributed to the shift away from the modernist Scandinavian aesthetic, which had been the standard at some schools since the 1950s, and toward personal expression in metal.

Smith's important commissions include a chalice for Trinity Episcopal Church in Lawrence, Kansas; an abbot's ring and pectoral cross made for St. Benedict's Abbey in Atchison, Kansas; and the chancellor's collar with mace for the University of Kansas. During his brief tenure in Costa Rica, he produced a gigantic bronze sculpture for the Supreme Court building in San José.

Throughout his career, Smith focused his energies on teaching. For his students, he created the Alpha Rho Gamma Club, the Greek letters forming the beginning of the word *argentum*, Latin for "silver." Under his direction, club members met educators, art historians, and commercial craftsmen, who provided them with guidance and opportunities in the field.[2] He was a founding member of both the Kansas Designer-Craftsman exhibitions sponsored by the University of Kansas and the Society of North American Goldsmiths. Of all these activities, Smith has been most proud of producing several generations of well-trained students imbued with the confidence to shape the future of silver. Smith packed up his bench and gave away his tools upon retiring in 2002.

Description: The elliptical vessel, with an asymmetrical emphasis, is soldered to a tall elliptical and angled base. The spoon consists of two overlapping oval forms that have been soldered together. The larger of the two has a shallow bowl, whereas the other serves as the handle.

History: Retained by artist until made a gift to the Museum.

Exhibitions and publications: None.

NOTES TO THIS ENTRY ARE ON PAGE 459.

365

Carlyle H. Smith (1912–2004)

Tea strainer

Lawrence, Kansas, 1949
Gift of Carlyle and Isabelle Smith
1993.594

L. 4⅞ in. (12.5 cm); W. bowl 2³⁄₁₆ in. (5.7 cm); Wt. 1 oz 8 dwt 4 gr (43.8 gm)

Marks: "925 SMITH" incised on handle.

Inscriptions: None.

THIS SILVER STRAINER was fashioned by Carlyle Smith within a few years of his arrival in Lawrence, Kansas. It displays a handle made from a polished brown mastodon fossil. The fossil—a fragment of a tooth discovered by Smith in the nearby Wakarusa River—was an unusual but sympathetic choice for artists of the period, who often chose wood, and especially ebony, as a warm complement to metal. The abstract piercings, the biomorphic shape of the bowl, and the carved handle make the strainer an exemplary piece of domestic silver from Smith's mature period.[1]

Description: A mastodon-tooth fragment, rounded and polished, serves as the handle to a deep biomorphically shaped bowl that displays piercings in an abstract pattern. The interior is gilded.

History: Retained by the artist until made a gift to the Museum.

Exhibitions and publications: None.

NOTE TO THIS ENTRY IS ON PAGE 459.

366

Valeri Timofeev (b. 1941)

Crosses beaker

East Stroudsburg, Pennsylvania, 1995
Museum purchase with funds donated by Dr. and Mrs. James Rabb
2002.64

H. 4 in. (12 cm); Diam. 3 in. (7.6 cm); W. base 2⅛ in. (5.4 cm); D. base 2⅛ in. (5.4 cm)

Marked: "Vt" within a square struck on side of base.

Inscriptions: None.

ENAMELING ON METAL dates to the fourth century B.C., when Greek goldsmiths adorned jewelry with cloisonné decoration. Plique-à-jour, the most difficult yet rewarding enameling tech-

nique, was not developed until the twelfth century. In this method, the artist uses the capillary action of liquid enamel to fill a fine wire framework. When fired, the enamel becomes a thin, translucent glass coat whose effects resembles those of stained glass.

Latvia-born Valeri Timofeev moved to Moscow, Russia, in 1967 to pursue his artistic education. There, he began work as a metalsmith and enamelist. By 1992 he received national recognition as one of a handful of contemporary artists to show their work at the Kremlin, in conjunction with an exhibition celebrating Faberge's 150th anniversary.[1]

In 1993 Timofeev immigrated to the United States, where his nationally exhibited work has garnered praise. He has won awards at the Philadelphia Craft Show (1995, 1996, 1998), Washington Craft Show (1997), and Crafts at the Castle in Boston (2001). His work is represented in the Rhode Island School of Design, the Newark Museum, and the Renwick Gallery of the Smithsonian American Art Museum.[2]

Timofeev employs an intricate geometry using cloison wires and color. In this beaker, the primary shape is the square formed by finely spaced cloison wires. Color adds its own pattern of crosses and diamonds, which are painstakingly applied in the form of enamel paste and then kiln fired up to thirty times. The process allows Timofeev to create dense passages of color that define the decorative scheme.

This complex design, a hallmark of Timofeev's work, recalls the Byzantine and Russian examples that served as his early sources of inspiration. The beaker departs from these early influences with a modern energy, rhythm, and rich coloration for which the artist is renowned.

Description: The cylindrical vessel is made of plique-à-jour enamel on an 18-karat gilded-silver body. The base is formed from twisted wire that has been wound tightly together at the base; single wires, or cloisons, shaped into decorative patterns, provide the framework for the enamel; the rim is applied. The base is composed of four narrow rectangular silver sheets that form shallow arches along their lengths. Soldered at each end, they form a square and support the base.

History: Purchased from the artist at the 2001 Crafts at the Castle show in Boston, Massachusetts; named as Director's Choice for the exhibition.

Exhibitions and publications: None.

NOTES TO THIS ENTRY ARE ON PAGE 459.

| 11 | 10 | 6 | 8 | 7 | 9 | | 2 | 1 | 4 | 3 | 5 |

367

Towle Manufacturing Company (est. 1882)

Robert J. King (b. 1917), designer

John Van Koert (1912–1998), director
of design

Contour place setting

Newburyport, Massachusetts, 1950–67
Gift of Mr. and Mrs. Charles Withers
1993.698.1–11

Serving spoon with egg-shaped bowl (1993.698.1): L. 9⅞6 in.
(24 cm); W. 2½ in. (6.3 cm); Wt. 3 oz 5 dwt 11 gr (101.8 gm)

Pie server (1993.698.2): L. 7⅞6 in. (19.2 cm); W. knife 3⅛ in. (8 cm);
Wt. 2 oz 10 dwt 19 gr (79.0 gm)

Serving spoon (1993.698.3): L. 8¾ in. (22.2 cm); W. bowl 1¹³⁄₁₆ in.
(4.6 cm); Wt. 2 oz 15 dwt 14 gr (86.5 gm)

Serving fork (1993.698.4): L. 9½ in. (24.2 cm); W. fork 1¹³⁄₁₆ in.
(4.6 cm); Wt. 3 oz 3 dwt 2 gr (98.1 gm)

Ladle (1993.698.5): L. 6⁵⁄₁₆ in. (16 cm); W. bowl 2⅜ in. (6 cm); Wt. 1
oz 17 dwt 19 gr (58.8 gm)

Knife with stainless blade (1993.698.6): L. 8⅞ in. (22.5 cm); W. ¾ in.
(1.9 cm); Wt. 2 oz 11 dwt 9 gr (79.9 gm)

Teaspoon (1993.698.7): L. 6⁷⁄₁₆ in. (16.3 cm); W. bowl 1¼ in. (3.1 cm);
Wt. 1 oz 4 dwt 21 gr (38.7 gm)

Soup spoon (1993.698.8): L. 6⅞ in. (17.4 cm); W. bowl 1⁷⁄₁₆ in.
(3.7 cm); Wt. 1 oz 11 dwt 19 gr (49.5 gm)

Demitasse spoon (1993.698.9): L. 4⅜ in. (11.1 cm); W. bowl 1³⁄₁₆ in.
(2 cm); Wt. 8 dwt 5 gr (12.8 gm)

Dinner fork (1993.698.10): L. 7⅝ in. (19.3 cm); W. fork 1⁵⁄₁₆ in.
(2.4 cm); Wt. 1 oz 17 dwt 22 gr (59 gm)

Luncheon fork (1993.698.11): L. 6¹⁵⁄₁₆ in. (17.7 cm); W. fork 1⅙ in.
(2.7 cm); Wt. 1 oz 10 dwt 17 gr (47.8 gm)

Marks: Lion rampant, enclosed within the script letter "T," all
within a rectangle; and "CONTOUR / TOWLE" in a rectangle
struck on all. "STERLING" in raised sans-serif lettering struck on
back of each handle.

Inscriptions: None.

See cat. no. 368.

Description: The handles have the appearance of a three-dimensional
brushstroke in which a long shallow indentation appears where the
pressure of the brush might have occurred; it is deeper toward the
center than at either end. The handle tips are gently upturned; the
knife handle is slightly curved toward sharpened blade. The forks
and spoons turn upward near each end. Each implement has a
matte brush finish.

History: Acquired between 1950 and 1967 by Charles C. Withers,
Towle Silversmiths president, and his wife, Margret (Craver) Withers; made a gift in 1993.

Exhibitions and publications: None.

Towle Silversmiths (est. 1882)

Robert J. King (b. 1917), designer

John Van Koert (1912–1998), director
of design

Contour beverage service

350

Newburyport, Massachusetts, 1953–about 1960
Museum Purchase with funds provided by The Seminarians
in memory of Nathaniel T. Dexter

2001.260.1–3

Pitcher (2001.260.1): H. 10⅓ in. (26 cm); W. 7 in. (17.8 cm); Diam.
base 3⁹⁄₁₆ in. (8.4 cm); Wt. 22 oz 13 dwt 21 gr (705.9 gm)

Creamer (2001.260.2): H. 4¼ in. (10.8 cm); W. 3¼ in. (8.4 cm);
D. 2⅓ in. (6 cm); Diam. base 1¹³⁄₁₆ in. (2.7 cm); Wt. 4 oz 11 dwt 1 gr
(141.8 gm)

Sugar bowl (2001.260.3): H. 3½ in. (8.8 cm); W. 3⅓ in. (8.6 cm);
D. 2¾ in. (7 cm); Diam. base 2 in. (5.1 cm); Wt. 5 oz 5 dwt 17 gr
(164.4 gm)

Marks: "TOWLE / STERLING / 128 / T / 350" on pitcher;
"TOWLE /STERLING / 115 / T / 350" on sugar bowl; and
"TOWLE / STERLING / T / 350" on creamer. All struck incuse
on bases.

Inscriptions: None.

TOWLE SILVERSMITHS has its roots in Newburyport, Massachusetts, where William Moulton II (b. 1664) first practiced his craft and where, for nearly two hundred years, at least one or two Moultons were engaged in the trade. The Towle name was introduced in 1857, when Anthony F. Towle and William P. Jones, apprentices under William Moulton IV (1772–1861), established Towle & Jones; over time that firm absorbed the Moulton business. The company underwent several name changes but had become generally known as Towle Manufacturing Company by 1882 and, soon after, as Towle Silversmiths.[1]

When Charles C. Withers was hired as president, the company diverged from their well-respected and large line of historically derived flatware and hollowware. Withers sought to inject a contemporary line into their silver offerings, and about 1949 he hired John Van Koert as head designer, based on the recommendation of Margret Craver (see cat. no. 335).[2] Van Koert set Towle on a path toward contemporary design as competition for modern-minded consumers grew among American and Scandinavian manufacturers.

The Contour pattern was the company's first foray into contemporary silver. Designed by Robert J. King (b. 1917) under Van Koert's leadership, it was launched with great fanfare in 1951. In a most unusual marketing strategy, Contour was featured center stage at an exhibition entitled "Knife/Fork/Spoon," held that year at the Walker Art Center in Minneapolis. The show was sponsored by the company, and (as might be expected) competing firms were not represented. Its stated mission was to consider the role of utensils from a wide range of cultures and periods to chart "the story of our primary eating implements and the development of their form." Historic and ethnographic objects were borrowed from leading American fine-art and natural-history institutions.

The exhibition arranged objects chronologically, from prehistoric stone knives and Pacific island horn spoons to sixteenth-century English flatware and, finally, Towle's Contour, which had been released about 1950. The pattern appeared on several pages of the exhibition catalogue, positioned as the apex in the evolutionary development of utensils. It was compared favorably to an unnamed floral flatware pattern, from the viewpoint of "good design," and was also featured in a table setting with Museum dinnerware designed by Eva Zeisel and glassware by Josef Hoffman, two high-profile artists whose inclusion conferred further status upon the flatware. To emphasize the Contour pattern's modernity and relationship to international art, it was compared with Konstantin Brancusi's sculpture titled *Bird in Space*; the text emphasized the "elimination of nonessentials" and "guarded use of ornamentation" expected of contemporary flatware.[3]

Towle's sponsorship of the exhibition, while exclusionary, was related to a trend in American museums that stretched back to the 1920s, when the Metropolitan Museum, the Museum of Modern Art, and the Institute of Contemporary Art in Boston had actively sought relationships with industry to improve or promote good design. Indeed, Towle initiated a number of silver exhibitions during the 1950s in an effort to educate consumers while drawing attention to the firm's products.[4]

This beverage service was released in December 1953, more than two years after the flatware was introduced. The beverage server was described as suitable "for coffee, for cocktails, for water, for any liquid, hot or cold."[5] At a time when many tableware manufacturers were reducing the number of elements in their services to attract busy consumers, the pitcher was an elegant form that could serve several purposes. It could be purchased singly for $200 or complemented by a sugar bowl ($75), creamer ($50), salt and pepper shakers ($50), or candlesticks ($35).[6]

The advertising copy for the service stated that Contour provided a "contemporary buffet ensemble for the connoisseur." For the consumer, the message was clear: Contour was the ultimate pattern of choice for the sophisticated American home.

Description: The silver beverage service is composed of a pitcher with lid, covered sugar bowl, and creamer that has a biomorphic shape and flat base. The pitcher handle is a translucent turquoise plastic.

History: Original owner unknown. Acquired by the Museum from Argentum, The Leopard's Head, San Francisco, California.

Exhibitions and publications: None.

NOTES TO THIS ENTRY ARE ON PAGE 459.

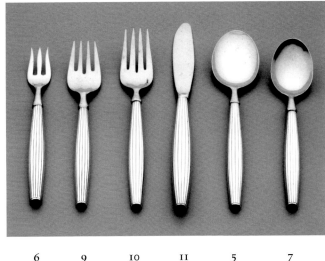

6   9   10   11   5   7

369

Towle Silversmiths (est. 1882), manufacturer

Earl Pardon (1926–1991), designer

William DeHart (active about 1949–1954), director of design

Contempra House flatware setting

Newburyport, Massachusetts, about 1954
Gift of Mr. and Mrs. Charles Withers
1993.699.1–11

Pie server (1993.699.1): L. 10⅜ in. (26.4 cm)

Salad fork (1993.699.2): L. 12½ in. (31.3 cm)

Salad spoon (1993.699.3): L. 12½ in. (31.3 cm)

Muddler (1993.699.4): L. 6 in. (15.2 cm)

Soup spoon (1993.699.5): L. 7 in. (17.4 cm)

Seafood fork (1993.699.6): L. 6⅛ in. (15.5 cm)

Teaspoon (1993.699.7): L. 6⅜ in. (16.3 cm)

Iced tea spoon (1993.699.8): L. 8¼ in. (21 cm)

Salad or dessert fork (1993.699.9): L. 6½ in. (16.5 cm)

Fork (1993.699.10): L. 7 in. (17.4 cm)

Knife (1993.699.11): L. 8⅜ in. (21.3 cm)

Marks: "contempra house," in lowercase sans-serif letters, above "STERLING HANDLE" in sans-serif capital letters, struck incuse on each handle. Stainless steel, melamine, or wooden implement affixed to each handle marked "TOWLE / STAINLESS."

Inscriptions: None.

4   8   1   2   3

EARL PARDON was one of the most influential American studio jewelers of the postwar era. Born in Memphis, Tennessee, Pardon attended the Memphis College of Art and studied with Dorothy Sturm (1910–1988), a remarkable artist and teacher who straddled the fields of modern painting, collage, and enameling.[1] Sturm introduced Pardon to enameling, which became his favorite mode of expression. In 1950 he was accepted as a participant in the silversmithing conference sponsored by Handy and Harman and, while there, broadened his appreciation for hollowware. The experience also brought him into contact with Margret Craver (cat. no. 335), with whom he developed a lifelong friendship.

In 1951 Pardon joined the Art Department of Skidmore College in Saratoga Springs, New York, fostering the development of such talented artists as Helen Shirk, Glenda Arentzen, Susan Hamlet, and Sharon Church. He retired in 1989.[2]

As part of the designer-craftsman trend that swept other silver manufacturers such as Reed & Barton (cat. no. 354), Pardon was invited to Newburyport in 1954 for a one-year appointment as designer-in-residence under Bill DeHart, another Handy and Harman participant. Pardon's interest in enamel was evident at this early date, and his chief contribution was the color note in enamel that energized Towle's new offerings. A subtle surprise in Pardon's Contempra House flatware was created by the circular dot of vitreous turquoise enamel on a recessed portion of the handle tip, which flashed as the diner handled the utensil.[3] Other enameled forms that Pardon developed include a Chinese- or Revere-style punch bowl and matching cups with enameled interiors as well as smaller candy or hors d'oeuvres dishes in biomorphic shapes and a variety of enameled colors, which found a ready audience.[4]

During Pardon's tenure with Towle, he and Craver occasionally collaborated. For the first visit by the Ancient and Honorable Artillery Company of Massachusetts to London in 316 years, Pardon designed a silver and enamel bowl for Queen Elizabeth II and an enameled cigar box for Sir Winston Churchill, for which Craver designed the lettering.

Following his experience at Towle, Pardon returned to Skidmore and focused almost exclusively on teaching and jewelrymaking. He perfected a lively geometric idiom, working in early years on a wire framework with enameled biomorphic shapes. Later he built modular, largely rectilinear sections of brightly colored enamel, which he combined with gemstones. His work demonstrates great color saturation and a refined sense of composition in the use of positive and negative space.

Description: Each utensil has a reeded silver handle, slightly convex in profile, that terminates in a recessed circular disk decorated with translucent turquoise enamel. The serving end of each is made of stainless steel, black melamine, or wood.

History: Acquired about 1954 by Charles C. Withers, Towle Silversmiths president, and his wife, Margret (Craver) Withers; made a gift in 1993.

Exhibitions and publications: None.

NOTES TO THIS ENTRY ARE ON PAGE 459.

Notes

333

1. *Young Americans* (New York: Museum of Contemporary Crafts, 1958), cat. nos. 14–15; *Fiber-Clay-Metal* (St. Paul, Minn.: Saint Paul Gallery and School of Art, 1959), cat. no. 183.

2. Bernstein's dual interest in metalsmithing and Jewish ritual silver can perhaps be best appreciated in an exhibition that he organized and whose catalogue he published, entitled *Sanctification and the Art of Silversmithing, Processes and Techniques: A Handbook for Museums* (Bronx, N.Y.: Judaica Museum, The Hebrew Home for the Aged at Riverdale, 1994).

3. Department files, Art of the Americas.

334

1. By the 1970s, Gebelein Silversmiths sold primarily antique silver and early examples of their own work; they undertook some conservation and repair work as well.

2. Robert Butler interview by Jeannine Falino, November 21, 2002.

335

1. The most comprehensive biographical information on Craver is in Jeannine Falino and Yvonne Markowitz, "Margret Craver: A Foremost 20th-Century Jeweler and Educator," *Jewelry: Journal of the American Society of Jewelry Historians* 1 (1996–97): 8–13. On Fleming, see "To the King's Taste," *Craft Horizons* 8, no. 23 (November 1948), 16–17.

2. Bennett graduated from the Sheffield school (now Sheffield Hallam University) in 1925. He worked for Omar Ramsden in London and was head designer at Garrard's, the royal jewelers, before returning to Sheffield to teach between 1936/7 and 1967. Bennett designed the Ascot Cup in 1936. "Sheffield Silver Set Chosen," *Sheffield (Eng.) Telegraph*, July 7, 1953; "Link with Year 1297, First Chain Designed for Town Trust," *The (Sheffield, Eng.) Star*, January 15, 1954.

336

1. Charles Crowley, "Exploration of issues and opportunities in a non-jewelry metalsmithing career," paper presented at "The Status of the Hand," Society of North American Goldsmiths Conference, 2000; typescript, department files, Art of the Americas.

2. Department files, Art of the Americas.

337

1. Katharine Richardson Wireman (1878–1966) was an illustrator who studied with Howard Pyle. See Henrietta Remington Shuttleworth, *Sunshine and Shadows: A Biography of Katharine Remington Wireman* (Riverton, N.J.: Richardson Press, 2000). Wireman drew illustrations for the *Saturday Evening Post* and the *Country Gentleman*, among other magazines. Virginia Wireman married James F. Cute (d. 1962) in 1943; her second marriage in 1965 was to Judge Thomas J. Curtin.

2. *The Philadelphia Inquirer Magazine*, April 30, 1950.

3. *Germantown (Pa.) Courier*, May 21, 1953; Prime was compiler and editor of *Three Centuries of Historic Silver: Loan Exhibitions under the Auspices of the Pennsylvania Society of the Colonial Dames of America* (Philadelphia: printed for the Society, 1938).

4. Among Cute's publications are "Care and Maintenance of Sterling Silver," *House Beautiful* (July 1954); "Collecting and Purchase of Sterling Silver," *House Beautiful* (December 1955); "Contemporary Silver," *House Beautiful* (April 1956).

5. Margret Craver, *Handwrought Silver* (New York: Craft Service Department, Handy & Harman, 1948), 11.

338

1. Biographical information is drawn from department files, Art of the Americas.

2. Bracelet (1995.783); demitasse service (2002.403.1–3); two rings (2002.404–5).

339

1. *Robert Ebendorf Retrospective Exhibition* (New Paltz, N.Y.: College Art Gallery, 1989), cat. nos. 2–4.

2. Department files, Art of the Americas.

340

1. "Modern Silver Design, Erik Magnussen Leads a Trend toward Plainer Patterns," *Good Furniture* 26 (June 1926), 291–92; Charles H. Carpenter Jr., *Gorham Silver, 1831–1981* (New York: Dodd, Mead, 1982), 256–64; Kathryn B. Hiesinger and George H. Marcus, *Landmarks of Twentieth-Century Design* (New York: Abbeville Press Publishers, 1993), 357; Venable 1994, 276–85; Mel Byars, *The Design Encyclopedia* (New York: John Wiley & Sons, 1994), 349.

2. In 1924 Frederik Lunning (1882–1959), sales chief for the Jensen Company, was responsible for opening the company's first American store in New York City. *Georg Jensen Silversmithy, 77 Artists 75 Years* (Washington, D. C.: Smithsonian Press, 1980), 17.

3. A similar example, retailed by Spaulding & Co. of Chicago, is illustrated in Venable 1994, fig. 9.28. For a period photograph of the dish without its cover, see "Silver in Modern Designs," *House and Garden* 52 (November 1927), 106.

341

1. The Cubic service is in the collection of the Museum of Art, Rhode Island School of Design. Much of the basic information on Magnussen has been drawn from Carpenter 1982, 256–64.

2. Advertisement, *The Jeweler's Circular* (July 5, 1928), 2–3. Karen Davies, *At Home in Manhattan: Modern Decorative Arts, 1925 to the Depression* (New Haven: Yale University Art Gallery, 1983), nos. 14–15; Alastair Duncan, *American Art Deco* (New York: Harry N. Abrams, 1986), 79–84; Alastair Duncan, ed., *Encyclopedia of Art Deco* (New York: E. P. Dutton, 1988), 114–15; Kathryn B. Heisinger and George H. Marcus, *Landmarks of Twentieth-Century Design: An Illustrated Handbook* (New York: Abbeville Press Publishers, 1993), no. 128; 108–9, 357.

3. Department files, Art of the Americas.

342

1. Quotation from *Sterling Silver by Gorham* (Providence, R.I.: Gorham Company, 1929), 266, courtesy Ulysses Dietz. For a cocktail set with twelve goblets, see Sotheby's, New York, sale 7568, December 1–2, 2000, lot 41. The cocktail shaker is illustrated in *Sterling Silver*. A set belonging to the Newark Museum has been published in Lowell Edmunds, *Martini Straight Up: The Classic American Cocktail* (Baltimore: Johns Hopkins University Press, 1989), 91.

[no notes on 343]

344

1. Department files, Art of the Americas.

345

1. The standing cup was made while the artist was on an eight-month sabbatical; department files, Art of the Americas.

2. Department files, Art of the Americas.

346

1. Lee Nordness, *Objects: USA* (New York: Viking Press, 1970), 188–89.

2. William Baran-Mickle, "Frederick A. Miller, A Precarious Balance," *Metalsmith* 13, no. 2 (spring 1993), 34–39; Jeannine Falino, "Obituary, Frederick A. Miller, 1913–2000" *Metalsmith* 20, no. 3 (summer 2000), 8.

3. Margret Craver, "An Ancient Method Goes Modern: Suggestions for the Metalworker," *Craft Horizons* 4, no. 4 (winter 1949), 15–17; "Fred Miller Makes a Silver Bowl by the Stretching Method," *Craft Horizons* 16, no. 6 (December 1956), 37–38.

4. Description of fabrication provided by Miller; department files, Art of the Americas.

[no notes on 347]

348

1. The pitcher is in the collection of the Yale University Art Gallery.

349

1. Barbara Dyer, "'A Thing of Beauty Is a Joy Forever': The Lovely Creations of a Silversmith," *Long Branch Daily Record*, April 6, 1966.

2. Doty 1987, 3.

3. Advertisements, department files, Art of the Americas.

4. Doty 1987. *Craft Horizons* 36, no. 1 (February 1976), 59. Petzal's silver is found in the collection of the Yale University Art Gallery and the Chicago Art Institute, among others.

350

1. For another example in this series, see Doty 1987, 40, cat. no. 50, where it is called a "covered bowl."

[no notes on 351–52]

353

1. For another example in this series, see Doty 1987, 54, cat. no. 82.

354

1. "Chronology," in *John Prip: Master Metalsmith* (Providence, R.I.: Museum of Art, Rhode Island School of Design, 1987), 49–50.

2. C. B., "Shop One," *Craft Horizons* 16, no. 2 (March/April 1956), 18–23.

3. John Prip to Jeannine Falino, June 1995.

4. W. Scott Braznell, "A 'New Way of Life': A Candelabrum from Reed & Barton's Contemporary Group," *Yale University Art Gallery Bulletin* (1997–98), 76–83.

5. John Prip, "John Prip and Reed & Barton . . . It's Been a Good Relationship. . .," *Craft Horizons* 24, no. 2 (May/June 1964), 51–52.

355

1. An undated photograph of the service, probably from a company catalogue and labeled no. 985, provides these prices. Information courtesy Jewel Stern. For published illustrations, see Shirley Lowell, "Designs in Contemporary Silver," *Home and Field* (February 1930), 32–35, 74; identical set is illustrated in Vanessa Brett, *The Sotheby's Directory of Silver, 1600–1940* (London: Sotheby's Publications, 1986), 347, cat. no. 1672.

356

1. According to the artist, Rollins had apprenticed with an unnamed jeweler who worked for the queen of England, probably at Garrard's, Crown Jewelers since their appointment to the post in 1843.

2. Jessie Ash Arndt, "Mrs. Kaufman, Modern Jill of Many Trades Proves Herself Mistress of Them All," *The Christian Science Monitor*, Tuesday, November 1945, 80 (shown with tray, location unknown); Virgina Marmaduke, "Silver, Not Diamonds, This Girl's Best Friend," *Chicago Sun-Times*, November 5, 1950, 64.

3. Department files, Art of the Americas.

4. *Montclair Art Museum Bulletin*, April 1949; Aline Louchheim, "Ancient Silversmiths' Art and Techniques Come to Life in Exhibit of Modern Sterling," *New York Times*, March 16, 1950; *Decorative Arts & Ceramics Exhibition* (Wichita, Kan.: Wichita Art Association, 1950), cat. no. 315; *American Church Silver* (Bloomfield Hills, Mich.: Museum of Cranbrook Academy, 1952), cat. no. 53.

5. Yolande Gwin, "A Rare Smith—A Woman Silversmith," *Atlanta Constitution*, October 16, 1959.

6. Regnier's career received renewed attention after 1980, when her silver was seen in the exhibition "St. Louis Silversmiths" at the St. Louis Art Museum. A 1948 tea service was illustrated on the cover of the accompanying catalogue. Deborah J. Binder, *St. Louis Silversmiths* (St. Louis, Mo.: St. Louis Art Museum, 1980), 35.

7. Jewelry by Regnier in the Museum's collection include a pair of clip-on earrings and ring (1988.147–48); an amethyst necklace (1989.70); and two brooches (1995.138–39).

[no notes on 357–58]

359

1. Seeler's unpublished manuscript, "Diary of a German Mother 1944 to 1945," focuses on her experiences and those of her children during the war; department files, Art of the Americas.

2. For an example of their collaborative work, see Lee Nordness, *Objects: USA* (New York: Viking Press, 1970), 184.

3. Margarete Seeler, *Enamel: Medium for Fine Art* (Pittsburgh, Pa.: Dorrance Publishing Co., 1997), introduction.

4. Many of Seeler's important works are illustrated in her books: Margarete Seeler, *The Art of Enamelling: How to Shape Precious Metal and Decorate It with Cloisonné, Champlevé, Plique-à-jour, Mercury Gilding, and Other Fine Techniques* (New York: Van Nostrand Reinhold, 1969); and Seeler, *Enamel*, 1997.

360

1. D. Kenneth Winebrenner, *Jewelry Making as an Art Expression* (Scranton, Pa.: International Textbook, 1953).

2. Conrad Brown, "Henry Shawah's Jewelry Is a Complement to Beauty," *Craft Horizons* 19, no. 5 (September/October 1959), 31–34.

3. These observations are drawn from the addendum to the artist's resume, department files, Art of the Americas.

361

1. Richard Reinhardt and Stanley Lechtzin, "Slow Is Fast, A Collaborative Dedication to Olaf Skoogfors," *Metalsmith* 7, no. 1 (winter 1987), 15–19; *Olaf Skoogfors, 20th-Century Goldsmith, 1930–1975* (Philadelphia and Washington, D.C.: Philadelphia College of Art and Renwick Gallery of the National Collection of Fine Arts, Smithsonian Institution, 1979).

2. *Jewelry by Olaf Skoogfors*, Museum of Contemporary Crafts, January 19–March 24, 1968, "Calendar," *Craft Horizons* 28, no. 1 (January/February 1968), 53; "Exhibitions," *Craft Horizons* 28, no. 2 (March/April 1968), 57–58; Lee Nordness, *Objects: USA* (New York: Viking Press, 1970), 221. No exhibition catalogue was produced for the Pforzheim exhibition; the Schmuckmuseum of Pforzheim owns a silver-gilt brooch with jade and pearls made by the artist in 1970.

[no notes on 362]

363

1. For a similar example by Skoogfors dated 1965, see Graham Hughes, *Modern Silver throughout the World, 1880–1967* (New York: Crown, 1967), 182–83, fig. 347.

364

1. Information on Smith's life drawn from numerous conversations, department files, Art of the Americas; Gary Nemchock, "Master Metalsmith: Carlyle H. Smith," *Metalsmith* 1, no. 3 (spring 1981), 10–14; and Richard Helzer, "A Legacy in American Metalsmithing," *Metalsmith* 14, no. 1 (winter 1994), 16–21. For Rose, see Jeannine Falino, "Augustus Rose and Antonio Cirino: Designers of the Society's Emblem," *Jewelry: The Journal of the American Society of Jewelry Historians* 1 (1996–97), 117.

2. Carlyle Smith interview with Jeannine Falino, Pittsburg, Kan., October 2002.

365

1. The Museum owns five works by Smith in addition to the two discussed here: a copper bowl made about 1934 (1003.592); three brooches (1993.595–97); and a rosary ring (1995.598).

366

1. Ellen Howards, "The *Plique-à-Jour* of Valeri Timofeev," *American Craft* 63, no. 2 (February/March 2003), 68–71. The vessel mentioned in the article's opening paragraph is not the work acquired by the Museum in 2001. Department files, Art of the Americas.

2. Department files, Art of the Americas; Kenneth R. Trapp, *Skilled Work: American Craft in the Renwick Gallery* (Washington, D.C.: Smithsonian Institution Press, 1998), 128.

368

1. Rainwater 1996, 206–7.

2. Craver married Withers in 1950; information courtesy Margret Craver Withers.

3. *Knife/Fork/Spoon: The Story of Our Primary Eating Implements and the Development of the Form* (Minneapolis, Minn.: Walker Art Center, 1951). The Museum of Fine Arts, Boston, was among the lenders. For MFA objects, see cat. nos. 17, 55, 69, 95. For flatware advertisements, see *House Beautiful*

93, no. 5 (May 1951), 90; 93; no. 6 (June 1951), 5, 93; and no. 9 (September 1951), 5. With other Towle flatware, *House Beautiful* 93, no. 12 (December 1951), 7.

4. *Knife/Fork/Spoon*, 47, 51–52. The exhibition traveled to the American Museum of Natural History; Dallas Museum of Fine Arts; Cincinnati Museum of Art; San Francisco Museum of Art; City Art Museum of St. Louis; J. L. Hudson Company of Detroit; and Cleveland Museum of Art.

5. A sampling of Towle exhibitions, some held at the Gallery of the Towle Silversmiths in Newburyport, include "The Story of Sterling" (1954 and 1956), with text by Kathryn C. Buhler; "'Upon this Occasion': A Loan Exhibition of Important Presentation Silver from Colonial Times to Today" (June 1–November 1, 1955); "The Odd and the Elegant in Silver" (October 8, 1956–September 27, 1957). All included historic silver borrowed from American museums. Unique among these Towle-sponsored shows is the traveling exhibition "Sculpture in Silver from Islands in Time" (New York: American Federation of Arts, 1955), in which ancient, medieval, and Renaissance silver sculptures were accompanied by contemporary works commissioned by the company. Among the artists were José de Creeft, Ibram Lassaw, Richard Lippold, José de Rivera, William Zorach, and David Smith; the sculptures were later donated to Harvard.

6. Advertisement, *House Beautiful* 95, no. 12 (December 1953), 106–7, described the "new Sterling Hollowware in *Contour*." The coffeepot and salt and pepper shakers of Contour were treated in Martin Eidelberg, ed., *Design 1935–1965: What Modern Was* (New York: Le Musée des arts décoratifs de Montréal in association with Harry N. Abrams, 1991), 200–1. Van Koert has been credited with the design of Contour, but it was created by Robert J. King (b. 1917), under his direction. See Kathryn B. Hiesinger and George H. Marcus, eds., *Design Since 1945* (Philadelphia: Philadelphia Museum of Art, 1983), 157, 217, cat no. V-20; Lee Nordness, *Objects: USA* (New York: Viking Press, 1970), 178. I am grateful to Jewel Stern for reminding me of this distinction. Julie V. Iovine, obituary, "John O. Van Koert, 86, Designer and Promoter of Danish Modern," *New York Times*, October 19, 1998.

369

1. Karen Blockman Carrier and Donna Riso Leatherman, eds., *Cobalt: The Art of Dorothy Sturm* (Memphis, Tenn.: Cobalt Publishing, 1988).

2. Jo Ann Goldberg, "Earl Pardon, Master American Jeweler," *Ornament* 10, no. 1 (1986); Sharon Church, "Color, Construction and Change, the Inventive Jewelry of Earl Pardon," *Metalsmith* 10, no. 1 (winter 1990), 18–24.

3. Because of the deep green-blue color, the design was dubbed "Jade." See "Annual Design Review," *Industrial Design* 3 (December 1956), 104; thanks to Jewel Stern for providing this reference. The flatware was available with or without reeding and with or without enamel; department files, Art of the Americas.

4. Enameled and epoxy-glazed bowls were produced concurrently by Reed & Barton and Wallace. For an advertisement that includes some of the enameled wares from Towle, see *House Beautiful* 99, no. 12 (December 1957), 81.

CHAPTER 7

KING SOLOMON'S TREASURE: SILVER IN LATIN AMERICA

Jeannine Falino

Silver played a unique role in the Spanish colonies of the Americas. It has come to represent stark contrasts: bright metal and dark mines, well-intentioned missionaries and abusive soldiers, foreign conquerors and vanquished natives. The Museum's collection of Latin American silver represents three major areas: Mexico; the Peruvian highlands, or the region that today straddles Peru and Bolivia; and Buenos Aires, Argentina. It encompasses ecclesiastical silver, whose production was centered in Mexico City and the Peruvian highlands; domestic silver, primarily represented by works from Peru and Argentina; and equestrian silver, best known through the colorful lives of the gauchos, also from Argentina.

The richly ornamented majesty of Latin American silver can be understood and appreciated only when set against the backdrop of complex historic events. Eager to gain a competitive advantage among European nations in the 1400s, Spanish monarchs Ferdinand and Isabella supported Christopher Columbus's plan to chart a westward route to Asia. There, they hoped to locate vast mineral deposits, just as Portugal had discovered in Africa. On December 22, 1492, Columbus arrived instead in the New World—continents unknown to Europeans. Landing in present-day Hispaniola, he was met by Taíno peoples wearing golden ornaments. Upon accepting the natives' gifts of gold jewelry, Columbus believed he had found new sources of riches. Within three weeks he hastened back to Spain, reporting his findings of "incalculable gold."[1] (Unbeknownst to Columbus, the ornaments given so freely by his hosts were in fact alluvial gold that had accumulated in the riverbeds for centuries.) Columbus's reports, published in more than twenty editions by 1500, sparked a gold rush, and Spanish explorers raced across the Atlantic to make their fortunes.[2] Thus the stage was set for Spain's energetic exploration and colonization of the Americas, efforts that were sanctioned by the Roman Catholic Church.

The Spanish did not find the rich gold deposits they sought. However, their efforts were rewarded about 1530, when significant veins of silver were found in Mexico and Peru. The fabulous yields underwrote the expansion of the Spanish empire and set the course of postconquest history in Latin America.

Speculators vigorously mined the less-precious metal, often with devastating consequences. Subjugated native peoples and, later, black slaves were forced to wrest the ore from the earth. Once refined, silver was minted into currency that symbolized the power of kings. It was transformed into sacred vessels that held the body and blood of Jesus Christ, and it was cast into utilitarian and decorative objects that gleamed silently from sideboards in comfortable homes, providing a source of not only beauty but also financial security for its owners. In the form of the Spanish *reale,* Latin American silver circulated throughout the Western world, including North America, where it was used as both currency and raw material. Silversmiths in the British colonies used the Spanish and other foreign coinage to supplement their supply of damaged or old-fashioned pieces of silver to melt in the crucible.

Fueling Columbus's reports were tales such as the biblical myth of King Solomon's gold. In the Old Testament story, "expert seamen" presented the king with gold from Ophir, a city whose location remained the subject of speculation; some believed it could be the source of the gold found by Columbus.[3] Others were tempted by tales of *el dorado,* or "the gilded man," in the Muisca culture of present-day Colombia. The Muisca incorporated gold into rituals celebrating the appointments of leaders. Covered in resin and gold leaf, the new ruler traveled on a raft accompanied by chiefs to the center of Lake Guatavita, where gold and emeralds were thrown into the sacred water as an offering to the gods. Spanish explorers plumbed and drained the lake several times in attempts to recover the precious metals believed to lie below the surface, but only a limited amount of worked silver and precious stones was recovered.[4] Still more compelling were the fabled seven cities of Cibola, which in 1542 explorer Álvar Núñez Cabeza de Vaca claimed to be located in the area of the present-day southwestern United States. Francisco Coronado sought this mythical kingdom in his travels through North America, a search that proved fruitless.[5]

Despite the lack of abundant surviving material evidence, ancient Mesoamericans were clearly knowledgeable about gold. Archaeological excavations have revealed that the earli-

FIG. 1 North and South America, 1535–1776.

est metalworkers in South America were based in present-day Peru about 1500 B.C. Their techniques migrated steadily northward to Mexico, where their presence is recorded about A.D. 800.[6] As for the metalsmithing skills of these early peoples, German artist Albrecht Dürer, himself the son of a goldsmith, wrote with amazement of the looted gold sent to Charles V by Hernando Cortez. Upon seeing the treasures in Brussels in 1519, Dürer remarked:

> I have seen the things which have been sent to the King from the new golden land: a sun all made of gold, a whole fathom wide, and a moon all of silver of the same size. . . . All the days of my life I have seen nothing that has gladdened my heart so much as these things, for I saw amongst them wonderful works of art, and I marveled at the subtle ingenuity of men in foreign lands.[7]

Likewise, the quality of wrought gold made in South America is known from descriptions of the brilliant ornaments worn by Atahuallpa, the thirteenth and last Incan king, and the roomful of gold he offered in 1532 to his captor, Francisco Pizarro, in exchange for his freedom. Despite twenty-four tons of gold and silver ornaments, jewelry, and statues brought

from throughout the Incan empire and melted down to obtain the ruler's release, Atahuallpa was executed in 1533.[8]

Soon after colonization began, Spain organized its territories into viceroyalties (fig. 1). The viceroyalty of New Spain was established in 1535 and encompassed Mexico, the western United States, and Central America. The viceroyalty of Peru, founded in 1542, originally embraced the whole of Spanish South America. Over time, it was broken into large parcels, including in 1710 the viceroyalty of New Granada, which was created by joining Colombia and the Caribbean Islands, and in 1776 the viceroyalty of Rio de La Plata, encompassing Argentina and Bolivia, to protect against the encroachments of neighboring Brazil.[9] Of these viceroyalties, silver-rich New Spain and Peru proved to be the most valuable.

The Roman Catholic Church was without doubt the most conspicuous consumer of silver in the New World. Its ambitious conversion program resulted in the construction of thousands of missions and churches requiring decoration, including ritual silver. Through the powers vested in the Church, Spain received a near monopoly to undertake the political and religious colonization of Latin America. In 1493, one year after Columbus's voyage, Pope Alexander VI issued *Inter caetera,* a bull authorizing Spanish occupation of the Americas. This was followed in 1508 with *Universalis ecclesiae regimini,* which directed the Spanish crown to oversee the establishment of churches for the conversion of indigenous peoples. In 1512 the two papal edicts were codified for secular use as the *Requerimiento,* which Spanish soldiers read to the natives they encountered. The document's friendly message of colonization and conversion was in fact a tool for subjugation, for any resistance was met with force, as sanctioned by the pope.

The combination of secular and spiritual rule in the Hispanic colonies enabled a seamless assimilation—missionaries converted indigenous peoples, and royal appointees brought them under Spanish jurisdiction.[10] The Church's efforts were rapid and dynamic; in Mexico alone, more than seven thousand churches were erected before 1700.[11] The silver mines provided the raw material for ecclesiastical ornament, which was used to sheath the surfaces of tabernacles, altars, and bible and missal stands and to create chalices, patens, and candlesticks employed in the celebration of Mass. In Lima, church decoration was especially lavish. In 1784 Spanish researchers Jorge Juan y Santacilia and Antonio de Ulloa captured the magnificence of churches there, observing:

> If the eye be directed from the pillars, walls, and ceiling, to the lower part of the church, it is equally dazzled with glittering

objects, presenting themselves on all sides: among which are candlesticks of massive silver, six or seven feet high, placed in two rows along the nave of the church; embossed tables of the same metal, supporting candlesticks. . . . In fine, the whole church is covered with plate, or something equal to it in value, so that divine service, in these churches, is performed with a magnificence scarce to be imagined.[12]

Second to the Church in consumption of silver were the Spanish colonists and creoles, or Spaniards born in the New World. Other consumers included successful mestizos, those of mixed European and native parentage, and a few respected indigenous families.[13] Many possessed large land tracts and great wealth, and they expressed their affluence through elegantly wrought silver objects, from serving plates and horse fittings to chocolate pots and chamber pots.

The veins of silver used by native peoples were all but exhausted by the early 1500s, when Hispanic settlers established the first colonial mines. In 1530 silver was struck in Sultepec and Zumpango, near Mexico City, in New Spain, and discoveries in Taxco and Zacatecas soon followed. But the spectacular find at Potosí, in Peru, caused the greatest sensation.[14] In 1545 at Cerro Rico ("rich mountain"), high in the Bolivian Andes, the Spaniards came closest to discovering a mythical city of gold. In sheer quantity, the silver found there exceeded their greatest expectations. Indeed, scholars believe that, between 1570 and 1650, Potosí produced more than half the silver in the world.[15] Such overwhelming production led to rapid and immense wealth, luxurious standards of living, and tremendous social turbulence that garnered for Potosí legendary status as one of the greatest boomtowns of all time.[16] Within twenty-five years, this barren highland town, located more than sixteen thousand feet above sea level at the base of the great mountain, grew from a desolate windswept precipice to a thriving metropolis of 120,000. In 1650 the population reached 160,000, far exceeding that of the viceregal capital of Lima to the west. Despite the town's altitude and isolation, the lure of immense riches attracted such vast numbers that, for a time, its population was said to rival those of the largest European cities. Site of the Royal Mint and Treasury and named by Charles V as the Villa Imperial de Potosí, the city grew to its zenith in the early 1700s, only to decline precipitously when the mines were depleted and Mexico's resources grew in importance. Other centers of silver production flourished through the late 1800s, but none reached the level of Potosí in size, importance, and extravagance.

Mined in vast quantities, silver became a common, albeit still valuable, material. The perception that the metal was everywhere led to exaggerated reports of streets lined with silver bars.[17] Yet, despite such hyperbole, even the most humble domestic forms, such as chamber pots, were subjects for the silversmith's hammer. Silver also lent itself to a particular style of architecture called plateresque, which was characterized by dense and lively surface decoration suggestive of silver plate. Many South American place names, such as Argentina ("land of silver" or "silvery one") and Rio de la Plata ("river of silver"), are based in part upon the metal's omnipresence within colonial culture.

The ceaseless drive for silver led to risky practices. Deeper and more dangerous mine shafts were built using imported iron to shore up passageways. Mercury, first used in 1555 to enable the separation of silver from ore, had deadly consequences for those who handled the poisonous element. The need for a large mining workforce led to forcible labor. First employed by the Spaniards as *mitas,* a seasonal or rotational form of labor that the Incas had used as tribute or tax system, native peoples who worked the mines at Potosí soon became a de facto enslaved population. An impoverished group, miners worked from morning until night in even the harshest weather conditions, suffering from mercury poisoning, silicosis, and accidents. As indigenous populations decreased due to sickness and death, they were replaced by enslaved Africans. In stark contrast to such hardships, Hispanic colonists enjoyed a period of extraordinary economic growth.[18]

Royal officials recognized the lamentable conditions of the laborers, but mining silver was paramount. The Spanish government ensured the extraction of the metal and its transport across the Atlantic to bolster the once-faltering Spanish economy.[19] The royal government's involvement in regulating the ore was directly related to the fiscal tax. Called *el quinto real,* or "the royal fifth," the tax provided funds critical to the Spanish monarchy but proved a vexation for those who extracted, refined, or otherwise handled silver. Without this payment, silversmiths could not receive the fiscal mark on their objects. In New Spain, and especially in Mexico City, where most workshops were located, silversmiths were expected to follow a strict hallmarking system that included location, assayer, and maker's touchmarks as well as the fiscal stamp proving payment of the *quinto real.* Many omitted touchmarks altogether to prevent tax officials from tracing pieces to their workshops. Indeed, surviving silver objects rarely carry all four marks; the greatest percentage of fully marked silver was fabricated in New Spain, whereas compliance in South America was erratic.[20] Examples in the Museum's collection demonstrate this pattern, for few bear touchmarks.

As in the establishment of hallmarks, Spanish colonists followed European precedents by creating a guild system, complete with rankings of master, official, and apprentice. The system was widely practiced among the various crafts in New Spain, but the metalsmithing guild was the richest and most successful. Well represented in all important cities of the viceroyalty, particularly Mexico City, the guild often displayed the most elaborate banners and lavish paraphernalia in civic and religious parades.

In the postconquest era, European and Spanish silversmiths introduced Western forms and ornamentation to the Hispanic colonies. Skilled native artists were engaged in workshops, but few have been identified due to the lack of hallmarks and records. In time, European hegemony in the field passed to new generations that included creoles, mestizos, and some blacks. In this manner, an energetic and eclectic interpretation of Spanish-inspired silver emerged to serve the church, state, and home.

The stylistic evolution of silver in Latin America followed principles of Renaissance and, later, Mannerist styles introduced by immigrant craftsmen from Portugal, Spain, and other European countries. Over time and through contact with local cultures and craftsmen, Western influences were subtly modified into a unique synthesis that can often be detected within the canon of European-based designs. For instance, feathers depicted in sixteenth-century silver may demonstrate an understanding of the material and the techniques of featherworking that would have been familiar to a person from a Mesoamerican culture. Native physiognomies sometimes appear, as do regionally based floral and animal representations. Many such features are rendered with an emphasis on detail that superseded European prototypes.

As in Europe, a stylistic progression from Mannerism to Baroque and Rococo designs took place in Latin America. Marked by profuse ornament and luxury, silver played both a physical and metaphorical role in colonial culture, especially in the religious realm. Silver served as one of the chief adornments for altars, sculpture, and architecture, often sheathing columns, entryways, and walls. This development was especially evident in the Peruvian highlands, where extensive and exuberant silver altar decorations prevailed. The workshops in this region were more provincial than those of New Spain, and the silver produced there demonstrates both the transfer of style throughout Spain's far-flung empire and the persistence of memory by local silversmiths, who blended their cultural tastes with European designs.

Like European decorative arts of the period, Peruvian silver emphasizes bilateral symmetry and a characteristic horror vacui that yielded a profusion of flowers, birds, figures, and strapwork. However, Peruvian craftsmen interpreted indigenous flora and fauna in a hyper-realistic regional manner and sometimes modeled Andean features on human figures. Grotesqueries included phytomorphic figures (sometimes called green men), mermaids and mermen, and androgynous and angelic characters. In addition to surface decoration, weight is also a distinguishing quality of Latin American silver. Many of the objects in this chapter are two or three times heavier than comparable examples made in North America or Europe.

With the establishment in 1785 of the Academia de San Carlos in Mexico City, Neoclassicism was introduced to Latin America, and a rational, cooler style of art prevailed. The era also heralded the end of the oft-cited golden age of mining, for most of the rich veins of silver in Mexico and Peru were depleted by the beginning of the 1800s. Silversmithing fell from favor as independence from Spain assumed precedence.

Over the last 150 years, the political turmoil and waning mining industry in Latin America have led to a decline in silversmithing. A reverse in this trend began in the 1930s, when American writer and designer William Spratling established a workshop in Taxco, Mexico, where he influenced a generation of Mexican silversmiths. Spratling single-handedly revived the craft by infusing it with new designs based loosely upon pre-Columbian imagery. His arrival coincided with that of American travelers who had realized the accessibility and affordability of their neighbor to the south. Burgeoning sales to tourists and American department stores fueled the early success of Spratling's endeavor and led to the lively industry that flourishes to this day.[21]

The Museum's collection is comprised of three major gifts. The first is a group of buried ecclesiastical silver discovered in 1879 by Mr. and Mrs. William H. Keith in St. Augustine, Florida. Made a gift to the Museum in 1928, these artifacts were only recently recognized as a rare and spectacular find. The bulk of the collection was presented as a gift by the Graves family in 1941. The family's patriarch, Edmund P. Graves, had conducted business in Argentina from 1898 to 1913 while his wife, Mary Warner Caldwell Graves, assembled an impressive silver collection.[22] Recently, the Museum's collection has been augmented by significant gifts from Landon and Lavinia Clay, longstanding advocates for pre-Columbian art in the Museum. Together, these works show a range of forms, techniques, and geographical sources made in Hispanic America from about 1600 to the early 1900s.

Several centuries of Spanish colonial activity in Central and

South America and Mexico have indelibly marked the region's language, art, architecture, and religion. Nevertheless, the overall effects of Spanish domination have been mitigated by the enduring strength and memory of indigenous peoples. The resulting Latin American world was and remains today one of multiple cultures and varied identities. The works of art in this chapter offer but one means of entry into the styles, forms, and preferences of its peoples.

Notes

The author offers special thanks to Vanessa Davidson for her assistance with this chapter, particularly her translations of Spanish-language texts and her review of the early manuscript. Cristina Esteras Martín, a scholar of Latin American silver, examined the Museum's collection and provided a wealth of observations for which we are deeply indebted. Gauvin Alexander Bailey of Clark University, Dennis Carr of the MFA, and Donna Pierce of Denver Art Museum provided insightful comments.

1. Some scholars have misidentified Taíno peoples as being Arawak. Irving Rouse, *The Taínos: Rise and Decline of the People Who Greeted Columbus* (New Haven: Yale University Press, 1992), 5, 142.

2. Portions of Columbus's *Diario del primer viaje (1492–93)*, now lost, were extracted by fellow traveler Fray Bartolomé de Las Casas and are cited in Fatima Bercht, ed., *Taíno: Pre-Columbian Art and Culture from the Caribbean* (New York: El Museo del Barrio and Monacelli Press, 1998), 170; Julie Jones, "Gold and the New World," in *El Dorado: The Gold of Ancient Colombia from El Museo del Oro, Banco de la República, Bogotá, Colombia* (New York: Center for Inter-American Relations and the American Federation of Arts, 1974), 12–14.

3. I Kings 9:27–28 NEB.

4 *The Gold of El Dorado* (London: Royal Academy, 1978), 18–23.

5. Cabeza de Vaca's 1542 report, published as *La Relación*, is treated in Cyclone Covey, trans. and ed., *Cabeza de Vaca's Adventures in the Unknown Interior of America* (Albuquerque: University of New Mexico Press, 1993), 13, 124. See also Michael Gannon, "First European Contacts," in Michael Gannon, ed., *The New History of Florida* (Gainesville: University Press of Florida, 1996), 16–39.

6. Warwick Bray, "Ancient American Metal-Smiths," in *Proceedings of the Royal Anthropological Institute of Great Britain and Ireland*, no. 1971 (1971), 25–43.

7. Cited in Jane Campbell Hutchison, *Albrecht Dürer: A Biography* (Princeton: Princeton University Press, 1990), 141. I am indebted to Thomas Rassieur for this reference.

8. *Encyclopedia Britannica* 2002, 1:661, 9:489–90.

9. Pedro Querejazu, introduction, in Pedro Querejazu and Elizabeth Ferrer, *Potosí: Colonial Treasures and the Bolivian City of Silver* (New York and La Paz, Peru: Americas Society Art Gallery, New York, in association with Fundación BHN, 1997), 8.

10. The eastern portion of South America was awarded by Pope Alexander VI in 1494 to Spain's rival, Portugal. Gabrielle G. Palmer, "Mestizaje," in *Cambios: The Spirit of Transformation in Spanish Colonial Art* (Albuquerque: Santa Barbara Museum of Art in cooperation with the University of New Mexico Press, 1992), 16. For the 1493 *Inter caetera* and *Requerimiento*, see James Muldoon, *The Americas in the Spanish World Order: The Justification for Conquest in the Seventeenth Century* (Philadelphia: University of Pennsylvania Press, 1994), 26–27, 40. For the papal bull of July 4, 1508, *Universalis ecclesiae regimini*, see J. H. Parry, *The Spanish Seaborne Empire* (London: Hutchinson, 1966). The position regarding colonization and conversion was generally known as the *Patronato Real*.

11. Richard E. Ahlborn, "The Ecclesiastical Silver of Colonial Mexico," in *Spanish, French, and English Traditions in the Colonial Silver of North America*, Winterthur Conference Report 1968 (Winterthur, Del.: Henry Francis du Pont Winterthur Museum, 1969), 19.

12. Jorge Juan y Santacilia and Antonio de Ulloa, *A Voyage to South America* (Tempe: Arizona State University, 1975), 181–82.

13. During the period of Spanish colonization, a stratified caste system, called the *sociedad de castas*, was established, based on racial characteristics. In this scheme, colonists and creoles were the most advantaged, whereas mestizos occupied a lower rank. Still lower were blacks, many of whom were enslaved specifically for mining. Edwin Williamson, *The Penguin History of Latin America* (London: Allen Lane, The Penguin Press, 1992), 144–46.

14. Mark A. Burkholder and Lyman L. Johnson, *Colonial Latin America* (New York: Oxford University Press, 1990), 54.

15. On the attempts by royal officials to maintain detailed records of production to levy the *quinto real* and the illegal smuggling from the mines, see Lewis Hanke, *Bartolomé Arzáns de Orsúa y Vela's History of Potosí* (Providence: Brown University Press, 1965), 36.

16. For the earliest history of Potosí, first advanced in the 18th century, see Bartolomé Arzáns de Orsúa y Vela, *Historia de la villa imperial de Potosí*; portions have been published in Hanke 1965; and Lewis Hanke, *The Imperial City of Potosí, An Unwritten Chapter in the History of Spanish America* (The Hague: Martinus Nijhoff, 1956), fn. 2. In addition to Querejazu and Ferrer, *Potosí*, see Peter Bakewell, *Miners of the Red Mountain* (Albuquerque: University of New Mexico Press, 1984).

17. On very special occasions, portions of streets were temporarily paved with silver bars; thanks to Donna Pierce and Cristina Esteras Martín for this information.

18. For the darker side of silver, see Richard Bushman, "The Complexity of Silver," in Falino and Ward 2001, 1–15. On the harsh conditions that continue today in Potosí mines, see John F. Ross, "Mountains of Pain," *Smithsonian* (November 2000), 142–51.

19. On the dangers to shipments, see Burkholder and Johnson, *Colonial Latin America*, 149.

20. The scarcity of fully marked silver, especially that made in South America, is evident in Esteras Martín 1992, 1992b.

21. For more than 1,200 marks, see Bille Hougart, *The Little Book of Mexican Silver Trade and Hallmarks* (Washington, D.C.: Cicatrix, 2001).

22. The Graves collection was placed on view in July–August 1941, shortly after its acquisition; *Antiques* 40, no. 3 (September 1941), 168. See also a press release issued by the MFA July 21, 1944; department files, Art of the Americas.

370

Chalice and paten (caliz y patena)

Mexico, about 1600
Gift in memory of Mr. and Mrs. William H. Keith
28.467, 28.469

Chalice (28.467): H. without base 7⅝ in. (19.5 cm); Diam. rim 3½ in.
(9 cm); Wt. (includes wooden base) 17 oz 8 dwt 23 gr (542.7 gm)

Paten (28.469): H. ⅜ in. (1 cm); Diam. 5³⁄₁₆ in. (13.2 cm); Wt. 2 oz 17
dwt 21 gr (90.5 gm)

Marks: "M" crowned, the Mexico City location mark, visible at base
of chalice bowl. Fragment of same mark on underside of paten.

Inscriptions: None.

DATING MEXICAN SILVER is somewhat easier than most Latin
American objects because of an assaying system established by
royal decree in the viceroyalty of New Spain. However, few
objects carry the full complement of required marks, and other
means are needed to fully understand the silver. Stylistic analysis of the form and the delicate, flat, Mannerist strapwork decoration of this chalice suggest a fabrication date of about 1600.
A published example of the crowned "M" Mexico City location
mark helps date the paten to the same period.[1]

The chalice is one of seven ecclesiastical items unearthed in
St. Augustine, Florida (see *History*) in the late nineteenth century. Long thought to be Spanish and only recently recognized
as Mexican, the vessels are a rare and early body of church silver made for Spain's North American colonies.[2] St. Augustine
was colonized by Spain in 1565, making it the oldest continuously occupied European settlement in the United States. The
town's strategic location on the Gulf Stream, where it protected Spanish vessels laden with South American silver en route
to Europe, prompted Spain to provide financial support, which
extended to the spiritual life of the inhabitants. From the beginning, religious and daily life in St. Augustine were interwoven.
Upon his arrival, founder Pedro Menéndez de Avilés (1519–1574)
brought "eight church bells and four ornaments for celebrating
Mass." When Spain became responsible for the colony, funding
for the clergy and the goods required for the celebration of
Mass were included in the annual budget for Florida's military
garrison. Between the late sixteenth and later eighteenth centuries, most sacramental goods were purchased from Mexico.
Proximity was a primary reason, for, in the age of sail, communication was slow. More compelling, however, was the financial
incentive—revenues collected in Mexico provided the budget
that sustained the Florida colony.

The early date of the chalice and its survival are remarkable given the many dangers through which it passed. How and when it came to be buried at some distance from the parish church of St. Augustine may never be fully determined, but the following events could account for some of its movements.[3]

In the seventeenth and eighteenth centuries, St. Augustine was often attacked by English soldiers. During some assaults, such as South Carolina's unsuccessful six-week siege in 1702, church goods were moved for safekeeping into a fortress called the Castillo de San Marcos. In 1763, when Florida was awarded to the British as a consequence of the Seven Years War (French and Indian War), all moveable church property was shipped to Havana, Cuba; an inventory from the next year records that these items included a *"copón* [cup] without a foot, silver and gilded on the inside," a description similar to the chalice in this entry. The Treaty of Paris in 1783 returned Florida to the Spanish, and the ecclesiastical goods were repatriated. An inventory taken in 1787 mentions chalices but lacks details that could identify this example.

St. Augustine joined the United States in 1821, and the parish found itself without financial support due to the separation of church and state under U.S. law. This stressful period was compounded by a largely anti-Catholic Protestant population that had emerged during the years of British occupation and renewed Spanish ownership. Chief among this group was District Attorney Alexander Hamilton Jr. (1786–1875), who argued that property of the Roman Catholic Church under the Spanish crown should pass to the U.S. government. Such rhetoric may have prompted church members to quietly relocate the chalice along with the rest of the ecclesiastical silver.

In 1823 Hamilton ran for the office of Territorial Delegate of Florida. Minorcan Catholics, an ethnic Spanish immigrant group affiliated with St. Augustine parish from the time of British occupation, sent a petition to President James Monroe protesting that Hamilton had threatened his opponents with unfavorable decisions on land claims. The name of Bernardo Segui appeared at the top of the document. Segui served as president of the Board of Wardens, which was incorporated that year by the Florida Legislative Council as trustee-proprietors of parish property. He also owned a plantation house on the land purchased in 1871 by the donors of these two objects. It is on this land that the church silver was discovered in 1879.

Church officials had reason to fear the loss of their silver, for the attitude of the Protestant majority was unsympathetic to their culture; upon seeing the communion objects at St. Augustine church in 1827, author and poet Ralph Waldo Emerson observed in his diary that they appeared to him as "great coarse toys." Church wardens had access to the church building and its furnishings, and it was not uncommon for them to house such items. Segui may have sought to protect the sacred silver items from falling into government hands.

Description: The chalice has a raised bowl with straight, slightly everted sides. The lower third is encircled with an applied molding that extends horizontally from the body; four small rings are soldered at equidistant points along the circle. The rings were originally intended to hold small bells that would have rung as the priest raised the chalice during Mass.[4] Below is a cup form with strapwork decoration that bulges slightly before tapering to a short trumpet-shaped stem having two flat graduated rings along a narrow stem. A larger baluster with additional strap decoration descends to smaller forms. The foot, long lost, has been replaced with a modern wooden base. The chalice, including the concealed central rod, has been gilded; some residual accretions from the period of its burial remain inside the bowl.

The circular paten has been raised into a shallow concave form; a center point has been incised as an asterisk on its underside. The concave side of the paten has been gilded.

History: The paten and chalice are among a group of seven ecclesiastical objects that were buried in St. Augustine, Florida, sometime after 1721, the date engraved on a cross (cat. no. 374) in the group. They were discovered in 1879 on Oneida Street in St. Augustine, on property owned by Mr. and Mrs. William H. Keith, located on the west side of Maria Sanchez Creek. They were placed on loan to the Museum in 1880 and given in memory of the couple in 1928.[5]

Exhibitions and publications: The paten, chalice, and five other items unearthed in St. Augustine were exhibited at the shop of silver and jewelry purveyors Bigelow, Kennard & Co. of Boston sometime after their discovery, according to an undated notice in department files.

NOTES TO THIS ENTRY ARE ON PAGE 507.

blood of Christ. The simple form is typical of those produced in viceregal Peru during the eighteenth century.[1] The horizontal emphasis of its decorative elements can be found in both ecclesiastical and secular forms.

Description: The raised vessel, with a low lid, is notable for its horizontal design elements. The flat-bottomed bowl is decorated with an applied projecting molding that is set beneath a lid, which has a similar rim. Three narrow knops define the baluster stem, which rises above a stepped base that splays outward. The stepped and scored lid with flange echoes the design of the circular base and is surmounted by a cast cross atop a small sphere. The interiors of the lid and the bowl have been gilded.

History: Collected in Buenos Aires, Argentina, by Mr. and Mrs. Edmund P. Graves between 1898 and 1913.

Exhibitions and publications: None.

NOTE TO THIS ENTRY IS ON PAGE 507.

371

Ciborium (copón)

Viceregal Peru, 1650–1700
Gift of Miss Ellen Graves, Mrs. Samuel Cabot, and Mrs. Roger Ernst in memory of their father and mother, Mr. and Mrs. Edmund P. Graves
41.373a–b

H. 7½ in. (19.1 cm); Diam. rim 3⅛ in. (9.3 cm); Diam. base 4 in. (10.2 cm); Wt. 16 oz 13 dwt 8 gr (518.4 gm)

Marks: None.

Inscriptions: None.

IN THE ROMAN CATHOLIC RELIGION, the ciborium is used to store the consecrated Host, which is mystically transformed into the body of Christ during the celebration of Mass. The interior gilding on this example is in keeping with church tradition that only the most noble metal could hold the body and

372

Aspersorium (acetre)

Colombia, 1675–1700
Gift of Mr. and Mrs. Samuel Cabot in memory of Helen N. (Mrs. Samuel) Cabot
41.360

H. 8⅝ in. (14.6 cm); W. rim 7½ in. (19.1 gm); D. rim 6⅞ in. (19.1 cm); Diam. base 4⁵⁄₁₆ in. (9.6 cm); Wt. 25 oz 5 dwt 10 gr (786.5 gm)

Marks: None.

Inscriptions: None.

A BOWL SUCH AS THIS, with tall curved handles, typically serves the Christian church as a vessel for holy water. It is usually paired with a hyssop, a small rod named for the herb used by the ancient Jews to sprinkle water on worshippers. The hyssop's long handle rested within one of the lobes at the vessel's rim. The priest carries the aspersorium and hyssop during church services, using them to sprinkle holy water on congregants.

Many such vessels have survived, although few retain their handles and accompanying hyssops. Examples were made throughout Latin America, and most share the lobed rim, cast handle loops, and simple foot seen on this example. Some have a taller, more elegant urn shape than this broad variant; still others more closely resemble large buckets. Published examples include highly repoussé and chased forms as well as simpler works bearing engraved dedications.[1]

372

With an emphasis on the large encircling planished lobes, this aspersorium recalls Portuguese two-handled cups of the seventeenth century. Such vessels may have been brought to Brazil, Portugal's South American colony, where they influenced silversmiths at work in the Spanish-speaking regions.[2] In New England, where sailing ships regularly departed for the Dutch colony Surinam, north of Brazil, among other distant ports, a lobed bowl made by Jeremiah Dummer has long intrigued scholars for its similarity to this distinctive form.[3]

With its lobed shape, answered from below by reverse curves that rise from the base, as well as its boldly chased strapwork, the aspersorium resembles at least two other published examples that have been attributed to Colombia.[4]

Description: The raised vessel is composed of a broad lower section that curves inward before extending upward and outward in a series of six large, repoussé demilunes, or scallops, that form the rim. Two gilded bosses, probably original, are cast with a face in the green-man style—here a man's face surrounded by a narrow band of petals.[5] Each head is surmounted by loops that originally served to secure the handle, now missing. The vessel was originally circular but is now elliptical.

Freely chased, flat, foliate decoration is set within the triangular and circular sections of the bowl, whereas the demilunes at the rim

are smoothly planished. A large tear in the vessel was repaired long ago, and the circular stepped foot may be a replacement.

History: See cat. no. 371.

Exhibitions and publications: "Exhibitions at Boston Museum," *Antiques* 40, no. 3 (September 1941), 168.

NOTES TO THIS ENTRY ARE ON PAGE 507.

373

Pair of altar cruets (vinajeras)

Peruvian highlands, 1675–1725
Gift of Miss Ellen Graves, Mrs. Samuel Cabot, and Mrs. Roger Ernst in memory of their father and mother, Mr. and Mrs. Edmund P. Graves
41.374a–b

41.374a: H. 4³⁄₁₆ in. (10.7 cm); W. 3½ in. (8.8 cm); Diam. rim 2 in. (5 cm); Diam. base 1³⁄₈ in. (3.6 cm.); Wt. 4 oz 17 dwt 13 gr (151 gm)

41.374b: H. 4³⁄₁₆ in. (10.7 cm); W. 3½ in. (8.8 cm); Diam. rim 2 in. (5 cm); Diam. base 1³⁄₈ in. (3.6 cm.); Wt. 4 oz 17 dwt 8 gr (155.4 gm)

Marks: None.

373

Inscriptions: Encircled letters "A" on one cruet and "V" on the other were cut from a sheet using a jeweler's saw and mounted on each lid.

THE LETTERS "A" AND "V" that surmount each small cruet stand for *agua* and *vino*, the Spanish words for water and wine, and reflect the cruets' role in the sacrament of Communion. During Mass, the priest pours a small amount of wine and water into the chalice, in accordance with the Roman Catholic belief that these liquids are miraculously transformed into the blood of Christ.

The mixing of water and wine in the communion chalice derived from the practice of the ancient Greeks, who diluted wine in this manner; Christians believed this act occurred during the Last Supper as well. Jewish precedent exists in the *chaburah*, a meal held once a week that customarily included a vessel containing water and wine. Early Christian converts continued the tradition. Descriptions of vessels for these beverages are mentioned as early as the eighth and ninth centuries, and by the eleventh century, records of these vials first appear. Most

ritual goods for Christian worship assumed specific shapes that varied little; cruets, however, were fashioned in a variety of forms. Each was usually distinguished by a jewel or letter symbol to easily discern the contents within.[1]

This pair, with plain bodies and simply cut letters, is a fine provincial example of the Baroque style from the turn of the eighteenth century in viceregal Peru.[2]

Description: Each vessel has a raised gourd-shaped body that tapers toward the rim. A cast circular foot and stem support each bowl. The foliate handles and snake-headed spouts are also cast. The lid is raised; a three-part hinge connects it to the handle.

History: See cat. no. 371.

Exhibitions and publications: None.

NOTES TO THIS ENTRY ARE ON PAGE 507.

374

374

Cross (cruz guión)

Probably Mexico, 1721
Gift in memory of Mr. and Mrs. William H. Keith
28.468

H. 12⅛ in. (33.2 cm); W. 7½ in. (18.2 cm); D. 3 in. (7.8 cm); Wt.
(including wooden base) 28 oz 7 dwt 6 gr (882.2 gm)

Marks: None.

Inscriptions: "+ SE ISIERON ESTE GION Y LAS SEIS BARAS
DE PALIO ANO DE 1721." (This cross and six canopy sticks were
made in 1721) in roman letters, engraved on cross, surrounding disk
of the Adoration of the Host. "IHS" engraved within the Host.
"+ SIENDO GORVERNADOR Y CAP.ᴬ GENᴬ EL Sᴿ Dᴺ
ANTONIO DEBENAVIDES." (Governor, captain general señor
sir Antonio De Benavides) in roman letters engraved around image
of Virgin Mary.

THE *cruz guión* was used to open processions for the bishop,
government, community, guilds, and other secular groups
that, in the Spanish colonial world, were often affiliated with
the church. The cross, mounted on a long staff, led the proces-
sion; the sticks, now lost, held aloft the canopy that served to
shield the priest or other high-ranking church members from
sun or inclement weather. The cross was made for, or more
likely commissioned by, Antonio de Benavides, who served as
general captain from 1717 to 1734 and was the twenty-eighth
governor of La Florida, the region so named by Juan Ponce de
León in 1513 and now the state of Florida.[1]

The term *guión* refers to the cross's role as a banner or sign.
It is thus distinct in purpose and design from the elaborate processional crosses called *cruz parroquial* that were usually carried by the priest within the church. Stylistically the former
can be identified by the baluster shape of the arms and their
smaller size.[2] In Latin America, where church and state were
intertwined from the start of exploration, the combination of
the sacred and profane was commonplace. The religious symbols on this cross suggest that it may have been intended for a
particular church. On the basis of its form, however, it is more
likely to have belonged to an affiliated fellowship *(cofradía).*

One mysterious aspect concerns the pine resin found within
the central boss. The unidentified silversmith who fashioned
the cross could easily have soldered the central sections together, yet he chose to fashion a friction-fit framework to enclose
an object; the pine resin was found within. An examination
of the resinous mass revealed no artifact, yet it is possible that

secular crosses were used as reliquaries. Technological developments may yet discern organic reliquary materials in the resin. Another theory relates to the ancient Mayans, who used resinous incense. Further research may indicate whether a lingering cultural impulse may have played a role in the placement of this unusual material within the cross.[3]

Description: The equal-sided cruciform structure surmounts a hollow cylinder that narrows toward the cross. The rod, which bears traces of gilding, has been lightly chased with foliate decoration. A baluster with scrolled projections separates the rod from the cross. Four chased "shooting" stars emanate from between each of the cruciform arms. A circular central boss is decorated on one side with a chased image of the Virgin Mary who, with elbows bent and hands together in an attitude of prayer, displays stylized roses in the folds of her cloak. The image is surrounded by engraved text. On the reverse, a removable circular frame also engraved with text holds a chased disk bearing the image of the Adoration of the Host, in which a consecrated Host, engraved "IHS" with a cross, floats above a chalice. A pair of angels flanks the chalice, and the scene is surrounded by rays of sunlight.

History: See cat. no. 370.

Exhibitions and publications: See cat. no. 370.

NOTES TO THIS ENTRY ARE ON PAGE 508.

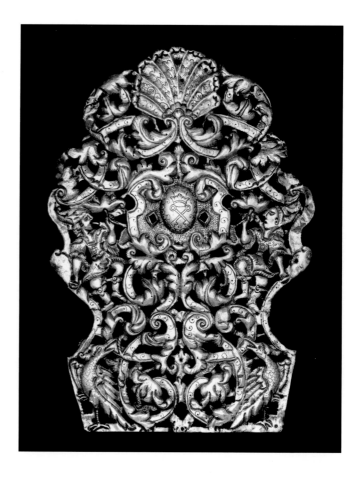

375

Plaque (mariola or maya)

Peruvian highlands, possibly La Paz or Lake Titicaca region of viceregal Peru, 1700–25
Gift of Landon T. Clay
1992.344

H. 21½ in. (54.7 cm); W. 15¹¹⁄₁₆ in. (40 cm); D. ⅜ in. (1 cm); Wt. 48 oz 4 dwt 13 gr (1500 gm)

Marks: None.

Inscriptions: None.

ORNAMENTAL PLAQUES such as this played an important role in Latin American churches of the colonial period. Made in large numbers, the plaques were attached at the rear to a wooden pole and set into a massive, stepped altarpiece that faced the congregation. When lit by candlelight and accompanied by silver candlesticks, altar frontals, paintings, and sculpture, they created a formidable, flickering presence. This example, the earliest of the group in the Museum's collection, features the

crossed papal keys and tiara associated with the papacy. The keys are an attribute of St. Peter, the first pope, who symbolically received the keys of the church from Christ. Their presence indicates that the plaque was probably made for a cathedral rather than a mission or church in Alto Peru. The delicate openwork pattern is a rare survival; the form was originally backed with velvet or silk to enhance its appearance.[1]

The figures on the plaque conflate several popular forms in Spanish colonial imagery. With their leafy hats, the characters are related to the so-called *hombres verdes*, or green men, whose forms spout verdant foliate decoration.[2] Their dress resembles that of archangels, with squared-neck garments, flaring sleeves, and prominent boots with bosses below the knee, as seen in paintings and sculpture.[3] The figures' broad noses, seen in profile, suggest that the silversmiths also blended images of indigenous peoples into the fanciful composite forms.

Description: The plaque is decorated in an overall, bilaterally symmetrical pattern of foliate strapwork fashioned as openwork decoration. A stylized scallop shell forms the peak; above the center is a raised oval reserve, oriented vertically, that bears a chased image of the crossed papal keys surmounted by a feathery two-tiered crown.

These symbols rest within a larger escutcheon framed by broken scrolls. The interior of the escutcheon has a punched background; two diamond-shaped holes once held precious stones. Two figures flank the central reserve, and two birds with long necks and slender beaks, possibly herons, flank the lower corners.

History: Original owner unknown. The plaque was part of a group of silver acquired in Bolivia and Argentina by Alphonse Jax, a private New York dealer; it was imported to the United States in 1975 and acquired by the donor at that time.

Exhibitions and publications: None.

NOTES TO THIS ENTRY ARE ON PAGE 508.

376

Plaque, possibly an altar frontal (*frontal del altar*)

Moxos or Chiquitos Missions, Paraguay, about 1730
Gift of Landon T. Clay
1992.343

H. 16¹¹⁄₁₆ in. (42.3 cm); W. 12 in. (30.3 cm); D. 1⁵⁄₁₆ in. (3.4 cm); Wt. 28 oz 18 dwt 17 gr (900 gm)

Marks: None.

Inscriptions: "MARIA" in overlapping letters chased on oval boss, near top of plaque. "IHS" in stylized foliate letters repoussé and chased on a large, circular central reserve.

BY VIRTUE OF ITS BOLD, repoussé central sun, this small plaque was probably the primary element in an altar frontal at a Jesuit church. The letters "IHS" displayed on the sunburst are a contraction of the ancient Greek spelling of Jesus, "ΙΗΣΥΣ," that, by the Middle Ages, was frequently seen in abbreviated form as "ΙΗΣ" and "HIS." The Society of Jesus, better known as the Jesuits, was formed in 1540 by Saint Ignatius of Loyola. The saint chose "IHS" as the order's emblem, with a cross above the *H* and three nails below, encircled by rays of sunlight. The rays refer to the consecrated Host, a symbol of the body of Christ and, by extension, the Jesuit brotherhood itself. Variations of this imagery were widely employed for many Roman Catholic ritual goods as well as for this particular religious order.[1] The curiously knotted quality of the lettering, strung along a taut ropelike line, may refer to the Flagellation, which, like the nails, is related to the Passion of Christ.

The Jesuits were the last such brotherhood to arrive in the Spanish South American colonies, establishing themselves in

the viceroyalty of Peru by 1568. This plaque was probably made for a Jesuit church in the Moxos or Chiquitos region in present-day Paraguay, where the Jesuits established missions in 1691. It may have been for a church dedicated to the Virgin Mary, for her name appears above that of Christ. The winged heart of Jesus, although not directly associated with Jesuit imagery, is shown here in its dual nature as both divine and human. Among the various angelic figures are nudes holding palm fronds as symbols of peace. The lower figure, with large sleeves and a hooded cowl, is probably a variant of an archangel.

Flanking the center of the plaque are pomegranates, a fruit with a hard exterior and tiny red corpuscles of juice within. During the Middle Ages, pomegranates were considered to be a symbol of the Passion and Resurrection of Christ. In this case, they can also be interpreted as a symbol for Granada, Spain, where the fruit can be found and whose coat of arms is dominated by its image. For the Spanish, the pomegranate was an important symbol of victory. Granada was the last major stronghold of the Moors, Muslims of mixed Spanish, Arab, and Berber descent who struggled against the Christians for control of the Iberian Peninsula for more than six hundred years. In

1492 Granada was reclaimed by Spanish monarchs Ferdinand and Isabella shortly before Columbus received their approval to seek a passage to China.[2] Thus the pomegranate carries multiple meanings for the Spanish. Beyond the symbol of the Passion, this unusual fruit served as a secular and, in this context, a particularly spiritual victory over the infidel Muslims.

The two curious figures wearing hats are fantastic androgynous figures that have been called mermaid-angels by Spanish scholars.[3] Shown from multiple viewpoints as they twist and turn, these winged creatures have female breasts and Andean features under their conquistador-style hats. Mayan speech scrolls emerge from their mouths, and a foliate tail completes the form. Although related to grotesqueries of the Mannerist era, these remarkable forms represent a unique fusion of European and local aesthetics.

Description: The rectangular, repoussé, and chased silver plaque bears, at center, a raised circular reserve with the letters "IHS" surmounted by a cross that straddles the letter *H*; below is a winged heart from which appear three nails. A sunburst radiates outward and downward to the rectangular plaque, which bears scrolled, foliate decoration. Among the elements on the plaque are a pair of nudes holding palm fronds; a single cherubim who flies over the name "MARIA"; two pairs of cherubim in each of the four corners; pomegranates; a pair of herons; two figures wearing hats; and a lower central figure with arms upraised. A hole used to secure the sheet to a frame appears in each of the four corners. Two diamond-shaped reserves suggest that precious stones may have originally adorned the plaque.

History: See cat. no. 375.

Exhibitions and publications: None.

NOTES TO THIS ENTRY ARE ON PAGE 508.

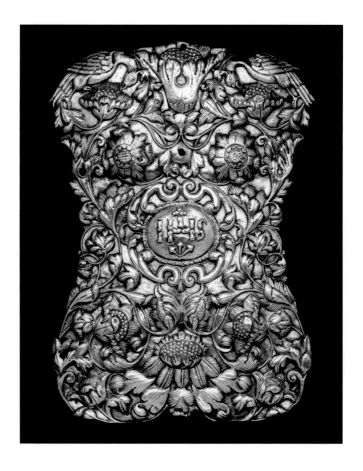

377

Pair of plaques (mariolas or mayas)

Moxos or Chiquitos missions, Paraguay, 1725–50
Gift of Landon T. Clay
1992.345–46

1992.345: H. 17¼ in. (43.8 cm); W. 12 in. (30.5 cm); D. 1⁵⁄₁₆ in. (3.4 cm); Wt. 28 oz 18 dwt 17 gr (900 gm)

1992.346: H. 16⅝ in. (42.2 cm); W. 12³⁄₁₆ in. (31.1 cm); D. 1⁵⁄₁₆ in. (3.4 cm); Wt. 25 oz 14 dwt 10 gr (800 gm)

Marks: None.

Inscriptions: "IHS" repoussé and chased on central elliptical boss.

A DYNAMIC BAROQUE ENERGY flourishes amid the formal symmetry of these plaques and the pair that follows (cat. no. 378). Derived stylistically from repoussé sconces of northern Europe, the heavily worked surface, hyper-realistic forms, and dense design mark these examples as a vigorous synthesis of European and native aesthetics. As with the previous plaque,

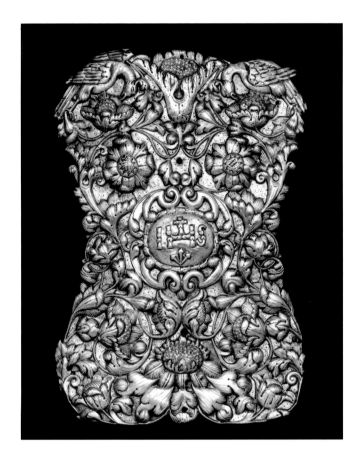

to the Passion of Christ.[1] The insistent repetition of the flower on these plaques is indicative of the Guaraní, who lacked a figurative tradition but emphasized pattern as a means of conveying a larger cosmology. Gauvin Bailey has advanced the theory that the Guaraní absorbed Roman Catholicism because their beliefs enabled them to see the spirit of their gods in many forms.[2] Given this perspective, it seems reasonable to assume that the plaques were made by native silversmiths working in a Western idiom to please the Jesuits while remaining faithful to their precontact worldview.

Description: The pair of shaped ornamental plaques has a bilaterally symmetrical design of flowers and birds, with a central elliptical boss. The letters "IHS" are chased on the boss, and a cross surmounts the broad letter *H*; below the letters are three nails that converge. The ellipse is surrounded by a scrolled mantling. Several holes appear along the central axis of each plaque.

History: See cat. no. 375.

Exhibitions and publications: None.

NOTES TO THIS ENTRY ARE ON PAGE 508.

this pair was probably made for a Jesuit church, possibly near Moxos or Chiquitos, home of the Guaraní peoples of Paraguay.

The intensely repoussé and chased flowers on these plaques, the following pair, and the missal stand (cat. no. 379) are rendered in a northern European–style composition typically composed of tulips and other cultivated Western blossoms. The silversmiths who produced these plaques appear to have depicted indigenous passion flower (*mburucuyà*), no doubt for their relevance to Guaraní society. Stylized drawings of the flower had been made by 1609 and 1610 that relate to the flowers depicted here. The Jesuits often adapted cultural elements of their hosts to convey the tenets of Christianity.

The passion flower was known for its sedative properties, and it was used by Guaraní shamans to achieve a dreamlike state. To gain coverts among the Guaraní, Jesuit priests assumed the messianic role of great shaman (*karai*). According to native beliefs, the flower was also thought to be favored by the Sun and linked with rebirth or resurrection. In Latin America, the Roman Catholic Church had appropriated the symbol for its own purposes, long before the arrival of the Jesuits, linking it

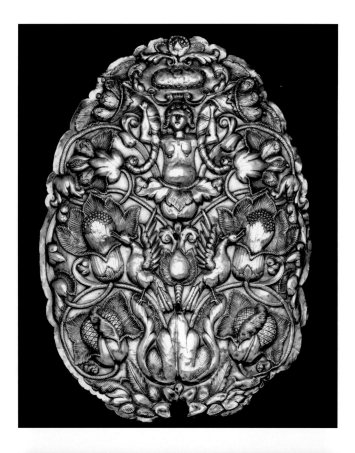

378

Pair of plaques (mariolas or mayas)

Moxos or Chiquitos missions, Paraguay, 1740–50
Gift of Landon T. Clay
1992.347–48

1992.347: H. 24⅜ in. (62 cm); W. 18⁵⁄₁₆ in. (46.5 cm); D. 2 in. (5 cm); Wt. 57 oz 17 dwt 10 gr (1800 gm)

1992.348: H. 24⅛ in. (61.2 cm); W. 17⅞ in. (45.4 cm); D. 1⅞ in. (4.8 cm); Wt. 57 oz 17 dwt 10 gr (1800 gm)

Marks: None.

Inscriptions: "IHS" engraved on elliptical boss, near tip of each plaque.

AN OLD WOMAN with drooping breasts forms the central decorative element of this plaque. She is the *hombre verde*, or green figure or grotesquerie, who emerges from a budlike form (see also cat. no. 376).

Description: Each almond-shaped plaque is bilaterally symmetrical. The flowers, a pair of long-necked birds, and a central figure have been repousséd and chased to create a form in high relief. The floral element appears to be the passion flower. Several holes appear along the central axis of the plaque.

History: See cat. no. 375.

Exhibitions and publications: None.

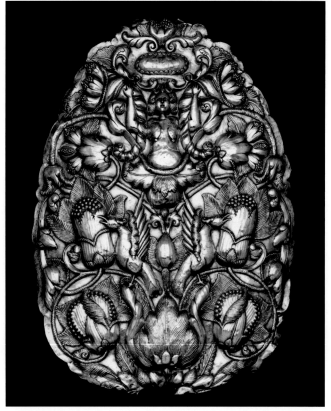

379

Missal stand (atril)

Probably Moxos mission, Paraguay, 1725–30
Gift of Landon T. Clay
2001.843

H. 11⅝ in. (29.4 cm); W. 13¹¹⁄₁₆ in. (34.8 cm); D. 10⅝ in. (26.8 cm);
Wt. including wooden frame 83 oz 11 dwt 20 gr (2600 gm)

Marks: None.

Inscriptions: "IHS" in raised letters chased within an elliptical boss
at center of stand.

THE BOLD FLORAL and figurative work on this missal stand is
similar to that seen in the preceding ornamental plaques. The
stand is perhaps most notable for its inclusion of the mountain
viscacha, an animal indigenous to South America. A member
of the chinchilla family, this small and timid plant-eating rodent
with large rabbitlike ears became a popular decorative element
in silver and textiles of the postconquest period.[1] The passion
flower is depicted as a strawberry-shaped fruit on the side of
the stand.

The missal stand is intended to support a copy of the liturgical book of the Roman rite that is used by the priest during
Mass. The stand would have been placed nearby on the altar

so that the officiant could refer to it as needed. Because of its orientation toward the congregation, the missal stand was finished on the front and two sides but left open and unfinished at the back.

Description: Formed of five sheets of silver with a simple replaced wooden framework, the slanted central portion of the stand has been repoussé with an elliptical boss on which is chased the Jesuit seal "IHS," with a cross above and three nails below.

Covered throughout with repoussé and chased decoration, the pattern is bilaterally symmetrical. Passion flowers and vines form the primary subject matter; a pair of *hombre verde*, or green men, flank the Jesuit seal, and a pair of viscachas emerges from the greenery below the seal. An angel-like grotesquerie emerges from a foliate bud located centrally on the lower skirt of the stand. Cast sphinxlike creatures are affixed to the two front corners, and three small floral elements are attached to the stand's upper edge.

History: See cat. no. 375.

Exhibitions and publications: None.

NOTE TO THIS ENTRY IS ON PAGE 508.

380

Circle of José María Rodallega (1741–1812)

Antonio Forcada y la Plaza (active 1790–1818), assayer

Chalice (caliz)

Mexico City, 1790–1812
Gift of E. L. Beck
19.119

H. 9⅜ in. (24 cm); Diam. rim 3 in. (7.7 cm); Diam. base 5¹¹⁄₁₆ in. (14.6 cm); Wt. 23 oz 13 dwt 23 gr (737.1 gm)

Marks: "FCDA" in roman capitals within a rectangle; "M" crowned within a shaped cartouche; and a fiscal mark of an eagle within a shaped reserve, all struck on side of cup, below midband, and on underside of rim. Zigzag graver's mark, incised by the assayer, visible on underside.

Inscriptions: "INRI" (*Iesus Nazarenus Rex Iudaeorum*, Jesus of Nazareth King of the Jews) and "SPQR" (*Senatus Populusque Romanus*, the senate and people of Rome), both in a banner, engraved on bowl.

THIS ELEGANT VESSEL lacks a maker's mark but is nearly identical in form and treatment to two other chalices attributed to the talented silversmith José María Rodallega of Guadalajara. It is fully gilded and ornamented with an elaborate display of emblems of the crucifixion, lamentation, and entombment of Christ.[1] A handsome product of the late Rococo style, the chalice appears to twist of its own accord, its base forming an elaborate skirt in motion. The bowknots and flattened foliate treatment around the base suggest the encroachment of Neoclassical taste that was first introduced in Mexico in 1785 with the formation of the Academy of San Carlos.[2]

The date of the chalice is based upon its almost certain fabrication in Rodallega's workshop, whose working dates overlap with those of assayer Antonio Forcada y la Plaza.[3] The assayer's abbreviated mark "FCDA" is stamped on the vessel, but the absence of the silversmith's touchmark, despite the crown's rigorous oversight of the guild in Mexico, prevents a secure attribution. The "M" crowned mark refers to the location of the assayer. The fiscal tax, as evidenced by the eagle mark, demonstrated payment of *el quinto real*.

Description: The tall and slender gilt chalice is composed of four separately formed elements that are held together by a threaded, gilded, silver rod secured to the calyx; a notched and gilded bolt secures the whole beneath the base. An applied scalloped midband bisects the bowl horizontally; the upper portion is slightly everted but unadorned. The calyx has been chased in a gently swirling design that is repeated in two baluster elements and in the tall base, which twists and expands outward to a splayed and scrolled rim.

The calyx, baluster, and portions of the base are chased with foliate decoration and bowknots; the background throughout has been given a fine punched treatment. Various elements of the Passion of Christ are repoussé and chased in swirling sections emanating from the calyx and base. On the bowl are a banner, hammer and pliers, pitcher, and mallet. In the panels on the base are chased images of a tomb, a spade and other tools, the column to which Christ was tied, a cross, a spear, and a sponge.

History: Unknown.

Exhibitions and publications: None.

NOTES TO THIS ENTRY ARE ON PAGE 508.

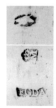

associated with Roman Catholic ritual silver. It may have been a personal cup belonging to a priest or one of his associates that was buried along with church goods to avoid seizure. It shares elements common among domestic vessels made in Spain and Latin America and appears to be closest in style to vessels made in Guatemala.[1]

Description: As with most vessels made in Latin America during this time, the cup was originally held together with a central bolt connecting the stem, base, and bowl. During an old repair, these elements were soldered together, rendering the vessel's weight greater than when it was originally fashioned.

History: See cat. no. 370.

Exhibitions and publications: See cat. no. 370.

NOTE TO THIS ENTRY IS ON PAGE 508.

381

Standing cup (copa)

Probably Guatemala, 1750–1800
Gift in memory of Mr. and Mrs. William H. Keith
28.466

H. 7¹¹/₁₆ in. (19.5 cm); Diam. rim 3¼ in. (9 cm); Diam. base 4⅛ in. (10.5 cm); Wt. 15 oz 1 dwt 11 gr (468.8 gm)

Marks: None.

Inscriptions: None.

THIS UNADORNED CUP was part of a cache of ecclesiastical communion goods discovered in St. Augustine, Florida, yet it does not display the small bowl and gilded interior typically

382

Pair of standing cups (copas)

Peru, 1850–1900
Gift of Landon T. Clay
2001.846–47

2001.846: H. 9¹³/₁₆ in. (24.8 cm); W. 7⅛ in. (18 cm); Diam. rim 5⅛ in. (13 cm); Diam. base 3¹¹/₁₆ in. (9.5 cm); Wt. 17 oz 2 dwt 8 gr. (532.4 gm)

2001.847: H. 9¹³/₁₆ in. (24.8 cm); W. 7⅛ in. (18 cm); Diam. rim 5⅛ in. (13 cm); Diam. base 3¹¹/₁₆ in. (9.5 cm); Wt. 17 oz 5 oz 3 gr (536.7 gm)

Marks: None.

Inscriptions: None.

LARGE STANDING CUPS such as these, with inordinately deep bowls, fanciful handles, and florid decoration, probably date from the mid- to late nineteenth century. These secular objects were often fashioned in pairs, and they may have served a matrimonial role in the Peruvian highlands.[1]

The pair of cast llamas that form the decorative handles are but two of many native and exotic animals that appear frequently on hollowware made during the nineteenth century in the Peruvian highlands and Argentina. These delightful figures were often added to the lips of *mate* cups and other drinking vessels. Dangling elements or bells, now lost, probably hung from a ring that forms an integral part of each cast handle.

382

Description: Each tall standing cup has a deep raised bowl with a rounded base and high everted sides. The slim, cast baluster stems are bolted into high stepped bases with splayed circular feet. Stylized floral designs are chased on the bowl and foot. Cast, scrolled foliate handles are surmounted by cast llamas, seen in profile, that face toward the cup.

History: Early history unknown.

Exhibitions and publications: None.

NOTE TO THIS ENTRY IS ON PAGE 508.

383

Mate cup

Argentina, 1800–50

Gift of Miss Ellen Graves, Mrs. Samuel Cabot, and Mrs. Roger Ernst in memory of their father and mother, Mr. and Mrs. Edmund P. Graves

41.391

H. 5 in. (12.7 cm); Diam. rim 1⅛ in. (2.9 cm); Diam. base 2⅜ in. (6 cm); Wt. 4 oz 2 dwt 3 gr (127.7 gm)

Marks: None.

Inscriptions: "C. [floral device] B" in script engraved on body.

MATE, unknown in North America, is celebrated throughout Latin America. A plant-based beverage, it possesses mild stimulants that offer benefits similar to those of tea. A product of the Paraná and Uruguay River basins of Paraguay, Uruguay, northern Argentina, and southern Brazil, mate is derived from *Ilex paraguarensis*, an evergreen tree related to holly that is a member of the family Aquifoliaceae.[1] In its dried state, mate is steeped in hot water and drunk with repeated infusions until its flavor has been exhausted.

Mate was used by the Tupi-Guaraní Indians of this region and the Quechuas of Peru before the arrival of the Spanish. The term originates in the Quechua word *mati*, which signifies the gourd from which the liquid was poured; it was this word that the Spaniards adopted. Because of an error in translation, mate has come to denote the drink itself. The Spanish term *yerba mate* indicates the dried leaves, even though the plant material is not an herb but is harvested from a tree.[2]

In preconquest days, mate was drunk, chewed, or ground into powder by indigenous peoples, who used it as a tonic, a medicine, and sometimes a ceremonial vomit-inducer. By the late sixteenth century, the Spanish colonists had become enamored of the plant and were major consumers of the drink. Indeed, mate became a highly valued commodity used as its own type of currency. The Jesuits, who had established missions among the Guaraní on the Paraná River, soon domesticated the plant and achieved significant financial gains from its cultivation. They also administered the drink to indigenous Indians who had fallen under the sway of alcohol, claiming to have returned many to productivity. During this period, the Jesuit name was so closely related to mate that the beverage was sometimes called "Jesuit tea."

Mate was originally drunk from a simple gourd, also called a calabash, that was cut in half and filled with liquid filtered through the drinker's teeth. Eventually, a utensil was used to push the herb away while drinking; it later became a pierced spoon. The *bombilla* (see cat. nos. 389–99), a slender tube with a pierced bulb at one end, was likely not introduced until the eighteenth century, when mate drinking became widespread throughout South America (see fig. 2).

Mate was enjoyed socially at all times of day by native peoples, creoles, and newly arrived Spaniards, who passed the cup from one drinker to another. The pleasures of mate *en familia* were recorded by botanist John Miers (1789–1879) in April 1819:

FIG. 2 Engraving of a young mate drinker (*Joven limeña tomando la yerba de un mate con su salvilla*) by Juan de la Cruz. From *Colección general de trajes de España* (Madrid, 1777), plate 36.

The *matesito* was handed round from one to another, each in his turn taking a sip through the long tin tube of the infusion of yerba, out of the little calabash, or *matesito*. . . . A fresh *matesito* was made for me, without a word being said respecting it. An old man threw out the leaves they were using, and pulled from under the hide on which he sat a small kid's skin, with the feet and tail tied into knots, so as to form a bag; in this he kept his store of yerba. He took out a small handful of the yerba, put it into the calabash . . . and filled it up with boiling water from a copper pot . . . then putting in the *bombillo*, or tin tube [they are generally of silver] he stirred it round, took a sip to ascertain its goodness, and then presented it to me, touching his hat at the moment I received it.[3]

The enjoyment of mate was enhanced, when possible, by ornamentation, first carved and painted and later in silver. As early as the eighteenth century, the mate cup was clad in mounts of silver, a precious metal that affected myriad aspects of colonial life. Silver gradually assumed the role originally played by the gourd; eventually entire cups were fashioned from it, although the shapes still echoed their botanical origins. Perhaps the greatest source of this form was Argentina, as were Uruguay, Bolivia, and Peru. Bombillas were produced separately, not en suite.

Description: The cast egg-shaped body with punched and engraved swagged decoration is supported by a tripod form of three cast legs having a strengthening ring. Two legs are chased; one is undecorated.

History: See cat. no. 371.

Exhibitions and publications: None.

NOTES TO THIS ENTRY ARE ON PAGE 508.

384

Mate cup

Chile or Cuyo, Argentina, 1800–50
Gift of Miss Ellen Graves, Mrs. Samuel Cabot, and Mrs. Roger Ernst in memory of their father and mother, Mr. and Mrs. Edmund P. Graves
41.400

H. 7 in. (17.9 cm); Diam. rim 1⅜ in. (3.6 cm); Diam. base 5 in. (12.7 cm); Wt. 8 oz 19 dwt 10 gr (279 gm)

Marks: None.

Inscriptions: None.

MATE CUPS such as this example are especially notable for the flora and fauna that balance on delicate wires and playfully sway with the slightest motion.[1] The footed salver that supports the whole is an element borrowed from the *sahumador,* or brazier, form that was designed to catch stray embers. The salver, however, is not a functional element in the mate cup, for the bombilla never rests on the tray; it typically remains within the bowl, which has a small opening that keeps it firmly in place as the cup is passed from one drinker to the next.

Rhinoceri are not native to South America, and their presence at the rim of the vessel is a fanciful expression that was

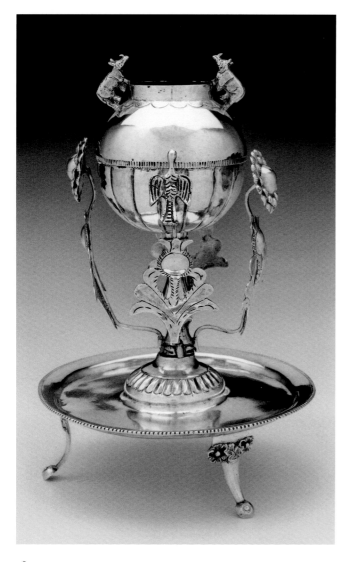

384

385

Mate cup

Uruguay, 1875–1900
Gift of Miss Ellen Graves, Mrs. Samuel Cabot, and Mrs.
Roger Ernst in memory of their father and mother, Mr. and
Mrs. Edmund P. Graves
41.389

H. 3⁵⁄₁₆ in. (9.3 cm); W. 4 in. (10.2 cm); D. 3¼ in. (8.2 cm); Wt. 2 oz
7 gr (62.7 gm)

Marks: None.

Inscriptions: None.

THE SMALL GROWTH at the side of this bottle gourd, as well
as the one in cat. no. 386, was commonly employed as a handle
on mate cups. Silver fittings were added to the finer examples.
These forms were particularly favored in Uruguay.[1] A separate
ring-shaped base, now lost but often made of silver, was intended to hold the cups upright when not in use.[2]

Description: The egg-shaped gourd has a stamped and engraved silver fitting affixed to the upper third of the body. A silver handle,
fitted to a fingerlike tendril of the gourd, extends to one side. The
cast two-part handle extends upward, in a C shape, toward the rim.
Decorated with foliate patterns, the handle terminates in the body
of a duck that perches on its tip.

History: See cat. no. 371.

Exhibitions and publications: None.

NOTES TO THIS ENTRY ARE ON PAGE 508.

probably prompted by prints or other images available by the
early nineteenth century.

Description: The spherical vessel is raised in two halves and overlapped horizontally at the center. The overlapping half is engraved
with a band of vertical decoration at the edge and soldered to the
lower portion. The rim of the bowl is flanked by two cast rhinoceri.
Four wires spring from the base of the baluster stem and extend
upward toward the sides of the bowl; at their tips are alternating
cast birds and flowers. A raised salver, with a beaded edge and a
raised center, supports the flowers and bowl. Cast floral tripod feet
support the salver.

History: See cat. no. 371.

Exhibitions and publications: None.

NOTE TO THIS ENTRY IS ON PAGE 508.

386

Unidentified makers and probably
Paulino Esperati (w. 1827–1855)

Mate cup

Possibly Uruguay, about 1820, with later additions made
in Buenos Aires, Argentina, 1827–55
Gift of Miss Ellen Graves, Mrs. Samuel Cabot, and Mrs.
Roger Ernst in memory of their father and mother, Mr. and
Mrs. Edmund P. Graves
41.394

385 (right), 386 (left)

H. 8¹¹⁄₁₆ in. (22.2 cm); W. 3¹³⁄₁₆ in. (9.7 cm); Diam. rim 1³⁄₁₆ in.
(3.1 cm); Diam. base 3⁵⁄₁₆ in. (8.5 cm); Wt. 8 oz 16 dwt 20 gr (275 gm)

Marks: "ESPERATI" in small roman capitals struck in lower section of bowl.

Inscriptions: None.

SIMILAR IN TREATMENT to the Uruguayan mate cup in cat. no. 385, this delightfully decorated example was likely originally made in the same manner. On at least one later date, it was given additional silver mounts.

The cowl-like silver mount that surrounds the rim, with its lightly engraved geometric surface, and the more decorative cast handle are much like those of the cup in the previous entry. Executed in a different hand is a silver mount with fanlike foliate decoration that adorns the base of the gourd. The whole rests on a tripodal support of three mermaids holding flowers. The bowl is marked "Esperati," probably for Paulino Esperati. Born in Mercedes, Uruguay, Esperati established himself in Buenos Aires by 1827 and was recorded as working there as late as 1855.[1] The baluster and circular base may be the work of a third silversmith who perhaps worked with him. The base is spun and decorated with a stamped foliate design that differs from that on the cup's central section.

The unusual assemblage of styles, hands, and techniques does not imply that an attempt was made to deceive. Rather, it appears that the vessel received attention at different times from craftsmen who probably worked in neighboring regions. Today the cup can be appreciated for these very features and for its rare maker's mark.

Description: The egg-shaped gourd has a silver mount covering its upper third, including the rim. A two-part cast foliate handle, surmounted by a swan, is mounted on a tendril of the gourd, at right angles to the bowl. A second artist may have chased the lower silver mount depicted as a leafy form. The whole is supported by a cast and turned baluster and three mermaids of indeterminate gender that are made of sheet silver with chased decoration. The circular splayed base has been spun, and its foliate treatment may have been mechanically executed. The handle bears old repairs.

History: See cat. no. 371.

Exhibitions and publications: Charles B. Heiser Jr., *The Gourd Book* (Norman: University of Oklahoma Press, 1979), 173.

NOTE TO THIS ENTRY IS ON PAGE 508.

387

Mate cup

Argentina, 1850–1900
Gift of Miss Ellen Graves, Mrs. Samuel Cabot, and Mrs. Roger Ernst in memory of their father and mother, Mr. and Mrs. Edmund P. Graves
41.397

H. 7³⁄₁₆ in. (18.2 cm); W. 3⁵⁄₁₆ in. (8.3 cm); Diam. rim 1 in. (2.6 cm); Diam. base 3³⁄₁₆ in. (8.1 cm); Wt. 4 oz 12 dwt 10 gr (143.7 gm)

Marks: None.

Inscriptions: None.

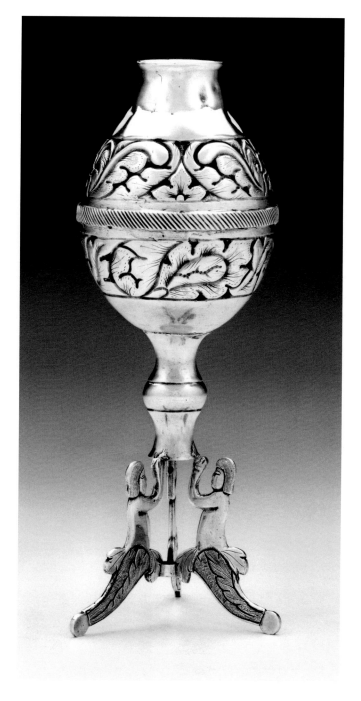

THIS MATE CUP and the following (cat. no. 388) exemplify the trend toward creating the vessel entirely of silver while maintaining the traditional gourd form. Silver mate cups were particularly unusual emblems of conspicuous consumption, for the metal's thermal conductivity created challenges for the user. Artists devised various methods, however, to distance the hot bowl from the rest of the form.

A floating tripodal support may have served the practical need of cooling the metal bowl so that it could be easily handled. Two design solutions are visible in these two examples. Here, the figures form a three-legged base and appear to support the baluster with their hands. In the other, three volutes spring from the baluster stem to support the bowl. Both vessels make only the smallest points of contact with the supporting framework, effectively minimizing heat transfer.

This example sports three fantastic androgynous figures,

sometimes considered to be mermaids or *hombres verdes,* "green men," who spring from foliate buds. They are less easy to classify, however, than the sturdy mermaids bearing bouquets seen on the example in cat. no. 386.

Description: Made entirely of silver, the bowl has an egg-shaped form that was fashioned in two parts; a geometric band hides the solder marks. A small baluster stem is supported by three grotesqueries held together by a small ring, to which they are soldered.

History: See cat. no. 371.

Exhibitions and publications: None.

388

Mate cup

Argentina, probably Buenos Aires, 1850–1900
Gift of Miss Ellen Graves, Mrs. Samuel Cabot, and Mrs. Roger Ernst in memory of their father and mother, Mr. and Mrs. Edmund P. Graves
41.399

H. 8⁵⁄₁₆ in. (21 cm); Diam. rim 1⁵⁄₁₆ in. (3.4 cm); Diam. base 3⅜ in. (8.6 cm); Wt. 10 oz 18 dwt 20 gr (340.3 gm)

Marks: None.

Inscriptions: None.

See cat. no. 387.

Description: The egg-shaped vessel has a large faceted pattern at the neck and broad foliate band across the center. Three volutes spring from a short baluster and support the bowl. The domed, splayed, circular base supports the whole.

History: See cat. no. 371.

Exhibitions and publications: Mrs. Hugh Allison Greenwood, "The Domestic Silver of Latin America," *Antiques* 41, no. 5 (May 1942): 304–7, 331, fig. 4.

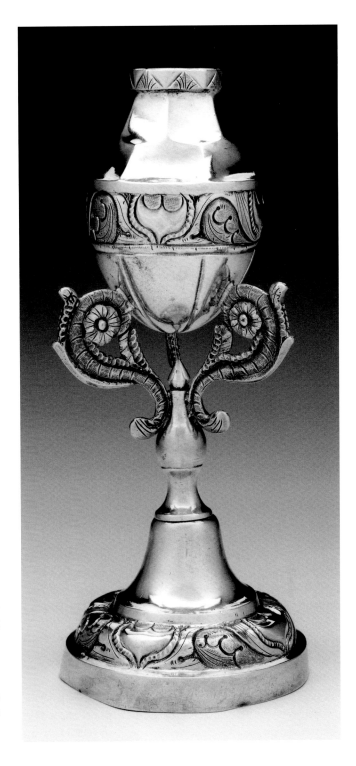

389

Bombilla

Argentina, probably 1850–1900
Gift of Miss Ellen Graves, Mrs. Samuel Cabot, and Mrs.
Roger Ernst in memory of their father and mother, Mr. and
Mrs. Edmund Graves
41.417

L. 9½ in. (23 cm); Wt. 1 oz 17 dwt 2 gr (57.7 gm)

Marks: None.

Inscriptions: None.

TRANSLATED AS "little pump," a bombilla is a specialized straw
having a pierced bulb at one end that is inserted in a mate cup
(cat. nos. 384–88). The bulb, designed to strain out the *yerba
mate*, is an ingenious element that is perhaps best described as
an inverse tea ball.

Made in a variety of patterns, bombillas share several distinctive features. All are slender and tubular and vary from about
eight inches in length to more than ten. Despite its length, the
bombilla sits comfortably inside the mate cup, whose narrow
mouth holds it in place while the cup is passed from one drinker to the next.

Consumers would have chosen their mate cups and bombillas separately; few, if any, were made as sets. However, due to
the narrow openings of many mate cups, it was probably necessary for the buyer to select both at the same time to ensure
that the bulb of the bombilla fit properly within the cup.

As with mate cups made entirely of silver, the thermal conductivity of silver bombillas may have posed problems for the
drinker. The unusually long straw, compared to the small mate
cup, may have cooled both the warm liquid and the cylinder
itself.

The bombillas in the Museum's collection have been organized into two groups according to their surface treatment.
Those in the first are ornamented with silver and gold wire;
those in the second feature a pinched and twisted pattern. Both
groups were probably made in Argentina, where they were
enjoyed by the middle class during the nineteenth century,
when mate drinking was most popular.

Description: The strawlike cylinder has three faceted and decorated sections between three heavily ornamented bands, a flattened
mouthpiece, and a pierced ball-shaped bulb.

History: See cat. no. 371.

Exhibitions and publications: Mrs. Hugh Allison Greenwood, "The
Domestic Silver of Latin America," *Antiques* 41, no. 5 (May 1942):
304–7, fig. 4.

390

Bombilla

Argentina, probably 1850–1900
Gift of Miss Ellen Graves, Mrs. Samuel Cabot, and Mrs.
Roger Ernst in memory of their father and mother, Mr. and
Mrs. Edmund Graves
41.416

L. 8⅞ in. (22.5 cm); Wt. 19 dwt 8 gr (30.1 gm)

Marks: None.

Inscriptions: None.

Description: The strawlike cylinder has bands of gold on an applied
silver molding, between which are incised lozenge designs, a plain
stem, and a pierced shell-shaped bulb.

History: See cat. no. 371.

Exhibitions and publications: None.

391

Bombilla

Argentina, probably 1850–1900
Gift of Miss Ellen Graves, Mrs. Samuel Cabot, and Mrs.
Roger Ernst in memory of their father and mother, Mr. and
Mrs. Edmund Graves
41.411

L. 8¹¹⁄₁₆ in. (22 cm); Wt. 17 dwt 7 gr (26.9 gm)

Marks: None.

Inscriptions: None.

Description: The strawlike cylinder has a stem decorated with ornamented wire that has been spirally wound between two applied
bands of same. A similar band has been applied just above the
spoon-shaped pierced bulb.

History: See cat. no. 371.

Exhibitions and publications: None.

392

Arantida (active about 1850–1900)

Bombilla

Argentina, probably 1850–1900
Gift of Miss Ellen Graves, Mrs. Samuel Cabot, and Mrs.
Roger Ernst in memory of their father and mother, Mr. and
Mrs. Edmund Graves
41.410

L. 9⅛ in. (23.1 cm); Wt. 1 oz 23 gr (32.6 gm)

Marks: "ARANTIDA" and "600," each within a rectangle, struck on flat side of bulb.

Inscriptions: "BM" owner's initials engraved near mouthpiece.

THE MAKER'S NAME "ARANTIDA" that appears on the bulb of this bombilla may be the same as that found on a portion of a bit dating to the end of the nineteenth century.[1]

Description: The strawlike cylinder has stem ornamentation with applied bands and alternating pinched and stamped decoration, a flattened mouthpiece, and a flattened pierced bulb form.

History: See cat. no. 371.

Exhibitions and publications: None.

NOTE TO THIS ENTRY IS ON PAGE 508.

393

Bombilla

Argentina, probably 1850–1900
Gift of Miss Ellen Graves, Mrs. Samuel Cabot, and Mrs.
Roger Ernst in memory of their father and mother, Mr. and
Mrs. Edmund Graves
41.412

L. 8⅞ in. (22.6 cm); Wt. 1 oz 3 dwt 14 gr (36.7 gm)

Marks: None.

Inscriptions: None.

Description: The strawlike cylinder has a pair of cast birds, two plain applied bands, and a flattened mouthpiece. A pierced shell forms the bulb.

History: See cat. no. 371.

Exhibitions and publications: None.

394

Bombilla

Argentina, probably 1850–1900
Gift of Miss Ellen Graves, Mrs. Samuel Cabot, and Mrs.
Roger Ernst in memory of their father and mother, Mr. and
Mrs. Edmund Graves
41.408

L. 9 in. (22.8 cm); Wt. 1 oz 22 dwt (32.5 gm)

Marks: None.

Inscriptions: None.

Description: The strawlike cylinder has two pairs of twisted incised sections and applied bands. The pierced bulb is flat on one side.

History: See cat. no. 371.

Exhibitions and publications: None.

395

Bombilla

Argentina, probably 1850–1900
Gift of Miss Ellen Graves, Mrs. Samuel Cabot, and Mrs.
Roger Ernst in memory of their father and mother, Mr. and
Mrs. Edmund Graves
41.415

L. 8⅛ in. (20.5 cm); Wt. 1 oz 4 dwt 21 gr (38.7 gm)

Marks: None.

Inscriptions: None.

Description: The strawlike cylinder is twisted and incised in two sections along the stem. The round mouthpiece is scored, and the pierced bulb is in the form of a flattened ball.

History: See cat. no. 371.

Exhibitions and publications: None.

395–99

396

Bombilla

Argentina, probably 1850–1900
Gift of Miss Ellen Graves, Mrs. Samuel Cabot, and Mrs. Roger Ernst in memory of their father and mother, Mr. and Mrs. Edmund Graves
41.413

L. 10¹³⁄₁₆ in. (27.5 cm); Wt. 2 oz 6 dwt 12 gr (72.3 gm)

Marks: None.

Inscriptions: None.

Description: The strawlike cylinder has several bands of twisted and incised ornament. The round mouthpiece is scored several times, and the pierced and shaped bulb has been repoussé.

History: See cat. no. 371.

Exhibitions and publications: Charles B. Heiser Jr., *The Gourd Book* (Norman: University of Oklahoma Press, 1979), 173.

397

Bombilla

Argentina, probably 1850–1900
Gift of Miss Ellen Graves, Mrs. Samuel Cabot, and Mrs. Roger Ernst in memory of their father and mother, Mr. and Mrs. Edmund Graves
41.405

L. 9⁵⁄₁₆ in. (23.6 cm); Wt. 2 oz 1 gr (62.3 gm)

Marks: None.

Inscriptions: None.

Description: The strawlike cylinder has one twisted and three plain bands, a flattened mouthpiece, and a pierced oval bulb.

History: See cat. no. 371.

Exhibitions and publications: None.

398

Bombilla

Argentina, probably 1850–1900
Gift of Miss Ellen Graves, Mrs. Samuel Cabot, and Mrs. Roger Ernst in memory of their father and mother, Mr. and Mrs. Edmund Graves
41.407

L. 11⅝ in. (29.4 cm); Wt. 2 oz 17 dwt 9 gr (89.2 gm)

Marks: None.

Inscriptions: None.

Description: The strawlike cylinder displays a spiral twisted section and several bands. It has a flattened mouthpiece and a shaped and pierced bulb.

History: See cat. no. 371.

Exhibitions and publications: None.

399

Bombilla

Argentina, probably 1850–1900
Gift of Miss Ellen Graves, Mrs. Samuel Cabot, and Mrs. Roger Ernst in memory of their father and mother, Mr. and Mrs. Edmund Graves
41.406

L. 8 in. (20.3 cm); Wt. 19 dwt 22 gr (31 gm)

Marks: None.

Inscriptions: None.

Description: The strawlike cylinder with flattened mouthpiece has a faceted stem and a spherical pierced bulb.

History: See cat. no. 371.

Exhibitions and publications: None.

CACAO PLANTS, the source of chocolate, originated in the Southern Hemisphere. This delicious drink was consumed by the Mayans as early as 150 B.C., and in the following centuries it became a popular beverage among many indigenous groups. The Spanish enthusiastically adopted it in the postconquest era.[1] To create a Western-style form of the traditional mate cup, colonists improvised by using gourds, nuts, wood, and other organic materials already in use, to which they added European-style bases, handles, and rims made of silver.[2] The form differs from indigenous mate cups, which have a narrow opening at the rim to hold the bombilla, or straw. The Peruvian *jicara*, or chocolate cup, features a wider rim that enabled the drinker to lift the vessel to the lips.[3] Footed cups such as this example were made throughout South America and differ markedly from another version called a *mancerina*, which was found primarily in New Spain. Designed more like a cup and saucer, the mancerina contained a circular receptacle at the center to receive a ceramic or glass cup and included a wide saucer to hold pastries.

The surface of some *jicaras* display elaborate designs. Many chocolate cups were made from coconut shells, an extremely dense nut that lends itself well to fine carving and polishing. A fine Mannerist scroll pattern has been lightly engraved on the surface. Close inspection reveals that the design is not aligned with the silver leaves that support the cup. Such discrepancies appear to be common among these vessels, suggesting that the carver and the silversmith worked independently.

The etymology of the present-day term *jicara* to describe such chocolate cups may be derived from the Nahuatl word *xicalli*. When adopted by the colonists and transformed into Creole, a Spanish dialect, the word may have been altered to *jicara*.[4]

400

Chocolate cup (jicara)

South America, possibly Peru, 1800–50
Gift of Miss Ellen Graves, Mrs. Samuel Cabot, and Mrs. Roger Ernst in memory of their father and mother, Mr. and Mrs. Edmund P. Graves
41.403

H. 5⅞ in. (15.1 cm); W. 3⅜ in. (8.5 cm); Diam. rim 2 in. (5.2 cm); Diam. base 2⅞ in. (7.4 cm); Wt. 4 oz 23 dwt 20 gr (144.4 gm)

Marks: None.

Inscriptions: None

Description: The cast tripod base has a clawlike foot that passes through a central baluster knop as well as cast and chased leaves that grace the base of the bowl; the whole is bolted to base. A silver band encircles the rim and is secured with a few small flat-headed nails.

History: See cat. no. 371.

Exhibitions and publications: None.

NOTES TO THIS ENTRY ARE ON PAGE 508–09.

401

Probably Gumersindo de Cañas (b. 1783)
José Joaquín Dávila (w. 1819–1823), assayer
Covered bowl or spice container (especiero)

Mexico City, Mexico, 1819–23
Gift of Kathryn C. Buhler in memory of Yves Henry Buhler
1984.184a–b

H. 5⅝ in. (14.3 cm); W. 8⅛ in. (20.6 cm); D. 3⁹⁄₁₆ in. (9 cm); D. base
2¹¹⁄₁₆ in. (6.9 cm); Wt. 18 oz 8 dwt 3 gr (572.5 gm)

Marks: "CAN," a portion of the maker's mark *CAÑAS*; "M"
crowned within a shaped cartouche; assayer's mark "DVLA"; and
a lion within a shaped oval, all struck from left to right on one side
of vessel.

Inscriptions: None.

THE IDENTIFICATION AND DATING of Latin American silver
is challenging due to the paucity of maker's marks. Fortunately, an assayer mark is often present. Assayers were bureau-
crats, and the years of their appointment are a matter of public
record. As a result, their marks can often provide a date range
for an object when little other evidence is available.

In the case of this covered bowl, the assayer's mark is that of
José Joaquín Dávila, who held his post between 1819 and 1823.[1]
The maker could be either Alejandro Antonio de Cañas (b.
1755) or Gumersindo de Cañas, for both men used the shaped
touchmark that bears their surname. Alejandro Cañas would
have been sixty-four years old by 1819, whereas Gumersindo
Cañas would have been only thirty-six. In addition, in the years
1823–24, the latter's mark appears more frequently with the
assayer's mark of Cayetano Buitrón (w. 1823–1824). It is therefore likely this vessel was made by the younger silversmith.[2]

The elliptical form of the bowl, its square foot, and its
graceful cane-shaped handles demonstrate the far-reaching
influence of the French Neoclassical style as disseminated by
Robert Adam, the English designer. Adam's work exerted a
powerful influence on the Academy of San Carlos in Mexico.
The shape of the bowl is based upon a conflation of the kylix
and kantharos, ancient Greek drinking vessels. In the evolution
of this new classical style, ellipses were preferred over circles,
and a greater variety of shapes, including lids, were created to
serve myriad purposes. A circular covered bowl with similar
handles, made by Paul Revere and now in the Museum's collection, demonstrates how the Neoclassical style found favor
throughout the Western world and its colonies during the early
years of the nineteenth century.[3]

Forms such as this bowl made in Latin America are also
called *especieros*, or spice containers. Smaller examples are
sometimes called *saleros*, or salt cellars.[4] Notable for its finely
planished surface and handsome cast and cold-worked finial,
this covered container would have served as a fine addition to
an upper-middle-class home in the viceroyalty of New Spain.

Description: The raised, broad, elliptical vessel is supported by
a short stem spreading to a splayed and stepped base and square
plinth. Two long strap handles are attached below, near the stem
and at the lid, and a leaf is chased at the upper join. The handles
rise upward to the base of the finial. A conforming friction-fitted lid has
one shallow step and rises to a height nearly equal to the depth of
the bowl. A large bud finial with spreading foliage has been cast and
cold-chiseled.

History: The donor inherited the object from her husband, whose
family used it for christenings during the nineteenth century.

Exhibitions and publications: None.

NOTES TO THIS ENTRY ARE ON PAGE 509.

402

Chocolate pot (chocolatera)

Probably Bolivia, 1850–1900
Gift of Landon T. Clay
2001.845

H. 10⅝ in. (27 cm); W. 13 in. (33 cm); Diam. rim 3½ in. (8.9 cm); Diam. base 4¹¹⁄₁₆ in. (12 cm); Wt. 41 oz 4 dwt 11 gr (1282.2 gm)

Marks: None.

Inscriptions: None.

LIKE MATE, chocolate became a beverage embraced by many settlers. Thomas Gage (1603–1656), an English-born Dominican friar, traveled in Mexico and Guatemala from 1625 to 1637 and recalled with pleasure his daily enjoyment of the beverage:

> A cup of chocolate well confectioned comforts and strengthens the stomach. For myself I must say I used it twelve years constantly, drinking one cup in the morning, another yet before dinner between nine or ten of the clock, another within a hour after dinner, and another between four and five in the afternoon, and when I was purposed to sit up late to study, I would take another cup about seven or eight at night, which would keep me waking till about midnight.[1]

The large size, lack of adornment, and thick handle of this chocolate pot are similar to those on pots made in the Peruvian highlands during the eighteenth and nineteenth centuries.[2]

The cacao-pod finial is an unusual addition. Typical of a Bolivian chocolate pot, the vessel has a thick chonta wood handle, set at an angle, and a pivoting section on top of the lid, which slid aside to accommodate a *molinillo* (or *molinet*), the utensil used to stir the liquid. The vessel's late date is also indicated by its lack of cast cabriole legs, a feature of earlier works.

This chocolate pot, like many produced in the region, was designed without the spout generally found in American and English versions. Thus, the entire lid was removed before serving.[3]

As with the *jícara*, the cup that holds the chocolate beverage (see cat. no. 400), the origin of the term *molinillo* may also be traced to the Nahuatl language. A *molinillo* was a utensil, usually a wooden stick with vertical grooves near its base. Inserted through a concealed hole in the lid, as in this example, it was used to whisk the liquid and dissolve the chocolate. The word was thought to originate with the Spanish word *molino*, meaning "mill," yet the tool does not work in a grinding fashion. The etymology may instead be derived from *moliniani*, a creolized Nahuatl word meaning something that moves, shakes, or waggles.[4]

Description: The large, raised, pear-shaped form has a handle socket attached at a slight angle to the body by an applied elliptical drop. A thick chonta-wood handle, circular in section and rounded at its thickened tip, is probably original.[5] The domed friction-fitted lid with flange has a cast finial in the shape of a cacao pod. The finial is soldered to a small disk that pivots to reveal a hole on the lid. The chain and bead that connect the lid to the body are probably old replacements. The concave foot ring is seamed. A double band of applied reeded decoration appears at the rim and on the lid.

History: See cat. no. 375.

Exhibitions and publications: None.

NOTES TO THIS ENTRY ARE ON PAGE 509.

Description: The raised shallow vessel has a center point and is embellished with lobes that softly radiate outward from the center point and evert slightly to form a narrow scalloped rim with applied molded edge.

History: Early history unknown.

Exhibitions and publications: None.

NOTE TO THIS ENTRY IS ON PAGE 509.

404

Elliptical serving bowl

Probably Mexico, 1775–1825
Gift of Mrs. W. L. McKee
16.22

H. 2⅜ in. (6.1 cm); W. 16⅛ in. (41 cm); D. 11⁹⁄₁₆ in. (29.3 cm); Wt. 38 oz 15 dwt 16 gr (1206.3 gm)

Marks: A very small head of a bearded man, in a shaped cartouche, struck on brim.

Inscriptions: "Pt" and "O" stamped on rim.

THE ELLIPTICAL FORM and deeply scalloped rim of this bowl relate to similar forms made of clay and silver in Spain, Portugal, and various parts of Spanish America from the 1750s to the 1830s. Although the bowl lacks local marks, it does bear a Lisbon symbol used from 1886 to 1938 that may have been added later. The tiny touchmark was used to indicate silverware of

403

Maker unknown

Antonio Forcada y la Plaza (active 1790–1818), assayer

Serving dish (fuente)

Mexico City, 1790–1818
Gift of Miss Evelyn Sears
61.1290

H. 2¾ in. (7 cm); Diam. rim 12⅞ in. (32.7 cm); Wt. 38 oz 15 dwt 19 gr (1206.5 gm)

Marks: Assayer's mark "FCDA" within a rectangle; location mark "M" crowned within a shaped cartouche; and fiscal mark of an eagle within a shaped cartouche, all struck from left to right on rim. Zigzag line left by assayer's graver visible on underside.

Inscriptions: None.

THE IRREGULAR AND SHALLOW scratches that radiate from the center of this lobed vessel indicate that it saw much use. Large forms such as this bowl, as well as the next two examples (cat. nos. 404–405), were rarely found in North America because of the great amount of silver required for their fabrication. In Mexico, however, where the silver-rich mines of Sultepec, Zumpango, Taxco, and Zacatecas yielded enormous quantities, these weighty vessels were the norm.[1]

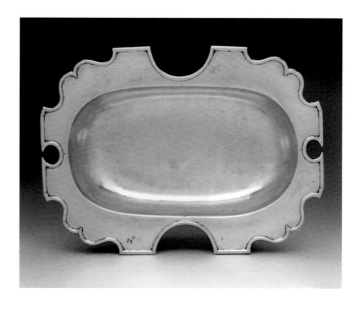

artistic or archaeological value.[1] The stamped letters "Pt" and "O" may indicate an owner's initials.

Several slightly larger and more elaborate versions have been published and identified as Mexican.[2] All share the same two-dimensional quality of the scrolled rim, although their deep, shaped bowls and applied rims accent bold curves. They exemplify the lively Baroque style as practiced in the Spanish-speaking Americas.

Description: The raised elliptical vessel has a deep flat bowl with steep sides and a broad flat rim finished with a rolled edge. The boldly scalloped rim has a wide hemispherical curve at the center of each length and a small, nearly circular curve on the shorter sides.

History: The bowl has a curious history of ownership in the early twentieth century that links two notable American silver scholars. The vessel, then called a Portuguese shaving basin, was lent to the Museum in 1914 by Francis Hill Bigelow (1859–1933). Bigelow placed it on loan for Englishman E. Alfred Jones (1872–1944), who had published his book entitled *The Old Silver of American Churches* the year before. The purpose of this loan is unclear, and we do not know anything about the donor's identity or her relationship to Bigelow or Jones.

Exhibitions and publications: None.

NOTES TO THIS ENTRY ARE ON PAGE 509.

405

Serving bowl (fuente)

Argentina, about 1890–1910
Samuel Putnam Avery Fund
34.62

H. 2³⁄₁₆ in. (7 cm); Diam. rim 15⅛ in. (38.4 cm); Wt. 50 oz 15 dwt 14 gr (1579.5 gm)

Marks: None.

Inscriptions: None.

STAMPING OF THE SORT seen on the rim of this large and heavy *fuente*, or deep bowl, was often a product of Argentinean silversmiths.[1] The speed at which the vessel was formed is evident in the narrow, spiral courses of raising that are visible in the bowl's interior and underneath, where numerous small fissures indicate improper raising, heating, and quenching.

Description: The raised circular vessel with center point has a deep, flat base in which the raising courses are evident. The bowl has sharply rising sides and a narrow rim, the latter stamped with two rows of small shield-shaped designs. A strengthening edge applied to the rim has also been stamped in a repeating pattern.

History: Early history unknown.

Exhibitions and publications: Mrs. Hugh Allison Greenwood, "The Domestic Silver of Latin America," *Antiques* 41, no. 5 (May 1942), 304–7, 331, fig. 6.

NOTE TO THIS ENTRY IS ON PAGE 509.

ance of silver in this region explains the use of a precious metal for such a humble vessel. The stylized floral decoration on the handle is similar to that commonly found on flatware made in the Peruvian highlands.[1]

Description: The large raised vessel has a tall applied foot ring and a wide base that swells outward before curving sharply inward and ending in an everted horizontal rim. Stamped and beaded decoration has been applied to the rim, and the handle displays stamped and engraved foliate decoration.

History: See cat. no. 375.

Exhibitions and publications: None.

NOTE TO THIS ENTRY IS ON PAGE 509.

406

Chamber pot (vaso de noche)

Bolivia, about 1850
Gift of Landon T. Clay
2001.844

H. 6½ in. (16.5 cm); W. 11 in. (28 cm); Diam. rim 8⁵⁄₁₆ in. (21 cm); Diam. foot 4⅞ in. (12.5 cm); Wt. 54 oz 12 dwt 5 gr (1698 gm)

Marks: None.

Inscriptions: "A A" in script stamped on underside.

THIS CHAMBER POT displays a classic squat form that was used in Europe and America, where it was commonly made of ceramic or a base metal such as pewter. Clearly, the preponder-

407

Container

Probably Peru, 1875–1900
Gift of Landon T. Clay
2001.841

H. 9⅜ in. (24 cm); W. 6 in. (15.2 cm); D. 6 in. (15.2 cm); Wt. 21 oz 11 dwt 13 gr (671.1 gm)

Marks: None.

Inscriptions: None.

THE TURKEY, native to both North and South America, has been the subject of countless images by indigenous and colonial peoples. Eighteenth- and early-nineteenth-century silversmiths were particularly fond of portraying it in the sculptural form of a *sahumador,* or brazier, that was used to perfume the air.[1] Often made in the shape of llamas, peacocks, and other animals, braziers featured hinged bodies that were opened by pressing on the tail or some other mechanical method. Embers glowed from within, and ash fell to a salver that supported the figure. Smoke escaped via small air holes cut into the back of the bird or, on filigreed forms, through wires.

In size, girth, and general appearance, this turkey-shaped container is similar to those described above. It can be opened in the same manner, revealing a small cavity such as those used for burning incense. However, this example lacks the air holes necessary to be effectively used as a brazier. Furthermore, it lacks a proper salver to catch stray embers.

Some scholars have speculated that hinged objects such as

FIG. 3 Spoon, probably Bolivia, about 1850–1900. Silver. Museum of Fine Arts, Boston; Gift of Miss Ellen Graves, Mrs. Samuel Cabot, and Mrs. Roger Ernst in memory of their father and mother, Mr. and Mrs. Edmund P. Graves (41.460).

407

this were made to serve a different purpose, perhaps to hold a store of incense or sweets. If they held the latter, they were called *confiteras*.[2] It seems more likely that they were made as echoes of an older way of life, retaining a vestige of function even as they took on a new decorative role. These vessels probably date to the late nineteenth century, by which time they were long separated from their original purpose.[3]

Description: The raised spherical form of a bird is hinged at the back; the cast head is soldered to the upper portion of the sphere. The fantail is used as a fulcrum when opening the body. The wings are made separately and attached with wire. The cast legs are soldered to the body and bolted to the base, which consists of a square plinth with a domed center. Cast leaves form the feet of the plinth. The whole is raised and chased.

History: Possibly part of the group of objects discussed in cat. no. 375.

Exhibitions and publications: None.

NOTES TO THIS ENTRY ARE ON PAGE 509.

408

Flint (pedernal)

Argentina or Peru, 1800–1900
Gift of Miss Ellen Graves, Mrs. Samuel Cabot, and Mrs. Roger Ernst in memory of their father and mother, Mr. and Mrs. Edmund P. Graves
41.430

L. 19⅞ in. (50.5 cm); Wt. 1 oz 19 dwt 8 gr (61.2 gm)

Marks: None.

Inscriptions: None.

THIS FLINT is illustrated without its wick, which would have been attached to the hook at the end of the chain and run through the small cylinder at center. The spark for the wick was provided by the stone flint, seen here in its setting, adorned with a cast silver cow.

The cylindrical wick holder was typical for South American flints, although animal- and bud-shaped examples were also produced. The cast cow ornament functioned as a grip or handle and is typical of many made in the nineteenth century.[1] The chain seems exceptionally long and may be a replacement. In silver and gold, such a flint would have served as a handsome personal accessory for a gentleman smoker or for use at the table in lighting candles, braziers, and the like.

Description: The cylindrical tube has foliate, bilaterally symmetrical decoration around its middle; foliate gold bands are soldered to the center and each end. A ring soldered at right angles to the center of the cylinder is used to secure the chain. One end of the chain is attached to a stone flint set in a silver mount with a cast form of a silver cow; the other end has a cone-shaped element that seats in the cylinder and is designed to hold the wick.

History: See cat. no. 371.

Exhibitions and publications: None.

NOTE TO THIS ENTRY IS ON PAGE 509.

409

Breast strap (pretal)

Argentina, 1890–1910
Gift of Miss Ellen Graves, Mrs. Samuel Cabot, and Mrs. Roger Ernst in memory of their father and mother, Mr. and Mrs. Edmund P. Graves
41.353

L. 48½ in. (117 cm); W. 2⅞ in. (7.4 cm); Wt. 33 oz 2 dwt 18 gr (1029.6 gm)

Marks: None.

Inscriptions: None.

It is a by-word that at Mexico four things are fair; that is to say, the women, the apparel, the horses, and the streets. But to this I may add the beauty of some of the coaches of the gentry, which do exceed in cost the best of the Court of Madrid and other parts of Christendom, for they spare no silver, nor gold, nor precious stones, nor cloth of gold, nor the best silks from China to enrich them. And to the gallantry of their horses the pride of some doth add the cost of bridles and shoes of silver.[1]

THE FIRST HORSES were brought to the Americas by the Spanish conquistadors in the sixteenth century, and they immediately became an essential resource for colonial and local populations. Highly valued commodities, horses were used for travel across rough terrain and on shorter pleasure trips, and some were engaged in more prosaic duties in domestic and farm life. The handsomest of these animals were the proud possessions of the landed gentry, who bred and dressed them for display.

409

410

Perhaps best known are the horses used by South American cowboys, or gauchos, for managing herds of cattle on the pampas, the vast, treeless plains south of the Amazon. Rivaling the American cowboy as the subject of romantic literature, legend, and music, the gaucho and his horse were especially renowned in Argentina. Their arrival was often heralded by the flash of silver and the jingle of spurs.

The Spanish brought with them a rich vocabulary and technical knowledge in the making and use of equestrian trappings, a result of some seven hundred years of occupation by the Moors, themselves highly skilled in the breeding, judging, and riding of horses. The gauchos required horses that were particularly suited to hard life on the pampas, and both man and animal were outfitted with a full range of riding equipment in leather, iron, and silver.

The breast strap was a large and showy piece. It was connected to the saddle with another strap that passed between the horse's legs, which was used to prevent the saddle from slipping. The cornucopia at the center of this example, also seen on the horse's bit that in the next entry (cat. no. 410), is a Neoclassical motif popular through the end of the nineteenth century.

Description: The cast and ornamented plaques include a central unadorned shield shape, flanked by cornucopia, and two floral bosses, interspersed with vertical bands. Linked and woven chains connect the whole to cast floral buckles at each end.

History: See cat. no. 371.

Exhibitions and publications: None.

NOTE TO THIS ENTRY IS ON PAGE 509.

Abelar (active 1890–1910)
Horse's bit (copas del freno)

Uruguay, 1890–1910
Gift of Miss Ellen Graves, Mrs. Samuel Cabot, and Mrs. Roger Ernst in memory of their father and mother, Mr. and Mrs. Edmund P. Graves
41.349

H. 2 in. (5.2 cm); W. 7⅛ in. (18 cm); L. 8⅛ in. (20.7cm)

Marks: "ABELAR" within a rectangle struck four times on silver portions.

Inscriptions: None

THE TOUCHMARK "Abelar" that appears prominently on the side of this horse's bit is that of a Uruguayan silversmith who also made a silver bombilla with a gold mouthpiece.[1]

Description: The decorative silver that flanks the curved iron curb is of a broken scrolled form that has been cold-chased with the design of a cornucopia and foliage.

History: See cat. no. 371.

Exhibitions and publications: None.

NOTE TO THIS ENTRY IS ON PAGE 509.

411

Pair of spurs (espuelas)

Chile, 1850–1900
Gift of Miss Ellen Graves, Mrs. Samuel Cabot, and Mrs.
Roger Ernst in memory of their father and mother, Mr. and
Mrs. Edmund P. Graves
41.355a–b

Each H. (including rowel) 4½ in. (11.5 cm); W. 3¹¹⁄₁₆ in. (9.5 cm); L.
9⁵⁄₁₆ in (23.6 cm). Dimensions do not include leather straps.

Marks: None.

Inscriptions: None.

EUROPEAN SPURS are generally small affairs in which rowels of
modest size are affixed to slender but sturdy frames of wrought
iron, steel, and occasionally silver.[1] For the horsemen of Latin
America, however, iron was an expensive commodity that was
generally shipped from Europe for use primarily as structural
supports in mine shafts. This example was undoubtedly costly.
The silver decoration has been applied to a wrought-iron framework. The spurs in the next two entries (cat. nos. 412–413) are
made entirely of silver, a popular alternative to iron or steel.

The niello arch seen here recalls the influence of the Moors,
who introduced this metalworking technique to Spain during
their seven-century occupation of the Iberian Peninsula. When
the rowels are large, as here, they are called *nazarenas* in South
America because the sharp barbs recall the crown of thorns
worn by Jesus of Nazareth. The pierced rectangular rowel box
is typical of examples made in Chile.[2]

Description: The iron spur is held in an openwork iron rowel box
fused on the exterior to a silver sheet. Alternating bands of silver

and copper in niello form a decorative arch pattern over an iron
framework; the leather straps survive.

History: See cat. no. 371.

Exhibitions and publications: None.

NOTES TO THIS ENTRY ARE ON PAGE 509.

412

Pair of spurs (espuelas)

Argentina, 1890–1910
Gift of Miss Ellen Graves, Mrs. Samuel Cabot and Mrs. Roger
Ernst in memory of their father and mother, Mr. and Mrs.
Edmund P. Graves
41.356a–b

41.356a: H. 2¹³⁄₁₆ in. (7 cm); L. 9⅜ in. (24 cm); W. 4⅛ in. (10.4 cm);
Wt. 14 oz 16 dwt 15 gr (461.3 gm)

41.356b: H. 2¹³⁄₁₆ in. (7 cm); L. 9⅜ in. (24 cm); W. 4⅛ in. (10.4 cm);
Wt. 15 oz 4 dwt 13 gr (473.6 gm)

Marks: None.

Inscriptions: None.

SPURS SUCH AS THESE were common in the late nineteenth
century. Variations are still being made today.

Description: A cast-leaf design forms the frame support for an iron
rowel. An applied foliate design appears on the arch.

History: See cat. no. 371.

Exhibitions and publications: None.

413

Spur (espuela)

Argentina, 1850–1900
Gift of Miss Ellen Graves, Mrs. Samuel Cabot, and Mrs.
Roger Ernst in memory of their father and mother, Mr. and
Mrs. Edmund P. Graves
41.357

H. 9 in. (22.9 cm); W. 3⅞ in. (9.8 cm); D. 4 in. (10.2 cm)

Marks: None.

Inscriptions: None.

Description: The spur is cast and finished in sections, with the silver rowel box designed as an openwork scroll that supports a star-shaped iron rowel. This mechanism is soldered to a circular, scalloped heel plate that, in turn, is soldered to the arch that surrounds the rider's shoe.

History: See cat. no. 371.

Exhibitions and publications: None.

414

Pair of men's stirrups (estribos)

Argentina, 1825–75
Gift of Miss Ellen Graves, Mrs. Samuel Cabot, and Mrs.
Roger Ernst in memory of their father and mother, Mr. and
Mrs. Edmund P. Graves
41.358a–b

41.358a: H. 9⅜ in. (24 cm); W 5½ in. (14 cm); D. 3⅛ in. (8 cm); Wt. 18 oz 2 dwt 20 gr (564.3 gm)

41.358b: H. 9⅜ in. (24 cm); W 5½ in. (14 cm); D. 3⅛ in. (8 cm); Wt. 18 oz 1 dwt 7 gm (561.9 gm)

Marks: None.

Inscriptions: "I.B.M." in script engraved inside each.

THIS STIRRUP DESIGN is unique to South America, where it was made primarily in Argentina. The form was called *campana*, or *corona*, because the stirrups look like bells or inverted crowns. It was thought that the shape originated in Brazil, migrated south to Uruguay, and finally reached Argentina, where it was adopted and made in great quantities because of the comfort it offered to the rider. A large amount of silver was required to make these stirrups, which also allowed the owner to display his wealth.[1]

Description: The stirrup is elliptical in section; its profile, in the shape of a bell or crown, has a lower scalloped edge, reeded midband, and engraved foliate decoration. Applied bands along the sides have additional floral decoration. The straps extend upward in an attenuated arch and terminate in a decorative end, or eye, from which the stirrup hangs.

History: See cat. no. 371.

Exhibitions and publications: None.

NOTE TO THIS ENTRY IS ON PAGE 509.

415

Ornament in the form of a lady's stirrup (estribo)

Argentina, 1850–1900
Gift of Miss Ellen Graves, Mrs. Samuel Cabot, and Mrs. Roger Ernst in memory of their father and mother, Mr. and Mrs. Edmund P. Graves
41.354

H. 3¹¹⁄₁₆ in. (9.5 cm); W. 3⅞ in. (10 cm); D. 8½ in. (21.5 cm); Wt. 12 oz 13 dwt 19 gr (394.7 gm)

Marks: None.

Inscriptions: None.

THE ORIGIN OF THIS FORM, a so-called lady's stirrup, is unclear, although apparently such objects were made in great quantities and variety during the mid- to late nineteenth cen-

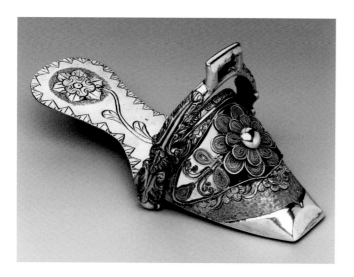

tury. The stirrup has a functioning arch and eye that enable it to pivot and hang. Such forms are rarely found in pairs, leading some scholars to argue that women who rode sidesaddle had need of only one stirrup. Nevertheless, this example and most others show no wear, and the small size precluded the use of a shoe. Rather than being a functional form, it was probably an elegantly worked souvenir, keepsake, or talisman.[1]

Description: The square-toe shoe has filigree floral decoration across the front; a long-stemmed flower on the sole sports a jagged engraved border; the workable arch and eye for stirrup feature cast and chased leafy ornament.

History: See cat. no. 371.

Exhibitions and publications: None.

NOTE TO THIS ENTRY IS ON PAGE 509.

416

Lamp (lámpara minera)

Possibly Bolivia, 1850–1900
Gift of Landon T. Clay
2001.842

H. 12⅜ in. (31.4 cm); W. 4⅜ in. (11.3 cm); D. 9⅝ in. (24.5 cm); Wt. 22 oz 17 dwt 23 gr (712.2 gm)

Marks: None.

Inscriptions: "B M," shaped from a sheet of metal, appear below cross on form.

THIS SO-CALLED MINER'S LAMP was unlikely used by miners, who worked in a cramped environment and were too poor to own such an elaborate form. It is possible that it belonged to "B M," the unidentified owner or manager of a mine. The hook and brace suggest that the lamp was hung over a large rod and secured in place. The animal and Christian elements are not uncommon in Latin American silver; the mining implements, which include a sledgehammer, shovel, and pick, suggest its relationship to a mine.[1]

The placement of the hinge at the front of the lamp seems curious, but it may have served to keep oil from spilling forward. When lit, the lamp would have cast a soft glow on the sconce where the above-mentioned symbols were arranged.

Description: The lamp is composed of a beaker-shaped hinged reservoir with an applied base and projecting wick holder that hangs

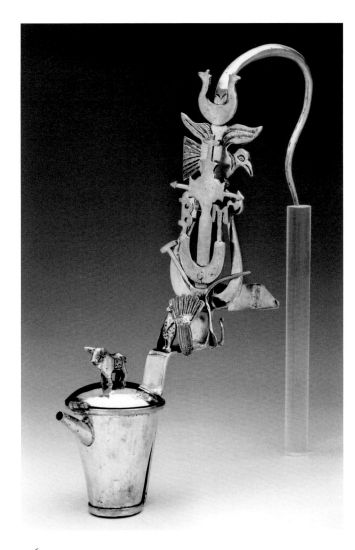

416

at the base of a tall sconce, which is ornamented with a variety of symbols. A silver framework supports the whole, beginning with a flat band soldered to the back of the lamp, rising upward to a wider frame. Above the sconce, a deep hook completes the frame. A U-shaped brace has been affixed to the back, presumably to assist in securing the lamp.

The lid of the lamp's reservoir is ornamented with a cast horned bull. Behind it, on a shallow step of the frame, is a small turkey with arrayed tail feathers. The sconce is composed of a series of emblems, letters, or symbols fashioned from a metal sheet and mounted to the framework, which has also been cast into several shapes. From top to bottom, they are a pair of llamas; a flying bird; a cross, the letters "B M"; and four mining tools. The framework is composed of the above-mentioned flying bird and a lyre.

History: See cat. no. 375.

Exhibitions and publications: None.

NOTE TO THIS ENTRY IS ON PAGE 509.

417

William Spratling (1900–1967), designer

Taller de las Delicias, workshop

Pair of salad servers

Taxco, Mexico, about 1945
Gift of Will and Alexandra Watkins in honor of Mymie Worrell Graham
2000.793.1–2

Spoon (2000.793.1): L. 12¾ in. (32.4 cm); W. 2¼ in. (5.7 cm); Wt. 4 oz 3 dwt 14 gr (130 gm)

Fork (2000.793.2): L. 13 in. (33 cm); W. 2¼ in. (5.7 cm); Wt. 3 oz 7 dwt 7 gr (104.7 gm)

Marks: "SPRATLING / MADE IN MEXICO" in sans-serif letters, within a circle, with "WS" incuse monogram at center, struck on back of spoon. "SPRATLING SILVER" oval touchmark in raised sans-serif letters struck on fork.

Inscriptions: None.

THE RENAISSANCE OF Mexican silversmithing that began in the 1930s was due to the efforts of the multitalented American artist and writer William Spratling. An unlikely candidate for this role, Spratling had attended the Art Students league in New York in 1919; studied architecture at Auburn University; and taught architecture at Tulane University from 1922 to 1929. His academic path was soon overshadowed by the bohemian life he led in the French Quarter of New Orleans, where he kept company with writers Sherwood Anderson and John

Dos Passos. Accompanied by his erstwhile roommate William Faulkner, Spratling embarked on a freighter trip to Europe, and the two men collaborated on a humorous book. While in New Orleans, Spratling also wrote articles, sketched, and exhibited his work locally.[1]

On his first visit to Mexico City, in the summer of 1926, Spratling met Mexican artist Diego Rivera. Through Rivera, he soon became acquainted with members of the city's artistic, archeological, and literary community, many of whom believed that Mexico, then emerging from the revolution of 1910, was on the verge of intense social, political, and intellectual change. He met Dwight L. Morrow, the influential United States ambassador to Mexico from 1927 to 1930; art historian René d'Harnoncourt; and artists David Alfaro Siqueiros, José Clemente Orozco, and Miguel Covarrubias, among others. For the next two summers, Spratling returned to Mexico to teach Spanish colonial architecture, explore the countryside, and deepen his friendships with Mexicans and American émigrés.[2]

By 1929 he left Tulane to settle in Taxco, a poor, mountainous Mexican town that had last seen activity as a mining center in the mid-eighteenth century. There he continued to write, sending a monthly column on local events to the *New York Herald Tribune* and publishing a book entitled *Little Mexico* to augment his lean income. A windfall came from Rivera, who, at Spratling's suggestion, had been engaged by Morrow to paint a mural in Cuernavaca. This commission enabled Spratling to purchase a home in Taxco on Calle de las Delicias (Street of Delights). As he ranged about his adopted country, Spratling drew and collected ancient artifacts and folk materials in all media, with which he decorated his new home.[3]

In Mexico, Spratling planned to support himself through writing, but soon he was in need of more substantive income. About 1933, encouraged by Morrow and inspired by the success of his friend Fred Davis, an American who operated a jewelry shop in Mexico City, Spratling established a workshop called the Taller de las Delicias (Atelier of Delights) down the street from his home. He began to create modernist designs for silver that were based on ancient and more recent folk materials of the region. His designs capitalized on the Mixtec and Zapotec jewelry that had caused a sensation in 1932, when they were discovered in a tomb at Monte Albán, galvanizing international interest in pre-Columbian metalwork.[4]

Employing local craftsmen who, until that time, had worked in a Spanish-colonial idiom, Spratling was able to create arresting and affordable jewelry, flatware, and hollowware. He obtained locally available materials, such as mother-of-pearl, amethyst, onyx, jade, tortoiseshell, and rosewood, using them as colorful and exotic accents. His bold designs, a striking fusion of varied pre-Columbian and Art Deco styles, quickly found favor among American tourists. With the success of this venture, Spratling expanded his operation to include textiles, furniture, and tinwork. His participation in *Contemporary Industrial and Handwrought Silver*, an exhibition held by the Brooklyn Museum of Art in 1937, conferred special status on his activities and stimulated American luxury stores such as Saks Fifth Avenue, Gump's, Neiman-Marcus, and Tiffany's to feature silver made at the Taller de las Delicias.[5] The town of Taxco prospered as Spratling's success gained momentum.[6] Widely copied in his own time, Spratling was the source of Mexico's remarkable comeback in silversmithing that continues today.

These hefty serving pieces, typical of Mexican-made silver, display a bold form. The raised dots on the ferrule evoke the pictographic language of the Mayan world and appealed to a sophisticated modernist sensibility for powerful composition and simplicity of form. The maker's marks incorporate the conjoined "WS" monogram that Spratling originally used as a brand on his horses.

Description: Each long-handled serving piece has a hammered inner bowl and planished exterior; the fork has been shaped into a form that complements the spoon and displays added piercing. The straight-sided broad rosewood handles narrow toward blunt downturned tips. The handles are joined to the bowls with a broad ferrule that has a Mayan-inspired collar in which three spheres of silver are arranged vertically on a wide band.

History: Mymie Worrell Graham, the original owner of these salad servers and the ladle that follows (cat. no. 418), was an American woman who moved to Mexico shortly after her marriage in 1930. From about 1935 to 1950, she operated a gift shop called Tesoros de Mexico at the Hilton Hotel in Mexico City, where she sold Mexican weavings and archeological materials. She acquired the salad servers for her personal use while in Mexico and made a gift to the donors shortly before they were given to the Museum.

Exhibitions and publications: None.

NOTES TO THIS ENTRY ARE ON PAGE 509.

418

William Spratling (1900–1967), designer
Taller de las Delicias, workshop
Ladle

Taxco, Mexico, about 1945
Gift of Stephen and Betty Jane Andrus in honor of Mymie
Worrell Graham
2000.789

L. 12½ in. (31.8 cm); W. 3¾ in. (9.5 cm); Wt. 5 oz 10 dwt 23 gr
(172.6 gm)

Marks: "SPRATLING / MADE IN MEXICO" in raised sans-serif
letters within a circle, with "WS" incuse monogram at center,
struck on back. "SPRATLING SILVER" in raised sans-serif letters, within an ellipse, appears indistinctly, slightly overlapping first
mark.

Inscriptions: None.

See cat. no. 417.

Description: The ladle has a hammered inner bowl and planished
exterior and a single pouring spout. A thick rattail drop attaches
the bowl to a wide handle ferrule with gadrooned decoration. The
broad rosewood handle has a downturned oval tip.

History: See cat. no. 417.

Exhibitions and publications: None.

Notes

370

1. Esteras Martín 1992b, 13.

2. Identification of the chalice and processional cross was provided by
Cristina Esteras Martín.

3. The history of St. Augustine parish and its related ecclesiastical silver is
drawn from research conducted by Susan R. Parker, "Sacramental items
unearthed in St. Augustine, Florida in 1879, donated by Keith family of
Boston and St. Augustine," prepared for the Museum of Fine Arts, Boston, June 2003, with funding from the St. Augustine Foundation; department files, Art of the Americas.

4. For other examples of Mexican chalices having intact bell decoration,
see Instituto de cooperacion iberoamericana, *Orfebrería hispanoamericana,
siglos XVI–XIX, obras civiles y religiosas en templos, museos y colecciones españolas* (Madrid: Museo de America, 1986), 33–34, cat. no. 8; and *Mexican Silver*
1993, 56, cat. no. 20.

5. For the full group, see Appendix 1.

371

1. For a similar ciborium, see Staatliche Museum 1981, 70, cat. no. 7; *Trois
siècles d'orfèvrerie Hispano-Américaine XVIIe–XIXe siècles des collections du
Musée d'Art Hispano-Américain Isaac Fernandez Blanco, Municipalité de Buenos Aires, Argentina* (Paris: Le Louvre des Antiquaires, 1986), 48, cat. nos.
13–14.

372

1. Staatliche Museum 1981, 102–4, cat. nos. 54–57; Esteras Martín 1992a,
306–7, cat. no. 132; Esteras Martín 1993, 87, 131, cat. nos. 13, 29.

2. Buhler and Hood 1970, 1:18–19, cat. no. 10. The Museum's collection
includes a related 17th-century two-handled silver cup from Oporto
(1985.998).

3. Surinam's connection to Boston was primarily based in the shipping
industry, but other relationships were more fraternal. Freemason Paul
Revere fashioned jewels for a Masonic brotherhood located in Surinam;
Revere Daybooks, 1:31.

4. For a similarly lobed chalice in the Tesoro de la Catedral, see *Oribes y
plateros en la Nueva Granada* (Bogotá: Banco de la Republica & Museo de
Arte Religioso, 1990), n.p.; Esteras Martín 1992b, fig. 25, mark ill. in cat.
no. 350.

5. The *hombre verde,* or "green man" as he is known in English and European imagery, has been discussed in popular and scholarly literature; see
Kathleen Basford, *The Green Man* (Cambridge, Eng.: D. S. Brewer, 1978),
9–24; and William Anderson, *Green Man: The Archetype of Our Oneness with
the Earth* (London and San Francisco: HarperCollins, 1990).

373

1. For the history of the form, see *Eucharistic Vessels of the Middle Ages*
(Cambridge: Busch-Reisinger Museum, 1975), 57–64, cat. no. 6.

2. For a related example, said to have been made in Cusco, see Carcedo
1997, 218, fig. II–124; Esteras Martín 1997, 150–51, cat. no. 35.

374

1. Archivo General de Simancas, *Titulos de Indias*, Catálogo XX del Archivo General de Simancas (Vallodolid: el Archivo, 1954), 345; Henry S. Marks, *Who Was Who in Florida* (Huntsville, Ala.: Strode Publishers, 1973), 33.

2. For comparison between the two forms, see Esteras Martín 1997, figs. 7, 12. For letter of August 12, 2001, see department files, Art of the Americas. For related examples, see *Mexican Silver* 1993, 62, 72, cat. nos. 33, 59.

3. Cristina Esteras Martín and Dorie Reents-Budet kindly offered these observations.

375

1. More elaborate examples of these symbols are found on a pair of plaques in the Museo de Arte Sacro de la Catedral de Santa Cruz de la Sierra, in Santa Cruz, Bolivia; Querejazu and Ferrer 1997, cat. no. 42.

2. For the discussion on Hispanic and Andean forms, see Ilmar Luks, "Tipologia de la escultura decorativa hispanica en la arquitectura andina del siglo XVII," *Boletín del Centro de Investigaciones Historias y Estéticas* (November 1973); William Anderson, *Green Man: The Archetype of Our Oneness with the Earth* (London and San Francisco: HarperCollins, 1990).

3. Archangels abound in Latin American religious imagery. For sculptural examples, see Gabrielle G. Palmer, *Cambios: The Spirit of Transformation in Spanish Colonial Art* (Albuquerque: Santa Barbara Museum of Art in cooperation with the University of New Mexico Press, 1992), 87, cat. no. 60. For a comparable painting, see Querejazu and Ferrer 1997, 45, fig. 8; and Fane 1996, fig. 53-3.

376

1. On the Jesuit seal, see F. L. Cross and E. A. Livingstone, eds., *The Oxford Dictionary of the Christian Church,* 3d ed. (Oxford: Oxford University Press, 1997), 819.

2. James Hall, *Dictionary of Subjects and Symbols in Art* (New York: Harper & Row, Publishers, 1979), 249.

3. The term *sirena-angel,* or mermaid-angel, has been used by Cristina Esteras Martín in reference to such forms.

377

1. John Vanderplank, *Passion Flowers* (Cambridge: MIT Press, 1996), 202; Gauvin Alexander Bailey, *Art on the Jesuit Missions in Asia and Latin America, 1542–1773* (Toronto: University of Toronto Press, 1999), 144–45, 178–82. The multiple symbolism of the passion-flower vine was adopted by the Roman Catholic Church soon after its arrival in Peru in the late sixteenth century; well before that date, the plant had been used by native peoples as a sedative and antispasmodic. Thanks to Gauvin Bailey for identifying the passion flower.

2. Bailey, *Art on the Jesuit Missions,* 144–45, 178–82.

[no notes on 378]

379

1. A likely rendition of a viscacha is in Rebecca Stone-Miller et al., *To Weave for the Sun: Andean Textiles in the Museum of Fine Arts, Boston* (Boston: Museum of Fine Arts, Boston, 1992), 96, cat. no. 75. For an image of a viscacha in metal, see Carcedo 1997, 157, fig. II-41.

380

1. For similar examples attributed to Rodallega, see Hector Rivero Borrell Miranda et al., *The Grandeur of Viceregal Mexico: Treasures of the Museum Franz Mayer* (Houston and Mexico City: Museum of Fine Arts, Houston and Museo Franz Mayer, 2002), 294–95, cat. no. 105; *Mexico: Splendors of Thirty Centuries* (New York: Metropolitan Museum of Art, published by Bulfinch Press, 1990), 418, cat. no. 190; Cristina Esteras Martín, "Plateria virreinal novohispana: Siglos XVI–XIX," in *El Arte de la Plateria Mexicana 500 Años,* exh. cat. (Mexico: Centro Cultural Arte Contemporáneo, A.C., 1989), 346–47, cat. no. 109. See also *Mexican Silver* 1993, 93, cat. 82.

2. Esteras Martín 1992a, 36.

3. Anderson 1941, 1:324–26.

381

1. Cristina Esteras Martín, *La Plateria en el Reino de Guatemala, Siglos XVI–XIX* (Guatemala: Fundación Albergue Hermano Pedro, 1994), 88, cat. no. 23. A taller example from Arequipa is published in Esteras Martín 1993, 69, cat. no. 3. See also *Mexican Silver* 1993, 67, cat. no. 43, for a similar form.

382

1. For similar pairs with identical cast handles and surviving pendants, see Taullard 1947, fig. 93; and Staatliche Museum 1981, 201, cat. no. 232.

383

1. Like tea and chocolate, mate is a stimulant. It contains caffeine, theobromine, and theophylline. A. Vasques and P. Molina, "Studies on Mate Drinking," *Journal of Ethnopharmacology* 18 (1986), 267–72.

2. Santacilia and Ulloa 1975, 229.

3. John Miers, *Travels in Chile and La Plata: Including Accounts Respecting the Geography, Geology, Statistics, Government, Finances, Agriculture, Manners and Customs, and the Mining Operations in Chile,* 2 vols. (London: Baldwin, Cradock, and Joy, 1826), 1:42–43.

384

1. For related examples, see Urgell 1988, 99–102, cat. nos. 38–42.

385

1. The regional attribution was suggested by Cristina Esteras Martín.

2. For examples of such bases, see Taullard 1947, fig. 255.

386

1. Adolfo Luis Ribera, *Diccionario de orfebres rioplatenses, siglos XVI al XX* (Buenos Aires: Fondo Nacional de las Artes, 1996), 136.

[no notes on 387–91]

392

1. For the mark by maker "Arantida," see Adolfo Luis Ribera, *Diccionario de orfebres rioplatenses, siglos XVI al XX* (Buenos Aires: Fondo Nacional de las Artes, 1996), 111.

[no notes on 393–99]

400

1. Thanks to Dorie Reents-Budet for sharing information on the early Maya.

2. For other examples of *jícaras* in this form and attributed to Alto Peru, Colombia, and Venezuela, see Staatliche Museum 1981, 232–34, cat. nos. 279–82; and Urgell 1988, 85, cat. no. 23. Scientific examination of the vessel walls was inconclusive regarding its material.

3. Sophie D. Coe and Michael D. Coe, *The True History of Chocolate* (London: Thames and Hudson, 1996), 120–21.

4. Coe and Coe, *True History of Chocolate*, 120–21.

401

1. Anderson 1941, 1:327–28; Esteras Martín 1992b, 84, no. 214. For a closely related example marked by assayer Cayetano Buitrón, see *Mexican Silver* 1993, 130, cat. no. 217.

2. Esteras Martín 1992b, 78, cat. nos. 197–98; 84, cat. no. 214.

3. Buhler 1972, 2:655, cat. no. 554.

4. Esteras Martín 1992a, 292–93.

402

1. J. Eric S. Thompson, ed., *Thomas Gage's Travels in the New World* (1648; reprint, Wesport, Conn.: Greenwood Press, 1981), 157.

2. Taullard 1947, figs. 98–99; Staatliche Museum 1981, 229–31, cat. nos. 274–79; *Orfebreria hispanoamericana, siglos XVI–XIX, obras civiles y religiosas en templos, museos y colecciones españolas* (Madrid: Museo de America, 1986), cat. no. 62; Jose Antonio del Busto Duthurburu, *Peruvian Silverwork: 2000 Years of Art and History, Enrico Poli Collection* (Lima: Banco del Sur, 1996), 243–44.

3. Gerald W. R. Ward, "The Silver Chocolate Pots of Colonial Boston," in Falino and Ward 2001, 61–88. See fig. 3 for a painting by Luis Melendez (1716–1780) entitled *Still Life of Chocolate Service*, about 1760, in the Museo del Prado, Madrid.

4. Sophie D. Coe and Michael D. Coe, *The True History of Chocolate* (London: Thames and Hudson, 1996), 120.

5. Chonta wood is a common name for a type of spiny palm trees, known by its scientific name *Aiphanes aculeata Willd*.

403

1. Mark A. Burkholder and Lyman L. Johnson, *Colonial Latin America* (New York: Oxford University Press, 1990), 126–27.

404

1. *International Hallmarks on Silver Collected by Tardy* (Paris: Tardy International Hallmarks on Silver, 1995), 338.

2. Anderson 1941, 2, fig. 87; *El Arte de La Plateria Mexicana 500 Años* (Mexico City: Centro Cultural/Arte Contemporaneo, A.C., 1989), cat. no. 56; *Mexican Silver* 1993, 80, cat. no. 74.

405

1. For an example with a similar border, see John Walker Harrington, "Spanish-American Colonial Silver," *International Studio* 90 (August 1928), 27, 31.

406

1. Staatliche Museum 1981, 182, cat. nos. 182–83. For an unadorned silver chamber pot, see Taullard 1947, fig. 27.

407

1. For a wide range of braziers, see Staatliche Museum 1981, 137–57.

2. For *confiteras*, see Mo 1992, 88–89, cat. no. 62; Fane 1996, 255–59, cat. no. 113.

3. This interpretation was advanced by Cristina Esteras Martín.

408

1. For related examples, see Taullard 1947, figs. 354, 357; and Staatliche Museum 1981, 221–24, cat. nos. 259–66.

409

1. J. Eric S. Thompson, ed., *Thomas Gage's Travels in the New World* (1648; reprint, Westport, Conn.: Greenwood Press, 1981), 157.

410

1. A bombilla marked "Abelar" was sold at auction in 1973; Adolfo Luis Ribera, *Diccionario de Orfebres Rioplatenses, Siglos XVI al XX* (Buenos Aires: Fondo Nacional de las Artes, 1996), 107.

411

1. *Equestrian Equipment* (Louisville, Ky.: J. B. Speed Art Museum, 1955), esp. "Spurs, the development of their commoner forms during the centuries" (chart).

2. Taullard 1947 figs. 308–9.

[no notes on 412–13]

414

1. Taullard 1947, figs. 294, 297.

415

1. Taullard 1947, fig. 295. For related examples and a similar conclusion, see Jose Antonio del Busto Durthurburu, *Peruvian Silverwork, 2000 Years of Art and History* (Lima: Bancosur, 1996), fig. 281.

416

1. For related examples, which are rare, see Querejazu and Ferrer 1997, fig. 50.

417

1. William Faulkner and William Spratling, *Sherwood Anderson and Other Famous Creoles: A Gallery of Contemporary New Orleans* (New Orleans: Pelican Book Shop, 1926); Sandraline Cederwall and Hal Riney, *Spratling Silver* (San Francisco: Chronicle Books, 1990), 13–14.

2. For a discussion of Spratling's contacts in Mexico, see Joan Mark, *The Silver Gringo: William Spratling and Taxco* (Albuquerque: University of New Mexico Press, 2000), 19–33. D'Harnoncourt worked with the Department of the Interior's Arts and Crafts Board, and later became director of the Museum of Modern Art. Penny Chittim Morrill and Carole A. Berk, *Mexican Silver, 20th-Century Handwrought Jewelry & Metalwork* (Atglen, Pa.: Schiffer Publishing, 1994), 54.

3. William Spratling, with foreword by Diego Rivera, *Little Mexico* (New York: Cape and Smith, 1932). Spratling was instrumental in bringing Mexican painters to the attention of Americans; see Morrill and Berk, *Mexican Silver*, 20–21.

4. Mark, *Silver Gringo*, 47–49; Taylor D. Littleton, *The Color of Silver: William Spratling, His Life and Art* (Baton Rouge: Louisiana State University Press, 2000), 254.

5. *Contemporary Industrial and Handwrought Silver* (Brooklyn, N.Y.: Brooklyn Museum, 1937); Littleton, *Color of Silver*, 260–63.

6. Cedarwall and Riney, *Spratling Silver*, 21.

[no notes on 418]

ADDENDA

419

Samuel Gray (1684–1713)

Fork

Boston, Massachusetts, about 1705–07
Gift of Catherine Coolidge Lastavica in memory of her great-grandmother Elizabeth Gardner Amory and in honor of her cousin John Lowell Gardner
2004.71

L. 4⅞ in. (11.4 cm); W. ⅞ in. (1.1 cm); Wt. 4 dwt 15 gr (7.2 gm)

Marks: "S G" in roman letters, within a heart, struck on back of fork and centered in an elliptical reserve on handle tip.

Inscriptions: "R C" in roman letters, within an irregular elliptical reserve, engraved at center of handle tip.

THE FORK CAME INTO USE late in Western cultures, joining knives and spoons as table utensils only in the 1500s. The form first appeared in Italy before being adopted by the English in the 1600s. The growing emphasis upon dining etiquette, particularly hygiene, may have influenced its creation and design. In 1611 Englishman Thomas Coryat observed its use, noting that "the Italian cannot by any means endure to have his dish touched with fingers, seeing all men's fingers are not alike

cleane. Herupon I myselft thought good to imitate the Italian fashion by this forked cutting of meate."[1]

Forks appeared on colonial American tables shortly thereafter, but in small numbers. In 1633 Gov. John Winthrop received a "case containing an Irish skeayne or knife, a bodekyn & a forke for the useful application of which I leave to your discretion," indicating that the proper use of the items was yet unclear.[2] Such utensils were enjoyed only by the wealthy, including Winthrop and a handful of well-to-do colonists such as Mary Browne (1674–1753), who owned a travel set of five miniature knives, forks, and spoons, which were stored in a shagreen case.[3]

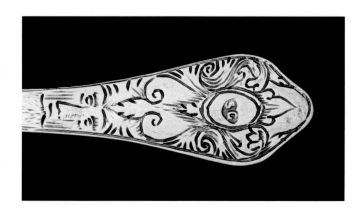

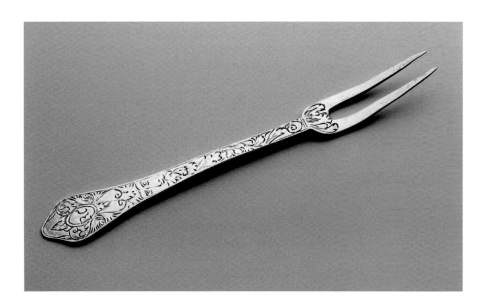

In colonial New England, forks were imported until the early 1700s, after which date a small number were made locally for privileged members of society such as Rebecca Chambers, whose initials grace this example by Samuel Gray. As a new and fashionable form, the fork would have been a desirable purchase made by her father, the Hon. Charles Chambers, Esq. (1650–1743), a member of His Majesty's Council, judge of the Court of Common Pleas, and treasurer for the County of Middlesex.[4]

This small fork may have been part of a set, originally accompanied by a spoon or knife (or both) as well as a traveling case. It bears a remarkable resemblance to a fork and spoon made by John Coney about 1700. All three are similar in weight and scale; they further share a two-tined form, trifid shape, and comparable engraved decoration, including the human face or "green man" in the foliate area and the position of the initials and makers' marks. Scholars have suggested that either Coney or Jeremiah Dummer may have been Gray's master. Indeed, the survival of these unusual examples, along with six forks among Gray's inventoried shop goods, supports a master-apprentice relationship with Coney. The fork is only one of three items that have been attributed to Gray.[5]

Gray began practicing his craft about 1705 and moved to New London by April 1707, the time of his marriage there to Lucy Palmes. Therefore, the fork may have been made beween 1705 and 1707.[6]

Description: The slender two-tined fork has an upturned trifid-shaped handle tip and is engraved throughout in a Mannerist style.

History: Engraved initials "R C" are probably those of Rebecca Chambers (1691–1729) of Charlestown, Massachusetts, m. 1711 Daniel Russell (1685–1763) of the same town. The fork probably descended to their son James Russell (1715–1798) and his wife, Katherine Graves (1717–1778), m. 1738; by descent to their daughter Rebecca Russell (1747–1816) and Judge John Lowell (1743–1808), m. 1778; by descent to their daughter Rebecca Russell Lowell (1779–1853) and Samuel Pickering Gardner (1767–1843), m. 1797; by descent to their son George Gardner (1809–1884) and Helen Maria Read (1819–1888), m. 1838; by descent to their daughter Elizabeth Gardner (b. 1843) and Charles Walter Amory, m. about 1864; thence to their great-grand-daughter, the donor.[7]

Exhibitions and publications: The Discerning Eye: Radcliffe Collector's Exhibition (Cambridge: Fogg Art Museum, 1974), no. 35; Kane 1998, 503; Sarah D. Coffin et al., *Feeding Desire: Design and Tools of the Table, 1500–2005* (New York: Assouline Publishing in association with Cooper-Hewitt, National Design Museum, Smithsonian Institution, 2006), 43.

NOTES TO THIS ENTRY ARE ON PAGE 522.

420

John Noyes (1674–1749)

Tankard

Boston, Massachusetts, about 1704
Gift of Catherine Coolidge Lastavica in memory of her great grandmother Elizabeth Gardner Amory and in honor of her cousin John Lowell Gardner
2003.784

H. 6⅛ in. (15.6 cm); Diam. base 5 in. (12.9 cm); Wt. 21 oz 7 dwt 14 gr (665 gm)

Marks: "I N" in roman letters within an ellipse struck to left of handle and on top of lid.

Inscriptions: "G / I * E" in a shield engraved on vessel, opposite handle; bust of a knight engraved above shield; foliate decoration surrounds the whole. "I W" in capital letters, below "G Gardner" in script, scratched on underside of lid. "This Tankard belonged / to John Gardner Great Grand / father of Saml P. Gardner and / was probably made prior to the / year 1700" in script inscribed on bottom.

420

THE SON OF A MINISTER, John Noyes was a member of the Third, or Old South, Church and later a founder of the Brattle Street Church; see cat. no. 97 for an account of Noyes's life and career. Less than thirty objects have survived bearing Noyes's mark. However, his level of accomplishment is clear from the variety of forms he fashioned, including candlesticks, forks, beakers, and salvers. All demonstrate a high degree of skill in casting, decorative details, and finishing. This tankard is one of nine known examples (another example is cat. no. 97); in each, the artist varied small details, such as the terminal and thumbpiece.[1]

The tankard formed part of a gift of family silver presented to the Museum, which included a fork by Samuel Gray (cat. no. 419) and eighteenth-century spoons by John Nelson (2004.73) of Portsmouth, New Hampshire, and Jonathan Trott (2004.72) of Boston.

Description: The raised flat-topped tankard tapers inward from an applied molded base; the rim is scored below applied molding. The base and lid bear evidence of center points. The stepped flat-topped lid has a broad scored rim and scalloped front. The cast scrolled thumbpiece descends to a five-part hinge with meander wire on molded hinge plates. The hollow seamed handle bears wear marks from lid and displays a cast cherub terminal over a vent hole. The upper handle is attached to the body with a long rattail drop.

History: The initials on the shield suggest that the tankard was made for the 1704 marriage of John Gardner (1681–1722) and Elizabeth Weld (1674–1770) of Salem, but the additional "I W" initials on the base may indicate that another Weld family member, such as Elizabeth Weld's older brother Joseph (b. 1671), had previously owned it. The tankard most likely descended from John and Elizabeth Gardner to their son John Gardner (1706–1784) and Elizabeth Putnam (1700–1764), m. 1730; to their son John Gardner (1731–1805) and Elizabeth Pickering (1737–1823), m. 1757; to their son Samuel Pickering Gardner (1767–1843) and Elizabeth Russell Lowell (1779–1853), m. 1799.[2] For continued history of descent to the donor, see cat. no 419.

Exhibitions and publications: Gourley 1965, no. 148; *The Discerning Eye, Radcliffe Collector's Exhibition* (Cambridge: Fogg Art Museum, 1974), no. 36; Kane 1998, 738.

NOTES TO THIS ENTRY ARE ON PAGE 522.

421

Paul Revere II (1734–1818)
Sugar bowl

Boston, Massachusetts, 1785
Gift of Mary E. W. Murphy
2004.2210

H. 10³⁄₁₆ in. (25.8 cm); W. base 3 in. (7.6 cm); Diam. rim 4⅛ in. (10.4 cm); Wt. 11 oz 2 dwt (345.3 gm)

Marks: "[pellet] REVERE" struck on bottom.

Inscriptions: "JAW" script monogram within an ellipse engraved on side of vessel; dragon's head crest on cover. "5440" scratched on underside of base.

Armorials: The Warren arms are engraved in an ellipse on one side: argent, a lion rampant; a chief checky argent and azure; and crest, a griffin's head couped.

THE RECENT ACQUISITION of a sugar bowl made by Paul Revere II for John and Abigail (Collins) Warren reunites the work with a large coffeepot the smith made in 1791 for the same couple. Given in 1895, the coffeepot was the Museum's first acquisition of Revere-made silver.[1] On June 24, 1785, Revere charged Dr. Warren £4.0.6 for the silver in this "sugar dish," which weighed 11 oz, 10 dwt, and an additional £3.15.0 for making and engraving it.[2] A teapot that Revere made in the same year for the couple remains on loan to the Museum from a private collection.

Dr. John Warren, a distinguished Boston physician, was

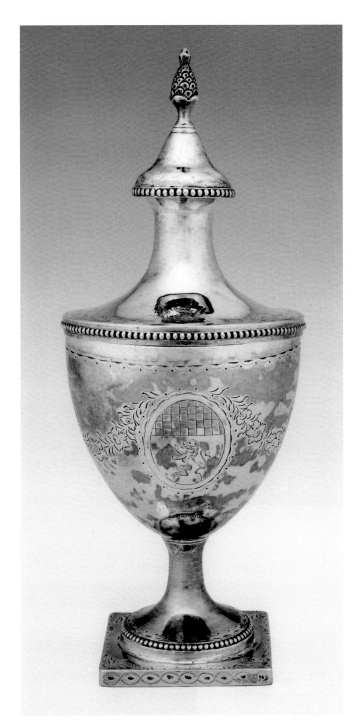

421

active in the Revolution as a surgeon general in the Continental Army and later was involved in many aspects of Massachusetts politics and cultural life. John and his older brother Joseph, a Boston physician who was killed at the battle of Bunker Hill, played an important role in medicine in Boston. In 1785 John and his family moved to a large house on property bordered by School, Tremont, and Washington streets, and he may have acquired this sugar bowl and other objects for use in his new home. He was a Mason and often patronized Revere, who engraved for him a certificate to award to attendees of his anatomy course at the American Hospital in Boston in 1780.[3]

Description: The tall urn-shaped sugar bowl is raised and rests on a flaring foot with a beaded edge. It is supported on a square base engraved with a border of ovolos and leaves at the corners and with a bright-cut chain of ovals around its edges. The high, separate, domed lid has a molded top, with a beaded edge demarcating the upper section, which is fitted with a pineapple or pinecone cast finial pinned in place, and a beaded edge. An encircling band of bright-cut sprigs adorns its lower end. The body is decorated with engraved garlands and ribbons and features the Warren coat of arms in an elliptical reserve on one side and the engraved owner's initials in an elliptical reserve on the other.

History: Made for Dr. John Warren (1753–1815) of Boston and his wife, Abigail (Collins) Warren, m. 1777; by descent to Joseph Warren, who lent the piece to the Museum on November 23, 1928; transferred to Mary W. Murphy (Mrs. Grayson M. P. Murphy), New York City, January 10, 1961; given by her in 2004.

Exhibitions and publications: Kane 1998, 826.

NOTES TO THIS ENTRY ARE ON PAGE 522.

422

422

Shepherd and Boyd (active about 1806–1830)

Robert Shepherd (1781–1853)
William Boyd (1775–1840)

Tablespoon

Albany, New York, 1809
The Estelle S. and Harris A. Solomon Collection—Gift of their daughter Carol Solomon Rothschild
2004.652

L. 9½ in. (24.1 cm); W. bowl 1¾ in. (4.4 cm); Wt. 1 oz 18 dwt 15 gr (60.1 gm)

Marks: "SHEPHERD & BOYD" in serrated rectangle struck on back of handle.

Inscriptions: "A MEMORIAL OF / Christ[r]. A Yates who died Nov[r] 8.th 1809" engraved on top of handle; "A.B." engraved on back of handle.

ROBERT SHEPHERD AND WILLIAM BOYD learned their trade from Albany silversmiths Isaac (1767–1855) and George Hutton (1773–1855). By the fall of 1806, the former apprentices had formed a partnership that produced a multitude of silver wares; they also sold a wide range of goods, from brass, lacquered, or gilt lamps to spectacles and hair powder.[1] Their silver follows

the late Neoclassical, or Empire, style and is often ornamented with bold gadrooning and figural finials.

Like their masters, Shepherd and Boyd made funeral, or memorial, spoons such as this. The practice of presenting an engraved spoon to friends of the deceased was common in the seventeenth and eighteenth centuries, particularly among the New York Dutch. The number of surviving spoons demonstrates that the tradition continued in Albany into the early nineteenth century.[2] Christopher A. Yates (1739–1809), son of Adam and Anna Gerritsen Yates and a member of Albany's politically prominent Yates family, died on November 8, 1809, at age seventy-one. He had married Catharina Waters on July 16, 1766, with whom he had seven children, including twin sons.[3] The "AB" initials on the back of the handle probably represent the person for whom the spoon was made.

This funeral spoon is part of collection of thirty-five pieces of eighteenth- and early-nineteenth-century American flatware given to the Museum in 2004 by the daughter of silver collectors Estelle S. and Harris A. Solomon.

Description: The tablespoon has a downturned coffin handle with a rectangular cross section and a pointed oval bowl with an incised pointed arch above a drop.

History: Given to the donor by her parents, Estelle S. and Harris A. Solomon, who collected colonial American silver spoons.

Exhibitions and publications: None.

NOTES TO THIS ENTRY ARE ON PAGE 522.

423

Jones, Ball, & Poor (active about 1847–1851)

John B. Jones (1792–1854)
True M. Ball (1815–1890)
George B. Jones (1815–1875)
Nathaniel C. Poor (1808–1895)

Water pitcher

Boston, Massachusetts, about 1849
Gift of John Herbert Ross and Barbara O'Neil Ross
2003.819

H. 12¾ in. (32.4 cm); W. 8½ in. (21.6 cm); Diam. rim 3¹⁵⁄₁₆ in. (10 cm); Diam. foot 5 in. (12.7 cm); Wt. 25 oz 18 dwt 12 gr (806.4 gm)

Marks: "JONES BALL & POOR [in rectangle] / BOSTON / PURE SILVER COIN" surrounding a center punch struck incuse on bottom.

Inscriptions: "H.S.W. / from / J.H.W." in Gothic letters within a reserve engraved below spout. "1849" engraved on bottom.

MUCH AMERICAN SILVER of the mid-nineteenth century was produced in relatively small shops and firms, which were often formed by short-lived partnerships. Such was the case in Boston, where a large number of partnerships were active in the industry. The firm of Jones, Ball, and Poor, which produced this handsome presentation pitcher in a florid Rococo-revival style, was in business only a few years under that name. However, firm members, along with other partners, were part of a continuous chain of operations that began in the early nineteenth century and culminated in today's Shreve, Crump & Low (see cat. nos. 212–16).

Description: The large raised pear-shaped pitcher is decorated with repoussé and chased floral ornament around the body. It is supported by an applied and raised stepped foot with a beaded edge. The applied scrolled handle is embellished with acanthus-leaf decoration at its upper and lower termini. A band of beaded decoration is at the rim; a reserve for the engraved inscription appears below the flaring spout, with an engraved bowknot below the inscription.

History: According to the donors, the engraved initials stand for Henry Sidney Waldo, who presumably presented the pitcher to an unidentified recipient about 1849; by descent to John Herbert Ross (1925–2002), the great-great-grandson of Henry Sidney Waldo.

Exhibitions and publications: None.

424

Clemens Friedell (1872–1963)

Punch bowl

Pasadena, California, 1912
Museum purchase with funds donated anonymously,
and from Shirley and Walter Amory, John and Catherine
Coolidge Lastavica, the H. E. Bolles Fund, the Michaelson
Family Trust, James G. Hinkle, Jr., and Roy Hammer, Robert
Rosenberg, Sue Schenck, the Grace and Floyd Lee Bell Fund,
and Miklos Toth
2003.730

H. 14¼ in. (36.2 cm); Diam. rim 17¾ in. (45.1 cm); Diam base 10¼
in. (26 cm); Wt. 103 oz 19 dwt 12 gr (3234 gm)

Marks: "STERLING / HAND CHASED BY / CLEMENS
FRIEDELL / PASADENA" engraved on edge of foot.
"STERLING / HAND CHASED BY / CLEMENS FRIEDELL
/ PASADENA / CAL." struck in reverse on inside of bowl.

Inscriptions: "POLO / CHALLENGE TROPHY [in repousséd Art
Nouveau-style lettering] / PRESENTED BY [in engraved capitals]
/ WILLIAM J. AND FRANK G. HOGAN [in repousséd letter-
ing] / PASADENA / CAL. [engraved]." inscribed on one side of
vessel. "WON / BY [in repousséd lettering]" above a blank reserve
on other side.

ONE OF A HANDFUL of independent California metalsmiths working during the Arts and Crafts period, Clemens Friedell practiced a lyrical form of silversmithing that retained elements of an Art Nouveau style. Born near New Orleans, Louisiana, Friedell was taken as a child to Vienna by his Austrian-born parents. There, he apprenticed to a Viennese silversmith for seven years, returning to the United States in 1892, at the age of twenty. Friedell did not find employment as a silversmith, however, until he was hired as a chaser for the Gorham Manufacturing Company, where he worked from 1901 to 1908. As a member of Gorham's most elite circle of craftsmen, he was probably assigned the task of chasing the company's Art-Nouveau-style Martelé line, among other designs. These experiences influenced Friedell's later work, which was characterized by similarly undulating forms and unplanished hammer marks. He also favored a floral decoration, often of repoussé flowers native to California, his home after 1911.[1]

After leaving Gorham, Friedell settled in the resort town of Pasadena, where he found a ready clientele among local society figures and wealthy Easterners who flocked there each winter. Friedell's first major client was likely the philanthropist Phoebe Hearst (1842–1919), for whom he created a monumental loving cup in 1912.[2] That the silversmith was capable of producing work in quantity and large scale is well demonstrated by the dining service he executed that year for Los Angeles brewer E. R. Maier. The service consisted of eighteen settings, numerous serving vessels, and a 28-inch-tall centerpiece.

In Pasadena, Friedell benefited from a steady demand for presentation silver, particularly in the form of trophies, ordered by the many sporting clubs active in the region as well as by the Tournament of Roses, which took place each December. The annual celebration, established in 1890 to promote the city as a winter destination, originally featured society events, a parade of flower-decked carriages, tugs-of-war, and ostrich races. It included football and other athletic events, including polo, which had been introduced on American soil in 1876 and whose popularity increased by the turn of the century. For the region's polo players and horsemen, Friedell created such trophies as this punch bowl as well as shield-shaped equestrian portraits mounted on wooden plaques.[3]

This presentation punch bowl, called the Hogan Challenge, was awarded by the Pasadena Polo Club about 1912–13. Friedell merged the Art Nouveau style of decoration into an Arts and Crafts aesthetic that incorporated regional interests, such as California poppies, and a visibly hammered appearance. Like Arthur Stone, who operated a larger workshop, Friedell exerted similar control over silver produced in his shop. His chief contribution was as a designer and chaser; he maintained an assistant who did most of the raising of the heavy-gauge sheets. Although Friedell did not exhibit widely, he received a gold medal at the 1915 Panama-California Exhibition at San Diego, where he exhibited a large punch bowl (possibly this example), equestrian plaques, and coffee sets. Friedell continued to fashion work in a similar style for clientele through the Great Depression. As Pasadena waned as a playground for the rich, however, he produced more domestic items rather than the ambitious loving cups and other trophy forms that had dominated his early career. By the 1930s and 1940s, he offered stock items in his store, a departure from previous years when the carriage trade had provided him with the luxury of creating bespoke silver. Friedell prospered far into the modern era by adapting to changing times. He maintained an active shop until sometime before his death in 1963.

Description: The large hand-raised vessel has a trumpet foot soldered to a broad bowl with an everted rim. Both the rim and the foot have a meandering scalloped edge reinforced with an applied flat exterior rim. Repoussé and chased floral decoration throughout features California poppies and trailing vines. A chased depiction of a polo player on horseback appears below the presentation inscription; the other reserve is flanked by mallets and pennants.

History: Fashioned as a presentation punch bowl for the Hogan Challenge, held by the Pasadena Polo Club. This competition may be the same as the Hogan Cup, which was awarded twice, in 1912 and 1913.[4] The donors of the punch bowl were club president Frank G. Hogan, who also served as president of the Tournament of Roses in 1911 and who owned a real estate and insurance company in Pasadena called the Hogan Company. The second donor was founding member Col. William J. Hogan.[5] Frank Braun was the likely winner of the trophy, as the vessel was consigned to auction by his granddaughter. Purchased by the dealer Argentum Antiques, of San Francisco, California, and acquired by the Museum in 2003.

Exhibitions and publications: Possibly the Panama-California Exhibition, San Diego, 1915; Philadelphia Antiques Show, April 2003; *MFA Annual Report*, 2003–4, 24.

NOTES TO THIS ENTRY ARE ON PAGE 522.

425

425

David Mason Little (1860–1923)

Teapot

Salem, Massachusetts, 1921
Gift of Selina F. Little in memory of Bertram Kimball Little
2004.710

H. 4⅞ in. (12.4 cm); W. 10¾ in. (27.3 cm); D. 5¾ in. (14.6 cm); Diam. foot 3¹⁄₁₆ in. (8.1 cm); Wt. 17 oz 9 dwt 24 gr (544.3 gm)

Marks: "LITTLE [enclosed in an ellipse] / SALEM / STERLING" and a small rooster, all incuse, struck on bottom.

Inscriptions: "MARGUERITE LITTLE YOUNG / FROM HER FATHER / 1921." in block letters engraved on bottom.

DAVID MASON LITTLE was trained as a naval architect and had a distinguished career of military service in the Spanish-American War and World War I; he was also elected mayor of Salem, Massachusetts, in 1900. Something of a polymath, Little enjoyed several hobbies, including photography and silversmithing, which he initially pursued in a studio in his home on Chestnut Street. Wishing to fashion a tea set for his wife, he sought the assistance of noted Arts and Crafts silversmith George C. Gebelein of Boston as early as 1907. Little soon became Gebelein's patron as well as his apprentice, helping the elder silversmith move in 1909 to a larger shop on Beacon Hill. There, Little maintained a bench while retaining his studio at home.[1]

Little produced teawares, vases, bowls, and tablewares as well as a delicately chased powder box now in the collection of the Peabody Essex Museum.[2] Most of his work was made for family members, such as this graceful, somewhat conservative teapot made for his daughter. In style, it is in harmony with the work of Gebelein, Arthur Stone, Karl Leinonen, Gyl-

lenberg and Swanson, and other Boston-area Arts and Crafts silversmiths.

Description: The raised globular teapot has a raised circular foot and a curved silver handle with wood insulators.

History: Made by the artist for his daughter Marguerite Little Young (1894–1975); her husband, Charles M. Young (1892–1984), gave it to their niece, the donor, after Marguerite's death in 1975; given in honor of the donor's father and the artist's son Bertram Kimball Little (1899–1933).

Exhibitions and publications: None.

NOTES TO THIS ENTRY ARE ON PAGE 522.

426

426

Arthur Stone (1847–1938)

Porringer

Gardner, Massachusetts, 1925
Gift of John Herbert Ross and Barbara O'Neil Ross
2003.817

H. 2⅛ in. (5.4 cm); W. 8½ in. (21.6 cm); Diam. rim 5¼ in. (13.3 cm);
Wt. 12 oz 9 dwt 15 gr (388.1 gm)

Marks: "Stone [with hammer mark] / STERLING" struck on bottom.

Inscriptions: "JHR" chased on handle. "JOHN HERBERT ROSS
/ MARCH 15–1925 / FROM / HIS GRANDPARENTS / Mary
Carney Vose Parker [in script imitating a signature] / Herbert
Parker [in script imitating a signature]." engraved on bottom.

As was common in Arts and Crafts silver, Arthur Stone's shop
used a colonial form—in this case, the porringer—but altered
it through the addition of chased decoration incorporating an
unusual Viking ship, which is used on both the bowl and the
elaborate handle. This porringer was a presentation piece, giv-
en to John Herbert Ross at his birth. Ross was a descendant of
Denman Waldo Ross, who was connected with Stone through
their mutual involvement in Handicraft Shop. The same donor
also gave the Museum an Arthur Stone plate (2003.818) decorated with three engraved groupings of elephants, which had been
given to John Herbert Ross on his first Christmas, in 1925.

Description: The large raised silver porringer has a circular bowl with
an everted rim, rounded sides, and a center punch; it is embellished
on the outside with an encircling band of six Viking ships, each riding on a band of stylized waves. The applied handle is decorated
with a Viking ship at center surrounded by pierced scrolled decoration evoking wavelike designs and stylized dolphins or other marine
forms; it incorporates the chased initials at the top.

History: Given to John Herbert Ross (1925–2002), Cambridge, Massachusetts, by his grandparents.

Exhibitions and publications: None.

427

Alexandra Solowij Watkins (b. 1933)

Three-piece tea set

Boston, Massachusetts, 1956–57
Gift of Miwa A. Watkins
2004.203.1–3

Teapot (2004.203.1): H. 5 in. (12.7 cm); W. 8¾ in. (22.2 cm); D. 6 in.
(15.2 cm); Diam. base 3⅝ in. (9.2 cm); Wt. 20 oz 15 dwt 20 gr
(646.7 gm)

Sugar bowl with lid (2003.203.2): H. 3¼ in. (8.3 cm); W. 5¼ in. (13.3
cm); D. 3½ in. (8.9 cm); Diam. base 2¼ in. (5.7 cm); Wt. 9 oz 2 dwt
7 gr (283.5 gm)

Creamer (2004.203.3): H. 3¼ in. (8.3 cm); W. 4⅝ in. (11.8 cm); D. 3¼
in. (8.3 cm); Diam. foot 2 in. (5.1 cm); Wt. 5 oz 5 dwt 5 gr (163.4 gm)

Marks: "STERLING / A. SOLOWIJ / ENTIRELY HAND /
WROUGHT" struck incuse on underside of teapot; same marks,
but in varying order, struck on underside of sugar bowl and
creamer.

Inscriptions: None.

Alexandra Solowij Watkins was born in Poland in 1933 and arrived at the School of the Museum of Fine Arts, Boston, in the mid-1950s, after training in Montreal. She designed and made this tea set and a chocolate pot (cat. no. 428) as part of her studies at the museum. Although after graduation, Watkins, as a foreign student, had to return to Montreal, the tea set was exhibited at the school and attracted the attention of an executive at Gorham Manufacturing Company of Providence, Rhode Island. The company hired her as a designer and provided the necessary immigration papers.

As a designer for Gorham, Watkins was one of several artist-craftspeople, including John Prip and Mary Ann Scherr, who collaborated with company designers to create modernist objects for mass consumption. One of her designs was a silver-plated "bateau" centerpiece (2004.205) produced in 1959–60. Watkins became an American citizen and later focused on jewelry, represented in the Museum's collection by a brooch (1995.749). Since 1968, she has been affiliated with the Atelier Janiyé gallery in Boston as a jeweler and, since 1982, as a co-owner.

Description: The raised round teapot rests on a simple circular base; it has an applied flaring spout and a C-shaped wooden handle. The detachable lid has a wooden finial set at a sloping angle. The covered sugar bowl is made en suite; it has two handles and a silver finial. The creamer has a simple spout and a single silver handle.

History: Made by the artist during her years at the School of the Museum of Fine Arts, Boston; given to the Museum by the artist's daughter.

Exhibitions and publications: None.

427

428

Alexandra Solowij Watkins
(b. 1933)

Chocolate pot

Boston, Massachusetts, 1957
Gift of Alexandra Solowij Watkins
2004.204

H. 3⅜ in. (8.6 cm); W. 6½ in. (16.5 cm); D. 4¼ in. (10.8 cm); Wt. 7 oz 8 dwt 23 gr (231.7 gm)

Marks: "A. SOLOWIJ / ENTIRELY HAND / WROUGHT / STERLING" struck incuse on underside.

Inscriptions: None.

Description: The round raised pot has a wooden handle placed at a right angle to the spout, which is formed by a shaping of the body of the pot. The hinged lid is placed opposite the spout and is operated with a teardrop-shaped thumbpiece attached near the hinge.

History: See cat. no. 427.

Exhibitions and publications: None.

429

Platter

South America, about 1780–1800
Gift of Lavinia and Landon T. Clay
2003.783

H. 2 in. (5.1 cm); W. 18¼ in. (46.4 cm); D. 13½ in. (34.3 cm); Wt. 63 oz 1 dwt 8 gr (1961.1 gm)

Marks: None.

Inscriptions: None.

LARGE AND WEIGHTY, this substantial platter, characteristic of much late South American silver, is unmarked, making it difficult to pinpoint the place of manufacture. It undoubtedly graced a dining table in a wealthy late-eighteenth-century home, for it shows signs of having been put to good use. Four additional South American silver platters were also given to the Museum by the same donors in 2003 (2003.779–82).

Description: The large, raised, oval platter is embellished with wavy chased decoration at the edge and has a decorative rim. It shows many signs of regular use.

History: See cat. no. 375.

Exhibitions and publications: None.

Addenda Notes

419

1. Thomas Coryat, *Coryat's Crudities Hastily Gobbled Up in Five Months Travells in France, Savoy, Italy, &c.* (London 1611), cited in Major C. T. P. Bailey, *Knives and Forks* (London and Boston: Medici Society, 1927), 6–7.

2. Cited in Alice Morse Earle, *Customs and Fashions in Old New England* (New York: Charles Scribner's Sons, 1893), 136.

3. Travel set of miniature silverware belonging to Mary Browne, Massachusetts Historical Society, Gift of Andrew, Peter, and Seabury Oliver, 1959, 0206.01–06.

4. Thomas Waterman, comm., "Charlestown Burying-Ground," *NEHGR* 5 (April 1851), 176.

5. For forks by John Coney and John Noyes, the only other surviving 18th-century Massachusetts examples, see Buhler 1972, 1:56, 113, cat. nos. 46, 92. See also the biography by Barbara McLean Ward in Kane 1998, 502–3.

6. Kane 1998, 502–3.

7. "D.," "Brief Memoirs and Notices of Prince's Subscribers," *NEHGR* 6 (July 1852), 274; "Record-Book of the First Church in Charlestown," *NEHGR* 23 (October 1869), 442, 444; T. C. A., "A Home of Olden Time," *NEHGR* 25 (January 1871), 37–52; The Church of Jesus Christ of Latter-day Saints, comp., *International Genealogical Index*, version 5.0 (Online: Intellectual Reserve, Inc., 1999–2003), http://www.familysearch.com (accessed 7/6/2004), film nos. 170519, 170460, 178134, 184764.

420

1. Kane 1998, 738.

2. T. C. A., "A Home of Olden Time," *NEHGR* 25 (January 1871), 37–52; George Walker Chamberlain, "The Early New England Coolidges and Some of Their Descendants," *NEHGR* 77 (October 1923), 302; *New York Times*, August 7, 1959, 23; Church of Jesus Christ of Latter-day Saints, comp., *International Genealogical Index*, version 5.0 (Online: Intellectual Reserve, Inc., 1999–2003), http://www.familysearch.com (accessed 7/10/2004), film nos. 170519, 455750, 456249, 458588; AFN:L9XB-LL; AFN:1J5D-HST; AFN:1J5D-J02.

421

1. Buhler 1970, cat. no. 388.

2. Revere daybooks, 2:33.

3. *DAB*, s.v. "John Warren"; *Sibley's Harvard Graduates*, 17:655–69; Falino and Ward 2001, 168–69, fig. 6.

422

1. Norman S. Rice, *Albany Silver, 1652–1825* (Albany, N.Y.: Albany Institute of History and Art, 1964), 75–76.

2. Waters 2000, 210, 420.

3. Stefan Bielinski, http://www.geocities.com/Heartland/Fields/2179/index.html?200511, Jeff's Geology webpage on Yahoo Geocities.

[no notes on 423]

424

1. Unless otherwise noted, Friedell's biographical details are drawn from Leslie Greene Bowman, "Arts and Crafts Silversmiths Friedell and Blanchard in Southern California," in Edgar W. Morse, ed., *Silver in the Golden State: Images and Essays Celebrating the History and Art of Silver in California* (Oakland: Oakland Museum History Department, 1986), 41–55.

2. Leonard Kreidt, "A Life Lined with Silver; Craftsman in Generous Gesture to City He Loves," *Pasadena Star News*, February 12, 1960, cited in Bowman, "Friedell and Blanchard," fn. 8.

3. For an example of these portraits, see Bowman, "Friedell and Blanchard," 44.

4. Correspondence, Museum of Polo and Hall of Fame, Lake Worth, Fla.; department files, Art of the Americas.

5. Correspondence, Pasadena Museum of History, Pasadena, Calif., and Museum of Polo and Hall of Fame; department files, Art of the Americas.

425

1. We are grateful to Selina Little for providing a wealth of biographical material on her grandfather; see department files, Art of the Americas. We are also grateful to Kelly H. L'Ecuyer for her assistance with this entry. See also Leighton 1976, 50–56.

2. Martha Gandy Fales, *Silver at the Essex Institute* (Salem, Mass.: Essex Institute, 1983), 58–60. Little's anniversary tea set made for his wife is also in the collection of the Peabody Essex Museum. Additional works by Little are in private collections. Selina Little has also given to the Museum an archive of ten period photographs Little took of his silver.

[no notes on 426–29]

Appendices 1–8: Church Silver

Jeannine Falino

Introduction

The Museum's collection of early Massachusetts church silver—including many objects on long-term loan—offers an unmatched resource for historians, curators, and collectors who can use these materials to study early works by American silversmiths, examine church history, and consider stylistic issues relating to changing forms, tastes, and patronage. This catalogue includes a number of objects owned by several Massachusetts congregations, discussed individually below, as well as a body of Spanish colonial objects from the Catholic church in St. Augustine, Florida. While the objects are catalogued individually under the appropriate maker or form, the following appendices summarize the history of each church and discuss the various objects owned originally by them, including the examples now in the Museum's collection.

The colonists who first arrived in Boston were nonconformist Puritans who suffered persecution in England under Charles I (1600–1649), who came to the throne in 1625. Soon afterward, William Laud, appointed by Charles I as Bishop of London, was ordered to zealously advance the position of the Anglican Church and prevent the growth of nonconformism in England. The ensuing Great Migration of the Puritans to the New World was a direct result of Charles's policy of intolerance, and by 1643, sixteen thousand people had arrived in the Massachusetts Bay Colony.

The Puritan hierarchy of church leadership included a pastor, whose work was to "attend to exhortation, and therein to administer a word of wisdom," and a teacher who "attend[s] to doctrine, and therein to administer a word of knowledge." Both were intended as church officers, and in many cases their roles overlapped, or were filled by one man. John Cotton, who arrived in 1633, served as teacher of the Boston church for nineteen years.

The third ecclesiastical rank was that of the elder, who assists the pastor and teacher in practical matters, tends to the sick, and provides leadership where needed. Last were the deacons, who were assigned to "receive the offerings of the church, gifts given to the church, and to keep the treasury of the church, and therewith to serve the tables which the church is to provide for; as the Lord's table, the table of ministers, and of such as are in necessity, to whom they are distributed in simplicity." Deacons were probably in charge of the communion silver, a fact proven out by silver given or bequeathed by some of these men.

Made before the separation of church and state was established, the history of these communion vessels is intertwined with the political and religious settlement of New England. Their desire to emulate the simplicity of the earliest Christian congregations had a radical effect on the shape and amount of church silver that was fabricated for their communion table. The new congregations replaced the Anglican chalice, used solely by the priest, with multiple beakers or cups, usually of a domestic shape, that were intended for the use of the covenanted congregation. This horizontal, democratic paradigm of Puritan church life also flourished in town meetings, where matters of interest to the community were discussed in a public forum.

Due to the engraved inscriptions and marks found on church silver, valuable information regarding the makers and the church's preferred forms of ecclesiastical silver can be gleaned. Each piece of church silver, with its particular form and accompanying engraved text, represents unvarnished, primary material that provides information on the religious and political leadership of Massachusetts from the very earliest years of its existence.

The donor of the silver, their standing in the community, and the reasons for their gift offer other avenues of inquiry. Unlike many examples of domestic hollowware whose owners are lost to us, church silver can offer concrete evidence of the patrons and their purpose of giving silver to their congregation. Silver was sometimes purchased with funds that came from a living donor, or in other cases, as a bequest. If specifically commissioned, church records sometimes list the cost, and the choice of silversmith. In other cases, the donor of the silver or the deacon, who sometimes ordered the silver, was related to the silversmith by blood or friendship, another means of illuminating the lives of working craftsmen and their symbiotic relationship to church and state.[1]

Notes

1. See Jones 1913; Barbara McLean Ward, "'In a Feasting Posture': Communion Vessels and Community Values in Seventeenth- and Eighteenth-Century New England," *Winterthur Portfolio* 23, no. 1 (spring 1988), 1–24;

Barbara McLean Ward, "Continuity and Change in New England Church Silver and Communion Practices, 1790–1840," in Falino and Ward 2001, 113–32.

Appendix 1. St. Augustine Church

St. Augustine is the oldest continuously occupied European settlement in the United States, Spain having colonized the area in 1565. Its strategic location on the Gulf Stream, where it could protect Spanish vessels en route to Spain with South American silver, prompted Spain to provide its financial support, which extended to the spiritual life of its inhabitants. Religious and daily life in St. Augustine were interwoven from the beginning, for its founder, Pedro Menéndez de Avilés (1519–1574), brought "eight church bells and four ornaments for celebrating Mass"[1] from Spain upon his arrival in San Augustine. When the crown became responsible for the colony, funding for the clergy and the goods required for the celebration of Mass were included in the annual budget for Florida's military garrison. Between the late sixteenth and later eighteenth century, most sacramental goods were purchased from Mexico. Proximity was a primary reason, for in the age of sail, communication was slow. Even more compelling, however, was a financial incentive, for revenues collected in Mexico provided the budget that sustained the Florida colony.

St. Augustine was often attacked by English soldiers during the seventeenth and eighteenth centuries, and on some of these occasions, such as during the unsuccessful six-week siege of the settlement in 1702 by South Carolina, church goods were moved into the fortress, called the Castillo de San Marcos, for safekeeping. Later, the silver was endangered when the colony became a pawn in war settlements. When Florida was awarded to the British in 1763 as a consequence of the Seven Years War (the French and Indian War, as it was called in North America), all moveable church property was shipped to Havana, Cuba.

Portions of the Museum's collection of church silver from St. Augustine Church was probably in Florida by the early 1600s.[2] An early chalice and paten were from Mexico, as may have been a cruz guion that was in the care of a church confraternity. The entire group in the Museum's collection may have been hidden at one point in St. Augustine's complex early history. A more likely scenario is that the objects were secreted sometime after 1821, when the Florida colony joined the United States. Under the separation of church and state as established by the American government, St. Augustine Church, as with others in the colony, found itself without a means of financial support.

This stressful period was compounded by their reception from the largely anti-Catholic, Protestant population that had emerged during the years of British occupation and renewed Spanish ownership. Chief among this group was District Attorney Alexander Hamilton Jr. (1786–1875), who argued that property of the Roman Catholic Church under the Spanish Crown should pass to the United States Government. Such rhetoric may have prompted church members to quietly relocate the chalice along with the rest of the cache in order to save it from potential seizure.

When, in 1823, Hamilton ran for the office of Territorial Delegate of Florida, Minorcan Catholics, an ethnic Spanish immigrant group affiliated with St. Augustine parish from the time of British occupation, sent a petition to Pres. James Monroe protesting that Hamilton had threatened those who opposed his election with unfavorable decisions on land claims. The name of Bernardo Segui appeared at the top of the petition. Segui served as president of the Board of Wardens that was incorporated in 1823 by the Florida Legislative Council as trustee-proprietors of parish property. He also owned a plantation house on the land purchased in 1871 by the donors. This is the same land where the silver was discovered in 1879.

Surely church officials had reason to fear the loss of their communion silver, for the attitude of the Protestant majority was unsympathetic to their culture; upon seeing the communion silver at St. Augustine church in 1827, author and poet Ralph Waldo Emerson observed in his diary that they appeared to him as "great coarse toys." Church wardens had access to the church building and its furnishings, and it was not uncommon for them to have housed such items. Segui may have removed the silver in an effort to protect these items, sacred to the Catholic faith, from falling into disrespectful government hands.[3]

The church silver consists of seven ecclesiastical objects that were buried in St. Augustine, Florida, sometime after 1721, the date engraved on a cross (cat. no. 374) in the group. They were discovered in 1879 on Oneida Street in St. Augustine, on property owned by Mr. and Mrs. William H. Keith on the west side of Maria Sanchez Creek. They were placed on loan to the museum in 1880 and given in memory of the couple in 1928.[4]

Exhibitions and publications: The paten, chalice, and five other items unearthed in St. Augustine were placed on exhibition at the shop of silver and jewelry purveyors Bigelow, Kennard & Co. of Boston sometime after their discovery, according to an undated notice in department files.

Notes

1. Esteras Martín 1992b, 13.

2. Identification of the chalice and processional cross was provided by Cristina Esteras Martín.

3. The history of St. Augustine parish and its related ecclesiastical silver is drawn from research conducted by Susan R. Parker, entitled "Sacramental items unearthed in St. Augustine, Florida in 1879, donated by Keith family of Boston and St. Augustine," prepared for the Museum of Fine Arts, Boston, June 2003, with funding from the St. Augustine Foundation. Department files, Art of the Americas.

4. The entire group consisted of the chalice and paten (cat. no. 370), a standing cup (cat. no. 381), and a cross (cat. no. 374). In addition, there are two vessels made of base metal and gilded silver (28.464–65) and one additional paten (28.470). Registrar's files, MFA.

Appendix 2. Arlington Street Church, Boston

The lack of an auspicious start in Boston did not prevent the Arlington Street Church from achieving a brilliant history and nurturing a lively and liberal-minded congregation that continues to thrive today. Latecomers to the well-established Congregationalist community of colonial Boston, the first wave of Scotch-Irish Presbyterians, largely of the artisan class, were warned out of Boston by the selectmen shortly after their arrival in 1718. However, the group persisted, and with the arrival of Rev. John Moorhead (minister 1729–1793) in 1729, a congregation was at last gathered. Church members first met in a barn on Long Lane at the corner of Bury Street that was expanded with time; in 1744 a proper meetinghouse was erected on the same site.[1]

Known and self-described as the "Church of the Presbyterian Strangers," the early members keenly felt their outsider status in Boston and were devoted to their church. Such sentiments were noted in an inscription on the first communion cup the church received in 1730 from Elizabeth Nichols, who gave thanks for "Gods wonderfull mercies to Her in a strange Land."[2]

Church silver was also given to commemorate important events in church life. The Museum's beaker by Jacob Hurd (cat. no. 86) was given by Brice and Ann Blair in honor of the new church building that was erected in 1744; three additional beakers were commissioned of Paul Revere II by the congregation in 1753, although the loss of church records prevents us from learning the reason for this large gift. In all, the church amassed seventeen pieces of American-made communion silver between 1730 and 1834, most of which was sold in 2002.[3]

The church shifted toward a Congregationalist theology in the late eighteenth century during the ministry of Jeremy Belknap (1787–1798). With the arrival of William Ellery Channing (1803–1842) in 1803, the membership made a second dramatic shift when it led the move among Congregationalist churches to Unitarianism. Channing was an influential leader in this regard, and his eloquent espousal of such liberal social and religious concepts as transcendentalism and abolitionism made the church an important gathering place for like-minded Bostonians.

In 1809 the church moved to a magnificent new structure in the Back Bay designed by Boston architect Charles Bulfinch. Its location at Arlington and Boylston streets gave the church its new name, which it bears to this day.[4]

Exhibitions and publications: MFA 1911, cat. nos. 509–12, 676, 871–73; Jones 1913, 78–80, pl. XXX; French 1939, no. 25; Kane 1998, 587.

Notes

1. The church's street location was later renamed Federal and Channing streets.

2. Jones 1913, 78.

3. Jones 1913, 78–79. For one of the three beakers, see cat. no. 111. The early records were lost when church member and loyalist, stationer William McAlpine, took them when he fled Massachusetts in the late 1770s. Jones 1913, 78–80, pl. XXX; Worthley 1970, 79–80. For church silver sold in recent years, see Christie's, New York, sale no. 1003, January 18, 2002, lots 319–33; Northeast Auctions, Portsmouth, N.H., August 3–4, 2002, lots 867–69.

4. Church history drawn from Harriet E. Johnson, comp., *Handbook of the Arlington Street Church* (Boston: Anchor Linotype Printing Company, 1929); Worthley 1970, 79–80.

Appendix 3. Brattle Street Church, Boston

The Brattle Street Church, also known as the Brattle Square Church, was the fourth congregational church to be established in Boston, and known in its own time as The Manifesto Church for its liberal positions on church membership and the reading of Scripture. The congregation was gathered in 1698, and the first meetinghouse erected on land on Brattle Street that had been conveyed to the church by Thomas Brattle. A church designed by Thomas Dawes and built in 1773 stood on the same site near Hanover Street, in the vicinity of Boston's Government Center.[1]

The Brattle Street congregation included an impressive roster of successful craftsmen, merchants, and Harvard graduates, beginning with Boston merchant and Harvard College treasurer Thomas Brattle (1658–1713), who entered the congregation in 1699 and served as its first deacon, Thomas Clark (1653–1704), and the merchant Stephen Minot (1662–1737). At least thirty-nine pieces of silver were accumulated by the church in the eighteenth century, a significant number for any Boston church. The quantity of church plate at the Brattle Street Church was due to the relative wealth of its membership and to its willingness to fund communion silver. In some instances, commemorative church silver acknowledged leading members such as Deacon Barnard, who received a tankard in 1700 "as an acknowledgement of . . . gratitude . . . for his service in the building of ye Meeting House." The tankard was fashioned by Noyes for twelve pounds, a price arranged by Thomas Brattle. On another occasion, the church "voted the Buying a Tankard of Deacon Draper, to be valu'd by Mr. Noyes & Edwards, & that it be paid for out of the Church Moneys."[2]

The Brattle Street Church was also filled with silversmiths. Beginning in 1699, Joseph Allen and John Noyes, the latter with his mother and siblings, joined the congregation. The next decade saw additional enrollment from the ranks of numerous silversmiths who may have gained some patronage from the church or its congregation. In addition to Allen and Noyes, silversmiths John Potwine, Andrew Tyler, Joseph Edwards, Samuel Edwards, John Dixwell, Edward Winslow, John Coney, and John Edwards entered the congregation between 1699 and 1741. Of these men, Noyes, Tyler, John Edwards, and Winslow received commissions for church silver. William Cowell Sr. was not a member, but, perhaps due to his apprenticeship with Allen and Edwards, he produced a tankard (cat. no. 40) for the church in 1705. Cowell's children were baptized at the Brattle Street Church, and his wife joined the congregation in 1715, the year before Cowell produced a fine baptismal basin for the church.[3] Unlike most churches that sought out silversmiths to fashion their communion plate, sometimes from great distances, Brattle Street Church had only to look within its congregation to find some of Boston's most distinguished craftsmen.

The ensuing decades saw the Brattle Street Church flourish as a center for Boston's most wealthy and successful townspeople. In 1746 the patriot John Adams called the church "Dr. Cooper's tasty society," a reference to Rev. Samuel Cooper, a quiet revolutionary in his own right, and his elite and powerful membership composed of such members as merchants John Hancock, Ebenezer Storer II (1729/30–1807), Gardiner Greene (1753–1832), Thomas Amory Jr. (1722–1784), Joseph Barrell (1739–1804), Isaac Royall, John Erving, and James Pitts. Adams advised joining the Brattle Street Church, so as to become known by members of Boston society having "more Weight and Consequence."[4]

By the early nineteenth century, however, the Brattle Street Church suffered dwindling membership and funds in the face of rapid growth among Boston's Trinitarian and Unitarian Congregational churches.[5] Having determined that they possessed far more communion plate than needed, the membership decided in 1839 to sell their excess silver at auction. The Museum's tankard by William Cowell Sr. (cat. no. 40) came from that sale. By 1870, the steady loss of congregants caused the church to revive its membership by commissioning a new church in the fashionable Back Bay district from architect Henry Hobson Richardson. However, before the move took place, the structure in Brattle Square suffered major losses during the fire of 1872.[6] The combination of expenses, losses from the old and new buildings, and other changes was damaging to the financial health of the church; the Richardson church was sold in 1876, and the congregation disbanded shortly thereafter.

About thirty-eight pieces of communion plate in all were commissioned by the Brattle Street Church. Today, less than twenty can be accounted for. The whereabouts of four tankards sold at the 1839 auction are known: the Museum's example by Cowell; one by Andrew Tyler, now at the Clark Art Institute; a third by John Edwards that was given to the First Church, Medford, and a fourth by Edwards in private hands. The church may have deliberately consigned the tankards, a domestic form, in order to save such ecclesiastical vessels as flagons, basins, and communion plates. Other pieces of church plate may have been lost in the great fire of 1872, as hinted by the inscription on a tankard by John Noyes relating that it had been "taken from the ruins after the fire of November 9th, 1872."[7] The Museum's fourteen pieces were received in 1913 from the Benevolent Fraternity of Churches, an urban ministry that cared for the silver after the dissolution of the Brattle church. In 1942 the Museum received the Noyes tankard made for Reverend Barnard, as noted above. With the acquisition of the Cowell tankard, the Museum now possesses sixteen pieces of Brattle Street Church's silver that recalls a lively chapter in Boston's religious life.

Exhibitions and publications: MFA 1906, cat. nos. 57, 73, 76, 97, 100–1, 108, 128, 178, 187, 207, 210, 221, 330; Jamestown 1907, cat. nos. 472–76; MFA 1911, cat. nos. 215–17, 283, 291, 362, 389, 421–22, 436, 499–503, 711–14, 724, 749, 796, 1004; Jones 1913, 67–71, 272–73, pl. XXVI and LXXXIX; Buhler 1972, cat. nos. 24, 71, 82, 87, 91, 93 100–1, 106, 272, 321, 425, 433, 452, 537; Kane 1998, 300–1, 350–51, 354, 414, 419, 421, 674, 692, 703, 738, 943, 977.

Notes

1. Walter Muir Whitehill, *Boston, A Topographical History* (Cambridge: Belknap Press of Harvard University Press, 1959), 28, 168. The Brattle Street Church was also known as the Fourth Church of Boston, Universalist. For information on the site of the early Brattle church and its membership, see *The Manifesto Church, Records of the Church in Brattle Square Boston with lists of Communicants, Baptisms, Marriages, and Funerals, 1699–1872* (Boston: The Benevolent Fraternity of Churches, 1902); Worthley 1970, 69–72. For the Dawes church, see Frederic C. Detwiller, "Boston's Patriot Architect," *Old-Time New England* 68, no. 249 (summer/fall 1977), 1–18; Frederic C. Detwiller, "Thomas Dawes's Church in Brattle Square," *Old-Time New England* 69, no. 255 (winter/spring 1979), 1–17.

2. Brattle Street Church possessed a quantity of silver exceeded only by the First Church of Boston, which owned forty-five pieces of communion plate. Other Boston churches fell far behind; Old South possessed twenty-nine, but fifteen was a more common number among Hollis Street, New South, and Long Lane churches.

3. James Jackson Minot, comp., *Ancestors and Descendants of George Richards Minot, 1758–1802* (n.c.: n.p., 1936), 12; John Coburn made communion plates for the church in 1764, although he was not a congregant.

4. See John A. Schutz's review of Charles W. Akers, *The Divine Politician: Samuel Cooper and the American Revolution in Boston*, in *New England Quarterly* 6 (1983): 297–99. For information on cabinetmakers and their patrons belonging to the Brattle Street Church, see Robert Mussey and Anne Rogers Haley, "John Cogswell and Boston Bombé Furniture: Thirty-Five Years of Revolution in Politics and Design," *American Furniture* (Hanover, N.H.: Chipstone Foundation and University Press of New England, 1994), 71–103.

5. According to Dr. Harold Worthley, Librarian, Congregational Library of the American Congregational Association, there were approximately fifty churches in Boston by the middle of the nineteenth century, a number that was considered too large to support the local population.

6. For quotations from the church regarding the auction, and some of the objects that were probably sold, and the fire of 1872, see Warren 1987, 33–36, figs. 18–19.

7. Christie's, New York, sale 8578, January 18, 1977, lot 75; Sterling and Francine Clark Art Institute, accession number TR524/80; Buhler 1979, 19–20, cat. 11.

Appendix 4. The First and Second Church, Boston

Rare, early, and accomplished examples of silver belonging to the First Church, Boston, form the core of the Museum's collection of ecclesiastical silver. These vessels help to document the formative years of the Congregational Church, then inseparable from the Massachusetts Bay Colony. They provide primary information about the colonial world, the name of the church, its sponsors, and the craftsmen who fashioned them, the latter being the first English-speaking silversmiths in the New World.

John Winthrop (1588–1649), first governor of the Massachu-setts Bay Colony, is perhaps the most distinguished early member of the First Church, Boston. Winthrop, a founding member of the church, spearheaded the colonization when he arrived in 1630 with a fleet of some dozen ships and established a community in Charlestown. Due to the scarcity of water, the group moved to Boston within a few months. Although First Church was not the earliest to be established in New England, it was soon considered the leading congregation in the Massachusetts Bay Colony. This was partly due to its early reputation as the governor's church, but it was soon enhanced by the inspired sermons and voluminous publications of its teacher, John Cotton (1585–1652), who arrived in 1633.[1]

Winthrop's gift of an English steeple cup, now missing its tall cover, is a cornerstone of the church's collection of early silver that includes a total of four domestic vessels of English and Dutch manufacture. In all, some forty-five pieces of church silver were fashioned for, given, or bequeathed to the communion table before 1796.[2]

As the congregation grew, the membership sought out Robert Sanderson and John Hull, mintmasters of the Colony and the first two silversmiths working in colonial Boston, for additional communion vessels. Hull and Sanderson began to fashion silver for the church beginning in 1647.[3] Several cups adorned with the simple initials "T / B C" highlight the membership's self-perception as The Boston Church, which at the time was the only Boston church in existence. When Second Church in the northern part of town was established in 1649, the First Church's self-image remained intact, as demonstrated by a beaker engraved "T / B ★ C / 1659" (cat. no. 70).

Many of the vessels given to First Church and many other congregational churches were gifts from its own leadership. Deacon Joseph Bridgham, a tanner, called a "righteous, merciful and publick-spirited man," bequeathed twenty pounds in 1708 to be "Invested in Plate for the Service of the Communion Table." His gift was used to purchase three wine cups by Jeremiah Dummer. Deacon John Williams, wine cooper and merchant, granted fifty pounds to the church in 1737. Through his legacy, a pair of mugs by Jacob Hurd was added to the service. Such wealthy donors and public officials as John Winthrop and Lydia Hancock are but two of many whose names grace the vessels given to Boston's First Church.

Close relatives and friends of the silversmiths provided a small but significant source of church silver. Among these were Anna Dummer and her father, Joshua Atwater, who gave a cup made by Anna's husband, Jeremiah Dummer. William Pollard fashioned a mug for First Church through the legacy of the tobacconist John Forland, who engaged Pollard's aunt, Mary

Pollard, as a housekeeper. The blacksmith Robert Hull gave a communion cup made by his son John, with partner Robert Sanderson, and engraved "The gift of a Friend." This inscription was also used for the Museum's example, which was given by the merchant Thomas Clarke (cat. no. 71).

As deacon of the First Church, Sanderson helped to solidify patronage of their shop, a relationship that they in any case dominated until about 1675 when Jeremiah Dummer, the first native-born silversmith and their first apprentice, began to work for himself. One wine cup was made for the church about 1675 by Sanderson's son, Benjamin (1649–1678/79). Aside from this example, the two beakers and five wine cups they fashioned make up all the colonial silver made for First Church before 1700.

A long roster of Boston silversmiths created vessels for the communion table in the first quarter of the eighteenth century. These craftsmen included Jeremiah Dummer, John Edwards (cat. no. 51), Benjamin Hiller, and William Pollard. A third wave of acquisitions came during the mid-eighteenth century, when John Coney, Daniel Henchman, and Jacob Hurd were engaged to produce additional vessels. A flagon by Samuel Bartlett of Concord and six pieces by Paul Revere added in the late colonial and early federal period completed the cycle of acquisitions for the church's communion table.

The Second Church of Boston, founded in 1649, merged with the First Church in 1970. The Museum's baptismal basin by Jacob Hurd (cat. no. 77) was among twenty pieces of church silver brought by the Second Church to the merger.

Exhibitions and publications: MFA 1906, cat. nos. 63, 87, 88–91, 102–03, 107, 135, 139–43, 148, 152, 165, 221, 250, 311; MFA 1911, cat. nos. 42, 227, 347–51, 393, 555–56, 561, 580, 584–86, 591, 594–96, 618, 631–32, 833, 896–99, 955, 957; Jones 1913, 19–43.

Notes

1. Richard D. Pierce, ed., *The Records of the First Church in Boston 1630–1868*, Publications of the Colonial Society of Massachusetts, Vol. 39 (Boston: Published by the Society, 1961), xv–xxvii; Worthley 1970, 53–58.

2. Jones 1913.

3. For the partnership of Hull and Sanderson, see Kane 1987.

Appendix 5. Malden, First Church

In May 1649 the First Church was gathered in Malden, and in 1739 it was organized as the First Parish, also called North Church, following the establishment of a second church that served the Second or South Precinct.[1] The communion service was placed on long-term loan to the Museum in 1911 and thus escaped damage when a fire struck the church in 1935; it was made a gift in 1991.

The liturgical silver made for First Church of Malden is composed almost exclusively of caudle cups that are closely matched in size and girth. In choosing this secular form, they affirmed the participatory and egalitarian role of the congregation in the communion service. Examples of such cups abound in communion services of the period, as the Congregational churches often strove to acquire multiples of such domestic vessels as beakers and caudle cups. This approach was typical of the reform churches, and in sharp contrast to the Anglican tradition derived from Roman Catholicism that asserted the primacy of priests as intermediaries between the laity and God, and for whom the chalice was reserved.

The decoration and inscriptions found on more lavish liturgical silver of the period are often indicators of the wealth of the donor, and the names of the ministers and members of the congregation engraved on the vessels can serve as a guide to their status. By contrast, the Malden communion silver is unornamented and unengraved. As in their selection of vessels, as described above, the simple, shorthand term "M : C : Plate," for "Malden Church plate," reinforces the communal nature of the service within the church community.

Although a number of churches used one or two caudle cups in their communion service, some of which originated in the homes of their congregants, others purchased sets outright. The First Church in Concord (gathered in 1636) was the first Massachusetts congregation to possess a large group of caudle cups, beginning in 1676. The Malden church probably began in the early 1700s with four vessels by Coney (cat. no. 27) and in 1728 engaged John Burt to produce cups similar to those already in use (cat. no. 20). A number of Connecticut churches favored this pattern, including the First Church in New Haven (gathered 1639), First Church, Stratford (gathered 1639), Whitehaven (United) Church in New Haven (gathered 1642), and First Church, Farmington (gathered 1652). Coney produced a pair of caudle cups for Farmington and four cups for the Concord churches, and of his generation, he appears to have received the most commissions for this form.

The Malden service includes one object having prior domestic ownership, a cann by Jacob Hurd. A spoon by Samuel Waters (cat. no. 180), probably used to mix water and wine, was the last piece of silver to join the communion service in the early nineteenth century.

Exhibitions and publications: Jones 1913, 257–58; Clarke 1932, nos. 26–27; MFA 1932, no. 15; French 1939, no. 87; Kane 1998, 251, 324, 590.

Notes

1. Worthley 1970, 339–242. Worthley notes that the churches reunited in 1792.

Appendix 6. Second Congregational Society of Marblehead

In the early years of its settlement, Marblehead was a rather unruly fishing community with a diverse and transient population composed of Newfoundlanders, along with Welsh, Irish, English, and Jersey (Channel Island) settlers. The economic and social development of the town was delayed due to a lack of initiative in the sale of the fish, which was controlled by merchants in Salem or Boston. The seasonal nature of fishing in a one-industry town, and the town's vulnerability to attack during the French and Indian wars, prevented the establishment of a stable society in Marblehead until 1713, when the Treaty of Utrecht brought a period of sustained growth to the region. Peace also brought a new generation of Boston and Salem merchants to Marblehead, who prospered as middlemen in the fishing industry.[1]

The First Congregational Society was formed in 1684 but played a minor role in the Marblehead community until the early 1700s. Membership was largely drawn from the local population until the early eighteenth century, when the new merchant group began to dominate church affairs. Disagreements between the two groups began in 1714, when a search for a new minister polarized the membership. John Barnard and Edward Holyoke were the chief competitors for the minister's position. Both men were Harvard graduates from respected Boston families, and in their liberal theology were evenly matched in their ability to serve the Marblehead community. However, the newer merchant families favored Holyoke due to the influence of Edward Brattle, whose brother Thomas was treasurer of Harvard College. When the older, conservative membership chose to defend Holyoke's competitor, John Barnard, the merchant group broke with the church. In 1716 they established the Second Congregational Society.[2]

Within the first year of its existence, the Second Church ordered a sizeable body of communion silver from John Burt and John Coney, who produced flagons, tankards, and beakers for the congregation. An impressive basin by Coney arrived in 1718, and a large bowl by Jacob Hurd in 1728. All twelve pieces acquired during Reverend Holyoke's tenure were inscribed with his name. Although such dedicatory inscriptions are found in ecclesiastical silver of the period, its uniform message illustrates the church's unequivocal support for its new minister. The names of the donors are unknown, except for Edward Brattle, whose name appears on a pair of beakers by Coney that were made about 1716, but there is little doubt that the affluence of the newly formed congregation made these rapid purchases possible. A tankard by Marblehead silversmith Thomas Grant was added in 1773, many years after the original group of silver was formed. One provincial, late-seventeenth-century English spoon may have entered the church service soon after it was gathered in 1716.[3] The size of the communion service and the variety of forms that were represented contrast sharply with those owned by First Church at the time of the controversy, which consisted of eight beakers, including five by Dummer, one by Hull and Sanderson, and an English beaker.[4]

Silver owned by the Marblehead church was among many loaned to the Museum of Fine Arts for a pioneering exhibition held in 1911 on ecclesiastical and domestic silver. The Marblehead silver remained on loan to the Museum afterwards and fortunately escaped the fire that consumed the church meetinghouse the following year. Pressing financial needs of the church were met when the silver was sold to the Museum in 1984.

The intense period of acquisition and wide variety of vessels that characterizes the Marblehead church silver indicate the level of prosperity of the newly arrived merchant class. Their choice of such nonliturgical forms as beakers and tankards demonstrates their commitment to Congregational methods of worship, even as the majestic flagons, a traditional ecclesiastical vessel, suggest their leanings toward the Anglican world they had left behind.

Exhibitions and publications: MFA 1911, 19, cat. nos. 167–68, pl. 6; Jones 1913, 259–68, pl. LXXXVII; MFA 1991, 18, 68, 91, cat. no. 48.

Notes

1. Christine Leigh Heyrman, *Commerce and Culture, The Maritime Communities of Colonial Massachusetts 1690–1750* (New York: W. W. Norton, 1984), 207–90.

2. During the ministerial controversy, a second debate regarding the Church of England was a source of friction. See Thomas C. Barrow, "Church Politics in Marblehead, 1715," *Essex Institute Historical Collections* 98, no. 1 (April 1962), 121–27. Holyoke became minister of the congregation in 1716 and resigned after twenty-one years of service to become president of Harvard College.

3. The bowl of the trifid-handled spoon (1984.213), dated to about 1700, carries the maker's mark "DA" with pellets above and below, all within a beaded circle. Three indistinct marks are on the back of the handle, among them possibly a tower (?) in a shield and a pinecone or tree incuse. The spoon is engraved "M.E."

4. For a complete listing of the Marblehead silver, including those not in the Museum's collection, see Jones 1913, 265–68, pl. LXXXVII.

Appendix 7. Medfield, First Congregational Parish (now First Parish, Unitarian, Church of Medfield)

The First Congregational Parish in Medfield was gathered in December 1651 and organized in 1814.[1] Of the three pairs of beakers owned by the church, the earliest by Zachariah Bridgen (cat. no. 7) was made in 1767. The second pair of vessels (cat. no. 148) has an oviform cup; one was made by Thomas Knox Emery, and its unmarked mate, identical in form and fabrication, is attributed to him as well. The final pair, also unmarked, was made in 1817 following the organization of the First Parish.[2]

Exhibitions and publications: Kane 1998, 208–18.

Notes

1. Worthley 1970, 359–61; "Medfield Silver Shown at Museum," *Medfield Suburban Press*, April 9, 1981.

2. The pair of unmarked cups are engraved "First / CHURCH OF CHRIST / in / Medfield" on the cup, and "1817" inside the foot ring (1980.488–89). Two London-made pewter collection plates, formerly on loan to the museum, were also part of the communion service.

Appendix 8. First Church in Newton, Massachusetts

The Massachusetts settlement variously named Nonantum, Cambridge Village, New Cambridge, and Newtown gathered in 1664 as the First Church in Newton. The majority of the church's silver was acquired between 1714 and 1757 during the ministry of Rev. John Cotton, the namesake and great-grandson of Rev. John Cotton of the First Church in Boston.[1] The church enjoyed a large congregation during the eighteenth and nineteenth centuries, but by the mid-twentieth century, with the passage of time and shifting populations, it sought unsuccessfully to merge with area churches. Its doors formally closed in 1972, at which time the ecclesiastical silver was given to the Museum, accompanied by silver plate, pewter, and various furnishings.[2]

Eighteenth-century Boston silversmiths represented in the church's collection include William Cowell Sr., John Edwards, Jacob Hurd, and the partnership of Samuel Minott and Josiah Austin (cat. nos. 2, 41, 52, 80). Three of the donors were from the Stone and Trowbridge families of Newton, each of whom served as deacons in the church.

The oldest vessel in the group is a mid-seventeenth-century English wine cup that predates the gathering of the Newton congregation. The esteem in which it was held can be inferred from the nineteenth-century mate that was made for it by Newell Harding & Co. (cat. no. 208).[3] Additional works by Thomas Aspinwall Davis (cat. no. 143), along with a body of silver plate, pewter, and other items dating from the late nineteenth and early twentieth centuries, round out the church's gift.[4] Taken together, they provide insight into the changing taste for ecclesiastical forms, which ranged from standing cups and tankards to a double-walled pitcher, a pair of cruets, and a number of bread plates. This collection attests to the vitality of the Newton congregation, and to their preference for Boston makers of church silver.

Exhibitions and publications: MFA 1906; MFA 1911, cat. nos. 281, pl. 8, 667, 736; Jones 1913, 322–25, pl. XCVIII.

Notes

1. Worthley 1970, 426–28.

2. Karen M. Jones, "Museum Accessions," *Antiques* 107, no. 1 (January 1973), 58.

3. The English wine cup (1973.24), bearing a leopard's head crowned and date letter "a" of cycle VII, is dated to 1618–19; the maker's mark is obscured. The cup is engraved "The Gift of Abraham White / to the Church of Christ in New=Town / in New England / 1731."

4. Museum accession numbers for the group gift are 1973.17–39, 1973.119, and Apparatus 1973.

Concordance

ACCESSION NUMBER	CATALOGUE NUMBER	ACCESSION NUMBER	CATALOGUE NUMBER	ACCESSION NUMBER	CATALOGUE NUMBER	ACCESSION NUMBER	CATALOGUE NUMBER
[18]77.61	248	41.399	388	65.1198	191	1973.411	140
01.64.49	142	41.400	384	65.1199	192	1973.481	179
14.516a	182	41.403	400	67.1072	98	1973.618	34
14.516b	182	41.405	397	68.57	102	1973.619	34
16.22	404	41.406	399	Res.69.2.1	210	1973.620	161
17.1079	149	41.407	398	Res.69.2.2	210	1973.621	161
19.5	251	41.408	394	Res.69.2.3a–b	210	1973.622	161
19.119	380	41.410	392	Res.69.2.4	210	1973.626	69
21.1258	203	41.411	391	Res.69.2.5	210	1973.643	119
21.1261	226	41.412	393	69.1291	247	1973.644	232
21.1262	226	41.413	396	69.1292	247	1973.645	215
28.466	381	41.415	395	69.1293	247	1973.735	81
28.467	370	41.416	390	69.1294	247	1973.736	81
28.468	374	41.417	389	69.1295	247	1974.434	73
28.469	370	41.430	408	69.1296	247	1974.455	59
29.915	153	54.512	207	69.1297	247	1974.456	175
32.381	42	54.513	205	1971.95	230	1974.497	31
32.385	147	54.514	202	1971.269	181	1975.28	1
Res.34.3	212	56.611	216	1971.313	223	1975.34	17
Res.34.5	188	58.1348	217	1971.319	100	1975.350	118
34.62	405	61.1290	403	1971.334	137	1975.394	120
41.349	410	62.202	206	1971.335	137	1975.649	155
41.353	409	62.203	206	1972.122	109	1975.650	155
41.354	415	62.204	206	1972.517	160	1975.651	155
41.355a	411	Res.63.27	258	1972.56	169	1975.652	177
41.355b	411	Res.63.28	319	1972.616	178	1975.669	238
41.356a	412	63.1041	219	1972.893	193	1975.670	238
41.356b	412	63.635a	151	1972.913	32	1975.671	238
41.357	413	63.635b	151	1973.15	74	1976.43	162
41.358a	414	Res.64.10.1	187	1973.17	41	1976.65	123
41.358b	414	Res.64.10.2	187	1973.18	2	1976.640	132
41.360	372	64.933	185	1973.19	80	1976.641	195
41.373a	371	64.934	185	1973.20	52	1976.642	195
41.373b	371	64.935	185	1973.21	95	1976.771	35
41.374a	373	64.936	185	1973.22	85	1977.19	306
41.374b	373	64.937	185	1973.23	143	1977.42	139
41.389	385	65.438	224	1973.28	143	1977.43	139
41.391	383	65.1195	191	1973.29	208	1977.44	139
41.394	386	65.1196	191	1973.123	26	1977.157	159
41.397	387	65.1197	191	1973.214	165	1977.193	218

ACCESSION NUMBER	CATALOGUE NUMBER	ACCESSION NUMBER	CATALOGUE NUMBER	ACCESSION NUMBER	CATALOGUE NUMBER	ACCESSION NUMBER	CATALOGUE NUMBER
1977.620	189	1978.472	245	1980.628	48	1983.134	72
1977.738	99	1978.679	135	1980.629	9	1983.162	133
1977.739	99	1979.156	266	1981.39	171	1983.163	133
1977.745	10	1979.157	265	1981.171	66	1983.210	12
1977.768	101	1979.169	294	1981.354	183	1983.223	89
1977.769	53	1979.171	295	1981.379a	260	1983.268	196
1978.198	30	1979.172	298	1981.379b	260	1983.331	243
1978.228	313	1979.173	297	1981.379c	260	1983.382	97
1978.229	313	1979.174	299	1981.379d	260	1983.550	64
1978.230	313	1979.175	301	1981.379e	260	1983.682	50
1978.231	313	1979.176	296	1981.379f	260	1983.760	129
1978.232a	292	1979.181	287	1981.379g	260	1984.51.4	211
1978.232b	292	1979.182	288	1981.379h	260	1984.109	78
1978.233	302	1979.183	285	1981.379i	260	1984.183	144
1978.234	310	1979.184	279	1981.379j	260	1984.184a	401
1978.235	318	1979.185	283	1981.379k	260	1984.184b	401
1978.236	318	1979.186	284	1981.379l	260	1984.204	15
1978.237	318	1979.187	282	1981.379m	260	1984.205	15
1978.238	318	1979.188	280	1981.379n	260	1984.206	36
1978.239	318	1979.189	286	1981.379o	260	1984.207	36
1978.243	307	1979.190	281	1981.403	234	1984.208	38
1978.244	329	1979.192	6	1981.427	21	1984.209	37
1978.245	330	1979.408	67	1981.504	16	1984.210	37
1978.246	304	1979.409	67	1982.172	271	1984.211	37
1978.247	312	1979.410	236	1982.176	190	1984.212	37
1978.248	316	1979.411	349	1982.177	190	1984.214	75
1978.249	317	1979.412	349	1982.183	88	1984.215	60
1978.250	314	1979.413a	350	1982.193	273	1984.460	233
1978.251	315	1979.413b	350	1982.194	273	1984.461	233
1978.252	305	1979.418a	352	1982.195	273	1984.462	233
1978.253	293	1979.418b	352	1982.359	152	1984.463	233
1978.254	311	1979.420	351	1982.360	152	1984.464	233
1978.256	320	1979.426a	353	1982.361	152	1984.465	233
1978.257	322	1979.426b	353	1982.362	152	1984.466	233
1978.258	321	1980.242	130	1982.363	152	1984.467	233
1978.259	326	1980.278	39	1982.364	152	1984.468	233
1978.260	324	1980.323	76	1982.443	253	1984.469	233
1978.261	323	1980.383	244	1982.452	277	1984.513	156
1978.262	325	1980.384	244	1982.503	68	1984.515	90
1978.263	328	1980.490	7	1982.651	22	1984.569	231
1978.264	327	1980.491	7	1982.799	44	1984.570	231
1978.265	331	1980.492	148	1982.800	49	1984.571	231
1978.306	278	1980.493	148	1983.21	242	1984.572	231
1978.307	291	1980.627	131	1983.129	166	1984.573	231

ACCESSION NUMBER	CATALOGUE NUMBER	ACCESSION NUMBER	CATALOGUE NUMBER	ACCESSION NUMBER	CATALOGUE NUMBER	ACCESSION NUMBER	CATALOGUE NUMBER
1984.574	231	1987.555	303	1990.323.2	355	1991.668	18
1984.575	231	1987.556	264	1990.323.3	355	1991.670	116
1985.16	13	1987.557	264	1990.323.4	355	1991.671	11
1985.56	262	1987.558	264	1990.323.5	355	1991.672	11
1985.102.4	222	1987.559	264	1990.348	29	1991.687	28
1985.327	23	1987.560	264	1990.349	96	1991.690	25
1985.410	46	1987.561	264	1990.363	239	1991.694	83
1985.411	47	1987.572a	346	1990.364	8	1991.744	308
1985.412	115	1987.572b	346	1990.365	8	1991.778	58
1985.413	115	1988.145	357	1990.366	8	1991.779	24
1985.691	157	1988.146	358	1990.367	55	1991.783	112
1985.938	92	1988.281	65	1990.466a	240	1991.784	200
1985.939	92	1988.533	335	1990.466b	240	1991.785	200
1985.940	93	1988.535a	345	1990.466c	240	1991.789	84
1985.941	93	1988.535b	345	1990.484	45	1991.790	108
1986.85	197	1989.60	356	1990.604a	334	1991.929	263
1986.86	197	1989.61	356	1990.604b	334	1991.1002	168
1986.678	114	1989.62	356	1990.625	249	1991.1011	110
1986.739	156	1989.166	145	1991.249	184	1991.1022	107
1986.740	156	1989.167	145	1991.250	184	1991.1037	173
1986.778	259	1989.168	145	1991.255	201	1991.1039a	360
1986.779	259	1989.169	145	1991.256	201	1991.1039b	360
1986.780	259	1989.170	145	1991.465	270	1991.1041	19
1986.781	259	1989.170	300	1991.493	27	1991.1084	163
1986.782	259	1989.171	145	1991.494	27	1991.1085	164
1986.796	257	1989.172	145	1991.495	27	1991.1086	164
1987.68	267	1989.173	145	1991.496	27	1991.1087	164
1987.69	268	1989.174	145	1991.497	20	1991.1088	164
1987.70	268	1989.175	145	1991.497	20	1991.1089	167
1987.71	254	1989.176	145	1991.499	87	1991.1093	174
1987.72	255	1989.515	105	1991.500	180	1992.27	14
1987.73	332	1989.810	221	1991.586	43	1992.230	82
1987.74	256	1989.811	309	1991.601	121	1992.231	82
1987.204	289	1989.812	309	1991.607	56	1992.265.1	339
1987.232.1	336	1989.813	309	1991.608a	57	1992.265.2	339
1987.232.2	336	1990.137	237	1991.608b	57	1992.268	126
1987.232.3	336	1990.138	237	1991.623	91	1992.269	54
1987.232.4	336	1990.139	237	1991.636	241	1992.271	128
1987.464	290	1990.140	237	1991.655	94	1992.273	125
1987.515	198	1990.141	237	1991.661	62	1992.274	5
1987.551	303	1990.142	237	1991.662	63	1992.275	5
1987.552	303	1990.143	237	1991.665	154	1992.276	113
1987.553	303	1990.216	61	1991.666	154	1992.277	113
1987.554	303	1990.323.1	355	1991.667	154	1992.286	122

ACCESSION NUMBER	CATALOGUE NUMBER	ACCESSION NUMBER	CATALOGUE NUMBER	ACCESSION NUMBER	CATALOGUE NUMBER	ACCESSION NUMBER	CATALOGUE NUMBER
1992.287a	362	1993.699.8	369	1999.13	124	2001.260.1	368
1992.287b	362	1993.699.9	369	1999.20	274	2001.260.2	369
1992.287c	362	1993.699.10	369	1999.21	275	2001.260.3	368
1992.343	376	1993.699.11	369	1999.63.1	225	2001.742.1	29
1992.344	375	1994.33	158	1999.63.2	225	2001.742.2	29
1992.345	377	1994.224a	250	1999.63.3	225	2001.743	170
1992.346	377	1994.224b	250	1999.64.19	209	2001.804	246
1992.347	378	1994.293.1	176	1999.64.22	204	2001.820.1	213
1992.348	378	1994.293.2	176	1999.89	77	2001.820.2	213
1992.386	261	1994.293.3	176	1999.90	70	2001.820.3	213
1992.387	276	1994.293.4	176	1999.91	71	2001.820.4	213
1992.511	4	1994.293.5	176	1999.92	51	2001.821	214
1992.512	3	1995.45	150	1999.131.1	363	2001.841	407
1993.61	127	1995.137	354	1999.131.2	363	2001.842	416
1993.120.1	235	1995.782.1	338	1999.132	361	2001.843	379
1993.120.2	235	1995.782.2	338	1999.133	141	2001.844	406
1993.128	104	1995.782.3	338	1999.134	141	2001.845	402
1993.218.1	138	1995.801	134	1999.135	359	2001.846	382
1993.218.2	138	1996.27.1	186	1999.250.1	342	2001.847	382
1993.218.3	138	1996.27.2	186	1999.250.2	342	2002.64	366
1993.218.4	138	1996.122.1	117	1999.250.3	342	2002.192a	228
1993.532	269	1996.122.2	117	1999.250.4	342	2002.192b	228
1993.593a	364	1996.240	194	1999.250.5	342	2002.192c	228
1993.593b	364	1996.242.1	341	1999.250.6	342	2002.225	86
1993.594	365	1996.242.2	341	1999.250.7	342	2002.226	111
1993.643	106	1996.242.3	341	1999.250.8	342	2002.628.1	272
1993.698.1	367	1996.242.4	341	1999.250.9	342	2002.628.2	272
1993.698.2	367	1996.243	227	1999.252.1	343	2002.628.3	272
1993.698.3	367	1996.263	220	1999.252.2	343	2002.628.4	272
1993.698.4	367	1996.401	79	1999.253	344	2003.730	424
1993.698.5	367	1997.56	252	1999.254a	340	2003.783	429
1993.698.6	367	1997.163	199	1999.254b	340	2003.784	420
1993.698.7	367	1997.260	103	1999.736	337	2003.817	426
1993.698.8	367	1997.305	33	2000.689a	146	2003.819	423
1993.698.9	367	1998.48	40	2000.689b	146	2004.71	419
1993.698.10	367	1998.188.1	229	2000.690	136	2004.203.1	427
1993.698.11	367	1998.188.2	229	2000.789	418	2004.203.2	427
1993.699.1	369	1998.188.3	229	2000.793.1	417	2004.203.3	427
1993.699.2	369	1998.188.4	229	2000.793.2	417	2004.204	428
1993.699.3	369	1998.188.5	229	2000.826	172	2004.221	421
1993.699.4	369	1998.188.6	229	2000.941	333	2004.652	422
1993.699.5	369	1998.189.1	229	2001.158	347	2004.710	425
1993.699.6	369	1998.189.2	229	2001.258a	348		
1993.699.7	369	1998.189.3	229	2001.258b	348		

Index

Abelar, *Horse's bit (copas del freno)*, cat. no. **410**, 501, 509

Altar cruets (vinajeras), pair of, cat. no. **373**, 468–69, 507

Anthony, Joseph Jr., *Camp cup*, cat. no. **135**, 171, 221

Aspersorium (acetre), cat. no. **372**, 467–68, 507

Austin, Josiah, 9, 34, 206, 213, 225 n.6; church silver, 10, 67, 530; *Creampot*, cat. no. **1**, 9, 161; *Tankard*, cat. no. **2**, 9, 10–11, 67, 151, 530

Bacall, Thomas. *See* Pear & Bacall

Bachelder, Josiah G., 183–84; Palmer & Bachelder, 184, 286, 311 n.7; *see also* Davis, Palmer & Co.

Bailey & Co., *Child's cup* (retailer), cat. no. **230**, 294, 313

Ball, Samuel S., 273, 275; *see also* John B. Jones & Co.; Jones, Lows & Ball

Ball, True M., 275, 277; *see also* Jones, Ball & Co.; Jones, Ball & Poor; Jones, Lows & Ball

Ball, Black & Co., 228–29, 293, 305, 311 n.7, 314 n.2; *Ewer* (retailer), cat. no. **189**, 242–44, 310

Ball, Tompkins & Black, 236; *Five-piece tea service* (retailer), cat. no. **185**, 236–38, 309–10

Banner holder, cat. no. 178, 218–19, 225

Barnum, Frances. *See* Smith, Frances (née Barnum)

Barron, Jane (née Carson), 333, 335, 362; with Frances Barnum, *Salad servers*, cat. no. **250**, 335–36, 401

Bernstein, Bernard, 411; *Elliptical bowl*, cat. no. **333**, 411, 457

Blanchard, George Porter, 399, 405 nn. 1 & 3; in Arthur Stone's workshop, fig. 5, 366; *Tea strainer*, cat. no. **330**, 399, 405

Boelen, Henricus, 12; *Spoon*, cat. no. **3**, 11, 139, 151

Boelen, Jacob, 11, 40, 105; *Pair of spoons*, cat. no. **5**, 13, 152; *Two-handled bowl*, cat. no. **4**, 12-13, 151

Bombillas, cat. no. nos. **389–399**, 488–92

Boyce, Gerardus, 231; *Pitcher*, 181, 231–32, 309

Boyd, William. *See* Shepherd and Boyd

Bramhill, Bartlett M. *See* Davis, Watson & Co.

Breast strap (pretal), cat. no. **409**, 500–501, 509

Brevoort, John, 14; *Tankard*, cat. no. **6**, 14-15, 152

Brigden, Zachariah, 5, 38, 70, 181, 289; chocolate pots, 50, 142; church silver, 15–16, 530; *Creampot*, cat. no. **9**, 18, 152; *Pair of wine cups*, cat. no. **7**, 15–16, 152, 530; *Set of three teaspoons*, cat. no. **8**, 17, 152

Brown, Charles, 397; *Demitasse spoon*, cat. no. **326**, 397, 405; *Dessert spoon*, cat. no. **327**, 398, 405; *Jelly spoon*, cat. no. **328**, 398; *Tea strainer*, cat. no. 329, 399

Brown, Seth E., 227, 296, 305; Shreve, Brown & Co., 271; *see also* Jones, Ball & Co.; Jones, Shreve, Brown & Co.

Buckley, Charles E. *See* Whiting Manufacturing Co.

Buel, Samuel, *Bowl*, cat. no. **136**, 172, 221

Bunker, Benjamin, 19; *Porringer*, cat. no. **10**, 18-19, 152

Burnett, Charles Alexander, 168, 173; *Four-piece tea service*, cat. no. **138**, 174–76, 221; *Teapot and creampot*, cat. no. **137**, 173–74, 221

Burt, Benjamin, 5, 6, 34, 62, 129, 172 n.4, 220; *Pair of Salts*, cat. no. **11**, 19–20, 126, 130, 152; *Teapot*, cat. no. **12**, 20–21, 152; *Teapot*, cat. no. 13, 21–23, 152

Burt, John, 8 n.17, 34, 59, 72, 129, 149; church silver, 26, 30–32, 88, 528–29; *Mug*, cat. no. **18**, 29–30, 154; *Pair of caudle cups*, cat. no. **20**, 32, 528; *Pair of flagons*, cat. no. **15**, 25–26, 153; *Porringer*, cat. no. **14**, 23–24, 153; *Tablespoon*, cat. no. **21**, 32–33, 154; *Tankard*, cat. no. **16**, 26–27, 153; *Tankard*, cat. no. **17**, 28–29, 153; *Two-handled cup*, cat. no. **19**, 30–31, 154

Burt, Samuel, 34, 129; *Teapot*, cat. no. **22**, 33–34, 81, 154; *Teapot*, cat. no. **23**, 34–36, 154

Butler, Robert A., 412; *Animal bowl*, cat. no. **334**, 412-13, 457

Callender, Joseph, 16; *Monteith and pitcher* (engraver), cat. no. **141**, 170, 180–82, 222, 226

Cañas, Gumersindo de, 494; probably, *Covered bowl or spice container (especiero)*, cat. no. **401**, 494, 509

Cann, John. *See* Cann & Dunn; Charters, Cann & Dunn

Cann & Dunn, 233; *Coffee urn*, cat. no. **182**, 232–33, 309

Carlson, David, 405 n.3; *Child's breakfast set*, cat. no. **309**, 386–87; *Miniature winged rocking chair with high back*, cat. no. **279**, 368–69, 404

Caron, Edgar L., *Bowl*, cat. no. **314**, 390, 405

Carson, Jane. *See* Barron, Jane (née Carson)

Cary, Lewis, 227, 234; *Creampot*, cat. no. 183, 233–34, 309; *Pair of covered pitchers*, cat. no. **184**, 234–36, 309

Chalice and paten (caliz y patena), cat. no. **370**, 465–66, 507

Chamber pot (vaso de noche), cat. no. **406**, 498, 509

Charters, Thomas Jr. *See* Charters, Cann & Dunn

Charters, Cann & Dunn, 233, 236; *Five-piece tea service*, cat. no. **185**, 236–38, 309–10

Chitry, Peter, 178; with William Gale, *Three-piece tea service*, cat. no. **139**, 170, 176–78, 221

Chocolate cup (jicara), cat. no. **400**, 493, 508–9

Chocolate pot (chocolatera), cat. no. **402**, 495, 509

Churchill, Jesse, 178–79, 181, 199–200, 227, 234; apprentices of, 179, 227, 309 n.2; church silver, 179, 234; *Pitcher*, cat, 140, 178–79, 222; *see also* Churchill and Treadwell

Churchill and Treadwell, 179, 227, 234; wine cooler, fig. 3, 181; *Monteith and pitcher*, cat. no. **141**, 170, 180–82, 222, 226

Ciborium (copón), cat. no. **371**, 467, 507

Coburn, John, 36, 38, 70, 95, 103, 129, 537 n.3; *Saucepan*, cat. no. **24**, 36-37, 154; *Strainer*, cat. no. 25, 37, 154

Coburn, Seth Storer, *Nutmeg grater*, cat. no. **26**, 38-39, 154

Coney, John, 4–5, 7, 24, 27, 31, 50, 81, 82, 137–38; apprentices of, 5, 82, 511; candlesticks, 149–50; church silver, 39, 40, 53–54, 78, 88, 526, 528; cups, 8 n.17, 39, 46, 78, 126, 528; family of, 38, 70; forks, 131, 511; monteith, 46, 141; porringers, 46–47, 78; tankards, 47, 50–51, 78; teapots, 48; *Baptismal basin*, cat. no. **36**, 53–54, 156, 529; *Chocolate pot*, cat. no. **35**, 48–50, 156; *Mug with added lid*, cat. no. **31**, 43–44, 155; *Pair of tankards*, 36, 50–51; *Pair of trencher salts*, cat. no. **34**, 47–48, 95, 155–56; *Porringer*, cat. no. **33**, 46–47, 155; *Punch bowl*, cat. no. **32**, 44–46, 98, 132, 135, 140, 155; *Set of four beakers*, cat. no. **37**, 52, 156, 529; *Set of four caudle cups*, cat. no. **27**, 39, 528; *Set of three spoons*, cat. no. **29**, 41–42, 110, 155; *Spout cup*, cat. no. **28**, 40–41, 154-55; *Tankard*, cat. no. **30**, 42–43, 155

Container, cat. no. **407**, 498–99, 509

Conyers, Richard, 4–5; *Tankard*, cat. no. **39**, 54–55, 156

Cooper, Francis W., 238–39; *see also* Cooper & Fisher

Cooper & Fisher, *Chalice and paten*, cat. no. **186**, 238–40, 310

Copeland, Elizabeth Ethel, 337; brooch, fig. 2, 338; *Box*, cat. no. **251**, 336; *Candlestick*, cat. no. 252, 337–38, 401

Cowan, William M. *See* Whiting Manufacturing Co.

Cowell, William Sr., 47, 118; church silver, 55–57, 526, 530; *Tankard*, cat. no. **40**, 55–57, 156, 526; *Tankard*, cat. no. **41**, 57, 156, 530

Cowell, William Jr., *Porringer*, cat. no. **42**, 58

Craver, Margret, 408, 413–14, 431, 453; influence